THE OXFORD HANDBOOK OF

PROFESSIONAL ECONOMIC ETHICS

THE OXFORD HANDBOOK OF

PROFESSIONAL ECONOMIC ETHICS

Edited by
GEORGE F. DEMARTINO
and
DEIRDRE N. MCCLOSKEY

OXFORD
UNIVERSITY PRESS

OXFORD
UNIVERSITY PRESS

Oxford University Press is a department of the University of Oxford. It furthers the University's objective of excellence in research, scholarship, and education by publishing worldwide. Oxford is a registered trademark of Oxford University Press in the UK and certain other countries.

Published in the United States of America by Oxford University Press
198 Madison Avenue, New York, NY 10016, United States of America

Library of Congress Cataloging-in-Publication Data
The Oxford handbook of professional economic ethics / edited by George F. DeMartino and Deirdre N. McCloskey.
pages cm
Includes bibliographical references and index.
ISBN 978-0-19-976663-5
1. Economics—Moral and ethical aspects. 2. Economists—Professional ethics.
I. DeMartino, George F. II. McCloskey, Deirdre N.
HB71.O854 2015
174'.4—dc23
2015005462

For the many virtuous economists who stay up nights worrying about the nature and consequences of their professional practice.

Contents

PART IV THE ETHICAL ENTAILMENTS OF ECONOMIC THEORY

1. *GENERAL ISSUES*

2. *ECONOMIC THEORY AND THE GREAT RECESSION*

PART V ETHICAL ISSUES IN ECONOMIC RESEARCH

1. *EXPERIMENTAL ECONOMICS*

2. *ECONOMETRICS*

3. *FIELD RESEARCH*

4. *CONFLICT OF INTEREST*

PART VI ETHICAL ISSUES IN APPLIED ECONOMICS

1. *DEVELOPMENT*

2. *ECONOMIC ADVISING IN GOVERNMENT AND BEYOND*

3. *FORENSIC ECONOMICS*

PART VII ETHICAL ISSUES IN ECONOMIC EDUCATION

PART VIII LOOKING AHEAD

Foreword

Discussing ethics makes economists uncomfortable, for some good reasons and some bad ones. Economics is ill-suited to discuss ethics in some ways, but very well-suited in others.

The best reason not to discuss ethics in economics is that we do not want to turn our debates into dueling ad-hominem attacks about unethical motivations for our arguments. Like other professionals such as physicians, we economists view ourselves as motivated by professional norms and not by crude self-interests that could be unethical. Moreover, we know that even if there are unethical motivations for an argument, this is not sufficient to disprove the argument—it still needs the kind of debate on theory and evidence that would have happened anyway if we had ignored ethics.

Nor do we want to allow declarations in economic debates that one position is morally superior to another. Economics is traditionally viewed as ill-suited to discuss competing ethical norms.

Yet economics is well-suited in other ways to address the very same concerns about discussing ethics. Whether we have a reputation for professionalism is not under our control—it is up to our audience to decide. We can do a better job convincing our audience of our professionalism by discussing self-interest openly rather than ignoring it. Our models of human behavior give insights into the need for professional norms. For example, sellers of a good whose quality is imperfectly observable will get a better price if they can convince buyers that the sellers obey ethical norms of not cheating on quality. The existence of a strong ethical norm that sellers don't cheat, along with some enforcement mechanism, would actually lead to a better outcome for sellers. It is economics that gives the paradoxical insight that your self-interest sometimes requires convincing everyone else that you are not responding too much to self-interest.

The belief that economics cannot adjudicate competing moral values is also overstated. Our normative analysis of what makes people better off is impossible without presuming some ethical positions. Take, for example, the concept of revealed preference: that if you chose A over B, then A must make you better off than B. Revealed preference analysis presumes that the individual does and should have the right to make her own choices and that she is the best judge of her own well-being. Most of our models make the same assumptions. Individual choice and autonomy are ethical values over which there has long been and still is a huge worldwide debate. If economists tried to do revealed preference analysis in a situation where there was actually coercion rather than choice, we should certainly take notice—and so we cannot avoid the global debate on individual choice.

So how should we economists confront our own ethical behavior and values? On our core ethical values of individual autonomy and consent, it seems straightforward. Whenever we apply models or analysis based on individual choice, shouldn't we also analyze whether individuals are indeed free to choose? There may be disagreement on how or whether to do this, but let's air those disagreements rather than avoid the topic of ethical values altogether.

The question of whether there is a profound tension between our professional norms and our self-interest deserves careful attention. Conflict of interest in economics gained much (unwanted) attention after the documentary *Inside Job* accused some finance economists of doing analysis favorable to financial industry interests while receiving undisclosed pay from those same interests. Even if you believe, as I do, that *Inside Job* was unfair to some of its targets, it did fuel a crisis of confidence in economists that we all have a strong interest in correcting. The response has been to strengthen the norms that we disclose possible conflict of interests in our research and policy recommendations; this is surely a good thing. An example from my own field of development is that researchers on foreign aid should disclose whether they are employees of or consultants to agencies dispensing foreign aid (or conversely, recipients of funding from anti-aid interests).

Yet the issue of conflict of interest is too complex to be so quickly dismissed by a simple disclosure requirement. A lot of attention has been focused on conflict of interest in academic research, where the norms were already fairly strong and were at least partly self-enforcing through reputational incentives. Conflict of interest is potentially more severe and the existing norms weaker in some of economists' other roles as government officials, as advisors to governments or international organizations or political candidates, as critics or advocates of political ideologies, or as public intellectuals shaping policy debates. Sometimes the conflict of interest is obvious and easily resolved, other times not so much. For example, it will be obvious that an economist advising a political party or serving as a political appointee has a conflict of interest in research or policy recommendations that support or oppose that party's positions. The economist should obviously disclose any such relationship to political parties or causes if it is not already public knowledge.

But the political role of economists brings with it a subtler ethical need for accountability. Again, research in our own field gives us some insight on this. We have a lot to say about how bad it is for agents to be able to play with other people's money. To return to finance examples, we know a lot about how bad it is for banks to socialize risk through taxpayer bailouts while keeping any rewards from those risky investments. Analogously, economists making risky policy recommendations allow the cost of our advice to fall on everyone else, with only weak individual accountability for economists ourselves. There are still hardly any positive or negative individual consequences of good or bad advice for the dispensers of advice. In this environment, we should consider the ethical implications of our overpromising on the payoffs to our recommendations or overstating the certainty with which our promises will be realized.

There is the hope, of course, that economists affiliated with opposing parties will tend to subject each other's overpromising and excess certainty to critical scrutiny on the traditional grounds of theory and evidence. Just as we think competition is a positive force in markets, competition among partisan economists should be a positive ethical force in keeping the debate healthy.

Yet sometimes competition is not as sufficient as it is assumed to be. Both sides may have a common interest in overstating the importance of economists' recommendations in general, such as overstating the importance of current policy decisions in any direction. Both sides may want to downplay competing explanations of outcomes from the economics literature, ones that suggest outcomes are also dependent on other forces far beyond the control of the current policy-makers, such as culture or history. So we are left with a possible self-interested bias on the importance of economists as policy advisors, even as we disagree with each other over particular policy proposals.

Economists on opposing partisan sides may also have a common interest in limiting debate to what is politically feasible for the current mainstream parties, avoiding viewpoints that pose a more fundamental challenge to the status quo.

These subtler biases are evident in my own field of economic development. On the status quo bias, development economists as public intellectuals seem to be expected to direct all their efforts to advising the current development establishment of rich country governments, aid agencies, philanthropic foundations, and non governmental organizations on how to end poverty. Even critics (such as this author) focus attention on the mistakes of this establishment and how to correct them. Public intellectuals who simply dismiss this establishment as irrelevant or inherently counterproductive—rightly or wrongly—have far more trouble getting a hearing. So self-interest of public intellectuals militates against fundamental challenges to the status quo, and, indeed, there are few such public intellectuals in the development field.

On the importance bias, public intellectuals in development (including this author) seem to have a common interest in exaggerating the importance and certainty of our own advice on how to end poverty even if we disagree on how to do so. Less "constructive" views that challenge how much we economists really do know are a threat to the status and power of economists as public intellectuals in the development field.

It seems to take a lot of ethical commitment to admit publicly to something so nihilistic and self-destructive as the limits to our knowledge and expertise as economists. Yet such ethical effort could really pay off for the field in unexpected ways. To take finance again, the audience for finance economists wanted them, above all, to give advice on how to find surefire high returns on investments. It took some courage to embrace theories that bluntly state finance economists are useless in helping you beat the market. Yet this freed the most courageous finance economists to develop principles under which financial markets work well for all their participants, such as the earlier admonition against banks socializing risks through unlimited taxpayer bailouts.

In development, there is a principle similar to "you can't beat the market": if there really is an easy and tangible solution *X* to end global poverty, why didn't *X* end global poverty already? Suppose development economists were ethically obliged to admit to their audiences an inability to find such easy answers if we do indeed have such inability. This could free us to develop and advocate the principles of a whole problem-solving system in which many different private and public entrepreneurs will discover the more difficult answers to the problems of poverty—as indeed economists (usually the ones not facing so much pressure for immediate and direct solutions) have already been doing for a long time. It could be surprisingly liberating for economists to overcome our importance bias to admit how little everyone actually needs us economists to run the economy.

This brief discussion of ethical issues for economists has chosen an idiosyncratic grab-bag of issues, and this selection and discussion probably reflects this author's own self-interested biases. But what this fascinating volume shows is that the open discussion of professional ethics in economics has great potential to provoke debate on many exciting questions and that there is no reason to continue inexcusable and counterproductive silence on the topic.

William Easterly

Acknowledgments

In addition to the contributors to this volume, many individuals provided invaluable support. At the Josef Korbel School of International Studies at the University of Denver, several students, including Matthew Farrell, Colin Gaiser, Eugenia Goh, Minsun Ji, Laura Roberts, Patrick Sutherland, Cecil Shapland and, in particular, Noelle Schaef and Michelle Woodruff, provided the editors with extensive research, editorial, and administrative assistance. The Earhart Foundation awarded a generous grant that allowed contributors to present their work at conferences and funded administrative support and honoraria. Emily Hinga of the Josef Korbel School of International Studies kept the books and managed to ensure that salaries and expenses were paid. Ilene Grabel provided consistent encouragement and advice, while Oxford University Press's Joe Jackson, Scott Parris, Terry Vaughn, and Cathryn Vaulman shepherded the project expertly from its inception through to its completion. Finally, Preethi Sundar at Newgen Knowledge Works provided outstanding editorial and production services.

The editors note with sadness the passing of contributor Thomas Mayer as this book was in press. Tom was an extraordinary person and a wonderful economist who advocated ethical economic practice and, more importantly, modeled it in his own work.

Contributors

Harold Alderman is Senior Research Fellow at the International Food Policy Research Institute (IFPRI), Washington, D.C.

Peter J. Boettke is University Professor of Economics and Philosophy at George Mason University (GMU), as well as the BB&T Professor for the Study of Capitalism, Vice President for Research, and Director of the F. A. Hayek Program for Advanced Study in Philosophy, Politics, and Economics at the Mercatus Center at GMU.

Jessica Carrick-Hagenbarth is a doctoral candidate in the Department of Economics at the University of Massachusetts, Amherst, and a Visiting Instructor in Economics at Middlebury College.

Jingnan Chen is Lecturer in Economics at the University of Exeter Business School.

Angelina Christie is Financial Economist in the Enterprise Risk Analysis Division, Economics Department at the Office of the Comptroller of the Currency, Washington D.C.

David Colander is Christian A. Johnson Professor of Economics at Middlebury College.

Herman Daly is Emeritus Professor in the School of Public Policy at the University of Maryland.

Jishnu Das is Lead Economist, Development Research Group, World Bank, Washington D.C., and Visiting Fellow at the Centre for Policy Research, New Delhi.

John B. Davis is Professor of Economics at Marquette University and Professor of Economics at the University of Amsterdam.

Erwin Dekker is Postdoctoral Fellow with the F. A. Hayek Program for Advanced Study in Philosophy, Politics, and Economics at the Mercatus Center and the Department of Economics at George Mason University.

George F. DeMartino is Professor of Economics and Co-Director of the Global Finance, Trade, and Economic Integration program in the Josef Korbel School of International Studies at the University of Denver.

Sheila C. Dow is Emeritus Professor of Economics at the University of Stirling, and Adjunct Professor of Economics at the University of Victoria.

William Easterly is Professor of Economics at New York University (joint with Africa House) and Co-Director of the Development Research Institute.

David Ellerman is a Visiting Scholar at the University of California, Riverside, and a Fellow of the Center on Global Justice at the University of California, San Diego.

Gerald Epstein is Professor in the Department of Economics and Co-Director of the Political Economy Research Institute (PERI) at the University of Massachusetts, Amherst.

Robert H. Frank is Henrietta Johnson Louis Professor of Management and Professor of Economics at Cornell's Johnson Graduate School of Management.

Alan Freeman is Co-Director of the Geopolitical Economy Research Group at the University of Manitoba, Canada.

Robert F. Garnett, Jr. is Chair and Professor in the Department of Economics at Texas Christian University.

Des Gasper is Professor of Human Development, Development Ethics, and Public Policy in the International Institute of Social Studies at Erasmus University Rotterdam, The Netherlands.

Rachel Glennerster is Executive Director of the Abdul Latif Jameel Poverty Action Lab (J-PAL) at Massachusetts Institute of Technology, as well as Scientific Director of J-PAL Africa and Co-Chair of J-PAL's education sector.

Sven Ove Hansson is Professor of Philosophy and Head of the Division of Philosophy at the Royal Institute of Technology, Stockholm.

Daniel Houser is Chairman and Professor in the Department of Economics and Director of the Interdisciplinary Center for Economic Science at George Mason University.

Ravi Kanbur is T. H. Lee Professor of World Affairs, International Professor of Applied Economics and Management, and Professor of Economics at Cornell University.

Arjo Klamer is Chair and Professor of Cultural Economics at Erasmus University Rotterdam, The Netherlands.

David M. Levy is Professor of Economics, Research Associate at the Center for Study of Public Choice, and Co-Director of the Summer Institute for the Preservation of the History of Economics at George Mason University.

Thomas Mayer was Emeritus Professor of Economics at the University of California, Davis, until his death in January 2015.

Deirdre N. McCloskey is UIC Distinguished Professor of Economics and History, Professor of English, and Professor of Communication, Emerita, at the University of Illinois at Chicago.

Julie A. Nelson is Professor of Economics at the University of Massachusetts, Boston, and a Senior Research Fellow at the Global Development and Environment Institute, Tufts University.

Robert H. Nelson is Professor in the School of Public Policy at the University of Maryland.

Kyle W. O'Donnell is a doctoral candidate at the Department of Economics at George Mason University, and a Visiting Lecturer of Economics at James Madison University.

Susan Offutt is retired Government Accountability Office (GAO) Chief Economist, US Congress Washington, D.C.

Sandra J. Peart is Dean of the Jepson School of Leadership Studies at the University of Richmond and Co-Director of George Mason University's Summer Institute for the Preservation of the History of Economics.

Shawn Powers is a Young Professional in the Education Global Practice at the World Bank, and was formerly a Senior Policy Manager at the Abdul Latif Jameel Poverty Action Lab (J-PAL).

Vijayendra Rao is Lead Economist of the Development Research Group at the World Bank.

Martin Ravallion is the Edmond D. Villani Professor of Economics, Georgetown University, and President of the Society for the Study of Economic Inequality.

Constantine Sandis is Professor of Philosophy at the University of Hertfordshire.

Tomáš Sedláček is a Czech Economist and University Lecturer at Charles University, Prague. He is the Chief Macroeconomic Strategist at ČSOB, a former member of the National Economic Council of the Czech Republic, and an economic advisor to former President Václav Havel.

Joseph E. Stiglitz is an American economist and a professor at Columbia University. He is also the co-chair of the High-Level Expert Group on the Measurement of Economic Performance and Social Progress at the OECD, and the Chief Economist of the Roosevelt Institute. A recipient of the Nobel Memorial Prize in Economic Sciences (2001) and the John Bates Clark Medal (1979), he is a former senior vice president and chief economist of the World Bank and a former member and chairman of the (US president's) Council of Economic Advisers. In 2000, Stiglitz founded the Initiative for Policy Dialogue, a think tank on international development based at Columbia University.

Nassim Nicholas Taleb is Distinguished Professor of Risk Engineering at New York University's Polytechnic Institute.

Edward R. Teather-Posadas is a doctoral candidate in the Department of Economics at Colorado State University.

Dennis F. Thompson is Professor of Government and Alfred North Whitehead Professor of Political Philosophy in the Faculty of Arts and Sciences, and Professor of Public Policy in the John F. Kennedy School of Government, Harvard University. He is also the founding Director of the University Center for Ethics and the Professions (now the Edmond J. Safra Center for Ethics).

Robert J. Thornton is Charles William Macfarlane Professor of Economics at Lehigh University and Associate Director of the Martindale Center for the Study of Private Enterprise.

Irene van Staveren is Professor of Pluralist Development Economics in the International Institute of Social Studies at Erasmus University Rotterdam, The Netherlands.

Robert H. Wade is Professor of Political Economy and Development in the Department of International Development at London School of Economics.

John O. Ward is Professor Emeritus in the Department of Economics, University of Missouri-Kansas City and Editor Emeritus, Journal of Forensic Economics.

Sharon D. Welch is Provost and Professor of Religion and Society at Meadville Lombard Theological School (Unitarian Universalist), Chicago.

Jonathan B. Wight is Professor of Economics and International Studies in the Robins School of Business at the University of Richmond.

Bart J. Wilson is Donald P. Kennedy Endowed Chair and Professor of Economics and Law at the Economic Science Institute, Chapman University.

Stephen T. Ziliak is Professor of Economics at Roosevelt University, Chicago, and Faculty Member of the Angiogenesis Foundation, Cambridge, MA.

PART I

INTRODUCTION

CHAPTER 1

INTRODUCTION, OR WHY THIS HANDBOOK?

GEORGE F. DEMARTINO
AND DEIRDRE N. MCCLOSKEY

Caminante, no hay camino. Se hace el camino al andar.
(Searcher, there is no road. We make the road by walking.)

—Antonio Machado, *Selected Poems*

ACADEMIC handbooks typically showcase the range of existing work defining mature fields of research. Handbooks catalogue what is taken to be representative, the best, or otherwise most important work in the field while pointing toward new areas of inquiry. They provide an opportunity to take stock, to map the field, and to identify the outstanding questions that deserve further attention.

Then why a handbook of professional economic ethics, of all things, when in fact there is no such field? You can look it up. Since its founding in 1885 and up to the present, the American Economic Association (AEA)—perhaps the most influential professional association of economists in the world—has never cultivated inquiry into professional ethics: what does it mean to be an ethical economist, or, what would it mean for economics to be an ethical profession? Never . . . as in, not once. The AEA's founders were on a mission to promote the influence of economists in public policy. Infected by the spirit of American Progressivism, they believed that professionals had a duty to promote the social good through the application of expertise to social and economic problems. Their ethical obligations began and ended with that duty. *Influence for economic experts*—that was the goal. The associated ethical burdens were taken to be trivial and obvious.

By the end of the 19th century, leading economists had concluded that achieving influence required the transformation of economics into a positivist science. They also believed, as many economists believe down to the present, that science required excision of all ethics talk from the field. Out with Richard T. Ely and his band of foggy-headed social gospel ministers who had founded the AEA; in with Charles F. Dunbar and the men of objective science who would achieve for the profession the standing it deserved.

The AEA is not alone in neglecting the professional ethics of economists. Of the several dozen economic associations existing today in the United States and among the leading associations in Europe and beyond, only a handful have promoted investigation of the ethical aspects of economic practice; indeed, very few even have rules covering disclosure of conflict of interest for their journals.[1] Beyond the associations, it is safe to say that it has never occurred to the majority of economists and certainly to most academic economists that their work involves complex ethical entailments warranting attention.

The goal of the Handbook surely can't be cartographic, then, since there is no terrain out there waiting to be mapped. The purpose is more audacious. We seek to lay down first tracks across a wilderness that we hope will evolve into a network of pathways through a cultivated field of inquiry. We have not sought to restrict our authors' destinations or the direction they take in getting there. Instead, we invited contributors to the volume to help us make the road by walking, *al andar*. Our method was simple: we tasked leading thinkers within economics and beyond to ruminate on those aspects of economic practice that they view as ethically fraught. We gave contributors free rein, holding no preconceptions about what kinds of conversations, questions, arguments, concerns, methods, and styles do and do not count as professional ethics. We hope readers will engage the essays herein with the same spirit of open-mindedness so that, together, we can generate the new field of professional economic ethics. The field is vital to our profession. But it is also and even more acutely vital to those whom economists purport to serve.

The Economist's Error: Professional Ethics Is Not a Code of Conduct

As a rule, economists are not enamored with the idea of The Profession. Chicago School economists in particular, and others, too, think of professions as forms of labor unions to protect the privileges associated with monopoly power (Friedman, 1962; and the Chicago oral tradition). The expectation is that as soon as an occupation claims for itself the status of a "profession," it begins to seek government protection in the form of certification, licensing, and other mechanisms restricting access to the market—all the while

[1] The notable exceptions include, in the United States, the National Association of Forensic Economics (NAFE) and the American Academy of Economic and Financial Experts (AAEFE); and, in Sweden, two associations of applied economists: Akademikerförbundet SSR and Civilekonomerna. Since 2011, a number of leading economic associations in Britain, France, Germany, and the United States have considered and some have adopted new conflict-of-interest disclosure rules for the journals they publish. But the new rules generally do not reach beyond disclosure to consider other ethical issues.

purporting to protect the public interest. In Friedman's words, "registration, certification, or licensure, almost inevitably becomes a tool in the hands of a special producer group to obtain a monopoly position at the expense of the rest of the public. There is no way to avoid this result" (1962: 148).

The economist's take on professional *ethics* is equally unflattering. The received view is that professional ethics entails a code of conduct that imposes on professionals and their clients the values that The Profession deems best. A professional code of conduct turns consumer sovereignty on its head—it puts the suppliers of a service in charge of just what they will sell (and who can sell it and under what terms), thereby circumscribing the freedom of consumers to satisfy their preferences for the particular services they think they need. The competition among suppliers that would otherwise protect consumers' interests is replaced by a producer cartel that dictates the terms of the transaction. Making matters worse, codes may induce unwarranted public trust in the profession, paving the way for scoundrels to profit from public naiveté. Leland Yeager (1976: 569) put it best:

> The more prevalent and well-based is the belief that people are generally decent and honest, the greater is the chance that culprits have to benefit from the presumption that they too have these virtues. They will enjoy a free ride on, while posing unfair competition with, the warranted credibility of other people.

There is some value in the economist's skepticism about the professions and codes of conduct. As good and loyal economists, we share it—although we would note, too, that a supplier has a legitimate interest in maintaining the quality of her product. But whenever an organized interest claims to know and to do what's best for you, watch out! Yet economists have made a basic yet consequential error that has stunted the development of ethical awareness in the profession. The error is to think of professional ethics as a tool to prevent the morally compromised from doing bad things. In the economist's view, professional ethics must entail ethical *legislation*, especially legalistic codes of conduct that are backed by sanctions in the form of certification or licensure. In other words, the economist thinks of codes as budget constraints, in the style of the "rules of the game" that Douglass North speaks of.

Properly understood, professional ethics is nothing of the sort. It is a conversation rather than a constraint, a dance rather than a pose. Professional ethics refers to a *tradition of critical inquiry* into the myriad questions that surround professional engagement. It entails reflection and debate, literatures, curriculum, texts, journals, and bulletins probing the nature of professional practice for its ethical substance. Professional ethics is intended to assist well-meaning professionals, and the profession as a whole, to do good—not to prevent charlatans from doing harm (DeMartino, 2011).

Professional ethics is an *activity*, not a rigid institution. It occurs in a profession only when reflective practitioners, ethicists, clients, and other members of the public wrestle with questions such as: just what ethical duties, obligations, and challenges attend the profession's practice? What virtues ought its practitioners and their clients cultivate in themselves and their peers? How can individual practitioners and the profession as a whole undertake their work responsibly? Defined in this way, very few professions today can claim professional ethics—although almost all proudly boast on their websites about codes of conduct. Economics must follow law, medicine, journalism, and the handful of other professions that struggle continuously with the ethicality of their practice. *Education, articulation, elucidation, and aspiration, not regulation, legislation, or condemnation*—these are the watchwords of the field that the Handbook seeks to announce and launch.

The Case for Professional Economic Ethics

But why the need for professional economic ethics when the profession has done quite well over the past century, thank you very much, without it? Surely there are risks associated with establishing the new field. Given the profession's proclivity to separate "us" from "them"—the mainstream from the backwater, the orthodoxy from the heterodoxy, Chicago from Cambridge, George Mason from the University of Massachusetts—isn't there a real danger that professional ethics might become the next weapon in the fight over who is and who is not a legitimate economist? *Preach free trade (or the raising of the minimum wage) or be damned as unethical!*

The case for economic ethics is simple and, we think, undeniable. Economists enjoy tremendous influence today over the life chances of others—innumerable others. That is the heart of the matter. The influence of economists arises from their expertise in a field vital to social well-being, freedom, and other valued goals. As economists know better than anyone, when you monopolize a resource that others need, you exert power over them. Moreover, in recent years, economists' influence has been amplified by institutional developments. Independent central banks, the multilateral development banks, and other international financial institutions are often in a position to set economic policy and even engage in social engineering without much oversight by elected officials or the public. Economists are at the helm of such institutions and occupy staff positions in the departments where the actual work gets done. Combined with its intellectual monopoly, institutional power enhances the ability of the economics profession to alter the course of human affairs—for the better, of course, but also, sometimes, for the worse.

Why also for the worse? In all but the simplest economies, even well-designed economic interventions impose harm on some agents. Sadly, Pareto improvements rarely present themselves, at any rate not with actual side payment. Most reform instead involves benefits to some and foreseeable costs to others. Indeed, as one of us argues (DeMartino, 2016), "econogenic harm," or the harm that follows from economists' interventions, is ubiquitous. The grander the economic intervention, the greater the scale of the project, the larger the number of losers and the greater the size of the aggregate losses. Large-scale development projects are a notable example (Kanbur, 2003; see Gasper, 2016). The regrettable fact is that the practice of economics harms even as it helps. That is the tragedy of economics. Economists are in the harm business. Economists usually know it and teach it every day. But what they don't consider carefully enough, or teach adequately, are the ethical entailments of the harm their practice induces.

There is a response available to our concern about econogenic harm. In the style of John Harsanyi, followed by Buchanan and Tullock, and then outside economics by John Rawls, one can argue that the better level of decision is "constitutional." That is, the question can be what sort of society we want to live in—a society in which every Kaldor-Hicks gain is second-guessed as entailing econogenic harm or a society in which market-tested innovations that promote the social good go forward, even though blacksmiths and buggy-makers are thereby unemployed? But such a reply should not be taken as a smart-aleck banishing of ethics. It, too, requires us to "struggle continuously with the ethicality of our practice."

Foreseeable harms can be damaging enough, to be sure, as foreseeable benefits can be uplifting. But in economics (and, indeed, in other professions), there are the unforeseen and unpredictable costs and benefits complicating professional practice. Economists operate on a terrain of *epistemic insufficiency* (McCloskey, 1990; DeMartino, 2013). They don't today and probably can't ever know enough to ensure the success of the policies and other interventions they advocate. Economies are complex whereas knowledge is partial, tacit, and widely dispersed. Economic policy entails predicting what will be the impact tomorrow (and next year and in 10 years) of an intervention undertaken today—and that is something that defies the capabilities of even the brightest economists in possession of the best-calibrated models. Making matters worse, there can be and generally is substantial slippage between the heady, pristine moment of policy design and the messiness of implementation. The poet said, "Between the conception and the creation/Falls the shadow." Economists are just one input in the drama of governance. In the policy domain, it is politics and not economic science that is in charge. The intrepid economist who risks advocacy quickly learns that, at best, she has influence but little ultimate control. And, in the absence of control lies the risk that the economist can do much harm as she tries to do good.

Influence over the lives of others, which can be immense, coupled with the risk of doing even substantial foreseeable and unforeseeable harm, implies that economic practice is ethically fraught. And yet the profession largely manages to ignore the attending burdens. Perhaps because economists understand that harm is universal in economics, the Hippocratic tradition appears to offer no insight into how economists should comport themselves. What does "do no harm" mean in a world where there are no free lunches and where all actions (including doing nothing) entail tradeoffs? And perhaps because economists often paint on big canvases, where they affect the lives of thousands or even millions of people all at once rather than individual clients one by one, clinical ethics seems largely irrelevant. The scale of economic interventions generates among economists a fear that serious and open engagement with professional ethical issues would paralyze them with doubt in those moments of human need when what is called for instead is focused audacity.

In our view and the view of many of the contributors to the Handbook, the implicit professional pact among economists to repress rather than engage the ethical concomitants of their work is ethically indictable. When the lives of so many are at stake, professional privilege and convenience cannot trump professional duties. Economists have secured the influence we've sought; hurray for us! The price to be paid for our privilege is open acknowledgment and careful examination of the ethical challenges of our work—in academia, government service, and the myriad other institutions and forums where we ply our craft.

But Isn't Ethics Just a Matter of Subjective Preference and Power?

Economists and calculators have long led the attack by the new clerisy on preaching the virtues.[2] The late Marc Blaug (1980: 132–133), for example, in many other respects a surprisingly sensible member of his profession, asserted that "There are no . . . methods for reconciling different normative value judgments—other than political elections and shooting it out at the barricades." By "methods for reconciling," he appears to mean "air-tight proofs such as the Pythagorean Theorem." Neatness reigns. The sort of amiable, casuistic reasoning-together that many in the rhetorical tradition recommend and that are practiced in courts of law and other fields of discussion, the trading of more or less good reasons, such as the stories of good or bad lives, ranging from the Hebrew Bible and Plutarch to the latest movie, are spurned by such a theory.

Schumpeter of Vienna and Harvard had earlier expressed an ethical philosophy similar to Blaug's: "We may, indeed, prefer the world of modern dictatorial socialism to the world of Adam Smith, or vice versa, but any such preference comes within the same category of subjective evaluation as does, to plagiarize Sombart, a man's preference for blondes over brunettes" (Schumpeter, 1954: 330). Hurrah-boo. Thus also, Lionel Robbins of the London School of Economics: "If we disagree about ends it is a case of thy blood against mine—or live and let live, according to the importance of the difference, or the relative strength of our opponents. . . . If we disagree about the morality of the taking of interest.. . . then there is no room for argument" (Robbins, 1932: 134).[3] And a fount

[2] Parts of what follow come from various of McCloskey's writings, such as *Knowledge and Persuasion in Economics* (1994).

[3] Amartya Sen (1987) says that such a view was "quite unfashionable then." Not, we think, among the reigning fashionistas of 1932.

of this attitude, again, Bertrand Russell (1977: 136; quoted in Perry): "As to ultimate values, men may agree or disagree, they may fight with guns or with ballot papers, but they cannot reason logically."

Such a theory, to which many economists subscribe, is called by philosophers "emotivism." Emotivism was believed by very many early 20th-century people, some under the influence of logical positivism, some under the influence of a falling away from religious faith. It is "the doctrine that all evaluative judgments and more specifically all moral judgments are *nothing but* expressions of preference" (MacIntyre, 1981: 11, italics in original). Or, as Hobbes wrote in 1651, "'Good' and 'evil' are names that signify our appetites and aversions (1982/1651: Part I, ch. 15, 82)." Emotivism, observe again, taken as a doctrine one *should* believe is, of course, self-contradictory because preaching against preaching is preaching. But logic is not the strong point of logical positivism or of those who have fallen away from religious faith.

Undergraduates and many of their professors become uneasy and start giggling when an ethical question arises. They regard such questions as having mainly to do with sex—thank you fundamentalists of the late 20th century—or with unargued authority, such as the Baltimore Catechism and the nuns who enforce it. The agreement to disagree that ended the wars of religion in Europe can be traced in their unease and in their stock remarks expressing it: "That's just a matter of opinion," "Religion should not be mentioned in polite conversation," "If we disagree about ends it is a case of thy blood against mine," "The only methods for reconciling different normative value judgments are political elections or shooting it out at the barricades." According to the emotivists, to be caught making ethical statements is to be caught in meaningless burbling. Shame on you.

We can do better than such obsolete philosophy. We can have a serious conversation about the goods and bads of our practice. We need to. Let the emotivists then make their case in the new agora we and our fellow contributors to the Handbook intend to construct. But be warned: in that new intellectual space, sneering won't do.

We Know ...

Yes, of course: paying attention to the ethical issues might substantially complicate the professional life of the economist. Yes, there are opportunity costs here. And yes, there are no guarantees that the profession would do much better in its mission to promote the public good were it to invest the time and energy necessary to construct the field of professional ethics. But objections such as these do not undermine the case for professional ethics. What they do is warn us against ethical simple-mindedness, and they alert us that good intentions will not suffice. They prepare us for what will be a daunting and risky undertaking. But what gain is there, we ask our fellow economists, without risk?

REFERENCES

Blaug, M. 1980. *The Methodology of Economics: Or, How Economists Explain*. Cambridge: Cambridge University Press.

DeMartino, G. F. 2016. "'Econogenic Harm': On the Nature of and Responsibility for the Harm Economists Do as They Try to Do Good." In *The Oxford Handbook of Professional Economic Ethics*, edited by G. F. DeMartino and D. N. McCloskey, pp. 71–97. New York: Oxford University Press.

DeMartino, G. F. 2011. *The Economist's Oath*. New York: Oxford University Press.

DeMartino, G. F. 2013. "Epistemic Aspects of Economic Practice and the Need for Professional Economic Ethics." *Review of Social Economy* 71(2): 166–186.

Friedman, M. 1962. *Capitalism and Freedom*. Chicago: University of Chicago Press.

Gasper, D. 2016. "The Ethics of Economic Development and Human Displacement." In *The Oxford Handbook of Professional Economic Ethics*, edited by G. F. DeMartino and D. N. McCloskey, pp. 534–557. New York: Oxford University Press.

Hobbes, T. 1982/1651. *Leviathan*. New York: Penguin Classics.

Kanbur, R. 2003. "Development Economics and the Compensation Principle." *International Social Science Journal* 2003(55): 175. First published online July 1, 2004. doi: 10.1111/1468-2451.5501019_2

MacIntyre, A. *After Virtue*. 1981. South Bend, IN: University of Notre Dame Press.

McCloskey, D. N. 1990. *If You're So Smart: The Narrative of Economic Expertise*. Chicago: University of Chicago Press.

McCloskey, D. N. 1994. *Knowledge and Persuasion in Economics*. Cambridge: Cambridge University Press.

Perry, J. F. "The Dream Hypothesis, Transitions, and the Very Idea of Humanity." Available at https://www.bu.edu/wcp/Papers/Teac/TeacPerr.htm

Robbins, L. 1932. *An Essay on the Nature and Significance of Economic Science* (second edition, 1935; third edition, 1983). London: Macmillan.

Russell, B. 1977. *Education and the Social Order*. London: Unwin Paperbacks.

Schumpeter, J. A. 1954. *History of Economic Analysis*. New York: Oxford University Press.

Sen, A. 1987. *On Ethics and Economics*. Malden, MA: Blackwell.

Yeager, L. B. 1976. "Economics and Principles." *Southern Economic Journal* 42(4): 559–571.

PART II

UNCERTAINTY, RISK AND PROFESSIONAL ECONOMIC ETHICS

CHAPTER 2

THE *SKIN-IN-THE-GAME* HEURISTIC FOR PROTECTION AGAINST TAIL EVENTS

NASSIM NICHOLAS TALEB
AND CONSTANTINE SANDIS

Agency Problems and Tail Probabilities

The chances of informed action and prediction can be seriously increased if we better comprehend the multiple causes of ignorance.[1] The study of ignorance, then, is of supreme importance in our individual and social lives, from health and safety measures to politics and gambling (Rescher, 2009). But how are we to act in the face of all the uncertainty that remains after we have become aware of our ignorance? The idea of *skin in the game* when involving others in tail risk exposures is crucial for the proper functioning of a complex world. In an opaque system fraught with unpredictability, there is, alas, an incentive and easy opportunity for operators to hide risk: to benefit from the upside when things go well without ever paying for the downside when one's luck runs out.

The literature of risk, insurance, and contracts has amply dealt with the notion of information asymmetry (see Ross, 1973; Grossman and Hart, 1983*a*, 1983*b*; Tirole, 1988; Stiglitz, 1988) but not with the consequences of deeper information opacity (in spite of getting close, as in Hölmstrom, 1979) by which tail events are impossible to figure out from watching time series and external signs: in short, in the "real world" (Taleb, unpublished), the law of large numbers works very slowly or does not work at all in the time horizon of operators, hence statistical properties involving tail events are completely opaque to the observer. And the central problem that is missing behind the abundant research on moral hazard and information asymmetry is that these rare, unobservable events represent the bulk of

1 A mathematical version of this paper has appeared in *Review of Behavioral Economics*, 2014, 1: 1–21.

the properties in some domains. We define a fat-tailed domain as follows: a large share of the statistical properties come from the extremum; for a time series involving *n* observations, as *n* becomes large, the maximum or minimum observation will be of the same order as the sum. Excursions from the center of the distributions happen brutally and violently; the rare event dominates. And economic variables are extremely fat tailed (Mandelbrot, 1997). Furthermore, standard economic theory makes an allowance for the agency problem but not for the combination of the agency problem, informational opacity, and fat-tailedness. It has not yet caught up to the fact that tail events are not predictable and are not measurable statistically unless one is *causing* them or is involved in increasing their probability by engaging in a certain class of actions with small upsides and large downsides. (Both parties may not be able to gauge probabilities in the tails of the distribution, but the agent knows which tail events do not affect him.) Sadly, the economics literature's treatment of tail risks or "peso problems" has been to see them as outliers to mention *en passant* while hiding them under the rug or removing them from analysis rather than as a core center of modeling and decision making, or to think in terms of robustness and sensitivity to unpredictable events. Indeed, this pushing under the rug of the determining statistical properties explains the failures of economics in mapping the real world, as witnessed by the inability of the economics establishment to see the accumulation of tail risks leading up to the financial crisis of 2008 (Taleb, 2009). The parts of the risk and insurance literature that have focused on tail events and extreme value theory, such as Embrechts (1997), accept the large role of the tails, but then the users of these theories (in the applications) fall for the logical inconsistency of assuming that they can be figured out somehow: this is naive Because they are rare, what do we know about them? The law of large numbers cannot be of help. Nor do theories have the required robustness. Alarmingly, very little has been done to make the leap that small calibration errors in models can change the probabilities (such as those involving the risks taken in Fukushima's nuclear project) from 1:1,000,000 to 1:50.

Add to the fat-tailedness the asymmetry (or skewness) of the distribution by which a random variable can take very large values on one side but not the other. An operator who wants to hide risk from others can exploit skewness by creating a situation in which he has a small or bounded harm to him while others face large harm, thus exposing others to the bad side of the distributions by fooling them with the tail properties.

Finally, the economic literature focuses on incentives as encouragement or deterrent but not on disincentives as potent filters that remove incompetent and nefarious risk takers from the system. Consider that the symmetry of risks incurred on the road causes the bad driver to eventually exit the system and stop killing others. An unskilled forecaster with skin in the game would eventually go bankrupt or out of business. But if shielded from potentially (financially) harmful exposure, he would continue contributing to the buildup of risks in the system.[2]

[2] The core of the problem is as follows. There are two effects: "crooks of randomness" and "fools of randomness" (Nicolas Tabardel, private communication). Skin in the game eliminates the first effect in the short term (standard agency problem), the second one in the long term by forcing a certain class of harmful risk takers to exit from the game.

Hence, there is no possible risk management method that can replace skin in the game in cases where informational opacity is compounded by informational asymmetry, as in the principal-agent problem that arises when those who gain the upside resulting from actions performed under some degree of uncertainty are not the same as those who incur the downside of those same acts.[3] For example, bankers and corporate managers get bonuses for positive "performance" but do not have to pay out reverse bonuses for negative performance. This gives them an incentive to bury risks in the tails of the distribution, particularly the left tail, thereby delaying blowups.

The ancients were fully aware of this incentive to hide tail risks and implemented very simple but potent heuristics (for the effectiveness and applicability of fast and frugal heuristics both in general and in the moral domain, see Gigerenzer, 2010). But we find the genesis of both moral philosophy and risk management concentrated within the same rule.[4] About 3,800 years ago, Hammurabi's code specified that if a builder builds a house and the house collapses and causes the death of the owner of the house, that builder shall be put to death. This is the best risk-management rule ever.

What the ancients understood very well was that the builder will always know more about the risks than the client, and the builder can hide sources of fragility and improve his profitability by cutting corners. The foundation is the best place to hide such things. The builder can also fool the inspector because the person hiding risk has a large informational advantage over the one who has to find it. The same absence of personal risk is what motivates people to only appear to be doing good rather than actually do it.

Note that Hammurabi's law is not necessarily literal: damages can be "converted" into monetary compensation. Hammurabi's law is at the origin of the *lex talonis* ("eye for eye," discussed later), which, contrary to appearances at first glance, is not literal. *Tractate Bava Kama* in the Babylonian Talmud[5] builds a consensus that "eye for eye" must be figurative: what if the perpetrator of an eye injury were blind? Would he have to be released of all obligations on grounds that the injury has already been inflicted? Wouldn't this lead him to inflict damage to other people's eyesight with total impunity? Likewise, the Quran's interpretation equally gives the option of the injured party to pardon or alter the punishment.[6] This nonliteral aspect of the law solves many problems of asymmetry under specialization of labor because the deliverer of a service is not required to have the same exposure in kind but must incur risks that are costly enough to be a disincentive.

[3] Note that Pigovian mechanisms fail when, owing to opacity, the person causing the harm is not easy to identify.

[4] Economics seems to be born out of moral philosophy (mutating into the philosophy of action via decision theory) to which was added naive and improper 19th-century statistics (Taleb, 2007, unpublished). We are trying to go back to its moral philosophical roots, to which we add more sophisticated probability theory and risk management.

[5] *Tractate Bava Kama*, 84a, Jerusalem: Koren Publishers, 2013.

[6] Quran, *Surat Al-Ma'idat*, 45: "Then, whoever proves charitable and gives up on his right for reciprocation, it will be an atonement for him." (our translation).

The problems and remedies are as follows:

First, consider policy makers and politicians. In a decentralized system, say municipalities, these people are typically kept in check by feelings of shame from harming others with their mistakes. In a large centralized system, the sources of error are not so visible. Spreadsheets do not make people feel shame. The penalty of shame is a factor that counts in favor of governments (and businesses) that are small, local, personal, and decentralized versus ones that are large, national or multinational, anonymous, and centralized. When large organizations or governments fail, everybody except the culprit ends up paying the cost, leading to national and international measures of endebtment against future generations or "austerity" programs.[7] These points against "big government" models should not be confused with the standard libertarian argument against states securing the welfare of their citizens, but only against doing so in a centralized fashion that enables people to hide behind bureaucratic anonymity. Much better to have a communitarian municipal approach: in situations in which we cannot enforce skin in the game, we should change the system to lower the consequences of errors.

Second, we misunderstand the incentive structure of corporate managers. Counter to public perception, corporate managers are not entrepreneurs. They are not what one could call agents of capitalism. Between 2000 and 2010, in the United States, the stock market lost (depending how one measures it) up to $2 trillion for investors, compared to leaving their funds in cash or treasury bills. It is tempting to think that since managers are paid on incentive, they would be incurring losses. Not at all: there is instead an irrational and unethical asymmetry. Because of the embedded option in their profession, managers received more than $400 billion in compensation. The manager who loses money does not return his bonus or incur a negative one.[8] The built-in optionality in the compensation of corporate managers can only be removed by forcing them to eat some of the losses.[9]

Third, there is a problem with applied and academic economists, quantitative modelers, and policy wonks. The reason that economic models do not fit reality (fat-tailed reality) is that economists have no disincentive and are never penalized for their errors. So long as they please the journal editors or produce cosmetically sound "scientific" papers, their work is fine. So we end up using models such as portfolio theory and similar methods without any remote empirical or mathematical reason. The solution is to prevent economists from teaching practitioners, simply because they have no mechanism to exit

[7] See McQuillan (2013) and Orr (2013); cf. the "many hands" problem discussed by Thompson (1987).

[8] There can be situations of overconfidence by which the CEOs of companies bear a disproportionately large amount of risk by investing in their companies, as shown by Malmendier and Tate (2008, 2009), and end up taking more risk because they have skin in the game. But it remains that CEOs have optionality, as shown by the numbers quoted. Furthermore, the heuristic we propose is necessary but may not be sufficient to reduce risk, although CEOs with a poor understanding of risk have an increased probability of personal ruin.

[9] We define "optionality" as an option-like situation by which an agent has a convex payoff (i.e., has more to gain than to lose from a random variable) and thus has a positive sensitivity to the scale of the distribution (i.e., can benefit from volatility and dispersion of outcomes).

the system in the event of causing risks that harm others. Again, this brings us to decentralization by a system where policy is decided at a local level by smaller units and thus has no need for economists.[10]

Fourth, the predictors. Predictions in socioeconomic domains don't work. Predictors are rarely harmed by their predictions. Yet we know that people take more risks after they see a numerical prediction. The solution is to ask—and only take into account—what the predictor has done (what he has in his portfolio) or is committed to doing in the future. It is unethical to drag people into exposures without incurring losses. Furthermore, predictors work with binary variables (Taleb and Tetlock, 2013)—that is, "true" or "false"—and they play with the general public misunderstanding of tail events. They have the incentives to be right more often than wrong, whereas people who have skin in the game do not mind being wrong more often than they are right, provided the wins are large enough. In other words, predictors have an incentive to play the skewness game (more on this below). The simple solution is as follows: predictors should be exposed to the variables they are predicting and should be subjected to the dictum "do not tell people what you think, tell them what you have in your portfolio" (Taleb, 2012: 386). Clearly, predictions are harmful to people because, by the psychological mechanism of anchoring, they increase risk taking.

Fifth, to deal with warmongers, Ralph Nader has rightly proposed that those who vote in favor of war should subject themselves (or their own kin) to the draft.

We believe *skin in the game* is a heuristic for a safe and just society. It is even more necessary in fat-tailed environments. Opposed to this is the unethical practice of taking all the praise and benefits of good fortune while disassociating oneself from the results of bad luck or miscalculation. We situate our view within the framework of ethical debates relating to the moral significance of actions whose effects result from ignorance and luck. We demonstrate here how the idea of skin in the game can effectively resolve debates about (a) moral luck and (b) egoism versus altruism while successfully

[10] *A destructive combination of false rigor and lack of skin in the game.* The disease of formalism in the application of probability to real life by people who are not harmed by their mistakes can be illustrated as follows, with a very sad case study. One of the most "cited" documents in risk and quantitative methods about "coherent measures of risk" set strong principles on how to compute the "value at risk" and other methods. Initially circulating in 1997, the measures of tail risk—although coherent—have proved to underestimate risk at least 500 million times (the number is not a typo). We have had a few blowups since, including Long Term Capital Management, and we had a few blowups before, but departments of mathematical probability were not informed of them. As we are writing these lines, it was announced that J. P. Morgan made a loss that should have happened every 10 billion years. The firms employing these "risk minds" behind the "seminal" paper blew up and ended up bailed out by the taxpayers. But we now know about a "coherent measure of risk." This would be the equivalent of risk managing an airplane flight by spending resources to make sure the pilot uses proper grammar when communicating with flight attendants in order to "prevent incoherence." Clearly, the problem is that tail events are very opaque computationally and that such misplaced precision leads to confusion. The "seminal" paper: Artzner, P., F. Delbaen, J. M. Eber, and D. Heath. 1999. Coherent measures of risk. *Mathematical Finance* 9(3), 203–228.

bypassing (c) debates between subjectivist and objectivist norms of action under uncertainty by showing how their concerns are of no pragmatic concern.

Reputational Costs in Opaque Systems

Note that our analysis includes costs of reputation as skin in the game, with future earnings lowered as the result of a mistake, as with surgeons and people subjected to visible malpractice who have to live with the consequences. So our concern is situations in which cost hiding is effective over and above potential costs of reputation, either because the gains are too large with respect to these costs or because these reputation costs can be "arbitraged" by shifting blame or escaping it altogether because harm is not directly visible. The latter category includes bureaucrats in nonrepeat environments where the delayed harm is not directly attributable to them. Note that in many domains the payoff can be large enough to offset reputational costs, or, as in finance and government, reputations do not seem to be aligned with effective track records. (To use an evolutionary argument, we need to avoid a system in which those who make mistakes stay in the gene pool, but throw others out of it.)

Forecasters

We can see how forecasters who do not have skin in the game have the incentive for betting on the low-impact high-probability event and ignoring the lower probability ones even if these are high impact. They can thus game their reputation. There is confusion between "digital payoffs" (i.e., payoffs linked to probability) and full distribution, called "vanilla payoffs" (i.e., payoffs in which the operator cares about expectation; see Taleb and Tetlock, 2013).[11] The crux is that if one earns money 99 percent of the time, but in pennies, and loses dollars 1 percent of the time, according to records he would be an excellent forecaster. But he would be bankrupt if he risked his own money by having skin in the game.

Application of the Heuristic

The heuristic implies that one should be the first consumer of one's product: a cook should test his own food, helicopter repairpersons should be ready to take random

[11] Money managers do not have enough skin in the game unless they are so heavily invested in their funds that they can end up in a net negative from the event. The problem is that they are judged on frequency, not payoff, and tend to cluster together in packs to mitigate losses by making them look like an "industry event." Many fund managers beat the odds by selling tails, say covered writes, by which one can increase the probability of gains but possibly lower the expectation. They also have the optionality of multitime series; they can manage to hide losing funds in the event of failure. Many fund companies bury hundreds of losing funds away in the "cemetery of history" (Taleb, 2007).

flights on the rotorcraft they maintain, hedge fund managers should be maximally invested in their funds. But it does not naively imply that one should always be using one's product: a barber cannot cut his own hair, the maker of a cancer drug should not be a user of his product unless he is ill. So one should use one's products *conditionally* on being called to use them. However, the rule is far more rigid in matters entailing systemic risks: simply that some decisions should never be taken by a certain class of people.

Heuristic Versus Regulation

A heuristic, unlike a regulation, does not require state intervention for implementation. It is simple contract between willing individuals ("I buy your goods if you use them" or "I will listen to your forecast if you are exposed to losses if you are wrong") and would not require the legal system any more than do simple commercial transactions. It is bottom-up.

The ancients and more-or-less ancients effectively understood the contingency and probabilistic aspect in contract law, and asymmetry under opacity, as reflected in the works of Pierre de Jean Olivi. Moreover, the foundation of maritime law has resided in skin-in-the-game unconditional sharing of losses even as far in the past as 800 B.C. with the *Lex Rhodia*, which stipulates that all parties involved in a transaction have skin in the game and share losses in the event of damage. The rule dates back to Phoenician commerce and caravan trades among Semitic people. We note that the idea is still present in Islamic finance commercial law (see Wardé, 2010).

Opacity and Risk Hiding

Here, we summarize in verbal form the mathematical argument concerning payoff skewness and lack of skin in the game presented elsewhere (Taleb, unpublished).

> A. *If an agent has the upside of the payoff of the random variable, with no downside, and is judged solely on the basis of past performance, then the incentive is to hide risks in the left tail using a negatively skewed (or, more generally, asymmetric) distribution for the performance. This can be generalized to any payoff for which one does not bear the full risks and negative consequences of one's actions.*
>
> B. *Furthermore, even if it is not intentional (i.e., the agent does not aim at probabilistic rent at the expense of the principal; which is at variance with the way agents are treated in the economics literature), by a survival argument, those agents without skin in the game who tend to engage in strategies that hide risk in the tail tend to fare better and longer and populate the agent population. So the argument is not one of incentive driving the agents but one of survival.*

We can sketch a demonstration of these statements with the following reasoning. Assume that an agent has a payoff as a proportional cut of his performance or the benefits to the principal and can get a percentage at year end, his compensation being tied to the *visible* income. The timing of the compensation is periodic, with no total claw back (subsequent obligation to completely return past compensation). The expected value to the agent is that of a stream, a sum of payoffs over time, extending indefinitely (or bounded by the life of the agent). Assume that a loss will reduce his future risk taking or even terminate it, in terms of shrinking of such contracts, owing to change in reputation. A loss would hurt the track record, revealing it, so to speak, and making such a stream of payoffs stop. In addition, the payoff of the agent is compounded over time as the contracts get larger in response to the track record.

Critically, the principal does not observe statistical properties, only realizations of the random variable. However, the agent has an edge over the principal; namely, that *he can select negatively skewed payoffs*. All he needs to do is to figure out the shape of the probability distribution, not its expected returns—nothing else. More technically, the expectation for the agent does not depend on the size of the loss: a small loss or a large loss are the same to him. So the agent can benefit by minimizing the probability of the loss, not the expectation. Minimizing one and not the other results in the most possibly negatively skewed distribution.

This result can be extended to include any situation in which the compensation or reward (in any form) to the agent depends on the probability rather than on the true expectation.

In an evolutionary setting, downside harm via skin in the game would create an absorbing state, without the system failing to be ergodic; hence, it would eliminate this class of risk takers.

Symmetrical Constraints in Moral Philosophy

We now turn to a philosophical approach to the problem. The skin-in-the-game heuristic is best viewed as a rule of thumb that places a pragmatic *constraint* on normative theories. Whatever the best moral theory (consequentialism, deontology, contractualism, virtue ethics, particularism, etc.) or political ideology (socialism, capitalism, libertarianism) might be, the "rule" tells us that we should be suspicious of people who appeal to it to justify actions that pass on the cost of any risk-taking to another party while keeping the benefits for themselves. At the heart of this heuristic lies a simple moral objection to negative asymmetry that lies at the heart of some of the oldest and most famous moral ideas, as illustrated in Table 2.1.

Of course, the clearest examples of any rule are likely to stem from a deontological approach, but the skin-in-the-game constraint is not committed to deontology. Indeed,

Table 2.1 Moral Symmetry

1 *Lex Talionis*: "An eye for an eye, a tooth for a tooth" (Exodus 21:24)	2 *15th Law of Holiness and Justice*: "Love your neighbor as yourself" (Leviticus 19:18)	3 *Silver Rule*: "Do not do unto others what you would not have them do unto you" (Isocrates and Hillel the Elder)	4 *Golden Rule*: "Do unto others as you would have them do unto you" (Matthew 7:12)	5 *Formula of the Universal Law*: "act only in accordance with that maxim through which you can at the same time will that it become a universal law" (Kant 1785: 4:421)

moral symmetry is one of the key ideas behind many forms of social contract theory (e.g., "I scratch your back, you scratch mine"), and different emphases on symmetry may also be found in consequentialism (which places the overall good above that of the agent) and virtue ethics (which looks for an ethical mean between excess and deficiency).

As worded, all of the principles in Table 2.1 are problematic. Take, for example, the fourth principle of reciprocity in Table 2.1. This "golden rule" seems to suggest that if I would like you to come up and kiss me, then I should go up to you and kiss you (regardless of whether *you* would like this). But whereas the precise principles may be faulted, the spirit of symmetry behind them (and arguably every moral tradition)[12] contains much insight. Indeed, the very plausibility of Derek Parfit's recent attempt to demonstrate that the best versions of the most popular normative theories converge (Parfit, 2012) must ultimately hang upon a common spirit of this kind. As we shall see, however, there can be positive asymmetries in our behavior as well as negative ones.

Altruism Versus Egoism

Psychological egoists claim that we always do what we most desire (Mandeville, 1714). Those who believe in the possibility of altruism tend to either deny this (Nagel, 1970) or to distinguish between self-centered desires and the desire to benefit others (Butler, 1726). So, although it is not false to think that whether or not we ever act altruistically is an empirical question (Slote, 1964), its answer will partly depend on a priori distinctions among notions such as "desire," "motivation," "reason," and so on. It is such distinctions, rather than experimental research, that allow us to recognize that whereas anyone who

12 See Blackburn (2001: 101).

Table 2.2 Egoism Versus Altruism

No skin in the game	Skin in the game	Skin in someone else's game
Selfish/egoistic	Neither egoistic nor altruistic	Selfless/altruistic
Negative asymmetry	Symmetry (neutral)	Positive asymmetry
Individualistic Morality	Conventional morality	Other-based morality

is not a sociopath will feel contentment in helping others, it would be perverse to help others *in order* to acquire this feeling (Sandis, 2012: 75; cf. Broad, 1930).

The most pragmatic way of distinguishing between egoists and altruists is to ask whether someone has ever voluntarily (a) paid a cost for someone else's benefit or (b) been willing to reap the rewards of risk while passing the cost to another. The first, altruistic, action is one where the agent has skin in another person's game (Taleb, unpublished), including the lives of future generations.[13] The second, egoistic act, is one where the person has no skin in the game. People we call "saints" are frequently disposed to act in the former way. Those who tend to act in the latter way we typically call "assholes." In reality, most of us are neither: we usually have skin in our own games and those of our loved ones, but nobody else's. On occasion, however, even the most average of people is liable to either slip up or rise to the occasion. Such moments are respectively marked by negative or positive asymmetries (see Table 2.2).

The middle column in Table 2.2 is the largest because most of the actions of the average person tend to fall within it. It is no wonder, then, that the "eye for an eye" reciprocity it epitomizes is—for better or worse—a conventional morality. To its left lies the sort of individualistic morality frequently associated with Nietzsche but most clearly ascribable to the "rational" normative egoism of Ayn Rand (1964) and many others who maintain that "greed is good." To its right lies the morality of self-sacrifice. This comes in all sorts of stripes: Christian, socialist, utilitarian, and so on. Needless to say, these divisions are never as sharp in practice as they are in theory. Rand's egoistic heroes, for example, subscribe to the symmetrical thought that one should never demand that others take a risk one wouldn't take oneself. Conversely, most welfare states are run by bureaucrats with no skin in the game. Both sides are fooling themselves.

The symmetrical constraint entails that we act wrongly when we open ourselves to great harm that could have reasonably been foreseen and avoided, but the wrongness isn't a moral one. We act immorally when we open *others* to great risk but are only willing to be considered as responsible for our actions if the risk turns out not to harm anyone. Such actions involve the malignant transfer of fragility and antifragility from one party to another with the aim of getting any possible benefits of our actions without

[13] Such altruism includes cases in which one voluntarily removes oneself from the social pool (e.g., through suicide or self-imposed exile) so as not to harm it. These should be distinguished from the agency problem in evolutionary theory.

being liable for any possible harms (Taleb, 2012). This agency problem is that of a negative asymmetry.

Those who are responsible for such transfers (most predictive analysts, economists, bankers, bureaucrats, consultants, editors, politicians, risk vendors, and sophists) attempt to justify their hypocrisy by appealing to bad luck and uncertainty. They offer excuses of the "we acted on information we believed was correct at the time" or "obviously it fell way short of expectations" variety but refuse to accept any liability for their actions and protest wildly at the mere thought that they should pay the cost. These may be contrasted with those who have skin in the game; that is, those who take risks for themselves and keep their downside. Typical examples are activists, artisans, citizens (as opposed to "*idiotes*"), entrepreneurs, traders, and writers. The greatest contrast, however, is with those who put their own skin in the game for the sake of others. We call such people heroes and saints, but they include not only knights and warriors but also some maverick artists, journalists, scientists, and writers who put their livelihood reputations on the line for the sake of others (Taleb, 2012). This all brings us to the so-called "problem of moral luck."

Moral Luck

Consider the case of two equally reckless drivers, only one of whom kills a pedestrian. According to Bernard Williams, the unlucky driver is morally guilty of something worse than the other driver (namely, manslaughter). Kantians, by contrast, maintain that both drivers would only be liable for reckless driving. Both views are confused. What we should say is that, from the moral point of view, a certain kind of reckless driving is as bad as manslaughter. When a person drives recklessly, he takes upon himself the risk of manslaughter and is accordingly responsible for it if it happens and for opening himself up to it (which is just as bad from a purely ethical point of view) if it doesn't (see Sandis, 2010). Hegel got it right, then, when he wrote not only that "[t]he laurels of mere willing are dry leaves that never were green" but also:

> It happens of course that circumstances may make an action miscarry to a greater or lesser degree. In the case of arson, for instance, the fire may not catch or alternatively it may take hold further than the incendiary intended. In spite of this, however, we must not make this a distinction between good and bad luck, since in acting a man must lay his account with externality. The old proverb is correct: "A flung stone is the devil's." To act is to expose oneself to bad luck. Thus bad luck has a right over me and is an embodiment of my own willing. (Hegel, *Philosophy of Right*, 119A)

We are not only responsible for the *known* of our actions and their effects but also for those that we *ought* be aware of (even if we are not). Our ignorance does not always relieve us of responsibility for things we have done because others can claim that, as rational beings, we *should* know what we were doing even if we did not.[14] Such is the knowledge involved in putting other people's lives at risk with no skin (of our own) in the game. Hegel's solution famously offers two aspects of any given act: *Tat* (deed) corresponding to the objective (which I am causally responsible for) and *Handlung* (action) corresponding to the subjective (which can be morally imputed to me); rights relating to the latter in turn divide into ones relating to various elements of the self, such as knowledge, intention, and purpose (PR 115, 117, 120; see also 118A).

Bad luck is no excuse when it could have been reasonably foreseen. Foresight should not be restricted here to a particular event. If I know that 1 in 1,000 actions of type A will have a tragic result, it is not acceptable to perform thousands of these actions on the grounds that for each one there is only a probability of 1/1,000 that something will go wrong. The greater the potential disaster, the smaller the probability has to be for an act that could bring it about to be immoral. There is an inverse symmetry between the acceptable probability of risk and the weight of the potential damage being assessed.

All action is, to varying degrees, *exposition* luck and must be judged accordingly. When we take a risk, we cannot wash our hands of the consequences for others and hide behind masks of expectation, intention, ignorance, luck, uncertainty, and so on. The central point bears repeating here: *asymmetry in taking risks without having skin in the game is unethical.* Any system deemed "too big too fail" not only encourages but demands that we live according to such skinless asymmetry. The real black swan event of the 21st century is not that any financial crisis occurred (which was predictable) but that there was no full-blown revolution against the governments that continue to encourage "idiotes" to gamble with other people's lives and money.

Objectivism Versus Subjectivism

The ethics of risk is frequently thought of as a branch of moral philosophy concerned with abstract principles that tell us how we ought to act when we lack (or do not know whether or not we lack) information that is relevant to our choice.[15] Far from being infrequent, such scenarios are the norm and can only be excluded in controlled thought experiments. In an important sense, then, all acts are performed under uncertainty, which is not to say that we never know what the consequences of our actions will be (see Prichard, 1932/2002: 233). This raises the problem of how we ought to act in the face of known ignorance. The skin-in-the-game ethic bypasses the issue, revealing it to be pragmatically irrelevant.

The worry is that of whether a person's obligation to perform (or omit from performing) some action depends "on certain characteristics of the situation in which he

[14] For a related point, see Thompson (1983).

[15] For instance, see Altham (1984), who makes a technical distinction between mere risk and general uncertainty.

is, or on certain characteristics of his thought about the situation" (Prichard, 1932: 84). Objectivists (such as Sidgwick and Parfit) claim that we ought to do whatever is *in fact* best, even when we cannot be reasonably expected to know what this is. By contrast, subjectivists (including Ross, 1939, and Prichard, 1932) claim that we ought to do whatever we *believe* will be best.

The difficulty of choosing between these positions is supposed to stem from two considerations that are in tension. On the one hand, we want to leave room for the thought that we can be unaware of what we ought to do. The fact that what we *believe* we ought to do and what we *actually should* do can come apart in this way seems to lend credence to objectivism. On the other hand, there is the procedural obstacle of the impossibility of stepping out of one's own mind in order to compare reality with one's impressions of it. Thus, the objective view appears to entail the absurd view that "although we may have duties, we cannot know but can only believe that we have; and therefore we are rendered uncertain whether we, or anyone else, has ever had, or will ever have a duty" (Prichard, 1932: 88–89).[16] A parallel absurdity is implied in this rhetorical question posed by Jonathan Dancy: "Suppose that, unknown... to me, someone has been buried alive in my garden during the night. Could this make it wrong of me to go away for a fortnight's holiday?" (Dancy, 2000: 57). Prospectivists, most prominently Michael Zimmerman, attempt to avoid this dilemma by arguing that we ought to perform whichever action it is most reasonable to *expect* will be the best.

Such academic debates have little pragmatic weight. All three views share the common mistaken assumption that they are each motivated by the same notions of "what one ought to do" when there are actually three different concepts at play:

1. *Objectivists* equate *what* we ought to do with whichever action turns out to be best. This is what we should *aim* at when we act.
2. *Subjectivists* equate what we ought to do with whatever we judge to be best. This the only way *through which* we can aim at what is best.
3. *Prospectivists* equate what we ought to do with what we can rationally expect to be best. This view attempts to reconcile objectivist and subjectivist intuitions that are only in tension because of the aforementioned assumption.

Whereas objectivists are concerned with the rightness of the things we do (typically thought to be universals), prospectivists and subjectivists are concerned with the rightness of our acts of *doing* these things (typically thought to be particulars). Yet it is possible that one rightly acts in doing something that results in negative value and, by the same token, that one acts wrongly in doing something that turns out positively.[17]

16 Ross 1930 rightly (but for the wrong reason) suggests that objectivists and subjectivists are talking at cross purposes. Cf. Zimmerman (2008: 1–2).

17 This point runs parallel to the distinction between a belief and a believ*ing* being justified (e.g., as introduced in the literature on Gettier cases).

Given that one can do the right thing for the wrong reason, the deontic question of *what* the right thing to do is should therefore be distinguished from the evaluative question of when one is acting right*ly*. The evaluative question is best answered via an account of how and when people and institutions are *liable* for choices they make under uncertainty. We have sought to answer the question (e.g., in the case of moral luck) via the skin-in-the game principle. Strictly speaking, this necessary (although insufficient) moral heuristic is not about action but about dispositions. Indeed, it relates directly to the virtue of being such that the system will not only *survive* uncertainty, randomness, and *volatility* but will actually benefit from it. Such a system is defined as *antifragile* (see Taleb, 2012).[18] Skin-in-the-game heuristics follow directly from the principle of antifragility.

Acknowledgments

The authors thank Jon Elster, David Chambliss Johnson, Gur Huberman, Raphael Douady, Robert Shaw, Ralph Nader, Barkley Rosser, James Franklin, Russell Roberts, Marc Abrahams, Andreas Lind, and Elias Korosis.

References

Altham, J. E. J. 1984. "Ethics of Risk." *Proceedings of the Aristotelian Society*. New Series 84(1983–1984): 15–29.

Blackburn, S. 2001. *Ethics: A Very Short Introduction*. Oxford: Oxford University Press.

Broad, C. D. 1930. *Five Types of Ethical Theory*. London: Kegan Paul.

Butler, J. 1726. "Sermons I and XI." In his *Fifteen Sermons Preached at the Rolls Chapel*, in *The Works of Bishop Butler*, edited by J. H. Bernard. London: Macmillan.

Dancy, J. 2000. *Practical Reality*. Oxford: Oxford University Press.

Dancy, J. 2002. "Prichard on Duty and Ignorance of Fact." In *Ethical Intuitionism: Re-evaluations*, edited by P. Stratton-Lake. Oxford: Oxford University Press.

Embrechts, P. 1997. *Modelling Extremal Events: For Insurance and Finance*. Springer.

Gigerenzer, G. 2010. "Moral Satisficing: Rethinking Moral Behavior as Bounded Rationality. *Topics in Cognitive Science* 2: 528–554.

Grossman, S. J., and O. D. Hart. 1983*a*. "An Analysis of the Principal-Agent Problem." *Econometrica* 7–45.

Grossman, S. J., and O. D. Hart. 1983*b*. "Implicit Contracts Under Asymmetric Information." *The Quarterly Journal of Economics* 123–156.

[18] One can, of course, render the virtue of the previous sentence into a principle about action ("act in whatever way renders you and the systems that you inhabit antifragile"), but such a principle treats antifragility as the ultimate end-in-itself, whereas it is best to treat it as a property whose value is derived from its effects.

Hegel, G. W. F. 1991. *Elements of the Philosophy of Right*, translated by H. B. Nisbet. Cambridge: Cambridge University Press.

Hölmstrom, B. 1979. "Moral Hazard and Observability." *The Bell Journal of Economics* 74–91.

Kant, I. 1785/2002. *Groundwork for the Metaphysic of Morals*, A. Zweig, edited by T. E. Hill, Jr. and A. Zweig. Oxford: Oxford University Press.

Malmendier, U., and G. Tate. 2008. "Who Makes Acquisitions? CEO Overconfidence and the Market's Reaction." *Journal of Financial Economics* 89(1): 20–43.

Malmendier, U., and G. Tate. 2009. "Superstar CEOs." *Quarterly Journal of Economics* 124(4): 1593–1638.

Mandelbrot, Benoit B. 1997. *Fractals and Scaling in Finance: Discontinuity, Concentration, Risk*. New York: Springer-Verlag.

Mandeville, B. 1714. *The Fable of the Bees*. London: J Roberts.

McQuillan, M. 2013. "The Severity of Austerity." *Times Higher Education* 30–35.

Nagel, T. 1970. *The Possibility of Altruism*. Princeton, NJ: Princeton University Press.

Orr, D. 2013. "It Wasn't Labour Who Spent Too Much, It Was the Banks. How Did We Forget This?" *The Guardian*, Saturday 5 January: 39.

Parfit, D. 2012. *On What Matters*, vols. *I & II*. Oxford: Oxford University Press.

Prichard, H. A. 1932/2002. "Duty and Ignorance of Fact." In *Moral Writings*, edited by J. MacAdam. Oxford: Oxford University Press.

Rand, A. 1964. *The Virtue of Selfishness: A New Concept of Egoism*. New York: Signet.

Rescher, N. 2009. *Ignorance: On the Wider Implications of Deficient Knowledge*. Pittsburgh: University of Pittsburgh Press.

Ross, S. A. 1973. "The Economic Theory of Agency: The Principal's Problem." *The American Economic Review* 63(2): 134–139.

Ross, W. D. 1930. *The Right and the Good*, rev. ed. 2002. Edited by P. Stratton-Lake.

Ross, W. D. 1939. *The Foundations of Ethics*. Oxford: Clarendon Press.

Sandis, C. 2010. "The Man Who Mistook His Handlung for a Tat: Hegel on Oedipus and Other Tragic Thebans." *Bulletin of the Hegel Society of Great Britain* 62: 35–60.

Sandis, C. 2012. *The Things We Do and Why We Do Them*. Palgrave Macmillan.

Slote, M. A. 1964. "An Empirical Basis for Psychological Egoism." *Journal of Philosophy* 61: 530–537.

Stiglitz, J. E. 1988. *Principal and Agent*. In *The New Palgrave: A Dictionary of Economics*, vol. 3. London: Macmillan.

Taleb, N. N. 2007. *The Black Swan*. Penguin and Random House.

Taleb, N. N. 2009. "Errors, Robustness, and the Fourth Quadrant." *International Journal of Forecasting* 25(4): 744–759.

Taleb, N. N. 2012. *Antifragile: Things That Gain From Disorder*. Penguin and Random House.

Taleb, N. N. unpublished. *Silent Risk*, manuscript.

Taleb, N. N., and P. E. Tetlock. 2013. On the Difference Between Binary Prediction and True Exposure with Implications for Forecasting Tournaments and Decision Making Research (June 25, 2013). Available at http://ssrn.com/abstract=2284964 or http://dx.doi.org/10.2139/ssrn.2284964

Thompson, D. F. 1983. "Ascribing Responsibility to Advisers in Government." *Ethics* 93(3): 546–560.

Thompson, D. F. 1987. *Political Ethics and Public Office*. Cambridge, MA: Harvard University Press.

Tirole, J. 1988. *The Theory of Industrial Organization*. Cambridge: MIT Press.
Wardé, I. 2010. *Islamic Finance in the Global Economy*. Edinburgh University Press.
Williams, B. 1993. *Shame and Necessity*. Cambridge: Cambridge University Press.
Zimmerman, M. J. 2008. *Living with Uncertainty: The Moral Significance of Ignorance*. Cambridge: Cambridge University Press.

CHAPTER 3

THE ETHICS OF ECONOMIC DECISION RULES

SVEN OVE HANSSON

Introduction

According to the received view, moral philosophy and the decision sciences are distinct disciplines with clearly demarcated subject areas. Moral philosophy is concerned with the choice of values to be used as guides in practical decision making. It does not tell us much about the means for realization of these values. The decision sciences take values as given and add no new values. Instead, they show us what to do to maximize the attainment of the given values, using for that purpose criteria of rationality that are assumed to be devoid of moral implications. The common decision-making rules that are used in economics are taken to be based on such value-free rationality criteria, which means that they tell us how to reach the goals we have chosen but they have nothing to say about what goals we should choose.

This conception of decision rules is based on the premise that instrumental rationality can at least in principle be perfectly separated from moral values and, more generally, from the ends and purposes of our actions. This is often called the Humean view of practical reasoning, despite the fact that it does not seem to have been endorsed by Hume himself (Hampton, 1995; Millgram, 1995). It is an important part of the self-understanding of economics and the decision sciences. If we can fully separate ends and means from each other, then we can presumably also give an objective answer to the question how best to further a given set of goals.

But can we? Or does our use of economic decision rules have implications that reach into the realm of values? Are the supposedly value-free, entirely rationality-driven decision rules in fact imbued with moral values? To answer that question we need to take a closer look at the various decision rules that arise in economic practice, and we also need to clarify what we use them for and what impacts they have on our decision making.

Let us begin with a very simple situation: Suppose that there is only one thing we want to achieve,[1] and we know to what extent each of our alternative actions will lead to its achievement. In such a situation we have no need for a decision rule—apart from the trivial rule "choose an option that will maximize goal achievement." Economic decision rules are intended to enhance our ability to deal with situations that differ from this uncomplicated case in at least one of the following two respects: Either we have *competing goals*, or we have *uncertainty* about how the goals can be achieved. Therefore, the question of whether the decision rules are value-free or value-laden has to be seen in relation to how we deal respectively with competing goals and uncertainty about goal achievement. In the second section the focus is on decision rules for competing goals and in the third section on rules for dealing with uncertainty.[2]

Decision Rules for Goal Conflicts

Three Types of Goal Conflicts

For our purposes it is useful to distinguish between three major types of competition or conflict among goals. The first are *intercategorical* goal conflicts, conflicts among goals that belong to different categories, that is, they are different in nature. This is perhaps the type of goal conflict that comes most easily to mind. Everyday life is full of conflicts of this type, many of which arise because our time and our money are limited. For instance, the goal of keeping down public expenditures may run into conflict with many, if not most, other social welfare goals.

The second category consists of conflicts among goals that may be similar in nature but concern the interests of different persons. They can be referred to as *interindividual* (interpersonal) goal conflicts. They are often presented as problems of distribution. Some examples are the distribution of wages in a company, of the time of physicians and nurses among patients in a hospital, of risks among soldiers, and of social resources in a society at large.

The third category comprises *intertemporal* goal conflicts, conflicts among goals to be satisfied at different points or periods in time. Some intertemporal problems refer to the same person or persons, for instance, a person's choice of whether to do tedious work now and have the next weekend free, or take free time now and defer the drudgery to next weekend. Many intertemporal goal conflicts refer to goals that involve partly but not completely overlapping sets of concerned persons. One example is the conflict between investment and future consumption. Investments will reduce current consumption, but may be expected to result in significantly higher consumption within a

[1] Or several goals, so constructed that the actions needed to achieve them coincide completely.

[2] This chapter is devoted to the use of decision rules to guide decisions. Decision rules can also be used as descriptive or analytical tools, for example, when a decision is described as being compatible with a certain rule. From this it does not follow that the rule was actually used.

decade or two. Many, but not all, of those who forego consumption today will benefit from the resulting higher future consumption. Obviously, intertemporal conflicts over longer time intervals, such as the conflict between the costs of climate change mitigation measures and the burdens of a less inhabitable planet some hundred years ahead, are interpersonal in addition to being intertemporal. (They can also be called intergenerational conflicts.) The interpersonal aspect of such a combined conflict may be at least as important as the intertemporal aspect. It would be a serious mistake to take it for granted that such problems can be solved with the same decision rules that we use for intertemporal conflicts in a single person's life.

The Reductive Approach

Let us begin with intercategorical goal conflicts, conflicts between different types of goals. Such conflicts are common enough. Many if not most of the decisions that we find to be difficult, both in private and public life, are difficult largely because we cannot easily weigh the different goals against each other. A parent considering divorce may face difficulty in comparing the effects on the children's welfare with those on her own freedom and quality of life. Politicians and public officials preparing decisions about infrastructure investments may have to weigh the advantages of improved transportation against the negative environmental impacts of a new road or railroad. But although these and many other comparisons may be very difficult to make, somehow we have to make them. A complete stalemate in all decisions that hinge on intercategorical comparisons is not an option.

Many proposals have been made to facilitate decisions involving difficult comparisons. A common recommendation is to systematize the decision by identifying all the advantages and all the disadvantages of each of the options that are open to us. The next, more difficult step is to compare the advantages and disadvantages, or weigh them against each other. A practical way to do this was proposed in lively terms by Benjamin Franklin in 1772 in a letter to the chemist Joseph Priestley:

> When these difficult Cases occur . . . my Way is, to divide half a Sheet of Paper by a Line into two Columns, writing over the one *Pro*, and over the other *Con*. Then during three or four Days Consideration I put down under the different Heads short Hints of the different Motives that at different Times occur to me for or against the Measure. When I have thus got them all together in one View, I endeavour to estimate their respective Weights; and where I find two, one on each side, that seem equal, I strike them both out: If I find a Reason *pro* equal to some two Reasons *con*, I strike out the three . . . and if after a Day or two of farther Consideration nothing new that is of Importance occurs on either side, I come to a Determination accordingly. (Franklin, 1970: 437–438)

Franklin struck out items or groups of items with equal weight. From this it is not a big step to assign to each item a number representing its weight, and to add up these numbers in each column. This is the decision procedure proposed by the moral philosopher Jeremy Bentham (1748–1832):

> Sum up all the values of all the *pleasures* on the one side, and those of all the pains on the other. The balance, if it be on the side of pleasure, will give the *good* tendency of the act upon the whole, with respect to the interests of that *individual* person; if on the side of pain, the *bad* tendency of it upon the whole.
>
> Take an account of the *number* of persons whose interests appear to be concerned; and repeat the above process with respect to each. *Sum up* the numbers . . . Take the *balance* which if on the side of *pleasure,* will give the general *good tendency* of the act, with respect to the total number or community of individuals concerned; if on the side of pain, the general *evil tendency,* with respect to the same community. (Bentham, 1780: 27–28)

Bentham used the word "utility" for "that property in any object, whereby it tends to produce benefit, advantage, pleasure, good, or happiness" (Bentham, 1780: 2). Therefore, moral theories based on this type of calculus are called "utilitarian." But neither Bentham nor any of his successors have been able to come up with a compelling method to actually measure the moral values of options. Modern utilitarian philosophers often refer to a hypothetical unit called "util" or "utile," and in the literature on utilitarianism we can read phrases such as "Suppose person A receives 3 units of utility and person B loses 2 units . . ." However, this is just a fictitious measure, not a real one. Its relationship to meters and liters is the same as that of a fire-spitting dragon to lizards and turtles.

But in spite of this, utilitarian calculations are performed in economics, namely in the discipline of cost–benefit analysis. This is an economic discipline that employs a collection of decision-facilitating techniques in which numerical estimates of advantages and disadvantages are established and weighed against each other. In a typical cost–benefit analysis, two or more options in a public decision are compared to each other in a calculation that is in a sense quite Benthamite. The most conspicuous difference is that in cost–benefit analysis the common currency is not a fictional util but instead a most real currency, such as dollars or euros. The basic methodology of cost–benefit analysis is to value all the different types of advantages and disadvantages in monetary terms, determine the amount of these advantages and disadvantages for the different alternatives, and then sum up the monetary values for each alternative. The result is a total value for each option under consideration, summing up consequences that may be very different in nature, such as economic costs, risks of disease and death, environmental damage, and so forth. The associated decision rule is to choose an option for which the highest total "economic" value has been calculated.

Arguably, cost–benefit analysis does exactly what Franklin achieved by identifying pairs of advantages and disadvantages that intuitively cancel out each other. But cost–benefit analysis has a major advantage over Franklin's method in terms of cognitive economy: the intuitive comparisons between different types of advantages and disadvantages do not have to be repeated again for each new decision. An example will clarify the difference: Suppose that in an analysis of traffic projects we have concluded, after considerable deliberation, that 5 minutes' daily reduction in travel time for 100,000 persons cancels out 100 cases of asthma. Presumably, it took us a lot of time and trouble to reach that conclusion. The next day we are confronted with a different but similar problem: Can 20 minutes' reduction in travel time for 1000 persons cancel out 4 cases of asthma? Applying Franklin's method would require us to start the whole intuitive process again. We are in a much better position if we have assigned numerical values in some unit (such as money) to a minute's time gain and to a case of asthma. All we have to do when a new case arrives is to apply these values in a new calculation.

But cost–benefit analysis is controversial. Probably the most common criticism is that some negative outcomes, in particular the loss of human lives, cannot be measured in money (Zelizer, 1978; Ashby, 1980; Baram, 1981; Kelman, 1981). It is indeed a rather odd activity to assign economic values to assets that do not have a market value. Prices arise on a market, and since values such as the "human life values" of cost–benefit analysis have no relation to a market, they are not prices. Obviously the assignment of a sum of money to the loss of a human life does not imply that someone can buy another person, or the right to kill her, at that price. Such a value means something else, namely either (1) that society tends to pay up to that sum to save a human life, or (2) that society ought to pay up to that sum to save a human life.

It is important to note that the incommensurability (unmeasurability) of lives in terms of money is only one of many incommensurabilities that cost–benefit analysis has to deal with. There is no definite answer to how many cases of juvenile diabetes correspond to one death, or what amount of human suffering or death corresponds to the extinction of an antelope species. Since such comparisons are technically effectuated in a cost–benefit analysis by assigning monetary values, the problem of incommensurability appears to be a problem of monetization. But even if money were removed from the analysis it would still be necessary to deal with comparisons between deaths, diseases, environmental damage, losses of cultural heritage, and so forth. Hence, the fundamental problem is not that we compare these disparate consequences of our actions in terms of money. Instead, the fundamental problem is that we compare them at all. But of course we have no choice, since such "impossible" comparisons are inherent in all major social decisions. Cost–benefit analysis has the advantage of bringing them to light and making the reduction from a multidimensional to a unidimensional decision problem extremely transparent. If we removed money from the analysis we would still have to deal with comparisons between deaths, diseases, and environmental damage. How should we, for instance, compare the value of saving the Indian tiger to the "tens to hundreds" (Nyhus et al., 2003) of people who are killed by wild tigers every year? This comparison is difficult enough in itself, and whether we make it by translating both values into money does not seem to have much impact on its difficulty.

The reason why monetary units are used in these calculations is of course that they are highly convenient for the purpose. Economic costs and gains are parts of almost all social decisions. Therefore, money is the only unit that is present in almost all decisions, irrespective of social sector. Furthermore, many of the goods and services that need to be taken into account in decisions are bought and sold on markets, and for them we can use market values in the calculations.[3] We need to add fictional values "only" for those items that do not have a market price.

But in spite of its practical advantages, the choice of money as a universal currency for all types of values may have an undesirable impact on our moral deliberations.[4] It has often been argued that certain types of goods should not be valued as market commodities. Instead they should be valued "in accordance with a particular set of norms" appropriate to their nature that differs from how we treat marketable commodities (Anderson, 1990: 72; cf. Anderson, 2000). Putting a monetary price on such objects can then incite us to treat them inappropriately (Titmuss, 1970). In particular, the assignment of an economic value to a human life has been conceived as sending a message that desecrates the value of life. Stuart Hampshire (1972: 9) has warned that the habits of mind engendered by this type of comparisons may lead to "a coarseness and grossness of moral feeling, a blunting of sensibility, and a suppression of individual discrimination and gentleness."

Irrespective of what type of unit is used for the comparisons, cost–benefit analysis and its associated decision rule have another feature that may be morally problematic. As already mentioned, the assignment of values to various aspects of decision outcomes is performed before the actual analysis of the different decision options, and it is assumed to be the same in different cost–benefit analyses.[5] Therefore, cost–benefit analysis is in fact a *two-tiered* process. In the first tier the money equivalents of outcomes such as lost lives, diseases, and different types of environmental damage are determined for cost–benefit analysis in general. In a second tier, these general values are applied to a specific problem, and a complete balance is obtained for each of the options in that decision. This is very different from Franklin's method, in which the comparative weighing of disparate effects took place on a case-by-case basis.

Most decisions involving incommensurable values are not performed in accordance with cost–benefit analysis. Instead they follow an *integrated one-tiered* process, in which the comparative impact of different aspects of the outcome is open to renegotiation in each particular decision. This is exemplified by a national budget process, in which policy goals in areas as diverse as natural security, crime prevention, healthcare, education, research, and social security have to be weighed against each other. This is done in an intuitive fashion, in a process driven by argumentation and negotiation from the

[3] The use of market prices is not morally neutral. Market prices may be influenced by morally indefensible preferences, and there are markets for goods and services whose sale is outright immoral (such as dangerous recreational drugs). However, this is not a specific problem for cost–benefit analysis but one that it shares with real markets. It will therefore not be treated here.

[4] The only common alternative to monetary units is QALYs, quality-adjusted life years, which is used in health care to evaluate the effects of treatments and other interventions.

[5] This appears to be in part due to practical considerations (the first tier is resource intensive) and in part due to a conviction that the calculation values should be the same in all applications. According to Kip Viscusi we should "spend up to the same marginal cost-per-life-saved amount for different agencies" (Viscusi, 2000: 855)

beginning to the very end. The outcome is reached without any explicit translation of one type of values into another.

The two-tiered method of cost–benefit analysis has created incentives to invent "objective" or otherwise uncontroversial ways to perform the first tier. One of the most common first-tier methodologies is contingent valuation. This is a survey-based method to create monetary values for nonmarket goods. It is commonly applied to environmental resources such as the preservation of a species or a natural reserve. People are asked for instance how much they would be willing to pay to preserve the giant panda. This methodology has been subject to severe criticism (Diamond and Hausman, 1994; Hausman, 2012). One of its most serious problems is that the sums mentioned in responses to these questions do not seem to differ in a credible way between questions referring to different objectives. For instance, in one study "willingness to pay to clean one lake is approximately equal to stated willingness to pay to clean up five lakes—including the one asked about individually" (Hausman, 2012). Some studies indicate that many respondents tend to report an amount that would not seriously disturb their normal expenditure and savings patterns, in other words, a sum corresponding to what they would normally be willing to pay to a charity (Beattie et al., 1998).

Another method, particularly common with respect to estimates of the value of life, is to derive values from willingness to pay for related goods. There is a long tradition in cost–benefit analysis of deriving the value of life from estimates of how much male workers are paid extra for working in occupations with a high risk of fatal accidents. These calculations are based on the assumption of a constant marginal value. However, it does not take much reflection to see that this is an untenable assumption. If a worker accepts a risk of 1 in 1000 of being killed in a mining accident next year, it cannot be inferred that he would take a 10 times higher risk against a 10 times higher premium, and it most certainly cannot be inferred that he would accept certainty of being killed against an amount that is 1000 times higher. Furthermore, such marginal values cannot necessarily be transferred to another population or another situation. It is difficult to justify the use of life values derived from marginal risk taking by male workers in cost–benefit analysis for another group that is exposed to a quite different type of risk. This was pointed out by Heinzerling (2000) when she criticized the use of these values to monetize the benefits for women of lifesaving screening to avoid breast cancer. Instead, women could have been asked how much they were prepared to pay for mammography, given realistic assumptions about the risk reduction it gives rise to. Their willingness to pay for reduced risks could then be used in a cost–benefit analysis. Although the use of such values would not have been unproblematic, it would at least have been much closer to the relevant context than the life value that was actually used (Hansson, 2007*a*).

The two-tiered structure of cost–benefit analysis ensures a sort of consistency that can be summarized as "the same life value for all purposes." The same monetary life value is used in transport planning, health-care priority-setting, environmental regulation, and all other areas in which such a value is asked for. However, it is far from evident that this type of consistency is desirable in all cases. We tend to pay more to save a life in some contexts than in others, and some of these differences may be morally justifiable. Many of us would be willing to pay more per life saved in a law enforcement program that reduces the frequency of manslaughter than what we would pay for most other lifesaving activities. There are plausible reasons to do so: We consider homicide a particularly unacceptable form of fatality; and we put a particular value on security against violent crime. Cost–benefit analysis as it is currently performed leads to a disregard of such values, which is of course another proof that it is a far from value-neutral tool. (It is possible to modify cost–benefit analysis so that it treats different deaths differently. That, of course, would not make it value free, only value laden in a different way.)

Since cost–benefit analysis aims at numerical calculations, it also tends to leave out aspects of future developments that can be predicted only in nonquantitative terms. This applies for instance to risks of cultural impoverishment, social isolation, and increased tensions between social strata (Hansson, 1989). Furthermore, owing to their aggregative structure, cost–benefit analyses often leave out social justice and other distributional aspects from the analysis even when they are accessible to quantitative treatment. In response to criticism of such limitations, cost–benefit analysts often point out that the factors that were left out could easily be included in the analysis. It is, for instance, not difficult to put a price on inequality and include it in a cost–benefit analysis, and the same applies to many other aspects that are commonly left out (Johansson-Stenman, 2005; Sen, 2000). However, such all-encompassing cost–benefit analyses are much more seldom performed than they are referred to in defense of the methodology.

Efficiency

Up to now we have discussed attempts to measure all aspects of a decision in one and the same value currency, in order to sum them up and maximize the outcome in terms of the aggregated value. But we have also seen that there are considerable problems with that method. The other major way to deal with plurality of goals is to refrain from reducing the goals to one shared value, and instead restrict the policy advice to what can be said without such a reduction. There are indeed cases when meaningful advice can be given without goal reduction. For a simple example, suppose that you need to borrow an extra table for a party. Your neighbor offers you to borrow one of three tables. You classify their properties as follows:

Table 1: right size, unstable, ugly
Table 2: right size, stable, ugly
Table 3: too small, stable, ugly

If these are all the aspects you wish to take into account then it would be difficult to deny that Table 2 is your best choice. The reason for this is that it *dominates* the other two options. An option dominates another if and only if it is better in at least one aspect and not worse in any aspect. If an option dominates all the other options, then it is the obvious choice.

You also need to borrow a large bowl, and fortunately your neighbor has three that you may choose among. You classify their relevant properties as follows:

Bowl 1: breakable, beautiful
Bowl 2: unbreakable, ugly
Bowl 3: breakable, ugly

Since Bowl 3 is dominated by each of the other two, it should not be your choice. However, neither Bowl 1 nor Bowl 2 dominates the other. To choose between the two you would have to weigh the two criteria against each other. And this is precisely the procedure from the previous section that we have now set out to do without. All we can say is in this case is that Bowl 1 and Bowl 2 are the two undominated options. Given your choice of these two decision criteria, you should therefore choose one of these two bowls, and not choose Bowl 3.

Another, more common way to express this is that the first and second alternatives in this case are the two *efficient* alternatives. An alternative is efficient in relation to a given set of goals if and only if none among the other options is an improvement in terms of one of the goals without also being a change for the worse in terms of at least one of the other goals (Sen, 1975; Le Grand, 1990, 1991). Efficiency is, of course, a central concept in economics. The different types of efficiency discussed in economics differ in the number and nature of the goals that they refer to. *Single-goal efficiency* is also called effectiveness. The concept of effectiveness is often used in technical contexts. For instance, the most effective cleaning agent is the one that removes most of the dirt. *Two-goal efficiency* can be of different types, the most common of which are cost efficiency and productivity. In cost efficiency, one of the goals is to minimize costs, and the other is usually the maximization of production. (In practice strivings for cost efficiency can take the form of minimizing costs relative to a fixed level of output, or maximizing production relative to some fixed cost.) If a health care unit is cost efficient, then we cannot produce the same health care for less money or improved health care for the same money. Productivity is usually conceived as efficiency with respect to the two goals of maximal production and minimal labor input. (In practice, productivity can be achieved by maximizing production volume relative to a fixed labor input, or minimizing labor input relative to a fixed level of output.[6]) Finally, *multi-goal efficiency* is most commonly referred to in discussions of the distribution of economic advantages among individuals. The welfare of each

[6] If the two goals are both measurable in numerical terms, then two-goal efficiency can be expressed as the (single) goal of maximizing a single number. In particular, if one of the goals is to maximize something and the other is to minimize something else (usually expenditure or effort), then we can refer to the ratio between the two numbers instead of using the general definition of two-goal efficiency. For instance, productivity can be characterized as maximization of the output per workhour. In cases when at least one of the goals cannot be expressed numerically, the more general definition cannot be replaced in this way. Such cases are rarely discussed in economics, but they are nevertheless common in social contexts. A young academic may have two goals: to qualify herself as a researcher and as a teacher. Even if these goals are not measurable in numerical terms we may talk about efficiency in the more general two-goal sense, but there is of course no way to reduce this instance of two-goal efficiency to the maximization of a single number.

individual can then be treated as a goal in itself. (See the subsection Interindividual Goal Conflicts).

It is essential to keep in mind that there is no efficiency per se, only efficiency in relation to specified goals. Claims that a certain activity is efficient or inefficient must always be specifiable in term of the goals referred to. Ambiguity in this respect has often led to confusion. For instance, around 1990 a lively debate took place on the efficiency of the slavery-based agricultural economy of the American South (Saraydar, 1989, 1990, 1991; Nye, 1990; Singh and Frantz, 1991; Schmidt, 1994). The plantation system appears to have been efficient in terms of cotton production per unit of labor input, that is, in terms of the two goals to maximize cotton production and to minimize labor input. However, it was far from efficient in terms of welfare production; much more welfare could have been produced with the same labor input (namely in an economy with a free workforce). To clarify this distinction it is necessary to replace unspecified efficiency claims by a precise analysis in which the goals to which efficiency refers are specified.

The injunction to be as efficient as possible should be counted among the economic decision rules, but it is often taken to be such a self-evident rationality requirement that its status as a decision rule is not recognized. Once we have realized that efficiency is always goal relative it becomes obvious that the requirement to be efficient is reasonable only to the extent that the particular efficiency concept to which it refers has sufficient coverage of goals. A good case can be made that we should be efficient with respect to the full set of goals for our endeavors. However, this does not imply that we should be efficient with respect to various subsets of the full set. Consider the following examples:

ECONOMIST: You are building this shieling in a very inefficient way. If you used modern saws you could have obtained the same result in less than half the time.
CARPENTER: Yes, but we also strive to maintain knowledge about old craft methods.

ECONOMIST: Running this factory with only 40 work hours a week is not at all efficient. Shift work would lead to much better use of the expensive investments in machinery.
MANAGER: We have refrained from introducing shift work because of its negative effects on worker welfare.

ECONOMIST: This farm is inefficient. You could produce more wheat per acre if you used more fertilizers.
FARMER: I know, but that would lead to nitrogen leaching and groundwater contamination.

In all these cases (and many others), claims that an activity is inefficient are based on a questionable delimitation of the goals that the activity should satisfy. Furthermore, in cases like these the choice of goals for a social activity is at least in part a moral choice. This brings us to an important way in which seemingly value-free statements about efficiency can in fact be value laden: A claim that an activity is inefficient is value laden to the extent that it is based on the exclusion of goals that might have led to another conclusion.

One possible response to this problem is to explicitly delimit the range of goals, for instance, to those that we consider to be central for economic analysis. If goals such as employee health, environmental quality, and preservation of cultural heritage are regarded as noneconomic, then we can describe the three cases above as cases in which (economic) efficiency clashes with other social goals. Under this approach, (economic) efficiency is not always desirable; in fact this is how laypeople often think about economic efficiency. However, this approach has the disadvantage of not helping us to do as much good as we can for health and the environment with the resources that we have at our disposal. An analysis that includes these goals might, for instance, reveal that we could achieve more for the environment without any sacrifice in terms of our other goals.

Such considerations would seem to lead us to include all relevant goal dimensions in efficiency analysis. But unfortunately, such a practice would create problems because of a phenomenon that may be called the *efficiency dilemma*. It consists in a conflict between goal coverage and decisiveness. On one hand, we want to base our efficiency analysis on a selection of goals that is as exhaustive as possible, so that all important considerations are included. This often leads to the inclusion of a rather long list of goals. On the other hand, we also want our search for efficient options to be of real help in decision making. This requires that the set of efficient options is as small as possible; if it (almost) coincides with the set of all available actions, then the whole exercise is (almost) of no help. Unfortunately, the more aspects we include, the larger can we expect the set of efficient alternatives to be. The reason for this is a very simple mathematical fact: Including an additional aspect in the analysis can make a previously inefficient alternative efficient, but not the other way around. To exemplify this, consider the following set of alternative ways to construct a new road: (Time gain refers to average gain in travel time for road users.)

Option 1: Time gain 5 minutes, cost €100,000,000
Option 2: Time gain 4 minutes, cost €110,000,000
Option 3: Time gain 3 minutes, cost €170,000,000

Here, Option 1 is the only cost-efficient option, and there seems to be no doubt that it should be chosen. But let us add a third dimension, environmental impact. It turns out as follows:

Option 1: Time gain 5 minutes, cost €100,000,000, large environmental damage
Option 2: Time gain 4 minutes, cost €110,000,000, medium environmental damage
Option 3: Time gain 3 minutes, cost €170,000,000, small environmental damage

When the additional dimension has been included, all three options are efficient, which means that efficiency analysis does not help us to make a choice. Unfortunately, this is a common situation. Owing to the efficiency dilemma, decisiveness in efficiency analysis is often achievable only at the price of limiting the number of aspects that are taken into account, and doing so threatens the moral adequacy of the conclusion.

Interindividual Goal Conflicts

In the previous two subsections we had intercategorical goal conflicts as examples. Most of what was said in those sections can be applied to interindividual goal conflicts as well, but the latter are in need of a special discussion because in practice, we treat them differently. The major difference is the assumption that there is one goal per person, usually referring to the welfare or the interests of that person. In a social context, this often means that a large number of goals will be involved.

Interindividual goal conflicts can be illustrated with the help of vectors representing distributions of the good. (We can leave open what the good is, but it may for instance be economic resources.) Thus in a three-person case we can compare vectors such as ‹16, 2, 2› and ‹6, 6, 6›, where the numbers represent the amount of good assigned to each of the three persons. In this particular example, if the numbers are utilitarian "utils," a utilitarian would prefer ‹16, 2, 2› to ‹6, 6, 6›, for the simple reason that the former vector has a higher sum (20) than the latter (18).

The other extreme in this case is to apply the concept of efficiency. Neither ‹16, 2, 2› nor ‹6, 6, 6› dominates the other, since the first individual is worse off in ‹6, 6, 6› and the other two are worse off in ‹16, 2, 2›. If these two are the only options that we can choose between, then they are both efficient. This type of efficiency is called Pareto efficiency. (The original term "Pareto optimality" is misleading and should be avoided.) Two major decision rules are based on this concept (Sen, 1987).[7] The *weak Pareto rule* recommends that we perform Pareto efficient changes (Pareto improvements) if we have a chance to do so, but it has no recommendations on what to do otherwise. Thus suppose that the current situation is ‹10, 3, 3› and we have a chance to change either to ‹21, 3, 3›, ‹9, 9, 9›, or ‹6, 3, 3›. The weak Pareto rule recommends a change to ‹21, 3, 3› since it is a Pareto improvement (someone gains and no one loses). It advises against a change to ‹6, 3, 3› since that would represent a Pareto loss. However, this rule is agnostic about a change to ‹9, 9, 9› since such a change is neither a Pareto improvement nor a Pareto loss.

[7] There is also a third, the so-called Potential Pareto Criterion or Kaldor-Hicks Criterion. According to this criterion, a policy change is commendable if it would have been possible for those whom it makes better off to compensate those who were initially worse off, so that in the end no one would lose and at least one would gain from the combination of the measure and the posterior redistribution. This criterion is often invoked in defense of cost-benefit analyses that are purely aggregative, that is, performed as if the distribution of benefits and detriments did not matter. It was originally justified by Nicholas Kaldor as follows: "In all cases, therefore, where a certain policy leads to an increase in physical productivity, and thus of aggregate real income, the economist's case for the policy is quite unaffected by the question of the comparability of individual satisfactions; since in all such cases it is *possible* to make everybody better off than before, or at any rate to make some people better off without making anybody worse off" (Kaldor, 1939: 550). However, the justificatory power of a transaction that does not take place is obviously nil (Raterman, 2012).

The *strong Pareto rule* recommends that we only perform Pareto improvements, and no other changes. It differs from the weak Pareto rule in advising against changes that are neither Pareto improvements nor Pareto losses. Thus, in our example it would advise in favor of a change to ‹21, 3, 3› and against changes to ‹9, 9, 9› as well as ‹6, 3, 3›. Opposition to change such as that from ‹10, 3, 3› to ‹9, 9, 9›, which increases both equality and total welfare, is of course not a morally neutral standpoint. To the contrary, it has immediate moral and political implications.

The weak (but not the strong) Pareto rule is plausible, given that we distribute "the good" to individuals. But if the ultimate goal is well-being, then we cannot distribute the ultimate good. Instead, we can (sometimes) distribute something that promotes wellbeing. Let us call that which is distributed "resources." The usefulness of weak Pareto efficiency in economic theory is based on a simple but remarkably powerful assumption on the relationship between resources and well-being: It is assumed that each individual's well-being increases when her resources increase. Nothing needs to be assumed about how much it increases. To see how this assumption works, again consider a small society with three individuals. Owing to our assumption there is for each of them a function from resources to well-being. Individual 1's function f_1 satisfies the simple criterion that for any two amounts x and y of resources:

$$f_1(x) < f_1(y) \text{ holds if and only if } x < y$$

In other words, more resources always generate more well-being, and fewer resources always generate less well-being. The same holds for the corresponding functions f_2 and f_3 of the other two persons. Now consider any two distributions of resources, represented by the vectors $\langle x, y, z \rangle$ and $\langle x', y', z'$. It is easy to show that $\langle x, y, z \rangle$ dominates over $\langle x', y', z' \rangle$ if and only if $\langle f_1(x), f_2(y), f_3(z), \rangle$ dominates over $\langle f_1(x'), f_2(y'), f_3(z') \rangle$. From this it follows that from the viewpoint of Pareto efficiency it makes no difference if we consider a set of resource vectors or the corresponding set of well-being vectors; the same changes will be Pareto improvements on both counts. This simple property of Pareto efficiency is a large part of the explanation of why it is such a useful tool in economics.

But the formal elegance of this conclusion is based on an assumption that is quite problematic both empirically and morally, namely the assumption that each individual's well-being depends exclusively on her or his own material resources. In actual life, each individual's well-being depends also on other factors, among them material resources that belong to other persons. Such dependencies can come in many variants. For a simple example, suppose that you live in a small village with three inhabitants. You have eight units of resources.

Case 1: The resource vector of the village is ‹8, 8, 8›.
Case 2: The resource vector of the village is ‹32, 30, 8›.

We might expect the well-being that you derive from your eight units of resources to be much lower in the second case, owing to the negative effects of the inferior comparative position (Hirsch, 1976; Hansson 2004). This contradicts the assumption just referred to that your well-being is strictly a function of (i.e., only depends on) the resources at your own disposal. Your relative position, that is, how the resources at your disposal relate to those of the other inhabitants, also has a role. Taking such "positional" effects into account would seem to be necessary not only descriptively but also from the viewpoint of moral philosophy, since the effects of being in an inferior position has moral implications (Wilkinson and Pickett, 2009). As soon as we allow for positional effects, Pareto efficiency on the two levels will no longer coincide. In particular, the well-being vector associated with ‹32, 30, 8› will not be an improvement over that associated with ‹8, 8, 8› since the well-being of the third individual is expectedly worse in the former case owing to positional effects.

Intertemporal Conflicts

Sometimes when summarizing the advantages and disadvantages of an option we find that they materialize at different points in time. For the smoker, the most important positive effect of smoking is immediate: she avoids the symptoms of nicotine withdrawal. The most important negative effect is the risk of serious disease that will typically materialize decades later. (About half of smokers die prematurely due to smoking [Boyle, 1997].) In climate and environmental policies, we often consider measures that cost money today but have their positive effects much later. Nuclear waste management provides what is perhaps the most extreme example of such temporal discrepancies: on one hand energy is produced to be consumed now, while on the other hand the potential damages from nuclear waste may materialize hundreds of thousands of years hence.

Intertemporal conflicts seldom come alone. They are often combined with both intercategorical and interindividual conflicts, and with uncertainty. We can see this from the two examples just mentioned. The smoker's decision whether to (try to) stop smoking is not only intertemporal. It is in most cases to some extent also an interindividual decision (i.e., unless she always smokes at sufficient distance from others to prevent secondary exposure, and no one else is affected by her welfare). It is also a decision under uncertainty since not all smokers are affected by serious smoking-related disease. The social decision on nuclear waste is intertemporal, intercategorical, and interindividual, and it takes place under uncertainty.

In a systematic treatment these components of decision problems should be discussed separately as far as possible. To begin with, let us consider purely intertemporal decisions, that is, decisions in which intercategorical, interindividual, and uncertainty-related aspects are either absent or so unimportant that we are justified in neglecting them. Such situations are in fact common, and as children we were all told how to deal with them:

CHILD: Father, I want to eat all the ice cream today.

FATHER: But then there will nothing left for tomorrow. Think of how sorry you will be then. Eat half of it, and save the other half for tomorrow.

The typical parents' advice in issues like this is to divide the limited resource in equal parts between the instances of consumption. The presumption seems to be that tomorrow's enjoyment is equally valuable as today's. The child would typically not be enjoined, for instance, to "eat two thirds today and leave a third for tomorrow, since having a good time tomorrow is not worth as much as having a good time today."

Moral philosophers have not spent much effort on (purely) intertemporal issues, but instead have focused on interindividual ones. However, some moral philosophers have commented on the intertemporal issues within a person's own life, and they have essentially given the same advice as the parent in the above ice cream example. For instance, Thomas Hobbes (1588–1679) regretted that "men cannot put off this same irrational appetite, whereby they greedily prefer the present good (to which, by strict consequence, many unforseen evils do adhere) before the future." (Hobbes, [1642] 1841: 48).[8] Henry Sidgwick (1838–1900) wrote that proximity in time "is a property which it is reasonable to disregard except in so far as it diminishes uncertainty."

> For my feelings a year hence should be just as important to me as my feelings next minute, if only I could make an equally sure forecast of them. Indeed this equal and impartial concern for all parts of one's conscious life is perhaps the most prominent element in the common notion of the *rational*—as apposed to the merely *impulsive*—pursuit of pleasure. (Sidgwick, 1907: 124; cf. 381)

More recently, Thomas Nagel proposed "a standpoint of temporal neutrality towards the events of our lives" (Nagel, 1970: 61). To the extent that other moral philosophers have expressed views on the matter, this is usually the view they have expressed.[9]

The major contribution of economics to the evaluation of future outcomes is the method of discounting future values. It was originally developed for money, and based on the assumption of a foreseeable, positive interest rate. For example, suppose that the interest rate is constantly 3 percent in real terms, and furthermore suppose that we want to have €100,000 in 10 years. Then it is sufficient to deposit €74,400 in the bank. We can therefore say that the "present cost" of having €100,000 10 years from now is €74,400. Alternatively, we can say that the "present value" of receiving €100,000 10 years from now is €74,400. With a similar argument, a loss €100,000 10 years from now corresponds to a loss of €74,400 today. In this way, we can "convert" future monetary value into current monetary value and vice versa.[10]

8 *De Cive*, Chapter 3, §32. In Latin: "homines exuere non possunt appetitum illum irrationalem, quo bona praesentia (quibus, arcta consequentia, multa adhaerent improvisa mala) prae futuris appetunt."

9 See also Rawls (1972: 422–423), Williams (1976), Ladmore (1999), Dickenson (1991), and Hansson (2007*b*, 2013).

10 More precisely, the value of a future good is assumed to be equal to the product of two factors. One of these is a time-independent evaluation of the good in question, that is, the value of having it now. The other factor represents the subject's "pure time preferences." It is a function of the length of the delay, and is the same for all types of goods. This can be summarized in the formula is $v_0(x) = v_t(x) \times 1/(1+r)^t$, where x is the object whose value we are converting, $v_0(x)$ its present value, $v_t(x)$ its value after t years and r the interest rate (Samuelson, 1937).

The practice of discounting has often been seen as at variance with the moral principle of temporal neutrality just referred to. That, however, is not necessarily true since the relationship between the two principles depends on how much money can buy at different points in time. If you can buy exactly as much of what you want to buy for €74,400 today as you can for €100,000 in 10 years, then discounting will be perfectly compatible with temporal neutrality in the moral sense. If you can buy more of what you want for €74,400 now than you can for €100,000 in 10 years, then discounting overrates future values, in comparison to what temporal neutrality prescribes. If it is the other way around, then discounting underrates future values. Which of these is the case is an empirical, not a conceptual question.

In cost–benefit analysis, discounting is the standard way to deal with intertemporal conflicts. It is routinely used for comparisons that are both intertemporal and interindividual. Suppose for instance that we discuss measures that would prevent an accident 15 years into the future in which 31 persons would die. With a 3 percent interest rate, the formula tells us to value the loss of 31 lives in 15 years the same way that we would value a loss of 20 lives today.[11]

However, although discounting is a reasonable practice for real market prices, it is much more problematic when applied to the calculation values for nonmarket entities that are used in cost–benefit analysis. Obviously, there is no interest rate for lives, and we cannot convert human lives today directly into human lives in the future. The same applies to other nonmarket goods such as environmental preservation. The only feasible way to defend discounting of nonmarket goods is indirect: they are discounted because they can be converted to money, and money can be discounted. Therefore, a justification for discounting for instance future losses in lives presupposes a series of three conversions:

1. From human lives today to money today
2. From money today to money in the future
3. From money at some future point in time to lives at that same future point in time

Let us consider each of these steps in turn. The first step is problematic for the reasons discussed in the subsection The Reductive Approach. It can be performed as a way to summarize how we in practice settle conflicts between incommensurables, but the process of doing so is very different in nature from the market mechanisms that give rise to prices in the ordinary sense of the word. The second step is a standard economic procedure. In the time spans that economists usually work with, it is both justified and indispensible. In longer time spans, its value is more uncertain since we cannot take for granted that the economy will function in the same way as today thousands of years ahead. But in the third step, the whole conversion breaks down. There is no ground whatsoever for projecting the tradeoffs that we make today between human lives and

[11] $31 \times 1/1{,}03^{15} \approx 20$.

money far off into the future. We have no reason to believe that our present priorities in these respects will remain the same over a longer period of time. (This is corroborated by historical experience. Although difficult to measure, our willingness to accept losses in lives seems to have decreased substantially; see Smith, 2005.)

It should also be noted that discounting of lives yields absurd results if applied to long time periods. Consider, as a simple schematic example, a hypothetical choice between the following two actions:

1. Killing one person now.
2. Performing an action today that will lead to the death of the whole population of the earth, 10 billion people, in the year 2800.

If we apply a discount rate of 3 percent, then the first of these actions will be worse than the second. The example is unrealistic, but it illustrates that even very large disasters count as almost nothing if they take place a couple of hundred years from now. (Lowering the discount rate only delays this effect. With a discount rate of 0.5 percent it will still be worse that one person dies today than that 10 billion people die in 4620 years.)

Summing this up, the common economic decision rule for future outcomes, namely to discount them, is sound in the short or medium run if applied to money and to goods with a monetary price. However, discounting is unjustified for goods without a price (even if a nonmarket monetary value has been assigned to it). The uncertainty component of intertemporal decision problems has not been discussed here; it is taken up in the subsection Uncertainty about the Future.

Decision Rules for Uncertainty

Up to now we have abstracted from uncertainty, that is, we have assumed that we know the consequences of the different options in our decisions. That is of course an idealization. In real life, uncertainty about future consequences is ubiquitous, and it is often the most important source of difficulties, disagreements, and irresoluteness in our decisions. The most common way to structure these difficulties is to assign probabilities to the various outcomes under consideration. This usually makes decision problems much easier to tackle. Consider, for instance, a company's decision on whether to buy one of its competitors. Someone points out: "It is possible that this acquisition will be stopped by the antitrust authorities." It is difficult to know what weight to assign to such a supposition. It is much easier to act on more specified information such as "according to our experts, there is a 90 percent probability that the acquisition will be stopped by the antitrust authorities."

The standard terminology distinguishes between decision making under uncertainty and decision making under risk. A decision is said to take place under risk if the probabilities of the relevant outcomes are assumed to be known by the decision maker. If these probabilities are unknown or only insufficiently known, then the decision is said to take place under uncertainty (Luce and Raiffa, 1957: 13). It should be noted that a decision "under risk" need not be one in which the probabilities are known. It is sufficient that they are assumed to be known. It should also be noted that the term "uncertainty" is ambiguous since it is used both in the sense just mentioned and as a general term also covering decision making under risk.

Expected Utility and Its Limitations

The standard rule for decision making under risk is expected utility maximization. The word "expected" refers here to probability-weighting, and the rule recommends the use probability-weighted values (statistical expectation values) for all outcome measures. If there is a probability of 0.7 to lose €1,000,000 then that is counted as a loss of €700,000. If there is a probability of 0.1 to gain $20,000 then that is counted as an income of $2000. It there is a probability of 0.01 of an accident that will kill 200 persons, then that is counted as equivalent with certainty that 2 persons will be killed. This is how both risks and uncertain benefits are dealt with in cost–benefit analysis.

The decision rule prescribing maximization of expected utility is often described as the "risk-neutral" decision rule. By this is meant that it puts neither too large nor too small an emphasis on undesired, uncertain outcomes. (Decision rules that put more emphasis on avoiding undesired outcomes than what expected utility maximization does are called risk averse, and those deviating in the opposite direction are called risk prone.) It is often assumed that deviations from risk-neutrality in this sense are irrational and that the expected utility rule is a requirement of instrumental reason, devoid of moral contents (Charnley, 1999, 2000; Durodié, 2003). However, that turns out to be far from true, and this for at least two major reasons.

The first reason is that probability estimates do not tell us all we need to know about the uncertainties we wish to take into account. To see that, let us first consider a simple, schematic example: A dime has been found among the property of a deceased cardsharp. We suspect that the coin may be unfair, but we have no clue to whether it is in that case biased toward heads or tails. Someone decides to toss the coin. If I have to assign a probability that it will yield heads, then I will say 0.5. This is the same answer that I would have given before someone tossed a coin that I knew to be fair. However, although the probabilities are the same, I am much more uncertain about the behavior of the cardsharp's coin than about that of the ordinary coin.

Suppose that we throw the coin and get heads 10 times in a row. If we had very good reasons to believe that the coin is fair, then we would see this as an unusual random event, and we would assign the probability 0.5 to the next throw yielding heads. But since it is a coin from the cardsharp's collection, we tend to see 10 heads in a row as a strong indication that the coin is biased in favor of heads. Therefore, we have good reasons to assign a probability higher than 0.5 to the event of this coin yielding heads when tossed an 11th time.

All this can be expressed in exact mathematical terms, but I will leave out that aspect here.[12] Instead, let us consider a highly important practical case, namely climate change. There is scientific uncertainty regarding the effects on the future climate of any possible future pattern of greenhouse gas emissions. We may specify this as uncertainty in the choice among several scientific models that yield different probabilities of climate events. The consensus or near-consensus of climate scientists is stated in the reports of the IPCC (Intergovernmental Panel on Climate Change). There is, however, a possibility that the IPCC's conclusions are too pessimistic. It is at least in principle possible that the greenhouse effect is completely counterbalanced by other mechanisms, so that no global warming disaster is approaching. On the other hand, there is also a possibility that global warming will accelerate much faster than what the IPCC predicts. Consider the probability of some specific potential effect of global warming (such as a large sea level rise within 20 years). For concreteness, we may assume that the probability of that event is 0.01 according to the IPCC, 0.9 according to the more pessimistic view, and 0 according to the more optimistic view. The standard approach in such situations is to use the appraisal that has the highest credibility. In our case, this means that decisions will be based on the IPCC's estimate that the probability is 0.01. However, although convenient, this approach is obviously flawed. In an adequate appraisal of the probability in question, the other two possibilities need to be taken into account. Unless the more pessimistic of the two is highly improbable, it could be seen as dangerously incautious not to take it into account (Hansson, 2006).

The second problem with the expected utility rule is that even if we actually know the probabilities, it does not follow that we have to base our decisions on probability-weighting and expected utility maximization. Suppose that an eccentric person offers you a bet that is based on repeated tosses of a fair coin of your own choice. If the coin yields heads n times in a row, then you have to give everything you own to the eccentric. Otherwise, he will pay you €100,000. According to the standard assumptions of expected utility maximization, there must be some n such that you are willing to play the game. However, it is not necessarily irrational to refuse the bet, simply on the ground that you are not willing to risk losing all that you own. In policy discussions the avoidance of very large catastrophes, such as a nuclear or chemical accident costing thousands of human lives, is often given higher priority than what is warranted by the statistically expected number of deaths. It has also been argued that as a matter of principle, serious events with low probabilities should be given a higher weight in decision making than what they receive in the expected utility model (O'Riordan and Cameron, 1994; O'Riordan et al., 2001; Burgos and Defeo, 2004).

In interindividual decision problems, there are additional moral reasons to deviate from the expected utility rule:

> In an acute situation we have to choose between two ways to repair a serious gas leakage in the machine-room of a chemical factory. One of the options is to send in the

[12] See Hansson (2008, 2009) for a formal treatment.

> repairman immediately. There is only one person at hand who is competent to do the job. He will run a risk of 0.9 to die due to an explosion of the gas immediately after he has performed the necessary technical operations. The other option is to immediately let out gas into the environment. In that case, the repairman will run no particular risk, but each of 10,000 persons in the immediate vicinity of the plant runs a risk of 0.001 to be killed by the toxic effects of the gas. (Hansson, 1993: 24, 2013: 27)

In this case, to maximize expected utility we would have to send in the repairman. However, that would be a morally repulsive decision. In this and many other cases, a rational decision maker may refrain from maximizing expected utility (minimizing expected damage) for a moral reason, namely to avoid being unfair to a single individual.

Alternative Decision Rules

One alternative to expected utility maximization is to completely disregard probabilities and focus entirely on avoiding the worst possibilities. This is done by using the maximin decision rule. It requires that we identify, for each alternative action, its security level, that is (the value of) the worst possible outcome that it can give rise to. We then have to choose an alternative with a maximal security level, thus maximizing the minimal outcome. This means that we completely disregard all but the worst possible outcomes of an action. Not surprisingly, the use of such a decision rule can have strange consequences.

> You are offered the choice between two investments. Option A yields a 99 percent chance of gaining €2000 and a 1 percent chance of gaining only €50. Option B yields a gain of €60 for sure.

The maximin rule recommends you to choose option B. As this example shows, the total neglect of chances and of all outcomes but the worst renders this rule unworkable in practice.[13]

An intermediate solution seems more promising. We can decide on the degree of cautiousness that we wish to apply. Mathematically it can take the form of a number c between 0 and 1, called the *cautiousness index*. 0 represents minimal and 1 maximal cautiousness. For each option x in the decision, let SEC(x) be its security value (the value of its worst possible outcome) and EU(x) it expectation value (expected utility). The rule requires that we choose an option with a maximal value of

$$c \times \mathrm{SEC}(x) + (1 - \mathrm{c}) \times \mathrm{EU}(x)$$

[13] The maximax rule (choosing an option whose best outcome is at least as good as that of any other option) has the same problem. Although maximax decision making is seldom recommended, it appears to be common in practice (DeMartino, 2011; cf. Hansson, 2006: 234n).

For $c = 0$ this coincides with the expected utility rule and for $c = 1$ with the maximin rule. We can of course select different values of c for different decision problems, depending on what degree of cautiousness we consider to be appropriate.[14]

The repertoire of available methods for decision making becomes larger if we replace the single probability function of the traditional model by a credal set, by which is meant a set of probability functions. The credal set is interpreted as consisting of the plausible probability functions. For a simple example, consider the following:

> There are two jars in the room. One of them contains 5 red and 95 black balls. The other contains 95 red and 5 black ones. Someone puts one of the jars—you do not know which—in front of you and asks: "If you draw a ball from this jar, what is the probability that it is red?"

A quite natural answer would be "It is either 0.05 or 0.95." More precisely, you hesitate between two probability functions, p_1 and p_2, such that p_1 assigns the probability 0.05 and p_2 the probability 0.95 to the ball you draw being red. Your credal set is then $\{p_1, p_2\}$. Similarly, in the above example of the cardsharp's coin, the credal set may, for instance, consist of all probability functions that assign a value between 0.3 and 0.7 to the coin yielding heads.[15]

Even more information can be encoded if we introduce second-order probabilities, that is, probabilities over probabilities. In the example of the two jars, it would be quite plausible to say that p_1 and p_2 are equally probable. We can then assign the (second-order) probability 0.5 to each of them. This and other, more elaborate representations of uncertainties allow for more sophisticated decision rules than the expected utility rule (Walley, 2000; Halpern, 2003; Hansson, 2016) but none of these constructions have gained much influence. Expected utility maximization is still the dominating economic decision rule for decision making under uncertainty.

Uncertainty about the Future

Finally, let us return to the issue that was left open in the subsection Intertemporal Conflicts, namely how to deal with intertemporal decisions in which there is uncertainty about the future. According to the standard approach to economic discounting, one of the functions of the discount rate is to reflect these uncertainties. However, a

[14] This type of index is usually called an optimism–pessimism index, but that is a misleading name. A person is pessimistic with respect to a possible undesirable event if she believes that its probability is high or its consequences large, or both. A person is cautious with respect to that same event if she is willing to take significant trouble to decrease its probability or limit its consequences, or both. Pessimism and cautiousness need not coincide.

[15] Higher or lower values do not seem to be technically feasible for coins (Gelman and Nolan, 2002).

few examples are sufficient to show that uncertainties about the future seldom have the structure of interest rates:

> The choice between a benefit now and the same benefit in 10 years' time is not the same for a person in her late 80s as it is for a healthy person in her 20s. A constant discount rate cannot reflect these differences.
>
> We know fairly well what effects a massive mercury spillage in a lake today will have on life in the lake a decade later. For spillages of most other chemical substances we do not have that information. Therefore the uncertainty of such events is much larger. A discount rate that is the same for all decisions cannot capture the difference.
>
> We have limited knowledge about the persistence of a particular substance in the environment: We know that its half-life in the environment is between 2 and 20 years, but we cannot say anything more precise. Then our uncertainty is small about its environmental concentration one month from now, large about its concentration in 20 years and small about its concentration in 400 years. A constant discount rate cannot reflect these differences.

The methods introduced in the previous subsection are much more useful than a discount rate to deal with uncertainty about the future. A person choosing between taking a long vacation trip now or taking it in 10 years can, for instance, think in terms of a credal set consisting of two probability functions: one in which she is alive and well in 10 years and one in which she is not. If she assigns second-order probabilities to them, then these probabilities will depend on her age and health status (contrary to a discount rate that is assumed to be the same for all persons and all decision problems). Similarly, when we are uncertain about the future effects of some environmental pollution, we can describe these uncertainties with the help of a credal set containing several probability functions corresponding to the possibilities that scientists hesitate between. Again, second-order probabilities can be used to represent the credibility of these different scenarios.

In general, discounting is unsuitable to represent our uncertainty about the future. Such uncertainty is much better represented by credal sets and second-order probabilities. The latter representation also has the advantage of leaving a choice open between different decision rules depending, for instance, on what degree of cautiousness we want to apply.

Conclusion

The use of decision rules has obvious advantages. Rules can simplify decision making and make it more consistent. But the employment of decision rules can also have negative effects. When using them we achieve simplicity by restricting the amount of information that we take into account in any particular decision. This may lead to disregard for aspects of the decision that should have been taken into account. In this way, the potential for a normative problem is inherent in the very notion of a decision rule. In a sense rules can be said to function as blinkers on a horse: They make it possible to move forward, but only at the price of leaving much unseen. This presentation has focused on some of the problems with common economic decision rules, and in particular on how their use makes value assumptions invisible that should instead have been brought forward and discussed.

So what should we do? There are two major strategies for improvement. One is to develop improved decision rules, for instance, rules that make the value assumptions visible (such as the cautiousness index of the subsection Alternative Decision Rules). The other strategy is to improve the way in which decision rules are used, for instance, by always clarifying to decision makers what aspects have been excluded from consideration and what the effects of including them might have been. In my view, these two strategies should be combined to develop a new style of policy advice that highlights the value issues instead of hiding them in the dark.

Acknowledgment

I thank George DeMartino for unusually helpful comments on an earlier version of this chapter.

References

Anderson, Elizabeth S. 1990. "Is Women's Labor a Commodity? *Philosophy and Public Affairs* 19: 71–92.

Anderson, Elizabeth S. 2000. "Why Commercial Surrogate Motherhood Unethically Commodifies Women and Children: Reply to McLachlan and Swales." *Health Care Analysis* 8: 19–26.

Ashby, Eric. 1980. "What Price the Furbish Lousewort?" *Environmental Science & Technology* 14: 1176–1181.

Baram, Michael S. 1981. "The Use of Cost-Benefit Analysis in Regulatory Decision-making Is Proving Harmful to Public Health." *Annals of the New York Academy of Sciences* 363: 123–128.

Beattie, J., Covey, J., Dolan, P., Hopkins, L., Jones-Lee, M., Loomes, G., Pidgeon, N., Robinson, A., and Spencer, A. 1998. "On the Contingent Valuation of Safety and the Safety of Contingent Valuation: Part 1–Caveat Investigator." *Journal of Risk and Uncertainty* 17: 5–25.

Bentham, Jeremy. 1780. *An Introduction to the Principles of Morals and Legislation.* London: T. Payne. (http://gallica.bnf.fr/ark:/12148/bpt6k93974k/f2.image.r=.langEN)

Boyle, P. 1997. "Cancer, Cigarette Smoking and Premature Death in Europe: A Review Including the Recommendations of European Cancer Experts Consensus Meeting, Helsinki, October 1996." *Lung Cancer* 17(1): 1–60.

Burgos, R., and Defeo, O. 2004. "Long-term Population Structure, Mortality and Modeling of a Tropical Multi-fleet Fishery: The Red Grouper Epinephelus morio of the Campeche Bank, Gulf of Mexico." *Fisheries Research* 66: 325–335.

Charnley, G. 1999. "President's Message." *RISK Newsletter* 19 (2): 2.

Charnley, G. 2000. "1999 Annual Meeting: Past President's Message: Risk Analysis under Fire." *RISK Newsletter* 20(1): 3.

DeMartino, George F. 2011. *The Economist's Oath: On the Need for and Content of Professional Economic Ethics*. Oxford: Oxford University Press.

Diamond, Peter A., and Hausman, Jerry A. 1994. "Contingent Valuation: Is some Number Better than No Number?" *Journal of Economic Perspectives* 8: 45–64.

Dickenson, Donna. 1991. *Moral Luck in Medical Ethics and Practical Politics*. Aldershot, UK: Avebury.

Durodié, Bill. 2003. "The True Cost of Precautionary Chemicals Regulation." *Risk Analysis* 23: 389–398.

Franklin, Benjamin. 1970. *The Writings of Benjamin Franklin, Vol. V, 1767–1772*, edited by Albert Henry Smyth. New York: Haskell House.

Gelman, Andrew, and Nolan, Deborah. 2002. "You Can Load a Die, but You Can't Bias a Coin." *American Statistician* 56: 308–311.

Halpern, Joseph. 2003. *Reasoning about Uncertainty*. Cambridge, MA: MIT Press.

Hampshire, Stuart. 1972. *Morality and Pessimism*. Cambridge, UK: Cambridge University Press.

Hampton, J. 1995. "Does Hume Have an Instrumental Conception of Practical Reason?" *Hume Studies* 21: 57–74.

Hansson, Sven Ove. 1989. "Dimensions of Risk." *Risk Analysis* 9: 107–112.

Hansson, Sven Ove. 1993. "The False Promises of Risk Analysis. *Ratio* 6: 16–26.

Hansson, Sven Ove. 2004. "Welfare, Justice, and Pareto Efficiency." *Ethical Theory and Moral Practice* 7: 361–380.

Hansson, Sven Ove. 2006. "Economic (Ir)rationality in Risk Analysis." *Economics and Philosophy* 22: 231–241.

Hansson, Sven Ove. 2007*a*. "Philosophical Problems in Cost-Benefit Analysis." *Economics and Philosophy* 23: 163–183.

Hansson, Sven Ove. 2007*b*. "Hypothetical Retrospection." *Ethical Theory and Moral Practice* 10: 145–157.

Hansson, Sven Ove. 2008. "Do We Need Second-order Probabilities?" *Dialectica* 62: 525–533.

Hansson, Sven Ove. 2009. "Measuring Uncertainty." *Studia Logica* 93: 21–40.

Hansson, Sven Ove. 2013. *The Ethics of Risk. Ethical Analysis in an Uncertain World*. London: Palgrave Macmillan.

Hansson, Sven Ove. 2016. "Representing Uncertainty. In *A Handbook of Formal Philosophy*, edited by Sven Ove Hansson and Vincent F. Hendricks. New York: Springer.

Hausman, Jerry. 2012. "Contingent Valuation: From Dubious to Hopeless." *Journal of Economic Perspectives* 26: 43–56.

Heinzerling, L. 2000. "The Rights of Statistical People." *Harvard Environmental Law Review* 24: 189–207.

Hirsch, F. 1976. *Social Limits of Growth*. Cambridge, MA: Harvard University Press.

Hobbes, Thomas. [1642] 1841. De Cive in English Works, Vol. 2, edited by William Molesworth. London: Bohn.

Johansson-Stenman, Olof. 2005. "Distributional Weights in Cost-Benefit Analysis–Should We Forget about Them?" *Land Economics* 81: 337–352.

Kaldor, Nicholas. 1939. "Welfare Propositions of Economics and Interpersonal Comparisons of Utility." *Economic Journal* 49: 549–552.
Kelman, Steven. 1981. "Cost-Benefit Analysis. An Ethical Critique." *Regulation* 5: 33–40.
Ladmore, Charles. 1999. "The Idea of a Life Plan." *Social Philosophy and Policy* 16: 96–112.
Le Grand, Julian. 1990. "Equity versus Efficiency: The Elusive Trade-off." *Ethics* 100: 554–568.
Le Grand, Julian. 1991. *Equity and Choice. An Essay in Economics and Applied Philosophy*. London: Harper Collins Academic.
Luce, Duncan R., and Howard, Raiffa. 1957. *Games and Decisions. Introduction and Critical Survey*. New York: John Wiley & Sons.
Millgram, E. 1995. "Was Hume a Humean?" *Hume Studies* 21(1): 75–93.
Nagel, Thomas. 1970. *The Possibility of Altruism*. Oxford: Clarendon Press.
Nye, John Vincent. 1990. "The Conflation of Productivity and Efficiency in Economics and Economic History—A Comment." *Economics and Philosophy* 6: 147–152.
Nyhus, P. J., Tilson, R. L., and Tomlinson, J. L. 2003. "Dangerous Animals in Captivity: Ex Situ Tiger Conflict and Implications for Private Ownership of Exotic Animals." *Zoo Biology* 22: 573–586.
O'Riordan, T., and Cameron, J., eds., 1994. *Interpreting the Precautionary Principle*. London: Earthscan.
O'Riordan, T., Cameron, J., and Jordan, A., eds. 2001. *Reinterpreting the Precautionary Principle*. London: Cameron May.
Raterman, Ty. 2012. "Regulation, Compensation, and the Loss of Life: What Cost-Benefit Analysis Really Requires." *Ethics, Policy and Environment* 15: 97–118.
Rawls, John. 1972. *A Theory of Justice*. Oxford: Oxford University Press.
Samuelson, P. A. 1937. "A Note on Measurement of Utility." *Review of Economic Studies* 4: 155–161.
Saraydar, Edward. 1989. "The Conflation of Productivity and Efficiency in Economics and Economic History." *Economics and Philosophy* 5: 55–67.
Saraydar, Edward. 1990. "The Inefficiency of Some Efficiency Comparisons. A Reply to Nye." *Economics and Philosophy* 6: 153–155.
Saraydar, Edward. 1991. "Productivity and X-efficiency." *Economics and Philosophy* 7: 91–92.
Schmidt, Volker H. 1994. "Some Equity–Efficiency Trade-offs in the Provision of Scarce Goods: The Case of Lifesaving Medical Resources." *Journal of Political Philosophy* 2: 44–66.
Sen, Amartya. 1975. "The Concept of Efficiency. In *Contemporary Issues in Economics*, edited by M. Parkin and A. R. Nobay, pp. 196–210. Manchester: Manchester University Press.
Sen, Amartya. 1987. *On Ethics and Economics*. Oxford: Basil Blackwell.
Sen, Amartya. 2000. "The Discipline of Cost-Benefit Analysis." *Journal of Legal Studies* 29(S2): 931–952.
Sidgwick, H. 1907. *The Methods of Ethics*. London: Macmillan.
Singh, Harinder och Roger Frantz. 1991. "The Conflation of Productivity and Efficiency in Economics and Economic History." *Economics and Philosophy* 7: 87–89.
Smith, Hugh. 2005. "What Costs Will Democracies Bear? A Review of Popular Theories of Casualty Aversion." *Armed Forces and Society* 31: 487–512.
Titmuss, Richard M. 1970. *The Gift Relationship: From Human Blood to Social Policy*. London: George Allen & Unwin.
Viscusi, W. K. 2000. "Risk Equity." *Journal of Legal Studies* 29: 843–871.
Walley, Peter. 2000. "Towards a Unified Theory of Imprecise Probability." *International Journal of Approximate Reasoning* 24: 125–148.

Wilkinson, Richard G., and Pickett, Kate. 2009. *The Spirit Level: Why More Equal Societies Almost Always Do Better*. London: Allen Lane.

Williams, Bernard. 1976. "Moral Luck." *Aristotelian Society, Supplementary Volume*50: 115–135.

Zelizer, Viviana A. 1978. "Human Values and the Market: The Case of Life Insurance and Death in 19th-Century America." *American Journal of Sociology* 84: 591–610.

CHAPTER 4

IN PRAISE OF IMPERFECT COMMITMENT

An Ethic of Power, Professionalism and Risk

SHARON D. WELCH

THERE is one point on which we have political consensus in the United States—there is little, if any, satisfaction with the economic status quo, and there are active calls for fundamental social and political change. Part of the challenge facing us, however, is not just the specific issue of economic policy but the means through which professionals address the making of public policy, and how we as a culture reckon with unpredictability, risk, and intrinsic epistemic fallibility.[1]

In this chapter I explore what it takes for economists, other professional policy advocates, and social activists to engage in forms of social analysis and political engagement that acknowledge the limitations of our knowledge of the world around us, and our inability to control complex social and economic processes.

Economists are likely unaccustomed to being addressed alongside social activists, to be sure. Here I will do just that. My reasons for doing so are twofold. First, there is a significant development within the world of social activism. Many of us are recognizing our need for the insights and expertise of economists as we move from social critique to the more difficult work of designing and implementing sustainable and equitable public policies. Second, there are equally significant developments within the world of economic theory and practice, with many economists recognizing a twofold intrinsic ethical challenge within policy implementation. This challenge is one shared with social activists: how to reckon with, responsibly and equitably, two factors: (1) the

[1] Reverend Dr. Lee Barker, president of Meadville Lombard Theological School, coined the term "in praise of imperfect commitment" to describe the vibrant, non-utopian model of social engagement that we are teaching Unitarian Universalist ministers and community activists at Meadville Lombard Theological School.

intrinsic unpredictability of our policy interventions and (2) the differential effects of policies—that which helps some, often hurts others.

The work that we do as activists and professionals can be fundamentally recast because of where we are now culturally and politically. We are immersed in a third wave of political engagement, an era that builds on two prior waves of progressive politics and yet has its own energy and challenges. The first wave was the forceful denunciation of manifold forms of social injustice—slavery, the oppression of workers and the secondary status of women—all forms of oppression defended as divinely ordained or part of the natural order of things. These struggles for social justice have been augmented by a second wave of activism, the work of identity politics, the resolute claim for the complex identities and full humanity of all groups marginalized and exploited by systemic oppression and silenced through cultural imperialism.[2]

These political tasks are ongoing, yet now occur within a third paradigm. Once we recognize that a situation is unjust, once we grant the imperative of including the voices and experiences of all peoples, how then do we work together to craft and implement just and creative social policies?

For far too long, activists like myself have exercised a form of the prophetic imagination that focused primarily on critiques of what is wrong, and visions of what might be right, and paid little or no attention to the third, most important and most difficult element of the prophetic role—the implementation of social policies that are just, sustainable and resilient. In contrast, professional economists have been very willing to design and implement grand policy solutions to pressing social problems without taking adequate account of the limits of their science and control over the world they seek to improve.

An example for activists of a full prophetic imagination that includes equal attention to critique, vision and implementation can be seen in the current work of the Unitarian Universalist Social Committee. In the 2012 annual report, UUSC's president and CEO William Schulz lays out clearly three elements of constructive social activism:

> First, engagement. We're eager to use the people power at our disposal to optimize our effectiveness. Our members, most of whom are associated with Unitarian Universalist congregations, are natural born activists. They're itching to get their hands dirty, be it on their computer keyboards taking online actions or by building an eco-village in Haiti.
>
> Second, innovation. Wherever we go in the world, we ask ourselves, "who's been forgotten and who is doing the most creative, groundbreaking work to transform and empower those forgotten populations." By finding the most innovative, entrepreneurial approaches to problems and crises . . . we encourage new solutions to old quandaries; we engage with communities of women or ethnic minorities, too often marginalized in their societies.

[2] For a thorough analysis of cultural imperialism and other forms of systemic injustice, see the definitive work of Iris Marion Young, *Justice and the Politics of Difference*. New edition with a Foreword by Danielle S. Allen (Princeton, NJ: Princeton University Press, 2011).

> Third, impact. . . . we're experimenting with different approaches to measuring impact because we know that at the end of the day the only thing that really counts is how many lives we've actually changed. (Schulz and Spence, 2012: 2)

A threefold form of prophetic engagement, with far more attention to implementation and impact than to critique or vision, is possible because of nuanced histories of successful social movements and empirical evaluations of the impact of policy interventions. This constructive form of prophetic engagement is leading activists to take seriously what economists have long known, the necessity of attention to implementation and impact. It may also lead economists to pay greater attention to what activists have long known—the imperative of learning from and with those that we professionals purport to understand and serve.

As we take seriously the role that we can play as economists and activists in designing and implementing just social policies, it is important to ground ourselves in two factors—the dynamics of social movements, and the particular role that professionals play in successful social analysis and political engagement.

First, let us look at some of the groundbreaking discoveries in the history of social movements. In his recent book, *The Honor Code: How Moral Revolutions Happen*, Kwame Anthony Appiah charts the transformation of "private sentiment into public norm" in the abolition of dueling in England, footbinding in China, slavery and the slave trade in England, and examines what may well be leading to a similar shift in the honor killing of women. In each case he finds that moral critiques were not enough. In fact, each practice had been discredited by religiously and philosophically based moral critiques decades before the practices came to be seen not just as wrong, but as unseemly.

Changes in behavior occurred only when a form of action that had been accepted for hundreds of years was seen not only as immoral, but as dishonorable, unworthy of respect, and unfitting for all, including elites (2010: 178).

In his massive study of the decline of various forms of physical violence, the social psychologist Steven Pinker explores what has led to significant changes in social norms. Pinker examines the history of the decline of slavery, capital punishment, and torture as accepted and routine forms of political and economic life. He also examines what he calls the ongoing "rights revolution:" "civil rights, women's rights, children's rights, gay rights and animal rights" (2011: xvi).

In each case Pinker finds a complex interaction of two phenomena—an expansion of the circle of sympathy, and an escalator of reason. In successful social movements, large numbers of people come to value the lives of people formerly ignored and devalued. Such emotional openness, however, to the dignity and struggles of others, is not enough for fundamental social change. Pinker writes that

> . . . the limited reach of empathy, with its affinity for people like us and people close to us, suggests that empathy needs the universalizing boost of reason to bring about changes in policies and norms . . . These changes include not just legal prohibitions against acts of violence but institutions that are engineered to reduce the temptations

> of violence. Among these wonkish contraptions are democratic government, the Kantian safeguards against war, reconciliation movements in the developing world, nonviolent resistance movements, international peacekeeping operations, crime prevention reforms . . . (691, 695).

Pinker is clear—empathy can be too easily limited to family, to tribe, to those near and dear. The challenge of the escalator of reason is to build on an expanded sense of sympathy and to find social behaviors, policy changes, rules, and laws that enable greater flourishing for the many, and not just the few (695). As we take up this work of the escalator of reason, finding what actually enables people to flourish in ways that are equitable as well as ecologically and economically sustainable is more a matter of critical experimentation and risk-taking than it is a matter of moral or ideological certainty. Take as a case in point the work of the feminist economists, J. K. Gibson-Graham.

Creative Experimentation

J. K. Gibson-Graham (Katherine Gibson, University of Western Sydney, and the late Julie Graham, University of Massachusetts, Amherst, writing as a single persona since 1992) have described a new political imaginary. They analyze, nurture, and celebrate the reality, opportunities, and challenges of community economies. People all over the world are finding ways of shaping their economic lives to recognize the power of interdependence, not a "common being" but a "being in common." J. K. Gibson-Graham describe different ways of "explicitly recognizing and acting on our interdependence:" "Employee buyouts in the United States, worker takeovers in the wake of economic crisis in Argentina, the anti-sweatshop movement, shareholder movements that "promote ethical investments and police the enforcement of corporate environmental and social responsibly," the living wage movement, discussions of a universal basic income, social entrepreneurship—all part of a "community economy" that "performs economy in new ways" (2006: 80–81). I would add to this list the growth of B Corporations (the most well known being Patagonia). According to an editorial in the January 2012 issue of *The Economist*, there are now several hundred corporations that have changed corporate laws to "create the legal framework for firms . . . to remain true to their social goals. To qualify as a B Corporation a firm must have an explicit social or environmental mission, and a legally binding fiduciary responsibility to take into account the interests of workers, the community and the environment as well as its shareholders" (2012: 1).

J. K. Gibson-Graham build on the insights of queer theory and political and feminist theory and organizing, emphasizing that shared questions often lead to different answers. Just as there is no one way to be a feminist, there is no single way to perform economic relations justly. There are, however, salient questions, choices to be made in each situation. Here the economy becomes the product of ethical decision making, different ways of answering the same questions:

> What is necessary to personal and social survival
> How social surplus is appropriated and distributed
> Whether and how social surplus is to be distributed and consumed, and
> How a commons is produced and sustained (88).

In making these choices, J. K. Gibson-Graham make a claim that is as unsettling for social activists as that of there being no preferred model of economic justice: it is as difficult for workers to live within community economies as it is for owners. Based on their research, they have found that for all of us, the challenge of new forms of subjectivity, sociality, and interdependence are "best shaped by practical curiosity as opposed to moral certainty about alternatives to capitalism" (159). J. K. Gibson-Graham call us to jettison the myths of the adequacy of our knowledge and the sufficiency of our control. For many progressives, this myth takes the form of a confusion of the epistemic privilege of the oppressed with the moral and strategic privilege of the oppressed. It is undoubtedly true that we cannot understand the contours of any social system unless we listen to the voices and know the histories and stories of all groups, those who are marginalized and excluded, as well as those who shape social policies and benefit from them. It is not true, however, that those who are oppressed intrinsically know how to design and implement social structures and policies that are generative and equitable. That exercise is one that requires—for all of us—risk, imagination, and accountability.

This exercise of creative experimentation in search of just social policies raises particular ethical challenges for those of us who are members of the professional managerial class. Beginning in the late 19th century and continuing into the 21st century, the professional managerial class has played a distinct role in capitalist societies. We are neither the primary owners of the means of production, nor the workers who produce goods directly. Rather, as managers in corporate and civil life, as health care workers, teachers, attorneys, and professors, we are the agents of social order. This may be a social order based on social control, and hence, be accompanied by relationships of either deference or hostility with marginalized groups, or, we can be in solidarity with the marginalized, agents of a social order based on justice, equity, and compassion (Barbara and John Ehrenreich, 1977: 13–15, 17–18, 22–26).

For professionals to serve as agents in solidarity with the poor and powerless it is essential that we take up collective, critical work that is both rigorous and open-minded. While we undoubtedly bring the rigor of historical and systemic analyses of social systems and policies to the work of crafting social policies, we often do not know with equal depth the lived experience of those outside of our social class. Few of us who are professional know first hand, for example, the costs and challenges of supporting a family on the current minimum wage. We do not know the hard choices that must be made by those trying to fund housing, food, shelter, and health care with extremely limited and fundamentally tenuous financial resources.

IMMERSION IN OTHER SOCIAL WORLDS

The economists Banerjee and Duflo have addressed this dilemma directly and challenge the way that the poor are characterized in much social theory and the implications of uninformed views for initiatives to combat poverty.

> The poor appear, in social theory as much as in literature, by turns lazy or enterprising, noble or thievish, angry or passive, helpless or self-sufficient. It is not surprise that the policy stances that correspond to these views of the poor also tend to be captured in simple formulas: "Free markets for the poor," "Make human rights substantial," "Deal with conflict first," "Give more money to the poorest," "Foreign aid kills development," and the like. These ideas all have important elements of truth, but they rarely have much space for average poor women or men, with their hopes and doubts, limitations and aspirations, beliefs and confusion. If the poor appear at all, it is usually as the dramatis personae of some uplifting anecdote or tragic episode, to be admired or pitied, but not as a source of knowledge, not as people to be consulted about what they think or want or do. (vii–viii)

In contrast to these reductive generalizations, Banerjee and Duflo, like J. K. Gibson-Graham, exemplify the fundamental insight articulated by Pinker as a core factor in the reduction of violence. The first step in fundamental social change is the expansion of the circle of sympathy, gaining a nuanced and realistic awareness of the conditions, constraints, and possibilities of lives different than our own. Banerjee and Duflo have pursued this work in their study of global initiatives to combat poverty. In 2003 they founded the Poverty Action Lab, and by 2010 researchers with the lab had studied "over 240 experiments in forty countries around the world . . . "(2011: 14).

Banerjee and Duflo claim that such immersion in the lives of the poor is necessary to craft economic policies that successful combat poverty. In so doing, they found that "the poor often resist the wonderful plans we think up for them because they do not share our faith that those plans work, or work as well as we claim" (35). They have concluded that there are good reasons for that mistrust: policies based on ideology that ignored the material constrains of people's lives. They give one striking example, a failed attempt to address the absenteeism among health care workers in the Indian Udaipur District by the NGO Seva Mandir. They cite the discovery by Neelima Khetan, the head of Seva Mandir:

> She had discovered . . . that what they [the nurses] were expected to do was crazy: Come to work six days a week. Sign in, then take your medicine bag and head out to one of the hamlets to do the rounds. Walk anywhere up to 3 miles to reach the hamlet, even if its 100 degrees Fahrenheit in the shade. Go from house to house checking on the health status of women of childbearing age and their children. Try to convince a few uninterested women to be sterilized. After five or six hours of doing this, walk back to the center. Sign out. Take a bus to go home, two hours away. (258)

Banerjee and Duflo see in this an endemic pattern that leads to the failure of social policies:

> The nurses' workload was based on an *ideology* that wants to see nurses as dedicated social workers, designed in *ignorance* of the conditions on the ground, that lives on, mostly just on paper, because of *inertia.* Altering the rules to make the jobs doable might not be sufficient to get the nurses to come to work regularly, but it has to be a necessary first step. (259)

Their work illustrates another intrinsic barrier to successful social change—expecting people to trust that change is substantive and long-lasting in a period of months, rather than years. Their research reflects the insight of John Paul Lederach, expert in conflict mediation and resolution, about the persistence and time constraints endemic to successful conflict resolution. Taking as an example a local police force that undertakes a system wide initiative to improve its relationship with the community it serves, Lederach states that

> . . . [the] test of authenticity of this change...will not lie at the level of the words spoken by the leaders or written on the side of the patrol cars, the distribution of the brochures announcing the program and the new guidelines, or the budget that paid for the training, which demonstrates the system's commitment to the change. Ultimately the authenticity litmus test will ride on how people experience the behavior of police officers in real-life situations. The great paradox is this: . . . Authenticity involves a long waiting period until people believe the change is real, but judgment of inauthenticity is continuous and immediate. (58)

In spite of these difficulties, Banerjee and Duflo find that incremental change is possible and can serve as the foundation for further substantive change, what they call the creation of a "virtuous cycle":

> If we resist the kind of lazy, formulaic thinking that reduces every problem to the same set of general principles; if we listen to poor people themselves and force ourselves to understand the logic of their choices; *if we accept the possibility of error and subject every idea, including the most apparently commonsensical ones, to rigorous empirical testing,* then we will be able not only to construct a toolbox of effective policies but also to better understand why the poor live as they do. Armed with this patient understanding, we can identify the poverty traps where they really are and know which tools we need to give the poor to help them get out of those. (272, italics mine)

Like J. K. Gibson-Graham, Banerjee and Duflo's immersion in the empirical study of communities that are different from their own has led them to make a shift "away from universal answers." These studies have led them to a conclusion similar to that held by J. K. Gibson-Graham: there will be more than one way to create community economies, more than one way to establish excellent health care, education, and environmental practices. Furthermore, what works in one situation may not work in another. As Banerjee and Duflo insist—attention to particularities of motivation, context, and resources are necessary to overcome the barriers of "ideology, ignorance, and inertia" (16).

Experimentation, Risk, and Responsibility

At this point we find a second shift in the imagination of economists and social activists that is equally momentous: experimentation requires risk and risk implies failure. There will be unintended consequences of our policy interventions, some positive, many negative. Looking for mistakes, examining them, learning from them—all sounds much easier than it is for many of us in the West, schooled as we are in heroic images of decisive battles between good and evil. As the Canadian First Nations author Thomas King writes, "If we had to have a patron story for North America, we could do worse than the one about Alexander the Great, who, when faced with the puzzle of the Gordian knot, solved that problem with nothing more than a strong arm and a sharp sword" (2003: 25).

Let me provide an example of how hard it is to make this shift to expecting, recognizing and learning from mistakes. In their account of the many ways in which a new generation of philanthropists are using their business skills to create social wellbeing and environmental justice, Matthew Bishop and Michael Green point out that "taking risks is the essence of philanthrocapitalism" (2009: 59). Not every venture will succeed, and ongoing critical analysis of the actual impact of economic initiatives is essential.

Despite their forthright acknowledgement of the necessity of critique, Bishop and Green interpret criticism as devastating indictment, rather than embracing it as an essential ingredient in effective social change. In their account of Laurie Garret's pertinent and serious examination of the approach of the Gates foundation to global health, published in *Foreign Affairs* in 2007, they describe the critique as an assault: "the brick bats came out again" rather than as just the kind of critical examination essential to determine which approaches to global health are most effective in particular situations: "her theme was that focusing on particular diseases—so-called stovepiping—was less effective than a broader approach based on building up the overall health care system of poor countries" (67).

Bishop and Green's aversion to critique is also seen in their rendition of the attempts by the Gates foundation to actively solicit critical feedback: "[Gates] has promised to be open about the foundation's failures, of which he expects plenty—given that taking risks is one of the philanthropist's comparative advantages . . . in 2007 he gave $105 million to the University of Washington to research the performance of global health work, including that of his foundation. It remains to be seen how willing the university will be to tell a major funding source that he is doing something badly (perish the thought)" (73).

What is behind this aversion to potentially transformative and even actively solicited critique? Bishop and Green are aware of a core element of this problem—the stories we tell ourselves. They quote the analysts Brainard and Chollett, who raise a central question: "Can a campaign achieve success where there is no Hollywood storyline—no heroes and villains and conclusive triumphs, only the slow struggle of well-meaning people to overcome the vagaries of nature and set the stage for future generations to lead modestly better lives?" (204).

At this point, a further shift in honor codes is necessary, feasible and actual. The necessary shift is this—that the measure of our success is not the perfection of our efforts but our honesty, humility, accountably, resilience, and audacity in the face of unintended consequences and ongoing challenges.

In *The Economist's Oath*, George DeMartino challenges economists to acknowledge that there are unforeseen and unforeseeable consequences to our economic interventions: "the economist operates in a world of uncertainty and epistemic insufficiency—where interpretive practice necessarily infuses the processes of knowing, error is inevitable, unintended consequences are the norm, ignorance is rife, and human subjectivity is not a temporary disability but an ineradicable condition of our being and acting in the world" (2011: 113–114).

DeMartino also points to another key dimension of openness to failure and risk—the differential impact of many policy initiatives:

> Economic interventions typically affect distinct groups of people differently. Some people are harmed by economic interventions that are understood to be beneficial in the aggregate . . . Mainstream economic theory demonstrates that policy changes often are of this sort—they yield net benefit in the aggregate while hurting some members of the economy . . . Should economists advocate for and enact policy that will harm some. . . .? While the affirmative answer to this question might in fact be warranted in at least some cases, the rush to the answer certainly never is . . . If an economist knows that some will indeed suffer lasting harm, [what are their ethical responsibilities?] Does it matter who in society will suffer—is there an ethical difference between the situation where those who stand to lose are the best off in society and the situation where those who stand to lose are the worst off? (111–113).

DeMartino claims that this is an intrinsic problem in economic decision making, and one not averted by either the oft-used "maxi-max" decision rule, nor by the prudential principle. While " . . . the maxi-max decision rule considers only the potential benefits from policy success and selects the policy that promises greatest reward, the prudential principle considers only the potential harm from policy failure and selects the policy that promises the least danger." The former ignores the potential costs associated with the risk of policy failure; the latter, the harm caused by the status quo (189).

It is here that Pinker's work is of utmost importance for economists and activists alike. Pinker claims that reductions in physical violence have occurred through a complex of factors, and that such reductions will stay in place only if the social and material conditions that led to the reductions are maintained (671). His work poses a challenge for those of us concerned with the reduction of various forms of structural violence, including the socially deleterious effects of poverty and increasing income inequality. I argue that it is well worth our while to apply the principles that have led to reductions in physical violence to the reduction of structural violence. In so doing, economists and social activists have much to learn from each other. Activists have long recognized the importance of the expansion of the circle of sympathy. Economists have long noted the importance of the escalator of reason—the importance of rational deliberation and evaluation of idealized social policies, paying attention to actual, not merely desired, impacts and effects.

As we combine the expansion of the circle of empathy with the escalator of reason, we encounter an ethical challenge—a recognition of the importance of redressing differential impacts of policy interventions. These concerns are shared by growing numbers of activists and economists, among them, the writer Nassim Taleb in his two books, *The Black Swan* and *Antifragile*. Given the differential impacts of our experimentation, Taleb articulates a clear ethical mandate: "No socialization of losses and privatization of gains" (374).

Taleb also urges us to a resolute embrace of the likelihood of mistakes and unpredictable consequences. In *The Black Swan*, he argues that the lesson of 9/11 is that there are positive and negative "events that stand outside the realm of the predictable" and our best response is to "adjust to their existence rather than naively try to predict them" (2010: xxv, xxvi). Taleb encourages us to focus on "robustness to errors" rather than on improved predictions, and claims that most significant strategies and discoveries come from "maximum tinkering and recognizing opportunities when they present themselves" (xxv). To thoroughly learn from mistakes requires a fundamental shift in the values of Western culture. In his most recent book, he writes of the importance of "daring to look our ignorance in the face" and being willing to "use error as a teacher" (2012: 11, 71). Taleb claims that this shift is momentous enough to warrant the new word, "antifragility."

"Antifragility is beyond resilience or robustness. The resilient resists shocks and stays the same; the antifragile gets better . . . " (3). Taleb claims that organizations can cultivate antifragility, and learn to work productively with, not in spite of, errors and failure.

> By grasping the mechanism of antifragility we can guild a systematic and broad guide to nonpredictive decision making under uncertainty in business, politics, medicine, and life in general—anywhere the unknown preponderates, any situation in which there is randomness, unpredictability, opacity, or incomplete understanding of things (4).

It is here that we have much to learn from the ecological theorists and practitioners Wes Jackson and Wendell Berry. Drawing from the impact of scientific and technological intervention on the natural world, Wendell Berry challenges the assumption that "in a time of great technological power that humans either know enough already or can learn enough soon enough to foresee and forestall any bad consequences." Jackson concurs, and calls for "an ignorance based science and technology in which practitioners would be ever conscious that we are billions of times more ignorant than knowledgeable and always will be." Furthermore, Berry asks us to consider the implications of such a world view for activists and professionals: "Acting on the basis of ignorance, paradoxically, requires one to know things, remember things—for instance, that failure is possible, that error is possible, that second chances are desirable" (2011: 3, 4). Given that premise, it is not surprising to see Wes Jackson claim "that by embracing an ignorance-based worldview, at least we go with our long suit" (4).

A New Honor Code

Let's back up. What do prophetic social engagement and rigorous economic analysis have in common? Let us return to our thesis—there is a promising convergence in current opportunities for constructive social analysis and political engagement for both social critics and professional economists. We are each equally challenged by the work of historians and empirical studies of policy interventions to take seriously two factors: (1) the differential impact of policy interventions that help some and harm others and (2) endemic patterns of failures of judgment and of policy creation and implementation that result in part from epistemic inadequacy.

Extensive and lasting social change occurs when people embrace a new vision of what is honorable (Appiah) and embody that vision in concrete social practices (Pinker). The move, however, from honorable goals to equitable practices is neither linear nor assured. Experimentation, risk taking, and mistakes are an inevitable part of the process. Here again we encounter a challenge to us both, economists and activists—the simple insight that it is far easier to rectify mistakes when you know that you are likely to make them. And, a corollary insight, it is far easier to see the mistakes of others than to acknowledge and reckon with our own. Daniel Kahneman describes his work as an attempt to address both concerns. Though we can rarely check ourselves, we can create an institutional culture in which we check each other. He states that " . . . it is much easier to identify a minefield when you observe others wandering into it than when you are about to do so" (417).

This cultural change requires two interrelated developments, "a richer language" for identifying errors of judgment and a culture that values " the skill of constructive criticism." In such a culture, Kahneman claims that "[Decisionmakers] will make better choices when they trust their critics to be sophisticated and fair. . ." (418).

Here we have a crucial component of a third wave of constructive political engagement—the emergence of a new honor code constituted by two factors: (1) compassion for the suffering of others and commitment to the common good; paying attention to who bears the cost of economic intervention and innovation, and who shares in the benefits; (2) risk taking and innovation that is honest and accountable, recognizing and learning from mistakes, failures, and unintended consequencesFor activists, this awareness calls us away from moral narcissism, the assumption that we have acted with moral integrity when we voice our most stringent critiques of what is unjust and share our heartfelt visions of what might be, yet fail to take up the more difficult task of the design, implementation, evaluation, and revision of alternative economic and social policies.[3] For economists and activists alike, the recognition of these two factors reminds us that there is no moral safe harbor, no course of action guaranteed to be free of risk, loss and negative side effects[4]. Our challenge is to forthrightly reckon with those tradeoffs and ways, as professionals, of bearing ourselves the costs of losses too often borne only by the most vulnerable and marginalized.

Given the realities of both unforeseeable consequences and differential effects, those who shape policy are better served by an ethic of risk than by an ethic of certainty and control. It is not easy, however, for many of us to embrace an ethic of risk, whether we are activists calling for change or professionals implementing desired change. The ethic of risk goes against deeply engrained religious and cultural values. Our moral and political imagination is often shaped by an ethic of control, a construction of agency, responsibility, and goodness that assumes that it is possible to guarantee the efficacy of one's action. This is a problem intrinsic in our culture's definition of responsible action. To be responsible means controlling events and achieving quick and predicted results. This understanding of responsible action leads to a striking paralysis of will when faced with complex problems. It seems natural to many people, when faced with a problem too big to be solved alone or within the foreseeable future, simply to do nothing, and possibly, even argue against partial remedies as foolhardy and deluded.[5]

There are, however, alternative understandings of responsible action in the face of complex and deep-seated social problems. In 1988 Dr. Katie Cannon published a

[3] I became aware of the concept of moral narcissism through conversations with Major Mark Schimmelpfenning (US Army, retired), who used it to describe what I have also criticized as a weakness in the peace movement. Too often activists such as myself have stopped with the critique of military action without taking upon ourselves the risk of implementing nonviolent responses to deadly conflict and crimes against humanity.

.[4] President Barack Obama warned us of the dangers of the illusion of a moral safe harbor in his discussion of the use of drone attacks to combat terrorism: "Our efforts must be measured against the history of putting American troops in distant lands among hostile populations. In Vietnam, hundreds of thousands of civilians died in a war where the boundaries of battle were blurred. In Iraq and Afghanistan, despite the extraordinary courage and discipline of our troops, thousands of civilians have been killed. So neither conventional military action nor waiting for attacks to occur offers moral safe harbor, and neither does a sole reliance on law enforcement in territories that have no functioning police or security services—and indeed, have no functioning law. Now, this is not to say that the risks are not real. Any U.S. military action in foreign lands risks creating more enemies and impacts public opinion overseas. Moreover, our laws constrain the power of the President even during wartime, and I have taken an oath to defend the Constitution of the United States. The very precision of drone strikes and the necessary secrecy often involved in such actions can end up shielding our government from the public scrutiny that a troop deployment invites. It can also lead a President and his team to view drone strikes as a cure-all for terrorism." Retrieved from http://www.nytimes.com/2013/05/24/us/politics/transcript-of-obamas-speech-on-drone-policy.html?pagewanted=all&_r=0

[5] For a further exploration of an ethic of risk, see Sharon D. Welch, *A Feminist Ethic of Risk: Revised Edition* (Minneapolis: Fortress Press, 2000).

groundbreaking exploration of "the moral wisdom found in the black women's literary tradition." She claimed that we find in the work of African American women a tradition of strength and persistence that is one of the richest heritages facing humankind. (Cannon, 1988: 75–98)

The ethic of risk, as expressed in the lives and writing of African American women and men, poses a foundational challenge to an ethic of control. The ethic of risk is characterized by three elements: a redefinition of responsible action, grounding in community, and strategic risk taking. Responsible action does not mean the certain achievement of desired ends but the creation of a matrix in which further actions are possible, the creation of the conditions of possibility for the ongoing implementation, and revision of desired social ends. This work requires the discipline and artistry of constructive critique, the ability to pay attention to actual rather than desired impact, and the creativity to undertake substantial and ongoing revisions in light of these effects. Responsible action as the creation of a matrix for further creative problem solving is sustained and enabled by participation in an extensive community, a community that offers support in struggle, constructive and ongoing critique, and constitutes the context for work that spans generations. Strategic risk taking entails making best judgments as to likely impact and differential consequences, and is vigilant in recognizing and addressing unintended consequences (Welch, 2000: 46–48).

Within an ethic of risk, the extent to which an action is an appropriate response to collective needs is constituted as much by the possibilities it creates as by its immediate results. Responsible action does not mean one group or individual resolving the problems of others. It is, rather, participation in generative communal work. Responsible action provides partial resolutions in the present and the inspiration and conditions for further partial solutions in the future.

There are six ethical values that can sustain us as we live out an ethic of risk.

Curiosity: Recall J. K. Gibson-Graham and their advocacy of practical curiosity rather than moral certainty about alternatives to unjust and unsustainable economic practices. They urge us to "start where we are and begin with what we have," eliciting new ways of performing economy justly, ways that might not work in all situations, yet can serve as a catalyst for other exercises in locally-grounded experimentations in nurturing greater flourishing for all members of a community.

Humility: As we move to a fallibility-based world view, we have much to learn from Buddhist understandings of responsible action. Within the work of engaged Buddhists we find a form of action founded on both knowing and non-knowing: knowing, from the best of all that we are, and all that we can see and can think about a situation, yet offering that knowledge as a gift, open to the transformation of insight and analysis in light of the gifts of others, and the surprising and unpredictable consequences of our wholehearted attempts to live justly and well (Welch, 2008: 93–101). As we lead, and as we govern, it is crucial that we recognize that any situation is intrinsically fluid, pregnant with multiple and unpredictable possibilities. Good and ill may emerge from the same action. The Buddhist teacher Pema Chodron states that the recognition of contingency can lead us to rigidity and denial. The Buddhist philosopher Stephen Batchelor, drawing on the teachings of Nagarjuna, philosopher monk who lived in India during the second century, states that through Dharma practice we may experience instead of rigidity and denial a freeing immersion in "the sublime contingency of self and things" and such immersion is a gift to the imagination, the will and the soul (Batchelor, 1997: 38; Chodron, 2006: 29).

Resilience and robustness in the face of error: The economist Julie Nelson advocates that policymakers learn from the lessons of "high-reliability" organizations—organizations that operate "within highly complex situations ... in which quick action is needed." Nelson gives as examples of high-reliability organizations aircraft carrier decks, nuclear power plants, healthcare organizations." She states that high reliability organizations are characterized by "a preoccupation with failure" ... They operate with a chronic wariness of the possibility of unexpected events ... they are reluctant to simplify interpretations and manifest a commitment to resilience ... developing the capabilities to detect, contain and bounce back from errors ... before they worsen and cause more harm" (2008: 6).

Audacity balanced with compassion: We may hone our collective imaginations and craft solutions that are bold, beautiful, daring, and compelling. Yet it is equally vital that audacity be combined with recognition of and compassion for those adversely affected by both unforeseen and unavoidable negative impacts of our audacious policy interventions. Such awareness leads to a basic commitment to fairness, expressed so clearly by Nassim Taleb: "no socialization of losses and privatization of gains." (2010: 374)

Humor: The final virtue—a resolute commitment to acknowledge and work with humor and grace, with the intrinsic limitations of our ability to know and control the world. It is possible to find cultural metaphors of energy, vitality, and power to replace the certitudes of Us Against Them on the Road to Certain Victory. Take, as one example, the words of the Texas journalist Molly Ivins, written shortly after the end of first Bush presidency.

> Fellow citizens, as we stagger toward the millennium, I can only hope that this modest oeuvre—as we often say in Amarillo—will remind you that we need to stop and laugh along the way. We live in a Great Nation, but those who attempt to struggle through it unarmed with a sense of humor are apt to wind up in my Aunt Eula's Fort Worth Home for the Terminally Literal-Minded, gibbering like some demented neoconservative about the Decline of Civilization ... Yours in the belief that the Founders were right all along, but that the results are a lot funnier than they intended. (1994: xi)

As Thomas King wrote in his astute comparison of indigenous and Western creation stories, "Want a different ethic? Tell a different story" (164). A new collective story of honest, creative, ironic and audacious political engagement has begun. As activists, as professionals who make and shape policy, this story may serve us well as we wholeheartedly live out our deepest hopes and unabashedly acknowledge our greatest limitations.

References

Appiah, Kwame Anthony. 2010. *The Honor Code: How Moral Revolutions Happen.* New York: W. W. Norton and Company.

Banerjee, Abhijit V., and Esther Duflo. 2011. *Poor Economics: A Radical Rethinking of the Way to Fight Global Poverty.* New York: Public Affairs.

Batchelor, Stephen. 1997. *Buddhism without Beliefs: A Guide to Contemporary Awakening.* New York: Riverhead.

Bishop, Matthew, and Michael Green. 2009. *Philanthrocapitalism: How Giving Can Save the World.* New York: Bloomsbury Press.

Cannon, Katie G. 1988. *Black Womanist Ethics.* Atlanta: Scholars Press.

Chodron, Pema. 2006. *Practicing Peace in Times of War.* Boston: Shambala.

DeMartino, George. 2011. *The Economist's Oath: On the Need for and Content of Professional Economic Ethics.* Oxford: Oxford University Press.

The Economist. Editorial. 2012. "B Corps: Firms with Benefits." *The Economist Newspaper Limited 2012.* Retrieved from http://www.economist.com/node/21542432/print January 7, 2012.

Ehrenreich, Barbara, and John Ehrenreich. 1977. "The Professional Managerial Class." *Radical America* 11(2): 13–15, 17–18, 22–26.

Gibson-Graham, J. K. 2006. *A Post-Capitalist Politics.* Minneapolis: University of Minnesota Press.

Ivins, Molly. 1994. *Nothing But Good Times Ahead.* New York: Vintage.

Jackson, Wes. 2011. "Toward an Ignorance-Based World View (LR81)." Salina, KS: The Land Institute. Retrieved from http://www.landinstitute.org/vnews/display.v/ART/2004/10/03/42c0db19e37f4

Kahneman, Daniel. 2011. *Thinking, Fast and Slow.* New York: Farrar, Straus and Giroux.

Kahneman, Daniel. 2013. "Foreword." In *The Behavioral Foundations of Public Policy,* edited by Eldar Shafir. Princeton, NJ: Princeton University Press.

King, Thomas. 2003. *The Truth About Stories: A Native Narrative.* Minneapolis: University of Minnesota Press.

Lederach, John Paul. 2005. *The Moral Imagination: The Art and Soul of Building Peace.* Oxford: Oxford University Press.

Nelson, Julie A. 2008. "*Economists, Value Judgments and Climate Change: A View from Feminist Economics.*" Medford, MA: Global Development and Environmental Institute, Tufts University.

Pinker, Steven. 2011. *The Better Angels of Our Nature: Why Violence Has Declined.* New York: Viking.

Schulz, William, and Chuck Spence. 2012. *Engagement, Innovation, and Impact: UUSC 2012 Annual Report.* Cambridge: MA: Unitarian Universalist Service Committee.

Taleb, Nassim Nicholas. 2010. *The Black Swan: The Impact of the Highly Improbable.* New York: Random House.

Taleb, Nassim Nicholas. 2012. *Antifragile: Things That Can Gain from Disorder.* New York: Random House.

Young, Iris Marion. 2011. *Justice and the Politics of Difference* (with a new introduction by Danielle S. Allen). Princeton, NJ: Princeton University Press.
Welch, Sharon D. 2000. *A Feminist Ethic of Risk: Revised Edition*. Minneapolis: Fortress Press.
Welch, Sharon D. 2008. *Real Peace, Real Security: The Challenges of Global Citizenship*. Minneapolis: Fortress Press.

CHAPTER 5

"ECONOGENIC HARM"

On the Nature of and Responsibility for the Harm Economists Do as They Try to Do Good

GEORGE F. DEMARTINO

> If it were known to be true, as a question of fact, that measures that cause misery and death to tens of millions today *would* result in saving from greater misery or death hundreds of millions in the future, and if this were the only way in which it could be done, then it *would* be right to cause these necessary atrocities.
>
> — J. J. C. Smart, 1973 (emphasis in original)

> Words matter.
>
> —Deirdre N. McCloskey, Oct. 4, 2010

Introduction

Professional practice often entails potential for harm to those professionals seek to serve, and to third parties. This is true in clinical medicine and public health, of course, but also in social work, engineering, law, and many if not most other professions. Partly in recognition of this fact, some professions have established bodies of professional ethics in hopes of promoting responsible behavior by their members—behavior that minimizes the avoidable harms and that helps them manage appropriately the unavoidable harms that may arise in the context of their practice. The medical profession is exemplary in this regard. In medical ethics, we find the term "iatrogenesis" or "iatrogenic harm" (from the Greek, "doctor-originating"), which refers to the adverse effects or complications associated with medical treatment. The concept of iatrogenic harm captures physician- or clinic-induced harms ranging from those associated with malpractice to the unpreventable consequences of well-intentioned and expertly delivered medical interventions.

Economists, on the other hand, generally do not give sufficient attention to the nature of economic harm or to the ways their own practice induces harm.[1] In fact, we have no language to discuss economist-induced harm. There is no parallel in economics to the concept of medical malpractice, of course; economists are not held legally liable for their mistakes, no matter how severe the effects. More broadly, there is no economic analogue to the concept of iatrogenesis. There should be. We need a concept, and a corresponding term, to name what is as-of-yet unnamed. Let us refer to the harm economists cause with the term "econogenesis," or "econogenic harm."[2]

The term iatrogenesis typically refers to physical and psychological harm—or to the *medical* harms associated with medical practice. But the concept is also used to capture other harmful effects of medical interventions. Meessen et al. (2003: 581) describe the impoverishment that accompanies "catastrophic health care expenditure" in the developing world as "iatrogenic poverty." Following their lead, we can distinguish between economic and noneconomic forms of econogenic harms. For instance, whereas adverse health effects of economic interventions—such as the rising alcoholism and dramatic declines in life expectancy that followed rapid privatization in Russia in the 1990s (Stuckler, King, and McKee, 2009)—have economic consequences, they are not in the first instance economic. We can therefore speak of "econogenic morbidity" or "econogenic mortality" in cases where economist-advocated interventions undermine public health.

Why do we economists fail to examine sufficiently economic harm in general and econogenic harm in particular? Several reasons come to mind. First, economists recognize that harm is a regular and likely ineradicable feature of economic practice. Any policy intervention that affects relative prices—which is to say, all interventions[3]—"benefits those on one side of the market, and damages those on the other" (Hicks, 1939: 706). It needs to be said plainly: *economists are in the harm business*. Almost always we cause harm as we try to do good. Hence, the Hippocratic directive "first, do no harm," if taken as an inviolable mandate or a decision rule, has no relevance in economics since it would imply that economists can do nothing at all.[4] Second, for more than a century the economics profession has been uncertain about and even resistant

[1] This claim will strike many economists as incorrect, if not absurd. The economist's toolkit includes cost-benefit analysis and the Kaldor-Hicks compensation test—both of which involve explicit recognition of the harms associated with economic interventions. I face a burden in what follows, then, to sustain the claim that these methods generally entail a simplistic account of harm—one that fails to recognize its internal heterogeneity, complexity, and often, its irreparability.

[2] In his remarkable book *Antifragile* Nassim Taleb argues for the generalized use across the professions—and especially within economics—of the concept of iatrogensis (see ch. 7). Econogensis strikes me as a better term; its adoption would help to bring badly needed attention to the harmful entailments of economic practice.

[3] Although the arguments that appear here apply with particular force to economic policy, they also apply to other economic interventions that economists design and advocate. These include, for instance, the design of government regulations, market structures, financial investment or corporate strategies, and more.

[4] Taking the Hippocratic directive as an absolute (which, it bears emphasis, neither physicians nor medical ethicists do) would prohibit economic adjustments that promote extraordinary aggregate gains or even substantial gains to those most in need. It would dictate that we do nothing at all, even when doing nothing prolongs avoidable misery.

to ethical matters in economic science (Sen, 1987). Discomfort with ethics manifests in part as mistaken presumptions that economists can bifurcate economics into its positive and normative components, and having done so, should privilege positive science over normative speculations. But, by its nature, and as we will see, harm does not yield to the bifurcation. Third, in comparison with many other professions that enjoy substantial influence over the life chances of others, economics has been particularly dismissive of the idea of *professional* ethics and especially of professional economic ethics.[5] This is so despite the fact that large numbers of economists (including the majority of economists employed in the United States) work outside of academia where they engage in applied work that bears on policy formation, regulation, and other government interventions; affect the outcome of legal disputes; provide consulting services to to private actors; influence financial market developments; and more (Lowenstein, 2000; DeMartino, 2011). Yet we have neither professional economic ethicists, nor texts, journals, newsletters, curriculum, regular conferences, or other forums that explore systematically what it means to be an ethical economist or what it means for economics to be an ethical profession.[6] Unfortunately, economists' disinterest in professional economic ethics deprives us of a tradition of careful inquiry into the nature of econogenic harm.

The neglect of economic harm in general and econogenic harm in particular allows economists to undertake their research, teaching, and applied work without sufficient worry about their impact on others. It allows economists to sleep too well at night—a happy circumstance for economists, to be sure, but far too dangerous for those the profession purports to serve.

Three issues concerning harm deserve more careful attention than economists tend to give them. They are (1) the complexity of the concept of harm, (2) the causes and prevalence of econogenic harm, and (3) the inadequacies in the predominant way that economists theorize harm. The following sections explore each of these matters in turn.

The Complex Nature of (Economic) Harm

Harm is an exceedingly complex concept.[7] First, harm is internally heterogeneous: a person (or group) can be harmed in many distinct ways (see Table 5.1). Harm can

[5] Only in 2011, in the wake of the unwelcome attention to the apparent misbehavior of prominent economists that was exposed in the film *Inside Job*, did the most important economic associations in the United States and elsewhere begin to explore the need for rules to govern conflict of interest disclosure among their members. This is a welcome development—but so far the new initiatives have failed to look beyond conflict of interest to other ethical issues, such as econogenic harm, that arise in the context of economic practice.

[6] The nonbinding code of the National Association of Forensic Economics (NAFE) and the interest of that organization's members in professional ethical issues stand as notable exceptions (see NAFE undated).

[7] And yet, sophisticated treatments of the concept of harm are surprisingly rare. But see Feinberg (1984), Sharpe and Faden (1998), Linklater (2011), and Shiffrin (2012). The discussion here does not begin to do justice to the complexity of the concept that is revealed in these texts.

Table 5.1 An Incomplete and Usefully Imprecise Taxonomy of Harmed or Harmful Conditions[8]

Physical:
Pain
Injury or dismemberment
Loss/diminution of physical or mental capacities
Death
Degradation of the physical environment
Psychological:
Emotional or psychological suffering; depression
Becoming fearful, insecure, or anxious
Becoming ashamed
Loss of Hope
Erosion of self-respect
Loss of capacity for creativity, playfulness, inventiveness, or fraternal feelings
Economic:
Loss of income, wealth, or welfare/utility
Loss of access to valued goods
Loss of genuine choice over valued goods
Loss of economic security
Loss of economic opportunities (to do, be, or become)
Loss of economic capacities (e.g., to earn a living)
Loss of control over one's economic activities and practices
Alienation from one's labor, output, or nature
Subjection to exploitation, discrimination, or deprivation
Social:
Loss of community
Loss of place in community (status, influence, or role as contributor)
Loss of respect, recognition, or honor
Loss of political efficacy
Loss of fraternity or meaningful connections with others
Erosion of social capital

[8] Feinberg, who defines harm as a "thwarting, setting back, or defeating of an interest" (Feinberg, 1984: 33), distinguishes between "harmed" and "harmful" conditions by reference to whether the condition compounds in its adverse effects. In his words, "A *harmed* condition of a person may or may not also be a *harmful* condition, depending on whether it has itself the tendency to generate further harm. A blistered finger may be to some small degree a harmed condition, but unless the finger is on the hand of a concert pianist or a baseball pitcher, it may not be at all harmful" (1984: 31).

It bears emphasis that neither the taxonomy of harm presented here nor the surrounding text is intended to be comprehensive or precise. Achieving those qualities would require a far lengthier treatment of harm than I can or need to provide here. My purpose is limited to demonstrating with an economy of words that harm is a viciously complex, heterogeneous, and contested concept that deserves more careful attention than economists tend to give it.

Table 5.1 Continued

Moral:
Erosion, inversion, and/or collapse of some important ethical or spiritual values, virtues, sensibilities, and norms
Autonomy:
Adaptive preference formation
Impairment in the pursuit of one's life plans
Treatment as mere means and not also as an end
Destruction of a valued way of life
Constriction of one's capabilities or feasibility set
Exacerbation of personal or systemic threats, risk, or instability
Assault on negative or positive rights/freedoms (coercion)
Denial of opportunity to participate in vitally important social, economic, or cultural processes

take the form of dismemberment or the loss of physical and mental faculties; psychological or emotional suffering; loss of income, wealth, or access to valued goods; exploitation; impairment in the pursuit of one's life plans; diminution in the capacity for creativity, inventiveness, or playfulness (Nussbaum, 1992); loss of respect, meaningful connections with others, community, or a valued way of life (Marglin, 2008); erosion of political efficacy (Sen, 1992); and more. Moreover, harm comprises objective and subjective components, and the two may not always align in the ways we might expect. Indeed, harm may occur without inducing any anguish or unhappiness. An example in the economic context is given by the case of "adaptive preference formation" in which the oppressed come to believe that they do not value important goods that are denied to them (Elster, 1982). The possibility of hidden harm complicates greatly judgments about the incidence and extent of harm and raises the thorny question: who should be authorized to ascertain when, how, and how badly an agent has in fact been harmed—the agent, her close associates, or some detached "harm expert"? Making matters worse, a harmful event might induce diverse, compound harms to individuals, families, and communities. For instance, an economic crisis causes various economic harms, of course, but also many of what I've listed here as psychological and social harms, along with harms to personal autonomy and freedom. The example of economic crisis also points us to the fact that whereas harm often manifests immediately upon the heels of the event that induces it, it can also linger well into the future (and even compound over time), affecting those not yet born at the time of the event. A Greek family in 2015 whose economic security is undermined as a consequence of the severe austerity measures now in place, which many economists endorse in response to the country's fiscal imbalance, may very well transmit substantially diminished health prospects (Stuckler and Basu, 2013) and economic capacities to future generations. Finally, for present purposes, we need to acknowledge the analytical problem that what is harmful to one person may prove to be benign or even beneficial to another owing to differences between the two (in their age and other physical attributes, intellectual abilities, familial obligations, degree of optimism and initiative, extent of integration into the community, and other characteristics).[9] For instance, unemployment may severely damage one agent who, for whatever reason, lacks the capacity to respond productively to the change in circumstances, and yet provide the impetus for another to attain new skills, start her own business, relocate to a more vibrant region, or otherwise change her life for the better. Divergent effects complicate the matter of assessing the occurrence and causes of harm, the causal significance of any harm-inducing event, the severity of the consequent harm, the responsibility for the harms suffered (and for harm avoidance and amelioration), and much else besides.[10]

Second, the concept of harm relates in complex ways to central features of human nature and social existence. Agents suffer harm when their welfare, agency, freedoms, liberties, or valued relationships are undermined. An adequate account of harm, then, presumes an adequate engagement with these salient features. For instance, a comprehensive account of harm almost certainly requires a good account of human needs, flourishing, subjectivity (and subjectivity formation), and of human connections with others and with their natural and social environment, let alone an adequate conception of human rights (civil, political, economic, social and cultural), freedoms, liberties, and responsibilities.

Third, once we have specified what does and what does not count as harm, we then have to explore carefully which harms are morally indictable and which are tolerable. If one participant beats another in a fair contest voluntarily and fairly played and judged—be it a sporting event, a political election, the pursuit of a coveted honor, award, good, life partner, or some form of economic competition—the victor may have harmed the vanquished by denying him the goal he sought.[11] The unsuccessful participant may feel the pain of loss acutely; he may be devastated and ashamed, with detrimental effects on the course of his life. But although such harm may earn for the unsuccessful contestant sympathy or concern for his welfare, it does not entitle him to our indignation or to redress. In short, not all victims of harm are rightly aggrieved by their hardship, and not all individuals or institutions that cause harm deserve opprobrium (Feinberg, 1984; Shiffrin, 2012).

[9] I am grateful to Robert Lepenies for suggesting this line of argument.

[10] See the magisterial four-volume work *The Moral Limits of the Criminal Law* by Joel Feinberg, especially volume one, *Harm to Others* (1984), for a comprehensive liberal account of harm. One cannot read Feinberg and retain any sense that the nature of harm, wrongful harm, and the act of harming are simple or obvious facts that can be easily identified, measured, and managed by professions that affect the lives of others. Nor can one continue to believe that harm is essentially a positive concept, devoid of normative content.

[11] For present purposes a "fair contest" refers to a contractarian judgment that society's members would choose to live in a world that permits all aspects of the contest including *inter alia* the degree of freedom to exit the contest altogether and the stakes associated with winning and losing. Although I cannot explore the matter here (but see DeMartino, 2011), economists too readily presume consent (or dismiss the need for consent) to policy regimes that are costly or even impossible to exit, and entail substantial risks to those who populate the economy—where the stakes for winning and losing are very high.

Fourth and finally, all of these antecedent matters are contested. Different philosophical and economic frameworks will and do disagree about just what events cause harm and what effects register as harm and as indictable harm. A libertarian and a utilitarian would be apt to disagree sharply about the causes and nature of harm, which harms are significant and which are *de minimis*, and which forms of harm are ethically worrisome.[12]

The foregoing discussion carries what is, for the economist, an inconvenient implication. Positive analyses of harm are thoroughly infused with normative judgments. We need to make normatively charged decisions about what counts as harm before we can begin to explore the supposedly positive questions of whether a policy has or has not induced harm and, if so, the magnitude of the harm. We then have to follow up the discovery of harm with normatively laden decisions about which harms are to be taken as ethically indictable or otherwise troubling and which are not. In regard to the matter of harm, then—if not everywhere else in economics—*the positive and the normative are inescapably linked.* Talk of harm is, necessarily, at once positive and normative (Feinberg, 1984). And it may be that the deeply normative character of the concept of harm helps to explain what is otherwise mysterious: why the economics profession has more often repressed rather than welcomed serious consideration of economic harm in general and econogenic harm in particular.

The Tragedy of Economics

The duty to engage economic harm is imposed on us by the problematic nature of economic science and practice. Harm to those economists purport to serve results most obviously from error in economic judgment—such as when an economist fails to anticipate the unintended adverse consequences of a proposed economic intervention. The position taken by US Federal Reserve Chair Alan Greenspan against financial regulation during the late 1990s and early 2000s qualifies, as indicated by his stunning admission before Congress in the fall of 2008 of his own naïveté in believing that liberalized financial markets would police themselves sufficiently so as to prevent irresponsible and destabilizing behavior. As the most severe economic crisis in the United States since the 1930s unfolded, Greenspan acknowledged that "I made a mistake in presuming that the self-interest of organizations, specifically banks and others, was such that they were best capable of protecting their own shareholders." Speaking of a "once in a century credit tsunami," he continued, "[t]hose of us who have looked to the self-interest of lending institutions to protect shareholders' equity, myself especially, are in a state of shocked disbelief" (Andrews, 2008).

[12] And so would feminist, Marxist, Keynesian, social, and neoclassical economists. Their respective judgments regarding harm would be driven in part by their competing conceptions about human and physical nature and about what makes for a good economic outcome (see DeMartino, 2000; thanks to Robert Lepenies for emphasizing this point in correspondence).

Greenspan is by no means exceptional among economists in making a consequential mistake. His failure reflects a deep and likely ineradicable knowledge problem in economics. Economists operate in a world of *epistemic insufficiency*, where they largely cannot be certain of the effects of the interventions they advocate (DeMartino, 2013; see also Colander, 2005).[13] The effects of economic policy interventions can be extraordinarily complex and dispersed, and they can extend indefinitely into the future. In this respect economics is closer to the field of environmental science than to clinical medicine or other fields that operate on smaller canvases, treating one client at a time, where the effects of an intervention are relatively contained. Environmentalists Bill Vitek and Wes Jackson (2008: 1) argue that humanity will always be "billions of times more ignorant than knowledgeable" about the physical world we inhabit. Their warning is just as apt in regard to economic phenomena. Epistemic insufficiency implies that even well-meaning and highly skilled economists risk imposing econogenic harm when they try to promote good economic outcomes (cf. McCloskey, 1990).[14]

The condition of epistemic insufficiency under which economists act entails an additional problem: economists cannot control the world in which they operate. There can be and often is substantial slippage between policy recommendation and policy effects owing to unforeseeable vagaries in policy making and implementation and in the responses of economic agents to policy interventions. Economists enjoy *influence without control*. This is the case even in the unusual instances in which economists occupy the role of social engineer—such as they arguably did in the restructuring projects of the 1990s in countries that were transitioning away from command economies, when leading economists at the international financial institutions, government agencies, and think-tanks were able to engage in institutional design on a vast scale. Economists sometimes wield just enough influence to be dangerous—call it the "Jeffrey Sachs in Russia Problem" (DeMartino, 2013). Not least, the policies that economists advocate can be and often are hijacked by special interests for their own ends or are otherwise undermined in execution by unforeseen contingencies or by the unpredictable response of the private actors populating the economy (cf. Friedman, 1972). In the policy arena, politics and not economic science is typically in charge. Moreover, the effects

[13] Nor can they be certain of the effects of policies that were implemented in the past. The conclusion that a certain economic intervention generated particular outcomes requires more than a good data set. It requires counterfactual analysis indicating what would have happened had the intervention not occurred. Presumably, there are cases involving discrete policy interventions of limited scale where the counterfactual may be fairly easy to discern. Most economic policy interventions, however, involve extensive and complex interactions—and in these cases specifying the counterfactual with any degree of certainty may be fairly impossible. This fact complicates all economic policy assessment and helps to account for the interminable nature of many policy disputes. It also confounds the task of tracing harms back to their causes. For insightful commentary on the difficulties of causal historical analysis, see Taleb (2010: 196–200).

[14] Economists are by no means alone in confronting epistemic insufficiency. Philip Tetlock's study of expertise across the professions provides remarkable evidence of consistent failure. In his words, "When we pit experts against minimalist performance algorithms—dilettantes, dart-throwing chimps, and assorted extrapolation algorithms—we find few signs that expertise translates into greater ability to make either 'well-calibrated' or 'discriminating' forecasts" (Tetlock, 2005: 20).

of any intervention will depend on innumerable factors about which the economist's knowledge is at best quite limited (cf. Hayek, 1978; Resnick and Wolff, 1987; McCloskey, 1990; Ruccio and Amariglio, 2003). All of this implies that economic practice is fraught with uncertainty and with the risk of perhaps substantial unintended and unforeseeable harm. The image we should keep in mind when we think about the position of the economic social engineer is of a 10-year old boy behind the wheel of a Hummer, careening down Main Street. Does the child have influence over what's about to happen? Absolutely. But does he enjoy control over those events? Don't bet on it—not your own livelihood and especially, as Taleb (2012) admonishes us, not anyone else's.

Harm resulting from error—or, more broadly, from the imperative facing the professional to act under conditions of epistemic insufficiency in a world that defies dependable prediction or control—is undoubtedly a universal problem in the professions. Its salience in economics represents a difference in degree rather than in kind (see Figure 5.1). If we theorize a continuum from the professional fields in which ignorance is manageable and domesticable, to those where it is unmanageable and consequential, we might place basic civil engineering near the benign pole and medical practice at a middling point.[15] In contrast, economics resides in the perilous zone, where dragons roam and ignorance is vast and dangerous.

Economists also cause harm in ways that may be (relatively) *sui generis*, at least in comparison with those professions that serve individual clients. Economic interventions generally entail disparate effects across society's members, as the Hicks passage cited above indicates. It is in the nature of complex economic systems that even well-designed economic interventions almost invariably cause harm to some economic actors. Think of the standard textbook advocacy of the removal of trade barriers and price supports. In these cases, which are representative of economic policy in general, some in society benefit from market liberalization while others necessarily suffer economic harm.

Economics is unlike many other professions in two important respects: the degree to which harm is inherent in its practice and the distribution of the harms its practice induces. In clinical medicine, for instance, the caregiver regularly confers benefits without inducing harm. When iatrogenic harm occurs it typically results from error, the limits to medical knowledge, incompetence, medical system failure, or malpractice. Moreover, iatrogenic harm afflicts principally the agent whose welfare the caregiver seeks to improve and perhaps those others who are closely related to the agent and who value his welfare. It is certainly not the norm in medicine (or medical research) to harm some without their consent for the benefit of others.[16]

[15] As concerns basic civil engineering I refer to certain of its mundane tasks, such as simple bridge building, and not adventurous projects like large-scale dam construction that involve much greater uncertainties and possibilities for unintended harm.

[16] Although there are instances of third-party harm and harm to some for the benefit of others in the context of public health, where medical decisions affect large groups of people rather than individual patients one at a time and where effects of interventions across a population can be disparate. (Even here, however, harming some for the benefit of others remains the exception rather than the rule). In part for this reason, public health ethics may offer a better guide in the formation of economic ethics than does (clinical) medical ethics.

Adequate knowledge	Moderate knowledge	Hic Sunt Dracones!
Engineering	Medicine	Economics

FIGURE 5.1 Severity of epistemic insufficiency.

In contrast, economists inescapably cause harm. Econogenic harm is an inherent feature of even successful economic interventions; it can and generally does occur even when the economist gets it right. Harm arises whenever a policy that may very well promote aggregate economic interests also worsens the absolute situation of some members of the economy, or substantially exacerbates inequality (see below). Although politicians claim that their preferred economic strategies benefit all of society's members, economists know better. In all but the simplest economies virtually all economic interventions have disparate impact, and many induce significant harm. This is the tragedy of economics: helping some routinely requires damaging others.

Taken together, the depth of epistemic insufficiency in economics and the harm-inducing nature of economic practice imply that economics faces a more urgent duty to engage the matter of harm than do those professions in which harm is a less pervasive feature of professional practice. So does the fact that econogenic harms, although substantial, are often indirect, postponed, and otherwise obscured. Unlike many other professionals, economists typically don't have to confront the people who are harmed by their practice, and they are generally unaware of the extent of and rarely held accountable for the harm (see Angner, 2006; Ravallion, 2009).

And yet, to repeat, we find no tradition of serious inquiry within the profession into the complex nature of economic or econogenic harm. What we find in the history of economic thought are fits and starts—periods such as the 1930s during which leading economists attempted to theorize carefully the ethical entailments of economic harm in the context of policy formation, and periods such as the present, in which economists have "a love-hate relationship" with the established procedures for assessing policy that generates harm (Kanbur, 2003). In general, economics treats harm too casually, perhaps out of an inchoate awareness that facing up to harm in a serious and rigorous way, attending carefully to the claims of those who will be adversely affected by economic interventions, would complicate economic practice to such a degree as to render it untenable.

The Kaldor-Hicks Potential Compensation Test

The predominant approach to harm assessment and mitigation in economics reflects the utilitarian framework from which economics draws its normative foundations. Standard neoclassical economics carries forward the consequentialism and welfarism of classical utilitarianism.[17] These features entail the evaluation of states of affairs by exclusive reference to the levels of welfare of the agents affected by such states. Welfare has been defined in neoclassical theory as levels of utility or, more recently, the extent of preference satisfaction (where existing preferences are generally taken as self-regarding and valid; Sen, 1987; DeMartino, 2000). Unlike classical utilitarianism, however, the consequentialist welfarism of neoclassical thought does not permit cardinal measurements of utility; hence, it disallows interpersonal utility comparisons or the summation of utility levels across distinct individuals. Contemporary welfarist social assessment depends instead on the Pareto criterion in the rare situations where the conditions for Pareto comparisons are met or, much more frequently, on the Kaldor-Hicks potential compensation test. Put simply, Kaldor-Hicks holds that some policy A is preferred to an alternative policy B if the winners under A can fully compensate the losers under A and while retaining net benefit.

The legitimacy of Kaldor-Hicks depends on the persuasiveness of a web of empirical, theoretical, and normative claims about what humans do and should value and about the nature of the harms they suffer as a consequence of economic policies. Neoclassical thought encompasses welfare reducibility of and *commensurability* across goods. Hence, rational agents are able to make comparisons across diverse goods, comparisons that depend exclusively on the extent of welfare the goods transmit. Neoclassical theory adds several restrictions on preferences orderings to ensure their tractability, but that also bias the analysis of harm. One is that preference orders are complete, ensuring that agents can welfare rank all bundles they confront. A second is that preference orderings are *continuous*. Continuity rules out a lexicographic preference ordering "which assigns priority to a good x if a bundle with less of that good is non-preferred regardless of how much of the other goods it contains" (Boadway and Bruce 1984, 182 fn 8). Continuity therefore implies *substitutability* among goods: the loss of a finite amount of one good *v* can always be fully offset in terms of welfare by the increased provision of a finite amount of some other good *w*.

Neoclassical welfarism and its associated assumption set yield an elegant account of harm, and its rectification. Harm is defined exclusively as a reduction in welfare resulting from a diminution in access to one or more goods that agents value. Moreover, commensurability and substitutability imply that agents who suffer harm from the loss of one good can remain at the same level of welfare—and hence, be rendered whole—through increased consumption of other goods. This claim implies in turn that all harms are *reparable* through adequate *compensation*, generally theorized as monetary transfers.

Consider workers who are displaced by a shift in economic policy, such as the removal of tariff protection for an industry employing them for which the country does not enjoy

[17] The term "neoclassical" is used here simply to refer to the standard textbook approach to economics and, in particular, to applied economics. The term is problematic since it is imprecise in what it includes and excludes and since economics today appears to be breaking with some of the central assumptions that guided economics through much of the 20th century. In what follows, I identify those aspects of neoclassical economic theory that are germane to the matter of how economists theorize harm.

a comparative advantage. In the standard economic treatment of the problem only the loss of workers' income registers in the harm accounting. In broader formulations other harms that are associated with unemployment can be figured in, of course.[18] These might include the increased incidence of physical and psychological ailments among the affected workers, increased rates of suicide and crime, and declining asset values (such as housing prices) that are consequent to the policy shift. In keeping with the utilitarian tradition, however, all such damages are treated as reducible to impacts on workers' welfare—as opposed to, say, their substantive freedoms. Full compensation simply requires finding the appropriate magnitude of monetary transfer that will restore the displaced workers to their previous levels of welfare. If full compensation is made, then the workers are taken to suffer no harm from the loss of employment—indeed, they are theorized as indifferent between their pre- and post-unemployment situations since full compensation implies that they have been made whole.

Unlike the Pareto criterion, the usefulness of which in economic application is limited because of conflicting preferences across people concerning possible social states, Kaldor-Hicks is taken to provide a tractable framework for reaching unequivocal judgments on economic policy decisions that entail harm. In Hicks' words, there is

> a perfectly *objective* test which enables us to discriminate between those reorganisations which improve productive efficiency and those which do not. If *A* is made so much better off by the change that he could compensate *B* for his loss, and still have something left over, then the reorganisation is an unequivocal improvement. (Hicks, 1941: 111, emphasis added)

The Kaldor-Hicks potential compensation test provides economists with a wonderfully elegant decision rule. The policy is preferred that is Kaldor-Hicks efficient.[19] Kaldor-Hicks yields a standard of assessment for the applied economist that appears to be minimally normative. The economist should advocate policy interventions that pass the Kaldor-Hicks compensation test and refrain from advocating policies that fail it. On this basis, for instance, economists typically preach the desirability of free trade. In Hicks's own view, "this criterion is more useful than any other as a basis on which to establish maxims of sound economic policy" (Hicks, 1941: 111). With Hicks, many economists believe themselves to be warranted in advocating policies that induce even

[18] This is the norm in cost-benefit analysis, where various effects of alternative policy interventions can be and are factored into policy assessment, such as through the use of contingent valuation, but typically only as determinants of individuals' levels of welfare. For the purposes of this chapter, it suffices to treat cost-benefit analysis as a means to operationalize the Kaldor-Hicks decision rule, and so I do not explore cost-benefit analysis separately here. A fuller treatment would need to examine the relevant practical, technical, and normative differences between them (see Boadway, 1974; Adler and Posner, 2006), and to explore the Coasian tradition as well.

[19] But see Scitovsky (1941), which demonstrates that Kaldor-Hicks assessments of policy options can yield indeterminate results. See also Little (1957: 93), who argues that Kaldor-Hicks is not a test of alternative social states at all, but is rather a more limited value-laden definition of "increased general economic welfare."

substantial harm to some in order to augment aggregate welfare (cf. Kanbur, 2003). Indeed, they do it every day.

Inadequacies of Kaldor-Hicks

Kaldor-Hicks raises several issues that pertain to harm, some of which have been long debated among economists.[20] One well-worn controversy concerns whether *potential* compensation is sufficient to warrant a policy intervention—or whether, as a condition for the economist's support, the losers under a Kaldor-Hicks efficient policy intervention must *actually receive* full compensation for their losses.[21] Hicks and Kaldor thought that potential compensation was generally sufficient; most economists follow their lead. In contrast, Amartya Sen (1987) ridicules the idea that potential compensation provides adequate justification, especially for a policy that benefits the rich but harms the poor. The eminent free trader, Jagdish Bhagwati, concurs:

> Sometimes I wonder whether the younger economists today are taught what Ian Little taught us—that it is not enough that there be potential compensation; compensation must actually be made. Otherwise, imagine a situation where the rich can compensate the poor while still getting richer, yet they do not. Surely, no people in their right minds, or certainly in their true hearts, would approve of the policy change, in that event. (1994: 21)[22]

In fact, full compensation rarely occurs, as Hicks understood (1939: 711). Absent actual compensation, Kaldor-Hicks policy adjustments generate anticipated harm (in comparison with the *ex ante* state of affairs), where the harm is in principle avoidable by foregoing the adjustment.[23] And yet economists tend not to think through carefully

[20] Several controversies surround the use of Kaldor-Hicks that I will not examine here. Marxian, Austrian, and other heterodox traditions largely reject the Kaldor-Hicks test—in part owing to their appreciation of the endogeneity of preference (and subjectivity) formation. See, for instance, Stringham (2001) for an Austrian critique of the use of Kaldor-Hicks in the judicial setting. See also 19 and Sen (1979) for critiques that have emerged within the tradition of welfare economics.

[21] We postpone for just a moment the vitally important question of whether all harms are in fact compensable.

[22] Bhagwati notes, however, that, in practice, compensating each victim of every policy change is infeasible. He advocates instead for a general safety net as a means to ensure compensation. See also Kanbur (2003: 32), who calls for automatic redistribution mechanisms and safety nets "to complement project-specific compensation," and Gasper (2016) for a human rights approach to manage justly harm-inducing policy adjustments.

[23] It can plausibly be argued, of course, that *not* implementing a Kaldor-Hicks-efficient policy also causes harm to those who would benefit from the state of affairs that the policy would yield. Hence, Kaldor-Hicks policy assessment requires a careful engagement with the ethical standing of competing claims—of those who would suffer relative to their current situation were the policy to be implemented and those who would suffer relative to their potential situation were the status quo to be preserved when an alternative state of affairs that benefits them is available. Thinking through this matter, economists

what might be their obligations to those who populate the economy when their practice routinely induces harms that are both foreseeable and preventable.

A second matter ought to be equally controversial, although economists to date have not given it the attention it is due. Are economists warranted in advocating all policy options that pass the Kaldor-Hicks test, irrespective of the matter of compensation? Or are there deontological (or other) limits on the policies that deserve their support? And if there are such limits, what are they?

A comparison with the field of public health might help to elucidate what is so disconcerting about the economist's mechanical embrace of Kaldor-Hicks. Is a physician warranted in causing harm to some to benefit others? For instance, is a physician warranted in corralling together in an isolation unit those who have been exposed to a dangerous pathogen during an epidemic, but who are as of yet asymptomatic, so as to reduce the risk of infection to the general public? Doing so might be taken to violate important rights (to mobility, to protecting and caring for oneself as one sees fit) and may also place the isolated individuals at much greater risk of illness and even death than if they were free to migrate away from the diseased site. Is it ethically appropriate for the medical profession to impose quarantines, then? Many of us—and certainly most economists—would answer in the affirmative. In this case, we tend to think it right (although surely regrettable) to impose potentially severe harms on some for the greater benefit of the broader population. If pressed to defend our view we would no doubt offer Kaldor-Hicks consistent arguments as justification.

But now consider an alternative case: is it ethically appropriate for a physician to snatch a healthy individual off the street in order to harvest organs from him, killing him in the process, in order to improve or perhaps even save the lives of many others? Less dramatically, is the physician warranted in merely extracting a kidney from an unwilling donor—a procedure that the donor will likely survive and that is certain to save the life of another? I presume that most economists would reject the legitimacy of organ snatching, whether or not compensation is paid, viewing the practice as an egregious violation of personal autonomy. We should take note, however, that harvesting body parts against the will of the donor is consistent with the utilitarian logic underlying J. J. C. Smart's claim that appears as the epigraph to this essay—and, under standard economic assumptions, it is likely to meet the conditions set forth in the Kaldor-Hicks compensation test. Does that fact make it a commendable policy?

The side-by-side consideration of the two similar cases suggests a difficult question: just what is the ethical difference between them? *Is there one*? Both cases involve harming some severely and against their will to benefit others—potentially many

would do well to consider carefully the arguments of theorists such as Feinberg (1984) and Shiffrin (2012) who claim that failure to provide benefits (generally) does not cause harm. Both privilege "not harming" over "benefitting" others. This line of argument creates perhaps insuperable obstacles to the use of the Kaldor-Hicks test in assessing competing interests when formulating public policy because it implies that benefits and harms are not (morally) commensurable—and hence not comparable via any simple metric.

others. Yet we intuit some sort of compelling ethical difference.[24] Asking the question, "just what is the difference?" requires us to pause and think. And that moment of hesitation, in which we reflect carefully about which harms physicians and public health officials can and can't impose on some for the benefit of others, gives us reason for hope for ethical medical practice.

In contrast, economists do not tend to hesitate. We are trained to apply Kaldor-Hicks reflexively whenever we face policy disputes, even when substantial harm will follow from the policy option that passes the test. In so doing, we fail to probe sufficiently whether the imposition of harm is appropriate. In possession of Kaldor-Hicks, economists do not typically ask themselves whether the cases they confront are the economic analogues to medical quarantines or to involuntary organ snatching. Instead, we make the error of reducing complex ethical judgment to what Radest (1997) calls "moral geometry," imposing a simplistic, mechanical formula to resolve the matter at hand when nothing less than deep, nuanced, and careful consideration will do. In possession of the convenient decision rule that Kaldor-Hicks provides, economists are seduced into treating individuals merely as means and not also as ends. On the state of ethical practice in the profession, Kant would despair. (White, 2006)

The Paretian Defense of Potential Compensation

The most compelling defense of potential as opposed to actual compensation warrants attention. Several theorists have offered an underdeveloped or proto-contractarian case for Kaldor-Hicks—it is that we all benefit by, and therefore have good reason to support, constitutional arrangements that encourage social innovations that promote rising incomes over time even if each of those innovations risks harm to some members of society[25]. This is a claim of the generalized benefits of efficiency: since we are all beneficiaries of a system that generates efficiency-inducing innovations, the harm that befalls any one of us from any particular innovation is ethically benign. Demanding actual,

[24] One is that those who have been exposed to a pathogen during an epidemic represent "innocent threats" to others, whereas unwilling organ donors presumably do not. This consideration weighs in favor of coercion in the case of epidemics but not in the case of organ transfers. But the concept of innocent threats provides little comfort or direction to economists using Kaldor-Hicks to assess economic policy. After all, those harmed by an economic policy shift (such as trade liberalization) do not generally represent a threat to others (under any common interpretation of the term "threat"): they occupy the position of unwilling organ donors rather than potential transmitters of disease. Hence, the innocent threat rationale cannot be used to sustain the harm that is imposed on them. See Nozick (1974) for a provocative although ultimately incomplete discussion of the ethics surrounding the treatment of innocent threats.

A possible response appears in the previous endnote, of course. It can be argued (though without the assistance of leading harm scholars) that the beneficiaries of trade restrictions do pose a threat to the welfare of those who stand to benefit from trade liberalization. But then the reverse is also true: the advocates of trade liberalization pose a threat to the welfare of those who benefit from trade restrictions.

[25] See DeMartino (forthcoming) for a more extensive examination of the Paretian defense of Kaldor-Hicks.

immediate compensation in those particular instances where one is hurt would amount to "double-dipping" since each of us is already compensated in the long run for the risk of harm we bear through the diffused benefits of innovation. The argument presumes hypothetical approval by all of us (or by our idealized representatives, operating behind a Rawlsian veil of ignorance) of an economic system that will necessarily harm members without compensation—not for the greater good of the greatest number, as a utilitarian would have it, but ultimately for the greater good of each and every one of us. The defense of potential as opposed to actual contribution is most securely grounded, then, in Pareto rather than Bentham (cf. Polinsky, 1972; Adler and Posner, 1999).[26]

Does this argument satisfy as a defense of an economic system that permits uncompensated, Kaldor-Hicks-consistent policy adjustments? That would depend in part on the nature of the harms that are associated with successive innovations and whether they are serially independent and relatively small in comparison with the associated benefits (Kanbur, 2003). If, for instance, today's winners are just as likely as today's losers to be tomorrow's losers, and vice versa, and if each of the successive harms is relatively minor (in a qualitative or quantitative sense) so that they are likely to be cancelled out by a series of prior or subsequent benefits, then each of us may be expected to benefit over time. If these conditions hold, and if the system on balance produces more socially beneficial innovations than alternative systems that entail less risk of harm, or that require compensation for every harm, then there is a reasonable basis for inferring hypothetical or tacit consent by rational actors to an arrangement that casts each of us occasionally in the role of loser (see Coleman, 1980; Posner, 1980).

Several objections have been and can be offered to the Paretian defense of uncompensated harms, however. One is that some economic innovations entail harms to agents from which they may never recover—either because of the qualitative nature of the harm (about which, more below) or its magnitude. This is the case, for instance, in large-scale development projects (like dam construction) that entail the forced relocation of large numbers of people (Gasper, 2016; Kanbur, 2003) or social engineering schemes that fundamentally alter a society's basic economic institutions. In cases like these, where the nature, depth, and extent of harm is such that the losers will never recover, economists cannot take normative cover in the contractarian defense of Kaldor-Hicks for the proposed policy—absent actual compensation—no matter the size of the aggregate welfare gains. A second objection is that, away from the blackboard and in real economies, the incidence of gains and losses tends to be serially correlated (cf. Adler and Posner, 1999). Being a loser today is correlated with having been a loser yesterday and with being a loser yet again tomorrow. Correlation follows from the obvious fact that those with the greatest economic and political power often use their

[26] Polinsky (1972: 409) writes: "By broadening the notion of compensation to include bundles of changes that have some effective randomness in distribution, it thereby becomes possible to leave particular individuals uncompensated and worse off for single changes, yet assure them that they can (mathematically) expect to be better off as a result of the entire bundle (with the probability of actually being made worse off set at a value approaching zero)."

influence to secure from among the set of available policy options those interventions that reflect their own, particular, and immediate interests. Moreover, even when elites refrain from exercising their influence to bias policy, they are typically in a much better position than others to insure themselves against or deflect the harms that would otherwise occasionally befall them.[27] This is not to deny that even the losers may secure some benefits from harm-inducing innovations. Workers who lose careers, status, income, wealth, political efficacy, and substantive freedom owing to trade liberalization may yet take advantage of lower consumer prices at Walmart, for instance. Instead, the claim is that a system that concentrates harms among some for the ultimate benefit of others fails to find cover in the Paretian defense. It certainly cannot be presumed to enjoy the universal consent of rational Rawlsian deliberators, let alone actual economic agents.

Compensable Versus Noncompensable Harm

The welfarist approach underlying Kaldor-Hicks tends to overlook conceptual distinctions that figure prominently in serious investigations of harm beyond economics and that ought to be engaged in analyses of economic harm.[28] One set of relevant issues (introduced earlier), which has been papered over in the consequentialist welfarism of neoclassical thought, is most important and also most difficult for economists to manage. It concerns the question whether all goods are to be theorized as *commensurable* and *substitutable* and whether, relatedly, all harms are viewed as *reparable* and, hence, *compensable*. The four concepts are analytically linked, but distinct (see Figure 5.2).

We took note above of central neoclassical assumptions concerning preferences. All goods are commensurable owing to welfarist reductionism; moveover, continuous preference orderings rule out lexicographic preferences. The implication for harm theory

McCloskey (2010) points out that the rule utilitarian tradition that runs from Mill and Sidgwick through Harsanyi, Buchanan, Tullock, and Rawls establishes a compelling case for the legitimacy of a constitution to govern economic interactions that permits uncompensated harms that yield generalized economic improvement. Also see Hicks (1939: 711–712; emphasis in original) where he summarizes the "hard-boiled attitude" of economists, which is "to reject all compensation on the ground that such risks *ought* to have been allowed for." If this line of argument is correct, then Kantian concerns evaporate.

[27] A Chicago School economist (but a friend nonetheless) replies: "But you know how I will answer this, in all seriousness and truth: fix the distribution of income and especially wealth directly. Don't use the price system to do the job!"

The objection has merit. Perhaps in a world with a fair distribution of income and wealth and where individuals enjoy relatively equal political efficacy, application of Kaldor-Hicks would be far less apt to penalize some routinely and severely for the benefit of others. Perhaps in *that* world, potential as opposed to actual compensation might suffice. Can we agree, then, to postpone reliance on Kaldor-Hicks (or at least refuse to take refuge in the contractarian defense of the decision rule) until that world is realized?

[28] A fuller treatment than is possible here would require examination of other harm-related conceptual distinctions that are sidestepped under the Kaldor-Hicks compensation test. Important distinctions include *inter alia* that between direct and indirect harm (McIntyre, 2011), doing and allowing harm (Howard-Snyder, 2008), and positive and negative harm (Friedman, 1962).

	Reparable Harm	Irreparable Harm
Commensurable, Substitutable Goods	Compensable Harm	Undefined
Incommensurable, Nonsubstitutable Goods	Noncompensable Harm: - Acknowledgement: Apology, Sympathy, Gratitude, Recognition, Respect, Honor	Noncompensable Harm: - Remedial Measures Unavailable or Inadequate

FIGURE 5.2 Compensable versus noncompensable harm.

is profound: with no lexicographic orderings, we are entitled to theorize all goods as substitutable, and all harms as compensable (residing in the northwest cell of Figure 2). Under this assumption set monetary transfer effects repair in the sense of rendering the harm victim whole.

What remains of Kaldor-Hicks if we relax these assumptions? Absent commensurability and substitutability, we can no longer presume universal compensability for harms. In that case, Kaldor-Hicks collapses as a viable decision rule. At the expense of stating the obvious, even potential compensation requires compensability. Nor can we presume that all harms are reparable: a cursory review of Table 1 should disabuse us of that conviction. For some harms, repair is out of the question (the southeast cell of Figure 2). Others might be reparable, wholly or in part, through noncompensatory mechanisms of private or public acknowledgment of the harms suffered (southwest cell).[29] Examples include socially sanctioned apology, the expression of genuine sympathy, or recognition for one's loss, such as attends the processes of truth-telling commissions in post-conflict situations. Moreover, harms suffered in the line of duty (e.g., by first responders to crises) or in public service more generally might warrant public displays of gratitude and respect, or the granting of public honors. Acts of acknowledgment—whether public and ceremonial or private and informal—may serve to heal the harmed agent in ways that attempted compensation might fail to do (Bouris, 2007).

Sometimes, of course, monetary transfers may occur in the context of acknowledgment; indeed, apology, sympathy, recognition, gratitude, respect, or honor might even manifest as a monetary transfer. The conjoint provision of acknowledgment and monetary transfer can lead to confusion in the minds of economists. The "sorry money" that is paid in New Guinea, as exemplified in a story recounted by Jared Diamond (2012), is illustrative. In the wake of a traffic accident that kills a child

[29] Reparability is a matter of degree. Acknowledgement might be appropriate for many instances and forms of harm, although the extent to which it ameliorates the harm would vary across cases.

but where the truck driver is exonerated of any wrongdoing, the relatively wealthy truck company owner gives money to the parents and says to them, "This money is nothing compared to your son's life, but I give it to show how sorry we are." Here money changes hands but there is no compensation. The simple example highlights the necessity of deciphering the social function of monetary transfers in instances of harm. Money transfers carry diverse meanings depending on the identities of the giver and receiver, the context in which the transfers occur, and the agents' respective purposes in giving and receiving. It is an elementary mistake to presume, with the economist, that all transfers represent monetary compensation—in which money substitutes for other lost goods—that has the capacity to render the harmed agent whole.

In her examination of bourgeois virtues (where she recounts and comments critically on Diamond's analysis of sorry money), McCloskey (forthcoming) discusses approvingly a historical trend in the Germanic north of Europe to commercialize disputes over injury or harm that might otherwise generate social conflict and disrupt economic progress. In place of honor-based, eye-for-eye justice, "Germanic law codes of early times encourage *cash* compensation for dishonor" (McCloskey, forthcoming). Payment for wrongs in the form of *wergelt*," which became the norm in northern Europe, helped to curtail costly feuds that otherwise might have disrupted commerce. In contrast, in the supposedly more advanced and mercantile south, a primitive approach to justice survived. "[F]rom Homer to El Cid to *The Godfather*, honor is absolute and wrongs are righted through altogether non-bourgeois forms of retribution that could and did disturb economic advancement."

A fundamental distinction needs to be drawn, however, between the bourgeois view of compensation that McCloskey recommends and the modern neoclassical view. Commercialization of harms need not presume that all harms are reparable and compensable. The virtue of payment for harms (in coins, cattle, and other goods, as was common under Germanic codes) can reside in its *instrumental effects*—keeping the peace, incentivizing and sustaining beneficial commerce, and promoting economic advance. The idea that those who harm must make amends in ways that are consistent with the social interest bears no likeness at all to the naïve, modern economic treatment of all harms as reparable and, indeed, compensable. They are not. Just ask the parents who are awarded damages for the wrongful death of a child whether they are indifferent between having their child and having the money. The payment (especially if accompanied by recognition of their loss, or apology) may dissuade them from taking revenge on the agent who caused the child's death, to be sure, but it does not compensate them in the sense of rendering them whole. The economist's mistake, and it is an egregious one, lies in subsuming all instances of transfer under the category of *compensation for reparable harms*—and in believing further that once compensation has been paid, the harm has been fully offset.

Sorry money and nonmonetary apology, recognition, and honor all reflect an awareness of a deep truth that economists have long repressed: not all harms are created equal, and not all are compensable.[30] A cursory review of the taxonomy given in Table 5.1 suggests that it is irresponsible and even callous to presume that all harms are reparable. Some rights violations, for instance, are generally viewed as too precious to repair, after the fact, with compensation (Rendleman, 2002). Alternatively, some harms, such as being dishonored, are not amenable to compensation at all: "Once lost, honor is extraordinarily hard, if not impossible, to regain . . . the very idea of [pricing honor] seems inconsistent with the concept" (McGowan, 2010: 589, 591).[31] It is therefore unfortunate that the standard economic assumptions regarding commensurability, substitutability, and reparability facilitate reliance on a convenient but simple-minded decision rule where nothing less than careful, difficult deliberation is required. The strategy of *presuming what should be explicitly investigated* suits the needs of economists in their pursuit of professional authority, tractable decision rules, and policy influence far more than the interests of those whom economists purport to serve.

Permanent damages to one's psychological or physical health, social standing, relationships, autonomy, and basic freedoms do not lend themselves to full repair—and certainly not by monetary compensation. But then, which harms are reparable, and which are not? Which reparable harms are compensable, and which are not? Which compensable harms should be compensated, and which should not? What is to be done when economist-advocated interventions potentially threaten or actually do cause noncompensable or irreparable harm, and what authority should the economist have in answering these questions? One looks to the economic tradition in vain for careful investigation of these vexing questions.

Rights Violations

There is a fundamentally important and ethically salient distinction to be drawn between those social innovations that occur without violating people's rights and those that do. The work of Nozick (1974) is illustrative in this regard. Nozick's libertarianism is founded on a "side-constraint" view of rights that holds that no individual (or institution) may violate the rights of others in order to achieve valued goals (such as economic

[30] It should be said that forensic economists and many in the field of law and economics tend to be far more careful in their judgments about the nature and complexity of harm, perhaps because the concept of irreparable harm is well established (although also contested) in the judicial setting. See, for instance, Keating, (2003).

[31] Kaldor (1939: 551) recognized that economic policies could induce "losses of a non-pecuniary kind," such as when "workers derive satisfaction from their particular kind of work, and are obliged to change their employment" or when "individuals feel that the carrying out of the policy involves an interference with their individual freedom." But Kaldor did not treat nonpecuniary harms as irreparable or noncompensable. Instead, he concluded simply that, in such cases, "something more than their previous level of money income will be necessary to secure their previous level of enjoyment." Unfortunately, the economics profession largely followed Kaldor in trivializing nonpecuniary harms by simply reducing it to a coefficient (greater than one) that is applied to lost income.

efficiency). Indeed, the side-constraint approach holds that one may not violate another's rights even when the purpose of so doing is to minimize rights violations in the aggregate. Rights are taken instead to be inviolable constraints on how we act toward each other and on how the institutions we create (such as corporations and the state) treat each of society's members.

In Nozick's account, actions by the state that promote Kaldor-Hicks efficiency but violate rights are ethically indictable despite their beneficial economic consequences for others or even for those agents whose rights are violated (cf. Friedman, 1962). A notable example is the takings associated with eminent domain—or the forced relocation that attends large development projects—whereby a government appropriates private property (or terminates communal access to common property) for public purposes. Harm appears here not just in the form of a loss of income or property, but also in the deeper Kantian sense of a rights violation (which may or may not cause a loss of income) that treats some persons merely as means. In libertarian and other rights-based frameworks, violations of this sort cannot be justified with compensation or with the promise of higher net income that results from the rights-transgressing act.[32] Nor can they be easily justified with a contractarian claim of rational assent to a regime that routinely violates rights (cf. Feinberg, 1986, ch. 22). From this perspective, there must be an explicit agreement among each of society's members to live under an arrangement that distributes harms and benefits without attention in each case to rights; or, failing that unanimity, each policy innovation must be probed to ensure that it does not violate anyone's rights. Only an *actual* voluntary bargain between an economic actor and the state (where, for instance, the agent willingly agrees to sell her property to the state) resolves the normative problem. Short of that kind of explicit bargain, Kaldor-Hicks efficient policy may very well entail substantial harm in the form of rights transgressions that Kaldor-Hicks cannot begin to theorize properly, validate, or compensate.[33]

[32] Confusion on this point may arise from the fact that Nozick's framework demands restitution for those whose rights have been violated. It might seem, then, that rights violations can be compensated for unproblematically via monetary payments. But, in the Nozickean framework, it is important to keep in view the distinction between the *economic consequences* of the rights violation, which can in principle be rectified, and the rights violation itself. It is not the case that the victim of a rights violation who has secured restitution for his or her economic losses is made whole. Were that the case, Nozick's side-constraint approach to rights would evaporate since all transgressions would be permitted provided compensation is paid after the fact. I thank Eugenia Goh and Patrick Sutherland for conversation that clarified for me this distinction.

[33] Like libertarianism, the rights-focused capabilities approach to equality and development (as freedom) of Sen (1992, 2000), Nussbaum (1992), and others also rejects the presumption that all harms are reparable and compensable. Capabilities scholars argue that the diverse beings and doings (or functionings) that people have reason to value are not necessarily commensurable and substitutable. Harm that takes the form of a diminution in one functionings domain—such as loss of self-respect or social standing—cannot be fully offset by increased performance in other domains—such as improved personal welfare. To live in a gilded cage is still to be enslaved, and the trappings of luxury in such a case cannot compensate for the loss of freedom that it entails.

On Inequality

In applying Kaldor-Hicks only agents' absolute losses and gains typically register in the economist's ledger.[34] Absent here is concern for economic inequality since a policy that increases inequality is just as apt to pass the Kaldor-Hicks potential compensation test as a policy that has the opposite effect. Indeed, the Kaldor-Hicks criterion is agnostic in regards to inequality. Applied economists typically ignore the question of whether increasing inequality in itself might harm the losers from a policy shift beyond the harm suffered by an absolute decline in their incomes. Hence, it is also ignored in calculating full compensation.[35] But economic inequality may induce all manner of harms, as countless theorists from Marx and Veblen to Sen and Stiglitz have by now argued at length.[36]

Kanbur (2003) notes that equality-minded economists can and do incorporate egalitarian considerations into Kaldor-Hicks assessments by weighting the losses and gains to the poor more heavily than losses or gains to the wealthy. On its face, the weighting procedure registers an appropriate concern for fairness by disqualifying some policy initiatives that favor the rich over the poor. But it does not disallow any policies that increase inequality per se, even egregiously, provided the absolute position of the poor does not deteriorate (such policy adjustments are theorized as Pareto improvements). Moreover, among the set of policies that harm the poor in absolute terms while also worsening inequality, the application of an egalitarian system of weights to gains and losses paradoxically yields a bias for policies that do the most to worsen income inequality.

Consider the two policy options in Figure 5.3, each of which benefits the rich but harms the poor. Both policies meet the conditions of Kaldor-Hicks since the gains to the winners more than offset the losses to the losers. If we impose egalitarian weights in which the losses to the poor are multiplied by a factor of three, then policy 1, which generates just a small increase in inequality, no longer passes muster. In contrast, policy 2, which substantially exacerbates inequality, would be deemed acceptable (and, indeed, wonderful). The example demonstrates the difficulty of reconciling Kaldor-Hicks with egalitarian concerns and especially with the view that relative inequality (above some threshold) is itself pernicious.

[34] A comprehensive treatment of economic harm would require a careful investigation of the matter of inequality. Here, I restrict myself to a few points that relate most directly to Kaldor-Hicks.

[35] Utility functions are generally (although not necessarily) defined in ways that rule out "envious" preferences.

[36] For instance, Sen (1992) claims that severe inequality can cause harm by diminishing levels of welfare or agency among the poor. The relatively poor in a wealthy society might lack self-respect, social capital, or political voice. Not all economists share the view that inequality causes harm, of course (see McCloskey, 2014). Many economists would view the connection between economic inequality and attendant social problems such as failed schools, racially biased incarceration policies, and the like as contingent rather than necessary. Moreover, some economists argue that inequality entails important economic and political benefits (see Friedman, 1962; Mankiw, 2013).

Policy 1		*Policy 2*	
Gains to the rich:	2	Gains to the rich:	20
Losses to the poor:	1	Losses to the poor:	1

FIGURE 5.3 Kaldor-Hicks test with egalitarian weights.

Conclusion

Economists cause harm. Econogenic harm can be predictable, preventable, direct, immediate, and visible, but it can also be unpredictable, unpreventable, indirect, postponed, and largely invisible. The harm can be massive, and it can routinely affect those who can least afford to bear it. But economists nonetheless strive to do good, in part by theorizing and advocating policies and other interventions that promise to eradicate suffering, promote prosperity and freedom, and achieve a range of other valued social goods and outcomes.

Recognition of the ubiquity of econogenic harm does not necessitate professional withdrawal from the policy domain or other arenas of economic practice—any more than recognition of iatrogenic harm requires physicians to retire from the field of medical practice. Not acting, too, causes harm—some of which might be substantial, avoidable, and irreparable. *Causing harm while answering the call to do good: that is the inescapable tragedy of economic practice.* And yet the economics profession has largely failed to wrestle with the complex nature of harm, investigate the pervasiveness and depth of econogenic harm, and explore carefully and openly its duties to those it purports to help but so often also damages.

The underlying assumptions and consequentialist welfarism of neoclassical theory have served as enablers for those looking to repress serious consideration of harm. Not least, neoclassical theory holds an account of the commensurability of all goods based on their respective contributions to welfare, a narrow conception of harm as the diminution in agents' welfare stemming from reduced access to goods that they value, and a contentious premise regarding the substitutability among goods that implies the reparability of harm. Commensurability, substitutability, and reparability ensure that any harm can be fully offset via monetary compensation. In this analytical and normative landscape the Kaldor-Hicks potential compensation test provides immense service to the economics profession by facilitating economists' influence in the always ethically charged field of policy formation while relieving them of the ethical burdens associated with even severe econogenic harm. Kaldor-Hicks is taken as a technical and objective tool that can solve ethical problems all the while ignoring the fact that, as McCloskey (2005: 23) might say, ethical judgment "does not inhere in a number."

A wide and largely unexplored terrain of inquiry into the nature of harm, economic harm, and econogenic harm awaits those economists who are prepared to make even minor departures from neoclassical theory's standard assumption set, welfarist normative framework, and decision rules. The terrain comprises both positive and normative questions and their necessary interdependence. The prospect of a new field of inquiry in economic harm and econogenesis, nested as it should be in a broader field of professional economic ethics, is unsettling, to be sure. There is the risk that it could generate professional confusion and even paralysis in a world that is badly in need of economists' interventions. But at the risk of hectoring, it needs to be said that the inquiry is imperative, despite the risks. A profession that is in the harm business—routinely generating substantial harm as a necessary byproduct of its efforts to promote the social good—has a deep, inescapable obligation to examine the nature of that harm and the ethical burdens that attend it.

Acknowledgments

Thanks to Jack Donnelly, Ilene Grabel, Robert Lepenies, and Deirdre McCloskey for their valuable comments on a prior draft of this paper; to Noelle Frampton, Eugenia Goh, Hanna Parakhnevich, Patrick Sutherland, and Michelle Woodruff for wonderful research assistance; to Mathew Adler, Jack Amariglio, S. Charusheela, Jonathan Diskin, Susan Feiner, Jonathan Feinstein, Craig Freedman, Daniel Hammond, Ravi Kanbur, Donald Katzner, Lewis Kornhauser, Ric McIntyre, Erik Olsen, Ceren Ozselcuk, J. Andres Ramirez, Mark Silverman, Jacinda Swanson, Paul Turpin, Jack Ward, Lucas Wilson, Peter Wissoker, and Richard Wolff for their thoughtful correspondence on themes explored in the paper; and to the participants at the 2013 SCEME Seminar in Economic Methodology in Cambridge, United Kingdom.

References

Adler, M. D., and E. A. Posner. 1999. "Rethinking Cost-Benefit Analysis." *Yale Law Journal* 109(2): 165–247.

Adler, M. D., and E. A. Posner. 2006. *New Foundations of Cost-Benefit Analysis*. Cambridge, MA: Harvard University Press.

Andrews, E. L. Oct. 24, 2008. Greenspan concedes flaws in deregulatory approach. *New York Times*: B1.

Angner, E. 2006. "Economists as Experts: Overconfidence in Theory and Practice." *Journal of Economic Methodology* 13(1): 1–24.

Bhagwati, J. Jan/Feb 1994. "Which Way? Free Trade or Protection?" *Challenge* 37: 17–24.

Boadway, R. W. 1974. "The Welfare Foundations of Cost-Benefit Analysis." *The Economic Journal* 84(336): 926–939.

Bouris, E. 2007. *Complex Political Victims*. Bloomfield, CT: Kumarian Press.

Colander, D. 2005. "From Muddling Through to the Economics of Control: Views of Applied Policy from J. N. Keynes to Abba Lerner." *History of Political Economy* 37(Supplement 1): 277–291.

Coleman, J. 1980. "Efficiency, Utility, and Wealth Maximization." *Hofstra Legal Review* 8: 509–551.

DeMartino, G. F. 2000. *Global Economy, Global Justice: Theoretical Objections and Policy Alternatives to Neoliberalism.* London: Routledge.

DeMartino, G. F. 2011. *The Economist's Oath: On the Need for and Content of Professional Economic Ethics.* London: Oxford University Press.

DeMartino, G. F. 2013. "Epistemic Aspects of Economic Practice and the Need for Professional Economic Ethics." *Review of Social Economy* 71(2): 166–186.

DeMartino, G.F. Forthcoming. "Harming Irreparably: On Neoliberalism, Kaldor-Hicks, and the Paretian Guarantee" (Will provide full citation before publication).

Diamond. J. 2012. *The World Until Yesterday: What Can We Learn from Traditional Societies?* New York: Viking.

Elster, J. 1982. "Sour Grapes—Utilitarianism and the Genesis of Wants." In *Utilitarianism and Beyond*, edited by A. Sen and B. Williams, pp. 219–238. Cambridge: Cambridge University Press.

Feinberg, J. 1984. *Harm to Others: The Moral Limits of the Criminal Law.* Oxford, UK: Oxford University Press.

Feinberg, J. 1986. Harm to Self: The Moral Limits of the Criminal Law, vol. 3. Oxford, UK: Oxford University Press.

Friedman, M. 1962. *Capitalism and Freedom.* Chicago: Chicago University Press.

Friedman, M. 1972. *An Economist's Protest: Columns in Political Economy.* Glen Ridge, NJ: T. Horton.

Gasper, D. 2016. "The Ethics of Economic Development and Human Displacement." In *The Oxford Handbook of Professional Economic Ethics*, edited by G. F. DeMartino and D. N. McCloskey, pp. 71–97. Oxford, UK: Oxford University Press.

Hayek, F. 1978. *New Studies in Philosophy, Politics, Economics and the History of Ideas*, London: Routledge.

Hicks, J. R. 1939. "The Foundations of Welfare Economics." *The Economic Journal* 49(196): 696–712.

Hicks, J. R. 1941. "The Rehabilitation of Consumers' Surplus." *The Review of Economic Studies* 8(2): 108–116.

Howard-Snyder, F. 2008. "Doing vs. Allowing Harm." *The Stanford Encyclopedia of Philosophy (Fall 2008 Edition)*, Edward N. Zalta (ed.), http://plato.stanford.edu/archives/fall2008/entries/doing-allowing/.

Kaldor, N. 1939. "Welfare Propositions of Economics and Interpersonal Comparisons of Utility. *Economic Journal* 49(195): 549-52.

Kanbur, R. 2003. "Development Economics and the Compensation Principle." *International Social Science Journal* 55(175): 27–35.

Keating, G. 2003. "Pressing Precaution Beyond the Point of Cost-Justification." *Vanderbilt Law Review* 56(3): 651–748.

Linklater, A. 2011. *The Problem of Harm in World Politics: Theoretical Investigations.* Cambridge, UK: Cambridge University Press.

Little, I. M. D. 1957. *A Critique of Welfare Economics, 2nd Edition.* London: Oxford University Press.

Lowenstein, R. 2000. *When Genius Failed: The Rise and Fall of Long-Term Capital Management.* New York: Random House.

Mankiw, N. G. 2013. "Defending the One Percent." *Journal of Economic Perspectives* 27(3): 21–34.

Marglin, S. A. 2008. *The Dismal Science: How Thinking Like an Economist Undermines Community*. Cambridge, MA: Harvard University Press.

McCloskey, D. N. 1990. *If You're So Smart: The Narrative of Economic Expertise*. Chicago: University of Chicago Press.

McCloskey, D. N. 2005. "The Trouble with Mathematics and Statistics in Economics." *History of Economic Ideas* 13(3): 85–102.

McCloskey, D. N. 2010. *Bourgeois Dignity: Why Economics Can't Explain the Modern World*. Chicago: University of Chicago.

McCloskey, D. N. 2010 (Oct. 4). "Bourgeois Dignity: A Revolution in Rhetoric." *Cato Unbound*, http://www.cato-unbound.org/2010/10/04/deirdre-mccloskey/bourgeois-dignity-revolution-rhetoric.

McCloskey, D. N. 2014. "Equality lacks relevance if the poor are growing richer." *Financial Times*, August 11. http://www.ft.com/cms/s/0/4c62ddaa-e698-11e3-9a20-00144feabdco.html#axzz3AIRKJid5.

McCloskey, D. N. Forthcoming. *Bourgeois Equality: How Betterment Became Ethical, 1600-1848, and Then Suspect*. Chicago: University of Chicago Press.

McGowan, D. 2010. "Irreparable Harm." Lewis & Clark Law Review 14: 577–596.

McIntyre, A. 2011. "Doctrine of Double Effect." *The Stanford Encyclopedia of Philosophy* (Fall 2011 Edition), Edward N. Zalta (ed.), http://plato.stanford.edu/archives/fall2011/entries/double-effect/.

Meessen, B., Z. Zhenzhong, W. Van Damme, N. Devadasan, B. Criel, and G. Bloom. (2003). "Iatrogenic Poverty." *Tropical Medicine & International Health* 8(7): 581–584.

National Association of Forensic Economics (NAFE). Undated. "Statement of Ethical Principles and Principles of Professional Practice National Association of Forensic Economics (NAFE)." Available at http://nafe.net/about-nafe/nafesethics-statement.html.

Nozick, R. 1974. *Anarchy, State, Utopia*. New York: Basic Books.

Nussbaum, M. 1992 (May). "Human Functionings and Social Justice: In Defense of Aristotelian Essentialism." *Political Theory* 20(2): 202–246.

Polinsky, A. M. 1972. "Probabilistic Compensation Criteria." *Quarterly Journal of Economics* 86(3): 407–425.

Posner, R. A. 1980. "The Ethical and Political Basis of the Efficiency Norm in Common Law Adjudication." *Hofstra Legal Review* 8: 487–507.

Radest, H. B. 1997. "First, Do No Harm! Medical Ethics and Moral Education." *Humanism Today* 11. https://web.archive.org/web/20020109023341/http://www.humanismtoday.org/vol11/radest.html.

Ravallion, M. 2009. "Evaluation in the Practice of Development." *The World Bank Observer* 24(1): 29–53.

Rendleman, D. 2002. "Irreparability Resurrected? Does a Recalibrated Irreparable Injury Rule Threaten the Warren Court's Establishment Clause Legacy?" *Washington and Lee Law Review* 59(4): 1343–1406.

Resnick, S. A., and R. D. Wolff. 1987. *Knowledge and Class*. Chicago: Chicago University Press.

Ruccio, D. F. and J. Amariglio. 2003. *Postmodern Moments in Economics*. Princeton, NJ: Princeton University Press.

Scitovsky, T. 1941. "A Note on Welfare Propositions in Economics." *Review of Economic Studies* 9: 77–88.

Sen, A. 1979. "The Welfare Basis of Real Income Comparisons." *Journal of Economic Literature* 17(1): 1–45.

Sen, A. 1987. *On Ethics and Economics*. London, UK: Blackwell.

Sen, A. 1992. *Inequality Reexamined*. Cambridge, MA: Harvard University Press.

Sen, A. 2000. *Development as Freedom*. New York: Anchor Books.

Sharpe, V. A., and A. I. Faden. 1998. *Medical Harm: Historical, Conceptual, and Ethical Dimensions of Iatrogenic Harm*. Cambridge: Cambridge University Press.

Shiffrin, S. V. 2012. "Harm and its Moral Significance." *Legal Theory*, 18: 357-398.

Smart, J. J. C. 1973. "An Outline of a System of Utilitarian Ethics." In *Utilitarianism: For and Against*, edited by J. J. C. Smart and B. Williams. Cambridge: Cambridge University Press, 1-74.

Stringham, E. 2001 (Summer). "Kaldor-Hicks Efficiency and the Problem of Central Planning." *The Quarterly Journal of Austrian Economics*, 4(2): 41–50.

Stuckler, D., and S. Basu. 2013. *The Body Economic: Why Austerity Kills*. New York: Basic Books.

Stuckler, D., L. King, and M. McKee. 2009, Jan. 1. "Mass Privatisation and the Post-Communist Mortality Crisis: A Cross-National Analysis." *The Lancet*, doi: 10.1016/S0140-6736(09)60005-2

Taleb, N.N. 2010. The Black Swan. New York: Random House.

Taleb, N. 2012. *Antifragile: Things That Gain from Disorder*. New York: Random House.

Tetlock, P. E. 2005. *Expert Political Judgment*. Princeton, NJ: Princeton University Press.

Vitek, B., and W. Jackson. 2008. "Introduction: Taking ignorance seriously." In *The Virtues of Ignorance*, edited by B. Vitek and W. Jackson, Lexington: University Press of Kentucky, 1–20.

White, M. D. 2006 (April). "A Kantian Critique of Neoclassical Law and Economics." Review of Political Economy, 18 (2): 235-252.

PART III

THE ETHICAL NATURE OF ECONOMIC PRACTICE

CHAPTER 6

ABOUT DOING THE RIGHT THING AS AN ACADEMIC ECONOMIST

ERWIN DEKKER AND ARJO KLAMER

WHAT to do? What is the right thing to do?

You are a young economist, starting your dissertation. Your professors are telling you that an empirical dissertation based on conventional economic theory offers the best chances for an academic position at a prestigious university. Yet, you are more interested in the intellectual history of economics and would like to explore new ideas in a qualitative way. What do you do? Do you compromise your own ideals for the sake of a good job or do you stick to your ideal inquiry and defy the well-intended advice of people whose help you may need?

You are an established economist with a chair at a reasonably good academic institution, and you are asked to participate in a discussion for a prestigious television program on a subject that is not your expertise. You realize that your academic colleagues will be critical of you and that your academic reputation will be compromised. Yet, you consider it your responsibility to contribute to the general discussion and exposure is a condition for your effectiveness in this regard. And you know that discussions on TV are basic and quite easy for you to handle. Would it, then, be right to accept the invitation?

What are you to do when your university is focusing more and more on governance, and is introducing a highly formalized tenure and promotion policy that compromises your sense of what an academic community is all about? Do you object or go along? Or would it be better to seek another job?

Is it right to do research without having a clue as to how it could matter for those who finance the research (such as taxpayers, or foundations)?

Dilemmas like these make up the daily life of academic economists. Being an academic economist requires responses to all kinds of challenges and the negotiation of various and sometimes conflicting values in adverse conditions. Each time, we are compelled to figure out what is the right thing to do. Should we put more effort into our teaching or should we concentrate on publishing in A-ranked journals? Should we seek public exposure or should we decline invitations for public speaking because it distracts too much from our research?

We suggest that in this daily figuring out of the right thing to do, we, academic economists, negotiate our moral position. Even when we try to be objective, we need to take stances on all kinds of issues, privileging certain actions over others, barring some actions altogether or engaging in activities that may not get the approval of our colleagues.

We take the "moral" in "moral" positioning to refer to human actions directed at some good. This is an Aristotelian interpretation that we see expressed in the work of philosophers such as Alasdair MacIntyre (1984), Charles Taylor (1989), Martha Nussbaum (2001), and Stuart Hampshire (1989). Recently, Deirdre McCloskey has developed such an interpretation in the economic context in her books *Bourgeois Virtues* (2006) and *Bourgeois Dignity* (2010). As Aristotle puts it at the start of his *Nichomachean Ethics*: "Every art and every inquiry, and similarly every action and pursuit, is thought to aim at some good; and for this reason the good has rightly been declared to be that at which all things aim."

What that good is remains to be seen, but as the title of Nussbaum's book announces, we should expect that our conception of the good will be fragile. Taylor points at the good life that humans try to realize or at the good society when our actions concern a common good. Moral philosophy, for Taylor, should focus on more than "what it is to do right, but also on what it is good to be" (1989: 3). As all these authors show, morality is more than respecting certain ethical principles or rules; it is more than obeying a catechism of do's and don'ts. It is about acting toward some, preferably articulated, good in accordance with the virtues. Moral actions are, as McCloskey never tires from pointing out, prudent, temperate, courageous, and just (the cardinal virtues) and faithful, hopeful, and loving (the theological virtues) (McCloskey, 2006). They will never be a matter of rational calculation, but rather a matter of practical wisdom (*phronesis*), involving experience, examples of good practices, beliefs, and a critical environment, among other factors (see also DeMartino, 2011: 218).

Take the student who is considering an intellectually challenging project when the economists in the department warn him that he will not get a job with such a project. There is no rule that tells him what the right thing to do is. Should he be "obedient" to his teachers, or at least "respectful," or should he follow his "passion"? He will weigh different values and may reflect on what his goals are in life, assess his talents, consider possible outcomes (and reckon the uncertainties involved), read about the lives of economists, perhaps study some articles and books on methodology, and take in advice from all kinds of people, including fellow students, parents, and friends.

The economics professor goes to the television studio even though he is aware of the damage to his academic reputation. He does so having weighed the options, taking into account his need for attention and recognition in the outside world, his sense of a public responsibility, and the pleasure that his daughter will have in being able to brag about her father at school.

The student and the professor practice what the ancient Greek philosophers called phronesis, or practical wisdom. It is what we humans do all the time. We do not apply formulas or use algorithms. Rather, we deliberate, weigh in our values, take into account feelings including our own, and grope for the right thing to do.

We wrote this chapter to shed some light on the fuzzy process of phronesis. Our striving is to raise awareness for ourselves, and hopefully for the readers as well, as to what we all do when we try to do the right thing. By doing so, we try to make sense of the moral positioning of economists with respect to dilemmas they face, as cited previously.

Our Aristotelian approach encompasses the ethical approach of George DeMartino in *The Economist's Oath* (2011) and some more. According to the oath that DeMartino articulates, economists are supposed to serve the interest of a community. That would constitute a good to strive for, in accordance with an Aristotelian perspective. But the oath does not make clear which community. The good to strive for remains inarticulate. Could it be that economists could serve different communities? What would be the consequences? When questioned in this fashion, economists are compelled to be more articulate as to the goods that they strive for. We think that to do so they are in need of a framework.

DeMartino does not claim that an oath is sufficient to guarantee a morally upright academic community. More is needed, as also our Aristotelian perspective informs us. More is needed for academic economists to be conscious, clear, and articulate about the goods they strive for, and about the virtues that are important to them. And a great deal of practice as well as a supportive and critical environment are needed to internalize these. The question, then, is rather what it takes to realize a supportive and critical environment and to foster the appropriate culture with the right habitus.

There Is No Chance of Being Value Free

The first challenge that we face is to counter the firmly established idea that scientific pursuit is value free, or should be so. From the very beginning of their studies students get the message that there is positive economics and there is normative economics. The latter involves values and should be left to others because economists as scientists should focus on positive economics, that is, on the study of things as they are. It is all about the distinction between what is and what should be. Note that the "should" is used in telling students what economics is about, and how it is practiced. It is not that economics is value free; it "should" be. Those people who mingle their economics with explicit value judgments are economic peddlers, as Paul Krugman characterized them (1994); they are not serious economists. Economics graduate students at the University of Chicago get the message loud and clear: serious economists do serious research; others go to Washington to advise policymakers (Klamer and Colander, 1990: 127–166). The admonishment to anyone aspiring to be a serious economist is clear. There is an unmistaken "should" implied.

When students get to work, they will run into values all the time and, with those, the "should's." For values are often articulated in the form of do's and don'ts. Do check the data, don't copy and paste, do be consistent, don't sneer, do use a model, do study math, do avoid speculation, don't be too philosophical, do go to conferences, don't be too critical at a conference seminar, do spend a great deal of time at the department, and don't take long vacations. (As to the last don't, the admonishment is here that people show their commitment and seriousness by working long hours and forgoing the time to take vacations.)

It is not just the practice of economics that is loaded with values; it is also the perspective that economists offer. Those values are readily apparent to people who are trained differently. Non-economists notice that economic methodology and vocabulary are far from neutral. If speaking in terms of efficiency, preferences, and profit maximization seems neutral to economists themselves, the terms may provoke visceral reactions in others. When economists instead of perceive the observation that there is a market for health care, or marriage, they will experience that others are disturbed or even offended. When economists stress that a performance is a product, the performers may be outraged. The easy thing to do in reaction is to call the others ignorant or downright stupid, but that is hardly the respectful thing to do. The appropriate course instead is to recognize that non-economists may operate on the basis of different values, different do's and don'ts that form the basis of different vocabularies that deserve economists' respect if not their acquiescence.

The Goods to Strive for

When considering the right thing to do, the important question to ask oneself is: "What is what I am doing good for?" Or, "to which good do I want to contribute?" The question is inspired by Aristotle's remark that all action is directed at some good. The question asks for the articulation of that good.

Economists will be quick to call upon the notion of utility. That notion, however, does not bring us any further toward the articulation of the goods we strive for. Utility is an abstract notion that encompasses everything that makes us better off. But some things are more important intrinsically than others. When we compromise on the most important thing, we compromise our integrity. Giving up an ice cream cone is qualitatively different from giving up our honesty.

Economists might reply that values, which are theorized along with our likes and dislikes as preferences, are revealed through the actual choices people make. With that move the critical question is sidestepped, which is, what counts as mere preference, and what counts instead as values that are central to our identities as moral persons? It also eliminates the process of deliberation—what preference to reveal—from our view. Economists' purpose in conflating values and preferences is apparently to get the model right, but that clearly is not the purpose when you or we are trying to do the right thing.

More generally methodology can never be the solution to the question "what is it good for." Methodology is invariably about prescriptions of means: about which rules the economist should follow. As we illustrated in the previous section, methodological maxims are of the "should"-type, but they prescribe how economic research should be done, not why we are doing research or what research and economic education are good for. The idea that methodology represents the solution to such problems is reminiscent of the shift that Max Weber analyzed from value-rationality (Wertrationalität) to instrumental-rationality (Zweckrationalität). It is a shift away from the ends, toward the means. More recently Flyvbjerg has used Weber's distinction to argue that a social science that aims to be relevant should reconsider value-rationality and seek to balance it with the dominant instrumental-rationality (Flyvbjerg, 2001).

So what is what you are doing good for? When the question came up in a seminar, a young economist responded with: "To let out what is in my head." "So what is that good for?" "I really would not know." "Why would anyone be willing to pay you for letting your ideas out?" "That is what amazes me every morning when I get up. I have no idea." This positioning of economists is in our experience quite typical. It is a good way to skirt the issue of the good to strive for. We kept pressing. "Why, then are you here at the seminar? Apparently, you are keen in sharing those ideas of yours." "Sure." "And you would not mind getting recognition for them, to get invited to present them at a conference, for example." "Sure." "So there is more than just letting your ideas out; you clearly are keen on contributing to the conversation of like-minded economists, of being part of that conversation." "Yes, I sure am." "And you probably do this because you are good at it." "I hope so."

In this probing we discover two types of goods this young economist is striving for. First of all he wants to be in the conversation with like-minded economists. We could call that a social good, as the conversation is something he shares with the other economists involved. And his own talent is a personal good, something he "owns" himself and that he is keen on developing and exploiting.

Social goods are one category of goods to strive for. They usually come in the form of relationships or membership in a club or community. Friendship is a good example. A group of colleagues, or a network of scholars involved in a particular research project, are other examples. They apply insofar as they constitute a good in and of themselves. If goods are pursued instead for their instrumental value, for their contribution to the pursuit of other goods, then the other goods should be articulated. When an economist suggests, for instance, that he is doing work for the income it yields, the question is what that income is good for. If the answer is "to support my family" then it is his family, and that is a social good.

In contrast to social goods, personal goods are something that someone "has" or "possesses" and that is of critical importance to that person. Like a talent. If someone becomes part of a community of researchers because that enables him to practice what he is good at, the personal good is the goal, rather than membership in that community.

There are two more categories of goods we need to distinguish. The first of these categories comprises societal goods, or goods that a society has in common. When an economist like Jan Tinbergen dedicates his work to social justice, he aims at a societal good, that is, social justice. Some economists more than others have similar goals in mind when they are doing their work. Outspoken liberal economists such as Hayek, Friedman, and McCloskey aim for freedom and prosperity; left-leaning economists such as Kenneth Arrow, John and James Galbraith, Amartya Sen, Herman Daly, and Samuel Bowles look for the realization of human dignity, basic equality, a decent life for those who met bad luck, or sustainable growth. Other economists may want to contribute with their work to the advancement of civilization. Other goals could be education, development in Africa, or the eradication of world hunger. All these goals pertain to a larger entity, like a society, the world, civilization, or nature.

The discussion with economists usually turns uncomfortable when we get to the fourth category of goods. This is the category of transcendental goods, or goods that transcend the social and the personal. These include goods such as Truth, Beauty, Enlightenment, the Muse in life, and Faith. When a Muslim student appeals to Allah before starting his essay, it is clear that he seeks a transcendental good with his scientific work. Other economists are not as outspoken and turn shy or often even hostile when this subject comes up. Even so, when we encounter theoreticians who dedicate their scholarly life to the search for a definitive proof of the existence of an equilibrium, we suspect that their goal transcends the social and the personal: they are reaching for the near impossible, as if they are seeking the Holy Grail (see Sedlacek, 2011 and Daly, 2016).

As Charles Taylor points out, articulating any of these goods will always be difficult. When the articulation is too confident, too explicit, there is the danger of its hardening into a dogma with the risk of blindness toward important occurrences and changes. But when people have no idea of the goods they are striving for, they may wonder how they keep the good course, how they can know what is the right thing to do. That is the reason why Charles Taylor stresses the importance of having at least an idea of what are the goods to strive for.

Whether we are considering individuals, groups of people, organizations, or societies, the goal values come first. They determine the purpose, that which they do is all about, what it is for. Not everyone will be conscious of what that good is, or be able to articulate it, but absent sufficient attention to the good, our actions become aimless and meaningless. Or as Carl Menger once put in his discussion of prudent behavior:

> All provident activity directed to the satisfaction of human needs is based on knowledge of [ends and means]. Lacking knowledge of the first, the activity of men would

> be conducted blindly, for they would be ignorant of their objective. Lacking knowledge of the second, their activity would be planless, for they would have no conception of the available means. (Menger, 1871/1950: 80)

Money is not an ultimate goal, notwithstanding what businessmen and even some in the arts world are suggesting. Money, or profit, is always a means to realize other values. After the seller of an art piece fetched a record price at an auction, the question arises regarding what to do with the money. Buy a yacht? What is that good for? To impress people? What is that good for? If we press the question "what is that good for," we arrive at one or more of the four realms of values that we specified above: personal, social, societal, and transcendental.

In one of the cases with which we began this chapter, a student has to figure out what the good is that he is striving for. Is it a transcendental good like true insight? Or is it a societal good like civilization? If so, this will make him lean toward pursuing his intellectual interests. In the case of our conflicted professor, if a contribution to societal discussions is in the end more important than his standing in the academic community, he will lean toward going to the TV studio despite the risk to his reputation that his appearance would entail.

If it only were so simple. Much more, however, is involved in the practice of phronesis.

Respecting and Internalizing the Right Virtues

In striving for our ultimate goods we want to be methodical, honest, fair to colleagues, courageous, and prudent. All these are qualities of our actions. The quality of prudence requires that we take into account the costs of our research, and have an eye for the practical side. A project that requires personal data of all people alive is not prudent. Neither is a project that requires the participation of all world leaders.

Being collegial is another virtue that is becoming for scholars. In our pursuit of truth or social justice we do well by being considerate of colleagues, involving them, taking their criticisms seriously, and recognizing their inputs. Courage is required as well. Going against the stream, defying prevailing wisdoms, and risking one's job doing so—all are signs of courage. That said, and as Aristotle reminds us, we can be too courageous, for example, when we risk losing all respect and our position, in pursuit of some trivial good, making it impossible to continue with our striving for the goods we deem to be most essential. There are times, then, when prudence must temper our courage so as to ensure our long-term ability to pursue the good. Judging the right balance between the two virtues of prudence and courage—to ensure that one does not back down too readily from risks that should be taken, but also that one does not risk all over trivial matters—requires an advanced level of practical wisdom that is terribly difficult to acquire. Below we will explore some of the most important issues and choices that all economists have to face.

In Which Conversation to Participate?

There is a tendency to speak of Science or Economics as if these are monolithic things. A chat with a few economists (and a look at the index of the *Journal of Economic Literature*) should cure us of such a monolithic perspective. You will notice that there all kinds of economists, doing all kinds of things. And it is just not the case that they share the same idea as to what Science is about.

For budding economists this means that they have to make consequential choices. They have to decide what kind of economics they want to do, and what kind economist they want to be. Following philosophers such as Hans-Georg Gadamer (2004), Richard Rorty (1979), and Wayne Booth (1988) and sociologists such as Randall Collins (1998), we suggest the metaphor of the conversation (Klamer, 2007). Think of what economists do as being in a particular conversation by contributing to it with papers and the like and by participating in it by way of seminars, conferences, blogs, mailing lists, and office talk. Accordingly, game theorists have their own conversation, as do cultural economists, general equilibrium theorists, and economists who advise policymakers. There are all kinds of conversations. The question that budding economists must ask themselves is this: In which conversation do I want to participate? Wayne Booth asked the same question differently: Whose company do I want to keep (1988)?

In *Speaking of Economics* (2007) Klamer elaborates on the metaphor of the conversation, shows its consequences, and explores the differences between all kinds of conversations that make up the discipline of economics. One conclusion is that aspiring economists need to learn about the rhetorical and social characteristics of a particular conversation and they need to be aware of the differences with other conversations. They need to know to whom they should pay attention, and what they should read (and what they can ignore) to be part of a particular conversation. They need to know how they can attract the attention of others to their own work, and how they can persuade their peers, a wider public, or policymakers. And they could ask themselves whether they can feel at home in that conversation, whether they like the company.

We all have tried conversations to find that they are not our cup of tea. One of us (Klamer) began his study within the conversation of econometricians with the expectation that he would learn how to do policy analysis well, only to discover that the conversation was mostly about statistics and linear algebra, and that it hardly addressed economic issues at all. So he moved on to the conversations of macroeconomists and methodologists, and ended up in the conversation of cultural economists. The other one of us (Dekker) is seeking to be part of conversations about the histories of ideas (and so has already resolved for himself the first of the dilemmas with which we started our exposition).

Whether the choice of conversation is moral or not remains to be seen. If people choose to quit the conversation of econometricians in favor of the macroeconomic conversation, they might do so simply because they prefer to discuss macroeconomics. But if their choice is based on a particular conviction—like the conviction that econometrics is an outdated method, or that macroeconomics is the subject to study in times of recession and high government debts—more is at stake. The question then could be whether it is right to stick to the conversation of econometricians. If an economist decides to move from macroeconomics to econometrics because of the relative status of econometrics or because it is easier to publish in that field then moral values are at stake as well. The economists might then be trading off social values (his status) against societal values (the relevance of his research for solving real-world problems) or transcendental values (the search for economic truth). And as any academic economist will tell you, changing conversations can be very costly, as the reputation built up in one community cannot be easily transferred to another.

The decision to abandon a conversation in pursuit of an important value does not mean that others who stick to the conversation are to be condemned for doing so. The temptation is great to disapprove of other conversations, to consider them irrelevant, misguided, senseless, boring, or even dangerous. From the perspective of one's own conversation all that may seem to be the case. But will those judgments hold when the perspective changes, and especially when the erstwhile critic is going to participate in the conversation that he had called into question? What do we know, really? How sure can we be of our judgments? How well do we know the conversations that we reject outright, or criticize? Recognition of what we do not know and cannot know, and the existence of a great variety of economic conversations should make us aware of our own limitations, and teach us to approach other conversations with some humility and respect, rather than to reject them outright.

The moral judgment that we stress here concerns one's own actions and choices. Sticking to conversations that one believes to be irrelevant, misguided, senseless, boring, or even dangerous would be the wrong thing to do. Just as it would be wrong to remain part of a conversation in which you no longer can realize your goals. Exit, however, is by no means the only option if we are dissatisfied with the tone or the direction of a conversation, we can also attempt to change the conversation. In that case we exercise what Hirschman has called voice (Hirschman, 1970).

Roles and Exemplary Validity

Moral positioning concerns, inter alia, our role in (academic) life.

Aristotle suggested that our moral positioning depends on the roles we assume in life. Each role requires a particular enactment of the virtues. A nurse will act differently from a soldier not only because the character of her actions differs but also because she tends toward different goods and especially the good of care whereas the soldier is more concerned with goods such as security and freedom. We should anticipate, then, that the moral positioning of an academic economist is different from that of a policy advisor because they, too, strive for different goods. We need to look into these differences when we consider the right thing to do for economists.

In this moral framing problems occur when people have to negotiate different roles and conflicting goods that they strive for. Loyalty matters in friendship, of course, but what if a friend does not qualify for tenure and you are on the tenure committee? Replacing "friend" with "colleague" does not eliminate the problem. The justice that you strive for as a member of the committee—treating all candidates equally and in accordance with the procedures and ruling standards—conflicts with the virtues of friendship. Such conflicts are what make tragedies work, such as *Antigone* by Sophocles or *The Assault* by Harry Mulisch.

In Aristotle's account of phronesis experience plays a vital role. In our pursuit of various goals we discover that we were misguided or that a particular good is even more worthy of our pursuit. There might not be a replacement for first-hand experience, but as with any type of moral education the study of examples might be helpful and enlightening. So what would such examples look like?

A good place to start is by studying the biographies of prominent economists. What made Hayek break away from his teacher Ludwig von Mises (Caldwell, 2004)? What was the relation of Chicago economists to the economic reforms in Chile under Pinochet (Valdés, 1995; Fischer, 2009)? What choices did Keynes make in the negotiations over the Bretton-Woods system (Skidelsky, 2003)? How did Central European economists respond to the rise of fascism (Dekker, 2013)? How did Hirschman balance his goals of influencing the economic debate on development with his societal goal of helping various South American countries develop (Adelman, 2013)? What motivated Tinbergen to set up a Central Planning Bureau in the Netherlands (Jolink, 2003)? And so on.

Traditionally the life of economists and their goals have not received much attention. But what can be learned from them is the practice of phronesis, the balancing act between various goods and the prudence required to achieve these goals. The examples of prominent economists have what Bernstein calls "exemplary validity"(Bernstein, 1983: 207–223). They help us in evaluating and judging in our own life as economists, not by providing general rules or universal maxims, but by moving from particular to particular.

The study of such examples also makes us aware, as Gadamer points out, that we as economists are part of a tradition in which a variety of goals has been pursued in a wide variety of manners (Gadamer, 2004: 282). Some of these goals were misguided or once achieved proved to be somewhat irrelevant, other goods proved harder to achieve than expected, while sometimes the means were ill chosen, as in Jevons sun-spot theory of the business cycle.

Biographies and life stories perhaps more than any other genre of economic writing help us find our path and direction. As MacIntyre points out: "It is through hearing stories about wicked stepmothers, lost children, good but misguided kings, (. . .) youngest sons who receive no inheritance but must make their own way in the world and eldest sons who waste their inheritance on riotous living (. . .) that children learn or mislearn what a child or what a parent is" (MacIntyre, 1984: 216). In the same way, stories for and about economists and intellectuals are valuable; they deserve to be told and taught.

Examples of such stories are few and far between within our economics curricula or graduate teaching. We prefer to teach methods instead: instrumental-rationality only. There are some fascinating examples available, however. Much of Robert Skidelsky's recent work is about the lessons we can learn from Keynes about both means *and* ends (Skidelsky, 2009; Skidelsky and Skidelsky, 2012). Sedlacek has analyzed the role of economic advisors in the Old Testament (Sedlacek, 2011). Hayek has frequently reflected on the position of the economist in society, in a dark moment even comparing it to that of Cassandra, the prophetess who was never believed (Hennecke, 2000). Bernstein has studied how American economists have dealt with their public purpose (Bernstein, 2001). And in his recent book Peter Boettke discusses a variety of economists and their moral positioning (Boettke, 2012).

Another source of such exemplars is the second-hand experience we receive from our economics teachers. It is they who help to guide us, and who show by example. They provide moral as well as scholarly inspiration. It is not for nothing that academic practice is still reminiscent in many ways of the master–apprentice system of guilds.

The Professional Economist?

Keynes called economics a moral science. He envisaged economics as a science that is dedicated to the realization of a good society. He saw himself as a gentleman who would engage in discussions with politicians, share insights with them, move in intellectual and artistic circles such as the Bloomsbury group, apply his ideas by trading in financial markets, and on top of all that he held an academic position at the University of Cambridge.

Jan Tinbergen saw the science of economics as an instrument for policy. He, too, envisaged contributing to a better and more just world, but insisted on the role of economists as engineers: they should point out the instruments that politicians could use to realize their objectives. To that end he founded in 1945 an institution, the Central Planning Bureau, which to this day provides "independent and neutral" economic advice to policymakers based on modeling techniques. Like Keynes, Tinbergen held a university professorship next to all kinds of other positions and activities.

Keynes and Tinbergen were economists in a way that would be almost inconceivable today. They both have reputations as excellent scientists and are recognized for major scientific contributions. Tinbergen even received the first Nobel Prize in 1969 that Keynes certainly would have received before him if he had been alive. Yet nowadays, a solid academic career is a condition sine qua non for a scientific reputation and recognition. To gain scientific distinction in economics people need to spend their working lives in university departments, preferably the best ones, where they are preoccupied with the rituals of academic life, including the writing of papers, participating in academic seminars, teaching preferably graduate students, and attending academic conferences. All other activities, including consulting and policy advising, have to be subsidiary. Klamer and Colander (1990) characterized this type of economist the *academic professional.*

One could conclude that times have changed and that economists now work differently from economists then. We suggest another perspective. Positioning oneself squarely in a university department is a moral position. Such a positioning is morally different from one in which economists apply their talents in political, intellectual, or commercial conversations. The academic professional will strive for different goods than the (popular) intellectual, the policy advisor, or the consultant.

The standard view has become that the good that the academic professional pursues is the most pure: truth and truth only. Economics is an autonomous discipline in which truth about the economy is uncovered or discovered. That has not always been the standard view; many economists of the early postwar generation studied and practiced economics to mitigate the effects of the business cycle or to fight unemployment (Klamer, 1984). For Aristotle the study of economic processes was primarily of importance in relation to his ethical theory. In his recent dissertation Dekker shows that many Austrian economists felt that they were contributing to and later defending their civilization (Dekker, 2013). Still others hope that a good basic economic education can help shape well-informed and critical democratic citizens. And recent popular economic books emphasize how economic insights can be used to improve our choices and the performance of those around us (Cowen, 2007).

For Keynes too, economics was a means to some other end. In his famous essay "Economic Possibilities for our Grandchildren" he formulates his vision as such:

> When the accumulation of wealth is no longer of high social importance, there will be great changes in the code of morals (. . .) The love of money as a possession—as distinguished from the love of money as a means to the enjoyments and realities of life—will be recognised for what it is, a somewhat disgusting morbidity, one of those semi-criminal, semi-pathological propensities which one hands over with a shudder to the specialists in mental disease . . . But beware! (. . .) Avarice and usury and precaution must be our gods for a little longer still. For only they can lead us out of the tunnel of economic necessity into daylight.

For Keynes, ultimately, noneconomic goods are most important: love, truth, and beauty. Keynes and the other economists referred to earlier were not doing economics for economics' sake; they were ultimately pursuing other goods. In our perspective that makes sense. Discovering economic truths might be an important good, but it is not the only one as we are sometimes prone to believe. Economics before the advent of the economics professional was primarily an instrument (a means), as it was for Keynes, to achieve other goods.

Richard Rorty once argued that: "[G]etting the facts right is merely propaedeutic to finding a more interesting way of expressing ourselves, and thus of coping with the world" (Rorty, 1980: 359). Economic knowledge in that sense helps us to cope with the world; it helps us to achieve other goods, rather than being a goal in itself. It makes us reconsider why and for whom we are studying economics; for which community we are working, and for whom we want to realize valued goods. Those questions, as our fourth dilemma suggests, cannot be answered without consideration of those who are enabling us to pursue economics.

Final Thoughts

We have made a first intervention by suggesting that the choices academic economists make are moral. Conventional wisdom among economists would relegate the moral to the domain of ethics, to the do's and the don'ts, to ethical rules such as "do not plagiarize" and "remain objective and disinterested in your research." The idea, apparently, is that we economists make rational choices when we conduct our objective research. But we disagree: we do not think that such framing is very helpful when it comes to all the deliberations and negotiations that make up daily economic practice. It is not that we sit down and make calculations or solve constrained maximization problems. The reality is rather that we do things we mention above: we talk, we read, we think, and we value.

So what are you to do when the administration pushes through measures that compromise your idea of what an academic community is about? It clearly depends: on what is the good you are striving for, on your values, and on your assessment of the consequences of doing one thing rather than another.

Most academic economists will care little or not at all about the benefits of their research to those financing the research. Working at a university rather than at a research organization is often valued because of the autonomy that a university is supposed to give its researchers. Even so, is it right for university economists to do their work without regard to its consequences for others? What is the economist's defense for professional autonomy when taxpayers demand accountability for the research money spent? What if taxpayers do not accept the usual justifications and want results that matter to them? Would the neglect of taxpayers up till then have been the right thing to do—or had academic economists shirked their social responsibility by neglecting to consider their duties to society?

To deal with all these moral questions, economists need to practice phronesis; the practical wisdom that involves the weighing of values and the assessing of varied circumstances. It should be expected from professionals that they are aware of the important values and consciously work on their abilities to realize such values. This requires self-knowledge and knowledge of the social contexts in which they operate. Most important is the continuous feedback of colleagues that is needed to stay focused, to evaluate past actions, and to correct bad or inappropriate judgments. The claim that economics is a positive science is no excuse to avert such interactions. Even if economics is not a moral science, practicing it is inevitably and necessarily moral.

References

Adelman, Jeremy. 2013. *Worldly Philosopher: The Odyssey of Albert O. Hirschman*. Princeton, NJ: Princeton University Press.

Bernstein, Richard J. 1983. *Beyond Objectivism and Relativism: Science, Hermeneutics, and Praxis*. Philadelphia: University of Pennsylvania Press.

Bernstein, Michael A. 2001. *A Perilous Progress: Economists and Public Purpose in Twentieth-Century America*. Princeton, NJ: Princeton University Press.

Boettke, Peter J. 2012. *Living Economics: Yesterday, Today, and Tomorrow*. Oakland: The Independent Institute.

Booth, Wayne C. 1988. *The Company We Keep*. Berkeley: University of California Press.

Caldwell, Bruce. 2004. *Hayek's Challenge*. Chicago: University of Chicago Press.

Collins, Randall. 1998. *The Sociology of Philosophies: A Global Theory of Intellectual Change*. Cambridge, MA: Harvard University Press.

Cowen, Tyler. 2007. *Discover Your Inner Economist*. New York: Dutton.

Dekker, Erwin. 2013. "The Viennese Students of Civilization: Humility, Culture and Economics in Interwar Vienna and Beyond." PhD dissertation, Erasmus University Rotterdam.

DeMartino, George F. 2011. *The Economist's Oath: On the Need for and the Content of Professional Economic Ethics*. Oxford: Oxford University Press.

Fischer, Karin. 2009. "The Influence of Neoliberals in Chile Before, During, and After Pinochet. In *The Road from Mont-Pèlerin: The Making of the Neoliberal Thought Collective*, edited by Philip Mirowski and Dieter Plehwe, pp. 305–346. Cambridge, MA: Harvard University Press.

Flyvbjerg, Bent. 2001. *Making Social Science Matter*. Cambridge, UK: Cambridge University Press.

Gadamer, Hans-Georg. 2004. *Truth and Method*. London: Continuum.

Hampshire, Stuart. 1989. *Innocence and Experience*. Cambridge, MA: Harvard University Press.

Hennecke, Hans Jörg. 2000. *Friedrich August von Hayek: Die Tradition Der Freiheit*. Düsseldorf: Verlag Wirtschaft und Finanzen.

Hirschman, Albert O. 1970. *Exit, Voice, and Loyalty*. Cambridge, MA: Harvard University Press.

Jolink, Albert. 2003. *Jan Tinbergen: The Statistical Turn in Economics 1903–1955*. Rotterdam: Chimes.

Klamer, Arjo. 1984. *Conversations with Economists*. Totowa, NJ: Rowman & Allanheld.

Klamer, Arjo. 2007. *Speaking of Economics: How to Get in the Conversation*. London: Routledge.

Klamer, Arjo, and Colander, David C. 1990. *The Making of an Economist*. Boulder, CO: Westview Press.

Krugman, Paul. 1994. *Peddling Prosperity: Economic Sense and Nonsense in the Age of Diminished Expectations*. New York: W. W. Norton.

MacIntyre, Alasdair C. 1984. *After Virtue: A Study in Moral Theory*. Notre Dame: University of Notre Dame Press.

McCloskey, Deirdre N. 2006. *The Bourgeois Virtues: Ethics for an Age of Commerce*. Chicago: University of Chicago Press.

McCloskey, Deirdre N. 2010. *Bourgeois Dignity: Why Economics Can't Explain the Modern World*. Chicago: Chicago University Press.

Menger, Carl. 1950. *Principles of Economics*. Glencoe, IL: The Free Press.

Nussbaum, Martha C. 2001. *The Fragility of Goodness: Luck and Ethics in Greek Tragedy and Philosophy*. Cambridge, UK: Cambridge University Press.

Rorty, Richard. 1979. *Philosophy and the Mirror of Nature*. Princeton, NJ: Princeton University Press.

Sedlacek, Tomáš. 2011. *Economics of Good and Evil: The Quest for Economic Meaning from Gilgamesh to Wall Street*. Oxford: Oxford University Press.

Skidelsky, Robert. 2003. *John Maynard Keynes: Economist, Philosopher, Statesman*. New York: Penguin Group.

Skidelsky, Robert. 2009. *Keynes: The Return of the Master*. Philadelphia: PublicAffairs.

Skidelsky, Robert, and Edward Skidelsky. 2012. *How Much Is Enough?* New York: Other Press.

Taylor, Charles. 1989. *Sources of the Self: The Making of Modern Identity*. Cambridge, MA: Harvard University Press.

Valdés, Juan Gabriel. 1995. *Pinochet's Economists: The Chicago School in Chile*. Cambridge, UK: Cambridge University Press.

CHAPTER 7

THE SOCIAL RESPONSIBILITY OF ECONOMISTS

PETER J. BOETTKE AND KYLE W. O'DONNELL

> I should perhaps add that I do not regard the general point at issue [conflict of interest] as having as much importance as you (and people generally) attach to it. In a debate it is the arguments that should matter rather than the motives which lead the parties to put them forward. I recognize that monetary interest may lead to bias. But the number of falsehoods put into circulation for the sake of money must be small compared with the number put forward "to serve the public interest."
>
> —Ronald Coase[1]

Introduction

In the wake of the global financial crisis that began in 2008, the economics profession was subjected to immense critical scrutiny for a number of supposed failings—intellectual, ideological, and ethical—which formed the basis for an emerging popular narrative about the *corruption of economics* that became engrained in the minds of numerous intellectuals, journalists, policymakers, and even various economists.

For one, some critics have alleged that a strong "groupthink" mentality existed among economists before the crisis, where methodological and analytical conformism took precedence over original ideas and critical thinking (see DeMartino, 2011: 166–168). This frame of mind lulled economists into an intellectual stupor, such that they accepted

[1] Quoted from a letter written by Ronald Coase to Edward W. Barrett, the Dean of the Columbia University Graduate School of Journalism, in response to allegations that his professional judgment had been affected by a conflict of interest (dated November 25, 1968). We thank Richard Epstein for permission to quote this letter.

the conventional wisdom without question simply because it was convention.[2] Owing to such unthinking conformism in economists' perspectives, the economics profession largely failed to predict the crisis despite abundant warning signs that now seem "obvious" in retrospect. Also, economists were said to have been biased by their ideological dispositions, particularly those inclined to favor free markets and limited government, which led them to advocate laissez faire and deregulatory economic policies without fully considering the potential costs and without empirical evidence for their positions.[3]

Perhaps most troubling of all, however, is the seeming insinuation that special interests had essentially paid economists (albeit indirectly) to produce research favoring their private interests without regard for, or even at the expense of, the public's interests. In this story, economists constructed and promoted simplistic, flawed, and even false economic theories catering to the vested interests of particular firms and industries, who could offer in return grants, funding, and other forms of support for academic research (see Zingales [2013] on the symmetry between the idea of regulatory capture and economists' capture by special interests). As a result of special interests' influence on economic research, a generation of policymakers and ordinary people were misled by these distorted ideas into adopting an array of economic policies that conferred private benefits upon vested interest groups at an enormous cost to society—namely deregulation, privatization, and various free market policies.[4]

Together, these factors comprise a popular narrative that many believe explains the wide acceptance of the vision of the self-correcting free market economy, and the apparent tidal shift towards free markets that began in the late 1970s and swept into the early 2000s—including a wave of financial deregulations in the late 1990s to 2000s. This narrative is portrayed in various popular media directed to broader audiences, such as documentaries like *Inside Job*, which won the 2010 Academy Award for Best Documentary Feature and brought an enormous amount of critical attention to the practices and conduct of the economics profession. If we consider this narrative from an ethical standpoint, each of the issues it raises appears problematical separately, and combined would certainly seem to constitute a serious ethical failure—at least when viewed through the lens of the popular narrative. Hence, alongside the increasingly popular belief in this narrative, there was growing debate, and much soul-searching, within the economics profession over professional economic ethics and the social responsibility of economists. This discussion gave rise, in part, to an increase in the demand for the economics

[2] Where "conventional" economics is commonly used in reference to some combination of the following basic elements: a highly formalized mathematical approach to economic theory, a substantive belief that idealized models of "perfect" markets describe reality, and a general presumption in favor of free markets and limited government intervention in the economy.

[3] Cf. Colander et al. (2009); Krugman (2009); Leonhardt (2008); and Stiglitz (2009).

[4] See for instance, Carrick-Hagenbarth and Epstein (2010, 2012), Flitter et al. (2010), and the work cited in fn. 3. In addition, it is important to note that this narrative does not necessarily require that individuals act on selfish or malevolent motives, and the vast majority of criticisms of the economics profession do not ascribe any moral or motivational defects to economists. Zingales (2013) argues that just as the most well intentioned regulators can be captured by special interests, so too can economists.

profession to adopt an ethical code of conduct, or a code of ethics.[5] If economists had to sign and abide by a professional code of ethics, then presumably the irresponsible adoption of false and unrealistic theories, and the advocacy of policies that benefit private interests at the expense of the public interest would be curtailed.

In response to such pressures, the American Economic Association (AEA) instituted a strict disclosure policy for all AEA journals, which mandates that authors of all submissions identify potential material, financial, political, and ideological conflict of interest. Although the AEA disclosure policy is relatively limited in comparison to some of the proposals for ethical codes—such as one modeled on that of the American Sociological Association[6]—it does attempt to address the most salient criticisms of the economics profession: namely, that economics research has been distorted by the pervasive, albeit marginal, influence of special interests on academic research. Perhaps it was also hoped that the AEA policy would allay, by extension, the more pernicious insinuations that some economists had essentially been paid to produce research to the liking of special interests.

Unfortunately, there are serious defects in the popular narrative, its diagnosis of both the financial crisis and the supposed corruption of economics, and its proposed solution, a professional code of ethics. Indeed, we cannot imagine a more inaccurate picture of contemporary history, economic theory, political economy, or the sociology of the economics profession. First, we did not experience a period of irresponsible deregulation leading up to the financial crisis of 2008. The financial crisis was not the result of free market forces at work. Rather, it was caused by the volatile combination of government manipulation of monetary policy and financial markets, and the accumulation of special interest policies that together led to the systematic misallocation of resources, which was followed by an inevitable crash and market correction (see Friedman, 2009; Taylor, 2009; Wallison, 2009). Second, the theory of the self-regulating market economy is the unassailable foundation of economic science—particularly as represented in the "mainline" of economic thought, which is defined by its core analytical propositions about the nature of spontaneous order and the institutional framework of a free and prosperous society (see Boettke, 2012). In addition, public interest theories of politics, implicit in the popular narrative, are hopelessly romantic (Buchanan, [1979] 1999). The inherent logic of democratic politics is to concentrate benefits on the well-organized

[5] For example, Gerald Epstein and Jessica Carrick-Hagenbarth wrote a letter, which was signed by nearly 300 economists, calling on the American Economic Association to adopt a conflict of interest disclosure policy as well as a professional code of ethics. Available at: (http://www.peri.umass.edu/fileadmin/pdf/other_publication_types/AEA_letter_Jan4.pdf). Also see Sewell Chan, "Letter Calls on Economists to Adopt a Code of Ethics," *New York Times* (January 4, 2011). Available at: (http://economix.blogs.nytimes.com/2011/01/04/letter-calls-on-economists-to-adopt-code-of-ethics). Also, see the debate in *The Economist* between several academic economists over the question: "Do economists need a code of conduct?" (January 7, 2011). Available at: (http://www.economist.com/economics/by-invitation/questions/do_economists_need_code_conduct).

[6] The letter in fn. 5 specifically proposes the ASA's code as its model. The ASA code of ethics is available at: http://www.asanet.org/images/asa/docs/pdf/CodeofEthics.pdf

and well-informed in the short run while dispersing the costs on the ill-organized and ill-informed mass of voters in the long run, *unless* the scale and scope of government is highly restricted.

We are also highly skeptical of claims that the economics profession has been corrupted by corporations and special interests, and biased in favor of deregulation and free market policies by financial and other incentives (see Carrick-Hagenbarth and Epstein, 2010, 2012; Flitter et al. 2010). First, there is no more justification for interpreting any apparent policy consensus among economists as a symptom of perverse incentives, ideological bias, or socialization (Carrick-Hagenbarth and Epstein, 2012) than as the outcome of a process of serious inquiry and critical discourse among researchers. Second, the idea that vested interests in business and the financial industry are necessarily supporters of laissez faire out of self-interest is incredibly naïve, and ignores much of the logic and empirical evidence of public choice, which shows that businesses and interest groups often seek out favorable regulation and legislation. In fact, this argument focuses almost all of its attention on the influence of private interests and laissez faire, while ignoring another obvious and likely more significant source of corruption in economics: the state's capture and politicization of the discipline.

Countering each of the subsidiary arguments that are deployed in the focal argument of the corruption of the economics profession would require a book, not an essay, so we will not attempt it here. Instead, we focus on the central argument of the corruption of economics itself, and the issue of whether a strict code of professional ethics would in fact solve the problem so identified. Our answer to this latter question is simple—signing or not signing a code of ethics would be symbolic at best, and largely irrelevant to the practice of economics, while the only hope for economic science in a politicized world is the open and continual contestation of ideas within the profession.

We do not necessarily need moral scientists to produce good science, but we do need good rules of scientific engagement to produce good science. What matters is that ideas are constantly subject to contestation by one's peers, and that the ideas that become part of the public discourse are subject to the contestation of democratic decision making. Just as the market process does not depend on the motivations of individual actors to generate socially beneficial outcomes, but on the institutions within which those actors pursue their self-interest, so too does the institutional framework shape the course of the scientific process and whether scientific knowledge progresses, stands still, or regresses. Thus, the question of the corruption of economics does not hinge on the ethics of individual economists—whether they are motivated solely by a lust for fame and recognition, or tireless truth-seekers—rather, it depends on the institutional structure within which economists *do* economics.

As we mentioned, if there is a case to be made for the corruption of economics, then the state, not corporations or private interests, is likely the most important culprit. Before directly addressing the issue of the corruption of economics, however, we propose a particular conception of the social responsibility of economists, and we argue that this perspective, which at first might seem bold or radical, focuses our attention on the most salient features of the problem at hand while framing the discussion of both positive and normative matters in a productive manner. To state our position plainly and succinctly: the *only* social responsibility of the economist is to maximize their career advancement within the scientific community of economists.

The Social Responsibility of Economists is to Maximize Their Scientific Career Advancement

Milton Friedman famously argued that, within the context of a free market economy, "there is one and only one social responsibility of business—to use its resources and engage in activities designed to increase its profits so long as it stays within the rules of the game, which is to say, engages in open and free competition, without deception or fraud" ([1962] 2002: 133).

Friedman's argument relies on the crucial distinction between intentions and outcomes, and on the particular institutional framework within which individuals plan and act to achieve their ends. The reason why Friedman can make his argument is that the businessman (i.e., entrepreneur or management of corporation) seeking to maximize profits—*within an institutional regime of private property and freedom of contract*—can do so only by satisfying the demands of consumers, which inadvertently helps to ensure that scarce resources are allocated to their most highly valued uses. Friedman challenged the belief that social justice and economic efficiency were mutually exclusive by explaining how, within the institutional context of a free market economy, there is no distinction between the aggressive profit-seeking firm and a socially conscious firm, since the most effective means of improving the welfare of society is seeking to maximize profits. Further, Friedman argued that the broader problem for society is to design or foster an institutional framework that directs profit-seeking behavior toward socially desirable outcomes. Thus, Friedman's argument is also valuable when discussing social, political, and economic reform, as it directs our attention away from the motivations and intentions of particular individuals, and instead focuses it on the institutional structure of society. Or to borrow terms from James Buchanan (cf. 1999), it redirects our attention toward the *constitutional* level of choice over alternative sets of rules, rather than the *post-constitutional* level of behavioral strategies and outcomes within the rules of the game as given.

We would like to suggest an analogous argument and approach to the ethical issues of the economics profession. The only social responsibility of the economist is to maximize their career advancement within the scientific community of economists (where career success can be understood in terms of publications, citations, awards, grants, academic positions, and other typical measures of scientific careers). In this argument, just as in Friedman's, the social desirability of the results of human action derives from the institutional context of human action, not from the moral character or motivations of individual actors. Instead of market competition within a regime of private property and freedom of contract, science operates against a backdrop of the constant contestation of ideas, where new and old ideas alike are continually subjected to debate and critical scrutiny. Indeed, the development and progress of scientific knowledge depends, in a fundamental sense, on the institutional framework of the scientific community.[7] That is, it must foster a contestable market for ideas within a professional incentive structure that rewards and punishes good and bad behavior accordingly.

In this setting, the career-maximizing economist[8] ensures that scientific knowledge is expanded and refined in a self-correcting process, such that scarce scientific resources (brain power, imagination, grants and funding, graduate students, administrative assistants, etc.) are continually allocated toward their most highly valued uses. Individual economists are able to propose, challenge, or defend ideas as they choose, while it is the scientific community of economists as a whole that ultimately judges their merit. Economists who consistently contribute to scientific knowledge, either by advancing original ideas or rooting out wrong ones, are rewarded with citations, grants, awards, endowed professorships, and so forth. Likewise, those who fail to do so, or worse, attempt to distort or deceive, are punished by similar means—heavy or undesirable teaching loads, being passed over for tenure or promotion, or even fired. These rewards and penalties are reinforced through the mechanism of scientific reputation, which is especially important in a profession where an individual's career rests so heavily on his or her intellectual integrity.

There is no doubt that the moral attitudes of the individual economists can raise or lower the enforcement costs of constructive rules of scientific engagement. But it is not necessary for the scientific process to work reasonably efficiently for the individual scientists to be "good"; they just need to exist in a contestable market for ideas. So while norms and rules like the AEA's disclosure policy can promote the disclosure of funding sources in research, what really ensures good scientific behavior is not the act of disclosure alone, but the constant contestation of ideas. If an economist was paid to produce distorted research favoring certain interests, as critics of the economics profession allege to have happened, they might be temporarily successful in passing off this deception. But there are systematic, self-correcting tendencies—within a contestable scientific market of ideas, and a professional structure of rewards and penalties for winning such contestations—for such deficient, deceptive work to be challenged and the offending economist disciplined. Bad scientific behavior among the biggest names in science will spur less famous, yet ambitious, younger economists to expose the distortion and blatant acts of self-deception, because to do so would earn them great professional stature.

Not only is good (moral) behavior not necessary, it also would not be sufficient—even the most noble individual could not provide the necessary self-correction within a

[7] Our argument is in line with the one developed by Thomas Leonard (2002) on how science must be structured to account for realistic motives of the scientists who compromise the community of scientists. As Leonard (2002: 141) put it: "Scientific rules, and the means for their enforcement, *constitute* the invisible-hand mechanism, so that scientific rules (sometimes) induce interested scientific actors with worldly goals to make epistemologically good choices."

[8] We use the phrase "career-maximizing economist" in an analogous sense to the idea of a "profit-maximizing firm."

scientific community dominated by monopolistic experts with false views, and where dissent is punished. When the requisite institutional conditions for a contestable scientific market do not exist or are distorted, the scientific process and knowledge can become distorted as well. For example, during Stalin's reign over the Soviet Union, biologists maximized their careers by accommodating and contributing to the false pseudoscientific theories of Lysenkoism; and while they might have avoided the gulag or an untimely demise, they were not advancing scientific knowledge. What is necessary is a set of rules of engagement that denies monopoly expert status to any one or group of scientists, and promotes a contestable market in science.

It should also be noted that "career-maximizing" does not imply that an economist who lacks conviction and who holds unorthodox views should uncritically follow the fads and fashions of the scientific community, or only pursue ideas that are "safe" and noncontroversial. Our moral and philosophical convictions can imbue research with a sense of purpose and direction, which, when combined with the rigor and discipline of economic theory, is more likely to generate interesting and impactful research than work lacking that same passionate philosophical drive. Indeed, part of the recipe for the successful careers of many economists is undoubtedly the driving force of their moral, ideological, and philosophical convictions, tempered by the disciplining logic of economics.

It does not matter ultimately who funds scientific research, or what the deep-seated motivations are of the individual scientist; what matters is that the scientific community has cultivated an environment of open, constructive discourse among practitioners, where critical dialogue is conducted in a serious manner. In such an environment, economists who seek to maximize their career success can do so only by engaging in the constant contestation of ideas, advancing better ideas, and challenging worse ones, and thereby contributing to the progressive development of scientific knowledge.

The Corruption of Economics: Institutional Problems Require Institutional Solutions

This perspective on the social responsibility of economists is useful when discussing the notion that the economics profession (even economic science itself) has been corrupted, and—if a problem can be identified—when examining the alternative remedies proposed.

Diagnosing the Problem

The most serious charge that critics have made is that corporate interests and wealthy foundations have distorted much of the university-based research agenda in economics through funding and grants for research; selection bias and pressure on academic hiring, publishing, and promotions; and even direct monetary rewards. This ranges from the more "simplistic" and invidious arguments that economists, motivated by their own private interests, hide behind a veneer of science to endorse theories (e.g., self-correcting market economy) and policies (e.g., financial deregulation) that promote the interests of corporations instead of the public interest.[9] The more sophisticated critics and commentators argue that even without such blatant acts of (self) deception, the incentives of academic research are skewed in a way that rewards economists who support certain special interests, on the margin, and results overall in a distortion of science (Zingales, 2013). We see several problems with this argument, however.

As rational choice economists, we have no doubt that some economists do follow the money, and that, on the margin, funding can influence research output. Yet, we think the predominant situation is the reverse, where the money follows the economists. In short, those special interest groups who would prefer a regime of financial deregulation seek out the best thinkers in the economics profession who independently have devised arguments for financial deregulation based on the theory and evidence. There is no distortion of ideas, let alone self-deception; instead, what we have is a matching model of economic ideas and funding sources. Again, the progress and integrity of science depends on the constant contestation of ideas, and within such an environment, the influence of funding is severely circumscribed, if not eliminated entirely.

The corruption of economics that matters does not come from corporate sponsorship of research, but rather from its politicization and the state's capture of the purpose of the discipline.[10] While critics of economics, including *Inside Job*, argue that the discipline has been corrupted by private interests, they say astonishingly little about the influence of political interests and the state in economics. This glaring, unjustified asymmetry poses a major defect in critics' arguments, and overlooks the really significant potential problem of "corruption" in the structure of production that links the scientific discipline of economics to political actors and policy outcomes.

At the base of this structure of production is the economics discipline itself, where research and critical discourse take place within the scientific community of economists. Here, the state is a big player (the biggest) in funding economics research. Yet, nothing is said in *Inside Job* about the role of the Federal Reserve in the funding of research in monetary economics and macroeconomics, the role of the international aid agencies (U.S. Agency for International Development [USAID], International Monetary Fund [IMF], etc.) in research in development and transitional economics, or the role of the National Science Foundation in research in basic economic theory. The only malevolent force in economic research discussed is the large financial corporations that have bribed economists and business school faculty, presumably, to provide cover for their special interest politics. If one accepts the argument that the source of funding affects the conclusions of

[9] In our view, *Inside Job* characterizes this rhetorical and substantive line of criticism.

[10] Economists from across the political spectrum and diverse ideological sympathies have identified and critically examined this trend (see Mises, 1949: 865–874; Rothbard, 1960; Bowles, 1974; Boettke 2012: 330–380).

scientific research, then it seems likely the case, at least prima facie, that the state is the most important source of corruption in economics. But again, even if politicized funding leads economists to distort their research in favor of the interests of the state, the state's *direct* influence on the economics discipline is constrained *within a contestable scientific market for ideas*. Further, although the public sector is the largest employer of PhD economists, only a small percentage of these economists actively engage in scientific research.[11]

Rather than the state's *direct* effect on economic *science* itself, the really crucial factor in the corruption and politicization of economics is the state's *indirect* influence on economic *praxis* through the political structure of policy production and social engineering. That is, the distortion of economic science arises from the links *between* the scientific community of economists, the economists *qua* policy engineers, and various noneconomist political actors, bureaucrats, politicians, and so forth. Moving beyond the scientific community (where the contestation of ideas limits distortions), but still within the economics profession proper, are the numerous economists who are engaged in the day-to-day design, implementation, evaluation, and analysis of public policy. Indeed, aside from the small fraction performing scientific research, the vast majority of public sector economists exists at this stratum of the structure of production—that of economic engineering.

Unfortunately, the institutional setting within which this practical policy work is done is radically different from the scientific community. The difference can even be seen in how these arenas are organized; in contrast to the relatively flat, "democratic" structure of contestable scientific markets in ideas, the practice of economic engineering conforms to a bureaucratic "hierarchy"—at the top, a few elite economists serve as high level advisors, descending below them are economists of increasing specialization, with the lowest ranked economists having a specific, constrained focus on a particular policy (see DeMartino, 2011: 24–25). Instead of the constant contestation of ideas in seminars, journal publications, and graduate teaching, we enter the realm of monopoly experts and the technocratic elite.

The Corruption of Economics is a Political and Institutional Problem

The corruption of economics, then, does not stem from faulty professional ethics or economic *science* itself, but from the practice and institutional context of economic engineering.[12] First, the realm of economic engineering contains filtering mechanisms

[11] By public sector employment we mean federal, state, and local government; various entities such as the Fed and Fannie Mae, Freddie Mac, and Sallie Mae; supranational agencies such as the World Bank and IMF; and public universities, and so forth. For more on the employment patterns of economists, and their professional activities, see DeMartino (2011: 19–34).

[12] See DeMartino (2011: 141–157) for more extensive discussion of the ethical challenges faced by economists acting as social engineers.

that skew the selection of practicing economic engineers toward certain shared characteristics—namely, their intellectual and scientific dispositions. Greg Mankiw (2006) captures the operation of this filtering process in the selection of high-level policy advisors and economic engineers from the ranks of elite macroeconomists, noting that:

> . . . it is remarkable that the new Keynesians were, by temperament, more inclined to become macroeconomic engineers than were economists working within the new classical tradition. Among the leaders of the new classical school, none (as far as I know) has ever left academia to take a significant job in public policy. By contrast, the new Keynesian movement, like the earlier generation of Keynesians, was filled with people who traded a few years in the ivory tower for a stay in the nation's capital. (Mankiw, 2006: 37)

Thus, macroeconomic engineering became dominated by economists who aligned themselves with a particular scientific perspective—Keynesian economics (both "Old" and "New"). Simply due to its selection process, the policy realm therefore reflected a greater homogeneity of economic perspectives than existed in the scientific community. Indeed, Keynesian economists dominated the policy realm for decades, even as Keynesian theories were subjected to serious challenges and debate within the scientific community.

This distortion arises from the filtering mechanisms of the policy realm, and not necessarily from any individuals being directly paid off to support the interests of another party. In fact, the matching model of funding and ideas in science bears a strong resemblance to this process, where political actors pursue those economists who have independently developed theories that support their ends. Unlike the contestation of ideas that limits the impact of funding on scientific research, however, no such intellectual competition exists in the political arena, a defect that is further compounded by the relatively narrow interests of political actors. Thus, while the split between the two schools had not been primarily political (economists on the left and right are New Keynesians), as Mankiw (2006: 37) explains, it is unsurprising that the New Keynesians have been more eager to lend their efforts to engineering policy, given that their theories lead them to conclude that government intervention and activist fiscal and monetary policies can have a positive effect on the economy. Meanwhile, New Classical economists have basically neglected policy work, given that their theorizing leads them to be much more skeptical about the value of managing the macroeconomy with fiscal and monetary policy.

Despite the fact that the policy realm is populated in large part by economists from the scientific elite (at least its new Keynesian representatives), there is no tendency for the actual policy process that emerges in this setting to reflect the current state of scientific knowledge. As Mankiw (2006: 43) admits, "The sad truth is that the macroeconomic research of the past three decades has had only minor impact on the practical analysis of monetary or fiscal policy." Instead, macroeconomic engineers have continued to employ conventional Keynesian models in policymaking, despite these models having been challenged and even rejected by the scientific community of economists. Mankiw (2006) places much of the blame on macroeconomists for not consistently connecting their advanced, abstract theories to practical applications of economic engineering. Yet, we think a more plausible explanation is that the most advanced macroeconomic theories paint a significantly more complex picture of the market economy, and simply do not yield strong or unambiguous implications for macroeconomic policy—in sharp contrast to the rather straightforward policy implications of hydraulic Keynesianism.

This brings us to what is, from our perspective, the ultimate source of the corruption of economics: *the political economy of economic expertise*. As public choice economics explains, there is a tendency for democratic politics to generate policies that favor highly organized special interest groups, and widely disperse the costs over numerous rationally ignorant voters, while self-interested political actors will attempt to expand their income, budget, influence, and power. Extending this logic to the field of economic expertise and policymaking, we see that political actors are likely to employ economists whose ideas comport with their goals—such as electoral success, bigger budgets and staff, more influence, and so forth. Because Keynesian ideas offer support to a relatively wide array of activities and interventions by the state, Keynesian economists will be more readily employed by political actors seeking to expand their budgets, influence, or even the patronage of interest groups by carving out favors and rents from Keynesian-inspired spending programs.

Ultimately, political actors are able essentially to pick and choose the particular economic theories and arguments that further their own self-interest (also see DeMartino, 2011: 39–41).[13] It is understandable if this discussion evokes an image of vested private interests "shopping" for sympathetic economic doctrine, as vocal critics allege to have occurred, corrupting the discipline of economic science itself. Though special interests have indeed been a pernicious influence on the economics profession, this problem does not stem from the corporate funding of research *within* the scientific community. Rather, it stems from the appropriation of economic doctrine by the state and political interests, *outside* of economic science proper.

A Professional Code of Ethics is an Ineffective Solution

In light of our alternative conception of the social responsibility of economists, and analysis of the notion that economics has been corrupted by special interests, we can examine the idea of a professional code of ethics for economists as a proposed solution to the corruption of economics. Our position, to be sure, is that a professional code of ethics for economists would be an almost entirely ineffective solution to the alleged problems of corruption in the economics profession.

[13] This extends to the political appropriation of economic statistics and econometrics as a tool for the state's purposes (see Rothbard, 1960).

The adoption of an ethical code would have a negligible impact on the professional behavior of economists, being largely redundant in promoting good practices, while having little if any power to constrain bad behavior. Because our intent is to further constructive discourse over these issues, and not to simply criticize and malign, we would like to highlight the better, more valuable aspects of the proposals for an ethical code of economists, before moving on to more critical discussion.

As we have argued, the corruption (i.e., politicization) of the economics profession is an institutional problem by nature, not an ethical one, and *institutional problems require institutional solutions*. The principal value of an ethical code for economists, therefore, is the discussion and debate that this idea has generated, and, in particular, that it begins to direct our attention to the *rules* of the scientific community and economics profession. If we, as professional economists, agree that there is in fact a problem of distortion and special interests in the economics discipline, and are to take seriously the task of reform, then we must look to the institutional framework of the economics profession—across the spectrum from pure science to the practice of engineering—as the appropriate target of critical analysis and reform. Whereas the value of this first aspect is conceptual in nature, there is another potential benefit of an ethical code that arises in practice, although it is of somewhat secondary value: collecting the various rules and practices that already exist in the profession, and compiling them into a central standardized form which can serve as a focal point for expectations about appropriate professional conduct. Still, it seems likely that a code of conduct is primarily valuable for instigating participation in the broader conversation over professional economic ethics.[14]

Aside from these limited benefits, however, there are (at least) three crucial issues that render ineffective the adoption of a code of ethics as a solution to the corruption of economics. In discussing these problems, it is helpful to frame the underlying problem that a code of ethics is intended to remedy—the corruption of economics by special interests—as a prisoners' dilemma game. In this perspective, implicit to many criticisms of the economics profession, players (economists) choose to cooperate (behave "ethically"; decline special interest bribes) or defect (accept bribes; distort research), which uniquely determines the game's (economic science) outcome. Unfortunately, the payoffs to players are structured such that the strategy "defect" strictly dominates "cooperate," and leads to the suboptimal equilibrium where all economists take bribes and distort their research, impairing economic science.

First, a professional code of ethics targets the wrong areas for reform—the behavior and ethics of individual economists—and pays insufficient attention to the rules and institutions of the economics profession. That is, to achieve its desired outcomes, an ethical code basically tries to encourage "good" behavior *within* the rules of the game, rather than altering the payoffs to different actions through constitutional choice *over* alternative rules. But if a prisoners' dilemma situation is perceived to exist, it must be

[14] To be sure, a code of conduct is not synonymous with professional economic ethics, and proponents for strengthening education and inquiry in the latter are not necessarily proponents of the former. See DeMartino (2011: 14–16).

recognized as an institutional problem, not a problem arising from defective personalities or morally corrupt people. To be effective, any potential efforts at reform must target institutions, not individuals: the institutional context within which economists *do* economics, not the moral quality or ethical character of individual economists; the incentive structure that individuals face, and its influence on choice, not the moral preferences or self-restraint of an individual; and, perhaps most importantly, how the institutional framework shapes the results of individuals pursuing their self-interest, not how much more or less selfish is an individual.

Second, the adoption of a professional code of ethics would almost certainly be a purely symbolic act—"cheap talk," more cynically speaking—as any such code would be practically unenforceable. For one, there are few, if any, enforcement mechanisms built into an ethical code, other than those that already exist in the economics profession. Still, the primary mechanism for enforcing a code of ethics is basically its appeal to the intrinsic moral beliefs and personal ethics of economists themselves, that is, the "honor system." Thus, adopting a code of ethics in response to a perceived prisoners' dilemma essentially amounts to asking that players promise not to defect, without actually modifying their incentives or constraints. At best, perhaps an ethical code might supplement the mechanism of scientific reputation in promoting good professional behavior, though its actual marginal value added is unclear, and potentially insignificant, given that a code of ethics would largely compile rules and norms already in practice. Further, it is not at all clear how ethical violations would even be identified to begin with, as they are undoubtedly highly difficult to detect and discern, let alone how alleged violations would be resolved.[15]

Third, the idea that adopting a professional code of ethics is necessary for the improvement of economic science fails to grasp the fundamental source of a robust, progressive scientific process—the constant contestation of ideas—and instead, misidentifies "good" ethical behavior by scientists with the source of "good" science. As we have repeatedly emphasized, however, the existence of a well-functioning scientific process does not depend on the morality or ethical character of its practitioners, but rather, on the constant contestation of ideas through open, critical discourse within the scientific community. In the context of a contestable market of ideas, whether or not a particular individual is a *good* moral or ethical scientist, and whether or not they are a good *scientist* who produces high-quality research, are essentially independent questions. Even if an ethical code were adopted that has "teeth" and effectively promotes "good" ethical behavior, it would nevertheless have an almost negligible impact on the efficiency of the scientific process. Where there exists a contestable scientific market in ideas, it would be largely redundant to adopt an ethical code, even a highly functional one, as a means

[15] In professions like medicine, practitioners who are found to have violated ethical rules can be sanctioned by having their license revoked, which essentially forbids them from practicing and can be a very serious threat. However, economists are not licensed, and we find (presumably along with many others) the idea of licensing social scientists to be thoroughly unattractive and disconcerting. (We thank George DeMartino for suggesting this point to us.)

of encouraging good professional practices and a progressive scientific process. At best, an ethical code would basically replicate the operation of other mechanisms and constraints that encourage good behaviors and outcomes. Outside of the constant contestation of ideas, on the other hand, whether or not an ethical code even exists is ultimately irrelevant to the efficiency of the scientific process, as an ethical code alone is powerless to effect desirable scientific outcomes. There is nothing in the intrinsic moral "goodness" of scientists alone, outside the contestation of ideas, to ensure that their work will tend to generate desirable results for science.

Finally, a code of ethics is an ineffective solution to the alleged corruption of economics because it ignores what is the principal source of that corruption—the politicization and appropriation of the purpose and practice of the discipline by the state. So long as government plays an active role in the economy, with economists as its principal engineers, then the economics profession will continue to be skewed by the influence of political interests, with significant rewards flowing to those economists who are the most efficacious servants of the state. Such a fundamental diversion between economic science and practice is wholly beyond the reach of a professional code of ethics, and its reform would require broader institutional changes in the political economy of the state, in particular, curtailing its scale and scope within definite constitutional limits.

A Plea for Humility and Radical Implications for the Reform of Economics

We believe that what the economics discipline is most in need of—to improve its scientific, ideological, and even moral status—is humility. Although such statements have become increasingly commonplace, almost obligatory, when discussing the intellectual and ethical concerns about economics, we believe that our position more consistently embraces humility as an intellectual, epistemological, and scientific virtue, relative to the proffered alternatives, including those favoring a code of ethics for economists. Our approach begins with economics having epistemic modesty, then reframes the economist as a humble student of society, not savior—and although our proposal is modest, in itself, such consistent economic humility leads to a vision of economics and the economist in society that is radically different from that which has dominated the discipline since the Keynesian revolution (cf. Boettke and Horwitz, 2005; Boettke, Coyne, and Leeson, 2006).

While the idea of a code of ethics for economists is sometimes seen as a reflection of intellectual humility, we argue that not only is there no inherent connection between these two notions, but that, in fact, they are deeply *at odds* with one another. The very idea that the economics profession should adopt a formal ethical code—as is common practice in other professions, such as medicine and engineering—implicitly presupposes a view of economists and their role in society that grants them a position of privilege and elevated status among the social sciences and even over humankind. Namely, the argument presumes the role (at least partial) of the economist in society is as social engineer, tasked with utilizing an array of social control mechanisms in order to solve the world's ills, guided by the engineering toolset of economic science. Note that inherent to perhaps one of the most seemingly modest codes proposed, a Hippocratic Oath for economists—first, *do* no harm—is the idea that economists do indeed *do*, in the first place, which reduces the room for debate over even such fundamental questions as whether or not it is *ever* appropriate for economists to *do anything* as social engineers at all. Rather than evoking images of a modest practical professional, the comparison of economists to doctors, engineers, and dentists evinces the hubris, not humility, of economists who perceive themselves as social engineers, or even "doctors to the world."[16] We can hardly imagine a more arrogant analogy than that between economist qua social engineer and medical doctor or civil engineer, which analogizes constructing a bridge from cement and steel to engineering society using the state's coercive apparatus of social control.

The concept of the economist as social engineer is inherently incompatible with the virtue of humility. At its core, this view elevates economists to a privileged position above society, from which they are purportedly revealed knowledge that enables them to design society at will. The economist as savior looks down on ordinary people as bricks and lumber that can be controlled, manipulated, and formed into a desired order. Adopting a code of ethics—which is in itself premised on economic engineering—would do nothing for the humility of economists who see social control and engineering as the purpose of their profession. To be sure, however, we are not merely concerned with the cultural or moral aesthetics of the lack of humility and arrogance of the economist qua engineer. Rather, we are concerned with the political economy of the technocratic system embodying such arrogance, where elite economic engineers are entrusted with an array of discretionary powers to intervene in the economy and society. Whether or not we attribute purely benevolent motives to the technocrats in charge, such a system lacks robustness to failures, has difficulty correcting errors, and mistakes by technocrats, no matter how well-meaning, can have serious and far-reaching consequences.

Indeed, the weight of failure alone should force us to reflect upon the self-ordained role of the economist as engineer—as well as the analogy to a doctor or civil engineer. A doctor's mistake can endanger the health of patients, and possibly even kill them. An engineer's error could lead to extensive property damage, and the loss of many lives.

[16] In an essay envisioning a future where social engineering had become a mundane element of society, Keynes (1931: 373) notably wrote that economic problems "should be a matter for specialists—like dentistry. If economists could manage to get themselves thought of as humble, competent people, on a level with dentists, that would be splendid!" Also, note that the letter to the AEA (fn. 5) specifically cites the role of the economics profession in policy and calls for a code of ethics as a means (in part) to strengthen public confidence in that role.

Yet, even the most disastrous failures of modern medicine and engineering undoubtedly pale in comparison to the damage that social engineering has caused, and is capable of causing, to the lives and well-being of ordinary human beings. As Milton Friedman argued, the Great Depression stands as a "testament to how much harm can be done by mistakes on the part of a few men when they wield vast power over the monetary system of a country" ([1962] 2002: 50). We are in complete agreement with Friedman, then, when he further argues: "Any system which gives so much power and so much discretion to a few men that mistakes—excusable or not—can have such far-reaching effects is a bad system" ([1962] 2002: 50). It is by this reasoning, then, that we are led to our critical views on the lack of humility in a profession of social engineers, in which this arrogance has arguably become institutionalized.

Therefore, as an alternative approach to correcting the alleged failings of the economics discipline, we argue for a restoration of epistemic modesty in economics; a modest view of the economist as humble student of society, or lowly philosopher; and the divorce of economics as a scientific discipline from the claims and practice of economic engineering.[17] At its core, this approach recognizes that there are strong limits to scientific reasoning and knowledge about society and the operation of social processes (see especially Hayek 1937, 1978).[18] This epistemic modesty is both a methodological input and an analytical output of economic theory. In order to generate meaningful insight and useful knowledge about the nature of social and economic order, it is incumbent on social science to adapt its methods and analytical tools around these irreducible epistemic limits, working within them rather than against them. This would mean that economists redirect their attention away from positivist theorizing in purely quantitative, empirically measurable terms, and instead construct theories that give substantial weight to qualitative data, predictions, and insights (see Hayek [1978] as well as Frydman and Goldberg [2007] for work in this direction). By reemphasizing the fundamental limits of scientific knowledge, economists would do much to restore epistemic modesty and intellectual humility to the claims of economic science. This would likely require, in part, that they content themselves to a position consonant with that of Friedrich Hayek (1978: 29), who preferred "true but imperfect knowledge, even if it leaves much indetermined and unpredictable, to pretence of exact knowledge that is likely to be false." If economists successfully eject epistemic hubris and scientism from the discipline, then economics would cease to be a principal tool of social control, emphasizing instead the complex nature of social phenomena and spontaneous order. This would dissolve the claims of central planning and social engineering to the mantle of "science," and cast serious doubt on their effectiveness as a means to constructing a rational social and economic order. Thus, scientific economists would perhaps be led to seriously consider, and potentially embrace, Hayek's (1988: 76) notion: "The curious task of economics is

[17] This approach draws principally on Boettke and Horwitz (2005) and Boettke, Coyne, and Leeson (2006).

[18] Our views owe much to the penetrating analysis and nuanced discussions about economics and knowledge of Friedrich Hayek (cf. 1937, 1945, 1948, 1978).

to demonstrate to men how little they really know about what they imagine they can design."

Thus, we believe that economists should view themselves as humble students of society, or lowly philosophers, whose principal task is to grasp the nature of spontaneous order in society and the market process, including the role of the institutional framework for such social processes, and to communicate these insights to the scientific community, students, policymakers, and the general public. In this role as lowly philosopher, the humble economist repudiates the scientistic posturing by would-be economic engineers who claim omniscience and the power to cure social ills through the mechanisms of state intervention and social control. Instead, the economist as humble philosopher embraces the role of cautionary prophet, whose task is filtering the claims of political entrepreneurs against the logic and means–ends analysis of economics—delimiting the scope of effective public policy. As a result of their epistemic modesty and humbled self-image, the economist as lowly philosopher is more inclined to focus upon the institutional structure of society as the crucial factor in generating desirable social outcomes. Hence, they turn their desires for social reform to the question of how to cultivate an institutional environment that fosters the wealth and well-being of society.

Of course, like the proposals for a professional code of ethics, recasting the economist as humble student has little power in and of itself to reform the economics profession. What matters is that this humble self-image is adopted as part of an economics that has epistemic modesty. Under these circumstances, it is the substantive content of economics itself that defines the rules of professional and intellectual humility, and provides the disciplining logic to enforce those rules. Where an economist oversteps those bounds—such as by claiming the support of "science" for a particular policy of social engineering—other economists will rush to point out the distortion, in order to improve their own career success, and thereby generate the self-correcting forces of economic science. If economists embrace this humbled role in society, and economics has epistemic modesty, then the problems raised by the corrupting influence of special interests, moral failings, and politics can be reduced, due to the much more limited notion of what economists *do*, and more importantly, what economists *are believed capable of doing*.[19]

Finally, if our approach still does not provide an adequate solution, then there is another even more direct step towards a fundamental solution to the corruption of economics: limiting the scope and scale of government. There are likely always going to be economists who possess the mentality of a savior of society, itching to wield state power to engineer society as they see fit. So long as the state continues to intervene in the

[19] Whether or not the economics discipline does accept a position of epistemic modesty, however, is not something that can be mandated or predetermined, but depends on its acceptance by the scientific community of economists. Nevertheless, such a result seems to us to be highly feasible, given that epistemic modesty has a more solid foundation in epistemology and modern developments in the philosophy of science, versus that of epistemic hubris. We are not claiming that epistemic humility comprises an ethical duty of economists per se, but merely argue that methodology matters—at most, economists have a *philosophical* duty to adopt methods that are appropriate to their field of inquiry, and to remain cognizant of their limits.

economy at its discretion, economics will continued to be distorted through the practice of policy and social engineering; indeed, the policy-engineering realm is the epitome of a corrosive institutional environment for science: a noncontestable market for ideas, with entrenched political interests, monopoly experts, and elite technocrats. The state will select for economists who are not constrained by epistemic modesty—even if such a position is widely adopted by the scientific community—and reward those who effectively serve the state, which reinforces the existing supply of economist-saviors and might even shift the supply curve to the right over time.[20] To sever the corrupting link between politics and science, then it may be necessary to limit the role of the state to providing the institutional infrastructure of economic order, thereby removing its role as an active player in the economy. If the government is confined to the background (yet vital) task of cultivating an institutional environment that promotes social and economic order, within well-defined constitutional constraints, then would-be economist-saviors lack the means to act on their visions, and even if their ideas persist, their ability to cause harm is diminished.

Conclusion

Thus, we have outlined an alternative conception of the social responsibility of economists, as well as proposed a "modest" approach to a solution to the corruption of economics that emphasizes what we might call "radical humility" as a disciplining force in economics. To state the argument in clear, concise terms: the social responsibility of the economist is solely to maximize their career within the scientific community of economists. Within an appropriate institutional environment—one that features the constant contestation of ideas and the mechanism of scientific reputation—the actions of career-maximizing scientists will tend to reward productive scientific behavior, punish bad behavior, and generate good scientific outcomes. Given these conditions, science is self-correcting and progressive, and scientific resources are allocated to their most highly valued uses. In our view, economics should embrace a radical humility, in which the economist is better understood as a humble student of society, or lowly philosopher, and economics has epistemic modesty. These conditions limit the economist to a

[20] Of course, it is important not to ignore the influence of popular ideas about the application and limits of science as a force for the deliberate improvement of the welfare of society, especially within the context of modern democratic politics. Indeed, Hayek (1978: 31) argues that the "conflict between what in its present mood the public expects science to achieve in satisfaction of popular hopes and what is really in its power is a serious matter because, even if the true scientists should all recognize the limitations of what they can do in the field of human affairs, so long as the public expects more there will always be some who will pretend, and perhaps honestly believe, that they can do more to meet popular demands than is really in their power." Similar reasoning also applies to the point raised in fn. 18—if a society rewards epistemic hubris and scientism, then these issues will likely continue to plague economics.

humble position in society and reduce the opportunities for the corruption of economics, and the potential harm from the economist qua social engineer.

Lastly, we would like to raise one final point pertaining to these general issues for further consideration, which relates our position back to Friedman's ideas about the social responsibility of business. Friedman argued that the only social responsibility of business is to maximize profits, not only because businesses would promote the broader interests of society by doing so, but also because the widespread acceptance of the doctrine that business does have other social responsibilities beyond maximizing profits would lead to the destruction of the market system and a free society. We believe that Friedman's argument and the problems he identifies extend beyond business and are directly applicable to the current discussion. Of particular interest, Friedman asks the critical questions: "If businessmen do have a social responsibility other than making maximum profits for stockholders, *how are they to know what it is? Can self-selected private individuals decide what the social interest is?*" ([1962] 2002: 133, emphasis added). Here, Friedman flips on its head the notion that individuals acting on selfish or undesirable motives will lead to bad outcomes, and instead casts critical attention to the problem of ostensibly well-intentioned individuals acting upon their own self-selected ethical ideals yet leading to bad outcomes. The non-maximum-profit doctrine of social responsibility is destructive because it is, in fact, deeply antidemocratic, relegating to private actors extraordinary discretion over what exactly *is in* the public's interest.

Translated to the realm of economic science, such a doctrine would not only fail to humble economists, but would also empower their self-ordained status as the high priests of society, giving them free rein to dictate the value scale of alternative ends for society and to employ the tools of social control as they see fit. We strongly believe that the potential harm—in terms of scientific knowledge and practical implications for the lives of ordinary people—caused by a self-referential, "ethical" science of economics far outweighs that which might arise from mere conflict of interest between the research of a scientist and their pecuniary interests. (Recall for a moment the introductory quote from Ronald Coase, from which we believe scientists of all stripes might benefit—particularly the proposition that "the number of falsehoods put into circulation for the sake of money must be small compared with the number put forward "to serve the public interest".) Thus, the constant contestation of ideas—combined with the career-maximizing view of the social responsibility of economists—is both necessary to direct "immoral" economists to act in ways that further social welfare, and a crucial prophylactic against the serious harms that might be caused by "ethical economists" attempting to impose their own unconstrained moral visions and ethical ideals on science and society.

References

American Sociological Association. 1999. *Code of Ethics and Policies and Procedures of the ASA Committee on Professional Ethics*. Washington, DC: American Sociological Association. Retrieved from http://www.asanet.org/images/asa/docs/pdf/CodeofEthics.pdf

Boettke, Peter J. 2012. *Living Economics: Yesterday, Today, and Tomorrow*. Oakland, CA: The Independent Institute, Universidad Francisco Marroquin.

Boettke, Peter J., Christopher J. Coyne, and Peter T. Leeson. 2006. "High Priests and Lowly Philosophers: The Battle for the Soul of Economics." *Case Western Reserve Law Review* 56(3): 551–568.

Boettke, Peter J., and Steven Horwitz. 2005. "The Limits of Economic Expertise: Prophets, Engineers, and the State in the History of Development Economics." *History of Political Economy* 35: 10–39.

Bowles, Samuel. 1974. "Economists as Servants of Power." *American Economic Review* 64 (2): 129–132.

Buchanan, James M. [1979] 1999. "Politics Without Romance: A Sketch of Positive Public Choice Theory and Its Normative Implications." In *The Logical Foundations of Constitutional Liberty*, edited by Jams M. Buchanan, pp. 45–59. Indianapolis, IN: Liberty Fund.

Buchanan, James M. 1999. *The Logical Foundations of Constitutional Liberty*. Indianapolis, IN: Liberty Fund.

Carrick-Hagenbarth, Jessica, and Gerald A. Epstein. 2012. "Dangerous Interconnectedness: Economists' Conflicts of Interest, Ideology and Financial Crisis." *Cambridge Journal of Economics* 36(1): 43–63.

Colander, David, Michael D. Goldberg, Armin Haas, Katarina Juselius, Alan Kirman, Thomas Lux, and Brigitte Sloth. 2009. "The Financial Crisis and the Systemic Failure of the Economics Profession." *Critical Review* 21(2–3): 249–267.

DeMartino, George F. 2011. *The Economist's Oath: On the Need for and Content of Professional Economic Ethics*. New York: Oxford University Press.

Epstein, Gerald A., and Jessica Carrick-Hagenbarth. 2010. "Financial Economists, Financial Interests and Dark Corners of the Meltdown: It's Time to Set Ethical Standards for the Economics Profession." University of Massachusetts Amherst, Political Economy Research Institute, Working Paper Series (239).

Flitter, Emily, Kristina Cooke, and Pedro da Costa. 2010. "Special Report: For Some Professors, Disclosure Is Academic." Reuters. Retrieved from http://www.reuters.com/article/2010/12/20/us-academics-conflicts-idUSTRE6BJ3LF20101220

Friedman, Jeffrey. 2009. "A Crisis of Politics, Not Economics: Complexity, Ignorance, and Policy Failure." *Critical Review* 21(2–3): 127–183.

Friedman, Milton. [1962] 2002. *Capitalism and Freedom*. Chicago: University of Chicago Press.

Frydman, Roman, and Michael D. Goldberg. 2007. *Imperfect Knowledge Economics: Exchange Rates and Risk*. Princeton, NJ: Princeton University Press.

Hayek, F. A. 1937. "Economics and Knowledge." *Economica* 4(13): 33–54.

Hayek, F. A. 1945. "The Use of Knowledge in Society." *American Economic Review* 35(4): 519–530.

Hayek, F. A. 1948. *Individualism and Economic Order*. Chicago: University of Chicago Press.

Hayek, F. A. 1978. "The Pretence of Knowledge." In *New Studies in Philosophy, Politics, Economics and the History of Ideas*, pp. 23–34. Chicago: University of Chicago Press.

Hayek, F. A. 1988. *The Fatal Conceit: The Errors of Socialism*. Chicago: University of Chicago Press.

Keynes, John Maynard. 1931. *Essays in Persuasion*. London: Macmillan.

Krugman, Paul. 9/6/2009. "How Did Economists Get It So Wrong?" *New York Times Magazine*: 36–43.

Leonard, Thomas. 2002. "Reflections on Rules in Science: An Invisible-Hand Perspective." *Journal of Economic Methodology* 9(2): 141–168.

Leonhardt, David. 10/23/2008. "Greenspan's Mea Culpa." *New York Times: Economix*. Retrieved from http://economix.blogs.nytimes.com/2008/10/23/greenspans-mea-culpa/?_r=0

Mankiw, N. Gregory. 2006. "The Macroeconomist as Scientist and Engineer." *Journal of Economic Perspectives* 20(4): 29–46.

Mises, Ludwig von. 1949. *Human Action*. Auburn, AL: Ludwig von Mises Institute.

Rothbard, Murray N. 1960. "The Politics of Political Economists: Comment." *The Quarterly Journal of Economics* 74(4): 659–665.

Stiglitz, Joseph E. 2009. "The Anatomy of a Murder: Who Killed America's Economy?" *Critical Review* 21(2–3): 329–339.

Taylor, John B. 2009. *Getting Off Track: How Government Actions and Interventions Caused, Prolonged, and Worsened the Financial Crisis*. Stanford, CA: Hoover Institution Press.

Wallison, Peter J. 2009. "Cause and Effect: Government Policies and the Financial Crisis." *Critical Review* 21(2–3): 365–376.

Zingales, Luigi. 2013. "Preventing Economists' Capture. The Tobin Project." Retrieved from http://www.tobinproject.org/books-papers/preventing-capture.

CHAPTER 8

THE ETHICAL ECONOMIST

Duty and Virtue in the Scientific Process

JONATHAN B. WIGHT

Introduction

> Now, what I want is, Facts. Teach these boys and girls nothing but Facts. Facts alone are wanted in life. Plant nothing else, and root out everything else . . . Facts, sir; nothing but Facts!
>
> —Charles Dickens (*Hard Times*, Chapter 1, 1854).

The image of an impartial scientist working to uncover value-free facts in an antiseptic laboratory is highly appealing. Unfortunately, this is not the way science actually works—nor should it (Shapin, 2010). For science to progress, economists must embody strong moral principles: they operate in an environment in which appeals to value matter a great deal in deciding which research projects get funded, which facts are collected, how they are collected, and how conclusions about truth are established. Almost every step of analysis requires value judgments in addition to professional norms. Being impartial is not the same as being value-free. Teachers and their students should be conversant in the ethical issues that arise in conducting positive research.

Two problems cause market failure in scientific research: (1) asymmetric information arises because knowledge creators know more about their methods and data than do knowledge consumers, and (2) research that is replicated and confirmed constitutes a public good, yet most people free-ride on that discovery process. In other professions, market failure is handled by a mix of approaches that often include the development of professional codes of conduct and external licensing. A doctor, for example, has substantially more knowledge than consumers and for that reason affirms in the Hippocratic Oath to put patient interests ahead of personal interests; a doctor can also lose a license for egregious behavior. Certified public accountants likewise profess an "obligation of self-discipline" and "unswerving commitment to honorable behavior, even at the sacrifice of personal advantage" (American Institute of Certified Public Accountants [AICPA], 2013). The same applies in engineering, architecture, law, and many other professions.

Unlike other professions, economists rely to a large extent on self-regulation to guide behavior. If this is to be successful, nonconsequentialist ethical principles of duty and virtue must be brought into the mix of self-interest and institutional rules. Adam Smith's ethical model, outlined in *The Theory of Moral Sentiments*, explains why self-control arising from moral commitment is superior to externally driven cost-benefit calculations of honesty (Smith, 1982*b*: 263). Amartya Sen likewise notes that moral commitment "drives a wedge between personal choice and personal welfare" that is not at work when moral conduct is grounded only in self-interest (1977: 329). Smith's model addresses why informal mentoring of junior colleagues in scientific norms is often provided even when the personal rewards are slight or negative.

To set the stage, this chapter first investigates the role of enlightened self-interest as an incentive for ethical conduct. The next section explores the ideology of science. In the section "Shadowing a Research Project," a PhD research project draws attention to the moral hazards in truth seeking and the ways in which positive economics relies on values and norms. The section "Moving Forward: Reclaiming Duty in Discipline," addresses proposed systematic reforms in the economics profession, and the final section concludes the chapter.

Self-interest as a Constraint on Unethical Conduct

Economists typically model behavior according to a consequentialist ethic in which self-interested outcomes are said to be the main motivator of action. Enlightened self-interest (concern for long-term reputation effects of one's behavior) can give rise to honest behavior in science, but it is unreliable unless costs and benefits motivate such conduct. Truth and self-interest are not always reliable bedfellows. Can one assume, to use the question posed by David M. Levy, "that scholars who pursue truth are made out of different stuff than we ordinary people, who, after all, seek not truth but happiness" (Levy, 2002: ix)? Levy proposes that economic researchers be modeled as maximizing their own wealth or status according to public choice theory. This casts a darker light on the scientific process because a funding donor can create incentives for researchers to find results that conform to a particular political agenda or ideology. The scientist becomes an "entrepreneur scholar of uncertain loyalties" (Mata, 2011).

The documentary movie *Inside Job* (2010) cites a particular case of noted banking expert Frederic Mishkin, who was paid $124,000 by the Icelandic Chamber of Commerce to co-author a study entitled, "Financial Stability in Iceland," which concluded that "financial fragility is not high and the likelihood of a financial meltdown is very low" (Mishkin and Herbertsson, 2006: 56). Two years later, the Icelandic financial system collapsed. It is facile in hindsight to suggest that Mishkin wrote what he did because he was paid to write it; someone of his stature presumably has much more to lose by being perceived as an industry hack. Paul Samuelson emphasized the quality of social respect: "In the long run, the economic scholar works for the only coin worth having—our own applause" (cited in Coase, 1994: 31). Nevertheless, Charles Ferguson, who wrote and produced the film, counters that the lack of transparency regarding who is funding economic research gives rise to pernicious incentives that are now ubiquitous:

> Over the past 30 years, the economics discipline has been systematically subverted, in much the same way as American politics—by money, especially from the financial services industry. Many of the most prominent economists in America are now paid to testify in Congress, to serve on boards of directors, testify in antitrust cases and regulatory proceedings, and to give speeches to the companies and industries they study and write about with supposed objectivity. (Ferguson, 2010)

Following the publicity of *Inside Job* and the publication of George DeMartino's, *The Economist's Oath: On the Need for and Content of Professional Economic Ethics* (2011)—both with scorching critiques of economists' alleged ethical lapses—the American Economic Association (AEA) issued new requirements for financial disclosure and data transparency when publishing research in its journals. An author must disclose all sources of financial research support and any sources of revenue from interested parties from consulting, fees, and so on exceeding $10,000 over the past three years, including payments to family members (American Economic Association [AEA], 2012). The AEA did not adopt an explicit code of ethics as exists in other professions in part because there is no mechanism for enforcing such a code—no licensing is required to sell economic services.

A major question remains: are the incentives in economics sufficient to promote ethical conduct? If the inducements for truth telling are weak, cheating can occur; indeed, a number of scientists, including some economists, have allegedly fallen off the truth wagon (List et al., 2001). In addition to the potential bias arising from funding sources, the growing pressure to publish creates a moral hazard because younger researchers in particular have an incentive to find publishable results in their first few years. The probability of producing publishable papers can be raised through fudging, falsification, or outright plagiarism. The benefits of successful cheating can be high, including lifetime employment through tenure.

On the other side of the ledger, researchers who are caught cheating face penalties of diminished reputation, ostracism, and even job loss. But the chances of being caught are often low. The peer-review process generally does not encompass attempting statistical replication. Hence, the probability of detecting errors in empirical work (whether through unintentional mistakes or outright fraud) is relatively low. A study by Dewald, Thursby, and Anderson (1986: 588) found that only a small sample of articles in one prestigious journal could be replicated, and inadvertent errors were "commonplace." The main reason for this, they stress, is not dishonesty, but simply a lack of time and attention. Until 2004 or even later, the top journals in economics did not require authors to presubmit their raw data and program code. Even after the rule was instituted, many journal editors have not enforced it, and replication remains difficult (McCullough, McGeary, and Harrison, 2008: 1408).

Even if replication were widely possible, the incentive for anyone to make the effort is generally low. Replication generally does not produce a publishable journal article unless it uncovers dramatic statistical aberrations or fraud. The recent paper by Herndon, Ash, and Pollen (2013), which found coding and other errors in Reinhart and Rogoff's (2010) influential paper, is an exception that demonstrates the value of replication in the search for truth. Generally, however, replication researchers may be labeled as unimaginative or untrusting of colleagues, and the results of replication experiments may be inconclusive for a number of reasons. The reward structure results in market failure, in the sense that published research that is replicated and confirmed constitutes a public good, yet most economists free-load on that discovery process (Dewald et al., 1986: 589).

Even if discovered, fabricators can use the easy alibi that unintentional errors arose and that these do not constitute unethical conduct. When deliberate falsification or plagiarism is proved, there is often only a "slap on the wrist" penalty of not being eligible for publication in that particular journal. Journal editors do not want to be sued for libel. Over half the editors in prestigious journals said that even in cases of plagiarism they would not report an author to his or her supervisors (Enders and Hoover, 2004). Nor is there a central licensing authority for reporting such misdeeds.

The standard view is that the potential loss of one's reputation is strong enough to discipline most behaviors. Relying on self-interest alone to control behavior produces a weak form of truth telling, however, because the agent only appears trustworthy because there is something to be gained from that charade; someone who *is* trustworthy does not depend on the circumstances for upholding that commitment. The discussion here raises the possibility that the incentives to cheat in economics may be large in some contexts, and the institutions for preventing cheating (e.g., replication and penalties) can often be weak.

Nevertheless, the number of cases of fraud in academic economic research appears to be low. In self-reported measures of impropriety on an anonymous survey, List et al. (2001: 166) find less than 5 percent of researchers admit to at least one instance of falsifying research data. How that translates into percent of published research is unknown because those who falsify may be more or less prolific than the average person or more or less inclined to cheat in particular cases. Researchers may also lie about how often they cheat. Research Papers in Economics (RePEc, 2013) publishes a list of alleged plagiarism offenders, and it is also surprisingly short. These results may be due to many cases of malfeasance yet to be discovered, or, as I suspect, to the fact that economists are generally honest for intrinsic reasons: they have consciously or unconsciously adopted the ideology of honesty and truth seeking in the presence of moral hazards.

Norms of Virtue and Duty

To overcome potential market failures, the science of economics relies on professionals who adhere to often unstated and instinctive codes of duty- and virtue-based ethics, in addition to enlightened self-interest. These internalized moral systems eschew computations of personal cost and benefit in favor of the acceptance of absolute moral norms of right and wrong. Adam Smith was quite clear in his view that scientific discovery is and ought to be driven by the intrinsic value of the process itself and not by a calculation of personal gain:

> Wonder, therefore, *and not any expectation of advantage from its discoveries*, is the first principle which prompts mankind to the study of Philosophy . . . and they pursue this study *for its own sake, as an original pleasure or good in itself*, without regarding its tendency to procure them the means of many other pleasures. (1982c: 51, emphasis added)

Frank Knight likewise described science as a moral code that should be observed as a "religion" to those who enter it. The "basic principle of science—truth or objectivity—is essentially a moral principle, in opposition to any form of self-interest" (Knight, 1947: 244). Ronald Coase also noted that scientists must adopt a vow of "integrity, competence and humility"—and sometimes courage (Coase, 1994: 33). These virtues should be identified and nurtured, not only because they may lead to personal success, but also because they are valued intrinsically as ideals to be upheld. Understanding and explaining the role that ethical mores play in economics research is a key part of mentoring junior colleagues and students (elaborated in the section "The Mentor's Role").

The Ideology of Science

The value of impartiality in truth seeking is a central tenet of the "spirit" of science, a term used by A. C. Pigou in defending himself against charges of political bias: "It is [a teacher's] duty to discover and teach what is true" (cited in Coase, 1994: 155n7). Schumpeter (1954) used the comparable term "ideology." Ideology can be defined as the characteristic set of beliefs of a particular group, culture, or class at a point in time; ideology contains value-laden ideas about what is important and proper. True scholars (in opposition to charlatans) consciously embrace the ideology of science founded on truth seeking. But scientists have other ideologies that they do not consciously choose and of which they may not even be aware. A child grows up absorbing the scents, sounds, and chatter of home life. Language is unconsciously acquired early in life, and language is an example of an ideological system bursting with ethical judgments and values. Speakers of English and other Indo-European languages, for example, use an egocentric spatial reference system, whereas speakers in many other languages use cardinal coordinates (Henrich, Heine, and Norenzayan, 2010: 8).

When scientists use words—as they must—those words are value-laden. For this reason, scientists strive to create their own vocabularies to break free from old connotations. Vilfredo Pareto and Arthur Pigou, in the early 20th century, were part of a positivist movement that strove to find words in economics that were, in their view, scientific rather than value-laden. To avoid using the word utility, Pareto coined the term *ophelimity* to represent relative satisfaction; meanwhile, Pigou favored the term *desiredness* "since it cannot be taken to have any ethical implication" (Pigou, 1962: 11). Nevertheless, their attempts to construct a neutral language failed, and moral appeals linger in economic terminology. "Efficiency," for example, represents the outcome in which the economic surplus is maximized, and the word efficiency is used *because* it provides a favorable connotation for that outcome. Kenneth Arrow notes:

> A definition is just a definition, but when the *definiendum* is a word already in common use with highly favorable connotations, it is clear that we are really trying to be persuasive; we are implicitly recommending the achievement of optimal states. (Arrow, 1963: 942)

One can likewise argue that the word "equilibrium" has similarly favorable connotations. Scientists like to believe that their efforts will make the world a better place, and that is indeed what motivated 38 percent of Nobel Prize winners in economics to enter the profession (Evans, Grimes, and Becker, 2012). It would indeed be surprising if the language of the discipline failed to reflect this motive.

In addition to language, humans absorb an orchestrated as well as random set of facts, theories, and beliefs about the world and how it works, constituting the important worldview of the scientist (Schumpeter, 1954). When combined with ideology and intuition, this prescientific outlook provides the milieu in which a researcher sets off to examine the economy. Worldview shapes the kinds of questions investigated and the methods employed. It also can shape the facts scientists are able to see. The famous duck/rabbit illusion illustrates the point. Seen in one way, the image is a duck; seen with another perspective, the same picture represents a rabbit. Ideological context can shape the way vision is interpreted: if asked around Easter, more children identify the drawing as a rabbit (Brugger and Brugger, 1993). Hence, "When something is discovered to be a 'fact,' it simply means that a larger number of those observers agree on what they see" (Welch, 2011).

A *paradigm* is a generally accepted viewpoint of how the world works; it is the conceptual framework within which scientific research is carried out. The familiar joke of lost car keys brings out the purpose and importance of a paradigm:

> It is midnight and a man is desperately looking under a street lamp for his lost car keys. A passerby offers to help. "Is this where you dropped them?" the passerby asks. "No, but this is where the light is," the man replies.

Paradigms cast the light that helps us search. But that reality should make us cautious. As one psychologist noted, "We cannot understand the world we see before we understand the tools we see it with" (Schreck, 2007). The assumption that a paradigm is impartial or free of values can impede scientific advance because it narrows the scope of vision. Thomas Kuhn, in *The Structure of Scientific Revolutions* (1970), wrote that revolutions in paradigms take place when more scientists begin to perceive the duck as well as the rabbit. The crisis of anomaly is resolved from a sudden and unstructured switch in *gestalt*—or holistic perception—that in hindsight may appear to be obvious.

Our brains process hundreds of bits of information per second. Most of it is lost to the conscious mind. For someone to pay attention, his mind must make a value judgment to pay attention. Another famous experiment in psychology illustrates this point. Subjects are asked to watch a video of basketball players and count the number of times the ball is passed between players wearing white. About half the subjects correctly count the number of passes but miss entirely the appearance of a large "gorilla" that strides across the court beating his chest (Chabris and Simons, 2010).[1]

Selective attention suggests that we see what we expect to see, thus introducing bias into data selection and collection. If someone asks you, "What time is it?" you will glance at your watch and say "about 2:30." But why did you not respond "2:31 and 15 seconds"? We subconsciously put the answer into a presumed context. We make a judgment that only a certain level of detail is desirable in this situation, and we round the minutes and cut out the seconds, a.m./p.m., and the time zone from the answer. The degree of specificity required, like the amount and timeliness of data collected, is a judgment that is addressed by the development of an economic model. The choices involved can be labeled professional or methodological, yet they raise ethical concerns, as shown in the following example.

Prior to the mid-20th century, history was largely taught as a compendium of facts about kings and wars. Names and dates of nobility filled textbook pages. What to observe and what to omit are, of course, professional judgments based on experience and expertise, but they also reflect social and ethical norms. Reporting in the past conveyed the value judgment that only leaders were important enough to write about. At some point in the mid-20th century, historians experienced a *gestalt* shift and suddenly could see the rest of humanity; books on the political, social, and economic histories of women and slaves soon appeared. The facts were always there but had gone unreported, like the gorilla in the video. Without theory, we do not know which facts to collect. But if ideology plays a part in selecting the theory, ideology plays a part in selecting the facts as well. Tjalling Koopmans, who pioneered the understanding of discount rates in natural resource use, was cautious about the rote application of scientific methods, as in selecting a discount rate: "[T]he problem of optimal growth is too complicated, or at least too unfamiliar, for one to feel comfortable in making an entirely *a priori* choice of [a time discount rate] before one knows the implications of alternative choices" (cited in

[1] The video can be seen at: http://www.youtube.com/watch?v=vJG698U2Mvo.

Nordhaus, 2007: 692). To Koopmans, in exploratory cases, scientists arrive at the facts after opting for the discount rate that will produce those facts.

The Keynesian Revolution of the mid-1930s is an example of a notable *gestalt* switch in economics. In the Preface to *The General Theory of Employment, Interest, and Money*, Keynes noted that "The ideas which are here expressed so laboriously are extremely simple and should be obvious. The difficulty lies, not in the new ideas, but in escaping from the old ones" (Keynes, 1964[1936]: vii). Kenneth Arrow builds on this: "There is no question that people, including economists, are motivated by their ideologies" (Arrow, 2000: 18). As one example, students self-select to enter graduate programs that reinforce their ideology (Colander and Klamer, 1987). Ideology is not a bad thing if it brings important issues to light. But being aware of ideology is necessary for thinking critically about one's own biases; according to Schumpeter:

> Now it should be perfectly clear that there is a wide gate for ideology to enter into this [scientific] process. In fact, it enters on the very ground floor, into the preanalytic cognitive act of which we have been speaking. Analytic work begins with material provided by our vision of things, and this vision is ideological almost by definition. It embodies the picture of things as we see them, and wherever there is any possible motive for wishing to see them in a given rather than another light, the way in which we see things can hardly be distinguished from the way in which we wish to see them. (1954: 42)

Scientific Method

Schumpeter argued that even though every economist enters with an ideology and a worldview, science provides a method of uprooting errors through the rules of investigation that are ideologically neutral. Ideas are subjected to rigorous competition in tests and replications. The method of science enables investigators to overcome their biases, provided they place truth seeking ahead of all else. But what does it mean to evaluate the truthfulness of a theory? Friedman (1966) argues that a theory should be judged not on the descriptive realism of its assumptions but on the accuracy of the model's predictions. Coase (1994) claims, however, that Friedman's approach interjects a normative conclusion that is neither objective nor accurate:

> When Friedman says that the "ultimate goal of a positive science is the development of a 'theory' or 'hypothesis' that yields valid and meaningful . . . predictions about phenomenon not yet observed," I cannot help mentioning that a science has no goals, only individuals have goals. (Coase, 1994: 18)

There is no scientific reason why prediction should be the ultimate measure of science. Some disciplines, such as biology, often have difficulty predicting the future because of the complexity of ecosystems (Nash, 2010). The fact that Darwin's model cannot project specific evolutionary events is no reason to discard a model that provides compelling analysis of past evolutions and qualitative insights into ongoing ones.

Similarly, economists can provide valid abstract deductions that are insightful for the analysis of public policies but that often are lacking in precision. Empirical testing can be revealing but is rarely conclusive because of data problems, modeling issues, and the pervasiveness of confounding events and evolving systems—namely, the emergence of novelty by combination (Georgescu-Roegen, 1971: 13). Natural experiments as well as laboratory experiments may offer some hope (List, 2007). Because of these issues, Coase argues that economists—as they actually go about doing research—choose the models they accept in an entirely different manner than Friedman suggests, based on whether a model is intuitively appealing:

> Economists, or at any rate enough of them, do not wait to discover whether a theory's predictions are accurate before making up their minds. Given that this is so, what part does testing a theory's predictions play in economics? First of all, it very often plays either no part or a very minor part. (Coase, 1994: 24)

The science of accepting or rejecting a model relies in many cases not on falsification but on discussion and debate—namely, the art of rhetoric (McCloskey, 1998). Coase observes that researchers operate in a market environment and "what we are dealing with is a competitive process in which purveyors of the various theories attempt to sell their wares" (Coase, 1994: 28). Intuitions (based on worldviews) may continue to play an important part of truth discernment. In a moment of unguarded honesty, C. E. Ferguson acknowledged that his continued belief in the neoclassical theory of distribution remained an article of faith—even after it had been shown mathematically to be untenable; hence, "it is difficult to unlearn that which one has learned" (Carter, 2012: 41).

The conclusion one draws from this account is that positive economics is more deeply steeped in value judgments about truth and method than many economists understand. Untangling some of the confounding forces may help researchers develop the virtuous habits needed to stay on course—that is, to put the religion of science ahead of all else. The education of an economist is, therefore, a serious undertaking that may be far more complex than we tend to realize (Dekker and Klamer, 2016; Coupé, 2004; Colander and Klamer, 1987).

Shadowing a Research Project

To explore the value-laden manner in which science must proceed, this section of the chapter shadows a researcher engaged in a specific project.

Choosing and Funding a Topic

Naomi is a graduate student in economics and is preparing to write her dissertation on unemployment. Why did Naomi choose to study economics, and particularly labor economics? Although it could be a random choice, more likely something in her past resonated with this area of study. Perhaps she took a class taught by a particularly engaging professor who communicated a passion for the subject. Naomi's choice of topic could require that she go against the advice of her academic mentor, developing *phronesis* or "practical wisdom," as illuminated by Dekker and Klamer:

> There is no rule that tells [her] what the right thing to do is. Should [she] be "obedient" to [her] teachers, or at least "respectful", or should [she] follow [her] "passion"? [She] will weigh different values and may reflect on what [her] goals are in life, assess [her] talents, consider possible outcomes (and reckon the uncertainties involved), read about the lives of economists, perhaps study some articles and books on methodology, and take in advice from all kinds of people, including fellow students, parents and friends (2016: p. 102).

Naomi's career will consist of extended rhetorical "conversations" with others about issues of mutual interest (Klamer, 2007). The choice of research topic is imbued with value judgments about what types of conversations and methods make for a fulfilling life.

In Naomi's case, her father had worked for a labor union, and, since childhood, her dinner table conversations had been filled with stories of the view that recessions were management's conspiracy to break the unions by creating a reserve army of unemployed. Naomi respected her father, but her economics training led her to two alternative approaches: the Keynesian model of sticky wages and the rational expectations model of clearing markets. Her dissertation was an opportunity to investigate the issues, but Naomi first needs to find financial support for her dissertation research. Not only must Naomi believe that her research program is personally valuable, she must also convince others who will pay for the research. Because there are far more research questions than funding available, the value judgments (or ideologies) of faculty mentors and donors often drive research agendas and may consciously or unconsciously affect what the researcher discovers.

Building a Model

An economic model is an attempt to describe the theory in a way that can be tested. To proceed, Naomi must decide whether she wishes to build a Keynesian-type model with sticky wages or a market-clearing model. As noted earlier, questions are value-laden because they arise out of a researcher's worldview—the mix of ideologies, beliefs, and random facts that Naomi possesses, either consciously or unconsciously. The type of model she builds is partially the result of that worldview, the influence of mentors, the values of donors, and her own intuition.

Defining Data

Naomi's model will be tested using data on unemployment rates over the business cycle. But what is meant by "unemployment"? It is impossible to define unemployment without introducing judgments that have both professional and ethical implications because economic data are socially constructed facts (Knight, 1947). They are value-laden because any definition requires a judgment about why and how we collect the data and what goals its collection will serve compared to alternative uses of funding. Economic data—their definitions, qualities, and interpretations—are ultimately a mix of objective and subjective features, and the happenstance that economists in the United States may reach consensus about how to calculate the unemployment rate in this locale does not remove the underlying ethical dimensions from the choices involved.

The Bureau of Labor Statistics (BLS) is charged in the United States with collecting data on unemployment. The rate of unemployment does not come from monitoring the number of people receiving unemployment checks. To do so would undercount those whose benefits have run out, those who may be ineligible, or those who may not apply. Instead, the BLS conducts a survey every month, sending interviewers out to 60,000 households across the country. Persons ready to work but without a job are classified as unemployed if they have actively looked for work in the prior four weeks. The BLS has a long list defining what the word "actively" means (BLS, 2012). But why is looking for work in the prior four weeks the right way to measure unemployment? After the recession of 2008, many laid-off workers struggled for years to find jobs. Defining unemployment more broadly—for example, having searched for work in the prior 12 weeks—would increase the measured rate of unemployment. Whatever definition is adopted will have ethical repercussions because it will raise or lower the measured unemployment rate and could cause a change in private expectations and spending, as well as in government policies.

If economists reach consensus on how to measure unemployment that does not mean that the relevant value judgments and ethical implications cease to be of interest. Many countries calculate unemployment rates in different ways, and many economists campaign to change the definitions of important variables. Five Nobel Prize winners along with other economists recently advocated a more nuanced approach to measuring human welfare (Stiglitz, Sen, and Fitoussi, 2009). Such debates cannot be settled by science without reference to the values and judgments of scientists. Nor is it possible to draw on the natural sciences to answer questions about humanly constructed terms. For example, does "subsistence" wage mean sufficient nutrients to prevent injury, or does it mean sufficient nutrients to produce normal biological functioning and growth (Levine and Rizvi, 2005)? Would subsistence include psychological maintenance? Adam Smith, when addressing this question, asserted that a "linen shirt" was part of subsistence consumption because appearing in public without it would bring shame:

> By necessaries I understand not only the commodities which are indispensably necessary for the support of life, but whatever the custom of the country renders it indecent for creditable people, even of the lowest order, to be without. (Smith, 1981[1776]: 869–870).

Economic terms therefore have social and ethical contexts. A religiously observant Jew offered pork to eat may have the nutrients to live, but it may not be a life considered worth living.

Even if there were a perfectly objective definition of economic variables, additional value-laden questions must be answered: how much data should be collected? Facts are not free, and it is expensive to be more accurate. If data quality were really important, the BLS could reduce the sampling error by surveying 120,000 households each month. If more timely data were important, the survey could be conducted once a week rather than once a month. The obvious rejoinder is that these changes would cost a lot of money that could be used to do other things that people find more important. Both the quality of economic data and its timeliness are not determined solely by professional norms, but also by value judgments of economic researchers and, more importantly, of politicians who may have quite different agendas.

Collecting Data

Naomi, the economics graduate student we have been shadowing, has at this point defined the data and determined how to collect them. She must now consider how the procedures for data collection are constrained by ethical choices in addition to economic choices. The survey method used by the BLS seems innocuous on its face, but quickly opens a proverbial can of worms. What are the ethical obligations of the interviewer to the interviewee? What are the privacy rights of those interviewed? What are the duties of an interviewer who happens to see someone in the household engaged in embarrassing or criminal behavior? Today, all universities require researchers of human and animal subjects to apply to an institutional review board (IRB) to determine if the methods of data collection are ethical. Hence, the facts we can obtain are limited to facts that are ethically possible to obtain.

Not all researchers have operated under this constraint. During World War II, Hitler's concentration camps engaged in experiments on human subjects in the name of furthering scientific knowledge. In one experiment, prisoners were involuntarily exposed to mustard gas to test the efficacy of antidotes, leading to the death of thousands. During the 1940s, the US Public Health Service engaged in medical research in Guatemala that exposed 1,300 prisoners and mental patients to sexually transmitted diseases without their consent; the purpose was to determine the effectiveness of penicillin (Associated Press, 2011). Routinely, the tombs of pharaohs are ransacked and their remains put on museum displays to raise revenues. This grave robbing is justified by the purported scientific value of learning about ancient peoples. But that is a slippery-slope argument: when should scientists adhere to the duty not to violate the dignity and rights of others? This issue also arises in the use of animals in testing. The positive economist is a truth-seeker who operates within certain deontological (duty-based) ethical parameters whose norms change over time.

The "Observer" Problem

A further difficulty confounds Naomi as data collector: the act of measuring the data sometimes changes the data. The "observer problem" is well-known in chemistry and physics. Endeavoring to measure the temperature inside a beaker (or something more complex like the location of a subatomic particle) requires using techniques that alter background circumstances. Whether the surveyor making a household visit for the BLS is male or female, young or old, or well- or poorly dressed could all potentially alter the responses (about 30 percent of surveys are done in person each month). Asking discouraged workers if they have sought work in the past four weeks might inspire them to get off the couch and look again, and surveying consumers about their confidence in the economy could interject ideas that did not previously exist. Most data surveys, like most temperature measurements, produce minor changes in the underlying data that, for most purposes, can be considered negligible. Yet the possibility of contaminating data should not be ignored.

Researchers must also consider the potential distortions caused by extracting only parts of relevant data from the surrounding environment. This is what happens when cartographers try to draw a two-dimensional map derived from a three-dimensional globe: inaccuracy must be introduced along at least one dimension of distance, shape, or size. The Mercator projection map (created in the mid-1500s) gave ship captains accurate guidance about coastal shapes so as to avoid wrecks but, in doing so, distorted land mass sizes. On the Mercator projection, Greenland is shown to be as large as Africa, when, in reality, Africa is 14 times larger. The issue of size versus shape is politically important for creating visual ideologies. By contrast, the Gall-Peters world map, which became popular in the 1970s, represents continental size accurately but distorts shapes and distances. The scientist as "observer" has to communicate the facts of the world, but sometimes the medium for doing so necessitates omitting or distorting facts—introducing (once again) value judgments about what aspects of the data are most important.

Analyzing Data

With information in hand, Naomi must now examine the data using statistical or other methods. If the theory is not falsified by the data, the theory is considered a candidate for the truth. One ethical dilemma encountered at this stage is that Naomi's incentives are almost always aligned with *not* falsifying her theory. She faces a moral hazard because her interests are not neutral with respect to her findings. Rewards go to those who discover what does work rather than what does not. To address this publication bias, economists have a fairly standard set of statistical techniques for determining whether a theory should be falsified.

Suppose, for example, that Naomi's research connects high unemployment rates with low high school graduation rates. One theory by Nobel Laureate James Heckman is that early childhood stimulation improves brain development and provides a lasting benefit to human capital in deprived children (Heckman, 2008). Building on this, Naomi hypothesizes that increased spending on childhood interventions (such as pre-kindergarten programs) could lead to higher high school graduation rates with a lag of 12 years. The null hypothesis is that it does not.

Statistical inference involves drawing conclusions about the properties of a population from a random sample of observations drawn from it. In this case, Naomi uses linear regression to fit the line (or, if diminishing returns are expected, she could use a quadratic form). In establishing a test for statistical significance, she can make two types of mistakes: a false positive would lead her to reject the null hypothesis that the slope is zero when really no positive relationship exists (type I error). A false negative would lead her to fail to reject the null hypothesis when really a positive relationship exists (type II error). Which type of mistake would one rather make: concluding that pre-K programs are effective at raising high school graduation rates when really they are not or concluding that they are ineffective when really they do work? This choice requires a value judgment with ethical implications.

Economists generally adopt the norm of avoiding false positives, which reflects the status quo bias: they desire to be at least 95 percent certain that the estimated slope is not due to chance. The benefit of the doubt is given to the null hypothesis that pre-K programs do not work. But who determines that a 5 percent false positive is the desirable standard of risk for this particular test? As it turns out, 5 percent was an artificial social criterion decided initially as a time- and space-saving heuristic. In the days before calculators, statisticians used slide rules and distribution tables. Because tables took up space, authors limited the range of values considered. Ronald Fisher's 1925 *Statistical Methods for Research Workers* emphasized the 5 percent criterion as a convenient compromise (Stigler, 2008: 12). William Gosset, the applied statistician who invented the small-sample probability test, rejected a rote application of the 5 percent probability test because it unscientifically disregarded the costs and benefits of possible errors (Ziliak and McCloskey, 2008).

This problem can be illustrated by analogy to truth seeking in courts. In a civil litigation, Rossi alleges that Galle caused damage to his car. Civil cases have a burden of proof based on the "preponderance" of the evidence. If more than half the evidence supports Rossi's version of events, the jury is instructed to rule in his favor. But that same jury would use a much stronger burden of proof ("beyond a reasonable doubt") if Galle were accused of murdering Rossi. Having different standards for truth in statistical studies reflects the reality that type I and type II errors generate different loss functions for society depending on the circumstances. If a food additive were suspected of causing serious fetal injury, society would likely prefer to reduce the chance of type II errors, compared to when the loss involves merely an upset stomach. Failing to consider these differences would be perverse. Establishing norms for tests of statistical significance should be debated among scientists and the public at large (Knight, 1947: 235).

A final point about statistical significance is that it can become a false god for researchers. If the initial data analysis does not provide statistical proof in support of the researcher's hypothesis, researchers may continue to explore by changing functional forms and trying new variable permutations. This may be unavoidable when dealing with complex phenomena whose structural relationships are not well understood. At the same time, researchers should be alert to the dangers of data mining—searching relentlessly for the results one wants to see and has an incentive to find (Coase, 1994: 27).

This has given rise to a call for principled rules in econometrics, as elaborated in the Symposium on Ethics in the *Eastern Economic Journal* (Peart and Levy, 2008; Levy and Peart, 2008).

Economic Inferences

Suppose that Naomi has determined that some of her variables are indeed statistically significant using appropriate norms. Statistical significance, by itself, is of little guidance for policy. A finding of *material* significance involves drawing different conclusions based on the economic importance of a policy variable, or what Ziliak and McCloskey call "oomph" (Ziliak and McCloskey, 2008: 43). Suppose a statistically significant finding of Naomi's research is that spending an additional $10,000 per pupil on pre-K intervention would reliably increase high school graduation rates from 60.0 percent to 64.0 percent 12 years later. That result may be scientifically dependable, but is it economically useful? Is this payoff from childhood intervention programs a big one or a small one? Economic significance is determined by the value judgment that the detected causation is not only positive, but also large. There is no scientific way of answering this except through reasoned debate.

Rhetoric in Economics

McCloskey, in several important papers and a book, *The Rhetoric of Economics*, argues that we must pull back the curtain of scientific modernism to reveal how economic thinking advances in practice ([1985]1998). What she notices is that before the statistical tests are begun, and certainly afterward when discussing materiality, economists are "spinning parables" or "telling stories" (McCloskey, 1993: 505). This notion comes from Adam Smith's theory of mind and language, in which persuasion is found to be the driving force behind exchange: "Men always endeavor to persuade others to be of their opinion even when the matter is of no consequence to them . . . And in this manner every one [including an economist] is practicing oratory on others thro the whole of his life" (Smith, 1982*a*: 352). Evolution may have favored the development of this type of reasoning (Mercier and Sperber, 2011: 72).

Persuasion often involves the use of metaphors, which link things we know to things that we do not know. When a listener says to a speaker, "I see what you're getting at . . .," the *I see* part is entirely metaphorical because there is no actual apparition. Economic metaphors abound: market equilibrium, spending multiplier, liquidity trap, price inflation, human capital, asset bubbles, and so on. Metaphors work by linking something known and tangible to a new and often figurative concept. Metaphors may be an essential part of innovation when exploring unknown frontiers: "Because metaphor involves extensive semantic possibilities, it compels the active engagement of the listener" (Klamer and Leonard, 1994: 30). Metaphors come packaged with contextual value judgments and ethical norms, yet McCloskey insists that metaphors are not illogical or unscientific; mathematics is itself an elaborate metaphor. The most famous metaphor in economics is the "invisible hand," which comes from Adam Smith laced with ethical content in its original form (Wight, 2007).

The rhetorical process is an inevitable and necessary part of learning and scientific advancement. Philosopher Kwame Appiah notes that a researcher is "left having to interpret the findings; they don't interpret themselves" (Appiah, 2007). As Naomi presents her working paper in seminars and conferences, she comes to see which arguments and metaphors work to convince her audiences. She develops new interpretations and ways of thinking (including new metaphors) about what she has discovered.

Research Dissemination

The next step in Naomi's scientific journey is to publish her research findings. Even if her results are compelling, that does not guarantee that she will be able to publish her results. If the organization funding her work chooses, in many cases it can block publication of unfavorable results. During the decades of the mid-20th century, hundreds of studies funded by tobacco companies linked cigarette smoking to illness. Only the few studies finding no correlations were published, while the rest were suppressed in internal files—part of a deliberate attempt to deceive the public about the science of smoking (Cummings, Brown, and O'Connor, 2007). Likewise, following the 2010 oil spill in the Gulf of Mexico, BP offered lucrative consulting contracts to marine scientists who would agree to let the company control their research findings about the disaster (Raines, 2010).

Companies and industries experience concentrated, focused gains and losses from research outcomes whereas the effects on citizens are often diffused. It makes economic sense for an industry to pay profusely for research that will bolster its interests, but it makes little sense for the public at large to do so. Hence, there is asymmetry in the incentives operating on the funding of science. One force mitigating the degradation of science to the highest bidder is the institution of external peer review. A reviewer's job is to provide the editor with objective advice as to the validity and importance of the paper. Because so much work is done at public conferences, and many subfields have a small number of active researchers, reviewers almost always know the name of the author (and the author may suspect who the reviewers are). Hence, double-blind review is nearly impossible. In recognition of this, the AEA changed its rules to single-blind: referees know the author but not the reverse. Even if anonymity were possible, one criticism of this process is that reviewers are also people who have their own reputations to protect. Entrenched experts may be unwilling to admit that their previous work needs to be overturned. One historian bleakly notes that:

> We like to continue to believe what we have been accustomed to accept as true, and the resentment aroused when doubt is cast upon any of our assumptions leads

> us to seek every manner of excuse for clinging to them. The result is that most of our so-called reasoning consists in finding arguments for going on believing as we already do. (Robinson, 1931: 41)

Adam Smith likewise complained that "those learned societies have chosen to remain, for a long time, the sanctuaries in which exploded systems and obsolete prejudices found shelter and protection, after they had been hunted out of every other corner of the world" (1981: 772). As with authors and editors, external evaluators need ethical virtues of integrity, self-control, humility, and open-mindedness.

Economic Knowledge Changes the World

Naomi's published findings on unemployment may alter the world Naomi set out to understand. Such changes are often unanticipated and undesirable. James Buchanan, who won the Nobel Prize for developing the Public Choice school, worried that his own research could corrupt civic virtues and alter the future by revealing that politicians act not in the common good but for their own good (Buchanan, 2000). And, similarly, in a well-known study, researchers discovered that exposing students to a course in positive economics reduced students' inclinations to cooperation (Frank, Gilovich, and Regan, 1993). Economic study, even purely positive in nature, can produce ethical aftermaths.

Economists like Naomi often go beyond trying to understand the world and delve into the normative realm of advocating change in public policies. If her findings support the hypothesis that early childhood intervention leads to higher rates of high school graduation, this could lead her to recommend expanding Head Start and other such programs. Public policy involves weighing values in addition to gathering facts, and it is not clear that economists have better ethical insights than the average citizen (e.g., in the tradeoff between equity and efficiency). Moreover, economists often overstate their claims to scientific knowledge as a basis for making policy recommendations. David Colander, historian of economic thought, notes that:

> [E]conomists have a tendency to convey more scientific certainty in their policy positions than the theory and evidence objectively would allow. Too many economists are willing to make seemingly definitive scientific statements about policy based on models, that they know, or should know, are highly imperfect. (2012: 1)

Having the virtues of humility and ego control are essential to not overstating one's findings in both positive and normative economics. This may be hard to develop in a culture that promotes the narrow outlook of closed-minded hedgehogs over the more humble, open-minded foxes (Berlin, 2013[1953]; Tetlock, 2006). In winner-take-all contests for celebrity, the media tend to reward overconfidence bred by a fervent ideology.

The Mentor's Role

Throughout this discussion,[2] hidden in the penumbra of interests and fiduciary responsibilities, is the mentor who oversees Naomi's project as faculty advisor, friend, and often co-author. At every step along the way, Naomi (an apprentice) has questions and concerns about substance and process. The advisor's role can be weak or strong, yet his or her attitude toward integrity is paramount. Does the advisor demonstrate respect or disdain for the IRB process? Is the advisor vigilant about accuracy or willing to fudge for convenience? Does the mentor show prudence and rectitude in how research funds are expended? How much courage is demonstrated in the mentor's willingness to tackle unpopular subjects?

Naomi's social interactions with her mentors and peers create spillovers of human capital that enhance her productivity and infect her with socially enforced moral norms. Mentors often pay a high cost in terms of their time. The expected payout for this could be jointly authored articles and a growing cadre of assistant professors carrying on the mentor's work and building the mentor's reputation. Mentoring is part of informal learning, however, a type of market exchange that may not derive only or mainly from self-interested motives. As Robert Lucas notes, "Most of what we know we learn from other people . . . but most of it we get for free" (1988: 38). Darwin argued that the origins of instinctive altruism may be governed by forces of evolution and group selection rather than rational reckoning of individual self-interest (1871: 159–160). Instead of calculation, cooperation may find its foundation in feelings of mutual sympathy (Gintis et al., 2005). This should not be taken to imply that individuals in groups evolved only or mainly through prosocial behaviors like benevolence because the instincts for punishment and justice are likely more significant.

The institutions or norms that govern how people jointly view and process issues of right and wrong constitute a form of moral capital in production. The mechanisms for enforcement and punishment are generally not legal but often work through shame, ridicule, or gossip. Properly socialized researchers get along in the academic tribe because they have internalized the ability to make moral discernments and to uphold them in their own conduct, generally in conformity with the prevailing norms of science. Social and moral capital are to some extent intertwined because one naturally tends to associate with those who share a similar ethical outlook (Smith, 1982*b*: 224–225).

This cannot be modeled by simply adding sociability or honesty into the subject's utility function because individual maximization is not the relevant psychological framework. Economic exchange is largely governed by unconsciously learned and enforced rules and norms (Hayek, 1979; V. Smith, 2004). Previous experiments in Ultimatum, Prisoners Dilemmas, Dictator, and Trust games confounded researchers who were dogmatically committed to the idea that behavior springs from calculations of self-interest

[2] This section draws on Wight (2009).

alone. Vernon Smith argues that, to understand these anomalies, researchers need to go beyond standard consequentialist ethics into a deeper understanding of psychologically embedded social norms as theorized by Adam Smith. In the world of moral sentiments

> *[T]he individual [is] not even defined except in a social context.* There is no cognitive individual psychology except as it is born of a person's social circumstances, out of the "social psychology" of his environs if you will." (V. Smith, 2013: 8, emphasis in original)

The social context for exchange in science matters because agents must understand the motives and intentions of other persons in order to judge the praiseworthiness of another's—and one's own—actions. It is in this psychological world that honor and duty exert a powerful influence over the conduct of science, especially in the socialization of young scholars by more seasoned advisors and collaborators.

Shared sentiments could lead a senior researcher to experience genuine empathy with a junior colleague, and thus the motive of ordinary benevolence could lead that person to aid Naomi in her research project even when there is no strong personal relationship or anticipated professional gain (e.g., the fourth reader on a dissertation committee). Another type of benevolence arises from habitually experiencing an alignment of sentiments that gives rise to affection. Smith states: "What is called affection, is in reality nothing but habitual sympathy" (1982*b*: 220). Habitual sympathy (as between a mentor and apprentice) can produce "contagious effects" that are akin to social externalities:

> This natural disposition to accommodate and to assimilate, as much as we can, our own sentiments, principles, and feelings, to those which we see fixed and rooted in the persons whom we are obliged to live and converse a great deal with, is the cause of the *contagious effects* of both good and bad company. (Smith, 1982*b*: 224, emphasis added)

Within the research environment, social relationships produce both constrained and genuine contagious effects. *Constrained sympathy* derives from convenience and utilitarian motives. The degree to which constrained sympathy evolves into feelings of genuine affection depends on the "*involuntary* feeling that the persons to whom we attach ourselves are the natural and proper objects of esteem and approbation" (Smith, 1982*b*: 224–225, emphasis added). Smith's model of human sociability anticipates discoveries in experimental economics in which authentic social relations grease the wheels of cooperation. Smith's model can be used to explain the proximate causes of how adaptation works to improve fitness, and hence multilevel selection, by reducing free-loading and cheating among members of a tribe (in this case, a scientific community):

> Those general rules of conduct, when they have been fixed in our mind by habitual reflection, are of great use in correcting the misrepresentations of self-love concerning what is fit and proper to be done in our particular situation. (1982*b*: 160).

A key activity within the economic research community is the construction of meaning and the enforcement of prosocial behaviors through overlapping institutions of culture. According to Wilson (2007: 237), a successful institution "adapts its members to their local environment, enabling them to achieve by collective action what they cannot achieve alone or even together" in the absence of that institution. Mentoring is one such key institution for establishing and enforcing the religion of science.

Moving Forward: Reclaiming Duty in "Discipline"

At its best, the economics discipline is a shared moral community of individuals who have chosen the pursuit of truth as an intrinsic virtue; in this world, truth must not be traded off in a utility-maximizing quest for career or money. Linking individual researchers to larger ethical principles is needed. Levy and Peart argue that a sense of community is essential for maintaining these ethical norms: "The larger role of statistical ethics is to remind the statistician that, even when he is a member of a research group or an expert witness, he is part of the larger statistical community," which presumably helps internalize the goal of truth seeking over personal gain (Levy and Peart, 2008: 112). The "ethical economist" may sound oxymoronic or self-contradictory, but it captures the essence of the argument: when the incentives for honesty are at times weak, scholars must develop the motive and the moral willpower to avoid temptation.

What it means to be a virtuous researcher in economics may be difficult to enumerate in a list of do's and don'ts, but, as Colander (2012) argues, we have to start with standards enforced not through licensing but through incubating social moral norms. How can such a community of disciples be cultivated and sustained? A virtue ethicist would likely argue that habits are the key to character. Habits must be ingrained at an early age and reinforced by the example of heroes and villains. Mentors and senior authors who work with economics students and junior colleagues set the habits and tone that may become internalized. The "master-apprentice system" provides a relevant metaphor for this experience (Dekker and Klamer, 2016: p. 111). Exemplars of courageous economic scholars should be celebrated, although this gets increasingly more difficult with the decline of the history of thought as a field in economics. Movies like the *Inside Job* can portray the problems associated with the appearance of impropriety by economic researchers, as well as provoke feelings of moral outrage at the consequences for the victims of scientific fraud and abuse. Learning the social norms of a profession arises as much from sympathetic feelings and positive personal affection for mentors as it does from fear of ostracism (Wight, 2009).

Although informal mentoring is the most important way that scientific norms of truth seeking can be inculcated, systematic global reforms are also needed. The great ship of orthodox economics sails ahead at full speed despite the warnings of ethical icebergs.

Turning this vessel toward a more sustainable ethical attitude requires institutional changes (DeMartino, 2011). First, and most important, creating and emphasizing a set of professional ethical norms for economists can, at the margin, improve ethical behavior through repetition and recall: indeed, this is the mechanism by which virtues become internalized as habits. Knowing that one is breaking the moral norms of the profession can at times prevent infractions (Mazar, Amir, and Ariely, 2008). This requires that norms be verbalized in writing and adopted by relevant economic associations (chiefly the AEA as the largest and most visible entity). DeMartino provides a starting point with the "Economist's Oath" to be proclaimed at graduation (2011: 232–233).

Second, researchers need to be educated about the roles that virtue and duty play in economic life, including academic life. Noted laureates such as Amartya Sen and Vernon Smith play an important role in enlarging the conversation toward a science of human choice within that wider ethical milieu and away from the ideology of narrow self-interest. Recognizing the existence and the utility of nonutilitarian ethical frameworks is a key step within positive economics, and one that needs also to be articulated to students. This could be institutionally reflected in a revised set of Voluntary Content Standards in Economics, initially adopted in 1998 and endorsed by a consortium including the Council for Economic Education (CEE), the National Association of Economic Educators, the Foundation for Teaching Economics, and the AEA's Committee on Economic Education. Here are two revisions that would be desirable. The existing Standard 2 asserts that decision making *requires* the use of "cost-benefit analysis" without specifying any necessary ethical safeguards (Siegfried and Meszaros, 1998: 145, emphasis added). A revised Standard 2 could read:

> Effective decision making can entail comparing the additional costs of alternatives with the additional benefits, assuming that duties, rules, or rights have first been carefully addressed. Most choices involve moral considerations about the choice of goals and frameworks of analysis. Benchmarks include marginal analysis, benefit-cost analysis, utility maximization, profit maximization, and non-consequentialist ethical frameworks.

The existing Standard 10 also discusses institutions and incorrectly relates the term to organizations like banks and unions and completely overlooks social norms (Sigefried and Meszaros,1998: 146). A revised Standard 10 could state that:

> Institutions evolve in market economies to help individuals and groups accomplish their goals. Social norms relating to ethical behavior and expected duties are examples of important institutions or "rules of the game." These institution help enforce property rights and create social cohesion essential to a market economy.

These proposed changes would call attention to the ethical norms necessary for economic exchange. Revisions to the Standards would be reflected in the teaching of 15,000 teachers of economics in secondary schools. CEE teachers reach perhaps 1 million students per year. CEE has previously shown support for ethics in economics through its publication of and national workshops on the teachers' manual, *Teaching the Ethical Foundations of Economics* (Wight and Morton, 2007).

Third, national philanthropies need to be further engaged in the project to reeducate the economics profession. The John Templeton Foundation has a core funding area in "Character Virtue Development," and the Liberty Fund periodically holds seminars that discuss Adam Smith's *Theory of Moral Sentiments* as a backdrop for understanding *The Wealth of Nations*. Additional sources of funding need to be explored to engage and motivate economists to learn about the new discoveries in the science of ethics. One possible theme for this is to reexamine the notion of efficiency as a standard for policy decision making. The modern-era definition of efficiency is based on the Kaldor-Hicks formulation in which compensation to losers is not required. This standard can only be defended in a society of democratic rights and legal safeguards for those injured. This is not the purview of pure science, but is rather one that requires moral judgments that are rarely discussed in textbook treatments. Workshops around the country on this and other ethical topics for junior faculty members could be funded by grants from philanthropies.

Fourth, universities can learn from the innovations of others. Martha Nussbaum at the University of Chicago trained judges and lawyers how to feel empathy as a necessary part of administering the law (Nussbaum, 1995). Echoing Adam Smith, she argues that "rational" decision on some matters of public policy require that the emotions be engaged. Professionals (including economists) may lack the emotional knowledge to treat people as complex individuals. The Supreme Court acknowledged that justice cannot be served when people are treated as a "faceless, undifferentiated mass" instead of "uniquely individual human beings" (quoted in Nussbaum, 1995: xv). As did Smith, Nussbaum uses great literature to evoke a deeper understanding of the social conditions surrounding human choice and exemplars of virtuous leadership.

Ravi Kanbur (2016) and DeMartino (2011) identify a similar approach at Cornell University to *exposure and dialogue programs* (EDPs) in the training of practitioners in economic development. Professional development workers are often insulated in five-star hotels while extreme deprivation exists a few blocks away. Following the EDP model, practitioners in development agencies could be required, as a prerequisite for hiring or promotion, to become immersed for a period of time in the lives of those addressed by public policies. Immersion works by expanding the moral imagination: people can more easily conceive of the experiences of others in this community and can more readily sympathize. Costs and benefits of various programs are brought into sharper clarity. Another way of saying this is that ideological preconceptions are broken down. However, too much immersion can result in one ideology being traded for another. A practitioner can "go local" and put the interests of some clients ahead of wider interests of other stakeholders. This is a risk that seems worth taking when economists become isolated from the people most affected by their policies.

Conclusion

Naomi has come a long way from her initial decision to study economics. She has chosen a specialized research question; gained funding; developed a model; defined, collected, and analyzed data; explored rhetorical ways of thinking and explaining her results; published her findings in a peer-reviewed journal; and engaged in public policy debates. At each step, professional norms, personal values, and ethical considerations permeate the work of discovery. This does not mean that Naomi cannot strive to be impartial or that her findings are invalid. Rather, it means that, "the conduct of inquiry cannot possibly be value-free. Inquiring is driven by action, and action is driven by values" (Hausman and McPherson, 2006: 296).

Whether a researcher desires it or not—or is even conscious of it or not—economics involves making numerous value judgments in carrying out positive research, entails normative persuasive arguments about the nature of truth, and produces outcomes that can be ethically important in their implications and repercussions. The long-standing distinction between positive and normative economics continues to provide a useful way of conceptualizing the division of labor: positive economics explains the world as it is, and normative economics explains how to make it better. Both activities are value-laden, but in different ways. The danger lies in thinking that positive economics is ethically empty when in reality it is overflowing with ideology and values—albeit often unexamined.

Some economists would argue, however, that the kinds of value judgments made in positive economics are of a substantially different kind—they are simply methodological. Widespread consensus makes these value judgments objective or neutral (Robbins, 1945; Blaug, 1996). This attitude is understandable and partially defensible: every science must at least temporarily have a paradigm within which to understand the world. But recall that Kuhn's scientific revolutions happen when people are able to see with new eyes. Conformity for the sake of conformity is unscientific. The questioning this article encourages is one of attitude or curiosity about the moral underpinnings of positive economics, not a rejection of technical analyses per se. It is a rejection of the possibility that economists are merely engineers or technocrats. As McCloskey notes:

> Modernism promises knowledge free from doubt, metaphysics, morals, and personal conviction; what it delivers merely renames as Scientific Method the scientist's and especially the economic scientist's metaphysics, morals, and personal convictions. (McCloskey, 1993: 488)

The conclusion that facts and values are entangled is not a cause for despair (Reddy, 2012). Rather, it is a call for more critical thinking, for recognition that it is better to debate the values behind economics than to sweep them under the rug of conformity. It is unscientific to ignore the ideologies that provide the raw materials for investigation and the ethical values that permeate data definition, collection, and analysis. It is unscientific to employ statistical tests by rote, ignoring loss functions and overlooking the role of rhetoric in convincing fellow researchers of the relevance of a theory. It is unscientific to ignore the funding and publication incentives that can distort research findings or to disregard the potential for market failure in the research academy.

Market failure is endemic in the research process, first, in regard to asymmetric information, and, second, because of free-riding in the production of public goods. Researchers cannot escape from ethics and particularly from internalizing nonconsequentialist approaches that constrain self-interest within a duty or virtue-ethics view of justice. The science of economics progresses not because ideologies and ethics are absent, but rather because the ideology and values of science are able to overcome competing ideologies and values. Enlightened self-interest through reputation building is a necessary and important contributor to this endeavor, but it is insufficient as an explanation for the rise of science. Market imperfections are also corrected with the aid of disciplined economists. A disciple is one who demonstrates the virtues of self-control and obedience to higher authorities and principles.

Rediscovering the role that ethical economists play in carrying out positive economics seems long overdue, and economic role models are the first line of defense in this engagement. Although informal mentoring is the main way that economists acquire the implicit moral norms of the profession, a formal and articulated set of ethical norms for economics seems long overdue.

Acknowledgments

The author wishes to thank George DeMartino, Jack Fiedler, Jim Monks, Erik Craft, Robert Dolan, Shakun Mago, Vance Pilkington, David Colander, David Levy, Sandra Peart, Candace Smith, Vernon Smith, and anonymous reviewers for comments on previous drafts and to participants at the Association for Social Economics panel on "Ethics and Professional Economic Practice—Has Anything Changed?" ASSA, January 2013, San Diego, California.

References

American Economic Association (AEA). 2012. "American Economic Association Disclosure Policy." Available at https://www.aeaweb.org/aea_journals/AEA_Disclosure_Policy.pdf, accessed September 7, 2014.

American Institute of Certified Public Accountants (AICPA). 2013. "Code of Professional Conduct." Available at http://www.aicpa.org/Research/Standards/CodeofConduct/Pages/et50.aspx, accessed April 5, 2013.

Appiah, K. A. 2007. "The New New Philosophy." *The New York Times Magazine*, Idea Lab: December 9, 34, 36.

Arrow, K. J. 1963. "Uncertainty and the Welfare Economics of Medical Care." *American Economic Review* 53(5): 941–973.

Arrow, K. J. 2000. "Three Nobel Laureates on the State of Economics." *Challenge* 43(1, January–February): 13–22.

Associated Press. 2011. "Panel Reveals New Details of 1940's Experiment." *The Capital*: August 30, section A, page 3.

Berlin, I. 2013[1953]. *The Hedgehog and the Fox: An Essay on Tolstoy's View of History*, 2nd edition. Princeton: Princeton University Press.

Blaug, M. 1996. *Economic Theory in Retrospect*, 5th edition. Cambridge: Cambridge University Press.

Brugger P., and S. Brugger. 1993. "The Easter Bunny in October: Is It Disguised as a Duck?" *Perceptual Motor Skills* 76: 577–578; cited in Eric W. Weisstein, "Rabbit-Duck Illusion." From MathWorld—A Wolfram Web Resource. Available at http://mathworld.wolfram.com/Rabbit-DuckIllusion.html.

Buchanan, J. M. 2000. "Is Public Choice Immoral?" In *The Collected Works of James M. Buchanan*, edited by G. Brennan, H. Kliemt, and R. D. Tollison (Vol. 13, pp. 79–89). Indianapolis: Liberty Fund Press.

Bureau of Labor Statistics (BLS). 2012. "Labor Force Statistics from the Current Population Survey: How the Government Measures Unemployment." Available at http://www.bls.gov/cps/cpshtgm.htm, accessed March 23, 2012.

Carter, S., 2012. C. E. "Fergusons's Lost Reply to Joan Robinson on the Theory of Capital." *Journal of the History of Economic Thought* 34(1): 21–41.

Chabris, C., and D. Simons. 2010. *The Invisible Gorilla: And Other Ways Our Intuitions Deceive Us*. New York: Crown Archetype.

Coase, R. 1994. *Essays on Economics and Economists*. Chicago: University of Chicago Press.

Colander, D. 2012. "Creating Humble Economists: A Code of Ethics for Economists." Presentation to the Allied Social Science Association meetings, January 7, 2012, p. 1.

Colander, D., and A. Klamer, A. 1987. "The Making of an Economist." *Journal of Economic Perspective* 1: 95–111.

Coupé, T. 2004. "What Do We Know About Ourselves? On the Economics of Economics." *Kyklos* 57(2): 197–216.

Cummings, K. M., A. Brown, and R. O'Connor. 2007. "The Cigarette Controversy." *Cancer Epidemiology Biomarkers Prevention* 16(June): 1070–1076.

Darwin, C. 1871. *The Descent of Man*. New York: D. Appleton and Company. Available at: Http://books.google.com/books.

Dekker, E., and A. Klamer, A. 2016. "About Doing the Right Thing as an Academic Economist." In *The Oxford Handbook of Professional Economic Ethics*, edited by G. DeMartino and D. McCloskey, pp. 101–115. New York: Oxford University Press.

DeMartino, G. F. 2011. *The Economist's Oath: On the Need for and Content of Professional Economic Ethics*. Oxford: Oxford University Press.

Dewald, W. G., J. G. Thursby, and R. G. Anderson. 1986. "Replication in Empirical Economics: The Journal of Money, Credit and Banking Project." *American Economic Review* 76(4): 587–603.

Enders, W., and G. A. Hoover. 2004. "Whose Line Is It? Plagiarism in Economics." *Journal of Economic Literature* 42(June): 487–493.

Evans, B. A., P. A. Grimes, and W. E. Becker. 2012. "What Led Eminent Economists To Become Economists?" *The Journal of Economic Education* 43(1):83–98

Ferguson, C. 2010. "The Director of 'Inside Job' Replies," Economists' Forum, October 14, 2010. Available at http://blogs.ft.com/economistsforum/2010/10/the-director-of-inside-job-replies/#axzz1UJ5C49lj, accessed on March 23, 2012.

Frank, R. H., T. D. Gilovich, and D. T. Regan. 1993. "Does Studying Economics Inhibit Cooperation?" *Journal of Economic Perspectives* 7(Spring): 159–171.

Friedman, M. 1966. "The Methodology of Positive Economics." In *Essays in Positive Economics*, edited by M. Friedman, pp. 3–46.Chicago: University of Chicago Press.

Georgescu-Roegen, N. 1971. *The Entropy Law and the Economic Process*. Cambridge, MA: Harvard University Press.

Gintis, H., S. Bowles, R. Boyd, and E. Fehr. 2005. *Moral Sentiments and Material Interests: The Foundations of Cooperation in Economic Life*. Cambridge, MA: MIT Press.

Hausman, D. M., and M. S. McPherson. 2006. *Economic Analysis, Moral Philosophy, and Public Policy*, 2nd edition. Cambridge: Cambridge University Press.

Hayek, F. A. 1979. "The Three Sources of Human Values." In Law, Legislation and Liberty, edited by F. A. Hayek (Vol. 3), pp. 153–176. Chicago: University of Chicago Press.

Heckman, J. J. 2008. "Schools, Skills, and Synapses." NBER Working Paper Series No. 14064. Available at http://www.nber.org/papers/w14064.

Herndon, T., M. Ash, and R. Pollin. 2013. "Does High Public Debt Consistently Stifle Economic Growth? A Critique of Reinhart and Rogoff." Political Economy Research Institute Working Paper 322, April. Amherst: The University of Massachusetts.

Henrich, J., S. J. Heine, and A. Norenzayan. 2010. "The Weirdest People in the World." *Behavioral and Brain Sciences* 33(2/3): 61–135.

Inside Job. (2010). Directed by C. H. Ferguson. New York: Sony Pictures Classics.

Kanbur, R. 2016. "Exposure and Dialogue Programs in the Training of Development Analysts and Practitioners." In *The Oxford Handbook of Professional Economic Ethics*, edited by G. DeMartino and D. McCloskey, pp. 697–713. New York: Oxford University Press.

Keynes, J. M., 1964[1936]. *A General Theory of Employment, Interest, and* Money. New York: Harcourt, Brace & World.

Klamer, A. 2007. *Speaking of Economics: How to Get in the Conversation*. London: Routledge.

Klamer, A., and T. C. Leonard. 1994. "So What's an Economic Metaphor?" In *Natural Images in Economic Thought: Markets Read in Tooth and Claw*, edited by Philip Mirowski, pp. 20–52. Cambridge: Cambridge University Press.

Knight, F. H. 1947. *Freedom and Reform*. New York: Harper and Brothers.

Kuhn, T. S. 1970. The Structure of Scientific Revoltions, 2nd edition. Chicago: University of Chicago Press.

Levine, D. P., and S. A. Rizvi. 2005. *Poverty, Work and Freedom: Political Economy and the Moral Order*. Cambridge: Cambridge University Press.

Levy, D. M. 2002. *How the Dismal Science Got Its Name: Classical Economics and the Ur-Text of Racial Politics*. Ann Arbor: University of Michigan Press.

Levy, D. M., and S. J. Peart. 2008. "Inducing Greater Transparency: Towards the Establishment of Ethical Rules for Econometrics." *Eastern Economic Journal* 34(1) (Winter): 103–114.

List, J. A. 2007. "Field Experiments: A Bridge Between Lab and Naturally-Occurring Data." NBER Working Paper 12992, March. Available at http://www.nber.org/papers/w12992.

List, J. A., C. D. Bailey, P. J. Euzent, and T. L. Martin. 2001. "Academic Economists Behaving Badly? A Survey on Three Areas of Unethical Behavior." *Economic Inquiry* 39(1/January): 162–170.

Lucas, R. E., Jr. 1988. "On the Mechanics of Economic Development." *Journal of Monetary Economics* 22(1):3–42.

Mata, T., 2011. "Bretton Woods, Past and Present: 1. Ethics in Economics." Institute for New Economic Thinking (September 11). Available at http://ineteconomics.org/blog/playground/bretton-woods-past-and-present-1-ethics-economics, accessed on March 23, 2012.

Mazar, M., O. Amir, and D. Ariely. 2008. "The Dishonesty of Honest People: A Theory of Self-Concept Maintenance." *Journal of Marketing Research* 45(6): 633–644.

McCloskey, D. N. 1993. "The Rhetoric of Economics." *Journal of Economic Literature* 21(2): 481–517.

McCloskey, D. N. 1998[1985]. *The Rhetoric of Economics*, 2nd edition. Madison: University of Wisconsin Press.

McCullough, B. D., K. A. McGeary, and T. D. Harrison. 2008. "Do Economics Journal Archives Promote Replicable Research?" *Canadian Journal of Economics* 41(4): 1406–1420.

Mercier, H., and D. Sperber. 2011. "Why Do Humans Reason? Arguments for an Argumentative Theory." *Behavioral and Brain Sciences* 34: 57–111.

Mishkin, F. S., and T. T. Herbertsson. 2006. "Financial Stability in Iceland." Reykjavik: Iceland Chamber of Commerce (May). Available at http://www.economicdisasterarea.com/wp-content/uploads/2010/08/Tryggvi-Herbertsson-Friedrich-Mishkin-Financial-Stability-in-Iceland.pdf, accessed on March 23, 2012.

Nash, S. 2010. "Ecosystem Resilience." *BioScience* (September): 571–575.

Nordhaus, W. D. 2007. "A Review of the *Stern Review on the Economics of Climate Change*." *Journal of Economic Literature* 45: 686–702, p. 692.

Nussbaum, M. 1995. *Poetic Justice: The Literary Imagination and Public Life*. Boston: Beacon Press.

Pigou, A. C. 1962. *The Economics of Welfare*, 4th edition. London: Macmillan.

Peart, S. J., and D. M. Levy. 2008. "Introduction to the Symposium on Ethics." *Eastern Economic Journal*, 34(1/Winter): 101–102.

Raines, B. 2010. "BP Buys up Gulf Scientists for Legal Defense, Roiling Academic Community." *Press Register* (Mobile, AL; July 16, section A, p. 1, 4.).

Reinhart, C. M., and K. S. Rogoff. 2010. "Growth in a Time of Debt." NBER Working Paper 15639 (January). Available at http://www.nber.org/papers/w15639.

RePEc. 2013. "RePEc Plagiarism Offenders." Available at http://plagiarism.repec.org/offenders.html, accessed March 26, 2013.

Reddy, S. 2012. "Facts and Values Are Entangled: Deal with It." Institute for New Economic Thinking. Available at http://ineteconomics.org/video/30-ways-be-economist/sanjay-reddy-facts-and-values-are-entangled-deal-it, accessed on March 23, 2012.

Robbins, L. 1945. *Essay on the Nature and Significance of Economic Science*, 2nd edition. London: Macmillan and Co.

Robinson, J. H. 1931. *The Mind in the Making*. New York: Harper and Brothers.

Schreck, M. T. 2007. Personal communication.

Schumpeter, J. A. 1954. *History of Economic Analysis*. New York: Oxford University Press.

Sen, A. K. 1977. "Rational Fools: A Critique of the Behavioral Foundations Of Economics." *Philosophy and Public Affairs* 6(4): 317–344.

Shapin, S., 2010. *The Scientific Life: A Moral History of a Late Modern Vocation*. Chicago: University Of Chicago Press.

Siegfried, J. J., and B. T. Meszaros. 1998. Voluntary Economics Content Standards for America's Schools: Rationale and Development. *Journal of Economic Education* 29(Spring): 139–149.

Smith, A. 1981. *An Inquiry into the Nature and Causes of the Wealth of Nations*, edited by R. H. Campbell and A. S. Skinner. Indianapolis: Liberty Fund.

Smith, A. 1982*a*. *Lectures on Jurisprudence*, edited by R. L. Meek, D. D. Raphael, and P. G. Stein. Glasgow edition. Indianapolis: Liberty Fund.

Smith, A. 1982*b*. *The Theory* of *Moral Sentiments*, edited by D. D. Raphael and A. L. MacFie. Indianapolis: Liberty Fund.

Smith, A. 1982*c* [1795]. *Essays on Philosophical Subjects*, edited by W. P. D. Wightman and J. C. Bryce. Glasgow edition. Indianapolis: Liberty Fund.

Smith, V. 2004. "Human Nature: An Economic Perspective." *Daedalus* 133(Fall): 67–76.

Smith, V. 2013. "Adam Smith: From Propriety and Sentiments to Property and Wealth." *Forum for Social Economics* 42(4): 283–297.

Stigler, S. 2008. "Fisher and the 5 Percent Level." *Chance* 21(4): 12.

Stiglitz, J. E., A. K. Sen, and J. P. Fitoussi. 2009. "Report by the Commission on the Measurement of Economic Performance and Social Progress." Available at http://www.stiglitz-sen-fitoussi.fr/documents/rapport_anglais.pdf, accessed on March 23, 2012.

Tetlock, P. E. 2006. *Expert Political Judgment: How Good Is It? How Can We Know?* Princeton: Princeton University Press.

Welch, T. 2011. Personal communication.

Wight, J. B. 2007. "The Treatment of Smith's Invisible Hand." *The Journal of Economic Education* 39(3): 341–358.

Wight, J. B. 2009. "Adam Smith on Instincts, Ethics, and Informal Learning: Proximate Mechanisms in Multilevel Selection." *Review of Social Economy* 67(1): 95–113.

Wight, J. B., and J. S. Morton. 2007. *Teaching the Ethical Foundations of* Economics. New York: The National Council on Economic Education.

Wilson, D. S. 2007. *Evolution for Everyone*. New York: Delacorte.

Ziliak, S. T., and D. N. McCloskey. 2008. *The Cult of Statistical Significance: How the Standard Error Costs Us Jobs, Justice, and Lives*. Ann Arbor: University of Michigan Press.

PART IV

THE ETHICAL ENTAILMENTS OF ECONOMIC THEORY

1. *General Issues*

CHAPTER 9

ETHICS IN RELATION TO ECONOMICS, ECOLOGY, AND ESCHATOLOGY

HERMAN DALY

The Problem of Ethics

Ethics is the ordering of multiple ends into a hierarchy with reference to some vision of the Ultimate End, however dimly we perceive it. The Ultimate End is that which is intrinsically good and does not derive its goodness by being instrumental to some other good. All other goods are instrumental to it indirectly and in varying degrees. Ethics is the problem of putting first things first, higher values ahead of lower values, and then, of course, *acting* according to that ordering of values in specific circumstances (Daly and Townsend, 1993: 17–24). The specific circumstances may be medical, economic, familial, and so forth, but the problem of ethics is basically the same—ethics is singular—knowing what goes in first place, second place, and so forth, putting it there, and acting accordingly, with enough knowledge of how the world works to avoid perverse unintended consequences. If we had a clear vision of the Ultimate End the process could be top down, but often it is only in the bottom up process of struggling to rank competing ends in specific situations that we get an insight into what the Ultimate End must be like for our consciences to approve the decisions.

We do not have a different Ultimate End and hierarchy of purposes for each area of life. Economic ethics, environmental ethics, medical ethics, and so forth are not different ethics (plural), but the same singular ethics applied in different circumstances. Consider the problem of separating "agricultural ethics" and "medical ethics." As Wendell Berry noted, agriculture is devoted to what we eat without considering its effect on our health, while medicine is devoted to our health without considering what we eat. A more coherent singular ethics would rank health high in the values hierarchy, and would judge both agricultural and medical practices accordingly. It would not have a different Ultimate

End and value hierarchy for agriculture and for medicine. Pluralizing ethics by differing professions leads to incoherence.

Another ethical incoherence comes from pluralizing the Ultimate End, in the sense of positing many "ultimate" ends of either equal or non comparable worth. In an age of pluralism there is considerable resistance to the notion of an Ultimate End—one often hears that one person's values are as good as another's, that there is no objective value, just subjective preferences, etc. This is incoherence equivalent to a denial of ethics in any operational sense. In the limit it means that any alternative can be "ethically" chosen simply by declaring it to be one of many "ultimate" ends. It is more than a grammatical error to treat ultimate as plural, and because ultimate must be singular, ethics, the prioritizing of plural ends with reference to the ultimate, must also be singular, or at least strive to be singular.

Economics and Ethics

So let us accept that "economic ethics" means common, singular ethics applied in economic circumstances of life. But even so, does it mean ethics applied by individuals in their actual economic behavior, or ethics applied to governing public economic policy, or the code of ethics of professional practitioners of the "science" of economics? The latter is the focus of this volume, so let us consider it first.

Trying to develop a professional ethics for economists presents special problems in addition to the general one discussed in the preceding text. It is difficult for a discipline that models human behavior on the assumption that atomistic self-interest is the fundamental motive (our approximation to the Ultimate End?) to then claim that its practitioners, unlike the rest of the human race, are differently motivated in the service of some professional "code of ethics" that presumably transcends self interest. And the claim of "value neutrality," itself a value, is completely unconvincing. The self-interest assumption is first applied by economists to individuals in the private sector, then via public choice theory to individuals in the public sector to "demonstrate" that the public interest is nothing but the private interests of those who work in the public sector. By logical extension academics and economics professionals who study private and public decisions should also be viewed as advancing their own self interests by their pretensions to objective study, in the same way that public officials advance their interests by pretensions about the public good. For economists to have a professional code of ethics different from self interest is therefore in contradiction with the discipline's basic assumptions about human motivation. Just as corporations supposedly exist only to maximize shareholder value (or is it CEO bonuses?), so the economics profession exists to maximize benefits to economists. Any "professional code of ethics" would be just another disguise by which to disarm those who would unmask the economists' pretensions. Instead of dealing with ethics in the service of the good, economists have attempted to design, in T. S. Eliot's words, "a system so perfect that no one needs to be good." Ethics would be unnecessary, as illustrated by Mandeville's "Fable of the Bees" and Adam Smith's "invisible hand."

The documentary film *Inside Job* about the 2008 financial collapse not only demonstrated the lack of a code of ethics for economists, but also left one doubting that the current discipline of economics is capable of anything transcending the self-interest of its own *homo economicus* assumption, logically internalized into the behavior of economists themselves. Many of the important economists interviewed seemed incapable of even recognizing the possibility of a conflict of interest between truthful analysis in the public interest and "consulting" for the interested client who is paying the fees.

A personal experience reinforces this point from another direction and is worth recounting as an insight into the professional ethics of economists. The *Growth Report (2008)* was a two-year study by the Commission on Growth and Development, a blue ribbon panel of 18 members from 16 countries, including two Nobel laureates in economics. It had many august sponsors, including mainly the World Bank, and can fairly be taken to represent the mainline consensus on economic growth, namely that it is our best approximation to the Ultimate End. The editors of the journal *Population and Development Review* asked me to review it. My review (Daly, 2008) was quite critical. I expected a debate, or at least a reply from the authors of the report, or chairmen of the Commission, whom the editor had quite properly invited to reply. They ignored it. Is this fact insignificant, or like Sherlock Holmes' dog that failed to bark in the night, might it be the clue to solving a mystery? Many issues and many people are deservedly ignored. But should economists ignore the question of whether growth still increases wealth faster than "illth," as it did in the past empty world, or whether in the new full world it has begun to increase illth faster than wealth? Is growth still economic in the literal sense, or has it become uneconomic? This is the main question not asked in the Report, and consequently raised in my review. Surely it is not a trivial question, and my discomfort at seeing it twice ignored transcends the mere personal pique that one feels at being brushed off. The failure of my critical review to initiate a dialog with the authors of the *Growth Report*, is, I believe, indicative of a deeper ethical failing within the economics profession. Ethics involves reasoning together in search of truth.

I tell this story because it illustrates the poor state of public discourse on economic matters (Daly, 2013). There were very few reviews of the Growth Report and no replies, rejoinders, etc. Why comment on someone else's work—there is not much academic credit in so doing, and besides you might make an enemy. Correcting errors through open debate is a fundamental part of the ethics that science proclaims, but because economics has only tenuous claims to being a science, why waste time on it? In any case consensus among experts is considered the hallmark of a mature science, so by prematurely declaring a consensus among "all *competent* economists," and avoiding public debate on fundamental issues, economists preemptively lay claim to the status of a mature science.

The advantage of a reputation as a "mature science" is that economists can profitably sell themselves as credibility-enhancing professional consultants to all sorts of interest groups. This at least is a professional ethics for economists that is highly consistent with the ethic of self interest postulated by economists for all other actors in the economy.

Economics is the problem of applying scarce means to attain as many ordered values as possible within physical limits, but with care not to waste resources by satisfying lower values to the neglect of higher values. Scarcity is imposed by our environment, which is finite, non-growing, and materially closed, though open to a fixed rate of flow of solar energy. It is also subject to the laws of thermodynamics. The big Ethical–Economic problem is to apply our limited ultimate means to serve a hierarchy of ends ordered with reference to the Ultimate End. Our ultimate means are low-entropy matter-energy—that which is required to satisfy our wants, but that we cannot produce in net terms but only use up (Georgescu-Roegen, 1972). We have two fundamentally different sources of low entropy: the solar flow and the terrestrial stock. They differ in their pattern of scarcity—the solar is flow limited but stock abundant; the terrestrial is stock-limited but temporarily flow-abundant. We can use up scarce terrestrial low entropy at a rate of our own choosing, in effect using tomorrow's fossil fuels today; but we must wait for tomorrow to receive tomorrow's energy from the sun. We cannot "mine" the sun. This fact is forcing upon us specific ethical questions that are new, even though the balancing of interests and the distribution of resources between present and future generations are traditional issues of singular ethics, and of economics.

The ethical question of balancing the interests of the present and the future also arises in the economics of education. A massive transfer of knowledge each generation is an unavoidable necessity. This transfer is not automatic. It requires two ethical decisions. The old must decide what knowledge is worth their effort to teach, and the young must decide what is worth their effort to learn. Some knowledge passes both ethical filters and becomes the basis for guiding the future and for discovering new knowledge. Other knowledge fails to pass one or both filters and is lost. Just as the world is always only one failed harvest away from mass hunger, so it is always only one failed generational transfer of knowledge away from mass ignorance.

What do we know about these two generational knowledge filters? What do they let pass and what do they filter out? I really don't know the answer, but I have one speculation, taken from E. F. Schumacher's reflections on Thomas Aquinas and Rene Descartes. Aquinas said that even uncertain knowledge of the highest things is worth more than certain knowledge of the lowest things. Descartes believed otherwise, that only knowledge that had the certainty of geometry was worth retaining, and uncertain knowledge should be abandoned even if it pertained to higher things. These two filters have very different selection biases. In their extreme forms they represent opposite errors of judgment about what knowledge to keep and what to jettison.

Which error are we most likely to commit today? I believe we overemphasize Descartes and pay too little attention to Aquinas. I take Aquinas' "higher things" to mean purposes, knowledge about right purposes. Lower things I take to refer to techniques—how to efficiently do something, assuming it should be done in the first place. We have overdeveloped our relatively certain knowledge of technique, and left underdeveloped our less certain, but more important, knowledge of right purpose. The old seem more interested in teaching technique than in purpose, and the young obligingly seem more interested in learning technique than purpose. So we develop more and more power, subject to less and less purpose. To paraphrase physicist S. Weinberg, the more science makes the universe comprehensible and subject to our control, the more it also seems to render it pointless, and the less our control is guided by purpose.

Ecology and Ethics

Let us consider another area—environmental ethics, or rather singular ethics related to environmental issues. Ecology and its parent discipline biology have in common with economics a fundamental commitment to self-interest. In economics self-interest via the invisible hand of competition is thought to lead to the common good. In biology the "selfish gene" via natural selection in a competitive environment is thought to lead to evolution and improved adaptation to the environment. There are of course countercurrents—the Adam Smith of *The Theory of Moral Sentiments*, and Peter Kropotkin of *Mutual Aid: A Factor of Evolution*. But the mainline thrust favors selfishness rewarded by adaptation and reproductive success, the latter seeming to play the role of Ultimate End in biology. Ecology, and by extension the biology, chemistry, and physics underlying it, seems even more barren ground for ethics than economics.

If the world we inhabit is an improbable ephemeral happenstance, long in coming and fated finally to dissolve, as naturalism teaches, and we as a part of it likewise are ephemeral chance happenings, then ethics is a sham. Ethics requires purposes, ordering of wants and actions relative to an objective value, final causation, teleology, and a perception of ultimate value—all the things that the reigning naturalism and materialism deny. The prevailing view is that all is determined by the ancient Epicurean vision of atoms moving in their determined pathways through the void, as reconstructed in modern scientific materialism. Anything that did not fit this theory was "explained" by Epicurus as caused by the "clinamen," an unaccountable "swerve" in the otherwise predetermined movement of atoms. This vision leaves no room for an Ultimate End and a hierarchy of values in reference to which actions are freely chosen, as required by ethics. Perhaps the clinamen should be recognized as the original "fudge factor." Ethics is doubly ruled out—if all is determined, then purpose is an illusion; if good and evil were nonexistent then there would be no criterion by which to choose ethically, even if choice were possible. Even pleasure, the proclaimed Ultimate End of the Epicurean, would be determined so it would be idle to advocate what could not be otherwise.

The idea of objective value or an Ultimate End scares us because we think, with some evidence, that it might lead to intolerance and persecution of those whose vision of ultimate value is different from ours. This is certainly a danger, but the larger danger is that in denying objective value we no longer have anything to appeal to in an effort to persuade. It is just my subjective preferences versus yours, and because there is by assumption no higher authority we have nothing to point to in order to persuade, nor accede to in being persuaded. There is no alternative but to fight, either with force or deceit.

A commitment to the reality of objective value, including our ability to reason together about it—however dimly it is perceived—is necessary to avoid arbitrary rule by force.

Some materialist biologists teach that morality and free will are illusions, but beneficial ones with survival value, they say, and therefore selected by their presumed contribution to reproductive success to fit our environment—our *randomly changing* environment, to be clear. However, they do not go on to consider the consequences of our (their) seeing through the illusions. Can an illusion be effective once it is exposed as an illusion? I doubt it. The consequences of drinking this poison were strikingly evident in the 1924 Leopold–Loeb trial of the two young Nietzschean–Darwinist nihilists who decided to prove to themselves that they were free from the illusion of objective morality by murdering a young man. The only defense their attorney, the famous Clarence Darrow, could muster for saving the admittedly guilty pair from execution was that their actions were determined, that in the great chain of strict causation "something slipped" (or swerved, as "explained" by the clinamen?). But why "slipped" if there is no objective norm to fall short of? Darrow was himself a determinist, and in principle should have been, and perhaps was, against any legal punishment, not just the death penalty, since for a determinist there can be no such thing as guilt.

A more basic reason why it is idle to speak of economic or environmental or medical or agricultural ethics is that the very foundation for any ethics at all is denied by philosophical materialists who seem to be in the ascendancy these days, at least in academia. If good and bad, better and worse, are meaningless concepts, as they are in a naturalist–materialist worldview, and if that worldview is dominant, then any discussion of ethics has to presuppose the prior rejection of the materialist worldview. Richard Dawkins, E. O. Wilson, Daniel Dennett, Christopher Hitchens, and most recently Alexander Rosenberg, have led the materialist attack on theism. The issue for now is not their atheism per se, but the worldview that leads them to it, namely philosophical materialism that not only rules out God, but also undercuts any notion of purpose, let alone an Ultimate End, required by ethics. One may say that Chance or Survival or Pleasure or Self Interest is the "ultimate end." But the materialists have been unsuccessful in demonstrating any convincing ethics based on such assumptions. Yet the materialists seem reluctant to give up on ethics, Rosenberg excepted. As a philosophical materialist Rosenberg is admirably consistent in disavowing any meaningful distinction between ethical and unethical behavior. Yet even he resorts to advocacy of "nice nihilism"—apparently as opposed to "nasty nihilism"—whatever those cutesy terms could possibly mean.

A quote from Leon Wieseltier's review of Rosenberg will illustrate the point:

> *Is there a god?* No. *What is the nature of reality?* What physics says it is. *What is the purpose of the universe?* There is none. *What is the meaning of life?* Ditto. *Why am I here?* Just dumb luck. *Is there a soul? Is it immortal?* Are you kidding? *Is there free will?* Not a chance! *What is the difference between right and wrong, good and bad?* There is no moral difference between them. *Why should I be moral?* Because it makes you feel better than being immoral. . . . *Does history have any meaning or purpose?* It's

> full of sound and fury, but signifies nothing." I take this cutting-edge wisdom from the worst book of the year, a shallow and supercilious thing called *The Atheist's Guide to Reality: Enjoying Life Without Illusions*, by Alex Rosenberg, a philosopher of science at Duke University. The book is a catechism for people who believe they have emancipated themselves from catechisms. The faith that it dogmatically expounds is scientism. It is a fine example of how the religion of science can turn an intelligent man into a fool. (Wieseltier 2011)

Unfortunately, scientism (scientific materialism as a worldview) has rotted the brains of many intelligent people, economists not excepted. They have carried the facile neo-Darwinist logic to the self-contradictory extent of explaining away explanation itself. Along the way they dispose of right and wrong and any notion of ethics. So it makes no sense to advocate any concept of ethics, much less any "code of professional ethics for economists," without first having rescued ethics itself from domination by scientism and "nice nihilism."

A similar problem was recognized and discussed long ago by Alfred North Whitehead under the term "lurking inconsistency." He expressed it in the following passage, which repays careful reading:

> A scientific realism, based on mechanism, is conjoined with an unwavering belief in the world of men and of the higher animals as being composed of self-determining organisms. This radical inconsistency at the basis of modern thought accounts for much that is half-hearted and wavering in our civilization. . . . . . It enfeebles [thought], by reason of the inconsistency lurking in the background. . . . . For instance, the enterprises produced by the individualistic energy of the European peoples presuppose physical actions directed to final causes. But the science which is employed in their development is based on a philosophy which asserts that physical causation is supreme, and which disjoins the physical cause from the final end. It is not popular to dwell on the absolute contradiction here involved. (Whitehead, 1925: 76)

In other words, our scientific understanding of nature is based on mechanism, on material and efficient causation with no room for final cause, for teleology or purpose. Yet we ourselves, and higher animals in general, directly experience purpose, and, within limits, act in a self-determining manner. Were that not the case we would not concern ourselves with ethics. If we are part of nature then so is purpose; if purpose is not part of nature then neither, in at least one significant way, are we. Whitehead (1925: 76) also put the contradiction more succinctly: "Scientists animated by the purpose of proving that they are purposeless constitute an interesting subject for study." Biologist Charles Birch (1990), a keen student of Whitehead, has restated the lurking inconsistency in his insightful book *On Purpose*: "[Purpose] has become the central problem for contemporary thought because of the mismatch in modernism between how we think of ourselves and how we think and act in relation to the rest of the world." Clearly, not all biologists are guilty of the lurking inconsistency.

The directly experienced reality of purpose or final cause must, in the view of materialism, be an "epiphenomenon"—an illusion that itself was selected because of the reproductive advantage that it chanced to confer on those under its spell. It is odd that the illusion of purpose should be thought to confer a selective advantage while purpose itself is held to be non-causative—but that is the neo-Darwinist's problem. The policy implication of the materialist dogma that purpose is not causative is *laissez faire* beyond the most libertarian economist's wildest model. The only "policy" consistent with this view is, "let it happen as it will anyway." Is it too much to ask the neo-Darwinist to speculate about the possibility that the survival value of neo-Darwinism itself has become negative for the species that really accepts it as a metaphysical worldview? Could this lurking inconsistency have lethal consequences?

Teleology has its limits, of course, and from the Enlightenment onward it is evident that materialism has constituted an enormously powerful research paradigm for biology. The temptation to elevate a successful research paradigm to the level of a metaphysical worldview is perhaps irresistible. But materialism too has its limits. To deny the reality of our most immediate and universal experience (that of purpose) because it doesn't fit the presuppositions of methodological materialism, is profoundly anti-empirical. To refuse to recognize the devastating logical and moral consequences that also result from the denial of purpose is anti-rational. To those of us who view science as a rational and empirical enterprise this is disturbing. That some others, already unembarrassed by the fact that their major intellectual purpose is to deny of the reality of purpose, should now want to concern themselves deeply with the relative valuation of accidental pieces of their purposeless world is incoherence compounded.

If purpose does not exist then it is hard to imagine how we could experience the lure of value. To have a purpose means to serve an end, and value is imputed to whatever furthers attainment of that end. Alternatively, if there is objective value then surely the attainment of value should become a shared purpose. Neo-Darwinist biologists and ecologists, who do not accept the reality of purpose, owe it to the rest of us to remain silent about valuation—and conservation as well.

Economists, unlike biologists, do not usually go to the extreme of denying the existence of purpose. They recognize purpose under the rubric of individual preferences and do not generally consider them to be illusory. However, preferences are thought to be purely subjective, so that one person's preferences are as good as another's. Unlike public facts, private preferences cannot be right or wrong—there is, by assumption, no objective standard of value by which preferences can be judged. Nevertheless, according to economists, preferences are the ultimate standard of value. Witness economists' attempts to value species by asking consumers how much they would be willing to pay to save a threatened species, or how much they would accept in compensation for the species' disappearance. The fact that the two methods of this "contingent valuation" give different answers only adds comic relief to the underlying tragedy, which is the reduction of value to taste weighted by income.

Economics too suffers from Whitehead's lurking inconsistency, but not to the extent that biology does. Purpose has not been excluded, just reduced to the level of tastes.

But even an unexamined and unworthy purpose, such as unconstrained aggregate satisfaction of uninstructed private tastes weighted by income—GDP growth forever—will dominate the absence of purpose. So, in the public policy forum, economists with their attenuated, subjective concept of purpose (which at least is thought to be causative) will dominate the neo-Darwinist ecologists who are still crippled by the self-inflicted purpose of proving that they are purposeless. Consequently GDP growth will continue to dominate conservation.

Whitehead's observation (1925: 76) that, "it is not popular to dwell on the absolute contradiction here involved," is even truer today, 85 years later. This willful neglect has allowed the lurking inconsistency to metastasize into the marrow of modernity. The Enlightenment, with its rejection of teleology, certainly illuminated some hidden recesses of superstition in the so-called Dark Ages. But the angle of its cold light has also cast a deep shadow forward into the modern world, obscuring the reality of purpose. To conserve Creation we will first have to reclaim purpose from that darkness. I say Creation with a capital "C" advisedly, and not in denial of the common facts of evolution. If our world and our lives are not in some sense a Creation, but just a purposeless happenstance—a random statistical fluke of multiplying infinitesimal probabilities by an infinite number of trials—then it is hard to see from where we will get the will and inspiration to care for it. Indeed, our decision-making elites may already tacitly understand that growth has become uneconomic. But apparently they have also figured out how to keep the dwindling extra benefits for themselves, while "sharing" the exploding extra costs with the poor, the future, and other species. Why not, if it is all just a purposeless happenstance? The elite-owned media, the corporate-funded think tanks, the kept economists of high academia, and the World Bank—not to mention Gold Sacks and Wall Street—all sing hymns to growth in harmony with class interest and greed. The public is bamboozled by technical obfuscation, and by the false promise that, thanks to growth, they too will one day be rich. Intellectual confusion is real, but moral nihilism, abetted by naturalistic scientism, may be the bigger problem. Such nihilism is hard to counter without strong appeal to the idea of purpose, of telos, and without raising its cosmic implications. Hence we are led, perhaps kicking and screaming for some of us, to eschatology.

Eschatology and Ethics

Eschatology is not the most popular field of theology. It deals with last things, the end of time and final purpose of Creation—not something of which we have any experience, so it is more an expression of hope than knowledge. Many Christian theologians believe that our hope, both individual and collective, ultimately lies in New Creation (Rom 8; 1Cor 15), which will be God's act at the end of the present creation (Polkinghorne, 2003; Wright, 2008; Moltmann, 2012). Most religions have an eschatology of some sort, and my focus on Christianity stems from my own religious commitments, which many will not share, including some Christians. However, the problems here discussed in the Christian context do not disappear in other contexts. Also, there are very many Christians in the world who do share these beliefs as a reasoned hope, and their views merit consideration. One can hardly understand the history and present of the West without understanding Christian thought. Furthermore, the issues raised are rather general. For example, one thing that science and Christianity agree on is that the present creation will ultimately die. The model for thinking about forever (whether personally or cosmically) is death and resurrection—New Creation, not perpetuity for the present creation, which would be both a Christian heresy and a scientific perpetual motion machine. Perhaps the cosmology of a "big crunch" followed by another big bang is to some extent an analogous secular eschatology of new creation. But New Creation in Christian theology will be a miracle, as was the first act of creation, or as the first fruit of the New Creation witnessed in the Resurrection. This doctrine is not emphasized from mainline Protestant pulpits today, perhaps from legitimate fear of identification with apocalyptic sects, left-behind rapture theology, and end-of-the-world fanaticism. But it remains foundational and biblical.

I will let the theologians sort out the conflicting eschatologies of different branches of Christianity, and of other religions (including the secular ones of Scientism, Marxism, and Growthism), and for now simply ask a question: what does the Christian belief in New Creation just outlined have to do with how we act in the world—specifically with the current economic/ecological crisis?

In God's New Creation death, decay, finitude and evil will, it is expected, be overcome. In the present creation they remain very real, built into its fundamental structure. We think that by building a modern Tower of Babel of unending economic growth and progress, we will reach heaven on earth, or maybe in space, and at least as a species escape death, decay, time, and entropy within the present creation. Furthermore, the secular intelligentsia assures us that the present creation (the Cosmos) is all there is, was, or ever will be, and in any case it is no longer considered a miracle, but the product of "Chance"—not Creation but "Randomdom" without any purpose. We now think that we understand this random evolutionary process and can control it in our quest for heaven on earth via genetic engineering, space colonization, and economic growth. Of course if we can control evolution it will no longer be random, inconveniently removing the principle on which our understanding of it was based. Scientists were always a bit embarrassed by so much appeal to chance, and would be pleased to offer an ethical criterion by which to choose our direction. But it is hard for them to appeal to a "moral compass" while denying any "magnetic north," any objective value that lures us toward itself. So let GDP growth and technology be a proxy for magnetic north, they say, since that is what all nations in fact put in first place. And GDP at least includes the goods of food, clothing, and shelter, which many still need—never mind the un-subtracted "bads" and the mistakenly added "anti-bads."

This idolatrous tower has collapsed before, and is badly out of plumb now. The basic reason is that, as creatures, we share subjection to entropy, evil, and finitude with the rest of this creation of which we are a part. Contrary to the dictates of "Randomdom,"

Christianity teaches that we are also made in God's image and charged with dominion and responsibility for this creation—but as mere creatures, and fallen ones at that, are not put in charge of constructing the New Creation. The current loss of faith in the New Creation has contradictory implications for economic and environmental policy. On the one hand people (many scientists) argue that this creation is all there is, so we better not undermine the intense seriousness of caring for it by allowing ourselves to hope for another gift,—a New Creation, after we have trashed this one. Be grateful for the temporary gift of life and enjoy it while it lasts, and be content with subsequent meaningless oblivion. On the other hand, we find it hard to be content. Without faith in the Creator, and the promise of ultimate renewal, we have no place to direct our gratitude, except dumb luck, and are irresistibly tempted to try to build a "new creation" ourselves. That seems to mean a modern Tower of Babel and the economic growth that supports it. As IBM forthrightly puts it in their advertisements, "let's build a smarter planet." They do not say: "let's make a smarter adaptation to the earth from which we were created and by which we are sustained." We are urged to change the planet, not ourselves! Indeed, many advocate escaping the doomed planet by colonizing space. Such techno-fantasies may constitute a secular eschatology that substitutes for the religious ones—salvation is replaced by the "singularity" and immortality as silicon-based information-bearing structures.

The net destructive consequence of the current scale and growth of the economy for the present creation that sustains it, is greatly downplayed, if not totally ignored. Death, decay, and entropy are permanent features in the present creation, and without faith in the New Creation, what final purpose is there beyond "eat, drink, and copulate, for tomorrow we dissipate"? We may well improve the material and social conditions in which we carry out these activities, and make it last a bit longer, but it all finally still dissipates unless there will be a radical renewal of the basic nature of creation. And who can renew creation other than the Creator?

Our attempt to reach heaven on earth by economic growth has led to the wholesale physical transformation of the earth into ourselves and our furniture—with ever less remaining for future generations and for other species. In my lifetime, the world population has more than tripled, and the populations of livestock, cars, houses, toasters, cell phones, and so forth have vastly more than tripled. These are all "dissipative structures," to use Prigogine's term, and they depend on environmental depletion and pollution for maintenance and replacement, much as human bodies do. The world has moved from empty to full—full of economy and empty of ecology. Remaining natural capital has now replaced man-made capital as the limiting factor in production. The fish catch is no longer limited by fishing boats, but by remaining fish and their habitats. Barrels of pumped crude oil are no longer limited by drilling and pumping capacity, but by remaining deposits, and perhaps more stringently by capacity of the atmosphere to absorb the CO_2 from burning the oil. But absorptive capacity is also natural capital. Sometimes sources are more limiting—sometimes sinks.

Yet the World Bank's *Growth Report* (2008) expects a four- to fivefold increase in the size of the world economy by 2050, and is eager to help this happen. They do not tell us by how much they expect the earth to grow by 2050! The social and environmental costs of the Tower of Babel are already growing faster than the production benefits, making us poorer not richer. Such uneconomic growth will not help the poor, yet we keep claiming otherwise. We hide the truth from ourselves by faulty accounting (treating natural capital consumption as income, adding rather than subtracting defensive expenditures), and by issuing mountains of debt, liens against the projected growth of real wealth that is unlikely ever to happen, but in which we put our faith. We misleadingly refer to these debts as "assets," or with slightly less dishonesty as "troubled assets" when they become devalued by the common sense realization that growth cannot redeem them. And then we make bets on which debts will be repaid and which will not. Those bets, incredibly, are then counted as additional assets!

If this sounds apocalyptic—well, that is why we are talking about eschatology! I have omitted the usual litany of ecological disasters consequent on growth not because they are unlikely, but just because they are well known. Why this destructive refusal to face reality? I think the answer is distressingly simple within the context of our present assumptions. Without growth the only way to cure poverty is by sharing. But redistribution is political anathema. Without growth to push the hoped for demographic transition, the only way to cure overpopulation is by population control—a second anathema. Without growth the only way to invest in environmental repair is by reducing current consumption—the third anathema. Three anathemas and you are out. Even if current policy manages to jump-start the growth economy for another round, we will soon enough have to move from a failed growth economy to a steady- state economy—from idolatrous efforts to build a substitute "new creation" or "smarter planet"—to humble stewardship and sharing of the present creation, with the poor, with future generations, and with other species, for as long as it lasts.

This stewardship of the present creation (caring for the poor, feeding the hungry, fallowing the land) would not be the New Creation, but a partial, hopeful anticipation of it reflected back into the present order. The consequence of the current lack of eschatological hope, the secular belief that this creation—nay, random happenstance—is all there is, or ever will be, is to get as much as you can while it and you last. Even our higher ethical impulse to love and care for others in the present creation is undercut by the ultimate futility of randomness, luring us toward its cold meaningless dissipation. Far from being an escape from present problems, eschatological hope for the New Creation is necessary to sustain both technological and political efforts to care for the gift of God's present creation. The New Creation will be a mysterious transformation of the present creation, we are told—somewhat like a tree is the transformation of a seed. Although the New Creation is God's act, not ours, it is the hopeful context in which our seed-saving actions can have ultimate meaning. Although emphasis in the New Creation theology is sometimes on the discontinuity with the present, there is also recognition of continuity—something from the old creation is transformed into the new, perhaps the broken pieces of our best efforts. And without a hopeful vision of the new, we are left with the losing game of transforming the old by our own efforts, with nothing but lame technological Gnosticism to confront the power of entropy, finitude, and evil. But as heirs to the New Creation, we are empowered to a limited degree to also be its proleptic agents, or maybe just its welcoming committee.

As stated several times, science and Christianity agree that the present creation, like we ourselves, will die. Without eschatological hope in New Creation we are left with, at best, an increase in longevity of the present creation, the much-discussed, though ill-defined, goal of "sustainability." Although that is a good thing, and I certainly advocate it, is it enough to inspire the enormous counter-cultural effort required to bring about even this restricted purpose? Christian belief in the *imago Dei* requires us to exercise responsibly our limited dominion over creation as its steward. But faith in the New Creation saves us from despair over our repeated failures, as well as over the ultimate impossibility of our preserving this Creation in the very long run.

Most scientists will, of course, not be happy with talk about miracles, with hope in the New Creation. Yet when faced with the ultimate heat death of the universe, and the meaninglessness implicit (and increasingly explicit) in their materialist cosmology, some scientists seem to flinch, and look for optimism, if not hope, somewhere within their materialism. They invent the hypothesis of infinitely many (unobservable) universes in which life may outlive our universe. They were led to this extraordinary idea to escape the implications of the anthropic principle—which argues that for life to have come about by chance in our single universe would require far too many just-so coincidences. To preserve the idea of chance as the only credible cause, and thereby escape any notion of Creator or Telos, they argue that although these fine-tuning coincidences discovered by scientists are indeed overwhelmingly improbable in a single universe, they would surely happen if there were infinitely many universes. And of course our universe is obviously the one in which the improbable events all happened. If you don't believe that Shakespeare wrote *Hamlet*, you can claim that infinitely many monkeys pecking away at infinitely many typewriters had to hit upon it someday.

Unfortunately the evidence for infinitely many universes, or monkeys for that matter, is lacking. Likewise, the only "evidence" that could be offered to support hope for a future miracle would be the occurrence of a similar miracle in the past. That of course would be the Creation itself. Science rightly tries to account for this Creation, as far as reasonable, in its own materialist terms, and of course understandably rejects "miracle" or God as an explanatory category. Whether fact-free postulation of infinitely many unobservable universes qualifies as a reasonable explanatory category, I will leave to the judgment of the readers.

The working hypothesis of scientific materialism, however fruitful it has been, should not be confused with an Ultimate Metaphysics of Chance. Nor does adding Darwinian natural selection to Mendelian random mutation mitigate the dominance of chance, since the selecting criterion of environmental conditions (other organisms and geophysical surroundings) is also considered to be a random product of chance. Mutations provide random change in the genetic menu from which natural selection picks according to the survival odds determined by a randomly changing environment.

This Metaphysics of Chance precludes explanation of some basic facts that, however, will not be silent: first, that there is something rather than nothing; second, the just-right physical fine-tuning "coincidences" set forth in the anthropic principle; third, the "spontaneous generation" of first life from inanimate matter before evolution can get started; fourth, the accumulation of an incredible amount of specified information in the genome of all the irreducibly complex living creatures that evolved from the relatively simple information in the first living thing (presumably by random change—ignoring that randomness destroys rather than creates information); fifth, the emergence of self-consciousness and rational thought itself (if my thoughts are ultimately the product of randomness why believe any of them, including this one?); and sixth, the innate human perception of right and wrong, of good and bad, which would be meaningless in a purely material world. Chance surely plays an important role in our world, but explaining all these facts "by chance" strains credulity at least as much as "by miracle."

Conclusion

We economists, and people in general, have a lot of serious rethinking to do about ethics, beginning with a critical review of the modern culture of scientism that emphasizes determinism and downplays purpose to such an extent that ethics disappears, and hope along with it. Scientism, Marxism, and Growthism have by a large margin failed to deliver on their secular eschatologies of heaven on earth. A cosmic metaphysics of hope, for example, the Christian theology of New Creation, conceives of ethics in the present creation as the lure of objective value from the future, drawing us already into anticipatory participation in New Creation. This view of course is in contradiction to the naturalism (philosophical materialism) of our time, but in harmony with the traditional spiritual wisdom of mankind. The former offers no basis for ethics; the latter still does.

References

Birch, Charles. 1990. *On Purpose*. Kensington, NSW: New South Wales University Press.

Daly, Herman. 2013. "A Further Critique of Growth Economics." *Ecological Economics* 88: 20–24.

Daly, Herman. 2008, September. "Growth and Development: Critique of a Credo." *Population and Development Review* 34(3).

Daly, Herman, and Kenneth Townsend, Eds. 1993. *Valuing the Earth*. Cambridge, MA: MIT Press.

Georgescu-Roegen, Nicholas. 1972. *The Entropy Law and the Economic Process*. Cambridge, MA: Harvard University Press.

Moltmann, Jürgen. 2012. *Ethics of Hope*. Minneapolis, MN: Fortress Press.

Polkinghorne, John. 2003. *The God of Hope and the End of the World*. New Haven, CT: Yale University Press.

Whitehead, Alfred. 1925. *Science and the Modern World*. New York: Macmillan.

Wieseltier, Leon. 2011. "Washington Diarist: The Answers." Review of *The Atheist's Guide to Reality: Enjoying Life Without Illusions*, by Alex Rosenberg. *New Republic*, December 14. Retrieved from http://www.newrepublic.com/article/washington-diarist/magazine/98566/science-atheism-meaning-life

World Bank. 2008. The Growth Report: Strategies for Sustained Growth and Inclusive Development. Washington, DC: Author.

Wright, N. T. 2008. *Surprised by Hope*. New York: Harper Collins.

CHAPTER 10

POISONING THE WELL, OR HOW ECONOMIC THEORY DAMAGES MORAL IMAGINATION

JULIE A. NELSON

WHAT IF . . . ?

LET'S begin with a thought experiment. *What if* the following were true?

- *What if* people might act out of social and other-regarding concerns, as well as reasonable self-interest in their economic lives, but are pushed by the economic theory of self-interested utility maximization to believe that it is permissible—and perhaps even appropriate—to be irresponsible, opportunistic, and selfish when participating in markets?
- *What if* business leaders might pay attention to the implications of their decisions for workers, communities, the environment, and others who are affected by their firm's actions, but economic theory encourages them to believe that they should—and in fact *must*—focus on getting every last dollar of profit possible?
- *What if* we all live in a world that is deeply interdependent, fundamentally unpredictable, and even rather dangerous, but economic theory lulls us into a false confidence that prevents us, as individuals and societies, from taking actions that might prevent dramatically harmful outcomes?
- *What if* the way in which economic theory has directed our attention towards self-interest and predictable "laws" and "mechanisms" has contributed in a major way to economic upheavals and human suffering, including financial crises, environmental deterioration, and a resource-starved care sector?

- *What if* the belief in the tenets of economic theory has become so widespread that even those who seek a more humane and sustainable world suffer from a severe dearth of moral imagination when it comes to commerce?
- *What if*, in short, economic theory creates myths that strengthen the hands of the most powerful, greedy, and short-sighted economic actors, while needlessly undermining normal human ethical sensibilities and normal human aspirations for a society that is prosperous, just, and sustainable?

If one follows the thought experiment and at least momentarily accepts these premises and the characterizations of economic theory, then the conclusion that there is something ethically troubling about a profession that promotes such an economic theory is inescapable.

But are these premises and the conclusion correct? This chapter argues that they are, and that contemporary mainstream economics, which centers on notions of utility- and profit-maximization and mechanism, is having hugely negative effects on human society. But many people will not agree. Among the objections that may immediately be raised to this line of argument are:

- Commercial life really doesn't require ethical concern.
- Commercial life really doesn't permit ethical concern.
- The assumptions of economic theory are required for scientific rigor.
- Economic theory is broader than that.
- So what if economics is narrow? Something else will fill the gaps.

This chapter examines each of these in turn.

"Commercial Life Really Doesn't Require Ethical Concern"

First, it may be argued that commercial and market behavior *really doesn't* require ethical concern. Economists, from Classical times up through Neoclassical and much present teaching, have tended to promulgate a vision of economic life as qualitatively similar to the phenomena studied by classical Newtonian physics. The image of economies as value-free, a-social, controllable systems whose "mechanisms" are driven by the "energy" of individual self-interest has become so much a part of the air we breathe and water we drink that it is rarely questioned.

Historically, Adam Smith's famous passage in *The Wealth of Nations* ([1776] 2001: 19), is, of course the most cited quote used by those who argue for this view: "It is not from the benevolence of the butcher, the brewer, or the baker, that we expect our dinner, but from their regard to their own interest. We address ourselves, not to their humanity but to their self-love, and never talk to them of our necessities but of their advantages." Although Smith himself was a much more sophisticated ethical thinker, this one passage has since been blown up into a whole philosophy about how individuals' pursuit of their own self-interest will be made, by the amazing mechanism of a self-regulating market system, to serve the common good. Perhaps nearly as often cited is Milton Friedman's assertion that "Few trends could so thoroughly undermine the very foundations of our free society as the acceptance by corporate officials of a social responsibility other than to make as much money for their stockholders as possible" (1982: 133). From such a perspective, explicit consideration of ethics is all or largely unnecessary.

These ontological beliefs about the nature of market-using, capitalist economies are not held only by very politically conservative economists, such as Friedman or others of the University of Chicago economics school. They also ground the thinking of many who are in favor of a greater role for community-feeling and action at a societal level. Political liberals who call on governments to serve the public interest by appropriately "intervening" in "the economy" are coming from the same basic perspective. This very phrasing suggests that the economy is imagined to be a freestanding, fundamentally private, mechanical, and ethics-free sphere, into which a public-spirited state must enter from the outside. Development economist Partha Dasgupta, for example, has set out a hard-and-fast dichotomy between the market sphere, in which he claims that self-interest is appropriate and "we should not worry about others," and the public sphere, in which concern for others is appropriate (2005: 247; 2007: 151). *Within* the market sphere, it seems, we are justified in adopting an attitude that has been described by Amartya Sen and Jean Drèze as "complacent irresponsibility" (Drèze and Sen, 1989: 276).

Before examining these beliefs more closely, let us examine how they have spread beyond the economics profession.

"Commercial Life Really Doesn't Permit Ethical Concern"

The belief, preached by economists, that capitalist or market-using economies are fundamentally systems set apart from human ethics is also shared by many who entirely condemn capitalist systems as immoral and a source of evil. To such critics, the (assumed) fundamentally selfish, profit-driven, and mechanical nature of these systems means that moral action within them is impossible. Classical economist Karl Marx, for example, followed Smith in adopting mechanical metaphors, creating among his followers firm beliefs in the "inherent dynamics of capitalism," the "logic of markets," and the "forces of capital accumulation."

The writings of sociologist and philosopher Jürgen Habermas have more recently been influential in disseminating this view. Habermas distinguished what he called the "lifeworld" arena of communicative action from the "system" arena driven by unconscious, objectifying forces (Habermas, 1981). The lifeworld, Habermas claimed, is the area of truly social public and private life, and the arena of norms, aesthetics, and conscious and deliberative action. Systems, on the other hand—in which Habermas included both economies and state bureaucracies—are "steered by" the nonhuman media of money or power (Habermas, 1981: 164). Within the latter, people are dehumanized— "stripped of personality structures and neutralized into bearers of certain performances" (308).

As a result of sharing the belief that capitalist systems are fundamentally mechanical, much of the "critical" literature tends to fall into a pattern of simple reactivity in prescribing solutions. If economists and capitalists are pro-growth, then critics must be diametrically anti-growth; if the conventional approach is pro-globalization and large-scale, then critics must be diametrically pro-local and small-scale; if current elites are pro-technology, critics must be diametrically Luddite and anti-technology; if policy debates focus on humans in industrialized societies, critics must diametrically venerate the wilderness, indigenous and nonhuman species; if those in control praise profits and private property, those who want change must advocate a complete disavowal of both (e.g., Norberg-Hodge, 2002; Bookchin, 2005; Watson, 2005). Or so it is thought. Salvation is therefore sought in some radically different sort of system—for example, worker-run, communitarian, nonmonetized, and/or local. Corporate leaders are demonized, and current-day economic systems are given up for lost.

But are these beliefs factually supported? Consider, for example, that a key element in Habermas's theory is a belief that money is a neutral, asocial medium. But this belief does not hold up under closer examination. Habermas claims that because money is backed up by "gold or means of enforcement" (1981: 270), it therefore does not require social, communicative agreements or legitimation (272). In fact, however, there hasn't been an international gold standard since the early 1930s, and money has long been a quintessential social construction: It has value precisely and only because (or when) people believe it has value. Those close to the actual management of national or regional monetary systems are, in fact, deeply concerned with issues of beliefs, expectations, credibility, reputation, legitimacy, and the problems of collective decision-making (King, 2004). Money and markets are thoroughly human and social creations.

In addition, as common-sense observation suggests, and research confirms, humans demonstrate pro-social as well as self-interested motivations in economic situations (Folbre and Nelson, 2000; Fehr, and Falk 2002), and diverge widely from the sort of decision-making assumed in models of "economic man" (Kahneman, 2003). Actual observation of human behavior, in business and markets as elsewhere, reveals a mix of motivations that can in regard to ethics often be summarized as "neither selfish nor exploited" (Margolis, 1982) or "pragmatic" (Dees and Cramton, 1991; Gentile, 2010). These terms describe most people's inclination to act in pro-social ways as long as they are confident that others will act pro-socially as well, but to retreat into self-defense if they perceive others as selfish and ready to exploit their goodwill.

Businesses and markets are, in fact, social organizations within which people have to cooperate, have to get along, and to which people bring their whole complex bundle of values and aspirations—for good or ill (de Goede, 2005; Nelson, 2006; Healy and Fourcade, 2007; Zelizer, 2011). Serious scholars are increasingly noticing that a regard for ethics is absolutely required for sustained economic functioning (even though the teaching of economics may simultaneous serve to undercut it) (e.g., Stout, 2011). In a world in which information is always too limited, and the future is always fundamentally unpredictable, short-term greed and opportunism crash the system rather than sustain it. Modern capitalist economies have probably functioned as well as they have, so far, only because many people in their daily lives have not bought into the "greed is good" mentality. The evidence tells us that to the extent real-world economies neglect issues of honor and integrity, the result is not a well-functioning machine, but rather a human-suffering-creating disaster (Smith, 2010). Although much maligned by people on the both the political right and left who believe that it is the essential nature of firms to maximize profits, many commentators—including many who have more direct experience than economists with the working of business organizations—emphatically reject this mechanical and ethics-free image of the firm. The long tradition of "corporate social responsibility," along with stakeholder approaches (Freeman, 1984) and approaches that investigate the roles of values and vision (Collins and Porras, 1994; Paine, 2002), offer richer perspectives.

The claim here is not that people or corporations can be counted on to always be good, moral, altruistic, or public-spirited. Such claims would be just as one-sided as assuming that they are always self-interested, greedy, and opportunistic.[1] The argument here is that people do not lose their status as social and ethical beings—with all the complexity and mixed motivation that implies—simply because they have entered the commercial realm. Likewise, business firms are not asocial machines operating in a vacuum, but are fully social entities with complex internal workings and that operate in deep interdependence with the ethical mores of the culture in which they participate.

Those who believe economists' ideas about commerce not requiring, or not permitting, ethical concern probably assume that such assertions originated in careful investigation of real-world markets and organizations. Nothing could be further from the truth. Rather, they grew out of a methodology-driven aspiration of economists to be more like physical scientists.

"The Assumptions Are Required for Scientific Rigor"

Perhaps it might be admitted that some of the premises of the opening statements of this chapter are true—that is, that individuals, firms, and the world really are more complex

[1] Note that the claim here is not that profits and ethics always coincide (e.g., Eisler, 2008), nor that capitalism creates its own requisite social norms (McCloskey, 2006). Such arguments go beyond the arguments of the current paper; they err on the side of presuming a too *close* relationship of economics and ethics.

than core economic theories allow. But then it may be argued—ethical ramifications notwithstanding—that the assumptions of self-interest, profit maximization, and mechanical control are required in order for the "science" of economics to be "objective" and "rigorous" (e.g., Persky, 1995; Caplin, 2008). These assumptions allow economic life to be studied using methods from fields such as geometry (involving theorem and proof) and especially classical Newtonian physics (involving maximization or minimization of mathematical functions using calculus and other tools). Even if the world is not a machine, "science" may seem to demand that we concentrate only on its machine-like aspects.

A key moment in the development of this belief occurred with John Stuart Mill's 1836 essay "On the Definition of Political Economy." In this essay, Mill attempted to carefully distinguish economics from the physical sciences and technology, from ethics, and from a more general study of social behavior. Those realms of human life were consigned by Mill to other disciplines, so that Political Economy could deal with "man [*sic*]. . . solely as a being who desires to possess wealth, and who is capable of judging of the comparative efficacy of means for obtaining that end" (1836: 38)—that is, as rational, self-interested "economic man." Mill believed that this separation of a very thin slice of human behavior for analysis was required by the nature of *science*—and the model for science, in his mind, was geometry. Mill, to his credit, argued that in any application Political Economy would need to be complemented by the insights of other sciences that had focused on other parts of human nature and other circumstances (58), and also by practical knowledge of specific experiences (68).

Unfortunately, however, what remained and flourished in later economic thought was not Mill's modesty, but rather his idea that Political Economy must become an axiomatic-deductive and mathematical enterprise in order to be "scientific." This approach received a big boost in the late 19th century when neoclassical economists (including Edgeworth, Jevons, Walras, and Pareto) found that they could formalize Mill's idea of the "desire for the greatest amount" of wealth in terms of the (Newtonian-physics-like) maximization of mathematical profit and utility functions. Alfred Marshall's systematization of the neoclassical approach, and economist Lionel Robbins (1935) precedent-setting definition of economics as the science of choice-making in the face of unlimited wants and scarce resources, further consolidated the mechanical view. The idea that analyzing the economic "machine" using mathematical tools yielded analysis that is "scientific," "objective," and "rigorous" continued to gain ground during much of the 20th century.

Yet the idea that abstract mathematical tools somehow on their own grant "objectivity" and "rigor" is an extremely odd one. Logic and mathematics assure that a model is internally consistent, which is a quite different thing from assuring that it says anything useful or relevant about the real world. The notion that objectivity is somehow guaranteed by a position of abstraction and detachment has been challenged by numerous philosophers of science (e.g., Keller, 1985; Longino, 1990; Sen, 1992; Kitcher, 2011). The opposite of science is not "softer" social sciences, or even art, literature, or spiritual practice—all of which are simply complementary modes of seeking understanding and expression of areas of human experience where more mathematical sciences cannot reach.

The opposite of science is dogma—the situation in which minds close around a particular set of beliefs and refuse to show curiosity about new evidence or alternative viewpoints. Yet the physics-imitating mode of hegemonic economic practice is precisely such a dogma, with its true believers remaining tightly wedded to particular metaphysical assertions about human psychology and organizational behavior long after other research has shown the assertions to be largely false and/or unhelpful. There are better alternatives. A more sensible notion of scientific rigor defines reliable knowledge as that which passes the test of evaluation by larger, more diverse communities that bring to bear a variety of perspectives (e.g., Keller, 1985; Longino, 1990; Sen, 1992; Kitcher, 2011). An economics profession that acknowledges the deeply social, interdependent, and uncertain aspects of economic life would, then, also be one that is more truly scientific.

"Economic Theory Is Broader than That"

But then again, it might be argued that the premises about human and organizational behavior being ethically richer are correct, but that the characterization of economic theory given in this chapter is false—that economic theory really is more broad, open, subtle, and engaged than pictured in the arguments just discussed.

To some extent this is a correct critique: The preceding characterization refers only to the core Neoclassical theories about utility-maximizing consumers and profit-maximizing firms that characterize the mainstream of economics in most Western (and increasingly Eastern) industrialized countries. The broader development of economic thought includes not only Neoclassical approaches but also heterodox approaches such as Institutional, Marxist, Austrian, post-Keynesian, social, and feminist economics. It also includes explorations at the edges of the mainstream, such as new institutional and behavioral economics. There certainly exist elective courses and graduate and professional seminars that do not conform to the narrow view.

But the reality is that the simplistic view of economics dominates at all levels of economics education, as attested to by the cookie-cutter content of the most popular K–12 teaching materials, standardized tests, university introductory and intermediate microeconomic and macroeconomic theory textbooks, and graduate "core" theory courses (Nelson and Sheffrin, 1991; Fullbrook, 2003; Maier and Nelson, 2008; Green, 2012). Despite protests by students (Fullbrook, 2003; Romero, 2011) and efforts to broaden economics education (Groenewegen, 2007; Goodwin, Harris et al. 2013, 2013; Morgan, 2014; Nelson, 2011*a*; Reardon, 2009), this hegemony continues.

The narrow view also dominates in economic policymaking, as attested to by the academic credentials and expressed views of most high office-holders. As discussed previously, simplistic views of the economy have also come to dominate thinking about commerce in fields such as sociology and philosophy, when the discussion turns to the "system" arena of economics; and in popular thought, as demonstrated by many discussions of economics in the media.

In this sense, what is or is not believed by individual, sophisticated economists is not particularly important. To the extent that anyone who calls him- or herself an economist still *allows* the radically simplistic and ethically harmful aspects of economic theory to be disseminated, without strenuous challenge, we participate in the damage.

"So What if Economics Is Narrow? Something Else Will Fill the Gaps"

Academic economists, it might be thought, are only responsible for *this* understanding of the economy. The fact that *this* understanding may be crowding out other understandings is not, it may be thought, our responsibility. Like Mill, we may believe that our bailiwick is "economic man," while somebody else's bailiwick is "ethics." Perhaps a purely public-interested state will arrange for public well-being. Or perhaps ethics may be thought of as the realm of philosophical theories of justice. Or the care of families or charitable work will provide a "haven in the heartless world" of competitive capitalism, or commonsense ethical sensibilities will hold sway in the street, even if they do not in the seminar room. Economics can stay as it is, perhaps, while something else takes up the slack.

A few recent examples, however, should lead one to doubt whether any of these "something else" factors envisioned as filling the gap is itself free enough from the poison, or from other flaws, to be an effective counterbalancing force.

The State

Do law and the state rein in the opportunism and greed encouraged by core economic theories? In a striking case of life imitating fiction, consider the 2005 United States court case "Re the Walt Disney Company Derivative Litigation." Former Disney president Michael Ovitz had been granted severance pay in an amount that the court acknowledged was "breathtaking" (2005: 6). A group of shareholders subsequently sued, alleging that when the CEO and board approved his pay and severance packages, they were self-serving and thus breached their fiduciary duty to act on behalf of the corporation.

The mechanical model says that "firms maximize profits," and profit maximization, or maximization of shareholder wealth, is widely (although erroneously) believed to be mandated by law and enforced by the courts, and/or enforced by market competition (see discussions in Nelson, 2006; Bratton, 2011; Nelson, 2011*b*). Meanwhile, economists' "principal-agent theory" has justified enormous growth in the compensation packages for corporate executives in the United States, based on the argument that they must be financially "incentivized" to work on behalf of their firms.[2]

The Disney case was, in fact, the classic sort of shareholder derivative suit that many imagine to be effective in *enforcing* profit maximization. The rhetoric of the decision makes it clear that presiding judge William B. Chandler believed that, as a metaphysical issue, increasing shareholder value is, indeed, the proper purpose of a corporation. But did Judge Chandler's ruling confirm that profit-maximization is legally enforceable—that is, that executives who take high compensation at the expense of shareholders should be reprimanded or punished by the courts? Far from it! The judge ruled *against* the shareholder plaintiffs, on the grounds that "[t]he redress for failures that arise from faithful management must come from the *markets*, through the actions of shareholders and the *free flow* of capital" and *not* from the courts (2005: 7, emphasis added). Concluding that the decision-makers' actions, while falling "significantly short of the best practices of idea corporate governance," did not constitute gross negligence, he invoked a longstanding tradition of deferring to the greater knowledge of a business's managers (2005: 3). Enforcement of "best practices," he said, should be left up to the free market.

That is, rather than asserting shareholder primacy as a principle enforceable in the courts, the court in *Disney* leaves the enforcement up to Chicago-style "self-regulating" markets. Following the Chicago line, this court found that there was no need for "interference" by any state organization—*including the court itself.* This is a rather stunning result: the law-and-economics approach at this point devolves into a situation where legal institutions themselves are largely seen as redundant. And what about *eBay Domestic Holdings, Inc. v. Newmark et al.* (2010), an even more recent case in which "the courts" confirmed that that the legal essence of a corporation is to make profits? Let's be clear about exactly who "the courts" was in this case: this same William B. Chandler, who has drunk deeply from the well of poisoned economic thought.

This is one extreme: The state eviscerated by the spread of narrow economic dogmas. Zelizer (2005, 2011) has called this "nothing but" thinking, in which a belief in rational self-interest and impersonal markets pervades all spheres. But the opposite extreme, of holding The State up as the icon of all that is good, true, and public-spirited (vis-à-vis presumably individualist markets) can be equally dangerous, as it relies on assumptions of state beneficence, state ability, and moral purity of state workers that also fly in the face of fact, history, and the complexity of human motivations. Rather than debates about which is more virtuous (or more evil), markets or states, a more mature ethical discussion would be about how to structure and encourage *both* sorts of institutions to promote *both* healthy levels of opportunities for individuals *and* beneficial levels of community solidarity and sustainability.

[2] Apparently, the feeling that one has a moral obligation to earn one's pay has gone out the window.

Theories of Justice

What are the ethical responsibilities of sovereign nations? How can we expect nations to behave, in regards to, for example, climate change? Here again, economic thinking is having a perverse effect. A number of scholars of economics, law, and politics have extended an "economic man" approach to thinking about governments, considering states as simply "economic man" writ large.

Eric Posner and David Weisbach's wildly mis-named 2010 book *Climate Change Justice*, for example, is a precisely argued exposition of such a position. They make national self-interest foundational: "we need to think about how to solve the climate problem in a way that even selfish states would agree to" (2010: 138). Any proposal must, by their lights, satisfy "the principle of International Paretianism: all states must believe themselves better off by their lights as a result of the climate treaty" (6). Distributional goals are set aside as the topic of some other discussion, to take place elsewhere. The stonewalling of international climate policy by the United States is excused as a case of the U.S. "just trying to exercise its bargaining power," which they regard as simply a "common state behavior" (114). Notions of collective responsibility are dismissed as being contrary to the "standard assumption" of individualism (101). They conclude that "an optimal climate treaty . . . could well require side payments" not to poor countries, but "to rich countries like the United States" (86).

But to whom are the assumptions of self-interest and individualism "standard"? They are standard—*and peculiar*—to those who think of the world in "economic man" terms. Envision a book along these lines called *Schoolyard Justice*. Picture a school playground in which a big, tough bully has taken control of all of the balls and bats, and refuses to share. What principle should be applied to straighten things out? Well, first, of course, we would have to grant the bully the right to keep all that he has amassed. Perhaps all the other kids could pool their lunch money, and bribe the bully to lend them a ball. That doesn't leave a whole lot of work for the "justice" part of the book title to do, does it?

However, not even Posner and Weisbach, it turns out, can completely ignore the fact that we need some elements of ethics in our behavior. Although their ideal treaty would be in the self-interest of every country, countries would afterwards, they argue, be under a strict ethical obligation to abide by the treaty (170). How convenient, for the countries that have been well-off all along.

Dogmatic economic poison in the form of "nothing but" thinking leads to a belief that nations will inevitably try to shape policy in ways that serve their own interests, where "interests" are largely defined in terms of short-run economic growth. Yet, if every nation sets this as a goal in climate change negotiations, we are—to use a particularly apt colloquialism—cooked. This situation is not at all helped by the fact that mechanical analogies have given economists an illusion of control that is wildly out of place when applied to complex natural systems and a highly uncertain future (Nelson, 2013).

The Caring Sphere

With the rise of industrialization during the Victorian era, a "separate spheres" ideology grew up. Industry and commerce came to be thought of as masculine realms of competition, rationality, and self-interest. The harsh edges of this dog-eat-dog existence were to be tempered, however—at least for the middle-class and rich—by the presence of "the angel in the house." The realm of households, wives, and children was envisioned as noneconomic, cooperative, emotional, and caring. The economic realm could go on being harsh *because* families would take up the slack. Or, in other versions, it may be thought that local communities, nonprofit organizations, or private charity will step in to take care of the ethical slack left by the mechanical economy.

In Chicago-style economics, one example of this is Gary Becker's (1981) "altruist": The self-interested actor in the market magically turns into the generous head-of-household as he steps through the door of the home. Another line of economics has adopted the "nothing but" assumption that people are just as rational and self-interested at home as elsewhere, resulting in models of household bargaining. A third line of argument divides motivations along occupational (and gender) lines: Although it is assumed that (mostly male) business executives and most other workers are self-interested and need to be incentivized with money to do their jobs, workers who provide personal care—such as nurses and child-care workers (mostly female)—are assumed to be motivated by love alone. In fact, some of this literature suggests that the way one gets the best workers in these latter fields is to pay them badly, because that is how one makes sure only people with genuine caring motivations take the jobs (see discussions in Folbre and Nelson, 2006; Nelson, 2011c). What seems to be forgotten in these discussions is that nurses and child-care workers need to eat. An intellectual bifurcation of the world into radically distinct non-caring and caring sectors is—among other ill effects— contributing to a massive shortage of resources in, and exploitation of, unpaid and low-paid caring labor (Folbre, 1994; Benería, 2003).

How long can this exploitation go on? A basic assumption behind the "separate spheres" model is that caring services—much like the services of the natural environment—arise effortlessly and endlessly, without any need for attention by those in power in economic and political life. But if all the incentives of money and respect are pointing toward the (presumed) "uncaring" sphere as the road to personal and family comfort, the patience of caring workers is sorely tried. "I love my job, but I'm about to leave it" is, in fact, a sentiment often found among low-paid caring workers (Modigliani, 1993)—and especially the most competent ones, who have other opportunities. If we lose the moral imagination that allows us to see people as possibly caring in and through their labor market roles, and as needing and meriting substantial financial resources in and because of caring work, we endanger the support system for our very lives.

Commonsense Ethical Sensibilities

Contemporary cognitive psychology and neuroscience have suggested that human behavior arises from "dual processes" in the brain: one process that acts quickly based on bodily emotional signals and another process that is slower and more deliberative. In relation to ethics, research suggests that moral judgment is—initially at least, and often entirely—more a matter of the former, or affective moral response, than of the latter, or moral reasoning (Greene, Sommerville et al., 2001; Haidt, 2001; Greene and Haidt, 2002). Moral reasoning, rather than being part of the process of coming to a judgment is more often—as a practical and empirical matter—involved in possible post hoc justifications of a judgment already arrived at intuitively. For questions of positive moral *action*—as opposed to moral judgment—emotional responses such as empathy, sadness, and shame seem to be particularly important, while the role of moral reasoning is particularly weak. Emotion is a motivator: One can be an expert on the many ways of formulating principles of justice, but if one does not *care* about acting justly, all the principles in the world will have no effect on behavior (Warren, 2000; Haidt, 2001: 112).

Yet the emotional aspects of moral judgments are not "anything goes"—that is, merely whims experienced, subjectively and randomly, by individuals. Rather, they tend to be formed out of the experience and knowledge of larger cultures (Haidt, 2001; Gigerenzer, 2007). Researchers have identified three clusters of moral intuitions that seem to function cross-culturally. Individualistic principles, such as the principle of individual freedom that implicitly underlies conventional economics (e.g., in the form of support for individual choice, Pareto Efficiency, and "free markets") is but one cluster. The second cluster revolves around community, loyalty, in-groups, hierarchy, and wise leadership. The third emphasizes divinity and purity (Haidt, 2006: 188; Gigerenzer, 2007: 187). Unlike individual goals that can be traded off, issues related to community and purity are usually perceived of as in some way non-negotiable and absolute—or, as put by Gigerenzer, "not up for sale" (2007: 206).

What is the effect, then, of conventional economic reasoning, which reinforces the idea that economic life is only about rational individual choice, impersonal money, and self-interested calculation? It both undermines the emotional base for much actual moral action and focuses attention away from norms related to community or sacredness. Research now suggests that putting people in an analytical rather than feeling frame of mind—for example, having people do calculations in advance of being asked to make a choice—can lead to a fading of ethical concerns and ethical emotions such as guilt (Zhong, 2011). People seem to act more generously when they are *not* given time to engage in ratiocination (Rand, Greene et al., 2012). Framing a decision as being merely "business" or "legal" or otherwise (presumably) "technical," it seems, now tends to draw our attention away from its moral aspects (Bazerman and Tenbrunsel, 2011). To the extent, then, that people associate economics with calculation and impersonality, the bodily responses we generally rely on to alert ourselves to ethical concerns may become even more suppressed. Also, to the extent that people seem to behave more self-interestedly as they believe others are doing the same (Margolis, 1982), economists' images of ubiquitous self-interest can become a self-fulfilling prophecy (Frank, Gilovich et al., 1993).

But defining economics around models of individual rational choice is only one option. A far better one, with a longer history, is to think of economics as being about how societies organize themselves to support human life and its flourishing (Nelson, 1993)—or about how they fail to do so. Such a "provisioning" definition of economics encompasses both markets and families, both money and care. The neurological and psychological research reveals that when we say that economics is about "rational choice in the face of scarcity," we stack the deck in favor of individualism and selfishness. Contrast this to saying that economics is about "who gets to eat and who does not." The latter packs a visceral punch and directs us toward investigating social relations.

Conclusion

Economists' self-assured pronouncements about basic economic "laws" and "mechanisms" have had a tremendous effect on the thinking of many noneconomists, including businesspeople, judges, sociologists, philosophers, and the public at large. In regard to ethics, this effect has been very negative, encouraging the belief that business and commercial life are intrinsically moral (due to the "invisible hand"), immoral (due to an elevation of greed and profit), or a-moral (due to a presumed a-social, mechanical nature). But the very image of the economy as mechanical was simply an invention of economists. The economy is, in reality, deeply social and dynamic, and is as moral or immoral as we make it through our own individual, business, and public actions.

This chapter is not an ad hominem ethical indictment of individual economists. The aspirations behind some of the most bizarre and harmful turns taken by the economics discipline may actually have been laudable at some place and time, and from some angle. For example, aspirations toward objectivity and individualism can indeed be good counteractives to sloppy assertions and overbearing communitarianism. It is not that economists as a group have sought to do harm (though some may be opportunistic), but the fact that the values pursued are *unbalanced* (Nelson, 1996) that has led to deep injuries to our moral imaginations. Economists share a general responsibility as a profession: To the extent we do not explicitly reject and combat the one-sided assumptions of neoclassical orthodoxy, and work to replace them with more ethical (and realistic) alternatives, we perpetuate the drinking of poisoned water.

To noneconomists, this chapter is intended to encourage a certain skepticism about economics as it has been taught, and also skepticism about the messages of many who call solely on government action or utopian transformation for ethical relief. It is meant to encourage moving beyond simplistic ideas into realizing that economic life is what we make it. Engagement with ethical issues could improve our economic lives, right here and right now.

References

2005. In Re The Walt Disney Company Derivative Litigation. *907 A.2d 693*, Delaware 2010. In eBay Domestic Holdings, Inc. v. Newmark, et.al. *C.A. No. 3705-CC*, Delaware.

Bazerman, Max H., and Ann E. Tenbrunsel. 2011. *Blind Spots: Why We Fail to Do What's Right and What to Do about It*. Princeton, NJ: Princeton University Press.

Becker, Gary S. 1981. *A Treatise on the Family*. Cambridge, MA: Harvard University Press.

Benería, Lourdes. 2003. *Gender, Development, and Globalization: Economics as if People Mattered*. London: Routledge.

Bookchin, Murray. 2005. "What Is Social Ecology?" In *Environmental Philosophy: From Animal Rights to Radical Ecology*, edited by M. E. Zimmerman, J. B. Callicot, K. J. Warren, I. J. Klaver, and J. Clark, pp. 462–478. Upper Saddle River, NJ: Pearson Prentice Hall.

Bratton, William W. 2011. "At the Conjunction of Love and Money: Comment on Julie A. Nelson, Does Profit-Seeking Rule Out Love? Evidence (or Not) from Economics and Law." *Washington University Journal of Law and Policy* 35: 109–115.

Caplin, Andrew. 2008. "Economic Theory and Psychological Data: Bridging the Divide." In *The Foundations of Positive and Normative Economics: A Handbook*, edited by A. Caplin and A. Schotter, pp. 336–372. Oxford: Oxford University Press.

Collins, James C., and Jerry I. Porras. 1994. *Built to Last*. New York: Harper Business.

Dasgupta, Partha. 2005. "What Do Economists Analyze and Why: Values or Facts?" *Economics and Philosophy* 21: 221–278.

Dasgupta, Partha. 2007. *Economics: A Very Short Introduction*. Oxford: Oxford University Press.

Dees, J. Gregory, and Peter C. Cramton. 1991. "Shrewd Bargaining on the Moral Frontier: Toward a Theory of Morality in Practice." *Business Ethics Quarterly* 1(2): 135–167.

de Goede, Marieke. 2005. "Resocializing and Repoliticising Financial Markets: Contours of Social Studies of Finance." *Economic Sociology: European Electronic Newsletter* 6(3): 19–28.

Drèze, Jean and Amartya Sen. 1989. *Hunger and Public Action*. Oxford: Clarendon.

Eisler, Riane. 2008. *The Real Wealth of Nations: Creating a Caring Economics*. San Francisco: Berrett-Koehler.

Fehr, Ernst, and Armin Falk. 2002. "Psychological Foundations of Incentives." *European Economic Review* 46: 687–724.

Folbre, Nancy. 1994. *Who Pays for the Kids? Gender and the Structures of Constraint*. London: Routledge.

Folbre, Nancy, and Julie A. Nelson. 2000. "For Love or Money—Or Both?" *Journal of Economic Perspectives* 14(4): 123–140.

Folbre, Nancy, and Julie A. Nelson. 2006. "Why a Well-Paid Nurse Is a Better Nurse." *Nursing Economics* 24(3): 127–130.

Frank, Robert H., Thomas Gilovich, et al. 1993. "Does Studying Economics Inhibit Cooperation?" *Journal of Economic Perspectives* 7(2): 159–171.

Freeman, R. Edward. 1984. *Strategic Management: A Stakeholder Approach*. Boston: Pittman.

Friedman, Milton. 1982. *Capitalism and Freedom*. Chicago: University of Chicago Press.

Fullbrook, Edward, Ed. 2003. *The Crisis in Economics: The Post-Autistic Economics Movement: The First 600 Days*. Economics as Social Theory Series. New York: Routledge.

Gentile, Mary C. 2010. *Giving Voice to Values: How to Speak Your Mind When You Know What's Right*. New Haven, CT: Yale University Press.

Gigerenzer, Gerd. 2007. *Gut Feelings: The Intelligence of the Unconscious*. New York: Penguin Books.

Goodwin, Neva, Jonathan Harris, et al. 2013. *Microeconomics in Context.* Armonk, NY: M.E. Sharpe.

Goodwin, Neva, Jonathan Harris, et al. 2013. *Macroeconomics in Context.* Armonk NY: M.E. Sharpe.

Green, Tom L. 2012. "Introductory Economics Textbooks: What Do They Teach about Sustainability?" *International Journal of Pluralism and Economics Education* 32: 189–223.

Greene, Joshua, and Jonathan Haidt. 2002. "How (and Where) Does Moral Judgment Work?" *Trends in Cognitive Sciences* 6(12): 517–523.

Greene, Joshua D., R. Brian Sommerville, et al. 2001, September 14. "An fMRI Investigation of Emotional Engagement in Moral Judgment." *Science* 293: 2105–2108.

Groenewegen, John, Ed. 2007. *Teaching Pluralism in Economics.* Cheltenham, UK: Edward Elgar.

Habermas, Jürgen. 1981. *The Theory of Communicative Action.* Boston: Beacon.

Haidt, Jonathan. 2001. "The Emotional Dog and Its Rational Tail: A Social Intuitionist Approach to Moral Judgment." *Psychological Review* 108(4): 814–834.

Haidt, Jonathan. 2006. *The Happiness Hypothesis: Finding Modern Truth in Ancient Wisdom.* New York: Basic Books.

Healy, Kieran, and Marion Fourcade. 2007. "Moral Views of Market Society." *Annual Review of Sociology* 33: 285–311.

Kahneman, Daniel. 2003. "Maps of Bounded Rationality: Psychology for Behavioral Economics." *American Economic Review*: 1449–1475.

Keller, Evelyn Fox. 1985. *Reflections on Gender and Science.* New Haven, CT: Yale University Press.

King, Mervyn. 2004. "The Institutions of Monetary Policy." *American Economic Review* 94(2): 1–13.

Kitcher, Philip. 2011. *Science in a Democratic Society.* Amherst, NY: *Prometheus* Books.

Longino, Helen. 1990. *Science as Social Knowledge: Values and Objectivity in Scientific Inquiry.* Princeton, NJ: Princeton University Press.

Maier, Mark H., and Julie A. Nelson. 2008. "Testing Economics: Does the National Economics Assessment Test High Schoolers on Economic Literacy or Economic Ideology?" *Dollars & Sense* 275: 24–28.

Margolis, Howard. 1982. *Selfishness, Altruism, and Rationality: A Theory of Social Choice.* Chicago: University of Chicago Press.

McCloskey, Deirdre N. 2006. *The Bourgeois Virtues: Ethics for an Age of Commerce.* Chicago: University of Chicago Press.

Mill, John Stuart. 1836. "On the Definition of Political Economy; and On the Method of Philosophical Investigation in That Science." *London and Westminster Review*: 1–29.

Modigliani, Kathy. 1993. *Child Care as an Occupation in a Culture of Indifference.* PhD dissertation, Wheelock College.

Morgan, Jamie. 2014. "Pluralism, Heterodoxy and the Prospects of a New Economics Curriculum." *Association for Heterdox Economics.*

Nelson, J. A. 2013. "Ethics and the Economist: What Climate Change Demands of Us." *Ecological Economics* 85(1):145–154.

Nelson, Julie A. 1993. "The Study of Choice or the Study of Provisioning? Gender and the Definition of Economics." In *Beyond Economic Man*, edited by M. Ferber and J. A. Nelson, pp. 23–36. Chicago: University of Chicago Press.

Nelson, Julie A. 1996. *Feminism, Objectivity and Economics.* London: Routledge.

Nelson, Julie A. 2006. *Economics for Humans*. Chicago: University of Chicago Press.
Nelson, Julie A. 2011*a*. "Broader Questions and a Bigger Toolbox: A Problem-Centered and Student-Centered Approach to Teaching Pluralist Economics." *Real-World Economics Review*, issue no. 58.
Nelson, Julie A. 2011*b*. "Does Profit-Seeking Rule Out Love? Evidence or Not from Economics and Law." *Washington University Journal of Law and Policy* 35: 69–107.
Nelson, Julie A. 2011c. "For Love or Money: Current Issues in the Economics of Care." *Journal of Gender Studies (Ochanomizu University)* 14: 1–19.
Nelson, Julie A., and Steven M. Sheffrin. 1991. "Economic Literacy or Economic Ideology?" *Journal of Economic Perspectives* 5(3): 157–165.
Norberg-Hodge, Helena. 2002. "Buddhism in the Global Economy." In *Mindfulness in the Marketplace: Compassionate Responses to Consumerism*, edited by A. H. Badiner, pp. 15–27. Berkeley, Parallax Press.
Paine, Lynn Sharp. 2002. *Value Shift*. New York: McGraw-Hill.
Persky, Joseph. 1995. "The Ethology of *Homo economicus*." *Journal of Economic Perspectives* 9(2): 221–231.
Posner, Eric A., and David Weisbach. 2010. *Climate Change Justice*. Princeton, NJ: Princeton University Press.
Rand, David G., Joshua D. Greene, et al. 2012, September 20. "Spontaneous Giving and Calculated Greed." *Nature* 489: 427–430.
Reardon, Jack, Ed. 2009. *The Handbook for Pluralist Economics Education*. London: Routledge.
Robbins, Lionel. 1935. *An Essay on the Nature and Significance of Economic Science*. London: Macmillan.
Romero, Jake. 2011. "The Trouble with Principles: Or, How to Not Lose Friends and Alienate People When Learning Economics." *Naked Capitalism*. Retrieved from http://www.nakedcapitalism.com/2011/12/the-trouble-with-principles-or-how-to-not-lose-friends-and-alienate-people-when-learning-economics-occupywallstreet-ows.html
Sen, Amartya. 1992. "Objectivity and Position." The Lindley Lecture, *University of Kansas*.
Smith, Adam. [1776] 2001. *An Inquiry into the Nature and Causes of the Wealth of Nations*. New York: P. F. Collier & Son.
Smith, Yves. 2010. *Econned: How Unenlightened Self Interest Undermined Democracy and Corrupted Capitalism*. New York: Palgrave Macmillan.
Stout, Lynn A. 2011. *Cultivating Conscience: How Good Laws Make Good People*. Princeton, NJ: Princeton University Press.
Warren, Karen J. 2000. *Ecofeminist Philosophy: A Western Perspective on What It Is and Why It Matters*. Lanham, MD: Rowman & Littlefield
Watson, David. 2005. "Against the Megamachine: Empire and the Earth." *Environmental Philosophy: From Animal Rights to Radical Ecology*, edited by M. E. Zimmerman, J. B. Callicot, K. J. Warren, I. J. Klaver, and J. Clark, pp. 470–495. Upper Saddle River, NJ: Pearson Prentice Hall.
Zelizer, Viviana A. 2005. *The Purchase of Intimacy*. Princeton, NJ: Princeton University Press.
Zelizer, Viviana A. 2011. *Economic Lives: How Culture Shapes the Economy*. Princeton, NJ: Princeton University Press.
Zhong, Chen-Bo. 2011. "The Ethical Dangers of Deliberative Decision Making." *Administrative Science Quarterly* 56: 1–25.

CHAPTER 11

ECONOMISTS' ODD STAND ON THE POSITIVE–NORMATIVE DISTINCTION

A Behavioral Economics View

JOHN B. DAVIS

Economists' Odd Stand on the Positive–Normative Distinction

There has been much change in recent economics ranging from theoretical innovation to new methods of research (Davis, 2008); indeed so much so that there seems to be less and less consensus today over how economics ought to be defined in terms of scope and essential content. I suggest, however, that one important unchanging aspect of economics remains especially central to its identity as a distinct discipline, if not to its definition: economists' positions on the positive–normative distinction. Here we see little disagreement among economists and little change in what economists think today from what they thought when Lionel Robbins asserted that interpersonal comparisons of utility implicitly involve ethical claims and should be excluded from the science of economics. Further, their view on the subject distinguishes them from most other social scientists who also differentiate the positive and the normative but generally do so in a far less severe way than economists.

Why has this part of the identity of economics so strongly resisted change when so much else in economics has undergone change? This question is even more perplexing in light of the fact that economists' position on the positive–normative distinction was rejected a half century ago by those who are far more expert on the subject, namely philosophers, who saw the positive–normative distinction as a naïve vestige of prewar logical positivism, and who, like other social scientists, have since worked with a far more nuanced view of the positive and the normative. Economists' view of the positive–normative distinction is thus an odd one: their position is basically indefensible but they remain steadfast in their conviction that it is correct at a time when they have changed their views of many other matters in economics. Thus amidst all this change, the positive–normative distinction is arguably now even more important to the identity of economics. Such a state of affairs calls out for more attention and investigation, despite the fact that as an official non-issue in economics few seem to see much reason to address it.

This chapter examines economists' odd stand on the positive–normative distinction. It first traces the distinction to logical positivism, and discusses the now well-established reasons that the standard view is indefensible, in order to show the exceptional status of the issue and its special importance to economics. But it is obviously not enough to review the longstanding critique of positivism because it has had little influence in economics for more than a half century. Thus the chapter sets out how economists' view of the positive–normative distinction might be explained by applying economic theory to economists: developing a behavioral economics account of economists' behavior on the subject. Just as behavioral economics is used to explain the choices of economic agents, so can it be used to explain the choices of economists as economic agents. Of course there are different ways this explanation could be developed because the various psychological heuristics that psychologists and behavioral economists have investigated are quite versatile in their application and interpretation. However, to provide what would count as a sort of mainstream behavioral economics explanation I rely on one of the most well demonstrated heuristics and widely employed types of arguments. Specifically, I apply the basic idea of reference dependence, and one of the main claims that prospect theory makes about human psychology, namely that people are loss-averse: a "salient characteristic of attitudes to changes in welfare is that losses loom larger than gains" (Kahneman and Tversky, 1979: 279). At the same time, the behavioral economics explanation of economists' behavior offered here is also modified from what prevails in many such explanations to reflect the disciplinary dimension of economists' behavior. Economists know they are members of the economics profession, and they socially identify with it. This needs to be part of what is involved in explaining how they interpret their choices. Behavioral economics explanations often ignore social identity effects because social identity is not involved in experiments that focus primarily on how psychological heuristics operate in general. But when we investigate decision makers in an explicit professional or disciplinary context, social identity should not be ignored. In the discussion that follows the goal is to explain the behavior of a representative type of decision maker: economists who value highly their identity as economists. This characterization clearly may not fit all individual economists.

The second section traces the standard view of the positive–normative distinction in economics back to positions that the logical positivists developed in the 1930s regarding facts and values, which drew on David Hume's earlier empiricist thinking and claims about the difference between "is" and "ought" statements.[1] I argue that Lionel Robbins essentially adopted the logical positivists' view in his famous definition and characterization of economics, employed it in his paradigmatic critique of interpersonal utility comparisons, and helped put in place the value neutrality view of the positive–normative distinction that most economists continue to hold. The third section reviews how philosophers' postwar rejection of logical positivism was associated with a rejection of the fact/value dichotomy and Hume's guillotine. The purpose here is to show that economists' understanding of the positive–normative distinction lacks reasonable foundations. The fourth section then looks at one of the many ways in which philosophers have subsequently rethought the relationship between facts and values, namely Hilary Putnam's fact–value "entanglement" view. Putnam's view is modified slightly in order to directly address Robbins' particular understanding of value neutrality as specific to ethical values. The fifth section turns back to the economics profession, and argues that economists embrace at least four ethical value judgments, despite their espousal of value neutrality. To explain this odd stance, the sixth section offers a behavioral economics explanation of economists' attachment to value neutrality. The seventh section concludes with brief comments on the identity of economics.

Before proceeding, let me add something here about what motivates this chapter. Probably because of their thinking about the positive–normative distinction, most economists believe being a good economist entails no ethical responsibilities other than honesty in research. That view is seriously mistaken by virtue of the tremendous influence economics has on people's lives. Thus one goal of this chapter is to try to encourage economists to reflect more on the ethical implications of their work. If economists were persuaded that economics is not value-neutral, then perhaps their contributions to economic policy might be ethically better informed and better suited to the purpose of improving policymaking.

Logical Positivism and the Fact–Value Dichotomy

Logical positivism, as derived from the interwar Vienna Circle (Hands, 2001: 72ff), had as its central principle a criterion of meaningfulness called the verifiability principle. The logical positivists classified all scientific statements or propositions either as analytic, which were tautological or true by definition (and thus trivially meaningful), or as synthetic a posteriori, which were meaningful in that they could be shown to be empirically true or false. They distinguished synthetic a posteriori propositions from synthetic

[1] Positivism and value neutrality have multiple origins in economics and social science, including Auguste Comte and his 19th and 20th century followers (see Mongin, 2006). I focus on the influence of the logical positivists because they were contemporaneous with Robbins and did much to set the tone for professional thinking on methodology in economics in the years that followed.

a priori ones, which also made claims about the world but were not subject to empirical verification. Immanuel Kant had argued that synthetic a priori propositions such as Newton's laws were universally true and thus meaningful. However, the logical positivists believed that synthetic a priori propositions could never be proved empirically true or false, and accordingly argued that allowing them to be regarded as scientific knowledge opened the door to a wide range of arbitrary claims about the world. It is worth noting that this view was developed at a time in Europe when racist and nationalist ideas were regularly claimed to be scientific, and that members of the Vienna Circle were among those personally exposed to violence and abuse in the name of such views. In any event, the verifiability principle claimed that scientific statements needed to be subject to empirical investigation to be seen as scientifically meaningful, and as a corollary all other statements were deemed "metaphysical." Its basis lay in positivist philosophies of science and especially in the empiricist thinking of David Hume.

Hume had made a distinction similar to the logical positivists' analytic–synthetic distinction 200 years earlier when he distinguished between matters of fact and relations of ideas (Hume, 1739, 1978). The fact–value dichotomy was a consequence of this distinction. Hume characterized statements that express matters of fact as "is" statements, and complained that "systems of morality" commonly switched from "is" statements to "ought" or "ought not" statements without ever explaining this "new relation" (Hume, 1739, 1978: 469–470). Thus Hume's Law, or the Humean guillotine as the fact–value dichotomy came to be called, is generally associated with the idea that one cannot infer statements about values from statements about facts. But behind this idea lies an even stronger claim, namely, that there are no matters of fact about values. For example, it can never be a fact that murder is morally wrong. Indeed if "ought" statements did refer to facts, then there would be a way of moving to them from "is" statements by linking sets of facts. So Hume's Law depended not so much on the different linguistic characters of "is" and "ought" statements as on his view that values and value judgments could never be matters of fact, a view he defended by differentiating between the origins of facts and values. Facts had their basis in the world in that they are ideas that "resemble" the world. In contrast, values are ideas that Hume believed had their basis in our minds and derived from our "passions" and "sentiments." This was not a very good argument, as there could be facts about our "passions" and "sentiments" just as there are facts about the world. But the association of facts with the world and values with the mind stuck, and from this it was subsequently inferred that facts are objective and could ground science, whereas values are subjective and had no place in science.

Thus when the logical positivists adopted Hume's Law and his empiricism, they also adopted his view that values were inherently subjective. Their primary goal had been to demarcate science from non-science (Boumans and Davis, 2010: 9ff). Thus it was not necessary to go on to characterize ethics, theology, literature, and so forth, which were clearly not science but instead metaphysical, nor was it necessary to see these domains as subjective in a pejorative sense. But early followers of logical positivism who discussed values and value judgments, such as A. J. Ayer (1946) and Charles L. Stevenson (1944), settled on precisely this meaning in a companion doctrine termed emotivism.

Following Hume, Ayer characterized value judgments and moral statements as expressions of our feelings and attitudes, or as "emotings." Stevenson was more subtle, and allowed that value judgments and ethical language could have both descriptive and emotive meaning, but believed the latter was nonetheless essential and independent of the former. The implication for both was that values and ethics occupied a domain in which persuasion and expression mattered, because they lacked objective basis. This meant that there was no way to say objectively that there was right or wrong or good or bad, and that language expressing such judgments was simply a matter of one expressing one's feelings to others.

This is basically the view that Robbins adopted in his famous definition of economics and critique of interpersonal utility comparisons as being motivated by value judgments (1932; Davis 1990, 2005).[2] Indeed, he went further than Ayer and Stevenson to treat ethical disagreements as not just expressions of feelings and attitudes, but also as irresolvable contests for power. Arguing that contests for power were always over either means or ends, and associating economics with the investigation of means and ethics with contests over values, Robbins asserted the following:

> If we disagree about ends it is a case of thy blood or mine—or live and let live according to the importance of the difference, or the relative strength of our opponents. But if we disagree about means, then scientific analysis can often help us resolve our differences. If we disagree about the morality of the taking of interest (and we understand what we are talking about), then there is no room for argument (Robbins, 1932: 134).

The problem with interpersonal utility comparisons for Robbins, then, was that they were essentially value judgments based on people's feelings of utility, and saying one person got more utility from some amount of consumption than another made a value judgment that credited one person with more power over consumption (Hands, 2012: 222ff). That person's subjective end, in effect, was counted more strongly than others' ends, and so to keep economics scientific and free of power contests interpersonal utility comparisons had to be excluded from economics. Interpersonal utility comparisons thus became the paradigm example of how values damaged economic science.

Robbins lived through the same period as the logical positivists, and was no less concerned than they that science might become a battleground for contesting ideologies. Thus he also thought it imperative to remove from science those grounds on which such contests might be played out, namely, wherever value judgments were made. The expression of this commitment was the idea that science is value-neutral. Of course the recommendation that science be value-neutral is a value judgment, so it might be

[2] David Colander and Huei-Chun Su (2015) argue that John Neville Keynes and John Stuart Mill played an important role in Robbins' thinking about the positive–normative distinction. The view in this chapter is that logical positivism in the 1930s was particularly influential in regard to the subjective nature of value judgments.

argued that Robbins' position was self-refuting. But it seems fair to say that his view of the matter was more nuanced. He presumably recognized that economists' investigation of means entailed making value judgments about how one ought to carry out one's investigations. These kinds of value judgments are what Mark Blaug termed methodological value judgments (Blaug, 1998), and though scientists can disagree about how science ought to be practiced, these values are generally not those that generate power conflicts, or at least not the kind associated with clashing social ideologies. Thus the values Robbins really wanted excluded from economic science were those associated with ethics and morality. Consequently, a corollary to his value-neutrality view is that methodological values employed in economics hold no special implications for ethical values. The former are essentially benign, and merely part of the everyday practice of science. It is important to keep this meaning of value neutrality in mind as we proceed, because saying there are methodological values in economics to refute Robbins' view targets something he accepted and found unproblematic, and because the truly fundamental issue behind the idea of value neutrality is that ethical values such as what is morally good or right cannot be a part of a scientific economics. This latter stronger view of value neutrality, however, is precisely what philosophers have rejected.

Philosophers' Postwar Rejection of Logical Positivism and the Fact–Value Dichotomy

The principal signpost in postwar philosophy's turn against logical positivism is W. V. Quine's attack on the analytic–synthetic distinction (Quine, 1953). Quine's basic point was that there are many propositions or statements in science that cannot be easily characterized as either analytic or synthetic a posteriori. He took this position partly because he thought the logical positivists had mischaracterized analytic statements—the language of mathematics and logic—which as true by definition and not as matters of fact were supposed to be independent of matters of fact or what can be shown to be empirically true about the world. Quine, who was influenced by American pragmatist philosophers, believed that mathematics and logic possessed many conventional elements. That is, they relied on customary value judgments that could reflect anything from claims about what good reasoning entailed to views about the value of mathematics and logic to society. Thus he thought it was wrong to say analytic statements were trivially true. How they were otherwise to be understood is a large philosophical question, particularly in regard to how matters of fact entered into the language of mathematics and logic, which need not be addressed here. What is important is that Quine's doubts about the logical positivists' view of analytic statements created doubts about the whole analytic–synthetic distinction, and this then stimulated philosophers' further reflection on the logical positivists' understanding of synthetic a posteriori statements.

The basic idea that synthetic a posteriori statements were true as a matter of fact seems straightforward and uncontroversial. The logical positivists took observation sentences to be paradigmatic examples, such as the sentence "the sky is blue," which could be verified by looking to see if as a matter of fact the sky was blue. This meant that each observation sentence was to be individually evaluated according to its correspondence to the world, and one carried out the evaluation of a set of empirical scientific claims sentence by sentence in sequential inspections of the world. By the late 1930s, however, even before Quine's critique, this simple model had undergone significant revision. Observation sentences clearly could not be evaluated individually, because not all the language used to express them corresponded to observational features of the world. For example, in physics terms such as "electron" and "charge" were not definitional (thus not derived from analytic statements), nor were they observable, and accordingly it was conceded by the logical positivists that they needed to be "taken as primitive" (Carnap, 1938), whatever that meant. Admitting theoretical or abstract terms in this way was nonetheless still thought to be consistent with the logical positivists' overall view if whole collections of observation sentences taken together could be said to produce successful predictions about the world.[3] Synthetic a posteriori statements, that is, were still essentially matters of fact, and the analytic–synthetic distinction still seemed to hold.

But the admission of theoretical or abstract terms and acceptance of the idea that individual observation statements could not be evaluated individually opened the door to an entirely different view of matters of fact that Quine's doubts about the analytic–synthetic distinction and thoughts about analytic statements now fostered. If analytic statements contained conventional elements that were important in determining the nature of mathematics and logic, it seemed fair to say that scientific theories contained conventional elements that were also important in determining what counted as a matter of fact. But this implied that synthetic a posteriori statements were no longer pure observation statements. Whereas the logical positivists had thought observation occurred through inspection of the world, the view was now that scientific conventions determined how that inspection was to be carried out. The concept of "inspection" was obviously far too simplistic as a representation of how scientists organized their empirical research. This meant that what counted as a fact reflected how a collection of sentences was assembled and investigated by scientists to produce an acceptable scientific theory. Scientific theories thus displaced scientific statements as the principal unit of understanding, and facts then provided evidence for theories according to how evidence was to be interpreted in a given theory. Thus the rejection of the analytic–synthetic distinction ultimately changed philosophers' understanding of science to being about theories rather than statements, and produced a more subtle view of what facts are. This raises the issue of what were the consequences of this shift for the analytic–synthetic distinction companion—the fact–value dichotomy.

[3] This predictionist extension of logical positivist thinking was also at the root of Milton Friedman's instrumentalist methodology for economics (Friedman, 1953).

Corresponding to the idea that there is no sharp line between analytic and synthetic statements is the idea that there is also no sharp line between facts and values—despite the clear differences that exist between some "is" statements and "ought" statements. This insight followed directly from the changed status of facts in post-positivist philosophy, and from the recognition that conventional aspects of scientific theories often depend on value judgments about how theories should be constructed. Such judgments can include value judgments about the significance of theoretical or abstract terms and about how evidence is to bear on theories' predictive capacities. At the very least, then, the fact that values underlie scientific practice and play a role in determining what counts as fact means that the fact–value dichotomy cannot be sustained. Note how this discredits Hume's argument about the linguistic difference between "is" statements and "ought" statements. Hume also reasoned in terms of individual sentences when he used this distinction to infer a metaphysical divide between facts and values. But when we think in terms of scientific theories rather than individual sentences, it turns out that these linguistic differences tell us very little about facts and values. Rather, the act of drawing a linguistic distinction between "is" statements and "ought" statements apparently conceals rather than reveals how values and facts are closely connected in scientific theories. Thus it cannot be argued that language alone tells us what is objective and subjective in science. For that matter, it is no longer clear what it means to talk about what is objective and subjective in science. There surely is something subjective in scientists relying on conventions and values to determine what counts as scientific knowledge. But is scientific knowledge then subjective or objective precisely because it depends on established conventions regarding scientific practice? I leave these important questions aside, and return to the main issue here: Robbins and value neutrality.

To be clear, the preceding argument applies specifically to what Blaug referred to as methodological value judgments, not to the sort of value judgments associated with ethics. So economists could still reject the analytic–synthetic distinction and the fact–value dichotomy while still maintaining a value neutrality that specifically identifies ethical values as the types of values that have no place in economic science. This is the view that I believe is enshrined in the textbooks. It separates positive economics, seen to be free of ethical commitments, from normative economics, which employs a value-neutral positive economics in ethically guided policy decision making. But philosophers question even this view of the fact–(ethical) value dichotomy. The following section presents Hilary Putnam's influential arguments on this score.

Putnam's "Entanglement" View of Facts and Values

Putnam makes an argument like Quine's, though not with respect to the classification of statements in science but rather with respect to the classification of concepts in language. Whereas Quine said many statements are neither purely analytic nor purely synthetic a posteriori, Putnam, addressing the associated fact–value dichotomy, says that many concepts we employ in ordinary language and science are neither purely descriptive nor purely normative but are somehow descriptive *and* normative. Further, Quine was critical of the logical positivists' intention to reform science by imposing a philosophical regime upon it using the analytic–synthetic distinction to demarcate science from non-science. Similarly, Putnam is critical of the logical positivists' intention to "*rationally reconstruct* our language . . . to make a "sharp and clear" distinction between value terms and descriptive terms" (Putnam, 2002: 24.). His basic position is that science develops within the confines of ordinary language, and replacing its natural form of expression with a regimented formal logical language, as, for example, was promoted in the logical empiricist program developed by Rudolph Carnap (1928), is likely to distort the meanings of the concepts we employ. In particular, Putnam argues, ordinary language concepts commonly "entangle" facts and values, where the criterion for "entanglement" is that these concepts cannot be understood and we cannot say what the fact of the matter is on subjects to which they are applied, unless we recognize the value judgments we make in using those concepts.

Consider, then, the logical positivists' idea of an observation term, such as would appear in observation sentences. On their view, observation terms are purely descriptive concepts, free of values, which have their meaning solely in virtue of how they correspond to some feature of the world. Putnam asks us to consider whether this view fits someone who aims to factually describe a Roman emperor, and uses "cruel" as observation term (Putnam, 2002: 24ff). It is clearly not the case that the term "cruel" simply corresponds to some feature of the world in the way that the term "blue" can be said to correspond to the color of the sky. It also not the case that "cruel" is an abstract theoretical term like "electron" that refers to nothing in the world, since clearly some Roman emperors actually had the characteristic of being cruel. Perhaps one might associate the property of being cruel with certain neurological states of human beings in order to still be able to treat "cruel" as a value-free observation term. But Putnam believes that this is not what most people are thinking of when they speak of cruelty. Cruel Roman emperors may well have been in certain brains states when they were cruel, but cruelty is generally described in psychological rather than neurological terms. The conclusion we need to draw, he then argues, is that cruelty is not a value-free concept. "Cruel" is still an observation term, but an "entangled" one that requires value judgments, so that we fail to accurately describe the behavior of cruel Roman emperors if we omit these value judgments. That is, our descriptions are objective because they reflect value judgments we make.

To be sure, the logical positivists were not much concerned with psychological descriptions, and instead focused on natural science terms with physics as their model. Thus they had little reason to be concerned about value-entangled terms such as "cruel," because natural science does not employ psychological descriptions where they tend to arise. Relatedly, the natural sciences generally employ highly specialized vocabularies, which lack the nuances of ordinary language. Thus it could be said in their defense that the issue was less a matter of reconstructing ordinary language, as Putnam charges, and more a matter of using technical scientific language precisely. Note, then, what this implies about economics. Putnam could be correct on the whole about the "entanglement" of facts and values in ordinary language, but his view could still be set aside by economists more or less in the spirit of logical positivism were they to model economics on the natural sciences. Consequently the issue would then be the nature of the vocabulary in economics.

Economic methodologists, in fact, have debated the issue of whether economics relies on ordinary language concepts—what has been referred to as "commonsensibles"—especially in connection with debate over whether economics is realistic (Guala, 2012; Hands, 2012). Is the important concept of preference, for example, an ordinary language term or commonsensible with potential value dimensions subject to Putnam's strictures, or is it an abstract theoretical term fully defined in axiomatic terms? What the truth of the matter is (if there is one) may be less important than whether economists elect to treat concepts in economics in a formal technical way on the model of the natural sciences. Then, even if the analytic–synthetic distinction and the fact–value dichotomy are flawed doctrines, as philosophers have argued, economists might proceed as if they were de facto acceptable principles by practicing economics in such a way as to exclude the interpretation of economic concepts most likely to give rise to value-entangled commonsensibles thinking. Note that many of those concepts that might fall into the ordinary language commonsensibles category—what are referred to as folk psychology concepts such as concern agent beliefs, preferences, and so forth—are like value-entangled descriptive terms. Thus the strategy economists could adopt to preserve the fact–value distinction is to insist that these are formal concepts, and that folk psychology has no place in economics. This view has recently been given especially strong statement in a critique of behavioral economics that claims that this approach relies on folk psychology and therefore is not scientific (Gul and Pesendorfer, 2008).[4] What, then, is the relevance of Putnam's entanglement view to economics?

First, suppose that in economics technically defined terms function as substitutes for ordinary language terms, do not operate per se like ordinary language terms, and are thus ostensibly immune to the entanglement critique. If Putnam is right that science develops within the confines of ordinary language, then it would still be reasonable to argue that technical terms' ordinary language associations are somehow preserved despite their redefinition. That is, the substitution of technical meanings for ordinary meanings must derive the former from the latter, or else the technical term is not a derivation but an entirely new concept. Then it could be argued that the fact–value entanglement that concepts have in ordinary language would be somehow implicit in technical concepts as well. Of course one could resist this view, and say that technical concepts such as the axiomatically defined preference concept are entirely new concepts and are not derived from ordinary language concepts despite their resemblance, though then

[4] Gul and Pesendorfer's argument is often seen as a defense of revealed preference theory, but the suggestion here is that its appeal might be more a matter of its implicit defense of value neutrality.

it would be difficult to say that their subject matter was still people's decision behavior. What would an axiomatically defined preference concept be about if it were not a formal representation of what people ordinarily understand (if less rigorously) by the meaning of the term "preference?" Most economists likely thus believe that the technical concepts in economics are derived commonsensible concepts.

Second, suppose that because technical concepts are not ostensibly value-entangled, the effect of their derivation from ordinary language is to produce fact–value entanglement in an indirect rather than a direct way, specifically at the level of the theories in which they are employed rather than at the concept level. That is, if terms are technical, the theories in which they operate are nonetheless about ordinary economic life, and this indirectly value-entangles those terms. Then the technically defined axiomatic preference concept could still be said to be value-free itself, but the economic theory in which it is employed could nonetheless be shown to exhibit the fact–value entanglement Putnam ascribes to concepts. This modification of Putnam's view consequently moves the analysis from how individual terms are evaluated to how the theories in which they appear are evaluated (as Quine argued). If his criterion for fact–value entanglement at the level of the concept is that we cannot understand what the concept describes unless we understand the value judgments we make in using it, then the modified Putnam criterion for fact–value entanglement would be that we cannot understand the explanations these theories provide unless we understand the value judgments we make in these theories.

Of course there are good reasons to be skeptical of this reformulated view. One could agree that technical vocabularies are derived from ordinary language, yet also argue against Putnam that their formal expression specifically suppresses or neutralizes the value associations of the latter. This was indeed essentially the rationale the logical positivists offered for their logical empiricism research program (Hands, 2001: 82ff). At the same time, it could be replied that post-positivist philosophy offers broad grounds for a reformulated Putnam entanglement view in the idea that theory construction involves many conventional elements and methodological values, so that theories, even when formulated in specialized vocabularies, clearly contain value judgments. But as methodological value judgments generally do not involve ethical value judgments, it remains an open question whether this reformulation of Putnam's view successfully challenges the standard value neutrality conception of economics in the stronger sense that says positive economics is free of normative ethical judgments. The following section accordingly puts this issue to the test by asking whether standard economic theory with its technical vocabulary nonetheless presupposes ethical value judgments.

Four Ethical Value Judgments Standard Economic Theory Makes

For the sake of the argument, then, let us assume that the concept of a preference in economics is not an ordinary language commonsensible and is a technical term that is ostensibly free of value associations. Further, it seems fair to say that in standard economic theory the concept of a preference is foundational to standard Walrasian equilibrium explanations of markets that are characterized as Pareto-efficient or Pareto-optimal, where that concept describes a particular relationship between individuals' preferences. Specifically, the first fundamental theorem of welfare economics (known as the Arrow–Debreu theorem) states that any Walrasian equilibrium, defined in terms of individual preference maximization, is Pareto-efficient (Mas-Colell et al., 1995, Chapter 16). If the standard view regarding the neutrality view holds, then this explanation should be value-neutral, and no ethical value judgments are made (though methodological value judgments are allowed). Is the first fundamental theorem of welfare economics indeed free of ethical value judgments?

One rationale for the Pareto concept was established when economists came to believe that cardinal interpersonal utility comparisons rested on value judgments, and should therefore be excluded from economics. Interpersonal utility comparisons had been previously employed to argue that low-income individuals gained more utility from a given additional income than high-income individuals lost were their income reduced by the same amount, so that transferring income from high-income to low-income individuals increases total utility. Robbins' critique of interpersonal utility comparisons was that they were based on ethical value judgments, so it followed that it could not scientifically be established that low-income individuals indeed gained more utility from additional income than high-income individuals lost from reduced income. Under the influence of his arguments, most economists ultimately rejected interpersonal utility comparisons and gave up the cardinal utility concept, making the Pareto concept the key welfare evaluation concept in standard economics. What the Pareto concept consequently does is rule out total utility-increasing income transfers between individuals by saying that no individual's preference satisfaction can be compared with that of any other individual. A state of affairs is accordingly Pareto-efficient when no individual can acquire greater preference satisfaction except at the expense of someone else. Note, then, that there are at least four important ethical judgments that this reasoning involves.

First, that Pareto judgments require that all individuals' preferences have the same weight in terms of preference satisfaction irrespective of their many other social characteristics is an ethical value judgment associated with saying what counts in judgments of well-being. Interpersonal utility comparisons presuppose a different weighting principle, namely, that utility satisfaction should also reflect people's income levels, on the grounds that more consumption for low-income individuals than for high-income individuals generates more total utility. Whether we look at preference satisfaction apart from people's social characteristics or at it in light of their social characteristics clearly involves making an ethical value judgment. Robbins' complaint that interpersonal utility comparisons are subjective only concerns their feasibility, and ignores the ethical issues associated with determining what counts. Further, though the ordinal meaning of preference underlying the Pareto concept is technically defined, clearly the concept is still connected to the commonsensible preference idea, as Pareto judgments concern how real-world preferences should be addressed in economic policy choices. Thus when the technical preference concept is used to explain efficiency, it makes an "entangled" ethical value judgment.

Second and relatedly, because Pareto judgments necessarily count all individuals equally in terms of preference satisfaction, distributional issues regarding the distribution of preference satisfaction are completely set aside. Distributional issues arise in ethics in connection with the concepts of fairness and justice. Preference satisfaction, however, is a well-being concept in ethics, where the focus is on what it is that makes people well off. It is a teleological ethical concept framed in terms of ends, whereas fairness and justice concern what is right, a deontological type of ethical concern. Thus when one employs Pareto judgments, one is effectively saying that distributional issues are not an ethical priority, or more strongly, that well-being is the only value priority. This by itself is an ethical value judgment. But the Pareto concept also makes an implicit ethical value judgment about what is fair or just. In cases where it is Pareto efficient to increase the preference satisfaction of one very well off individual though all other individuals are not as well off, the implicit ethical judgment made is that it is fair or just to do so (or at least not unfair to do so). Thus Pareto reasoning is not only "entangled" with the ethical issue regarding whose well-being counts, but also with ethical issues regarding the relation of teleological to deontological ethics.

Third, Pareto efficiency judgments ignore the content of preferences, and this also, we can see, indirectly constitutes an ethical value judgment. Put aside the case of preference satisfaction that results in harm to others, such as involved in racist or sadistic preferences, as these would violate Pareto judgments. Rather consider frivolous preferences that cause no one harm, such as are associated with such things as fashion, sports loyalties, and hobbies. On the standard view, the satisfaction of these preferences is a Pareto improvement that increases well-being. But if we say that some preferences are truly frivolous (allowing we can disagree over which ones), then it is hard not to conclude, as Thomas Nagel did (1986, Chapter 9), that our preferring things in itself has no moral content. What we should say is that we attribute value to what we prefer in virtue of the valuable nature of those things themselves. If we say instead that preference satisfaction is always valuable irrespective of the value of the things preferred, then what we are in effect arguing is that the freedom to satisfy one's preferences is what is valuable, as argued by libertarians (Nozick, 1974). So remaining agnostic about the content of preferences implicitly makes an ethical judgment that freedom to prefer what one prefers trumps all other values. Thus though the Pareto concept is a technical term in economics, the analysis which it employs entangles its meaning with the value of freedom, and moreover with one particular interpretation of the concept of freedom.

Fourth, the Pareto principle provides a specific welfare conception of well-being, that is, well-being explained in terms of preference satisfaction. But there are many other welfare concepts of well-being that are put aside, and this thus constitutes an ethical value judgment. Within the utility welfare framework itself, cardinal utility is a measure of well-being that can be explained in terms of desire satisfaction. Another conception of welfare well-being is subjective happiness, where this can be understood in terms of individuals' reports of perceived happiness. However, one can also speak of well-being using concepts not framed in terms of welfare at all. An example of the latter is the idea of a just society, as when one says one's well-being is greater in a just society. As noted previously, the Pareto principle says nothing about justice, so it is not only selective in its welfare basis for well-being, but also excludes non-welfarist well-being ideas. Multiple ethical value judgments on multiple levels are thus made when one uses the Pareto concept, despite the fact that economists generally regard the Pareto concept as a value-neutral, descriptive technical term.

If we take the concept of preference satisfaction and Pareto efficiency judgments as foundational to standard economics theory, then, the reformulated Putnam fact–value entanglement view accurately describes that theory. As a technically defined idea, the preference concept may be ostensibly value-free, but the role it plays in explaining equilibrium outcomes as Pareto-efficient requires numerous ethical value judgments. Economists consequently promote one ethical vision of the world while claiming that economic science is a positive value-neutral subject, and extol the positive–normative distinction while systematically violating it. How are we to understand this odd combination of beliefs? One might reply that economists pay little attention to philosophers and arguments such as the preceding one, and are simply unaware of how untenable their thinking is on facts and values. Their professional practice is highly empirical in emphasizing data and evidence, and perhaps they would revise their views on this subject were they more exposed to these issues. But this seems an inadequate response because though it is understandable that philosophers' arguments might be remote for economists, the ways in which ethical judgments operate in Pareto thinking are not any more difficult to understand than many other complex conceptual issues in economics. Moreover, economists are surely aware that Pareto-based policy recommendations are ordinarily contested from other ethical perspectives. Thus the section that follows offers a behavioral economic analysis of economists' steadfast attachment to the positive–normative distinction.

A Behavioral Economics Interpretation of Economists' Value Neutrality View

Behavioral economics investigates the psychological dimensions of economic decision making. From an economics of scientific knowledge perspective (Hands, 2001: 365ff), economists themselves can be said to engage in economic decision making to the extent that their research and scientific activity have economic motivations. Economists clearly recognize that some types of research are more conducive to career advancement than others, so it seems reasonable to say that economic motivations have an influence on economists' research choices. Accordingly it makes sense to ask whether the economically motivated decisions economists make also have psychological dimensions. Taking prospect theory (Kahneman and Tversky, 1979) as our guide for how to understand the psychological dimensions of choice means that we should see choices as being framed by reference points.

> An essential feature of the present theory is that the carriers of value are changes in wealth or welfare, rather than final states. This assumption is compatible with basic principles of perception and judgment. Our perceptual apparatus is attuned to the evaluation of changes or differences rather than to the evaluation of absolute magnitudes. When we respond to attributes such as brightness, loudness, or temperature, the past and present context of experience defines an adaptation level, or reference point, and stimuli are perceived in relation to this reference point. (Kahneman and Tversky, 1979: 277)

But though current wealth or welfare constitutes a generic sort of adaptation level or reference point appropriate to economic choices in general, in more specific choice contexts reference points presumably more closely reflect the nature of those choices. What sorts of reference points, then, might operate in regard to economists' research choices?

When we ask how economists make choices as economists, that is, with an awareness of being economists, their professional social identity might function as a powerful reference point for the choices they make. In social identity theory, when one acts on a social identity, one acts as a representative agent of that social identity (Tajfel et al., 1971). In behavioral economics terms, then, when economists are economically motivated to make research choices that they believe a representative economist would make, one such research choice they would likely make would be to support the standard value neutrality view, because, as textbooks demonstrate, that view is generally seen as representative of standard economics. In effect, just as economists recognize that some types of research are more conducive to career advancement than others, so they would recognize that contesting the standard value neutrality view would likely be inimical to career advancement. This explanation offers one way of understanding the odd circumstance that economists remain attached to a position that philosophers and other social scientists have long rejected as indefensible. That their position is indefensible is irrelevant for them, because the choice to support value neutrality is a psychological one motivated by career and identity considerations, not one motivated by a reasoned evaluation of the position itself.

Returning to prospect theory, we also find that the theory provides a way of saying something about economists' degree of attachment to value neutrality. "Strictly speaking, value should be treated as a function in two arguments: the asset position that serves as reference point, and the magnitude of the change (positive or negative) from that reference point" (Kahneman and Tversky, 1979: 277). The interpretation then given to the value function that substitutes for the standard utility function is that people generally exhibit loss aversion.

> A salient characteristic of attitudes to changes in welfare is that losses loom larger than gains. The aggravation that one experiences in losing a sum of money appears to

> be greater than the pleasure associated with gaining the same amount. (Kahneman and Tversky, 1979: 279)

Economists' value function, when we address the research choices they make that concern value neutrality, would exhibit loss aversion if they felt that those arguments they might make that would potentially undermine value neutrality "loom larger" as losses than arguments they might make that reinforce the position as gains. That is, when their social identity as economists acts as a reference point for the choices economists make, and an important component of this social identity is the value neutrality position, then a way of understanding the strength of their attachment to the position is to say economists feel that their standard economics social identity would likely be jeopardized by giving any more than cursory attention to the subject. Indeed, the sense that the position could suffer losses is probably well-founded in that economists are presumably aware that their view of value neutrality is not shared by many outside economics. Consequently investing in potential gains to the position by making further arguments for it is not attractive. To avoid potential losses relative to their social identity as economists, the best course of action is to ignore the subject altogether.

A behavioral economics explanation of economists' attachment to value neutrality accordingly not only tells us why economists remain attached to an indefensible position, namely, that as a social identity reference point its content and meaning are simply irrelevant to them as economists; it also tells us, when we impute a prospect theory representative value function to economists, that on loss aversion grounds any discussion of the subject should be avoided if at all possible.

Ironically, behavioral economists also generally subscribe to the standard value neutrality view, and see prospect theory as providing an "adequate descriptive model" for explaining choice behavior under risk (Kahneman and Tversky, 1979: 263; cf. Heukelom, 2011). Indeed, the value function that prospect theory employs as a replacement for the standard utility function basically has the same preference-based welfare characteristics, so that it can be argued that prospect theory also makes ethical value judgments such as reviewed in the previous section. This does not mean that a behavioral economic analysis of economists' attachment to value neutrality should be set aside. It rather means that behavioral economics' analysis applies reflexively to itself as well, so that following the expanded reading of Putnam's argument provided earlier we should say that prospect theory is no less value-entangled than standard utility theory.

Concluding Comments on the Identity of Economics

Previously I argued (Davis, 2008) that over its history economics has regularly reproduced itself as a core-periphery structure in which rival approaches compete in the periphery to occupy the core and be identified with economics, and core positions in economics change over time. A core-periphery account accordingly provides an account of the identity of economics whereby the discipline can undergo change but retain recognizably distinct core content. One issue this view leaves open is why some approaches and not others come to occupy the core of the discipline. Presumably part of the answer concerns the social uses of economics (though surely not all successful approaches are socially useful). But another part of the answer might concern how dominant approaches selectively admit and filter content adopted from peripheral approaches. For example, game theory came into the core of economics in the 1980s but only in the form of noncooperative game theory. Thus though over the long history of economics the core of the field has been occupied by very different types of approaches, in the short run changes in the core are generally gradual. On a filter view, however, the adoption of content from peripheral approaches in the long run can be either consistent with core views or ultimately disruptive of them. If game theory is an example of the former case, then experimentalism might be an example of the latter, as evidenced by the evolution of Vernon Smith's thinking about standard theory. Smith began his experimental work expecting to confirm most economic standard assumptions, and this helped introduce experimental research into economics. Over time, however, he increasingly found himself disconfirming them (Smith, 2010), and this can be seen as having had a disruptive effect on standard economics. This state of affairs can possibly be due to the filtering processes in a discipline working nonmonolithically on a variety of levels with limited forward-thinking. It is perfectly possible, then, that new ideas seen initially to be consistent with existing core conceptions later turn out not to be.

What might we say in this regard with respect to value neutrality? It is probably fair to say that all the new approaches in economics today basically share standard theory's value neutrality position. Behavioral economics is not unique in this regard. Thus with this barrier to entry missing some of their contents (or indeed entire approaches) could enter the core of economics in the future. But there is an important difference between the new approaches in economics and standard theory on value neutrality. Whereas the basis for value neutrality in standard economics lies in Robbins' arguments, the new approaches in economics with their different conceptual origins, often in other sciences, not only lack clear connection to Robbins' thinking, but also appear to lack any specific arguments in favor of value neutrality. The value neutrality doctrine in economics has a specific history and a tight set of connections to general equilibrium theory and Pareto judgments. But the new approaches in economics generally operate with different theoretical foundations, and their attachment to the doctrine appears to be largely conventional. So it is not clear what basis the doctrine might retain in economics should these new approaches or elements from them become part of core economics. Of course this does not imply that economics will change its odd stand on value neutrality. But it might be a mistake to assume things will never change in this regard. What is called for, it thus seems, from those who would like to see economics adopt a more enlightened view of ethical values in economics, is careful attention to how the new approaches in the field address the issue, on the assumption that their interpretation of the matter might ultimately supplant the standard view.

Acknowledgments

Thanks for helpful comments on an earlier version of this paper go, without implication, to Dave Colander, Ricardo Crespo, George DeMartino, Wade Hands, Philippe Mongin, and session participants at the June 2013 Rotterdam International Network for Economic Method meetings and the June 2013 Vancouver History of Economics Society annual meetings where the paper was presented.

References

Ayer, A. J. 1946. *Language, Truth, and Logic*, 2nd ed. London: Gollancz.

Blaug, Mark. 1998. "The Positive-Normative Distinction." In *The Handbook of Economic Methodology*, edited by J. Davis, W. Hands, and U. Mäki, pp. 370–374. Cheltenham, UK: Edward Elgar.

Boumans, Marcel, and John Davis. 2010. *Economic Methodology: Understanding Economics as a Science*. Basingstoke, UK: Palgrave Macmillan.

Carnap, Rudolph. 1928. *Der Logische Aufbau der Welt*. Leipzig: Felix Meiner Verlag. (English translation by Rolf A. George, *The Logical Structure of the World. Pseudoproblems in Philosophy*. University of California Press, 1967.)

Carnap, Rudolph. 1938. "The Foundations of Logic and Mathematics." In *International Encyclopedia of Unified Science*, Vol. 1, part 1, pp. 139–214. Chicago: University of Chicago Press.

Colander, David, and Huei-Chun Su. 2015. "Making Sense of Economist's Positive Normative Distinction." Paper presented at the History of Economics Society annual meetings, June.

Davis, John. 1990. "Cooter and Rappaport on the Normative." *Economics and Philosophy* 6(1): 136–146.

Davis, John. 2005. "Robbins, Textbooks, and Value Neutrality." *History of Political Economy* 37(2): 191–196.

Davis, John. 2008. "The Turn in Recent Economics and Return of Orthodoxy." *Cambridge Journal of Economics* 32 (May): 349–366.

Friedman, Milton. 1953. *Essays in Positive Economics*. Chicago: niversity of Chicago Press.

Guala, Francesco. 2012. "Are Preferences for Real? Choice Theory, Folk Psychology, and the Hard Case for Commonsense Realism." In *Economics for Real: Uskali Mäki and the Place of Truth in Economic*, edited by A. Lehtinen, J. Kuorikoski, and P. Ylikoski, pp. 137–155. London: Routledge.

Gul, Faruk, and Wolfgang Pesendorfer. 2008. "The Case for Mindless Economics." In *The Foundations of Positive and Normative Economics: A Handbook*, edited by A. Caplin and A. Schotter, pp. 3–39. Oxford: Oxford University Press.

Hands, D. Wade. 2001. *Reflection without Rules: Economic Methodology and Contemporary Science Theory*. Cambridge: Cambridge University Press.

Hands, D. Wade. 2012. "Realism, Commonsensibles, and Economics: The case of Contemporary Revealed Preference Theory." In *Economics for Real: Uskali Mäki and the Place of Truth in Economics*, edited by A. Lehtinen, J. Kuorikoski, and P. Ylikoski, pp. 156–178. London: Routledge.

Heukelom, Floris. 2011. "Behavioral Economics." In *The Elgar Companion to Recent Economic Methodology*, edited by J. B. Davis and D. W. Hands, pp. 19–38. Cheltenham, UK: Edward Elgar.

Hume, David. 1739. *A Treatise of Human Nature*, edited by L. A. Selby-Bigge, 2nd ed. revised by P. H. Nidditch, 1978. Oxford: Clarendon Press.

Kahneman, Daniel, and Amos Tversky. 1979. "Prospect Theory: An Analysis of Decision Under Risk." *Econometrica* 47: 263–291.

Mas-Colell, Andreu, Michael D. Whinston, and Jerry R. Green. 1995. *Microeconomic Theory*. Oxford: Oxford University Press.

Mongin, Philippe. 2006. "Value Judgments and Value Neutrality in Economics." *Economica* 72: 257–286.

Nagel, Thomas. 1986. *The View from Nowhere*. Oxford: Oxford University Press.

Nozick, Robert. 1974. *Anarchy, State and Utopia*. New York: Basic Books.

Putnam, Hilary. 2002. *The Collapse of the Fact/Value Dichotomy and Other Essays*. Cambridge, MA: Harvard University Press.

Quine, W. V. 1953. "Two Dogmas of Empiricism." In *From a Logical Point of View*. Cambridge, MA: Harvard University Press.

Robbins, Lionel. (1932) 1935. *An Essay on the Nature and Significance of Economic Science*, 2nd ed. London: Macmillan.

Smith, Vernon. 2010. "Theory and Experiment: What Are the Questions?" *Journal of Economic Behavior and Organization* 73: 3–15.

Stevenson, Charles. 1944. *Ethics and Language*. New Haven, CT: Yale University Press.

Tajfel, Henri, Michael Billig, Robert Bundy, and Claude Flament. 1971. "Social Categorization and Intergroup Behavior." *European Journal of Social Psychology* 1: 149–178.

CHAPTER 12

THE COMPLEX ETHICAL CONSEQUENCES OF "SIMPLE" THEORETICAL CHOICES

ROBERT H. FRANK

MANY economists are reluctant to confront ethical issues directly, saying that whether an action is good or bad requires value judgments best left to philosophers. But that disclaimer rings hollow. Economics, after all, was founded by moral philosophers, and links between the disciplines remain strong. Today's economists are actually well positioned to contribute useful insights on ethical questions.

Adam Smith, the father of modern economics, was a professor of moral philosophy at the University of Glasgow. His first book, *A Theory of Moral Sentiments*, was published more than 15 years before his celebrated *Wealth of Nations*, which was itself peppered with trenchant moral analysis.

Then, as now, there were two competing schools in moral philosophy—consequentialists and deontologists. Consequentialists believe that the right course of action is the one that leads to the best overall consequences. Deontologists concede that consequences matter, but also stress that fundamental moral principles must be followed, irrespective of consequences. Smith himself clearly had consequentialist leanings, but there have always been serious scholars in both camps. Smith's spirited approach for tackling moral questions remains alive and well in economics.

In this chapter, I explore several areas of economics teaching and research (both abstract and applied) that have ethical substance, and that merit more careful thinking by a profession that is committed to recognizing and meeting its ethical duties. In the process, I'll attempt to defend three simple claims: (1) that the emphasis on narrow self-interest in economic models has had some regrettable side effects; (2) that economic analysis can help shrink the scope of disagreement about important moral questions, a point I'll illustrate by examining some of the concrete economic costs of the recent rise in income inequality; and (3) that the emphasis on ordinal preferences has handicapped our thinking about a broad range of ethical choices. Each of these claims bears not just on "doing good economics," but also on the broader responsibilities of economists as members of society.

The Corrupting Influence of the Self-Interest Model

A powerful attraction of economic models is their ability to predict people's behavior. Rational choice models assume specific preferences and then ask what options people will choose when confronted with specific constraints. The rich diversity of human preferences forces formal modelers to simplify, and perhaps the most common simplifying assumption is that people are self-interested. Most economists concede that other motives also matter, of course, but many argue that this particular assumption comes at little cost in realism. In the words of Gordon Tullock, for example, "the average human being is about 95% selfish in the narrow sense of the term."[1]

This self-interest assumption underlies the rational choice model's prediction that people will always defect in one-shot social dilemmas. Suppose, for example, that Tom and Bill must choose whether to cooperate or defect in a one-shot prisoner's dilemma. Tom knows that the best outcome overall would result if both parties cooperated, but he also understands that Bill's material incentives favor defection. And he knows that if Bill defected while Tom cooperated, Tom would get the lowest possible payoff.

So if Tom predicts that Bill will defect, he becomes more likely to defect himself, if only in self-defense. By encouraging such a prediction, it is plausible to conjecture that the economist's self-interest model makes Tom more likely to defect.

Economists might respond that their instruction has made Tom better able to survive in the bitterly competitive social environment we inhabit. Yet relatively high cooperation rates are often observed even in dilemmas involving complete strangers. A cooperation rate of more than 74 percent, for example, was observed in one study in which participants were allowed to communicate briefly about unrelated subjects before playing a one-shot prisoner's dilemma.[2]

Experiments from that same study found that economics majors were more than twice as likely to defect as students majoring in other subjects. Again, if studying the self-interest model encourages students to predict defection, that finding is hardly surprising. And many other studies have also found that economists are less likely than others to cooperate in social dilemmas.[3]

[1] Quoted in Mansbridge (1990: 12).

[2] Frank, Gilovich, and Regan (1993*b*).

[3] See, e.g., Marwell and Ames (1981); Carter and Irons (1991); Laband and Beil (1999); and Wang et al. (2011).

Many economists argue that the only promising way of dealing with social dilemmas is to eliminate them by changing people's material incentives—as, for example, by taxing congestion or pollution. But that's not always possible. For instance, it will never be practical to catch and punish violators who pour damaging toxins down their basement drains at midnight. In such cases, society's best bet may be to encourage people to cooperate, despite the edge they could gain by defecting.

Are those who are most responsive to such appeals hapless chumps? Not necessarily, at least if you believe that people are reasonably good at identifying people who won't defect in one-shot dilemmas. That's because someone with that ability can reap the substantial economic gains made possible by mutual trustworthiness.

For example, consider someone with a thriving local business who has an opportunity to open a branch outlet in a distant city. She's confident the business would succeed there, but cannot manage it herself and knows that any hired manager would be able to loot the business with impunity. She also knows that the gains from looting would exceed any salary she could pay the manager and that because there are many reasons besides looting that the business could fail, there would be no practical possibility of punishing a looting manager. But if she could hire a trustworthy manager, she could pay him a premium salary and still prosper. The important practical question, then, is whether she can identify such a manager.

To think about this question, imagine that you've just returned from a crowded concert to discover that you've lost an envelope containing $10,000 in cash that had been in your coat pocket. Can you name someone, not related to you by blood or marriage, who you feel sure would return the envelope (which has your name and address on it)? If so, then you can solve the social dilemma inherent in the branch outlet problem just discussed simply by hiring someone you've identified as trustworthy.

Cooperation can be a viable strategy even if people's ability to identify trustworthiness isn't perfect. Experimental evidence suggests that people are reasonably good at estimating what even near strangers will do in one-shot social dilemmas. In the aforementioned experiments in which the base rate of cooperation was 74 percent, subjects were asked to predict whether their partners would cooperate or defect. Because the base rate of defection was only 26 percent, an uninformative prediction would have been right 26 percent of the time by chance. Yet predictions of defection proved correct 58 percent of the time.[4]

If economics training boosts defection rates directly, it will also tend to boost them indirectly. That's because each time someone defects, he increases the base rate of defection in the relevant population, which increases others' estimates of the likelihood their partners will defect. Once the dust settles, the total losses from higher defection rates could be substantial.

Although self-interest is surely an important human motive, it is not the only motive. Those who cannot put self-interest to one side under the right circumstances are

[4] Frank, Gilovich, and Regan (1993*a*).

unlikely to prosper in most social environments. Economists should take care not to give the impression that defection is the "right answer" to the question of what a person should do in a one-shot social dilemma.

Is Rising Income Inequality a Bad Thing?

Most people earn their income by selling their services in labor markets. An attractive feature of this system is that it provides strong incentives to work hard and develop valued skills. The resulting higher incomes serve not just the direct interests of workers and their families; they also boost tax revenues, making better public services possible for everyone.

These attractions notwithstanding, most economists are reluctant to claim that the market-determined distribution of income is morally just. But rather than confront this issue directly, most seem content to relegate it to philosophers and others.

Many moral philosophers address inequality by invoking principles of justice and fairness.[5] But because they have been unable to forge broad agreement about what these abstract principles mean in practice, that approach has made limited progress. The more pragmatic cost–benefit framework favored by Smith is more promising, for it turns out that rising inequality has created concrete gains and losses that we can quantify. Rough estimates suggest that rising inequality has produced significant losses and few gains, even for its ostensible beneficiaries.

Recent research on psychological well-being has taught us that beyond a certain point, across-the-board spending increases often do little more than raise the bar for what is considered adequate. A CEO may think he needs a 10,000-square-foot mansion, for example, just because most of his peers have one. Although they might all be just as happy in more modest dwellings, few would be willing to downsize on their own.

People do not exist in a social vacuum, and economists have long recognized that demand depends heavily on context. As Adam Smith wrote in *The Wealth of Nations*, "A linen shirt, for example, is, strictly speaking, not a necessary of life. The Greeks and Romans lived, I suppose, very comfortably, though they had no linen. But in the present times, through the greater part of Europe, a creditable day-labourer would be ashamed to appear in public without a linen shirt, the want of which would be supposed to denote that disgraceful degree of poverty, which, it is presumed, nobody can well fall into without extreme bad conduct."[6]

[5] Notably, John Rawls (1971).

[6] Smith (1776: 715–716). More recently Thorstein Veblen (1899), James Duesenberry (1949), and others have emphasized the importance of social determinants of demand.

Community norms define clear expectations not just about what people should spend for clothing but also for many other important consumption categories. Because spending in every category also depends directly on income, changes in the distribution of income will inevitably give rise to changes in patterns of spending, which in turn will change the norms that shape expectations.

During the three decades immediately after World War II, incomes rose at about the same rate—slightly less than 3 percent a year—for families up and down the income ladder. Because income growth was balanced, spending growth was also balanced. But the pattern has been markedly different since the early 1970s. Since then, virtually all significant income growth has accrued to the top quintile of the income distribution, and gains have been similarly concentrated within even that group. This change has spawned a multitude of "expenditure cascades," whose first step is increased spending by top earners.

The rich have been spending more simply because they have so much more money than they used to. Their spending has shifted the frame of reference that shapes the demands of those just below them, who travel in overlapping social circles. So this second group, too, spends more, which shifts the frame of reference for the group just below it, and so on, all the way down the income ladder. These cascades have made it substantially more expensive for middle-class families to achieve basic financial goals.

Using census data for the 100 most populous counties in the United States, Adam Seth Levine, Oege Dijk, and I found that the counties where income inequality grew fastest also showed the biggest increases in symptoms of financial distress.[7] For example, even after controlling for other factors, these counties had the largest increases in bankruptcy filings.

Divorce rates are a second reliable indicator of financial distress, as marriage counselors report that a high proportion of couples they see are experiencing significant financial problems. The counties with the biggest increases in inequality also reported the largest increases in divorce rates.

Long commute times are a third footprint of financial distress, because families who are short on cash often try to make ends meet by moving to where housing is cheaper—in many cases, farther from work. The counties where long commute times had grown the most were again those with the largest increases in inequality.

In both cross-section and time-series data for Organisation for Economic Co-operation and Development (OECD) countries, increased income inequality is associated with longer hours of work.[8] This pattern is also consistent with the hypothesis that growth in inequality makes it more difficult for middle-income families to make ends meet.

The middle-class squeeze has also reduced voters' willingness to support even basic public services. Rich and poor alike endure crumbling roads, unsafe bridges, an unreliable rail system, and cargo containers that enter our ports without scrutiny. And many

[7] Frank, Levine, and Dijk (2010).

[8] See, e.g., Bowles and Park (2005).

Americans live in the shadow of poorly maintained dams that could collapse at any moment.

Economists who say we should relegate questions about inequality to philosophers often advocate policies, such as tax cuts for the wealthy, that increase inequality substantially. That greater inequality causes real harm is beyond doubt. But are there offsetting benefits?

There is no persuasive evidence that rising inequality bolsters economic growth or enhances anyone's well-being.[9] Yes, the rich can now buy bigger mansions and host more expensive parties. But the fact that the average American wedding now costs more than $30,000—roughly, a threefold increase since 1980—appears to have made no one any happier.

In short, the economist's cost–benefit approach—itself a longstanding important arrow in the moral philosopher's quiver—has much to say about the effects of rising inequality. We need not reach agreement on abstract philosophical principles of fairness to recognize that growing income dispersion has imposed considerable harm without generating significant offsetting benefits.

Although fairness may be difficult to define precisely, no one argues that rising inequality is required in the name of fairness. So maybe we should just agree that rising inequality is a bad thing—and ask whether something might be done about it.

Ethical Choice Depends on Intensity of Preference

Economists rightly believe that it is difficult to aggregate utility across people for the purpose of reaching welfare judgments. That skepticism led many in the profession to abandon the notion of cardinal utility if favor of an ordinal representation of preferences.

But that step came at a price. It led many economists to believe, or at least say they believe, that it is impossible to weigh one person's experience against another's. In an extreme example, some would insist that we have no basis for saying that when McCloskey is struck violently on the arm with a stick, she experiences a greater injury than when DeMartino is bit on the arm by a disease-free mosquito. Yet any reasonable observer must believe that McCloskey suffered greater pain. By ignoring such interpersonal differences in intensity of preference, we ignore information that could inform many important ethical judgments.

Yet economists have always had a very powerful way of aggregating intensity of preference across individuals. That would be the basic cost–benefit model, which constitutes the foundation of consequentialist moral theory. Economists are generally more

[9] For a survey of the relevant evidence, see Frank (2011, Chapter 10).

proficient in its use than the practitioners of other disciplines, and can add considerable value by applying it to ethical questions.

Many, perhaps even most, interesting ethical questions take the following simple form: "Can someone perform an action even though it will result in harm to others?" If gains and losses were really incommensurable across persons, that question would always be impossible to answer. But as Ronald Coase demonstrated, the use of willingness to pay often renders the relevant comparisons tractable.[10]

In Coase's example of the factory owner whose machinery disrupted the neighboring doctor's practice, the best solution to the problem was easily identified by comparing the factory owner's monetary cost of soundproofing his machines to the doctor's monetary cost of moving to a quiet location.[11] The incomes of the two parties were completely irrelevant for that comparison, although their incomes would clearly be affected by how the law chose to assign responsibility for noise damage.

But sometimes the incomes of parties affected by harmful activities play a direct role in determining the least costly solution to the problem. Suppose, for example, that Tom likes to play his trumpet late at night, which disturbs his neighbor Sam. Should the law restrain Tom's playing? To keep the discussion simple, let's suppose that legislators are considering only two options—banning music after 10:00 pm on weeknights or banning it after 11:00 pm. To decide which alternative would ameliorate the problem at lower cost, legislators would need two pieces of information: (1) the value to Tom of being able to continue playing until 11:00 rather than having to stop an hour earlier and (2) the value to Sam of having Tom stop playing at 10:00 rather than an hour later.

Tom would obviously like to be able to continue playing until 11:00, but how strongly does he feel about it? In cost–benefit analysis, the answer to this question is simple in principle, if not always easy to come up with in practice. It's the largest amount he'd be willing to pay to maintain his right to play until 11:00. Similarly, Sam's valuation of the right to have quiet starting at 10:00 would be the largest amount he'd be willing to pay to secure that right. Of course, if the two parties were simply asked how much they were willing to pay, they'd have clear incentives to overstate their responses if they knew that the timing of the noise ordinance depended on them. So as a practical matter, we often try to infer how much the respective parties would be willing to pay from indirect behavioral evidence—perhaps by comparing property values in otherwise similar communities whose noise ordinances kick in at different times.

But practical measurement problems would be the least controversial aspect of any proposal to base the solution to a noise problem on a comparison of the amounts that affected parties are willing to pay to have their way. Far more troubling would be the fact that willingness to pay depends so heavily on ability to pay. How much people would be willing to pay for an extra hour of quiet, or for the right to continue playing music for an extra hour, depends on many things—including their feelings about music, the

[10] Coase (1960). The examples discussed in this section are developed more fully in Frank (2011, Chapters 6 and 7).

[11] Coase (1959).

thickness of their apartment walls, and their work schedules. But willingness to pay also depends heavily on income. Holding all else constant, the more people earn, the more they're willing to pay to have their way.

The upshot is that Coase's approach to solving the noise problem will tend to tilt heavily in favor of the solutions preferred by those who have the most money. Suppose, for example, that Tom feels extremely strongly about being able to practice until 11:00, but his meager income enables him to pay at most $8 a day for the right to do so. And suppose that Sam is really not much disturbed by Tom's playing in the evening, but because he is extremely wealthy he'd be willing to pay $15 a day for the right to silence after 10:00. The Coase framework would then hold that the efficient solution to the problem would be to adopt an ordinance that prohibits noise after 10:00 pm. Yet when I poll students about what should be done in this example, most say the noise curfew should begin at 11:00.

When the 1960 Coase paper first appeared, much of the negative reaction from critics on the left was prompted by the perception that measuring costs and benefits by willingness to pay was morally tone-deaf, a gross violation of the principle that citizens should have equal rights irrespective of their incomes. But despite the intuitively compelling attraction of this statement, it's misguided. It accounts for our repeated failure to take actions that could benefit everyone.

Suppose, for example, that a community must decide whether to switch the format of its public radio station from all music to all talk. The two formats cost the same and all voters are indifferent between them except for the following three: One wealthy voter favors the switch and, with equal intensity, two poor voters oppose it. But because of their income differences, the rich voter would be willing to pay $1,000 to see the change enacted, while the poor voters would be willing to pay only $100 each to prevent it. Should the switch be made?

According to standard cost–benefit analysis, the benefit of making the switch is the $1,000 the rich voter would be willing to pay for it. Its cost is $200, the sum of what the two poor voters would be willing to pay to avoid it. The net benefit of making the switch is thus $800. The cost–benefit rule recommends adopting all options whose benefits exceed their costs. This rule thus says unequivocally that the format switch should be made.

Critics object, however, that using the cost–benefit test to resolve such issues offends the aforementioned important democratic value that each citizen's interests are entitled to equal weight in the eyes of the law. In the example just discussed, each interested party was assumed to feel equally strongly about the format switch. So why, critics ask, should the preferences of one wealthy voter trump those of two poor voters?

The question has obvious rhetorical force. There *is* something troubling about the prescription of cost–benefit analysis in such cases. This concern has made many governments reluctant to rely on it. Executive orders issued during the Clinton administration, for example, instructed federal agency heads to temper the results of cost–benefit analysis by distributional considerations.[12] If we were to completely temper willingness

[12] Clinton Executive Order 12866, 3 CFR 638 (1993).

to pay by ability to pay, the cost–benefit test in our radio example would become a simple head count. The proposed switch from all music to all talk would fail by a 2-to-1 margin.

Is that the right outcome? The question is not whether the prescription of cost–benefit analysis is troubling in some way, but whether some alternative decision rule would yield a better outcome.

One obvious consequence of abandoning cost–benefit analysis in this example is that failure to switch formats results in a net loss of $800—the difference between the $1,000 benefit forgone by the rich voter and the $200 in combined losses avoided by the two poor voters. That loss could easily be avoided. For example, the switch could be made conditional on the rich voter's payment of additional taxes of, say, $500, which could then be used to reduce the taxes of each poor voter by $250. Relative to the status quo, this move would improve the welfare of each voter.[13]

The rich voter may complain about having to pay extra taxes. But from her perspective, the alternative would be even worse. The $1,000 benefit she gets from the format switch is more than enough to compensate her for the additional levy. Similarly, although the two poor voters will not be pleased about losing their preferred all-music format, the alternative would be worse for them, too. By their own testimony, each is more than adequately compensated for the format change by the $250 tax reduction. Without the income transfer, all parties lose.

Some object that the government cannot legitimately impose such transfers. ("It's your money, and the government has no right to take if from you and give it to the poor!") But although this objection is commonly attacked on equity grounds, it's perhaps more transparently vulnerable on efficiency grounds.

In a democratic society, the interests of poor voters will receive attention one way or another. As in the example just discussed, ruling out income transfers often means that those interests will be addressed in other, more costly ways. Permitting such transfers, by contrast, creates the possibility of crafting policies that will advance the economic interests of rich and poor alike. Yet we cannot identify or implement those policies unless we're free to rely much more fully than we do now on willingness to pay; and this freedom can often be purchased only at the expense of a greater willingness to employ income transfers.

Before Coase, negative externalities were almost always discussed in terms of perpetrators and victims. But as Coase made clear, externalities are reciprocal in nature. The factory owner's noise makes life more difficult for the doctor, yes. But forcing the factory owner to eliminate the noise would make life more difficult for him. The two

[13] I am assuming, for the sake of this example, that the preferences underlying these willingness-to-pay values faithfully represent the underlying interests of those who hold them. As Sen (1977), Elster (1985), and others have argued, people often want things that don't serve their interests, while those who suffer deprivation sometimes lose the capacity to desire goods that they would otherwise recognize as valuable. Evidence of such divergences should of course be taken into account in cost–benefit analysis.

parties confront a problem because their aims are not fully compatible. And they have a shared interest in solving that problem in the least costly way.

That's an important insight for consequentialist ethical theory. As long as redistribution among the relevant parties is a practical possibility, a necessary condition for deeming an action to be ethical is that it be economically efficient—in the standard sense of creating the greatest surplus of benefit over cost, where cost and benefit are based on conventional willingness-to-pay measures.[14] Any action that fails to meet that test is one that fails to grant all affected parties the opportunity to pursue their respective visions of the good life to the fullest extent possible.

Concluding Remarks

I have argued that the emphasis on narrow self-interest in economic models appears to have undermined cooperation in one-shot social dilemmas. Economists would do well to refocus on the moral sentiments that figured so prominently in Adam Smith's thinking, and remind students that few employers are looking to hire or promote people who lack those sentiments. No one should be encouraged to believe that employers are completely without insight about potential employees' moral character.

I then attempted to show that intelligent application of cost–benefit analysis can help promote more widespread agreement about important moral questions. Regarding the question of whether rising income inequality is a bad thing, for example, agreement has been difficult to reach because people lack shared understandings of concepts like fairness that have been emphasized by philosophers. But even if we set fairness concerns to one side, plausible estimates suggest that rising inequality has created large costs and no significant benefits. That knowledge should surely inform the judgment about whether rising inequality has been a bad thing.

Finally, I argued that our profession's emphasis on ordinal preferences has handicapped our thinking about a broad range of ethical choices. The basic cost–benefit model suggests that in the absence of compelling barriers to redistribution, a necessary condition for an action to be ethical is that it be economically efficient. Anything that makes the economic pie larger necessarily makes it possible for everyone to receive a larger slice than before. That's not to say, of course, that all economically efficient actions are ethical. Many economically efficient actions are ethically offensive for distributional reasons. But surely efficiency does merit a more prominent role in discussions about ethical choices.

[14] Again, those measures should be adjusted, when appropriate, to reflect evidence that preferences and interests fail to coincide.

REFERENCES

Bowles, Samuel, and Yongjin Park. 2005. "Emulation, Inequality, and Work Hours: Was Thorsten Veblen Right?" *Economic Journal* 115: F397–F412.

Carter, John R., and Michael D. Irons. 1991. "Are Economists Different, and If So, Why?" *Journal of Economic Perspectives* 5: 171–177.

Coase, Ronald H. October 1959. "The Federal Communications Commission." *Journal of Law and Economics* 2: 1–40.

Coase, Ronald H. October 1960. "The Problem of Social Cost." *Journal of Law and Economics* 3: 1–44.

Elster, Jon. 1985. *Sour Grapes*. New York: Cambridge University Press.

Frank, Robert, Thomas Gilovich, and Dennis Regan. July, 1993*a*. "The Evolution of One-Shot Cooperation." *Ethology and Sociobiology* 14: 247–256.

Frank, Robert, Thomas Gilovich, and Dennis Regan. Spring 1993*b*. "Does Studying Economics Inhibit Cooperation?" *Journal of Economic Perspectives* 7: 159–171.

Frank, Robert H. 2011. *The Darwin Economy*. Princeton, NJ: Princeton University Press.

Laband, David N., and Richard O. Beil. 1999. "Are Economists More Selfish than Other "Social" Scientists?" *Public Choice* 100: 85–101.

Mansbridge, Jane (ed.). 1990. *Beyond Self-Interest*. Chicago: University of Chicago Press.

Marwell, Gerald, and Ruth E. Ames. 1981. "Economists Free Ride, Does Anyone Else?" *Journal of Public Economics* 15: 295–310.

Rawls, John. 1971. *A Theory of Justice*. Cambridge, MA: Belknap Press of Harvard University Press.

Sen, Amartya K. 1977. "Rational Fools: A Critique of the Behavioral Foundations of Economic Theory." *Philosophy and Public Affairs* 6(4) Summer: 317–344.

Smith, Adam. *The Theory of Moral Sentiments*. Retrieved from http://www.excellentfuture.ca/sites/default/files/Theory%20of%20Moral%20Sentiments%20Adam%20Smith.pdf

Smith, Adam. *An Inquiry into the Nature and Causes of the Wealth of Nations*. Electronic Classics Series 2005, edited by Jim Manis. Retrieved from http://www2.hn.psu.edu/faculty/jmanis/adam-smith/Wealth-Nations.pdf

Wang, Long, Deepak Malhotra, and J. Keith Murnighan. (2011). "Economics Education and Greed." *Academy of Management Learning & Education* 10(4): 643–660.

CHAPTER 13

GOOD, EVIL, AND ECONOMIC PRACTICE

TOMÁŠ SEDLÁČEK

In recent years there has been seen a growing effort to introduce ethics into economics. While this in itself is a welcomed effort, this makes it look like the body of economics is an ethical vacuoid, that it is ethically empty and this empty space simply needs to be filled with desirable ethics. The task at hand is more complicated: economics already has ethics, ethics of its own, ethics that it has been forging and preaching for decades and centuries. In order to make economic ethics aligned with our ethics (the ethics that we want) the task is then to replace already existing ethics with a new one.

So, while economics has been trying to pretend to be positivist, value-free, neutral, objective, analytical, technical scientific discipline, this paper will in fact argue that economic ethics has become a dominant moral school of today.

Old-new Prayer

There is an old prayer Lead me into the land of uprightness (Psalm 143: 10, King James Bible).

This is, surely, a strange quote to start an economic debate. "Lead us into the land of growth," or "plenty," or "prosperity" or "GDP growth" or "growth of utility/profit" would be much more likely silent prayers that one might hear under the analytical talk of professional economists and people who believe in the economy and live upon it today. I have started with this strange quote from a very old book just to show how our focus has shifted to a different goal, but the principle of the wish, the "prayer," remains.

Such language may come as a shock to the reader. Why should one expect to find a discussion of scriptures and prayer in a discussion of the ethics of an economist? Economics should be a positive, value-free science, and economists are the technicians of the economic machine: theirs is not to dictate its use, but merely to write its instruction manual. How could scriptures and prayer—things that we typically associate with the *normative* category of "religion"—possibly offer us any clue to the workings of this machine?

The contention of this chapter is that this is precisely the problem. The claim to positivity does not do away with moral categories or normative statements; instead, it hides them in the region of assumptions, which (consciously or not) affect our decision making. Or, more precisely: the claim to positivity masks the way in which *the claim to positivity is itself a normative claim* ("Economics *should be* a positive science" is itself a normative statement). Once this is understood, the perceived distance between religion and economics collapses, and the economist becomes a bizarre sort of spiritual guide. At the same time, economics itself becomes imbued with a sort of "religious" significance.

The goal of this vein of inquiry, one might say, is to understand the religious dynamic of the economist. What we find in this attempt is that our conventional view, in which the economist studies the mechanics of a value-free economic apparatus and communicates them to policymakers and public to use according to their more normative aims, becomes reversed: this "value-free" economic apparatus actually *gives the economist* a set of norms that are perceived and communicated as positive, impersonal "laws." Economics therefore does not avail itself of any normativity—instead, the normative process is merely *reversed*, with the *economy* deciding on the norms. Economics is no ethical vacuum, but a treasure trove of hidden ethical assumptions. We economists have thus become priests of the path to affluence[1]—not only technically, but also *morally*. And we must be aware of this—that is, we should fully know that we are creating a new sort of ethics, economic ethics.

(Economic) Body without a Soul?

The proper question to ask is not "does the economy work or not?" but rather, "does it work the way we *want it* to work?" The trouble is, the first question appears to be positivistic, while the second has a normative component to it (how *should* it work?) that must be addressed first. Nevertheless, even the first question is, in fact, implicitly normative, only our norms (what do we expect of economics?) have never been openly questioned. To make a mental image: a zombie will *work* very well (in its own definition), be very effective (it even reproduces by eating, so no time wasted here, they eat *and* re-produce at the same time), but without a soul, with an intent agenda and ethics of their own, the "system" will not work the way we "souled human beings" would *like it to work*. Zombies do not have a soul, they are just (animal) bodies at work, and while "undead" they do have a "life" and agenda of their own, detached from human life and a human agenda. Has the economy lost a human soul, having an agenda and life of

[1] As, for example, Richard Nelson shows in *Religion of Economics*.

its own, one that we can neither understand nor control? Have we been so concerned with its functionality that we have been unable to detect the presence or absence of a soul, intent, goal, *telos*? And if it has a soul and will of its own, what then is the soul of economics?

What Are the Beliefs and Ethics of Economics?

Even though economics appears to be a value-free and normative science, economics has beliefs and thus ethics of its own. But where are they hidden, if we are to be "positivists" and not talk about them? I will try to argue that we have put our soft, normative, ethical, and philosophical beliefs into the assumptions, and then we silently started believing in our own (allegedly "technical," yet ethical, philosophical, and theological) assumptions. For example, it is fine to technically say "let's assume human beings are rational." The problem begins when, later on in the evening in a pub, we actually say to our friends that "human beings *are* rational." This seems harmless at first, but something significant is taking place here. Saying "let's *assume I have* a million dollars" is not the same as "I *have* a million dollars." The problem is obvious—we started believing our own assumptions, the very myths we ourselves created. And here we find the beliefs and ethics of economics. The normative component of economics is in the *is* (the human being *is* rational—but what we really mean is that we *want* it to be so in our model case, which is a proxy for reality).

We economists (and whoever else believes in our economics) actually seem to believe in a basic triangle of three myths/beliefs—the (mysterious) *invisible hand* of the market, the (mysterious) *homo economicus*, and the (even more mysterious) *animal spirits*. Between these three points of the triangle lie our beliefs. We will treat each of these points individually.

Let us take, for example, the belief that human beings are rational-utility-maximizing-agents-able-to-calculate-order-and-measure-their-utility. This is not a mere innocent assumption; it has become a moral imperative (its OK to behave like that, in fact, one *should*; it's for the benefit of not just the actor, but the whole society—as the concept of the invisible hand teaches us). We economists pretend we are not telling people *what to believe* and *what to do*, but in fact, we are doing the exact opposite. We believe not to believe, but even that is nothing more (or less) than a belief. Notice how often we are asked to teach these *beliefs* ("this *is* how the economy functions") and *ethics* ("this *is* what should be done")—and how readily we do.

In daily language, we often substitute the words *think* and *believe*. To say "I *think* this is the way the economy works, this is good for society and this is bad" is the same as to say "I *believe* this is the way the economy works . . . ". How strange, when one thinks about it, that in our rational world which thinks of itself as void of beliefs, the two words that seem to be exact opposites (*think* and *believe*) are in fact very close to each other, often substituted freely, in daily talk.

We believe that we are teaching students of economics "to think like an economist." We should instead understand that we are teaching them "to believe like an economist." Of course, the natural question becomes: which one? Should they *think* (or believe) like Keynes, or Friedman, or Smith, or Mill or (to take a more extreme example) like Veblen, Schumpeter, Weber, or even Marx? Or was Marx not an economist? And where is the line?[2]

It is noteworthy that this ability needs to be taught: it is not natural per se to think like an economist. We *want* it to *become* a natural way of thinking, of believing, of looking at life, society, and social interaction, but natural it is not. It needs to be taught.

To a skilled dancer, the moves *become* natural, and he or she moves in a different way, even when not dancing. But the feeling of natural is a result of training, training that is itself not natural.

The very sentence "economics should be a positive science" is revealing when deconstructed. First, and most importantly, notice that this crowning claim of positivism is in fact a normative statement (*should be*). Second, this claim (more appropriately "request") also means that economics *is not* a positive science. If economics were a positive science, then a statement like the one above would be redundant (you do not hear pleas like this in physics). For why should we want it to be positive, if it were already so? Again the normative is located in the *is* (in assumptions and claims), it is in the reductionist approach (*what* you reduce to *what, what* is represented/proxied by *what*, and *what* becomes important [and what does not] in explaining the behavior of the world). So the models themselves appear positive and hard, but they cannot exist without the underlying assumptions—that all-too-rarely explored region to which we have "crowded out" the normative and the "soft."

In *The Hitchhiker's Guide to the Galaxy* by Douglas Adams, a computer is asked to answer the "ultimate question of the meaning of life, universe and everything." It computes for millennia and then comes with the only possible right, objective, scientific, positivist answer: the answer to the ultimate question is "42." Of course, that is the essence of the joke: this number alone makes no sense. Why? Because we do not know the context, the assumptions, the beliefs, the process. We get meaningless (but correct) answers like this when we ask a *soft* question of a *hard* science. My claim is that we see this in economics all too often. The "truth" does not lie in the results of the model; it lies in the surrounding (soft) context. Without the context, our analytical answers are equivalent to "42."

[2] Robert Frank (1993) has written about how economic students are "trained" in Econ 101 to become closer to the rational actor that the theory presumes. Khurana and Gintis (2008) also examine the same effect on MBA students who are taught the Friedmanian argument that the social responsibility of managers is to maximize profits, full stop.

Invisible Hand of the Market: The Unorchestrated Orchestrator?

Did we not once, when mankind was younger, believe in a Divine Orchestration (by a Divine Orchestrator)? This belief is far from gone; in fact, we have only substituted it with an Unorchestrated Orchestrator. To see this in action, one need only try to read economic commonplaces literally. When we do so, we find that they are quite religious: It is the "market" that will orchestrate us ("disturbed" by politics and regulation), lead us into the future, and become Providence that provides for us—generating more and more (of whatever we discover we want or feel we need). We call this economic growth.

Economics brings with it a body of ethics and beliefs. "The will of the market be done, on earth as it is in theory!" has become our prayer. Many hard-core economists believe in this Unorchestrated Orchestrator and our most important charge (like with gods) is that we should not meddle with its (or their) will. Not only are we to *give in* to its will, so to speak, but *its will* should become *our* will ("we wish your will be done"—whatever it is). Laissez-faire, laissez-passez! Let it be, let it work (itself)! No matter what you do, do not meddle and, above all, do not moralize *it*. In fact, let *it* moralize you, let the markets tell the policymakers what to do, let *it* choose the way. In this, economics has become normative— normative backwards. We are not supposed to give *it* norms or values; *it* will give *us* norms and values.

And what sort of values, one asks, does the economics give us? It tells us how to be rational (that is: profit maximizing), that it is good for everybody to be egoist, that we should be egoist, that we should be maximizing our utility, that we should not care about the effects of our business on others (that is the work of invisible hand of the market which turn the most malicious intents into public benefit), that we should care only about what could be immediately profitable to us, that real gifts do not exist ("there is no free lunch"), that we should cynically look at the world, that every act which appears altruistic is in fact profit seeking in disguise, be efficient, be hard working, etc. These are the key principles of economic ethics.

But back to the unorchestrated orchestrator. Although we economists talk about rational market actors and rational markets (the markets are even more rational than the sum of its participants) we actually believe the markets to be mysterious. They often have a logic of their own and what we really cannot explain, we "explain" with the "animal spirits." (Notice the frequent usage of the dubious term "market sentiments," which only really means irrational "market moods" or "feelings.") Furthermore, we economists pretend to know what is the true, "real" value of things, and we have our models to calculate it. Yet, in doing exactly this, we also imply that the markets are wrong in setting the "real" price. This is the true meaning of any statement such as "the current market ***price*** is higher/lower than its ***value***. Thus the imperative: Sell! Buy!" But how can we know what the real, fundamental, "ontological" ***value*** is, when only the price manifests? This statement collides with the belief that markets are rational (if value does not equal price, then markets are wrong). Uttering such a statement (which one hears all the time) means that the analyst must be in some way smarter than the market and have some secret insight into the *real value* (usually through some model), which the market has no access to or does not follow or believe in. (If it did, it would not diverge from it.) If markets *were* right, the price would always reflect its value – and there would be no word such as overvalued or undervalued in a vocabulary of an analyst. Note that the analyst often comments on the *present* discrepancy between price and value (the stock *is* overvalued), not on the future. In this case we often talk of "bubbles"—but a "bubble" means nothing less than that the markets are consistently and for prolonged periods of time *wrong*— misjudging the value. A true believer in markets should not even talk of bubbles, because doing so means that he or she understands something that the market (where people bet with their real money) does not. Talk of bubbles implies that the analyst is right where the market is wrong. The whole irony is emphasized when we realize that these models which come up with the "real, ontological"value of things (which deviates from market price) and which thus show how "irrational" or even ignorant the markets are, are based on the assumption that the markes are rational.

Growth as a Moral Solution

"Give us today our daily bread, and deliver us from evil" has been modified to "give us more and more and thus deliver us from evil." Our current system of *market democracy* (note that markets here come first, then democracy—this seems to reveal how we prioritize) is perceived as structured in such a way that it collapses when it does not grow. This is the fear, even *threat*, that one hears from most economists. So we must sacrifice whatever we need to in order to grow. The fundamental question is this: is economic growth a *result* of market democracy or has growth become a *conditio sine qua non* of market democracy?

Isn't the recent debate on growth (austerity vs. stimulation), to take a current example, also (or primarily) a moral debate? The imperative "we must grow" (otherwise markets—and with them our whole society—will collapse; there will be "financial Armageddon" . . . what stronger religious and mythical language could we use?) isn't really anything other than the statement "we want to be richer" in disguise. For we do not *have to* grow, we *want to* grow.[3] And the only way we measure *this growth* is in GDP, that is, in riches. The system is believed to need growth; it is believed to be unsustainable without growth.[4] That is *why*, officially, we "must" grow. And, as the argumentation often goes,

[3] Notice how often we substitute the word *I want* with the imperative *I must* in everyday language: we say *I have to* go now, where we should truly say *I want to* go now.

[4] This is why it is more appropriate to talk of a crisis of *growth-capitalism* rather than a crisis of capitalism as such.

we don't want growth for ourselves, but for the poor (the alleged trickle-down effect), for other countries, and so on. Even here we, unnoticed yet very quickly, argue ethically.

Growth has become the solution for our moral problems connected with economics. Imagine a situation where three people are sitting around a table, but on the table are only two beers. How should we divide it so as to be fair? Should we auction so that the richest person will have it and the poorest person around the table go without? Or should the lady have the right to have it? Should one who never tasted beer, or should an alcoholic, get the beer? Should the younger or the older? Should we share? This is, basically, an ethical question of diving national wealth—a question that has been, so far, solved by a magical third beer appearing—that is, growth. Problem solved: each can now have a beer, without any complaints or dilemmas.

The problem facing us today is that the third beer did *not* appear. And so we have to answer the ethical question of just distribution (of the cake which is for now, alas, not growing) *without* the trick. But this is a question that we have ceased to ask, because growth took care of it in our stead. We thus have become dependent on growth – yes growth makes everything easier, the problem is that it is not omnipresent in time and space. And it is unpredictable and flickering. Here it would be useful to stress that the desire for more is one of the oldest archetypes of mankind. It is one with which we have wrestled since time immemorial. It also serves as an example of the fundamental inseparability of ethics and economics—of how religious beliefs are interwoven with economics, and vice versa. Until now I have tried to show how much belief there is in economics. Now let's view the relationship from the opposite angle, asking how much economics there is in our (religious or traditional) beliefs.

The Ancient Archetype of Consumption

When dealing with consumption, and with wanting more and more even in a saturated situation, one is dealing with the most ancient religious and spiritual archetypes of our civilization. Even the original sin can be read from this economic perspective.[5]

The first ever case of consumption appears in the first book of the Bible, in Genesis. Here Eve and Adam consumed something they did not *need* nor really *want*. For most medieval theologians, the original sin was often considered to be of a sexual nature for some strange reason, for we read almost nothing of sex in the first chapters of Genesis[6]. On the contrary the word "eat" or consume appears 17 times from Genesis 2:4 to 3:19 (see, e.g., the New International Version translation). Hence there are good grounds for the "economic" interpretation of the original sin as a "sin of (over)consumption." Didn't

[5] For more on this please see *Und Schopping-center* and *Economics of Good and Evil*", chapter "The Need for Greed."

[6] The only one time one reads about sex is with a positive connotation: be fruitfull and multiply (Gen 1:28).

they, after all, live in Eden, the paradise of plenty? Yet it was not enough. This reflection can be also used to answer the question, How much is enough? Even in the spiritually and materially perfect Eden human beings felt discontent. The feeling of enough seems to never come from external, the word enough has to come from the inside.

The curse that Eve and Adam received was fundamentally economic, involving demand and supply. Eve was cursed by the "curse of demand": you will desire, you will want, but your desires will not be with you; they will be disjointed, somewhere else, and they will rule over you. You will never stop wanting. Your desire, your demand for more than you need or own or what has been given to you, a desire you could not control even in the perfect garden of plenty, will now never cease—and will control you. Your desires for more than is appropriate will be much more painful in the world of scarcity.

Adam then got the "curse of supply," or curse of labor. To paraphrase again: you will work by the sweat of your brow, production will not come easy to you, and even with the technology of the 21st century, you will not be able to be productive enough to provide for all the desires and demands, which will be ever-growing and never-ending.

And in fact this is the voice that we still hear today: demand more, because it is an imperative of our survival, *and* produce more, be more productive, more efficient in order to feed it.

It is interesting to see how this ancient curse echoes even today. We are still driving ourselves to desire more (desires that are not ours but manufactured elsewhere and that rule over us) and driving ourselves to produce more. In the words of Frank Knight, "The chief thing which the common-sense individual wants is not satisfactions for the wants he had, but more, and better wants."

Greed Is Good and Doubly-Holy Consumption

In one way, the silent unspoken moral philosophy of economics justifies exactly that—greed (considered evil by almost all religion) is in fact good (this is the point of Bernard Mandeville's *Fable of the Bees: or, Private Vices, Public Benefits*). What we perceive as evil is goodness in disguise. Note that in this economic interpretation, greed is not only good for the greedy, but also for the rest of society. In a more radical reading of the (in)famous line from the movie *Wall Street* "greed is good" (as controversial as it might sound), the problem today is really that there is not enough of it, that we need more desire for more. One can also see it in the discourse on consumption: consume more! Consuming is not good just for the consumer. In consuming the consumer performs a doubly-holy act since consumption is also vital for the economy, society, progress, and other valued goals. You not only help yourself, but you help others as well—an "egoist" thus becomes an "altruist" at the same time.

We should take note of the fact that when properly read, the ultimate argumentation for *egoism* is the resulting unintended *altruism; indeed, under the economist's logic* they become inseparable. The very argument is of a moral sort: the butcher of Adam Smith *is* (unknowingly) promoting the public good—and *that is why* his egoism should be fostered and not limited. The trick is *not* to think of the public good, but of one's own only. Otherwise, and ironically, the public good would not be achieved. If economics were truly egoist, or "ethics/value free," then no further argumentation, beyond personal egoism, would be necessary. But it is. Let's take the famous example of Adam Smith:

> It is not from the benevolence of the butcher, the brewer, or the baker, that we expect our dinner, but from their regard to their own interest. We address ourselves, not to their humanity but to their self-love, and never talk to them of our own necessities but of their advantages. He [the butcher] generally, indeed, neither intends to **promote the public interest, nor knows how much he is promoting it.** By preferring the support of domestic to that of foreign industry, he intends only his own security; and by directing that industry in such a manner as its produce may be of the greatest value, he intends only his own gain, and he is in this, as in many other cases, led by an **invisible hand** to promote **an end which was no part of his intention** . . . By pursuing his own interest he **frequently promotes that of the society more effectually than when he really intends to promote it.**[7]

So the butcher *does* serve the common good. If we were concerned only with our own interest, *why should we care* if it helps the society and others? The same argument can be heard later from Milton Friedman when it comes to the selfish-yet-socially-beneficial behavior of a profit-only-maximizing firm: "The social responsibility of business is to increase its profits."[8] The story goes that the firm seeks nothing other than its own egoistic aim, and yet in the pursuit of that aim it serves the public good.

So it is not only economic rationality that we teach our students in the classes of economics; it is also (or perhaps primarily) a specific sort of unnoticed, undercurrent (and thus uncensored) sort of ethics: not merely to "think like an economist" but also to believe like one and to act like one. Of course, you can put a lot of mathematics on top of it, but what lies beneath is ethical teaching of the purest form.

This is the "good news," the economic gospel that we tell the world: greed is good, it does not work against us, but for us. I do not want to dispute whether that economics ethic is proper or sinister—but merely to show the point that it *is* ethics that lies underneath economics and our teachings. This fact should be addressed and talked about in quite open fashion. We should stop pretending that we are value free and ethically

[7] Smith, *An Inquiry into the Nature and Causes of the Wealth of Nations*, 266 (1.2.2; 4.2.9). Emphasis mine.

[8] Or more extensively Friedman ends his article quoting his book *Capitalism and Freedom*: "there is one and only one social responsibility of business–to use it resources and engage in activities designed to increase its profits so long as it stays within the rules of the game, which is to say, engages in open and free competition without deception or fraud."

neutral. We are, in fact, exactly the opposite. Appearances are deceiving in this regard. While the vast majority of moral schools and philosophies try to somehow limit or discipline our wants, desires, demands, powers, consumption (except perhaps Nietzsche), we celebrate self-interest and greed, telling ourselves that these sentiments promote the public good. We, too, are moralists.

Displaced Ethics?

It is not sufficient to say, however, that we have merely disguised our ethics under "positive" science and math. The further point must be made that in doing so, we have effectively transferred the responsibility to engage our ethical precepts away from ourselves.[9] As the Austrian philosopher Ivan Illich points out, today ethics has moved from people to institutions. Institutions have become bearers of ethics in a highly specialized and detached society that, still, needs (or more precisely, *wants*) moral coordination. We no longer have to personally care for the sick, elderly, and poor, for instance—institutions do that in our stead, for us, vicariously, so to speak.

I have always found it ironic that economists who believe in the power of the spontaneous markets constantly want to change the institutions that govern (and thus constitute) the markets. They never seem to be happy with the way these institutions are. From a psychoanalytical perspective, one feels that the spontaneous urge and power of the markets is constantly being limited, held back, even suppressed by some Other—in this case institutions. For example, one gets the feeling when reading F. A. Hayek that formal and informal institutions both *enable* and also *limit* markets. This can only mean, again, that some of the institutions are good, and some are bad. So it is not a fight of the (good) economy *against* the (bad) institutions, regulations and so on, but *some* parts of the economy, battling with *some* parts of institutions and regulations.

Who would claim that there is something natural about our institutions? And even if we accept Hayek's reading of spontaneous institutions, why is the current stage considered natural? Was the state of capitalism more "natural" a hundred years ago, or will it be more natural a hundred years from now? And what can we do to make the institutions *more* natural? The system, it seems, cannot be left as it is. And that goes for the change of the system as well. The state we are in is not a natural status quo, but a result of the market-shaping-institutions, the work of politicians, lawyers, *and* economists.

Lets take an example of a semi-informal institution: GDP. On a practical and personal level, we do not really care. Who of us knows if his or her "personal GDP" was higher or lower from year to year (say, 2010/2011 inflation adjusted)? And if so, by exactly what percent? And here I don't want just rough estimates, but accurate to a decimal point. This information is easy to find (we have just to look at our tax documents), and yet few

[9] Slavoj Žižek has made this point from the beginning of his writing career—see his *The Sublime Object of Ideology*, Verso, 1989.

of us actually know. We do not know, because we do not care. Yet, when we elevate this number from a personal level (which should concern us most) to an abstract macro level, some magic appears: this number gains extreme prominence and importance. Especially when its growth is low or even negative, we are instructed by economists in what we must do and even sacrifice to restore the economy's health.

At the level of formal institutions, one can talk of "sinful structures" in which the individuals are all doing well and according to their best intentions, yet the result of their coordinated activity is some evil. This evil is of a collective nature and lies in institutions and is created by the structure. A small technical increase in some remote interest rate can have devastating effects on the lives of thousands of villagers, for instance—and the decision can be made by a well-meaning person, regularly devoting half of her income to charity, as the anthropologist David Graeber points out.[10]

Golden (C)age—Economics before Ethics

But it's not that economists are so greed-driven that we have completely forgotten how to think ethically; rather, what we seem to believe is that we will grow affluent enough to be ethical—*growth* is the answer to our moral problems. In fact, even classical economists talk about the Golden Age in this sense. The notion that economics *can save the world and contribute to ethics* has taken a form of social hope par excellence. David Hume believed that "if nature gifted us with a surplus of material possessions and everyone had enough of everything, then it would be certain that every virtue would blossom in that blessed state."[11]

John Stuart Mill, one of the fathers of economics,[12] famously stated: "I confess I am not charmed with the ideal of life held out by those who think that the normal state of human beings is that of struggling to get on; that the trampling, crushing, elbowing, and treading on each other's heels, which form the existing type of social life."[13] Sometime in the future, when we get past this kind of social life, we will achieve what Mill calls a *steady age*, when "no one desires to be richer."[14]

Thus we are led *by* economics, by the "existing type of social life," *to* ethics. Or more precisely, when ethics becomes sufficiently cheap, it is no longer a concern.

[10] See David Graeber, *Debt: The First 5000 Years*. Melville House, 2011.

[11] In Hume, *Selections*, 203–204.

[12] First published in 1848, Mill's work quickly became the bible of nineteenth-century English economics. The editor of a recent edition titles it *Principles of Political Economy with Some of Their Applications to Social Philosophy*, ix.

[13] Mill, *Principles of Political Economy*, 4.6.2.

[14] Mill, *Principles of Political Economy*, 4.6.2 (ibid).

Through this undesirable current system, we are to be spontaneously led to a new, remote-yet-approaching desirable one, the Kingdom is the making.

John M. Keynes takes on this point a hundred years later, expecting the "greatest change our material development has ever had": "If the economic problem is solved, mankind will be deprived of its traditional purpose . . . For many ages to come the old Adam will be so strong in us that every-body will need to do some work if he is to be contented . . . for three hours a day [of work] is quite enough to satisfy the old Adam in most of us!"[15]

And thus:

> When the accumulation of wealth is no longer of high social importance, there will be great changes in the code of morals. We shall be able to rid ourselves of many of the pseudo-moral principles which have hag-ridden us for two hundred years, by which we have exalted some of the most distasteful of human qualities into the position of the highest virtues . . . I see us free, therefore, to return to some of the most sure and certain principles of religion and traditional virtue—that avarice is a **vice**, that the exaction of usury is a **misdemeanour**, and the love of money is **detestable**, that those walk most truly in the paths of virtue and sane wisdom who take least thought for the morrow. We shall once more value ends above means and prefer the good to the useful. We shall honour those who can teach us how to pluck the hour and the day virtuously and well, the delightful people who are capable of taking direct enjoyment in things, the lilies of the field who toil not, neither do they spin.[16]

Here the fathers of economics in unison adopt religious language to convey the ethical goals that economic affluence is to achieve. The introductory quote with which we started, "lead us into the land of upright," thus gains new relevance. It is the market that is to lead us into the land of righteous: it has become our shepherd. It is the market that is to transform us, naturally eliminate vice, and give us, in a way, a "new heart" in which doing good becomes easy and spontaneous.[17] It is no longer the Divine that makes us divine (in the image that we would like to see ourselves) but the current system of the economy, which is based on (as Keynes puts it) *vice* and *misdemeanor* and in which the love of money (a term used by St. Paul)[18] is appropriate, even necessary. Keynes is claiming that the system does not honor goals, but means—a means that the system itself has become (as a means to golden age of not just riches but, most importantly, *morality*). But another point is perhaps even more interesting when it comes to ethics of economics. Economic ethics becomes *primarily* economic and *then* ethical. The ideal state is to be so rich that altruism becomes easy, painless, and trivial. In the ideal state, ethics is

[15] Keynes, *Essays in Persuasion*, 358–373.

[16] Keynes, *Essays in Persuasion*, 358–373 [emphasis mine].

[17] How economics as "dismal science" of Thomas Malthus gained such an optimistic outlook is a subject with which I deal in *Economics of Good and Evil* in the chapter entitled "Progress, New Adam and Sabbath Economics," specifically in the sections "Dreams of the End of Avarice" and "The History of Progress: The Golden (c)Age" on pages 235–237 and 232–234 respectively.

[18] 1 Timothy 6:10, Bible

affordable. Here we find a paradox: ethics is possible only when it dies; when it is diminished; when, economically speaking, ethics becomes so affordable, so cheap that it is no longer perceived as a sacrifice.

This is the heaven, the ultimate aim toward which everything in economics is directed. Every single calculation is built upon this dream. This is the unspoken creed of economists—to follow the path toward this (ethical) goal.

Still, questions remain. The first among them is this: Is this dream real? How much affluence is needed for this new Adam to rise? Is the affluence gained in the last 80 years since Keynes wrote these words leading us to more justice? In a society where all are rich, perhaps less petty robbery occurs and less violence, but what about big structural, financial "systemic sins," some of which the current financial crisis revealed? And what sort of panic will this affluent society revert to if, due to some business cycle, bursting bubble, or other crisis, the level of riches decreases? Can the Unorchestrated Orchestrator of the markets guide us under these conditions? And even if, in the long run, we will make it to the ideal society as a civilization, will this be before we die in the short run, immersed in our egoism that seems to promise this *future* heaven on earth—both in terms of affluence and in terms of morality? Note that in Keynes' vision (and the visions of the other fathers of economics and contemporary economists) affluence is not the ultimate goal per se. No, affluence is a (almost technical) doorstep or gate—a prerequisite to a just and peaceful society. This, by the way, is the principal idea of European integration: to have peace (the ultimate goal) through trade (a vanishing mediator, a transitory goal).

Now (at least) one more question remains: What sort of justice or ethics will it be? Why (and how) should we care for others even *if* it does not cost us *anything*? Where does or will our idea of justice (spontaneously?) come from? From economics? Who and what will guide us, in justice, once the guidance of the Unorchestrated Orchestrator of the markets has ceased and is no longer needed, for its role has been fulfilled?

And finally, will we be happy in this state of bliss if we, according to founding legends of our civilization could not be long-term happy in the perfect states and gardens of creation?

What Can Be Done?

If economics is to have a future that will be meaningful for humanity, we need to nurture its soul. Our current way of practicing economics must yield to a new *human*omics. I offer the following as suggestions with the aim of returning to the undead body a spirit and a meaning, and of reopen the debate about what it is that we want the economy to achieve.

Responsibility

We should be aware of and openly debate the values and ethical teachings of economics. We should not pretend to operate above values systems, and our teachings should be subject to as much care as we typically show when religious and moral schools are concerned. We must realize that economics as a system carries values, and so do we as individual economists. We have to bear the burden of being responsible—both systematically and personally—for actions with results that impact the lives of others. It is not acceptable to pretend that most of our economic practice as economists and our economic activities as economic actors have no ethical relevance. When we affect others, as our economic practice and activities do, we face ethical responsibilities whether we recognize them or not.

Broadening the Field

Economics, as a field, should be broader. It has become the narrowest field, most reductionist, in the social sciences, although it was considered at one time imperial. Without appropriate context, and adequate scientific, philosophical, and social awareness, economic models are misleading and blinding. It is also my view that in economics, the history of the field should be studied first and only later the current mainstream academic fashion. This would help economics from being so often religiously mono-paradigmatic and would allow the usage of different metaphors for different purposes. Just imagine how closed contemporary philosophy would look if we first dogmatically started teaching the current prevailing philosophical thought and only in later years, as an appendix, talked of the history of philosophy as a sort of a set of alternative schools.

Humility

The way we teach economics to students makes it look like we understand it. This stands in contrast to philosophy, sociology, anthropology, and other subjects concerned with human knowledge about humans, where students are taught primarily to handle the subject very humbly, and are taught a variety of schools and diversity of approaches, methods, and paradigms with the aim of understanding that we do *not* fully understand, that we are dealing with a difficult and internally controversial subject. On the contrary, in economics we are trying to pretend certainty in the face of fundamental uncertainty.

Less Exactitude

"Exactness is a fake," said Alfred North Whitehead, the key mathematician of the last century. It is definitely treacherous. The feeling that we can predict and can understand the system is not only not helpful, it is also dangerous—and in a way that contributed to the financial collapse of 2008. The problem with financial institutions was not that they knew too little about things that are possible to know, but that they felt they had sufficiently understood such things. With a bit more uncertainty, financial models that offer exact estimates would have never developed, and banks would not have been lending so much on the edge that the edge cut them. If the government would not eternally believe that "next year we will grow" then national debt levels would not be so high—for we take on high levels of national debt *only* with the firm belief (but in reality it is little more than a hope) that GDP will rise in the future and that we will be able to pay back our debts with increased revenue.

The fascination with exactness, especially of future predictions, can also be dangerous as it eliminates uncertainty and the need to create reserves. If such a prediction, upon which actors have acted, is wrong, it could lead to sinister results. Government expenditure, for example, could be based on last year's income, so as to be certain how much money is on hand.

Short-termism versus Growth vs Stability

Economics started as a field by debating the ends of economics, that is, asking the question, "where is the system heading?"—and evaluating whether or not we like the answer. Today, it seems, the debate is concerned only with short futures of exact fetishized statistics elevated to meta-numbers (as we showed in the case of GDP) that are meaningless without the appropriate context. In my view economics should concern itself with where the system is heading. The eternal and endless GDP growth should not be our aim; instead we should define the goal of economics as the stationary state—the end of growth—within which we fulfill other goals as well. Growth does happen and it is good when it does, but if we believe it *should* happen all the time and at high rates, that belief itself can destroy us. For far too long we have been selling stability in order to buy growth. So we got what we wanted: a very fast growing economy that is very unstable. What needs to become the imperative for the coming years is to do the reverse: to sell growth (if and when it occurs) in order to buy back stability.

One role of the political economy is to stabilize the manic–depressive tendencies of the economy, individuals, and markets. In other words, political economy should attempt to decrease the amplitude of business cycles. This inevitably means not only running deficits and aiming for low interest rates (in our manic–depressive metaphor this means giving antidepressants to the economy) so as to promote growth, *but also* running fiscal surpluses and high interest rates to slow down (so as to stabilize) the growth of GDP when it is excessive. It is thus not the role of economists to only speed up GDP growth, but also to slow it down during the manic upwards phases of the business cycle. The less popular responsibility is often forgotten.

The responsibility of economists is to contribute to stable economies, not necessarily growing economies (all the time). It is stability that should be our highest priority, with growth demoted to priority four of five. This is obviously a normative statement, and economists need to learn to accept that, rather than ignoring responsibility and hiding (even if unknowingly, unconsciously) behind a feigned positivism.

If living in the land of righteous is the aim, as Keynes and others put it, then let us define what we mean and aim for that instead of the land of growth. *That* is the moral responsibility of economics: to limit itself.

References

Adams, Douglas. 1995. *The Hitchhiker's Guide to the Galaxy*. New York: Ballantine.

Frank, Robert H., Gilovic, Thomas, and Regan, Dennis T. 1993. "Does Studying Economics Inhibit Cooperation?" *Journal of Economic Perspectives* 7(2): 159–171.

Friedman, Milton. 1962. *Capitalism and Freedom*. Chicago: University of Chicago.

Graeber, David. 2011. *Debt: The First 5000 Years*. New York: Melville.

Holy Bible: New International Version. 2001. Grand Rapids, MI: Zondervan.

Hume, David, and William, Charles. 1927. Hendel. *Hume: Selections*. London: n.p.

Keynes, John Maynard. 1963. *Essays in Persuasion*. New York: W. W. Norton.

Khurana, Rakesh, and Gintis, Herbert. 2008. "What Is the Purpose of Business?" BizEd (January–February).

Knight, Frank H. 1935. *The Ethics of Competition and Other Essays*. New York: Harper & Brothers.

Mandeville, Bernard, and Harth, Phillip. 1970. *The Fable of the Bees*. Harmondsworth: Penguin.

Mill, John Stuart. 1965. *Principles of Political Economy with Some of Their Applications to Social Philosophy*. N.p.: RKP.

Mill, John Stuart. 1848. *Principles of Political Economy, with Some of Their Applications to Social Philosophy*. London: J. W. Parker.

Nelson, Robert H. 2001. *Economics as Religion: From Samuelson to Chicago and beyond*. University Park: Pennsylvania State University Press.

Sedláček, Tomáš. 2011. *Economics of Good and Evil: The Quest for Economic Meaning from Gilgamesh to Wall Street*. Oxford: Oxford University Press.

Sedláček, Tomáš. 2012. Chapter "Shopping, Hopping, or Hoping for Growth?" In *Und Schopping-center, Das Lesebuch Und Nachdenkbuch*. Comp. Kurt Schneider, Hannes Ch. Steinmann, and Bernhard Bugelmayer, pp. 138–151. Wien: EKAZENT.

Smith, Adam, and Playfair, William. 1995. *An Inquiry into the Nature and Causes of the Wealth of Nations*. London: W. Pickering.

The Bible: King James Version. 2008. Glasgow: Collins.

Wall Street. 1987. Dir. Oliver Stone. Perf. Michael Douglas, Charlie Sheen, Daryl Hannah, Martin Sheen, and Hal Holbrook. Twentieth Century Fox Film Corporation.

2. *Economic Theory and the Great Recession*

CHAPTER 14

ALTERNATIVE ETHICAL PERSPECTIVES ON THE FINANCIAL CRISIS

Lessons for Economists

IRENE VAN STAVEREN

INTRODUCTION

ACADEMIC interpretations of the financial crisis often refer to "thick concepts," as Amartya Sen calls them, which have both descriptive and normative value. As Ricardo Crespo and I argued in an ethical analysis of the financial crisis (Crespo and van Staveren, 2012), we see references in the literature to "hiding risky situations," "excessive liberalization," "extremely high bonuses," "irresponsible loans," "failing control," "regulatory capture," "perverse incentives," "moral hazard," "too rosy assessments," and "excessive liquidity related to consumerism" (Blundell-Wignall, Atkinson, and Lee, 2008; Narayan, Ferri, and Brem, 2008; Acemoglu, 2009; Hart and Zingales, 2009; Nothwehr and Manning, 2009; Schneider and Kirchgässner, 2009).

Neoclassical theory, with its efficient market hypothesis, normal probability distributions of risk, and a self-interested logic of principal–agent interaction, reflects a particular underlying ethics. This is a specific form of the ethical a framework of utilitarianism, which foregrounds a highly subjective, individualist interpretation of utility. This, I will argue in the next section, is part and parcel of the underlying causes of the crisis (see also Crespo and van Staveren, 2012). In the following section, I want to briefly discuss two other ethical frameworks, namely deontology and the ethics of care. The reason for doing so is that the ethics of the crisis and financial reform can also be understood by reference to alternative ethical frameworks. The recognition of such alternatives by professional economists will help to demonstrate what alternative behavioral paths are available for successful financial sector reform. The last part of the chapter presents two case studies in alternative finance, which emerged in response to the crisis. These case studies show how an ethics of care may translate into a meaningful and economically sound alternative in the financial sector, and induce more appropriate behavior by financial sector professionals. The chapter concludes that regulation may be important to prevent crises and to guide financial reform after a crisis, but emphasizes that a caring ethical approach is just as important for economists, precisely because it generates less crisis-prone behavior in finance, and informs financial innovation toward more stable and sustainable finance, supporting the real economy instead of endangering it.

Utilitarian Economics Contributing to the Financial Crisis

Neoclassical economic rationality, embedded in utilitarianism, only considers the best way of satisfying preferences, regardless of the specific content of those preferences and whether this satisfaction causes harm to others. The moral characteristics of the behaviors just before the crisis mentioned in the introduction are preferences or individual maximizing strategies that have no place in utilitarianism. In utilitarianism, the highest moral good is utility or, in contemporary interpretations, preference satisfaction. As explained by the founder of utilitarianism, Jeremy Bentham (1789), an action is considered morally just if and only if no alternative action generates greater happiness for those involved. Utilitarianism is therefore a consequentialist ethics: the good is evaluated strictly in terms of consequences. In the aggregate, utilitarianism considers everyone's utility as equal; hence, it applies the impartiality criterion. The content of the good, however, remains hidden in the black box of preferences where individual agents are concerned: we neither know nor care what people prefer, or what will yield happiness. Utilitarianism is a subjective and individualist ethics, which allows for preferences that may do good or bad to others, to society or the environment, and even to the individual's long run objective wellbeing, as is for example the case with altruism or, alternatively, addictions (van Staveren, 2001).

At the level of the firm, maximizing utility requires the maximization of profits, and all (legally allowed) strategies that achieve that end are deemed to be legitimate (Graafland, 2009). In this domain utilitarianism is an ethics driven by markets: competition on unregulated markets dictates firms' strategies for profit maximization, through innovation, cost reduction, and economies of scale, which are selected through cost–benefit analyses. Moreover, the ethics of utilitarianism may involve the specification of rules, as in rule-utilitarianism (Broome, 1991), that when generally followed serve to maximize aggregate utility. Such rules allow agents to make decisions in environments when it is not practical for them to calculate the full set of consequences of their actions. Such rules may include behavioral rules in finance, for instance, which are individually rational. But as we've now learned, when the same rule is followed by many agents at the same time, the result may be collectively irrational because the behaviors may generate self-fulfilling prophesies that drive financial values quickly in the same direction without correction by the market.

The length of the time period over which utility is maximized depends on the individual's or society's time horizon and discount rates. Long-term consequences may or may not have an important weight owing to existing preference orderings, and the discount rates that are used to calculate costs and benefits when comparing alternative courses of actions.

It is important to note that utilitarianism is not necessarily self-centered: the interests of others can be taken into account, as enlightened self-interest, when this is necessary to maximize one's own utility. Or one can derive utility from increasing someone else's happiness when doing so yields a warm glow, so to speak. But in both cases, utility maximization remains selfish in the sense of its individual happiness-orientation: what matters in the end is one's own utility, for which someone else's utility may or may not be instrumental.

Under the system of a capitalist market driven by immediate shareholder value, and with volatile, unpredictable financial markets, utility maximization's time horizon is reduced to the short run. In such a market, professionals, firms, investors, and consumers can no longer patiently pursue the maximization of a lifetime utility function; instead they apply bounded-rationality to a long series of short-run utility maximization opportunities. This is because preference satisfaction is granted only in the short run—that is, a series of short runs such as quarters or at most a year, in which financial results are produced, announced, and transferred into rewards that satisfy shareholder value. The underlying utilitarian ethic of economic rationality, hence, is also limited to short term rewards: the contribution to the good by capitalist markets is expressed by the rewards accumulated over a series of short run maximization periods, while the bad are reflected by the losses incurred, including negative externalities when unregulated markets fail. This is an inconsistency in the utilitarian framework.

If we evaluate the financial crisis according to such bounded-rational, serial short-run decisions, combined with utilitarian ethics, we find that the individuals and firms that gained in various short run periods, either because they directly maximized their returns or followed rules that helped them to maximize returns, did "the right thing." But the crisis generated only a few ultimate winners and many more losers. That may be as a consequence of irrational behavior: not maximizing one's preferences even though the constraints would have allowed for a higher level of preference satisfaction. Or it may be because preference satisfaction and rule-following did not result in utility maximization, owing to unforeseen events, even though the behavior was in line with cost–benefit analysis based on available information of credit rating agencies, interest rates, financial product diversification, and so forth. However, much of the behavior leading up to the crisis can be considered rational in terms of utilitarianism, because agents did follow rational rules with the available information to maximize their returns, thereby satisfying their preferences.

The utilitarian ethics underlying the behavior of financial professionals, consumers, investors, and regulatory bodies appeared to have been unable to signal in a timely fashion that things were going wrong. I will argue in this chapter that the utilitarian ethics underlying much of the behavior leading up to the crisis had marginalized other ethical approaches, such as an ethics based on principles and an ethics built on intrinsically valuable relationships. In the remainder of this chapter, I will try to show what these alternative approaches are and how they can be expressed in finance.

Two Alternative Ethical Approaches for Financial Sector Analysis and Behavior

Deontology, also referred to as duty-based ethics, is concerned with acting in accordance with appropriate, inviolable principles or rules. These principles or rules are taken to be intrinsically right, irrespective of their outcomes. Deontological ethics is therefore not concerned with bringing about preference satisfaction or happiness, but with ensuring "justice," "rights," or some other ultimate value. A dominant form of deontological ethics is expressed in the Kantian categorical imperative. It states that one should act according to that maxim by which you can at the same time will that it should become a universal law (White, 2009). A more individual-oriented interpretation of its universalist implication is that one should act toward others as you would like and expect others to behave toward you. Hence, deontology is not an individualist ethics, as is utilitarianism, but a social and universalist ethics: it is concerned with justice, with what is considered as right for a society as a whole (White, 2009).

In the financial sector, a deontological ethics is reflected in regulation that ensures the protection of rights, duties and justice by central banks, governments, and the sector itself. Regulation by definition works by rule-setting and rule enforcement. These may be rules operating within banks, such as credit limits for consumer loans; rules embedded in risk models, which come into action at a predefined threshold of certain market values of assets; or the values of certain variables of a bank's financial healthiness, such as its capital ratio. From a deontological perspective, such rules codify the duty of agents not to pursue courses of action (such as taking on excessive risk) that violate the rights of others (such as their creditors). Another important type of regulation is by the state and its related authorities. There are the regulations that are imposed by central banks, guided by internationally established rules for international financial markets set by the so-called Basel Committee, in which the central banks are represented. Other public regulatory bodies include the European Monetary Union and ministries of finance. Their actions are clearly visible—the former in its reactions to the euro crisis and the latter in their deciding on and managing the bail-outs of failing banks in the recent financial crisis. In addition, there are also private regulatory bodies that help the market to value assets such as credits, entire banks, and even a country's bonds. These bodies are rating agencies, which give ratings of the financial reliability of actors or products in the financial sector.

Clearly, deontology as institutionalized in financial regulation failed as a moral guide in the financial sector. Property rights were destroyed and other injustices resulted from the behavior of financial actors who disregarded their moral duties not to violate the rights of others. Obviously, it is not merely the amount of regulation that matters, but the quality of regulation. From a deontological perspective, financial sector regulation should be regarded as just or fair and hence, universally supported throughout the sector. Otherwise, it fails to achieve its chief purpose. Regulation failed in particular in terms of two of the moral connotations listed in the introduction: excessive liberalization of the financial market, which allowed some actors to take risks that undermined the rights of others; and failed control of banks, partly through regulatory capture. Rules that came into being after the 1929 crisis had been removed by a strong bank lobby in the United States (Igan, Mishra, and Tressel, 2009), and new rules to govern new financial strategies and products, such as short-selling, credit default swaps, and derivatives, were not yet introduced even though these assets were being traded increasingly. Without a stronger commitment to the sanctity of rules, both in terms of rule setting and rule enforcement, deontology has limited moral capacity to prevent the next financial crisis. Moreover, rules alone are too limited to address the day-to-day ethical dilemmas in financial decision making. Rules can conflict, they can come in effect too late, and they may not take important feedback effects in the long run into account.

Unlike deontology, which relies on external enforcement of moral behavior in the form of inviolable rules, the ethics of care helps us to understand agents' behavior and firms' strategies from a deeper ethical sense. It is concerned with ethical reflection and deliberation by agents whenever they have the space to make different choices. The ethics of care was first developed by Carol Gilligan (1982), who studied gender differences in moral reasoning. The ethics of care is attentive to the interpersonal level, where ethics is concerned with sustaining human relationships and preventing harm to others (Waerness, 2009). In the words of care ethicist Virginia Held: "Whereas justice protects equality and freedom, care fosters social bonds and cooperation" (Held, 2006: 15). And it is here where the other moral terms that we have seen in the introduction will come into the picture—terms concerning hiding risk, excessive bonuses and other perverse incentives, construction of securities that no one understands, too rosy credit ratings, and the consumerism encouraged by extremely low interest-rate policies. These moral dimensions of the crisis have much less to do with regulation than with the responsibility of the agents involved vis-à-vis other agents and organizations. The ethics of care enables a fundamental shift in the parameters of the financial market. "With the ethics of care and an understanding of its intertwined values, such as those of sensitivity, empathy, responsiveness, and taking responsibility, we could perhaps more adequately judge where the boundaries of the market should be" (Held, 2006: 119). It is important that economists learn about the ethics of care in their education, both at university and later as professionals. This would allow them to see beyond utility maximization and its limitations and to seek more varied roles for the government in relation to the financial market beyond that of protector of rights or rule maker and keeper, as Held rightly argues.

In the ethics of care, preventing harm to others is contextualized. It is not abstract, as is the rule of non-intervention or a set of rules based on principles. Instead, it stems from and is inherent in the relatedness of actors. Preventing harm to others therefore requires taking responsibility for the consequences of one's actions, not only as an individual but also through institutions, and responsibility for preventing the system in which one functions to turn into an uncontrollable chaos causing harm to all involved. Care also involves sympathy, in the sense of being able to place oneself in the shoes of others, as explained by Adam Smith. Sympathy is not limited to particular others known to oneself, nor an abstract, generalized other that is similar to oneself as in the categorical imperative—it also extends to concrete others whose circumstances are imaginable owing to the general information one has about their context (Benhabib, 1987). Preventing harm to others, then, requires contextualization to be able to know how others are in their concrete situation and what our responsibilities to them would be.

When applied to the economy, the ethics of care is expressed through efforts to minimize harm in day-to-day practices that have possible harmful effects on others, whether these would come from free markets, government regulation, intra-firm self-interested behavior, power-seeking strategies, or any other behavior in any economic sector. Possible harmful effects of behavior abound because of imperfect markets, risk alongside uncertainty, and a wide variety of motives including harmful ones. Uncertainty is particularly important in this regard. Uncertainty, which goes beyond risk because the probabilities of possible future events are unknown, significantly influences financial markets. Keynes, of course, already knew this, as Skidelsky (2009: 75) notes: "Keynes believed that in many situations market participants face irreducible uncertainty. They have no basis on which to calculate the risks they face in making an investment. They are plunging into the unknown." This condition implies that any economic sector is always in transition and may face discontinuities and disruptions, as Keynes noted, and does not jump from equilibrium to equilibrium, whether by free market forces or state interference. And in transition, rules are often not applicable or not yet established. This fragility of economic life and human fallibility in economic decision making under conditions of uncertainty induce harm and call forth government regulation that is, although necessary, utterly insufficient (see also Hellwig [2008] on systemic risk regulation). It is precisely such fragility and fallibility to which a caring attitude responds, by contextual reasoning. Such contextual reasoning is also what Keynes pictured as the most adequate response to financial crises. He stated, as recounted by Skidelsky (2009: 76) that the cures "are not meant to be definitive; they are subject to all sorts of special assumptions and are necessarily related to the particular conditions of the time." Hence, with the current renewed attention to Keynesian policy responses to financial instability, I suggest that economists also begin to apprehend the underlying contextual ethics of such responses, as a sensible alternative to utilitarianism as well as deontology.

Case Study on "Caring Capital Financing"

This section presents a case study of a new capital funding product that a major Dutch bank has developed in response to the crisis and that has attracted much attention from investors and regulators worldwide[1]. An example of a caring financial innovation, it was developed by two senior bankers in the context of regulatory pressure, limited liquidity in a hesitant capital market, in a cooperative bank structure with a client-value orientation. The case study points out that a caring attitude partly depends on an enabling institutional context.

Rabobank, a top-three Dutch bank and market leader in savings, mortgages, and agricultural lending in the Netherlands, has issued an innovative form of senior debt, called the Senior Contingent Note (SCN), as a response to the crisis.[2] In the first instance, the SCN is in a way to raise capital for the bank through bonds. The value of the bond does not appear on the balance sheet unless the bank's equity capital ratio were to fall below 7 percent. In that very unlikely case the bank's core capital will be strengthened as the bank will receive 75 percent of the value of the outstanding SCNs. Hence, those who bought the bond will lose 75 percent of their investment.[3] In exchange for that risk, the interest rate that bond holders receive includes a risk premium.

Rabobank is the only large Dutch bank that did not need state support, that kept a healthy equity capital ratio and its triple A rating throughout the crisis, merely dealing with collateral damage spilling over from other banks that were hit seriously by the crisis.[4] Rabobank is a cooperative bank, so it cannot raise capital through issuing shares, and it is not listed on the stock market.[5] Although about 85 percent of Rabobank's

1 This case study is based on information released through the media, a presentation for investors, and an interview I held with the two key informants who developed the security at Rabobank's capital funding department, Treasury Rabobank Group, Utrecht, May 18, 2010. See also Van Staveren (2013).

2 The transaction date was March 12, 2010, at the amount 1.25 billion euro for a 10-year fixed rate senior contingent note priced at an annual coupon of 6.875 percent. It was twice oversubscribed and sold to major investors across the world.

3 In the past, convertible bonds were labeled as Tier 2 capital and institutional lenders were often supported in a bailout (Levinson, 2010). With new SCNs in the new situation after the crisis, it is less likely that regulators will protect these types of capital.

4 The cost of its bad loans in 2009 was nearly 2 billion euro, which was 0.33 percent of its balance total of 608 billion euro. On December 31, 2009 its equity capital ratio was 12.5 percent. Rabobank has always been profitable since its start more than a century ago, including in the crisis years 2008 and 2009.

5 The bank has 1.8 million members, which is a non-financial membership for any client but involves no claim on the equity of the 147 local banks. It is globally number one in several countries in the food and agri-business and has 623 foreign offices in 48 countries. The maximum bonus for senior management and executives is 30 percent of salary and half of the bonus is transferred only after three years.

activities are in the Netherlands, about half of its capital is raised abroad. The major way in which the bank raises its capital is simply through retained profits. Another recent innovation of the bank has been to raise capital and at the same time involve members more closely, as capital providers to the bank through the issuance of certificates to its members (Rabobank clients can become members of the member council of their local branch). But this is a small scale initiative through the local, independent branches; the SCN targets large investors such as pension funds and globally operating investment funds.

The SCN was not developed at the international branch of the bank where the financial traders are based, in the fast world of short-term transactions and the balancing act between long term obligations and short-term liquidity. Instead, the new type of bond was developed at the treasury of the bank, as part of its long-term funding strategy. The challenge during the crisis was how to gain access to liquidity in a drying up market (which hit Europe especially hard due to defaulting governments, such as that of Greece) while staying true to the bank's conservative capital position (for which it had been criticized before the crisis as being not profitable enough, but later earned the bank its triple-A rating throughout the crisis). In a market, crisis risk and uncertainty are the major factors that investors are worried about. Moreover, during a crisis, risks turn into uncertainties, as rating agencies cannot assign reliable probabilities to the chances of default for institutions or even for individual products.[6] The strength of Rabobank is precisely its prudence—its higher than average equity capital ratio, as compared with most other banks, which gave it a boring image in the booming years before the crisis. This asset—prudence—was the basis for developing the SCN. The product was developed internally with consultation of a few large investors. Whereas Rabobank initially planned a 100 percent core capital strengthening with the new product, investors made clear that that would be deemed unacceptable by the market. A different case of Lloyd's in London half a year earlier,[7] but with similarities, has led to the current 75 percent ratio of the SCN to be added to the balance sheet in case the bank's equity capital ratio falls below 7 percent. The investors run a risk and, unlike typical shareholders, do not benefit from riskier projects undertaken by the bank that may bring in more short-term profits. Instead, they will demand that the bank either increase its buffers or raise the premium on newly issued contingent notes. The interest rate was not discussed at these sounding board meetings with investors, until the last week before the transaction on March 12 2010 in a meeting with four major investors. The interest among institutional investors as well as private investment funds was overwhelming, both nationally and internationally (London, Paris, Frankfurt,

[6] The top three international rating agencies, including Standard and Poor's, which together have more than 90 percent of the market, did not want to assign a rating to the SCN since they preferred to await new international regulation coming from Basel.

[7] Lloyd's is a listed bank, which failed to raise sufficient capital through issuing new shares. Hence, it issued contingent notes that would be turned into equity in case of predefined stress. It is different from the Rabobank case because Rabobank is not a listed bank and therefore has no shares.

New York), so much so that the transaction of the 10-year fixed rate Senior Contingent Note, priced at an annual coupon of 6.875 percent, was twice oversubscribed. Its issuance generated 1.25 billion euros.

Prudence—putting the responsibility for risk taking where it should be, namely the providers of capital—made it possible to find a market for this product. But it was also the pressure coming from regulators that led to the development of the SCN. Without the crisis and the subsequent call for (re-)regulation of banks and financial markets, it would not have been developed, at least, not now and not in this form. Regulators in the Netherlands and Europe are discussing implementing a bank tax, with equal rates across all banks, to form a fund that in case of need would become a lender of last resort. However, such a fund does not solve the problem of moral hazard, and does not reward conservative banks for their conservative positions and subsequent higher capital ratios. Therefore, a second reason for developing the SCN was to influence regulation, as both Basel III agreements and European Union law were being crafted and are still in the making. In other words, rather than focusing on lobbying against a bank tax (which they also did to some extent), the SCN represents a different type of incentive for banks and by banks, to increase their core capital in case of crisis, but with the great advantage that it reduces moral hazard by providing an incentive for the issuing bank to keep its equity capital ratio up by keeping risks manageable. In case of a bank having an inadequate capital ratio, the 75 percent shift of the loan to the balance sheet would imply that the equity capital ratio would be increased automatically, based on the rule imposed by the SCN, so that the bank does not (immediately) require financial support by the state, and hence is not a burden on taxpayers. This characteristic of contingent capital allows banks to increase their capital ratio in a more effective way than through issuing new shares because the prices of shares are currently very low and demand for them is inadequate. Moreover, a contingent capital product like SCNs would help to reduce the likeliness of another crisis. In particular, SCNs reduce the chances of crisis caused by excessive risk-taking by banks (as is the case with the current crisis). It does this by forcing banks to keep risks relatively low to prevent the equity capital ratio from falling too much by leveraging too much. The SCN can also be seen as a strategic move to influence regulation, which indeed did raise attention from regulators all over the world. This feature of the development of SCN hence can be characterized as taking a long-run and systemic view: it involves the banking sector itself recognizing the dangers associated with financial market volatility and the need to undertake effective responses—all of which signal an attitude of responsibility. This is not the kind of self-sacrificing responsibility that entails risking one's survival, but the kind of responsibility that reflects a liberal attitude of accepting the consequences of one's individual actions on the whole, including financial sector participants (such as clients and investors) and also nonparticipants who bear negative externalities (such as taxpayers). This is the responsibility that Adam Smith wrote about, that does not constrain markets, but rather, supports the effective functioning of markets. The SCN, and hence, the economists in the bank who developed it, express this responsibility because it is a self-regulating instrument that prevents banks from taking excessive risks and diminishes the need for costly bail-outs and compensation of clients' deposits in times of crisis. It is, in the end, a mechanism that puts the risk where it should be, on the shoulders of the capital providers of banks, rather than on its clients or the taxpayer. It is therefore a good illustration of how an ethics of care can function in the financial sector.

Finally, why was it a cooperative bank that developed this innovation? Why did it not emerge within equally big banks listed on the stock exchange, such as ABN Amro or ING? This has only indirectly to do with the cooperative structure of the bank. The idea did not come from the member council, not the local ones, and not from the central membership council. So, as much as the bank is driven by client value through close contact with its members and other clients, this did not play a role in the SCN. But it was the lack of access to capital through shares that drove the bank's treasury to be innovative and to develop a product that would on the one hand build on its conservative position and on the other hand even strengthen its image in the market as a prudent bank, by providing an extra buffer for its capital ratio. In other words, the other banks did not develop such a contingent note simply because their equity capital ratios were too low. In the words of one of the interviewees: "we do not have the shareholders pressure, which is an enormous benefit" and thereby it also "protects against moral hazard internally" and "pushes to be creative to raise capital if you can't do it through equity." This confirms Keynes' insight that it is the capitalist system based on equity capital that generates the uncertainty and subsequent systemic risk in financial markets. Skidelsky (2009: 84) reminds us: "Under capitalism, uncertainty is generated by the system itself, because it is an engine for accumulating capital goods whose rewards come not now but later. The engine of wealth creation is at the same time the source of economic and social instability."

In conclusion, the contingent capital product of Rabobank may be characterized as a caring form of capital financing because it is a form of self-regulation that lowers the risk of default, while reinforcing the bank's good rating. This, in turn, lowers the costs of capital funding, which makes it a solid product not only for the bank but also for the financial market, without the moral hazard of shifting risk to clients and tax payers. The SCN therefore carries a positive externality as compared to share-based capital funding which has a negative externality—it reduces systemic uncertainty in the financial sector. It therefore provides a good illustration to the economics profession on how to follow an alternative ethics, rather than utilitarianism, and still act economic rationally. Indeed, the use of an ethics of care may be more rational in light of financial uncertainty and the ever-shorter time horizons of financial markets.

Case Study on Gender Differences in Financial Behavior

During the crisis, but also well before it broke out, women fund managers in the United States performed better than their male colleagues (Chang, 2010). Chang refers to an internal study done by AsiaHedge that concludes that female fund managers in the AsiaHedge Composite Index scored 73 percent better than their male colleagues between 2000 and 2007, and a report by Hedge Fund Research that shows that women performed 56 percent better than men in the period 2000 until May 2009. Moreover, during the height of the crisis in the second half of 2008, men lost twice as much money as did women. A recent study on mutual fund management in Egypt shows that women perform better than men in an emerging market (Ahmed Azmi, 2008). A study among 649 fund managers in four countries confirms that women are more risk averse than men (Beckmann and Menkhoff, 2008). A large study on gender differences in the mutual funds industry in the United States does not find statistically significant performance differences, but it does show that female fund managers follow more stable investment styles and show higher performance persistence (Niessen and Ruenzi, 2005). Linked to this, a recent survey by a major UK investment bank, among 2000 wealthy clients in 20 countries, showed not only that women are more risk averse in their investing, but also that they place more importance on financial discipline than do men (Barclays Wealth, 2011).

These gender differences in financial performance are supported by many studies on risk in experimental economics, showing that on average women take less risk than men (see Croson and Gneezy [2009] for an in-depth review of experimental research on gender and risk).[8] As a consequence, under conditions of high volatility women perform better than men because they take lower risk or take more time to study risks or include a wider variety of risk factors than men do. This might imply that under conditions of relative stability of financial markets men perform better than women, although this is not necessarily the case (see, e.g., van den Bos, Harteveld, and Stoop, 2009). A famous study by Barber and Odean (2001) using survey data from 35,000 US households on their portfolio investment behavior has shown that women performed even better under normal conditions of financial markets, controlling for risk diversification in portfolio choice. Men traded 45 percent more often than women, who tried less to beat the market. Their patience prevented them from unnecessary and costly trading. Hence, women's transaction costs were lower, leading to higher net returns on investment. In couples, men's returns

[8] A recent report by the Deutsche Bundesbank on gender and age composition in boards of banks finds that banks increase their levels of risk when there are more women on the board (Berger, Kick, and Schaeck, 2012). This contradicts the findings of most empirical and experimental research on gender and risk attitudes. The report does not give an explanation for its findings but admits that there may be a relationship with age and experience for which it did not control. I suggest that the result may well be a consequence of men's reaction to the entry of women on boards. They may exhibit typical macho behavior, signaling to the women that they are "real men," increasing their levels of risk. This potential explanation is supported by a recent study with data from online chess playing (discussed later in the text) with 15,000 players (15 percent women) and 1.4 million games. It found that when men play against women, they choose more aggressive strategies, even though such strategies reduce their winning probability (Gerdes and Gränsmark, 2010). Further analysis into male reactions to women entering a male domain is necessary before any conclusions can be drawn on whether a change in risk profile of a bank is driven by an increase in women on the board or by an over-reaction of the males on those boards to the entry of women in a traditionally all-male domain.

were 1.4 percent lower, whereas comparing the behavior of singles, men earned 2.3 percent less in returns. The finding of less trading by women was recently confirmed in a survey among 2000 wealthy individuals (Barclays Wealth, 2011). The report also indicated that women use somewhat different strategies of financial discipline than do men: they more often use cooling-off periods and they more often avoid information about markets that may lead them to deviate from their long-term strategies. Hence, women seem to be less overconfident than men in their investment behavior.

Moreover, women seem to behave more contextually, which is a central tenet of the ethics of care. A survey among fund managers found that women change their strategy more often when they are ahead of or behind the market—"they try to perform closer to the market development than men" (Beckmann and Menkhoff, 2008: 377). A study on pension fund investment indicates that women tend to diversity their portfolio slightly more than men, and are less likely to sell when markets are down (Vanguard, 2011). However, in a study using a large database on chess playing, it was found that men adapt their strategy when playing against women, whereas women do not (Gerdes and Gränsmark, 2010). Apparently, men are more sensitive to a gender difference between players than are women. Men appear to play a more aggressive strategy when playing against women, and this effect is even stronger when a male player is on objective grounds (measured with the Elo rating system) weaker than a female player. This reaction to women by male players reduces their winning probabilities, controlling for various other factors: a solid strategy has a 1.5 percentage point higher probability of winning as compared to an aggressive strategy, a difference that is statistically significant. Again, this points to overconfidence among males in risky, strategic settings.

The findings reviewed above are not necessarily driven by nature—these are precisely the key features of the investment strategy of Warren Buffet, portrayed recently in a book under the title *Warren Buffett Invests Like a Girl—and Why You Should, Too* (Lofton, 2011).[9] Moreover, it is not only experimental economists and other academics who have found gender differences in financial behavior. The financial sector itself is increasingly aware of these differences, though only very slowly following up on these, with the top of the sector protecting its interests by keeping the circle of hiring and promotion largely within the old boys' network.[10] The nurture explanation suggests that women's socialization into societal norms about proper behavior for women as compared to men leads them to take lower risks, to have more self-restraint, and to react more contextually to changes in the market. This is supported by a recent study by Booth and Nolen (2012), who found that girls in single-sex schools exhibit

[9] Lofton gives the following three-point advice to investors based on Buffett's experience and attitude: (1) Value and cultivate your relationships with people; (2) Learn from the masters, but be willing to question them; and (3) Be fair and operate in an ethical manner.

[10] An interesting example of a sector response to the insight of higher female financial performance is a new private equity fund set up by three women in the Netherlands, Karmijn Kapitaal, investing only in medium scale firms that have women on the board. See: http://www.karmijnkapitaal.nl/en/

the same levels of risk in games as boys, whereas girls in coed schools take lower risk levels.

Adolescent females, even those endowed with an intrinsic propensity to make riskier choices, may be discouraged from doing so because they are inhibited by culturally driven norms and beliefs about the appropriate mode of female behavior—avoiding risk. But once they are placed in an all-female environment, this inhibition is reduced. No longer reminded of their own gender identity and society's norms, they find it easier to make riskier choices than women who are placed in a coed class (Booth and Nolen, 2012:F74).

The nature dimension finds support in the empirical literature too. This has been analyzed in particular in neuroeconomics. A key study is among 17 male London City traders, testing for the relationship between two hormones, testosterone and cortisol, on the one hand and financial decision making and returns on the other hand (Coates and Herbert, 2008, and for a more general interpretation see Coates, Gurnell, and Sarnyai, 2010). Testosterone is known in the literature for the "winner effect" because it increases confidence and risk taking. Cortisol is sensitive to situations of uncontrollability and uncertainty, while it also affects the immune system. The traders traded in many assets but mostly in German interest rate futures, closing their trades at the end of the day, and were followed for eight consecutive business days. Saliva samples were taken twice a day (at 11 a.m. and 4 p.m.) and profits and losses were recorded at the same time. The study found that daily testosterone was significantly higher when they made above average profits. Also, on days of higher morning testosterone levels, traders made higher profits for the rest of the day than on lower testosterone days. The authors conclude that "because the days of high 11 am testosterone were different for each trader, thereby ruling out any general market effects on both testosterone and profits and losses, our results suggest that high morning testosterone predicts greater profitability for the rest of that day" (Coates and Herbert, 2008: 6168). On cortisol, the study found that the more volatile a trader's profits and losses, the higher were his average daily cortisol levels as well as the standard deviation in cortisol. This suggests, according to the authors, "that individual levels of cortisol relate not to the rate of economic return, as does testosterone, but to the variance of return" (Coates and Herbert, 2008: 6169). Cortisol rose in 38 percent of the subjects' days, sometimes up to 500 percent. Also, cortisol correlated strongly and positively with the volatility of the interest rate of the German Bund, while testosterone did not. The authors signal potential negative effects for financial markets from their findings. First, when testosterone is chronically elevated, the literature indicates that it no longer has positive effects, but instead increases impulsivity and harmful risk taking, as well as euphoria and mania, and becomes addictive. This may exaggerate a market's upward movement. Second, chronically elevated levels of cortisol stimulate anxiety and a tendency to find threat and risk where none exist, which may exaggerate a market's downward movement. Together, the behavioral effects of these hormones may strengthen market volatility, and "help explain why people caught up in bubbles and crashes often find it difficult to make rational choices" (Coates and Herbert, 2008: 6171).

The mentioning of "people" in the last quote is interesting, given the fact that the sample only contains males. It may well be, of course, that women would express similar behavioral reactions to similar levels and changes in the two hormones. But the fact is that women's testosterone levels are much lower than men's, whereas, even though their cortisol levels are similar, women's bodies react much more than do men's bodies to higher cortisol levels with the secretion of the hormone oxytocin, which counters the production of cortisol and promotes nurturing and relaxing emotions (Nazario, n.d.). A study on oxytocin and altruism among a double-blind placebo-controlled sample of 96 male students in a public goods game has shown that receiving oxytocin (through a nose spray) positively correlates with the willingness to cooperate and the expectation that others will cooperate (Israel et al., 2012). This suggests that oxytocin indeed may have positive economic effects in a context of uncertainty, stress, and anxiety-based herd behavior. In line with these findings, a review article on the neurological foundations of economic choice concludes that the cognitive control processed by the dorsolateral prefrontal cortex of the brain is impaired during stress and depleted with repeated use (Fehr and Rangel, 2011). The authors conclude that "this predicts that subjects are more likely to make short-sighted decisions under stress" (Fehr and Rangel, 2011: 24). So, in order to reduce increasing risk levels and market volatility in financial markets, a better gender balance on trading floors seems meaningful, both physically by replacing some male traders with female traders, and chemically, by administering oxytocin to male traders when market volatility increases.

Experimental game theory has also consistently shown than women are more cooperative than men (Croson and Gneezy, 2009). This has been shown with well-known games that test for attitudes that have moral as well as social dimensions, such as the dictator game, the ultimatum game, the prisoner's dilemma, and the public good game. Moreover, varying game conditions, such as a change in the members of the group or information about players, appear to have more effect on women's than on men's strategies. This suggests that women's reasoning in complex situations is more contextual than men's. Such contextual reasoning in complex social settings, involving ethical implications, is a major characteristic of the ethics of care. Indeed, Croson and Gneezy (2009: 464) conclude: "we believe, as suggested by Gilligan (1982), that men's decisions are less context-specific than women's."

The ethics of care is attentive to the interpersonal level, where ethics is concerned with sustaining human relationships and preventing harm to others (Waerness, 2009). In the financial sector, this can be done, for example, by recognizing the limited financial means of some people; recognizing risks that individuals, families or firms run; or recognizing how certain institutions that emerged, like systems of reward, may tempt people to behave irresponsibly in the knowledge that this will not be punished. Context, then, refers to livelihood, risk, and perverse incentives. In the ethics of care, preventing harm to others is contextualized and requires taking responsibility for the consequences of one's actions. Hence, put in this frame, the ethics of care can be used to analyze the financial system and banks operating in that system.

There is only very limited empirical literature testing for gender differences in moral behavior in firms (see, for a few studies, Robinson et al., 2000; Dreber and Johannesson, 2008). However, a recent experimental study with 96 MBA students (33 percent female) on buyer–seller information asymmetry has done a revealing test for understanding gender differences in ethical behavior before the outbreak of the financial crisis (Kray and Haselhuhn, 2011). The study finds that male participants more often identify with the interests of a buyer or a seller, changing their attitude toward sharing of asymmetric information, depending on whether they were assigned the seller's role or the buyer's role. Female participants more often identify with what they consider to be a fair relationship between buyer and seller, that is, revealing asymmetric information, irrespective whether they take the buyer's role or the seller's role. The differences were found to be statistically significant and indicate that women's ethical attitude in a market relationship is more cooperative and oriented toward "fair play," whereas men's ethical attitude is more competitive and oriented toward protecting the interests of the market side that they represent. These results have led the authors to test gender differences in financial decisions.

Borrowing the metaphor from Kray and Haselhuhn (2011), would a hypothetical Bernadette Madoff have committed the same infamously unethical actions as the real Bernie? The current research suggests not, and importantly, offers an explanation as to why not. Though men and women may share common social and achievement motivations, they appear to differ in the extent to which their experiences and beliefs are called on to set ethical standards. By relying more heavily on their motivations, men derive considerable leeway in setting ethical standards, rendering them more vulnerable to ethical lapses (Kray and Haselhuhn, 2011: 12).

The literature indicates, then, that women are not only, on average, more cooperative than men, but that they also let their behavior be guided more by what they perceive as morally good in relation to particular others in a particular context as compared to men. This suggests that women would be more inclined than men toward responsible behavior when relationships with others are involved.

This is not something that is acknowledged in firms, however. A recent paper by Lyda Bigelow et al. (2012) analyzed whether investors have equal confidence in female and male CEOs. The experimental set-up among 222 MBA students used hypothetical descriptions of CEOs that differed only in the sex of the CEO. The experiment has shown that "despite being identical in the experiment, the abilities and experience of female CEOs were evaluated more negatively than those of male CEOs" (Bigelow, 2012: 20). The authors suggest that the market does not see gender diversity in top management as a predictor of potentially better performance owing to gender-biased perceptions about female leadership.

The implication of this case study for the economics profession is that more women at the top—in universities and research institutions as well as in other institutions where economists hold institutional power such as the International Monetary Fund (IMF) and banks—will probably be a stabilizing factor for the economy in general and the financial sector in particular. Not because they would naturally be more caring—the

SCN in the Rabobank case study was developed by two men—but because a combination of socialization and a bit of biology has made it more likely for women to be more risk averse, less overconfident in a competitive environment, and more flexible in their market strategies as well as their management styles. Hence, more women and more learning by males of women's economic behavior would help to balance the economics profession far beyond the sex ratio in top positions.

Conclusion

This chapter has reviewed two alternative ethical approaches to "doing finance"—both of them are yet poorly understood in the economic literature. Economists often mistake mainstream economics to be a morally neutral science. They are so convinced that they tend to see ethics in economics as comprising only deontology, because it entails acting in accordance with a rule or principle recognized to be right and just, even if it compromises the ultimate goal of utility maximization. In doing so, they fail to recognize that the "utility maximization" that neoclassical economics seeks is itself value laden and utilitarian in nature. Deontology has come out stronger after the crisis, often in the shape of a compliance attitude in the sector, both by regulators and in banks. The intention of this chapter is to present an alternative to this dichotomous view of deontology constraining utility maximization. The alternative is the ethics of care. This is not an entirely new ethics in finance but resonates in the sector with its emphasis on integrity. The two case studies, one on careful financial asset development and one on gender differences in finance, illustrate the value of the ethics of care in finance. This ethics serves to introduce not only more stable and sustainable financial sector practices, "caring finance," but also as an analytical framework for economists to understand behavior that does not fit a utilitarian set of assumptions or a deontological approach—"caring economics."[11]

References

Acemoglu, Daron. 2009, January. "The Crisis of 2008: Structural Lessons for and from Economics." *Policy Insight* no. 28. Washington, DC: Centre for Economic Policy Research.

Ahmed Azmi, Rania. 2008. "Mutual Funds Performance: Does Gender Matter in an Emerging Market." Mimeo, University of Portsmouth.

Barber, Brad, and Terrance Odean. 2001. "Boys Will Be Boys: Gender, Overconfidence, and Common Stock Investment." *Quarterly Journal of Economics* 116(1): 261–292.

[11] 'Caring for Economics' was the title of my PhD dissertation in 1999. It was published two years later as *The Values of Economics* (van Staveren, 2001).

Barclays Wealth. 2011. "Understanding the Female Economy: The Role of Gender in Financial Decision Making and Succession Planning for the Next Generation." London: Barclays Wealth and Ledbury Research.

Beckmann, Daniela, and Lukas Menkhoff. 2008. "Will Women Be Women? Analyzing the Gender Difference among Financial Experts." *Kyklos* 61(3): 364–384.

Benhabib, Seyla. 1987. "The Generalized and the Concrete Other: The Kohlberg-Gilligan Controversy and Moral Theory." In *Women and Moral Theory*, edited by Eva Feder Kittay and Diana T. Meyers, pp. 154–177. Totowa, NJ: Rowman & Littlefield.

Bentham, Jeremy. 1970. [1789]. *An Introduction to the Principles of Morals and Legislation*, critical edition edited by J. H. Burns and H. L. A. Hart. London: Athlone Press.

Berger, Allen, Thomas Kick, and Klaus Schaeck. 2012. "Executive Board Composition and Bank Risk Taking." Discussion Paper No. 03/2012. Deutsche Bundesbank.

Bigelow, Lyda, et al. 2012. "Skirting the Issues: Experimental Evidence of Gender Bias in IPO Prospectus Evaluations." Working Paper. Retrieved from http://ssm.com/abstract=1556449

Blundell-Wignall, Adrian, Paul Atkinson, and Se Hoon Lee. 2008. "The Current Financial Crisis: Causes and Policy Issues." In *Financial Market Trends*. Paris: OECD: 1–21.

Booth, Alison, and Patrick Nolen. 2012, February. "Gender Differences in Risk Behaviour: Does Nurture Matter?" *The Economic Journal* 122: F56–F78.

Broome, John. 1991. *Weighting Goods*. Oxford: Basil Blackwell.

Chang, Susan Arterian. 2010, April 5. "Outsiders and Outperformers: Women in Fund Management," *The Finance Professional's Post*. http://post.nyssa.org/nyssa-news/2010/04/outsiders-and-outperformers-women-in-fund-management.html

Coates, J. M., and J. Herbert. 2008. "Endogenous Steroids and Financial Risk Taking on a London Trading Floor." *Proceedings of the National Academy of Sciences* 16(105): 6167–6172.

Coates, John M., Mark Gurnell, and Zoltan Sarnyai. 2010. "From Molecule to Market: Steroid Hormones and Financial Risk-Taking." *Philosophical Transactions of the Royal Society of London B: Biological Sciences* 365: 331–343.

Crespo, Ricardo, and Irene van Staveren. 2012. "Would We Have Had this Crisis if Women Had Been Running the Financial Sector?" *Journal of Sustainable Finance and Investment* 1(3–4): 241–250.

Croson, Rachel and Uri Gneezy. 2009. "Gender Differences in Preferences." *Journal of Economic Literature* 47(2): 448–474.

Dreber, A., and M. Johannesson. 2008. "Gender Differences in Deception." *Economics Letters* 99: 197–199.

Fehr, Ernst, and Antonio Rangel. 2011. "Neuroeconomic Foundations of Economic Choice—Recent Advances.," *Journal of Economic Perspectives* 25(4): 3–30.

Gerdes, Christer, and Patrik Gränsmark. 2010. "Strategic Behavior across Gender: a Comparison of Female and Male Expert Chess Players." IZA Discussion Paper no. 4793. Bonn, Germany: Institute for the Study of Labor.

Gilligan, Carol. 1982. *In a Different Voice. Psychological Theory and Women's Development*. Cambridge MA.: Harvard University Press.

Graafland, Johan. 2009. "Utilitarianism." In *Handbook of Economics and Ethics*, edited by Jan Peil and Irene van Staveren, pp. 555–563. Cheltenham, UK: Edward Elgar.

Hart, Oliver, and Luigi Zingales. 2009. "How to Avoid a New Financial Crisis." Working Paper, University of Chicago.

Held, Virginia. 2006. *The Ethics of Care. Personal, Political, and Global*. Oxford: Oxford University Press.

Hellwig, Martin. 2008. "Systemic Risk in the Financial Sector—an Analysis of the Subprime-Mortgage Financial Crisis." Jelle Zijlstra Lecture 6. Wassenaar, the Netherlands: Netherlands Institute for the Advanced Study in the Humanities and Social Sciences.

Igan, Deniz, Prachi Mishra, and Thierry Tressel. 2009. "A Fistfull of Dollars: Lobbying and the Financial Crisis." IMF Working Paper WP/09/287. Washington, DC: International Monetary Fund.

Israel, Salomon, Ori Weisel, Richard P. Ebstein, and Gary Bornstein. 2012. "Oxytocin, But Not Vasopressin, Increases both Parochial and Universal Altruism." Discussion Paper no. 598, Hebrew University of Jerusalem.

Kray, Laura, and Michael Haselhuhn. 2011. "Male Pragmatism in Ethical Decision Making." Working Paper. Berkeley, CA: Institute for Research on Labor and Employment.

Levinson, Marc. 2010. "Faulty Basel: Why More Diplomacy Won't Keep the Financial System Safe." *Foreign Affairs* 89(3): 76–88.

Lofton, Louann. 2011. *Warren Buffett Invests Like a Girl—and Why You Should, Too.* New York: The Motley Fool.

Narayan, V. G., Fabrizio Ferri, and Lisa Brem. 2008. "Executive Pay and the Credit Crisis of 2008." 9-109-036 Study Case. Boston: Harvard Business School.

Nazario, Brunilda. n.d. "Why Men and Women Handle Stress Differently." WebMD Feature. Retrieved from http://www.womanscopenewsmagazine.com/top-stories/2013/04/25/today-is-take-your-child-to-work-day/;http://women.webmd.com/features/stress-women-men-cope

Niessen, Alexandra, and Stefan Ruenzi. 2005. "Sex Matters. Gender and Mutual Funds." Paper of the Department of Corporate Finance & Centre for Financial Research. University of Cologne.

Nothwehr, Erin, and Tim Manning. 2009. "Regulatory Failures and Insufficiencies that Contributed to the Financial Crisis and Proposed Solutions." University of Iowa Center for International Finance and Development. Retrieved from http://blogs.law.uiowa.edu/ebook/sites/default/files/Regulatory_Failures_0.pdf

Peil, Jan, and Irene van Staveren, Eds. 2009. *Handbook of Economics and Ethics.* Cheltenham, UK: Edward Elgar.

Robinson, R. J., R. J. Lewicki, and E. M. Donahue. 2000. "Extending and Testing a Five Factor Model of Ethical and Unethical Bargaining Tactics: Introducing the SINS Scale." *Journal of Organizational Behavior* 21: 649–664.

Schneider, Friedrich, and Genhard Kirchgässner. 2009. "Financial and World Economic Crisis: What Did Economists Contribute?" Discussion Paper 2009-14. Universität St. Gallen, Department of Economics.

Skidelsky, Robert. 2009. *Keynes. The Return of the Master.* London: Allan Lane.

Van den Bos, Ruud, Marlies Harteveld, and Hein Stoop. 2009. "Stress and Decision-making in Humans: Performance Is Related to Cortisol Reactivity, Albeit Differently in Men and Women." *Psychoneuroendocrinology* 34: 1449–1458.

Vanguard Retirement Centre Research. 2011. "The Great Recession and 401(k) Plan Participant Behaviour. Valley Forge: The Vanguard Group Inc.

Van Staveren, Irene. 2001. *The Virtues of Economics—an Aristotelian Perspective.* London: Routledge.

Van Staveren, Irene. 2014. "The Lehman Sisters Hypothesis." *Cambridge Journal of Economics* 38(5): 995–1014.

Van Staveren, Irene. 2013. "Caring Finance Practices." *Journal of Economic Issues* 47(2): 419–425.

Waerness, Kari. 2009. "The Ethics of Care." In *Handbook of Economics and Ethics*, Jan Peil and Irene van Staveren, pp. 138–143. Cheltenham: Edward Elgar.

White, Mark D. 2009. "Immanuel Kant." In *Handbook of Economics and Ethics*, Jan Peil and Irene van Staveren, pp. 301–307. Cheltenham, UK: Edward Elgar.

CHAPTER 15

ECONOMISTS' ETHICS IN THE BUILD-UP TO THE GREAT RECESSION

ROBERT H. WADE

> There is a certain hubristic attitude among economists—we are the queen of the social sciences because we use numbers and data
>
> John Taylor, professor of economics, Stanford, 2010
>
> Charles Ferguson (director of *Inside Job*): "A medical researcher writes an article saying 'To treat this disease, you should prescribe this drug'. Turns out doctor makes 80 percent of personal income from the manufacturer of said drug. Doesn't that bother you?"
>
> John Campbell (chair of Harvard University's economics department): "I think . . . It's certainly important to disclose the, um . . . The, um . . . Um . . . Well, I think that's also a little different from the cases we're talking about here, because, um . . . Um . . ."
>
> Daron Acemoglu, professor of economics, MIT, 2013. Quoted in Freeland, 2
>
> The recent crisis gives no reason to abandon the core empirical 'rational expectations/sticky price model' developed over the past 30 years—whether you call this type of model 'dynamic stochastic general equilibrium', 'new Keynesian', or 'new neoclassical"

George DeMartino (2011, 2013) argues that the "epistemic community" of US economists has long exercised far more influence over peoples' life-chances than other social scientists (sociologists, political scientists, anthropologists, for example). He offers several reasons why economists exercise this added influence. First, their discipline gives answers to questions about appropriate policies and institutions as they affect material welfare of whole societies and the world at large. Second, the culture of the discipline encourages them to believe that their science is very reliable, including for knowing the future with statistical probability (as in Lawrence Summer's dictum, "the laws of economics . . . are like the laws of engineering"), and therefore to claim high confidence in their knowledge and prescriptions. DeMartino calls this assumption of highly reliable knowledge, "epistemic sufficiency". Third, economists believe that the mathematical formalism which unifies the discipline means that noneconomists, without access to mathematical formalism, cannot match the truth of economists' knowledge; so if noneconomists disagree with them, either they do not understand the theory or their objective is not to enhance the material welfare of others. DeMartino calls this assumption of superior knowledge vis-à-vis noneconomists, "epistemic asymmetry".

DeMartino further argues that any profession that exercises high influence over the life-chances of others should make explicit to its members the ethical principles by which they should exercise their influence, whether directly or indirectly; and to institutionalize processes through which to formulate and constantly engage with the ethical principles that should guide the behavior of its members. He concludes that—in contrast to medicine and engineering, two other professions that exercise far-reaching influence over the life-chances of others—the epistemic community of US (and other) economists has largely failed to grapple with these ethical principles. In the absence of ethical restraints its members have too often confidently advocated policies on the assumption that the optimal outcomes will materialize, only to find that their prescriptions bring about unanticipated, harmful effects that catch them off guard.

This chapter takes as its context the views of mainstream economists—mainly American and British—in the years preceding the Great Crash of 2008. It argues that they contributed to the build-up of financial fragility through their assumption of both epistemic asymmetry (or hubris) and of epistemic sufficiency (or close-mindedness, or selective inattention to data and arguments which would upset their way of seeing things). It argues, second, that they also contributed to the build-up of financial fragility through undisclosed conflict of interests, involving collusion between economists and financial organizations, such as ostensibly independent academic economists advocating financial deregulation when they were undisclosed directors of investment funds (see epigraph 3). It argues, third, that the discipline has long demonstrated ethical failings by refusing to formulate and teach ethical principles for guiding economists as they prescribe policies that may affect the welfare of millions of people and the health of the biosphere. Since the Crash there is not yet much sign of improvement.

Epistemic Confidence in the Build-Up to Crisis in 2007–2008

We start with some reminders of the confidence with which distinguished mainstream economists over the 2000s presumed the ability of market economies to sustain full-employment equilibrium.

Robert Lucas, one of the founding fathers of modern neoclassical macroeconomics, and Nobel laureate, gave the presidential address to the American Economic Association in 2003: "My thesis in this lecture is that macroeconomics . . . has succeeded: *Its central problem of depression prevention has been solved, for all practical purposes*, and has in fact been solved for many decades" (Lucas, 2003, emphasis added). Ben Bernanke, Princeton professor and at the time a member of the board of governors of the US central bank (subsequently the chair), said in a 2004 speech to a gathering of prominent economists:

> One of the most striking features of the economic landscape over the past twenty years or so has been a substantial decline in macroeconomic volatility . . . Several writers have dubbed this remarkable decline in the variability of both output and inflation "the Great Moderation."

Bernanke expected the Great Moderation to continue, thanks to continued good management of the economy, especially through monetary policy. He overlooked the income distribution and debt trends that, little more than three years later, culminated in plunging the US economy and then much of the Western economy into what may be a decade-long recession.

In May 2006 Anne Krueger, First Deputy Managing Director of the International Monetary Fund (the top-ranking American), announced that

> *In recent times the world economy has rarely been in better shape than it is today* . . . the Fund has yet again revised upwards its expectations for global growth . . . growth in the United States remains rapid . . . there are signs of an upturn in those parts of Western Europe, including France and Germany, where growth has been sluggish . . . There are . . . significant downside risks to our central forecasts. [She then enumerated several risks, such as geopolitical developments like a major terrorist attack, an outbreak of avian flu, or a disappointing outcome of the Doha trade round; all her risks were exogenous to the US and European economies. She concluded:] *The global economy appears to be more resilient in the face of shocks than it was even a short time ago* (emphasis added).

Through 2007 the tone of leading economists remained upbeat. In May 2007 the chief economist of the Organisation for Economic Co-operation and Development (OECD), Jean-Philippe Cotis, reported that earlier, in the autumn of 2006,

> . . . the OECD took the view that the US slowdown was not heralding a period of worldwide economic weakness, unlike, for instance, in 2001. Rather, a "smooth" rebalancing was to be expected, with *Europe taking over the baton from the United States* in driving OECD growth.

Cotis went on:

> Recent developments [in the few months before May 2007] have broadly confirmed this prognosis. Indeed, the *current economic situation is in many ways better than*

> *what we have experienced in years . . . Our central forecast remains quite benign* . . . [we expect the OECD to show] strong job creation and falling unemployment (7, emphasis added).

Prominent economists remained relaxed about the rise of US and other Western countries' current account deficits (the other side of rising private debt-to-GDP ratios). In December 2007 Anatole Kaletsky, a well-known British economist, declared:

> The remarkable decline in economic instability during the past 20 years—which has been well documented by academic researchers and has been titled "the great moderation"—is closely connected to the abandonment of fixed exchange rates and the deregulation of financial markets . . .
>
> [L]arge trade deficits [in OECD economies] have done none of the economies concerned any visible harm. On the contrary, among the large OECD countries, *those with persistent trade deficits have mostly had the healthiest economic conditions* . . . while the countries with big surpluses, most notably Japan and Germany, have been falling behind in all these respects. This is no coincidence, because *large trade deficits, far from being a cause of economic dislocations, have actually been a consequence of rapid economic growth* (emphasis added).

The celebrated American guru of supply-side economics, Arthur Laffer, announced to his Icelandic audience in November 2007 that Iceland's combination of fast economic growth with a large trade deficit and rising foreign debt represented success, not danger. "Iceland should be a model to the world," he declared. Less than a year later Iceland's financial system imploded, causing the biggest slump of GDP in the 33 member states of the OECD and propelling Iceland into the league of the 11 biggest financial crashes in history. Laffer somehow overlooked the dangers facing a tiny economy of 310,000 people which by 2007 supported three of the world's 300 biggest banks, with the second highest ratio of bank assets to GDP in the world after Switzerland—on the basis of only seven years' experience of international banking (Wade, 2009; Wade and Sigurgeirsdottir, 2012).

All through the credit boom of the 2000s economic theory blinkered economists to dangers in plain view. Of course, features of economic theory had their effect through wider institutional and cultural forces, notably the triumph of market individualist ideology in much of the West over the last decades of the 20th century, including in social democratic political parties. Political leaders translated the ideology into policy prescriptions, as in Labour Chancellor Gordon Brown's declaration to the Confederation of British Industry in November 2005 that his policy on financial regulation could be summarized as "not just a light touch but a limited touch."

Politicians' confidence in market individualistic ideology and its policy prescriptions owed much to the confidence of economists, who carried high moral authority.

Heterodox Dissenters

To identify the misleading features of economic theory it helps to understand the approaches of those who did see a big crisis coming. A substantial number of business journalists and business-oriented economists warned publicly through the 2000s that a housing bubble was under way (Foster and McChesney, 2012). *Business Week* said in August 2002 "A credit crunch could set in if a rate rise triggers a wave of defaults by holders of adjustable mortgages." The *Economist* magazine declared in June 2005, "The worldwide rise in house prices is the biggest bubble in history. Prepare for the economic pain when it pops." The political analyst Kevin Phillips issued many warnings, including in 2006 that houses had become "tools of speculative finance" and that "the United States had exchanged a stock-market bubble for the larger credit bubble," presaging financial collapse.

But warning of a housing bubble and even of a more general financial crisis is one thing; warning of protracted recession and high unemployment is another. The Dutch economist Dirk Bezemer searched the academic and media literatures for people whose warnings met the following exacting criteria (2009a, 2009b).

- They forecast not just a real estate crisis but a finance-induced recession substantially more severe than a "normal" recession.
- They gave an account of the mechanism from which the warning was derived.
- They included a time period.
- They put the warning in the public domain.

Bezemer identified only 12 people in the vast literature who met these criteria. They included Dean Baker, Wynne Godley, Fred Harrison, Michael Hudson, Eric Janszen, Steve Keen, Jakob Brochner Madsen and Jens Kjaer Sorensen, Kurt Richebacher, Nouriel Roubini, Peter Schiff, and Robert Shiller. All are identified as, in one way or another, heterodox economists.

Heterodox means outside the neoclassical school. The various heterodox schools include "Austrian" economics (whose adherents are mostly American); feminist economics; ecological economics; Marxist economics; Marxisant economics; Sraffian economics; development economics (or a sub-school within it); complexity theory; evolutionary economics; and post-Keynesian economics. For all their differences they all reject the concept of equilibrium and most reject Ricardian comparative advantage theory as the foundation of international economics.[1]

Let us consider features of neoclassical theory that led neoclassical economists to fix their attention on the Great Moderation and overlook or downplay indicators of coming crisis.

[1] See Keen (2011, chapter 18) for a review of non-neoclassical approaches.

The Blinkers of Neoclassical Economics

Neglect of Finance

To an outsider it is amazing to realize that neoclassical macroeconomic theory assigns a marginal role to finance. It treats finance like oil in the engine—the engine will not turn without it but it has no role in making the engine turn. Or in another metaphor, finance is "the veil of money" over the "real" economy, meaning that finance passively accommodates the supply side of the economy, where the determinants of output and employment are located. Debt is repaid instantly and without default. The models do include money supply and the interest rate, but depict them as determined by the real side rather than imposing their own dynamic on the real side.[2]

Christina Romer, former chair of the Council of Economic Advisors for President Obama, expressed this neoclassical understanding when she said in 2008:

> Just as there is no regularity in the timing of business cycles, there is no reason why cycles have to occur at all. The prevailing view among economists is that there is a level of economic activity, often referred to as full employment, at which the economy could stay forever.

The statement quoted above from the OECD chief economist, Jean-Philippe Cotis, in May 2007, "Our central forecast remains quite benign," was based on the OECD's "small global forecasting" model. Dirk Bezemer notes that the model has no place for "credit flows, asset prices or increasing net worth driving a borrowing boom, nor interest payments indicating growing debt burdens, and no balance sheet stock and flow variables that would reflect all this" (2009: 19). The Bank of England's macro model of the economy long excluded the same variables and concentrated on "real" exchanges (Arestis and Sawyer 2002).

Joseph Stiglitz generalizes:

> This crisis ... was a credit crisis, but few of the macroeconomic models modelled credit; neither banks (particularly surprising in models used by banks) nor securitization were typically incorporated into the analysis. While in normal times, credit and money are highly correlated, this is not so in the unusual times surrounding crises, which is when we need to turn to models for guidance. (2011: 2)[3]

[2] The models expounded in Michael Wickens. 2008. *Macroeconomic Theory: A Dynamic General Equilibrium Approach*, Princeton University Press, have no financial sector.

[3] See also Arestis, P. 2009. "New Consensus Macroeconomics and Keynesian Critique." In *Macroeconomic Policies on Shaky Foundations: Wither Mainstream Macroeconomics?*, edited by E. Hein, T. Niechoj, and E. Stockhammer. Marburg, Germany: Metropolis-Verlag.

Bezemer found that the 12 prescients differed from neoclassical economists in that they focused on (1) the distinction between financial assets and real-sector assets, (2) credit flows that finance both types of assets, and (3) the resulting debt levels relative to income. Starting from the proposition that financial stability (at the micro and macro levels) is based on a sustainable relationship between income streams and debt service, they put at the center of their mechanism of crisis the fast rise in credit over the 1990s and 2000s—the fast rise in private debt-to-income (GDP), including debt of households, financial companies, and nonfinancial companies. In the United States the ratio rose from about 70 percent in 1960 to about 265 percent by 2008—far above any previous level since the Second World War.

Looking back it is clear, first, that the high level of private debt-to-income was the main *proximate* cause of the US financial crash of 2007 and ensuing economic slump; and second, that rising debt-to-income was made possible by financial innovations such as subprime mortgages and securitization. Rising private debt financed a boom in demand, up to a level from which collapse in the growth of debt triggered a collapse of private demand, as private debtors struggled to repay by cutting consumption and investment, causing income streams to collapse.

As for why debt-to-income rose through the 2000s we cannot get far without encountering another set of variables largely overlooked by the neoclassical school: income distribution, and in particular, a strong shift from wages to profits and a strong concentration of income in the top few percentiles of the household distribution and in giant funds (such as pension funds), especially in the United States and United Kingdom (Wade, 2011, 2012).[4] On the one hand, rising income concentration produced a tidal wave of surplus capital not into consumption or investment but into asset markets prone to rapid price rises, especially stocks and real estate; then rising asset prices generated the collateral on which the wealthy and the funds could base more borrowing to buy more assets. On the other hand, even as the middle class shrank (the number of families with income between 75 percent and 150 percent of the median fell), middle class consumption boomed through the 2000s—financed partly by cutting savings and mostly by increasing borrowing. Goldman Sachs and other such firms supplied the financial instruments that matched up the demand from the top for assets in which to hold and multiply wealth with the demand from lower down the income distribution for borrowing to supplement stagnant incomes. This is the mechanism by which private debt reached a level far above the capacity to repay out of income. In essence, what we commonly call the debt crisis of 2007 and beyond is an epiphenomenon of a wages crisis, and behind that, a radical shift in the balance of power in society from "labor" to the owners and managers of capital.

Circumstances in the international economy also contributed to the build-up of financial fragility. Neoclassical theory assumes that exchange rates are driven by trade flows, and hence change slowly and in an equilibrating direction; so that countries

[4] See the film, *The Flaw*, directed by David Sington, 2010. The title comes from Alan Greenspan's admission in late 2008 that he had discovered a flaw in his life-long ideology of free markets.

running external deficits will experience depreciation of the external value of their currency, and those running surpluses will experience appreciation. In the real world the exchange rates of major economies turn out to be driven more by capital flows, making them volatile and prone to move in directions which make trade imbalances bigger rather than smaller.

The neglectful treatment of finance, and the linked neglect of both income distribution and the role of capital flows in driving exchange rates, are some of the main features of neoclassical macroeconomics which blinkered economists to dangers in plain view. But these blinkers themselves stem from more fundamental features of neoclassical theory. To understand how economists could ignore rising financial fragility through the 2000s we should look to these more fundamental features. They include self-adjusting equilibrium as the conceptual center of the model of the market system; deduction from a priori premises; the future assumed to be knowable in terms of probabilistic risk; and macroeconomics on microeconomic foundations.

Autonomous Self-adjusting Equilibrium System

The neoclassical way of seeing the economy, society, and politics teaches economists to believe that the market economy is (a) autonomous from the state, and (b) largely self-adjusting. The state should only "intervene" in the system in the event of "market failure", and then only if the benefits of intervention will clearly exceed the costs. This conception imposes a strong presumption against state intervention, including intervention to constrain private financial firms' lending and borrowing, and intervention to "distort" pre-tax income distribution by using taxes and transfers to achieve objectives decided through a political rather than market process. Competition ensures that the system equilibrium is at or close to full employment, and that economic growth in excess of population growth is "natural," except when institutions such as the state or trade unions distort the workings of the system. Hence the market economy—with a little help from the external agent, the state—is the best social system because of the conditions that pertain in equilibrium.

Neoclassical theory encourages adherents to believe that financial markets themselves keep debt within sustainable limits, on the assumption that market agents will detect overborrowing and cause the stock price of overborrowed organizations to fall. Likewise, the theory teaches that financial markets themselves tend to keep trade imbalances within limits, on the assumption (mentioned earlier) that exchange rates are driven mainly by trade flows, not capital flows; and therefore that exchange rates will adjust slowly and in direct response to trade imbalances (Harvey, 2012). These are but two of many self-correcting mechanisms built into the neoclassical market model.

In contrast, the heterodox schools are less wedded to the assumption of an autonomous, self-correcting market system. Here one finds theoretical work based on the assumption that the economy is a system that is dynamic, nonlinear, and reflexive, in the sense that beliefs about what will happen influence what does happen. The post-Keynesian school, for example, sees exchange rates as being largely determined by institutional investors adjusting their capital portfolios in response to actual and expected rates of return. This mechanism can explain how exchange rates often move in the *wrong* direction for reducing trade imbalances. Investors may borrow in the currency of a low interest rate country (Switzerland, Japan) and buy the currency of a high interest rate country that allows free capital mobility (Iceland, Hungary, Brazil), appreciating the target country's exchange rate even when it is running a large trade deficit. And investors' decisions may change quickly, whiplashing the exchange rate (UNCTAD, 2009).

Of course, the neoclassical journals are full of criticisms of the market system; but they concentrate on failures of the price mechanism due to specific reasons such as incomplete information, price distortions, financial repression, increasing returns, monopoly. Few neoclassical economists have focused on (1) persistent unemployment due to lack of demand (which would challenge the whole theoretical edifice built on the premise that economics is the study of choices in conditions of *scarcity*); (2) conflicts between employers and employees, producers and consumers, producers and producers, or between classes and within classes; (3) income and wealth concentration and (4) different types of market-based economies, such as the "coordinated" type represented by Germany and Japan and the "liberal" type represented by the US and Great Britain.

Deductive Rigor

Neoclassical economics is based on the epistemological premise that the economy is understandable through deductive reasoning from a specific set of a priori premises; that the reasoning should be in mathematical form; and that models are not just useful tools but are capable of yielding comprehensive and universal explanations and prescriptions. Phenomena not explicable by deductive reasoning are rendered of marginal importance. By the early 1990s more than 90 percent of the articles in the top-ranked half dozen economics journals were expressed mostly in algebra, calculus, and econometrics. By contrast, verbal exposition dominated more than 90 percent of the articles in the top-ranked journals of the 1920s; and fell to about a third by the 1960s as the neoclassical revolution kicked in (Hodgson, 2009).

John Hicks' *Value and Capital* (1946), one of the seminal works in microeconomics, illustrates the tradeoff between mathematical formalism and real world observation. Hicks made an explicit defense of a priori reasoning on grounds that it was legitimate to build a theoretical edifice on the basis of certain assumptions about firms and consumers which were chosen (over alternative assumptions) *because* they were necessary for the development of tractable mathematical models with determinate solutions. The key assumption was that firms faced *decreasing* returns to scale, and hence limits to their growth. This assumption was necessary to present the economy as a perfectly competitive system in equilibrium. Hicks was clear that the assumption was a heuristic device.

Without it, "the stability conditions become indeterminate; and the basis on which economic laws can be constructed is therefore shorn away," he said (84).

Later generations of economists tended to forget Hick's instrumental justification for assuming decreasing returns (that it is necessary for equilibrium solutions to mathematical models) and to presume that it depicts the real world—and hence that the real world has a strong tendency to self-adjusting full-employment equilibrium.

A corollary of the assumption of decreasing returns is the marginal productivity theory of income distribution, which says that factors of production (including labor) are paid—in equilibrium—at their marginal productivity; with the further corollary that state "intervention" to change income distribution generally causes inefficient resource allocation. The marginal productivity theory of income distribution tended to anaesthetize neoclassical economics to problems of rising income inequality over the 1990s and 2000s, including the link from rising inequality to financial fragility as the financial sector grew to connect the savings glut in giant funds and at the top of the household income distribution with the demand for credit on the part of the majority of families on stagnant incomes.

Knowable Future

In the past few decades neoclassical economists have developed a microeconomics of "rational expectations," whose basic proposition is that "outcomes do not differ systematically . . . from what people expected them to be . . . In their efforts to forecast prices, investors comb all sources of information" (Sargent, 2008). Hence banks and nonfinancial corporations can know the future (such as credit events) in terms of statistical probabilities—they can calculate on the basis of past events the probability of future financial conditions. The premise of the knowable future has scant empirical backing, but it is used because it is necessary to solve equations pertaining to the theory of the firm and the theory of financial markets. And it is also used because it carries the agreeable implication that *corporations, including banks and other financial firms, can manage risks so as to prevent future problems for themselves. Therefore, government regulation constitutes an external* interference *that tends to slow down the self-equilibrating tendencies of the system.*

More specifically, the premise implies that financial regulation *should* enable gambles to be taken on all possible future states of the world, because this will make for complete markets and enhance efficiency. Statistical and actuarial techniques for establishing probabilistic risks of possible future outcomes can be trusted safely to equate credit default insurance premiums with the expected value of payments.

Hence regulators such as Alan Greenspan, chair of the US Federal Reserve, asserted that complex financial instruments represented new and effective tools of risk management, and that the growth of trade in these instruments made the economy *more stable.* And the International Monetary Fund (IMF) justified its earlier-quoted optimism about the outlook for the world economy as of 2006 with the claim that "developments in the global financial system have played an important role, including the ability of the United States to generate assets with attractive liquidity and risk management features" (2007).

This line of argument encouraged the proliferation of substantially unregulated derivatives, such as credit default swaps, based on mortgages, car loans, student loans, and the like. Without this proliferation of derivatives the credit boom over the 2000s would have been much smaller, the financial crash much milder.

None of the heterodox schools identified earlier assume that the future is knowable in terms of probabilistic risk. They operate with an assumption closer to the Keynes–Knight concept of nonquantifiable uncertainty, which implies that beyond narrow and short-term horizons the future is unknown, not reducible to probability distributions. The question is how decision makers make decisions and act in conditions of uncertainty (Keynes covered up ignorance with the hazy phrase "animal spirits"). The assumption of uncertainty rather than probabilistic risk is crucial for understanding the volatility of investment and speculation; but it is also difficult to formalize (Kahneman, 2011).

Macroeconomics on Micro Foundations

With the neoclassical school in the saddle, macroeconomics has come to be largely an extrapolation of microeconomics; and moreover, a microeconomics based not on meticulous observation of how people, businesses and governments behave, in the spirit of Alfred Marshall or A. C. Pigou, but on deduction from axioms some of which have no basis in evidence, such as the axiom that the future is knowable in terms of statistical probabilities.

The *preanalytic* assumption is that macroeconomics must have microeconomic foundations, in the sense that macroeconomic propositions, to be considered valid, must be logically derivable from microeconomic propositions about individual agents in conditions of scarcity; and those that cannot be so derived are put on the margins. The assumption rules out the premise of post-Keynesian theory, that microeconomic theory must be consistent with post-Keynesian macroeconomic theory of business cycles, sustained unemployment, excess capacity, income distribution, the nature of money, the role of credit in driving consumption and economic growth, and so on.

However, the microeconomic takeover of macroeconomics has provoked some opposition even within the neoclassical school, including from one of the most eminent, Nobel Prize laureate Robert Solow. Here is Solow's critical summary of this approach, commonly known as "real business cycle" theory or "Dynamic Stochastic General Equilibrium" theory (see epigraph 1). The prototypical macro model, he said, contains

> . . . a single, immortal household—a representative consumer—that earns wages from supplying labor. It also owns the single price-taking firm, so the household receives the net income of the firm. The household takes the present and future wage rates and present and future dividends as given, and formulates an optimal infinite-horizon

> consumption-saving . . . plan . . . The firm looks at the same prices, and maximizes current profit by employing labor, renting capital and producing and selling output . . .
>
> The theory actually imagines that the model economy is disturbed from time to time by unforeseen shocks to the technology and the household's tastes . . . There is nothing pathological or remediable about observed fluctuations . . . [A]fter one of them has happened, the economy is already making optimal adjustments, given its technology and the inter-temporal preferences of its single inhabitant or identical inhabitants. *There is no role for macroeconomic policy in this world . . . the best [the government] can do is to perform its necessary functions in the most regular, predictable way, so as not to add unnecessary variance to the environment* (Solow 2001, emphasis added. Quoted in Keen, 2011: 257)

Solow here confirms that neoclassical economics attempts to model the entire economy by extrapolating from microeconomic theory about the behavior of individual consumers and firms. There is little room for "emergent properties" of an economy—phenomena that arise from our interactions with each other and the environment rather than from the properties of the units in isolation.

Consequences for Economic Policy

The combination of the several features described above—finance as neutral, inherent tendencies of the free-market economy to full-employment equilibrium, the future as probabilistically knowable, knowledge constrained by mathematical formalism, and the microeconomic takeover of macroeconomics—lead prototypical neoclassical economists to be politically conservative in major economic and financial policy debates, while seeing themselves as rigorous scientists driven by evidence rather than ideological predilection. They tend to see state and market as opposed, so that "more state" implies "less market," and vice versa. Moreover, and following from the above features, they see the state, and the public sector more generally, as a source of not just inefficiency but also of instability, in contrast to the private sector with its built-in self-adjustment mechanisms through the price system. They see the political domain as dominated by personal interest more than by moral concern, and without the built-in checks to personal interest provided by competition in a market; and so they discount the significance of political actors having to justify their actions in terms of a notion of the common good whose characteristics are decided through political debate, as corporate actors do not have to.

It follows from the foregoing that neoclassicals tend to urge that the state (in economic and financial realms) be as small as possible in order to reduce inefficiency and instability, and urge government to withdraw from management of the economy beyond those actions consistent with maintaining a "level playing field." They are keen on expanding the fee-seeking private supply of "public goods" such as health care and education; and strongly in favor of free trade. Also, it almost goes without saying, they tend to be hostile to labor unions, collective bargaining, and minimum wage legislation, seen as inefficiency-producing interferences in the market that lower the rightful ("equilibrium") share of profits in national income. They see trade unions, in particular, as rent-seeking organizations, trying to get a bigger share of the pie rather than make the pie grow.

Alan Budd, Special Advisor at the UK Treasury in 1979–1981, explained how the Thatcher government sought to create a neoclassical structure in Britain by first creating mass unemployment, disguising the strategy as an anti-inflation strategy. Interviewed in 1991 he said,

> The nightmare I sometimes have . . . is that there may have been people making the actual policy decisions, or people behind them, or people behind them, who *never believed for a moment that this was the correct way to bring down inflation. They did, however, see that it would be a very, very good way to raise unemployment, and raising unemployment was an extremely desirable way of reducing the strength of the working classes . . . What was engineered there in Marxist terms was a crisis of capitalism which re-created a reserve army of labour and has allowed the capitalists to make high profits ever since* (emphasis added).

He said this a month after Tory Chancellor Norman Lamont stated in parliament (May 6, 1991), "Rising unemployment and the recession have been the price that we have had to pay to get inflation down. That price is well worth paying." In fact, the rate of retail price inflation when Mrs. Thatcher left office in November 1990 was identical to the rate when she took office in May 1979, at 9.2 percent.

Why Has Neoclassical Economics Remained So Dominant?

Let us consider why neoclassical economics has remained so dominant since the 1960s (relative to other schools listed earlier), and continues little challenged even after the revelations of the current Western financial crisis and recession.

Social Coordination without Power

The first reason is the powerful moral and aesthetic attraction of the teleological vision of a market system that coordinates itself so well that little superior (state) power is needed. The vision resonates strongly with cultural values that are "beyond negotiation" in the West, such as freedom defined as the absence of state coercion, individualism, hard work, self-discipline, self-reliance, incentives, science—values at the center of the conservative world view, which have more qualified status in the progressive world view.

Mathematical Formalism

Second, this vision is expressed in mathematics. Economics achieves its status as the most consensual and unified of all the social sciences because it centers on the method of mathematical formalism. Since a high degree of mathematical ability is necessary to master the modelling techniques there is a prevailing assumption that only the brightest can become (neoclassical) economists, as distinct from institutional economists, sociologists, historians, and so forth. Mathematization has recruited people who are less driven to try to explain how the world actually works or how policy could make it work more efficiently or more fairly, and more motivated to prove themselves masters of an arcane craft.

Mark Blaug, one of a small number of experts in the history of economic thought, minced no words when he wrote in 1997,

> Modern economics is sick. Economics has become an intellectual game played for its own sake and not for its practical consequences for understanding the economic world. Economists have converted the subject into a sort of social mathematics in which analytical rigor is everything and practical relevance is nothing.

Evaluative Standards

Third, the high degree of consensus (compared to other social sciences) about what constitutes quality gives rise to a high degree of consensus about the ranking of journals and economists. Recruitment and promotion according to these rankings generate positive feedback. Non-neoclassical journals, such as the *Cambridge Journal of Economics*, *Journal of Economic Issues*, and *Journal of Post Keynesian Economics* are far down the totem pole. By one commonly used ranking (based on 1998 citations), they occupy ranks 77, 108, and 113 respectively among economics journals (Kalaitzidakis et al., 2003).[5] In the eyes of many neoclassicals, it is better not to publish than to publish in such low-ranked journals. At the top of the discipline the dominance of American economics is captured in the fact that 86 percent of the Nobel Prizes in economics awarded between 1980 and 2007 went to US-based professors.

Socialization of Students

Economics in the United States produces more PhDs than political science, anthropology, history, philosophy, and English (as of 2005), and its share of PhDs in all subjects

[5] The *Journal of Post Keynesian Economics* is one ahead of the *Journal of Real Estate Finance and Economics*. The top six are *American Economic Review, Econometrica, Journal of Political Economy, Journal of Economic Theory, Quarterly Journal of Economics,* and *Journal of Econometrics. The Economic Journal* is 18.

has remained constant while these other subjects lost share and the share of the natural sciences rose (Lamont, 2009). Both graduate and undergraduate students are "socialized" to believe in the neoclassical vision and the high importance of formalism, and discouraged from studying history or other social sciences, or even from acquiring in-depth knowledge of real economies. Michele Lamont, who studied how academics in six (non-natural science) disciplines evaluate research proposals and published work, reports that "This ascendance of mathematical economics has translated into a homogenization of the core courses in every major institution, which has further solidified its position" (Lamont, 2009: 100).

Geoffrey Hodgson (2009) reports, "Most economists are interested in mathematical models. They are taught tools of analysis rather than the intellectual, historical and institutional contexts in which analytical questions arise." Indeed, they may be taught that knowing about real-world economies, as distinct from mathematical models, is not important. David Colander (2005) investigated the views of 231 graduate students at the seven top-rated US economics departments, and found that (in the early 2000s) only 9 percent thought that "a thorough knowledge of the economy" was "very important" for success. Broken down by year of study he found that 15 percent of first- and second-year graduate students thought it "very important," while fewer than 1 percent of fourth- and fifth-year students thought it very important—suggesting that the already low level of interest in real-world economies among the first and second year students had been thoroughly beaten out of them by the fourth and fifth years.

Students of mainstream economics get little exposure to the literature on financial crises. David Colander reports that even well *after* the current slump began,

> The core macroeconomic courses teach DSGE [Dynamic Stochastic General Equilibrium] modelling almost exclusively . . . Not only are the writings of Thornton or Bagehot missing, the writings of Keynes, Minsky, Hicks, Clower, Leijonhufvud, Gurley, Davidson, Goodhardt, or even Friedman, to mention just a few of those whose writings could also have contributed to a better understanding of the crisis, are missing as well. *Most students who have graduated in the past twenty years would never have even heard of half of them, let alone read them*" (2011, emphasis added).[6]

The Cambridge University Economics Department, the base of Keynes and his collaborators, teaches virtually no Keynesian economics at graduate or undergraduate level. One of its few heterodox members said in July 2012, "What is most pathetic about my faculty is that the teaching of macro continues as if the crisis had not happened" (personal communication).

On the other hand, neoclassical microeconomics sanctions much more of a "self-maximizing" principle of behavior than in the population at large. The famous

[6] Geoffrey Hodgson reports that in the first half of 2009 he "tried without success to find the work of Keynes or Minsky on any reading list available on the web of any macroeconomics or compulsory economic theory course in any of the top universities in the world" ("The great crash of 2008 and the reform of economics").

experiment by Gerald Marwell and Ruth Ames gave economics graduate students, and others, the opportunity to contribute their earnings to a charitable pot or keep the money for themselves. The economics students contributed about 20 percent of their earnings to the pot, while the others gave between 40 and 60 percent. On examination the economics students were substantially less able to articulate the concept of "public interest" (Marwell and Ames, 1981).

To what extent does economists' embrace of neoclassical views about the world—including the emphasis on individualism, freedom from state-imposed constraints, deductive reasoning, equilibrium, the neglect of income distribution and social classes—come from self-selection into economics (such that those with predisposing beliefs and preferences tend to choose economics) and to what extent from socialization as they study economics? Self-selection is suggested by the mechanism Emil Durkheim proposed, in 1912, for the origin of religious belief—as a way for social groups to experience themselves as groups. When people experience themselves as members of a community they feel bigger, bolder, more purposeful, and they identify that sense of transcendence with the supernatural. They believe in God because they belong to a certain social group, not the other way around, said Durkheim. Students of economics wanting to join the epistemic community of economists learn a set of beliefs about The Market, analogous to God, as a condition of acceptance.

However, the evidence is mixed: some studies find in favor of "selection," others in favor of "socialization." Colander's evidence on the difference in beliefs of first- and fourth-year graduate students suggests a strong socialization effect. So does an experiment by Raul Lopez-Perez and Eli Spiegelman (2012), designed to identify factors that determine the propensity to lie (such as religion, gender), and to isolate the "pure" preference for honesty by eliminating other motivations, such as altruism or fear of getting caught. Using a sample of university students, they find that sociodemographic characteristics and gender make no difference, while major subject of study makes a big difference. Humanities students lied a bit less than half the time; "others" (mainly sciences) lied about 60 percent of the time; business and economics, 77 percent of the time. So people who study economics are less likely to tell the truth for its own sake; also, the experimenters found that the difference reflects a strong socialization (not just selection) effect.

Another study also finds a strong socialization effect (Racko, 2011). It compared economics undergraduate students at the orthodox, hard-nosed Swedish School of Economics in Riga, Latvia with a control group comprised of economics undergraduate students at the two leading Latvian universities. The two sets were selected so as to be homogeneous at the start in terms of demographic characteristics (such as gender, age, ethnicity, parental occupations, family income, etc.); and also in value orientations. The study tracked the students over two years, 2005–2006 and 2006–2007. The Swedish School's courses put heavy emphasis on mathematics and econometrics, and included virtually no noneconomics courses, in contrast to the Latvian universities.

Having been much the same at the start, the value orientations were strongly divergent after two years. The Swedish School students gave much higher normative value to "instrumental rationality" and the goals achievable through self-interest, including income, status, power, and hedonism. They gave less normative value to "socially oriented self-transcendence goals." In other words, by the end of their second year many more of them endorsed individualistic ideology, thanks to socialization.

What the Wealthy Want to Hear

The fifth reason neoclassical economics has become and remains so dominant is that, put crudely, it says what the wealthy want to hear—more so than any of the other schools (with the partial exception of the Austrian). The wealthy want to hear about the self-adjusting stability of the market economy partly because this enables them—and investment banks and similar financial entities—to practice a big conceit: to wrap their activities in adherence to the rhetoric of free markets in order to obscure the mega state subsidies received by "too big to fail" financial entities, and in order to justify sky-high profits and bonuses, and, recently, the need to prevent new regulations (Tett, 2012: 24).[7] The neoclassical presumption—that Adam Smith's "invisible hand" of self-interested agents interacting in a market produce the social optima—resonated with the boom years' assumption that anything vaguely legal was acceptable, including rigged markets, avoided taxes, embellished expense claims, and unearned bonuses. But even a cursory reading of *The Wealth of Nations* and especially *The Theory of Moral Sentiments* would have required the rejection of that conclusion.

Governments have used the same smokescreen of the beneficent invisible hand to obscure how their policies have facilitated an unprecedented concentration of wealth and power. In the United Kingdom even leaders of Labour Party governments declared themselves entirely relaxed about people becoming filthy rich.

Patronage

The sixth reason is an intensification of the fifth: neoclassical economics has remained so dominant because of corporate and government patronage. Corporations and governments go beyond merely using what economists say, to commissioning them to say what they want them to say—directly through consulting fees, indirectly through grants to think tanks, university departments, and research funding bodies. Many leading academic economists live in the revolving door between academia, government, big business, and big finance (Wedel, 2009). They are invited to explain public issues in the media or to act as government advisors, while simultaneously receiving undisclosed money from banks and corporations. For example, the French economist Olivier Pastre writes articles and co-produces a French radio show on economic questions, and takes as a main theme the dangers of France leaving the euro. He is described only as a "professor of economics

[7] Gillian Tett. June 29, 2012. "Libor Affair Exposes Big Conceit at the Heart of Banking." *Financial Times* 24.

at the University of Paris VIII." His board memberships in three financial organizations and chairmanship of IMBank (Tunisia) are not mentioned (Lambert, 2012).[8]

A substantial body of research since the 1980s has shown that researchers' pharmaceutical affiliations bias research outcomes in favor of the sponsoring affiliations, and it would be surprising if the same were not true for academic economists. Though the evidence is too thin, it is plausible that conflict of interest help explain why few mainstream economists called for stronger regulation of financial derivatives and restrictions on hedge funds, or warned of growing risks of a major financial crisis.[9]

The OECD's high-level Financial Markets Committee was an engine room for promulgating to the world through the 2000s the virtues of self-regulated financial markets. The committee had substantial presence of people who worked for financial firms, meant to attend in their personal capacity as experts. But the cost of their time was paid by their companies, not by the OECD.

[8] Lambert quotes French economist Jean-Herve Lorenzi defending non-disclosure: "The issue is whether the way you earn your living influences your judgement. It doesn't – 2 + 2 is 4 whether you work for a university or for a bank." Lorenzi is introduced in public forums as chairman of the Cercle des Economistes, without mention of his membership or advisory roles in at least nine French companies.

[9] Take as two cases in point the reports of Frederic Mishkin and Richard Portes about Iceland's banks. By 2006 tiny Iceland's three main banks had shot from domestic obscurity to enter the list of the world's 300 biggest banks in just a few years, to the point where their assets amounted to over eight times GDP and most of their lending was in foreign currency. The IMF Article IV consultation report for that year rang the alarm bell, as did a Danish bank in a public report. The banks faced a "mini crisis" as their supply of short-term borrowing on international markets dried up. In May 2006, at the same time as the IMF's report became available, the Iceland Chamber of Commerce published a report attesting to the stability of the Icelandic banks, co-authored by Frederic Mishkin, a leading US monetary economist, and an Icelandic economist closely affiliated to the governing right-wing political party (2006). Mishkin and his collaborator batted away almost all the worries. For example, it dismissed worries about Iceland's large current account deficits (running at more than 15 percent of GDP) by saying, "There is generally a better case for Iceland's current account imbalances being a reflection of *optimal policies* than is true for many other countries" (chapter 3, emphasis added). It answered the question, "Is the financial supervisory authority monitoring risk sufficiently?" in just four sentences, the last of which reads, "Although concerns about the risks of rapid growth in new business areas for the banks are not unwarranted, the FSA's awareness of the potential risk and the fact that Iceland has high-quality governmental institutions provide some comfort about the safety and soundness of Iceland's banks" (chapter 4). The report does not note that the FSA's total staff—for supervising three of the world's 300 biggest banks and a dense set of regional banks which were honeypots for politicians—was 46, and its offices approached behind a fast-food joint in Reykjavik. Mishkin was paid a fee of $135,000 from the Icelandic Chamber of Commerce (*The Wall Street Journal*, 2008).

The following year, in November 2007, the Iceland Chamber of Commerce published a report co-authored by the British economist Richard Portes and another Icelandic economist. It too gave a firm endorsement of the stability of the Icelandic banks and the soundness of their business model. It too gave scant attention to the question of the capacity of the central bank to act as lender of last resort, though it noted that if all three of the big banks failed the central bank would have to borrow abroad, or the government would have to guarantee the banks' own borrowing, "which would probably also be feasible, although borrowing what would amount to almost a year's worth of tax revenues for the central government would stretch its credit lines" (40). Iceland's bank assets to GDP were then the second highest in the world, just below Switzerland's. Portes was paid £58,000 by the Chamber of Commerce (as reported in Iceland's *Special Investigation Commission Report to Parliament* in April 2010). Neither economist disclosed their fee. See further Wade and S. Sigurgeirsdottir (2012).

A study of 19 US academic financial economists found that 15 of the 19 regularly worked in some capacity with private financial organizations, and that over the period 2005–2009 13 of the 15 did not disclose these ties in any academic publications seen by the study (Carrick-Hagenbarth and Epstein, 2012). Another study, by Reuters, of 96 testimonies by academics to the Senate Banking Committee and the House Financial Services Committee between late 2008 and 2010 found that a third of the testimonies gave no indication of the academics' private financial affiliations, as they sought to influence the biggest overhaul of financial regulation since the 1930s.

Those who enjoy status and profits under the neoclassical paradigm may actively obstruct researchers who favor heterodox approaches. For example, leading heterodox economist Steve Keen—one of Bezemer's 12—applied for funding to the Australian Research Council for research on models of debt deflation nine times between 1996 and 2011, and was turned down nine times (in Keen, 2011: 257). Departments dominated by neoclassical economists tend to vote against hiring heterodox economists, on grounds that they are not "competent," and on grounds that their presence will lower the reputation of the department and thereby worsen their own access to research funding.

That being said, it is likely that the majority of economists believe in the neoclassical paradigm not because of corporate patronage and ease of access to research funds, but because they are deeply socialized into its mathematically elegant world view, and see themselves as members of an elite group, superior to other social scientists. As Durkheim's and also Pierre Bordieu's research would lead us to expect (Bordieu, 1989), neoclassical economists are aware of their dominant position among economists and of the status of economics as queen of the social sciences, and fearful of abandoning the "normal" conceptual and normative ideas of the paradigm even in response to easily observable events—such as frequent financial crises and collapses of output around the world—lest they be alienated from the group. Robert Shiller, one of the Bezemer 12, admitted that, during his tenure on the advisory panel of the Federal Reserve Bank of New York from 1990 to 2004, he warned about the housing bubble "very gently and felt vulnerable expressing such quirky views. Deviating too far from consensus leaves one feeling potentially ostracized from the group, with the risk that one may be terminated" (Shiller, 2008: 5). Durkheim could not have put it better.

Economists' Ethics in the Build-Up to the Great Recession

This chapter has been an extended reflection on Daron Acemoglu's observation, "There is a certain hubristic attitude among [neoclassical] economists—we are the queen of the social sciences because we use numbers and data" (epigraph 2). It has suggested that the characteristic "hubristic attitude" stems, first, from the fact that economists have more influence over others' life-chances than all other social scientists; second, from the fact that the relationship between economists and those they purport to serve (including the general public) is characterized by a high degree of epistemic asymmetry compared to other social sciences, reflecting their monopolization of knowledge derived from mathematical formalism inaccessible to most people; and third, from the fact that economists operate on the assumption of a high degree of epistemic sufficiency, or confidence in the rightness of the neoclassical theory.

We have seen here how economists of the great neoclassical mainstream failed, almost completely, to spot the signs of an impending great crash and long slump. Of the small number of economists who did publish informed warnings, with analytical underpinnings, all were identified by the profession as "heterodox," according to Dirk Bezemer's research. They operated outside the frame of neoclassical economics.

Why did neoclassical economists generate false confidence in the stability of the market system and fail to warn of impending debt-induced recession? Let us recap. First, the most important proximate reason is that they use macro models in which money supply and interest rates accommodate or adapt to real sector conditions rather than impose their own dynamic on real sector conditions (hence modeling the financial sector is unnecessary). In consequence, they largely ignored the build-up of household debt in the United States, United Kingdom, and several other Western economies.

Second, at a deeper level, neoclassical economics presents a teleological vision of a moral social order based on a market economy whose participants are not big enough to influence (i.e., "distort") market outcomes, which self-adjusts so well that no external superior authority (the state) is needed to provide more than a framework of rules and infrastructure not providable by private profit-seeking.

This vision of an autonomous, self-adjusting market economy is buttressed by the emphasis on deductive rigor; by the assumption that the future is statistically knowable; and by the assumption that only macroeconomic theory rigorously derived from microeconomic theory can be accepted as valid (not the other way around).

The paradigm supports the comforting belief that debt and debt-based instruments are generally correctly priced, in line with "fundamentals"; so debt and risk are, by and large, good, and to be encouraged. The central mechanism of the current crisis—debt levels, based on bubbling asset values, rose far above what could be serviced from incomes, and the collapse of asset bubbles triggered the collapse of demand as debtors tried to repay debt or defaulted—is largely beyond its scope. The paradigm directed believers' attention elsewhere, to the real economy and the Great Moderation. And it directed them to be unworried about trade imbalances and exchange rate changes, since trade flows tend to drive exchange rates toward equilibrium. As Alan Greenspan said in 2007, "I would place the U.S. current account [deficit] far down the list of imbalances to worry about (347)," as though US external debt was unrelated to US internal debt. In the same spirit Alan Greenspan declared that the US central bank—and other central banks—should not try to lean against the wind as bubbles formed, but "mitigate the fallout when it occurs and, hopefully, ease the transition to the next expansion."

The bottom line is that neoclassical theory generates tranquil equilibrium growth, and so cannot explain crises or long periods of depressed output except as the result of external shocks, not as a result of processes inherent to a capitalist economy. Indeed, John Kenneth Galbraith suggested that even just by describing their object of study as "the market system" rather than "capitalism" economists have committed what he called "a not wholly innocent fraud," because "market system" entails "no adverse history . . . in fact no history at all. No individual or firm is dominant. No economic power is evoked. There is nothing here from Marx or Engels. There is only the impersonal market, a not wholly innocent fraud" (2004: 6–7, 12).[10]

RETHINKING?

The crash of 2008 and the ensuing long slump and high unemployment in Western economies—more than six years long at the time of writing (mid-2014)—should have delivered a rebuke to neoclassical economists and induced a softening of "hubristic attitude," including more attention to learning from other highly influential professions—such as medicine and engineering—about how they engage with ethical issues.

But there is not much sign of rethinking within neoclassical circles. One distinguished British economist exclaimed in late 2011, "Keynes was a disaster. Skidelsky [a leading latter-day Keynesian] should be locked up. Krugman [Nobel laureate and proponent of Keynesian demand stimulus] has lost all respect in the economics profession" (personal communication).

In 2010, well after the recession began, Ben Bernanke—quoted earlier celebrating the Great Moderation and by then Alan Greenspan's successor as chairman of the US central bank--admitted that "Standard macroeconomic models . . . did not predict the crisis, nor did they incorporate very easily the effects of financial instability." Yet he went straight on to defend neoclassical macroeconomics, on grounds, first, that "the recent financial crisis was more a failure of economic engineering and economic management than . . . of economic science"; and second, that modern macroeconomics works well for non-crisis times. "Do these failures of standard macroeconomic models mean that they are irrelevant or at least significantly flawed? I think the answer is a qualified no . . . *The standard models were designed for non-crisis periods, and they have proven quite useful in that context*" (16–17, 3, emphasis added).

This is strange. It implies that the conditions prior to the crisis—the Great Moderation for which the models allegedly worked well—did not contain vital causes of the crisis. It is more plausible to argue, given that recessions and depressions have occurred repeatedly, that a crucial test for the worth of a theory or model is that it be able to predict recessions and depressions as a possible outcome of mechanisms

[10] Galbraith's point stands even once one recognizes that today's capitalism is very different from the kind of economy where the ownership of the means of production was clear (Arkwright's Weaving Company was owned by Mr. Arkwright), for which the term was coined.

internal to the model. Yet neoclassical macroeconomics has no such theory. Its models imply a long recession is impossible, and turn their back on the theories of Keynes, Kalecki, Hyman Minsky, Charles Kindleberger, and Paul Sweezy, which long ago showed how financial crises and long recessions can be generated endogenously by mechanisms within the theory of capitalism. At a minimum, macro models must recognize that the financial sector is as real as the real sector, and incorporate balance sheets and flows of funds. Indeed, the distinction between the so-called "real sector" and the "financial sector" has substantially broken down, because the real sector nowadays is heavily financialized, to the point where many large "real sector" companies make more money from debt instruments than from selling goods or services.

In another sign of non-learning, the American Economic Association at its annual meeting in 2011 sponsored a session on "the 50th anniversary of rational expectations," which turned out to be a celebration rather than a wake. When one of the proponents was asked what economics would be like in 50 years he was adamant that rational expectations and equilibrium would still be at the heart of the discipline (Keen, 2011: 456–457).

Not all neoclassical economists have been so mulish. Olivier Blanchard, chief economist of the IMF, declared in a paper published in 2009 that "there has been enormous progress and substantial convergence . . . The state of Macro is good." By 2011 he changed his mind, when he said that the crisis "forces us to do a wholesale re-examination of those [standard macro] principles" (in Arestis, 2009).

However, knowledgeable insiders agree with David Colander, quoted earlier, that rethinking has hardly started. The celebrated British monetary economist Charles Goodhart observed in 2009 that the standard macro models "were, by construction, 'fair weather models' only. When rough weather, in the form of financial turmoil, blew in, in August 2008, I expected one consolation to be growing appreciation among mainstream economists of the shortcomings of their models" (2009). By late 2013 he found little evidence of growing appreciation (personal communication). Cambridge University non-neoclassical economist Philip Arestis reports that "The majority of [neoclassical] proponents . . . have not, and will not, give up easily."

It is one thing for a profession to make honest mistakes: error alone does not imply unethical behavior. It is quite another for a profession to refuse to acknowledge and learn from its mistakes—especially those with grave consequences for others. When the lives of so many are at stake, a profession has a duty to root out its failings, to examine critically and openly its own practice, and to demand of itself that it do better. So far, we see only small signs of this within neoclassical economics.[11]

Clearly, hosting a disproportionate density of high-IQ professionals and students is no levee against misconceived theory unconnected to disciplinary ethics.

[11] However, the American Economic Association, which had long resisted discussion of ethics, adopted at its annual meeting in 2012 a policy of disclosure of financial ties and other conflict of interest covering papers published in its journals. The policy calls on other journals to require the same; and for economists to apply the same disclosure principles in media interviews, government testimony, and the like. The change has begun to cross the Atlantic, as mild codes have been adopted by some European economic associations.

References

Arestis, P. 2009. "New Consensus Macroeconomics: A Critical Appraisal." *Economics Working Paper Archive* wp_564. The Levy Institute, Bard College.

Arestis, P., and Sawyer, M. C. 2002. "The Bank of England Macroeconomic Model: Its Nature and Implications." *Journal of Post Keynesian Economics* 24(4): 529–545.

Bernanke, Ben. 2004. "The Great Moderation: Remarks by Governor Ben. S. Bernanke at the Meetings of the Eastern Economic Association, Washington, DC, February 20." Washington, DC: Federal Reserve Board.

Bernanke, Ben. 2010. "On the Implications of the Financial Crisis for Economics," Conference co-sponsored by the Center for Economic Policy Studies and the Bendheim Center for Finance, Princeton University, Princeton NJ. Washington, DC: US Federal Reserve Board.

Bezemer, Dirk. 2009*a*. " 'No One Saw This Coming': Understanding Financial Crisis through Accounting Model." Faculty of Economics, University of Groningen.

Bezemer, D. 2009*b*. "No One Saw This Coming—or Did They?" VoxEU.org, 30.

Blanchard, O. J. 2009. "The State of Macro." *Annual Review of Economics* 1: 209–228.

Blanchard, O. J. March 2011. "The Future of Macroeconomic Policy: Nine Tentative Conclusions. In *iMFdirect, IMF's Global Economic Forum* 13. Washington, DC: International Monetary Fund.

Blaug, Mark. 1997. "Ugly Currents in Modern Economics." *Options Politiques* 18(17): 3–8. Reprinted in *Fact and Fiction in Economics: Models, Realism, and Social Construction*, edited by U. Maki. Cambridge, UK: Cambridge University Press, 2002.

Bordieu, Pierre. 1989. "Social Space and Symbolic Power." *Sociological Theory* 7(1): 14–25.

Budd, Alan. 1991. Interview by Adam Curtis, http://cheltenham-gloucesteragainstcuts.org/2013/04/09/former-thatcher-adviser-alan-budd-spills-the-beans-on-the-use-of-unemployment-to-weaken-the-working-class-sound-familiar/.

Carrick-Hagenbarth, Jessica, and Epstein, Gerald. 2012. "Dangerous Interconnectedness: Economists' Conflicts of Interest, Ideology and Financial Crisis. *Cambridge Journal of Economics* 36(1): 43–63.

Colander, David. 2005. "The Making of an Economist Redux." *Journal of Economic Perspectives* 19(1).

Colander, David. 2011. "Is the Fundamental Science of Macroeconomics Sound?" American Economic Association, Annual Conference, Denver, CO.

Cotis, J-P. 2007. "Editorial: Achieving Further Rebalancing." *OECD Economic Outlook* 1: 7–10.

DeMartino, George. 2011. *The Economist's Oath: On the Need for and Content of Professional Economic Ethics*. New York: Oxford University Press.

DeMartino, George. 2013. "Epistemic Aspects of Economic Practice and the Need for Professional Economic Ethics." *Review of Social Economy* 71(2): 166–186.

The Economist. June 16, 2005. "The Global Housing Boom: In Come the Waves."

Foster, John Bellamy, and McChesney, Robert. 2012. "The Endless Crisis." *Monthly Review* 64(1): 7–8.

Freeland, Chrystia. May 24, 2013. "Some Cracks in the Cult of Technocrats." *International Herald Tribune*.

Galbraith, J. K. 2004. *The Economics of Innocent Fraud*. Boston: Houghton Mifflin.

Goodhart, C. 2009. "The Continuing Muddles of Monetary Theory: A Steadfast Refusal to Face Facts. In *Macroeconomic Policies on Shaky Foundations: Wither Mainstream*

Macroeconomics? edited by E. Hein, T. Niechoj, and E. Stockhammer. Marburg, Germany: Metropolis-Verlag.

Greenspan, A. 2007. *The Age of Turbulence*. New York: Penguin.

Harvey, John. 2012. "Exchange Rate Behaviour during the Great Recession." *Journal of Economic Issues* 46(2): 313–321.

Hicks, John. 1946. *Value and Capital*, 2nd ed. Oxford: Oxford University Press.

Hodgson, Geoffrey. 2009. "The Great Crash of 2008 and the Reform of Economics." *Cambridge Journal of Economics* 33(6): 1205–1221.

Iceland Special Investigation Commission. 2010. *Special Investigation Commission Report to Parliament*, Vol.1, section 4.4.5.

IMF. 2007. *World Economic Outlook*. Washington, DC: International Monetary Fund.

Kahneman, Daniel. 2011. *Thinking, Fast and Slow*. Farrar, Straus and Giroux.

Kalaitzidakis, P., Stengos, T., and Manuneas, T. 2003. "Ranking of Academic Journals and Institutions in Economics." *Journal of the European Economic Association* 1(3): 1346–1366.

Kaletsky, Anatole. December 2007. "Is Global Finance Out of Control?" Robert Wade vs Anatole Kaletsky. *Prospect* 20–24.

Keen, Steve. 2011. *Debunking Economics—Revised and Expanded Edition: The Naked Emperor Dethroned?* London: Zed Books.

Krueger, Anne. 2006. "A Remarkable Prospect: Opportunities and Challenges for the Modern World Economy." Lecture at Claremont McKenna College, May 2.

Laffer, Arthur. 2007. "Overheating Is Not Dangerous." *Morgunbladid*. November 17.

Lambert, Renaud. March 2012. "Economical with the Truth." *Le Monde Diplomatique* (English) 1–2.

Lamont, Michele. 2009. *How Professors Think: Inside the Curious World of Academic Judgment*. Cambridge, MA: Harvard University Press.

Lopez-Perez, Raul, and Spiegelman, Eli. 2012. "Do Economists Lie?" Working Paper 4/2012, Departamento de Analisis Economico, Universidad Autonoma de Madrid.

Lucas, Robert. 2003. "Macroeconomic Priorities." *American Economic Review* 93(1): 1–14.

Marwell, Gerald, and Ames, Ruth. 1981. "Economists Free Ride, Does Anyone Else?" *Journal of Public Economics* 15: 295–310.

Mishkin, Frederic, and Herbertsson, T. 2006. *Financial Stability in Iceland*. Iceland Chamber of Commerce.

Phillips, Kevin. 2006. *American Theocracy*. New York: Viking.

Portes, Richard, and Baldursson, F. 2007. *The Internationalisation of Iceland's Financial Sector*. Iceland Chamber of Commerce.

Racko, Girts. 2011. "On the Normative Consequences of Economic Rationality: A Case Study of a Swedish Economics School in Latvia." *European Sociological Review* 27(6): 772–789.

Romer, Christine. 2008. "Business Cycles." In *The Concise Encyclopedia of Economics*, 2nd ed., edited by D. R. Henderson. Indianapolis, IN: Liberty Fund, Inc.

Sargent, T. 2008. "Rational Expectations." *The Concise Encyclopedia of Economics*, 2nd ed., edited by D. R. Henderson. Indianapolis, IN: Liberty Fund, Inc.

Shiller, Robert. February 11, 2008. "Challenging the Crowd in Whispers, Not Shouts." *New York Times*, B5.

Solow, Robert. 2001. "From Neoclassical Growth Theory to New Classical Macroeconomics." In *Advances in Macroeconomic Theory*, edited by J. H. Dreze,. New York: Palgrave. Quoted in Keen (2011: 257).

Stiglitz, J. March 22, 2011. "A Balanced Debate about Reforming Macroeconomics." In *iMFdirect, IMF's Global Economic Forum*. Washington, DC: International Monetary Fund.

Taylor, John. 2010. "Macroeconomic Lessons from the Great Deviation." In *NBER Macroeconomics Annual 2010*, Vol. 25, edited by Daren Acemoglu and Michael Woodford. Cambridge, MA: National Bureau of Economic Research.

Tett, Gillian. June 2012. "Libor Affair Exposes Big Conceit at the Heart of Banking." *Financial Times*, 24.

UNCTAD. 2009. "Reform of the International Monetary and Financial System." *Trade and Development Report 2009*: chapter IV.

Wade, R. 2011. "The Economy Has Not Solved Its Problems." *Challenge* 54(2): 5–41.

Wade, R. 2009. "Iceland as Icarus." *Challenge* 52(3): 5–33.

Wade, R. 2012. "Why Has Income Inequality Remained on the Sidelines of Public Policy for So Long?" *Challenge* 55(3): 21–50.

Wade, R., and Sigurgeirsdottir, S. 2012. "Iceland's Rise, Fall, Stabilisation and Beyond." *Cambridge Journal of Economics* 36(1): 127–144.

The Wall Street Journal. May 28, 2008. "Mishkin Resigns: A Look Back."

Wedel, Janine. 2009. *Shadow Elite: How the World's New Power Brokers Undermine Democracy, Government and the Free Market*. New York: Basic Books.

PART V

ETHICAL ISSUES IN ECONOMIC RESEARCH

1. Experimental Economics

CHAPTER 16

ETHICS AND ADVANCES IN ECONOMIC SCIENCE

The Role of Two Norms

JINGNAN CHEN, ANGELINA CHRISTIE, AND DANIEL HOUSER

INTRODUCTION

THE past two decades have seen a remarkable increase in the use of experimental methods in economics.[1] Many prominent contributions to economic theory (Laibson, 1997; Camerer, 2003; Charness and Dufwenberg, 2006) have been motivated by the findings of economics experiments, and advanced by further experimentation (see, e.g., Houser and Kurzban, 2002; Xiao and Houser, 2005). This iterative process indicates a sense of trust in both experiments and the experimenters who conduct them. This trust hinges on two key norms that guide the design, analysis, and reporting of economic experiments in both the lab and the field. These norms help to ensure adherence to the key ethical standard of "transparency"[2] (Levy and Peart, 2009).

All researchers are judged in some part by the novelty of their investigations. What sets experimentalists apart from other economists is the fact that an experimentalist's reputation is built heavily on the degree to which his or her results can be replicated. In other words, another researcher at another institution using a different subject pool should be able to reproduce the results of an experiment using the same design, procedures, instructions, and monetary incentives as the first researcher. As a result,

[1] This chapter expands on Houser (2008). Some sections of this chapter are drawn from that earlier work.

[2] There is a large body of experiments that has established regularities in individual decision making and in market interactions, see, for example, Davis and Holt (1993), Camerer (2003), and Plott and Smith (2008).

researchers must be extraordinarily transparent when publishing results: they must publish, either in the main article or at a publicly available hyperlink provided in the article, a full description of procedures, a copy of the instructions, screenshots (if software is used), and all parameters used in the design. Replication is the primary quality that enforces standard practices in experimental economics.

Our goal in this chapter is to demonstrate how ethical norms in experimental economics have contributed to advances in economic science. While our review focuses largely on laboratory experiments, we note in the conclusion that our discussion applies with equal force to experimental studies conducted in the field.

Experimental Economics: A Success Story

Experimental economics, which dates back to the early 1960s, was founded by Vernon Smith. Smith was recognized for this contribution with the Nobel Prize in Economics in 2002, "for having established laboratory experiments as a tool in empirical economic analysis, especially in the study of alternative market mechanisms."[3]

Until recently, the field of economics has lacked a body of behavioral principles that have survived controlled experimental tests (and thus can be used to explain the naturally occurring observational data). Writing in 1987, Smith called much of economic theory "ecclesiastical[4] theory": "it is accepted (or rejected) on the basis of authority, tradition, or opinion about assumptions, rather than on the basis of having survived a rigorous falsification process that can be replicated."

While economists traditionally use logical parables to describe human action and rationality, the experimental economics research program has also been driven by the desire to rely on empirical regularities. Likewise, experimental economists seek testable and tested results that could be just as, if not more, informative to our economic analysis of competing institutions, individual behavior, or proposals for human betterment. Smith also embarked unintentionally on the testing of the standard neoclassical economic model of human rationality, in which a human agent is a self-interested utility-maximizer, acting independently and taking into account full and relevant information.[5]

[3] http://www.nobelprize.org/nobel_prizes/economics/laureates/2002/

[4] See also Nelson, Robert Henry. *Economics as Religion: From Samuelson to Chicago and beyond* (University Park: Pennsylvania State University Press, 2001).

[5] V. L. Smith, in his "Constructivist and Ecological Rationality in Economics," *The American Economic Review* 93(3): 465–508 (2003), refers to standard neoclassical economic model as "standard socioeconomic science model." See E. Roy Weintraub, "Neoclassical Economics" in *The Concise Encyclopedia of Economics* (2007) for a definition of neoclassical economics. http://www.econlib.org/library/Enc1/NeoclassicalEconomics.html

Smith (1987) notes that most economic data collected by government or private agencies is for nonscientific purposes. In contrast, experimental economists gather data using laboratory- and field-experimental studies for scientific purposes. The laboratory approach to economics has given the economist direct professional responsibility for data generation and collection.

The use of laboratory methods to evaluate policy proposals, and as a testing ground for institutional design, has recently lead to revolutionary changes in economic and other behavioral sciences. The evaluation of policy proposals in the lab has brought forth an experimental development economics (e.g., Karlan, 2005; Duflo, Glennerster, and Kremer, 2007; Banerjee and Duflo, 2008), experimental political science (Druckman et al., 2006; Morton and Williams, 2010), and experimental finance (Sunder, 2007; Noussair and Tucker, 2013). Now, policymakers can test their proposals in the lab, which is a relatively low-cost method for "making a mistake," prior to implementing large-scale high-cost programs that are not always easily reversible in the natural environment. It can also allow policymakers and politicians to maintain their reputation by testing their proposals prior to implementation. Institutions such as the World Bank are also adopting the use of experimental methods for testing proposals or policies (McKenzie and Woodruff, 2008).

The use of experimental economic evidence, from both the lab and field, by academic scholars, government policymakers, and decision makers in the private sector points to the success of the experimental revolution in economics. This revolution was made possible by the presence of norms that guided the development of experiments over the past 50 years. These norms have in turn laid a strong foundation for its success into the future. In our view, two key norms, "simplicity" and "availability of data and procedures," are primarily responsible for the increasing importance of experimental economics. We review each in the text that follows.

Simplicity of Design—The First Norm

By "norms in experimental economics," we here refer to informal rules guiding the decisions of scholars who use designed investigations to inform economic hypotheses. The first key norm for experimental economists is simplicity: experimentalists adopt the simplest design that can address their research hypothesis. An experimental design is "simple" if it provides (1) ease of replication and (2) straightforward interpretations of outcomes. The importance of the former is discussed further later. The latter point (2) is not meant to suggest that sophisticated econometric or statistical analysis is or should be avoided in experimental economics. Rather, it means that the analysis procedures should be appropriate and defensible given the design, and that the design should be chosen in view of such considerations.

Personal Exchange Experiments: Simplicity Leading to Advances in Knowledge

The importance of simplicity of design is best demonstrated by experiments with ultimatum (Güth et al., 1982), dictator (Kahneman et al., 1986; Forsythe et al., 1994), and trust games (Berg et al., 1995), which have exploded in recent decades.[6] These games are popular because they model key features of many economic situations, and these experiments are fairly easy to run.

In a typical ultimatum experiment, subjects are paired with an anonymous other. Then, a Proposer (first-mover in the game) makes an offer to split a pie (say $10). The Responder (the second mover in the game) can either accept or reject the offer. If the Responder rejects the offer, both get nothing. If Responders maximize their own money payoffs, they should accept any offer. If Proposers also maximize and expect Responders to maximize, they should offer the smallest possible amount. The equilibrium behavior is simple to compute, and the ultimatum game is well suited to study and measures social preferences rather than strategic thinking. "Measuring social preferences in money terms is important because concepts such as fairness and trust figure prominently in private negotiation and public policy" (Camerer, 2003: 43).

Ultimatum games are a way to test whether self-interest outweighs ethical values (fairness, trust, and reciprocity) in personal exchange environments (albeit anonymous in the experiments). The overwhelming results from many ultimatum game experiments have demonstrated behavioral regularities that do not support the theoretical predictions of the standard economic model based on self-interested utility-maximizer. Proposers offer on average 30 percent–40 percent of the money (many offer 50 percent), and the Responders reject small offers of 20 percent or lower half the time. As a result, the ultimatum games have been replicated many times, varying many of the important conditions of the game to test the robustness of original results. Studies of methodological variables—repetition, stakes, and anonymity—have tested the robustness of ultimatum rejections that conflict with economic theory (Roth et al., 1991; Bolton and Zwick, 1995; Knez and Camerer, 1995; Slonim and Roth, 1998; List and Cherry, 2000). Among the variables affecting the behavior in ultimatum games, culture and structure have proved to be two of the most influential.

Here, it is important to make the point that the simplicity of the game has been critical in allowing these advances in knowledge. Specifically, it has helped to eliminate confounds and thus produce new theory to explain decisions in a clean and coherent way. This would not have been possible in other less simple environments. Also, owing to the simple start, it was possible to build on this and create more sophisticated environments.

[6] Güth, et al. (1982) on ultimatum bargaining has been cited 2514 times; Berg et al. (1995) canonical trust game has been cited 2434 times (Camerer and Weigelt, 1988, is an earlier game in the same spirit, cited 411 times); the first dictator game experiment (albeit hypothetical) by Kahenman, Knetsch, and Thaler (1986) has been cited 2279 times, later studied with real stakes in Forsythe et al. (1994), which has been cited 1101 times (according to Google Scholar citations as of March 2013).

Note that simplicity is tricky in experimental economics. The double auction is simple at the aggregate level (supply and demand, buying and selling in a very natural environment), but very complex at the individual level (it remains unknown why people make the decisions they do in that game). Some of this "simplicity" discussion should indicate this, that is, that there is simplicity at multiple levels, and the key is to be simple in a way that enables you to answer the relevant question in a cogent way.

To explain other-regarding (or social) preferences demonstrated in ultimatum, dictator, and trust games, new theories have been proposed that could help organize the existing data from experiments. The new theories of inequity aversion (Bolton, 1991; "inequality-aversion" in Fehr and Schmidt, 1999; "ERC"—equity, reciprocity and competition—in Bolton and Ockenfels, 2000) and Rabin's (1993) "fairness equilibrium" approach helped rationalize the two seemingly contradictory findings that people sometimes behaved non-selfishly and other times tended to conform to the self-interested prediction.

These new theories generated new predictions, which were tested experimentally, leading to new behavioral results (e.g., Blount, 1995; Engelmann and Strobel, 2004; Falk et al., 2008). For example, Engelmann and Strobel (2004) led to the "comment" studies by the original authors whose theories were tested (Fehr et al., 2006 [comment]). Likewise, Bolton and Ockenfels (2006 [comment]) demonstrate how any possible theoretical or experimental inconsistencies are "settled in the lab" (Engelmann and Strobel, 2006 [reply]), further cementing the ethical culture of scientific inquiry using experimental economics methods. Subsequent new theories of reciprocity try to account for new observations and behavioral regularities (Charness and Rabin, 2002; Dufwenberg and Kirchsteiger, 2004; Charness and Dufwenberg, 2006; Falk and Fischbacher, 2006; Cox et al., 2007).

"The emotional reaction to unfairness which is highlighted by the ultimatum game can work at many levels" (Camerer, 2003: 44). Xiao and Houser (2005)[7] introduce a novel structural variable of emotion expression by the responders in the ultimatum games. The authors find that when responders can convey their feelings to the proposer concurrently with their decisions, rejection of unfair offers is significantly less frequent as compared with the treatment in which expressing emotions directly to proposers is prohibited. These data support the view that costly punishment might itself be used to express negative emotions. They further suggest that future studies will benefit by recognizing that human demand for emotion expression can have significant behavioral consequences in social environments, including families, courts, companies, and markets.

A similar iterative process of scientific inquiry—again made possible precisely owing to simplicity of design—has also occurred with dictator game experiments. Dictator games are ultimatum games in which the Responder (the second mover) does not have the ability to reject the offer. The Proposer is the first mover and the only decision maker in the

[7] The Xiao and Houser (2005) study on emotion expression in punishment behavior in ultimatum games has been cited 188 times, indicating a growing interest in economics of emotion (Google citations March, 2013).

game, that is, the dictator. He or she decides how the pie is split, and whether to contribute anything to the matched counterpart. The Proposer's decision on this point is final.

The first dictator game experiment in economics was introduced by Kahneman, Knetsch, and Thaler (1986), who gave subjects a choice (albeit hypothetical) between dictating either an even split of $20 ($10 each) with another student, or an uneven split ($18, $2) that would favor themselves. Three-quarters opted for the equal split ($10, $10). Forsythe et al. (1994) later conducted the dictator game experiments with real stakes and allowed the dictators to send any amount they wanted, rather than choosing one of the two options. In their experiments, the dictator contributions are less generous than in Kahneman et al. (1986), but nonetheless positive, with a mean allocation of 20 percent of the endowment. Camerer (2003: 57, table 2.4) compiles statistics from subsequent dictator game experiments that replicate earlier results, finding that more than 60 percent of subjects usually pass a positive amount of money, with a mean transfer of approximately 20 percent of the endowment.

Unselfish behaviors discovered (and widely replicated) in especially simple environments have inspired theoretical advances. Among the competing models of unselfishness are inequality aversion (Bolton and Ockenfels, 2000; Fehr and Schmidt, 1999), models of altruism (Andreoni and Miller, 2002; Cox and Sadiraj, 2005), egocentrism (Cox et al., 2002, 2008), and Rawlsian "social welfare" preferences (Charness and Rabin, 2002).

For example, Cox et al. (2007) propose a tractable model of other-regarding preferences based on one's emotional state, which is affected by status and reciprocity relation with another person. They then apply their model to past experimental data on various types of two-person games. Their first application is to dictator games. They assert that their model highlights well the unconditional altruism in dictator game data.

In addition to theorists who are inspired by findings from experiments, experimentalists also develop new designs to shed further light on, for example, "unselfish" behavior. One example is novel experimental design of the dictator game—the "taking game"—by Bardsley (2008). Bardsley, who is also interested in theoretically driven tests of unselfish giving in dictator games, changes the game slightly by allowing the dictator "taking options." Thus, he is able to test whether social, or other-regarding, preferences are sensitive to the presence of the opportunity to take from the counterpart, rather than just give or share a particular endowment. He finds that most subjects' generosity can be reserved if they are allowed a sufficient opportunity to take. He concludes that giving in dictator games is driven by the experimental demand characteristics and the choice set available to the subjects in the experiment. These aspects can cue the subjects to the acceptable or expected behavior in the lab.

Another advance inspired by the simplicity of dictator game experiments is List (2007). List conducts similar "taking" experiments, in which he varies the amount of allowed taking to further test the social preferences explanation for dictator giving. His study replicates the results obtained in Bardsley (2005, an earlier unpublished version of Bardsley, 2008) and further finds that subjects do not ubiquitously choose the most selfish option in the choice set. In addition to concerns raised by Bardsley, List emphasizes the importance of institutions, as rules of the game, which specify the allowed or restricted set of choices. In particular, he provides evidence that the restrictions of the action set have a profound effect on behavior: when taking (negative quadrant) is in the permissible set, the distribution of offers in the positive quadrant (giving) shifts. He further posits that these behavioral changes are consistent with the framework introduced in Levitt and List (2007).

Consider also the simple investment game experiments proposed by Berg, Dickhaut, and McCabe (1995), another very simple environment that has been used—in various forms—to shed substantial light on many issues surrounding principal–agent relationships. In the investment/trust game, the first mover is the investor, who has an endowment X, which he can keep or invest. The investor is anonymously paired with a second mover, the trustee. If the investor chooses to invest an amount T, he keeps $X-T$. The investment of T also earns a return $(1+r)$, such that the trustee receives $T(1+r)$. The trustee, after receiving $T(1+r)$, must decide how much of this amount to send back to the investor. Because the investor is not guaranteed to receive anything back from the trustee, the amount T sent is a measure of the trustee's trust that the second mover will reciprocate in a similar manner by returning some amount back. This blind "trust" includes uncertain return.

Berg et al. (1995) report that investors, on average, sent 50 percent of the endowment $X = \$10$, while the average amount repaid was about 95 percent of what was invested, T, or a third of $T(1+r)$, with a wide dispersion. These results have been generally replicated in various places with some variation. For example, Willinger et al. (2003) find that the French trust much less than the Germans, while both return on average 40 percent. Ensminger (2002) finds little trust and trustworthiness among Orma herders in Kenya.

The simplicity of the Berg et al. (1995) design was unquestionably critical in enabling its use in multiple ways and to inform multiple scientific questions. Indeed, closely related designs that preceded it in spirit—but lacked its simplicity—failed to gain the attention and widespread use of the Berg et al. investment game.

Market Experiments: Complexity Revealed through Simplicity of Design

Vernon Smith understood, at a very early stage, the importance of simplicity in design. Indeed, in his first published experimental study of market behavior, Smith (1962) reports results of simple experimental games that shed light on neoclassical competitive market theory. In contrast to the first experimental supply and demand study of Chamberlin (1948), Smith operationalized a multilateral auction-trading process characteristic of organized stock, bond, and commodity exchanges.[8] This trading

[8] In Chamberlin (1948), buyers and sellers were permitted to simply circulate freely around the classroom and engage in bilateral negotiations. Each trader's attention is thus directed to only one trader with whom he or she is bargaining. In contrast, in Smith (1962) each trader's bid or offer is directed to the entire trading group one offer/bid at a time.

process is now widely known as a double auction (DA) institution. The trading process in Chamberlin's experiment took the form of unstructured bilateral negotiations by students. The major characteristics of Smith's first true market experiments were the publicity of all bids, offers, and transactions, and the prohibition of collusion by any participants.

The two studies, Chamberlin's and Smith's, reveal different market outcomes. In Chamberlin, the outcomes systematically deviated from competitive predictions. In Smith, markets can converge to efficient, competitive outcomes even with a small number of traders who initially know nothing about market conditions. In Smith's interpretation of Chamberlin's results, we do not observe convergence to a competitive equilibrium. The reason is that there is less opportunity for traders to gain experience and to modify their subsequent behavior.[9]

It is worth noting that Smith (1962) provides readers a most detailed and careful description of all procedures, parameters, and conditions of each experimental treatment (the general importance of this is discussed in the fourth section). First, the group of subjects is randomly divided into two subgroups, buyers and sellers. Each buyer privately receives a notecard with a number on it, which represents the maximum price he or she is willing to pay for one unit of the fictitious good. This price is also the induced value of one unit of the good to the buyer. In other words, the buyer can make a profit by buying one unit of the good at a price lower than his stated (induced) value on the notecard—the maximum reservation price. These reservation prices of all buyers generate a demand curve that defines the set of possible demand quantities at each hypothetical ruling price. Further, each seller also privately receives a notecard with a number on it, which represents the minimum price he or she is willing to accept for one unit of a good. This price also indicates the induced cost of one unit of the good to the seller. Hence, the seller can make a profit by selling one unit at a price higher than his or her stated (induced) cost on the notecard—the minimum reservation price. The minimum reservation prices of all sellers generate a supply curve that defines the set of possible supply quantities at each hypothetical ruling price.

The apparent simplicity of design and procedures enables anyone to run a similar experiment in an attempt to replicate previous results or to study further modifications of the environment. The design of this particular market experiment is simple but no simpler than necessary, meaning that the goal of simplicity is to address the research question at hand. For example, as Smith (1962) describes, no collusion among traders was allowed, and all purchases were for final "consumption," meaning no speculative purchases for resale in the same or later periods. These two conditions generate a particular simplified environment that allows the study of the equilibration process in a purposefully narrow and controlled way.

[9] In Chamberlin's experiments, markets lasted for one period. In Smith's experiments, the same group of subjects traded in a sequence of market periods, each with identical supply-and-demand structures, allowing for learning to take place.

Smith's DA market experiments generated competitive prices and quantities under a robust set of circumstances: different subject pools (students at all levels, business persons, government regulators, citizens of Russia and China, and academics) and complex multiple market supply and demand environments. In fact, the DA markets provide a benchmark against which the performance of other institutions can be studied, compared, and evaluated. Sealed bid-offer call markets and posted offer markets have been shown to converge to the market clearing equilibrium, although DA tends to converge more rapidly and reliably to efficient allocation levels (Smith et al., 1982; Ketcham et al, 1984)[10]. The interest in the results of DA market experiments was further enhanced by its similarity to the trading rules of major securities markets, maintaining its practical applicability.

According to Smith (2010), "the challenge of the DA empirical results has not yielded game theoretic models that predict convergence to a static competitive equilibrium." While static competitive market equilibrium theory has performed well under DA trading rules, the theory did not predict the weak conditions under which these outcomes would prevail. Consequently, the simplicity of the DA trading institution and a controlled simple environment of publicity and private information of buyers and sellers of Smith (1962) have nonetheless revealed the underlying complexity of the individual dynamic learning and market convergence process. This emphasizes the important point that simplicity of design can be, and often is, associated with complexity of individual decision patterns and strategic behavior.

Smith (1962) suggests a potential modification of this simple experiment: "There is nothing, however, to prevent one from designing an experiment in which purchases for resale are permitted if the objective is to study the role of speculation in the equilibrating process. One could, for example, permit the carry-over of stocks from one period to the next." Later, Smith and his co-authors would run a series of such experiments that would become the standard experimental model for studying asset markets (Smith, Suchanek, and Williams, 1988).

Smith, Suchanek, and Williams (SSW hereafter) conducted an experimental study of asset-price bubbles that would define and motivate research on asset markets for decades.[11] What has attracted numerous researchers[12] to the experimental method of studying asset market behavior is the ability of well-designed and simple experiments to observe and exogenously control key aspects of a market. In the now canonical SSW design,[13] the student subjects buy and sell an asset over fifteen 2- to 6-minute periods in a single closed book continuous DA market. The asset may not be sold short or bought on a margin in a baseline market. It pays a random, discretely

[10] See Davis and Holt (1993) for an in-depth discussion of results.

[11] For a collection and aggregation of stylized results from 41 published and 20 working papers on experimental asset markets see Palan (2013).

[12] Current number of citations of Smith, Suchanek, and Williams (1988) exceeds 880 on Google Scholar.

[13] Earlier experiments in which the traded item was a proper asset that generated dividends for asset holders were originated by Forsythe, Palfrey, and Plott (1982) and continued by Plott and Sunder (1982), and Friedman, Harrison, and Salmon (1984).

and uniformly distributed dividend with positive expected value at the end of each period, and has no terminal value. In the SSW experiment, all traders receive the same dividend value (common dividend payout) at the end of the period, as opposed to different dividend values for different groups of traders as in Friedman, Harrison, and Salmon (1984).

Smith and co-authors study the question of how traders come to have rational expectations, or common priors, about the value of the asset. As they state on p. 1120 (SSW): "In an experiment we *cannot* control expectations when the theory provides no explicit implementable model of expectations, but we can control the dividend structure and trader knowledge of it." The authors are again very careful to report with full transparency all the procedures (PLATO computerized double-auction mechanism as in Williams and Smith, 1984) and instructions used in the experiment, carefully describing each step of the decision making of the asset trader. As we maintain in this chapter, it is precisely this culture of scientific method transparency and replication that has led to consistent norms of conducting experiments and reporting experimental results by experimental economists.

The now-stylized results of SSW's asset market experiments are (1) exchanges of assets in large volumes occur even with common probabilistic dividend payout; (2) the modal outcome was a market characterized by a price bubble measured relative to dividend value; and (3) the traders' expectations are adaptive, and the adaptation over time is to rational expectations equilibrium outcomes. These early results have become "stylized" because they have been replicated in numerous subsequent studies. Palan (2013) discusses 32 empirical observations and results in experimental studies of asset price markets. He concludes that "despite criticism directed at the SSW design (e.g., against the declining fundamental value, the deterministic length of the market, or the perfect knowledge about the asset's expected value), it is the best-documented experimental asset market design in existence and thus offers a superior base of comparison for new work."

Noussair and Tucker (2013), in the same special issue of the *Journal of Economic Surveys*, concisely distill some of the more influential results in the study of asset market behavior and experimental finance in general. Their survey reveals the subsequent complexity of the studies in experimental finance and the gradual buildup of designs that originated from the fairly "simple" experimental asset markets discussed above. In fact, as we assert, it is the simplicity of initial asset market experiments, and the fairly straightforward results that they have produced, which paved the way for the new and more complex studies of financial markets and testing of financial theory. Having reviewed the long-standing lines of research in experimental finance, Noussair and Tucker conclude that it is experimental finance that will push into the areas of financial engineering and market regulation in the future.

Particularly worth noting is that this entire literature, and the tremendous scientific advances contained therein, were inspired by and extended the original Smith (1962) double auction experiment.

Availability of Data and Procedures—The Second Norm

The second norm is (1) all published data are made publicly available and (2) so are the experimental procedures.

For the first point, readily available published data are crucial for advancing economic research. The reason is that fellow researchers can review, reanalyze the existing findings, discover regularities, and thereafter extend the original research (or even open up new arenas).

One example illustrating the use of published data is meta-analysis, in which the authors collect all the relevant available data for a certain topic and investigate the robustness of the results. The authors explore new patterns that cannot be easily examined within the scope of a single paper, as well as other factors (e.g., geographical, methodological, data analytical, and cultural factors, etc.) that may influence the result, but would be difficult to discern without different sets of data. Oosterbeek et. al (2004) report meta data analysis of ultimatum games from 37 papers with 75 results. The authors find that the average offer rate is around 40 percent, and the average rejection is rate is 16 percent. Both rates vary with regard to the size of the pie; likewise, the use of strategy method has a negative impact on the responders' willingness to accept. Additionally, while responders' behavior differs across countries, cultural differences are not the main contributor.

Engel (2011) uses data from dictator games spanning the past 25 years and compares multiple specifications of statistical models for analyzing dictator game data. The author concludes that the Tobit model and hurdle models can provide additional insight into the behaviors in the dictator game. Johnson and Mislin (2011) gather 162 replications of trust games in an effort to identify the effect of experimental protocols and geographic variations on the measure of trust and trustworthiness. The authors discover that both payment method (whether it is random or according to choices made in the game) and matched counterpart (whether it is computer or real person) affect trust (as implied by the amount sent) in the game. Trustworthiness (as measured by the amount returned) is impacted by three factors: the size of the multiplier, experience of partners' role, and whether the subjects are students. Johnson and Mislin also uncover geographic differences in willingness to trust between Africa and North America. Most of the aforementioned discoveries would not have been possible without the wide availability of related data sets.

Reanalysis of published research prevents premature acceptance of empirical results, and is crucial for advancing economic research. Convenient public access to published data promotes and encourages such practices. There are famous examples of this even from outside of the experimental economics literature. For instance, Levitt (1997) published an influential paper arguing for the causal effect of police on crime. Levitt argued that police substantially reduce violent crimes, but that the effect is smaller for property crime. The author employs the timing of electoral cycles as an instrumental variable in his estimation process. After closer examination, however, McCrary (2002) points out that there is a weighting error in Levitt's estimation procedure that could lead to incorrect references to the main findings; if weights on crimes with different variability over time are used correctly, the author suggests, there is no significant impact of police on any type of crime. As a response, Levitt (2002) admits the coding error, and provides further evidence (including alternative instrumental variables and stronger statistical tests) that supports the original finding.

An example from within experimental economics is Holt and Laury (2002). Holt and Laury propose an experimental procedure to elicit individual risk attitudes. Using the data collected with this procedure, the authors assert that greater incentives lead to greater risk aversion. They then introduce a flexible utility function with variable risk aversion (compared to constant risk aversion). Harrison et al. (2005), however, point out that the effect of increased stakes on lottery choice is possibly confounded by an order effect where prior experience with one task affects behaviors in subsequent tasks. With new sets of experiments, the authors demonstrate that with proper order effect control, the original findings of Holt and Laury are significantly smaller. As a rebuttal, Holt and Laury (2005) collect new data without the order effects, confirm that scaling up real payments does result in a significant increase in risk aversion, and offer a new finding that scaling up hypothetical payment does not trigger a significant change in risk attitude given that there is no order effect. As evidenced from the above examples, reanalysis strengthens the credibility of the economic findings, while published data that are publicly available pave the way.

Experimental procedures should also be made publicly available. How experiments are conducted is crucially important for replication and transparency in economic science. In particular, the published results must be supported by a discussion that would allow the procedures to be replicated. The procedural discussion includes not just a description of the formal experimetrics procedures (Houser, Schunk, & Xiao, 2007), but also the procedures by which the data were generated. Usually, this entails publishing at least the experiment's instructions, either in the journal or on a website that the published article references.

Indeed, journals are progressively requiring any submission of experimental economics papers to provide additional materials related to experimental procedure. As the *Journal of Political Economy* put forward on its data policy section.[14]

For experimental papers, we have a more detailed policy, including requirements for submitted papers as well as accepted papers. We normally expect authors of experimental articles to supply the following supplementary materials (any exceptions to this policy should be requested at the time of submission):

1. The original instructions . . .
2. Information about subject eligibility or selection, such as exclusions based on past participation in experiments, college major, etc . . .

[14] For the complete policy, please see http://www.press.uchicago.edu/journals/jpe/datapolicy.html?journal=jpe

3. Any computer programs, configuration files, or scripts used to run the experiment and/or to analyze the data . . .
4. The raw data from the experiment . . .

The requirement for complete transparency is well justified. Burnham et al. (2000) conducted an extensive form two person trust game in the laboratory. The treatments differ by only one word in the instructions: instead of using "counterpart" to refer to the matched individual, in one treatment, the authors substitute "counterpart" with "partner," while in the other treatment, "opponent" is used in place of "counterpart." Burnham et. al. find a significant difference in both trust and trustworthiness behaviors across treatments. In addition, Johnson and Mislin (2011) indicate that experimental payment procedures also play a role in affecting behaviors in the experiment. Evidently, transparency of experimental protocol (including instructions, recruitment information, software packages) is quite necessary.

It is worth noting that with the growing use of computers in assisting economic experiments, experimental economists have coordinated on a software package, *z*-tree (Fischbacher, 2007), which allows for easier replication of others' results. The reason is that *z*-tree allows researchers to share or modify the program while keeping the same interface. This plays an important role in helping to rapidly advance the science, as it ensures that substantive investigations are not confounded due to interface differences.

REWARD, REPLICATION

The development of the laboratory approach to economics has provided economists with a direct responsibility for a source of scientific data by controlled processes that can then be replicated by other experimentalists.[15] As Davis and Holt (1993) state, the laboratory methods offer two chief advantages: replicability and control. Davis and Holt define *replicability* as the capacity of other researchers to reproduce the experiment, and thereby verify the findings independently. They also note that the notion of replication should be distinguished from the conventional use of the term in econometrics: in econometrics it refers to the capacity to reproduce results with a given data set; in an experimental context, it is the capacity to create an entirely new set of observations (see Roth, 1994).

As Smith (1987) astutely points out: "interest in replicability of scientific research stems from a desire to answer the question 'Do you see what I see?'" Replication and control allow economic scientists to reduce the error in our common knowledge of economic processes. Smith identifies three component questions that can help to identify when the research study may fail to be replicable. These are: (1) *Do you*

[15] This section draws heavily from Houser (2008).

observe what I observe? (2) *Do you interpret what we observe as I interpret it?* (3) *Do you conclude what I conclude from our interpretation?* In answering the first question, one can say that one has replicated someone else's previous experiments if one is unable to reject the hypothesis that one's experimental data came from the same population as the previous one. In other words, the experimenter, his/her subjects, and/or procedures are not significant treatment variables. In answering the second question, the interpretation of observations requires theory, formal or informal, or an empirical interpretation of the theory in the context that generated the data. As the theory is not always developed directly in terms of what can be observed (e.g., assuming risk aversion that is not directly observable), failure to replicate may be due to differences in interpretation that result from different meaning ascribed to the theory. Lastly, in answering the third question, even if the data and the interpretation are the same, different conclusions may arise as a result of different model specifications. This type of problem is inherent in nonexperimental methods, which at best can estimate the parameters of a prespecified model, but cannot credibly test one model or theory against another.

Experimentalists understand that incentives matter. Norms in experimental economics persist due to the fact that they are rewarded in two primary ways. First, an inspection of the experimental literature reveals that most published research is consistent with the two norms. Thus, research that follows the code might have a relatively easier time being placed. Second, leading journals are willing to publish new experiments on previously investigated questions, but typically require that the new study use an improved design. This creates an incentive for experimentalists to compete over design innovation, leading to increasingly efficient procedures.

The structure of rewards promotes a culture of replication. Often, the replication is exact in the sense that it involves analyzing data generated using exactly the design that appeared in the original research. The link between innovation and replication arises due to the fact that, when differences between new and old results on the same question are found, it is necessary to return to and replicate the original design. If the research team does not recover the original results with their implementation of the original design, then they must explore the possibility that there are nuisance effects (perhaps subject pool differences or unrecognized procedural variations) that caused the disparate outcomes.

Owing to the culture of replication in experimental economics, the incentives to behave outside the norms in collecting and reporting data are mitigated. Further reducing such incentives is the fact that economics experiments are not generally result dependent. For example, the value of "wind-tunnel" experiments lies in their ability to inform policy debates, regardless of the direction of their findings.

The fact that experimentalists can choose the generating process for the data they eventually report, and thereby help to ensure result-independent, replication-robust interest in their findings, maintains investigators' indifference over outcomes. As discussed by Levy and Peart (2009), indifference over outcomes promotes a scientific culture of truth-seeking.

This scientific culture has consequences for the way ideological clashes are resolved in experimental economics. An example is how to interpret the replicated finding that measures of trust are positively correlated with measures of market performance (Henrich et al., 2001). Does trust promote markets, or do markets promote trust, or both or neither? There are scholars on all sides of this debate, and as always, the issues will be sorted out through a process of reporting data generated by competing but complementary research paradigms. Indeed, an experimental economist's point of view is to proceed scientifically and "settle it in the lab." This reflects a sense of trust among members of the experimental community, a trust that stems from and reinforces the norms of experimental economics.

Conclusion

We have presented a rather sanguine view of research practice in experimental economics. This partially contrasts with the views expressed by Roth (1994), who fretted about the failure to report pilot experiments and insufficient attention to failed treatments, evidently worrying that these impede the discovery of "robust empirical regularities" (Roth, 1994, especially p. 188, first full paragraph). Two decades and several Nobel prizes later, there is little evidence that such reasonable but mundane concerns (routinely repeated across empirical sciences) have impeded scientific progress in economics. The reason is the two norms we have discussed, and especially replication, which ensure exciting but false findings gain little traction. Moreover, the last decade of research with "field experiments" has done much to identify those lessons from the lab which extend to natural environments of interest, as well as those that do not (see, e.g., Harrison and List, 2004).

While our review has focused on laboratory experiments, the norms we discussed are of course equally well practiced by those conducting experiments in the field. Indeed, descriptions of procedures in field experiments are often quite extensive because, unlike labs, each field setting is unique. The uniqueness of a field environment, combined with the logistical and pecuniary costs of implementing some field experiments, means that replication of field experiments can be (much) more difficult than replication of studies conducted in a university laboratory. On the other hand, those same costs make it difficult to explore multiple designs and, consequently, published data have often been generated by the initial design implementation. Consequently, greater difficulty with a field experiment's replication may be partially offset by increased confidence that the results are generalizable: the design was not likely tailored to the specific environment with an eye toward producing any particular result.

In sum, experimental economics is a norms-based field, with standards, guidelines, and rules of behavior that are enforced both formally and informally. It is a field taught largely through apprenticeship. Graduate students spend hours in a laboratory administering experiments in order to learn proper procedures and discipline. There are some sources that codify portions of the experimental approach. Standards on how to conduct economic experiments have emerged from practice and been codified into ethical norms and methods in experimental economics (Smith, 1976, 1982, 1987; Plott, 1982; Friedman and Sunder, 1994; Friedman and Cassar, 2004). The widespread use of experimental economics methods has come about as a result of ethical research practices, a culture of truth-seeking among experimentalists using a scientific methodology that allows for independent verification and replication of results.

References

Andreoni, J., and Miller, J. 2002. "Giving According to GARP: An Experimental Test of the Consistency of Preferences for Altruism." *Econometrica* 70(2): 737–753.

Banerjee, A. V., and Duflo, E. 2008. *The Experimental Approach to Development Economics*. No. w14467. Cambridge, MA: National Bureau of Economic Research.

Bardsley, N. 2008. "Dictator Game Giving: Altruism or Artifact?" *Experimental Economics* 11(2): 122–133.

Berg, J., Dickhaut, J., and McCabe, K. 1995. "Trust, Reciprocity, and Social History." *Games and Economic Behavior* 10(1): 122–142.

Blount, S. 1995. "When Social Outcomes Aren't Fair: The Effect of Causal Attributions on Preferences." *Organizational Behavior and Human Decision Processes* 63(2): 131–144.

Bolton, G. E. 1991. "A Comparative Model of Bargaining: Theory and Evidence." *The American Economic Review* 81(5), 1096–1136.

Bolton, G. E., and Ockenfels, A. 2000. "ERC: A Theory of Equity, Reciprocity, and Competition." *The American Economic Review* 90(1), 166–193.

Bolton, G. E., and Ockenfels, A. 2006. "Inequality Aversion, Efficiency, and Maximin Preferences in Simple Distribution Experiments: Comment." *The American Economic Review* 96(5): 1906–1911.

Bolton, G. E., and Zwick, R. 1995. "Anonymity versus Punishment in Ultimatum Bargaining." *Games and Economic Behavior* 10(1): 95–121.

Burnham, T., McCabe, K., and Smith, V. L. 2000. "Friend-or-Foe Intentionality Priming in an Extensive Form Trust Game." *Journal of Economic Behavior & Organization* 43(1): 57–73.

Camerer, C. F. 2003. *Behavioral Game Theory: Experiments in Strategic Interaction*. Princeton, NJ: Princeton University Press.

Camerer, C., and Weigelt, K. 1988. "Experimental Tests of a Sequential Equilibrium Reputation Model." *Econometrica: Journal of the Econometric Society* 56(1), 1–36.

Chamberlin, E. H. 1948. "An Experimental Imperfect Market." *The Journal of Political Economy* 56(2): 95–108.

Charness, G., and Dufwenberg, M. 2006. "Promises and Partnership." *Econometrica* 74(6): 1579–1601.

Charness, G., and Rabin, M. 2002. "Understanding Social Preferences with Simple Tests." *The Quarterly Journal of Economics* 117(3): 817–869.

Cox, J. C., Friedman, D., and Gjerstad, S. 2007. "A Tractable Model of Reciprocity and Fairness." *Games and Economic Behavior* 59(1): 17–45.

Cox, J. C., Sadiraj, K., and Sadiraj, V. 2002. "Trust, Fear, Reciprocity, and Altruism." University of Amsterdam, Working Paper.

Cox, J. C., Sadiraj, K., and Sadiraj, V. 2008. "Implications of Trust, Fear, and Reciprocity for Modeling Economic Behavior." *Experimental Economics* 11(1): 1–24.

Cox, J., and Sadiraj, V. 2005. "Direct Tests of Models of Social Preferences and a New Model." University of Arizona Working Paper.

Davis, D. D., and Holt, C. A. 1993. *Experimental Economics*. Princeton, NJ: Princeton University Press.

Druckman, J. N., Green, D. P., Kuklinski, J. H., and Lupia, A. 2006. "The Growth and Development of Experimental Research in Political Science." *American Political Science Review* 100(4): 627.

Duflo, E., Glennerster, R., and Kremer, M. 2007. "Using Randomization in Development Economics Research: A Toolkit." *Handbook of Development Economics* 4: 3895–3962.

Dufwenberg, M., and Kirchsteiger, G. (2004). "A Theory of Sequential Reciprocity." *Games and Economic Behavior* 47(2): 268–298.

Engel, C. 2011. "Dictator Games: A Meta Study." *Experimental Economics* 14(4): 583–610.

Engelmann, D., and Strobel, M. 2004. "Inequality Aversion, Efficiency, and Maximin Preferences in Simple Distribution Experiments." *The American Economic Review* 94(4): 857–869.

Engelmann, D., and Strobel, M. 2006. "Inequality Aversion, Efficiency, and Maximin Preferences in Simple Distribution Experiments: Reply." *The American Economic Review* 96(5): 1918–1923.

Ensminger, J. 2002. "Experimental Economics in the Bush." *Engineering and Science* 65(2): 6–16.

Falk, A., Fehr, E., and Fischbacher, U. 2008. "Testing Theories of Fairness—Intentions Matter." *Games and Economic Behavior* 62(1): 287–303.

Falk, A., and Fischbacher, U. 2006. "A Theory of Reciprocity." *Games and Economic Behavior* 54(2): 293–315.

Fehr, E., Naef, M., and Schmidt, K. M. 2006. "Inequality Aversion, Efficiency, and Maximin Preferences in Simple Distribution Experiments: Comment." *The American Economic Review*, 96(5): 1912–1917.

Fehr, E., & Schmidt, K. M. (1999). A theory of fairness, competition, and cooperation. *The quarterly journal of economics*, 114(3), 817-868.

Fischbacher, U. 2007. "z-Tree: Zurich Toolbox for Ready-Made Economic Experiments." *Experimental Economics* 10(2): 171–178.

Forsythe, R., Horowitz, J. L., Savin, N. E., and Sefton, M. 1994. "Fairness in Simple Bargaining Experiments." *Games and Economic Behavior* 6(3): 347–369.

Forsythe, R., Palfrey, T. R., and Plott, C. R. 1982. "Asset Valuation in an Experimental Market." *Econometrica: Journal of the Econometric Society* 537–567.

Friedman, D., Harrison, G. W., and Salmon, J. W. 1984. "The Informational Efficiency of Experimental Asset Markets." *The Journal of Political Economy* 92(3), 349–408.

Friedman, D., and Cassar, A. 2004. *Economics Lab: An Intensive Course in Experimental Economics*. London: Routledge.

Friedman, D., and Sunder, S. 1994. *Experimental Methods: A Primer for Economists*. Cambridge, UK: Cambridge University Press.

Güth, W., Schmittberger, R., and Schwarze, B. 1982. "An Experimental Analysis of Ultimatum Bargaining." Journal of Economic Behavior and Organization 3(4): 367–388.

Harrison, G., Johnson, E., McInnes, M., and Rutstrom, E. 2005. "Risk Aversion and Incentive Effects: Comment." *The American Economic Review* 95(3): 897–901.

Harrison, G. W., and List, J. A. 2004. "Field Experiments." *Journal of Economic Literature*, 42(4): 1009–1055.

Henrich, J., Boyd, R., Bowles, S., Camerer, C., Fehr, E., Gintis, H., and McElreath, R. 2001. "In Search of *Homo Economicus*: Behavioral Experiments in 15 Small-scale Societies." *The American Economic Review* 73–78.

Holt, C., and Laury, S. 2002. "Risk Aversion and Incentive Effects." *The American Economic Review* 92(5): 1644–1655.

Holt, C., and Laury, S. 2005. "Risk Aversion and Incentive Effects: New Data without Order Effects." *The American Economic Review* 95(3): 902–904.

Holt, C. A. 2006. *Markets, Games, and Strategic Behavior.* Pearson Addison Wesley.

Houser, D. 2008. "A Note on Norms in Experimental Economics." *Eastern Economic Journal* 34: 126-128.

Houser, D. and Kurzban, R. 2002. "Revisiting Kindness and Confusion in Public Goods Experiments." *The American Economic Review* 92(4): 1062–1069.

Houser, D., Schunk, D., and Xiao, E. 2007. "Combining Brain and Behavioral Data to Improve Econometric Policy Analysis." *Analyse and Kritik* 29: 86–96.

Johnson, N. D., and Mislin, A. A. 2011. "Trust Games: A Meta-analysis." *Journal of Economic Psychology* 32(5): 865–889.

Kahneman, D., Knetsch, J. L., and Thaler, R. 1986. "Fairness as a Constraint on Profit Seeking: Entitlements in the Market." *The American Economic Review* 76(4), 728–741.

Karlan, D. S. 2005. "Using Experimental Economics to Measure Social Capital and Predict Financial Decisions." *The American Economic Review* 95(5), 1688–1699.

Ketcham, J., Smith, V. L., and Williams, A. W. 1984. "A Comparison of Posted-Offer and Double-Auction Pricing Institutions." *The Review of Economic Studies* 51(4): 595–614.

Knez, M. J., and Camerer, C. F. 1995. "Outside Options and Social Comparison in Three-Player Ultimatum Game Experiments." *Games and Economic Behavior* 10(1): 65–94.

Laibson, D. 1997. Golden Eggs and Hyperbolic Discounting. *The Quarterly Journal of Economics*, 112(2), 443-478.

Levitt, S. 1997. "Using Electoral Cycles in Police Hiring to Estimate the Effect of Police on Crime." *The American Economic Review* 87(3): 270–290.

Levitt, S. 2002. "Using Electoral Cycles in Police Hiring to Estimate the Effects of Police on Crime: Reply." *The American Economic Review* 92(4): 1244–1250.

Levitt, S. D., and List, J. A. 2007. "What Do Laboratory Experiments Measuring Social Preferences Reveal about the Real World?" *The Journal of Economic Perspectives* 21(2): 153–174.

Levy, D. M., and Peart, S. J. 2009. "Inducing Greater Transparency: Towards the Establishment of Ethical Rules for Econometrics." *Eastern Economic Journal* 34(1): 103–114.

List, J. A. 2007. "On the Interpretation of Giving in Dictator Games." *Journal of Political Economy* 115(3): 482–493.

List, J. A., and Cherry, T. L. 2000. "Learning to Accept in Ultimatum Games: Evidence from an Experimental Design that Generates Low Offers." *Experimental Economics* 3(1): 11–29.

McCrary, J. 2002. "Using Electoral Cycles in Police Hiring to Estimate the Effect of Police on Crime: Comment." *The American Economic Review* 92(4): 1236–1243.

McKenzie, D., and Woodruff, C. 2008. "Experimental Evidence on Returns to Capital and Access to Finance in Mexico." *The World Bank Economic Review* 22(3): 457–482.

Morton, R. B., and Williams, K. C. 2010. *Experimental Political Science and the Study of Causality: From Nature to the Lab*. Cambridge, UK: Cambridge University Press.

Noussair, C. N., and Tucker, S. 2013. "A Collection of Surveys on Market Experiments". *Journal of Economic Surveys*, 27: 395–397.

Oosterbeek, H., Sloof, R., and Van de Kuilen, G. 2004. "Cultural Differences in Ultimatum Game Experiments: Evidence from a Meta-analysis." *Experimental Economics* 7(2): 171–188.

Palan, S. 2013. "A Review of Bubbles and Crashes in Experimental Asset Markets." *Journal of Economic Surveys* 27(3), 570-588.

Plott, C. R. 1982. "Industrial Organization Theory and Experimental Economics." *Journal of Economic Literature* 20(4): 1485–1527.

Plott, C. R., and Smith, V. L. (eds.) 2008. *Handbook of Experimental Economics Results*, Vol. 1. Amsterdam: North-Holland.

Plott, C. R., and Sunder, S. 1982. "Efficiency of Experimental Security Markets with Insider Information: An Application of Rational-Expectations Models." *The Journal of Political Economy* 663–698.

Rabin, M. 1993. "Incorporating Fairness into Game Theory and Economics." *The American Economic Review* 83(5), 1281–1302.

Roth, A. E. 1994. "Let's Keep the Con Out of Experimental Econ: A Methodological Note." *Empirical Economics* 19(2): 279–289.

Roth, A. E., Prasnikar, V., Okuno-Fujiwara, M., and Zamir, S. 1991. "Bargaining and Market Behavior in Jerusalem, Ljubljana, Pittsburgh, and Tokyo: An Experimental Study." *The American Economic Review*, 1068–1095.

Slonim, R., and Roth, A. E. 1998. "Learning in High Stakes Ultimatum Games: An Experiment in the Slovak Republic." *Econometrica* 569–596.

Smith, V. L. 1962. "An Experimental Study of Competitive Market Behavior." *The Journal of Political Economy* 70(2), 111–137.

Smith, V. L. 1976. "Experimental Economics: Induced Value Theory." *The American Economic Review* 66(2), 274–279.

Smith, V. L. 1982. "Microeconomic Systems as an Experimental Science." *The American Economic Review* 72(5), 923–955.

Smith, V. L. 1987. "Experimental Methods in Economics." *The New Palgrave: A Dictionary of Economic Theory and Doctrine*, edited by J. Eatwell, M. Milgate, and P. Newman. London: Macmillan Press.

Smith, V. L. 2010. "Theory and Experiment: What Are the Questions?" *Journal of Economic Behavior and Organization* 73(1): 3–15.

Smith, V. L., Suchanek, G. L., and Williams, A. W. 1988. "Bubbles, Crashes, and Endogenous Expectations in Experimental Spot Asset Markets." *Econometrica: Journal of the Econometric Society* 56(5), 1119–1151.

Smith, V. L., Williams, A. W., Bratton, W. K., and Vannoni, M. G. 1982. "Competitive Market Institutions: Double Auctions vs. Sealed Bid-Offer Auctions." *The American Economic Review* 72(1): 58–77.

Sunder, S. 2007. "What Have We Learned from Experimental Finance?" In *Developments on Experimental Economics* (pp. 91–100). Berlin and Heidelberg: Springer Science+Business Media.

Williams, A. W., and Smith, V. L. 1984. "Cyclical Double-Auction Markets with and without Speculators." *Journal of Business* 57: 1–33.

Willinger, M., Keser, C., Lohmann, C., and Usunier, J. C. 2003. "A Comparison of Trust and Reciprocity between France and Germany: Experimental Investigation Based on the Investment Game." *Journal of Economic Psychology* 24(4): 447–466.

Xiao, E., and Houser, D. 2005. "Emotion Expression in Human Punishment Behavior." *Proceedings of the National Academy of Sciences of the USA*, 102(20): 7398–7401.

CHAPTER 17

THE MEANING OF *DECEIVE* IN EXPERIMENTAL ECONOMIC SCIENCE

BART J. WILSON

INTRODUCTION

Two principles distinguish experimental economic science from other experimental social sciences. First, we experimental economists pay our participants based on the decisions they make. Incentives matter. Not only might it seem hypocritical not to practice what we preach, but we are also concerned that the experiment's rewards are salient and achieve dominance. Smith (1982*b*: 931, 934) explains:

> In order that subject rewards in a laboratory experiment have motivational relevance such rewards must be associated indirectly with the message actions of subjects. This is called *Saliency*: Individuals are guaranteed the right to claim a reward which is increasing (decreasing) in the goods (bads) outcomes . . . of an experiment . . .
>
> A condition sufficient to guarantee that we have not lost control over preferences . . . [is called] *Dominance*: The reward structure dominates any subjective costs (or values) associated with participation in the activities of an experiment.

Note the subtle ethical imperatives: "must be," "guarantee," and "the right to claim." The integrity of our experimental conclusions rests on the soundness of our methods. A casual perusal of experimental papers reveals that the average salient earnings in economic experiments, that is, excluding any payment for showing up on time, range roughly from US$10 for an hour-long session to US$40 for a two-hour-long session.

Second, we do not use deception, not out of any deontic aversion to dishonesty, but rather because we are "concerned about developing and maintaining a reputation among the student population for honesty in order to ensure that subject actions are motivated by the induced monetary rewards rather than by psychological reactions to suspected manipulation" (Davis and Holt, 1993: 23–24).[1] Again, our concern is for the integrity of the inferences from our observations.

Although there is apparent wide agreement on what it means to maintain salience and achieve dominance of rewards, the same is not true of deception. Hertwig and Ortmann (2008) open their answer to the question of *What is deception?* by uncontentiously positing that "[d]eception is not easily defined" (61). Krawczyk (2013) conducts a survey of experimental economists and confirms that there is no clear agreement in practice on what deception is. My goal in this chapter is to shine a little light on the subject.

Is "What Is Deception?" a Perspicuous Question?

Like ordinary people, economists are serial nominalizers. If people do not sign up for retirement plans, it is because of hyperbolic discounting; if someone bids aggressively in a first-price auction, it is because of risk aversion; if proposers offer more than the minimum increment in an ultimatum game, it is because of fairness; etc., etc. So it is not surprising that when it comes to the ethics of experimental economists, we pose the question as about *deception*, the noun.[2]

Perhaps the form of the question befuddles us. As Wittgenstein (1958) recognized, "the mistake we are liable to make [is]... that we are looking for a 'thing corresponding to a substantive'" (5). A thing is something we classify by its boundaries, its features. Is this pest a termite or an ant alate? Well, let's look at the wings, antennae, and waist. Is this procedure deception by commission or omission? Well, let's look at the experimenter's behavior and/or the participants' perceptions of the experiment (Ortmann and Hertwig, 2002; Hertwig and Ortmann, 2008). But deception isn't a thing like a household pest is a thing; it's a conceptualization of what we *do* and so it doesn't have boundaries that make it readily identifiable. I know I have a termite problem and not an ant problem if the specimen on the floor has fore and hind wings of equal size, beaded antennae, and a broad waist. In contrast, we cannot envision all the forms of deception that we may encounter because there is no finite set of characteristics by which to classify it.

That doesn't deter us from trying to categorize the features of deception. Ortmann and Hertwig (2002) propose a boundary with the imperative that "default assumptions should be avoided" (113). They explain by example what a default assumption is: "One default assumption participants may reasonably have is that the initial interaction with

[1] As good practicing utilitarians, experimental economists are consummate consequentialists.

[2] I am no exception. My list of protocols to the Institutional Review Board includes the statement that "I adhere to the principle of never using misinformation or deception in my research."

the experimenter (upon entering the laboratory) is not yet part of the experiment" (113). The difficulty with creating this boundary, as they mention in an endnote, is (126):

> Admittedly, this statement is difficult to operationalize. In the words of one referee, "How will we know what range of default assumptions might be entertained by a given sample pool." One sensible approach to assessing default assumptions would be appropriately constructed pilot sessions.

Invoking appropriateness does not take us far, for it adds yet another unclear feature as to what deception is.

In his survey of experimental economists, Krawczyk (2013) makes the distinction between instructional statements to participants that "may be likely to change at least some subjects' behavior" and those that convey "complete information" (3). Ortmann and Hertwig's referee would ask, "How will we know what complete information is and what would change some subjects' behavior?" Complete information amounts in practice to what economists themselves need to know to solve the mathematical representation of a problem presented to experimental participants. Not only is this odd—delimiting the meaning of dishonesty by the current reach of positive economic analysis—but it also rules out as honest inquiry questions not deducible from economic theory. As we shall see, there are many questions regarding changes in participant behavior that are not covered by complete knowledge. Must an experimenter be deemed dishonest by a charge of deception to explore them?

No, but we do avoid pinning a scarlet *D* on an experimenter by posing the question as *What is deception?*. Listen to the tone of questioners in seminars and conferences and watch the body language of the presenter. To question a procedural detail as deceptive comes rather close to calling into question the ethical character of a person, and in everyday conversations that carries strong emotional force. Posing the question as *Is that not deception?* softens the charge and puts the focus on the procedural detail, not the experimenter and his or her moral character. But here's the rub. The experimenter is responsible for each and every detail of the experiment. The experimenter did what he or she did for a reason, to answer a specific question. It is the experimenter of whom we can ask questions and inquire about what is in fact the case or not the case. So rather than work with the nominalization of the problem, let's let the action of a verb do the work and pose the question like we generally do for ethical infractions: Who did what to whom?

Did the Experimenter Deceive the Participants?

Notice how this question differs from *What is deception?*. We are not trying to settle what deception is by covering all the positively creative ways that we can construct an experiment. We are asking a question of a specific case, of something that has happened, of what someone did, and the answer to this question rests on the meaning of the word *deceive*. I propose that we use pithy definition no. 1 from Dictionary.com: to mislead by a false appearance or statement.

Two elements must be established with this definition to attaint an experimenter as having done something to deceive a participant. First, the experimenter must have wrongly led or wrongly guided. Whatever assistance the experimenter gave the participants to make decisions, some component of what the experimenter *did* must have been wrong. Second, as in a court of (common) law, establishing wrongness of actions consists in assessing evidence with reference to objective criteria. What criteria might these be? A false appearance or a false statement.

Consider the case of Ortmann and Hertwig's default assumption. Instead of posing the question in terms of the default assumptions of the participants, let's examine the experimenter's action with the following yes-or-no questions directed to the experimenter.

QUESTIONER: As the participants entered the laboratory, did you collect data as a part of this experiment?

EXPERIMENTER: Yes.

QUESTIONER: Do you collect data as part of every other experiment of yours as participants enter the laboratory?

EXPERIMENTER: No.

QUESTIONER: That seems peculiar and difficult to reconcile as a genuine appearance. Why did you choose as part of this experiment to collect data as the participants enter the laboratory?

At this point, like in all research, we must rely on the integrity of the experimenter. In the subsequent sections I consider several economic experiments and answer the question, Did the experimenters mislead the participants by false appearance or statement?

Kim and Walker (1984)

Let's start with a straightforward case. In this public goods experiment with voluntary contributions Kim and Walker instruct their participants that "[t]here are exactly 100 people involved in this experiment, including yourself" (16). They disclose to the reader, however, that "[w]e did not in fact use 100 subjects in the experiment . . . Instead, we used only five subjects" (19). By their own admission Kim and Walker misled their participants by false statement.

Burnham, McCabe, and Smith (2000)

Krawczyk (2013) includes this experiment as an example of "deception by omission" for the use of a "surprise continuation" of the session. In the words of Burnham et al., though, "[t]here was no deception. Subjects were given the instructions for Single play [of an extensive form trust game] with no mention of whether there would be other experiments. After Single play, subject were paid and told that today they would be part of a second experiment" (64). Burnham et al. instructed their participants on how to play their trust game and how their decisions mapped into cash payoffs. After the participants made their decisions, the experimenters paid the participants as they said they would. Then they told the volunteers that they could participate in a second experiment.

A false statement about the second experiment would be informing the participants upfront that there would be one and only one play of an extensive form trust game and then springing the surprise second experiment on them. Burnham et al. made no such false statement, but is the surprise second experiment a false appearance? At first blush this case reminds us of Ortmann and Hertwig's default assumption. Is the surprise continuation part of this experiment? Yes. Is the surprise continuation part of every other experiment of yours? No. But these answers don't appear as peculiar in tandem. Why? Because entering the laboratory in the Ortmann and Hertwig example is a necessary part of conducting an experiment in a laboratory. It appears in every experiment and so guiding participants to their seats as if it does not matter constitutes a false appearance—not unlike treating a confederate as if he or she is not a confederate is a false appearance.[3] The key, I argue, is what did the experimenters *do* and the appearance thereof. The experimenters collected data as the participants entered the laboratory. In other experiments they do not do this. The appearance is the same in both cases but former's appearance is a false one because as they collected data they appeared not to be doing something when in fact they were.

A surprise second experiment is not necessary for a project, so what would the experimenters do if they didn't conduct a surprise second experiment? Exactly the same thing as when they conducted the first experiment plus a surprise second experiment, just without the second experiment. There was no false appearance that there was only one experiment when in fact there was a second experiment. Nor was there a false appearance to the second experiment. The second experiment simply appeared. The surprise continuation does not constitute leading the participants because there is nothing to lead the participants to. That the experimenters knew something at the start of the experiment that the participants did not is not a matter of the experimenters *doing* anything to mislead the participants by false appearance or statement.[4]

[3] Krawczyk (2013) reports some agreement among his respondents that the use of confederates is deceptive. The average rating is 5.08 on a 0–7 scale (with 0 representing not deceptive at all).

[4] The editor raises the interesting question as to what the experimenters would have done had a participant inquired at the start of the experiment whether there would be a second or third experiment. To deny that there would be a subsequent experiment would be to mislead by false statement. So to avoid deceiving the speculating participant the experimenter would have to plead the 5th. This question raises a separate, but related issue with conducting surprise experiments, namely the negative externality of participants second-guessing the experimenters. Recall Davis and Holt's reasoning for not deceiving participants, an expectation among the participants that they are not being deceived by the experimenter. I submit that one reason why experimental economists consider a surprise continuation to be deceiving a participant is that both can lead to second-guessing of future experiments by repeat

Holt and Laury (2002)

This well-cited article for measuring risk aversion pushes the boundaries of the previous case. Here is what they said to the participants in what they called the "Option A/B" choice:[5]

> You will make ten choices and record these in the final column, but only one of them will be used in the end to determine your earnings . . . After you have made all of your choices, we will throw this die twice, once to select one of the ten decisions to be used, and a second time to determine what your payoff is for the option you chose, A or B, for the particular decision selected. Even though you will make ten decisions, only one of these will end up affecting your earnings, but you will not know in advance which decision will be used.

The second throw of the die is the realization of the lottery that has been randomly selected for payoff. After all decisions have been made, the experimenters passed out another page of instructions. This is the first paragraph of the second set of instructions:

> Now, we will provide you with the chance to make another choice, with much higher potential payoffs, as you can see from the sheet we are passing around. As always, we will pay you the exact amount you earn in this part, and we have the cash required. If you choose to participate in this round, we will not pay you what you just earned in the Option A/B choice that you just finished, i.e. you can choose which one you want to count, and to be added to your earnings from all previous parts. The procedures are exactly as before, after you make your ten decisions, we throw the die once to determine which decision is to be used, and then we throw the die to determine the payoff for that decision.

Unlike Burnham et al., Holt and Laury did not complete the first experiment. They wished to avoid having the realized wealth from the first lottery affect the choices in the second lottery with much higher stakes. Did Holt and Laury mislead their participants by false statement? Holt and Laury said that they "will throw this die twice" for the first experiment, but they never did because all of the participants chose to forego their first experiment earnings. They also said that "only one of these [Option A/B decisions] will end up affecting your earnings." If we were to ask Holt and Laury what they would have *done* had a participant elected not to participate in the second experiment, we would have to take them at their word if they said that they would have executed the first experiment lottery and subsequently dismissed the participant. At some point with these questions we reach bedrock and can't avoid relying on the integrity of the scholars,

participants. A procedure may invite second-guessing but that doesn't make it deceptive. Not all digits are thumbs. Let's be precise about the everyday meaning of *deceive* and its application to experimental economic science.

[5] Accessed at http://people.virginia.edu/~cah2k/highdata.pdf on February 15, 2014.

and this makes it difficult to conclude that Holt and Laury misled their participants by false statement.

Gunnthorsdottir, Houser, and McCabe (2007)

In 1997, "a good decade between first sessions and eventual publication," Gunnthorsdottir, Houser, McCabe, and Holly Ameden were interested in how the disappointment of expectations in the early rounds of a public goods experiment contributed to the standard decay of voluntary contributions (see, e.g., Isaac and Walker, 1988).[6] The stylized facts of the voluntary contributions mechanism for public goods is that some people start the experiment contributing all of their tokens to the "Group Account," others contribute none, and some others hedge splitting their tokens between the Group and Private Accounts. Over time, however, the full contributors stop fully contributing and the hedgers stop hedging. What if, Gunnthorsdottir et al. surmised, the full contributors met other full contributors in the first period, would their contributions still decay over time?[7]

Since full contributors aren't identifiable ex ante by a mark on their foreheads, they designed a procedure by which a pool of participants would first decide their contributions and then the software would allocate the individuals to proper subsets of four-person public goods. In the baseline condition the software randomly assigned participants to different subgroups of four people. In the other condition, the software assigned the four highest contributors to one group of four, the next four highest contributors to another group, and so on. To hold constant the expectations of whom the participants may be meeting, the experimenters did not inform the participants in either treatment on how they were being matched. Here are their exact instructions for both conditions:[8]
Each period proceeds as follows:

> First, decide on the number of tokens to place in the private and in the public account, respectively. Use the mouse to . . .
>
> Second, once everyone has submitted his or her investment decision, you will be assigned to a group with 4 members (including yourself). Your total group investment will then be determined and your experimental earnings calculated.
>
> Third, you will receive a message with your experimental earnings for the period. This information will also appear in your Record Sheet.
>
> A new period will begin after everyone has acknowledged his or her earnings message.
>
> After the last period, you will receive a message with your total experimental earnings (sum of earnings in each period).

6 Daniel Houser (personal communication, February 18, 2014).

7 Their answer is no, they sustain high contributions without decay.

8 I received a copy of the instructions by contacting the first author.

Rigdon et al. (2007) applied a similar procedure to a two-person extensive form trust game. In the baseline condition, first movers were randomly matched with second movers. In the sorting condition, more trustworthy second movers were matched with more trusting first movers. Their instructions for both conditions state that "[t]he joint decisions made by you and your counterpart for that period will determine how much money you will earn in that period. After each period you will be re-paired."[9] My co-authors and I adopted a similar one-time matching mechanism in Wilson et al. (2012). Our instructions said nothing about how the participants were matched (and not one of 144 participants at two different universities ever asked).[10] For the first 13 periods only two avatars appeared on each of the 12 participant screens, and in period 14 two pairs joined them out of nowhere to form a sextet.

Not once in the instructions of these three experiments did the authors mislead the participants. The experimenters created an exercise in which they simply did not inform the participants on how the pairs or groups were formed. A false statement in these experiments would be explicitly telling the participants that the experimenters randomly formed the groups when in actuality they sorted according to the participants' actions. In all three experiments the task was what it was; there were no false appearances or false statements.

And yet something about this bothers many economists:[11] *This must be deception by omission because had the participants known about the matching algorithm, they would have acted differently*. Yes, if the authors had informed the participants of the matching mechanism, this knowledge would have likely changed their decisions, but that is beside the point and misses the point. These authors are not interested in how people behave when they know how they are being matched. What people do knowing how they are matched is a different and, I submit, a less interesting question than what people do when they have no idea of how they are matched.

The unexamined assumption for claiming deception in these experiments is that because the experimenter knows something that the subject does not, that somehow the experimenter is lying to the subjects. Experimenters know a lot about their participants' tasks that their participants do not: what the Nash equilibrium is, how the last session performed, why this is an interesting question, etc. Participants in the canonical double auction experiment, for example, are typically not told what all the values and costs are. In fact, the point of that experiment is to demonstrate that the participants can realize

9 Available in a working paper dated February 15, 2006.

10 Answering this question in the other two designs requires a stoic response. Having conducted the sorting trust game version probably a hundred times in workshops and courses, inevitably a student will ask, "How are we matched?" Or, "Are we matched randomly?" My reply is to simply reread the relevant sentences from the instructions.

11 One referee for Wilson et al. (2012) expressed his or her concern thusly: "A more pertinent issue would seem to concern whether or not telling subjects how their groups are formed is a deceptive practice or at least something that spells long run loss of control. It seems to me what is done is OK, but perhaps questionable. There is this design feature subjects are not told about but which if they knew about it would possibly have changed their behavior in the early stages."

nearly 100 percent of the gains from trade even without knowledge of the supply and demand arrays (Smith, 1982*a*). Not telling the participants about all the costs and values, moreover, is not a "loss of control" in the experiment. To wit, we experimenters are expressly interested in observing what people do without that knowledge.[12]

Not providing information in and of itself is insufficient grounds to conclude that the experimenters have deceived the participants. The nontrivial difference between misleading by false appearance or statement and simply not providing information in an experiment is *a matter of fact that can be demonstrated to be false.* We cannot articulate a general rule on knowing things (by experimenters or participants) that delineates when experimenters have deceived their participants and when they have not. We can, however, examine what the experimenters *did* in guiding their participants through the experiment and judge the evidence of those actions as involving a false appearance or false statement. Rather than attempting to classify experimental procedural details as deception or not, I propose a negative test of experimenter actions: Did the experimenters mislead the participants by false appearance or statement?

Acknowledgments

I thank George DeMartino, Andreas Ortmann, David Rojo Arjona, and Vernon Smith for constructive comments that have improved this chapter.

References

Burnham, Terence, Kevin McCabe, and Vernon L. Smith. 2000. "Friend-or-Foe Intentionality Priming in an Extensive Form Trust Game." *Journal of Economic Behavior and Organization* 43(1): 57–73.

Davis, Douglas D., and Charles A. Holt. 1993. *Experimental Economics.* Princeton, NJ: Princeton University Press.

Gunnthorsdottir, Anna, Daniel Houser, and Kevin McCabe. 2007. "Dispositions, History and Contributions in Public Goods Experiments." *Journal of Economic Behavior and Organization* 62(2): 304–315.

Hertwig, Ralph, and Andreas Ortmann. 2008. "Deception in Experiments: Revisiting the Arguments in Its Defense." *Ethics & Behavior* 18(1): 59–92.

Holt, Charles A., and Susan Laury. 2002. "Risk Aversion and Incentive Effects." *American Economic Review* 92(5): 1644–1655.

Isaac, R. Mark, and James M. Walker. 1988. "Group Size Effects in Public Goods Provision: The Voluntary Contributions Mechanism." *Quarterly Journal of Economics* 103(1): 179–199.

[12] Logico-deductive economic theory cannot handle this open question because there is nothing from which to deduce outcomes. This may make some economists uncomfortable, and perhaps they conflate this feeling that something is wrong with the notion that experimenter has done something wrong.

Kim, Oliver, and Mark Walker. 1984. "The Free Rider Problem: Experimental Evidence." *Public Choice* 43: 3–24.

Krawczyk, Michał. 2013. "Delineating Deception in Experimental Economics: Researchers' and Subjects' Views." Faculty of Economic Sciences Working Paper, University of Warsaw.

Ortmann, Andreas, and Ralph Hertwig. 2002. "The Costs of Deception: Evidence from Psychology." *Experimental Economics* 5(2): 111–131.

Rigdon, Mary L., Kevin A. McCabe, and Vernon L. Smith. 2007. "Sustaining Cooperation in Trust Games." *Economic Journal* 117(522): 991–1007.

Smith, Vernon L. 1982*a*. "Markets as Economizers of Information: Experimental Examination of the Hayek Hypothesis." *Economic Inquiry*, 20 (2): 165–179.

Smith, Vernon L. 1982*b*. "Microeconomic Systems as an Experimental Science." *American Economic Review* 72(5): 923–955.

Wilson, Bart J., Taylor Jaworski, Karl Schurter, and Andrew Smyth. 2012. "The Ecological and Civil Mainsprings of Property: An Experimental Economic History of Whalers' Rules of Capture. *Journal of Law, Economics and Organization* 28(4): 617–656.

Wittgenstein, Ludwig. 1958. *The Blue and Brown Books*. New York: Harper & Row.

2. *Econometrics*

CHAPTER 18

HONESTY AND INTEGRITY IN ECONOMETRICS

THOMAS MAYER

INTRODUCTION

HONESTY and integrity are of greater importance in applied econometrics and in the provision of data than in other parts of economics. If an overly enthusiastic theorist tries to give his hypothesis an unwarranted boost, readers have a readily available defense against being deceived; they can read it carefully enough to spot the error. Similarly, if an economist tries to support her hypothesis by claiming that financial crises generally occur before business cycle turning points you can look at the historical data and see that this is wrong. But if you are told that a certain regression coefficient is 0.809 it would generally be too difficult and laborious to ascertain whether this is true. Here the reader is at the author's mercy. And so he is with respect to plagiarism.

The credibility of econometric results are of central importance for economics. If economics is to tell us anything about the external world, and not just about the operations of a particular formal model, models have to be tested empirically by the accuracy of their predictions (broadly interpreted) and such tests are overwhelmingly econometric testsd Are these tests done honestly enough that we can trust their results to discriminate among various models? Strangely, although we teach our students that self-interest governs human behavior, we do not ask whether honest reporting is in an economist's self-interest, and if not, consider the implications of this for the credibility of our own work.[1]

Applied econometricians (whom I will from now on just call "econometricians"), like other economists, may be dishonest in at least three ways. They may take credit for work done by others or they may misstate the results of their own work. Referees may also

[1] There is, however, one organization, the Association for Integrity and Responsible Leadership in Economics and Associated Professions, concerned with the honesty and integrity of economists. It is very small.

abuse the refereeing process by using it to reward friends and punish enemies, or by failing to do an adequate job. Because such refereeing abuses are linked to "honesty" and "integrity" only by the referee not letting the editor know that she failed to do an adequate job, I will not discuss them.[2] I will emphasize the misstating of results because from a consequentialist viewpoint, though not from a deontological one, that is probably the most damaging and also probably the most common way dishonesty occurs in econometrics. (I cannot justify my consequentialist bias here, but whether plagiarism is a more or a less heinous crime than is misstating one's results is fortunately not a central issue.)

But before discussing either plagiarizing or misstating results one needs to ask what one means by honesty and integrity in econometrics.

The Meaning of Honesty and Integrity

Because I am an economist and not a philosopher I will use a pragmatic and not a "deep" definition of honesty by characterizing it as a certain behavior—not lying—that is helpful in advancing our knowledge. But not telling lies is not sufficient because it does not imply that one is telling enough of the truth, and is therefore compatible with misleading readers. This is where integrity comes in.[3] In legal proceedings the prosecution has to provide the defendant with any favorable evidence for the defense that it has. Doesn't integrity call for the econometrician to obey a similar rule? This would require her to mention all or at least some of the alternative regressions she has run that do not support her conclusion, but are as (or more) plausible than the ones that do support it. Integrity does not let you get away with: "Oh well this procedure does not seem quite right to me,

[2] For a detailed discussion of plagiarism see Lafayette (1992).

[3] Instead of trying to present a definition of integrity, here are some delineating examples of how I am using this term. Suppose you believe that you can present an idea as a simple, verbal argument but you dress it up in complex mathematics to impress referees. Unless in the process you distort the argument, that is consistent with integrity, though bad practice. Or suppose you are more likely to check for keypunch errors when you get a result that negates your hypothesis than when it supports it. This is acceptable because a result that contradicts your hypothesis seems to you less plausible, and hence more likely to be due to a keypunch error, than one that is consistent with what you consider to be true. But if you present the results of a regression that supports your hypothesis without mentioning that another nine equally plausible regressions you ran disconfirmed it, that shows a lack of integrity. Similarly, if in the text you cite evidence that supports you, but relegate what you think are serious arguments that contradict this evidence to a footnote in an appendix you lack integrity. And the same is true if you do not mention or if you dismiss with a wave of the hand that someone has previously made the same point as you do, and did it just as well. Similarly, if you dimly see a fallacy in your argument, but refuse to think about it for fear of what you may find, then you lack integrity. Refusal to share your data is usually contrary to proper scientific behavior and unethical, but represents a lack of integrity only if you do so because you are afraid that it would allow someone to disconfirm your analysis (see Gelman, 2011). Otherwise it may just indicate laziness.

but all the same I will use it, because it is used by many authors in leading journals, and if they can get away with it, so can I."

And how about the assumptions of the model? Those that are part of the generally accepted paradigm, or else are obviously true, need not be mentioned, but there is a fuzzy line between these and other assumptions that might cause readers to reject the conclusion if they were told about them. Is an econometrician who hides them in footnotes or an appendix lacking integrity? And does integrity require at least a certain minimal care to avoid errors? I believe that the answer to both these questions is "yes," but how far should these requirements be pushed?

Another definitional problem is to distinguish errors due to ignorance from those due to dishonesty or lack of integrity. Here is an example. Economist A tests her hypothesis that the price elasticity of demand is higher in recessions than in expansions. Her regressions yield a coefficient with the right sign, but its *t*-value is only 1.2. Can she salvage all her work by arguing that she has *dis*confirmed the hypothesis that the price elasticities of demand are higher in expansions? Having read Ziliak and McCloskey (2008) she knows that this is wrong, but she also knows that this error is not unusual. So she goes ahead with it. Clearly, she is being dishonest. Economist B, who is not familiar with the literature, does not know that failure to obtain a significant coefficient does not imply that the converse hypothesis is correct, also publishes her new hypothesis that the elasticity does *not* increase. She is not dishonest. Economist C has read enough to know that there is a dispute about whether the insignificance of a coefficient confirms the converse of the initial hypothesis. But he does not bother to investigate any further and publishes his claim that the elasticity does not increase. Is he dishonest? Not really, but he is exhibiting a lack of integrity because he is leaving unresolved a critical issue he could have resolved.[4]

And then there is the question of whose honesty or integrity is being discussed. One possibility is that of an individual econometrician, taken as given the criteria that prevail in econometrics, that is, not the formal rules laid down by theoretical econometricians and by textbooks, but the criteria used by applied econometricians as they go about their work. These, as discussed later, may be more forgiving, and permit such errors as interpreting failure to confirm a hypothesis at the 5 percent significance level as disconfirmation, or ignoring the unreliability of the underlying data.[5] Because the magic of

[4] Another problem I am not discussing is the postmodernist criticism of the notion of objective truth and of the importance of honesty. Paul Feyerabend (1977) has given many examples of great scientists who have fudged their evidence. But his argument relies on what may well be a cherry picked sample. Besides, there is the proverb: "what Jupiter may do an ox may not do". Furthermore, suppose a prevailing paradigm has encountered serious problems, but so has a new, competing paradigm that we now take as correct. A scientist who succeeds in converting his contemporaries to the new paradigm only by fudging the evidence is probably more likely to be considered a great scientist by future generations than one who is unconvincing because he does not fudge. But when one takes into account the damage that a general disposition to fudge does to science as a whole, it is far from obvious that fudging enhances the growth of scientific knowledge.

[5] In practice it can be hard to distinguish between lack of integrity and merely poor workmanship. Perhaps the best way is that lack of integrity results in errors biased in favor of the author's thesis, while bad workmanhip results in asymptotically unbiased errors. The prevailing use of digital databases may

group-think is able to transform a statement that any single member of the group on his or her own would feel uneasy about into a statement about which the group as a whole has no qualms, something more than individual honesty is needed for an econometric paper to be considered trustworthy.[6] And for users of econometric results, unlike for moralists, what counts is the honesty and integrity of econometric papers, not that of individual econometricians who are somehow isolated from group influence.

The problem is that the criteria we use to define acceptable results are not passed on to us from on high, but are set by a group containing members who have a (presumably unconscious) incentive to set the goal posts so that that particular papers they have written are acceptable. As a result, standards are set too low with respect to faults and shortcuts that are common. The downward drift will be checked both by economists criticizing each other's papers and by the unpleasantness of the cognitive dissonance that results from using criteria that seem too loose to you.

The bias that group-think can generate might seem to imply that econometricians should avoid all group-think. But this is naïve. Given the usual time constraints and the number of criteria to be applied, critically considering all your econometric criteria is the counsel of perfection. Moreover, the criteria are part of a field's paradigm, and it is a hallmark of science—according to Thomas Kuhn, (1970) *the* hallmark—that there be an agreed-up paradigm; that way progress is made. But such a relaxed view of econometrics ignores that econometricians are maximizers, and that stating the truth is not the only argument in their utility functions. And if Dan Ariely (see later) is right and people have a strong preference for cheating only in minor ways, so that they can still regard themselves as basically honest, adopting criteria that are easy to meet and that other researchers have used is very appealing. Even if your reason tells you that were you to subject these criteria to closer examination they might not stand up, your intuition, which wants you to accept them so that you can publish your paper, will tell you to do so. And much evidence shows that intuition is the master and reason the servant (see Haidt, 2012). To be sure, science has a countervailing mechanism; it just takes one scientist to see through the delusion and write a paper showing it. But she would have to convince the referee(s) of a journal, and then the readers of that journal, that she is right. Because in many cases these referees and readers have published papers that lose value if she is right, that can be an uphill struggle.

Whether that struggle is won or lost may depend not only on the rationality of the argument, but also on its emotional—and careerist—appeal. If the proposed revision

seem to eliminate the need to check one's data. But that assumes that the database has been carefully checked by its originator. I once found two errors in a then widely used database, and when I informed the commercial supplier of that database my letter did not elicit any response, suggesting a "who cares?" attitude that is incompatible with integrity. Faraji Kasidi, H. Chaturvdi, and Rahul S. Sigh (2010) discuss the reliability of some Indian databases. Cargill (2012) shows that widely used data on central bank independence are unreliable.

[6] We have here an example of emergence. The decision-making units, individual econometricians, determine the aggregate, that is the papers that are being published, but this aggregate partially determines the decisions that individual econometricians make.

promises to bestow prestige on the limited number of researchers who have the skills needed to employ it, their emotions will urge them to accept it, while the emotions of those who lack theses skills will tell them to reject it. Referees and editors feel these emotions too. A paper that is critical of currently employed procedures, while offering no alternative procedures but just warning readers to be skeptical about a certain type of paper, may be hard to publish, or if published may be ignored. No conspiracy is implied here; nobody colludes, but the results do not differ all that much from those of an imperfectly adhered to conspiracy.[7]

One example where the stand-patters have won is the need to confirm the results that one's regression program generates by running the regression also on other programs. McCullough and Vinod (1999) have shown that the results obtained by regression analysis are frequently sensitive, and substantially so, to the particular regression program used. Because they published this paper in the widely read *Journal of Economic Literature* (and published similar results in several other journals) it would be reasonable to expect that many economists who previously published regression analyses would now publish papers showing what happens if one uses a different program. But this did not happen. By implicit common consent the unwelcome news went down the memory hole. And this is so not just in economics. Similarly, Aris Spanos (2008) and others have challenged the propriety of fitting a hypothesis to the data without first investigating the functional form of the data. But their challenge appears to have had little impact.

Moreover, if it is hard to determine whether a certain criterion has been met, that criterion is less likely to have bite. Thus Ariely's theory predicts that any criterion that is not expressible as a hard number, for example, having a sample large enough to justify the assumption of a normal distribution, may be eroded over time as many successive researchers each fall slightly short of it. If a referee has seen many papers in good journals in which normalcy is assumed even though $N \geq 25$, she is not likely to reject a paper because it has an N of 24. The publication of that paper then encourages referees to pass papers with an N of 23. Mark Blaug (1980: 256) has famously described much of econometrics as "playing tennis with the net down." This is less likely to be noticed if the net is not dropped all at once, but is lowered slightly after each volley.

Two Positive Theories of Honesty

The traditional way economists approach the problem of dishonesty is to apply utility-maximization theory and say that the extent of dishonesty depends on four factors: the benefits obtained from being dishonest, the probability of being caught, the cost if caught, and the degree of risk aversion. This theory does not deny that social cohesion, religious beliefs, and so on affect the extent of dishonesty. Instead, it either claims that

[7] For a game theory model of the interaction between journals, authors, and readers see Zelder (2008).

for the phenomena to be explained, for example, differences in the degree of honesty between, say used car dealers and dentists, the differences that are due to "tastes," such as the degree of social cohesion, account for so little of the variations in honesty that they can without significant loss be impounded in the error term, or else that economists can treat these differences as exogenous and leave it to others, for example, psychologists to deal with them. And the same applies to differences in honesty over time.

Another way, that of behavioral economics, is to open the box of tastes, and to explain differences in tastes. Dan Ariely (2012) provides an outstanding example with his "fudge factor" theory of honesty. Ariely first amends the traditional utility function by adding a specific taste variable for honesty, one that is to be explicitly considered instead of being impounded along with other tastes in a general and unanalyzed constant. This taste variable, which is grounded in the fundamental human desire for self-respect, is to see oneself as a basically honest person. He then argues on the basis of substantial evidence from behavioral economics that this factor has much more to tell us about the prevalence and characteristics of honest behavior than do the factors considered by traditional economic theory:

> Behavior is driven by two opposing motivations.... [W]e want to view ourselves as honest, honorable people.... On the other hand, we want to benefit from cheating.... Clearly these two motivations are in conflict. How can we secure the benefits of cheating ... and still view ourselves as honest, wonderful people? This is where our amazing cognitive flexibility comes into play.... [A]s long as we cheat by only a little bit, we can benefit from cheating and still view ourselves as marvelous human beings. This balancing act is ... the basis of ...the "fudge factor theory." (Ariely 2012: 27)

Thus, though Ariely does not discuss this, you are also more likely to adjust the regressors included in your regression equation to obtain the result you want than you are to claim results from a regression you never ran. It is when there are gray areas and when we are left to score our own performance—conditions not so uncommon in econometrics—that we are most tempted to cheat (Ariely, 2012: 65). Moreover, Ariely (2012: 172) points out that the more creative we are the easier it is for us to find rationalizations. And applied econometrics does not lack creative people. Moreover, when we see our friends being flexible in what they allow themselves to do, this makes us more flexible too, and so does a belief that others (e.g., our university or department, or our collaborators) also benefit when we cheat (Ariely, 2012: 195, 206, 226).

I will use Ariely's theory of honesty, but with one modification. Ariely argues that the empirical evidence shows that the factors stressed by the traditional economic theory of honesty—the size of the potential gain, the danger of being caught, and the potential punishment—are unimportant in determining whether a person is dishonest. This may well be so when discussing dishonesty of a representative agent. But I have to worry about heterogeneous agents. Suppose only 10 percent of econometrics papers involved some cheating that is serious enough to change the results substantially. Although for a general theory of dishonesty the fact that there are potential gains from cheating may be unimportant, to the reader of econometric papers the fact that 10 percent of the results are distorted is not.

Econometricians as Maximizing Agents

I will therefore drop the common and very comforting assumption that the utility function of econometricians contains just one argument, the maximization of human knowledge. The additional arguments I include are income, leisure (which enters here only indirectly via income) and self-esteem. The close relation between publications and income allows one to substitute (quality weighted) publications for income. Self-esteem depends on many variables, but the relevant ones for the purpose at hand are your own and other people's appraisal of your publications and of your honesty. It is therefore not surprising that a recent survey of economists (Attema et al., 2012) found that the respondents would on average be willing to sacrifice about three quarters of a thumb for an article in the *The American Economic Review* (AER). The respondents also stated that on average they expected an additional AER article to raise their salaries by 8 percent. (However, one should be cautious about taking these results at face value. The response rate was only about 6.5 percent, and on an issue like this those who responded may well be less typical of the universe than is usual in surveys.)

The Incentive to Publish and Honesty and Integrity

Let us now see the extent to which the urge to publish reduces honesty and integrity by encouraging stealing, fraud, and the manipulation of results.

Taking Credit for the Work of Others

The opportunity to take credit for the work done by one's research assistants and junior collaborators is much smaller in economics than in most natural sciences, because economics does not have the large, hierarchic labs of the natural sciences with their masses of post docs and junior assistants whose work is often intended to be fused into the overall work of the lab. Typically in economics a research assistant does not carry out independent, self-contained research. There is thus little question about who owns the research, though a faculty member may be less than forthright in acknowledging a research assistant's contribution.

However, when a junior and a senior professor collaborate, the latter (who is likely to vote on the assistant professor's tenure) can exploit his powers by doing less than his share of the work, at the potential costs of a bad conscience and of acquiring a reputation as an undesirable co-author.

The story is different for PhD dissertations. Here a dissertation supervisor may suggest, or more than merely "suggest," to a graduate student that her name as well as the student's appear on the resulting paper. This might occasionally be justified because the supervisor may have provided the idea for the dissertation, or provided a solution when the student got stuck.

But given that so many graduate students cannot think of a dissertation topic, trying to steal good ideas from graduate students is likely to result in slim pickings. But in some cases it may succeed. When it does and is not caught the potential costs to the plagiarist of such misbehavior is only a bad conscience. However, in many universities there is, at least formally, not just a single supervisor for each dissertation, but a committee. Normally its chairman is the only one heavily involved. But peripheral members may stay informed enough to discover at least the more flagrant cases where a graduate student is pressured into a jointly authored publication, and they may let the rest of the department know. This seems to suggest that exploitation of dissertation writers is likely to be only an occasional problem. But that may be too optimistic a view. A study of US graduate education found that 36 percent of recent PhD's, 30 percent of graduate faculty, and 41 percent of graduate deans "agreed with the statement that 'major professors often exploit doctoral candidates'" (Sovacool, 2008: 278). Even though the term "exploit" is vague enough to include other things besides plagiarism, this does suggest that stealing the work of doctoral candidates is more common than I have previously suggested.

Another problem, one that has received more discussion, is referees stealing from papers they review (see LaFollette, 1992), and more generally, economists stealing ideas from working papers they read. The chance of being caught is small because there are many genuine cases of simultaneous discovery. Moreover, the line of demarcation between honest research and plagiarism is not always clear.[8] If endowed with a sufficiently pliant imagination a plagiarist may convince herself that she did not *really* steal the idea; that prior to reading the paper she had more or less thought of the essence of it herself, and that the paper had at most clarified what was in her own mind.

Apart from stealing ideas (which in the United States is not copyright infringement) there is the hard-core plagiarism of copying verbatim a paper or significant parts of it, something which in the United States is copyright infringement. An editor of one journal has reported that his journal "sometimes receives a full paper already published by someone else," with only the name of author(s) changed (Karabag and Berrgren, 2012: 172).

There are now computer programs that allow editors to catch this (Enserink, 2012). But once potential infringers learn how these programs work they may be able to defeat

[8] For a good discussion of the difficulty of defining plagiarism see Clarke (2006).

them. Moreover, what is really important is to prevent the stealing of ideas, not of wording. However, stolen wording suggests stolen ideas.

In addition to plagiarizing from working papers and dissertations in progress, one can, of course, also plagiarize from previously published papers or books. But the temptation to do this is not as great as it may seem at first glance. Suppose you plagiarize a recent paper in a good journal. There is a substantial chance that the editor or one of the referees has read it, or that should your submission be published, someone who has read the original paper will catch it. If you try to avoid that by plagiarizing a paper that is old enough to have been forgotten, you will likely be told that both the terminal date of your regressions and your econometric techniques are out of date. If, to escape these problems, you plagiarize from a recent paper in an obscure journal you may avoid detection, but there is a reason why the paper was published in an obscure journal, and putting your name on it is not likely to make it publishable in a good journal. Even so, plagiarizing from an obscure journal may be tempting to someone teaching in a school that insists on a publication for tenure, any publication, never mind its quality.

You can also reduce the probability of being caught by plagiarizing from a paper in a foreign language. But that limits your choice greatly both because many papers in foreign journals are published in English, and there is perhaps also the cost of having to learn the foreign language.

In addition to outright plagiarism there is what might be called "self-plagiarism"—submitting to another journal more or less the same paper, or a substantial part of a paper, you have already published elsewhere, in the hope that the referees have not read the earlier version. This is justified if the two journals have very different readerships, so that a second publication may help to break down undesirable disciplinary barriers. For example, in writing a paper for *Public Choice* you may develop a statistical test that would be of interest to theoretical econometricians who would never see it in *Public Choice*. But otherwise it just wastes readers' time and journal space. It is dishonest because it misleadingly puffs up the author's C.V. A less annoying version of self-plagiarism is to use verbatim in a new publication one or more paragraphs from your earlier publication, a relatively harmless manifestation of laziness.

Finally, there is a sneaky trick that, though not plagiarism in a formal sense, operates like it. This is to cite in a footnote the paper whose basic insight you duplicate, so that you cannot be accused of plagiarism, but to make it sound as though the previous paper did not contain the essence of your paper. I suspect that this device is used mainly when an author who has already completed much of her paper discovers a previous paper that is essentially the same as her's.

There are no hard data on the frequency of plagiarism. That one hears about it only infrequently does not mean that it occurs only infrequently.[9] In a survey that Enders

[9] As best I can recollect I have heard only about three actual cases of plagiarism in economics (and am suspicious about a fourth case) in the more than 60 years I have been an economist. Two of them were so clumsy that one wonders whether the perpetrators cared about being caught, and in the third the perpetrator could have avoided discovery by taking an elementary precaution. Although this sample is much too small to draw a reliable conclusion, it is consistent with the disturbing hypothesis that only

and Hoover (2006: 94) sent to (mainly academic) American economists, 24 percent of all respondents (and 43 percent of full professors) reported that their work has been plagiarized. But that is not a reliable estimate. As Enders and Hoover (2006: 93) themselves point out, those who believed that that they had been plagiarized are much more likely than others to respond to the survey. Moreover, probably not everyone who believes that he or she had been plagiarized actually was, as coincidental discoveries do occur. On the other hand, some economists may have been plagiarized without their being aware of it. In another survey Enders and Hoover (2004: 489) asked journal editors to estimate the number of plagiarized papers that they received during a typical year. Seventy-one percent replied "none," while 2 percent replied "four or more." But editors, too, probably did not catch all instances of plagiarism.

A remarkable finding of the Enders and Hoover survey was the reluctance to punish plagiarizers severely; fewer than half of the editors responding to the survey (and they may be a biased sample) would make the incident public or inform the plagiarist's superior, for example, her dean. However, 83 percent reported that they would definitely, or were likely to, ban a plagiarist from future publication in their journal (Enders and Hoover, 2004: 490). Yet, occasionally the punishment could be severe. In one case the plagiarist lost his endowed chair, was reduced in rank to assistant professor, and was suspended without pay for a semester (Enders and Hoover, 2006: 100).[10]

In another survey Laband and Piette (2000) asked American academic economists to estimate the frequency and severity of certain unacceptable practices.[11] Three of these practices relate to plagiarizing the work of others and one to self-plagiarism. The respondents, who take such self-plagiarism surprisingly seriously, estimate it to be the most common of the eleven sins discussed in the survey, and rank the frequency of the other types of plagiarism fairly low. Not surprisingly, they rank the seriousness of plagiarism lower than that of dishonestly reporting results. But it is surprising that they are not more concerned about economists undertaking research based on papers they rejected as referees and on ideas they heard about from colleagues. The former has the potential for an obvious abuse of the refereeing process, and the latter for inhibiting the free exchange of ideas that is such a valuable part of an university environment. And they are surprisingly tolerant of failing to provide the data for replication, a tolerance that is mirrored in the way economists behave.

Plagiarism does damage in several ways. One way is that by allowing someone to publish without having to do research it reduces the incentive for productive work. And it does this also by reducing the citation counts of the original paper. Further, it fosters

shameless stealing is uncovered, and that there might be many cases of more cautious and therefore undiscovered stealing.

[10] In a survey of members of the European Economic Association covering, not just plagiarism, but all types of scientific misconduct only 23 percent of those who observed the misconduct reported it or talked informally about it to other scholars (Feld, Necker, and Frey, 2012: 16).

[11] There were 728 respondents in their sample (about a 25 percent rate of response) which was taken in 1996. They provide data on many additional practices.

inappropriate career advancement for plagiarizers (Clarke, 2006). Last, but not least, it is dishonest.

Outright Fraud

What is to prevent an economist from taking some hypothesis, and instead of bothering to test it, present "results" pulled out of thin air and thus obtain whatever results and regression diagnostics he wishes? The potential damage done to the discipline of economics is, of course, much greater than that done by plagiarism. If not discovered it introduces false information, and may invalidate the work of others who use these spurious results in their own work, and it can also result in misleading policy advice. Moreover, if the fraud is discovered it damages the reputation of economics, and more generally, gives demagogues ammunition in their war against science.

One disincentive for such fraud is, of course, the loss of self-respect that anyone committing it should feel. Let us hope that this alone is sufficient to deter most economists. But what suffices for most need not suffice for all. Moreover, fraud need not be as stark as just described, and still be damaging. Someone might say to herself: "I have done much work on this paper and have great confidence in its results. But the referee will block publication unless I add the result of an additional test that has very little relevance, and would be hard to undertake. O.K., so I'll just make it up" (see Crocker, 2011; Anonymous, 2012b: 238; *Nature*, 2012a). Bad enough, but further, the slope that leads from such a "minor" infraction to publishing a paper based entirely or largely on spurious data may be slippery. It seems probable that somewhere in sliding down it many authors would stop, take stock, and realize the immorality of what they are doing. But would all?

Fortunately, the moral repugnance for fraud is—at least to a minor extent—reinforced by fear of being caught. But how likely is it that a culprit will be caught? Even a major contribution is highly unlikely to be checked or replicated.[12] Checking and replication require much work and earn much too little prestige to attract many economists, as neither provides much opportunity for demonstrating one's cleverness. And if checking confirms the paper's conclusions nearly all journals will consider the checker's results not worth publishing. Even if checking or replication does demonstrate an error, many if not most journals are unlikely to publish it.[13] This is a common problem not just in

[12] Replication (also known as "conceptual replication" or by other names) differs from checking. According to the definitions I am using a checker merely tries to duplicate the author's steps with the same data, essentially seeing if the author made an arithmetic or computational error. A replicator looks to see whether the author's results hold up under at least slightly different conditions, for example, using a different sample of countries, or changing the wording of the questionnaire slightly. This terminology is unfortunately not standardized and readers have to check which definitions an author is using (see Fuess, 1996).

[13] *The Quarterly Journal of Business and Economics* has announced its openness to replication studies, and, to a lesser extent to papers that check the work in previously published papers. *The Industrial and Labor Relations Review* has also indicated its willingness to publish replication studies of extraordinarily important papers. And the *Journal of Political Economy* created a special "Confirmation and

economics but also in the natural sciences (see Crocker and Cooper, 2011; Yong, 2012), even though, as Jennifer Crocker and M. Lynne Cooper (2011: 1182) point out, "replication is the cornerstone of a cumulative science." Fortunately, there is now a website for replications in economics, http://replication.uni-goettingen.de.

Moreover, even if someone would like to check an econometrics paper, unless a paper meticulously describes its data sources and programs (and most papers don't) it usually cannot be checked unless the author provides this information to the potential checker. Some economics journals now require authors to submit their data or data sources along with their papers, so that in principle potential checkers could obtain the data that way. However, it is far from obvious that the journals check whether all the necessary data have been submitted. The one study I have located gives a strongly negative answer (McCullough, McGeary and Harrison, 2003). Moreover, book publishers and editors of collective volumes do not, as far as I know, require the submission of data.

An alternative way fraud might be discovered is through statistical tests that have been developed for just this purpose (see Uri Simonsohn, 2012: 21). But there is the danger that purveyors of fraudulent work will develop tricks to fool them.

How likely is it then that outright lying accounts for a significant proportion of published econometrics papers? Nobody knows. Given the potential gains from such lying and the weak safeguards against it, the apparently general presumption that this problem is trivial can have only three bases. One is a subjective opinion that our colleagues are too honorable to behave like that. But that is not convincing. Another is that I (and presumably the readers) have not heard any rumors about such lying, and unless it is rare we would have heard them, if only because even econometricians occasionally get tipsy. Possibly, but again hardly convincing evidence. The third basis is wishful thinking. Some researchers have tried to estimate the frequency of fraud by asking scientists both to confess how often they themselves have committed scientific fraud and how often they have observed scientific fraud by others. Danielle Fanelli (2009: 1), in a meta-analysis of studies of scientific fraud, found that a "a pooled weighted average of 1.97% percent of scientists admitted to have fabricated, falsified or modified data at least once." On questions asking about colleagues the corresponding number was 14.12 percent. These estimates are not persuasive. On the one hand, having "modified" data does not necessarily imply fraud. On the other hand, people are not likely to admit that they committed fraud. And the number generated by asking whether they have observed fraud by colleagues does not tell us much, because it depends not only on the proportion committing fraud (which is the number we want), but also on the probability that others can spot instances of fraud, as well as on the allowance, if any, that the respondents made for the fact that they cannot observe all instances of fraud by their colleagues. Also, note that the data relate to scientists as a whole, and not just to econometricians.

Contradictions" section (See Fuess, 1996) which, however, has withered on the vine. Feus (1996) argues that the quantity of submissions of replication papers to the *Quarterly Journal of Economics and Business* suggests that journals can cultivate replication papers.

Reporting Distorted Results

Distorting results differs from what I have called "fraud" because the econometrician actually generated his results instead of just making them up. But in doing so he chooses his data or his techniques so that they give him the particular results he wants, and does not tell readers that he has done that. It is special pleading in the disguise of objectivity. Put another way, he demonstrates that the data can be shown to be consistent with his hypothesis, but not necessarily that they should induce us to accept it. That today was colder than yesterday is *consistent* with the hypothesis of a cooling trend, but it hardly *compels* us to accept it.

Why Are Results Biased?

There are many reasons why econometricians present distorted results. One that is seldom encountered in popular discussions, but may well be the biggest, is to make their results seem more important and publishable. This may involve distorting the regression diagnostics, such as *t*-values, rather than the substantive results. But publishability can also be given a boost by distorting substantive results. Suppose your hypothesis is that *x* affects *y*, but your regressions show a significant but only a very slight effect. A referee's "So what?" can be as fatal as her: "This is wrong."[14]

Another reason for presenting biased results is the wish to have your results conform to your ideology. Indeed, this possibility is a major argument of those who claim that economics is not a science. Cognitive dissonance is unpleasant, so when we estimate, say the effect of increasing the minimum wage on employment we want our result to be consistent with what our expectations, emotions, and our friends tell us about the minimum wage (see Haidt, 2012). Even before they run their regressions those who thrill to *Wall Street Journal* editorials already *kno*w that minimum wage increases cause substantial unemployment, while those who thrill to Paul Krugman's blog *know* that they do not. And the data had better agree, or else they will be sliced and diced until they do.

Such slicing and dicing is not *always* unreasonable. Suppose when you fit a demand function for money the coefficient of the interest rate is positive. Is it reasonable to stop there and claim that the demand function for money is upward sloping? Isn't it more reasonable to assume that your regression equation is misspecified and redo it with different control variables, ones that may be no more a priori plausible, but avoid reaching an invalid result for the demand for money? Unfortunately, such "rational bias" is not the only type of bias. Value judgments, political attachments, and self-interest may well play a larger role. How much do such ideological prejudices pollute the scientific purity of our econometric results? Much has been said (I am tempted to say "shouted") about this question, but empirical evidence is scarce and conflicting. Fuchs, Kruger, and

[14] Or, suppose you get a result that is far from the accepted view. The referee may believe that you must have made a mistake somewhere, and even though she cannot spot it, she is tempted to reject your paper for what she would otherwise have considered only some minor blemishes.

Poterba (1998) found a substantial effect of economists' ideological commitment on their econometric estimates, while I found a much smaller effect (Mayer, 2010).

Not just ideology but also other extraneous factors can influence an econometrician's preference for one type of result over another. They include the wish to obtain results that are consistent with her previously published results, thus showing the high quality of her previous papers. Consistency of results also helps to make you a leader of a school. Leaders lead; they do not smother the obvious truth that our side is right in the vapors of "on the one hand, but on the other." Moreover, the position you have previously taken on important issues also affects who your friends are, so that you are likely to experience social pressure to proclaim that the results of your current study are congruent with the views of your friends. Scientists are not just truth seekers, but also social beings.

In citing these reasons why an econometrician has an investment in her results coming out one way and not the other, I do not claim that she will purposefully manipulate her data or methods, or use a sledgehammer to pound square pegs into round holes. But the wish is father to the thought, and recent work in psychology has stressed how easily our emotions can dominate our conscious thoughts. And Ariely's compromise of pounding the pegs not all the way in, but pushing them just a bit too hard is usually available. The main reason why such emotive factors play a larger role in economics than in, say, physics, is probably not that economists are less "scientific" than physicists, but that in economics it is much harder to obtain results that compel.

Many people attribute bias in economics primarily to something else: corruption. They see corporations as buying academic economists—who conceal their conflict of interest—to speak for them.[15] No doubt that may occur, but how often? I doubt that more than a small percentage of academic economists thus sell out. This need not necessarily indicate economists' nobility of mind, but merely that a sale requires, not just a willing seller, but also a willing buyer, and I doubt that many corporations see academic economists as influential enough to bother with.[16] However, they may be willing to buy a few of those economists who have great prestige or whose names are well known by the public, so that some corruption does occur. And if other economists do not speak up because they prefer to concentrate on their academic research rather than participating in political discussions the public is likely to interpret what the few bought economists are saying as the consensus of the profession. But casual observation at least suggests that this threat may not be all that great, perhaps because there are so few economists whose names the public knows well. However, some of these may sell out, without necessarily feeling guilty, because as Bazerman and Tentrunsel (2011: 21) point out, "well

[15] In a study of 19 financial economists who were members of groups that had put forward proposals for financial reform Gerald Epstein and Jessica Carrick-Hagenbarth (2010) found that most did not mention their affiliations with financial institutions in their papers on finance.

[16] The film *Inside Job* indicts only a very small sample of financial economists, and besides, only a small proportion of economists are financial economists. As Colander (2011) points out, academic economists who are eager to earn additional money can do so much better than accepting occasional corporate largess by leaving academia for jobs in business or finance. Still, even receiving only occasional payments is nice.

replicated research . . . [shows] that when people have a vested interest in seeing a problem in a certain manner they are no longer capable of objectivity."

Moreover, the influence of money can seep through subtle channels. Suppose I am reviewing a book by a senior officer of a trade association that sponsors luxurious conferences or hands out generous research grants. Consciously or unconsciously that might induce me to be more willing to endorse its message. And as long as I have not yet received any goodies I have no conflict of interest that can readily be reported. Or suppose a corporation hires an economist who it has reason to believe will take its side on a certain issue to write a paper on it. Suppose further that in the absence of a payment this economist would not have worked on this topic. Even if this economist is incorruptible and reaches exactly the same conclusion as he would have had the other side been paying him, money does talk in this instance. Another example is an economist who writes an article that favors some business interests who are not paying her, in the (perhaps unconscious) hope that demonstrating a pro-business attitude will result in some corporation hiring her to write an article supporting it on some issue. In the first of these articles she does not have any direct financial interest that needs revealing. All in all, the requirement that conflict of interest be revealed, though useful, does not suffice to eliminate all the baleful influence of corporate money on economics.

All the same, seeing corporate money behind every case in which an economist takes the same side as a corporation is naïve. There is a well developed theory showing that, given certain conditions, the free market solution is optimal. And the temptation to see corruption instead of honest disagreement on facts and theories fosters intellectual laziness and should be resisted. Unless one has evidence one should not accuse one's opponents of dishonesty, if only because such accusations tend to lower the probability that the debate will be correctly resolved.

There is, however, a very different type of sellout that may perhaps be more tempting to academics. This occurs when an academic tries to advance his career by coming up with conclusions that conform to the beliefs of influential faculty members of his own department, or of a department from which he hopes to receive an offer. Though no comparable data on economics departments are available, a study of social psychologists found that more than one third of them stated that they would discriminate against conservatives in their hiring decisions (Inbar and Lammers 2012: 6). It would be surprising if this had no effect on the expressed views of social psychologists. Because economists are generally more conservative than other social scientists their hiring decisions are probably less biased against conservatives than social psychologists', and in some departments probably biased in favor of conservatives. Even so, although I lack relevant data, I would guess that a careerist economist would probably be well advised to reach liberal conclusions.

Ways of Distorting Results

Unfortunately, it is often easy to bias one's findings to support or reject a hypothesis. Hypotheses are usually formulated in theoretical terms, such as "money" or "the price level" that have alternative measurable counterparts. They also involve empirically unobservable conditions such as before ceteris paribus". To test such hypotheses how does one implement the ceteris paribus clause? And how does one define "money"? Is it M_1, M_2, or M_3, and which price index best measures inflation? Moreover, hypotheses usually do not specify time lags. Last but not least, what control variables should be introduced? Thus if you ask whether the death penalty lowers, leaves unaffected, or raises the homicide rate, you can get whatever answer you want, depending on your control variables. In other words, the theoretical hypothesis itself is not testable.[17] What is testable are particular, more or less arbitrary, specifications of it. That any one of these specifications fails the test is not sufficient evidence against the hypothesis itself because it may not be the correct specification. To reject the hypothesis itself all plausible specifications would have to fail. And testing all is often not feasible. Similarly, the fact that one particular specification passes the test is not sufficient evidence for it, because it may be a wrong specification.

Often by suppressing all the failed specifications and arbitrarily presenting one successful specification (a procedure called "data mining" or "fishing") one can claim success, but it is a spurious success. Edward Leamer (1983) calls the presentations of the results of just one of the many regressions that a researcher ran "whimsical." as Someone with different priors who has used the same data may be able to present very different results. There is by now an extensive literature on the bias that such whimsical testing generates and on the higher t-values that should be required to offset this bias (see Giles 2014), but it has been largely ignored by applied econometricians. The failure to make such an adjustment should arouse suspicion.[18]

Presenting only one's best results can be defended. Thus Hoover and Perez (2000, 13) have tellingly argued that it is entirely necessary. Because economic theory usually does not point to a particular specification we have to test several: "the first use of statistical models is to draw on the resources of the data itself to cover the weakness of economic theory itself." And as (Glaeser 2008) points out presenting only significant results relieves the reader from having to plough through a multitude of insignificant a regression results. But is this an excuse for not letting the reader know how many specifications have been tried that *a priori* seem just as likely as the selected one?

Another potential justification is that presenting only the best results is valid in a verificationist framework; the data are used to show only that the hypothesis might be valid; as it is sometimes put: "the data do not reject the hypothesis". But verificationism has been replaced by falsificationism. Finally, if data mining is dishonest it is dishonest only

17 This problem of testing a hypothesis without at the same time testing a number of subsidiary hypothesis (the Quine – Duhem problem) has been discussed extensively by philosophers of science (see Ladyman, 2002).

18 But it is not necessarily dishonest. Authors may not be aware that methods of adjustment exist and should be applied, or they may be unable to use them because, strange as it may seem, they do not know how many variants they tested. To satisfy their own curiosity they may run some variants that they thinks are not really appropriate, but might be willing to treat their results as valid and superior to their other variants if their diagnostics are markedly superior to those of their previously preferred variants. Should these regressions be counted?

for the profession as a whole, and at least arguably not for the individual econometrician who is only doing something generally considered appropriate.[19]

The problem of econometricians presenting only those regressions that favor their conclusions has been substantially ameliorated in recent years by their often publishing the outcome of numerous robustness tests. But though this tells us that their results are robust with respect to certain differences in specification there may be other reasonable specifications with respect to which the claimed results are not robust, but the researcher does not tell us about.

How frequent is data mining that presents only the results that the econometrician wants? Little hard information is available, but I have the general impression that it is common.[20] The temptation is great even if it does not matter to the econometrician whether her regressions support or reject the hypothesis. Because she wants her tests to be decisive one way or another, she has a bias toward the specification with the best diagnostics. The cost of choosing this specification frequently seems minor because there is no compelling evidence which specification is the true one. And in the more common case where the econometrician has a stake in whether the hypothesis is confirmed, the temptation for suppressing unfavorable results is even greater.

Hoover's (2012) method of data mining avoids this problem because he sets out strongly restrictive rules that a specification has to pass, such as having superior diagnostics, not just for the entire period under examination, but also for both halves of it. This is very similar to the ideal method of formulating a hypothesis on one set of data and estimating it on another. But such testing requires extensive samples that are often not available. It is too early to tell whether Hoover's method, or the emendations of it in the subsequent literature, will catch on.

Another way of making an otherwise failed research project seem successful is to misuse significance tests. As already discussed, interpreting failure to disconfirm a hypothesis as confirmation of its converse can turn an inconclusive result into a seemingly conclusive one. Similarly, results that are trivial because the regression coefficient of the strategic variable is too small to matter can be made to seem important by confusing statistical with substantive significance. How frequent are these abuses? Ziliak and McCloskey (2008) claim that they pollute most of the econometric papers published in the AER in the 1980s and 1990s. Others have found much fewer, but still substantial

[19] Edgar Feige (1975) has suggested that to avoid the bias introduced by data mining authors should be required to submit their papers in two stages. The first would be their research plan before they have run their regressions. Only after this has been accepted by the journal would they be allowed to run these regressions and then resubmit their papers which could not deviate from their prior plans. But this proposal has some serious problems. First what is to prevent authors from secretly testing prior to the initial submission? Second, having to pre-register every regression, including exploratory ones, seems like excessive regulation that would stifle creativity. (Cf. Angus Deaton 2012)

[20] In a survey taken in the early 1990s (Mayer, 1995) I found that data mining made almost one third of the respondents (academic economists) either skeptical or distrustful of econometric results. Brodeur et al. (2012) provide current evidence that econometricians do data mine for acceptable *t* values. This problem is far from unique to economics.

misuses of significance tests (see O'Brien, 2004; Kramer, 2011; Mayer, 2012; in response to the latter see McCloskey and Ziliak, 2013 and a reply by Mayer, 2013).

To what extent these mistakes are either conscious attempts to burnish failed research projects, or are due to ignorance about the proper use of significance tests cannot be determined, but I suspect that many are due to an unwillingness to ask questions that would elicit an unwelcome answer, that is, to an institutionalized lack of integrity grounded in group-think.

Some Proposals for Enhancing Honesty and Integrity

How can the honesty and integrity of academic economists be enhanced?

Plagiarism

One way to reduce plagiarism would be to act more decisively when plagiarism is discovered. There is little justification for treating plagiarism by a colleague as merely an unfortunate manifestation of a nervous breakdown that calls for psychotherapy rather than punishment, while treating plagiarism by a student as a manifestation of evil that deserves at least suspension.

A second way is to rely on moral pressure and to admit that there is not *very* much that can be done about plagiarism, because stealing ideas, unlike stealing exact wording, is legal. And that law cannot be changed because it would be much too difficult to determine with the degree of certitude required by law when an idea has been stolen rather than independently discovered, or when two published ideas are really the same. But although economists cannot determine whether something is legal they can determine what the economics profession considers inappropriate behavior, and how to respond to it. When it is a matter of meting out legal penalties, such as revocation of tenure, lawyers are determinative. But if a potential plagiarizer believes that nearly all his colleagues think plagiarism deserves contempt he is less likely to plagiarize. Similarly, if an economist believes that the trick of alluding only in a footnote to a prior paper that fully anticipates him will also earn him the contempt of his colleague, he is less likely to do this.

A third way would be to require PhD candidates to take a course in professional ethics. Such a course need not consist of wishy-washy appeals to "be good." Presumably many students who enter PhD programs are idealistic, but that idealism and its accompanying rectitude are sometimes worn away by the day-to-day realities of academia. An ethics course could help to preserve some earlier idealism. And since any bad examples that are thus avoided prevent other bad examples there is a multiplier process. Moreover, such a course could demonstrate how seemingly minor transgressions can seriously undermine our understanding of the economy. It could also discuss specific problems in which ethical behavior is far from clear. Suppose that a research assistant has strong reasons for believing that his supervisor is stealing the ideas of a paper she is refereeing, but he is not certain. Should he report this even though there is a danger that doing so means damaging an innocent person's career? Beyond that, it could do good by teaching students about their own biases. A student who in such a course has read Ariely (2012) is less likely to treat his own transgressions as harmless.

The obvious disadvantage of a required ethics course is that it adds one more requirement to an already overcrowded PhD schedule.[21] Moreover, even if an ethics course would be useful, seeing one's dissertation supervisors and other role models act ethically might well be more useful and perhaps suffice. But that might be more difficult to achieve than adding another course. None of this means that there is an overwhelming case for an ethics course, but it would seem worth trying.

Fraud

The only feasible way to reduce fraud is to detect it. And that means having journals check say, every tenth paper. They should then not only announce when a paper's results cannot be verified but provide sufficient detail to let readers surmise whether the paper has been constructed out of whole cloth. Alternatively, graduate students could be required to do such checking as part of their econometrics courses and the results could be made public. This would also protect against careless errors, and could be extended to guard against excessive data mining.

Cheating

Because rules about cheating, for example, about suppressing negating evidence, or sampling until the desired result appears and so forth, are less clear than the rules that determine plagiarism and outright fraud, it is with regard to cheating that a professional ethics code is most likely to be effective. George DeMartino (2009, 2011) has advocated setting out the principles of professional ethics for economists. He distinguishes professional ethics from a formal code of conduct, a code that might restrict competition.[22] Professional ethics, on the other hand:

> . . .at its best comprises attentiveness of a profession to the ethical issues that arise in the conduct of its work. It comprises not a simple set of rules that can be tacked

[21] Some schools have courses on how to write dissertations or do other research into which an ethics course could be incorporated.

[22] A code of conduct may even have perverse effects by transforming an ethical issue into one of merely satisfying a minimal standard (see Bazerman and Tenbrunsel, 2011: 114–115, who also stress the greater importance of informal rules than formal rules).

> to the cubical wall but a lively tradition of scholarship, critical inquiry, debate and investigation into the ethical nuances of professional conduct. It involves means by which a profession promotes ethical awareness and transmits ethical and practical wisdom from one generation of practitioners to the next. And when we take this sort of expansive view of professional ethics, we find that economics lacks virtually all of its components (DeMartino, 2009: 7).

By contrast, the American Statistical Association; the National Association of Forensic Economists; and to cite one foreign example, the leading association of German economists, the Verein für Socialpolitik, have adopted codes of conduct, as have many other professional associations, such as those of accountants, engineers, historians, and statisticians. And the American Economic Association has shown concern about ethics by adopting rules for disclosing conflict of interest for papers in its journals.

That does not necessarily mean that attention to ethical issues, whether in the form of a course in ethics or of lively discussion in economic journals of ethical issues pertaining to economics, would reduce cheating more than anything else would. David Colander (2011) has argued that "the most serious ethical problem of economics" is a lack of humility. This seems right, but inducing sufficient humility would be a Herculean task, more difficult (utopian?) than generating ethical discussions and guidelines.

The journals should also do their part in fostering honesty. The recent requirement of some journals that authors disclose conflict of interest is a move in the right direction. But we do not know if the journals will enforce this adequately. They should enforce it by (as already mentioned) checking, say, every tenth paper, and rejecting any that cannot be verified from the data provided (which would also guard against fraud), preferably only after it has gone through all the revisions, so that an author who does not provide all the data would face a substantial delay before she can resubmit the paper elsewhere. In addition, to discipline data mining, journals should also require more robustness tests.[23]

In Conclusion

Insufficient integrity in econometric research is a serious problem, not just something that some left-wing (and occasionally some right-wing) ideologues fulminate about. A recent example is work by Reinhart and Rogoff purporting to show that a public debt to GDP ratio in excess of 90 percent slows economic growth substantially. Among objectionable features of their work are a long delay in providing their data, an error in

[23] Ideally they might consider requiring a table that shows the results for all the regressions bearing on the main results that have been run. But it would be hard to specify these regressions and there would also be no way of enforcing such a requirement.

their calculation that caused them to omit some data points, their weighting of their observations when calculating averages, and sometimes the confounding of mere correlation with causality. I am not accusing them of intentional misconduct; rather I am accusing the profession as a whole of adopting mores that are too lax, and of showing too little concern about whether prevailing practices are truth-seeking. As Lawrence Summers (2013: 1) remarked: "Anyone close to the process of economic research will recognize that data errors like the ones they made are distressingly common."

The American Economic Association or some other professional organization or perhaps the National Science Foundation should therefore work toward raising standards by, for example, requiring more robustness tests and by checking, say, every tenth paper.

Should there be additional punishment, perhaps even prison sentences, for those who commit scientific fraud? Given the high pay-off to publications in terms of tenure and salary to those who commit it, law-and-economics considerations suggest that there should be. But considerations of justice suggest that those who yield only to great temptations are less reprehensible and therefore deserve less punishment than those who yield even to small temptations.

Acknowledgments

I am indebted to Yanos Zylberg for helpful comments.

References

Anonymous. 2012a. "Face Up to Fraud." *Nature* 481(19): 237–238.

Anonymous. 2012b. "Fraud-Detection Tool Could Shake Up Psychology." *Science* 337(6): 21–22.

Ariely, Dan. 2012. *The (Honest) Truth about Dishonesty*. New York: HarperCollins.

Attema, Arthur, Werner, Brower, and Job van Exel. 2012. "Your Right Arm for a Publication in the AER?" Working Paper, Erasmus University, Rotterdam, The Netherlands.

Bazerman, Max, and Ann Tenbrunsel. 2011. *Blind Spots*. Princeton, NJ: Princeton University Press.

Blaug, Mark. 1980. *The Methodology of Economics*. New York: Cambridge University Press.

Brodeur, Abel, Mathias LÉ, Marc Sangnier, and Yanos Zylberberg. 2012. "Star Wars: The Empirics Strike Back. Working Paper No. 2012-29, School of Economics, Paris.

Cargill, Thomas. 2012. "A Critical Assessment of the Measures of Central Bank Independence." *Economic Inquiry* 51(1): 260–272.

Clarke, Roger. 2006. "Plagiarism by Academics: More Complex than It Seems." *Journal of the Association for Information System* 7(2): 91–120.

Colander, David. 2011. "Creating Humble Economists." Middlebury Economics Working Paper 11-03.

Crocker, Jennifer. 2011. "The Road to Fraud Starts with a Single Step." *Nature* 479: 151.

Crocker, Jennifer, and M. Lynn Cooper. 2011. "Addressing Scientific Fraud." *Science* 334(2): 1182.

Deaton, Angus. 2012. "Your Wolf Is Interfering with My t-Values." *Royal Economic Society, Newsletter* 152: 3–4.

DeMartino, George. 2009. "On the Need for Professional Economic Ethics." *Challenge* 52(July–August): 6–15.

DeMartino, George. 2011. *The Economist's Oath*. New York: Oxford University Press.

Enders, Walter, and Gary Hoover. 2006. "Plagiarism in the Economics Profession: A Survey." *Challenge* 49(September–October): 92–107.

Enders, Walter, and Gary Hoover. 2004. "Whose Line Is It? Plagiarism in Economics." *Journal of Economic Literature* 42(June): 487–493.

Enserink, Martin. 2012. "Fraud Detection Tool Could Shake up Psychology." *Science* 337(6): 21–22.

Epstein, Gerald, and J. Carrick-Hagenbarth. 2010. "Financial Economists, Financial Interests and Dark Corners of the Meltdown: It's Time to Set Ethical Standards for the Economics Profession." Working Paper Series, No. 239, Political Economy Research Institute, Amherst, MA.

Fanelli, Daniele. 2009. "How Many Scientists Fabricate and Falsify Research? A Systematic Review and Meta-analysis." *PloS One* 4(5): e5738.

Feige, Edgar. 1975. "The Consequences of Journal Editorial Policies and a Suggestion for Revision. *Journal of Political Economy* 83: 61291–61296.

Feld, Lars, Sarah Necker, and Bruno Frey. 2012. "Scientific Misbehavior in Economics—Evidence from Europe." Working Paper, Walter-Euken Institute and University of Freiburg.

Feyerabend, Paul. 1977, *Against Method*, London, New Left Books.

Fuchs, Victor, Alan Krueger, and James Poterba. 1998. "Economists' Views about Parameters, Values and Policies: Survey Results in Labor and Public Economics." *Journal of Economic Literature* 36(September): 1387–1425.

Fuess, Scott. 1996. "On Replication in Business and Economic Research: The QJBE Case." *Quarterly Journal of Business and Economics* 35(2): 3–13.

Gelman, Andrew. 2011. "Open Data and Open Methods." *Chance* 24(4): 51–53.

Giles, David. 2014. "More on Step-(Un)wise Regressions and Pre-testing," Econometrics Beat: Dave Giles' Blog" 7/22.

Glaeser, Edward. 2008 "Researcher Incentives and Empirical Methods," in Andrew Caplin and Andrew Schotter, *The Foundations of Positive and Normative Economics*, New York: Oxford University Press.

Haidt, Jonathon. 2012. *The Righteous Mind: Why Good People Are Divided by Politics and Religion*. New York. Pantheon Books.

Hoover, Kevin. 2012. "The Role of Hypothesis Testing in the Molding of Econometric Models." Working Paper, Economics Department, Duke University.

Hoover, Kevin, and Stephen Perez. 2000. "Attitudes towards Data Mining." *Journal of Economic Methodology* 10(December): 195–210.

Inbar, Yoel, and Joris Lammers. 2012. "Political Diversity in Social and Personality Psychology." *Perspectives on Psychological Science* 20(10): 1–8.

Karabag, Solmaz, and Christian Berggren. 2012. "Retraction, Dishonesty and Plagiarism: Analysis of a Crucial Issue for Academic Publishing, and the Inadequacy of Responses from Leading Journals in Economics and Management Disciplines. *Journal of Applied Economics and Business Research* 2(3): 172–183.

Kasidi, Faraji, H. Chaturvedi, and Rahul Sing. 2010. "Detecting Data Error and Inaccuracy: A Case Study of Indian FDI Inflow." *Margin—Journal of Applied Economic Research* 4(4): 405–425.

Kramer, Walter. 2011. "The Cult of Statistical Significance: What Economists Should and Should Not Do to Make Their Data Talk." RATSWD Working Paper 176, German Data Forum, Berlin.

Kuhn, Thomas. 1970. *The Structure of Scientific Revolutions*. Chicago: University of Chicago Press.

Laband, David, and Michael Piette. 2000. "Perceived Conduct and Professional Ethics among College Economics Faculty." *American Economist* 44(Spring): 24–33.

Ladyman, James. 2002. *Understanding Philosophy of Science*, London: Routledge.

Lafollette, Marchell. 1992. *Stealing into Print*. Berkeley: University of California Press.

Leamer, Edward. 1978. *Specification Search: Ad Hoc Inferences with Nonexperimental Data*. New York: John Wiley & Sons.

Leamer, Edward. 1983. "Let's Take the Con out of Econometrics." *American Economic Review* 73(March): 31–43.

Mayer, Thomas. 1995. *Doing Economic Research*. Aldershot, UK: Edward Elgar.

Mayer, Thomas. 2010. "The Role of Ideology in Disagreements among Economists: A Quantitative Analysis." *Journal of Economic Methodology* 8(2): 253–273.

Mayer, Thomas. 2012. "Ziliak and McCloskey's Criticism of Significance Tests: An Assessment." *Economic Journal Watch* 9(3): 256–297.

Mayer, Thomas. 2013. "Reply to Deirdre McCloskey and Stephen Ziliak on Statistical Significance." *Economic Journal Watch* 10(1): 87–96.

McCloskey, Deirdre, and Stephen Ziliak. 2013. "Statistical Significance in the New Tom and the Old Tom: A reply to Thomas Mayer." *Economic Watch*, 9(3): 298–308.

McCullough, B. D., and H. D. Vinod. 1999. "The Numerical Reliability of Econometric Software." *Journal of Economic Literature* 37(June): 633–665.

McCullough, B. D., A. M. Kerry, and D. H. Harrison. 2003. "Lessons from the JMCB Archive." *Journal of Money, Credit and Banking* 38(4): 1093–1107.

O'Brien, Anthony. 2004. "Why Is the Standard Error of Regressions So Low Using Historical Data?" *Journal of Socio-Economics* 33(November): 565–570.

Simonsohn, Uri. 2012. "Just Post It: The Lesson from Two Cases of Fabricated Data Detected by Statistics Alone." Working Paper, The Wharton School, University of Pennsylvania.

Sovacool, Benjamin. 2008. "Exploring Scientific Misconduct: Isolated Individuals, Impure Institutions, or an Inevitable Idiom of Modern Science?" *Bioethical Inquiry* 5(4): 271–282.

Spanos, Aris. 2008. Review of Stephen T. Ziliak and Deirdre, McCloskey's, "The Cult of Statistical Significance: How the Standard Error Costs us Jobs, Justice and Lives." *Erasmus Journal of Philosophy and Economics* 1(Autumn): 154–164.

Summers, Lawrence. 2013. "Larry Summers: Reinhart-Rogoff Debacle Shows No Policy Should Be Based 'On a Single Statistical Result.'" *Huffington Post Business* May 11.

Yong, Ed. 2012. "Bad Copy." *Nature* 485(17), May: 299–300.

Zelder, Martin. 2008. "Why the Con Has Not Been Taken Out of Econometrics." *Eastern Economic Journal* 34(1): 115–125.

Ziliak, Stephen, and McCloskey, Deirdre. 2008. *The Cult of Statistical Significance: How the Standard Error Costs Us Jobs, Justice and Lives*. Ann Arbor: University of Michigan Press.

CHAPTER 19

LADY JUSTICE VERSUS CULT OF STATISTICAL SIGNIFICANCE

Oomph-less Science and the New Rule of Law

STEPHEN T. ZILIAK AND DEIRDRE N. MCCLOSKEY

> This statistical significance always works and always doesn't work.
>
> —Stephen Breyer, Associate Justice, U.S. Supreme Court

We have an ethical problem in economics and other sciences in using null hypothesis statistical significance testing without a loss function—a test that avoids asking, "how big is a big loss or gain from the null?" Statistical significance is not equivalent to economic significance, nor to medical, clinical, biological, psychometric, pharmacological, legal, physical, or any other kind of scientific significance—those functions of gain and loss. The mistake is evident when one reflects that the estimated payoff from a lottery (of, say, $1 million) is not the same object as the odds of winning that lottery (odds of, say, 1 in 2 million chances). Yet a widespread failure to make the distinction between an estimate of economic consequence and an estimate of its probability—between the meaning of an estimated average and the random variance around it—is killing people in medicine and impoverishing people in economics (Ziliak and McCloskey, 2008). The ethical problem created by a test of statistical significance is made worse by the method's blatant illogic at the foundational level, a fact unacknowledged by the bulk of decision makers depending on it.

The Statistically Significant Median Is Not the Message

In sciences from accounting to zoology, the errors from null hypothesis significance testing without a loss function—without some quantitative standard of meaningful gain or loss separate from the probability of its occurrence—pile up daily. Adam Smith noted that "whatever praise or blame can be due to any action, must belong either . . . to the . . . affection of the heart . . . or . . . to the external action . . . which this affection gives occasion to . . . or to the . . . consequences which . . . proceed from it" (Smith, 1790 [2009]: Part II, Sect. iii). How *much* unemployment, or inflation, or toxic asset bailout is too much? That is the scientific, and ethical, question. We are not doubting "the affection of the heart" of the average econometrician. We find him instead neglecting Smith's second and third elements of an ethical judgment. Most significance testers—for instance, 80 percent in economics and 90 percent in breast cancer epidemiology, we have found—fail to take the correct "external action" with their evidence. And they neglect the ethical, economic, and other "consequences." They are testing by an ethically irrelevant criterion.

By the 1930s, the null hypothesis significance test at the 5 percent level was considered so sophisticated in economics, psychology, and medicine "that these studies might be raised to the ranks of sciences," according to Ronald A. Fisher, the inventor and steady advocate of the test of two standard deviations (Fisher, 1925: Preface). He wrote, "Personally, the writer prefers to set a low standard of significance at the 5 percent point, and *ignore entirely* all results which fail to reach this level" (Fisher, 1926: 504). Fisher kept saying so up to his death in 1962, exerting a great influence on others. The sociologist Robert Merton would have considered the cult he initiated, based on merely statistical significance, to be a social pathology of science—a "bureaucratization of knowledge" (quoted in Ziliak and McCloskey, 2008: 243). "Adherence to the rules," Merton wrote, "originally conceived as a means, becomes transformed into an end-in-itself" (Merton, 1949: 199).

The core problem is that statistical significance is neither necessary nor sufficient for testing an ethical, scientific, commercial, or material fact in a court of law or of scientific and business opinion. An insignificant coefficient can be substantively significant and important to real people or ecosystems if, for example, the possible loss from ignoring it (as in "ignore entirely," as Fisher urged) is large enough. And a statistically significant coefficient might be, economically speaking, irrelevant to the choice problem if, for example, the significance is caused by merely having a very large sample size or if the variable to which the coefficient is attached is not in any case a policy tool.

What people want from the analyst is a demonstration of "oomph," of meaningful effect size, whether large or small. Probability comes in only as an inquiry into the odds of various levels of oomph. What we have in statistical sciences today, by contrast, is a table of Student's t-statistic distributed on a scale of Fisher's p-value, ranging in probable error from .05 in economics and medicine to, in some parts of particle physics, $p < .00000001$ (but see Ziliak, 2013; most physics does *not* use such tests, but rather "interocular trauma": does the result hit you between the eyes?). A reported finding of "significant" or "not significant" does not answer the scientific question, which is always How Big along a scale agreed to by other scientists or clinicians of How Big *Is* Big.

The need to consider the human meaning of effect sizes, our "oomph," throughout the distribution was well described by Stephen Jay Gould in "The Median Isn't the Message"

(Gould, 1985). In July 1982, Gould learned that he "was suffering from abdominal mesothelioma, a rare and serious cancer usually associated with exposure to asbestos." He was told by his doctor that the *median* survival time after discovery of the rare cancer is eight months.

> What does "median mortality of eight months" signify in our vernacular? I suspect that most people, without training in statistics, would read such a statement as "I will probably be dead in eight months". . . . [But] it isn't so, and . . . attitude matters [to recovery]. The distribution was . . . strongly right skewed. . . . I saw no reason why I shouldn't be in that small tail, and I breathed a very long sigh of relief. . . . I had read the graph correctly. . . . I didn't have to stop and immediately following Isaiah's injunction to Hezekiah—set thine house in order: for thou shalt die, and not live.

He recovered and survived for another 20 years—more than 30 times the median survival time. Oomphful, for sure.

Unhappily, for the past 90 years in fields infected by Fisher's rule, the merely "statistically significant" median or mean is the sole message in economics and most other branches of science, ignoring the oomph. Since the first large-scale survey of best practice significance testing in economics, covering the 1980s in the *American Economic Review*, the significance mistake has gotten worse, not better (Ziliak and McCloskey, 2008; cf. McCloskey and Ziliak, 1996).

Matrixx Inverted: High Court Rejects Significance at the 0 Percent Level

A new rule of law, handed down in 2011 by the Supreme Court of the United States, might help (Supreme Court, 2011*b*). The high court ruled that companies can no longer conceal from investors relevantly bad news about their products by claiming that the adverse effects are not "statistically" significant at the 0.05 or any other level. Companies must consider the human meaning of over- or underestimation. Statistical significance without a loss function is no longer the rule of securities law. Substance, effect size, oomph, is. On March 22, 2011, in *Matrixx Initiatives, Inc. v. Siracusano*, No. 09-1156, the Supreme Court rejected Fisher's rule by a 9–0 vote.

The case involved a homeopathic medicine called Zicam, a zinc-based cold remedy produced by Matrixx Initiatives. When swabbed or sprayed in the nose, the drug is expected to reduce incipient colds. But it also causes some users to lose permanently their sense of smell (and thus of taste), a condition called *anosmia*. The loss function here is a function, then, of a high probability of stopping a cold balanced against a low probability of losing all taste of food and not smelling the flowers or your lover ever again.

When a doctor appeared on the *Good Morning America* television show in 2004 explaining the dangers of zinc-based treatments, Matrixx stock price plummeted. The company replied, though, that the adverse effect reports were not statistically significant. The company assured investors that revenue from Zicam, a hundred million dollar a year seller, was expected to grow vastly—by "50 and then 80 percent" (Supreme Court, 2011*b*: p. 3).

In the January 10, 2011, oral arguments before the Supreme Court, Justice Sotomayor chastised counsel for the petitioners (petitioning, that is, to have an appeals-court ruling against Matrixx reversed [Supreme Court, 2011*a*]). "Mr. Hacker" was chastised for neglecting to respond to technical briefs on the subject that had been authored and filed by *amici* of the court. Many of the friends of the court, the Justice said, "did a wonderful job." (Full disclosure: we were two of the *amici* [McCloskey and Ziliak, 2010]. As is common in such matters, though, the "wonderful job" was mostly done by Allan Ingraham, an economist who drafted the brief for a law firm on the basis of our writings.)

Investors in Matrixx stock had filed suit against the company in a federal district court. They told the court that the company had failed to disclose the bad news it had received from expert nose doctors. But the district court dismissed the suit on the basis that investors did not prove "materiality," which meant, under then-existing precedents, statistical significance. Statistical significance had long since become part of securities law: if it is statistically "insignificant" then, however illogical, it is materially insignificant, too. The Court of Appeals for the Ninth Circuit then reversed the district court's decision, reasoning in a narrow fashion "that whether facts are statistically significant, and thus [under the then-existing rule of law] material, is a question of fact that should ordinarily be left to the trier of fact—usually the jury."

The Justices went deeper. They disagreed with the definition of materiality invoked by the district court in the first place. The Justices said that the district court "erred when it took liberties in making that determination on its own." "Something more is needed," Justice Sotomayor wrote for the unanimous Court, and the something, she said, should address the "source, content, and context" of the bad news. *Matrixx v. Siracusano* presented the Court with the question whether plaintiffs can sustain a claim of securities fraud against a company neglecting to warn investors about bad news that is *not* statistically significant. Nine to zero it ruled that they can.

The Court is not well known for economic or statistical sophistication. But, in this case, it got it right. The precedent, now the law of the land, should be followed, we believe, for all statistical reporting, nine to zero, from climate change research to randomized field experiments in developing nations. In other words, loss functions matter. Oomph is what we seek. And oomph, not the level of Student's *t*, is the new rule of law.

What a Reasonable Investor or Impartial Spectator Might Say

The Court examined the expectations of a "reasonable investor." Would undisclosed bad news be likely to negatively affect the "total mix" of information considered by a reasonable investor? If yes, then the report must be disclosed, regardless of statistical significance or insignificance. Sotomayor wrote for the Court (Supreme Court, 2011*b*),

> medical professionals and researchers do not limit the data they consider to the results of randomized clinical trials or to statistically significant evidence [unhappily the movement for "evidence-based medicine" may falsify her claim]. . . . The FDA similarly does not limit the evidence it considers for purposes of assessing causation and taking regulatory action to statistically significant data. In assessing the safety risk posed by a product, the FDA considers factors such as "strength of the association," "temporal relationship of product use and the event," "consistency of findings across available data sources," "evidence of a dose-response for the effect," "biologic plausibility," "seriousness of the event relative to the disease being treated," "potential to mitigate the risk in the population," "feasibility of further study using observational or controlled clinical study designs," and "degree of benefit the product provides, including availability of other therapies.". . . [The FDA] does not apply any single metric for determining when additional inquiry or action is necessary.

To the theory of the attorneys for Matrixx that statistical significance set the standard for disclosure, over and above "background noise," Justice Breyer (Supreme Court, 2011*a*: 22) replied to a Mr. Hacker, "Oh, no, it can't be. I mean, all right—I'm sorry. I don't mean to take a position yet." [Laughter.]

> JUSTICE BREYER. But, look—I mean, Albert Einstein had the theory of relativity without any empirical evidence, okay? So we could get the greatest doctor in the world, and he has dozens of theories, and the theories are very sound, and all that fits in here is an allegation he now has learned that it's the free zinc ion that counts.
>
> MR. HACKER. But. . . .
>
> JUSTICE BREYER. And that could be devastating to a drug even though there isn't one person yet who has been hurt.

To Hacker's argument that statistical "significance" is the way to truth, Breyer snorted, "This statistical significance always works and always doesn't work." In the same session, Sotomayor (citing *amici*) said that what counts as "statistical importance can't be a measure because it depends on the nature of the study." Justices Kagan and Ginsberg argued that small numbers of humanly meaningfully large effects can be materially relevant, independent of the level of statistical significance. Thus, the loss function. Loss of smell is bad enough, but suppose (a small number of) people died? Kagan referred to a situation in which a small number of instances of blindness were known to be associated with the use of a contact lens solution. The FDA, she noted, would not wait around for statistical significance to make a determination or to investigate further into the facts of such black swans. Chief Justice Roberts sympathized with the test of expectations of a "reasonable investor," concluding that statistical significance was not necessary for establishing causation or belief in association. Sotomayor, in the Court's decision again (Supreme Court, 2011*b*: 1–2, 11):

> We conclude that the materiality of adverse event reports cannot be reduced to a bright-line rule. Although in many cases reasonable investors would not consider reports of adverse events to be material information, respondents have alleged facts plausibly suggesting that reasonable investors would have viewed these particular reports as material. . . . Matrixx's argument rests on the premise that statistical significance is the only reliable indication of causation. This premise is flawed.

SIGNIFICANCE IS NOT MATERIAL

The *Matrixx* decision is consistent with the high court's prior rejection of a bright-line rule in a fact-finding and economically important situation. Citing *Basic v. Levinson* (1976), a case involving a bright-line definition for what is meant by "merger negotiations," Justice Sotomayor argued (Supreme Court, 2011*b*) that "we observed [in Basic] that 'any approach that designates a single fact or occurrence as always determinative of an inherently fact-specific finding such as materiality, must necessarily be overinclusive or underinclusive.' "

Consider a pill that is thought to be effective at relieving pain but at the cost of an increased risk of heart attack. Suppose a well-designed experiment is conducted on a sample of adult humans: half taking the drug, the other half taking another and competing drug. The significance tester—in search of a single, determinative fact—then poses the question: "Assuming there is no real difference between the two pills, what is the chance that the data—showing some amount of difference—will be observed?" If the chance of seeing a difference in adverse effect larger than the one observed is less than or equal to 5 percent, it is declared to be statistically significantly different from the null hypothesis of "no difference"—without saying how much that difference is or how one should view it. But it is an ethically flawed procedure, and before the Justices spoke it was accepted by American law.

In the early 2000s, around the time that Matrixx and Zicam were getting into trouble, a much larger producer, Merck, a pharmaceutical company, got into billions of dollars of trouble with their Vioxx pill. Vioxx-takers began to die from heart disease and heart attacks. In a clinical trial, the Merck scientists reported that Vioxx takers risk a big adverse effect—death. Yet the p-value came in at 0.20, meaning that a 4:1 or higher odds of experiencing a major cost (such as death) is not worthy of policy consideration because it is not "statistically" significant at $p = .05$, or higher than 19:1 odds (see Ziliak and McCloskey, 2008, chapter 3). Therefore the company neglected the adverse outcomes. Therefore they committed the error of under-inclusiveness, a deathblow to science and lives, an error caused by unnecessary adherence to a bright-line rule of statistical significance.

We Need Something More

What the Supreme Court did not say is that the test of significance gives us the *wrong* information, period. The test gives a probability of finding a larger difference than that observed in the sample on offer, assuming that treatment and control drugs are actually the same. But that is "the fallacy of the transposed conditional" (Ziliak and McCloskey, 2008). What we really want to know is the probability of a hypothesis being true (or at least practically useful), given all the data we've got—not the other way around. We want to know the probability that the two drugs are *different* and by how much, given the available evidence. The significance test—based as it is on Fisher's fallacy of the transposed conditional—does not and cannot tell us that probability. The power function, the expected loss function, and many other decision-theoretic and Bayesian methods descending from William Sealy Gosset (known in the trade as "Student," as in Student's *t*) and Harold Jeffreys, now widely available, do (Ziliak, 2008).

A "significant" result does not in any way answer the How Much question, the question of how much or how valuable the difference in magnitude is (such as loss of smell or sight, or relief from pain, or nipping a cold in the bud). The significant result cannot demonstrate economic, medical, or any other importance for the obvious reason that it does not address it. In other words, we want to know the probability of detecting a *large and practically important difference* when the difference is truthfully there. We need exploratory methods, a power function, an expected loss function, and, ideally speaking, a series of independently repeated experiments controlling for random and real error.

Here are four small but important improvements suggested by Gosset and a lengthy list of first-rate statisticians after him:

1. *Visualize the data, the whole distribution.* Visualizing uncertainty leads most people—highly trained econometricians included—to make better science, approaching the standard of most physics, biology, geology, and the rest of the non-Fisherian sciences in examining interocular trauma (Soyer and Hogarth, 2012). For key variables, a scientific article would do better to present graphical and other representations of the whole distribution *on axes of effect size and their likelihood.* In that way, other scientists can judge by eye whether Big is Big or Small is Small in a meaningful metric of gain and loss. At present, it is nearly impossible to extract such information from the usual computer dump of six regression specifications, complete with asterisks on "significant" variables.

Gosset himself was a visualizer. He conveyed to fellow statisticians the then-novel idea of "kurtosis" (e.g., the highly non-normal variation of Gould's cancer-patient survival data) with ink drawings of two kangaroos face-to-face illustrating long tails and a platypus with a short, asymmetric tail (Student, 1927: 160). As Gould learned first-hand, the median is not the message. An ethical economist will graph it out.

2. *Report power and real type I error, not the nominal.* Power is protection against merely statistical significance. Power asks, "What in the proffered experiment is the probability of correctly rejecting the null hypothesis, concluding that the null hypothesis is indeed false when it is false?" If the null hypothesis is false, perhaps another hypothesis—at some other effect size than literally and exactly zero—is true. The power function graphs the probability of rejecting the null hypothesis as a function of various assumed-true effect sizes, 0 or 3 or 2,034. The further the actually true effect size is away from the null, the easier it is going to be in an irritatingly random world to reject the null, and the higher is the power going to be.

To calculate a power function, one needs a random sample, a fixed level of significance (type I error of, say, .05), and one or more measures of effect size different from the null and from the result obtained. The effect size is the assumed efficacy in God's eyes, so to speak, which we should be in the business of uncovering. If you have a very large sample, there is no problem of power. With $n = 10{,}000$, even weak effects will show through a cloud of skepticism. Everything will be significant and with high power—although in that case the significance of an effect, or for that matter its power, is not itself much of an accomplishment. If you are a Fisherian, though, a large sample *becomes* your problem. You will be deluded into thinking you've proved oomph before you've considered what it is.

Suppose a pill does in fact work to the patient's benefit, although with sampling uncertainty. What you want to know—and are able in most testing situations to discover—is with how much power you can reject the null of "*no* efficacy" when the pill is in truth efficacious *to such-and-such a clinically interesting degree.* In general, the more power you have, the better. You do not want by the vagaries of sampling to be led to reject what is actually a *good* pill. That way lies the ethical disaster of death or discomfort for the patients (a death rate that, in fact, the best medical statisticians have calculated and found large in criticizing the reliance on "significance" alone).

Power is powerful because hypotheses are plural, and the plurality yields overlapping probability distributions. In a random sample, a sleeping pill Napper may on average induce 3 extra hours of sleep on the airplane, plus or minus 3. But, in another sample, the same scientist may find that the same sleeping pill induces 2 extra hours of sleep, plus or minus 4 (after all, some sleeping pills contain stimulants, causing negative sleep). The traveler would like to know from her doctor before she takes the pill exactly how much confidence she should have in it. She reasonably wants to know, "With what probability can I expect to get the additional 2 or 3 hours of rest on my overnight to Heathrow? And with what probability might I actually get *less* rest?"

Scientists express "real" type I error as the ratio of the p-value to the power of the test. Thus, an alleged $p = .05$ will turn out actually to be an alarming "real" p of .20 if the power of the test is only .25. An alleged $p = .10$ is really .33 if the power of the test is .30. Dozens of power studies have shown how often this is indeed the case for small effect sizes. Mosteller and Bush (1954, cited in Ziliak and McCloskey, 2008) were the first to have assessed the amount of statistical power in the social sciences. The psychologist Jacob Cohen was the first to conduct a large-scale, systematic survey in psychology (Cohen, 1962, cited in Ziliak and McCloskey, 2008). He surveyed 70 articles published in the *Journal of Abnormal and Social Psychology* for 1960, excluding minor case reports, factor-analytic studies, and other contributions for which the calculation was impossible. He found little power in the tests—and little use for psychologists.

According to a large-scale study by Joseph Rossi (1990) of top psychology journals, the real rate of false rejections of null hypotheses is equally grim: "More than 90 percent [of more than 6,000] of the surveyed studies had less than one chance in three of detecting a small effect"—as against the Fisherians' false claim of 5 percent error. Decision makers need to know that the real rate of false rejection is, for small effect sizes, at best .05 divided by .17, or about 29 percent; and, for medium-sized effects, .05 divided by .57, or about 9 percent. Reporting the *real* level of type I error has the advantage of allowing the reader to approximate how many "false" rejections of the null will occur for every "true" or correct rejection. Real type I error adjusts the p value upward, by basing the value on the rate of true rejections—which is certainly more relevant than a baseline of nothing at all. Most Fisher tests reject with a power of less than 50 percent, with the predictive accuracy of your local psychic.

Freiman et al. (1978) found that if the authors of the 71 original medical studies they examined had considered the power of their tests, the studies would not have ended "negatively." That is, they would have found that the therapy was capable of producing "important therapeutic improvement." Freiman et al. reckoned that if 50 of the 71 studies published in the *New England Journal of Medicine* had paid attention to power and effect size and not merely to a one-sided, qualitative, yes/no interpretation of "significance," they would have *reversed* their conclusions. Astonishingly, they would have found up to "50 percent improvement" in "therapeutic effect." The premature negative results were published in *Lancet*, the *British Medical Journal*, the *New England Journal of Medicine*, the *Journal of the American Medical Association*, and other elite journals. Effective treatments for cardiovascular, cancer, and gastrointestinal patients were abandoned because they did not attain statistical significance at the 5 percent level.

The Fisherian tests of significance—the only tests employed by the original authors of the 71 medical studies—literally could not see the beneficial effects of the therapies under study, even though staring at them. The point about hearts and cancer is the same as the Gosset point about Guinness beer (Ziliak, 2008), which is the same as the Neyman and Pearson point about justice, which is the same as the McCloskey point about purchasing power parity (McCloskey, 1985), which is the same as the Ziliak point about black unemployment rates (Ziliak and McCloskey, 2008), which is the same as the Jeffreys (1939) point about p-values.

Yet high power is no permanent shield against other kinds of oomph-ignoring errors rife in the sciences obsessed with significance testing. To estimate the power function, one needs to define, among other things, a domain of relevant effect sizes different from the null. And that decision, as Gould recognized when he was diagnosed with cancer, is about oomph. The 2003 article on Vioxx is proof of what can go wrong when the oomph of the test is not attended to, even if the power of the test is. In the study on which Vioxx was marketed, "A sample size of 2780 patients per treatment group was expected to provide 90 percent power to detect a difference of 2 percentage points between treatments for the primary safety variable" (Lisse et al., 2003: 541). But the authors did not estimate the power of their test to reject the hypothesis of no harmful cardiac effect between Vioxx and naproxen. Pretending to be excessively gullible, they ignored an 8:1 cardiac damage or death ratio, a magnitude or "safety variable" of some importance.

3. *Define, report, and examine the expected loss function.* Scientists and their clients wish to have relevance, not reports of amateur philosophy derived from positivism c. 1920, which is the method on offer in much of the statistical sciences. They wish for standards that will help them, say, minimize the maximum loss of jobs, income, profit, health, or freedom in following this or that hypothesis as if true. The validity of the loss function is not sensitive to the degree of risk-aversion felt by an investigator. It need not be, to mention the automatic objection from Fisherian statisticians, "subjective." "Loss" is, in the Gossetian tradition of statistics, the value of a sacrifice, and it may be positive or negative, properly addressing the *economic* meaning of significance. So even the gambler who sees nothing but blue sky—a real risk lover—will distinguish maximum losses from minimum, big wins from small. Adjusting the levels of type I and type II error is usually sufficient for handling differential attitudes toward risk. The problem is that today's statistical experts do not employ the loss function or type II error at all. In his last year, the great statistician and economist Leonard Savage asked, "When is one [statistical] expert, real or synthetic, to be preferred to another?" He replied: "Employ, until you have further experience, that expert whose past opinions, applied to your affairs, would have yielded you the highest average income" (Savage, 1971: 145–146). Substitute "highest average income"—or rather add to it—other concerns, such as "highest average quality" or "highest rate of patient survival" or "lowest number of heart attacks" or "highest average rate of minority student graduations," or, in less practical studies, "highest acceptance rate of my results among my scientific colleagues," and you have what we are claiming here.

In any case, without a power and loss function, a test of statistical significance is meaningless, no better than a table of random numbers. Pretending to afford a view from everywhere, statistical significance is, in fact, a view from nowhere. In its desire to maximize precision in one kind of error from sampling (often enough, by the way, it is applied not to samples but to populations, the urn of nature spilled out on the floor), it turns away from the human purposes that motivated the research in the first place. Savage noted in his *Foundations* (1954) a part of the problem we are highlighting: "Many [scientists following in the footsteps of Karl Pearson and R. A. Fisher] have thought it natural to extend logic by setting up criteria for the extent to which one proposition tends to imply, or provide evidence for, another. . . . It seems to me obvious, however, that what is ultimately wanted is criteria for deciding among possible courses of action." Following Fisher's words precisely, significance testers do not think at all about "possible courses of action," holding themselves to be ethically harmless (they mistakenly believe) from possible courses of action. As Fisher declared late in his career, explicitly rejecting the loss functions introduced 30 years earlier by Gosset, Wald, Egon Pearson, and others:

> *Finally, in inductive inference we introduce no cost functions for faulty judgments*, for it is recognized in scientific research that the attainment of, or failure to attain to, a particular scientific advance this year rather than later, has consequences, both to the research programme, and to advantageous applications of scientific knowledge, which cannot be foreseen. . . . *We make no attempt to evaluate these consequences, and do not assume that they are capable of evaluation in any currency.* (Fisher, 1955: 75, emphasis added)

4. *Consider the choice of sample size, experimental design, and its implications for external validity*. For example, is the experiment repeated once, twice, 12, or 30 times, or is it not repeated at all? People need to know. The Chinese eyeglass experiment, described by Ziliak and Teather-Posadas (2016), did not need to grow to 19,000 schoolchildren before concluding that prescription eyeglasses help at school. We already knew it. As in the Tuskegee Syphilis Trial, a leave-out group is unethical if we already know. In the Vioxx clinical trial, younger people with stronger hearts were overrepresented, and elderly people with weaker hearts were underrepresented. Thus, Gosset's recommendation of stratification, balance, repetition, and opportunity cost in experimental design (Ziliak, 2014, 2011; Ziliak and Teather-Posadas, 2014).

Oomphful Economics

The economic approach to the logic of uncertainty—pioneered by Gosset at Guinness—is a better way forward. Bruno De Finetti (1971) [1976] said that "The economic approach seems (if not rejected owing to aristocratic or puritanical taboos) the only device apt to distinguish neatly what is or is not contradictory in the logic of uncertainty" (pp. 486–487). The new rule of law should help.

References

De Finetti, B. 1971 [1976]. "Comments on Savage's "On Rereading R. A. Fisher." *Annals of Statistics* 4(3): 486–487.

Fisher, R. A. 1925 [1928]. *Statistical Methods for Research Workers.* New York: G. E. Stechart.

Fisher, R. A. 1926. "Arrangement of Field Experiments." *Journal of Ministry of Agriculture* 33: 503–513.

Fisher, R. A. 1955. "Statistical Methods and Scientific Induction." *Journal of the Royal Statistical Society, Series B (Methodological)* 17(1): 69–78.

Freiman, J. A., T. Chalmers, H. Smith, and R. R. Kuebler. 1978. "The Importance of Beta, the Type II Error and Sample Design in the Design and Interpretation of the Randomized Control Trial: Survey of 71 "Negative" Trials." *New England Journal of Medicine* 299: 690–694.

Gould, S. J. 1985. "The Median Isn't the Message." *Discover* 6(June): 40–42.

Jeffreys, H. 1939 [1967]. *Theory of Probability.* Third revised edition. London: Oxford University Press.

Lisse, J. R., M. Perlman, G. Johansson, J. R. Shoemaker, J. Schectman, C. S. Skalky, M. E. Dixon, A. B. Polis, A. J. Mollen, and G. P. Geba. 2003. "Gastrointestinal Tolerability and Effectiveness of Rofecoxib [Vioxx®] versus Naproxen in the Treatment of Osteoarthritis." *Annals of Internal Medicine* 139(October): 539–546.

McCloskey, D. N. 1985. "The Loss Function Has Been Mislaid: The Rhetoric of Significance Tests." *American Economic Review*, Supplement 75(2, May): 201–205.

McCloskey, D. N., and S. T. Ziliak, with Edward Labaton et al. Counsel of Record (ed.). 2010. *Brief of Amici Curiae Statistics Experts Professors Deirdre N. McCloskey and Stephen T. Ziliak in Support of Respondents* (vol. No. 09-1156, pp. 22). Washington DC: Supreme Court of the United States.

McCloskey, D. N., and S. T. Ziliak. 1996. "The Standard Error of Regressions." *Journal of Economic Literature* 34(March): 97–114.

Merton, R. M. 1949 [1957]. *Social Theory and Social Structure.* New York: Free Press.

Rossi, J. 1990. "Statistical Power of Psychological Research: What Have We Gained in 20 Years?" *Journal of Consulting and Clinical Psychology* 58: 646–656.

Savage, L. J. 1954 [1972]. *The Foundations of Statistics.* New York: John Wiley & Sons [Dover edition].

Savage, L. J. 1971 [1974 posthumous]. "Elicitation of Personal Probabilities." In *Studies in Bayesian Econometrics*, edited by S. Fienberg and A. Zellner, pp. 111–156. North-Holland.

Smith, A. 1790 [2009]. *The Theory of Moral Sentiments.* New York: Penguin. Introduction by Amartya Sen.

Soyer, E., and R. Hogarth. 2012. "The Illusion of Predictability: How Regression Statistics Mislead Experts." *International Journal of Forecasting* 28(3): 695–711.

Student. 1927. "Errors of Routine Analysis." *Biometrika* 19(1/2): 151–164.

Supreme Court of the United States. 2011*a*. Oral arguments in Matrixx Initiatives, January 10. Available at http://www.supremecourt.gov/oral_arguments/argument_transcripts/09-1156.pdf

Supreme Court of the United States. 2011*b*. Matrixx Initiatives, Inc., et al., No. 09-1156, Petitioner v. James Siracusano et al., On Writ of Certiorari to the United States Court of Appeals for the Ninth Circuit, March 22, 2011. 25 pp., syllabus.

Ziliak, S. T. 2008. "Guinnessometrics: The Economic Foundation of 'Student's' *t*." *Journal of Economic Perspectives* 22(Fall): 199–216.

Ziliak, S. T. 2011. "W.S. Gosset and Some Neglected Concepts in Experimental Statistics: Guinnessometrics II." *Journal of Wine Economics* 6(2): 252–277.

Ziliak, S. T. 2013. "Junk Science Week: Unsignificant Statistics." *Financial Post*: June 10.

Ziliak, S. T. 2014. "Balanced Versus Randomized Field Experiments in Economics: Why W. S. Gosset aka 'Student' Matters." *Review of Behavioral Economics* 1(1): 167–208.

Ziliak, S. T., and D. N. McCloskey. 2008. *The Cult of Statistical Significance: How the Standard Error Costs us Jobs, Justice, and Lives.* Ann Arbor: University of Michigan Press.

Ziliak, S. T., and E. R. Teather-Posadas. 2016. "The Unprincipled Randomization Principle in Economics and Medicine." In *Oxford Handbook on Professional Economic Ethics*, edited by G. Demartino and D. N. McCloskey, pp. 423–452. New York: Oxford University Press.

3. *Field Research*

CHAPTER 20

BALANCING RISK AND BENEFIT

Ethical Tradeoffs in Running Randomized Evaluations

RACHEL GLENNERSTER AND SHAWN POWERS

Introduction

There has been a dramatic rise in the use of randomized evaluations, particularly in development economics, in the last 20 years. This research has tested everything from the provision of additional textbooks in schools to providing information to voters on their elected officials. With the rise of the use of this methodology have come questions about how and when the approach can be used ethically.

While the use of random assignment to answer social and economic questions is increasingly common, it is not new. An early example examined questions of energy policy in 1966 (quoted in Levitt and List, 2009). This was followed by a series of negative income tax experiments in the United States starting in the late 1960s and the Rand Health experiment completed in 1982. There have been changes, however, in how the tool has been used: in particular, researchers have increasingly engaged in intense collaborations with small-scale implementers, who can be more flexible and responsive than traditional government partners. There have been practical and methodological innovations that have introduced new ways to randomize, enabled us to measure spillovers, improved our ability to measure outcomes such as corruption and empowerment, and helped us maximize statistical power under tight budget constraints (see, e.g., Miguel and Kremer, 2004; Olken, 2007; Bruhn and McKenzie, 2009; Barios et al., 2010; and Abadie and Imbens, 2008). One consequence of the innovations in measurement is that random assignment has been used to examine questions in new subject areas, such as women's empowerment (Chattopadhyay and Duflo, 2004) and building trust in post-conflict communities (Casey, Glennerster, and Miguel, 2012).

This work has not taken place in an ethics regulation vacuum. In 1974, the United States put into place a framework for medical and nonmedical research involving human subjects. The ethical guidelines produced under this framework (the Belmont Principles) are similar to other ethical regulatory guidelines around the world, such as the Tri-Council Policy Statement in Canada and the National Statement on Ethical Conduct in Human Research in Australia.

We begin this chapter with a discussion of the Belmont Principles because we consider them a sound basis for judging the ethical issues we will discuss later. Next we discuss whether and in what dimensions randomized evaluations of social programs raise different ethical questions from other research and evaluations and other forms of program provision.

In the fourth main section we discuss some of the practical issues that arise in applying the Belmont Principles to running randomized evaluations, especially in developing countries. We include in this discussion issues that are common to randomized and nonrandomized research. Throughout this chapter we draw on the experience and examples of researchers affiliated with our organization, the Abdul Latif Jameel Poverty Action Lab (J-PAL), who have collectively implemented hundreds of randomized evaluations in developing and developed countries. However, the opinions expressed here are our own and do not necessarily represent a consensus of all J-PAL affiliated researchers or the Massachusetts Institute of Technology.

A theme throughout the chapter is the importance of balancing risks and benefits: a tradeoff that is central to the ethical guidelines enshrined in the Belmont Report. Because researchers may have an incentive to see the tradeoff in a way favorable to the continuation of their research, it is important to have well-functioning institutions to oversee the assessment of risks and benefits. In the final section we discuss the extent to which these systems are in place for social sciences internationally and the ways in which they could be improved.

A Framework for Thinking About the Ethics of Randomized Evaluations

The Belmont Report, which was issued in 1978 by the US National Commission for the Protection of Human Subjects of Biomedical and Behavioral Research, provides the basis for decisions about the ethics of research carried out or funded by most federal departments or agencies. (Code of Federal Regulations, title 45, sec. 46.101).[1] Most US universities draw on this report and subsequent guidance from the Office for Human

[1] Retrieved from http://www.hhs.gov/ohrp/humansubjects/guidance/45cfr46.html#46.101 (Accessed August 15, 2013).

Research Protections (OHRP) to establish human subject procedures covering all research carried out by their faculty and staff, whatever the location or funding source.[2]

Though the principles set out in the report were formulated in the United States, they are reasonably general and are the basis of many other institutional review structures around the world.[3] Since 1978, hundreds of thousands of research studies have been evaluated against these principles, building up a considerable bank of experience in how to apply them in practice.[4] While medical research, with the attendant level of potential risk, was clearly in the mind of those writing the principles, the principles explicitly cover nonmedical studies and recognize that the level of scrutiny and safeguards should be adjusted to the level of risk.

We start by briefly describing the main principles, the ethical traditions on which they are based, and how they are related to principles in economics, in order to discuss how and when randomized evaluations are compatible with these guidelines.[5] The three principles set out in the Belmont Report are:

- *Respect for Persons*: People's right to make their own decisions must be respected. In particular, participants in research must give informed consent to participate in the research. As discussed in the fourth main section, in some cases where the risks are minimal and the costs high, the requirement for informed consent can be waived. If the risks of a particular study are high, however, more detailed procedures may be required to ensure that participants fully understand the risks before giving informed consent. Those who find it hard to understand risks or cannot easily refuse to participate (such as prisoners) need extra protection. Providing very high levels of incentives to participate in a study could potentially undermine a subject's ability to assess risk, requiring careful oversight.
- *Beneficence*: Researchers should seek to increase people's well-being and avoid knowingly doing harm, for example, by subjecting participants to unnecessary and painful tests or increased stress. However, avoiding all risk can be harmful to society in general if it prevents research that could have widespread benefits. Thus the overall benefits of the research to society always need to be balanced against the risks. Researchers should seek to maximize possible benefits and minimize possible harm.

[2] Entities that do research outside of universities have adopted a variety of approaches to ethical oversight. Some organizations, such as Innovations for Poverty Action and Abt Associates, maintain their own internal IRBs, which follow OHRP standards. Others, such as Mathematica Policy Research, use external IRBs accredited by the Association for the Accreditation of Human Research Protection Programs (AAHRPP), a voluntary organization.

[3] For example, the Australian guidelines similarly include principles of justice, beneficence, and respect, although they also include a "research merit and integrity" principle. The three main principles underlying Canadian ethics review are respect for persons, concern for welfare, and justice.

[4] PubMed, a database of medical research, reports more than 325,000 medical trials registered between 1978 and 2013.

[5] The Commission was established in the United States following concerns about unethical research conducted during and after the Second World War. The report can be accessed from the website of the US Department of Health and Human Services: http://www.hhs.gov/ohrp/humansubjects/guidance/belmont.html.

- *Justice*: There should be fairness in the allocation of risks and benefits between different groups of people. It is important to avoid a situation where one group bears all the risk and another stands to reap all the benefits. For example, it would be unjust if a potentially risky vaccine were tested on prisoners and once approved was made available only to the rich.

The principles reflect a melding of two different traditions in ethics: a rights-based approach and a utilitarian approach. The respect for persons principle reflects the view that people should have the right to pursue their own happiness and make their own choices, including those about risks and benefits. Welfare economics, which comes more from the utilitarian tradition, similarly enshrines a respect for individual preferences and finds that (under conditions such as full information and no externalities) allowing individuals to make their own choices maximizes individual utility. The practical implication is that it is better to regulate the provision of information to study participants than to regulate whether someone can participate in a program or study.

Nevertheless, the Belmont Principles do allow for exceptions to this freedom to participate because of the fear that some individuals may not assess risk rationally. This perspective has echoes in behavioral economics, which finds that people tend to weigh risks inconsistently, "overweighting" short-term incentives and "underweighting" long-term risks.

The beneficence principle comes squarely from a utilitarian tradition in explicitly discussing tradeoffs between risks and benefits and thus has strong parallels with welfare economics. The principle recognizes that there may be cases in which research benefits society as a whole even though risks may be taken by a few individuals, much as an economist would discuss the concept of maximizing expected social welfare. While regulatory systems have increasingly relied on more rigid rules for assessing the ethics of research in a way that is much more in line with a rights-based approach than a utilitarian one, the Belmont Report and Common Rule nearly always include a caveat that where the benefits outweigh the costs, waivers can be given.

Simple utilitarianism is sometimes criticized for not taking the equitable distribution of costs and benefits into account. As a result, many ethical systems put some constraints on a simple criterion of maximizing aggregate social welfare. In the Belmont Principles this comes in two forms. First, as discussed previously, respect for persons means that the individual bearing the risk can decide to opt out of research, even though it may be beneficial to society as a whole. Second, the justice principle addresses the issue of equitable distribution directly. The justice principle has a parallel in the economic concept of Pareto improvement. Though a policy may maximize social welfare, it is not a Pareto improvement if it increases total welfare by raising benefits for some while imposing costs on others. In practice, there are virtually no situations in which we can guarantee that no one will be made worse off by an action or policy change. Thus Pareto improvement is rarely a criterion for judging policy options. Nor does the justice principle go as far as requiring Pareto improvement; it does not say that each individual must, in expectation, gain. Instead, the principle looks at groups: for example, if women in Ethiopia take risks for the study, then women in Ethiopia should (in expectation) gain from the results of the study.

Applying these principles is not always straightforward, and in practice research poses tradeoffs among different ethical claims. For example, the Belmont Report notes that finding effective treatments for childhood diseases justifies medical research involving children, even when the children in a particular study do not benefit directly. However, when research presents "more than a minimal risk without immediate prospect of direct benefit to the children involved," then different claims under the principle of beneficence come into conflict. These tradeoffs require value judgments. For this reason researchers in many institutions must answer to Institutional Review Boards (IRBs), so that the researchers themselves are not the last word on the ethics of a study. In the discussion that follows, we attempt to clarify the ethical tradeoffs involved in RCTs, but the fact that there are so many tradeoffs underscores the importance of having an appropriate institutional framework that can balance risks and benefits in an objective way. We return to questions about how well the existing institutional frameworks (particularly outside the United States) operate at the end of this chapter.

What Is Different, Ethically, About Randomized Evaluations?

As we noted in the introduction, the increasing use of randomized evaluations in economics has been associated with an increase in discussion about ethical issues. As we discuss specific ethical questions that arise during the conduct of some randomized evaluations, it is worth understanding what is different, and what is not different, ethically, about RCTs.

To answer this question we need to consider the counterfactual: what are we judging RCTs against? In what follows, we have to consider both what is different about the evaluation as well as what is different about the implementation of the program because of the involvement of researchers. We focus on four aspects of randomized evaluations that have ethical implications: their potential to answer policy-relevant questions by cleanly identifying causal impact; collection of primary data on individuals and communities; close collaboration between researchers and implementers; and the randomized methodology itself, which may change how programs are delivered.

Potential to Answer Policy-Relevant Questions by Cleanly Identifying Causal Impact

The ability to cleanly identify causal impact is a key reason that randomized evaluations have become an increasingly popular tool of economists and social scientists. There is surprisingly little high-quality evidence on the effectiveness of alternative ways to reduce poverty. Often the only evidence we have is based on comparisons of outcomes before and after the program started. However, this type of time series evidence implicitly assumes that all the changes that happen over time are the result of the program, which is a strong assumption. Another common form of evidence used by practitioners to inform program design and policy is comparisons of outcome between program areas and non-program areas. But programs are often introduced in particular areas at particular times for specific reasons. For example, a new education initiative may be piloted in schools with enthusiastic or motivated principals. Outcomes in these schools may exceed those in other schools for reasons that have more to do with the motivated principal than the particular program. In contrast, if a program is randomly assigned to a particular set of schools, communities, or individuals, we can be confident that the only systematic difference between the treatment and comparison group is that one has access to the program and the other does not. With sufficient sample size, this allows us to measure the causal impact of the program on outcomes.

Randomized evaluations are not the only methodology that allows social scientists to identify the causal impact of a policy and program. Quasi-experimental approaches such as instrumental variables or regression discontinuity can be very effective methodologies in the right situation. However, the use of quasi-experimental approaches is often constrained by the need to find a quirk that leads to near-random variation in how a program is implemented. For example, regression discontinuity designs can be used only if a program has a cutoff score for deciding eligibility and this is strictly enforced. [6] Randomized evaluations, in contrast, can be designed explicitly to answer very specific questions of importance to those designing antipoverty programs.

Why is this relevant to ethical considerations? The reason is that risks and benefits of research always have to be balanced. The more likely a research project is to be able to answer a question in an unbiased way, and the more important that question is to designing more effective policy, the higher the benefit to conducting the research for a given risk, or similarly the more risk it is acceptable to take. Of course, just because a study generates a great deal of benefit does not mean we should take on more risk for the sake of it. The Belmont Principles are clear that researchers should seek to minimize risk where they can. But it is ethical to take on some risk if it is necessary to achieve the benefit, and good identification of the causal impacts of relevant programs is an important benefit.

[6] A regression discontinuity design is an empirical technique that exploits a discontinuity based on a cutoff value of a continuous variable. For example, a means-tested program may provide support to people below a given threshold of income, and no support to those above the threshold. This creates an opportunity to estimate the program's impact: those immediately above and below the cutoff are likely to be quite similar (provided that the variable used in the means test is not easy for people to manipulate), except that one group receives the program and the other does not. In this example, involving a researcher may cause the means test to be enforced more rigorously than it would have been in the absence of an evaluation.

Critics of randomized evaluations will argue, however, that though randomized evaluations answer questions in an unbiased way, they may be too small scale and too specific in the questions they ask to provide useful information to those wanting to design more effective policy. Again, this is relevant to ethics: if the information generated is not of wide benefit to society then it is harder to justify any risk of harm involved in the evaluation. This contention, articulated, for example, by Ravallion (2008) and Deaton (2010), rests on the suggestion that understanding the impact of one program in one context at one time may be uninteresting because there is little reason to believe the results will generalize to other contexts. It is fine to test the effectiveness of a vaccine on a specific population and assume that it will generalize to others, but the way in which people respond to social and economic programs is so mediated by local institutions that generalization from one small context to another is difficult.

One response is to run RCTs on large representative samples. For example, a randomized evaluation of teacher performance pay in Andhra Pradesh, India, tested the program in a representative sample of school in a random sample of districts across the state, which has a population of 84 million people (Muralidharan and Sundararaman, 2011). It can be expensive to run an RCT on a randomly selected representative sample of a larger population, as it involves a much more dispersed focal population. As always, these costs need to be compared to the benefits. But it is good practice for researchers to test programs in areas that are similar to conditions found in a wider population so that it is more plausible that results will generalize.

Another response to this criticism is to test whether in fact similar effects are found from implementing the same policy or program in different contexts in order to build up a theory and evidence base of when results generalize and when they do not. We cannot and should not test every approach in every geographic, cultural, or economic setting, but if we observe similar results emerging in different contexts, we can be more confident about the generalizability of the findings.

An increasing number of studies do this. A program providing assets, livelihoods training, and other services to the "ultra-poor" is being tested in seven different countries, and preliminary results suggest similar impacts (Innovations for Poverty Action, 2013). A remedial education program was first tested in two cities in India with very different education systems (Banerjee et al., 2007). It was then tested in a rural context in India (Banerjee et al., 2010a) and is now being tested in Ghana. Again, very similar results have been found in all of these contexts. Studies of basic microcredit products have found broadly similar results in urban India (Banerjee et al., 2010b), rural Morocco (Crépon et al., 2011), rural Mongolia (Attanasio et al., 2011), and the Philippines (Giné and Karlan, 2011). In contrast, evaluations of similar programs designed to provide information to local communities and empower them to improve service delivery have produced very different results in different contexts (Glennerster and Kremer, 2011). A program to encourage communities in Uganda to press for better health services was very effective (Bjorkman and Svensson, 2009), while a similar program in India to encourage communities to press for better government education services had no effect (Banerjee et al., 2010a). Whether it was the sector, the county, or the details of the program that made the difference is unclear.

Some studies seek to test more fundamental questions about human behavior on the assumption that these are more likely to generalize (although it is still necessary to test this assumption). For example, how does charging a small copayment for health prevention products change demand? Do people exhibit evidence of sophisticated procrastination and are they willing to pay for commitment devices? Randomized evaluations have found similar results on these questions in many different contexts, (Kremer and Holla, 2009; Glennerster and Kremer, 2011). This type of study arguably has wider social benefits because the results are less likely to be context dependent.[7],[8]

Collection of Primary Data

Researchers working on randomized evaluations will, in most cases, collect primary data on individuals and/or communities. The collection and storage of these data places an ethical obligation on researchers to ensure that subjects provide informed consent for data to be collected and that the data will be treated confidentially. The collection and storage of primary data is far from unique to randomized evaluation, but complying with ethical standards represents one of the main areas where researchers working on RCTs interact with ethical regulations.

Economists have been complying with ethical standards in this area long before RCTs became popular, but important issues still arise (Alderman, Das, and Rao in this volume), especially as new forms of data are collected and data are collected in new ways. We discuss the practical ethical issues that arise for randomized and nonrandomized studies when collecting primary data in the fourth main section.

Close Collaboration with Antipoverty Programs

One of the biggest changes to how development economists work, which has come alongside the rise of randomized evaluations, is that researchers have become intimately involved in the design and implementation of antipoverty programs. The intensity of involvement of researchers varies considerably between studies. At one end of the spectrum, researchers may develop an idea for a new program (based on the results of previous research), design an evaluation to test the idea, and manage both the implementation of the program and the evaluation. At the other end of the spectrum, researchers can evaluate programs that others have designed and that have, for

[7] When testing a more general principle, we might want to combine evidence from lab-based randomized evaluations (which have the advantage of being less expensive to run) with field-based evaluations, which are more realistic and thus likely more reliable gauges of how people will respond to actual policies and programs.

[8] The creation of the American Economic Association's registry for RCTs (www.socialscienceregistry.org) is designed to make it easier to systematically assess the extent to which results generalize by making it easier to find all the studies conducted that test a given proposition.

reasons other than evaluation, been implemented with an element of randomization. How should ethical guidelines be applied across this spectrum of cases? Do they apply only to data collection or do they also apply to the program being implemented? The issue here is not randomization itself. Researchers using nonrandomized techniques may be involved in the design of the programs they evaluate. However, the increased use of randomized evaluations has been strongly associated with an increase in researchers' involvement in the design and implementation of programs as an integral part of their research.

Unfortunately, this is an area where the Belmont Report and subsequent guidance is less clear, at least as far as economic and social research is concerned. A distinction is made between practice (which is not governed by the regulations) and research (which is). The Belmont Report discussion is written from a medical perspective and a footnote explains that "Because the problems related to social experimentation may differ substantially from those of biomedical and behavioral research, the Commission specifically declines to make any policy determination regarding such research at this time" (HHS 1978, fn 3). In the biomedical sphere the report says that even standard medical practice, when it is subject to systematic investigation, is covered by the guidelines. As we discuss later, if this were translated into economic research to mean that any program being systematically evaluated would itself have to follow research guidelines, this would prevent a great deal of economic work going forward (this is presumably why the committee refused to extend this rule to economic and social work). Many other guidelines are also not very clear about the distinction between research and practice in the areas of economic and social research. Canada's Tri-Council Policy Statement has among the clearest definitions of research, while still being close in spirit to other definitions. It states, "For the purposes of this Policy, 'research' is defined as an undertaking intended to extend knowledge through a disciplined inquiry or systematic investigation" (Canadian Institutes of Health Research et al., 2010, p. 15).

In the world of development the lines become even more blurred because government and nongovernment organizations regularly conduct evaluations that are not considered to fall under research guidelines. Data are collected and analyzed by these organizations and conclusions drawn from the results but this is not considered research.

The Nature of Researcher Responsibility in Project Implementation

The collaboration between researchers and implementers raises a host of important questions about the ethical regulation of this interaction. Most fundamentally, if researchers are involved in implementation, do the same ethical standards apply to them in their role as implementers (or partners in implementation) as apply to them in their role as researchers? At one level, it seems obvious when reading the Belmont Report that they do. In the canonical case of a medical trial, the risk of harm that is being balanced against the likelihood of benefit is often the risk that the vaccine or medicine being tested causes harm. In other words, it is in large part the risk of harm from the implementation that the guidelines are designed to address. But it is just as clear that we cannot always hold researchers accountable for the ethical issues raised by the program they are evaluating.

Angrist et al. (1990) examined the impact of serving in the Vietnam War by using the draft lottery to identify individuals who were more and less likely to serve in the armed forces. If we took the Belmont Principles for biomedical research coverage literally here, the program was being systematically investigated and thus the draft would fall under the guidelines. However, from a practical standpoint, the researchers clearly had no ethical responsibility for the war and their IRB had no jurisdiction to require informed consent before men were drafted. Similarly, when the Government of Colombia held a randomized lottery to give vouchers to students to attend private school (Angrist et al., 2002) or the Indian Supreme Court decided that one-third of local village councils should be headed by women, and some states picked villages through a lottery (Chattopadhyay and Duflo, 2004), research ethical guidelines did not apply to the implementation of the program. The randomization was done for reasons other than evaluation, such as fairness, and initially the agencies involved were not even aware that an evaluation was taking place. In these cases, the ethical guidelines apply only to the data collection efforts of the researchers.

But this distinction between cases where researchers are responsible for implementation and where they are not can be difficult to make in practice. If the implementation was going to go ahead without the evaluation in any case, but the researchers work closely with the implementer on the logistics of implementation to enable an element of randomization, do the researchers take on responsibility for the ethics of the program? Does the entire program itself now come under review by the IRB? Or only those elements of the program that researchers modified to generate knowledge through systematic inquiry? What if in the process of designing the evaluation the researchers make some minor suggestions that they hope will improve the program? What if the final decision about program design is with the implementer, and the implementer takes advice from many people (including the researchers)?

There are no simple answers to these questions, and different review boards take somewhat different positions. Some want to understand the risks and benefits of the program implementation even if it would have taken place without the researchers' involvement. Other review boards are interested mainly in the evaluation aspect of the research, especially if the program would go ahead in the absence of an evaluation.

One rationale to regulate implementation is that it is difficult to judge the level of researcher involvement and the degree of change in implementation resulting from research, so a more inclusive policy is preferable. Another, more cynical rationale is that a key objective of IRBs is to keep the name of their organization out of the newspaper, and even the association of one of their researchers with a program that has negative effects is bad publicity. Thus an IRB may want to stop evaluation of a risky program even if the program would go ahead without researcher involvement and there are large social benefits to understanding the risks.

In our view, if the definition of research is generating knowledge through systematic investigation, then only the elements of the program that were changed to allow for systematic investigation are research. However, because researchers may be tempted to define those changes narrowly, it is good practice to provide information on the whole program to the review board as well as setting out the counterfactual—that is, what would have happened if the program was not being evaluated.

Though the world of implementing poverty programs in resource-poor settings is messy and complex and full of difficult tradeoffs that have ethical implications, the fact that researchers are now engaging with these issues, often quite directly, is in our view a very positive development. The experience of directly implementing programs and/or working closely with those who do has influenced researchers' understanding of and interest in the challenges of implementation in developing countries (Banerjee, 2007). And if we think research is a valuable endeavor and generates important lessons, then researcher involvement in these questions should be encouraged. The complex tradeoffs that implementers make would not disappear if researchers retreated from the field of policy implementation. Thus, as we consider how to regulate this nexus of research and implementation, we must be careful to avoid overregulation.

Potential Harm from Overregulating Researcher Involvement in Implementation

There are costs, and indeed even risk of harm, involved in applying research guidelines to implementation simply because a researcher is involved. In particular, IRBs often impose tighter consent requirements to participate in a study than are used to determine participation in most programs. This may be a consequence of the assumption that "randomized evaluation" means "medical trial" and therefore one-size-fits-all consent requirements are applied that do not take risk (or the lack of it) into account. A real example makes the point.

In a study on the educational impacts of mass school-based deworming in Kenya, the IRB overseeing the study decided at one point that written parental permission should be required before deworming drugs could be given to children. If the program had not been part of a study, this requirement would probably not have been in place given the World Health Organization (WHO) recommendation in support of mass school-based deworming and its conclusion that the risks are negligible. Acquiring written consent from parents is difficult in Kenya, and the result was that some children in the treatment group did not receive deworming pills. Given the low level of risk, it could be argued that imposing written consent imposed harm and was not in line with ethical principles. Interestingly, this was not a case of US rules being imposed inappropriately on a developing country, as the requirement for written consent was imposed by the Kenyan review board.

Overly burdensome informed consent requirements could also make it difficult to work with a wide range of implementers and evaluate a wide range of important projects. Imagine a program designed to reduce child marriage. Such a strategy has risks: maybe if the family keeps a girl in school until the legal age of marriage, it will be harder to find a suitable partner for her. The implementing organization, however, does not want to start its program by warning about the risks of delaying marriage. Households are free to participate in the program and know the local marriage market well (certainly better than an IRB committee does). Stressing the risks at the outset of the program and documenting consent to continue from all households whether or not they participate in the program could undermine the partners' efforts to encourage families to delay marriage. Should the researcher refuse to work with such an organization?

Overregulation and peer pressure could also stop researchers from evaluating programs that are being carried out but might have a risk of harm. A naïve reading of the researchers' ethical obligation to avoid harm might be interpreted as meaning that researchers have an ethical obligation to ensure the program they are evaluating never does any harm to anyone. But we can never guarantee that no one will lose as a result of a program. If microcredit helps women start new businesses, existing businesses may be hurt. Even if we modify this criterion to say researchers should evaluate only programs where most participants will gain in expectation, this is not, in our view, a correct reading of the Belmont Principles.

Imagine there is a program that is quite commonly implemented but that a researcher is concerned may have harmful effects. The researcher does not have enough evidence to convince those running the program that it is harmful and should be shut down. Surely society would benefit if the researcher volunteers to evaluate the program and, if it has negative effects, help prevent more people from being hurt? In other words, it might well be that the benefits of gathering evidence of harm through a research program would outweigh the potential risks to those who take part in the research. In other words, such research could be compatible with the Belmont Principles.

The key criteria for moving forward, ethically, when a research believes that a program may be doing harm to the average participant would be: there is no hard evidence that the program is harmful (if there were we could use that evidence to have the program shut down without the evaluation); that all those taking part in the study are warned of the potential risks; and that the evidence generated is likely to be effective in reducing the prevalence of the program in the future if the results show it causes harm.

Some research may involve interventions that are socially desirable but have negative impacts on research subjects, such as programs intended to improve tax collection or regulatory enforcement. For example, McKenzie (2013) discusses an evaluation of government policies to get more large, informal firms registered for tax purposes. Should an IRB approve such a project? In our view, as long as the methods used do not themselves raise ethical concerns and the potential benefits to society plausibly outweigh the costs borne by the research subjects, it should.

Finally, it is important to make a distinction between cases in which the researcher goes in thinking that a program may well be causing harm to the average participant and those cases in which the researcher finds that harm is being caused even though this was not anticipated at the outset. Criticizing researchers who happen to find the program they evaluate has negative impacts would create publication bias, which would be damaging to society as a whole.

Who Regulates Researchers Involved in Implementation?

Ethical regulation of research involving human subjects covers activities that are research, which are not always synonymous with involvement of researchers. For example, a researcher may know the evidence on what is an effective approach to addressing a particular problem and may advise governments to take up this approach or may even establish an organization to scale it up .[9] This work is not covered by human subjects regulation. A more complicated situation is where a researcher advises a government on the design of a program or sets up a nongovernmental organization (NGO) to implement programs initially with no research objectives. Later he decides that the program provides a good opportunity to test some important questions. Following the preceding discussion, research would be defined as any changes in the program that were the result of the program being subject to systematic investigation. In our experience, however, the fact that researchers are involved in the design of the program (even for nonresearch purposes) or running the implementation makes it more likely that the program itself will be subject to research guidelines. This raises the question of why researchers involved in implementation should be regulated differently than others undertaking exactly the same activities.

The problem is that the process for regulation of implementation tends to be very different from those developed for research. Implementation regulation tends to be less codified, less transparent, and less consistent across countries. For example, if implementation is carried out by a government agency there are usually many layers of required approval, but there are rarely stated principles by which proposals are evaluated. On the other hand, in democracies at least these processes are potentially more accountable than IRBs. Similarly, most governments have procedures for regulating the activities of NGOs or other implementers with which researchers work. Should researchers work only in countries and sectors where there are well-functioning reviews of implementation agencies? Such a position would have many drawbacks: it would raise the difficult question of who decides whether the local review process is adequate, and it would prevent us learning about and improving policies in the least functional societies where there is often a strong need for policy improvement and evidence to support it.

Though the principles of the Belmont Report probably represent a decent basis for judging the ethics of implementation, most of those reviewing development projects are not even aware of them. This can lead to jurisdictional conflicts as research review boards and implementation review processes disagree on the appropriate way forward. What if a government wants to implement a program that monitors attendance of teachers and does not want to give teachers a right to opt out of the program—do they have the right to impose this view against the view of an IRB committee in a foreign university? What if the government simply wants all teachers to be required to answer the survey, but is happy for the individual answer to be anonymized and thus ensure that no

[9] Rachel Glennerster is on the board of Deworm the World, an organization devoted to scaling up school-based deworming programs. These activities, though they involve humans, are not research.

action is taken against individual teachers? One response is to say that the government can go ahead, but the researcher has to withdraw when there is disagreement between the two authorities. However, this fails to take into consideration the often strong leverage that comes with foreign researcher involvement: for example, funding may disappear if the foreign researcher leaves, putting the government in a difficult position.

When Researchers Change Who Receives a Program and How

One area where randomized evaluations are different from other research is the way the research methodology directly affects who receives services under the program and, sometimes, how these services are delivered. This is one of the clearest areas of researcher responsibility. Such research-generated changes in program allocation may occur in nonrandomized studies (see endnote 6 for an example). But randomized evaluations tend to have more implications than other methodologies for who receives benefits.

Critics of randomized evaluations have charged that allocating benefits randomly treats research subjects "merely as means to some end" (Ravallion, 2012). In this view, having a methodology dictate who receives benefits might be seen as treating people as objects for experimental manipulation. If done only for the amusement of the researcher with no general benefit this would violate the principles of Justice and Respect for Persons. But as discussed previously, randomized evaluations, if designed well, can generate wider benefits to society that need to be compared to any potential harm caused by changing the allocation of beneficiaries. There is nothing intrinsically unethical about allocation being determined in part on the basis of evaluation needs.

A more subtle objection is that random allocation of resources is a form of mistargeting (Barrett and Carter, 2014). In the absence of an experiment, implementers would likely want to provide the intervention to the individuals, households, or communities most in need. But in an experimental setting, even if researchers are careful to ensure that the entire sample population being allocated into treatment and control groups meets some criterion of "needy," there is always more information available on the ground that could help target the neediest of the needy. By allocating treatments randomly, the research in effect throws this information away.

The potential harm caused by changes in allocation of beneficiaries due to randomization will depend on the type of randomization methodology involved and the context. We therefore take the different randomization methodologies one by one.

Treatment Lottery

Under the treatment lottery, a sample frame is chosen and units are randomly chosen from it to be offered access to the program being evaluated. Unlike some other methods of randomization, in a treatment lottery some participants in the study are never given access to the program. Is this ethical? The treatment lottery approach is often used when there are insufficient funds to provide the policy or program to all those who could benefit from it. For example, a program may target coffee farmers in Rwanda but have funding to cover only two hundred farmers, far fewer than the number of all eligible farmers. A lottery is used to decide who receives access to the program. In assessing the potential harm from this approach, we have to ask: how would allocation of the program be decided in the absence of the evaluation? Would the program have tried to assess which were the two hundred neediest or most suitable farmers? Or would the program have decided to work in a district with roughly two hundred eligible farmers? Or accepted farmers on a first-come, first-served basis?

The potential for less optimal allocation of the program to arise as a result of evaluation is an issue mainly when program implementation is highly targeted and there is no ability to expand the geographic scope of the program. In our Rwanda example, if the program was planning to target the two hundred most suitable farmers in one district, it may be possible instead to target the most suitable farmers in two districts and then randomly pick two hundred of these for the program, without significantly diminishing the accuracy of the targeting of the program. There will be specific farmers who would have got the program if it had remained in one district who do not get it because of the evaluation, but this is not unethical because (a) guaranteeing that no specific individual is worse off is not a required or feasible standard for judging ethics; instead the standard is whether coffee farmers in Rwanda in general are or are not likely to be negatively impacted by the research and (b) we do not know whether the program will have a positive effect so we do not know that any individual farmer is worse off for not receiving the program. This geographic expansion with little change in targeting criteria is probably the most common way in which treatment lottery evaluations are introduced. When targeting is already very precise and it is not possible simply to expand to a wider geographic area, using a lottery around the cutoff is one possible approach (see later).

Randomized Phase-in

Under a randomized phase-in methodology, the final allocation of the program is usually kept exactly as it would have been in the absence of the evaluation, but the order in which different people or groups are phased in to the program is altered. This approach is often used where a phase-in is planned from the start. If the phase-in in the absence of the randomized evaluation were carefully designed to target the neediest, or those who would benefit most, early, then introducing a randomized phase-in will generate some costs that have to be weighed against the benefits of the evaluation. In practice, it is rarely the case that implementers determine the order of roll out based on a careful assessment of need. The order of phase-in is usually determined by logistical considerations—for example, the first people or communities to receive the program are those nearest the implementer's headquarters or nearest the road. By randomizing the order of the phase-in we create logistical complications for the implementer (which are an important cost of evaluation), but rarely does this approach lead to less needy communities jumping the queue over more needy communities.

Treatment Lottery Around a Cutoff

Unlike a simple treatment lottery, this methodology explicitly recognizes that some potential participants may be more qualified than others and is used when programs have explicit criteria for ranking eligibility. The methodology takes potential participants who are near the cutoff for eligibility and randomly selects who will be accepted into the program.

There are three slightly different ways to do a lottery around a cutoff. Eligibility can be expanded to those who would previously have been ineligible, and access to the program within this group can be randomized. Or the group that is to be randomized can come out of those who would previously have been just above and those who would have been just below the eligibility cutoff. Or the randomization can occur only among those who would previously have been eligible, thus reducing the total access to the program. Usually the methodology does not change the number of beneficiaries, but in most cases it involves accepting some people into the program who are less qualified than some others who are not accepted into the program. Is this ethical?

In assessing the tradeoff between costs and benefits of using a lottery around the cutoff, there are a number of issues to keep in mind. First, it is unlikely that the program is known to be beneficial, or else the evaluation would not be occurring. There are degrees of uncertainty—the stronger the evidence that the program is beneficial, the greater is the concern about "denying" people access. Another key question is whether the benefits of the program are likely to be higher for those who are more qualified.

For example, imagine the methodology is being used to evaluate the effect of giving access to consumer loans to people in South Africa (Karlan and Zinman, 2010). The bank has a scoring system for deciding who is creditworthy. The assumption is that those who score highly will use the loan wisely and will be able to repay the bank, making both the bank and the participants better off. The scoring system is also meant to weed out those who would be a bad risk and would not be able to repay. Potentially bad risks do worse if they are given a loan and cannot repay it because they acquire a bad credit record (although if they would never otherwise have been eligible for a loan from any lender it is not clear a poor credit record hurts them).

But do the researchers, or the bank, know that the scoring system is good at determining who is a good risk and who is a bad risk? Maybe the system is good enough to detect the very good risks and the very bad risks, but does it do a good job of selecting people around the cutoff? It is also possible that the credit scoring system may be discriminating against people who are good risks but happen to live in a poorer neighborhood. In this case, using a lottery may actually reduce the harm of discrimination. If there is uncertainty about the quality of the scoring system, a lottery around the cutoff can be a very good reason to do a randomized evaluation because it helps generate knowledge about how good the scoring system is and whether the cutoff has been placed at the right point.

In the bank example, if the evaluation finds that those just below the cutoff do just as well as those above it, then the bank will be encouraged to extend its loans to more people, and those just below the cutoff will gain, as will the bank. There is a risk that the cutoff was at the right place and that those below the cutoff will get into debt as a result of being offered a loan they cannot repay. This risk has to be taken into account when designing the study. The risk can be ameliorated by randomizing only above the cutoff (lottery among the qualified) but this has other risks: the evaluation cannot tell if the cutoff was too high, and it reduces access among the qualified more than in other designs. It is also possible to narrow the range around the cutoff within which the randomization takes place so that the bank never lends to anyone who has a very bad score. But this also has downsides: less would be learned about where the cutoff should be and, for a given size program, there would be less statistical power and hence less precision in the impact estimate.

The better the evidence there is that the cutoff is well measured and targets the program well, the more careful researchers should be with a lottery around the cutoff. For example, there is a strong evidence base suggesting that weight-for-age and arm circumference are good criteria for judging which children need a supplemental feeding program. Researchers may therefore decide that randomizing around the cutoff for a supplemental feeding program is not appropriate.

Encouragement Designs

Under randomized encouragement designs, the evaluation does not alter who is eligible for the program: those who meet any program eligibility criteria in both treatment and comparison groups can take up the program. Instead, some randomly selected individuals or communities may be given more information about the program, or they may be given help in signing up for the program or a small incentive to sign up. A necessary condition for this type of evaluation is that the encouragement does not directly affect the outcome of interest (except through encouraging take-up of the program). If this criterion is satisfied, the encouragement approach allows researchers to estimate the impact of the program on those who are induced to take it up.

Encouragement designs ease some of the ethical and political concerns that may arise when randomized evaluations restrict or alter access to the program being evaluated. Everyone can have access to the program; the researcher simply makes it easier for some to have access than others. But this difference with other forms of randomization is really a matter of degree. If it becomes easier for some people to get access to the program, the researcher is still potentially (if the program works) giving a benefit to some over others. Thus the process of balancing the risks and benefits of the evaluation applies even in this case.

Common Tradeoffs and Practical Ethical Questions

In this section we discuss the practical issues and tradeoffs researchers face when undertaking randomized impact evaluations. As we have made clear, many of these issues are far from unique to those conducting randomized trials, but they are important and worth discussing. Any researcher collecting primary data on human subjects needs to consider issues of confidentiality and informed consent. Respect for persons means that in most cases we have to explain any risks and ask consent from those participating in the research. These requirements may seem obvious and simple, but researchers have to make difficult decisions about how to keep personal information confidential and how to ask for consent (see also Alderman, Das, and Rao in this volume). We also discuss when researchers may, for reasons essential to the social value of the research, not fully inform or even deceive respondents.

Confidentiality of Primary Data

Unless researchers get explicit permission from the subject, they have a duty to ensure that any private information collected on individual human subjects is kept confidential. (The exception to this rule is if data are already publically available). This means that only researchers involved in the study and those responsible for their oversight have access to information that could identify individuals, including names, addresses, telephone numbers, e-mail addresses, numbers related to government identification numbers or programs, account numbers, vehicle identifiers, full-face photos, and any other information that could be used for this purpose. IRB protocols typically require that survey responses be numbered and that a code linking names and numbers be stored securely and separately from the survey data (in a separate locked file cabinet or in password-protected files on password-protected computers). The exact systems that will be used to ensure confidentiality have to be explained when the study is reviewed by an IRB.

When using paper surveys it is standard to have all identifiers on the first one or two pages of the survey. All sheets in the paper survey have a unique ID, and as soon as some basic checks have been performed by a field supervisor, the first page(s) containing identifying information are detached and stored separately from the rest of the survey, providing rapid anonymity. At some stages during the analysis it is usually necessary to match identifiers and the main answers to the survey, but this analysis is done in secure conditions.

Two developments have necessitated a change to this standard protocol. First, data are increasingly being collected electronically, and the equivalent to "ripping the front page off the survey" had to be developed. Often identifiers and survey content can be separated only after the data are downloaded from the electronic data collection device. In some cases, this downloading takes place over the Internet or phone system. However, to balance these challenges, most electronic data collection systems can be made password-protected so that access to identified data is restricted. Similarly, encryption software allows the data that are sent over the Internet or phone system to be made confidential. Encryption software has also allowed researchers to share identified data more easily within the research group. Given that these systems are new, however, different protocols have been developed for different institutions about the appropriate handling and sharing of electronic data.

The second technological development is the increasing use of geo-positioning data. Because geo-positioning data can be used to identify an individual it counts as confidential data; however, it is much more integral to analysis than, for example, a person's name. Thus a greater part of analysis now includes handling confidential data, making encryption and other safeguards much more important.

Researchers are also faced with a difficult dilemma when deciding how much geo-positioning data to include when they publish their data. Geo-positioning data allow researchers to study, for example, the spillover effects of an intervention on those who live or work nearby. It may therefore be necessary to have access to these data to replicate research. Economic datasets that include geo-positioning data also allow researchers to use existing data to answer new questions by linking different datasets together. For example, researchers can link rainfall data with economic data, or link economic data sets collected at different times to create community-level panels.

How should we balance the risk that publishing geo-positioning data will make it possible to identify individual subjects with the real benefit from being able to link different datasets together? We have to consider what is the likelihood that it will be possible to identify individuals if the data are made accurate to half a mile, one mile, five miles. We also need to consider the likelihood of harm to the subjects if it is possible to identify them from the geo-positioning data. What benefits will be given up if the geo-positioning data are published only at a very high level of aggregation?

The answers depend crucially on the context of the particular study: how densely populated an area is, what other questions are included in the dataset, what proportion of people are being interviewed, and how accessible the data are to those who could potentially use it to harm participants. For example, it would not be appropriate to put on the web data with geo-positioning variables accurate to within two miles on HIV status of farmers in rural Montana. The low density of the population would make it relatively easy to identify individual subjects, neighbors would have access to the Internet and could look up the data, and HIV status is a sensitive piece of information. At the other end of the spectrum, a survey that measured child height in rural Rwanda is unlikely to risk harm even if geo-positioning data are released down to one mile. Many children are likely to live within a one-mile radius, most of those who would interact with the subjects would not be able to figure out which child was being referred to in a given survey even if they could access the data, and the people the child interacts with can observe their height anyway so the survey results are not revealing any private information.

Given the huge variation in risks, blanket rules about publishing geo-positioning data are unlikely to be optimal. Unfortunately, fear of being accused of releasing confidential information is leading researchers to strip most useful geo-positioning data from datasets before publication.

Informed Consent for Data Collection and Exposure to Experimental Treatment

Usually when data are collected on research participants, human subject rules require that the participants give their informed consent. In other words, the researchers need to explain who they are and what the research is about and ask whether the respondent agrees to participate. The exceptions are if the data being collected are already public or if the risks are negligible and the burden of getting consent outweighs the benefits. Examples of data that are public are previously collected primary data, or noting down public behavior (such as whether people who walk down a public street are wearing a hat). Risks are often viewed as sufficiently minimal and informed consent is not usually required if personal identifiers are not collected. For example, we want to record how the weather affects people's mood. We stand on a street corner and ask people whether they are feeling happy or sad, both on cloudy and sunny days. If we do not collect responders' names, ages, addresses, or telephone numbers, informed consent may not be required.

A more complicated question is what kinds of consent are required from research subjects. Some gray areas include the necessity of oral versus written consent, consent to provide information versus consent to be part of the program being evaluated, informed consent in clustered randomized evaluations, and occasions where some suspension of informed consent may be required for methodological reasons.

Written versus Oral Consent

Informed consent rules designed in developed countries are not always sufficiently adapted to local needs. For example, some IRBs require written consent from subjects to participate in any study, even if the risks are low and literacy rates are low. It is important to take the local context into account here. The costs of gaining written consent may be very high in areas with very low levels of literacy. Specifically, it may require finding a literate member of the community, having her sit down with the respondent to read the consent form, and asking the respondent to then make his mark on a special consent form. Similarly, Zywicki (2007) presents cases where IRB processes have made consent forms more technical and less readable, making it difficult for people with lower levels of education to understand them. In this volume Alderman, Das, and Rao discuss additional complications with written consent in developing country contexts.

There is also a danger that overly stringent consent rules could lead to perverse results by preventing people from receiving services that could help them. This is one area where existing guidelines impose higher burdens on researchers than implementers would face in the absence of an evaluation, with the potential to cause real harm. An example comes from a study of a potentially life-saving medical treatment in an undisclosed country in Africa that was shut down because researchers were unable to secure signed consent forms in advance (Zywicki, 2007) even though in the absence of the study signed consent would probably not have been required.

Suspension of Informed Consent for Methodological Reasons

The obligation to acquire informed consent can be waived if the risks are low and full knowledge by participants could lead to behavioral responses that undermine the usefulness of the research. The use of mystery clients is a good example. An enumerator may come into a store and ask the price of a good or service, attempt to register a crime, bargain for the price of a taxi ride, or interview for a job. In all these cases the purpose of the study is likely to be undermined if, prior to the interaction, the enumerator explains that the interaction is part of a study and asks for informed consent. In most of these cases the risk to the subject is small, although cases where bribes or illegal behavior is involved need to be regulated much more closely. Some authors have argued that suspension of informed consent has been given too readily (Ravallion, 2012; Barrett and Carter, 2014).

Who Is the Subject of a Randomized Evaluation and Thus from Whom Do We require Informed Consent?

Cluster randomized evaluations (those in which treatment is randomly assigned at the school, community, or some other level above the individual) pose further complications because they raise the question of who is the subject of the study. Is it only those individuals on whom data are collected or is it everyone in the cluster who receives the intervention?

McRae et al. (2011) argue that in certain types of medical cluster randomized evaluations, patients are not, in fact, research subjects and hence protections such as informed consent do not need to be applied at the patient level. These conditions occur in a relatively narrow set of interventions, such as training for healthcare providers, in which the patients are not directly intervened upon by investigators, do not interact with investigators, experience no manipulation of their environment that may compromise their interests, and do not provide identifiable personal information. In the case of training, the healthcare providers themselves are the research subjects, and they are responsible for deciding what is ethical to do for the patient, so the researchers themselves do not have ethical accountability for a change in the patient's treatment as a result of the intervention.

This discussion links to the previous one on whether the researcher is responsible for the program intervention or just the study. If we think the researcher is responsible only for the study, then informed consent is required only of those on whom we collect data. If the researcher is responsible for the program in general, and if we believe that ethical research standards apply to implementation, then we need informed consent from everyone affected by the program. In cluster trials, community-level consent is often sought from "gatekeepers" in political or administrative positions (e.g., village heads) or through community meetings. In most program evaluations by economists when the program is available to all members of a community, individuals are still required to opt in. This opting in (after appropriate briefing from the implementer) can be considered a form of informed consent. We need to be much more careful when subjects cannot opt out of an intervention. for example, if the study involves adding chlorine to a municipal water supply (Hutton, 2001).

When Is Informed Consent Not Sufficient?

Even if a researcher intends to gain informed consent from participants, IRBs reserve the right to rule that a study should not go ahead. What justifies regulators denying an informed choice to individuals in this way? The assumption must be that the individual is unable to make a rational assessment of the risk. There are three main examples where this claim is made.

First, in the language of the Belmont Principles, participants may be potentially vulnerable. It may be hard to judge whether prisoners are fully free to decide on participation or are being coerced or feel they are being coerced. Similarly, children may not be able to judge risks effectively, and their parents may not always have their best interests at heart. Therefore, the IRB takes more responsibility for judging risks and benefits for these vulnerable populations.

Second, when the risks are very high a research regulator may not permit a study to go forward because in his view the risks outweigh the benefits. This view that "the regulator knows best" has been criticized in the United States in recent years by patients' groups who argue that research regulators and medical regulators are too cautious about what drugs are tested and whether patients can try untested drugs. Patient advocates take the position that as the risks are borne by the patients, they should have the last word, and only they can judge the tradeoff between the risk of treatment versus the potential gain of a cure. Regulators point out that assessing risk is difficult and they have particular expertise in assessing the likely benefit of treatment. In most economic and social evaluations there is less need for technical knowledge to assess risks than in medical programs. Nevertheless it is worth keeping in mind that lab experiments suggest humans are not always good at assessing risks and that experts judge risks differently than laypeople (see Kahneman, 2011: 137ff for discussion). Whether experts make better decisions about risk is not as clear.

The third argument for regulators to overrule an individual's choice is that an inducement to participate is so high that it undermines the ability of individuals to make a rational decision about risks and benefits. This argument is controversial because imposing preferences on others is likely to reduce welfare. Behavioral economics has, however, generated evidence that some people exhibit present bias and that people's choices are not always consistent over time. Some people even understand that they face this inconsistency and are willing to pay to restrict their own future choices. This inconsistency could provide support for regulation.

On the other hand, we need to be careful that we are not, as researchers, falling into a self-interested trap of our own. Imagine an industry that regulates itself and whose regulations state that it is unethical to pay those people whose time, ideas, and effort are key to the industry's success. If this were any industry other than our own, we might criticize such regulation as unethical cartel behavior designed to drive down costs. It certainly has an uncanny resemblance to regulations stating that universities should not pay athletes who generate such large revenue for them.

We therefore have offsetting considerations to keep in mind. Large upfront payouts may distort people's ability to judge risks, and taking up a lot of people's valuable time and giving no benefit is an imposition. With these considerations, how do we judge how much payment is too much? As with so many of the issues discussed here, there is no simple answer. The amount will clearly depend on the wealth and income of the individuals we are working with. The prevailing daily wage for the average participant is often a good benchmark for judging whether an inducement is large. If a survey takes half a day to answer, we may give a monetary or nonmonetary gift equal to half a day's wages. More commonly, an inducement will be much less than that, almost a token gift. It may be culturally appropriate to give a small gift when coming to someone's house and spending considerable time there. Alternatively, if people are close to indifferent about completing a survey, a small amount might tip the balance in favor of participation.

Another key consideration is what the inducement is designed to influence. Is it linked to participation in the survey or participation in the program? Is the inducement an integral part of the program, or is it designed to entice people to participate in a program that entails risks participants might otherwise be unwilling to take? Ethical issues arise mainly where we are using the inducement to offset a risk of harm from the program. Unlike in medical trials, inducements in economic and social studies usually are either given for participation for the survey and delinked from participation in the program or are the potential benefit of the program itself.

For example, an ongoing study in Sierra Leone by Rachel Glennerster and Tavneet Suri evaluated a program that introduced a new variety of rice seed. Farmers were randomly chosen to be surveyed and were offered an inducement of Maggi bouillon cubes (used to flavor stews) as a token of thanks for participating in a survey, which lasted roughly two hours. Half of the farmers were then randomly chosen to be offered the new rice seed at different prices ranging from free to full market price. Farmers were free to accept or reject the new rice seed independent of their participation in the survey. The seed was bred to have higher yield and shorter maturity but had no health risks. The risk was that yield would be lower than for traditional varieties because farmers did not know how to grow the new rice as effectively. Thus, there is a second inducement to participate, namely, for some the benefit of receiving below market price seed. This latter is an integral part of the program and would take place in the absence of an evaluation.

It could be argued that the poor face no real choice about whether or not to participate in a program. They are so desperate they will accept any resources whatever the risk involved. But in fact, the poor take up some opportunities and turn down others. In the rice example not all farmers took the subsidized rice, and a few did not accept the free rice (Banerjee and Duflo [2011] have a good discussion of this point).

Thus though there are reasons to worry about whether very high inducements to participate in a study may undermine people's ability to make rational choices, this is really a concern only when there are significant risks to participation that the inducement is trying to overcome. Even here we need to keep in mind the principle of respect for persons, which implies that we should make sure that people are fully informed of the risks and let them make the judgment of whether it is worth their while to participate.

Misleading Respondents

Another important and difficult question is when it is permissible for researchers to use tactics to elicit information from research subjects that they might not be willing to provide if asked directly, and to what extent deception is a legitimate approach to elicit this information. Historically, social scientists have argued against deception in laboratory experiments to protect the "public good" of subjects' trust. Different researchers may use a common pool of participants, for example, students on a university campus, and the integrity of the study requires subjects to take instructions at face value. If participants are deceived once, this may change their behavior in future experiments, and Jamison, Karlan, and Schechter (2008) find some empirical support for this concern.

But the main ethical consideration is whether it is appropriate from the standpoint of the participants, not from the standpoint of future researchers. In the field, misleading respondents may be necessitated when researchers need to collect information about socially undesirable or illegal behavior. There are ways to address "social desirability bias," without outright deception. For example, we may ask respondents to evaluate a political speech. We may not tell the respondents that our aim is to judge attitudes to gender, as this might influence how they respond to our questions. But we are not deceiving them: we say we want to learn about people's response to politicians and we do; we just don't highlight that we want to know about the response to the gender of the politician. The informed consent document will need to be approved, but there is little risk of harm and a good reason to not fully explain the full motivation of the research.

In other cases researchers have used more overt forms of deception. In a study by Bertrand and Mullainathan (2004) researchers randomly assigned African American–sounding or white-sounding names to the curriculum vitae (CVs) of fictional job candidates. The researchers submitted the CVs in response to published job openings in two US cities. They then tracked the difference in callbacks for interviews between apparently African American and white candidates with otherwise identical CVs as a measure of racial discrimination.

Another form of deception is a use of trained actors in real-world settings. A study in Kenya and Uganda by Dizon-Ross and coauthors (2013) sought to determine whether health workers distribute subsidized health products to targeted recipients. The researchers sent actors into clinics to ask for subsidized products for which they were clearly ineligible (i.e., men asking for insecticide-treated bednets intended for pregnant women). The researchers obtained a waiver of the consent requirements for the clinic visits because the research design would have been compromised if the health workers knew they were being observed and the protections against identifying the clinics or workers were deemed adequate. In this volume, Alderman, Das, and Rao also discuss the use of "standardized patients," actors who are trained to portray standardized versions of medical cases.[10]

Is it ethical for researchers to mislead respondents in these ways? To answer this question researchers and IRBs must weigh the social value of the research and the risks of harm from misleading respondents. In all of the preceding examples there is an excellent case to be made for the social value of the research: gender and racial discrimination and poor delivery of health services are serious social problems in the societies where these studies took place. In each case, the risks of harm from the research were small. For example, the costs imposed on firms in the discrimination study were the time required to read and respond to an additional application, which are likely small. In the Kenya and Uganda case the anonymity of the clinic staff who inappropriately sold nets was preserved and action was not taken against them. The greatest potential risk to human subjects may be from the researcher intentionally or unintentionally revealing information about the respondents, which is why confidentiality of information, as discussed previously, is essential.

Gaps in and Concerns with the Existing Institutional Framework for Ethics Review

As we have seen, the ethics of experimental research in economics poses constant tradeoffs among competing ethical claims and values. Many of these tradeoffs come down to weighing the benefits of the knowledge generated by research against the potential or actual costs borne by research subjects, ranging from the opportunity cost of their time to the risk of being harmed by an intervention under study; and also against any violation of respect of persons or injustice that the research might entail. We have concluded that the Belmont Principles provide a good basis for judging these tradeoffs. But this still leaves open the question of who should judge whether the benefits outweigh the risks in any particular case, whether the existing institutions designed to regulate these tradeoffs are doing this well, and ways in which these institutions can be improved.

The primary responsibility for ethical research rests with researchers themselves. Yet researchers are human and are affected by the incentives they face. For example, psychological research shows that people's judgments are subject to "halo effects": a positive or negative evaluation in one dimension (e.g., the potential professional benefits to the researcher) tend to bias our perceptions in other dimensions (e.g., the ethics of a research project).[11] This tendency may cause even well-intentioned

[10] Friedman (2011) provides a useful discussion of the ethical tradeoffs involved with this type of deception in light of the Belmont Principles.

[11] For a discussion of halo effects, see Kahneman (2011), pp. 82ff.

researchers to overweigh the benefits and underweigh the costs of a research project. Thus IRBs can be useful as an institutional safeguard by double-checking a researcher's judgment. In a similar way, most developing countries have some sort of review of development projects that review the implementation side of projects being evaluated. However, IRBs also have their own incentives and information constraints, which do not necessarily mean they will produce rulings or systems that are optimal for society.

In this section we discuss gaps and problems with the existing institutional review system for randomized evaluations carried out in developing countries. As we made clear earlier, many of the ethical issues arising in the context of randomized evaluations are the same as those that arise with nonrandomized evaluations. Thus most of the gaps and concerns raised here apply with equal force to nonrandomized evaluations.

Missing Institutional Structures

If we think that institutional review boards are useful for checking the tradeoffs inherent in most research involving human subjects, then logically these institutions should exist wherever this type of research takes place. In fact, the coverage of IRBs for economic and social research is rather patchy. Most US universities with researchers undertaking social research in developing countries (whether randomized or not) have functioning IRBs to review research involving human subjects. However, many European universities that do not have medical schools do not have IRBs. In some cases research organizations do not have IRBs, but there are national medical IRBs. Some of these medical IRBs do cover nonmedical research, some explicitly do not, and many are ambiguous on the point. In a few of the poorest countries no review boards exist even for medical studies.

Over the last few years there has been considerable progress in establishing IRBs that explicitly deal with social and economic research involving human subjects. This move has been motivated primarily by researchers working on randomized evaluations of social programs seeking approval mechanisms for their studies. Thus, for example, both the Paris School of Economics and the Institute for Financial Management and Research (IFMR) in India established IRBs in 2009. As Alderman, Das, and Rao discuss in this volume, World Bank staff are actively discussing the creation of an ethical review board (currently the Bank relies on its member countries' regulations and its internal review system for projects). That the increasing use of randomized evaluations should have spurred the creation of IRBs is somewhat surprising, as presumably many of these institutions collected data from human subjects long before randomized evaluations became popular.

An additional spur to the creation of IRBs is the relatively new requirement instituted by the American Economic Association that papers involving the collection of data on human subjects must disclose whether they have obtained IRB approval.

Lack of Clarity on the Mandate and Coverage of Existing Institutions

In many countries it is unclear whether economic and social studies fall under the jurisdiction of medical research boards. This ambiguity causes confusion and stress on the part of researchers, although it may to some extent be deliberate.

What should the criteria be for an economics study falling under the jurisdiction of a medical research board? Some boards state that "health" studies fall under their jurisdiction. But what defines a health study? One in which any question about health is asked (that would include most economics and social science studies)? Or one in which a health intervention is tested (note that a health intervention would include a short message service [SMS] message encouraging people to get their child immunized)?

If a medical review board is the only IRB available in the country, one could argue that it is effective to build on this existing institution to provide coverage for economic and social research. However, it is important that if medical review boards extend their jurisdiction in this way, they should bring on experts to help them assess economic and social research and adapt their procedures to take into account the different needs of this research.

In addition to medical research boards, many countries require that researchers get research permits before they begin a study. In most cases, "evaluations" are exempt from these requirements for approval of research. Why this seemingly arbitrary distinction between evaluation and research? The standard definition of research versus evaluation is that research generates general lessons, whereas evaluation is more directly related to a specific project. But why would a study that is sufficiently well designed that it produces general lessons generate more risk and thus need more regulation than a poorly identified evaluation? This is not just a developing country issue. Developed countries also restrict regulation to systematic study designed to generate general knowledge. The implication is that it's fine to harm subjects if your study is not systematic and you only hope to learn about your own program. A cynical answer is that countries understand that the processes for acquiring research approvals are often so dysfunctional and delayed that requiring them for all evaluation work would prevent most organizations from undertaking most evaluations. This lack of evaluation would have negative consequences on the quality of projects in the country. It might also reduce the number of projects, as some implementers and donors might refuse to run or fund projects if evaluations were so hard to do.

An alternative explanation is that as most countries have a process by which NGOs and other development agencies report and receive approval for their activities (including their evaluation work), there is no need to require duplicate approval for these activities. The research approval process is designed to catch those activities that do not fall under this alternative reporting system. Thus, for example, a randomized evaluation of a project run by an NGO will be reported through the NGO activity approval process. But a survey conducted by a foreign researcher for a randomized or nonrandomized evaluation unrelated to an NGO project might need a research permit because otherwise the government would have no way of knowing of its existence.

In an ideal world, greater clarity about what work requires human subject approval and what falls under medical research boards would be useful. However, in the short run, pushing for clarity might lead medical research boards and research approval committees to define their jurisdiction as widely as possible. Given the limited capacity of many of these institutions to review economic and social studies, there is some danger to this approach. Indeed, it is quite likely that, knowing the limitations of these institutions, the lack of clarity is a deliberate strategy on the part of governments.

Overregulation and a Reliance on Rules versus Discretion

Niskanen's (1996) model of bureaucratic behavior assumes that regulators and bureaucrats seek to maximize their budget. This raises the concern that once IRBs are established they will succumb to regulatory creep—expanding their regulation beyond the areas they were originally established to regulate. In addition to this concern, though IRBs are meant to weigh the risks and benefits of a study, their own incentives are likely to weigh the risks more heavily than the benefits. Those reviewing studies gain little of the upside if a study generates important knowledge for the world, while they face the downside risk of approving a study that ends up causing harm. This is likely to make IRB reviewers overly cautious about what they approve, compared to what is socially optimal. Zywicki (2007) suggests that IRBs are overly sensitive to Type II errors (allowing potentially dangerous research to go forward) and insufficiently sensitive to Type I errors (incorrectly rejecting, delaying, or modifying a proposal because the board improperly overstated the risks to human subjects). Schrag (2011) documents many cases of what he describes as overreach by IRBs.

For individuals seeking to minimize effort and the risk that they will be blamed for a bad decision, rules provide greater comfort than discretion. It is easier to justify a past decision by pointing to a rule than by explaining a judgment of costs and benefits as assessed at the time. But given that risks and benefits are likely to vary considerably between studies, rules risk undermining the Belmont Principles.

We discuss two examples of rules that have emerged in judging the ethics of studies involving human subjects. We argue that in most cases applying these rules to randomized or nonrandomized evaluations of economic and social programs in developing countries makes little sense.

Rules and HIPAA Consent Requirements

In 1996 the Health Insurance Portability and Accountability Act (HIPAA) introduced a set of privacy and security rules that regulate the storage and transfer of personally identifiable health data in the United States. The regulations were designed to ensure the confidentiality of medical records that were increasingly being stored electronically. Procedures were established to gain consent for transferring health information from one user to another (e.g., if a specialist was to transfer test results to a general practitioner). Anyone who has visited a doctor in the United States will know that he or he will be asked to sign very detailed HIPAA release forms, which are so long and dense that very few people read them.

But if HIPAA regulates the storage and transfer of medical data, and a research study involves collecting information on a person's health, and transferring this from the enumerator to the researcher, do subjects of the study have to sign an HIPAA release form? Some IRBs have concluded that they should. But these forms are arguably too dense to be effective in the United States, let alone in countries with much lower levels of education. Arguably, having a page and a half of dense jargon read to someone is a less meaningful form of acquiring consent than a few clear sentences. Consent forms should be tailored to the particular study—how big are the risks that data will become publically available? How damaging would it be to the subjects if they did become publicly available? How can these risks be appropriately explained given the context?

Rules and Geo-positioning Data

A second area where, in our view, unhelpful guidelines have emerged is in the publication of geo-positioning data. The problem with geo-positioning data is that they can reveal the identity of a respondent even when other identifying information, such as name and address, have been stripped from the data prior to public release. As we argued previously, including geo-positioning data in published datasets makes them much more valuable to other researchers. The risk that releasing geo-positioning data will enable an individual to be identified, as well as the potential harm caused if someone were identified, vary considerably according to the context and content of the dataset.

HIPAA rules suggest an appropriate level of disaggregation for geo-positioning data linked to individual medical records for the United States. The main clause says that geo-positioning data should not be released at a level lower than a state. An exception is made for geographic areas formed by the first three digits of a zip code that contain more than 20,000 individuals. This rule is often now used for data that are not as sensitive as medical records and are not from the United States. We believe that applying this rule to these other situations is not in line with the Belmont Principles because it fails to take into account the different levels of risk of harm and benefits associated with different datasets. Applying the rule outside of the United States also defies common sense. States are very different sizes in different countries. The state of Uttar Pradesh includes 200 million people; do we really think that prohibiting the publication of any geo-positioning data more precise than the entire state is needed to keep respondents' responses confidential? If that were the case it would be a breach of confidentiality to say that a randomized evaluation of an education program took place in Jaunpur district in Uttar Pradesh.

Limited Expertise in Social Sciences

Review boards that were established originally as medical review boards, or draw their members mainly from the medical sciences, often do not have enough expertise in the social sciences to properly judge the risks and benefits involved in a given study

(Dingwall, 2012). In particular, Dingwall argues that problems arise when boards fail to take into account the much lower risk involved in many social science studies than in many medical trials. What makes sense when regulating the provision of a new, untested drug may not make sense when testing the effect of doubling the number of government-approved textbooks in a class.

Schrag (2011) argues that IRBs with medical backgrounds tend to apply standards from medical experiments without considering the differences between medical and social science research. Take the example of requiring written consent to take part in a study. If the study is designed to test a new vaccine whose risks are as yet unknown we may want to require written consent from participants even in a context with high levels of illiteracy where this involves finding a literate person the participant knows to carefully read the consent document to the participant and observe and validate his approval mark. However, oral consent may be sufficient when the risks of a study are minimal, as might be the case with an evaluation of a textbook distribution program. If a review body commonly addresses medical trials, it may have a blanket rule that written consent is always required.

There are also cases where IRBs impose rules from professional ethics documents even to those not covered by these rules. For example, there is a wide perception that US research rules require compensation to those harmed in the course of research and that treatment should be offered to those who are found to have medical issues. Doctors may have such responsibilities but these are not requirements under the common rule.

Medical reviewers may not appreciate the need for socioeconomic questions in a questionnaire. In one case, a review board rejected the inclusion of questions about assets in research about how regularly patients took their medications. The rationale was that asking about assets was too intrusive. From an economist's standpoint, questions about assets are standard. They are included to allow evaluators to test for heterogeneity of results by socioeconomic status: did the project work better for the rich than the poor? The same review board rejected the inclusion of questions about madrassa education. Again, in Muslim countries it is standard to distinguish between years of madrassa and non-madrassa education because of the very different subject matter covered in the different school systems. Given the program being evaluated required reading non-Arabic script and many madrassas only teach Arabic script, approval was given after appeal for this question to be included. However, this example highlights how differently economists and medical researchers think about these questions. Indeed, there are questions that medical and public health researchers routinely ask that social scientists might consider quite intrusive: about sexual activity or bowel movements. It is therefore important to have on review boards people who are experienced in running surveys of a given type and know which questions are sensitive and which are not.

It is worth noting that participants are always free not to respond to questions that make them uncomfortable. If we imposed a standard that no questions should be asked that might make someone uncomfortable, we would never have studies on important topics such as domestic violence.

Basic Competency Concerns

Any regulatory approval process creates rents and rents can generate rent-seeking behavior (Krueger, 1974). Very large sums of money, years of preparatory work, and academic reputations are on the line when a study is considered for IRB approval. The risk of rent-seeking behavior, which does not necessarily take the form of explicit requests for bribes, and how the risk can be moderated, should be taken into account when setting up regulations.

The major competency concerns that arise, however, are timeliness of approvals and inappropriate harsh requirements. Even if delays are simply an issue of bad management and not an attempt to extract rents from researchers, they nevertheless come with a high price. Zywicki (2007) notes that one of the costs of poor IRB regulation is that some research is never attempted for fear of derailment by institutional review. We could add that some studies may not be attempted because the required timeline for IRB approval would not allow researchers to act on time-sensitive opportunities. This is a particular issue for randomized evaluations where researchers have to coordinate their research with the timeline of implementers who may themselves be constrained by deadlines such as impending elections or agricultural planting seasons. The costs of IRB review due to "paths not taken" are difficult to observe and quantify.

One response is to establish competing IRB approval processes so than no one body has a monopoly on approvals and there are competitive pressures to provide good service to researchers (Zambia, for example, has two national approval bodies). The competing bodies must be composed of people with sufficient reputational capital to ensure that the competition does not lead to studies being approved when they should not be, but we are unaware of any cases where this has been a problem.

Capacity Development and IRBs

Some IRBs either explicitly or implicitly treat research studies involving local researchers more favorably, arguing that this promotes capacity building. In our view because protection of human subjects and capacity building of local researchers are distinct objectives they should be treated separately and capacity building should not be a criteria by which to judge research proposals by IRBs. The sole concern of IRBs should be research subjects and those who might benefit from the research findings.

Conclusion

While there has been debate in other social science disciplines about the appropriateness of existing ethical guidelines for social sciences, economists have not been very active in this debate until recently. The increased use of randomized evaluations of social programs in developing countries, however, has sparked more debate among economists about whether the existing systems of ethical oversight are adequate.

We conclude that many of the important ethical issues that arise when conducting randomized evaluations are far from unique to randomized evaluations. It is relatively rare that randomization itself raises difficult ethical issues (although we discuss examples where this may be the case). Alongside the use of randomized evaluations, however, has come a change in the way development economists work. Researchers have become much more involved in the details of program and policy implementation. Intense partnerships have developed between researchers and implementers that can blur the researcher/implementer distinction. It is possible that this change in role is in part responsible for the increased attention to ethical issues. It is certainly the case that many development economists are involved in designing projects that have direct consequences for the lives of thousands of people in developing countries. Whether we view this as a good or dangerous trend depends on whether we think that development economists are well equipped to advise on project design. One important but difficult question that arises from this trend is whether researchers who are designing programs should be regulated as researchers or as implementers. Current regulations are somewhat unclear, with the result that programs influenced by researchers are often regulated both as research and as programs.

Finally, we have concluded that though the principles behind ethics regulations are reasonable and balanced, they are not always well implemented. In countries that have established medical review boards, simply extending these to cover social and economic research comes with risks. All too often IRBs apply rules that make sense for medical trials or are derived from medical professional ethics rules without taking into account the much lower risk involved in economic and social studies. Real costs in research forgone are incurred when regulatory bodies are slow and overweigh risks.

References

Abadie, Alberto, and Guido Imbens. 2008. "Estimation of the Conditional Variance in Paired Experiments." *Annales d'Economie et de Statistique* (91–92): 175–187.

Angrist, Joshua. 1990. "Lifetime Earnings and the Vietnam Era Draft Lottery: Evidence from Social Security Administrative Records." *American Economic Review* 80(3): 313–336.

Angrist, Joshua, Eric Bettinger, Erik Bloom, Elizabeth King, Michael Kremer, and Juan Saavedra. 2002. "Vouchers for Private Schooling in Colombia: Evidence from a Randomized Natural Experiment." *American Economic Review* 92(5): 1535–1558.

Attanasio, Orazio, Britta Augsburg, Ralph de Haas, Emla Fitzsimons, and Heike Harmgart. 2011. "Group Lending or Individual Lending? Evidence from a Randomised Field Experiment in Mongolia." IFS Working Papers W11/20, Institute for Fiscal Studies.

Banerjee, Abhijit. 2007. "Inside the Machine." In *Making Aid Work*, edited by A. Banerjee, pp. 123–166. Cambridge, MA: The MIT Press.

Banerjee, Abhijit, and Esther Duflo. 2011. *Poor Economics: A Radical Rethinking of the Way to Fight Global Poverty*. New York: Public Affairs.

Banerjee, Abhijit, Shawn Cole, Esther Duflo, and Leigh Lindon. 2007. "Remedying Education: Evidence from Randomized Experiments in India." *The Quarterly Journal of Economics* 122(3): 1235–1264.

Banerjee, Abhijit, Rukmini Banerji, Esther Duflo, Rachel Glennerster, and Stuti Khemani. 2010a. "Pitfalls of Participatory Programs: Evidence from a Randomized Evaluation in Education in India." *American Economic Journal: Economic Policy* 2(1): 1–30.

Banerjee, Abhijit, Esther Duflo, Rachel Glennerster, and Cynthia Kinnan. 2010b. "The Miracle of Microfinance? Evidence from a Randomized Evaluation." Working Paper, MIT, June 30.

Barios, Thomas, Rebecca Diamond, Guido Imbens, and Michal Kolesar. 2010. "Clustering, Spatial Correlations and Randomization Inference." NBER Working Paper No. 15760. Cambridge, MA: National Bureau of Economic Research.

Barrett, Christopher B., and Michael R. Carter. 2014. "A retreat from Radical Skepticism: Rebalancing Theory, Observational Data and Randomization in Development Economics." In *Field Experiments and Their Critics*, edited by D. Teele, pp. 58–77. New Haven, CT: Yale University Press.

Bertrand, Marianne, and Sendil Mullainathan. 2004. "Are Emily and Greg More Employable than Lakesha and Jamal? A Field Experiment on Labor Market Discrimination." *The American Economic Review* 94(4): 991–1013.

Bjorkman, Martina, and Jakob Svensson. 2009. "Power to the People: Evidence from a Randomized Field Experiment on Community-Based Monitoring in Uganda." *The Quarterly Journal of Economics* 124(2): 735–769.

Bruhn, Miriam, and David McKenzie. 2009. "In Pursuit of Balance: Randomization in Practice in Development Field Experiments." *American Economic Journal: Applied Economics* 1(4): 200–232.

Canadian Institutes of Health Research, Natural Sciences and Engineering Research Council of Canada, and Social Sciences and Humanities Research Council of Canada. 2010. *Tri-Council Policy Statement: Ethical Conduct for Research Involving Humans*. December.

Casey, Katherine, Rachel Glennerster, and Edward Miguel. 2012. "Reshaping Institutions: Evidence on Aid Impacts Using a Preanalysis Plan." *The Quarterly Journal of Economics* 127(4): 1755–1812.

Chattopadhyay, Raghabendra, and Esther Duflo. 2004. "Women as Policy Makers: Evidence from a Randomized Policy Experiment in India." *Econometrica* 72(5): 1409–1443.

Crépon, Bruno, Florencia Devoto, Esther Duflo, and William Parienté. 2011. "Impact of Microcredit in Rural Areas of Morocco: Evidence from a Randomized Evaluation." Working Paper, École Polytechnique, March 31.

Deaton, Angus. 2010. "Instruments, Randomization, and Learning about Development." *Journal of Economic Literature* 48: 424–455.

Dingwall, Robert. 2012. "How Did We Ever Get into this Mess? The Rise of Ethical Regulation in the Social Sciences." In *Ethics in Social Research* (Studies in Qualitative Methodology, Vol. 12), edited by Kevin Love, pp. 3–26. Bingley, UK: Emerald Group Publishing.

Dizon-Ross, Rebecca, Pascaline Dupas, and Jonathan Robinson. 2013. "Governance and Effectiveness of Public Health Subsidies." Mimeo, Stanford University.

Friedman, Jed. 2011. "Sometimes It Is Ethical to Lie to Your Study Subjects." *Development Impact Blog*, June 29. Retrieved from http://blogs.worldbank.org/impactevaluations/sometimes-it-is-ethical-to-lie-to-your-study-subjects

Giné, Xavier, and Dean Karlan. 2011. "Group versus Individual Liability: Short and Long Term Evidence from Philippine Microcredit Lending Groups." Working Paper, Yale University.

Glennerster, Rachel, and Michael Kremer. 2011. "Small Changes, Big Results: Behavioral Economics at Work in Poor Countries." *Boston Review* 36(2): 12–17.

Hutton, J. L. 2001. "Are Distinctive Ethical Principles Required for Cluster Randomized Trials?" *Statistics in Medicine* 20(3): 473–488.

Innovations for Poverty Action. 2013. "Ultra-Poor Graduation Pilots." Retrieved from http://www.poverty-action.org/ultrapoor.

Jamison, Julian, Dean Karlan, and Laura Schechter. 2008. "To Deceive or Not to Deceive: The Effect of Deception on Behavior in Future Laboratory Experiments." *Journal of Economic Behavior & Organization* 68: 477–488.

Kahneman, Daniel. 2011. *Thinking, Fast and Slow.* New York: FSG.

Karlan, Dean, and Jonathan Zinman. 2010. "Expanding Credit Access: Using Randomized Supply Decisions to Estimate the Impacts." *The Review of Financial Studies* 23(1): 433–464.

Kremer, Michael, and Alaka Holla. 2009. "Pricing and Access: Lessons from Randomized Evaluations in Education and Health." In *What Works in Development? Thinking Big and Thinking Small*, edited by Jessica Cohen and William Easterly, pp. 91–119. Washington, DC: Brookings Institution Press.

Krueger, Anne. 1974. "The Political Economy of the Rent-Seeking Society." *The American Economic Review* 64(3): 291–303.

Levitt, Steven, and John List. 2009. "Field Experiments in Economics: The Past, the Present, and the Future." *European Economic Review* 53:1–18.

McKenzie, David. 2013. "Doing Experiments with Socially Good but Privately Bad Treatments." *Development Impact* blog, May 27. Retrieved from http://blogs.worldbank.org/impactevaluations/doing-experiments-socially-good-privately-bad-treatments

McRae, Andrew Charles Weijer, Ariella Binik, Angela White, Jeremy M Grimshaw, Robert Boruch, Jamie C Brehaut, Allan Donner, Martin P Eccles, Raphael Saginur, Merrick Zwarenstein, and Monica Taljaard. 2011. "Who Is the Research Subject in Cluster Randomized Trials in Health Research?" *Trials* 12(183): 1–12.

Miguel, Edward, and Michael Kremer. 2004. "Worms: Identifying Impacts on Education and Health in the Presence of Treatment Externalities." *Econometrica* 72(1): 159–217.

Muralidharan, Karthik, and Venkatesh Sundararaman. 2011. "Teacher Performance Pay: Experimental Evidence from India." *Journal of Political Economy* 119(1): 39–77.

Niskanen, William A. 1996. *Bureaucracy and Public Economics*, 2nd edition. Northampton, MA: Elgar.

Olken, Benjamin. 2007. "Monitoring Corruption: Evidence from a Field Experiment in Indonesia." *Journal of Political Economy* 115(2): 200–249.

Ravallion, Martin. 2008. "Evaluation in the Practice of Development." World Bank Policy Research Working Paper No. 4547.

Ravallion, Martin. 2012. "Fighting Poverty One Experiment at a Time: A Review Essay on Abhijit Banerjee and Esther Duflo, Poor Economics." *Journal of Economic Literature* 50(1): 103–14.

Schrag, Zachary. 2011. "The Case Against Ethics Review in the Social Sciences." *Research Ethics* 7(4): 120–131.

US Department of Health and Human Services (HHS). 1978. *Belmont Report: Ethical Principles and Guidelines for the Protection of Human Subjects of Research.* Report of the National

Commission for the Protection of Human Subjects of Biomedical and Behavioral Research. Retrieved from http://www.hhs.gov/ohrp/humansubjects/guidance/belmont.html

Zywicki, Todd J. 2007. "Institutional Review Boards as Academic Bureaucracies: An Economic and Experiential Analysis." George Mason Law & Economics Research Paper No. 07-20. Retrieved from SSRN: http://ssrn.com/abstract=983649

CHAPTER 21

CONDUCTING ETHICAL ECONOMIC RESEARCH

Complications from the Field

HAROLD ALDERMAN, JISHNU DAS, AND VIJAYENDRA RAO

INTRODUCTION

IN 1993, anticipating the imminent majority government by the African National Congress, researchers in South Africa sought to establish a baseline of economic welfare in order to guide and assess the new government's progress. However, as the [then] Central Statistics Office was widely distrusted, the project was undertaken by a wide consortium of social scientists, health specialists, labor union representatives, and members of civil society convened by the Southern Africa Labour and Development Research Unit (SALDRU). To no surprise, the process of designing a survey by committee generated a number of lively debates. One, in particular, was in regards to documenting informed consent.

Many participants felt strongly that it was imperative that the survey teams not only inform the respondents of the research nature of the survey and the goal of confidentiality but also that the respondent had to indicate that he or she understood this with their signature. Others felt that in the prevailing political climate and with the limited literacy in rural areas this requirement would doom the project. Not only would a significant share of the sample decline to participate, but as this group would be self-selected the sample would no longer be representative of the population. Consensus, not voting, was a means for decision making among the team designing the survey, but casual observation suggested that the views of the social scientists differed from those in health fields, with economists offering an additional nuance, that answering the questions in the survey instrument was a form of revealed preference and thus implicit consent, a view that eventually prevailed. In the event, few respondents refused to be interviewed.

This incident serves as an introduction to some of the themes of this chapter. It illustrates that many of the practical issues confronted in designing ethical field trials also need to be considered in a wider range of data collection. It also hints that there are some glitches when translating the experience of research guidelines in clinical environments into fieldwork undertaken by economic and other social sciences.[1] We group these issues into three broad categories, cautioning readers that more often than not, we pose questions but have relatively little to say definitive about potential solutions.

Our first category considers the objectives of balancing transparency and confidentiality. Researchers familiar with the act of conducting a survey in a remote village are aware that there is seldom a single "respondent." Even in the confines of his or her home, the survey respondent typically faces the entire family, with neighbors "dropping in" and a curious set of faces looking in from the window. How to maintain confidentiality in these settings, and what confidentiality *means* in a context where certain information is public—and therefore "OK" to share—but other information is not (and the researchers seldom knows which is which) is an ethically complicated question. The ethical ambiguity is heightened in cases where such confidential information implicates certain members of the family in behaviors that, at least in the eyes of the surveyor, fall outside the moral norms of society. We present a specific case study—surveys on domestic abuse—that takes on this issue.

The second category relates to trust between the surveyor and the surveyed and again goes to the issue of informed consent, and the sharing of information from the survey with the surveyed population. There are three fundamental issues that we address in this context. First, surveys are never isolated from the social history of the surveyed population. For instance, *any* survey on vaccinations among certain populations in India will have to tackle the surveyed populations' perceptions, and in particular, whether they believe that the survey will lead to follow-up action from the government, and if so, what these actions may be. In particular, the link between mandated government action on vaccination and previous experience with drastic population control policies has often led to a fundamental "trust deficit" that impinges and defines survey evidence to this date. See, for instance, Jegede (2007) on the Nigerian boycott of the Polio Vaccination Campaign or Hussain et al. (2012) on continuing misinformation about polio vaccines in India leading to population resistance.[2] Further, the act of surveying in itself could

[1] Stark (2012), however, reports that the question of obtaining signatures of informed consent—not of consent per se—was also controversial when the National Institutes of Health was drafting its guidelines for research on human subjects.

[2] Hussain et al. (2012) note, for instance: "Though most respondents supported the eradication program and vaccinated their children, many did not seem informed why the program had intensified the frequency of vaccination. Families described that when they asked the door-to-door vaccination teams why they visited them so often, they were usually not given an adequate response. Though the presence of medical interns helped, members of the vaccination team were observed sometimes providing dubious etiological explanations to the families: telling them that polio was "special" and needed a constant boost which other vaccines did not. One clinician who worked with routine immunization services explained that many patients did not understand why, whereas they vaccinated with BCG at fifteen days, DPT at one and a half months, and received a measles injection twice, they had to vaccinate for polio almost twelve times a year until they were about six years old."

change the surveyed populations' behavior in the future; a hypothesis for which there is now some evidence (see Das and Leino, 2011; Zwane et al., 2011).

Second, what does informed consent really mean in a low literacy setting? Is consent really informed consent when the respondent does not fully understand the context of the research at hand? The broad notion of informed consent has, to our minds, an implicit social contract where the researcher believes that survey information will provide a better basis for decision making or deepen our understanding of the needs of the surveyed populations in the future. Actions stemming from the research will arguably help improve the lives of at least a subset of the surveyed population. But what should we do in cases where the surveyed population itself engages in practices that are not beneficial—and even harmful—to a broader population of individuals? We have in mind here, for instance, surveys of service providers, including teachers, doctors, and licensing organizations. A number of studies in low-income countries have revealed that the behavior of such agents deviate sharply from that which professional ethics in their chosen profession would dictate and the neutrality of the survey team in these circumstances is ethically indeterminate. Our second case-study presents the ethical dilemmas in this case using research on the behavior of health care providers. We illustrate these problems using ongoing research on the interactions between health care providers and their patients in low-income settings, highlighting the difficult decisions that researchers face in such instances.

Our third category relates to review boards in low-income countries and the *absence* of such a board at the World Bank, an organization that routinely conducts more than 500 surveys in low-income countries every year. This scale, and the fact that all of the authors of this chapter have conducted surveys and trials as World Bank staff (two are still working in that capacity at the time of this writing), motivate the inclusion of this topic in the chapter.

This chapter concentrates on practical issues of data collection and of communication with respondents and participants both in observational studies and in impact evaluations of interventions. This largely reflects the expertise of the authors and the large number of surveys that they have conducted over the previous three decades. Each of us has faced the problems that we highlight here in several instances. We have struggled with the answers, and in most cases, muddled through trying to keep the best interests of poor people around the world in view in making our decisions. Our hope here is that by recounting the issues of surveying populations in low-income countries, we do justice to the tough problems that researchers face and the need for a negotiated solution in each case. Many times, these problems (and their solutions) fall in the interstices of the human subjects courses that we take, and more often than not, these departures and a relative lack of guidance are part and parcel of surveying populations today. We recognize, of course, that there are many related ethical considerations in the choice of field studies to undertake and in the assignment of treatments and control groups in evaluation-based designs. Some of the key issues in such studies are extensions of the data collection themes in this chapter. Other issues, both in regard to the economic content of techniques employed and of the ethical challenges in setting up such empirical economic studies are well developed elsewhere (Barrett and Carter, 2010; Deaton, 2010; Ravallion, 2012; Glennerster and Powers, 2016) and will be secondary focuses here.

Balancing Transparency and Confidentiality

Participants in field trials and observational surveys have a recognized right that the information they provide will remain confidential. Field conditions, however, often put pressure on the best intentions of researchers. For example, it is difficult to arrange a one-on-one interview in a village setting. Moreover, by its very nature, it is impossible to do so in a focus group. A noted illustration of this challenge was reported by Nancy Scheper-Hughes, who was run out of the village where she had conducted an award winning anthropological study after the study was perceived as overly negative and after observers deduced in which village she had worked and with whom she had interviewed despite her efforts to provide anonymity (Scheper-Hughes, 2000).[3] This successful unraveling of attempted concealment of identities was achieved long before the design of current search engines that make a concerted effort at reidentification likely to be successful.

Although generally this is a minor concern for data collection it brings out the practical complexity of standard, though slightly conflicting, principles of research ethics beyond the voluntary nature of participation: the more or less categorical admonition to "do no harm" and the somewhat more utilitarian concern that the risk to participants in research be vanishingly small relative to the anticipated value of the research. But as illustrated in the following case study on research regarding domestic violence, this is not always what prevails. This case study comes from a survey conducted by one of the authors in 1992, which was one of the first attempts to collect quantitative data on domestic violence in the Indian subcontinent and, therefore, conducted without the advantage of the experience of other researchers (Rao, 1997, 1998; Bloch and Rao, 2002).

Case Study: Domestic Violence

When a man hits his wife it is, usually, a private act about which the wife feels great shame and is thus reluctant to reveal, particularly to an outsider. Thus, asking such questions in a survey raises various ethical concerns. Mindful of the sensitivity of the issue—and on the recommendation of various women's activists who had worked on the

[3] This incident was highlighted in an essay challenging the goal of anonymity on the grounds it is "usually impossible to ensure" and "often undesirable to try to do so" (Walford, 2005).

subject—in 1992 a team of social workers with specific experience in gender issues was hired to conduct field work. The team was strictly instructed to have all respondents sign an informed consent form and to ensure that interviews with women were conducted in private and behind closed doors at a time of day when men were away in the fields. They were also instructed to inform respondents that the survey was being conducted by the University of Michigan (where the principal investigator [Rao] then worked).

The informed consent form had a general statement explaining that questions would be asked about the lives of women, that all responses would be kept confidential, and that respondents should feel free to stop the interview at any stage if they felt uncomfortable with the questions. The first ethical question raised by this is—was this enough? Is documented "informed consent"—which followed the strict guidelines of the University of Michigan's Institutional Review Board (IRB)—meaningful? In practice, more than half the people in the sample (consisting of married women of reproductive age) were illiterate. Consequently, proof of consent was obtained by thumbprint. Both signatures and thumbprints in the rural Indian context are associated with interactions with the state, which makes it very likely that the majority of respondents viewed the survey, regardless of the information they received from the interviewer, as associated with the government. Given this, almost all respondents likely viewed it as a precursor to some kind of benefit or intervention rather than as merely an interview. This raises two important questions: First, what is the meaning of "consent" when it is conveyed by signing a consent form in a context where the process of signing the form is very similar to interactions with the government? Second, with the consequent expectation of the possibility of assistance (which the interviewers know is not forthcoming) what is the ethical response to observations of egregious abuse?

In this particular case no one who was approached refused the survey and everyone who started the survey completed it. Many women who had suffered violence were hesitant to speak about it but did so with encouragement from the social worker interviewers. In many cases this was a cathartic experience for the respondents who had never had the opportunity to share their trauma with a sympathetic stranger. We heard several heart-wrenching stories of wife abuse that surprised us by the length of their duration and severity. In some instances the violence was current and ongoing, particularly with younger wives with alcoholic husbands or who were stuck in the middle of dowry disputes. But, at the end of the conversation, the survey team simply walked away without being obliged to intervene or to help in any way. A claim can perhaps be made—and is often made by researchers of domestic violence—that the very act of having women share their stories of trauma is healing, but the claim seems a little self-serving.

Most surveys in most developing countries with high levels of illiteracy face similar ethical concerns and survey researchers are acutely aware of these concerns. Often there is an expectation of help that underlies a respondent's consent to the survey. In cases where the survey is collecting relatively benign information, say on demographic characteristics, or consumption patterns, this is perhaps less of an issue, particularly because respondents have usually been subject to such survey questions in the past. But when the survey is trying to obtain information on particularly traumatic events, the question of what constitutes consent and the ethics of the obligation to intervene and help becomes particularly acute.

Collecting information on issues that are private, shameful, or imbedded within struggles for power in the surveyed population potentially violates an even more serious ethical principle than informed consent: the principle of "do no harm." Despite all our efforts to keep the interviews private, it was impossible to keep the nature of our questions a secret. When outsiders come to a village they are objects of curiosity, and people wonder what they are doing there. This can have serious consequences for respondents.

After completing the survey interviews the team of social workers started conducted focus group discussions with the female respondents. One of these was held in the home of an older woman whom the survey team had befriended. A group of about eight women had gathered for the discussion at about 11 in the morning. Given the dense clustering of homes in the village we could not keep the location of the group discussion a secret. About half an hour into the discussion a man burst in to the room (the door was unlocked) and furiously walked over to one of the women and hit her in the head screaming "get back and do your work you -----, how dare you ignore your children. You should be at home cooking, not talking to these people." He then grabbed her right ear and pulled her out the room. We knew from our interview with her that the woman was a victim of domestic violence. Clearly our interview had made her husband angry enough that he had come back home from the fields to "punish" his wife publically and make the point that talking to us would have adverse consequences. The very act of conducting the interviews had raised the risk of violence against our respondents.

Could this have been prevented? It is not clear how. The survey team was experienced with women's issues. The sample size was small (fewer than 200 women) so the PI was able to supervise the survey personally. All existing protocols on informed consent had been followed. Every effort was made to keep the interviews (especially the individual interviews) confidential. But the very act of asking questions of this nature is fraught with risk for the respondent. And asking about traumatic events makes concerns about the nature of informed consent in low literacy populations even more acute.

Such concerns are common to any effort to collect information on domestic violence and other issues that are private, involve some shame, and are embedded within power relationships. Cognizant of these concerns, and also of the importance of collecting representative data on domestic violence, the World Health Organization (WHO, 2001) has developed a set of ethical guidelines that they follow in collecting their influential data on domestic violence in several developing countries.[4] There has been an explosion of research on the topic and a vast expansion in the availability of data on domestic

[4] The guidelines are: (1) The safety of respondents and the research team is paramount, and should guide all project decisions. (2) Prevalence studies need to be methodologically sound and to build on current research experience about how to minimize the under-reporting of violence. (3) Protecting confidentiality is essential to ensure both women's safety and data quality. (4) All research team members should be carefully selected and receive specialized training and ongoing support. (5) The study design must include actions aimed at reducing any possible distress caused to the participants by the research. (6) Fieldworkers should be trained to refer women requesting assistance to available local services and

violence over the last decade. The Demographic and Health Surveys, which have collected nationally representative data on domestic violence for a variety of countries, state that they follow a modified version of the WHO guidelines (Kishor and Johnson, 2004). However, given the extremely large samples involved (ranging from 2000 to 90,000), it seems fair to ask if such guidelines can be effectively implemented at reasonable cost.

What Does Privacy Mean?

Beyond the difficulty of conducting private interviews illustrated with the challenging example of studying domestic violence there are more general issues of privacy to consider. For example, once data are collected the researcher often has limited say in regards to the subsequent dissemination of the data. Indeed, although the ethical rationale for privacy is readily apparent, there are also ethical considerations that encourage wide data access. For instance, students, particularly in low-income countries, generally have limited access to research grants and other funds that could be used to collect data that will further their research. From this perspective broad access is less extractive than exclusive rights to use a data set granted to a single research team, often from outside the countries where the data has been generated. Moreover, as field research is not as easily replicated as are clinical studies, public posting of data provides a check against inadvertent research errors or excessive data manipulation. Thus, it is common policy that funders of research require that the data collected as part of the project be made publically available within a specified period.[5]

Implementing data access, however, poses a few practical issues. Although individual identifiers are generally stripped out of data that are publically posted, community identifiers often are not. For example, global positioning system (GPS) coordinates are frequently used in data analysis and are valuable for steps such as determining the distance from the household to a school or clinic. Because, in principle, GPS data can be used to locate a household, it is common practice to either use a shifter to disguise the original site or to convert GPS information to commonly used distances and then to remove the raw indicator. Still, a determined researcher can likely use location data to extract information as to the likely households that participated in the survey and undermine the

sources of support. Where few resources exist, it may be necessary for the study to create short-term support mechanisms. (7) Researchers and donors have an ethical obligation to help ensure that their findings are properly interpreted and used to advance policy and intervention development. (8) Violence questions should be incorporated into surveys designed for other purposes only when ethical and methodological requirements can be met.

[5] The research department at the World Bank has such a policy. In addition, the World Bank strongly encourages governmental statistical offices to make data collected using instruments it has designed, such as the Living Standards Measurement Survey, publically available. It often provides a draft letter of data protocol for the country statistical director as part of technical assistance. However, the ultimate decision on data access to such surveys remains within the statistical office and is governed by local laws and the preference of the government.

guarantee of anonymity. Fortunately, however, such steps increase the required effort and thus plausibly make the exertion not worth undertaking.

There are also times when the research actually may want to retain the identity of the household in the data set. Not only is a baseline-resurvey approach a standard research tool, panels are increasing used to identify long-term impacts of programs (see, e.g., Maluccio et al., 2009) or the dynamics of investments in children (see Helmers and Patnam, 2011). To reduce attrition in such panel data sets, researchers commonly ask for names of individuals who will be in a position to help locate the initial respondents (and, not infrequently, their children) in the future. As the team conducting follow up research may be quite distinct from the original research team—and, indeed, the initial survey team may not have even conceived of the topic of the follow-up study and thus would not have discussed the subject of the new research with the respondent—the validity of the initial confidentiality agreement ultimately rests on the chain of trust between the respondent, the initial researchers, the repository of the data, and the subsequent users of the archived data.

Trust and Communication: Informed Consent and a Two-Way Exchange of Information

Trust is also at the core of the concern for deception in laboratory experiments conducted by economists. Jamison, Karlan, and Schechter (2008) note that deception or misdirection is generally proscribed in protocols for laboratory experiments in economics in contrast to, say, psychology and offer guarded evidence that this reflects, in part, the potential costs of lost trust. They claim, further, that this particular concern has little overlap with purview of ethical review boards.

Does the observation that participant pools at universities may be influenced by deception have any relevance for field work? Mistrust, particularly of distant governments and of strangers, is ubiquitous and ignoring the influence of the various social constructs that have evolved to reinforce social cohesion is likely to result in misleading research. This point was made apparent to one of the authors of this essay (Alderman) in a futile attempt to elicit time preference in rural Gambia using standard instruments in a survey pretest; the virtually infinite discount rate implicit in the respondents' preference for small immediate payments over larger future payments said much about trust but little about intertemporal utility.

The absence of trust undermines the ability to implement protocols for informed consent. Although researchers must provide the respondents a background on the purpose of the data collection, there is no guarantee that even when this is clearly communicated the respondents will take the reason at face value. As many respondents will have little familiarity with research it is not surprising that they will try to understand the surveyors' motive in terms closer to their own experience and concerns. This natural tendency fuels speculation—often with rather creative proposals. An example of fairly benign attempts to place research in the framework of local concerns comes from one of the author's (Alderman) study of allocation of time between farmers' own fields and landlords' as part of his Master's thesis research during Indira Gandhi's emergency in 1976. At the time, the teacher reported that his neighbors believed that this work was preparation for the return of the Raj; noteworthy, a local school teacher indicated that this was perceived locally as a worthy endeavor. More worrisome, however, such speculation may be a fertile area for manipulation, as tragically noted in regards to some thwarted interventions such as polio inoculations in Nigeria (Jegede, 2007). Although outright refusal to participate in research is relatively rare, at least in rural contexts, strategic responses can be influenced by the perceived motives of the survey team, for example, in regard to collecting information believed to be useful for taxation. Thus, informed consent, with or without written documentation, again reduces to trust.

But to whom do the researchers owe their primary responsibility? This is at the heart of ethical research but is not without its ambiguities. We discuss here, in some detail, the particular case of poor service provision by doctors in low-income countries, a topic on which one of the authors has led survey design for the last decade.

Case Study: Health Care Providers in Low-Income Countries

In early 2003, researchers at the World Bank started collecting unique information on teachers and health care providers to help guide key policy decisions, ranging from regulatory concerns—should unqualified health care providers be allowed to practice—to specific investments for public providers. The initial surveys focused on the availability of staff and resources in "frontline" clinics, documenting both high levels of absence and a leaky funding pipeline from ministries to schools or clinics.

Using these facts as a starting point, in a series of papers Das and Hammer (2005, 2007b)—henceforth, DH—and Das, Hammer and Leonard (2008) ask questions about health care provider quality and prices, an agenda squarely within the discipline of the organization of firms and industries. They soon discovered that there were no data and no established method for assessing provider quality in these settings. Many different measures had been proposed—ranging from the availability of medicines to the quality of infrastructure or to patient satisfaction—but these data had seldom been validated against other measures of the quality of medical advice and theoretically, they held little promise. The availability of medicines—a widely used measure of health care *quality*—for instance, is high in a commercial chain pharmaceutical in the United States, but few individuals would go to one if they had chest pains; at most *free* medications was a measure of subsidies rather than the quality of care.

Over 3 years, DH developed protocols that would measure both the technical *competence* of providers (that is, how much they knew about medical conditions) and their *practice* (that is, what they do when an actual patient comes to them). Measurements of competence were based on medical *vignettes* (tests based on hypothetical patients given to doctors) and fell within standard protocols for surveys of firms, an activity with a clear precedent and well-defined notions of "informed consent." Measurements of practice, on the other hand, required them to observe doctors with their real patients and here things became trickier.

To consider why, think of the kinds of clinics they were visiting. Because their sample was selected from a list of all providers in select neighborhoods, they were sitting with providers ranging in expertise from those with a degree from the United Kingdom to those who had no medical education at all. In many cases, "clinics" were small one-room affairs facing the main road. The doctor sat behind desk and one or two benches for the patients spilled over into the street. Patients sat on the bench, and the doctor saw the one who was sitting closest to him. As DH document, the average interaction lasted three minutes, the doctor asked three questions, performed 1 exam and gave three medicines. In many cases, these medicines would be taken from a bottle that contained a large number of pills (bought from one of the "wholesale" markets for medicines in Delhi), put in a mortar, crushed together and dispensed in a small piece of paper. There was no hint of privacy, and none was expected: Every patient observed the full doctor–patient interaction, and only in cases where a woman's examination required her to undress did the doctor use a second room, separated from the main clinic by a curtain. The time spent with patients was low on average, and among the busiest doctors, each interaction lasted 30 seconds. On the data front, the key challenge that the surveyors had to meet was maintaining similar data quality irrespective of the doctor's practice. From the viewpoint of the analysis down the line, data on clinical practice that emerged from crowded clinics where interactions are short and doctors may be "seeing" multiple patients at the same time had to be as accurate as data from a clean and well kept clinic where patients were seen one by one in private.

In one notable example, the two researchers and a surveyor approached a doctor's clinic in a low-/middle-income locality. On seeing them approach, the "doctor" promptly got up and disappeared before the researchers could reach the clinic, leaving behind three patients—one at the table, one lying down on a bench with an oxygen mask, and a third waiting behind. The researchers then sat in a tea-stall for 30 minutes, until the doctor reentered the clinic. They then split up and approached the clinic from different directions and managed to talk to the provider. The provider was forthcoming, and immediately gave consent to observing interactions between him and his customers—as long as the researchers went to his *real* job, which was selling bolts and other industrial material in a hardware shop! The medical practice, he insisted, was a sideline: "I only do this for charity, because these poor people don't have others to go to. Who knows, maybe one day soon, I will decide to close this up and go somewhere else. So what is the point of sitting here with me? Come with me to my real shop, and you can sit there all you want." Notably, the provider's clinic had been in operation for more than a decade and there were close to 60 other medical clinics in the same locality, with similar prices at his level of quality. Ultimately, it took us four visits to this provider to convince him of the anonymity of the survey as well as the benefits of allowing us to collect these data within the context of a broader democratic debate on health care.

On the ethical front, several issues were raised. To begin with, what would "privacy" mean in this context? There was a concern that by observing interactions we could be violating the privacy of the doctor–patient interaction. Yet, in a context where such privacy was violated by the very nature of the practice and was expected neither by the doctor nor the patient, it appeared to us that further observation by a silent observer would not be detrimental to the patient or the provider as long as informed consent was obtained. And here the researchers ran into further problems. Technically, informed consent would require them to approach both the patient and the provider. That makes sense when there is a separate waiting room and patients can be "enlisted" prior to the actual interaction, neither of which held in this context. In the pilot phase, explaining the informed consent form to the patient in every case took an average of 5–6 minutes and DH could not do this prior to the actual interaction; in many cases, this turned out to be a distraction to the doctor and to other patients. DH started asking patients what they thought of the informed consent, and they reported it to be a bother at the time of the interaction; the suggestion from patients and doctors instead was for us to take the consent from the doctor and elicit the patient's feedback only if (a) the patient specifically requested information on the observer or (b) the doctor wanted to examine the patient in private (again, mostly female patients). Both patients and doctors agreed that this would be a far more efficient way of proceeding, as it would retain the sanctity of the interaction and cause no disruptions to the practice. DH's eventual decision was to take informed consent from the provider ("We will be sitting with you for the duration of your practice today and taking some notes. During this time, we will observe your interactions with patients, but at no time will we ask questions from you about these interactions. If you, or the patient, feel that you would rather not have the observer present for a particular interaction, please let us know and we will leave the room") and, in the case of private examinations, DH decided to omit the observation entirely (for survey purposes, this happened in fewer than 0.5 percent of cases).

The researchers' final ethical dilemma was the identity of the observer. At the beginning of the study, DH thought that they could use trained nurses and/or doctors for the observation, but the ethics of this were difficult to handle. Specifically, in many cases (more on this later), the doctor diagnosed the patient incorrectly, gave the wrong medicines, and may have engaged in behavior detrimental to the patient (such as using an unsterilized injection). Doctors as observers now faced a dilemma that could not be resolved. On the one hand, they were required in their role as doctors to inform on the interaction and provide better care to the patient. On the other, they could not break the sanctity of the provider–patient relationship *unless* the observed provider actively solicited a second opinion. Eventually, DH had to give up on this idea and use nonmedical personnel who had no medical judgment regarding the quality of the interaction to conduct the observations.

The results from this study were startling in what they disclosed. DH demonstrated empirically the very low levels of effort that providers exerted in their clinical interactions. They were also able to show that effort was a key component of medical care quality—public sector providers were more *competent* than unqualified private sector providers, but because of abysmally low effort levels (an average interaction of 90 seconds) actually provided medical advice that was *worse* than that provided by unqualified providers. The results opened up a substantial debate on the practices of the medical sector and the importance of incentives in the profession, a debate that eventually led to an incentive-based design in India's quest for universal health coverage.

Clearly, the researchers muddled through. DH made several decisions that reflected both their own prior beliefs that the study was critical to understanding the nature of health care delivery in India and to provide information for better policy that would eventually help the poor. Each of the three key decisions—"violating" privacy, informed consent only from providers— and not using medical personnel could rightly be criticized using strict definitions from human resource subjects' courses. Yet, when DH asked the fundamental question "how could this study be done with full privacy, informed consent from every patient and medical personnel as observers," people who were commenting could offer no alternative; they even heard the view that "such data should not be collected because all the ethical protocols cannot be strictly followed." Yet, DH were not harming either the patient or the doctor, the data that they collected played (and continue to play) an important role in improving the lives of the poor, and subjects in the research (both doctors and patients) agreed with the study protocols. And, in many cases, patients actively welcomed our research on medical practices. It appears to us that we have little guidance in such situations.

Addressing deeper questions regarding the validity of diagnoses obtained by patients and differences between doctors in the treatment of patients raises further issues pertaining to the ethics of research on survey delivery. Specifically, the DH studies using interactions with real patients were still subject to biases in estimations of practice quality across doctors due to unobserved case and patient selection. For instance, it could be argued that lower process quality among public doctors reflected a different patient or sickness profile. Furthermore, the DH method, when combined with their inability to use medical personnel in the observation stage, did not provide any information on the accuracy of diagnoses; the researchers suspected that the accuracy of diagnosis was low, but could not validate their suspicions with data.

Therefore, in 2010, Das et al. (2012) deployed *standardized patients*—surveyors recruited from the local community and extensively trained to portray standardized presentations of limited cases—in a sample of health care providers in Delhi and the rural regions of an Indian state. Such standardized patients (SPs) are widely recognized as the "gold standard" in measurements of quality, but the use of SPs in large samples of randomly selected providers, many of them with low medical training, had not been previously attempted.

In Delhi, the study sought informed consent from all providers (where the providers knew that a standardized patient would be sent, but did not know the date) and follow-up surveys showed (a) a single case of adverse interaction between the provider and the patient (out of 230 interactions) and (b) less than a 1 percent detection rate for the SPs. On the basis of this pilot, the study was rolled out in the rural district *without* informed consent from providers, who were all part of a larger study (with informed consent) similar to that in the DH Delhi studies. The reasons for the lack of informed consent stemmed primarily from the remoteness of the sampled populations. In rural villages, most patients were known to the doctor and although unknown patients often presented to the providers, the combination of announcing the SP study *and* a remote rural setting would have raised suspicions, invalidating the study design. The study was cleared through Institutional Review Boards at Harvard University and Innovations for Poverty Action. For the purposes of the discussion, we note that the study demonstrated, for the first time, the very poor diagnoses rates in Indian health care (the correct diagnosis of unstable angina was provided to 12 percent of patients) and the complete lack of correlation between the quality of care and the availability of equipment and medicines or patient load. Further, the study also confirmed the earlier DH results that quality in the public sector was *worse* than among completely untrained private sector providers (see Das et al., 2012).

Despite the official clearance from IRBs, again, there are tricky issues that arise in the use of informed consent and the nature of the study. Had the researchers been forced to inform providers of the arrival of SPs, detection rates would have been high in the rural context and the study could not have been completed. In the course of the study, careful safeguards ensured that all data were anonymous *and* that no provider even knew that they had participated in such a study. Therefore, it is difficult to argue that there was any harm to either patients or providers through the course of the study, but a strict interpretation of informed consent "at all costs" was not possible in this context.

This issue relates to a wider debate over the use of stealth surveys by anonymous observers sent to ascertain the quality of services.[6] Other examples from the literature pertain to the use of false shoppers or patients who observe the activities of a doctor, teacher, or other agent but who do not seek their consent or inform them directly of the purpose of the visit. In such situations a researcher is presumably seeking an assessment of average quality of services and not that of a specific individual. Thus, the information is expected to remain anonymous and not to be used to punish the individual or seek damages. In partial contrast, employers may use stealth clients to monitor performance, usually with the employee informed that he or she may be observed in this manner. Researchers are sometimes advised to use a similar strategy of informing potential subjects (participants seem an inappropriate label in this circumstance) that they may be observed without indicating who will be studied or when this might occur. However, it is not clear that there are always practical means to communicate this to the service providers (we return to the logistics of communication later). Moreover, this may lead to strangers, often easy to recognize in a remote rural setting, receiving higher quality

[6] See a blog by Jed Friedman on this subject, http://blogs.worldbank.org/impactevaluations/sometimes-it-is-ethical-to-lie-to-your-study-subjects

services than usual. Thus, the clearest ethical guideline for such types of research pertains not to the rights of individuals being observed, but to the interests of the wider community that these individuals are expected to serve, as any such stealth visits should be designed in a manner that does not crowd out or otherwise reduce access for the general population.

Further Discussion on Communications with Subjects Beyond Informed Consent

Survey respondents or trial participants are not only expected to be informed of the purpose of the study, but they are also generally expected to be informed of the results. Chambers (2001), among others, makes the point that surveys take the time of respondents and to a degree interviews are, therefore, extractive, even if the consent to be interviewed is voluntary.[7] Communication of the results as they pertain to the community then can be viewed as a minimal compensation for participation, although even the process of an interview serves a degree of communication because the interview may raise awareness of health or other concerns even in the absence of a direct intervention. The advice to share results is, however, more practical for focus groups than for broad surveys. The statistical power of surveys is determined by the interplay of the number clusters or communities included in the sample and the number of respondents in each cluster. Transport costs—which are often inputs into software used for survey design—are a key factor in determining these two elements of sampling. These costs will also be a factor in the ability of a research team to hold community level meetings to disseminate results. However, this obstacle is reduced in the case of panel data collection in which repeated visits to the community provide opportunities to share observations. Still, there is a challenge to communicate research results from a survey in which the community is a cluster in a larger sample when the results are not designed to be representative at the cluster level.

Rather than—or in addition to—sharing results, respondents can be compensated more directly with cash grants or small gifts in kind. The former, however, are hard to track and may end up with members of the field team instead of the households. Gifts may be in the form of items useful for the households, such as soap, a flashlight, or daris (light blankets commonly used in India and Pakistan) or they may be a collective good for the community such as a repair to a school roof. Although such gifts are modest relative to the cost of data collection, they may be significant relative to the daily wage of poor households, and thus increase the incentive for the members of the household to seek to provide the information that they believe the survey team would like to receive. This may

[7] However, this observation does not, by itself, imply that such data collection is unethical; taxes are also extractive yet viewed by most economists as justifiable to fund public goods even if they entail various distortions that economists seek to minimize. The value of the tax on the respondent's time, then, is a function of the public value of research.

be due to the fact that a gift is offered as much as it is to the value of the gift per se (Ariely, 2008). Whether this compensation biases the data collected is an area for research.

Even in the absence of direct payments, survey design can lessen the burden on respondents both by paring down the size of the survey instrument (a practical consideration for quality as well) and by scheduling the data collection in seasons and times of day that least interfere with work, although it is difficult to envision what time fulfills that recommendation in regards to a child care provider.

Generally, individuals who have a threatening but treatable ailment that is found in the course of a clinical trial are removed from that trial and given appropriate therapy.[8] This stands in partial contrast to communication with respondents in observational studies, for example, in regard to whether they or their children are malnourished or anemic. Arguably there are few curative (rather than preventative) therapies for stunting, although there clearly are recommended practices to address the heighted risk of mortality attendant to severe acute malnutrition as indicated by low weight for height (wasting) or low upper arm circumference. The former measure of weight for height requires comparison to international reference tables which can be carried in the field or built into computerized data capture; similarly upper arm circumference cutoffs for acute malnutrition can be assessed in the field with the data routinely collected in many household surveys.

Protocols for Demographic and Health Surveys advise direct advice on anemia for individuals deemed at risk and referrals to clinics for severe cases.[9] However, neither acute malnutrition nor anemia can be treated in a single visit and in many contexts knowledge of the status is ineffective without the presence of a health system that facilitates regular interaction between health workers and the individual at risk.

Communication at the Cluster Level

One of the authors of this chapter submitted a randomized cluster-based trial of deworming that analyzed data from more than 30,000 children derived from registers at child health days in Uganda. The paper was initially rejected primarily because it was not a double-blind study. A letter was sent to the journal suggesting that scale trials should have different methodologies than clinical trials. The journal's "hanging committee"—their choice of title—agreed and the paper was eventually published (Alderman et al., 2006). Do we need a similar modification of agreed on ethical guidelines for large-scale and cluster-based studies? This is not just a question for economic programs; the issue has been mooted in various health journals, sometimes in an expected benefit, expected risk framework (Winkens et al., 1997; Osrin et al., 2009). Nor is the issue of how scale influences informed consent raised only with controlled trials. Scale affects consent

[8] This may set up an incentive for willful ignorance in which a researcher avoids ascertaining information such as parasite loads or anemia before the final stages of a trial.

[9] Some techniques for assessing anemia such as Hemocue© require additional analysis not generally conducted in the field.

even in observational studies because a community leader is often the initial contact before individuals are approached for their consent. Whether the community leader represents the full interests of the population is often doubtful. In the SALDRU data collection mentioned previously, much of the non-response from the initial sample was due to a landowner refusing access to his tenants or hired laborers.

In the case of a cluster-based trial, often a local official or community leader provides consent for the cluster. Indeed, in most observational studies, as well as many impact evaluations, the central government's approval is considered binding on the community. Local officials are often relatively powerless to decline involvement in a survey undertaken when the central government is a partner in the study or when participation in an impact evaluation has been approved at a higher level. Similarly, households may feel compelled to follow the lead of the community leader.

In some cases individuals themselves can opt out by not taking up the service offered. This take-up provides important practical information, and the difference between the intention to treat and the treatment on those taking up the treatment is an important aspect of the analysis. But in many cases all members of the cluster share some opportunities and risks. As communities are generally heterogeneous in their needs, the consent of one individual, even if this person was chosen by consent of the community, does not cover the risks for all individuals affected by the intervention. In principle, a researcher seeking consent can stratify by gender, caste ethnicity, and so forth and seek consent from a representative of each stratum. In practice, this is rare.

In a similar manner, as some interventions change power relations in a community—either as a direct goal or as an indirect outcome—refusal for participation may perpetuate inequality and thus be unethical on a criterion rather different than that which guides clinical trials. Imagine, for example, excluding a community from an evaluation of an improvement in access to education in the American South in the 1950s because the local mayor declined or dropping an experiment to mediate inheritance claims of widows in Sub-Saharan Africa on the view of a single male dignitary. At the very least, the results of the study of those communities that did not opt out will be biased. More generally, the option of having a representative decide on participation in cluster-based trials is clearer in medical trials where power relations and distributions of resources are not central.[10]

Review Boards in Cross-Country Research

Ethical review boards, often multidisciplinary, have been standard for a sufficiently long time for their overall rules of operation to be well worked out to the satisfaction of legal advisors as well as ethicists (Stark, 2012). There are even a number of companies that

[10] However, this approach of using a representative to prove consent in cluster trials is generally advocated for low-risk interventions.

provide ethical review services on a commercial basis. Many health journals require that submissions indicate the nature of the review process that the study utilized, although this is not commonly required by economic journals even in the case of trials, never mind in the case of observational studies.[11] The World Bank generally follows the lead of the WHO as to ethical guidelines and has a link to these guidelines for applicants to funds approved by the research board. However, it does not have either an internal board dealing specifically with ethical research on human subjects or a policy on the utilization of external boards.

Discussions among staff as to the need for such a policy have stressed, among other things, the reputational risk for the Bank. Yet, it seems to us that a review board that simply mimics boards in universities and the private sector would be a missed opportunity for the World Bank in an area where it has decades of field experience in a large number of countries. Three particularities of the World Bank make it fundamentally different from other research institutions.

First, unlike most American and European universities, the bulk of the research that the World Bank engages in is in low-income countries, rather than on the United States and Europe. As we have sought to demonstrate through this chapter, the legal framework; the experience of fieldwork; and the organization of communities, households, and firms is very different in each of the countries in which we have worked. Consequently, a biomedical model of ethics largely developed in the United States (for instance, all researchers in the United States are required to clear a human subjects course designed by the National Institutes of Health) has serious limitations when applied to much of the research undertaken at the World Bank. As one example, there is a criterion that you can't withhold known efficacious treatments from people. But what if you know that it is efficacious on one dimension but not on another? This is may be the case with deworming—we know the effect on health, but not on education for instance.

Second, much of the research at the World Bank is undertaken jointly with its "operational" arm in projects that are run by the governments of the concerned countries. Every operational project is subject to a number of "safeguards" designed to protect the vulnerable and ensure that environmental concerns are adequately addressed. Every such project also generates a large amount of data, ranging from surveys of beneficiaries and households to bespoke monitoring and information systems that track resources and aid. An open question is whether projects that also have a research arm—perhaps asking the simple question of whether project resources reached the intended beneficiaries—should be subject to further IRB clearance when the project itself is not.

Third, it has also been pointed out that the presence of an internal review board would hardly suffice when a researcher conducts a study in one of its 188 member countries and the internal board's view is not in accord with local boards. Therefore, although having an internal board might facilitate reviews by host country panels, this would not

[11] Economic journals are also less likely to solicit letters criticizing research design or even challenging the published results.

supersede the need for local clearance. On the other hand, not every country has a board that is functional and diligent. Thus, local review may also not be sufficient. Whether one should privilege the views of the local board of the World Bank's internal board in these cases remains an open question. One option is that the union of the recommendations of both a local board (if any) and that of an external board might be prudent.

By highlighting these three issues we do not, by any means, wish to argue for World Bank exceptionalism when it comes to ensuring that research is carried out in an ethical manner consistent with the goals of the institution. Quite the opposite. The World Bank should be equally ethical in its research, but given the vast experience it has accumulated, it should actually be a leader in addressing the issues that arise in the contexts it works in. We feel that the World Bank is actually in a unique position to lead in the creation of an institutional review board that can move beyond the Eurocentric biomedical model that is currently in use. The process of creating such a review board could bring up many questions that researchers working in low-income countries face, and over time, these issues could be addressed by a panel of ethical experts backed by the considerable experience of researchers in the institution.

For instance: Is a different process of review needed for observational data collection as opposed to reviews for research that involve trials or treatments to a group of participants? Or, how should reviews that vet questionnaires and are often cumbersome because, in principal, redesign after pretesting requires additional clearance, be handled? Various types of data collection involving focus groups or other qualitative techniques are inherently open-ended and thus cannot easily be preapproved. How should the review process take this into account? These are all difficult questions and they add to the considerable ethical complexities that we have all faced in the field and tried to document here. At this stage, we feel that the Bank should start from the beginning by first documenting the kinds of issues that have arisen in both Bank projects and Bank research, perhaps by looking at a random set of publications and projects within the institution. Such a step would enable the creation of a database of ethical issues that we feel have been insufficiently addressed by the current IRB process—not surprising given the very different contexts that researchers in low-income countries work in. Our hope is that the conversations around such a process would generate valuable insights into how to proceed—not just so that World Bank research is "covered" by an ethical approval, but so that that institution can become a global leader in thinking of ethical research in resource-poor settings.

Conclusion

This chapter presents no objections to or modifications of standard guidelines and protocols for research ethics. We do, however, argue that these protocols are tools, the application of which in the field relies on trust between the research and the community, among other things. That is, the guidelines are imperfect substitutes for trust; the guidelines can assist a researcher in handling the burden of that trust but they cannot eliminate ambiguities.

Among the ambiguities is the question: To whom is the researcher obligated? This question needs to be confronted, for example, in cases of conflict of interests within a household or within a community—conflicts that seldom arise between participants in medical trials. They occur quite clearly in the situation of domestic violence illustrated previously, but also in cluster-based studies where individuals are asked to speak for the larger community. They also arise between principals and their agents or between service providers and their clients.

Economists generally seek Pareto improvements where actions harm no one and help some. No harm, of course, also lies at the very core of research ethics. Economists know that Pareto improvements are rare outside a classroom discussion. Fortunately, no harm is the norm in research. But as we attempt to illustrate here, researchers in the field do have to be acutely aware that there are times when they need to go beyond existing protocols in order to judge whose welfare are they obligated to protect.

Acknowledgments

The authors wish to thank Gero Carletto, Jed Friedman, and Varun Gauri for shared insights on the topic.

References

Alderman Harold, Joseph Konde-Lule, Isaac Sebuliba, Donald Bundy, and Andrew Hall. 2006. "Increased Weight Gain in Preschool Children due to Mass Albendazole Treatment Given During "Child Health Days" in Uganda: A Cluster Randomized Controlled Trial." *British Medical Journal*, 333: 122–126.

Ariely, Dan. 2008. *Predictably Irrational. The Hidden Forces that Shape Our Decisions.* New York: HarperCollins.

Barrett, Christopher, and Michael Carter. 2010. "The Power and Pitfalls of Experiments in Development Economics: Some Non-random Reflections." *Applied Economic Perspectives and Policy* 32(4): 515–548.

Bloch, Francis, and Vijayendra Rao. 2002, September. "Terror as a Bargaining Instrument: A Case Study of Dowry Violence in Rural India." *American Economic Review* 92(4): 1029–1043.

Chambers, Robert. 2001. "Qualitative Approaches: Self-Criticism and What Can Be Gained from Quantitative Approaches." In *Q-squared: Combining Qualitative and Quantitative Methods in Poverty Appraisal*, edited by Ravi Kanbur. New Delhi: Permanent Black Press: 28–34

Das, Jishnu, and Jeffrey Hammer. 2005. "Which Doctor: Combining Vignettes and Item Response to Measure Doctor Quality." *Journal of Development Economics* 78: 348–383.

Das, Jishnu, and Jeffrey Hammer. 2007b. "Money for Nothing: The Dire Straits of Medical Practice in India." *Journal of Development Economics* 83(1): 1–36.

Das, Jishnu, Jeffrey Hammer, and Kenneth Leonard. 2008. "The Quality of Medical Advice in Low-Income Countries." *Journal of Economic Perspectives* 22(2): pp. 93–114.

Das, Jishnu, Alaka Holla, Veena Das, Manoj Mohanan, Diana Tabak, and Brian Chan. 2012. "The Quality of Medical Care in Clinics: Evidence from a Standardized Patient Study in a Low-Income Setting." *Health Affairs* 31(12): 2274–2784.

Das, Jishnu and Jessica Leino. 2011. "Lessons from an Experimental Campaign for Evaluating the RSBY." *Economic and Political Weekly*. August 6th 2011 Volume XLVI (32: 85–93.).

Deaton, Angus. 2010. "Instruments, Randomization, and Learning about Development." *Journal of Economic Literature* 48(2): 424–455.

Glennerster, Rachel, and Shawn Powers. 2016. "Assessing Risk and Benefit: Ethical Considerations for Running Randomized Evaluations, Especially in Developing Countries." In *The Oxford Handbook of Professional Economic Ethics*, edited by George DeMartino and Deirdre McCloskey, pp. 367–401. New York: Oxford University Press.

Helmers, Christian, and Manasa Patnam. 2011. "The Formation and Evolution of Childhood Skill Acquisition: Evidence from India." *Journal of Development Economics* 95(2): 252–266.

Hussain, R. S., S. T. McGarvey, T. Shahab, and L. M. Fruzzetti. 2012. "Fatigue and Fear with Shifting Polio Eradication Strategies in India: A Study of Social Resistance to Vaccination." *PLoS ONE* 7(9): e46274.

Jamison, Julian, Dean Karlan, and Laura Schechter. 2008. "To Deceive or Not to Deceive: The Effect of Deception on Behavior in Future Laboratory Experiments." *Journal of Economic Behavior and Organization* 68: 477–488.

Jegede, A. S. (2007.) "What Led to the Nigerian Boycott of the Polio Vaccination Campaign?" *PLoS Med* 4(3:): e73. doi:10.1371/journal.pmed.0040073.

Kishor, Sunita, and Kiersten Johnson. 2004. *Profiling Domestic Violence: A Multi-Country Study*. Calverton, MD: ORC Macro.

Maluccio, J. A., J. Hoddinott, J. R. Behrman, R. Martorell, A. R. Quisumbing, and A. D. Stein. 2009, April. "The Impact of Improving Nutrition during Early Childhood on Education among Guatemalan Adults." *Economic Journal* 119(537): 734–763.

Osrin, David, Kishwar Azad, Armida Fernandez, Dharma S. Manandhar, Charles W. Mwansambo, Prasanta Tripathy, and Anthony M. Costello. 2009. "Ethical Challenges in Cluster Randomized Controlled Trials: Experiences from Public Health Interventions in Africa and Asia." *Bulletin of the World Health Organization* 87(10): 772–779.

Rao, Vijayendra. 1997, "Wife Beating in Rural South India: A Qualitative and Econometric Analysis." *Social Science and Medicine* 44(8): 1169–1180.

Rao, Vijayendra. 1998. "Wife-Abuse, Its Causes and Its Impact on Intra-Household Resource Allocation in Rural Karnataka: A "Participatory Econometric" Analysis. In *Gender, Population, and Development*, edited by M. Krishnaraj, R. Sudarshan, and A. Sharif. Oxford: Oxford University Press.: 94–121

Ravallion, Martin. 2012. "Fighting Poverty One Experiment at a Time: Poor Economics: A Radical Rethinking of the Way to Fight Global Poverty: Review Essay." *Journal of Economic Literature* 50(1): 103–114.

Scheper-Hughes, Nancy. 2000. "Ire in Ireland." *Ethnography* 1(1): 117–140.

Stark, Laura. 2012. *Behind Closed Doors: IRBs and the Making of Ethical Research*. Chicago: University of Chicago Press.

Walford, Geoffrey. 2005. "Research Ethical Guidelines and Anonymity." *International Journal of Research & Method in Education* 28(1): 83–93.

Winkens, R. A. G., J. A. Knottnerus, A. D. M. Kester, R. P. T. M. Grol, and P. Pop. 1997. "Fitting a Routine Health-care Activity into a Randomized Trial: An Experiment Possible without Informed Consent?" *Journal of Clinical Epidemiology* 50(4): 435–439.

World Health Organization. 2001. *Putting Women First: Ethical and Safety Recommendations for Research on Domestic Violence against Women*. Geneva, Switzerland: Department of Gender and Women's Health, Family and Community Health, World Health Organization.

Zwane, Alix Peterson, Jonathan Zinman, Eric Van Dusen, William Pariente, Clair Null, Edward Miguel, Michael Kremer, Dean. Karlan, Richard Hornbeck, Xavier Giné, Esther Duflo, Florencia Devoto, Bruno Crepon, and Abhijit Banerjee. 2011. "Being Surveyed Can Change Later Behavior and Related Parameter Estimates." *PNAS* 2011 108 (5:) 1821–1826.

CHAPTER 22

THE UNPRINCIPLED RANDOMIZATION PRINCIPLE IN ECONOMICS AND MEDICINE

STEPHEN T. ZILIAK AND EDWARD R. TEATHER-POSADAS

OVER the past decade randomized field experiments have gained prominence in the toolbox of economics and policy making. Yet enthusiasts for randomization have perhaps paid not enough attention to conceptual and ethical errors caused by complete randomization.

Many, but by no means all, randomized experiments are being conducted by economists on poor people in developing nations. The larger objective of the new development economics is to use randomized controlled trials (RCTs) to learn about behavior in the field and to eradicate poverty.[1] The number of randomized trials in economics is increasing in the United States and Europe, too (Levitt and List, 2009). The study by Herberich, Levitt, and List (2009) is representative of the work being done. They believe that a whole-hog return of randomized trials to agriculture—including crop yield and variety trials—could "return" to "glory" (1259) a field they take to be all dried up (but see, e.g., Ziliak [2011*b*, 2014] and Meyers et al. [2011]).[2]

Not everyone admires randomized trials in economics, foreign or domestic. Angus Deaton (2007) calls the leaders of the randomization movement in development economics *randomistas*. Deaton does not believe that randomization of treatments and

1 For example, Banerjee and Duflo (2011), Duflo, Glennerster, and Kremer (2007), and Karlan and Appel (2011).

2 Herberich, Levitt, and List do not seem to realize that randomized field experiments began in agricultural economics starting with Student's (1911, 1923) rejections of them in favor of deliberate and balanced designs.

controls can solve the fundamental identification problem of econometric parameter estimation, and he—like William Easterly (2009), Dani Rodrik (2008), Sanjay Reddy (2012), and others—questions the macroeconomic validity of their one-off, small-market experiments. "Randomization is a metaphor and not a gold standard," Heckman and Vytlacil (2007: 4836) have noted. "Student's" collaborator, the experimental maltster and barley farmer, Edwin S. Beaven, observed long ago (1947: 293) in a reply to Ronald A. Fisher (1925 [1928], 1935) that, "Many of the 'randomized' plot arrangements appear to be designed to illustrate statistical theory . . . Only a trifling number of them so far have demonstrated any fact of value to the farmer."

Mr. Beaven, we believe, was right. Randomization is not the purpose of an experiment in business or economics. Profit is. Or quality assurance is. Or growth is. Randomization is not, and, in fact, as one of us has shown, randomized field experiments were tried and rejected in an economic context more than a century ago by the pioneer of randomized trials in economics.[3] Between 1904 and 1937, William Sealy Gosset, aka Student (1876–1937)—the same "Student" of Student's test of statistical significance—designed a large number of barley yield and variety experiments for his employer, Arthur Guinness & Sons Ltd., Dublin, comparing the relative performance of random and balanced designs in order to advance the beer and Guinness's bottom line.[4]

Balanced designs are deliberate, systematic allocations of treatments and controls to the experimental units. Student (1911, 1923) discovered the advantage of balancing allocations symmetrically with respect to relevant strata or blocks (in drug trials, e.g., important strata include body weight and age). He also discovered the advantage of balancing allocation of treatments with respect to nonrandom fixed effects (observed and unobserved) that are known in advance to spoil randomized experiments by creating a source of uncontrolled heterogeneity and variance in experimental units. For example, in crop yield trials, the confounding variable is differential soil fertility—a big source of variance in the object of interest. Student's balanced designs defeated the completely randomized whenever the experimental result really mattered; that is, whenever economic differences between treatments were high enough for the farmer and Guinness brewer to care. Beaven, Jerzy Neyman, Egon Pearson, and Sir Harold Jeffreys, among others, admitted the superiority of Student's balanced designs (see also Heckman and Vytlacil, 2007). Given the history and outcome of the Student-Fisher debates on randomization, the trouble with RCTs in medicine and pharmacology (Altman et al., 2001), and the high cost of producing what are after all ambiguous results from large, unbalanced, and unrepeated experiments, we find that the loss of experimental knowledge after Student is nontrivial.

There are, in addition, prudential and other ethical implications of a practice that deliberately withholds already-known-to-be best-practice treatments from one or more human subjects. Randomized trials often give nil placebo or no treatment at all to

[3] See Ziliak (2008, 2010*a*, 2011*b*, 2014); Ziliak and McCloskey (2008, ch. 20–22).

[4] See Student's (1942) collected papers, edited by Egon S. Pearson, and especially therein Student (1911, 1923, 1938) and Gosset (1936).

vulnerable individuals, withholding (in the name of science) best treatments from the control group.

We present new evidence from a 25-question survey of randomization, statistical significance, and validity that was applied to all the full-length articles employing randomization techniques and published by the *American Economic Review*, 2000–2009, and, for comparative purposes, the *New England Journal of Medicine*, 2000–2002.

George DeMartino (2011) notes that economists need a handbook of ethics (such as this one) because economists—and the methods and policies we promote—affect human lives. The use of field experiments in economics and medicine is not itself objectionable. The objection is that no principle can be discerned behind randomization.

Blinded Me with Science: The Chinese Children's Eyesight Experiment

A recent example of a randomized and controlled field experiment in both economics and medicine is "Visualizing Development: Eyeglasses and Academic Performance in Rural Primary Schools in China" (Glewwe, Park, and Zhao, 2012).

The development economists wished to know if wearing corrective eyeglasses might enable sight-defective kids to perform better at school. The economists were inclined to believe "yes," that wearing eyeglasses would help. In contemporary medical ethics, one would say there is no basis for a randomized trial in this instance because "clinical equipoise" does not exist, meaning that the scientific community is not indifferent between treating and not treating sight-defective people with eyeglasses (Freedman, 1987; Altman et al., 2001; Howick, 2011). But too many randomized trials are, we find in our survey, violating even this simple norm of conduct.[5] Although many thousands of schoolchildren from rural China were discovered on investigation to be sight defective and lacking in corrective glasses at the time the experiment began, not all of those children were provided with glasses.

Thousands of schoolchildren—up to one-half of the 19,000 student sample—were randomly chosen to be experimental "controls" in the eyesight experiment (it is difficult to determine from the study precisely the number of students selected for the control group). Students randomly selected to serve as "controls" were not supplied with corrective eyeglasses nor any other eye care, however sight defective and prepared they were to benefit from the best-practice treatment, if given.

[5] None of the studies in our survey of the *American Economic Review*, 2000–2009, considered equipoise and "no-treatment" controls from the perspective of actual study participants—an odd fact about a discipline that is otherwise devoted to maximum welfare, freedom of choice, and methodological individualism. Clinical researchers have paid far more attention to the role of individual values and preferences: see, for example, Alderson (1996) and the Bayesian approaches of Kadane (1986) and Lilford and Jackson (1995).

Students in the control group were recruited, followed, and tracked, just as the "treatment" group was, but under no circumstance were the "controls" to be given corrective eyeglasses (Glewwe et al., 2012: 8). "The lack of rigorous studies on the impact of providing eyeglasses to students with visual impairments in developing countries led to the implementation of the Gansu Vision Intervention Project in 2004 in Gansu Province in northwest China."

Why were thousands of poor Chinese schoolchildren with defective eyesight recruited and followed for a full calendar year (8) and yet not given corrective eyeglasses to wear at school? Because the experimental economists (by subfield, "development" economists) wished to "test" against nil placebo whether wearing corrective eyeglasses might improve children's educational performance.

No one is sure why economists and their sponsors at the World Bank, National Institutes of Health (NIH), and Spencer Foundation had any doubt about the null hypothesis, which is blindingly obvious (Glewwe et al., 2012: acknowledgments). Helen Keller said, "It is a terrible thing to see and have no vision." We wonder why the sample size had to grow to 19,000 students before the trial was considered valid. Conduct the eyesight/school productivity experiment on yourself, in your own classroom ($n = 1$). Take off your glasses and try to read a smattering of Malthus or mathematics scribbled over there on the blackboard. If you are far-sighted instead of near-sighted, there is a difference. But the large negative effect is still there; sight-defective professors need glasses to improve their scholastic work and so do sight-defective children. If you are still in doubt after $n = 1$, ask your teenage baby sitter: "Does wearing glasses help?" (we mean for school, not vanity). Regardless, you do not need 19,000 schoolchildren from any nation to reject the null hypothesis of "no help."

To test the hypothesis that eyeglasses help at school, the authors of the Eyesight Experiment argued, along with most other experimental economists, that there is a need for a no-treatment control group, meaning that some of the kids can't have the glasses.

Some data were dropped for fear of spoiling the experimental design. "Unfortunately," the authors write, "in a few cases students in control townships were given eyeglasses because, after providing the eyeglasses in the treatment townships, the remaining funds were used to buy eyeglasses for students with poor vision in the paired control township. This occurred in two control townships in Tianzhu and three control townships in Yongdeng" (Glewwe et al., 2012: 8). In remaining townships, the "randomization was done according to the plan" (Glewwe et al., 2012: 8), the authors of the China study state. But one ought to question a practice that elevates abstract method over ethics and the chance to really help.

Substituting syphilis for short-sightedness, we are reminded of the Tuskegee Syphilis Experiment (1931–1972) wherein doctors employed by the U.S. Department of Public Health were, they believed, advancing science by deliberately *not* treating hundreds of syphilitic African-American men in Macon County, Alabama (Jones, 1992; Gray, 1998). "The doctors [from the U.S. Department of Public Health] were sure that untreated syphilis was a deadly problem and that treatment [penicillin] was efficacious, that they wanted to prove it beyond question by control group comparisons and autopsies that would rule out any other possible explanation" (Gray, 1998: 94). Short-sightedness is not deadly, but it is highly treatable.

In medical ethics, such "no-treatment" studies violate "the personal care principle" (Royall, 1991)—an oath accepted by physicians to provide the best available treatment. "No-treatment" control groups are thus ethically suspect. In economic ethics, "no-treatment" disturbs, for example, the general rules of conduct laid down by Adam Smith's (1759 [1791, 2009]: 280) impartial spectator who cannot accept the utilitarian reply that the deliberate sacrifice of today's children is for the betterment of tomorrow's. A transcendental theorist of justice, rights, and duties—such as the followers of John Rawls and John Rawls himself—would agree with Smith. And so, too, would Amartya Sen (2006: 217), who judges experiments much like Smith did, not from behind a veil of ignorance but empirically using the "comparative" (217) method:

> Investigation of different ways of advancing justice in a society . . . or of reducing manifest injustices that may exist, demands comparative judgments about justice, for which the [transcendental Rawlsian] identification of fully just social arrangements is neither necessary nor sufficient. To illustrate the contrast involved, it may well turn out that in a comparative perspective, the introduction of social policies that abolish slavery, or eliminate widespread hunger, or remove rampant illiteracy, can be shown to yield an advancement of justice.[6]

In truth, the development economists could have used their millions of dollars of funds to simply purchase eyeglasses for each of the thousands of untreated children discovered by them.[7] This would not serve a purpose for abstract research, but it would serve a higher purpose, Sen would agree, by helping poor and needy schoolchildren with best-practice (and affordable) treatment. To illustrate, at the time of the eyeglass experiment in China, one pair of correctives cost on average the equivalent of about US$15 (nominal 2012 dollars; Glewwe et al., 2012: 28). Lower prices for glasses were then available in China, for as low as US$2 per pair per student. So with an expenditure equal to or less than the cost of the experiment, the World Bank, NIH, and other grant money could have been used a lot more efficiently and a lot more justly by empowering thousands of additional students. (Needless to say, the authors conclude from their study that corrective eyeglasses give a significant boost to school performance.)

[6] For Rawls (1971: 83) inequality is permissible if and only if the inequality can be shown to benefit the least advantaged persons. The treatment/no-treatment inequality does not.

[7] We were not able to determine the cost of the eyesight experiment. But randomized trials are rarely low cost. Johnston et al. (2006: 1319) report in *The Lancet* on 28 large-scale trials costing $335 million or $12 million for the average trial. Only six of the trials (21 percent) resulted in measurable improvements for trial participants, and only 4 of the 28 trials (14 percent) resulted in cost savings to society. By 2004, the U.S. National Institutes of Health was investing $3 billion annually (1319) in these and other large-scale clinical trials.

The authors decided not to work at all with children and schools located in remote areas of rural China, meaning that the poorest of the poor did not get eyeglasses from the experiment. "Primary schools with less than 100 students were excluded from the project to avoid high travel costs to a few very remote schools. Students in such schools are only 6 percent of primary students in the two counties. . . . This leaves six pairs of townships in Yongdeng and six pairs (plus the poorest township, the one randomly assigned to be treated) in Tianzhu for which the randomization was done according to the plan."

The Mostly Random Rise of Randomized Trials in Economics

"I am a huge fan of randomized trials," Hal Varian (2011) told *The Economist*. "[T]hey are well worth doing since they are the gold standard for causal inference," he asserts without proof. Economists working for Varian, the chief economist of Google, "ran about 6,000" randomized trials at Google in 2010 alone. A leading *randomista*, the John Bates Clark Award-winning economist Esther Duflo has told *The New Yorker* that field experimentalists (such as her and her colleagues at MIT) have borrowed from medicine a " 'very robust and very simple tool' . . . they subject social policy ideas to randomized control trials, as one would use in testing a drug. 'This approach,' Duflo claims, 'filters out statistical noise; it connects cause and effect' " (quoted in Parker, 2010: 79–80). List (2008) agrees with the drug-testing analogy, and so do many others in the current generation.

Levitt and List (2009) go further and assert that the introduction of randomized treatments and controls—of completely randomized blocks—laid the "foundation" for good experimental design (Levitt and List, 2009: 3). Artificial randomization of treatments and controls is, they claim, the only "valid" justification for use of Student's test of statistical significance.[8]

The authority of today's randomization school seems to derive from uncritical acceptance of assertions by Ronald A. Fisher in *The Design of Experiments* (1935) and *Statistical Methods for Research Workers* (1925).[9] Levitt and List consider this quote from Fisher (1935) the foundation of experimental method:

[8] Levitt and List (3); contrast Ziliak (2008, 2011*b*, 2014), Ziliak and McCloskey (2008), and the unanimous rejection of statistical significance by the Supreme Court of the United States in *Matrixx Initiatives, Inc. v. Siracusano*, No. 09-1156, on March 22, 2011 (Ziliak, 2011*a*).

[9] The advocates of RCTs in economics appear to be innocent of the real sources of randomized trials in medicine, the field they claim to imitate. For example, in addition to their neglect of Student, none of the new generation makes any mention of A. Bradford Hill and his immense influence on the use of RCTs in medicine. See the recent symposium introduced by Iain Chalmers (2003). Chalmers (922–924) neglects Student, too, repeating the popular but incorrect Fisherian history of randomized trials.

> The validity of our estimate of error for this purpose is guaranteed by the provision that any two plots, not in the same block, shall have [via complete randomization of treatments, controls, and varieties] the same probability of being treated alike, and the same probability of being treated differently in each of the ways in which this is possible.

"The thoroughness of Fisher's insights are exemplified by this passage," Levitt and List write, "concerning what constituted a valid randomization scheme for completely randomized blocks" (Levitt and List, 2009: 3).

To Fisher and today's *randomistas*, blocks (or strata) have the same probability of being "treated alike" only when treatments and controls are randomly assigned to the experimental unit. Yet Duflo, Banerjee, Karlan, List, Levitt, and others—following Cochrane (1976), Rubin (1990), and Street (1990)—do not explain why Fisher is to be believed.

The enthusiasm for randomized trials is not limited to academics. The World Bank asserts in a research guidebook that randomized trials are the most "rigorous" type of assessment (World Bank, 2004: 23). The United Nations Food and Agriculture Organization (FAO) published, back in 1999, a 234-page Statistical Manual for Forestry Research, "Design and Analysis of Experiments" (Jayaraman, 1999). On randomization the FAO sounded the usual bell:

> Assigning the treatments or factors to be tested to the experimental units according to definite laws or probability is technically known as randomization. It is the randomization in its strict technical sense that guarantees the elimination of systematic error. It further ensures that whatever error component that still persists in the observations is purely random in nature. This provides a basis for making a valid estimate of random fluctuations which is so essential in testing of significance of genuine differences. . . . Through randomization, every experimental unit will have the same chance of receiving any treatment.

Three Big Losses Caused by Randomization

But the FAO and World Bank are, like many academics, not as aware as they might be of several big losses caused by randomization. Randomization in the design of an experiment is normally achieved by using a random number generator to allocate treatments and controls to experimental units. For example, a barley farmer may wish to test the hypothesis that, other things equal, crop yield is importantly higher when crops are fertilized—with the unfertilized crops serving as controls. There are at least three reasons why the rational statistician would rather balance and stratify treatments and controls rather than completely randomize over the experimental unit.

1. Randomization leads to Simpson's Paradox, reversing the sign of causal effects. Let *T* be a treatment in an experiment to be tested against control *P*, the company or industry standard, a sugar pill, or—as in many field experiments in economics—no treatment at all.

Suppose you run an experiment on $n = 160$ adults, randomly assigning the treatment *T* to some of the randomly chosen adults and control *P*—which, as in the Chinese eyeglass experiment, economists often equate with "no treatment at all"—to the others in the sample, whom we will call the control group.[10] Here are the aggregate results:

Results for all Participants

		S	F	Total	Success Rate
Treatment	*T*	40	40	80	50 percent
	P	32	48	80	40 percent

where S = treatment success (e.g., an unemployed person gets and keeps a job for a certain number of months while receiving either all treatment *T* or all control *P*), and where F = treatment failure (e.g., the unemployed did not get a job, the sight-defective student did not scholastically improve).

The aggregate results appear to show that treatment *T* works much better than the control *P*—a 50 percent success rate versus a 40 percent success rate. But the aggregate results assume that the participants are homogeneous in all important fixed factors and covariates (income, gender, race, skill level, education, etc.). When the units of the experiment are made more homogeneous, by disaggregating the data into strata by gender, for example, the results are as follows:

Results for Stratum 1 (Men)

		S	F	Total	Success Rate
Treatment	*T*	36	24	60	60 percent
	P	14	6	20	70 percent

Results for Stratum 2 (Women)

		S	F	Total	Success Rate
Treatment	*T*	4	16	20	20 percent
	P	18	42	60	30 percent

Note: Results for stratum 2 = Aggregate results—Stratum 1

But now, after controlling for the heterogeneity caused by gender difference, the balance of evidence has shifted, reversing the result of the experiment. The treatment *T* is not the best, most successful treatment after all—not when judged from

[10] The data were supplied by Lindley (1991: 47–48), but Lindley does not mention that Simpson's Paradox can be caused by artificial randomization of treatments and controls.

the perspective of just two relevant strata, male and female. For both men and women, the disaggregated data show that the control *P* dominates the treatment *T* (i.e., the percentage success rate is higher in the control group), thus making it clear that treatment *T* is effective for the whole sample but harmful for both men and women.

Something is wrong. It is called *Simpson's Paradox*, a common defect of statistical studies and especially of randomized controlled trials. In summary, if the experiment is not prudently stratified to eliminate heterogeneity bias, the randomized trial can mislead investigators. For example, in the Chinese eyesight experiment, complete randomization suggests that 73 percent of the boys accepted glasses when offered but only 66 percent of the girls accepted (Glewwe et al., 2012: 30). Further analysis of the sample shows, however, that boys were offered glasses 8.5 percent more frequently than girls. Thus, a stratified sample might serve to reduce or eliminate the apparent difference in propensity to accept eyeglasses. Regardless, the authors uncovered a much larger strata of difference, one that spoiled the external validity of their study: the social position of parents. Turns out that children of schoolteachers and village cadres were much less likely than average to accept the eyeglasses when offered:

> children in households headed by a schoolteacher or a village cadre were less likely to accept glasses . . . These effects are very large, with schoolteachers' children 22.4 percentage points less likely, [and] village cadres' children 35.2 percentage points less likely, to accept them. Perhaps these local authority figures decline program benefits to avoid being perceived as manipulating the program for personal benefit. Alternatively, it would be strange, and ironic [the authors admit], if these authority figures had more doubts about the merits of eyeglasses.

2. *Randomization raises the probability of imbalance, biasing estimation and tests of significance and possibly reversing the impact of treatments and controls.* A second major flaw in randomized trials is caused by a related design failure—the failure to control for allocation imbalance and systematic error. Imbalance can occur for at least two reasons: first, the treatments might be given disproportionately to one strata and not to the others, as in our example, where the treatment *T* was given disproportionately to men (60 men, 20 women). Second, imbalance can occur when there are unobserved omitted variables in the system that are large with respect to the output of interest and yet are systematic and not able to be artificially randomized.

Consider a classic example from agricultural economics and experimental statistics: designing a yield trial to compare the estimated yield per acre of barley variety A (the treatment) versus barley variety B (the control) when there is differential soil fertility cutting across the farm plot, the experimental unit. We need some way or other to allocate seeds A and B to rows and columns of the plot (or plots—plural—ideally speaking, in a small sample of independent and repeated experiments; Ziliak, 2011*b*, 2014). Suppose each plot is divided into blocks or subblocks. For simplicity, imagine that each block gets a unique "treatment," A or B, determined by a random coin flip: head for A and tail for B. The problem with random assignment of treatment and control to natural soil is that, by a series of chance coin flips, the recommended allocation of As and Bs could turn out highly imbalanced with regard to a major variable of crop growth; namely, soil fertility:

A A A A A A B B
A A A A A A B A
. . . . etc. (i)

⟶ Direction of increase in soil fertility (higher yielding soil)

And a second series of random flips could produce an imbalanced allocation of this sort:

B B B B B A A B
B B B B B A A A
. . . etc. (ii)

⟶ Direction of increase in soil fertility (higher yielding soil)

How precise are the estimated differences in average yields, A-B, or B-A, if fertility on the left side of the field is systematically lower than fertility on the right? Layouts such as (i) and (ii)—although randomly chosen by the field experimentalist—produce biased mean squared errors and parameter estimates with respect to this major source of fluctuation—differential soil fertility (cf. van Es et al., 2007; Meyers et al., 2011). Likewise, in the Chinese eyesight experiment, the randomized sample is found to be highly imbalanced with respect to a large nonrandom effect: the differential behavior of the schoolchildren's parents, which varies greatly, the authors found, by occupational level and social status. Thus, as Heckman would note, the eyeglass experiment suffers also from selection bias.

Student proved the point first, as we've noted, in Guinnessometrics and agronomy. In example (i), the As are bunched up and growing in the very worst soil; thus, the yield of the Bs will be artificially high, and the real treatment difference, A-B, will be undetermined. Student and collaborators found again and again, in repeated trials, that deliberate balancing—through adding to the "apparent" error, that is, to type I error in ANOVA terms, actually *reduces* the real error of the experiment, minimizing type II error and errors from fixed effects such as nonrandom soil heterogeneity.[11]

As Student showed (1911, 1923, 1938), examples (i) and (ii) suggest that whenever there is a systematically variant fertility slope (or other temporal or secular source of local and fixed effect, as there so easily could have been in the Chinese experiment) that cannot be artificially randomized, then the systematic source of fluctuation cannot be ignored without cost: differences in yield will be correlated by local and adjacent fertility slopes. Random layouts analyzed with Student's test of significance will yield on average more

[11] Student (1938: 364–372).

biased differences, A-B and B-A, and less ability to detect a true difference when the difference is large. By 1923, Student's solution became perfectly balanced. The ABBA layout is:

```
A B B A A B B A
A B B A A B B A        (iii)
A B B A A B B A
. . . etc.
```

One virtue of the ABBA *non*randomized design is that it minimizes bias caused by differential soil fertility. Student found that the "principle of maximum contiguity" (as he called it) takes full advantage of the correlation of variables by twinning, in the manner of Noah's Ark, and holding other things equal. Given the built-in symmetry of ABBA, no matter what the trajectory or magnitude of differential fertility gradients, A's and B's are equally likely to be grown on good and bad soil. Random throws of seed do not have this virtue, biasing mean yield differences, A-B.

Yet ABBA brings additional statistical and economic advantages, too.[12] On the supply side, with ABBA, the ease and cost of sowing, harvesting, and calculating basic statistics on yield is plot-wise and block-wise reduced. Compare the rows and columns of ABBA with the random rows and columns in (i) and (ii), and it's easy to appreciate Student's sensitivity to supply-side economic conditions.

With ABBA, there is no need for chaotic tractor driving while planting seed in randomly dispersed blocks, and thus with ABBA there is a lot less measurement error and loss of material at harvest and counting time (see Beaven, 1947, for details). Imagine harvesting and counting up the mean difference in yield of strip A minus strip B, block by block, in the ABBA field versus the randomized field, and one can appreciate further still the efficiency of Student's balanced solution. As Student told Fisher in the letter of 1923, "There must be essential similarity to ordinary [in this case, farming] practice."[13] After all, "[t]he randomized treatment pattern is sometimes extremely difficult to apply with ordinary agricultural implements, and he [Student] knew from a wide correspondence

[12] Student's ABBA design is, formally speaking, *chiasmus*—one of the most powerful design patterns in the history of language, music, religion, and science. What is chiasmus beyond the symmetric Greek symbol for chi, X, from which the term derives? Lanham (1991: 33), defines chiasmus as "The ABBA pattern of mirror inversion." Unaware of Student's use of ABBA, a rhetoric professor, Richard Lanham, explains: "Chiasmus seems to set up a natural internal dynamic that draws the parts closer together . . . The ABBA form," he notes, "seems to exhaust the possibilities of argument, as when Samuel Johnson destroyed an aspiring author with, 'Your manuscript is both good and original; but the part that is good is not original, and the part that is original is not good' " (33). Good, original, original, good: the ABBA form. James Joyce, another famous Dubliner in Student's day, wrote chiasmus in *Portrait of the Artist as a Young Man*. Other examples of chiasmus are by John F. Kennedy ("Ask not what your country can do for you; ask what you can do for your country") and by Matthew 23:11–12 ("Whoever exalts himself will be humbled, and whoever humbles himself will be exalted"). In science, supply and demand and the double helix are two notable examples revealing the power of balanced chiasmus.

[13] Pearson (1938: 163–164); Pearson shows how to adjust ANOVA and Student's test of significance to accommodate the ABBA structure.

how often experimenters were troubled or discouraged by the statement that without randomization, conclusions were invalid" (Pearson, 1938: 177).

Fisher refused to admit the economic and statistical advantages of Student's ABBA and other balanced designs (see, e.g., Fisher and Yates [1938], which fails to mention Student's methods). In Student's (1938: 366) last article—which he worked on during the final months and days of his life and until the day he died—he said to Fisher,

> It is of course perfectly true that in the long run, taking all possible arrangements, exactly as many misleading conclusions will be drawn as are allowed for in the tables [Student's tables], and anyone prepared to spend a blameless life in repeating an experiment would doubtless confirm this; nevertheless it would be pedantic to continue with an arrangement of plots known before hand to be likely to lead to a misleading conclusion. . . .
>
> In short, there is a dilemma—either you must occasionally make experiments which you know beforehand are likely to give misleading results or you must give up the strict applicability of the tables; assuming the latter choice, why not avoid as many misleading results as possible by balancing the arrangements? . . . To sum up, lack of randomness may be a source of serious blunders to careless or ignorant experimenters, but when, as is usual, there is a fertility slope, balanced arrangements tend to give mean values of higher precision compared with artificial arrangements.

As far back as 1926, Student (1926: 126) explained the flaws of randomization to agricultural economists:

> Generally speaking, . . . the population of large-scale yields with which we are concerned is a population of "differences", i.e., some such question as the following is asked: "By how much may we expect the yield of variety B to exceed that of variety A if they were sown alternatively on the same soil in the same season?" . . . That being so, it is clear that the observed differences will not represent the true differences even in the same sample plots as two crops cannot occupy the same place at the same time. Observed differences will miss the mark not only because the experimental soil and the weather experienced by *the experiment may not be random samples of the soil and weather to be explored, but also because the actual plots laid out for the two varieties will usually differ in fertility. This is one of the largest sources of errors in field experiments.* (Student, 1926: 126; emphasis added).

Despite these warnings, today's *randomistas* follow R. A. Fisher. They have not yet perceived that Student's balanced designs and small series of independently repeated experiments continue to dominate randomized experiments.

In general, Student's Imbalance and Simpson's Paradox can spoil results from any randomization scheme, including instrumental variables with nonexperimental data, which is said to solve the problem of omitted variable bias. Angrist and Krueger (2001: 72) are, for example, mistaken when they assert:

> One solution to the omitted variables problem is to assign the variable of interest randomly. For example, social experiments are sometimes used to assign people to a job training program or to a control group. Random assignment assures that participation in the program (among those in the assignment pool) is not correlated with omitted personal or social factors. . . . Instrumental variables offer a potential solution in these situations.[14]

3. *Randomized controls fail at the margin of economics—and ethics, too.* Third, if randomization of treatments and controls has economic and/or ethical advantage over balanced or other systematic designs, then pure randomization would win at the margin.

Decisions based on randomized allocations would be, other things equal, more valuable at the margin than would alternative, deliberately made decisions using systematic or what is known as balanced designs of experiments. Ethically speaking, if randomized controls are preferred, it would be easy to prove that withholding best-practice treatment raises the well-being and life chances of participants assigned to the untreated control group.

That is not always the case. Consider making a decision at the margin of the Chinese eyeglass experiment. Suppose you, the development economist, have $15 to spend on each study participant, and you have now to choose one of two options to spend it:

Option 1: You supply a pair of prescription eyeglasses (costing $15) to all sight-defective children you encounter in your study, given that they do not have eyeglasses of their own. You follow them in school and note the improvement.

Option 2: You flip a fair coin each time you meet a sight-defective child in the study. If the coin turns up heads, give the child a pair of eyeglasses; if tails, do not supply the glasses; instead, spend the money tracking and reporting on untreated students.

Does Option 2—the option and method frequently employed by today's randomizers—feel ethically correct? Or does the ethical mandate of the personal care principle (or, alternatively, of the impartial spectator) dominate "no treatment" at the margin? Our "feelings" for the untreated children or other subjects of economic and medical trials may not be the decisive factor. But they are certainly one of the deciding factors that the ethical economist must consider. In Part II, Section III of *The*

[14] See also Angrist and Pischke (2009: 15–17).

Theory of Moral Sentiments, "On Merit and Demerit; or, Of the Objects of Reward and Punishment," Adam Smith (1759 [1791, 2009]) observes:

> Whatever praise or blame can be due to any action, must belong either, first, to the intention or affection of the heart, from which it proceeds; or, secondly, to the external action or movement of the body, which this affection gives occasion to; or, lastly, to the good or bad consequences, which actually, and in fact, proceed from it. These three different things constitute the whole nature and circumstances of the action, and must be the foundation of whatever quality can belong to it.

What is missing now is a sense of balance in both ethics and statistics. A balanced ethics would give, for example, best-practice treatment to the control group while trying out on willing others a novel and promising treatment about which not much is known. Casey Mulligan (2014) agrees that if research workers insist on using a no-treatment option, the cost of that decision should be shared by them, with skin in the game, such as by paying more cash money to people who are willing to be randomly chosen for their "no-treatment" control group. Currently, most randomized trials fail to meet a basic postulate of welfare economics, Pareto efficiency (see, e.g., Johnston et al., 2006). The defensive answer that is often heard in reply is that "Policy makers have to be convinced of the initiative. How can we convince policymakers that investment in [Project X] is worthwhile?"[15]

The So-Called Randomization Principle Is Not a Principle

Other economic statisticians have gone far beyond mere randomization and randomized controlled trials (Kadane, 1986). For example, statisticians have long known that stratification, or blocking, is a first necessary step to improving the precision and efficiency of a study based on pure randomization. Student (1911) used blocking and stratification before the synonymous words existed in the statisticians' vocabulary. As W. Edwards Deming (1978: 879), an admirer of Student, noted, "Stratification is equivalent to blocking in the design of an experiment."

[15] Martin Ravallion, a former director of research at The World Bank, has been a critic of randomized trials. He told the authors that he would defend the Chinese eyesight experiment and other experiments like it on, he said, "consequentialist" grounds (Ravallion, 2014). "Actually, I think the consequentialist argument is key," he argues. But the ends do not justify the means for at least two reasons. First, the means of withholding best treatment from impoverished people today to possibly help unknown others in the future is not justified by any ethic save vulgar utilitarianism, which both Ravallion and we reject. Second, the ultimate ends of the experiment are, Hayek and others would note, evolving and unknown in the developing Chinese economy.

Box, Hunter, and Hunter (1978 [2005]: 92) explain that "A block is a portion of the experimental material (the two shoes of one boy, two seeds in the same pot) that is expected to be more homogenous than the aggregate (the shoes of all the boys, all the seeds not in the same pot). By confining comparisons to those within blocks (boys, girls), greater precision is usually obtained because the differences associated between the blocks are eliminated." Blocks are strata.

Deming (1978), who, before turning to manufacturing, did a long stint at the U.S. Department of Agriculture, agreed with Student's larger point: complete random sampling and randomized experiments are at best preliminary steps to scientific study. Complete randomization has a purpose when the investigator knows little or nothing at all about strata or when the cost of being wrong is negligible. Said Deming (879):

> The primary aim of stratified sampling is to increase the amount of information per unit of cost. A further aim may be to obtain adequate information about certain strata of special interest. One way to carry out stratification is to rearrange the sampling units in the frame so as to separate them into classes, or strata, and then to draw sampling units from each class. The goal should be to make each stratum as homogeneous as possible, within limitations of time and cost.[16]

Likewise, in his book, *Planning of Experiments*, David Cox (1958) recommends "completely randomized arrangement . . . [only] in experiments in which no reasonable grouping into blocks suggests itself"—that is, when ignorance prevails, or priors are flat.

Normally speaking, ignorance does not prevail, and real economic and statistical gains can be found by stratifying. Deming (1978) and Tippett (1958) simplified Student's (1911, 1923) proof that stratification (blocking) can reduce sample size requirements by 40 percent or more, holding variance constant.[17] And, as Tippett noted, "At the worst"—assuming the rare case that calculated variance between strata is zero—"sampling in strata is no better than random sampling, but it is never worse."

According to Levitt and List (2009: 4), Fisher and MacKenzie (1923) is the second classic article to use randomization in the design of a field experiment. This is a remarkable achievement given that randomization does not appear even once—randomization is neither used nor mentioned—in the article by Fisher and Mackenzie. "Fisher's fundamental contributions were showcased in agricultural field experiments. In his 1923 work with MacKenzie, Fisher introduced . . . randomization (Fisher and MacKenzie, 1923)," Levitt and List write. But that is not so; what they are claiming is not true. In fact, it is precisely the absence of careful planning that made the 1923 Fisher and Mackenzie

[16] Deming (1978: 879). Deming said he learned the technique from Neyman (1934). In the seminal article, Neyman proves mathematically and empirically the statistical and economic advantages of stratified sampling over random sampling (Neyman, 1934: 579–585). Neyman credits the idea of "purposive selection" to earlier writers, such as Bowley and Gini and Galvani.

[17] Deming (1978: 880–881), Tippett (1958: 356). In a Riesling vine-and-wine experiment, Meyers, Sacks, van Es, and Vanden Heuvel (2011) used blocking, balancing, and repetition (at $n = 3$ vineyards) to reduce sample size requirements by up to 60 percent.

experiment infamous—famous in the bad sense—eliciting negative comments from Student, Yates, Cochrane, and others.

As late as 1923—the same year that Student was comparing random with balanced designs on farm fields across England and Ireland—Fisher had not given much thought to the statistical design of experiments. Cochrane (1989: 18) notes that: "Fisher does not comment [in Fisher and Mackenzie (1923)] on the absence of randomization or on the chessboard design. Apparently in 1923 he [that is, Fisher] had not begun to think about the conditions necessary for an experiment to supply an unbiased estimate of error."

Yates (1964: 310–311) goes further. Like Cochrane, Yates observes that in 1923 Fisher did not possess any theory of experiments, random or balanced. Says Yates (310–311) of Fisher's and Mackenzie's 1923 manure experiment:

> Twelve varieties of potatoes were grown with two types of potash (sulphate and chloride) and also without potash. Half the experiment also received farmyard manure. There were three replicates of each variety on each half, each varietal plot being split into three in a systematic manner for the potash treatments. The actual layout (Fig. 1) [by Fisher and Mackenzie] illustrates [Yates said] how little attention was given to matters of layout at that time.[18] It is indeed difficult to see how the arrangement of the varietal plots [designed by Fisher and Mackenzie] was arrived at.

Thus, Fisher's design in 1923 was neither randomized nor balanced: "the arrangements for the farmyard manure and no farmyard manure blocks are almost but not quite identical, and some varieties tend to be segregated in the upper part and others in the lower part of the experiment" (Yates, 1964: 310–311). "Consequently," wrote Yates, "no satisfactory estimate of error for varietal comparisons can be made [in the Fisher and Mackenzie experiment]. . . .To obtain a reasonable estimate of error for these interactions," he said, "the fact that the varietal plots were split for the potash treatments should have been taken into account. This was not done in the original analysis" (Yates, 1964: 310–311). *Randomistas* want their readers to believe otherwise.

Yates continued (Yates, 1964: 311–312): "The principle of randomisation was first expounded in [Fisher's textbook] *Statistical Methods for Research Workers* [1925]"—not in Fisher and Mackenzie (1923).[19] In other words, an article that Levitt and List claim for the canon in the history of randomization neither mentions nor uses randomization. In addition, randomization was proved to be inferior to balanced designs, and anyway, it is not even a principle. "I don't agree with your controlled randomness," Student told Fisher in a letter of October 1924 (Gosset, 1962). "You would want a large lunatic asylum for the operators who are apt to make mistakes enough even at present," Student said of Fisher's so-called principle. "If you say anything about Student in your preface you

[18] But compare Student (1911, 1923), two seminal articles omitted by Yates.

[19] The case for random arrangement is made by Fisher (1925 [1928], sections 48 and 49, "Technique of Plot Experimentation" and "The Latin Square": 229–237); for the full story, see Ziliak and McCloskey (2008: ch. 20–22).

should I think make a note of his disagreement with the practical part of the thing." Significantly, Fisher did not make a note.

Survey of Randomization, Significance, and Validity in Economics and Medicine

To better understand randomization in practice, we designed a survey of randomization, statistical significance, and validity as used in RCTs in economics and medicine. We put 25 questions to published articles, eliciting Yes, No, and Not Applicable answers, where "Yes" indicates that the study corrected for or at least acknowledged the potential costs of randomization bias and the cult of statistical significance. Several of the survey questions are directly comparable with surveys of significance testing in general, as conducted and reported by Ziliak and McCloskey (2008; McCloskey and Ziliak, 1996). The survey questions are drawn from the past century of best-practice experimental statistics, from the works of William S. Gosset aka "Student" to James J. Heckman, not including Ronald A. Fisher.[20] Given our ethical concerns about randomization, we also inquire whether each study established a no-treatment control group when in fact known treatments were available at the time of the study (Question 1).

Tables 22.1, 22.2, and 22.3 present survey results for the last decade of publishing randomization studies in the *American Economic Review* (AER), January 2000–December 2009. We compare the AER results with the population of full-length articles using randomization techniques and published in the *New England Journal of Medicine* (NEJM), 2000–2002.

Here are the results from our survey:

- All of the articles published in the AER (100 percent) fail to provide any information at all as to the balance or lack of balance of covariates and treatments in their experiment (Table 22.2, Questions 4a and 4b). That is a lot of occasions for effect reversal from Simpson's Paradox, from Student's Imbalance, and from other systematic errors of judgment under conditions of uncertainty.
- A mere 14 percent of the AER articles stratified the sample, producing, as Student, Deming, and Cox noted long ago, a lack of confidence in randomly generated results (Table 22.2, Question 3); practice was better in the NEJM (40 percent

[20] Excluding Fisher's philosophy from the survey design is natural. The reason is not because he was not a major figure in the development of statistics. Clearly, he was. It's because Fisher's philosophy and rhetoric was, as we have noted elsewhere (Ziliak, 2010*a*,*b*, 2011*b*, 2014; Ziliak and McCloskey, 2008: ch. 20–23), a major cause of today's randomization and significance school.

Table 22.1 Results of *New England Journal of Medicine* Survey of Randomization, Significance, and Validity (2000–2002), Ranked by Percent Yes

Survey Questions	Number of Applicable Articles	Percent Yes
Does the study...		
7. Do diagnostic tests to assess "internal validity"?	234	0
7a. If the study does diagnostic tests to asses "internal validity" does it: do nothing (0), plots residuals for test of normally distributed error terms (1), or tests for independence of error terms (2)?	234	0
16. Acknowledge that statistical significance (or the lack of it) is not decisive?	234	0
18. Specify a loss function or otherwise stipulate the meaning of effect sizes, such that the reader can assess the how "large is large" and how "small is small" questions?	234	0
19. If it does not specify a loss function, does the study discuss otherwise the implications of being wrong about the preferred hypothesis?	234	0
21. Seek mainly to demonstrate substantive significance?	234	0
23. Consider the validity of other types of evidence, that is, evidence not based upon formal experiment and artificial randomization?	234	0
5. Replicate a previous RCT or other types of empirical study?	234	1
9. Discuss its design relative to previous studies of the same?	234	1
13. Include cost and benefit data, such that one can determine the real net benefit of the experiment- adverse effects included?	234	1
17. Recognize that statistically insignificant results might have large and important substantive effects?	234	1
14. Include cost and benefit data such that the reader can estimate the net benefit of accepting the preferred hypothesis?	234	6
12. Compare results (such as effect sizes, magnitudes of coefficients, etc.) with previous studies?	234	14
2. Strive to test and estimate multiple treatments?	234	26
25. Provide conflict of interest information?	234	39
3. Design balance covariates (confounding variables) prior to experimentation? Or, if the study is an observational study, does it stratify the sample prior to data collection?	234	40
15. Explain the choice and implications of sample size?	234	48
20. Discuss the power of the test?	234	48
22. Mimic conventional best practice, in both experimentation and implementation, in the industry for the "treatment" in question?	234	51
1. Eschew the use of placebo control and no treatment?	234	52

Table 22.1 Continued

Survey Questions	Number of Applicable Articles	Percent Yes
6. Test hypotheses (or treatments and controls) at multiple places?	234	82
8. Does the study test the favored model on sub- populations or strata and/or test for robustness of estimates across different periods of time?	234	83
4a. Does the study discus questions of balance for sample strata and covariates?	234	84
4. Eschew balancing (and/or stratifying) after experimentation?	234	88
24. Is the study sponsored by a government, firm, or other non-academic entity?	234	93
4b. Does the study give estimated magnitudes of balance (or imbalance) in table, chart, or other form?	234	93
10. Defend the design of the experiment; for example, does it explain why it's using artificial randomization? Or, does the study explain eligibility criteria for participants' inclusion?	234	99
11. Provide sufficient details to allow replication- including details on how and when treatments and controls were actually administered?	234	100

Note: "Percent Yes" is the total number of Yes responses divided by the relevant number of articles.

Source: All full-length articles that use randomization published in the *New England Journal of Medicine*, January 2000–December 2002.

Table 22.2 Results of *American Economic Review* Survey of Randomization, Significance, and Validity (2000–2009), Ranked by Percent Yes

Survey Questions	Number of Applicable Articles	Percent Yes
Does the study . . .		
4a. Does the study discuss questions of balance for sample strata and covariates?	80	0
4b. Does the study give estimated magnitudes of balance (or imbalance) in table, chart, or other form?	80	0
16. Acknowledge that statistical significance (or the lack of it) is not decisive?	80	0
17. Recognize that statistically insignificant results might have large and important substantive effects?	80	0
18. Specify a loss function or otherwise stipulate the meaning of effect sizes, such that the reader can assess the how "large is large" and how "small is small" questions?	80	0

(*continued*)

Table 22.2 Continued

Survey Questions	Number of Applicable Articles	Percent Yes
19. If it does not specify a loss function, does the study discuss otherwise the implications of being wrong about the preferred hypothesis?	80	0
21. Seek mainly to demonstrate substantive significance?	80	0
25. Provide conflict of interest information?	80	0
20. Discuss the power of the test?	80	1
23. Consider the validity of other types of evidence, that is, evidence not based upon formal experiment and artificial randomization?	80	1
7. Do diagnostic tests to assess "internal validity"?	80	5
7a. If the study does diagnostic tests to asses "internal validity" does it: do nothing (0), plots residuals for test of normally distributed error terms (1), or tests for independence of error terms (2)?	80	5
15. Explain the choice and implications of sample size?	80	5
5. Replicate a previous RCT or other types of empirical study?	80	11
3. Design balance covariates (confounding variables) prior to experimentation? Or, if the study is an observational study, does it stratify the sample prior to data collection?	80	14
6. Test hypotheses (or treatments and controls) at multiple places?	80	20
22. Mimic conventional best practice, in both experimentation and implementation, in the industry for the "treatment" in question?	60	20
10. Defend the design of the experiment; for example, does it explain why it's using artificial randomization? Or, does the study explain eligibility criteria for participants' inclusion?	80	23
12. Compare results (such as effect sizes, magnitudes of coefficients, etc.) with previous studies?	80	26
14. Include cost and benefit data such that the reader can estimate the net benefit of accepting the preferred hypothesis?	80	29
8. Does the study test the favored model on sub-populations or strata and/or test for robustness of estimates across different periods of time?	80	36
13. Include cost and benefit data, such that one can determine the real net benefit of the experiment-adverse effects included?	80	44

Table 22.2 Continued

Survey Questions	Number of Applicable Articles	Percent Yes
2. Strive to test and estimate multiple treatments?	80	46
1a. Eschew the use of placebo control and no treatment? (All Field Experiments, not Laboratory)	21	48
9. Discuss its design relative to previous studies of the same?	80	60
24. Is the study sponsored by a government, firm, or other non-academic entity?	80	69
1b. Eschew the use of placebo control and no treatment? (All Experiments, Field and Laboratory)	49	73
4. Eschew balancing (and/or stratifying) after experimentation?	80	88
11. Provide sufficient details to allow replication- including details on how and when treatments and controls were actually administered?	80	98

Note: "Percent Yes" is the total number of Yes responses divided by the relevant number of articles.

Source: All full-length articles that use randomization published in the *American Economic Review*, March 2000–December 2009, excluding the *Proceedings*.

Table 22.3 Difference in Results Between *New England Journal of Medicine* and *American Economic Review* Survey of Randomization, Significance, and Validity, Ranked by Percent Yes, NEJM Minus AER

Survey Questions	Absolute Percent Difference
Does the study...	
4b. Does the study give estimated magnitudes of balance (or imbalance) in table, chart, or other form?	93
4a. Does the study discuss questions of balance for sample strata and covariates?	84
10. Defend the design of the experiment; for example, does it explain why it's using artificial randomization? Or, does the study explain eligibility criteria for participants' inclusion?	76
6. Test hypotheses (or treatments and controls) at multiple places?	62
9. Discuss its design relative to previous studies of the same?	59
20. Discuss the power of the test?	47
8. Does the study test the favored model on sub- populations or strata and/or test for robustness of estimates across different periods of time?	47
15. Explain the choice and implications of sample size?	43

(*continued*)

Table 22.3 Continued

Survey Questions	Absolute Percent Difference
13. Include cost and benefit data, such that one can determine the real net benefit of the experiment- adverse effects included?	42
25. Provide conflict of interest information?	39
22. Mimic conventional practice, in both experimentation and implementation, in the industry for the "treatment" in question?	31
3. Design balance covariates (confounding variables) prior to experimentation? Or, if the study is an observational study, does it stratify the sample prior to data collection?	26
24. Is the study sponsored by a government, firm, or other non-academic entity?	24
14. Include cost and benefit data such that the reader can estimate the net benefit of accepting the preferred hypothesis?	23
1b. Eschew the use of placebo control and no treatment? (All Experiments, Field and Laboratory)	22
2. Strive to test and estimate multiple treatments?	20
12. Compare results (such as effect sizes, magnitudes of coefficients, etc.) with previous studies?	12
5. Replicate a previous RCT or other types of empirical study?	10
7. Do diagnostic tests to assess "internal validity"?	5
7a. If the study does diagnostic tests to asses "internal validity" does it: do nothing (0), plots residuals for test of normally distributed error terms (1), or tests for independence of error terms (2)?	5
1a. Eschew the use of placebo control and no treatment? (All Field Experiments, not Laboratory)	4
11. Provide sufficient details to allow replication- including details on how and when treatments and controls were actually administered?	2
4. Eschew balancing (and/or stratifying) after experimentation?	1
17. Recognize that statistically insignificant results might have large and important substantive effects?	1
23. Consider the validity of other types of evidence, that is, evidence not based upon formal experiment and artificial randomization?	1
16. Acknowledge that statistical significance (or the lack of it) is not decisive?	0
18. Specify a loss function or otherwise stipulate the meaning of effect sizes, such that the reader can assess the how "large is large" and how "small is small" questions?	0
19. If it does not specify a loss function, does the study discuss otherwise the implications of being wrong about the preferred hypothesis?	0
21. Seek mainly to demonstrate substantive significance?	0

Note: "Absolute Percent Difference" is the absolute difference between the "Percent Yes" responses in the AER and the "Percent Yes" responses in the NEJM per question.

stratified), but that still leaves 6 of every 10 medical studies at risk of misleading conclusions from Simpson's Paradox and Student's Imbalance.

- None of the AER articles (0 percent) and less than 1 percent of the NEJM articles focused on substantive "size matters/how much" questions (Table 22.1 and Table 22.2, Questions 16–21). *Randomistas* base experimental conclusions exclusively on tests of statistical significance that reach or fail to reach the arbitrary 5 or 10 percent level of significance, ignoring the "oomph" (Ziliak and McCloskey, 2008).
- 11 percent of the AER articles and only 1 percent of the NEJM articles replicated a previous experiment, suggesting that more attention might be paid to establishing the external validity of randomized trials (Table 22.1 and Table 22.2, Question 5).
- None of the NEJM articles (0 percent) and only 5 percent of the AER articles did any graphing or other diagnostic tests on the distribution of error terms and of correlations to determine by how much their data depart, if they do, from the normal assumptions of internal validity (Table 22.1 and Table 22.2, Question 7).
- None of the NEJM articles (0 percent) and only 1 percent of the AER articles considered other sources of evidence before concluding that their statistically significant finding from one randomized set of data is "valid" (Table 22.1 and Table 22.2, Question 23); this finding confirms what the randomizing experimentalists themselves, from Banerjee to List, have claimed: they do not value evidence produced by other types of studies—econometric, historical, and other (contrast Harrison [2011], who does).
- Only 5 percent of the AER articles explain the choice and likely implications of their sample size selection and thus of the power of their tests (Table 22.2, Question 15 and Question 20). The Guinness Brewery and Student himself would be puzzled: don't we need to know the economically most efficient way of learning?
- Only 1 percent of NEJM articles include data on costs and benefits related to the experiment such that one might estimate the net benefit of the authors' favored hypotheses (Table 22.1, Question 13); authors of the AER performed better (although not exemplary) in this regard, with 44 of 80 or little more than half of the economics articles providing basic information about cost and benefit (Table 22.2, Question 13).
- More than two-thirds (69 percent) of the AER studies were sponsored by a government, business, or private grant-making agency, but none of them (0 percent) made a conflict-of-interest statement (Table 22.2, Questions 24 and 25).[21]

We see these and other problems played out in the works of our colleagues. On the question of validity, for example, consider the article by Salazar-Lindo et al. (2000) published in the NEJM. The article is the end result of a four-year study to test the benefits of a drug, racecadotril, for treating acute watery diarrhea in children. The authors studied

[21] On January 5, 2012, the American Economic Association adopted "extensions to [seven added] principles for author disclosure of conflict of interest," including disclosure of bank and corporate sponsorship, if any. See Epstein and Carrick-Hagenbarth (2016).

exclusively male infants (aged 3–35 months) with diarrhea, but they extrapolate their results onto adults, a leap of faith. They rely on controlled tests, although we applaud them for using the next-best alternative treatment for diarrhea rather than "no treatment," as economists are prone to do with poor people in studies from eyeglasses to mosquito nets (surprising in a field emphasizing the next-best alternative as the definition of cost).

The work by Salazar-Lindo et al. (2000) compares favorably with a study in the United Kingdom of antenatal steroids and infant mortality, first published back in 1972. "The outcome of interest was infant mortality due to complications of immaturity [in the womb]" (Howick, 2011: 18). Pointless debates about the "significance" and "insignificance" from a number of independently randomized controlled trials dragged on until 1995, delaying marketing of the steroid for pregnant mothers and causing many preventable deaths. In a systematic review of the combined studies (four in the final analysis), Patricia Crowley discovered that 1,000 of the premature babies (and their mothers) received the antenatal steroid and about the same number, 1,000, received a placebo. Of the babies who received the steroid, "70 died, while 130 [about twice as many] died in the placebo group" (Howick, 2011: 19).

In Fehr and Goette (2007; in the AER), the authors seek to find the effect of transitory wage changes on workers' labor supply by studying two Swiss bicycle messenger services and artificially manipulating the commission paid to messengers. But, as usual in both the AER and NEJM, there are no diagnostic checks for validity, whether internal or external. And there is no evidence of balance and stratification. Fehr and Goette studied bicycle messengers at two companies in Switzerland. Should readers assume their merely statistically "significant" findings are representative of the whole Swiss labor force? What, if anything, can we learn about American or Belgian or Indian bicycle messenger services?

Of the 80 articles using randomization techniques in the AER over the past decade, 21 of 80 or 26 percent are controlled field experiments wherein subjects are randomly selected by economists and offered one of two or more treatments, including a "no-treatment" or nil placebo control group in one-half (52 percent) of the real-world trials (Table 22.2, Question 1a). By "no treatment," we mean those studies in which a preferred treatment (a low-cost HIV test, a food voucher, a pair of eyeglasses) is experimentally withheld from a control group. For example, Jensen and Miller (2008) withheld food vouchers from poor Chinese farmers, and Thornton (2008) withheld HIV test vouchers from randomly selected African villagers living in Malawi.

The practice of giving no treatment at all appears to be more pronounced in the field journals of development and applied economics. For example, in 2013, in a sister journal, *American Economic Journal: Applied Economics*, edited by Esther Duflo, seven of the nine (i.e., 77 percent) RCTs published offered no treatment to the control group. Again, we found some pushback against "no treatment," and, again, the pushback came not from the economists but from the moral conscience of local teachers and staff cooperating with the economists. Fairlie and Robinson (2013: 215), for example, is a randomized controlled experiment designed to see if having a computer at home affects student academic success: "In discussing the logistics of the study with school officials, school principals expressed concern about the fairness of giving computers to a subset of eligible children. For this reason, we decided to give out computers to all eligible students. Treatment students received computers immediately, while control students had to wait until the end of the school year. Our main outcomes are all measured at the end of the school year, before the control students received their computers." The practice of withholding best-practice treatment from the control group is equally pronounced in drug and medical experiments. Of the 234 randomized trials published in the NEJM, nearly half (48 percent) offered participants in the control group a placebo or no treatment at all (Table 22.1, Question 1). None of the studies we examined discusses or justifies the practice of withholding best treatment from the control group.

In short, it would seem that a large majority of randomized field trials in economics and medicine are—economically, experimentally, and ethically speaking—out on a limb.

The Impartial Spectator Against *Homo Experimentalis*

In a recent opinion piece published by *Science*, "*Homo Experimentalis* Evolves," John List (2008) celebrates the randomized field experiments for which he is known:

> The fundamental challenge in the social sciences is how to go beyond correlational analysis to provide insights on causation. . . . Increasingly, insights on causation are also gained through the use of controlled experimentation. In this approach, causation is usually identified through randomization, much like controlled experiments used in drug trials. This approach combines the most attractive elements of the laboratory and of naturally occurring data: randomization.

The ethics of *Homo experimentalis* are thus constrained by an erroneous conception of scientific method and by an unexamined behaviorism. What would the impartial spectator say about RCTs? Testing the null hypothesis is not ethical if the randomized "control" is already known to be meaningfully less effective than best-practice treatment. Justice requires best-practice treatment, and proper benevolence should nudge it along. Prudence dictates due concern for efficiency and consistency, which have been shown to be lacking in randomized allocations of treatments and controls.

In Section III of *The Theory of Moral Sentiments*, "On Self Command," Smith observes (280):

> The man who acts according to the rules of perfect prudence, of strict justice, and of proper benevolence, may be said to be perfectly virtuous. But the most perfect knowledge of these rules will not alone enable him to act in this manner: his own passions are very apt to mislead him; sometimes to drive him and sometimes to seduce him to violate all the rules which he himself, in all his

> sober and cool hours, approves of. The most perfect knowledge, if it is not supported by the most perfect self-command, will not always enable him to do his duty.

We have shown here that RCTs in economics (and in medicine, too) routinely violate the rules of perfect prudence, strict justice, and proper benevolence.

In medicine, the alleged justification for RCTs is based on the idea of equipoise (Freedman, 1987). Equipoise is a suspended state of belief, an "indifference" between two or more treatments. When equipoise exists, the mainstream medical community argues that a null hypothesis can be formed and tested using an RCT (e.g., Royall, 1991). "There is widespread agreement that ethics requires that each clinical trial begin with an honest null hypothesis" (Freedman, 1987: 141). We believe we have rejected the argument from equipoise and thus blind randomization using theory and evidence illustrating Simpson's Paradox (a big problem), Student's Imbalance (a bigger problem), and ethical-economic thinking at the margin (the biggest problem of all).

At their best, RCTs are, as David Cox noted, preliminary studies designed under desperation to alleviate pure ignorance and find something, anything. Deming agreed and noted that randomized studies offer no conclusions of real-world importance, save possibly to help discover the categories and covariates to be stratified and balanced in a more relevant experiment. At their worst, RCTs are—like Tuskegee and Milgram (Milgram, 1974)—conclusive only in the moral stratum. On average, they do not filter out noise from signal.

In field experiments, we are in a sense serving two different and powerful masters; the one, the warm glow in our hearts, our desire to help people in the real world, and to make a positive difference in their lives; the other, the cold and exclusively selfish tug for academic fame, wealth, and longevity. The one tug is active the other passive in its main appeal to our passions and reasons, thus affecting our self-command. Which master is recommended by the spectator is, we believe, now evident. Randomization + statistical significance = validity is a popular but false equation; the result is not equal to the cause and hasn't been since Student. Randomized trials are neither necessary nor sufficient. And they're often unethical.

Acknowledgments

We thank the editors, George DeMartino and Deirdre N. McCloskey, and Tim Harford, Jason Houle, Gary Langer, Casey Mulligan, Martin Ravallion, Flora S. Ziliak, and James P. Ziliak for comments on a previous version of this manuscript. Our thanks also to Julian Alston and Koen Deconinck for comments made at the 6th Annual Conference of the American Association of Wine Economists, Princeton, New Jersey, June 2012.

References

Alderson, P. 1996. "Equipoise as a Means of Managing Uncertainty: Personal, Communal, and Proxy." *Journal of Medical Ethics* 22(3, June): 131–139.

Altman, D. G., K. F. Schultz, D. Moher, M. Egger, F. Davidoff, D. Elbourne, P. Gotzsche, and T. Lang. 2001. "The Revised CONSORT Statement for Reporting Randomized Trials: Explanation and Elaboration." *Annals of Internal Medicine* 134: 663–691.

Angrist, J. D., and J. -S. Pischke. 2009. *Mostly Harmless Econometrics.* Princeton: Princeton University Press.

Angrist, J. D., and A. B. Krueger. 2001. "Instrumental Variables and the Search for Identification: From Supply and Demand to Natural Experiments." *Journal of Economic Perspectives* 15(4, Fall): 69–85.

Banerjee, A., and E. Duflo. 2011. *Poor Economics: A Radical Rethinking of the Way to Fight Global Poverty.* New York: Public Affairs.

Beaven, E. S. 1947. *Barley: Fifty Years of Observation and Experiment.* London: Duckworth.

Box, G. E. P., W. G. Hunter, and J. S. Hunter. 1978 [2005]. *Statistics for Experimenters.* New York: John Wiley & Sons.

Chalmers, I. 2003. "Fisher and Bradford Hill: Theory and Pragmatism?" *International Journal of Epidemiology* 32: 922–924.

Cochrane, W. G. 1976. "Early Development of Techniques in Comparative Experimentation." In *On the History of Statistics and Probability*, edited by D. B. Owen, p. 126. New York: Marcel Dekker.

Cochrane, W. G. 1989. "Fisher and the Analysis of Variance." In *Fisher: An Appreciation*, edited by S. E. Fienberg and D. V. Hinkley, pp. 17–34. New York: Springer-Verlag.

Cox, D. 1958. *Planning of Experiments.* New York: Wiley.

Deaton, A. 2007. "Evidence-Based Aid Must Not Become the Latest in a Long String of Development Fads." In *Making Aid Work*, edited by A. Banerjee, pp. 60–61. Cambridge, MA: MIT Press.

DeMartino, G. 2011. *The Economist's Oath: On the Need For and Content of Professional Economic Ethics.* New York: Oxford University Press.

Deming, W. E. 1978. "Sample Surveys: The Field." In *International Encyclopedia of Statistics*, edited by W. H. Kruska and J. M. Tanur, pp. 867–884. New York and London: Free Press (Macmillan).

Duflo, E., R. Glennerster, and M. Kremer. 2007. *Using Randomization in Development Economics Research: A Toolkit.* MIT Department of Economics and J-PAL Poverty Action Lab.

Easterly, W. 2009. "The Civil War in Development Economics," AidWatch: Just Asking That Aid Benefit the Poor. Blog of William Easterly. Available at http://aidwatchers.com/2009/12/the-civil-war-in-development-economics/

Epstein and Carrick-Hagenbarth. 2016. "Consideration on Conflict of Interest in Academic Economics." In *The Oxford Handbook of Professional Economic Ethics*, edited by G. DeMartino and D. McCloskey, pp. 475–490. New York: Oxford University Press.

Fairlie, R. W., and J. Robinson. 2013. "Experimental Evidence on the Effects of Home Computers on Academic Achievement Among Schoolchildren." *American Economic Review: Applied Economics* 5(3, July): 211–240.

Fehr, E., and L. Goette. 2007. "Do Workers Work More If Wages Are High? Evidence from a Randomized Field Experiment." *American Economic Review* 97(March): 298–317.

Fisher, R. A. 1925 [1928]. *Statistical Methods for Research Workers*. New York: G. E. Stechart.

Fisher, R. A. 1935. *The Design of Experiments*. Oliver & Boyd: Edinburgh.

Fisher, R. A., and W. A. Mackenzie. 1923. "Studies in Crop Variation: II. The Manurial Response of Different Potato Varieties." *Journal of Agricultural Science* 13: 311–320.

Fisher, R. A., and F. Yates. 1938. *Statistical Tables for Biological, Agricultural and Medical Research*, Sixth edition. Edinburgh: Oliver and Boyd.

Freedman, B. 1987. "Equipoise and the Ethics of Clinical Research." *New England Journal of Medicine* 317(3): 141–145.

Glewwe, P., A. Park, and M. Zhao. 2012. "Visualizing Development: Eyeglasses and Academic Performance in Primary Schools in China." Working Paper WP12–2 (January) Center for International Food and Agricultural Policy Research, University of Minnesota.

Gosset, W. S. 1936. "Co-operation in Large-scale Experiments." *Supplement to the Journal of the Royal Statistical Society* 3: 115–136.

Gosset, W. S. 1962. *Letters of William Sealy Gosset to R. A. Fisher. Vols. 1–5*. Eckhart Library, University of Chicago. Private circulation.

Gray, F. D. 1998. *The Tuskegee Syphilis Study*. Montgomery: New South Books.

Harrison, G. W. 2011. "Randomization and Its Discontents." *Journal of African Economies* 20: 626–652.

Heckman, J. J., and E. J. Vytlacil. 2007. "Econometric Evaluation of Social Programs, Part I: Causal Models, Structural Models and Econometric Policy Evaluation." In *Handbook of Econometrics 6B*, edited by J. J. Heckman and E. Leamer, pp. 4779–4874. Amsterdam: Elsevier.

Herberich, D. H., S. D. Levitt, and J. A. List. 2009. "Can Field Experiments Return Agricultural Economics to the Glory Days?" *American Journal of Agricultural Economics* 91: 1259–1265.

Howick, J. 2011. *The Philosophy of Evidence-Based Medicine*. Oxford, UK: Wiley and Sons.

Jayaraman, K. 1999. *A Statistical Manual for Forestry Research*. Bangkok: United Nations Food and Agriculture Organization.

Jensen, R. T., and N. H. Miller. 2008. "Giffen Behavior and Subsistence Consumption." *American Economic Review* 98(4): 1553–1557.

Johnston, S. C., J. D. Rotenberg, S. Katrak, W. S. Smith, and J. S. Elkins. 2006. "Effect of a U.S. National Institutes of Health Programme of Clinical Trials on Public Health and Costs." *Lancet* 367: 1319–1327.

Jones, J. H. 1992. *Bad Blood: The Tuskegee Syphilis Experiment*. New York: Free Press.

Kadane, J. B. 1986. "Progress Toward a More Ethical Method for Clinical Trials." *The Journal of Medicine and Philosophy*: 385–404.

Karlan, D., and J. Appel. 2011. *More than Good Intentions: How a New Economics is Helping to Solve Global Poverty*. New York: Dutton.

Lanham, R. 1991. *A Handlist of Rhetorical Terms*. Los Angeles: University of California Press.

Levitt, S. D., and J. A. List. 2009. "Field Experiments in Economics: The Past, the Present, and the Future." *European Economic Review* 53: 1–18.

Lilford, R., and J. Jackson. 1995. "Equipoise and the Ethics of Randomization." *Journal of the Royal Society of Medicine* 88(Oct.): 552–559.

Lindley, D. 1991. *Making Decisions*. New York: Wiley.

List, J. 2008. "Homo Experimentalis Evolves." *Science* 11(321–5886): 207–208.

McCloskey, D. N., and S. T. Ziliak. 1996. "The Standard Error of Regressions." *Journal of Economic Literature* 34(March): 97–114.

Meyers, J., G. Sacks, H. van Es, and J. Vanden Heuvel. 2011. "Improving Vineyard Sampling Efficiency via Dynamic Spatially Explicit Optimisation." *Australian Journal of Grape and Wine Research* 17: 306–315.

Milgram, S. 1974. *Obedience to Authority: An Experimental View*. New York: Harper/Collins.

Mulligan, C. 2014. "The Economics of Randomized Experiments." The New York Times, Economix blog, March 5, 2014. Available at http://economix.blogs.nytimes.com/2014/03/05/the-economics-of-randomized-experiments/

Neyman, J. 1934. "On the Two Different Aspects of the Representative Method: The Method of Stratified Sampling and the Method of Purposive Selection." *Journal of the Royal Statistical Society* 97: 558–625.

Parker, I. 2010. "The Poverty Lab." *The New Yorker* May 17, pp. 79–80.

Pearson, E. S. 1938. "Some Aspects of the Problem of Randomization: II. An Illustration of Student's Inquiry into the Effect of 'Balancing' in Agricultural Experiment." *Biometrika* 30: 159–179.

Ravallion, M. 2014, March 24. Two letters of correspondence to authors: Comments on Ziliak's and Teather-Posadas's "The Unprincipled Randomization Principle in Economics and Medicine." Washington, DC: Georgetown University.

Rawls, J. 1971. *A Theory of Justice*. Cambridge: Belknap Press.

Reddy, S. 2012. "Randomise This! On Poor Economics." *Review of Agrarian Studies* 2(2): 60–73.

Rodrik, D. 2008. "The New Development Economics: We Shall Experiment, but How Shall We Learn?" Brookings Development Conference, Harvard University, John F. Kennedy School of Government.

Royall, R. M. 1991. "Ethics and Statistics in Randomized Clinical Trials." *Statistical Science* 6(1 February): 52–62.

Rubin, D. 1990. "Comment: Neyman (1923) and Causal Inference in Experiments and Observational Studies." *Statistical Science* 5: 472–480.

Salazar-Lindo, E., J. Sebastian-Hart, et al. 2000. "Racecadotril in the Treatment of Acute Watery Diarrhea in Children." *New England Journal of Medicine* 343(7): 463–467.

Sen, A. 2006. "What Do We Want from a Theory of Justice?" *Journal of Philosophy* 103(5 May): 215–238.

Smith, A. 1759 [1791, 2009]. *The Theory of Moral Sentiments*. New York: Penguin. Introduction by Amartya Sen.

Street, D. 1990. "Fisher's Contributions to Agricultural Statistics." *Biometrics* 46: 937–945.

Student. 1911. "Appendix to Mercer and Hall's Paper on The Experimental Error of Field Trials.' *Journal of Agricultural Science* 4: 128–131." In *Student. Student's Collected Papers*, edited by E. Pearson and J. Wishart, pp. 49–52. London: Biometrika Trust.Student. 1923. "On Testing Varieties of Cereals." *Biometrika* 15: 271–293.

Student. 1926. "Mathematics and Agronomy." *Journal of the American Society of Agronomy* 18. Reprinted in *Student's Collected Papers* (1942), edited by E. S. Pearson and J. Wishart, pp. 121–134. London: University College London.

Student. 1938 [posthumous]. "Comparison Between Balanced and Random Arrangements of Field Plots." *Biometrika* 29: 363–378.

Student. 1942 [posthumous]. *Student's Collected Papers*, edited by E. S. Pearson and J. Wishart. London: University College London.

Thornton, R. L. 2008. "The Demand for, and Impact of, Learning HIV Status." *American Economic Review* 98(5): 1829–1863.

Tippett, L. 1958. *The Methods of Experiments*. New York: Wiley.

van Es, H. M., C. P. Gomes, M. Selman, and C. L. van Es. 2007. "Spatially-Balanced Complete Block Designs for Field Experiments." *Geoderma* 140: 346–352.

Varian, H. 2011, April 27. "Are Randomized Trials the Future of Economics? Federalism Offers Opportunities for Casual [sic] Experimentation." *The Economist*. Available at http://www.economist.com/node/21256696

World Bank. 2004. *Monitoring and Evaluation: Some Tools, Methods, and Approaches*. Washington, DC: The World Bank.

Yates, F. 1964. "Sir Ronald Fisher and the Design of Experiments." *Biometrics* 20: 307–321.

Ziliak, S. T. 2008. "Guinnessometrics: The Economic Foundation of 'Student's' *t*." *Journal of Economic Perspectives* 22(Fall): 199–216.

Ziliak, S. T. 2010*a*. "The *Validus Medicus* and a New Gold Standard." *Lancet* 376(9738, July): 324–325.

Ziliak, S. T. 2010*b*. "Significant errors—Author's reply [to Stephen Senn]." *Lancet* 376(9750, October): 1392.

Ziliak, S. T. 2011*a*. "Matrixx v. Siracusano and Student v. Fisher: Statistical Significance on Trial." *Significance* 8: 131–134.

Ziliak, S. T. 2011*b*. "W. S. Gosset and Some Neglected Concepts in Experimental Statistics: Guinnessometrics II." *Journal of Wine Economics* 6: 252–277.

Ziliak, S. T. 2014. "Balanced Versus Randomized Field Experiments in Economics: Why W. S. Gosset aka 'Student' Matters." *Review of Behavioral Economics* 1(1): 167–208.

Ziliak, S. T., and D. N. McCloskey. 2008. *The Cult of Statistical Significance: How The Standard Error Costs Us Jobs, Justice, and Lives*. Ann Arbor: University of Michigan Press.

4. Conflict of Interest

CHAPTER 23

PROFESSIONAL DISEQUILIBRIUM

Conflict of Interest in Economics

DENNIS F. THOMPSON

Introduction

The economics profession has been slow to adopt rules regulating conflict of interest, and the rules it has finally adopted are weaker than those of other professions. The rules mandate only limited disclosure, and avoid completely any other kind of regulation. Some economists still resist even this modest regime of disclosure (Pritchett, 2011). In medicine, physicians and researchers are required under certain conditions to refuse some kinds of research support, accept monitoring, or forego participation in some stages of research and treatment (Institute of Medicine, 2009: 62–96; Perlman, 2010). In other academic professions, the rules are usually less elaborate but still require more than disclosure. For example, the American Sociological Association's code instructs members to avoid personal gain from confidential information obtained from reviewing a manuscript or serving on a proposal review panel (American Sociological Association, 1999).

It may be tempting to try to explain the resistance in terms of assumptions about self-interest that economists accept in their own models. Some might say that economists are more likely than other academics to think that maximizing their income is a commendable aim, and more interested in seizing opportunities for extra compensation. Regulations that threaten to diminish these supplemental sources of income are naturally resisted, and given these assumptions, easily justified. Furthermore, regulations are seen as unnecessary because bias can be kept in check through competition in the marketplace of ideas, where professional reputations are at stake. Bias disappears at this professional equilibrium.

Yet, like many economic explanations, this conjecture is no doubt too simple. The motivations of economists, like those of other professionals, are mixed, and the variation among economists, like that among other groups, is great. Some economists resist conflict of interest regulation because they believe it is wrong on the merits. Instead of trying to explain the motives of the resisters, we should address the reasons that they give or could give for it. That is a more constructive way to understand conflict of interest, and to clear away the misconceptions about it.

The case for conflict of interest regulation is by no means obvious, and the objections to it are not only self-interested. If we wish to create and sustain an effective regime of regulation, we need to understand more fully its ethical basis—the nature of conflict of interest itself, the risks it creates, and the methods by which it can be regulated. To appreciate the significance of conflict of interest in economics, we need to put the ethics of economists in the context of ethics of the professions more generally.

Paradoxes of Conflict of Interest

Unlike norms prohibiting other unethical conduct, rules regulating conflict of interest are themselves ethically problematic. They seem to make unethical demands even while promoting ethics. This gives rise to two different but related paradoxes.

The ethical norms that proscribe typical wrongs such as lying, cheating, and stealing directly address the conduct they are supposed to prevent. The rules regulating conflict of interest do not directly prohibit bias or other forms of research misconduct they are intended to check. They focus the ethical judgment on the researcher, rather than the research; they attend to the way the research came about, rather than to its validity. On its face, this approach seems a version of a classic logical fallacy—the argumentum ad hominem. It appears to advocate rejecting the truth of a proposition because of the motives of the person who asserts it. This seems not only illogical but also unfair—to the researcher, the profession, and ultimately the public who might benefit from the knowledge. We should examine research and scholarship on its merits, a critic would say, not the character, motives, or associations of the researchers and scholars. Even if conflict of interest rules are necessary to keep the profession ethical, they seem to require judgments that are in this sense unethical.

The second paradox grants that the professional is a legitimate object of ethical judgment, but points to a tension between the appearance and reality of the professional's conduct. Conflict of interest rules are at least partly about appearances. Having a conflict of interest does not mean that you are influenced improperly, only that your decisions may be reasonably perceived as being improperly influenced. That is what is distinctive about the rules, and part of their ethical justification. Yet in personal ethics, we do not usually believe that appearances should matter that much, certainly not as much as reality. It looks unfair (even unethical) to judge professionals according to how they appear to be acting rather than how they are actually acting. Conflict of interest rules set an ethical standard that seems to treat professionals unethically.

On closer examination, these paradoxes turn out to be only apparent. Both arise as a result of misconceptions about the purposes of conflict of interest regulation. They can be resolved by clarifying the meaning of conflict of interest and the justification for its regulation. The first results from a failure to recognize that bias is not easily detected, and that the purpose of regulation is not only to prevent bias but also to preserve public confidence. The second results from a failure to appreciate the ethical basis of appearances, and to distinguish among the various publics that judge them.

The Concept of Conflict of Interest

A conflict of interest is a set of circumstances that are reasonably believed to create a substantial risk that professional judgment of a primary interest will be unduly influenced by a secondary interest.[1] The primary interest refers to the purpose of the professional activity, such as the integrity of the research. The secondary interest is typically financial gain. The conflict creates a presumed risk, based on past experience in other relevant cases, not on an assessment of the risks only in a current case. Each of these three elements requires some explanation.

The *primary interest* that conflict of interest policies seek to protect varies according to the purpose of the activity. In the case of economics and similar academic disciplines, they include maintaining the integrity of research and the education of students and future scholars. These should be the primary interest both for individuals in a professional role and for professional associations and educational institutions.

Describing exactly what the primary interest is for professionals and for various institutions may be controversial. Sometimes primary interests conflict with each other. In medicine, for example, researchers may confront a choice between the welfare of the patients in a research protocol and the successful completion of the research. In economics, the dilemmas are usually not so acute. They typically involve decisions about how to balance the demands of teaching and research, or how much to simplify technical findings for public consumption. (The expanding use of randomized control trials in development economics, however, is beginning to raise ethical issues that are more similar to those in medical research.)

In any case, the important point is that the conflicts among primary interests differ fundamentally from conflicts between primary and secondary interests—the kind that are the object of conflict of interest regulation. In the case of conflicts between primary interests, neither can be said in advance to have priority. That is not so with conflicts

[1] This definition of the concept, now widely used in the literature and policy statements, was proposed in Dennis F. Thompson, "Understanding Financial Conflicts of Interest," *New England Journal of Medicine* 329: 573–576 (August 19, 1993). See Institute of Medicine, pp. 45–48.

between primary and secondary interests: the premise of conflict of interest regulation is that the primary interests should dominate secondary interest. They should have decisive weight in the professional decisions any individual or institution make.

Secondary interests include the desire for professional advancement, recognition for personal achievement, favors to friends and family, assistance to one's students and colleagues, and most saliently, financial gain. Most secondary interests, including financial gain, are, within limits, perfectly legitimate (often desirable) goals. The secondary interests are objectionable only when they have greater weight than the primary interest in professional decisions.

Conflict of interest rules typically focus on financial gain, not because it is more corrupting than the other interests but because it is relatively more objective, fungible, and quantifiable. It is therefore more effectively and fairly regulated than other secondary interests. That point is neglected by those who try to dismiss concerns about conflict of interest on the grounds that it is arbitrary to single out financial conflicts, or that it is futile to try to regulate conflicts because they are so pervasive.

The *conflict* that is to be regulated is not an occurrence but a set of circumstances that create or increase a risk that primary interests will be compromised as a result of the pursuit of secondary interests. The claim that there is a conflict of interest expresses a tendency. It is based on common past experience: we have learned that under certain circumstances professional judgment about a primary interest is at risk of being unduly influenced by a secondary interest. Rules that control this danger, even if the threat is actualized in relatively few cases, are intended to protect against this risk. Therefore, a conflict of interest exists whether or not a particular individual or institution is actually influenced by the secondary interest. In any particular case, individuals may be said to have a conflict of interest even though their decisions do not actually impede primary professional goals or violate primary professional obligations.

The Purposes of Conflict of Interest Policies

Institutions, professional associations, and governments on behalf of the public establish policies to address the problem of conflict of interest. The policies try to ensure that professional decisions are made on the basis of primary, not secondary interests. To the extent that they are effective in this specific goal, they serve two general purposes.

Integrity

First, conflict of interest policies help maintain the integrity of professional judgment (Association of American Medical Colleges, 2008; Institute of Medicine, 2009: 48–50).

They seek to minimize the risk of undue influence from secondary interests, which should be irrelevant to the merits of decisions about the conduct of research, teaching, and consulting. Bias is the most obvious way in which integrity can be compromised[2]. Notice that the bias they target is financial, not political or methodological. Some critics of the economics profession understandably regard the latter as even more troubling. They allege that a bias in the profession in favor of the free market solutions contributed to the financial crisis (Leonhardt, 2008; Kaletsky, 2011). But the purpose of conflict of interest policies is much more limited. They are not intended to address methodological or ideological bias.

No doubt some financial bias can be detected by the normal process of professional review and criticism. Economists are not shy about pointing out the biases of their colleagues. The principle expressed in the first paradox is right as far as it goes: to protect against bias, we should assume that most professionals are honest, and we should start by looking at the results of the research on the merits, not the motives. But because of the circumstances in which professionals now work and the increased influence they have on public policy, maintaining professional integrity requires more. The first paradox can be resolved by recognizing that both of the principles it expresses can be valid: assess both the content and the circumstances of research.

Conflict of interest policies do not assume that all or even most professionals will let financial gain actually bias their research, only that there is a significant chance that some will. It is often said that no economist would rationally risk his or her reputation for the relatively small gains that are usually received from consulting or research support. No doubt few if any would do so consciously. But the bias that conflict of interest policies target is almost always unconscious. Studies of drug company influence on medical professionals suggest that even very small gifts can create favorable attitudes that result in persistent biases of various kinds (Katz et al., 2003; Adair and Holmgren, 2005). Perhaps economists demand a higher price. They may not be swayed as easily as doctors by gifts, honoraria, and one-time research support, but surely they are as susceptible, if not more so, to the influence of the continuing relationships that give them access to data, investment opportunities, and board memberships, all of which promise larger and continuing gains. These relationships are less transparent, and give rise to influences that harder to detect, even by the individuals being influenced. More generally, a growing literature on unconscious bias shows that even well-educated and self-aware professionals are vulnerable to unconscious bias that results from financial support of their activities (Gilovich, 1991; Loewenstein et al., 1992; Babcock et al., 1995; Institute of Medicine, 2009: 359–366).

It is difficult to investigate bias because economists with financial interests related to their research do not typically disclose their affiliations. A study of 19 prominent

[2] Institute of Medicine, 2009, 24–25, 39, 41, 43,107. Violations of other standards of professional practice, such as timely publication of research, fair treatment of students and post-docs, and appropriate acknowledgement of ideas and sources, are also risks the integrity of the profession, but they are covered by other kinds of rules.

economists found that 15 had close financial connections to organizations that took public positions on financial reform but "infrequently and inconsistently" disclosed their affiliations in relevant publications (Carrick-Hagenbarth and Epstein, 2012). A more recent study by Luigi Zingales (2012) found that, in a sample of "quality" papers, those that favor industry views are much more likely to be cited and to be published.[3] He identified numerous sources of bias in the publication process, including the board affiliations of editors, the greater resources devoted to studies that reach positive conclusions about a company or industry, and the greater access to data given to economists who are known to write favorably about a company or an industry. These economists tend to act like the regulators who (as other economists have shown) are often "captured" by the industry with which they are associated.

Although the evidence of bias in economics is so far limited, the studies of other professions should give economists pause. By now, there is a considerable body of evidence showing that biomedical research funded by the industry companies is more likely to produce results favorable to the companies, and less likely to report negative findings. "Strong and consistent evidence shows that industry-sponsored research tends to draw pro-industry conclusions" (Bekelman et al., 2003; Brennen et al., 2006; Campbell et al., 2007; Institute of Medicine, 2009: 104–108; Zinner et al., 2009). The correlations certainly do not show that the bias is deliberate, nor can other explanations be completely ruled out. But the connection is striking, and the tilt toward the sponsors in the results is manifest, whatever its cause.

Is economics different? Harvard economist John Campbell, who appeared in the film *Inside Job* attempting to defend the profession against charges of ignoring conflict of interest, acknowledges the need for more disclosure. But he draws a distinction between "fields like medicine, where researchers can suppress data that don't support their or their sponsors' desired outcomes, and economics, where most research is based on publicly available information."[4]

It is probably true that most of the source data in economics is publicly available — though only for those economists and others who know where to look and how to use the data. But the various forms of preparation of the data—creating subsets, operationalizing the measures, trimming extreme responses—are much less accessible. In statistical

[3] Zingales (2012) also finds that economists who serve on boards are four times more likely than other expert economists to believe that executive compensation accurately reflects the marginal contribution, and that shareholders should not have a say about the compensation.

[4] Quoted in Ben Casselman, "Economists Set Rules on Ethics," *Wall Street Journal*, January 9, 2012. A Cambridge University economist defends the profession by: "I don't think economics is particularly bad compared to other professions . . . doctors routinely prescribe drugs . . . without telling the patient that [they have] been to a nice conference in Bali that was funded by a particular drug company whose drug [they are] prescribing at the moment . . . I don't think that we can blame the economists too much for being exceptionally kind of sinister in this regard," Ha-Joong Chang, "No Worse than Doctors," in Institute for New Economic Thinking, History of Economics Playground, Bretton Woods, Part I: Ethics in Economics, "Are there conflicts of interest in economics today?" September 11, 2011. Available at: http://ineteconomics.org/blog/playground/bretton-woods-past-and-present-1-ethics-economics

studies, the researcher in effect creates a derived database, which is rarely made public. Economists may be more inclined to share all their research materials than medical researchers (who are often limited by proprietary restrictions). But even when everything is public, researchers rarely bother to try to replicate other studies. Replication may be even less common in economics than in medical science (Hamermesh, 2007). Furthermore, financial interests presumably reinforce the well-known bias in favor of publishing positive results (Ioannidis, 2005; Dwan et al., 2008). Under these conditions, then, the normal process of scholarly review is not a very reliable method for exposing bias resulting from financial interest.

Furthermore, much influential work by economists is not peer-reviewed. Research takes the form of policy papers, congressional testimony, expert reports or other forms of public statements that even if based on research are not actually published as research or subject to the rigors of disciplinary review. A striking example is the now infamous report co-authored by Frederic Mishkin (who was also featured in *Inside Job*). Just before the Icelandic banking system collapsed, the paper sought to reassure investors and others that the Icelandic banking system was stable. Mishkin did not disclose that he received $124,000 from the Icelandic Chamber of Commerce, which published the report (Mishkin and Herbertsson, 2006).

The consulting reports and other public statements by economists generally have a more immediate effect than do the results of clinical research. When those results lead to new drugs or devices, the applications are subjected to years of testing and review before they can be approved for use. The conclusions of economists are not mediated by a similarly extended process of testing. They are not certified for safety and effectiveness.

There are also economic reasons to doubt that the marketplace of economic publication works smoothly to expose bias. As economist Paul Seabright observes, this particular "marketplace for ideas suffers major market failure, including a very major problem of externalities since ideas compete for a scarce and almost open-access resource which is the limited attention of decision-makers" (Seabright, 2011). Given this scarcity, a small number of experts are able to command monopoly power. The "buyers of expertise" tend to use unreliable indicators of quality, and many "don't even want quality in the sense of theories that are true: they want theories that [only] look true but advance the buyer's own interests in the wider world." In this kind of market, reputational incentives do not operate dependably to produce objective and impartial results.

Perhaps partly for these reasons, one of the profession's most distinguished economists, Joseph Stiglitz, called attention more than a decade ago to the ethical obligations of economists who act as advisors both in private and public life.[5] He noted that "ethical norms require disclosure of significant conflict of interest, reflecting the precept of honesty." He stated that "it is immoral not to disclose the conflict of interest, so that

[5] Stiglitz, 2000. For a general argument that advisors bear more responsibility for the consequences of their advice than is commonly assumed, see D. F. Thompson, *Restoring Responsibility: Ethics in Government, Business and Healthcare* (Cambridge University Press, 2005), "The Responsibility of Advisers," pp. 33–49.

those affected can take appropriate precautions." He criticized colleagues who "take advantage of inside information obtained as an advisor for profit" or "directly use connections generated in [their] advisory role for profit." He called for greater disclosure, but also noted that it "does not totally eliminate, the danger that advice would be driven by self-interest."

One reason that disclosure does not eliminate the problem is that the conflicts in economics are typically more diffuse than those in medicine. In this respect, economics *is* different from medicine, but in a way that makes the problem more insidious and the need for more far-reaching regulation greater. Economists in their research publications do not usually promote a particular product or company in which they have holdings. But some publish analyses or give testimony about regulatory rules that could have substantial if indirect effects on their own investments. The problem has been most evident in the financial industry but is increasingly prevalent in the world of information technology, where economists not only consult but also sit on boards of companies that benefit from policies they advocate (e.g., regarding the economics of intellectual property). Even harder to detect is the subtle cognitive bias that comes from having close and continuing connections to the industry about which you are writing. The more you work for an industry, the more you see the world its way. In many cases, there are few experts on the industry, and all have industry ties. The industry captures the economists not through direct grants supporting their research, but through a gradual process in which economists, already predisposed to favor market solutions, come to thoroughly adopt the perspective of the particular industry.

Confidence

Prevention of bias is not the only purpose of the rules, not even the most important one. Conflict of interest policies are necessary to sustain public confidence in professional judgment and the profession as a whole.[6] This is the more comprehensive goal because it justifies applying the rules to everyone, even those known to their friends and colleagues as models of integrity. Here the point is to minimize or eliminate circumstances that would cause reasonable persons to suspect that professional judgment has been improperly influenced, whether or not it has in the particular case. The second paradox—the ethical tension between reality and appearance— dissolves when we recognize that the concern for appearances has an ethical basis.

[6] Kelch, 2002. In their letter to the president of the American Economic Association, some 300 economists urged the adoption of a code of ethics by noting: "As the economics profession serves a prominent role in economic policy, the public's confidence in the integrity of the profession will, in part, depend on how the issue of potential conflict of interest is addressed" (Sewell Chan, "Letter Calls on Economists to Adopt Code of Ethics, *New York Times* [January 4, 2011]). Available at http://economix.blogs.nytimes.com/2011/01/04/letter-calls-on-economists-to-adopt-code-of-ethics/

When a professional accepts financial support from interested corporations under certain conditions (as specified by conflict of interest rules), the public is ethically justified in believing that the professional's judgment has been improperly influenced and also justified in then acting on that belief. The professional is guilty of failing to take into account the reasonable reactions of citizens. That is an ethical violation in itself.[7]

The justification for the confidence goal should be distinguished from the type of argument (common in discussions of rule utilitarianism) that judges particular acts by appeals to general rules. In a rule utilitarian argument, an overly broad rule is justified by showing that the costs of judging each case of a conflict are greater than the costs of wrongly judging some cases. The confidence argument differs in two respects. First, it counts as a cost, not simply the risk that a case might be wrongly decided, but also the likelihood that the public will perceive the case to have been wrongly decided. Public confidence could be undermined, and misconduct by others encouraged, even if a case were rightly decided but not so perceived. Second, the rationale for the policy recognizes that many of the people who are affected by the work of professionals (such as economists' policy recommendations) are not in a position to assess their motives and therefore to make any judgments about costs and benefits of regulating the conflicts.

Prompted in part by highly publicized scandals and the threat of greater governmental regulation, the medical profession began early to adopt conflict of interest policies (Institute of Medicine, 2009: 35–41; Murray and Johnston, 2010). Presumably, most medical professionals believed that the conduct exposed in the scandals was not typical, and that most of their colleagues were honest. But they recognized that the profession depends on public trust, and that the absence of regulation could jeopardize it.

The negative publicity that followed the financial crisis seems to be having a similar effect on the economics profession. Even though it is not plausible to claim that the absence of conflict of interest rules was a cause of the crisis, the increase in public criticism of economists and the apparent decline in confidence in the profession has caused many leading economists and their major professional association to take the problem of conflict of interest more seriously than they had before. It might be noted that in Gallup surveys, doctors still rank high in public confidence (just below the military personnel and nurses) (Gallup, 2012). The surveys do not ask about economists, but some within the profession have begun to worry that if economists were included now, they might well rank in the bottom third, somewhere in this descending list: lawyers, stockbrokers, telemarketers, lobbyists, or car salespeople (Hollenbeck, 2014).

The medical profession recognized that the public whose confidence they need is not limited to patient and research subjects, who may have other concerns on their mind.

[7] The potential effect on the conduct of others is the principal reason that Thomist ethics has traditionally treated appearing to do wrong under certain conditions as a distinct wrong. The wrong is called "giving scandal" and is defined as providing the "occasion for another's fall." It is considered a sin if one's otherwise permissible action is of the kind that is in itself conducive to sin, and it remains sinful whether or not one intends it to have any effect on others [Thomas Aquinas, *Summa Theologiae* (New York: McGraw-Hill, 1972), Vol. 35, pp. 109–37].

The part of the public that is no less important includes legislators, foundation heads, editorial writers, and other opinion leaders. To the extent that these leaders begin to distrust the profession, they are likely to be less generous in providing research support and more insistent on greater external regulation of the research they do support. That began to happen in biomedical research. In the absence of policies supported by the profession and the institution in which professionals work, the actions of only a few individuals can fuel public distrust, with consequences that spill over on to colleagues, students, and the profession as a whole. The credibility of economics in the public sphere can be undermined by a minority of economists pursuing their private interests. If the profession shows indifference toward conflicts, the distrust increases further. Once trust is lost, it is difficult to restore.[8]

The Use and Misuse of Appearances

Appearances thus matter. But it is a mistake for conflict of interest policies to state, as many do, that professionals should avoid "even the appearance of a conflict of interest."[9] In an important sense, all conflict of interest are appearances. They are, to be sure, not just any kind of appearance, only those that are defined by rules that specify the circumstances that give rise to reasonable suspicions. All conflict of interest involve perceptions or appearances because they are specified from the perspective of people who do not have sufficient information to assess the actual motives of a professional and the effects of these motives on the professional work. Contrasting actual with perceived conflicts is a confusion and leads to two problems.[10]

First, the contrast encourages the mistaken idea that the appearance is not as problematic as the actual conflict. Emphasizing the contrast can undermine the rationale for regulating any conflict of interest because it suggests that there is no conflict unless the professional was actually motivated to favor secondary over primary interests. When a professional's judgment is actually distorted by financial interests, the violation is no longer simply a conflict of interests, but emphatically the victory of the wrong interest. It becomes another, different kind of offense—scientific misconduct (such as falsification or fraud), abuse of power (such as mistreatment of students), or criminal activity (such as bribery or extortion).

Second, separating apparent from real conflicts leads to overly broad and excessively subjective judgments, which can be used to raise questions about conduct that is

[8] "Numerous scholars have noted that trust is easier to destroy than create" (R. M. Kramer (1999). Trust and Distrust in Organizations: Emerging Perspectives, Enduring Questions," *Annual Review of Psychology* 50: 593–594 (1999).

[9] As does the sociologists' code: American Sociological Association, section 9.

[10] The term "potential conflict" has some of the same problems if it is used as equivalent to apparent or perceived conflict. But it is appropriate if used to indicate uncertainty about whether a particular circumstance fits the rule specifying a conflict, or a case not yet decided under the rule.

perfectly proper. When the appearance is detached from the actual conflict, apparent conflicts can be found everywhere by anyone. This misuse of appearances is partly why the second paradox and the objection to the use of appearances gains traction. With a loose notion of perception or appearance, circumstances that are suspicious only to uninformed people or muckraking reporters can be the basis of indiscriminate charges of conflict of interest. Charges of conflict of interest should be limited to circumstances specified by rules that are objectively grounded in past experience and interpreted by reasonable persons on the basis of relevant and publicly available facts. Then, when circumstances appear to create a conflict, there really is a conflict.

Misplaced Objections

Economists are not alone in resisting conflict of interest policies. Even in medicine, many objections have been raised against the increasing regulation.[11] To some extent, the objections draw their force from the paradoxes described earlier. But as should now be clear, they do not undermine the case for conflict of interest policies if their meaning and purpose are correctly understood.

The most vigorous resistance to conflict of interest rules arises when they are applied to an individual. When professionals are accused of having a conflict or violating a conflict of interest rule, they often take offense. They respond indignantly that they would never let financial interests influence their decisions; they care too much about their professional reputation to succumb to such temptations. This objection to regulation misses the point, as should be evident from the meaning of a conflict of interest. Because the conflict is a set of circumstances that refer to a generic risk rather than the individual decision in a particular case, the existence of a conflict of interest does not imply that any particular individual is improperly motivated.

Some who are charged with a conflict react by declaring that their work speaks for itself, that anyone who believes the work is biased should prove it by pointing to specific errors or distortions in the publications. Judge my decision—the results of the research, the content of the lecture, the merits of my testimony—not my financial motives. But again, as we have seen in considering the first paradox, judging only results is not sufficient in the circumstances where the results have extensive and often immediate effects on many people. Many of those affected by professional decisions are not in a position to judge their validity. Those who are competent to judge may not be able to do so until after the damage has been done. Moreover, the objection completely ignores one of the main

[11] Among the critics in the medical field are: K. Rothman, "Conflict of Interest: The New McCarthyism in Science," *JAMA* 269: 2783 (1993); T. Stossel, "Regulation of Financial Conflicts of Interest in Medical Practice and Medical Research: A Damaging Solution in Search of a Problem," *Perspectives in Biology and Medicine* 50 (2007): 54–71; and T. Stossel, "Has the Hunt for Conflicts of Interest Gone Too Far? Yes," *British Medical Journal* 336: 476–477 (2008).

purposes of conflict of interest policies—maintenance of public trust. Even valid decisions and honest research may not be widely accepted as such if the decisions are made and the research is conducted under conditions in which secondary interests are salient.

Another objection accepts that motives are relevant, but claims that it is not fair to generalize in the way conflict of interest rules do. If you insist on considering motives, the objection goes, then you should actually examine them. This appeals to a version of the second paradox, and fails when it is dissolved. Conflict of interest rules are by their nature designed to avoid the need to investigate individual cases in the way the objection assumes. It is both impractical and unethical to base the policy on a requirement to examine the motives of particular individuals.

First, it is usually impossible for the potentially affected parties to determine with any degree of confidence that a particular decision was improperly motivated. Generally, there are multiple considerations that influence the decisions that professionals make. Students, research assistants, colleagues, policymakers, citizens, and others who are affected by the decision but do not know the decision maker are not in a position to assess motives in particular cases. Even if they know the decision maker, they would find it very difficult to determine whether secondary interests motivated a decision. As already noted, the decision makers themselves are not always fully aware of their motivations.

Second, it is improperly intrusive to conduct the kind of investigation that would be necessary to determine how much influence each of the various interests had in a professional decision in any particular case. Fair hearings could not be held, and reliable conclusions reached, without distracting many people from their other important work, and without risking violations of the rights of privacy and the academic freedom of the many individuals who may be involved.

Standards for Assessing Conflicts

Conflicts are not binary. They can be more or less severe. The severity of a conflict depends on (1) the likelihood that professional work in the relevant circumstances tends to be unduly influenced by a secondary interest; and (2) the seriousness of the harm or wrong that could result from such influence. Both of these assessments are based not mainly on the particular case in question, but on other cases in similar circumstances.

In assessing the likelihood, we may assume that within a standard range the greater the value of the secondary interest (e.g. the size of the financial gain), the more probable its influence. Although absolute value is important, the secondary interest should generally be measured relative to typical income for the relevant class of professionals, and relative to the scale of the practice, projects, and institutional budgets. Most economists are presumably adept at making this kind of calculation. But as will become clear later, the disclosures required by the new rules of the American Economic Association (AEA) do not provide the data that would be necessary for making it.

Scope of conflict refers to the duration and depth of the relationship that generates the conflict. Longer and closer associations increase the scope. A continuing relationship as a member of the board or limited partner, for example, creates a more serious problem than the acceptance of a one-time grant. Consulting agreements that extend for years or honoraria that span years of speaking engagements are also more problematic. The scope also depends on how close the compensated activity (research or advice) is to the core purpose (the primary interest) of the institution providing the compensation (the secondary interest). Evaluation of government contractors is more likely to create conflicts than general advice about government reorganization.

The extent of discretion—how much latitude a professional enjoys in the making of major decisions—partly determines the range of the probabilities. The more closely the research methods follow conventional practice, the less room there is for judgment, and hence for improper influence. Also, the less independent authority the professional has in a particular case, the less latitude there is for improper influence. A conflict involving a research assistant, for example, is generally less severe than one involving a principal investigator. A professional may also enjoy less independent authority if there is a large team overseeing the research and if there is a mechanism for external auditing. In general, because most economists have more discretion and independence than do most medical researchers, this factor is likely to be correspondingly more significant in economics research.

In assessing the seriousness of a conflict, we should consider first the value of the primary interest. Some relationships that present a conflict of interest also advance primary aims of research and teaching, and thus the primary aims of the profession and the institution in question. In some situations, it may therefore be necessary to accept a conflict of interest in order to avoid the cost of interfering with the pursuit of a primary interest. For example, some important research may not be possible without support from a source that creates a conflict, or without access that comes only with a close connection to the company that is the subject of the research. At the same time, these commercial relationships can undermine the very primary values that they are intended to promote. They can have damaging effects on the integrity of the research, teaching, or consulting. In weighing these costs, we consider the possibility of harm to students, colleagues and the public, damage to the objectivity of the research and education, and the loss of confidence in the judgment of the individual professional and collaborators. Even if the conflicts are not prohibited, they should generally be managed, not merely disclosed.

The greater the scope of consequences, the more serious is the conflict. Beyond its impact on the research of a particular individual, a conflict may have effects on the research and teaching of colleagues. A bank's sponsorship of a research project on the financial services industry could reasonably raise questions about the work of other colleagues in the researchers' institution, especially if the research is on similar subjects, and could weaken their ability to raise funds for other sources. A professor's close connections with an industry could cast doubt on the objectivity of his classes. Students might, for example, discount his criticisms of the industry because they suspect he is overcompensating for his relationship with it. The close connections could also have negative effects on the careers of his teaching assistants, and the collegial culture of the institution.

Finally, a conflict is more serious the less extensive the accountability of the professional. In many large healthcare organizations, the decision of a physician is reviewable by colleagues or authorities who do not themselves have conflict of interest. That is less common in the case of medical researchers, and still less in the case of economists. The results of the research may of course be subject to peer review, but as we have noted that process is not always adequate. Moreover, some economic advice and consultant reports are not public at all, or not public in time or in a form that could be effectively reviewed.

Even if professionals are accountable for particular decisions, a further problem remains. The accountability does not usually extend to the cumulative effects of their research and other work. The informal norms and policies of a profession and the institutions in which professionals work represent judgments that, no less than explicit decisions in particular cases, may be improperly influenced by secondary interests. As a result of the distribution of research support, the overall agenda of research may be skewed in various ways—for example, more heavily focused on the financial services industry than the subject warrants on the merits. The peer review process, however inadequate, is a better check on the results of particular research projects than it is on the direction and significance of the research in a field as a whole.

Procedures for Dealing with Conflicts

The standards should guide the choice of procedures and the way in which they are deployed. In general, the more severe the conflict, the more rigorous the procedures should be. Three major types of procedure are commonly used to deal with conflict of interest: disclosure, management, and prohibition.

Disclosure

Disclosure is intended to provide information about the secondary interests that could influence the work of professionals to the detriment of their primary interests. The key question in establishing disclosure policies is: Who should disclose what to whom?

The standard for disclosure should be what the affected persons should want to know to assess the severity of the conflict of interest. Specifically, information should be disclosed that is relevant to evaluating the value and scope of the interests and the extent of discretion and accountability (as indicated in Table 23.1).

Disclosure is the most common way of dealing with conflicts. It is the only method stipulated in the new policy of the AEA (American Economic Association, 2012).

Table 23.1 Severity of Conflict of Interests

Likelihood of Undue Influence	Seriousness of Harm or Wrong
Value of Secondary Interest	Value of Primary Interest
Scope of Conflict	Scope of Consequences
Extent of Discretion	Extent of Accountability

Authors are required to disclose the source of support for the research reported in the article under consideration, any other financial support received by the author or close relatives from interested parties, any paid and unpaid positions in organizations whose interests are related to the article, and whether any person or organization has the right to review the article prior to publication. Because the amount of the support does not have to be disclosed, readers have no way to assess its relative significance. They are told only that the support sums to at least $10,000 in the previous three years, a misleading cue in cases in which the support amounts to a large proportion of the author's income.[12] Furthermore, although the AEA "urges" its members and other economists to apply the same standards to their other public work, disclosure is required only for the five journals published by the Association.

Even if the disclosure requirements were more robust, they would not adequately deal with the problem. As is now widely recognized in other professions, disclosure itself is not a sufficient method of dealing with conflicts (Institute of Medicine, 2009: 67–78). The chief difficulty can be brought out by asking a simple question: What is anyone supposed to do with the information that is disclosed? Many of the people affected by the research have no way of assessing what the disclosure means, and no alternatives if they were to conclude that disclosed conflict is not acceptable.

In circumstances that involve personal relationships in medicine, a physician's disclosure of conflicts evidently causes some patients and research subjects to become more trusting, even when they should be wary. The physician seems more honest simply because he or she reveals the conflicts (Institute of Medicine, 2009: 77–78, 368–369). Studies of advice-giving have found that disclosure tends to increase "the bias in advice because it leads advisors to feel morally licensed and strategically encouraged to exaggerate their advice even further."[13] Recipients of advice may be more trusting than they should be simply because the advisor seems forthcoming about the conflicts.

[12] Cain et al., 2005. "Each author of a submitted article should identify each interested party from whom he or she has received significant financial support, summing to at least $10,000 in the past three years, in the form of consultant fees, retainers, grants and the like" (American Economic Association Disclosure Policy, http://www.aeaweb.org/aea_journals/AEA_Disclosure_Policy.pdf[http://www.aeaweb.org/aea_journals/AEA_Disclosure_Policy.pdf)

[13] Also see: "When Sunlight Fails to Disinfect: Understanding the Perverse Effects of Disclosing Conflicts of Interest," *Journal of Consumer Research*, 37(5): 836–857 (2011).

It is possible that in the impersonal and distant relationships involved in publication and public statements, as in much of economics, the effect could be the opposite. Some who are affected by the research may, as a result of disclosure, look at it more critically, but then, because many do not have the competence to assess it, become simply more suspicious, perhaps even dismissing conclusions that are in fact valid. More generally, when the public sees the extensive conflicts that pervade the profession, they may well think worse of it than before. Disclosure can undermine confidence in the profession and research professionals produce—the very confidence that conflict of interest policies are intended to maintain. In either of these ways—encouraging too much trust or too much distrust—disclosure can be counterproductive.

The implication is not that disclosure is undesirable but that it is insufficient. If disclosure is to have a positive effect, it must be accompanied by procedures for interpreting and explaining the significance of the information that is disclosed. Interpretation and explanation are especially necessary for the more diffuse kinds of conflict mentioned earlier. It may not be realistic to expect editors of journals to offer interpretative comments on the individual disclosures for the articles they publish, but they could provide periodic reviews that examine the patterns of interests disclosed, discussion of the general categories that in their view create the greater risks, and reports on incidents in which the disclosures led to reconsideration of the assessment of the research. Similar but simpler reviews in the general media could help policymakers and the public understand better the significance of various kinds of information disclosed. A more wide-ranging proposal would institute a system of ratings, in which individual economists would be ranked according to the degree of their independence from financial interests related to their research and consulting (Zingales, 2012).

It would be a step forward if the economics profession were to pursue these and other methods for making disclosure more effective, but effective disclosure is not sufficient for many kinds of conflicts. Some call for more rigorous management, and even outright prohibition.

Management

Management techniques are necessary when disclosure is inadequate and prohibition of the activity is not a desirable option (as when the research is important and no other source of support available). Management of conflicts is relatively common in medical research, but rare in economics. It should be given more serious consideration by the profession.

Management includes various methods: divesting, creating blind trusts, limiting participation of conflicted professionals to the parts of the project in which they have unique expertise, pooling multiple sources of support, and establishing independent oversight bodies (Institute of Medicine, 2009: 79–87; Perlman, 2010). Some of these are too cumbersome and in any case probably unnecessary for individual research projects in economics. But major collaborative projects receiving large amounts of support for longer term research may well require some form of sustained management. Medical research continues to flourish under these constraints, and there is no reason why economics would not do the same.

One problem with management is that managing in any of its forms has a tendency to turn into merely permitting. Blind trusts are often not as opaque as they might seem, and controlling current conflicts does not reach the conflicts that arise from anticipation of future benefits. The oversight, if conducted by colleagues and continued for a long time, tends to become perfunctory. Management is also sometimes adopted simply because it is a less draconian measure than prohibition, even when prohibition is warranted. If management is to be appropriately applied and effectively implemented, it will have to be managed well itself.

Prohibition

With this method, the professional who has a serious conflict of interest is not permitted to accept support from any sources determined to be related to the research or other public statements. A few economists have voluntarily followed this practice in their own professional activities.[14] But the profession as a whole has not adopted it, and the AEA ethics code does not propose anything like it. Although most economists would probably be reluctant to decline all such support, the profession should be able to identify some circumstances in which interested support should not be accepted. At a minimum, the profession could establish ethical norms that would, for example, proscribe publishing research on companies in which the author has a financial interest. Ethical norms can have an effect even if they cannot be legally enforced. If the AEA cannot bring itself to establish such norms, universities and eventually the government are increasingly likely to do so.

Prohibition usually operates in conjunction with disclosure. Institutional officials do not know what to prohibit until the relevant financial interests are disclosed to someone in authority. Prohibition may refer to specific individuals but it can also express a general policy. For example, a rule could state that no member of a committee of the AEA dealing with ethics issues may have an ongoing financial relationship with any corporation that has a financial interest in the research of economists. Prohibition can also be applied in degrees: for example, an economist with stock in a bank could be prevented from serving as principal investigator for research that involves the banking industry but might be permitted to serve as a consultant to those who are conducting the research.

Although any of the methods for dealing with conflicts may be used alone, they are usually, and more effectively, combined in various ways. Even when disclosure is not sufficient —as we have seen is usually the case—it may be still be essential as

[14] Zingales (2012) reports that he declines compensation for publications from companies with an interest in the subject.

part of a comprehensive policy. Some level of disclosure is necessary for both management and prohibition of conflict of interests. Even when some aspects of a relationship are prohibited, management techniques will usually be needed for other aspects.

Conclusion

Like other professionals, economists face serious challenges today—the discouraging job market for young academics, questions about the relevance of professional education, doubts about the value of professional advice, and increasing difficulty in funding major research. Economists also confront their own special problems. In the aftermath of the financial crisis, their methods and mindsets have come under increasing criticism. The criticism has come as much from members of the profession as from the public (Colander et al., 2009). In comparison to these challenges, the problem of conflict of interest may seem less significant. But in an important sense, conflict of interest is the most serious challenge because none of the others can be adequately met if conflicts are not well controlled and seen to be so. Confidence in the profession more generally would continue to erode. Dealing successfully with the other problems depends on the capacity of economists to make, and be seen to make, decisions on the basis of the primary goals of the profession,—maintaining the integrity of research and teaching. Failure to deal with the challenge of conflict of interest is likely to undermine efforts to address the other serious problems the profession faces today. Economists could then look forward to a persistent professional disequilibrium.

References

Adair, R., and L. Holmgren. 2005. "Do Drug Samples Influence Resident Prescribing Behavior? A Randomized Trial." *American Journal of Medicine* 118: 881–884.

American Economic Association. 2012, January 5. "American Economic Association Adopts Extensions to Principles for Author Disclosure of Conflict of Interest." *American Economic Association Publications Office*, press release. Retrieved from http://www.aeaweb.org/PDF_files/PR/AEA_Adopts_Extensions_to_Principles_for_Author_Disclosure_01-05-12.pdf

American Sociological Association. 1999. *Code of Ethics and Policies and Procedures of the ASA Committee on Professional Ethics*. Washington, DC: American Sociological Association, section 9.

Association of American Medical Colleges (AAMC). 2008. *Report of the AAMC Task Force on Industry Funding of Medical Education to the AAMC Executive Council*. Washington, DC: Association of American Medical Colleges. Retrieved from http://www.aamc.org/research/coi/industryfunding.pdf

Babcock, L., G. Loewenstein, S. Issacharoff, and C. Camerer. 1995. "Biased Judgments of Fairness in Bargaining." *American Economic Review* 85: 1337–1342; and Institute of Medicine, 359–366.

Bekelman, J. E., Y. Li, and C.P. Gross. 2003. "Scope and Impact of Financial Conflicts of Interest in Biomedical Research: A Systematic Review." *JAMA* 289: 454–465.

Brennan, T. A., D. J. Rothman, L. Blank et al. 2006. "Health Industry Practices That Create Conflicts of Interest: A Policy Proposal for Academic Medical Centers." *JAMA* 295: 429–433.

Cain, Daylian M., George Loewenstein, and Don A. Moore. 2005. "The Dirt on Coming Clean: Perverse Effects of Disclosing Conflicts of Interest." *Journal of Legal Studies* 34(1): 1–25.

Campbell, E. G., R. L. Gruen, J. Mountford, L. G. Miller, P. D. Clearly, and D. Blumenthal. 2007. "A National Survey of Physician–Industry Relationships." *New England Journal of Medicine* 356: 1742–1750.

Carrick-Hagenbarth, Jessica, and Gerald A. Epstein 2012. "Dangerous Interconnectedness: Economists' Conflicts of Interest, Ideology and Financial Crisis." *Cambridge Journal of Economics* 36 (1): 43–63.

Colander, David, Hans Föllmer, Armin Haas, Michael Goldberg, Katarina Juselius, Alan Kirman, Thomas Lux, and Brigitte Sloth. 2009. "The Financial Crisis and the Systemic Failure of Academic Economics." *Critical Review: A Journal of Politics and Society* 21 (2): 249–267; also referred to as the Dahlem Report.

Dwan, K., D. G. Altman, J. A. Arnaiz, J. Bloom, A-W Chan, et al. 2008. "Systematic Review of the Empirical Evidence of Study Publication Bias and Outcome Reporting Bias." *PLoS ONE* 3: e3081.

Gallup. 2012, February 17. "Honesty/Ethics in the Professions." Retrieved from http://www.gallup.com/poll/1654/honesty-ethics-professions.aspx

Gilovich, T. 1991. *How We Know What Isn't So: The Fallibility of Human Reason in Everyday Life*. New York: The Free Press.

Hamermesh, Daniel S. 2007. "Replication in Economics." *Canadian Journal of Economics* 40(3): 715–733.

Hollenbeck,Frank. 2014. "The Sad State of the Economics Profession." Mises Daily. Retrieved from https:/mises.org/library/sad-state-economics-profession.

Ioannidis, J. P. A. 2005. "Why Most Published Research Findings Are False." *PLoS Medicine* 2(8): e124.

Kaletsky, Anatole. 2011, September 11. "Ideology Caused the Crisis." *Institute for New Economic Thinking, History of Economics Playground, Bretton Woods, Part I: Ethics in Economics, "Are there conflicts of interest in economics today?"* Retrieved from http://ineteconomics.org/blog/playground/bretton-woods-past-and-present-1-ethics-economics;

Katz, D., A. L. Caplan, and J. F. Merz. 2003. "All Gifts Large and Small: Toward an Understanding of the Ethics of Pharmaceutical Industry Gift Giving." *American Journal of Bioethics* 3: 39–46.

Kelch, R. P. 2002. "Maintaining the Public Trust in Clinical Research." *New England Journal of Medicine* 346: 285–287.

Leonhardt, David. 2008. "Greenspan's Mea Culpa". New York Times, October 23, retrieved from http://economix.blogs.nytimes.com/2008/10/23/greenspans-mea-culpa/

Lo, Bernard, and Marilyn J. Field, Eds. Institute of Medicine, Committee on Conflict of Interest in Medical Research, Education and Practice. 2009. *Conflict of Interest in Medical Research, Education and Practice*. Washington, DC: The National Academies Press.

Loewenstein, G., S. Issacharoff, C. Camerer, and L. Babcock. 1992. "Self-serving Assessments of Fairness and Pretrial Bargaining." *Journal of Legal Studies* 12: 135–159.

Mishkin, Frederic, and Tryggvi T. Herbertsson. 2006. *Financial Stability in Iceland*. Reykjavik, Iceland: Icelandic Chamber of Commerce.

Murray, Thomas H., and Josephine Johnston, Eds. 2010. *Trust and Integrity in Biomedical Research: The Case of Financial Conflicts of Interest*, Part I. Baltimore, MD: Johns Hopkins Press.

Perlman, David. 2010. "Current Regulations, Comparison of Guidelines, and Considerations for Policy Development." In *Trust and Integrity in Biomedical Research: The Case of Financial Conflicts of Interest*, edited by Thomas H. Murray and Josephine Johnston, pp. 217–240. Baltimore, MD: Johns Hopkins University Press.

Pritchett, Lant. 2011, January 7. "Do Economists Need a Code of Conduct?" *The Economist*. Retrieved from http://www.economist.com/economics/by-invitation/questions/do_economists_need_code_conduct

Seabright, Paul. 2011, January 7. "Do Economists Need a Code of Conduct?" *The Economist*. Retrieved from http://www.economist.com/economics/by-invitation/questions/do_economists_need_code_conduct

Stiglitz, Joseph E. 2000. "Ethics, Economic Advice, and Economic Policy." Paper originally presented at a conference at the Interamerican Development Bank in Washington, D.C. in December 2000, which is included in this volume.

Zingales, Luigi. 2012. "Economists' Capture." Presentation at the Conference on Institutional Corruption, Safra Center for Ethics, Harvard University, February 4.

Zinner, D. E., D. Bolcic-Jankovic, B. Clarridge, D. Blumenthal, and E. G. Campbell. 2009. "Participation of Academic Scientists in Relationships with Industry." *Health Affairs*, 28(6): 1814–1825.

CHAPTER 24

CONSIDERATIONS ON CONFLICT OF INTEREST IN ACADEMIC ECONOMICS

JESSICA CARRICK-HAGENBARTH[1]
AND GERALD EPSTEIN

Introduction

Professions aspire to serve moral ideals. For example, medicine, law, and journalism claim to promote well-being, justice, and truth, respectively. Economics has long styled itself on the hard sciences as a way to uncover the laws and workings of the economic world. Academic economists try to produce knowledge about the functioning of the economy and its impacts on society. The practical applications of economics are generally found in the policy realm, where, ideally, policymakers use economic ideas to attempt to make policies more effective. Nevertheless, professionals can find themselves caught between the moral ideals of the profession and their own self-interest. Such tensions create the possibility for conflict of interest.

> Conflict of interest is a problem only in a certain domain, one in which we do not want ordinary self-interest to guide the decisions of those on whom we depend; instead, we want those on whom we depend to be 'independent,' 'impartial,' 'unbiased,' or the like. This is the domain in which professions flourish. Why? If we think of a profession as a number of individuals in the same occupation voluntarily organized to earn a living by openly serving a certain moral ideal and a morally permissible way beyond what law, market, and morality would otherwise require, then the answer is obvious. Insofar as a profession is successful at serving its chosen moral

[1] Many thanks to George DeMartino for invaluable conversation and comments, and to Joao Paulo de Souza, Peter Skott, and Patrick Sutherland. All errors are our own.

> ideal, the profession provides an alternative to self-interest (the typical motive in an ordinary market). (Davis and Stark, 2001: 4).

A conflict of interest is present if a situation can potentially bias a person because of a clash between the person's self-interest and that of the profession or public. A conflict of interest can also occur when a person's responsibility to another party (such as a client) limits his or her ability to carry out his or her responsibility to a third party.

As we discuss in the text that follows, some high-profile academic economists dance between academic positions and private positions convinced that the steps they take in one arena do not influence their steps in the other. This unwitting ballet has left academic economists open to deserved criticism, either for naiveté or actually contributing to the Great Financial Crisis of 2008. This criticism has led to a rethinking of professional ethics in economics and, more specifically, conflict of interest in economics.

In this chapter we argue that the economics profession needs an effective policy to deal with conflict of interest. We focus here on academic economists to keep the issue within manageable proportions. We maintain that an appropriate conflict of interest policy for academic economists would, at a minimum, require the *disclosure* of relevant, significant conflict of interest. In addition, the policy should require the *avoidance* of conflicts that undermine academic economists' roles as credible producers and teachers of knowledge about the functioning of the economy to the best of their abilities. Economists need to discuss when disclosure is sufficient, and when instead an economist should avoid a conflicted activity altogether. Given there is no existing institution that is dedicated solely to economics and capable of disciplining transgressions of a conflict of interest policy, we argue that universities, the professional economic organization, funders, and publishers must work together to reinforce a norm of disclosure and, when necessary, avoidance of conflict of interest. Universities have the ability to monitor and discipline conflict of interest. The professional association for economists can create a conflict of interest policy that is specific to the issues economists face. This policy can be used by universities when making decisions regarding avoidance and disclosure. Ethical behavior can be further reinforced by publishers requiring disclosure of all potential conflict of interest in both submission and publication of articles. If university conflict of interest policies are to play a main role in regulating disclosure of academic economists for the profession, it is essential that they require that disclosure is made, not only privately to the university, but also to the public in all publications, presentations, Congressional testimony, and media appearances and interviews.

In what follows we first describe why we believe there should be a conflict of interest policy for academic economists, drawing on the experience of the buildup and subsequent fallout from the Great Financial Crisis of 2008. We then discuss the question of disclosure and avoidance of conflict of interest. Among other aspects, we investigate the appropriate locus of responsibility for monitoring and enforcing such rules. Subsequently, we review and indicate some shortcomings in the new American Economic Association (AEA) policy on professional conflict of interest. Finally, we describe the changing norms in regard to conflict of interest in the field of economics.

Ultimately, we argue that the profession must adopt and codify rules addressing conflict of interest, requiring disclosure and avoidance when necessary.

The Economics Profession's Need for a Conflict of Interest Policy

There is reason to worry that some academic economists hold additional positions whose income and responsibilities compete with that of their academic role. Such positions in the private sector include ownership of businesses, executive positions, board positions, consultant positions, and positions as affiliated experts. Many economists also take on temporary roles, such as providing Congressional testimony, consulting, and otherwise providing their expertise on an ad hoc, for-hire basis.

Rightly or wrongly, academics and the media interpret academic affiliation as a seal of objectivity and credibility regarding information conveyed in articles, interviews, or Congressional testimony. Limited evidence suggests that academic economists often do not disclose their private financial affiliations when writing or appearing in the media, giving government testimonies, or in journal articles (Flitter, Cooke, and Da Costa, 2010; Carrick-Hagenbarth and Epstein, 2012).

Conflict of interest or the appearance of conflict of interest can harm both the economic profession's reputation and the public. There was widespread disbelief in the wake of the failure of the majority of financial economists to predict or even perceive economic fragility leading up to the Great Financial Crisis of 2008. Disbelief was followed by outrage when the Oscar-winning documentary *Inside Job* publicly highlighted a link between influential academic economists, private financial affiliations, and economists' contribution to the economic catastrophe (Ferguson, 2011). A Reuters study that evaluated 82 academics testifying before Congress from 2008 to 2010 on financial regulation found that around a third of the time these academics did not disclose their financial affiliations (Flitter, Cooke, and Da Costa, 2010). Public distrust of the economics profession was reflected in negative comments that appeared in news and blog articles debating a code of ethics in 2010 in *The New York Times, The Economist*, and other locations.[2]

In our work we found evidence of potential conflict of interest among prominent academic financial economists that were so widespread they appeared to border on

[2] For example, this is a comment on a blog post on the economist.com, "Failure of mainstream economics academic community as a whole to warn of the properties bubble in the USA in 2006 was nothing sort of criminal. Whether through incompetence or complicity, the US economic academia has lost ALL its academic standings because of this. Economics as a rigorous, scientific, academic study has about as much credence as Astrology" (Anjin-San [pseud] 2011, emphasis in original). Another example is this comment on the *New York Times* blog *Economix*, "One would think that these economists would not need to sign a letter stating there is no conflict of interest, however, in this day and time, particularly after the economic crisis of 2007/2008, it is quite evident that unless these people do sign this letter, none of us in America can any longer trust them one iota" (Bradford, 2011).

a norm (Epstein and Carrick-Hagenbarth, 2010; Carrick-Hagenbarth and Epstein, 2012). We studied the private financial affiliations of 19 prestigious academic economists who were members of two groups promoting their views on financial reform over the period 2005–2009. Fifteen of these economists had private financial affiliations over this period ranging from owning their own firms to working as consultants. The most common affiliation was holding a board position. Egregiously, the majority of the economists we studied failed to disclose their private financial affiliations in their academic publications, testimonies, or media writings and interviews related to financial reform. Those who did disclose their private financial affiliations did so sporadically and infrequently.

Some have argued that such conflict of interest are of little import to the profession because they affect only a minority of economists. Even supposing that failure to disclose potential conflict of interest is limited to a handful of prestigious financial economists, these are the economists with the most influence, who set standards for the field. They are regularly interviewed in the media, receive awards, and are looked to for advice when making policies. It is central that they disclose any potential conflict of interest because they have an inordinate impact on the profession's reputation, the profession itself, and on policy.

The apparent professional indifference to the fact that leading academic economists have and yet fail to disclose potential conflict of interest motivated our letter to the AEA before its annual meeting in January of 2011. We, along with more than 300 economists who signed, urged the AEA to adopt a code of ethics promoting, and where possible, requiring the disclosure of potential conflict of interest for the economics profession. We chose the AEA because it is by far the most influential economic association in the United States. Beyond economics, almost all American professions have treated ethics seriously and, at minimum, have adopted a code of ethics to guide members. Professional associations in sociology, anthropology, political science, physics, and chemistry have established codes, just to name a few.

The AEA responded to external and internal criticism of the profession's lack of attention to conflict of interest by creating a committee in January 2011 to discuss disclosure in economics over the following year. This did lead to the eventual passage of a conflict of interest policy, requiring disclosure in all AEA journals and suggested disclosure in economists' professional lives (see section on The American Economic Association and Disclosure). Yet not altogether unsurprisingly, considering the economic profession's historical disregard for ethics, many economists demonstrated a lack of interest in redressing this issue, even once the matter of failure to disclose conflict of interest was brought to their attention. For example, when the AEA committee on disclosure asked for input from the profession on disclosure guidelines in their journals they received responses from "only a handful of its 18,000 members" over the period January 2011 to July of the same year (Cooke and Flitter, 2011; and personal communication from Robert Solow, chair of the advice committee). This indicates that although there has been significant public attention to economists' conflict of interest, economists' historical inattention to ethics may be an obstacle to integrating ethics and ethical practice into the profession.[3]

It is also likely that most academic economists do not think private financial affiliations bias their economic analyses. The relevant psychology literature has identified what is now called an "ethical blind spot"—a tendency for people to see themselves as unbiased or as less biased than others. "This research [on self-serving biases in judgments of what is fair] shows that when individuals stand to gain by reaching a particular conclusion they tend to unconsciously and unintentionally weigh evidence in a biased fashion that favors that conclusion. Furthermore, the process of weighing evidence can happen beneath the individual's level of awareness, such that a biased individual will sincerely claim objectivity" (Dana, 2009: 358–359; see also Bazerman and Tenbrunsel, 2011). Dissonance reduction, which Bowles uses to explain one way in which preferences and values are modified, can also be used to understand why people facing two competing obligations may conclude they are not biased (Bowles, 1998). Dissonance occurs when one's actions and one's values are at odds. Often a person will resolve the tension by unconsciously rearranging his or her opinions and values, or adopting new opinions and values to resolve the tension inherent in his or her otherwise conflicted situation.

As Dana presents in *How Psychological Research Can Inform Policies for Dealing with Conflicts of Interest in Medicine*, there have been a number of experiments and surveys that have been used to identify blind spots (Dana, 2009). For example, in a survey of 264 Stanford students, respondents claimed that they were less likely to be biased than the average American, than their average classmate, and than the average airport traveler (Pronin, Lin, and Ross, 2002). Even when confronted with probable bias, people (including medical faculty) averred their objectivity (McKinney et al., 1990; Pronin, Lin, and Ross 2002). In studies of bias in medical residents with links to industry, it has been found that individual residents claim less bias than that of their colleagues. For example, one study of medical residents found that 61 percent declared that industry connections did not affect their own prescribing pattern, yet only 16 percent stated the same about their fellow residents (Steinman, Shlipak, and McPhee, 2001). Another study based on a review of medical literature of industry ties and bias in residents confirmed the same result (Zipkin and Steinman, 2005).

The tendency for academics to hold more than one role is being intensified by an increasing melding of industry and academia. Medicine provides an example. Much of medical training is done in academic medical centers and teaching hospitals, both of which are under growing financial pressure due to the cost of new technologies and the

[3] Of course, there are exceptions, economists that have been working on the issues of ethics in economics beginning with Adam Smith in the *Theory of Moral Sentiments* and including many current economists, such as George DeMartino in *The Economist's Oath*, Charles Wilber and Amitava Dutt in *Economics and Ethics*, Nancy Folbre in *The Invisible Heart* and "Ethics for Economists," Deidre McCloskey in *The Bourgeois Virtues*, and Amartya Sen in *On Ethics and Economics*—to name just a few (Sen, 1991; Smith, 2000; Folbre, 2002, 2010*b*; McCloskey, 2007; Wilber and Dutt, 2010; DeMartino, 2011).

adoption of new medical informatics systems (Research and Medicine, 2009). A survey by Campbell et al. (2007) with a 67 percent response rate found that of the 459 department chairs who responded, 60 percent had some affiliation with industry, in capacities such as consultants, members of scientific advisory boards, as paid speakers, officers, founders, and as members of corporate boards of directors.

This tendency reaches beyond that of the medical discipline. Reduced funding and the promotion of a business model for public universities are creating a similar melding of education and business.

> Universities now urge their faculty members to seek corporate sponsorship and privatize the gains from their research. Following the money often means abandoning any pretense of objectivity. It deincentivizes the pursuit of risky, creative ideas that have little chance of gaining funding. It can also lead to downright corruption. Many studies document the impact of financial incentives on the results of drug trials, the development of new genetic engineering methods (in which genes themselves can be patented), and even researcher participation in insider trading. (Folbre 2010a: 118)

Affiliations between academics (as well as universities) and private business proliferate in such an environment, blurring the line between the ideals of public education and the needs of business. In this environment a norm of academics holding business affiliations in addition to their university positions has emerged.

The examples and evidence provided here reasonably establish that potential conflict of interest arise among academic economists. Furthermore, the recent exposure of such potential conflict of interest has exacerbated public distrust of the economics profession. This problem should be faced. Economists, despite whatever resistance they have to dealing with conflict of interest, must debate, adopt, and codify a set of best practices for dealing with conflict of interest. Grounding such a discussion in the broader field of ethics in economics would strengthen the analysis.

Disclosure and Avoidance

If we assume many academic economists will take on positions beyond that of professor, then we are evaluating a world where it may make little sense to try and advocate for the "pure academic economist" even if it were desirable. We must create practical rules that address the reality of the academic economist. Conflict of interest can be dealt with in various ways. Here we are going to talk about two of them: disclosure and avoidance.[4] Disclosure occurs when an academic economist thinks she or he may have a potential

[4] For a more extended discussion of how conflict of interest are dealt with see the Introduction to Davis and Stark (2001).

or real conflict of interest and reveals that fact to all parties involved. Avoidance occurs when she or he must make a decision about which position or project to keep and from which she or he must recuse her- or himself.

We suggest that academic economists should always disclose potential conflict of interest in their papers, in their testimonies, and in the media. The AEA has recently addressed this issue and made similar suggestions in their disclosure policy. This raises the question, if disclosure is a given, when should academic economists avoid conflict of interest altogether? The strength of rules regarding avoidance depends on the profession. For example, journalists in many situations are not allowed to have any conflict of interest, while judges are prohibited from seeing cases that include family members or former firm partners (Luban, 2001).

The severity of a conflict of interest can be evaluated on both a qualitative and a quantitative scale. The qualitative scale takes into account the types of jobs economists hold. For example, one could rank the positions according to responsibility: founders, executive positions, board positions, and consultants. The quantitative scale generally entails an income threshold. The Harvard Medical School and the University of California, Berkeley, in addition to having quantitative cutoffs for potential conflict of interest, also use qualitative rules. For example, the Harvard Medical School policy prohibits their full-time faculty from holding executive positions in for-profit businesses of a biomedical nature and the University of California, Berkeley policy states that it reviews and often does not allow tenured professors to hold executive positions (Harvard Medical School, 2012; University of California, 2001).

Quantitative scales have the benefit of establishing precise boundaries where a review of the person's potential conflict of interest is necessary. Traditionally the quantitative scale is set as a dollar amount, though some have argued for using a percentage of income as the cutoff. In either case the type of position held by the academic economist is not relevant but rather the total dollar amount or the percentage of their total income they receive from the additional position. Quantitative rules are most common in the conflict of interest policies we reviewed here, including those of the AEA guidelines for journal submission and the University of Massachusetts policy. Often the threshold mirrors the U.S. Public Health Service regulations for funding research (U.S. Public Health Services, 2012, sec. Part 50—Policies of General Applicability).

Who Should Monitor and Enforce Conflict of Interest Policies?

In 2008 a national scandal broke out when Senator Grassley (R, Iowa), investigating pharmaceutical company funding and academic researchers, requested the disclosure statements for Drs. Joseph Biederman, Thomas Spencer, and Timothy Wilens. The three were nationally renowned psychiatrists at Harvard Medical School. These psychiatrists were treating children for bipolar disorder with antipsychotic drugs that had yet to be FDA approved for pediatric use at that time, while receiving funds from the manufactures of the drugs (Silverman, 2011).

In their disclosure statements the psychiatrists grossly underreported their payment from the pharmaceutical sector. According to Grassley, the doctors had disclosed several hundred thousand dollars of income over the period from 2000 to 2007, but when asked to resubmit these disclosure statements Drs. Biederman and Wilens disclosed about $1.6 million each and Spencer about $1 million over the same time period (Senate, 2008). These doctors have since been reprimanded and have submitted a letter of apology (Kowalczyk, 2011). Responding to these events the Harvard Medical School drafted a new conflict of interest policy that in certain cases requires professors not only to disclose conflicts of interest but to avoid them altogether (Yu, 2011).

This story shows both the weakness and the strength of conflict of interest policies. The weakness is that they must be known and monitored in order to function properly. The strength is that even when they don't function properly, having clear rules in place makes it easier to retroactively deal with conflict of interest problems. Unethical action can be discovered after the fact and disciplined. Yet there must be some institution that is responsible for monitoring the conflict of interest policies and punishing violators.

Who should manage academic economists' conflict of interest? Should conflict of interest be addressed at the institutional or the professional level? These two levels are the most obvious at which to manage conflict of interest in economics. In the case of the academic economist the institutional level is the college or the university and the professional level would most likely be through the AEA. One of the main arguments for managing conflict of interest at the university level is that universities have a greater capacity to punish transgressors than does the professional association, which does not license economists and consequently has few tools for enforcement. That said, university conflict of interest policies tend to be specific to the university and cover all disciplines, whereas a professional code would be specific to the economics discipline and set consistent rules for all economists.

While academics are subject to their university conflict of interest policies, generally these policies do not require disclosure to the public. A notable exception is Columbia University's conflict of interest policy, which "requires individuals to disclose outside financial interests that relate to any of their research, including unfunded research, to peers and members of the public. These disclosures must be made in publications, reports, talks, or other presentations of research" (Columbia University, 2009). Columbia University provides a model that university conflict of interest policies should follow. The public should be alerted when academics have conflict of interest. This benefits not only the public but also the university because the university is protected from scandals that reflect badly on it.

Academic economists are often required by their university rules to disclose significant outside positions. University conflict of interest policies most often focus on financial income, such as ownership, equity in a business, wages, and salary. Frequently conflict of interest policies define a specific income or equity stake above which staff is required to submit disclosure statements for review, often following the US Public Health Service (PHS) definition of a significant conflict of interest. The previous $10,000 dollar threshold of wages or salary for a significant conflict of interest was revised down to $5000 in 2012 (U.S. Public Health Services 2012, sec. Part 50—Policies of General Applicability).

We illustrate such rules by evaluating a small group of universities' conflict of interest policies for their income threshold that defines a significant financial conflict of interest. For example, following the change to the PHS policies, Stanford and Columbia Universities reduced their income threshold from $10,000 to $5,000 for the reporting of a significant financial conflict of interest in August of 2012 (Columbia University, 2012; Stanford University, 2012). Ohio State University has two thresholds: a $10,000 threshold for all faculty and a $5,000 threshold for any faculty with PHS-funded research (Ohio State University, 2012). Our home university maintains the $10,000 dollar for review of a potential conflict of interest (University of Massachusetts Amherst and Boston, 1997). The University of Chicago has a zero percent threshold for disclosure and requires all financial interests to be disclosed to the university annually, including equity, wages, and salaries earned outside of the university (The University of Chicago, 2007).

Universities generally convene a panel when cases are flagged for review following a submitted disclosure statement showing an outside position is above a certain income level, or requires a certain responsibility that seems as if it might interfere with the faculty member's primary job (service to the university). The review process yields a decision whether the potential conflict is considered likely to create bias or the appearance of bias. The panel then decides the appropriate steps for the academic: no action is needed, the affiliations need to be managed, or the faculty member is prevented from taking the outside position. If the review process finds that the conflict of interest may cause bias or the appearance of bias but that it can be mitigated, a management plan is created. These plans can include steps, such as public disclosure of private financial affiliations, independent monitoring, and required holding of stock for a significant period. If it is decided that the bias cannot be mitigated then the review process can result in the prohibition of holding both the university position and the outside position.

University conflict of interest policies have two weaknesses. First is the problem of their relative invisibility. For example, anecdotal evidence from conversations with University of Massachusetts Amherst academics suggests many professors are unaware of the university's conflict of interest policy. Such evidence is perhaps supported by a study done at the University of California San Francisco and Stanford University that interviewed 34 professors of medicine. Fewer than half of the faculty participants could accurately state the conflict of interest policies even with staff at both universities dedicated to enforcement of the policies (Boyd, Cho, and Bero, 2003). Medicine is a discipline with an active field of professional ethics. If half the academics of these two universities in medicine have difficulty remembering rules regarding conflict of interest policies it is probable that academic economists would have an equal or greater problem stating their university's conflict of interest policy. Second, university conflict of interest policies were in place long before academic economists' conflict of interest issues came to light. While economists may have been disclosing their conflict of interest to the university, it seems this information was not known by the public. Thus, although disclosure to the university is important, disclosure must also be made to the public when relevant. Universities need to treat conflict of interest more seriously and transparently.

The alternative to managing conflict of interest at the university level is to monitor and manage them at the professional level. Economics faces two problems of professional oversight. First, because economists are not licensed and membership in the professional association is voluntary, the professional organization has no way to punish transgressions (Homan, 2010; Lahart and Whitehouse, 2011). If an economist were to violate such a code there would be no codified legal sanctions the AEA could take. Second, the primary US professional economic organization has shown little interest until recently in creating a code of ethics that deals with conflict of interest. The AEA, founded in 1885, has never adopted a full professional code of ethics even though the issue was brought before the AEA's secretary several times in the 1930s and since. Traditionally, the AEA has argued that the issue was outside its realm of expertise and that it had no ability to enforce sanctions (Coats, 1986; DeMartino, 2011).

Yet, professional level conflict of interest policies can establish a baseline standard of conduct for the economics profession and serve to reinforce university conflict of interest policies. Indeed, the AEA could develop and advocate university adoption of an appropriate economic conflict of interest policy. Although there is no body that is charged with protecting the public from academic economists' conflict of interest, university and professional conflict of interest policies together could begin the process of creating a minimum norm of disclosure. Such disclosure could then be monitored and inappropriate conflict of interest could be dealt with at the university level. In addition, journals, other publishing institutions, and funders could require disclosure and decide appropriate responses, including non-publication if the conflict of interest is deemed likely to cause bias. As mentioned previously, the AEA as well as the National Bureau of Economic Research (NBER) have elaborated disclosure guidelines for their authors.

The American Economic Association and Disclosure

Critiques of and responses to conflict of interest had already made disclosure an issue at the annual AEA meeting in 2011. The discussion of disclosure resulted in the decision to form a committee that would debate disclosure guidelines. Robert Solow chaired the committee; the other committee members were Derek Bok, David Card, William Nordhaus, and Nancy Stokey.

In January of 2012, the committee released the new guidelines addressing disclosure for the seven AEA journals at the annual AEA meeting in Chicago (American Economic Association 2012*b*). Although, these journals already had limited guidelines for disclosure, the AEA took a step forward by considering the topic of disclosure more systematically and issuing new guidelines that both augmented the scope of and provided greater specificity to the existing disclosure guidelines. The *Journal of Economic Perspectives* provides an example of the previous policy on disclosure, "Authors of articles appearing in the *Journal of Economic Perspectives* are expected to disclose any potential conflict of interest that may arise from their consulting activities, financial interests, or other nonacademic activities"(*Journal of Economic Perspectives*, 2011: i–ii). In particular, the new guidelines do make some motions toward prescribing behavior for the profession as a whole. Nevertheless, for the most part the new guidelines are confined to the seven AEA journals and in no way replace the need for a professional code of ethics dealing with conflict of interest for economists.

The first three AEA guidelines outline when and how authors should disclose potential conflict of interest to the journal publishers. Guideline 1 requires that all sources of funding for the research examined in the paper be disclosed in the article submission. If there is not outside funding, this fact should also be noted (American Economic Association, 2012*b*). Similarly guideline 2 requires each author to identify all parties that provided financial support over the previous three years amounting to $10,000 or more, "in the form of consultant fees, retainers, grants and the like" (American Economic Association, 2012*b*). According to the guidelines authors should also disclose in kind compensation, including access to data. Ten thousand dollars per year was the threshold for the definition of a conflict of interest by the U.S. Public Health Service (PHS) until its recent revision to $5,000. Thus the use of the $10,000 amount was fairly standard for university conflict of interest policies, and by spreading it over three years it is similar to the current U.S. PHS guidelines. It should pick up most major positions the authors hold. Guideline 3 requires authors to disclose all positions they hold, paid or unpaid, as a board member, officer, or director of any relevant profit, nonprofit, or advocacy firm. "A "relevant" organization is one whose policy positions, goals, or financial interests relate to the article" (American Economic Association, 2012*b*).

Guideline 4 applies these disclosure requirements to spouses and close relatives (American Economic Association, 2012*b*). This is an important guideline but is weakened by that fact that it does not adequately define close relatives. For example, the newly revised NBER guidelines on disclosure specify that the investigator must report on the relevant relationships of his/her spouse and dependent children. Guideline 5 requires authors to disclose all people who reviewed the article when submitting the article (American Economic Association, 2012*b*). This provision strikes us as sufficient to ensure that the publisher knows whether outside interests reviewed the conclusions and inferences of the article.

Although the first five guidelines are specific about the authors' obligation of disclose to AEA journals when submitting papers, the recommendations are vaguer about the AEA journals' obligations of disclosure to the public. For example, the sixth guideline states, "For published articles, information on relevant potential conflict of interest will be made available to the public" (American Economic Association, 2012*b*). This guideline has a weakness in that a relevant potential conflict of interest is not defined. Although the guideline itself does not delineate how the potential conflict of interest will be disclosed to the public, more recent text accompanying the guidelines explains that whatever is included in the disclosure statement will be made public (American Economic Association, 2012*a*). Each article will include the disclosure statement in the acknowledgments. If the disclosure statement is large, a brief summary will be included in the acknowledgments with a link to the full disclosure online. This is an excellent protocol. It has the advantage of transparently and reliably stating what and where disclosed information can be reviewed.

Perhaps most important for the profession as a whole is the last guideline, guideline 7. It reads:

> The AEA urges its members and other economists to apply the above principles in other publications: scholarly journals, op-ed pieces, newspaper and magazine columns, radio and television commentaries, as well as in testimony before federal and state legislative committees and other agencies. (American Economic Association, 2012b)

This recommendation is not restricted to the AEA journals and is an important step in establishing ethical standards of disclosure for economists in their academic and public writings and appearances.

These guidelines are a significant step forward for the economics profession. Yet, for these guidelines to be effective, it will be important for the AEA to design means to monitor compliance.

Changing Norms

Some professional organizations had moved forward on the issues of ethics and disclosure prior to the recent surge of interest. For example, in the United States the National Association of Forensic Economists (NAFE) first adopted a code of ethics in 1992 (Brookshire, 2003) and currently follow their 2004 published statement of ethical principles (National Association of Forensic Economics [NAFE], 2004; DeMartino, 2011;). The Swedish Association of Graduates in Business Administration and Economics created a code of ethics in 2007 (Civilekonomerna, 2012). However, other professional organizations were inspired by the recent interest and changes by the AEA on disclosure. For example, the OFCE (*Observatoire Français des Conjonctures Économiques*, French Observatory of Economic Affairs), an important French research institute, recently created a code of ethics based on the AEA guidelines (*Le Monde Economie*, 2012). In 2012 the French Association of Economic Science created a working group to discuss norms of conduct for economic researchers and professors. The German Association for Social Policy, which represents economic and social scientists, adopted a code of ethics in

September of 2012 requiring transparency in the event of conflict of interest (Verein für Socialpolitik, 2012).

Among funders of research, the NBER has led the way on disclosure. The NBER substantially strengthened its rules on disclosure of conflict of interest in 2012. The new Research Financial Conflict of Interest Policy requires all research funding as well as other significant financial or material interests related to NBER published research papers of $5000 or greater be disclosed both to the NBER and, on request, to readers.

Individually, academic economists have also taken steps toward greater disclosure. For example, in 2011, some economists began to post outside activities and disclosure statements on their websites. In fact, of the 19 economists in our previous study, 10 had put up disclosure statements as of May of 2011 (Carrick-Hagenbarth and Epstein, 2012).

Conclusion

Changes such as these are positive, particularly because there is the pressure and opportunity for academic economists to take on a greater number of affiliations. Disclosure policies need to ward against becoming solely bureaucratic exercises. The creation of a professional field of economics—which DeMartino (2011) calls for—would foment such discussion. Conflict of interest policies must also be monitored and enforced to be effective. Such policies can be enforced both informally, by the creation of a norm of disclosure and the ostracization of those who do not follow the norms of ethical conduct, and formally, through university and journal enforced conflict of interest policies. If universities are to take on the role of regulator they must protect not only the university but also the public. Norms of ethical conduct for academic economists can be strengthened by buttressing university conflict of interest policies with professional conflict of interest policies and with guidelines for conflict of interest in journal article submissions and publications, and in all other activities and venues where economists offer their professional expertise.

References

American Economic Association (AEA). 2012*a*. "American Economic Association Disclosure Policy." Retrieved from http://www.aeaweb.org.silk.library.umass.edu:2048/aea_journals/AEA_Disclosure_Policy.pdf

American Economic Association (AEA). 2012*b*. "Press Release: American Economic Association Adopts Extensions to Principles for Author Disclosure of Conflict of Interest." Retrieved from https://login.silk.library.umass.edu/login?url=http://www.aeaweb.org/PDF_files/PR/AEA_Adopts_Extensions_to_Principles_for_Author_Disclosure_01-05-12.pdf

Anjin-San [pseud]. 2011. "Comment on 'A Code of Conduct Would Undermine the Rigor of Economic Discourse.'" *The Economist: Do Economists Need a Code of Conduct? Entry*

2011/01/07. Retrieved from http://www.economist.com/economics/by-invitation/guest-contributions/code_conduct_would_undermine_rigor_economic_discourse

Bazerman, Max H., and Ann E. Tenbrunsel. 2011. *Blind Spots: Why We Fail to Do What's Right and What to Do about It*. Princeton, NJ: Princeton University Press.

Bowles, Samuel. 1998, March 1. "Endogenous Preferences: The Cultural Consequences of Markets and Other Economic Institutions." *Journal of Economic Literature* 36(1): 75–111.

Boyd, Elizabeth A., Mildred K. Cho, and Lisa A. Bero. 2003. "Financial Conflict-of-Interest Policies in Clinical Research: Issues for Clinical Investigators." *Academic Medicine* 78(8): 769–774.

Bradford, Lisa. 2011. "Comment on 'Letter Calls on Economists to Adopt Code of Ethics.'" *Economix*. Retrieved from http://economix.blogs.nytimes.com/2011/01/04/letter-calls-on-economists-to-adopt-code-of-ethics/

Brookshire, Michael L. 2003. "A History of the National Association of Forensic Economics, 1986-2001." *Litigation Economics Review* 6(1): 22–32.

Campbell, Eric G. 2007, October 17. "Institutional Academic–Industry Relationships." *JAMA* 298(15): 1779.

Carrick-Hagenbarth, Jessica, and Gerald Epstein. 2012, January. "Dangerous Interconnectedness: Economists' Conflicts of Interest, Ideology and Financial Crisis." *Cambridge Journal of Economics* 36: 43–63.

Civilekonomerna, The Swedish Association of Graduates in Business Administration and Economics. 2012. "Yrkesetiska Riktlinjer." Retrieved from http://www.civilekonomerna.se/portal/page/portal/Om_oss_About_us/sokresultat/visa?element_id=8165

Coats, A.W. 1986. *Economists in International Agencies: An Exploratory Study*. Westport, CT: Praeger Publishers.

Columbia University. 2012. "Policy on Financial Conflicts of Interest and Research" Revised, effective as of August 24th, 2012." Retrieved from http://evpr.columbia.edu/files/evpr/imce_shared/FCOI_Research_Policy.pdf

Cooke, Kristina, and Emily Flitter. 2011, July 8. "Economists Display Little Interest in Ethics Code." *Real Clear Markets*. Retrieved from http://www.realclearmarkets.com/news/reuters/finance_business/2011/Jul/08/economists_display_little_interest_in_ethics_code.html

Dana, Jason. 2009. "How Psychological Research Can Inform Policies for Dealing with Conflicts of Interest in Medicine." In *Conflict of Interest in Medical Research, Education, and Practice*, edited by Bernard Lo and Marilyn J. Field. Washington, DC: National Academies Press: 358–374.

Davis, Michael, and Andrew Stark, Eds. 2001. *Conflict of Interest in the Professions*. New York: Oxford University Press.

DeMartino, George F. 2011. *The Economist's Oath: On the Need for and Content of Professional Economic Ethics*. New York: Oxford University Press.

Epstein, Gerald, and Jessica Carrick-Hagenbarth. 2010. "Financial Economists, Financial Interests and Dark Corners of the Meltdown: It's Time to Set Ethical Standards for the Economics Profession." *Political Economy Research Institute Working Paper Series*. Number 329: 1–39.

Ferguson, Charles. 2011. *Inside Job*. Sony Pictures Classics.

Flitter, Emily, Kristina Cooke, and Pedro da Costa. 2010, December 20. "Special Report: For Some Professors, Disclosure Is Academic." *Reuters*.

Folbre, Nancy. 2002. *The Invisible Heart: Economics and Family Values*. 1st ed. The New Press.

Folbre, Nancy. 2010*a*. *Saving State U: Fixing Public Higher Education*. New York: The New Press.

Folbre, Nancy. 2010*b*, November 8. “Ethics for Economists.” *Economix Blog*. Retrieved from http://economix.blogs.nytimes.com/2010/11/08/ethics-for-economists/

Harvard Medical School. 2012. “Interim Policy Statement on Conflicts of Interest and Commitmen.” *Harvard Medical School*. Retrieved from http://hms.harvard.edu/content/interim-policy-statement-conflicts-interest-and-commitment

Homan, Timothy R. 2010. “Economics Professors Will Consider Code of Ethics.” *Bloomberg*, December 31. Retrieved from http://www.bloomberg.com/news/2010-12-31/economics-professors-to-consider-ethics-code-disclosure-of-ties-to-banks.html

Journal of Economic Perspectives. 2011. “Front Matter.” 25(1): i–ii.

Kowalczyk, Liz. 2011, July 1. “Three Harvard Psychiatrists Violated Conflict of Interest Rules.” *White Coat Notes: Boston.com*. Retrieved from http://www.boston.com/Boston/whitecoatnotes/2011/07/three-harvard-psychiatrists-violated-conflict-interest-rules/s9wmaqq-zLx9HnpYOsitegL/index.html

Lahart, Justin, and Mark Whitehouse. 2011, January 7. “Economists' Group May Revamp Ethical Guide.” *Wall Street Journal*, sec. Economy. Retrieved from http://online.wsj.com/article/SB10001424052748704415104576066611532847124.html

Luban, David. 2001. “Law's Blindfold.” In *Conflict of Interest in the Professions*, edited by Michael Davis and Andrew Stark. New York: Oxford University Press.: 23–48.

McCloskey, Deirdre N. 2007. *The Bourgeois Virtues: Ethics for an Age of Commerce*. Chicago: University of Chicago Press.

McKinney, W. Paul, David L Schiedermayer, Nicole Lurie, Deborah E Simpson, Jesse L Goodman, and Eugene C Rich. 1990, October 3. “Attitudes of Internal Medicine Faculty and Residents Toward Professional Interaction with Pharmaceutical Sales Representatives.” *JAMA* 264(13): 1693–1697.

Le Monde Economie. 2012. “Dogmatisme, Conflits D'intérêts, La Science Économique Suspectée.” Retrieved from http://lemonde-emploi.blog.lemonde.fr/2012/04/03/dogmatisme-conflits-dinterets-la-science-economique-suspectee-dans-le-monde-economie/

National Association of Forensic Economics (NAFE). 2004, October 8. “Statement of Ethical Principles and Principles of Professional Practice.” Retrieved from http://nafe.net/about-nafe/nafes-ethics-statement.html?searched=ethics+rules&advsearch=oneword&highlight=ajaxSearch_highlight+ajaxSearch_highlight1+ajaxSearch_highlight2

Ohio State University. 2012. “Faculty Financial Conflict of Interest.” Retrieved from http://orc.osu.edu/regulations-policies/coi/policies-procedures/

Pronin, Emily, Daniel Y Lin, and Lee Ross. 2002, March 1. “The Bias Blind Spot: Perceptions of Bias in Self Versus Others.” *Personality and Social Psychology Bulletin* 28(3): 369–381.

Research, Education, and Practice Committee on Conflict of Interest in Medical, and Institute of Medicine. 2009. *Conflict of Interest in Medical Research, Education, and Practice*, edited by Bernard Lo and Marilyn J. Field. Washington, DC: National Academies Press.

Sen, Amartya. 1991. *On Ethics and Economics*. New York: Wiley-Blackwell.

Senate. 2008. “154 Congressional Record S5029 – Payments to Physicians.” June 4rth. Retrieved from http://www.gpo.gov/fdsys/pkg/CREC-2008-06-04/pdf/CREC-2008-06-04-pt1-PgS5029-2.pdf.

Silverman, Ed. 2011. “Harvard Docs Disciplined For Conflicts of Interest.” *Pharmalot*. Retrieved from http://www.pharmalot.com/2011/07/harvard-docs-disciplined-for-conflicts-of-interest/.

Smith, Adam. 2000. *The Theory of Moral Sentiments*. Amherst, NY: Prometheus Books.

Stanford University. 2012. “Faculty Policy on Conflict of Commitment and Interest (RPH 4.1).” Retrieved from http://rph.stanford.edu/4-1.html

Steinman, Michael A., Michael G. Shlipak, and Stephen J. McPhee. 2001, May. "Of Principles and Pens: Attitudes and Practices of Medicine Housestaff Toward Pharmaceutical Industry Promotions." *The American Journal of Medicine* 110(7): 551–557.

The National Bureau of Economic Research. "Research Financial Conflict of Interest Policy." Last modified November 2012. Retrieved from http://www.nber.org/COI/NBER_ResearchFCOI_Policy.pdf

The University of Chicago. 2007. "Outside Professional and Commercial Interests of Faculty/Conflict of Interest Policy." Retrieved from http://researchadmin.uchicago.edu/policies_compliance/conflict_interest/

University of California. 2010. "University of California Policy on Disclosure of Financial Interests and Management of Conflicts of Interest Related to Sponsored Projects." Retrieved from http://researchcoi.berkeley.edu/review.html.

University of California. 2001. "Conflict of Commitment and Outside Activities of Faculty Members." Retrieved from http://researchcoi.berkeley.edu/review.html

University of Massachusetts Amherst and Boston. 1997. "Conflict of Interest Relating to Intellectual Property and Commercial Ventures Policy". University of Massachusetts Amherst and Boston. Retrieved from http://www.umass.edu/research/conflict-interest-relating-intellectual-property-and-commercial-ventures-policy

U.S. Public Health Services. 2012. *Electronic Code of Federal Regulations: Title 42: Public Health. Electronic Code of Federal Regulations.* Retrieved from http://www.ecfr.gov/cgi-bin/text-idx?c=ecfr&sid=f67ea01984581d3934103b5074c05500&rgn=div5&view=text&node=42:1.0.1.4.22&idno=42#42:1.0.1.4.22.6

Verein für Socialpolitik. 2012, July 21. "Der Ethikkodex Des Vereins Für Socialpolitik (The Code of Ethics of the Association for Social Policy)." Retrieved from http://www.socialpolitik.org/vfs.php?mode=ethik&lang=1

Wilber, Charles K., and Amitava Dutt. 2010. *Economics and Ethics: An Introduction.* Basingstoke, UK: Palgrave Macmillan.

Yu, Xi. 2011, July 2. "Three Professors Face Sanctions Following Harvard Medical School Inquiry." *The Crimson.* Retrieved from http://www.thecrimson.com/article/2011/7/2/school-medical-harvard-investigation/.

Zipkin, Daniella A., and Michael A. Steinman. 2005. "Interactions Between Pharmaceutical Representatives and Doctors in Training." *JGIM: Journal of General Internal Medicine* 20(8): 777–786.

PART VI

ETHICAL ISSUES IN APPLIED ECONOMICS

1. Development

CHAPTER 25

ETHICS, ECONOMIC ADVICE, AND ECONOMIC POLICY

JOSEPH E. STIGLITZ

INTRODUCTION

IN this chapter I wish to discuss the ethical dimensions of a variety of issues in development and international economics that I confronted as a member and chairman of the Council of Economic Advisers under President Clinton and as chief economist of the World Bank.[1,2] Economists have long bought into the importance of self-interest not only in explaining behavior, but also in yielding efficient outcomes. But economists have also long been aware of the limitations of these perspectives. Not only does the self-interest/market paradigm often fail to generate efficient outcomes, but even when it does, these outcomes may not comport with notions of social justice. Still, in the realm of economic policy, governments typically justify foreign aid and other policies aimed at poorer countries in terms of their own self-interest: how such policies increase world incomes, thereby increasing the country's own exports, or contribute to global political stability, from which all benefit. Such arguments deflect attention from the moral justification for these policies.

Ethics in the relationship between developed and less developed countries dictate that the developed countries treat the less developed countries fairly, aware of their

[1] The author is University Professor at Columbia University. He previously served as senior vice president and chief economist of the World Bank and as Chairman of the US Council of Economic Advisers under President Clinton.

[2] This paper was prepared for the Inter-American Initiative on Social Capital, Ethics and Development, December 2002; earlier versions were presented in 2000 at a meeting in Milan sponsored by the Vatican in connection with the Jubilee, and at a conference at the Interamerican Development Bank in Washington, DC. The content has not been significantly updated since the original drafting. Before publication in 2013, I inserted an occasional footnote or parenthetical remark on how matters have evolved since then.

disadvantaged economic position, and acknowledging that taking advantage of one's own economic power will inevitably hurt the poor within developing countries. We have seen several instances where, in global economic relationships, this precept has been grossly violated: an international trade agenda set to advance the interests of the more developed countries, at least partially at the expense of the less developed—so much so that on average the world's poorest region was actually worse off at the end of the last round of trade negotiations; and an international environmental agreement that provided that those rich countries that today are polluting more be entitled to continue polluting more into the future.[3]

There are other dimensions to globalization that illustrate the same violation of basic ethical precepts. Consider the argument made for free capital mobility: it increases world efficiency. Never mind the devastation that it might bring to small, poor countries—and the poor within those countries—that are not able to withstand the seemingly irrational vicissitudes of investor sentiments and the consequent reversals of capital flows! But globalization in these factor movements is much like globalization in trade: there we saw the powerful tell the less developed countries to open their markets to the goods of the more industrial countries, while keeping their own markets closed. The factor that the developed countries export is capital, while the factor that the developing countries have in abundance is labor. From an economic perspective, global efficiency can be attained by free mobility of labor every bit as well as it can be attained through free mobility of capital. But the developed countries are not arguing that there should be free mobility of labor. They are not offering to open up their doors to the poor of the world. The reason is obvious: they are aware of the social dislocation—and the consequent political pressure—that such migration would bring about. But they simply cannot put themselves in the shoes of the developing countries. And they are unsympathetic when the developing countries raise precisely the same objections to opening up their countries to the factors and goods that are in abundance in the developed world.[4]

I shall conduct my discussion at the level of pragmatic ethics, that is, I shall not try to derive the ethical principles from first-order considerations. Rather, I shall explore the implications of certain widely held ethical precepts for the conduct of international economic relations and, by extension, the conduct of development and other economists who operate in this environment. By the same token, I shall evaluate certain actions,

[3] In the case of international trade agreements, there was the hope that the round of negotiations begun in November, 2001 at Doha would rectify the imbalances of earlier trade agreements; it was even called the *development round*. But in the more than a decade since the inauguration of this round, the developed countries reneged, so much so that the round no longer deserves that epithet. Indeed, some of the bilateral and so-called "partnership" agreements have been as or even more unbalanced than the agreements of the past. So, too, there was hope for a global agreement affecting climate change in which the developed countries lived up to their moral responsibilities. But this has not been forthcoming, either.

[4] Interestingly, more than a decade after the IMF attempted, in Hong Kong in 1997, to change its charter to enable it to force countries to liberalize their capital markets, the Fund recognized that capital market restrictions can be an important tool for countries to help stabilize their economy.

ascertaining which can be viewed as *principled actions.* I shall not undertake the far more ambitious goal of defining a set of principles for action, though to be sure, my remarks are intended as a prelude to that task. I will use this occasion to raise questions as much as provide answers.[5]

I focus on five concepts in particular: honesty, fairness, social justice (including a concern for the poor), externalities, and responsibility. Although the meaning of most of these terms should be self-evident, let me briefly comment on each. Honesty goes beyond the dictate to refrain from outright lying; it comes closer to the dictum of telling the truth, the whole truth, and nothing but the truth. Misrepresentation—asserting that there is evidence for some proposition when there is none—violates the principle of honesty.[6] Fairness includes what economists call horizontal equity—either treating everyone the same (e.g., not discriminating on the basis of race or gender), or, to the extent that it is desirable to treat those in different circumstances differently (e.g., the aged and the handicapped may need special treatment), treating those in similar positions similarly. The hard question, of course, is, What are meaningful differences, differences that could justify differences in treatment? Favoritism—including giving special treatment to special interests—is thus a violation of the ethical norm of fairness. Social justice includes helping those in need, and doing so in ways that enhance their sense of dignity and the ability to assume individual responsibility for themselves. "Externalities" entail that individuals should not impose costs on others. Littering is, in this view, "wrong," a violation of an ethical norm. Responsibility is the ethical norm that individuals should take responsibility for their own actions and for the consequences of those actions.

Ethical issues arise in every aspect of economics and economic policymaking. We recognize, for instance, the ethical problems posed by *conflict of interest;* and that the multitude of positions that individuals have also makes such conflict of interest inevitable. Today, modern ethical norms require disclosure of significant conflict of interest, reflecting the precept of honesty. It is not commonly viewed to be immoral to take actions, in the role of a fiduciary, or to provide advice, from which one might oneself benefit. But it is immoral not to disclose the conflict of interest, so that those affected

[5] Much of what I have to say could be justified in terms of more general principles, for example, Kant's categorical imperative, or the Rawlsian analysis of social justice. The latter may be particularly useful in approaching the issues of equity discussed below: What kind of international social and economic order would one want behind the veil of ignorance, not knowing whether one would be born in a developed or developing country? Toward the end of this chapter, I shall try to put some of the ethical precepts into a broader context: the rules and norms that facilitate cooperative social interactions.

[6] Honesty is a precept that can be taken as a value on its own, or as *instrumental*: actions taken on the basis of distorted information may lead to adverse results. Presumably, one of the reasons for dishonesty is to induce others to take actions that, were they to know the truth, they would not. Thus, not disclosing fully the risks of capital market liberalization—and purporting that there are gains from such liberalization when there is little evidence that there are such gains—may induce countries to liberalize when, were they provided with more accurate information, they would not. Even if the country would have, in any case, liberalized its capital markets, the distorted information may lead it not to provide the safety net that it would have provided, were it fully aware of the risks.

can take appropriate precautions. The modern theory of agency recognizes that agents do not in general *adopt* the interests of those (the principal) whom they are supposed to be serving as their own; it is the responsibility of the principal to design incentive structures that align those interests, as much as possible. But it is wrong for the agent, for instance, to steal, to accept kickbacks from clients, or to engage in a host of other corrupt practices.

Advisors face ethical issues. Government bureaucrats and elected officials face ethical issues, such as those associated with corruption. Governments face ethical issues in the design of programs; and international institutions face ethical issues. I begin this chapter by subjecting the role of economic advisor to ethical analysis: What does it mean to be an *ethical* economic advisor? The question is an important one, because the international financial institutions are actively involved in providing economic advice. In doing so, do they behave ethically? I then examine specific issues: ethics in the treatment of developing countries by developed countries, for example, ethics in the areas of trade, global environmental policies, debt forgiveness, growth strategies, crisis management, and finally, ethical issues in population policy.

The Ethics of the Economic Advisor

Most professions have clear ethical principles. In medicine, these are embedded in the Hippocratic Oath, which includes doing no harm. In a sense, the ethical norms seek to mitigate the adverse consequences of the unbridled pursuit of self-interest, in particular those that arise whenever there are agency problems (where, because of lack of information, one party can take advantage of another). Violating these ethical principles harms the entire profession (there is, in this sense, an externality). It destroys trust. It is, for instance, unethical for a doctor to prescribe a medicine because he receives a kickback from the manufacturer. The patient, not knowing the reason a doctor prescribes a particular medicine over another, assumes the doctor is prescribing the medicine in the best interest of the patient. Thus, actions that could lead to a conflict of interest between the professional and the person for whom he or she is providing a service are unethical. Since a central part of the service being provided by most professions is information, honesty is a critical virtue.

There is a large economic cost to the destruction of trust. In simplistic models, individual self-interest leads to efficient outcomes; individuals act, and are expected to act, in their self-interest. But in modern theories in which information imperfections and incomplete markets play an important role, self-interested behavior in general does not yield efficient outcomes. Equilibria based on trust can yield better outcomes than those in which trust is absent. The patient, for instance, will be induced to get second and third opinions, because he will doubt the disinterested nature of the doctor's advice, if he believes that the doctor has a large financial stake in that advice. There is thus an *instrumental* argument for ethical behavior.

Some principles governing the behavior of economic advisors are straightforward. Clearly, there is an ethical mandate not to take advantage of inside information obtained as an advisor for profit, or to *directly* use connections generated in an advisory role for profit.[7] Furthermore, there are ethical (and often legal) norms for disclosure. Transparency mitigates, but does not totally eliminate, the danger that advice would be driven by self-interest. A consultant to a firm that had a short position in the stock of the firm would have an incentive to provide advice that would lead to the decrease in the market value of the firm. Few firms would allow the consultant to maintain such a position *were they to know about it.* Similarly, a consultant hired to advise a firm on the choice of a supplier should not have a financial interest in one of the suppliers, and if he does, he should disclose it; to not do so would be unethical.

But there are less straightforward implications as well, and it is these to which I want to call attention. First, honesty requires full disclosure of the limits of knowledge. Indeed, this has become an explicit part of the norms of good science. In the hard sciences one always presents the range of estimates, the confidence intervals with which certain results are held. The recognition of these uncertainties is even more important in the social sciences. Different propositions are held with different degrees of confidence. For instance, economists can claim with considerable certainty that hyperinflation has adverse effects on the economy. We can claim with some confidence that capital market liberalization is associated with greater risks, particularly for small, open, developing economies. On the other hand, *honesty* would dictate that an advisor recommending capital market liberalization reveals the absence of empirical evidence proving that capital market liberalization leads to faster growth (or at least after any supposed evidence is ambiguous and weak), and that economic theories supporting capital market liberalization are disputed. He would qualify any argument that capital account liberalization is helpful in inducing foreign direct investment by pointing out that the developing country that has been most successful in recruiting foreign direct investment—China—has not liberalized its capital account.

Second, *honesty* requires revealing that there is more than one Pareto-efficient policy. There are tradeoffs, with different policies affecting different groups differently, imposing different risks on different segments of society. Economic advice should focus on ensuring the *efficiency* of policies (to put it technically, to ensure that the economy is on the Pareto frontier), but it is the responsibility of political processes to choose the points on the Pareto frontier. When an economist recommends a particular point on the frontier as if it were the only efficient policy, he is using the cover of his supposed economic expertise to advance a political position. This is a misrepresentation. It becomes

[7] The most famous instance in recent years of an alleged violation of this ethical norm was in Russia, where two of the American advisors were accused of using their inside connections to obtain licenses for friends to establish funds. (Subsequent to the publication of the original version of this chapter, an in-depth of analysis of these events was provided by David McClintick, and severe penalties were imposed on Harvard University and Andrei Shleifer.) See McClintick, David. 2006. "How Harvard Lost Russia." *Institutional Investor*, January.

a particularly serious misrepresentation when the advisor, or interests with which he is affiliated, might be expected to benefit disproportionately from the particular policies being pursued. For instance, if there are a range of policies, some of which are more advantageous to those in the financial market, it would be unethical for an advisor representing financial interests not to disclose the fact that the particular policy he advocates would be particular advantageous to those groups.[8]

But in the public sphere today, there is a problem of "revolving doors," which are a manifestation of exactly these kinds of ethical conflicts. Individuals have what might be viewed as a *contingent* interest. Those who serve special interests well while in public service often get rewarded with lucrative positions after public service. Many governments are aware of the conflict of interest to which this gives rise. To mitigate the inevitable, related ethical issues, they insist that those who leave government service do not, for a period of time, enter into the employ of those where there might be a conflict of interest. Or, governments restrict the kinds of activities in which former public servants can be engaged. Certainly without such rules (but even with them) it would be unethical to give advice that favors those interests, without disclosing both the consequences for those groups and what might be viewed as the contingent interest of the advisor. (To be sure, the firms hiring these "devoted" public servants claim that they do so not as a reward for past services but on the basis of demonstrated acumen while in public service. It should be obvious that it is virtually impossible to draw the line between the two.)

Third, concern for social justice should make an economic advisor particularly attentive to the consequences of policies for the poor. Information does affect action, and although economists have a moral responsibility not to impose their values, they also have a moral responsibility to ensure the information is available on the basis of which *moral* policy decisions—for instance, decisions that reflect the principles of social justice—can be made.[9] If a policy imposes risks on the economy, then the advisor should point that out, especially if the risks are borne disproportionately by the poor. To the extent possible, there is a moral responsibility to think creatively about what kinds of policies might enhance the opportunities for the poor, allowing them to take more responsibility for their own well-being. Similarly, since there is a moral imperative to be concerned with future generations, economists should be attentive to the policies' affect on the environment, and should provide information that can lead to better environmental policies.[10]

[8] In the context of the Great Recession brought about by the financial crisis, the documentary movie *Inside Job* highlighted the many conflict of interest of several key economists in policy-making position and/or who had taken prominent public positions.

[9] I realize that there is a fine line that I am treading: I argued earlier that the economist should, in effect, distinguish the economist's role in defining opportunity sets from the political task of choosing among the points in the opportunity set. But the information supplied about the points in the opportunity set—for example, their impact on the poor—can affect the choices made. Someone not sharing the *values*, not concerned for the poor, might argue not only that providing that information is irrelevant, but also that it distorts the political process of decision making.

[10] We should thus view "green accounting" not just as a matter of providing a *good* accounting framework, but as a *moral* issue.

These are general precepts that apply to all policy advisors. I have argued that one of the advantages of the institutional structure of the Council of Economic Advisers in the United States is that it reduces the scope for conflict of interests.[11] The members are appointed for a short term and return to academia. Thus their incentive is to provide relatively accurate information, advice that will stand up to the scrutiny of their *academic* peers. The norms of the economics profession require making most of the distinctions I have alluded to, including distinguishing between special interests and general interests, efficiency effects and distribution effects. (Furthermore, US government regulations require that they dispense of all financial interests or put them into blind trusts; and in any case, few have substantial financial interests.)

One of the main activities of the international financial institutions is giving advice. In assessing the way that international financial institutions dispense advice, I feel that all too often they fall short on all counts described above. They push a particular set of policies, as loan conditionalities, rather than outlining the range of policies and trade-offs and then encouraging the countries themselves to take responsibility for choosing among alternative policies. They fail to clarify the uncertainties associated with the policies they promote, making assertions about the policies' efficacy that cannot be supported by evidence. Most importantly, at least in the past, they have not only failed to pay due concern to possible adverse effects of the policies on the poor, but they also have not even disclosed the likely risks. They have continually pushed policies entailing "pain," seemingly almost oblivious to who within the country has to bear that pain. Many of their policies seem to disproportionately benefit financial interests, and they fail both to point this out, and to disclose what I have viewed as the *contingent* interests of their staff—evidenced by the fact that many staff members leave the International Monetary Fund (IMF) or World Bank to work for private financial institutions.[12]

Facing Moral Dilemmas as an Economic Advisor

This brings me to perhaps the hardest moral question facing the policy advisor. What should he do when confronted with a policy that he believes is, in some sense, "immoral"? Should he speak out, but thereby risk possibly losing influence? Is silence a form of complicity? There are no easy answers, but a couple of examples may help illustrate the nature of the dilemma. When President Lyndon B. Johnson's economic advisors tried to forecast where the economy was going (and therefore what kinds of

[11] See Stiglitz, Joseph. 1997. "Looking Out for the National Interest: The Principles of the Council of Economic Advisers." *American Economic Review* 87(2): 109–113.

[12] In 2002, the number two person in the IMF moved directly from the IMF to take the vice-chairmanship of Citibank Group.

macro-policies would be required to sustain noninflationary full employment), they were confronted with the following problem: The government was spending more on the Vietnam War than it would admit to. On the one hand, the advisors could pretend that the official numbers were correct, thereby recommending a clearly misguided fiscal policy. On the other hand, they could choose not to use the official numbers and instead to use more accurate numbers, but this would violate the "confidences" of government. But maintaining this confidence was in itself morally questionable: in democratic societies, one might argue there is a moral imperative for openness and transparency; after all, a public official is the "servant" of the people and the people have a right to know what the government is doing.

A few years later, President Ronald Reagan's economic advisor, Martin Feldstein, faced a similar problem. He had long argued for the importance of high national savings. Yet Reagan had pushed a tax cut that resulted in huge deficits, potentially undermining the future prosperity of the country. A few economists predicted that, contrary to all the evidence, the tax cut would generate enough growth so that there would not be a deficit. Intellectual honesty would require discussing the absence of evidence for that conclusion, and the risks associated with the high deficits. In this instance, Feldstein took a strong public stand, pointing out the potential adverse consequences of the policy; but in doing so, he undermined the effectiveness of the Council of Economic Advisers within the Reagan administration.

I faced a similar dilemma as chief economist at the World Bank. I believed the policies pursued by the IMF in the wake of the East Asia financial crisis would lead to deeper, longer recessions and depressions than necessary. I believed that the financial interests of the foreign creditors were placed above the concerns for the poor and small businesses. The policies pushed by the IMF, I believed, would almost surely wreak havoc on their lives and livelihoods. I tried, quietly and within the institutional processes, to change the policies, or at least to promote open discussion of the policies (given my belief that the errors were so obvious that any open discussion would quickly bring about a reversal of course). But with the great institutional rigidities (and the powerful special interests and their ideologies), I not only could not reverse policies, but I also could not even engender open discourse. It seemed to me that there was a basic moral issue: How could I remain silent? I felt a strong moral obligation to speak out, and at the very least, to point out the risks of these policies.

The moral stance of those who worked hard to quash public discussions had irreconcilable contradictions. They argued that open discussion could undermine confidence in the policies, and the lack of confidence would impede the desired effects. Thus, speaking out was, in their minds, *wrong*, because without the confidence, capital would continue to flow out of the country, and this capital outflow would further weaken the economy, hurting the poor. They were arguing, in effect, not only for a lack of openness and transparency, but also for a kind of dishonesty: asserting that the policies were likely to be more effective than the evidence warranted. The dangers of this stance should be obvious. In almost every arena, government could argue that dishonesty, partial truths, are "means" that justify the ends. To be sure, the Treasury or IMF may believe in their cases. But the Department of Defense may argue the same thing about every aspect of its activities (from the toxicity of Agent Orange to the true magnitude of the threat of an enemy[13]). Such positions are not only dangerous and undermining of democracy, but are also ultimately self-defeating. Repeated assertions of this kind destroy the credibility of government. In the economic arena, they are particularly problematic, because the predictions will frequently be proven wrong, and the *ex post* excuses always seem absurd. Indeed, the IMF's overconfident forecasts have created a lack of credibility that itself contributes to the lack of efficacy of the Fund's policies. In the end, this lack of credibility made my decision easier: whether I spoke out or not would have little effect on the confidence in the policy; but speaking out might have some effect on the policy chosen, thereby averting, or at least reducing, the recessionary consequences.

In general, there is no easy answer to these moral dilemmas facing the policy advisor. Each situation is different. One must make a critical judgment about which actions will most likely bring about the actions that one believes are morally right. In some cases, resignation may be the most effective answer; but even when that is contemplated, there is an important issue of timing. A well-timed resignation can sometimes bring about change more effectively than any amount of argumentation. The resignation is often seen as a costly move, and as such, the fact that a public official—who has often worked hard to obtain the prominent position—is willing to undertake such a measure provides an effective signal concerning the depth of feeling on the issue.[14]

Ethics and International Economic Policy

I have argued that, though we expect individuals to act by and large in their self-interest, there are circumstances in which we say such behavior is *unethical*. So too for countries. We expect countries, by and large, to pursue policies that are in the interests of their citizens. But there are limits—behaviors that are unethical, or border on the unethical. To some, for a rich and powerful country to go back on its word is simply *real politick:* what can anyone do in retaliation? Some would go further, and say for government officials not to do so would be abrogating their responsibilities to their citizens, whose welfare they are supposed to be maximizing. If they can do so by lying, cheating, or stealing, so

[13] A point that was brought out even more forcefully by the events leading to the Iraq War, sometime after this speech was delivered.

[14] A case in point, which emerged after the original version of this chapter was completed: Ravi Kanbur served as the director of the World Bank's decennial World Development Report on poverty. The version that he submitted for consideration emphasized not only income poverty, but also lack of voice and insecurity. The US Treasury (and in particular the Secretary of Treasury) insisted on the more narrow focus; with Kanbur's resignation, and the resulting civil society protest, the report that emerged reflected the original vision.

be it. Again, however, one can argue against such behavior on instrumental grounds. In today's world even a powerful country needs the cooperation of others, and if it develops a reputation for mistreating others—for dishonesty, for breaking its word—it will find it more difficult eliciting that cooperation. The lack of trust has even more important consequences in the international arena than in the arena of domestic economics; in the latter, legal enforcement mechanisms can provide a partial substitute for trust. In the international arena, that is not the case.

In the following subsections, I review several recent issues in international economic policy through the lens of *practical ethics*. Each of these issues can be approached in other ways, and I do not intend to provide a comprehensive treatment of any of them. I do believe, however, that approaching these issues from an ethical perspective provides new insights—including insights into why it is that some of these issues have taken on such moral overtones.

Debt Forgiveness

Debt forgiveness has become the subject of enormous public discussion.[15] There seems something peculiar about very poor countries transferring money to richer countries year after year. Many countries have to spend a huge fraction of their export earnings to service their debts, leaving little remaining to spend on improving the plight of the poor. The debt overhang impedes growth and poverty reduction. Without debt forgiveness, prospects for these countries are bleak.

Here, I do not want to address the economic issues, but rather the moral issues and dilemmas. There are four, in particular, that have not received sufficient attention. The first concerns *fairness* among developing countries. The amount of resources transferred from the rich to the poor will, in any case, be limited. The question is, Who will receive these funds? The funds used for debt forgiveness could have been used to aid other needy countries, in particular countries that are equally poor, but had repaid their debt. It seems unfair, to say the least, that those who have lived up to the terms of the loan contract should be in the same or worse position than those who do not.

The second issue revolves around the moral responsibility of the lenders. Consider loans made to Mobutu Sese Seko in his heyday. The lenders knew of his corruption. They knew that the money would not go to the people in the country. At best, it was Cold War lending, pure and simple. At worst, it was lending to ensure that Western companies could continue to exploit the rich natural resources of that country. Why should the people of Zaire—who had no say in the choice of Mobutu as their leader—have had to pay for the money that was given to him, and which he squandered? Doesn't the moral responsibility lie with the lender? (Such debts have come to be called *otiose* debts, with many critics of the lending policies suggesting that there is no *moral* obligation on the

[15] This chapter was written at the time of the Jubilee movement, which successfully called for large-scale debt forgiveness for the world's poorest countries.

part of the debtor to repay the debt, and that there is a moral obligation on the part of the creditor to forgive the debt.) In any case, every loan is a voluntary transaction between the lender and the borrower; as such, if a loan is made that shouldn't have been, the lender is as much at fault as the borrower. Indeed, in a fundamental sense, he may be more to blame: lenders have better knowledge of risks, and they typically have been rewarded for those risks by interest rates that are in excess of the safe interest rate, sometimes considerably so.

The case just described seems like an easy one, where the moral responsibility of the lenders cannot be avoided. But there are cases that might seem slightly more problematic. Consider the 1998 IMF loan to Russia. In that case, there was an elected government, though one for which there was considerable evidence of corruption. It was perfectly clear at the time that Russia's exchange rate was overvalued; the overvalued exchange rate was having an adverse effect on their economy; the IMF-imposed contractionary policies (part of the conditionalities imposed for assistance) caused a deep plunge in its economy leading to enormous increases in poverty (from 2 percent under the previous regime to almost 50 percent by 1998); and the policies of privatization and free capital outflows that the Fund also had pushed led to a few oligarchs accumulating huge amounts of wealth. Should the IMF have lent billions of dollars to the country knowing what it did? They knew full well that there was a high likelihood the funds would simply enable a few oligarchs to take more money out of the country, and that it would saddle the country with increased indebtedness. They knew that the poor taxpayers would eventually have to pay back the funds borrowed. And they knew that, in any case, lending was unlikely to facilitate the resumption of growth (and indeed, by sustaining the exchange rate at an overvalued level, actually had an adverse effect on growth). If the IMF did lend the country money, and if the money then was, in effect, used to enable oligarchs to take more of their wealth out of the country on more favorable terms, and if the economic polices failed, what is the moral obligation of the citizens of the country to repay the loan, or of the Fund to forgive the loan? What is the moral responsibility for their misguided advice, for their complicity in providing funds where there was such a high likelihood of abuse?

The third issue concerns the nature of the debt contract, and the advice given to the countries. In well-functioning capital markets, the risk associated with any contract is divided among the parties, with the party most able to bear the risk bearing the risk disproportionately. But capital markets do not work as well in practice as they do in theory. It is the developing countries that bear the brunt of the risks associated with exchange rate and interest rate changes, and it is large changes in exchange rates and interest rates that have led many of the countries to their current predicament. The international financial institutions, of course, have the opportunity—I might say the obligation—to design contracts that reflect an appropriate sharing of the risk burden, but they have failed to do so. And they have failed, in many cases, to advise the country of the risks associated with the borrowing policies that they recommended. For instance, prior to the Russian 1998 crisis, the IMF advised Russia to borrow in dollars, seemingly because the interest rate was lower. But the IMF, of all institutions, believes in well-functioning markets and should have also pointed out that if markets were working well, then the differences in interest rates (between the dollar and ruble rates) reflected the risk of exchange rate change, and that if Russia did borrow more in dollars, the consequences in the event of a devaluation (which at the time seemed highly likely) would be very severe. The moral weight for debt forgiveness seems greater because of these poorly designed contracts and the incomplete, and in some cases, misguided advice.

The fourth issue relates to the conflict of interest that I brought up earlier in this chapter. One of the functions of the large bailout loans has been to provide funds with which Western banks can be repaid. There are potential conflict of interest (at the individual[16] and organizational levels[17]): much of the benefits to these loans arguably go to the banks and other Western financial interests, with the costs being borne by workers and others within the country. Ethical advice and lending practice would require that this be pointed out. When there has not been adequate disclosure, what is the *moral* obligation of the borrower to repay, or of the lender to forgive?

Ethical issues associated with repaying debts, and debt enforcement, are longstanding and complicated. Over time, there has clearly been a change in ethical views. Debtor prisons were employed in the 19th century in Britain. Most people today would view such treatment as cruel punishment, unethical, no matter how strong the incentives for repayment it provides. Similarly, bonded labor, sometimes used as a debt enforcement mechanism in developing countries, is not only illegal in most countries, it is also unethical—just a step away from slavery. For a country to march into another to enforce a debt contract would also today be viewed as unethical, though it occurred several times in the 19th century. At the individual level, usurious interest rates and the imposition of other "conditions" associated with loan-sharking are viewed as unethical. The extensive conditionalities imposed by the IMF in the context of the loans to countries in desperate need for funds raise similar questions: When do such conditionalities represent an abuse of power, and in that sense, are they unethical? These are questions I briefly touch upon later.

Providing Loans

In approaching the problem of whether to give a country a loan, a simple question needs to be posed: Will the country, as a whole, be better off with the loan than without it, taking into account that it will be more indebted? If there is a reasonable chance that the country will be worse off, the *moral* case (as well as the economic case) is questionable. The incentives of the lending institution and its staff and the incentives of the borrowing

[16] That is, many of those responsible for making the loans have, and will have, connections with the financial institutions being bailed out.

[17] That is, finance ministries (US Treasury) and central banks, with close ties to the financial community in the advanced industrial countries—the lenders—are responsible for the lending decisions.

government may differ markedly from these *moral* dictates. The government may feel that the money will give it a chance to survive; if the money fails to work, it will be someone else's problem. To return to the IMF loan to Russia, one of the arguments for giving the money was that it would enhance the political survival of Boris Yeltsin, whom the United States and the IMF viewed as a friend. More to the point, the downfall of Yeltsin would be seen as a failure of IMF and US Treasury policy. The incentives of the IMF and the US Treasury did not necessarily, in this sense, coincide with the interests of Russia, though to be sure, the IMF and US Treasury might have thought that they were in a better position to make the appropriate political judgments than were the voters in Russia. (The discrepancy between individual and organizational incentives has been emphasized in the organizational literature; for instance, the theory of escalating commitment points out that the cost to an individual of abandoning a strategy that he has advocated may be greater than the cost to the organization.).

To provide another example: in the recent Argentina debacle, at the time of the August 2001 loan, even IMF Board members were skeptical that the money was going to make any difference. The country would be left more in debt, but the likelihood that it would enable the country to survive for more than a few months without a major default or devaluation was slim. It could conceivably be viewed, however, in the interests of a very senior official, who was about to depart. Not lending would have precipitated a crisis then and there, and it would have made apparent that the policies he had pushed had been a dramatic failure. If there was even a small chance that the program might work, his policies might be vindicated. If they failed, he did not bear the costs: it was the people in the country that bore the increased indebtedness. So cynical had some of the Board members become at this juncture that they talked about the $8 billion as a going away present for the departing official; the money was likely to hold things together until he left the Fund, sparing him the immediate embarrassment, but not much longer.

In short, there are reasons to believe that the interests of the borrowing government and lending institution (IMF) may differ markedly from those of the people in the country. The IMF and its staff would like to persuade others that they are unlike other public and private institutions: although they recognize the role of rent seeking and distorted incentives especially in governmental institutions, they themselves believe that they are immune from such distortions. There is little in the way of theory or evidence to support such a view. When money was lent to a country for reasons other than promoting the development of the country (e.g., to maintain friendship with the ruling government in the Cold War), the ethical case for debt forgiveness is enhanced; the moral obligation for repayment is reduced.

Of course, in the case of private lending, there may not even be a pretense that it is in the long-run interests of the country. The lenders may make their money up front and often don't have to bear the full risk of the loan going bad—especially if they can syndicate the loan and/or if they can count on a bailout by the IMF.

So far, I have emphasized that there are numerous instances in which loans have been given when they arguably should not have been, raising ethical issues about repayment. There are similar issues when there are circumstances in which one might argue that loans should be given but the money is withheld, or conditions are imposed, taking advantage of the weakened position of the borrower. Ecuador provides a possible example. Providing money at a critical stage to a country facing a liquidity crisis because of a series of adverse shocks, including low oil prices, a weak agricultural position because of El Niño, or a disease affecting shrimp—one of its major export crops—would have made economic sense and would have been the *ethical* thing to do. And because of Ecuador's oil reserves, its long-term financial position was more positive. It might have enabled the survival of a democratically elected government. But the IMF had been extensively criticized for large bailouts; there was pressure for a policy of "bail-ins"—private sector participation. It was too risky to try this new strategy on rich and powerful countries like Brazil and Russia; weak countries like Romania and Ecuador were chosen for the experiment, with adverse consequences for both.

Developed Countries' Trade Policy

The riots in Seattle brought home the extent of dissatisfaction with the way that international trade negotiations have been conducted, and are likely to be conducted in the future.[18] The agenda had been set by the rich and powerful countries, to reflect vested interests in their countries. And the outcomes had reflected their economic power. Indeed, by one calculation, sub-Saharan Africa was actually worse off after the Uruguay round of trade negotiations (which was completed in 1994) than before. The United States pushed for liberalization of financial services and information technology and for more extensive protection of intellectual property. It was less concerned about other services, such as marine and construction, or even the potential adverse effects of the rigid enforcement of intellectual property on those in the developing countries whose lives depended on the availability of cheap drugs. In trade negotiations with Korea (and other countries), it pushed for rapid financial and capital market liberalization, knowing full well the risks that those policies imposed on the country.[19] The welfare of the US financial community was put above the welfare of the developing countries' workers. In dragging its feet in negotiations leading up to the admission of China to the World Trade Organization, the United States went so far as to argue that China was not a developing country—though the World Bank (and every other international agency) classifies it as such.

[18] For a moment, with the signing of the agreement marking the beginning of the Development Round trade negotiations in Doha in November, 2001, it seemed that the West had become aware of the imbalance, and that the inequities would be rectified. What happened in the subsequent years showed, however, that that was not to be the case.

[19] This policy was pushed by the US Treasury, even though the Council of Economic Advisers not only warned about the risks imposed by the policy and the dubious benefits to the country, but also argued that there were few benefits to the United States as a whole. The policy was another example of special interests having sway.

At one level, it is natural for a country to pursue its own interests. But, as I asked earlier, at what point does this pursuit of a country's own interest (or, as is more frequently the case, special interests within one's country) at the expense of the poor, become a *moral* issue?

There is one aspect of these discussions that particularly troubles me as an economic advisor: when the arguments used for the US position border on hypocrisy and dishonesty. For instance, while the United States (and the IMF) lectured developing countries on the evils of subsidies and the virtues of free trade, Western governments maintained huge subsides and trade barriers in agriculture, the areas of comparative advantage for many developing countries. The United States and Europe accused others of dumping—and under that ruse created new trade barriers—even though few economists would characterize what the countries were doing as dumping. It would have been better to be more honest and forthright, to admit that political pressures at home forced us to have policies that were hard to justify.

Global Externalities: The Global Environment

We teach our children early on that it is wrong to litter. This is an example of an externality, an action by one individual that affects others and for which that individual does not bear the costs. Government policies are designed to limit the extent of externalities, but they are imperfect. Social control mechanisms—a sense of what is right and wrong, ethical presuppositions—are more effective. The actions of those in one country similarly have effects on others, and given the absence or weaknesses of international law, there is a need for reliance on ethical norms. For instance, it is wrong for a country to locate a garbage dump on its boundary so that the downward wind pollutes the air of its neighbor.

The realization that we all share the same planet, that its resources are limited, and that bad policies can squander those resources, leaving future generations at risk, has come about only slowly. There is now general recognition of the *dangers* of global warming, and the Rio and Kyoto conventions are testimony to this global concern. But there is a deeply troubling aspect of the framework of these conventions. It is based on cutbacks in current emission levels. It is hard to detect an underlying principle of equity: the developed countries seem to have the right to pollute more than the less developed countries (on a per capita basis) simply because they have polluted more in the past. Is there any moral justification for such a policy? There are alternative frameworks, involving, for instance, agreements to undertake common policies (e.g., universal taxes on carbon emissions) that would seem to have a stronger ethical basis. The ethical stance of the United States, the largest emitter of greenhouse gases, both on a per capita basis and absolutely, is even harder to comprehend.[20] It claims that it need not do anything because the developing countries have not bound themselves to doing anything, even

[20] Since this chapter was written, China has overtaken the United States as the largest emitter of greenhouse gases, though the United States still remains, by far, the largest polluter on a per capita basis.

though the build-up of greenhouse gases is largely due to the advanced industrial countries, and even though, were they to make a commitment not to emit at levels that exceed those of the United States on a per capita basis, it will be decades before that constraint will be binding.

Intergenerational Equity, the Environment, Population Policy

There are moral dimensions not only to how we treat others who are alive today, but also how we treat future generations. By using up natural resources, without leaving compensating endowments of physical capital, we leave future generations more impoverished. This violates principles of intergenerational equity or social justice. Many developing countries today are exploiting their limited natural resources, without adequate provisions for the future. There are accounting frameworks (green accounting) that are designed to encourage better intergenerational equity. Governments should be encouraged not only to use such accounting frameworks, but also to set aside funds or to invest in physical and human capital.

Perhaps the most important determinant of environmental degradation (including that related to carbon emissions) is population growth. Population growth imposes a wide variety of externalities (a point recognized long ago by Edgeworth[21]). Countries with high rates of population growth have a hard time increasing incomes (per capita), and thus face a greater prospect of increasing poverty. Indeed, in the last decade of the last century, in the race between improving standards of living and population growth, the latter won: while the percentage of the population in poverty fell, the absolute number of people living in absolute poverty increased. Those with large families not only have a hard time feeding their children (and childhood malnutrition has lifelong effects), but they cannot afford to educate them, thereby condemning another generation to poverty and suffering. We now have the means of controlling population. I would argue that there is a moral obligation for governments to pursue such policies.

Crises

Earlier, I briefly alluded to the moral dilemmas I saw when confronting the East Asia financial crisis. I do not want to address here the problem of parsing out "blame" for the crisis and the failed management of the crisis. I want to focus on the *ethics* of

[21] Edgeworth, Francis Ysidro. 1925. *Papers Relating to Political Economy*. London: Macmillan.

international advice and assistance. To be sure, policies within the affected countries did contribute to the crisis: corruption and inadequate financial regulation played their part. But that is not the issue. The issue is how to intervene in the crisis in ways that minimize the damage, particularly to the poor, providing at the same time the foundations for correcting the underlying problems. The IMF failed to do this.[22] The interests of foreign creditors were put ahead of the concerns for the workers and small businesses, with devastating effects, from soaring unemployment to plummeting wages. These parties were innocent bystanders; it was not their borrowing that had led to the crisis. Food subsidies for the poor were cut, just when they were most needed. The political and social unrest—with many people dying—was predictable, and predicted.

What is the moral responsibility for those who push for the policies that had such disastrous consequences? Especially when their prior advice, encouraging and even demanding rapid capital market liberalization, was probably the single most important factor contributing to the occurrence of the crisis in the first place? And, even more so, when the policies put forward fail to have the predicted outcomes, the IMF and the US Treasury shifted blame to the country—and in doing so contributed further to investor flight. As Jeffrey Sachs pointed out, it was like crying fire in a crowded theater. Not only is doing so bad economic policy, and an abuse of the trust and confidence placed in the institutions. It is also arguably a fundamentally *immoral* act, just as crying fire in a crowded theatre—knowing that doing so might generate a riot and needless death—would be an immoral act. These are questions that all too seldom have been raised within international institutions or the governments that dominate their policies. But they are the questions that are increasingly being asked by ordinary citizens both in the developing world and in the more advanced industrial countries.

The governments in power, which acquiesced in those policies, bear some responsibility, but they often view themselves as having no choice—and indeed, were told that they did not in effect have any choice. The outside advisors did have a choice in the advice they prescribed. Indeed, there was controversy about the appropriateness of different policies. Thus, the issue is not whether the affected countries themselves and their governments bear some responsibility; they do. Rather, my concern here is the moral culpability of the IMF, which it has yet to recognize.

[22] The IMF has claimed that the quick recovery of several of the countries affected by the crisis is proof that its medicine works. A closer look at the pattern of recoveries does not support this conclusion, as I argue elsewhere. The country that has been the most assiduous follower of the IMF prescriptions, Thailand, years after the crisis still had a GDP below the pre-crisis level, and almost 40 percent of loans were still nonperforming. Malaysia had a quick recovery, but never had an IMF program. Indonesia, too, remained in a deep recession for years, partly attributable to the riots that were inspired by the failed IMF policies, partly attributable to the fact that those policies led to massive bankruptcies from which the country was slow to recover, and partly due to the strategy of restructuring the financial system, which led to runs that undermined the entire private banking system. Korea's relatively quick recovery in part was due to the fact that it did not listen to the IMF at key points: had it followed their advice in disposing of the so-called excess capital in the chip industry, it would have missed out on the global turnaround in that market that fueled the recovery. The growth in Russia and Brazil was because of the devaluations, which the IMF policies only delayed.

I want to briefly refer to several of the ethical dimensions of the IMF's behavior. First, in providing its advice, advisors did not act honestly in conveying the risks and uncertainties and in presenting the range of alternatives. Second, there is the issue of the trade-off between devaluations and interest rate increases and moral issues concerning responsibility. The IMF held that only by increasing interest rates could they forestall further declines in the exchange rate. In fact, the high interest rate policies were ineffective in forestalling the decline in the exchange rate, and may have actually contributed to it: by helping to deepen the recession/depression, capital was induced to flee, rather than be attracted into the country. But this mistake in economic judgment[23] should not be confused with the deeper moral issue. At the root of the crisis in several of the countries was excessive borrowing abroad. Those borrowing could have—and most economists would say, should have—obtained "cover" (effectively insurance) against a change in the exchange rate. No government guarantees its exchange rate; and there is no such thing as fixed exchange rates. Exchange rates change; the only difference in regimes concerns the frequency, magnitude, and more generally the rules that govern those changes. The market was, in effect, telling borrowers that there was a risk of devaluation (in equilibrium, the difference in interest rates at home and abroad is equal to the expected rate of change of the exchange rate, plus a risk premium). The stance of the IMF, once the crisis occurred, was to bail out those who had gambled on the exchange rate not changing (who had not bought cover), at the expense of the innocent bystanders. In a sense, those who *caused* the crisis, by borrowing excessively abroad in the short term, were let off the hook (at least partially), at the expense of those who were only engaged in normal business borrowing. Put this way, the bailout raises disturbing moral issues, beside the broader *moral hazard* issues that have been extensively discussed (the pattern of IMF inspired bailouts reduce the incentive of those borrowing abroad to obtain cover as well as the incentives of lenders to engage in due diligence in assessing credit worthiness.)

[23] There were other mistakes in economic judgment: the IMF concluded (without deep empirical work) that allowing the exchange rate to fall would harm the economy more than letting interest rates rise. In fact, in several countries, this was almost surely not the case. For instance in Thailand, those who borrowed abroad were the real estate firms (and those who had lent to them), who were already dead, in the wake of the collapse of the real estate bubble, and for whom a further fall in the exchange rate would have had little effect (though it may adversely affect the amount that foreign creditors could obtain); and exporters, who would gain as much in earnings as they would lose on their balance sheet. Perhaps the reason that they did not go into a close empirical evaluation of the effects was that that was not really their concern; they were more focused on the impact of the countries' ability to repay the loans to the creditors that they represented in the advanced countries (e.g., US and European banks). But this change in mandate from the purposes for which the institution was created—to help sustain a country in the face of a threatened downturn—and this obfuscation of the true objective of the policy (if correct) is itself deeply troubling, and raises moral issues.

Growth and Poverty Reduction Strategies

Today, everyone pays obeisance to the importance of reducing poverty. The IMF changed the name of its program for developing countries from Enhanced Structural Assessment Facility (ESAF) to incorporate the words "poverty and growth." Trickle-down economics—whereby one justifies programs that make the rich still richer by arguing that the benefits eventually trickle down to the poor—is no longer in fashion. But putting rhetoric aside, there is an active debate concerning economic policies. The position of the US Treasury and the IMF can be characterized as "trickle-down plus": growth is necessary and almost sufficient for reducing poverty, and consequently the best strategy for helping the poor is to adopt growth-maximizing reforms—the same neoliberal agenda, with its emphasis on privatization and liberalization, that prevailed over the past two decades, augmented by education and health. The modifications in the traditional formula represent important steps in the right direction. But the underlying prescription is faulty in several respects. The fact of the matter is that the countries that have been most successful in development over the past half a century—the countries of East Asia—have not followed the Washington Consensus policies. And many of the countries that have followed the Washington Consensus policies have not done particularly well (though the "doctor" claims that the prescriptions were not followed sufficiently closely). *Honesty* should have dictated full disclosure: the evidence in favor of the Washington Consensus policies is at best mixed; and failing to provide such honesty raises moral issues.[24]

But perhaps more important, concern for the poor should have dictated greater attention to the consequences of the policies for poor, and an awareness that the countries that have done the best job of reducing poverty have gone well beyond a reliance on trickle-down economics. Some examples help illustrate what I have in mind:

- The countries that have done best in improving the plight of the poor have had an explicitly pro-poor growth strategy that goes beyond simply paying lip service to education and health.
- Unless the poor are given assets—such as in land reform—they are likely to remain mired in poverty. But land reform may challenge vested interests. It is curious that although those who currently own large amounts of wealth in many of the poor countries acquired this wealth in ways that have little legitimacy (e.g., through the exercise of brute force by colonial masters), taking wealth away from these individuals is viewed as an abrogation of basic values of "property rights."

[24] Interestingly, in the 1996 World Development Report: "From Plan to Market" on transition, the most successful transition—that of China—is given short shrift, being relegated largely to "boxes." Was this because its success—including its success in reducing poverty—ran so counter to the prevailing orthodoxy?

- The disparity between the ownership of resources (such as land) and labor results in institutions, like sharecropping, that lead to attenuated incentives and reduced output. Under sharecropping, tenant farmers face, in effect, a tax rate of 50 percent (or more). Although the IMF speaks out strongly against high tax rates, and their enervating effects on effort, it has not spoken out as strongly in favor of a land reform that reduces these agency problems and increases economic efficiency at the same time that it increases equity.
- Some of the economic reforms advocated by the IMF and the US Treasury have dubious effects on growth, but increase the country's vulnerability to shocks. (Capital market liberalization represents the most obvious example.) It is the poor who inevitably bear the brunt of the downturns, regardless of the lip-service paid to the importance of creating safety nets. Honesty would require observing that even in the most developed countries, safety nets for farmers and the self-employed are inadequate.
- Even the benefits of trade liberalization become questionable unless accompanied by measures that enable the creation of new enterprises and jobs. But IMF packages often have accompanied trade liberalization measures by high interest rates that would make job creation a virtual impossibility, even in a well-functioning market economy. The point is a simple one: trade liberalization often leads to a loss of jobs. The free market ideology argues that this enables a flow of resources from less efficient uses to more efficient uses. Were that the case! The problem is that in many less developed countries markets do not work well (that is part and parcel of being less developed). Unemployment rates are high. Job creation is difficult. Moving labor from low productivity jobs to unemployment decreases a country's GDP and increases poverty. But often, that is precisely the effect of IMF packages combining liberalization with high interest rates.
- And even if the country is successful in creating new jobs, the poor may be adversely affected, because greater openness can lead to greater sensitivity to shocks from the outside world, the brunt of which is borne by the poor. Insecurity is one of the major problems facing the poor, and policies that increase that sense of insecurity adversely affect the plight of the poor.
- Privatization programs have often had adverse effects, particularly on the poor. The rapid privatization programs have led to privatization of monopolies, without regulatory oversight; and these monopolies, though they may or may not have proven more efficient in production, have sometimes proven more efficient in exploiting consumers. Privatization has proven an important vehicle for both corruption and increasing inequality, a point brought out forcefully by the experiences in Russia. Indeed, one of the incentives for rapid privatization was that those that received state assets below market value then made a contribution (not just in terms of finance, but also in terms of the even more valuable organizational support and media coverage) to support Yeltsin's reelection. The silence in the face of the corrupt loans-for-share deal spoke loudly: the means seemingly justify the end!

- The IMF has taken a particularly narrow (and peculiar) definition of good budgetary policy, in which foreign aid is not included, or is discounted, as a revenue source. The alleged reason for this is that foreign aid is volatile, and therefore cannot be counted upon. The World Bank analyzed this allegation, and showed that tax revenues were even more volatile. Hence, according to Fund logic, tax revenues should not be included in revenues either, in which case no country is in budgetary balance. More to the point, the appropriate response to volatile income flows is flexible expenditures. Countries build new schools and health clinics as they receive the money; when the aid stops, so does the construction. In long discussions with the Fund, I have never seen an adequate justification for the Fund's stance. But the consequences should be clear. It means that an increase in foreign aid may not result in more schools or health clinics, only more money going to the country's reserves.

The economics of these policies has long been debated, both within the economics profession and within civil society. My point in raising these issues is not to rehearse that debate, but to emphasize the moral dimension. The budgetary stance of the Fund means that fewer schools and clinics are built, to the detriment of the poor. Other policies described above increase the risks faced by the poor. In some cases, such as capital market liberalization, these policies seem of questionable benefit to the country as a whole, though they might bring benefit to the financial communities both within the country or, more likely, abroad. But there have been sins of omission as well as commission: land reform would have arguably increased both equity and efficiency.

In retrospect, as we look back at the colonial policies, at the unfair trade treaties foisted on Japan, at the Opium Wars, we shudder at their seeming lack of moral justification. We look with derision at writings describing the White Man's Burden, especially in light of its legacy in Africa and in so many other places in the colonial world. We no longer use military power to open markets or to enforce debt contracts, but the advanced industrial countries do use their economic power. They use their economic power to forge international agreements in which disproportionate benefits accrue to the developed countries, and in which, the less developed countries are sometimes even worse off. In this section, I have asked whether the same objections raised to colonialism could, in fact, be applied to the economic policies foisted on these countries. Even when they help the poor, are there alternative policies that might have helped them even more, or that would have imposed less risk on them? Have the international institutions that have pushed these policies been honest in portraying these risks? Have they been dishonest in exaggerating the evidence concerning their economic benefits? (Certainly, the benefits promised from economic reform in Russia have far exceeded what has been delivered.) Perhaps we should ask, Will our children's children look at current economic relationships with the same shock—the same sense of moral outrage with—which we look at the colonial experience? The experiences in Seattle and Washington, and extensive conversations with young people around the world, suggest that we may not have to wait for these reactions: the youth of today are questioning the moral legitimacy of these policies. The defenders of these policies claim there is no alternative; there is a single recipe for success. In this they are wrong, and if there was a single *best* recipe, the countries that have succeeded in simultaneously growing and reducing poverty would have given credence to the view that it is not the one that the international institutions have prescribed, with their inadequate attention to democratic, equitable, and sustainable development.

A General Perspective

Ethics has to do with an individual's relationship with other individuals, with the community and with society more broadly. Ethics involves the recognized moral rules required to live together in well-functioning communities. It is *wrong* to murder or assault or otherwise cause harm to another. But in modern societies harm to others can be done in a variety of ways—when an individual litters, he harms the environment, and hence injures the well-being of anyone who values the environment. Simple maxims such as "do unto others as you would have them do unto you" or "don't do unto others as you would not have them do unto you" and touchstones such as Kant's categorical imperative provide widely accepted guidelines, though to be sure, the world is complex enough that the application in particular circumstances may not be obvious, or even unambiguous. Earlier, we observed that from today's vantage point, we look on slavery with abhorrence, and view colonialism—and the colonial mentality—as a violation of basic ethical norms. But is one person's—or one country's—imposition of his will on another, by force of economic power more acceptable than an imposition by force of military power? In the 19th century, the two were often intertwined, with military power being used to enforce economic obligations. Today, matters are, perhaps, more subtle, but does this make them any more acceptable? In ordinary life, it would be viewed as a breach of ethical norms to take advantage of an individual's temporary misfortune, but at the international level, this is sometimes seen as simply the natural state of affairs. Should the imposition of conditions on the countries that needed finance in the 1997–1998 crisis—conditions that were unrelated to the crisis, or to the repayment of the loan—be considered a breach of ethical norms? Even if it is (at least from the perspective of the party imposing the conditions) for the good of the other party?

Many ethical precepts are concerned with actions that undermine "community." The development process, no matter how well it is carried on, typically undermines some traditional values, some aspects of traditional culture. But if carried on in the wrong way, it can have a devastating effect. The way that the transition from communism to a market economy was carried out in Russia was a disaster, by any account, with poverty soaring and output falling, while a few people garnered huge riches for themselves. No wonder there has been a complete erosion in the sense of community, in basic norms of behavior, matched by the growth of "mafia" activity. Economists have begun to talk about these ideas in terms of the concept of social capital. One of the reasons for the difference between China's successful transition and Russia's failure is the relative preservation of social capital in the former and its destruction in the latter.[25] But we also know that economic policies play a critical role: transitions accomplished through Bolshevik means, or with Bolshevik speed, or with the Bolshevik lack of concern for building social consensus, are more likely to lead to an erosion of social capital. In the case of Russia, the rapid privatizations helped erode what little social capital was left over from the communist reign: they resulted in a few individuals seizing control of vast assets formerly owned by the state, with free capital mobility almost inviting them to take their ill-begotten gains abroad, while the state claimed it did not have enough resources even to pay pensions.

We often talk about the "social contract." The social contract is never formally written down, but it can nonetheless still be broken, or be perceived to be broken. Hyperinflation is widely criticized because it undermines the social contract. What happened in Russia has been widely viewed within as a violation of the social contract. While the IMF argued during the midst of the 1997–1998 crisis that not repaying creditors was a violation of the sanctity of contracts, even though bankruptcy is a central institution in capitalism, they seemed to pay little attention to the violation of an even more important contract, the social contract.

If, as a result of the erosion of the social contract, there is a weakening of social cohesion, in ways that lead to more violence, more corruption, and more crime, then what is the culpability of those who have contributed to this evisceration of social capital? To what extent should they be held *morally* responsible for the consequences, especially when these consequences are the predictable—if not inevitable, at least highly likely—result of their actions?

I am raising here some fundamental issues: earlier, I argued that economic policies often give too little attention to their effect on the poor, to the sense of security. I suggest that this is a violation of basic ethical precepts. But economic policies are typically even less concerned with their impact on the community, on traditional social safety nets and traditional relationships. "Flexible labor markets" mean that employers should feel free to discharge workers as soon as they are not needed; there is no moral obligation to see workers through the hard times. Any policy that undermines the sense of community, social norms, a country's culture and pride, can, from this perspective, be viewed as a violation of ethical principles.

Individual and Institutional Responsibility

The thesis that I have advanced so far is that policies toward and within developing countries can be looked at from an ethical perspective, in terms of how they comport

[25] See A. Hussain, N. Stern, and J.E. Stiglitz. 2000. "Chinese Reforms from a Comparative Perspective." In *Incentives, Organization, and Public Economics: Papers in Honour of Sir James Mirrlees*, edited by Peter J. Hammond and Gareth D. Myles, 243–277. Oxford: Oxford University Press.

with basic precepts of moral behavior; and so too can the behavior of those who are called on to provide economic advice to developing countries. In these terms, we have seen that many of the actions undertaken by governments and recommended by outsiders, including the IMF, do not fare well. There have been large—and some might argue unnecessarily large—adverse consequences for the poor. Take for instance the full toll that the IMF's handling of the Asian crisis has had. It was not only the increase in poverty, but also that the cutbacks in social and health expenditures in, say, Thailand, exacerbated the economic downturn. And this led to an increase in the incidence of AIDS, and the poverty itself led to an increase in the trafficking of children.

In American jurisprudence, in many states, there is the principle of contributory negligence. All parties that had a role in the adverse outcome are held, in part, responsible. Similar issues arise in the realm of ethics. To be sure, the governments made the final decision about what policies were to be pursued. But the governments were often pushed to undertake the policies by the IMF, and felt that they had little room for maneuver. Here, we do not have to parse the blame. What we can say unambiguously is that the IMF and others who supported those policies—and especially those like the US Treasury who *pushed* those policies—bear considerable moral culpability for the outcomes.

In the Holocaust, the world also came to an understanding that those who stand idly by when they see others commit (what they view as potentially) heinous acts also bear a certain moral responsibility. The institutions in our society that are the guardians of our morals have an especial responsibility for taking up these issues. This is particularly important given the inadequacies in our system of global governance, where the voices of the poor and the voices of poor countries are barely heard, even in matters that affect their lives and livelihoods, where democratic principles are systematically ignored. The good news is that throughout the world today, there is a growing recognition of the importance of these issues. It is an opportune time for those with moral authority to raise their voices and join the chorus of the concerned.

Concluding Remarks

The past half-century has shown that with growth, development is possible, but far from inevitable. It has shown too that growth with poverty reduction is possible, but it is far from easy. There are a host of ongoing policy debates about the best way to pursue poverty reduction and growth. My concern in this chapter has not been to rehearse that debate—though inevitably I have had to touch on some of the more controversial issues—but to suggest that there are dimensions of that debate that can be usefully examined from a *moral* dimension, from precepts concerning such values as honesty, fairness, and a concern for the poor. Some might argue that such language speaks to the heart, and not just the head. But I argue that decisions about public policies inevitably need to speak both to the heart and the head, that it is important to think deep and hard about the moral dimensions of our economic decisions. One can, and indeed one should, combine this kind of moral analysis with a hardheaded analysis of the consequences and risks associated with alternative policies. Indeed, the lack of such a moral demand has all too often allowed ideology to have sway—an ideology that dishonestly claims more favorable and more certain benefits than the evidence would support, an ideology that suppresses meaningful democratic discussions of alternative courses of action, and that ignores, or at least puts insufficient weight on, the adverse consequences to the poor. Thus, I see the new humanism as a complement to hard economic reasoning, not antithetical to it; and I see the two working together as holding the greatest promise for a future international economic order based on social justice.

CHAPTER 26

NEOCLASSICAL ECONOMICS AS THE NEW SOCIAL ENGINEERING

The Debacle of the Russian Post-Socialist Transition

DAVID ELLERMAN

INTRODUCTION: THE RUSSIAN DEBACLE

THIS chapter considers the role that neoclassical economics, as represented by a few elite professors and the principal Western advisory institutions of the World Bank and International Monetary Fund (IMF), played in the post-socialist transition in the former Soviet Union and East Europe. The transition to a market economy in China was markedly different in that the "standard" shock therapy advice offered by neoclassical economics was largely ignored in favor of a robust pragmatism and gradualism. And the results were also markedly different.

According to the pro-market Stanford economist John McMillan, in his 2002 book *Reinventing the Bazaar: A Natural History of Markets*, Russia's production fell by 19 percent in the first year of shock therapy (1992) with a further 12 percent and 15 percent in the ensuing two years. It bottomed out at about 50 percent drop in gross domestic product (GDP). In contrast, from the start of incremental reforms in early 1980s, China averaged 8 percent per capita growth *for two decades*—which has continued (at various rates). In short, Russia experienced a debacle while China went through the greatest growth episode in modern history.[1]

[1] As McMillan put it: "The experiences of China and Russia could hardly have been more different. In China, reform was followed by world-record growth for twenty years. In Russia, incomes plummeted. Differences in their initial conditions . . . account for some of the differences in responses to reform. But much of it is accounted for by their policies" (2002: 206).

How Did Russia Arrive at Its Disastrous Policies?

> The amount of reliance on foreigners' advice highlights the difference between shock therapy and gradualism. Russia leaned on lawyers, economists, and bankers from the West for advice on how to privatize state firms, develop capital markets, and reform the legal system. . . . China by contrast called little on foreign consultants (McMillan, 2002: 207–208)

Who is to blame? In his review of McMillan's book, Harvard's Gregory Mankiw wrote:

> If McMillan is right that shock therapy was the problem, then the economics profession must accept some of the blame. Our profession lent some of its best and brightest to the transition effort, such as my former colleague Jeffrey Sachs. Most of these advisors pushed Russia to embrace a rapid transition to capitalism. If this was a mistake, as McMillan suggests, its enormity makes it one of the greatest blunders in world history. (Mankiw, 2003: 257)

Yet the main economists involved, principally the "Harvard boys" Jeffrey Sachs, Lawrence Summers, and Andrei Shleifer, as well as the leading advisory institutions such as the IMF and World Bank that espoused the standard Western economics advice (some version of shock therapy) have suffered *no professional or ethical accountability* for "one of the greatest blunders in world history."

The problem lies not just in the arrogant misdeeds of a few individuals but in the whole orientation of neoclassical economics as the new "scientific" basis for social engineering on a vast scale.

Social Engineering and Socialism

While neoclassical economics is seen as directly opposed to socialism, there is a deeper connection that can be seen by reviewing some of the intellectual history of socialism following the path laid out by Friedrich Hayek (1944, 1979) and Karl Popper (1961, 1962).

During the 19th century, the progress of the natural sciences was apparent to all, and that progress was translated into engineering triumphs over nature. The biological sciences were also starting to register successes that translated into major improvements in public health and disease control. Hence it was an easy matter to extrapolate the "march of science and technology" into the social world. As the scientific method would be applied to human affairs, then surely, it was thought, this would lead to better understanding of society which, in turn, would lead to the engineering of a better society for the future.

These ideas were developed in the first half of the 19th century by the French school of scientism or positivism founded by Henri de Saint-Simon and Auguste Comte. They saw the rise of a "social physics" that would have the scientific certitude of the law of gravity (Hayek, 1979: 255) and that would then translate into the engineering of a better society. Even the word "socialism" in its modern sense was first used by this school (Hayek, 1979: 282). In Germany, these ideas were blended with Hegelianism and were eventually developed with the greatest effect by Karl Marx. As the saying goes, "the rest is history."

I wish to extract from this thumbnail sketch only one idea—the idea that socialism would represent *the rational reconstruction of society on scientific principles.* The scientific treatment of the social world would be the inevitable end result of the triumphal march of the natural and life sciences carried over into the human sciences. As the march of science has led to the civil engineering of nature and to the medical control of many diseases, so the march of the social sciences would inevitably lead to the social engineering of society to achieve a prosperous and peaceful future for all. That vision of a socially engineered future was always a key part of the vision of "scientific socialism"—indeed, that phrase was first used by this French scientistic school (Hayek, 1979: 320). It was exactly that idea of rationally reconstructing society on scientific principles that ironically guided the advice of neoclassical economics to the post-socialist countries.

Yet that aspect of the socialist idea is now almost lost. It was not Saint-Simonism that entered history as a brute reality but Marxism. And it was the specific flavor of Marxian communism—namely state ownership of the means of production and state planning of the economy—that has become historically associated with "scientific socialism." Thus the main historical lesson that is too narrowly drawn from the recent collapse of communism is the failure of state ownership and state control of the economy.

The lesson that has *not* been drawn is the failure of the idea of "utopian social engineering" (Popper, 1961, 1962). Instead the idea of social engineering has survived largely unscathed but dressed in the different garb of modern neoclassical economics. The lesson drawn is that *Marxist* economics failed, and that neoclassical economics is scientifically triumphant. Social blueprints based on Marxism have been shown to be abject failures. Social blueprints or "models" based on the science of economics are thus seen as simply the application of science to reconstructing society both in the transition and the developing countries. Hence the major development institutions such as the World Bank and the IMF are simply being "scientific" when they base their social engineering schemes on the models provided by the "best and brightest" of the economics profession (Ellerman, 2003).

What Is Wrong with Social Engineering?

The Pragmatic Critique

History offers few "crucial experiments," but the contrast between the Russian and Chinese transitions is probably the best one could ask for to contrast a socially engineered shock therapy approach with a pragmatic incremental, step-by-step, or staged approach to institutional change. As the Yeltsin reformers such as Anatoly Chubais did use rather "Bolshevik" methods to try to storm the ramparts during the few windows of opportunity, Stiglitz (1999) and Reddaway and Glinski (2001) have called this "market Bolshevism." A wise commentator has put the matter well:

> We have a fearful example in Russia today of the evils of insane and unnecessary haste. The sacrifices and losses of transition will be vastly greater if the pace is forced . . . For it is of the nature of economic processes to be rooted in time. A rapid transition will involve so much pure destruction of wealth that the new state of affairs will be, at first, far worse than the old, and the grand experiment will be discredited.

These words are as true today as when they were written. And they were written by John Maynard Keynes (1933: 245) about the original Bolshevik transition, not today's market Bolshevik transition in the opposite direction.

What was the alternative strategy? In this case, the incremental non-Bolshevik/Jacobin alternative has long found its sophisticated expression in the work of the late Albert Hirschman about incremental reform-mongering change driven more by endogenous pressures, bottlenecks, and linkages rather than by exogenous "carrots and sticks" embedded in IFI loan conditions.[2] The reform experience in China—which has never had an IMF program—represents something like this incremental approach in practice; crossing the river groping for the stepping stones rather than jumping over the chasm in one last "great leap forward." As Deng Xiaoping put it in 1986:

> We are engaged in an experiment. For us, [reform] is something new, and we have to grope around to find our way. . . . Our method is to sum up experience from time to time and correct mistakes whenever they are discovered, so that small errors will not grow into big ones. (Quoted in Harding 1987: 87)

[2] See the "two basic approaches" in Hirschman (1973: 247–248), where he contrasts an ideological, fundamental, and root-and-branch approach to reform with an incremental, step-by-step, piecemeal, and adaptive approach.

When the experiments had positive results, the method was to catalyze the process. As another Chinese reformer Hu Qili put it at the same time: "We allow the little streams to flow. We simply watch in which direction the water flows. When the water flows in the right direction we build channels through which these streams can lead to the river of socialism."[3] One of the important misformulations of the transition alternatives was: fast versus slow. "Incremental" might be misleading if it is construed as "slow," as the Chinese reforms were hardly slow.

> China's gradualism turned out to be a speedier route to markets than Russia's shock therapy . . .
>
> The fastest route from a planned economy to functioning markets, it turns out, was not frenetically tearing down the old institutions, starting with a clean slate, and enacting top-down reforms. It entailed letting the new economy grow up around the old one, maintaining some stability to let people create new ways of doing business. (McMillan, 2002: 210)

This advice was not just "20–20 hindsight" about how "it turns out." The following was written in the middle of the transition debates in 1992 and published in 1993:

> After the collapse of the socialist idea in the late 1980s and early 1990s, the question of institutional change strategies came to the forefront. Broadly speaking, two opposed strategies emerged. The Big Bang approach advocated just drawing a big X over the old half-reformed institutions and then legislating new "ideal" institutional forms.

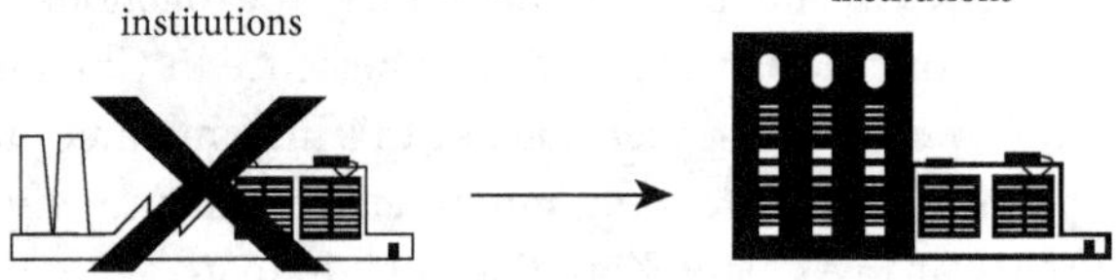

Big Bang Approach to Institutional Change.

[3] Quoted in Harding 1987: 318. Thus do Chinese "socialists" instruct market Bolsheviks on the non-Bolshevik methods of institutional transformation. A related "pave the paths" metaphor is used by Christopher Williams (1981: 112). In a complex of new buildings, let grass grow between them, see where footpaths develop, and then pave the paths. Whilst voicing Hayek's ideas about the market as a spontaneous order, many market Bolsheviks such as Václav Klaus at the same time labored to totally stop "spontaneous privatization" instead of trying to find the closest socially acceptable channel so that those spontaneous forces could grow from a stream to a river (Ellerman, 1993).

> The old *de facto* property rights embodied in the half-reformed institutions would not be recognized in any significant way, and the new *de jure* property rights would be legislated by the new "revolutionary" democratic government.
>
> What is wrong with moving in one great leap to some desired ideal form? Nothing—if institutional change could actually take place in that manner. But it usually does not. People will resist and "drag their feet" in countless ways when their *de facto* property rights are canceled or trivialized. The imagined great leap breaks down in chaos. Instead of disappearing overnight in favor of the new ideal institutions, the de-legitimated old institutions break down in favor of a shadowy anarchy of *ad hoc* opportunistic forms. The Big Bang becomes a Big Bust.
>
> The alternative is a strategy of incremental institutional change. Instead of an imagined great leap forward over the chasm between socialism and capitalism, incentives would be devised to move people incrementally but irreversibly from the existing quasi-reformed institutions towards the "ideal" institutions. Instead of just negating the *de facto* property rights of managers and workers, they can arrive at a nearby set of legitimized *de jure* property rights by moving in the right direction.
>
> 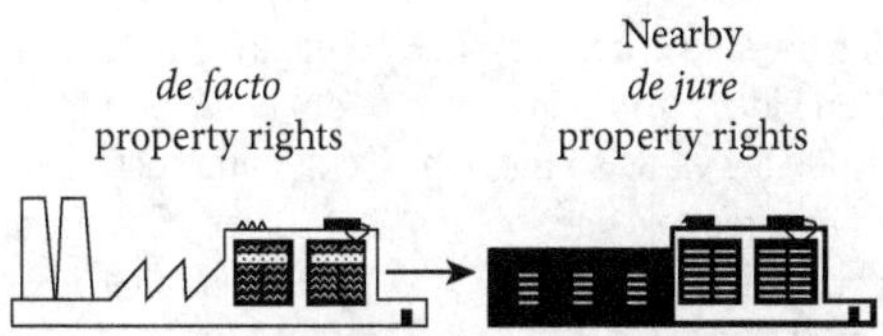
>
>
> Alternative Incremental Approach to Institutional Change
>
> . . . [T]he Russian mass privatization program is a Big Bang program, while the Chinese reforms in agriculture and industry are the clearest example of a thoroughgoing incremental approach. (Ellerman, 1993: 27–28)

Murrell (1992) explored the connections between incrementalist strategies and conservative political philosophies. In Lau, Qian, and Roland (2000), the Chinese "two-track" system of reforms is analyzed where a second track, step, or stage is inaugurated and can then grow to eventually render the earlier stage obsolete. Black et al. (2000) use the word "staged" in much the same sense. In Joseph Stiglitz's *Whither Reform?* (1999), the two "ideal types" were compared in Table 26.1 as a "battle of metaphors."

Another part of the incremental approach, also evident in China, is the willingness to allow bottom-up experiments in different parts of the country and then foster horizontal learning and the cross-propagation of the successful experiments. In contrast, the Bolshevik/Jacobin approach stops "imperfect" bottom-up experiments like the Russian lease buyouts (Ellerman, 2003) and then legislates the brave new world of "ideal institutions" from the capital city to be applied uniformly across the country. But the transition from socialism to a market economy had not happened

Table 26.1 "Battle of Metaphors"

	Shock Therapy	Incrementalism
Continuity vs. Break	Discontinuous break or shock—razing the old social structure in order to build the new.	Continuous change—trying to preserve social capital that cannot be easily reconstructed.
Role of Initial Conditions	The first-best socially engineered solution that is not "distorted" by the initial conditions.	Piecemeal changes (continuous improvements) taking into account initial conditions.
Role of Knowledge	Emphasizes explicit or technical knowledge of end-state blueprint.	Emphasizes local practical knowledge that only yields local predictability and does not apply to large or global changes.
Knowledge Attitude	Knowing what you are doing.	Knowing that you don't know what you are doing (Benziger, 1996).
Chasm Metaphor	Jump across the chasm in one leap.	Build a bridge across the chasm.
Repairing the Ship Metaphor	Rebuilding the ship in dry dock. The dry dock provides the Archimedean point outside the water so the ship can be engineered to blueprint without being disturbed by the conditions at sea.	Repairing the ship at sea. There is no "dry dock" or Archimedean fulcrum for changing social institutions from outside of society. Change always starts with the given historical institutions.
Transplanting the Tree Metaphor	All at once transplantation in a decisive manner to seize the benefits and get over the shock as quickly as possible.	Preparing and wrapping the major roots one at a time (*nemawashi*) to prevent shock to the whole system and improve chances of successful transplantation.[4]

before in history so the situation *clearly* called out for experimentation and pragmatism.[5] Instead the World Bank, IMF, and Western advisors succumbed out of their own arrogance and "la rage de vouloir conclure"—the rage to conclude—(Hirschman, 1973: 238–240) to the social-engineering Bolshevik/Jacobin mentality (complete with cold-warrior moral

[4] See Elster et al. (1998) for the use of Otto Neurath's "rebuilding the ship at sea" metaphor in this context and Morita (1986) about *nemawashi*.

[5] Deng Xiaoping's pragmatism, "It is not important if the cat is black or white, but that it catches the mice," was echoed by Ralf Dahrendorf's 1990 call "to work by trial and error within institutions" (41; quoted in Sachs, 1993: 4). Dahrendorf's book was a deliberate updating of Edmund Burke's anti-Jacobin tract *Reflections on the Revolution in France* (1937, orig. 1790). Sachs argued against Dahrendorf's pragmatism noting that: "If instead the philosophy were one of open experimentation, I doubt that the transformation would be possible at all, at least without costly and dangerous wrong turns" (Sachs, 1993: 5). To avoid "costly and dangerous wrong turns," Sachs promoted the scheme of privatization through voucher investment funds as if that were a tried and true model for a transformation that, in fact, had never taken place before.

fervor to wipe the slate clean of past evils) and supported Moscow legislation to apply the dreamed-up "ideal solutions" across all of Russia.

The Autonomy Critique

In addition to that critique of large-scale social engineering based on the wisdom of pragmatism, there is another principled objection to social engineering based on the humanist conception of autonomy. Humans are, in essence, autonomous beings, and the very idea of treating persons as being the objects of social engineering is inherently heteronomous. This is essentially a Kantian argument and it finds its normative expression in the version of the Kant's categorical imperative that persons should always be treated as ends in themselves and never simply as means.

One prominent economic model to engineer a human relationship is called "agency theory" which models the principal–agent relationship (e.g., the employment relation). The problem is not straightforward because the agent may have much more information than the principal about the tasks the principal wants to be performed and the principal's monitoring of the agent may be rather imperfect. The job of the agency-theory economist is to design the carrots and sticks of the agency contract taking into account the information asymmetry so that when the agent follows his own self-interest, he will in fact be performing the tasks desired by the principal. The slogan and mantra is: "get the incentives right."

From such relatively simple micro-situations, the social engineers of the economics profession then generalize the methodology to the grand problems of institutional design—seeing an institution as being like a complex multiperson contract. The key to institutional design is again to "get the incentives right" so that the various agents will "do the right thing" by following their self-interest within the designed incentive structure of carrots and sticks. In short, this is one of the ways that the idea of science-based social engineering—rationally reconstructing (a post-socialist or developing) society on scientific principles—has been reborn without any taint of association with Marxism or socialism.

It's the "How"—Not the "What"

There are inherent flaws in the economic theory of institutional design as "getting the incentives right."

One problem is the question of "what versus how." At the individual or social level, the question of *how* people do something is more important than simply *what* physical behaviors take place. For a new reform law to represent an effective and sustainable institutional change, it is crucial how the law was arrived at. Did the law evolve out of the experience, the debates, and the conflicts of the people,[6] or was the law passed by the government simply as a requirement to get a loan from the World Bank or IMF? That "how" question is much more important than the "what" question of the technical details of the law. But the major development agencies have no time for historical processes that might end up anyway with a "flawed" law. The "market Bolsheviks" (Reddaway and Glinski, 2001) have to use the "window of opportunity" to get the government to pass the "correct law" drafted by the best and brightest experts in the field. The conditionalities in the loan contract have to be crafted with the right carrots and sticks so that the client government will "do the right thing" by passing the law.

This criticism might be formulated using a notion of (psychological) "ownership." Unless the law is a product of the authentic internal processes in a country, the government and the people will have no "ownership" of the law; it will have little effect. Yet to the social engineering approach, it is a question of the "what" that is in the law. The "correct law" is like the correct answer to a mathematics problem; it is still correct no matter how it is obtained. Whatever might evolve out of the experience of a transition or developing country will be "marred" by the circumstances of its birth. From the social engineering viewpoint, if those people knew what they were doing, they wouldn't be in such a mess in the first place. Why settle for some second- or third-best product of the internal processes in such a country when they can have the first-best product imported from the advisory institutions of the first world? Don't governments want the very best for their people? Hence it is the "professional duty" of the social engineers to see that their clients get the "best" laws.

The Fundamental Conundrum of Trying to Engineer Autonomy

This ownership of laws and policies refers to the How, and not the What. Perhaps the efforts of the World Bank to engineer "ownership" were just clumsy initial attempts that will eventually be perfected. Is there any problem, in principle, with engineering "ownership"?

This brings us to the fundamental problem in the social engineering approach. There is a basic conundrum that occurs across a wide spectrum of human affairs,

[6] For instance, Machiavelli writing as a civic republican in his *Discourses on Livy* noted the quality of laws that arose out of the conflicts between the nobility and the people. "I maintain that those who blame the quarrels of the Senate and the people of Rome condemn that which was the very origin of liberty, and that they were probably more impressed by the cries and noise which these disturbances occasioned in the public places, than by the good effect which they produced; and that they do not consider that in every republic there are two parties, that of the nobles and that of the people; and all the laws that are favorable to liberty result from the opposition of these parties to each other, as may easily be seen from the events that occurred in Rome" (Discourses, Book I, Chapter IV).

which might be called the "helping-self-help conundrum" (Ellerman, 2005). *Autonomy cannot be heteronomously engineered.* Inside-out change cannot be imposed from the outside in. Genuine social change is a form of social learning writ large. Yet this basic helping-self-help conundrum cuts across any educational enterprise whether writ large or small. As the late philosopher of education, David Hawkins, put it:

> If we ask how the teacher-learner roles differ from those of master and slave, the answer is that the proper aim of teaching is precisely to affect those inner processes that, as Hegel (and the Stoic philosophers before him) made clear, cannot in principle be made subject to external control, for they are just, in essence, the processes germane to independence, to autonomy, to self-control. (Hawkins, 2000: 44)

Therein lies the flaw in all the modernized social engineering of economic theory. It is not a matter of "getting the incentives right" so that the agents will "do the right things." Unless doing the right thing is simply a physical behavior like digging a ditch, then the external control provided by even the best of incentive structures will not reach "those internal processes . . . germane to independence, to autonomy, to self-control."

It is not a matter of just getting the incentives right since the problem lies in the heteronomous *source* of the incentives. The motivational source in other human wills is familiar in the notions of oppression and coercion.

> "The nature of things does not madden us, only ill will does," said Rousseau. The criterion of oppression is the part that I believe to be played by other human beings, directly or indirectly, with or without the intention of doing so, in frustrating my wishes. (Berlin, 1969: 123)
>
> In this sense "freedom" refers solely to a relation of men to other men, and the only infringement of it is coercion by men. This means, in particular, that the range of physical possibilities from which a person can choose at a given moment has no direct relevance to freedom. (Hayek, 1960: 12)

Natural events on Robinson Crusoe's island might lead to hardship and suffering but never coercion or oppression. Or as Tawney put it, "Hunger and cold cause misery, but men do not revolt against winter or agitate against the desert" (1964: 102). Thus in the juxtaposition of self with "other" as a source of motivation, "other" refers to other human wills.

Any incentives that could be socially engineered would have to be external and thus heteronomous. Any human activities where independence, autonomy, and self-control have a role must be based on internal motives. Søren Kierkegaard eloquently made both points about the importance of the How over the What, and the impossibility of externally ("objectively" in his language) engineering an internal (or "subjective") result. The god Mars was said to have a special armor that made him invisible. Thus Kierkegaard likened the attempt to "objectively" bring about a "subjective" result to the attempt to have Mars put on the armor of invisibility to see what he looked like (1992: 174). It was an impossibility, as the means would defeat the end.[7]

Building new institutions and developing economically are not just physical behaviors that can be imposed from without by "getting the incentives right" but are human activities that can only be grown from within. The economic historian Richard Tawney put it well after visiting China in 1930:

> To lift the load of the past, China required, not merely new technical devices and new political forms, but new conceptions of law, administration and political obligations, and new standards of conduct in governments, administrators, and the society which produced them. The former could be, and were, borrowed. The latter had to be grown. (Tawney, [1932] 1966: 166)

The social engineering to "get the incentives right" is a means that will only defeat the ends. But, unfortunately, that is the standard approach of neoclassical economics to institution-building and development assistance.

In view of human beings' autonomous potential, there is a certain ultimate futility in trying to engineer humans into a heteronomously imposed blueprint. The point surfaced in the Reformation doctrine of the liberty of conscience. When Martin Luther addressed those who would try to "engineer" religious belief in his time, he might as well be addressing the social engineers of our day:

> Besides, the blind, wretched folk do not see how utterly hopeless and impossible a thing they are attempting. For no matter how much they fret and fume, they cannot do more than make people obey them by word or deed; the heart they cannot constrain, though they wear themselves out trying. For the proverb is true, "Thoughts are free." Why then would they constrain people to believe from the heart, when they see that it is impossible? (Luther, [1523] 1942: 316)

It is perhaps no surprise that Auguste Comte, following Henri de Saint-Simon, repeatedly attacked the liberty of conscience as a "revolting monstrosity" (Hayek, 1979: 257) with no role in a scientifically engineered society. Saint-Simon and Comte would have loved agency theory.

But it should be noted that the Reformation did not lead directly to concepts of autonomy, freedom, and tolerance but to a multitude of new authoritarian "right churches" instead of the one big "wrong church" of Rome.

[7] For instance, there is the old insight that the "civil sword would make a nation of hypocrites but not a single Christian" (Gooch, 1959: 74–75) And "getting the incentives right" in a package of IMF or World Bank conditionalities can make a government full of hypocrites but not a single true reformer. There is now a whole literature on the problems of providing external incentives to try to achieve inward psychological results, e.g., Lepper and Greene (1978), Lane (1991), or Kohn (1993).

Concluding Remarks

Has the basic lesson been learned today about the problems in a heteronomously imposed social order—or has the "lesson" simply been that communism was based on the "wrong church" of Marxian economics rather than on the "right church" of neoclassical economics?

Aside from a few individual exceptions, the prognosis is that the bulk of the mainstream economics profession and the major development institutions will continue to worship at the shrine of social engineering dressed in the garb of modern economics. Those advisory institutions tend to be the instruments of the new "White Man's Burden" (Easterly, 2006), the attempt of the advanced industrial world to impose certain institutional models (e.g., American-style Wall Street capitalism) on the developing world—which, if history is any guide, will not be to the ultimate benefit of the supposed "beneficiaries."

Genuine assistance in the post-socialist transition or in economic development does not operate according to the linear logic of a big engineering project where the more resources and expertise are pushed into one end of the pipeline, the more "transformation" and "development" will come out the other end. Genuine help, that fosters rather than smothers self-help, is a limited, subtle, and indirect matter. Today's thundering giants of the development industry—such as the World Bank—are totally unsuited for limited, pragmatic, and indirect assistance. And precisely for that reason, they will continue to operate according to the "right church" of neoclassical economics and according to the engineering logic that the greater the resource-incentives (carrots) and power (sticks) that are applied to the problem to make people "do the right thing," the greater the "results."

We have already seen in the 20th century the major world movement of "scientific socialism," and we have seen in the closing decade of that century the ignominious failure of that heteronomous social order. It should be a time of triumph for the humanist vision of autonomous development; it should be a time to build a bulwark against the abuses of scientism and social engineering in the future. But the lack of any accountability within the economics profession for "one of the greatest blunders in world history" is not a promising start. To this observer, it seems that the main "lessons learned" are far too narrowly drawn, and that the fundamental lesson has hardly been learned at all.

References

Benziger, V. 1996, July–August. "The Chinese Wisely Realized That They Did Not Know What They Were Doing." *Transition* 7 (7–8): 6–7.

Berlin, Isaiah. 1969. *Four Essays on Liberty*. Oxford: Oxford University Press.

Black, Bernard, Reinier Kraakman, and Anna Tarassova. 2000. "What Went Wrong With Russian Privatization." *Stanford Law Review* (52): 1–84.

Burke, Edmund. 1937 (1790). "Reflections on the French Revolution: In a letter intended to have been sent to a gentleman in Paris." In *The Harvard Classics: Edmund Burke*. C. Eliot, pp. 143–378. New York: Collier.

Dahrendorf, Ralf. 1990. *Reflections on the Revolution in Europe: In a letter intended to have been sent to a gentleman in Warsaw*. New York: Random House.

Easterly, William. 2006. *The White Man's Burden: Why the West's Efforts to Aid the Rest have done so much ill and so little good*. New York: Penguin Press.

Ellerman, David. 1993. "Management and Employee Buy-Outs in Central and Eastern Europe: Introduction." In *Management and Employee Buy-Outs as a Technique of Privatization*, edited by D. Ellerman, pp. 13–30. Ljubljana, Slovenia: Central and Eastern European Privatization Network. [Available at: www.ellerman.org]

Ellerman, David. 2003. "On the Russian Privatization Debates: What Has Been Learned a Decade Later?" *Challenge* 46 (3 May–June): 6–28. [Available at: www.ellerman.org]

Ellerman, David. 2005. *Helping People Help Themselves: From the World Bank to an Alternative Philosophy of Development Assistance*. Foreword by Albert O. Hirschman. Ann Arbor: University of Michigan Press.

Elster, J., C. Offe, and U. Preuss. 1998. *Institutional Design in Post-communist Societies: Rebuilding the Ship at Sea*. Cambridge: Cambridge University Press.

Gooch, G. P. 1959. *English Democratic Ideas in the Seventeenth Century*. New York: Harper & Row.

Harding, Harry. 1987. *China's Second Revolution: Reform after Mao*. Washington, DC: Brookings Institution.

Hawkins, David. 2000. *The Roots of Literacy*. Boulder: University Press of Colorado.

Hayek, Friedrich A. 1944. *The Road to Serfdom*. Chicago: University of Chicago Press.

Hayek, Friedrich A. 1960. *The Constitution of Liberty*. Chicago: University of Chicago Press.

Hayek, Friedrich A. 1979. *The Counter-Revolution of Science: Studies on the Abuse of Reason*. Indianapolis: Liberty Fund.

Hirschman, Albert O. 1973. *Journeys toward Progress*. New York: W.W. Norton.

Keynes, John Maynard. 1933. National Self-Sufficiency. In *The Collected Writings of John Maynard Keynes*. D. Moggeridge, pp. 233–246. London: Cambridge University Press: (Originally published in the 1933 *Yale Review*.)

Kierkegaard, Søren. 1992. *Concluding Unscientific Postscript to Philosophical Fragments*. Vol. I, Howard and Edna Hong (eds. and translators). Princeton, NJ: Princeton University Press.

Kohn, Alfie. 1993. *Punished by Rewards*. Boston: Houghton Mifflin.

Lane, Robert E. 1991. *The Market Experience*. New York: Cambridge University Press.

Lau, Lawrence, Ying-Yi Qian, and Gerard Roland. 2000. "Reform without Losers: An Interpretation of China's Dual-Track Approach to Transition." *Journal of Political Economy* 108(1), 120–143.

Lepper, Mark R., and David Greene, Eds. 1978. *The Hidden Costs of Rewards: New Perspectives on the Psychology of Human Motivation*. Hillsdale, NJ: Lawrence Erlbaum.

Luther, Martin. 1942 (orig. 1523). "Concerning Secular Authority." In *Readings in Political Philosophy*, edited by Francis W. Coker, pp. 306–329. New York: Macmillan.

Machiavelli, Niccolò. 1940 (orig. 1513). *The Prince and the Discourses*. New York: Random House.

Mankiw, N. Gregory. 2003, March. Review of: *Reinventing the Bazaar* by John McMillan. *Journal of Economic Literature* XLI: 256–257.

McMillan, John. 2002. *Reinventing the Bazaar: A Natural History of Markets*. New York: W. W. Norton.

Morita, A. 1986. *Made in Japan*. New York: E. P. Dutton.

Murrell, Peter. 1992. "Conservative Political Philosophy and the Strategy of Economic Transition." *Eastern European Politics and Societies* 6(1): 3–16.

Popper, Karl R. 1961. *The Poverty of Historicism*. New York: Harper Torchbooks.

Popper, Karl R. 1962. *The Open Society and its Enemies: The High Tide of Prophecy: Hegel, Marx, and the Aftermath*. New York: Harper and Row.

Reddaway, P., and D. Glinski. 2001. *The Tragedy of Russia's Reforms: Market Bolshevism Against Democracy*. Washington, DC: United States Institute of Peace Press.

Sachs, Jeffrey. 1993. *Poland's Jump to the Market Economy*. Cambridge, MA: MIT Press.

Stiglitz, Joseph. 1999. *Whither Reform?* 1999 ABCDE Conference, Washington, DC: World Bank. Reprinted in *Joseph Stiglitz and the World Bank: The Rebel Within*, edited by H.-J. Chang, 2001, pp. 127–171. London: Anthem Press.Tawney, Richard H. 1964. *The Radical Tradition*. New York: Minerva Press.

Tawney, Richard H. 1966 (1932). *Land and Labor in China*. Boston: Beacon Press.

Williams, Christopher. 1981. *Origins of Form*. New York: Architectural Book Publishing Co.

CHAPTER 27

THE ETHICS OF ECONOMIC DEVELOPMENT AND HUMAN DISPLACEMENT

DES GASPER

Introduction: Beyond the Economist's Oath

Economic development raises painful ethical questions. The example we consider in this chapter is the displacement of people from their homes and livelihoods, and the associated ethical conundrums. The questions cannot be adequately answered by the conventional methods of economics. This does not mean that economists can conveniently leave the ethical questions purely for an often absent notional "colleague" from another discipline or an authorized decision maker. The latter often readily resorts to the recommendations generated by the conventional methods of economics. In market-based societies these methods, the expression of a private business rationality, are accepted as common sense, even as neutral or natural; they are familiar, apparently precise, and part of a larger world view that proffers impersonal justifications. Yet development processes in which (to use the formulation by Michael Cernea) the same groups consistently reap the gains while other groups consistently suffer the pains are immoral.

Nor may the professional economic ethics presented in George DeMartino's *The Economist's Oath* suffice, relevant though it is in embodying a stance of accepting responsibility and accountability. The proposed Oath appears based on an analogy to the medical Hippocratic Oath. But most economists do not work as clinicians in direct contact with individual suffering or needy patients. Instead they work as employees or advisors to power-holders—governments, businesses, banks, international agencies—whose actions impact thousands, millions, even sometimes hundreds of millions of persons, including often beyond any single legal jurisdiction. Sometimes they become power-holders themselves. If engaged in research they, unlike medical scientists or other social scientists, rarely have direct contact with ordinary people; instead typically they process statistics produced by other agencies. The Oath's acknowledgment of economists' great potential influence, including great potential to advance actions that seriously harm many people, and of corresponding ethical obligations—to consult, reflect, think deeply about the limits of their own arguments, and seek to minimize harm—are strongly to be welcomed. The means for seeking to respect these ethical obligations must take partly different forms than those normal for medical practitioners or field anthropologists, to reflect the more indirect and generalized mechanisms through which economists typically work.

First, economists' methodologies, not only their personal use of tools, must come under ethical scrutiny. Notably, economic cost–benefit analysis as an approach to evaluation of public choices is enormously ethically deficient for many cases and purposes (see, e.g., MacIntyre, 1977; Shue, 2006; Penz et al., 2011), both in theory and (especially) in use. The relationship of economics research and advice to nonutilitarian ethical systems, including those of human rights and human development thinking, demands close attention in economics training and practice (see, e.g., Gasper and St. Clair, 2010). Good practice by economists cannot draw only on distinctively economic concepts (DeMartino, 2011: 105).

Second, the ethically aware self-consciousness required of economists must include attention to their societal insertion and roles, and the forms of their relationship to publics and not only to those who pay for their services. In this context, we need attention to procedural requirements set by values of human rights and democracy, and to the roles of social movements and agencies that seek to articulate and defend such rights and to counterbalance the pulls of payment-for-service.

Third, often the do-no-harm principle cannot be fulfilled: not only cannot all consequences be foreseen, but ethically desirable material progress depends on development projects that inevitably displace some people, and full remedial compensation appears not always possible. Hence, a principle of free, prior, and informed consent would give every group (including rich groups) a veto over changes that bring them net costs. In some cases, displacement of one disadvantaged group might be necessary for major improvement in the lives of much larger and equally or more disadvantaged groups. *The Economist's Oath* sometimes highlights the principle "do no harm," but the oath presented in its final chapter (p. 232) involves a more feasible commitment: to minimize harm. How?

Relevant thinking about dangers, ideals, constraints, and how still to pursue the ideals, has been undertaken in the field of development ethics since at least the 1950s (see, e.g., Goulet, 1960, 1971; Malley, 1968; Berger, 1974; Gasper and St. Clair, 2010; Penz, Drydyk, and Bose, 2011). However the majority of economists have remained content with principles of utilitarianism, as transmuted into the format of economic cost–benefit analysis, which not merely adopts the Kaldor–Hicks principle of potential compensation rather than actual compensation but measures gains and losses in terms of willingness and ability to pay, thus ignoring both nonmonetizable values and the value of those people with little or no ability to pay. I have called this stance "money-tarianism" (Gasper, 2004). The language of human rights, for example, remains unknown in nearly all economics teaching, and is deliberately avoided by the most powerful international development agency, the World Bank (McNeill and St. Clair, 2009; Gasper et al., 2013). It is also absent from the index of *The Economist's Oath*.

Development projects displace an estimated 10–15 million people per year who are directly forced to vacate their location of residence or work when it is requisitioned for or made uninhabitable by other activities. The issue has been considered in work on development ethics, including with special reference to dams projects. In recent years it has been examined in depth, as by the World Commission on Dams (2000), in reaction to increased pressures to put "international competitiveness first, at the expense of intra-national distributive justice" including by downplaying the social costs of projects (Penz et al., 2011: 255). Similarly, as enormously disruptive and land-using new technologies of open-cast mining have spread, a body of work on rights-based approaches to proposed mining projects has emerged.[1]

Chris de Wet asks "Does Development Displace Ethics?" In his view the notion of compensation fails and the clash between the right to development and the rights of potential displacees cannot be well resolved (de Wet, 2009). Eviction is inherently such a disruptive and stressful event, and resettlement such a complex and uncontrollable exercise, that displacees cannot in general be adequately compensated, given what they require and what development managers can deliver. De Wet's view reflects a mood of depression in the literature on dams, displacement, and forced resettlement, after decades of research that has revealed enormous victimization, and decades of discussion of remedial guidelines that then in practice become diluted and often largely ignored.

This chapter considers two complementary lines of response. First is the ethic of responsibilities proposed by Peter Penz and colleagues regarding development-induced displacement (Penz et al., 2011). They build a system of ethical guidelines for local, national, and international responsibilities, with special reference to dam projects; it is based on a synthesis of core values that they believe constitute a widely officially accepted "human development ethic." Such work goes beyond DeMartino and may evoke optimism through being able to identify reasonable principles, not highly specific to a particular philosophical and cultural tradition but still with important implications. What give principles force, however, are bases of power, such as through the embedding of the principles in social movements (cf. Stammers, 2009).

So, second, we will consider the human rights–based approaches that have been elaborated to deal for example with conflicts over proposed new mining projects. This literature is more upbeat than that over dams, given some emblematic cases of local success and recent national cases of advance (Bolivia and Ecuador; Bebbington et al., 2008a,

[1] The largest gold mine in the world, the Grasberg mine in West Papua, for example, reportedly generates 700,000 tons of waste per day and could eventually affect about 100 square miles of territory (Earthworks and Oxfam America, 2007).

2008b). The work has both an explicit ethical basis and a focus on the social and political dynamics of conflicts. Proponents of a human rights–based approach argue that it helps us in explaining and transforming mining conflicts (Echave et al., 2009). It can help to explain, because if core rights are not respected then conflict is (more) likely to ensue or intensify. It can help to transform, by indicating how respect for human rights and their institutionalization can establish bases for mutually fruitful local dialogue and cooperation. Some experiences suggest the value of processes of encounter, of building trust and legitimacy, and joint search for solutions, but also the need for backing for local resistors from national and international movements of change. Here too the global language of human rights has a key role: its relatively widely agreed legitimacy and partial institutionalization can help in establishing the required processes of respectful encounter, negotiation, and alliance building, locally, nationally, and internationally.

Economic Development and Human Displacement: Does Development Displace Ethics?

A widely cited figure for the scale of development-forced displacement in the early 21st century was 15 million people per year, up from perhaps 10 million per year in the late 20th century (de Wet, 2009; Oliver-Smith, 2009). The estimates come originally from Michael Cernea, doyen of displacement studies, the first sociologist in the World Bank and for many years a lonely voice there. "These figures do not include the even broader processes of incidental and indirect displacement" (Penz et al., 2011: 2).[2] Displacement on such a scale is likely to continue. The rapid growth of mega-cities brings displacement within and adjacent to the cities, and also requires transfers of food, energy, and water from far away, which bring demands for new large dams (Scudder, 2005).

Displaced people are subject to many types of risk: landlessness, joblessness, homelessness, marginalization, food insecurity, increased morbidity, loss of access to common property resources, and social disarticulation (Cernea, 2000). In addition, those who are displaced or at risk of displacement are profoundly stressed by their exclusion from knowledge and control about what will happen to them. From a distance, unfortunately, we can be rather sure about what that will eventually be, if past practice continues. For "the record of dismal failures and concomitant pain and suffering for the displaced continues with depressing regularity," notes another veteran of displacement studies (Oliver-Smith, 2009: 17), citing also Cernea (2009).[3] In general, of low- and

[2] Penz et al. (2011) define different types of displacement, direct or indirect, by eviction or threat or inducement; including the case where people do not migrate but are barred access to local resources on which they have traditionally relied.

[3] See, e.g., the record in India, reviewed in detail in Perspectives (2008), which estimated well over sixty million people displaced since 1947.

middle-income countries only those that have had to take donor loans with conditions concerning procedures and compensation have undertaken careful assessment of options and serious compensation in development projects. Even where compensation exercises exist: "Overwhelming evidence documents pervasive and multidimensional distortions of compensation in practice" (Cernea, 2008: 56).

The losses, resulting vulnerabilities, and rending of structures and meanings are not equally shared. Some people, very largely already worse off, lose—drastically—so that others, largely already (much) better off, may gain. Thirty-six of the forty-four dam resettlement cases reviewed by Scudder (2005) showed direct material losses to the displaced. Economic cost–benefit analysis requires only potential, not actual, compensation, of victims; whether to compensate is left for determination by those in power. Penz et al. note that for the method's creators the "gains and losses from public projects were implicitly thought to be widely dispersed gains and losses that are relatively small for everyone" (2011: 76). Displacement shatters this assumption. But in the predominant implicit theory of citizenship, one's rights flow from and are secondary to being a member of a viable and thriving nation. In the same way that a conscript soldier's family may in many cases get little compensation if he strays "into the way of a bullet," a community is widely considered duty-bound to bear the sacrifice if they happen to be located "in the way of development" (Blaser et al., 2004; Dwivedi, 2006).

Dwivedi (2002) identified a set of alternative current responses to potential dam-induced displacement, a classification that is adopted with modified labels by Penz et al. (2011): (1) "reformist-managerial" ("managerialist" for Penz et al.); (2) "radical-movementist" ("radical-structuralist"), and (3) "institutional" ("responsibility").[4] In reality, the most prevalent approach has lain outside this list: it has been to crush or sweep aside those who stand "in the way of development." We may call that the "bulldozer" approach (no. 4). Managerial reformists see development projects and therefore displacement as necessary, and as matters to be decided at national level; but they at least seek in a second stage of consideration to minimize displacement's undesirable features. Contrary to Dwivedi (2002: 730), though, not all managerialists are managerial-reformists. Many are not interested in a second stage, of amelioration; instead they administer the bulldozer. At the opposite pole, the "radical structuralist" approach says there are no solutions under capitalism, and "movementist" approaches insist on the veto rights of local peoples. Such approaches are skeptical about the quantity and quality of the claimed benefits and estimated costs of development projects, as well as outraged at the typical distribution of actual costs and benefits across different groups. In between the poles, the responsibility approach of Penz et al. "rooted in development ethics is [proposed as] a productive way of starting to bridge the gap between movementist and managerial [reformist] concerns"

[4] See also Dwivedi, 2006, Ch. 9.

(2011: 288). It holds that local people have extensive rights, but not of veto; and seeks to work out the rights and duties of each of a wide range of actors, both national and international.

Responding to the prevalence of "bulldozer" development, displacement has been discussed in the literature on development ethics since its outset, as in classic statements by Denis Goulet (1971) and Peter Berger (1974). But, says de Wet (2009), in reality development displaces ethics as well as people: decision makers in development-forced displacement and resettlement projects find themselves unable to refuse projects that they are at the same time unable to ethically justify. There is arguably an inherent clash between rights to development and the livelihood rights of inhabitants in the affected locality who face displacement. New projects that will promote human well-being in the aggregate and will benefit, directly or eventually, large numbers of poor people, inevitably bring costs to many people whose homes and workplaces lie "in the way of development." And, for the following reasons, for many of those people the costs will be irreparable.

Why are the costs so often irreparable? First, contingent but very probable factors increase the exposure of the at-risk inhabitants: projects will be rushed and politically driven. Moreover, at-risk populations come typically from weaker and often ethnically distinct groups who are easily denigrated, pushed aside—for example, because they lack formal legal title to land—and forgotten (Oliver-Smith, 2009). The worldwide record of treatment of displaced populations involves large-scale dispossession, not just "displacement."

Second, fundamental features of resettlement mean it is very likely to bring irreparable damage to the displaced. Displacement involves not just loss of place and of economic assets; it typically also brings losses of organization, identity, and meaning (de Wet, 2009; Downing and Garcia-Downing, 2009). The stresses of involuntary relocation and resettlement—physiological, psychological, and sociocultural, according to the famous Scudder–Colson model derived from their studies of the impacts of the Kariba Dam on the Zambezi River—are permanent rather than temporary. There are stresses of having moved, not only stresses of the move. Costs of loss of meaning are major, and not only for displaced indigenous peoples; they affect many displaced persons. Some people lose their tranquility, their sense of purpose, their psychological grip; some become mentally ill. Social disintegration is hard to avoid because earlier social balance was the product of long trial and error. Disintegration cannot readily be subsequently tidied up, remedied, or counterbalanced by a bit of economic investment (Downing and Garcia-Downing, 2009).

Third, continues de Wet, the complexities of resettlement are enormous and uncontrollable. Administrative, cognitive, and material limits mean that compensation adequate for disrupted population groups often cannot be ensured even if the will existed. Suitable alternative land or jobs may not be available. And both official agencies and popular groups lack capacity to understand, to negotiate, and to find creative solutions. "[Cernea finds that resettlement] projects are consistently underfinanced because of a failure to understand the nature and extent of losses and needs" (Oliver-Smith, 2009: 17). We saw that Scudder (2005) found sufficient compensation in only 8 out of 44 large dam cases that had been studied; and in only 3 of the cases had the displaced people shared in the net gains from the project.

Faced with such profound conflicts and scarcities of understanding and capacity, ethics too is displaced, concludes de Wet. It cannot give us guidance that will justify us in sleeping quietly. All it can tell us is that projects that are purely for minority interests should be rejected. Projects for the greater public good can be accepted, but with sadly no assurance that the victims can and will be adequately protected—though we must try our best to ensure it, including by studying the particularities of each case and by seeking to widen sympathies across society.

What of creative innovation to find mutually beneficial solutions, as the policy analysis literature exhorts (e.g., Forester, 2009)? The chapter on creative problem-solving in *The Oxford Handbook of Public Policy* opens with the challenge set by a prospective dam (Winship, 2006). The site of the prospective Orme Dam in Arizona, at the confluence of two rivers close to a fast growing metropolis, fulfilled the standard engineering, aesthetic, and economic criteria for constructing an inspiring structure that would be a cathedral of the nation and simultaneously a vast economic enterprise. The government was willing to pay enormously for the site. But the potential resulting lake would cover the ancestral homeland of the Yavapai people. The price was irrelevant to them: "The land is our mother. You don't sell your mother." In the 1970s United States, unlike in many other countries or in the United States of the previous century, the indigenous group had a strong enough legal and political position to block the project. During the following decade, new-style engineers joined the government agency responsible, the Bureau of Reclamation, engineers who had trained not only to plan huge dams but to conceive of alternatives and to compare them through economic cost–benefit analysis. An equally economically attractive alternative design emerged: a series of smaller dams that avoided displacement of the Yavapai. Note that although cost–benefit analysis was required to persuade economists and engineers, it did not itself address the concerns of the Yavapai, so that other elements of fresh thinking were needed for a solution that satisfied all parties despite their very different values.

De Wet is aware of such possibilities in some cases, but he considers that they are too rarely available to offer much relief (2009: 89). As implied by the Orme Dam case, however, the very complexity of such development enterprises, exceeding the capacity of any government to control, can provide opportunities for advance through new ideas if space is created for various actors to participate, meet, argue, and generate and share such ideas (Dwivedi, 2006, Chapter 10; Oliver-Smith, 2009). Social movements may have more potential here to influence attitudes, the identification of alternatives, and the whole terms of engagement, than do journal discussions among academics or conclaves only of politicians, planners, and economists (Baviskar, 2006).

A Proposed Ethics of Harm Avoidance and Reduction: The Penz–Drydyk–Bose Synthesis

Penz, Drydyk, and Bose's *Displacement by Development—Ethics, Rights and Responsibilities* (2011) offers a systematic ethical response to displacement dilemmas: a reply to the ethical blindness of economic cost–benefit analysis, the rigidity and veto powers created by simple human rights formulations, and the pessimism articulated by de Wet. The lead author, Peter Penz, is originally a welfare economist. The second author, Jay Drydyk, is a former President of the International Development Ethics Association.

Penz's early work explored the normative criterion of consumer sovereignty, which underlies market-based evaluation and cost–benefit analysis (Penz, 1986). From identification of strengths and weaknesses in the criterion, including its acceptance of the existing distribution of purchasing power, he proceeded to identification, building, and testing of a possible alternative public policy criterion. Here he arrived at a conception of basic human needs as intersubjectively established societal priorities, derived from core criteria of health (physical and mental), social inclusion, and happiness. Testing of this conception was done by application of the various criteria to the performance of several different ideal-type economic systems. Penz's work had a major influence on the seminal *A Theory of Human Need* (1991) by Len Doyal and Ian Gough, probably the best known modern statement on needs ethics and needs-based policy, and also contributed indirectly to the theoretical foundations for the UNDP "Human Development Approach," which was launched in 1990, by a team including Paul Streeten, Penz's former PhD supervisor.

Penz, Drydyk, and Bose synthesize such ideas and much more, to provide a massive elaboration of a development ethic that offers guidance on displacement issues. They seek thereby to ground more solidly, amend, and extend the principles presented by the World Commission on Dams: accountability, efficiency, equity, sustainability, and participatory decision making. Much of their argumentation is within a human rights framework, delineating rights and responsibilities. They use in effect a conception of rights known as "goal-rights" (Sen, 1982): the fulfillment of identified rights has finite weight, like the achievement of other goals, not an overriding status. Rights fulfillment must be balanced against other goals, including not least the fulfillment of other rights. A right to property, for example, is no argument against a duty to pay taxation to support shared systems of law, education, public health, and infrastructure—and systems for compensation to displaced people. Penz and colleagues' stance is also pragmatic methodologically. Rather than seeking to adopt and apply any single ethical theory, or simply to rely on intuition or regnant community values,[5] they follow an intermediate approach

[5] The formulation in DeMartino's Oath—"to enhance the capabilities of that community to undertake those innovations that it deems desirable and achievable" (p. 232)—leaves some risk that the "community" voice is that of elite groups.

that "focuses on generalizable principles, but does not commit itself to a particular normative theory" such as utilitarianism, Kantianism, or Rawlsianism (Penz, 2003: 142).

Penz and colleagues' proposal follows in the footsteps of the World Commission on Dams and has three elements:

1. The development for which the displacement is required must be shown to satisfy the values of "responsible development" (2011: 13), namely not merely economic growth but (a) promotion of human well-being and security, and respect for (b) equity, (c) participation and empowerment, (d) cultural freedom, (e) environmental sustainability, and (f) (other) human rights including respect for fair procedure.
2. The treatment of displaced people must itself satisfy those values: the displaced people "should not be victimized; . . . on the contrary, they should share in the benefits of the projects that displace them; and . . . they should be empowered rather than disempowered by the process" (2011: 13).
3. Procedures for adjudication of claims and disputes must be provided, on an ethically justified basis, including participation by those affected and with adjudication completed at each stage before proceeding to the next.

The proposed values of responsible human development derive from a principle of "non-maleficence"—a core value of "minimizing harm and neglect" (2011: 118)—that matches the commitment in DeMartino's Oath to "[take] care to minimize harm" but is more refined.[6] Similarly to rule-utilitarianism, the principle is used for judging systems of moral ideas rather than as a direct prescription to all individual agents. As a principle to guide policy, it goes further than only avoiding directly doing harm, to include trying to reduce and prevent avoidable harm, and so can be called a principle of harm reduction, minimization or avoidance. From this core value Penz et al. argue toward the more specific (sets of) values mentioned earlier, that have all become widely adopted in international organizations and international declarations.

Penz et al. (2011: 289) hold that such "a development ethics approach offers a fundamental and necessary shift in focus from a conception of development that is rooted in aggregate welfare to one that foregrounds not only distributive justice but also self-determination." A style of development that suppresses the latter two values is very unlikely in the long run to promote aggregate welfare either, for it sows seeds of social malaise and conflict. Penz et al. are perhaps overly sanguine, though, on the extent of value consensus, including around the interpretation of distributive justice. Reviewing several large global value surveys, Kates et al. (2006) found that whereas large majorities worldwide are concerned about the weak (children, the elderly, sick, and disabled), views are divided about poverty. Large majorities in Pacific Rim countries, including

[6] DeMartino (2011: 123-6) discusses treatments of non-maleficence in medical ethics and environmental ethics.

the United States and China, blame poverty on laziness and lack of willpower, whereas majorities elsewhere stress lack of fair opportunities as the main cause.

Penz and colleagues' ethic seeks to minimize displacement, by ensuring realistic inclusive assessment of its costs and alternatives, but can permit it when there is equitable compensation. In contrast to the "bulldozer ethic's" positing of a duty of sacrifice by the unfortunates who live "in the way of development," Penz et al. stress that sacrifices required by any development projects that are in the general interest must be shared equitably not arbitrarily, that is, not be imposed disproportionately on those who happen to live in a project location. If the project is justified then the polity can afford to provide adequate compensation to those who suffer from the project (provided that their holdings were legitimate, and that priority goes to compensation for the most needy), and it must ensure their ability to share in project benefits. When identification of damage on a per individual basis is difficult, compensation may be paid instead to a local community or regional government.

Element 3 of the proposal, on participation, follows the World Commission on Dams. Whereas when the people at risk of displacement are "Indigenous and Tribal Peoples," ILO Convention No. 169 of 1989 and the 2007 UN General Assembly Declaration on Rights of Indigenous Peoples give them a *veto* right, the World Commission proposed instead for *all* peoples a right of *participation* and negotiation at all stages of project planning and decision-making, including on the type of project and whether it was justified; "within these procedures, development does not proceed from one stage to the next unless adequate commitments to deliberation, negotiation and adjudication have been made, fulfilled and verified" (Penz et al., 2011: 113). When the required consultation, search for alternatives, assessment of social and environmental costs, etc. have not been competently completed, then adjudication authorities—notably the courts—should have the power to halt a project. In this way the World Commission sought to advance beyond the managerialist versus movementist impasse. Displacement could sometimes be found necessary, but the assessment must be through broad and fair consultation and deliberation. A government, even if fairly elected, does not have the right to do whatsoever it chooses; its proposals on major issues should be tested by extensive public discussion that meets requirements set in deliberative democracy theory.

"Rather than leave forced development to an administrative process that paternalistically determines what the displaced are entitled to, the approach that commends itself is one of negotiation between the two parties of developers and the potentially affected, with access to adjudication based on explicit rules . . . " (Penz et al., 2011: 235). Such rules are to draw from international law and conventions. The principles of just process are the most disputed; managerialists may more readily accept principles on paper of compensation and of sharing in benefits, but typically become quiet on a share in decision making, for that impinges on their authority and on how the paper principles are really used. The World Commission's proposal has hardly been adopted. International funding organizations, led by the World Bank, sidelined its work, and national governments followed suit. To national governments the relevant independent adjudicators are, by definition, themselves; even if a Ministry of Water or of Mines might perhaps be deemed a partisan stakeholder, governments deem an Office of the President, Ministry of Finance, or National Assembly to be the legitimate representative of the general interest.

Besides the rights of the people at risk, Penz, Drydyk, and Bose examine the responsibilities of the agencies whose actions may harm or benefit them, responsibilities that derive from the rights of the vulnerable and are binding specific duties. They stress the difference from charity of this responsibility to compensate for harm done. Penz et al. identify four salient rights and the associated responsibilities. First comes people's right to receive good reasons. It brings responsibilities for all agents in the public sphere, to facilitate and abide by the outcomes of fair public deliberation, and to block proposals that violate the "values of responsible human development." Second is a right to avoid victimization, which brings counterpart public responsibilities to identify all types of losses (definite and potential) and losers, and to try to prevent or mitigate losses. Third is the right to equitably share in benefits, which brings accompanying public responsibilities for making such arrangements. This right to benefit-sharing sometimes renders acceptable what might otherwise be adjudged as high demands for compensation. Further, non-niggardly compensation is sometimes justifiable as fruitful investment. Fourth comes a right to empowerment, which implies some responsibilities on others to provide timely and adequate information and to ensure fair representation of, negotiation with, and accountability to those affected by a project. Penz et al. consider how such responsibilities are distributed amongst public, private, civil society, and community agencies, both national and international. Where a damage-doer is clearly identifiable, it must pay the compensation. Thus, "the risks involved in relocation should be borne primarily by the development agent" (2011: 220). Where the damage-doer is not sharply identifiable, compensation becomes a government responsibility, including sometimes a responsibility of foreign governments, on the principle that the relevant government level is one that covers the relevant damage-doers (e.g., corporations that have foreign headquarters) and that can tax them. Their book illustratively applies these principles to India's famous Narmada Valley dams. Penz, Drydyk, and Bose conclude:

> ... the development ethics approach allows for greater flexibility, breadth and appropriateness by drawing on more than international law as its foundation. By basing our approach on several key principles of "good development" and by enumerating rights of non-victimization, benefit-sharing, good reason and empowerment, we are able to consider displacement as more than an individual project phenomenon. It allows us to examine the roles of private capital, civil society, and both national and international development strategies as part of the evaluation of particular situations. (Penz et al., 2011: 298)

Who will sustain these complex and protracted processes of assessment, negotiation, and adjudication? Essential partners for the forms of analysis described by Penz et al. are social movements and civil society organizations that support and represent (in deeds as well as in words) the claims of the weakest groups in national and global society (Goulet, 2005). While codes of practice on displacement have gained some support from intergovernmental funding agencies, shifts in funding from multilateral to private banks and to less socially concerned foreign governments and investors who are less apt to be embarrassed or shamed have partly sidelined the painstakingly achieved ethical codes for investments (Johnston and Garcia-Downing, 2004). The role of social movements is therefore crucial (Khagram, 2004), although continued adequate State capacity and authority remain essential too. Penz et al. consciously try to move beyond just appeals to any enlightened technocrats in donor organizations and government Ministries, which was the orientation that Dwivedi (2002) argued had fundamentally limited the work of, for example, Cernea. We need therefore to clarify the roles for social movements in influencing norms, exerting pressure and increasing capacity, and the international connections that provide essential support to local movements for human rights.

Situating, Locally and Globally, Human Rights for Participation in Decision-making

Human rights thinking directly responds to the neglect of those who are most vulnerable and excluded. But it has long faced the dilemma discussed by de Wet: the clash of different rights, each deemed absolute (Gasper, 2009). Further, while rights thinking tries to set firm standards and limits, we saw that in practice compensation arrangements typically are undermined and even ignored. Besides the dramatic undercounting of human and environmental costs, projects often systematically underestimate other costs, exaggerate benefits, and manipulate other aspects of assessment in order to get approval. Project choice often involves partisan manipulation rather than application of even a utilitarian or money-tarian ethic.[7]

"Human rights based approaches" (HRBAs) have therefore moved on, firstly to stress the rights to equitable procedures and accountability in decision-making (Newell and Wheeler, 2006), including to check counts and estimates, and secondly to incorporate insights from conflict resolution theory (Menkel-Meadow, 1996). Required are not simply declarations of particular rights but a "human rights culture" which includes the principles of accountability, transparency and the like, and, underlying those principles, sufficient feelings of mutual respect and community. Conflict theory suggests that without mutual interaction of the stakeholders the essential bases of respect, trust and

[7] See, e.g.: Flyvbjerg (2008) on large construction projects worldwide; Porter et al. (1991) for a typical large development project in Kenya; Singh (1990) on cost overruns and performance shortfalls in dam construction in India; and Alvares and Billorey (1988) and Dwivedi (2006) on omissions and double-counting, etc., in the Narmada dam appraisals.

co-operation are unlikely to be achieved, but that such processes usually require a long time and that negative situations cannot be easily reversed.

HRBAs in mining, for example, have been elaborated and disseminated by the Oxfam group. Oxfam Australia in particular has advocated a principle of "free, prior and informed consent" (FPIC) of local communities in disputes over new investments in their localities. It has, like the World Commission on Dams, extended this principle beyond only indigenous peoples, who already have such standing in certain intergovernmental declarations, to insist that: "Non-indigenous, project-affected peoples have the right to consultation and negotiation in decision-making processes in ways that are consistent with the principles underlying the right to FPIC" (Oxfam Australia, 2010: 3). First, Oxfam Australia has presented FPIC as an implication of various basic human rights, and held that, like those basic rights, it therefore "cannot be overridden on the grounds of protecting national interest or state ownership of subsoil resource rights" (Oxfam Australia, 2007: 9). Second, and taking us beyond disputes over which agreed international document has which areas of application and which degree of force, Oxfam Australia has proffered to companies and governments a principle of prudence: "pursuing projects without obtaining the consent of local communities and Indigenous Peoples is not financially sustainable" (Oxfam Australia, 2007: 4). Projects require a local "social license" in order to operate satisfactorily, not only a government license. Rio Tinto Zinc reportedly, if ambiguously, states "that it recognizes the need to respect the ability of non-indigenous local communities [too] to withhold consent" (cited by Oxfam Australia, 2007: 13).

The *casus classicus* cited by Oxfam Australia to illustrate mining companies recognizing and respecting the right of communities to FPIC was the Tintaya mine in Peru. Let us look at that case, to consider how far it illustrates FPIC, Penz and colleagues' proposed arrangements of negotiation and arbitration, and/or relevant other principles.[8] The case is used to raise hypotheses, rather than investigated in depth in its own right. In the altiplano of southern Peru the state-run Tintaya copper mine opened in the 1980s after expropriation of 2400 hectares from a peasant community. The community officially filed its objection, to no avail. The mine was privatized in the 1990s, and eventually acquired by a group that became part of BHP Billiton, an Australian-British conglomerate that is one of the two largest mineral groups in the world. It aggressively expanded operations and more than doubled the mine's landholding. Widespread local dissatisfaction with its methods led to a 2001 report by the Peruvian NGO CooperAcción, which found that the land acquisitions had often been irregular: extremely underpriced, arranged in deals with local leaders who had no authorization to sell, and leading to forced evictions and loss of livelihood. The communities obtained support from Oxfam America to commission the Oxfam Mining Ombudsman based in Australia to examine

[8] This discussion draws especially on Echave et al. (2006, 2009) and Merino (2008). Tintaya is an open pit mine at over 4,000 meters elevation in Cusco region. In 1999 it processed more than 16,000 metric tons per day of skarn Cu ores (http://www.infomine.com/minesite/minesite.asp?site=tintaya).

their grievances. Until it was closed in 2009, this Ombudsman unit investigated grievances concerning Australian mining companies.

In early 2002 the Tintaya Dialogue Table (*Mesa de Diálogo de Tintaya*) was established, including BHP Billiton, the five Quechua-speaking local communities, and the mayor of the province, plus the National Coordinating Committee of Communities Affected by Mining (CONACAMI), its regional counterpart (CORECAMI), and representatives of Oxfam America and CooperAcción. The local communities insisted that central government agencies must not be invited. This reflected the national history of dispossession and exclusion, as a result of which the state is typically not trusted as a protector of local community interests and is seen locally as the ally of the mining company (Merino, 2008: 40). The Dialogue Table was co-funded by participants. Several months were used for familiarization, and brought acknowledgment that problems existed that needed to be tackled jointly, plus agreement to undertake a set of joint review studies. In the following phase, commissions to undertake the studies were formed, led by representatives of the local communities and by CORECAMI, and went to work from late 2002. The Land Commission evaluated, modified, accepted and then supervised the company's proposal to acquire and develop land to resettle displaced people. The Environment Commission conducted and commissioned a series of studies on the mine's impacts on the physical environment and on human and animal health. It found that some grievances were correctly attributable to the mine but some were not. The Human Rights Commission contracted with an independent institute to investigate other alleged human rights violations related to the mine, such as cases of eviction and violence, and to make recommendations. These eventually included that the mining company should publicly accept responsibility for various adverse impacts on the lives of local people; provide assistance in confirmed cases of individual violations; and invest in general support to local communities, including investment in better company–community relations. The Sustainable Development Commission looked at longer term development options for the area and promoted preparation of plans by communities. A Coordination Commission helped to maintain momentum and trust. Reflecting the considerable progress that was achieved, an agreement was signed in late 2004: to record the specific agreements in these various areas; to consolidate the Dialogue Table as a standing body for ongoing negotiation and follow-up; and to commit (modest) company funds for the remedial activities. In addition the company agreed to commit up to 3 percent of pre-tax profits to the provincial government's programs, and to support local community projects in other ways.

In assessing this case one must be aware of the desire of both the company and the national and international NGOs involved to present an inspirational model. Some exaggerations may have entered the literature for wider publics. The research literature describes the ups and downs, tensions, and limitations in the process. For Arellano (2008: 35) this is simply a case where "an individual mining company uses the rhetoric of promoting local development to gain local support through clientelism, offering local communities . . . infrastructure development, marginal jobs and other benefits in exchange for a peaceful coexistence." Tintaya is also not an example of FPIC for a major new investment; the case concerns not whether to permit or close a mine, but the rectification of an existing investment, through institutionalized trust-building and negotiation. Further, the area has a long tradition of mining activity, and agriculture is for survival only, so that mining is locally accepted as centrally important. Even so, by 2012 the local communities were less easily placated. In that year the central government declared a state of emergency in response to local unrest, objections to ongoing pollution, and campaign demands that the mining company now share not 3 percent but 30 percent of its profits: a serious sharing of gains, not only crumbs.[9]

Nevertheless the Tintaya Dialogue Table did represent an atypical advance—the transformation of an emergent conflict before it could deepen into violent actions that would make dialogue impossible; and BHP Billiton committed itself to "seek prior consent" for new projects on communities' lands, not only get central government clearance (Echave et al., 2006: 46). The key features deserve attention. One is that participation by local communities in the negotiation was voluntary; it felt self-initiated and non-coerced. Second, vitally, "mechanisms . . . now exist in the international sphere that, when used correctly, can be very helpful for communities" (Echave et al., 2006: 39). "There is no doubt that the presentation of the case involving the five communities near the Tintaya mine to the Mining Ombudsman's Office in Australia [had] worried the mining company" (Echave et al., 2006: 30). BHP Billiton reacted by serious investment of resources and of high-level attention in order to safeguard its image, legitimacy and profits. It responded to the demand from communities and NGOs for more intensive citizen participation. "The launch of the Dialogue Table . . . [paved] the way for binding decisions . . . " (Echave et al., 2006: 45). The role of Oxfam was vital, including in enhancing the readiness and skills for mutual listening and open negotiation, of both the mining company and the local communities. Some mining managers and some local leaders were sent to India to observe localities where mining companies and local communities had found ways to acceptably coexist.

Large-scale mining projects offer to local communities definite negative effects in the short run—including environmental damage and loss of access to some lands and waters—in return only for promises of possible longer term benefits that depend on many uncertain factors and that are often (and overwhelmingly so in Peru) not corroborated by known prior experiences (Tanaka, 2007; Merino, 2008). The local community will surely bear many costs, but lacks assurance on its share in economic benefits, including because of the national state's insistence on national priorities and on state sovereignty over natural resources. Conflict frequently emerges nowadays where local rights explicitly claimed by communities were ignored by the duty bearers: the mining company and the state, which have typically proceeded exclusively in terms of the perspectives of, respectively, pursuit of short-term profit and maximization of national monetized net product. Transformation of conflict is possible where there are "duty bearers committed to make institutional changes by negotiating the differences between

[9] In 2006-7 the mine was sold to Xstrata. On the 2012 unrest see e.g. *Peruvian Times*, 1 June 2012, http://www.peruviantimes.com/01/business-federation-calls-population-to-reject-mine-protests/15885/

the mining company and the local communities, and where meaningful participation from the communities took place" (Merino, 2008: 41; drawing on Echave et al., 2006, 2009 and Tanaka, 2007). In particular, fruitful transformation is helped when some allies of the local communities have connections to the countries where the mining companies are based, and can capture attention there for the dispute (Merino, 2008). Besides exerting pressure, a key role of the external facilitators is to help strengthen amongst the conflicting parties their willingness and ability to listen, mutual respect, and readiness and skills to negotiate. At Tintaya, the principle of local consent too was implicit as a priority concern, even if not an absolute commitment, in the agreement between the mining company and the communities.

Analysis of the Tintaya case that seeks a blueprint for harder cases certainly risks over-optimism; but it shows a set of relevant factors and linkages. The Tintaya negotiations did not rely on injection of substantial new material and financial resources to the region. It instead involved strategic application of intellectual and organizational resources by several NGOs—local, national, and international—that triggered counterpart intellectual and organizational contributions from the mining company, leading to a somewhat more equitable and sustainable allocation of the material benefits being generated by the mine. As in the Orme dam case, application of these additional intellectual and organizational resources extended the set of identified alternatives, to show possibilities that were mutually beneficial compared to a conflict scenario. And the processes of mutual familiarization allowed convergence on mutually agreeable compromises rather than the sort of ongoing conflict over the division of potential benefits that is likely when the bargaining partners lack mutual consideration and respect.

A model emerges of an institutionalized consensus-building approach, based on a combination of ethical and economic pillars (Merino, 2008). First, the local community must have the right to participate in all the phases of projects that will have a major effect on its environment, living conditions and human security. Such participation helps to guarantee that communities benefit from extractive industry in their localities. Second, whether or not local communities have "indigenous" status and whatever is or is not stated yet in international law, there is widespread demand from communities to decide if they want projects on their lands, and a principle of agreement-building should be incorporated for new projects, to prevent or transform social conflicts. Without a "social license" from the communities, projects face major extra risks and costs. Recognition of this principle should motivate recognition of the equally necessary "corporate license" (de Wet's phrase): the investor business's commitment to respect local needs and rights. Views are divided over whether the local community should have not only a right of meaningful participation and ample compensation but a formal right of veto. A veto right might sometimes inhibit meaningful negotiation. The Tintaya case suggests also how it may be unnecessary when well-structured negotiations can create a path that is mutually beneficial as compared to one of confrontation. In the absence of local community vetoes Penz et al. (2011) stress the necessity of access, when required, to neutral competent mediation and arbitration.

A Human Rights Approach: Responsibility Ethics Advanced by Social Movements

We saw a note of despair in some of the anthropological literature on displacement. The record shows sharply conflicting immediate interests, severe victimization of weaker groups, and little respect for paper guidelines. Economic cost–benefit analysis is ready to systematically sacrifice the interests of groups with lesser economic weight for those with greater weight. Simple formulations of human rights allow veto of what would be widely beneficial steps, by small groups who reject them. Professional codes that call for attention to the interests of all, or of "the community," are relevant but insufficient responses, even when they also acknowledge the ubiquity of conflicts and the prevalence of injustices (DeMartino, 2011: 232). We need something more complex.

We saw greater optimism in a literature on principles that builds them into a proposed structured approach to decision making. That literature—represented by the World Commission on Dams and taken further by Penz, Drydyk, and Bose—is not only about paper principles for use by technocrats, including "econocrats" (Self, 1975). It stresses, first, why an approach that does not respect norms of distributive justice and self-determination is unlikely to securely and sustainably achieve the development goals that "managerialists" profess. (The recent stages of the Tintaya case may well illustrate this.) This proposition, of the growing ineffectiveness of bulldozer development in a world of widespread human rights expectations, represents a warning as well as a theorem: exploitative development is likely to generate local, national, and international resistance. Second, this literature leads econocrats into a sphere of negotiation that recognizes values neglected in the pleasurably self-contained calculus of economic cost–benefit analysis. Third, what gives potential force to paper principles is their backing by social movements: local movements and external movements that represent and support the claims of the weak, plus effective articulation between these organizations. Social movements channel expressions of value, identity and emotions, and demands for respect, not only calculations of material "interests" (Guha, 1989; Stammers, 2009).

The somewhat greater optimism we saw in parts of the literature on mining reflects some cases of success that show such movements powerfully at work. The purported success story we looked at, around the Tintaya mine in Peru, concerned how to reasonably accommodate a mine in a locality, in a case that does not threaten displacement of most of the population. To generalize from Tintaya to other mining cases is problematic, and more so if we seek lessons for non-mining cases. Large dams demand displacement of entire communities, not just a few settlements. De Wet argued that experience shows there is no reliable way to adequately compensate those communities: the administrative systems cannot cope, there are few alternative jobs, people's life-worlds are destroyed. And, in a case like India's Narmada Valley dams, the bigger economic stakes bring the involvement of higher levels of government who are unwilling to concede any authority to social movements and civil society organizations, local or foreign. Correspondingly, for social movements to attain major impact they must become able to influence and even enter national government. As Bebbington et al. (2008a: 905 put it:

> ... reading across [country] cases [including Bolivia, Ecuador, Guatemala, Peru] suggests that if movements are to shift public debates in ways that stand much chance of translating into significant change in the governance of mineral expansion, this is far more likely to occur if these movements become part of government. Such a move requires articulation between activism, social movements, and political parties.

We can extend this line of argument to highlight, as in the Risse-Sikkink (1999) model of the spread of human rights norms, the role of international movements that pressurize national governments, including through foreign governments, foreign investors and international financial institutions (IFIs). Risse and Sikkink's influential model describes the entry and absorption of international human rights norms concerning civil and political rights into the domestic practices of many countries that originally rejected the norms as Northern interference in their realm of sovereign self-determination. Influenced by ideas in the "global human rights polity," domestic critics seek not only to directly impact national governments and other possible rights violators or delinquent duty-bearers, but also to spread information and appeals back to the global human rights polity, which then brings intensified pressures to bear on violators and duty-bearers. This is "the boomerang effect." The model of change includes processes of socialization, as human rights ideas gradually become internalized as a language of justification. Risse and Sikkink propose that such interactions typically generate a "spiral model" of change, proceeding through five stages (but with possible loops-back or standstills). At several of the stages the "boomerang effect" is at work, building pressure to move to the next stage. Foreign actors are, it is true, less likely to express criticism over uncompensated or inadequately compensated displacement than they are over torture or military coups. However, human rights "principles"—of non-discrimination, participation and inclusion, accountability and rule of law—as well as civil rights norms are highly relevant in the negotiations over projects that would displace people, more so than any norms about particular levels of compensation. Such human rights principles are now declared in most development cooperation lending. Pressure from social movements and civil society organizations also on foreign private companies that aim to exploit resources is sometimes a significant weapon in campaigns for justice. The presence of funders who are less embarrassed by human rights criticisms, such as perhaps organizations from China presently, can weaken the mechanism; but international campaigns can influence corporations even when they are not formally constrained by IFI codes. A new statement of the model (Risse, Ropp, and Sikkink, 2013) refines its formulation, on the basis of widespread testing, and extends its range of application to a wider set of human rights.

The model involves connections between a series of agents, national and international. It thereby requires languages of mobilization that have cross-group and global appeal (cf. Khagram, 2004): hence the centrality of the language of human rights. Sometimes the campaigns are driven by an absolutist conception of rights that philosophers may find naïve. Inevitably, local activists employ less sophisticated formulations than do policymakers, legal theorists, or academicians. But, presenting cases as involving bedrock values can provide energy and legitimacy for social movements and social entrepreneurs to fight for "a seat at the table." Once at the table they have a chance to re-frame the terms of the debate: to change the vision of what are available alternatives and long-term interconnections, the vision of who are one's interlocutors, and even the interlocutors' conceptions of themselves. Absolutist formulations may help in mobilization and getting this place at the negotiation table, which then provides a learning space to promote the mutual respect and acceptance (especially from the duty-bearers' side) that are essential for flexibility and rethinking (Forester, 2009).

A human rights-based approach (HRBA) relies thus on promoting reasonableness and mutual adjustment by the parties. There are no guarantees that an HRBA will work, especially if it offers just a listing of human rights norms that may conflict with each other. Nor can such an approach substitute for relevant technical knowledge, good technical options, and suitable institutional structures. But a human rights perspective helps by encouraging, sometimes even forcing, greater recognition of "the other" by powerful groups, leading them at least to a more enlightened practice of self-interest. Human rights campaigns that increase duty bearers' degree of reasonableness can thereby increase readiness by the marginalized to come to stable accommodations, when they feel they are taken seriously and will gain a worthwhile share. This is what the proposals by the World Commission on Dams and Penz et al. rely on—not a technocratic method or a formal and absolute veto for local communities but rather the right to be closely involved, well compensated, and treated with respect, which if not fulfilled will bring problems for the duty-holders.[10] The approach stresses human rights principles of recognition, accountability, and participation, not only human rights norms about living standards; for in the absence of the principles the norms can be marginalized and undermined: ". . . the right to claim accountability is fundamental to making other social and economic rights real" (Newell and Wheeler, 2006: 7).

Full compensation is in fact impossible when the displaced or potentially displaced are treated merely as objects; nothing then can compensate for loss of homeplace and identity. But during more participatory interaction the definitions of "I" and "we" can become modified. The "I" and the community "we" are now more than damaged objects whose wounds are to be patched or who are to be sacrificed for a greater good. They are agents who choose, fulfilling their fundamental human right to share in choosing, including choosing who they are. They may identify ways in which they can advantageously grow into new roles, modified personas. This understanding of people, as meaning-making

[10] Sen (2009) similarly stresses the contributions of reasoned debate in the public arena towards establishing mutual awareness and recognition, communicating respect, and thus constituting a framework of cooperation.

agents, takes us far beyond the model of sovereign (provided they are monied) consumers with given preferences, which underlies economic cost–benefit analysis.

A case like Tintaya does not illustrate application of a disembedded philosophical formula. Rather it shows the working of processes of encounter, trust-building, legitimacy-building, and joint search for solutions, supported by pressures provided through the transnational "boomerang effect." The mechanisms may be summed up, with apologies to Theodore Roosevelt, as "speak softly and carry a big boomerang." They go beyond the Risse–Sikkink model, and give a scenario of possible change through the combination of local processes of encounter that lead to dialogue and a global human rights language of legitimacy that encourages alliances wider than narrow interest groups. The global language facilitates the institutionalization of the local processes. So, using Dwivedi's terms, we need both "movementism" and an "institutional"/"responsibility" approach. Social movements supported by civil society bodies are the engines to force progress, toward a more justifiable allocation of rights and responsibilities between various organizations and institutions; and the movements and networks involved must be international as well as local.

Displacement is an ethical problem. Where some observers fear it has no ethical solution, others suggest not just that the problem—obviously—is political (too), but that progress may be made through local and international mobilization, as triggers for democratic deliberation. A human rights–based approach synthesizes these necessary features, for it is both an ethical discourse and a political strategy, which mobilizes groups and builds alliances nationally and internationally. That Dwivedi's influential 2002 review article of the literature on development-induced displacement never once used the term "human rights" serves as an indicator of how rapidly human rights approaches have evolved and spread in recent years, with stress on human rights procedural principles and a de-absolutized treatment of human rights provision standards. The approach functions as both a language of protest and a framework for deliberation. Human rights thinking seems to have a central role in motivating and binding the intranational and international alliances that are needed, because of its relative familiarity, forcefulness, and established institutionalization; and it can add a further vital ingredient, a stress on establishing the dialogical spaces and processes that are essential for increasing the levels of mutual understanding and trust between duty holders and the alliances that campaign for poor people at risk, and for strengthening the bases for shared creative thinking and for acceptable compromise.

Conclusion: Economists as Professionals with Human Responsibilities

We began by noting how a professional economic ethics, one that takes seriously the obligation to seek to minimize harm, must examine the mechanisms by which economists influence people's lives, and must remember that compared to the face-to-face work of medical practitioners these mechanisms are more generalized and indirect. Economists must examine, therefore, their methods and methodologies and how these are used, including also by engineers, politicians, administrators, and businessmen. We noted in particular the deep ethical inadequacy of economic cost–benefit analysis that relies on the potential compensation principle in projects whose distribution of benefits is sharply skewed to the disadvantage of groups who are already disadvantaged. That the already disadvantaged groups could potentially be compensated for their further disadvantage engineered by the project, out of the gains generated by the project, is significant but not a sufficient basis to consider the project acceptable. To not require their actual compensation for major losses is to endorse unethical victimization of blameless groups and a concealed promotion of privilege.

Economists should include in their analyses attention to the actual distribution of costs and benefits, and to how far courses of action are consistent or inconsistent with universally declared human rights standards and principles, in the same way that other professions are expected to. Just as economists should highlight the uncertainties regarding the data and predictive theories they use, and the extent to which these uncertainties can affect conclusions, equally we must highlight the ethical assumptions of any valuation method used. However, the assumption in nearly all economic cost–benefit analyses that distribution can be ignored cannot be exonerated simply by stating it, as it leads in many cases to sanctioning proposals that infringe nationally and internationally endorsed human rights. We must be aware of, and explicit about, the special circumstances required for the Kaldor–Hicks criterion of potential compensation to be an ethically legitimate criterion of improvement. Stated relatively indulgently these conditions include that the criterion is applied exclusively to projects that bring only minor shifts in distribution, and that projects do not have a systematic tendency to disadvantage the same groups again and again; and, more strictly, that, in addition, the existing distribution of purchasing power is acceptable, for it influences the market values for required compensation. Economists should point out in addition the riskiness, in addition to the ethical questionability, of project plans that disproportionately provide gains to some groups, typically already privileged, and disproportionately impose pains on other groups, typically already underprivileged; such projects build insecure social foundations.

The notion of a profession includes the idea of recognition of responsibilities that correspond to the special status and influence of the profession's members. Economists must consider responsibilities to the publics whom they affect, as well as responsibilities to those who hire them. To suggest some required elements of an adequate professional economic ethics with special reference to economic development, this essay has drawn on ideas from human rights theory. Since important values can conflict, we recognized that assertion of human rights standards regarding mandatory outcomes and of a do-no-harm principle are not always adequate. We referred therefore also to other work in development ethics, regarding the meaning of "responsible development," and to procedural human rights values, which are articulated as the so-called human rights principles including accountability, inclusive participation, and the right to receive good reasons.

As indicated at the outset, economists cannot leave ethical questions purely for an often absent notional "colleague" from another discipline or for an authorized decision maker who is rarely master of the issues at stake and the methods in play. A narrowly disciplinary definition of professional role is a way of abandoning ethics. We would find it unacceptable for doctors, and should find it unacceptable for economists too.

Acknowledgments

For helpful discussions, materials, and suggestions I thank Chris de Wet, Jay Drydyk, the late Ranjit Dwivedi, John Forester, Lenny Merino, Peter Penz, P. V. Poruthuyil, George DeMartino, and seminar audiences in Lima, Ithaca, Ottawa Porto Alegre, and Cambridge, UK.

References

Alvares, C., and R. Billorey. 1988. *Damming the Narmada*. Penang: Third World Network/ APPEN.

Arellano-Yanguas, J. 2008. "A Thoroughly Modern Resource Curse? The New Natural Resource Policy Agenda and the Mineral Revival in Peru." Working Paper 300, IDS Sussex.

Baviskar, A. 2006. Foreword. In R. Dwivedi, *Conflict and Collective Action*, pp. xi–xxvi. Delhi: Routledge.

Bebbington, A., L. Hinojosa, D. H. Bebbington, M. L. Burneo, and X. Warnaars. 2008a. "Contention and Ambiguity: Mining and the Possibilities of Development." *Development and Change* 39(6): 887–914.

Bebbington, A., D. H. Bebbington, J. Bury, J. Lingan, J. P. Munoz, and M. Scurrah. 2008b. "Mining and Social Movements: Struggles over Livelihood and Rural Territorial Development in the Andes." *World Development* 36(12): 2888–2905.

Berger, P. 1974. *Pyramids of Sacrifice*. New York: Basic Books.

Blaser, M., H. A. Feit, and G. McRae, eds. 2004. *In The Way Of Development: Indigenous Peoples, Life Projects and Globalization*. London and New York: Zed Books.

Cernea, M. 2000. "Risks, Safeguards, and Reconstruction." In *Risks and Reconstruction*, edited by M. Cernea and C. McDowell, pp. 11–55. Washington, DC: World Bank.

Cernea, M. 2008. "Compensation and Investment in Resettlement." In *Can Compensation Prevent Impoverishment?*, edited by M. Cernea & H. M. Mathur, pp. 15-91. New Delhi: Oxford University Press.

Cernea, M. 2009. "Financing for Development: Benefit-sharing Mechanisms in Population Resettlement." In *Development & Dispossession*, edited by A. Oliver-Smith, pp. 49–76. Santa Fe, NM: SAR Press.

DeMartino, G. 2011. *The Economist's Oath*. Oxford: Oxford University Press.

de Wet, C. 2009. "Does Development Displace Ethics? The Dilemma of Forced Resettlement." In *Development & Dispossession*, edited by A. Oliver-Smith, pp. 77–96. Santa Fe, NM: SAR Press.

Downing, T., and C. Garcia-Downing. 2009. "Routine and Dissonant Cultures: A Theory about the Psycho-socio-cultural Disruptions of Involuntary Displacement and Ways to Mitigate Them without Inflicting Even More Damage." In *Development & Dispossession*, edited by A. Oliver-Smith, pp. 225–253. Santa Fe, NM: SAR Press.

Doyal, L., and I. Gough. 1991. *A Theory of Human Need*. New York: Macmillan.

Dwivedi, R. 2002. "Models and Methods in Development-induced Displacement." *Development and Change* 33(4): 709–732.

Dwivedi, R. 2006. *Conflict and Collective Action: The Sardar Sarovar Project in India*. Delhi: Routledge.

Earthworks and Oxfam America. 2007. *Golden Rules: Making the Case for Responsible Mining*. Oxfam America.

Echave, J. de, K. Keenan, M. K. Romero, and A. Tapia. 2006. *Dialogue and Management of Conflicts on Community Lands: The Case of the Tintaya Mine in Peru*. Lima: CooperAcción.

Echave, J. de., A. Diez, L. Huber, B. Revesz, X. Ricard, and M. Tanaka. 2009. *Minería y Conflicto Social*. Lima: CIES-ACDI-IDRC.

Flyvbjerg, B. 2008. "Public Planning of Mega-projects: Overestimation of Benefits and Underestimation of Costs." In *Decision-making on Mega-projects*, edited by H. Priemus, B. Flyvbjerg, and B. van Wee. Cheltenham: Edward Elgar.

Forester, J. 2009. *Dealing with Differences*. New York: Oxford University Press.

Gasper, D. 2004. *The Ethics of Development—from Economism to Human Development*. Edinburgh: Edinburgh University Press.

Gasper, D. 2009. "Human Rights, Human Needs, Human Development, Human Security." In *Ashgate Research Companion to Ethics and International Relations*, edited By P. Hayden, pp. 329–355. Aldershot, UK: Ashgate.

Gasper, D., and A. L. St. Clair, eds. 2010. *Development Ethics*. Aldershot, UK: Ashgate.

Gasper, D., A. L. St. Clair, and A. V. Portocarrero,. 2013. "The Framing of Climate Change and Development: A Comparative Analysis of the Human Development Report 2007/8 and the World Development Report 2010." *Global Environmental Change* 23: 28–39.

Goulet, D. 1960. "Pour une éthique moderne du développement." *Développement et Civilisations* 3 (September): 10–23.

Goulet, D. 1971. *The Cruel Choice*. New York: Atheneum.

Goulet, D. 2005. "Global Governance, Dam Conflicts, and Participation." *Human Rights Quarterly* 27: 881–907.

Guha, R. 1989. *The Unquiet Woods: Ecological Changes and Peasant Resistance in the Himalaya*. Delhi: Oxford University Press.

Johnston, B. R., and C. Garcia Downing. 2004. The Pehuenche: human rights, the environment, and hydrodevelopment on the Biobio River, Chile. In *In the Way of Development: Indigenous Peoples, Life Projects, and Globalization*. M. Blaser, H. Feit, and G. McRae, eds., pp. 211–231. London: Zed.

Kates, R., A. A Leiserowitz, T. M. Parris, 2006. *Great Transition Values—Present Attitudes, Future Changes*. Paper 9, Great Transition Initiative.

Khagram, S. 2004. *Dams and Development—Transnational Struggles for Water and Power*. Ithaca, NY: Cornell University Press.

MacIntyre, A. 1977. "Utilitarianism and Cost-Benefit Analysis." In *Values in the Electric Power Industry*, edited by K. Sayre, pp. 217–237. Notre Dame: IN: Notre Dame University Press.

Malley, F. 1968. *Le Père Lebret: L'économie au service des homes*. Paris: Cerf.

McNeill, D., and A. Lera St. Clair. 2009. *Global Poverty, Ethics and Human Rights: The Role of Multilateral Organisations*. London and New York: Routledge.

Menkel-Meadow, C. 1996. "The Trouble with the Adversary System in a Post-modern, Multi-cultural World." *William and Mary Law Review* 38: 5–44.

Merino, L. 2008. *Community Right to Participate in Mining Policies with Reference to Tintaya and Rio Blanco Mining Conflicts in Peru*. The Hague: Institute of Social Studies.

Newell, P., and J. Wheeler. 2006. Introduction. In *Rights, Resources and the Politics of Accountability*, edited by P. Newell and J. Wheeler, pp. 1–36. London: Zed.

Oliver-Smith, A. 2009. "Development and Dispossession." In *Development & Dispossession: The Crisis of Forced Displacement and Resettlement*, edited by A. Oliver-Smith, pp. 3–23. Santa Fe, NM: SAR Press.

Oxfam Australia. 2007. *Free, Prior and Informed Consent: The Role of Mining Companies*. Carlton: Oxfam Australia.

Oxfam Australia. 2010. *Guide to Free, Prior and Informed Consent*. Carlton: Oxfam Australia.

Penz, P. 1986. *Consumer Sovereignty and Human Interests*. Cambridge, UK: Cambridge University Press. Reprinted 2008.

Penz, P. 2003. "Development, Displacement and International Ethics." In *A Moral Critique of Development*, edited by P. Quarles van Ufford and A. K. Giri, pp. 139–152. London: Routledge.

Penz, P., J. Drydyk, and P. Bose. 2011. *Displacement by Development—Ethics, Rights and Responsibilities*. Cambridge, UK: Cambridge University Press.

Perspectives. 2008. *Abandoned: Development and Displacement*, 2nd ed. Delhi: Perspectives Team, Hindu College, Delhi University.

Porter, D., B. Allen, and G. Thompson. 1991. *Development in Practice*. London: Routledge.

Risse, T., and K. Sikkink. 1999. "The Socialization of International Human Rights Norms into Domestic Practices: Introduction." In *The Power of Human Rights—International Norms and Domestic Change*, edited by T. Risse, S. C. Ropp, and K. Sikkink, pp. 1–38. Cambridge, UK: Cambridge University Press.

Risse, T., S. C. Ropp, and K. Sikkink, eds. 2013. *The Persistent Power of Human Rights—From Commitment to Compliance*. Cambridge, UK: Cambridge University Press.

Scudder, T. 2005. *The Future of Large Dams: Dealing with Social, Environmental, Institutional and Political Costs*. London: Earthscan.

Self, P. 1975. *Econocrats and the Policy Process: The Politics and Philosophy of Cost Benefit Analysis*. London: Macmillan.

Sen, A. K. 1982. *Choice, Welfare and Measurement*. Oxford: Basil Blackwell.

Sen, A. K. 2009. *The Idea of Justice*. London: Penguin.

Shue, H. 2006. "Ethical Dimensions of Public Policy." In *The Oxford Handbook of Public Policy*, edited by M. Moran, M. Rein, and R. E. Goodin, pp. 707-726. Oxford: Oxford University Press.

Singh, S. K. 1990. "Evaluating Large Dams in India." *Economic and Political Weekly* 17(March): 561–574.

Stammers, N. 2009. *Human Rights and Social Movements*. London: Pluto Press.

Tanaka, M. 2007. "The Mining Conflicts Cannot Be Resolved, but Only Transformed." *Economia y Sociedad*. Lima: CIES.

Winship, C. 2006. "Policy Analysis as Puzzle Solving." In *Oxford Handbook of Public Policy*, edited by M. Moran, M. Rein, and R. Goodin, pp. 109–123. Oxford: Oxford University Press.

World Commission on Dams. 2000. *Dams and Development*. London: Earthscan.

CHAPTER 28

HOW CAN WE BETTER ADDRESS THE GAPS IN OUR KNOWLEDGE ABOUT DEVELOPMENT EFFECTIVENESS?

MARTIN RAVALLION

INTRODUCTION

ANYONE who doubts the potential benefits to development practitioners from evaluation should study China's economic reforms. In 1978, the Communist Party's 11th Congress broke with its ideology-based view of policymaking in favor of a pragmatic approach, which Deng Xiaoping famously dubbed "feeling our way across the river." At its core was the idea that public action should be based on evaluations of experiences with different policies— "the intellectual approach of seeking truth from facts" (Du Runsheng, 2006: 2). In looking for facts, a high weight was put on demonstrable success in actual policy experiments on the ground. The first major application was to rural reform. Although there had been much dissatisfaction with collectivized farming, there were competing ideas as to what needed to be done. The evidence from local experiments was eventually instrumental in persuading even the old guard of the Party's leadership (many of whom still favored collectivized farming) that household contracts

This is a revised and extended version of a paper, "Evaluation in the Practice of Development," published in the *World Bank Research Observer* 2009. For helpful comments and related discussions on this topic, the author is grateful to Francois Bourguignon, Asli Demirguc-Kunt, Gershon Feder, Jed Friedman, Emanuela Galasso, Markus Goldstein, Bernard Hoekman, Beth King, Danny Leipziger, David McKenzie, John Rust, Luis Seven, Lyn Squire, Dominique van de Walle, and Michael Woolcock.

could deliver higher food output. The evidence had to be credible. A new research group did field work studying the local experiments—though they were certainly not randomized experiments—in using contracts with individual farmers. The evidence might not be conclusive by today's scientific standards, but it helped to convince skeptical policymakers (many still imbued in Maoist ideology) of the merits of scaling up the local initiatives (Xiaopeng Luo, 2007). The rural reforms that were then implemented nationally helped achieve probably the most dramatic reduction in the extent of poverty the world has yet seen.

Unfortunately we still have a long way to go before we will be able to say that this story from China is typical of development policymaking elsewhere. (And China still has much that it could do to enhance the credibility of its own efforts at evidence-based policymaking.) This chapter argues that we underinvest in rigorous (experimental and non-experimental) evaluations of development interventions *and* that the evaluations that are done currently are not as useful as they could be. Distortions in the "market for knowledge" about development effectiveness leave persistent gaps between what we know and what we want to know and the learning process is often too weak to reliably guide practice. The outcome is almost certainly less overall impact on development goals, including poverty reduction.

The chapter first examines why we might see too few evaluations, pointing to issues of incentives, such that gaps in our knowledge about development effectiveness come to persist, and the ethical and political sensitivities posed by evaluation. The chapter then identifies a number of things that need to change in current approaches to evaluation if the potential to inform development practice is to be fulfilled. Examples are given from recent research, although a number of these issues remain under-researched. It is hoped that the discussion will help change that.

Why Might We Underinvest in Rigorous Evaluations?

The focus of this chapter is the problem of assessing the impact of a development project, where "impact" is measured against explicit counterfactual outcomes (such as in the absence of the project); the essential characteristic of a rigorous evaluation is that it includes a credible strategy for identifying the counterfactual. The topic embraces both ex ante and ex post evaluation (and possibly both for the same project). Ex ante evaluation is a key input to project appraisal. Ex post evaluation can sometimes provide useful insights into how a project might be modified along the way, and is certainly a key input to the accumulation of knowledge about development effectiveness, which guides future policymaking.

There are good reasons why not everything that is done in the name of development gets evaluated. Rigorous evaluations are rarely easy. Practical and logistical difficulties abound. Special-purpose data collection and close supervision are typically required.

The analytic and computational demands for valid inferences can also be daunting and require specialized skills. However, there are also reasons to doubt that the market for knowledge about development effectiveness works well. The outcome of these market failures is almost certainly that we underinvest in rigorous impact evaluations.

Knowledge Market Failures

Suppliers and demanders of knowledge about development effectiveness typically do not have the same information about the quality of the evaluation—giving an example of what economists call "asymmetric information," which is a well-known source of market failure.[1] In the present context, development practitioners cannot easily assess the quality and expected benefits of an impact evaluation, to weigh against the costs. Short-cut methods promise quick results at low cost, though rarely are users well informed of the inferential dangers. Because it is often hard for practitioners to know whether research is reliable or not, there is a real risk that rigorous evaluations are driven out by non-rigorous ones of doubtful veracity.

Two examples illustrate the asymmetric information problem in this context. The first is from Organization for Economic Co-Operation and Development (OECD, 2007), which outlines an approach to "ex ante poverty impact assessment" that claims to assess the "poverty outcomes and impacts" of a project in just 2–3 weeks at a cost of $10,000–$40,000, which, as the authors point out, is appreciably less than standard impact evaluations. The OECD paper proposes that a consultant fills in a series of tables giving the project's "short-term and long-term outcomes" across a range of (economic and non-economic) dimensions for each of various groups of identified "stakeholders," as well as the project's "transmission channels" through induced changes in prices, employment, transfers, and so on. Many readers (including many practitioners) would not know just how hard it is to make such assessments in a credible way, and the OECD paper offers no guidance to readers on what degree of confidence one can have in the results of such an exercise.

The second example is found in the advocacy and use of recall methods in surveys to make up for missing baseline data. Many more impact evaluations could be done, and at lower unit cost, if evaluators could avoid the need for baseline data using objective socioeconomic surveys and rely instead on retrospective subjective questions on how outcomes have changed, asked post-intervention.[2] The problem is that that we will rarely know whether the results are reliable. In one exception, Ravallion (2014) tested a rapid-appraisal, "shoestring," method using subjective recall for welfare changes. The recall data were collected at the end of a full-scale evaluation of a large World Bank supported poor-area development program in China. Qualitative recalls of how living standards have changed were found to provide only weak and biased signals of the changes

[1] The classic reference on this problem is Akerlof (1970).

[2] See, for example, the positive discussion of such methods in Bamberger et al. (2006).

in consumption as measured from contemporaneous surveys. Importantly, the shoestring method was unable to correct for the selective placement of the program favoring poor villages.

Another important feature of the market for knowledge is the degree of control that individual project managers (including staff in both aid agencies and governments) have over what gets evaluated and how much is spent on evaluation. This can be thought of as a noncompetitive feature of the market for knowledge about development effectiveness, in that the project manager effectively has the power to block the supply of knowledge. The decision about whether resources should be invested in data and research on a specific project or policy is often made by (or heavily influenced by) the individual practitioners involved, or by political stakeholders whose incentives need not be well-aligned with knowledge demands. The portfolio of evaluations is almost certainly biased toward programs that work well; managers of weak programs try to avoid rigorous evaluation, which threatens to expose the program's weaknesses. Lighter "evaluations" are often easier to manipulate to show seemingly positive results.

Decentralized decision making about evaluation generates another source of market failure: the benefits from the rigorous evaluation of a development project spillover to other projects, which typically do not share in the cost of doing that evaluation. Development is a learning process, in which future practitioners benefit from current research. The individual project manager will typically not take account of these external benefits when deciding how much to spend on evaluation. This is what economists call an "externality." An implication of the externalities in the market for knowledge about development effectiveness is that we tend to underinvest in research that can draw useful lessons for other projects and settings besides that of the specific evaluation.

Certain types of evaluations are likely to be more prone to these sources of market failure. It is typically far easier to evaluate an intervention that yields all its likely impact within one year (say) than an intervention that takes many years. It can be no surprise that credible evaluations of the longer-term impacts of (for example) infrastructure projects are rare. Similarly, we know very little about the long-term impacts of development projects that do deliver short-term gains; for example, we know much more about the short-term impacts of transfer payments on the current nutritional status of children in recipient families than about the possible gains in their longer-term productivity from better nutrition in childhood. So future practitioners are often poorly informed about what works and what does not. There is a "myopia bias" in our knowledge, favoring development projects that yield quick results.

We probably also underinvest in evaluations of types of interventions that tend to have diffuse, widespread benefits. Impacts for such interventions are often harder to identify than for cleanly assigned programs with well-defined beneficiaries, as one typically does not have the informational advantage of being able to observe nonparticipants (as the basis for inferring the counterfactual). It may also be hard to fund evaluations for such interventions because they often lack a well-defined constituency of political support.

The implication of all this is that, without strong institutional support and encouragement, there will probably be too few evaluations, particularly of the long-term impacts of development interventions and of broader sectoral or economy-wide reforms. And the evaluations that do get done will focus too much on *internal validity*—whether valid inferences are drawn about the impact of that specific project in its specific setting—relative to *external validity*—whether valid inferences are drawn for other projects (scaled up versions of that project in the same setting or similar projects in different settings). The fact that long-term evaluations are so rare (yet it is widely agreed that development does not happen rapidly) and that we clearly know too little about external validity suggest that the available support is currently insufficient *or* it is misallocated.

Ethical Objections to Evaluation

Even when incentives of project staff are aligned with the need for proper evaluation, at times the delivery runs into ethical and political objections. These have been stronger for social experiments, largely stemming from the fact that some of those to which a program is randomly assigned will almost certainly not need it, while some in the control group will. But the problem goes well beyond social experiments. If one finds a valid comparison group in any evaluation then this must include equally needy people to the participants, in which case it might be argued that the only ethically acceptable option is to help them, rather than just observe them passively for the purposes of an evaluation. Versions of this argument have stalled evaluations in practice. Often, some kind of "top-down" political or bureaucratic force has been brought in; for example, state-level randomized trials of welfare reforms in the United States in the 1980s and '90s were mandated by the federal government. However, we also need to study more closely the ethical or political objections. They should be taken seriously but they are not necessarily persuasive.

The ethical objections to impact evaluations are clearly more persuasive if eligible people have been knowingly denied the program for the purpose of the evaluation *and* the knowledge from that evaluation does not benefit them. However, it would seem that the main reason in practice why valid comparison groups are possible is typically that fiscal resources are inadequate to cover everyone in need. Although one might object to that fact, it is not an objection to the evaluation per se. Furthermore, knowledge about impacts can have great bearing on the resources available for fighting poverty. Citizens benefit from good evaluations, which weed out defective antipoverty programs and identify good programs.

One defense against the ethical objection to evaluation is to propose randomization "conditional on observables;" in other words, one first selects participants based on the available data, and only then randomly assigns the intervention. This is an attractive idea, but one must also flag caution as it may well be seen as a lame response, given that the set of "observables" to the evaluator is only a subset of what is observable on the ground (which is, after all, the reason for randomizing in the first place). At the local level, there will typically be more information—revealing that the program is being assigned to some who do not need it and withheld from some who do. The political consequences, and feasibility of doing a social experiment, will vary from one setting to another.

The *ex-ante* ethical concerns about evaluation need to be weighted properly against the benefits, as discussed further in Ravallion (2016, ch.6). Those benefits will be greater if the evaluations meet the knowledge needs of citizens and policymakers. Later this chapter will discuss how that might be assured.

The Role of Development Agencies and Donors

Increasingly evaluations receive support beyond what is demanded by the immediate practitioners. There has been substantial growth in donor support for impact evaluations in recent years. Donor governments are increasingly being pressed by their citizens to show the impact of development aid, which has generated extra resources for financing impact evaluations. The resources available do not always seem to go to rigorous and strategic evaluations. Nonetheless, there is now a broader awareness of the problems faced when trying to do evaluations, including the age-old problem of identifying "causal" impacts. This has helped make donors less willing to fund weak proposals for evaluations that are unlikely to yield reliable knowledge about development effectiveness.

However, it remains that what gets evaluated is still only a modest fraction of what gets done on the ground in the name of development. (Currently it appears that only about 10 percent of World Bank lending operations have impact evaluations.) That may always be the case, given the costs of evaluation. More worrying, though is that it is a decidedly *nonrandom* fraction. Typically, a self-selected sample of practitioners approaches the funding sources, often with researchers already in tow. This process is likely to favor projects and policies that are expected to have benefits by their advocates.

All this makes it very important that new efforts by the development community to support impact evaluations of development policies—to address the market failures discussed earlier—should start from those knowledge gaps, not from a researcher's prior preference for one sort of data or method. That is not always the case. For example, although the recent enthusiasm for randomized controlled trials (RCTs) (also called social experiments)—see, for example, Banerjee (2007), Duflo and Kremmer (2005), and Banerjee and Duflo (2011)—has generated some interesting new research, it is not based on any clear strategic assessment of how this particular method would fill the knowledge gaps of highest priority. Nor is there any obvious reason why doing more social experiments would help correct for the distortions that generated those knowledge gaps. Randomization is clearly feasible only for a nonrandom subset of policies and settings; for example, it is rarely feasible to randomize the location of infrastructure projects and related programs, which are core activities in almost any poor country's development strategy. And even for the types of programs for which randomization is an option, it will be adopted more readily in some settings than in others, given that social experiments raise ethical and political concerns, as discussed previously. A better idea would be to randomize what gets evaluated rigorously and then choose a method appropriate to each sampled intervention, with randomization as one option.

The extra attention to evaluation also needs to come with efforts to strengthen incentives for evaluation among staff in development agencies and donor governments. It is not clear that the extra resources are having as much impact as they could on the incentives facing project managers and governments. Donor support needs to focus on increasing marginal private benefits from evaluation, or reducing marginal costs; too often the support seems inframarginal.

The incentives of managers and operational staff need to be aligned better with sustained development impact than at present. Currently staff are primarily assessed using easily observable bureaucratic and procedural measures, such as the volume of disbursements (as discussed in Ravallion, 2015, with reference to the World Bank). Accountability for past results also seems weak. While client countries feel the effects of a staff member's work for years or even decades, the development professional has often transferred to other countries and tasks. It is clearly possible to improve the incentives in development agencies. Over and Ravallion (2012) have made a concrete proposal whereby development professionals would acquire a visible and abiding stake in the success of the projects in which they invest their time and effort throughout their career, and that accumulated development impact would become a factor in their professional recognition and financial compensation. Tying staff and managerial assessment to evaluative efforts would probably also help in supporting those efforts going forward, as the results will matter more than they do now.

The rest of this chapter explores how we might assure that future evaluations are relevant to the needs of development practitioners. Although better approaches to evaluation will not, on their own, solve all the problems in the market for knowledge, recognizing those problems is the starting point for thinking about what constitutes good evaluation.

How Can We Do Better in Filling Key Knowledge Gaps?

The archetypal formulation of the evaluation problem aims to estimate the average impact on those to which a specific program is assigned (the participants) by attempting to infer the counterfactual from those to which it is not assigned (nonparticipants). Although this is an undeniably important and challenging problem, solving it is not sufficient for ensuring that evaluation is relevant to the knowledge needs of development practitioners.

Questions for Evaluations

Evaluations should not take the intervention as predetermined, but must begin by probing the problem that a policy or project is addressing. Why is the intervention needed?

How does it relate to overall development goals, such as poverty reduction? What are the market, or governmental, failures it addresses? What are its distributional goals? What are the trade-offs with alternative (including existing) policies or programs? As Devarajan et al. (1997) argue, researchers can often play an important role in addressing these questions. This involves more precise identification of the policy *objectives* (properly weighing gains across different subgroups of a population, and different generations); the relevant *constraints*, which include resources, information, incentives, and political economy constraints; and the *causal links* through which the specific intervention yields its expected outcomes.

This role in conceptualizing the case for intervention can be especially important when the capacity for development policy making is weak, or when it is captured by lobby groups, advocating narrow sectoral interests. The ex ante evaluative role for research can also be crucial when practitioners have overly strong priors about what needs to be done. Over time, some practitioners become experts at specific types of interventions, and some may even lobby for those interventions. The key questions about whether the intervention is appropriate in the specific setting may not even get asked.

Evaluators themselves can also become lobbyists for their favorite methods. Too often it is not the question that is driving the evaluation agenda but a preference for certain types of data or certain methods; the question is then found that fits the methodology, not the other way around. Starting with the question, not the method, often points the researcher toward types of data and methods outside the domain traditionally favored by the researcher's own disciplinary background. For example, some of the World Bank's research economists trying to understand persistent poverty and the impacts of antipoverty programs have been drawn to the theories and methods favored in other social sciences such as anthropology, sociology, and social psychology; see, for example, the collection of papers in Rao and Walton (2004). Good researchers, like good detectives, assemble and interpret diverse forms of evidence in testing empirical claims.

As already noted, rigorous impact evaluations require credible strategies for identifying the counterfactual—taking proper account of the likely sources of bias, such as when outcomes are only compared over time for program participants, or when participants and nonparticipants are compared at only one date; for a survey of the (experimental and nonexperimental) methods available for this task see Ravallion (2008). This is all about internal validity, which has been the main focus of researchers working on evaluations. This discussion will flag some issues that have received less attention and matter greatly to the impact of an evaluation.

The choice of counterfactual is one such issue. The classic evaluation focuses on counterfactual outcomes in the absence of the program. This counterfactual may fall well short of addressing the concerns of policymakers. The alternative of interest to policymakers is rarely to do nothing, but rather to spend the same resources on some other program (possibly a different version of the same program). A specific program may appear to perform well against the option of doing nothing, but poorly against some feasible alternative. For example, in an impact evaluation of a workfare program in India, Ravallion and Datt (1995) showed that the program substantially reduced poverty among the participants relative to the counterfactual of "no program," but that once the costs of the program were factored in (including the foregone income of workfare participants), the alternative counterfactual of a uniform (untargeted) allocation of the same budget outlay would have had more impact on poverty. Formally, the evaluation problem is essentially no different if some alternative program is the counterfactual; in principle we can repeat the analysis relative to the "do nothing counterfactual" for each possible alternative and compare them. But this is rare in practice.

Nor is it evident that the classic formulation of the impact evaluation problem yields the most relevant impact parameters. For example, there is often an interest in better understanding the *horizontal impacts* of a program: the differences in impacts at a given level of counterfactual outcomes, as revealed by the joint distribution of outcomes under treatment and outcomes under the counterfactual. We cannot know this from a randomized evaluation, which reveals net counterfactual mean outcomes only for those treated. Instead of focusing solely on the net gains to the poor (say) we may ask how many losers there are among the poor, and how many gainers.

Counterfactual analysis of the joint distribution of outcomes over time is useful for understanding impacts on poverty dynamics. This approach is developed in Ravallion et al. (1995) for the purpose of measuring the impacts of changes in social spending on the intertemporal joint distribution of income. Instead of only measuring the impact on poverty (the marginal distribution of income) the authors exploit panel data to distinguish impacts on the number of people who escape poverty over time (the "promotion" role of a safety net) from impacts on the number who fall into poverty (the "protection" role). (This is possible only if one can identify how impacts vary with household characteristics; the discussion will return to this issue in discussing impact heterogeneity below.) Ravallion et al. apply this approach to an assessment of the impact on poverty transitions of reforms in Hungary's social safety net.

Spillover Effects

A further way in which the classic impact evaluation problem needs to be adapted to the requirements of policymakers concerns its assumption that impacts for direct participants do not spillover to nonparticipants. Only under this assumption can we infer the counterfactual from an appropriate sample of the nonparticipants. Spillover effects are recognized as a concern in evaluating large public programs, for which contamination of the control group can be hard to avoid owing to the responses of markets and governments, and in drawing lessons for scaling up based on an RCT; for further discussion see Mofitt (2003, 2006).

An example of spillover effects can be found in the Miguel and Kremer (2004) study of treatments for intestinal worms in children. The authors argue that a randomized design, in which some children are treated and some are retained as controls, would seriously underestimate the gains from treatment by ignoring the externalities between treated and "control" children. The design for the authors' own evaluation avoided this problem by using mass treatment at the school level instead of individual treatment (using control schools at sufficient distance from treatment schools).

Spillover effects can also arise from the way markets respond to an intervention. Consider the example of an *Employment Guarantee Scheme* (EGS) in which the government commits to give work to anyone who wants it at a stipulated wage rate; this was the aim of the famous EGS in the Indian state of Maharashtra and in 2006 the Government of India implemented a national version of this scheme. The attractions of an EGS as a safety net stem from the fact that access to the program is universal (anyone who wants help can get it) but that all participants must work to obtain benefits and at a wage rate that is considered low in the specific context. The universality of access means that the scheme can provide effective insurance against risk. The work requirement at a low wage rate is taken by proponents to imply that the scheme will be self-targeted to the income poor.

The EGS is an assigned program, in that there are well-defined "participants" and "nonparticipants." And at first glance it might seem appropriate to collect data on both groups and compare their outcomes either by random assignment or after cleaning out observable heterogeneity. However, this classic evaluation design could give a severely biased result. The gains from such a program are very likely to spill over into the private labor market. If the employment guarantee is effective then the scheme will establish a firm lower bound to the entire wage distribution—assuming that no able-bodied worker would accept non-EGS work at any wage rate below the EGS wage. So even if one picks a perfect comparison group, one will conclude that the scheme has no impact, as wages will be the same for participants and nonparticipants. But that would entirely miss the impact, which could be large for both groups.

Spillover effects can also arise from the behavior of governments. Chen et al. (2009) find evidence of such spillover effects in their evaluation of a World Bank supported poor-area development program in rural China. When the program selected certain villages to participate, the local government withdrew some of its own spending on development projects in those villages, in favor of non-program villages—the same set of villages from which the comparison group was drawn. Ignoring these spillover effects generated a non-negligible underestimation of the impact of the program. Chen et al. show how, under certain assumptions, one can estimate the maximum bias due to the specific type of spillover effects that arises from local government spending responses to external development aid. In the case of the poor-area program in China that Chen et al. study, their results suggest that the spending responses of local governments to the external aid entail that the standard "difference-in-difference" method may well capture only two-thirds of the true impact.

Heterogeneity

Practitioners should never be happy with an evaluation that assumes common (homogeneous) impact. The impact of an assigned intervention can vary across those receiving it. Even with a constant benefit level, eligibility criteria entail differential costs to participants. For example, the foregone labor earnings incurred by participants in workfare or conditional cash transfer schemes (via the loss of earnings from child labor) will vary according to skills and local labor-market conditions.

By recognizing the scope for heterogeneity in impacts and the role of contextual factors one can make evaluative research more relevant to policymaking. For example, in the aforementioned evaluation of a poor-area development program in rural China, Chen et al. (2009) found low overall impact, but considerable heterogeneity, in that different types of households benefited more than others, with the relatively better educated among the poor achieving the highest returns to the project's investments. The policy implication is that choosing different beneficiaries would have greatly increased the project's overall impact; indeed, the study estimated that an alternative process of beneficiary selection that better exploited the heterogeneity in impacts could have led to a fourfold increase in the project's overall rate of return. By developing a deeper understanding of such heterogeneity, evaluations can help develop better projects.

Heterogeneity of impacts in terms of observables is readily allowed for by adding interaction effects between the intervention and observables to one's model of outcomes. However, not all sources of heterogeneity are observable, and participants and stakeholders often react to factors unobserved by the researcher—confounding efforts to identify true impacts using standard methods, including randomized experiments; this is what Heckman et al. (2006) refer to as "essential heterogeneity." With some extra effort, one can also allow for latent heterogeneity in the impacts of an intervention (using a random coefficients estimator in which the impact estimate contains a stochastic component). Applying this approach to the evaluation data for *PROGRESA* (a conditional cash transfer program in Mexico), Djebbari and Smith (2005) found that they can convincingly reject the assumption of common (homogeneous) effects made by past evaluations of that program.

When there is such heterogeneity, it can be of interest to policymakers to distinguish marginal impacts (from small program expansions or contractions) from the average impacts that have received the bulk of attention. Following Björklund and Moffitt (1987), the marginal treatment effect can be defined as the mean gain to units that are indifferent between participating or not. This requires that we model explicitly the choice problem facing participants (Björklund and Moffitt, 1987; Heckman and Navarro-Lozano, 2004). We may also want to estimate the joint distribution of outcomes under treatment and outcomes under the counterfactual, and a method for doing so is outlined in Heckman et al. (1997).

Portfolio Effects

When people ask about "development impact" they are often referring to the impact of some set of development policies and projects; let's call it a "development portfolio." The portfolio of interest may be various things that are (ostensibly) financed by the domestic resources of developing countries. Or it might be a set of externally financed projects spanning multiple countries—a portfolio held by a donor country or international organization, such as the World Bank.

Yet the bulk of the evaluative work today is assessing the impact of specific projects, one at a time. Each such project is only one component of the portfolio. (And each project may itself have multiple elements.) As evaluators we worry mainly about whether we are drawing valid conclusions about the impact of that project in its specific setting, including its policy environment. The fact that each project happens to be in some development portfolio gets surprisingly little attention.

How useful will all this evaluative effort be for assessing development portfolios? Assessing a development portfolio by evaluating its components one by one and adding up the results requires some assumptions that are hard to accept. For one thing, it assumes that there are negligible *interaction effects* among the components. Yet the success of an education or health project (say) may depend crucially on whether infrastructure or public sector reform projects (say) within the same portfolio have also worked. Indeed, the bundling of (often multisectoral) components in one portfolio is often justified by claimed interaction effects. But evaluating each bit separately and adding up the results will not (in general) give us an unbiased estimate of the portfolio's impact. If the components interact positively (more of one yields higher impact of the other) then we will overestimate the portfolio's impact because of the double-counting of benefits; negative interactions yield the opposite bias (Ravallion, 2016, ch. 6).

For another thing, it assumes that we can either evaluate everything in the portfolio or we can draw a representative sample, such that there is no *selection bias* in what is assessed. If the components are in fact roughly independent (as implicitly assumed) then ideally we should be evaluating a random sample of all the things in the portfolio, so as to make a valid overall assessment. (When interaction effects are also present one might need to sample differently.) I have not heard of development projects being randomly sampled for evaluation.

We need to think creatively about how best to go about evaluating the portfolio as a whole, allowing for interaction effects amongst its components, as well as among economic agents. This is not going to be easy. Standard tools of impact evaluation will have to be complemented by other tools, such as structural modeling and cross-country and cross-jurisdictional comparative work. We will need to look at public finance issues such as fungibility and flypaper effects (whereby external aid sticks to the sector or ministry to which it is initially allocated). And we will probably be looking at *general equilibrium effects* (sometimes called "feedback" or "macro" effects), which can overturn the partial equilibrium picture that emerges from standard impact evaluations. There is scope for more eclectic approaches, combining multiple methods, spanning both "macro" and "micro" tools for economic analysis. The tools needed may not be the favored ones by today's evaluators. But the principle of evaluation is the same, including the key idea of assessing impact against an explicit counterfactual.

External Validity

Arguably the most important thing to learn from any evaluation relates to its lessons for future policies (including reforms to the interventions being evaluated). External validity is highly desirable, but it can be hard to achieve. We naturally want research findings to have a degree of generalizability, so they can provide useful knowledge to guide practice in other settings. Thus empirical researchers need to focus on questions that tell us about *why* a policy or program has impact; the chapter will return to this question. However, too often impact evaluations are a "black box"; under certain assumptions, they reveal average impacts among those who receive a program, but say little or nothing about the economic and social processes leading to that impact. And only by understanding those processes can we draw valid lessons for scaling up, or for taking the same project to other settings. Research that tests the theories that underlie the rationales for policy or program intervention can thus be useful in practice.

When the policy issue is whether to expand a given program at the margin, the classic estimator of mean-impact on the treated is actually of rather limited interest. For example, we may want to know the marginal impact of a greater duration of exposure to the program. An example can be found in the study by Ravallion et al. (2005) of the impacts on workfare participants of leaving the program, relative to staying (recognizing that this entails a nonrandom selection process). Another example can be found in the study by Behrman et al. (2004) of the impacts on children's cognitive skills and health status of longer exposure to a preschool program in Bolivia. The authors provide an estimate of the marginal impact of higher program duration by comparing the cumulative effects of different durations using a matching estimator. In such cases, selection into the program is not an issue, and we do not even need data on units who never participated.

Relatedly, one must recognize the importance of *context* since this can be key to drawing valid lessons for other settings. Relevant contextual factors may include the circumstances of participants, the economic, cultural and political environment, and the administrative context. Unless we understand how such factors influence the outcomes of an intervention, the evaluation will have weak external validity. The next section returns to this issue.

Given that we can expect in general that any intervention will have heterogeneous impacts—some participants gain more than others—serious concerns can arise about the external validity of RCTs. The people who are normally attracted to a program, taking account of the expected benefits and costs to them personally, may differ systematically from the random sample of people who got the trial.[3] The RCT may well have evaluated a very different program to the one that is actually implemented on the basis of that RCT.

[3] This is sometimes called "randomization bias"; see Heckman and Smith (1995). Also see Moffitt (2004).

External validity concerns about impact evaluations can also arise when certain institutions need to be present to even facilitate the evaluations. For example, when randomized trials are tied to the activities of specific nongovernmental organizations (NGOs) as the facilitators, there is a concern that the same intervention at national scale may have a very different impact in places without the NGO. Making sure that the control group areas also have the NGO can help, but even then we cannot rule out interaction effects between the NGO's activities and the intervention. In other words, the effect of the NGO may not be "additive" but "multiplicative," such that the difference between measured outcomes for the treatment and control groups does not reveal the impact in the absence of the NGO. Furthermore, the very nature of the intervention may change when it is implemented by a government rather than an NGO. This may happen because of unavoidable differences in (inter alia) the quality of supervision, the incentives facing service providers, and administrative capacity.

A further external validity concern is that, while partial equilibrium assumptions may be fine for a pilot, general equilibrium effects can be important when the pilot is scaled up nationally. For example, an estimate of the impact on schooling of a tuition subsidy based on a randomized trial (such as for Mexico's *PROGRESA* program) may be deceptive when scaled up, given that the structure of returns to schooling will alter. Heckman et al. (1998) demonstrate that partial equilibrium analysis can greatly overestimate the impact of a tuition subsidy once relative wages adjust, although Lee (2005) finds a much smaller difference between the general and partial equilibrium effects of a tuition subsidy in a slightly different model.

A special case of the general problem of external validity is *scaling up*. There are many things that can change when a pilot program is scaled up: the inputs to the intervention can change, the outcomes can change, and the intervention can change; Moffitt (2006) gives examples in the context of education programs. The realized impacts of scaling up can differ from the trial results (whether randomized or not) because the socioeconomic composition of program participation varies with scale. Ravallion (2004) discusses how this can happen in theory, and presents results from a series of country case studies, all of which suggest that the incidence of program benefits becomes more pro-poor with scaling up. Trial results could over or under estimate impacts on scaling up. Larger projects may be more susceptible to rent seeking or corruption (as Deaton, 2006, suggests; also see the discussion in Deaton, 2010); alternatively, the political economy may entail that the initial benefits tend to be captured more by the non-poor (Lanjouw and Ravallion, 1999).

Evaluative research should regularly test the assumptions made in operational work. Even field-hardened practitioners do what they do on the basis of some implicit model of how the world works, which rationalizes what they do, and how their development project is expected to have impact. Existing methods of rapid ex ante impact assessment evidently also rely heavily on the models held by practitioners. Researchers can perform a valuable role in helping to make those models explicit and (where possible) helping to assess their veracity.

A case in point is the questionable assumption—routinely made by both project staff and evaluators—that the donor's money is actually financing what recipients claim it is financing. Research has pointed to a degree of fungibility in development aid, whereby the marginal use of public finds is unlikely to be the specific project that is being evaluated. Yet an assessment of "aid effectiveness" is (presumably) just that—an evaluation of the impact of the aid, not the project per se. These are two different evaluation problems.

Assessments of aid effectiveness need to take a broader view of public spending, as advocated by Devarajan et al. (1997). How broad it needs to be is unclear. There is some evidence that external aid sticks to its sector (the aforementioned "flypaper effect"); see van de Walle and Mu (2007). The existence of fungibility and flypaper effects points to the need for a sectoral approach in efforts to evaluate the impacts of development aid.

What Determines Impact?

The preceding discussion points to the need to supplement standard evaluations by information that can throw light on the factors influencing measured outcomes. That can be crucial for drawing useful policy lessons, including for redesigning a program and scaling up. The relevant factors relate to both the participants (such as understanding program take-up decisions and how the outcomes are influenced by participants' characteristics) and program context (such as understanding how the quantity/quality of service provision affects outcomes and the role of local institutions in influencing outcomes). This section elaborates on some of the ways that we might learn more about how a program does, or does not, have impact, so as to better address the issues raised earlier.

An obvious approach to understanding what factors influence a program's performance is to repeat it across different types of participants and in different contexts. Duflo and Kremer (2005) and Banerjee (2007) have argued that repeated RCTs across varying contexts and scales should be used to decide what works and what does not in development aid. Even putting aside the aforementioned problems encountered in social experiments, the feasibility of doing a sufficient number of trials—sufficient to span the relevant domain of variation found in reality for a given program, as well as across the range of policy options—is far from clear. The number of RCTs needed to test even one large national program could well be prohibitive. It is questionable whether this is feasible for filling the existing gaps in our knowledge about development effectiveness.

Nonetheless, even if one cannot go as far as Banerjee et al. would like, it can be agreed that evaluation designs should plan for contextual variation. Important clues can often be found in the geographic differences in impacts. These can stem from geographic differences in relevant population characteristics or from deeper location effects, such as agro-climatic differences and differences in local institutions (such as local "social capital" or the effectiveness of local public agencies). An example can be found in the study by Galasso and Ravallion (2005) in which the performance of Bangladesh's

Food-for-Education program in reaching the poor was assessed across each of 100 villages in Bangladesh and the results were correlated with characteristics of those villages. The authors found that the revealed differences in performance were partly explicable in terms of observable village characteristics, such as the extent of intra-village inequality (with more unequal villages being less effective in reaching their poor through the program). Failure to allow for such location differences has been identified as a serious weakness in past evaluations; see, for example, the comments by Moffitt (2003) on trials of welfare reforms in the United States.

The literature suggests that location is a key dimension of context. An implication is that it is less problematic to scale up from a pilot within the same geographic setting (with a given set of relevant institutions) than to extrapolate the trial to a different setting. In one of the few attempts to test how well evaluation results from one location can be extrapolated to another location, Attanasio et al. (2003) divided the seven states of Mexico in which the *PROGRESA* evaluation was done into two groups. They found that results from one group had poor predictive power for assessing likely impacts in the other group.

Useful clues for understanding overall impacts can sometimes be found by studying impacts on what can be called "intermediate" or "structural" measures. The typical evaluation design identifies a small number of "final outcome" indicators and aims to assess the program's impact on those indicators. Instead of using only final outcome indicators, one may choose to also study impacts on certain intermediate indicators of behavior. For example, the intertemporal behavioral responses of participants in antipoverty programs are of obvious relevance to understanding their impacts. An impact evaluation of a program of compensatory cash transfers to Mexican farmers found that the transfers were partly invested, with second-round effects on future incomes (Sadoulet et al., 2001). Similarly, Ravallion and Chen (2005) found that participants in a poor-area development program in China saved a large share of the income gains from the program. Identifying responses through savings and investment provides a clue to understanding current impacts on living standards and the possible future welfare gains beyond the project's current life span. Instead of focusing solely on the agreed welfare indicator relevant to the program's goals, one collects and analyzes data on a potentially wide range of intermediate indicators relevant to understanding the processes determining impacts. Good practice in such cases is to report impacts on all the indicators collected, to avoid concerns about data mining.

This also illustrates a common concern in evaluation studies, given behavioral responses, namely that the study period is rarely much longer than the period of the program's disbursements. However, a share of the impact on peoples' living standards will usually occur beyond the disbursement period. This does not necessarily mean that credible evaluations need to track welfare impacts over much longer periods than is typically the case—raising concerns about feasibility. But it does suggest that evaluations need to look carefully at impacts on partial intermediate indicators of longer-term impacts even when good measures of the welfare objective are available within the project cycle. The choice of such indicators will need to be informed by an understanding of participants' behavioral responses to the program. That understanding will be informed by economic theory and data.

In learning from an evaluation, one often needs to draw on information external to the evaluation. Qualitative research (intensive interviews with participants and administrators) can be a useful source of information on the underlying processes determining outcomes; see the discussions of "mixed methods" in Rao and Woolcock (2003). One approach is to use such methods to test the assumptions made by an intervention; this has been called "theory-based evaluation," although that is hardly an ideal term given that identification strategies for mean impacts are often theory based. Weiss (2001) illustrates this approach in the abstract in the context of evaluating the impacts of community-based anti-poverty programs. An example is found in a World Bank evaluation of social funds (SFs), as summarized in Carvalho and White (2004). Although the overall aim of a SF is typically to reduce poverty, the study was interested in seeing whether SFs worked as intended by their designers. For example, did local communities participate? Who participated? Was there "capture" of the SF by local elites (as some critics have argued)? Building on Weiss (2001), the evaluation identified a series of key hypothesized links connecting the intervention to outcomes and tested whether each one worked. For example, in one of the country studies, Rao and Ibanez (2005) tested the assumption that a SF works by local communities collectively proposing the sub-projects that they want; for a SF in Jamaica, the authors found that the process was often dominated by local elites.[4]

In practice, it is very unlikely that all the relevant assumptions are testable (including alternative assumptions made by different theories that might yield similar impacts). Nor is it clear that the process determining the impact of a program can always be decomposed into a neat series of testable links within a unique causal chain; there may be more complex forms of interaction and simultaneity that do not lend themselves to this type of analysis. For these reasons, theory-based evaluation cannot be considered an alternative to assessing impacts on final outcomes by credible (experimental or non-experimental) methods, although it can still be a useful complement to such evaluations, to better understanding measured impacts.

Project monitoring data bases are an important, underutilized, source of information for understanding how a program works. Too often, however, the project monitoring data collected and the information system used have negligible evaluative content. This is not inevitably the case. For example, Ravallion's (2000) method of combining spending maps with poverty maps can allow rapid assessments of the targeting performance of a decentralized antipoverty program. This illustrates how, at modest cost, standard monitoring data can be made more useful for providing information on how the program is working and in a way that provides sufficiently rapid feedback to a project to allow corrections along the way.

[4] For a fuller discussion of the evidence on the performance of community-based "participatory" development projects see Mansuri and Rao (2012).

The *Proempleo* experiment in Argentina provides an example of how information external to the evaluation can carry important insights. *Proempleo* was a pilot wage subsidy and training program for unemployed workers. The program's evaluation by Galasso et al. (2004) randomly assigned vouchers for a wage subsidy across (typically poor) people currently in a workfare program and tracked their subsequent success in getting regular work. A randomized control group located the counterfactual. The results indicated a significant impact of the wage-subsidy voucher on employment. But when cross-checks were made against central administrative data, supplemented by informal interviews with the hiring firms, it was found that there was very low take-up of the wage subsidy by firms. The scheme was highly cost effective; the government saved 5 percent of its workfare wage bill for an outlay on subsidies that represented only 10 percent of that saving. However, the cross-checks against these other data revealed that *Proempleo* did not work the way its design had intended. The bulk of the gain in employment for participants was not through higher demand for their labor induced by the wage subsidy. Rather the impact arose from supply side effects; the voucher appears to have had credential value to workers—it acted like a "letter of introduction" that few people had (and how it was allocated was a secret locally).

This could not be revealed by the evaluation, but required supplementary data. The extra insight obtained about how *Proempleo* actually worked in the context of its trial setting also carried implications for scaling up, which put emphasis on providing better information for poor workers about how to get a job rather than providing wage subsidies.

Spillover effects also point to the importance of a deeper understanding of how a program operates. Indirect (or "second-round") impacts on nonparticipants are common. A workfare program may lead to higher earnings for nonparticipants. Or a road improvement project in one area might improve accessibility elsewhere. Depending on how important these indirect effects are thought to be in the specific application, the "program" may need to be redefined to embrace the spillover effects. Or one might need to combine the type of evaluation discussed here with other tools, such as a model of the labor market, to pick up other benefits.

An extreme form of a spillover effect is an economy-wide program. The classic evaluation tools for assigned programs have little obvious role for economy-wide programs in which no explicit assignment process is evident, or if it is, the spillover effects are likely to be pervasive. When some countries get the economy-wide program but some do not, cross-country comparative work (such as growth regressions) can reveal impacts. That identification task is often difficult, because there are typically latent factors at country level that simultaneously influence outcomes and whether a country adopts the policy in question. And even when the identification strategy is accepted, carrying the generalized lessons from cross-country regressions to inform policymaking in any one country can be highly problematic. There are also a number of promising examples of how simulation tools for economy-wide policies such as Computable General Equilibrium models can be combined with household-level survey data to assess impacts on poverty and inequality.[5] These simulation methods make it far easier to attribute impacts to the policy change, although this advantage comes at the cost of the need to make many more assumptions about how the economy works.

In both assessing impacts and understanding the reasons for those impacts, there is often scope for a "meso" level analysis in which theory is used to inform empirical analysis of what would appear to be the key mechanisms linking an intervention to its outcomes, and this is done in a way that identifies key structural parameters that can be taken as fixed when estimating counterfactual outcomes. This type of approach can provide deeper insights into the factors determining outcomes in ex post evaluations and can also help in simulating the likely impacts of changes in program or policy design ex ante.

Naturally, simulations require many more assumptions about how an economy works.[6] As far as possible one would like to see those assumptions anchored to past knowledge built up from rigorous ex post evaluations. For example, by combining a randomized evaluation design with a structural model of education choices and exploiting the randomized design for identification, one can greatly expand the set of policy-relevant questions about the design of a program that a conventional evaluation can answer; examples using the *PROGRESA* evaluation data can be found in Todd and Wolpin (2002, 2010), Attanasio et al. (2004), and de Janvry and Sadoulet (2006). This strand of the literature has indicated that a budget-neutral switch of the enrolment subsidy in *PROGRESA* from primary to secondary school would have delivered a net gain in school attainments, by increasing the proportion of children who continue onto secondary school. While *PROGRESA* had an impact on schooling, it could have had a larger impact. However, it should be recalled that this type of program has two objectives: increasing schooling (reducing future poverty) and reducing current poverty, through the targeted transfers. To the extent that refocusing the subsidies on secondary schooling would reduce the impact on current income poverty (by increasing the forgone income from children's employment), the case for this change in the program's design would need further analysis.

Many of these observations point to the important role played by theory in understanding why a program may or may not have impact. However, the theoretical models found in the evaluation literature are not always the most relevant to developing country settings. The models have stemmed mainly from the literature on evaluating training and other programs in developed countries, in which selection is seen largely as a matter of individual choice among those eligible. This approach does not sit easily with what we know about many antipoverty programs in developing countries, in which the choices made by politicians and administrators appear to be at least as important to the selection process as the choices made by those eligible to participate. We often need a richer theoretical characterization of the selection problem to ensure relevance.

[5] See, for example, Bourguignon et al. (2003) and Chen and Ravallion (2004).

[6] For a useful overview of *ex ante* methods see Bourguignon and Ferreira (2003).

An example of one effort in this direction can be found in the Galasso and Ravallion (2005) model of a decentralized antipoverty program; their model focuses on the public-choice problem facing the central government and the local collective action problem facing communities, with individual participation choices treated as a trivial sub-problem. Such models can also point to instrumental variables for identifying impacts and studying their heterogeneity.

An example of the use of a more structural approach to assessing an *economy-wide* reform can be found in Ravallion and van de Walle (2008). Here the policy being studied was the de-collectivization of agriculture in Vietnam and subsequent efforts to develop a private market in land-use rights. These were huge reforms, affecting the livelihoods of the vast majority of the Vietnamese people. Ravallion and van de Walle develop models to explain how farmland was allocated to individual farmers at the time of de-collectivization, how those allocations affected living standards, and how the subsequent reallocations of land among farmers (that were permitted by the subsequent market-oriented agrarian reforms) responded to the inefficiencies left by the initial administrative assignment of land at the time of de-collectivization. Naturally, many more assumptions need to be made about how the economy works—essentially to make up for the fact that one cannot observe nonparticipants in these reforms as a clue to the counterfactual. Not all of those assumptions are testable. However, the principle of evaluation is the same, namely to infer the impacts of these reforms relative to explicit counterfactuals. For example, Ravallion and van de Walle assess the welfare impacts of the privatization of land-use rights against both an efficiency counterfactual (the simulated competitive market allocation) and an equity counterfactual (an equal allocation of quality-adjusted land within communes). This type of approach can also throw light on the heterogeneity of the welfare impacts of large reforms; in the Vietnam case, the authors were able to assess both the overall impacts on poverty and identify the presence of both losers and gainers, including among the poor.

Does Published Knowledge Reliably Guide Development Practice?

The benefits from evaluations depend in part on their publication, which is the main way they feed into development knowledge. Development policymaking draws on accumulated knowledge built up in large part from published findings. At the same time, publishing in refereed journals is important to a researcher's credibility and career prospects. Thus publication processes—notably the incentives facing journal editors and reviewers, researchers, and those who fund research—are relevant to our success in achieving development goals.

There are reasons for questioning how well the publication process performs in helping to realize the social benefits from rigorous evaluations. Three issues stand out. First, the cost of completing the publication stage in the cycle of research can be significant and it is hard to reduce these costs; writing the paper the right way, documenting everything that was done, and addressing the concerns of referees and editors all take time. Practitioners are often unwilling to fund these costs, and even question the need for publication. Again a large share of the benefits is external, to which individual project staff naturally attach low weight.

Second, received wisdom develops its own inertia through the publication process, with the result that it is often harder to publish a paper that reports unexpected or ambiguous impacts, when judged against current theories and/or past evidence. Reviewers and editors are likely to apply different standards according to whether they believe the results on a priori grounds.

In the context of evaluating development projects, the prior belief is often that the project will have positive impacts, for that is presumably the main reason why the project was funded in the first place. Then a preference for confirming prior beliefs will tend to bias our knowledge in favor of finding positive impacts. Negative or non-impacts will not get reported as easily. When there is a history of research on a type of intervention, the results of the early studies will set the priors against which later work is judged. An initial bad draw from the true distribution of impacts may then distort knowledge for some time after.

A third source of bias is that the review process in scientific publishing (at least in economics) tends to put greater emphasis on the internal validity of an evaluative research paper than on its external validity. The bulk of the effort goes into establishing that valid inferences are being drawn about causal impacts within the sample of program participants. The authors may offer some concluding (and possibly highly cautious) thoughts on the broader implications for scaling up the program well beyond that sample. However, these claims will rarely be established with comparable rigor to the efforts put into establishing internal validity, and the claims will rarely be challenged by reviewers.

These imperfections in the research publication industry undoubtedly have feedback effects on the production of evaluations. Researchers will tend to work harder to obtain positive findings, or at least results consistent with received wisdom, so as to improve their chances of getting their work published. No doubt, extreme biases (in either direction) eventually will be exposed. But this takes time.

Researchers have no shortage of instruments at their disposal to respond to the often distorted incentives generated by professional publication processes. Key decisions on what to report, and indeed the topic of the research paper, naturally lie with the individual researcher, who must write the paper and get it published. In the case of impact evaluations of development projects, the survey data (often collected for the purpose of the evaluation) will typically include multiple indicators of "outcomes." If one collects 20 indicators (say) then there is a good chance that at least one of them shows statistically significant impacts of the project even when it had no impact in reality. A researcher keen to get published might be tempted to report results solely for the significant indicator. (Journal reviewers and editors rarely ask what other data were collected.) The dangers to knowledge generation are plain.

The threat of replication by another researcher can help assure better behavior. But in economics, replication studies tend to have low status and are actually quite rare. Thus, as Rodrik (2009) points out, there will be little or no incentive for researchers to carry out the great many repetitions that would probably be called for in the agenda for mass RCTs proposed by Banerjee (2007) and Duflo and Kremer (2005), given that professional journals would have little interest in such replications of the same intervention and method in different settings.

There are a number of things that journals can do to help ensure better behavior in the interests of scientific progress. Researchers do not typically have a strong incentive to make their data publicly available for replication purposes. Some professional economics journals have adopted a policy that the data sets used in accepted papers should be made available this way, although enforcement does not appear to be uniformly strong. Another thing that can be done is for journals to insist on the existence of an ex ante analysis plan, giving details on the hypotheses, data and proposed tests *prior to* actually collecting the data and doing the analysis.[7]

The individual researcher can face a trade-off between publishability and relevance. Thankfully, the fact of being policy relevant is not in itself an impediment to publishability in most journals, though any research paper that lacks originality, rigor, or depth will have a hard time getting published. It is by maintaining the highest standards that we assure that relevant research is publishable, as well as being credible when carried to policy dialogues. However, it must be acknowledged that the set of research questions that are most relevant to development policy overlap only partially with the set of questions that are seen to be in vogue by the editors of the professional journals, at any given time. The dominance of academia in the respected publishing outlets is understandable, but it can sometimes make it harder for researchers doing work more relevant to development practitioners, even when that work meets the standards of more academic research. Academic research draws its motivation from academic concerns that overlap imperfectly with the issues that matter to development practitioners. Provided that scholarly rigor is maintained, the cost to a researcher's published output of doing policy relevant research might not be high, but it would be naïve to think that the cost is zero.

Communication and dissemination of the published findings on development effectiveness can also be deficient. Researchers sometimes lack the skills or personalities needed for effective communication with nontechnical audiences. Having worked very hard to ensure that the data and analysis are sound, and so pass muster by accepted scientific criteria, it does not come easily for all researchers to translate the results into just a few key policy messages, which do not seem to do justice to all the work involved. The externality problem can also arise here, whereby social returns from outreach exceed private returns. A research institution will often need to support its researchers with specialized staff, with strong communication skills.

[7] For a sobering example see Casey et al. (2011); also see the discussion in McKenzie (2012).

Conclusions

We under-invest in the knowledge needed for enhancing development effectiveness. Weak incentives facing key decision makers—stemming from externalities, asymmetric information and noncompetitive features of the market for knowledge—entail that too few rigorous evaluations of development interventions get done. This problem appears to be severe for evaluations of projects that yield benefits over long periods and for efforts in rigorously understanding the lessons that can be drawn for other projects and settings. Evaluations also raise ethical objections that can have political salience; these objections need not be conclusive, but they do need to be taken seriously.

Although donor support for evaluation in developing countries is helping, there is still a long way to go. Existing support could also be made more effective if it was aimed at changing private incentives to evaluate, by either raising the marginal benefits or lowering marginal costs facing project managers. The process of knowledge generation through evaluations is probably also affected by biases on the publication side, which distort the incentives facing individual researchers in doing evaluations.

None of this is helped by the fact that even the most rigorous methods found in practice often fall well short of delivering credible answers to the questions posed by practitioners. Those questions start at the outset of the project cycle, and even embrace the rationale for the intervention. They include understanding why the intervention might have greater impact for some participants, and in some settings, than others. They include the lessons for both the intervention under study and (importantly) future interventions. The classic estimate of the mean impact on those treated is of limited utility for addressing these issues.

Nor is the task helped by the fact that researchers have at times overstated what their favorite method can deliver for practitioners, and have often chosen what they evaluate according to whether their favorite method is feasible, rather than whether the question is important to development. There are even signs that interventions are being chosen, or designed, to fit certain preferred evaluation methods. At the same time, exaggerated claims are sometimes made by non-researchers about what can be learnt about development effectiveness in a short time with little or no credible data.

Looking forward, an effort is needed to develop approaches to evaluation that can throw more useful light on the external validity of findings on specific projects (including implications for scaling up) and can provide a deeper understanding of what determines why an intervention does, or does not, have impact. A broader sectoral approach to assessing aid effectiveness is also needed. There is still much to do if we want to realize the potential for evaluative research to inform development policy by "seeking truth from facts."

REFERENCES

Akerlof, George. 1970. "The Market for 'Lemons': Quality Uncertainty and the Market Mechanism." *Quarterly Journal of Economics* 84: 488–500.

Attanasio, Orazio, Costas Meghir, and Ana Santiago. 2004. "Education Choices in Mexico: Using a Structural Model and a Randomized Experiment to Evaluate PROGRESA." Working Paper EWP04/04, Institute of Fiscal Studies, London.

Attanasio, Orazio, Costas Meghir, and Miguel Szekely. 2003. "Using Randomized Experiments and Structural Models for Scaling Up: Evidence from the PROGRESA Evaluation." Working Paper EWP04/03, Institute of Fiscal Studies, London.

Bamberger, M., J. Rugh, and L. Mabry. 2006. *Real World Evaluation*. London: SAGE.

Banerjee, Abhijit. 2007. *Making Aid Work*. Cambridge, MA: MIT Press.

Banerjee, Abhijit, and Esther Duflo. 2011. *Poor Economics: A Radical Rethinking of the Way to Fight Global Poverty*. New York: PublicAffairs.

Behrman, Jere, Yingmei Cheng, and Petra Todd. 2004. "Evaluating Preschool Programs When Length of Exposure to the Program Varies: A Nonparametric Approach." *Review of Economics and Statistics* 86(1): 108–132.

Björklund, Anders, and Robert Moffitt. 1987. "The Estimation of Wage Gains and Welfare Gains in Self-Selection." *Review of Economics and Statistics* 69(1): 42–49.

Bourguignon, François, and Francisco Ferreira. 2003. "Ex-ante Evaluation of Policy Reforms Using Behavioural Models." In *The Impact of Economic Policies on Poverty and Income Distribution*, edited by Francois F. Bourguignon. and Luiz Pereira da Silva. New York: Oxford University Press.

Carvalho, Soniya, and Howard White. 2004. "Theory-Based Evaluation: The Case of Social Funds." *American Journal of Evaluation* 25(2): 141–160.

Chen, Shaohua, Ren Mu, and Martin Ravallion. 2009. "Are There Lasting Impacts of Aid to Poor Areas? Evidence from Rural China." *Journal of Public Economics* 93: 512–528.

Deaton, Angus. 2006. "Evidence-based Aid Must Not Become the Latest in a Long String of Development Fads." *Boston Review* July. Retrieved from http://bostonreview.net/BR31.4/deaton.html

Deaton, Angus. 2010. "Instruments, Randomization and Learning about Development." *Journal of Economic Literature* 48: 424–455.

De Janvry, Alain, and Elisabeth Sadoulet. 2006. "Making Conditional Cash Transfer Programs More Efficient: Designing for Maximum Effect of the Conditonality." *World Bank Economic Review* 20(1): 1–29.

Devarajan Shantayanan, Lyn Squire, and Sethaput Suthiwart-Narueput. 1997. "Beyond Rate of Return: Reorienting Project Appraisal." *World Bank Research Observer* 12(1): 35–46.

Djebbari, Habiba, and Jeffrey Smith. 2005. "Heterogeneous Program Impacts of PROGRESA." Mimeo, Laval University and University of Michigan.

Duflo, Esther, and Michael Kremer. 2005. "Use of Randomization in the Evaluation of Development Effectiveness." In *Evaluating Development Effectiveness*, edited by George Pitman, Osvaldo Feinstein, and Gregory Ingram. New Brunswick, NJ: Transaction.

Du Runsheng. 2006. *The Course of China's Rural Reform*. Washington, DC: International Food Policy Research Institute.

Galasso, Emanuela, and Martin Ravallion. 2004. "Social Protection in a Crisis: Argentina's *Plan Jefes y Jefas*." *World Bank Economic Review* 18(3): 367–399.

Galasso, Emanuela, and Martin Ravallion. 2005. "Decentralized Targeting of an Anti-Poverty Program." *Journal of Public Economics* 89(4): 705–727.

Galasso, Emanuela, Martin Ravallion, and Agustin Salvia. 2004. "Assisting the Transition from Workfare to Work: Argentina's *Proempleo* Experiment." *Industrial and Labor Relations Review* 57(5): 128–142.

Heckman, James, Hidehiko Ichimura, Jeffrey Smith, and Petra Todd. 1998. "Characterizing Selection Bias Using Experimental Data." *Econometrica* 66(5): 1017–1098.

Heckman, James, L. Lochner, and C. Taber. 1998. "General Equilibrium Treatment Effects." *American Economic Review Papers and Proceedings* 88(2): 381–386.

Heckman, James, and Salvador Navarro-Lozano. 2004. "Using Matching, Instrumental Variables and Control Functions to Estimate Economic Choice Models." *Review of Economics and Statistics* 86(1): 30–57.

Heckman, James, and Jeffrey Smith. 1995. "Assessing the Case for Social Experiments." *Journal of Economic Perspectives* 9(2): 85–110.

Heckman, James, Jeffrey Smith, and Nancy Clements. 1997. "Making the Most Out of Programme Evaluations and Social Experiments: Accounting for Heterogeneity in Programme Impacts." *Review of Economic Studies* 64(4): 487–535.

Heckman, James, Serio Urzua, and Edward Vytlacil. 2006. "Understanding Instrumental Variables in Models with Essential Heterogeneity." *Review of Economics and Statistics* 88(3): 389–432.

Lanjouw, Peter, and Martin Ravallion. 1999. "Benefit Incidence and the Timing of Program Capture." *World Bank Economic Review* 13(2): 257–274.

Luo, Xiaopeng. 2007. "Collective Learning Capacity and the Choice of Reform Path." Paper presented at the IFPRI/Government of China Conference, "Taking Action for the World's Poor and Hungry People," Beijing.

Mansuri, Ghazala, and Vijayendra Rao. 2013. *Localizing Development. Does Participation Work?* Washington, DC: World Bank.

McKenzie, David. 2012. "A Pre-Analysis Plan Checklist." Development Impact Blog, World Bank.

Miguel, Edward, and Michael Kremer. 2004. "Worms: Identifying Impacts on Education and Health in the Presence of Treatment Externalities." *Econometrica* 72(1): 159–217.

Moffitt, Robert. 2003. "The Role of Randomized Field Trials in Social Science Research: A Perspective from Evaluations of Reforms of Social Welfare Programs." Cemmap Working Paper, CWP23/02, Department of Economics, University College London.

Moffitt, Robert. 2004. "The Role of Randomized Field Trials in Social Science Research." *American Behavioral Scientist* 47(5): 506–540.

Moffitt, Robert. 2006. "Forecasting the Effects of Scaling Up Social Programs: An Economics Perspective." In *Scale-Up in Education: Ideas in Principle*, edited by Barbara Schneider and Sarah-Kathryn McDonald. Lanham, MD: Rowman & Littlefield.

Organization for Economic Co-Operation and Development (OECD). 2007. *A Practical Guide to Ex Ante Poverty Impact Assessment.* Development Assistance Committee Guidelines and Reference Series, OECD, Paris.

Over, Mead, and Martin Ravallion. 2012. "Recognizing and Rrewarding the best Development Professionals." Development Impact Blog, World Bank.

Rao, Vijayendra, and Ana Maria Ibanez. 2005. "The Social Impact of Social Funds in Jamaica: A Mixed Methods Analysis of Participation, Targeting and Collective

Action in Community Driven Development." *Journal of Development Studies* 41(5): 788–838.

Rao Vijayendra, and Michael Walton, Eds. 2004. *Culture and Public Action*. Stanford: Stanford University Press.

Rao, Vijayendra, and Michael Woolcock. 2003. "Integrating Qualitative and Quantitative Approaches in Program Evaluation." In *The Impact of Economic Policies on Poverty and Income Distribution: Evaluation Techniques and Tools*, edited by Francois J. Bourguignon and Luiz Pereira da Silva, pp. 165–190. New York: Oxford University Press.

Ravallion, Martin. 2000. "Monitoring Targeting Performance when Decentralized Allocations to the Poor Are Unobserved." *World Bank Economic Review* 14(2): 331–345.

Ravallion, Martin. 2004. "Who Is Protected from Budget Cuts?" *Journal of Policy Reform* 7(2): 109–122.

Ravallion, Martin. 2006. "Looking Beyond Averages in the Trade and Poverty Debate." *World Development* (special issue on *The Impact of Globalization on the World's Poor*, edited by Machiko Nissanke and Erik Thorbecke), 34(8): 1374–1392.

Ravallion, Martin. 2007. "How Relevant Is Targeting to the Success of an Antipoverty Program?" Policy Research Working Paper 4358. Washington, DC: World Bank.

Ravallion, Martin. 2008. "Evaluating Anti-Poverty Programs." In *Handbook of Development Economics*, Vol. 4, edited by Paul Schultz and John Strauss. Amsterdam: North-Holland.

Ravallion, Martin. 2014. "Can we Trust Shoestring Evaluations?" *World Bank Economic Review* 28(3): 413–431.

Ravallion, Martin. 2015. "The World Bank: Why it is Still Needed and Why it Still Disappoints." Center for Global Development Working Paper 400, Washington DC.

Ravallion, Martin. 2016. *The Economics of Poverty*, New York: Oxford University Press.

Ravallion, Martin, and Shaohua Chen. 2005. "Hidden Impact: Household Saving in Response to a Poor-Area Development Project." *Journal of Public Economics* 89(11–12): 2183–2204.

Ravallion, Martin, and Gaurav Datt. 1995. "Is Targeting through a Work Requirement Efficient? Some Evidence for Rural India." In *Public Spending and the Poor: Theory and Evidence*, edited by Dominique van de Walle and Kimberly Nead. Baltimore: Johns Hopkins University Press.

Ravallion, Martin, Emanuela Galasso, Teodoro Lazo, and Ernesto Philipp. 2005, Winter. "What Can Ex-Participants Reveal about a Program's Impact?" *Journal of Human Resources* 40(1): 208–230.

Ravallion, Martin, and Dominique van de Walle. 2008. *Land in Transition: Reform and Poverty in Rural Vietnam*. London: Palgrave Macmillan and Washington, DC: World Bank.

Ravallion, Martin, Dominique van de Walle, and Madhur Gaurtam. 1995. "Testing a Social Safety Net." *Journal of Public Economics* 57(2): 175–199.

Rodrik, Dani. 2009. "The New Development Economics: We Shall Experiment, but How Shall We Learn?" In *What Works in Development? Thinking Big and Thinking Small*, edited by Jessica Cohen and William Easterly. Washington, DC: Brookings Institution Press.

Sadoulet, Elisabeth, Alain de Janvry, and Benjamin Davis. 2001. "Cash Transfer Programs with Income Multipliers: PROCAMPO in Mexico." *World Development* 29(6): 1043–1056.

Todd, Petra, and Kenneth Wolpin. 2002. "Using a Social Experiment to Validate a Dynamic Behavioral Model of Child Schooling and Fertility: Assessing the Impact of a School Subsidy Program in Mexico." Penn Institute for Economic Research Working Paper 03–022, Department of Economics, University of Pennsylvania.

Todd, Petra, and Kenneth Wolpin. 2010. "Ex-Ante Evaluation of Social Programs." *Annales D'économie et de Statistique* 91: 259–286.

van de Walle, Dominique, and Ren Mu. 2007. "Fungibility and the Flypaper Effect of Project Aid: Micro-Evidence for Vietnam." *Journal of Development Economics* 84(2): 667–685.

Weiss, Carol. 2001. "Theory-Based Evaluation: Theories of Change for Poverty Reduction Programs." In *Evaluation and Poverty Reduction*, edited by Osvaldo Feinstein and Robert Piccioto. New Brunswick, NJ: Transaction.

2. *Economic Advising in Government and Beyond*

CHAPTER 29

CONFESSIONS OF A POLICY ANALYST

ROBERT H. NELSON

Introduction

In June 1975 I became a career civil servant in the federal government, working at the headquarters of the Washington Department of the Interior. To be more precise, I became a member of the Economics Branch of the Office of Policy Analysis in the Office of the Secretary of the Interior. The full Office of the Secretary included the Secretary of the Interior, the several Assistant Secretaries of the Interior and their staffs, the Solicitor (the chief legal officer), the Department budget office, and various other Secretarial staff offices such as mine. The roughly 500 employees of the Office of the Secretary oversaw the operations of the National Park Service, Bureau of Reclamation, Bureau of Land Management, Bureau of Indian Affairs, Fish and Wildlife Service, Geological Survey, and other agencies in the Interior Department (all together containing about 70,000 employees spread over the United States).

The largest part of the activity of these agencies takes place in the American West, where the federal government still owns about 50 percent of the total land area and is therefore intimately involved with many aspects of western land and natural resource governance. The State of California, for example, remains today 45 percent federally owned land. Created in 1849, the Interior Department historically played a large role in the development of the West and is still responsible for administering much of the federal land and resource role there. I remained a staff member of the Office of Policy Analysis for 18 years, leaving the Interior Department in the summer of 1993 to become a professor of environmental policy in the School of Public Policy of the University of Maryland, still my current position (where I have now been for more than 20 years). (Nelson, 1989*b*).

I have a PhD in economics from Princeton University (1971) and vaguely expected when I entered graduate school that I would spend my career in a university economics department (my father had been a college professor of economics and then business administration for about 20 years). I found graduate economic education disappointing, however. It provided me a valuable credential (without which I could not hold my current job) and, no small matter, offered me a student deferment from the military draft in the late 1960s when the Vietnam war was raging. After I finished graduate school, I did not think that I learned much, however, about how the American economy actually worked, nor did I learn much about how to improve public policy (an important goal for me in going to economics graduate school in the first place). Rather, graduate economics education at Princeton was preoccupied with mathematical modeling, sophisticated econometrics, and other demonstrations of high reasoning power that would impress other members of the economics profession. It was institutionally and culturally remarkably barren, given the central role that the economy has in the wider workings of any modern society. Having majored in mathematics as an undergraduate (at Brandeis University), graduate education in economics at Princeton fortunately came fairly easily for me, and I did well, so I did at least have considerable spare time to pursue a variety of interests outside economics.

I would not write about it explicitly in these terms for another 20 years but even then Princeton economics felt "religious" to me. Mainstream economic analysis was a closed system of elaborate reasoning from simple assumptions, reminiscent almost of medieval scholastic theology. Economics professors tended to think that economics could explain the whole world—it was far removed from Marxism in the specifics of the analysis but there was a similar strong economic determinism. Ideas themselves almost never came up as key causal elements themselves in explaining economic outcomes, something that persists to this day in the mainstream economics profession. (Although he was an economic historian during his academic years in Germany, Max Weber's analysis of religion and the rise of capitalism is encountered in the contemporary American university only in the sociology and intellectual history departments.) The study of economic history and the history of economic thought were increasingly being marginalized at Princeton and other leading economics departments, a trend that would only grow stronger in the decades to follow. Even the economic roles of the law and other institutions in society seldom came up in the 1960s as important factors in explaining the workings of an economic system (fortunately this has changed and economists today do give considerable attention to the large economic importance of institutions). Economists in the 1960s—and still today—are trying to persuade society that they are true scientists (the *Economist* magazine recently referred to this as "physics envy"). A better analogy, however, is that they are priests of a modern secular religion of economics. Again, while such thoughts were already entering my mind in my days in economics graduate school at Princeton, it would be another 20 years before I would write explicitly about professional economics in these terms (Nelson 1991, 2001, 2010).

Mainstream Voices of Concern

Few current economists are as critical in their assessment of their profession or explicitly use my kinds of religious analogies in describing its workings. But I should note that there is a surprising undercurrent of discontent today even in the economics mainstream, normally suppressed but that occasionally breaks out into print (Akerlof and Schiller, 2010; McCloskey, 2007, 2011). The Spring 2012 issue of the *Journal of Economic Perspectives* (a leading journal published by the American Economic Association intended specifically to address policy matters), for example, contains the following remarks by Timothy Taylor, its longtime and highly regarded managing editor. As Taylor writes, "a wise colleague once said to me that jargon and technical expressions always have two uses: (1) to streamline and clarify the communication of concepts between specialists; and (2) for specialists to identify themselves as an in-group while impressing and excluding others." The latter serves the important purpose within economics of feeding "the inner glow of being within the charmed circle of jargon-users" (Taylor, 2012: 32). Thus, all too often, the technical displays of economic experts become an end in themselves, something to be understood in sociological terms rather than of improving real-world economic understanding.

Further reinforcing Taylor's observations, in the same Spring 2012 issue of the *Journal of Economic Perspectives*, the current editor, David Autor, a professor of economics at MIT, explains—remarkably enough in light of mainstream economic practices—that the journal does not normally allow use of the leading quantitative methods of economics in its pages, implicitly conceding that much of the more sophisticated modeling and empirical work of the profession is too abstract and unreliable to be applicable for actual policy purposes. Frequently, the more technical statistical articles in mainstream economics journals, Autor says, offer "the juxtaposition of strong claims [to scientific findings] with weak evidence." It is common that "the main empirical inferences [are] . . . dependent on functional forms or choices of control variables" that are somewhat arbitrary; much different results would often be obtained if the problem were specified differently, as could plausibly be done in many cases. For the *Journal*'s purposes, therefore, its publication policy was to present only empirical "findings that are almost immediately apparent from a scatter plot or table of means." Empirical results acceptable for purposes of policy discussion in the *Journal* should be "almost immediately self-evident in tabular or graphic form" (Autor, 2012: 14). That serves as a necessary protection against the false advertising so common to the economics profession today in its typical mainstream publications.

One possibility is that current economists are simply unaware of the large gap between mainstream economics and the real world—and are unwilling to make much effort to find out about all this. More likely, many of them are aware and simply do not care enough to do much to try to help to resolve the problem—either in setting their own research agenda or in seeking changes in the wider practices of the economics profession.

Being an economics professor in a top university is a comfortable, prestigious, and high-paying form of employment (typically with an annual salary in the range of $150,000 or more). Why upset the apple cart? Economists can always rationalize their behavior by arguing that, even if we are still awaiting them, fundamental theoretical advances must precede policy applicability—as was the case historically in physics and other natural sciences. This expectation of future policy applications of economic theory is, to be sure, itself an article of—as I would say—(religious) economic faith.

All this amounts to a large ethical failure on the part of the contemporary economics profession. The economist George DeMartino thus finds that "there is an urgent need for [a] professional economic ethics." It is not only intellectually but ethically objectionable when large numbers of professional economists show a deep "naiveté and hubris regarding economic science and the capacities of the economics profession" that leads to "dangerous" behavior in confidently offering strong policy conclusions about matters that in fact they know little about factually and conceptually. Economists wading blindly into areas of real world concern, DeMartino finds, "have made extraordinary errors over the past decade" (DeMartino, 2011: 4–5). The financial crisis of 2008 and the Great Depression that followed defied almost any conventional economic understanding offered in the years prior to the crisis (Lo, 2012). Over a longer time frame, development economists at the World Bank and other international institutions for many years offered professional policy advice to the poorer nations of the world that they would themselves end up disavowing a mere decade or two later (Easterly, 2007).

Coming to the Department of the Interior

Not surprisingly, given such increasingly skeptical views on my part about the economics mainstream even as I completed my PhD, I left the university world in 1972, first to work for two and a half years at a public policy foundation, The Twentieth Century Fund (now The Century Fund), and then moved to the Interior Department in 1975. I needed a job (relations had become strained at the Twentieth Century Fund) but another consideration in joining the Interior Department was that, given my disappointing graduate school experiences, I still needed an education in real-world economics and public policy. I thought a good way to learn might be to enter directly into government service, where I could observe how things really worked there. That turned out to be a good idea. My original commitment in my own mind was for only two years in government but, given that it turned out that I liked the job and was actually learning a lot, I extended for another two years, and then another two, and so forth until I finally ended up remaining at the Interior Department until 1993.

My Princeton PhD in economics, ironically, was probably a significant factor in my being hired for the Interior job. In fact, the job description sent out to potential job candidates was for an "economic expert" who could perform technical analyses of matters of economic concern to Interior policy officials. Although I had not yet learned this in 1975, the officially stated version of my expected role at the Interior Department closely reflected the lingering influence of American intellectuals from the progressive era (typically dated from 1890 to 1920) and their commitment to the "scientific management" of American society (Nelson, 1995*b*).

According to the "progressive" political philosophy, for example, there should be a clear separation of "politics" and "science." The democratic political process would supply the values and set the basic policy directions for American society but the implementation should then be assigned to professional experts—such as I was officially hired to be in joining the Interior Department in 1975. Economic policy analysts such as I should operate in a "value-free" manner because we were to function as technical experts who would bring to bear scientific skills and knowledge that was itself independent of any personal values and beliefs. The American federal civil service, also supposedly making appointments according to strictly objective criteria and otherwise remaining insulated from politics, was established in the progressive era, yet another way that my life story has reflecting the influence of progressive-era thinking that has continued—if increasingly under challenge—into our own times.

My Actual Interior Role

These circumstances of my hiring soon raised the first ethical dilemma for my government service as an economic policy analyst. I was hired to be a value-neutral expert who should function simply as an economic technician of sorts. My relationship to the Interior leadership should be as, say, a computer technician hired to fix a problem is related to the owner of the computer. It turned out, however, that this was a serious mischaracterization of the way my job in the Office of Policy Analysis was actually turning out. Economic policy analysts in government, as I was discovering, were not simply told to study the technical means of implementing a given policy and to report the scientific results back to their superiors. Rather, economic policy analysts often functioned themselves as strong advocates for particular policy positions. They had an important internal political role themselves in the workings of the Interior Department, as well as making their expertise available.

Most of my Interior work the first few years involved policy issues relating to the management of government-owned forests, rangelands, coal reserves, and other natural resources in the American West (Nelson, 1983). Many private ranchers, for example, graze their cattle on the publicly owned rangelands. Government economists in practice are not merely asked to calculate the "fair market value" as a basis for charging a reasonable grazing fee but become themselves strong internal advocates in government for charging such fees (which would be significantly higher than historic grazing fees). On federal forests, many federal timber sales returned such low sale revenues (in public auctions of the rights to harvest the timber) that they could not even cover the federal administrative costs of holding the sales. In opposition to the traditional policies of the federal forest agencies such as the U.S. Bureau of Land Management in the Interior Department and U.S. Forest Service in the Department of Agriculture, government economists such as I campaigned actively in government for the curtailment or outright elimination of such "below-cost" (money losing for the government) timber sales.

It was similar with many of the dams being constructed by the Bureau of Reclamation, another Interior agency. Interior economists and other policy analysts in the Office of the Secretary of the Interior were the leading internal proponents within the Interior Department for curtailing or eliminating such dam construction as wasteful "pork barrel" spending that involved higher costs to society than the benefits realized. Despite the arid climate of the American West, there was no real shortage of water. Indeed, large acreages of the West were irrigated with subsidized water from Bureau of Reclamation dams, including the Central Valley of California, one of the mainstays to this day of agricultural production in the United States. As with the grazing fee, government economists were leading in-house proponents in the Interior Department of charging more for farmer use of the water.

Probably even more important as a matter of the overall economic consequences, there were large potential economic gains to society from transferring water from rural agricultural use to urban use. Rural agriculture then received 90 percent of the water in the American West but this water would have been at least an order of magnitude more valuable if it had been available to supply metropolitan housing and other urban water needs. Longstanding institutional barriers in the water law of the West, however, prevented any such transfer of the water from lower value to higher value uses. Government economists such as myself in the Office of the Secretary (other economists in the office such as Robert Davis—possessor of a Harvard economics PhD—and Richard Wahl had a more important role in this area than I did) here again assumed the leading Interior role as advocates for "water marketing"—pushing strongly for a transformation of the institutions of western water law to allow formal buying and selling of water rights (Wahl, 1989).

There were many more such examples. Indeed, strongly advocating such "economic" approaches to government policy proved to be my most important role as an Interior Department economic analyst for all my 18 years there. It seldom took much sophisticated technical analysis, moreover, to identify the superior economic policy. For me at least, ways to improve government economic results were mostly pretty obvious, once I had had the time and experience to grasp the full factual, historical, and institutional details of the situation. I think this was true for most other professional economic colleagues of mine in the Office of Policy Analysis, although they differed considerably in their taste for economic policy entrepreneurship within the Department and their willingness to confront the sometimes unpleasant bureaucratic tensions that might arise as a result of being a strong internal advocate for policy change.

The Economist in Government

Many other professional economists were also entering the federal government in the 1960s and 1970s and a few of them were soon writing about similar experiences (Nelson, 1987, 1989*a*). As a former director of the Bureau of the Budget in the Johnson administration and later chairman of the Council of Economic Advisors in the Carter administration, Charles Schultze was among the most prominent of such economists. Rejecting outright the traditional "progressive" concept of a value-neutral, scientific role for expert professionals such as economists in government, Schultze was already writing in 1968 that "political values permeate every aspect of the decision-making process in the majority of federal domestic programs. There is no simple division of labor in which the 'politicians' achieve consensus on an agreed on set of objectives while the [economic and other professional] 'analysts' design and evaluate—from efficiency and effectiveness criteria—alternative means of achieving those objectives" (Schultze, 1968: 2–3). Rather, as Schultze would later clarify, the actual role of the professional economist in government is to be an internal (and to some extent external) "partisan advocate for efficiency" (Schultze, 1982).

Shortly after leaving the Council of Economic Advisors (CEA), a former staff member reminisced on his 1970s experiences there:

> [As professional economists at the CEA], we were not expert political strategists ... even if we had been, we were not in a position to actually play the role. On the other hand, I think it's an exciting and intriguing kind of role.... I think it was, as a practical matter, hard for us not to try to play amateur political strategist and think about how could we get this thing through that group, who would accept what, and what kind of friends and allies you needed to do what. So I guess we all played that in varying degrees, and I think some [CEA] staff people did quite a lot of it ... tried to get through to the right people and sway their views [to get them to adopt the right policies]." (Allen, 1977: 67–68)

As I could affirm from my own experiences at the Interior Department, this was an accurate description of a typical economist role in government. Almost no former government economists wrote, however, about the ethical issues that such observations raised. In the overall progressive scheme under which we were hired, and that justified the very existence of our policy offices, government economists were to function as technical experts who would undertake value-free (and politically neutral) applications of economic science. In reality, however, we were bringing a strong value system to bear and using the opportunity created by our (sometimes high level) government positions to advance these particular economic values. One might describe such economists as a special breed of unelected "economic politician" in government, admittedly motivated not mainly by narrow self-interest (although obviously this could happen) but to advance the economic value system that had been reinforced in economics graduate school. Economists were not the only important professional participants in American government who operated as unofficial political advocates. The judiciary in the United States in the 1960s and 1970s was actively interjecting itself into almost every area of Interior Department land and resource policymaking—as indeed was then happening over much of the federal government—all the while claiming misleadingly that it was simply applying neutrally and impartially "the law." For judges, much like economists, as we are now coming to understand, the ultimate source of their legitimacy in society all along has been religious (Levinson, 1988; Nelson, 2001).

Probably more than most government economists, I had an introspective awareness about my actual function in government and recognized the resulting tensions with official progressive assumptions about professional economic roles—as I eventually wrote about in a 1987 review article on "The Economics Profession and the Making of Public Policy," published in the *Journal of Economic Literature* (another journal of the American Economic Association) (Nelson, 1987). Ethically, one might ask: Should I have resigned from the Interior Department, concluding that I was acting under false pretenses—that I could not in all honesty continue to function as an internal "value politician," as I actually was, in the false guise of providing progressive "value-neutral" expertise. It was not only that my official job description emphasized my own Interior role in value-neutral "scientific" terms but that I sometimes had to describe myself in these (as I knew misleading) terms to others during my years in government. If asked what an economic policy analyst did in government, and why economists like myself should play a meaningful role in internal Interior Department decision making, I would have to revert to the official language—the progressive and "scientistic" terminology of value-neutral expertise—of my original job description.

If I had been more candid, and confessed my actual political role at Interior in explicit terms, it might well have undermined my own legitimacy and effectiveness in government (as an economic policy advocate). Other non-economists in the Interior Department with opposing policy views admittedly were often skeptical of the official self-portraits of top government economists. At least as long as we did not confess, however, there was not much they could do about it.

An Antidote to American Politics as Usual

In those days, how did I justify ethically to myself my own actual political and value advocacy role at the Interior Department, even as I was supposed to be a "value-neutral" technician? In terms of the progressive value system of scientific management under which the Interior Department and much of the rest of the federal government supposedly operated, I was in fact behaving as a progressive heretic. My own thinking at the time went something like this. The ordinary workings of democratic politics in the

United States obviously left much to be desired. Members of Congress wanted to be reelected, which frequently meant maximizing the narrowly economic and other benefits that they could deliver to their own constituents. American politics was also becoming more expensive, which meant that candidates for federal office needed increasing amounts of money to run effective campaigns. That meant turning to organized interest groups or to individually rich and powerful individuals as a source of campaign finance money—and often accommodating the sources of this money in some fashion if they then happened to be elected. Congressional staff ultimately had to play by similar rules as well. The top political appointees within the Interior Department faced similar incentives and often behaved in a similarly "political" fashion (sometimes they came to the Department from prior Congressional careers).

The various agencies of the Interior Department had many skilled and motivated employees at the working career level. But they tended to be risk averse. Generous pensions and other policies encouraged lifetime employment for the government civil service. Its members typically considered that the American political system, whatever its deficiencies, was a given and its wider basic problems were not their responsibility. As long as they were well enough compensated, they would do the best they could under the—sometimes unfortunate—circumstances of American government. The result was that most career employees at the Interior Department played by the rules of the game, as set by Congress and the political leadership of the Interior Department (and in a few especially important instances, set by the White House).

According to the official progressive political philosophy, American government should serve "the public interest"—the best interests of the whole nation. In practice, this was admittedly difficult to define operationally. But the Interior Department and many of its agencies, including the public land management agencies with which I was mostly working, were not even attempting to achieve this result. They were intentionally taking care of the private needs of the local constituents within each district and otherwise carrying out the details of political deals made in the halls of Congress and in the executive branch. As James Buchanan, Gordon Tulloch, and other members of the "public choice" school of economics (which originated in the 1960s) were arguing with much validity, the ethics of the private market place—the individual pursuit of self-interest—also applied widely to the ethics of the behavior of individual actors in American government and politics (Buchanan and Tulloch, 1962).

In the 1970s and 1980s I was observing such self-interested behavior in government first hand at the Interior Department. It was not a pretty sight. American progressivism was an American version of European democratic socialism, often showing a similar attraction to large doses of government economic planning and management. One major problem, however, was that the implementation of any such planning and management had to pass through the workings of the American democratic process. In that process, at least as structured in the United States, the end result ironically was often in basic conflict with core progressive values themselves. Indeed, what passed in the 1970s and 1980s in the American political arena as "progressive" might well have often been described more accurately as "anti-progressive." So-called American progressive politics had actually become fundamentally conservative, designed in large measure to protect the particular beneficiaries of the welfare and regulatory state as they had established their claims on government over the course of the twentieth century—all in the name of the progressive cause (for discussion of this on a worldwide basis, see Scott, 1998).

Unlike most federal civil servants, I never intended to remain permanently in government. As I noted previously, I had come to government to get a better policy education and to gain some real-world experience (my plan in this respect was working). I was making the decision to continue working at the Interior Department for no longer than two years at a time. I was, as the remarks above would suggest, unhappy with the workings of American government. This was admittedly not an altogether "value-free" observation; rather, it was a value judgment that I was making, informed by my own values (many of which I shared in significant respects with other professional economists). Putting it even more candidly, I thought my own "economic values" were superior to—were more ethical than—the contrasting private values that were all too often being served in the routine workings of American democratic politics.

In a certain sense, I saw myself as actually committed to the old fashioned—if now increasingly contested in practice—progressive ideal that the role of government is in fact to serve the public interest. Although many American politicians continued publicly to defend their actions in such progressive terms, this was, as I saw matters, frequently a false front. In actually serving narrower and often private purposes, American progressive politicians were frequently betraying their own outwardly professed ideals.

It was not necessarily the case, however, that these people were themselves deficient in moral character. Rather, to a significant extent, they were operating in a world of American democratic politics where they felt—probably reasonably enough—that they had little choice. Many people rejected the American political world outright as unethical—resembling too closely the sale of government to the highest bidder—and therefore were unwilling to enter politics at all. Those who did enter electoral politics were obviously willing to live with it—perhaps thinking that their own participation was at least better than the alternatives.

It was easy to see my personal job situation in the Interior Department as almost a random historical accident. Whatever my official job description, in practice it had turned out that I had considerable flexibility to function as an internal professional entrepreneur for public policies (mainly but not exclusively involving economic matters) that I thought would be of overall benefit to the nation. Surprisingly often, moreover, it did not require much economic knowledge or other forms of technical understanding to identify such policies. It did not take a sophisticated economic analysis to see the large inefficiencies of many Interior Department policies. Rather, given the workings of American democratic politics, these policies had never really been intended in the first place to serve a broader national interest. To understand the outcomes of the American government decision-making processes (even its economic outcomes), political insight was therefore at least as important as economic insight.

Involvements with Federal Energy Leasing

One dramatic example in which I was personally involved occurred in the early 1980s. The Pauley Group had purchased a federal oil lease off Santa Barbara, California in the 1960s. Following the negative fallout for nearby oil development from the Santa Barbara oil spill in 1969, and concluding that it would in any case be uneconomic to develop the lease at the low oil prices of that time, the company had voluntarily surrendered the lease back to the Interior Department (there were costs to holding an oil and gas lease, and in addition undeveloped leases could not be held for more than 10 years). The rapid rise of oil prices in the mid-1970s after OPEC, however, combined with new more promising exploration results in the area, had caused Pauley to regret its earlier decision. Failing in its efforts to win the lease back in court, Pauley sought help from Congress in the form of special legislation to give the lease back to the company.

With Pauley wielding strong political influence with Democratic Senator Alan Cranston and others in the California Congressional delegation, and elsewhere in the Congress, as well as at the highest levels of the Interior Department (now part of a Republican administration), this legislation was well on track to pass. I was alerted to these circumstances by another Interior (PhD) economist in my office who was more directly involved with the oil and gas program. With both of us considering this an abuse of the democratic political system, I alerted an old friend who happened then to be a producer for NBC Weekend News in New York. Once the situation received nationwide publicity on a Sunday NBC Evening News broadcast, the legislation was soon permanently derailed. The federal government later resold this Santa Barbara lease for more than $25 million (a financial gain for the federal government, I might note, that substantially exceeded the total salary payments I would receive in all my years in the federal government).

As I was aware at the time, I was in effect making an ethical decision—what was my higher loyalty, to the national interest as I saw it in denying Pauley the leases, or to the Republican political leadership of the Interior Department that employed me (although I was a career employee hired by a previous Republican administration) but that I now saw as acting in concert with Congress to achieve an unethical result (it was not a question of economic efficiency, since Pauley now wanted to develop the lease, as would any new purchaser at 1980s oil prices). In a certain sense it was contest between my values as an individual (and as an economist) and the conventional political standards of Washington. In this case, owing to some quite unusual personal circumstances, enabling me to marshal the force of the national media, I happened to find a way to prevail. Many other economic professionals in government have had to make similar choices, sometimes involving even far higher economic stakes than in my case.

Other ethical dilemmas can arise. Sometimes, as a matter of successful policy advocacy, the economist in government may strengthen his internal "political" influence by presenting his or her policy conclusions as a "technical" result, based on a "scientific" analysis. In reality, the justification for the policy may actually be that it serves the economist's commitment to the economic value system grounded in efficiency, while political leaders in their current decision making roles give little heed to efficiency consequences. The government economist, however, cannot argue explicitly that he or she is committed to superior values, as compared with the political leadership. It is sometimes therefore necessary—if they want to prevail—for government economists to assert that their policy conclusions are derived from their superior expert skills. In the modern age, science has replaced God as the ultimate source of truth and social legitimacy (at least in the public arena). Medieval priests once instructed rulers in the commands of God; American economists now instruct political leaders in the commands of "economic science." Efficiency is the operative measure of the rate of economic progress, and the real religion of American public life in the twentieth century was the religion of economic progress (Nelson, 2001, 2010).

One might reasonably ask, assuming a professional economist is convinced of the correctness of his view, is he or she behaving ethically in advocating this view in a misleadingly technical economic dress? Can a good end justify a questionable means? That is to say, the economist in government is accorded a certain amount of prestige—and thus decision making influence—because at least some people in government defer to the scientific status of economics. In practice, asserting that a policy recommendation is technically grounded in economic expertise increases the likelihood that the argument will be heard and perhaps even followed. But what if the policy recommendation is actually grounded in little more than ordinary common sense, once economic efficiency is taken as the correct value to be served?

The Interior Department manages the vast coal reserves—about a third of the total reserves of the United States—owned by the federal government in the American West. In the late 1970s there was growing interest in developing some of these reserves—especially in the Powder River Basin in Wyoming—on a large scale for the first time. For one thing, much of the western coal was unusually low in sulfur content, making it possible to comply with Clean Air Act requirements established by the Environmental Protection Agency (EPA) in the 1970s without having to build expensive sulfur removal systems ("scrubbers"). So I was convinced that development of this western federal coal was both economically and environmentally advantageous for the nation. I was further convinced that the Interior Department should offer Wyoming leases for sale containing large amounts of coal, leaving it to the market to decide which specific coal deposits could most efficiently be developed (the leases would contain "diligence requirements" that they be returned to the government if the leases were not developed within 10 years).

The Interior political leadership in the Carter administration, however, thought that the government should plan much more precisely for the total required amounts of coal and then lease only those specific coal deposits that were needed for this purpose. It was another legacy of the progressive era: Because the coal was government owned, its development should be carefully planned and scientifically managed by the government—in this case the Interior Department. Several Interior Department economists, including myself, were tasked with doing a technical economic analysis to determine the total amount of federal coal reserves needed to meet current western coal demands. Other government analysts would then determine the specific coal tracts to be leased, cumulatively adding up to this overall needed quantity. It was in effect an exercise in central economic planning, if occurring on a small scale for one particular segment of the economy managed by the Interior Department (of admittedly significant national energy importance), but otherwise not unlike the central economic planning of many past European socialist nations.

This posed an ethical dilemma for me. I did not believe that the central planning task I was being assigned was technically feasible, that it reflected a naïve progressive planning mentality that underestimated the unpredictability of events and overestimated the government's ability to anticipate and control them (Nelson, 1983). Should I have simply refused to be part of the comprehensive "scientific" planning for the development of federally owned coal in the West? Perhaps. But I went ahead and helped to develop estimates of the future objective "need" for western coal, and the share of this that should be provided by the federal government, based on its ownership of much of the coal in the West. These estimates were developed with the help of a large computer modeling exercise undertaken by a private consulting company under contract to the Department of Energy (ICF Consulting), working with the Interior Department. In the end, many of the future energy price and use estimates proved wildly inaccurate, as has often turned out to be the case for such comprehensive planning calculations in government over the years. The scientific planning appearance, however, served at the time as an important part of the public case then being made by the Interior Department leadership to advance leasing of federally owned coal in the West, a policy that I favored. In effect, as one might say, it was necessary to put on a public show of the development of a progressive "scientific" leasing policy—however misguided the effort necessarily would be in practice—if any federal coal was to be leased at all (itself an outcome to be desired). My government economist role in this instance was to help in providing the required scientistic "PR."

Thus, although I did not initiate it, I was in effect going along with, and even contributing to, an exercise in misrepresenting the actual precise validity of an ostensibly scientific policy result, partly because in my view it was helping in the American political system to yield the correct economic policy conclusion. Top Democratic political leaders in the Interior Department demanded a technical "scientific" justification and would not have heeded my contrary skeptical views. Much of the American public, including some federal judges with powerful holds on Interior Department policymaking, had similar "progressive" views. So I sought to accommodate a widespread American economic naiveté in the interest of a better—a more efficient—national use of the federally owned coal resource. Was this ethical?

Some policy economists in government have been less scrupulous, going so far as to take the initiative themselves to dress economic policy conclusions in a technical economic garb that actually adds little or nothing to the policy results. But what if this is the only way in the flawed American political system to "sell" a policy that in reality serves the national interest? Here again, there is an ethical dilemma: Can the attainment of a genuinely desirable economic policy justify using a misleadingly "scientific" means of economic presentation and advocacy within the government (and in the wider public arena as well)? It may also be that many government economists have actually persuaded themselves that they are doing a valid scientific analysis in order to discover the best policy. So they never have to confront their own expert misrepresentations to the political leadership and the wider American public.

Policymaking in government is often a question of luck and timing, a lesson illustrated by another involvement of mine with the coal leasing efforts of the Interior Department. With the arrival of the Reagan administration, James Watt became the Secretary of the Interior. Coming from Wyoming, Watt was knowledgeable about the Interior Department, was a law school graduate and was in some other respects well equipped to be Secretary. He had a self-defeating tendency, however, to make unnecessary enemies with clumsy statements in public and other actions. He was, remarkably enough for such a high level political appointee, tone deaf to much of the discourse of American public life. Those who simply disagreed with him in conventional policy terms—typically advocates of a "progressive" orientation—were quick to take advantages of the large political weaknesses he thus had created for himself.

In any event, Watt's Interior Department was accused of selling a Wyoming coal lease in 1982 for less than its fair market value (harking back to memories of the 1920s Teapot Dome scandal, also involving a federal energy lease in Wyoming). Congress established a commission to investigate the situation. It did not make much money available, however, so the Commission had to be largely staffed by civil servants detailed from federal agencies, including several from the Interior Department, including myself. I ended up as the lead economist in writing the eventual Commission report.

After they had gathered, the Commission members decided to examine not only the specific Wyoming lease sale but the manner of operation of the entire federal coal leasing program. By then I was closely familiar with this program, having worked on its design since 1978, along with other members of the Office of Policy Analysis who had played a key role in the development of the Interior program. Our new staff roles at the Commission allowed mainly Interior economists such as myself to advance many of the policy conclusions of our previous years of coal policy study to the five members of the Commission. One might reasonably ask whether we faced an ethical conflict of interest in being asked to evaluate a program we had helped significantly to design. I decided to ignore this issue at the time, partly because I had not sought the position, partly because there was little similar expertise in federal coal leasing available from any other source that would be available to the commission, and partly because I saw the situation as an unexpected opportunity to advance further improvements in federal coal leasing policy that I favored. More influenced by economic arguments, the Commission recommended, for example, that the federal government not attempt to centrally plan the development of federally owned coal and instead should adopt policy measures to make greater use of market forces (United States Commission on Fair Market Value Policy for Federal Coal Leasing, 1984).

By then, the Interior Department was a beleaguered agency. Watt had made yet another maladroit public statement that had been captured in a television video (relating awkwardly to the "cripple" status of one member of the Commission), and had been forced by the Reagan administration to resign. The great majority of our staff-level professional economic proposals for coal leasing were accepted by the commission members, incorporated into the final report, and then soon officially adopted by the new leadership team at the Interior Department. A few professional economists in government had in effect substantially designed and brought to realization a new federal coal leasing program. But political and economic events are unpredictable; OPEC was collapsing at this time, oil prices were plummeting, and the demand for new federal coal leases was declining correspondingly. Our economist "dream" coal leasing program therefore never was put to a practical test (Sanzillo, 2012).

Defending Progressive Values

So, despite my skepticism about many details of the progressive agenda, I had come by the 1980s to see myself more broadly in surprisingly old-fashioned progressive terms, as an opponent of the more recent corruptions of the American political system (progressivism had itself been a counter-reaction to the many corruptions of American politics of the late nineteenth century). Ironically, however, this required that I become a politician of sorts myself. As a further irony, the source of my political legitimacy within the Interior Department was due in significant part to my supposedly value-neutral and nonpolitical expert status as an economic professional. Complicating the situation still further, I seldom used any elaborate technical expertise in my economist roles in government. Rather, my greatest contributions as a professional economist to the Interior Department reflected precisely the fact that I could practice politics in a less crassly "political" way; that is to say, I did not have to be elected, would not have minded leaving the Interior Department (or the government altogether) to change jobs, and thus could have greater independence from the normal forces of democratic electoral politics.

At least in my own mind, I thought that this made it possible for me to show a greater commitment to the actual public interest. It was by the advancement of my own ethical values—in many areas closely reflecting the historical values of economic professionalism—that I contributed the most to my social usefulness as a government economist, rather than by the application of any technical economic skills. As I would later come to write about all this, economic professionals in government are like the members of a priesthood surrounded by ordinary flawed politicians who have a weaker commitment to the true progressive service of the national interest (Nelson, 2001). Priests of many other kinds have served similar roles historically in instructing the lay leadership of their times in matters of the higher truths of religion (in my case in the truths of progressive economic religion).

Thus, professional values, as I concluded, are higher values in American life than ordinary political values, as I was seeing American politics as usual in the Interior Department in the 1970s and 1980s. Of course, during my years in government, I could not say any such thing in public in defense of my own government role. I could not say that professional decisions should override decisions reached through American democratic politics as usual. As noted previously, many American judges are like that as well. In many rulings, especially the most consequential decisions the judiciary makes, judges are another special unelected form of politician who, owing to their personal and professional values (to some degree formed during their legal education) and their lifetime tenure (at least in the case of federal judges), are free to serve higher values than those that dominate ordinary democratic politics. The important role of legal, economic and other professionals—and the higher values that they hope to serve—seems to be an important part of the informal workings of the American political system as a whole.

In the United States there is an outward official commitment to democracy as the "voice of the people" which is the ultimate source of social authority and political legitimacy (the modern substitute for the legitimizing authority of God in the medieval order). At the same time, however, many Americans seem to recognize implicitly (and for some people it is more explicit) that the system of American democratic decision making is deeply flawed. Inevitably, "the people" know little or nothing about the specifics of the great majority of government actions being taken. The system of political representation prescribed by the Constitution is now 200 years old, and has broken down in the face of the challenges of twentieth (and now twenty-first) century government. The original progressives early on in the twentieth century made a heroic effort to adapt American governance to the new demands of the century without changing the basic American constitutional structure (although they did make at least one important change—the constitutional amendment for the direct election of Senators in 1912).

The basic progressive approach was to create new powerful professional roles in government that are themselves undemocratic, such as the creation of many professional—"expert" —offices and agencies within the executive branch of government. Among the most important of such institutions, in this case still dominated by economic professionals, is the Federal Reserve System, created in 1913. Indeed, the Federal Reserve's "nonpolitical" policy making sometimes rivals even the Supreme Court in its overall policy influence on American society.

At least this was the way I had come to see the workings of the American governing system by the 1980s from my observation point in the Interior Department. Some observers admittedly might suggest that this was a self-serving justification for my own illegitimate "freelance" interventions in the government decision making process. But I disagreed, regarding my economic entrepreneurial and policy advocacy roles at the Interior Department in the 1970s and 1980s—my role effectively as a special, a "professional" internal political player—as ethically justified. Sometimes political and economic systems work only because informal adaptations are made. If every official guiding principle is strictly and rigorously followed, a political system might not work as well and might even break down altogether. As I learned in the 1970s, for example, private property rights to land have evolved for centuries mostly outside the official formalities of the law (Nelson, 1977). In the former Soviet Union, many students of its economy once described how the informal existence of black markets was an essential corrective to the failings of what was nominally a centrally planned economic system. Going strictly by the book might have been economically very damaging.

In the United States, the large decision making role of legal, economic, and other professionals amounts to a system of participation in policymaking by elites given substantial independence from politics, based ideally on the good judgment of these elites and their own best assessments of the policy needs of the nation. In some cases professional economists are the relevant top officials themselves. In the Interior Department, however, economists such as myself did not have any final decision making authority. But we were able—at least in some cases—to play an influential role in the decision making process. In the worst cases, admittedly, professional elites may simply act to advance their own interests. In this sense, a high level of professional ethics is essential to the informal workings of the American governance system, as I was learning about it during my Interior Department years. The professional legal, economic, and other priesthoods must behave honestly and honorably, if the greater good is to be served by the undoubted real policy making powers they possess in the overall American governing scheme.

The Ethics of Growth, Progress, and Efficiency

An obvious question arises at this point: What more precisely was the understanding of the national interest that I worked to serve as a professional economist in the Interior Department? The original progressives assumed that it would be possible to identify an actual "public interest" that could be spelled out explicitly in the democratic process and that government expert professionals would then work to implement. In the decades after World War II, however, David Truman, Charles Lindblom, Theodore Lowi, and other leading American political scientists effectively debunked this idea as simplistic and ill-conceived, as wholly impractical for any real-world situation. For myself, then, were the "economic values" I was seeking to advance merely a cover or euphemism for what in practice amounted to my own personal values and political opinions, and nothing more?

As I was thinking about such questions in the 1970s and 1980s, I had two main answers. First, I was convinced personally that my own value system was reasonably representative of the broader mainstream of American values. Interior (and other government) policymaking was simply failing to reflect such core American values, owing to the structural and other weaknesses of the American constitutional system, and especially to the manner in which the U.S. Congress is organized and functions. Thus, I could justify my Interior political role as a small corrective effort—at least in those particular areas of Interior Department policymaking in which I was involved—to the failings of American democratic politics in serving widely shared American values. This depended of course on my own skill and effectiveness as a participant in the internal decision making—the internal politics—of the Interior Department (Leman and Nelson, 1981). As I have noted, I served exclusively in a staff role but staff often play a significant part in reaching the final results of government decision making.

Along the range of mainstream American values, I saw myself in particular as a leading advocate in government for the values of economic growth, progress, and efficiency. The progressive-era political philosophy has been described by historians as the "gospel of efficiency." Indeed, the distinguished American political scientist Dwight Waldo wrote in 1948 of the progressive era that "it is yet amazing what a position of dominance "efficiency" assumed, how it waxed until it had assimilated or over-shadowed other values, how men and events came to be degraded or exalted according to what was assumed to be its dictate." Waldo found that "every era has a few words that epitomize its world-view and that are fixed points by which all else can be measured. In the Middle Ages they were such words as faith, grace and God; in the eighteenth century they were such words as reason, nature and rights; during the past 50 years in America they have been such words as cause, reaction, scientific, expert, progress—and efficient" (Waldo [1948] 1984: 19–20). These "progressive" values were no longer as automatically assumed in American life in the second half of the twentieth century but they were still core values for many Americans in the years when I was working at the Interior Department. As leading government advocates for efficiency, professional economists such as myself were in effect seeking to revive and to advance in practice some of the core values of the original progressive agenda.

I should say that another leading value for me was social equality, if perhaps more equality of opportunity than equality of result. Still another important personal value, perhaps more so than for the typical professional economist in government, was individual freedom and personal liberty. In trying to be a strong advocate for such values in the Interior Department, I thus saw myself as working to defend these mainstream American values against the strong countervailing forces within American politics as usual. Again, as the public choice school of economics has emphasized, the normal incentives in government often work to frustrate the achievement of the government goals most Americans would seek (Holcombe, 2012).

Thinking about Dismantling the Interior Department

The routine operation of the market, by contrast, increasingly seemed to me in my Interior years to be typically a more effective agent of economic progress. The pursuit of higher profits might be only correlated in a rough fashion with economic progress and efficiency. But there was at least a correlation. You could say in very broad terms that the workings of the market broadly served to increase the total economic pie, while the workings of politics were more concerned with redistributing this pie—and the redistributive acts might in practice bear some relationship to objective needs for public assistance but were often equally or more closely controlled by the raw distribution of political power in America. Some government interventions might advance the overall public interest but many conferred a political benefit on a favored form of private activity (Olson, 1965).

I was increasingly thinking this way toward the end of the 1970s as I was approaching five years of seeing American government in action from my insider Interior Department perspective. Government service was proving to be a good education, as I had originally hoped it would be. If judged by objective efficiency standards and the broader national values that I myself sought to advance, my rough ballpark estimate was that about half the Interior Department could be abolished to the benefit of the whole nation (Nelson, 1995*a*). Some of the existing Interior functions might be eliminated altogether, some transferred to other parts of the federal government, some transferred to state and local levels, and some privatized outright (Nelson, 1995*b*).

Happenstance then again came into play with the election of Ronald Reagan. It seemed to me that the Reagan administration might be more sympathetic to reducing the responsibilities of the Interior Department along these lines. Indeed, the Reagan team that arrived at Interior in 1981 was pleased to find that there were at least some career insiders already thinking on at least a similar wavelength. This again raised the ethical question of the relationship between political appointees and career professionals such as economists in a federal agency. I had entered the Interior Department under a Republican administration, remained in my career position for the four Carter Democratic years, and now again was seeing the arrival of a new Republican administration (which would eventually last through two presidencies until the Clinton administration arrived in 1993 near the end of my Interior career).

It might seem that it would be difficult for a government economist to work as an internal professional policy advocate under different national administrations possessing different political philosophies. It might also seem that a new administration might be reluctant to work with high-level policy personnel who had served a previous administration of another party. For me at least, such potential tensions worked out in the following way. First, after a few years at the Interior Department, I had an institutional memory that was useful for any incoming team, whatever its politics. I could explain the lay of the land at Interior—often involving matters as much historical and institutional as economic—in a helpful way.

Equally important, there were many policy issues that did not break down along traditional party lines in the American political system. Both parties, for example, would be judged in part by the electorate in terms of their economic success in advancing growth and efficiency (the former admittedly typical easier to assess for the average voter than the latter). Political appointees also varied in their approach to their responsibilities; a few had a strong idealist streak, and others were committed mainly to their own career advancement. It was possible to appeal to the more idealistic on grounds of the national interest that would be served by a particular policy.

It helped that I was permitted to have a considerable freedom to choose myself the policy areas to which I committed my greatest energies. This was not part of my official job description but it worked something like this. I had to select policy areas that I could see were of interest to the current political team. I could also usually see fairly easily what kinds of policy conclusions and recommendations might be politically acceptable to this team. I also typically had a pretty good idea where I might be coming out myself on how to realize my own bottom line policy goals such as efficiency. As an economic policy analyst in the Interior Department, the greatest challenge was not to discover the most efficient policies in the first place but to identify a politically and bureaucratically feasible path by which a more efficient policy might actually come to be realized.

My real job thus might have been described as that of an economic "policy entrepreneur," rather than an expert economic analyst. In my entrepreneurial role, I simply chose to work—to "invest" my time and energy—in those policy areas that satisfied the two aforementioned criteria: (1) the top political leadership of the Interior Department was interested in the policy area and would appreciate any favorable policy results achieved; and (2) the policy outcome that I would work to advance in the Interior Department was one that I could also endorse myself, based on my own economic and other personal values. In other words, I attempted to avoid any possible ethical tensions by seeking to identify and commit my efforts to win–win policy situations—a win politically for the current political people in the Department, and a win for me personally in terms of advancing my own ideals and values for public policy.

In the Reagan administration, this initially suggested that a promising area for me to work would be the deregulation, decentralization, and privatization of appropriate Interior Department responsibilities. It proved more difficult in practice, however, than I had expected. As a candidate, Ronald Reagan had endorsed the "Sagebrush Rebellion," the western protest movement during the late Carter years against federal land management that sought a transfer of large areas of federal lands to the western states. As noted previously, I broadly thought myself that the federal government, still owning about 50 percent of the land in the American West, was overextended and might well divest itself of some of its western responsibilities. On much of the federal western domain—the "public lands"—the most important decisions typically concern matters such as the number of cows that will be allowed to graze in particular pastures, building of local roads, levels of timber harvests, leasing of land for oil and gas drilling, building and maintaining hiking trails, prevention and fighting of forest fires, determining areas that will be available to off-road recreational vehicles, and other such routine land management details. Outside the West, such matters are instead state and local responsibilities paid for by state and local governments. Why not do the same in the West?

It turned out, however, that the West did not actually want to take ownership of the public lands. The Sagebrush Rebellion, as I now discovered, was mainly western rhetorical posturing for political effect. Under the normal workings of Congress, the presence of the public lands serves to justify the transfer of large federal revenue streams to the rural West (much like the role of farm subsidies historically in the Midwest). With the Reagan administration in office, western Republicans would be able to control more effectively the actions of the Interior Department and other federal land management agencies. Maintaining the status quo offered both the federal money and the western control over federal actions. Perhaps the wisest statement ever made about the relationship of the federal government and the West was made by Wallace Stegner many years ago—that the real western viewpoint is that the federal government should "get out, and give us more money" (Nelson, 2012*b*).

Top Republicans in western states thus passed the message to the new Reagan team at the Interior Department in the early 1980s that any large transfers of federal lands and other responsibilities to the states would be unwelcome. However desirable it might seem in terms of abstract Republican political principles of federalism, it would simply cost the western states too much money. When I naively offered some practical means in the early 1980s by which the Interior Department might actually undertake a transfer of some federal responsibilities to the states, high level political officials patiently explained to me that the earlier Republican political rhetoric about a Sagebrush Rebellion and other proposals for decentralization had not actually been serious. I would eventually write about all this in a 1984 article in *Regulation* magazine on "Why the Sagebrush Revolt Burned Out" (Nelson, 1984).

Economic Progress as a Religion

By the mid-1980s I had been at the Interior Department for ten years. My first years had been absorbed in learning about the historical and institutional details of the Interior Department and in working in particular policy areas, as described previously. But I was now seeing old issues and discussions being repeated and was looking for new challenges. My attention therefore shifted in two respects. I began to spend a considerable part of my time working with the Bureau of Indian Affairs and the policy issues it was facing (though this was a fascinating experience, I will have little to say about this side of my Interior career in this chapter). I also decided that I needed to think more seriously about the economic values that I had been advancing for the previous 10 years. What were these economic values more specifically? Why were they so important? How could I justify my own efforts in government to advance efficiency and other economic values as against other value systems that I could see were also well represented at the Interior Department? The original progressives had effectively assumed that a national values consensus existed and could be identified, but this was another aspect of the progressive vision that would not be historically sustainable.

What if, I began to ask myself, and despite my own longstanding views to the contrary, economic growth, progress, and efficiency might conceivably be the wrong values? In any case, whatever the eventual verdict, I could not be sure without thinking more deeply about this matter. Almost no one in the United States would have questioned the enormous benefits of economic progress at the opening of the twentieth century. The terrible scale of the human destruction on the battlefields of World War I, however, first raised some significant doubts. Then, the horrors of World War II and the Holocaust, including the development of the atom bomb with the new power potentially even to destroy human life on earth, significantly increased these doubts. By the 1960s, not long before I arrived in the Interior Department, the environmental movement was raising still further doubts about "progress"—and the progressive understanding of the proper relationship of human beings and nature (Carson, 1962).

The original progressives had seen nature as a "natural resource" to be exploited for human benefit, as an object to be used to serve the core values of economic growth, progress and efficiency. Environmentalists now argued, however, that nature had an "intrinsic" value independent of any human benefits and that human beings were themselves now behaving in an unethical—in traditional Christian language, a "sinful"—fashion in their callous treatment of the natural environment. For some species, it even meant their complete extinction from the earth. The Wilderness Act was enacted in 1964, effectively establishing a national system of environmental "cathedrals" defined by the exclusion of human impacts from these areas as far as was practically feasible.

For environmentalists, they saw that economic transgressions against nature were typically justified in the progressive language of economic efficiency. One leading environmental philosopher even went so far as to write an article in 1991 in a well-respected journal, *Environmental Ethics*, addressing the question of "Why Environmentalists Hate Mainstream Economists" (Norton, 1991). My greatest concern in my early Interior years was the failings of interest group politics in the American democratic system. Even then, however, I had recognized that environmentalists were often among the strongest opponents of the economic values I was seeking in those days to advance in the Interior Department.

This raised yet another ethical question. It was one thing to work to solve the interest-group problems of the American political system; it was quite another to oppose a competing value system—a competing religion, as I would eventually come to think and write about such matters from the 1990s onwards. Any attempt to justify my own actions ethically in this respect could only be done by venturing into broader questions of political philosophy and even theology broadly understood. I began a more complicated—and intellectually challenging—journey to address this subject in the second half of the 1980s.

It was not only environmentalists, moreover, who were raising questions about the whole progressive value system in American life. Karl Jacoby in 2001 wrote of the progressive movement of the early twentieth century that it reflected the values of an elite in American society that sought to impose its own vision on other Americans who often did not share these values. Ordinary farmers and other rural Americans often disagreed with the "scientific" solutions that progressive planners and scientific managers were seeking to impose on them. In the American West, there long were strong rural protests, for example, against the vast areas of national forests placed during the Theodore Roosevelt administration under the national management of the Forest Service, seeking to advance progressive values as imposed by a new elite of expert forestry professionals. As Jacoby explains, from the rural American perspective,

> What made [progressive] conservation so controversial in such locales was the fact that it ultimately concerned far more than mere questions of ecology—how many trees to cut and where, what animals to hunt and for how long. In redefining the rules governing the use of the environment, [the progressive] conservation [movement] also addressed how the interlocking human and natural communities of a given society were to be organized. Conservationists might present themselves as dispassionate technicians concerned only with solving neatly confined scientific problems, but their proposals contained profound social implications. With their emphasis on the need for expert oversight of the environment, conservationists endeavored to concentrate the decision-making power of the state in the hands of a corps of highly trained technocrats. Conservation thus expanded far beyond natural resource policy, not only setting the pattern for other Progressive Era reforms but also heralding the rise of the modern administrative state. (Jacoby 2001: 5–6)

By the late 1980s, I was beginning to think more about the fact that a rapid rate of economic progress will create many losers as well as winners. In favoring reliance on markets, economists make a powerful social value judgment that the market-driven benefits of economic progress will necessarily outweigh the costs borne by the losers in society. Charles Schultze once thus commented that the greatest "advantage of the market as a means of social organization is its 'devil take the hindmost' approach to questions of individual equity"—and by equity he meant a wider range of social impacts that the measured distribution of income alone. As Schultze further explained, the ethics of markets could be contrasted with a social value judgment of "do no direct harm" to anyone — as was typically sought in the ordinary workings of American democratic "politics" (Schultze, 1977: 72; 21). If such a "political" ethic of avoidance of any losing parties had prevailed throughout American society, many of the most efficient actions in the market and in government might well have been blocked.

Partly by excluding consideration of such "equity" impacts in the social decision calculus, however, it was possible for professional economists to render a positive verdict on economic progress, and for American society to advance rapidly along the route of progress. The conflict between the pursuit of economic progress and American democratic politics as usual was thus also a disagreement about core national values to be served by government in the United States. Indeed, many other social values were in effect being sacrificed to economic efficiency and progress. Such values were automatically excluded by the conventions of the economics profession that guided mainstream economic calculations of social benefits and social costs. The social costs typically excluded by economists included, among others:

1. The loss of community when the market, operating nationally and internationally, renders a negative verdict on the mainstays of the local economy—and, if they want to have a job, many people have little choice but to move away to another

place, likely to be a painful process for them. (Economists don't enter the pain into their benefit–cost calculations.)

2. The individual financial and psychic losses when a person loses a job, and has to look for another one, owing to the workings of market forces.
3. The individual sense of anxiety about possible losses of a community or a job, even when such losses never actually occur.
4. The sense that a precious social asset is devalued by the very fact of entering it into the price system (occasionally, as in the case of prostitution, government may intervene to limit such costs but there are no restrictions in the great majority of cases).
5. The loss of personal freedom when economically efficient actions require collective organization by governments—often large governments such as the national government in Washington, DC—that then must employ powers of coercion to collect income and other taxes to fund these efforts (including even from many people opposed to the actions).
6. The sense of personal powerlessness when large private organizations are the winners in the market, leaving many people to work as small cogs in a large and often impersonal business enterprise where their own contribution to the overall outcome (even assuming it is highly beneficial) is difficult to identify.
7. The sense of personal, community, and national disappointment when a person realizes that he or she is a relative loser (or belongs to a group of relative losers) in the competition for greater profits, higher paying and more prestigious jobs, and other indicators of social rank, as established by market and other economic successes.
8. The sense of personal loss when homes, streets, farms, and other historic reminders of the past are swept aside by the workings of the market (or by "efficient" government actions and programs).
9. The sense of individual and community loss when plant and animal species habitats, wild areas, and other parts of nature are transformed from their earlier "untouched" condition to become "natural resources," sources of the energy and other material requirements to power a modern economy.
10. The feelings of loss when the defense of private property rights is perceived to encourage strong feelings of individual possessiveness and a weakened sense of communal bonds (violating, among other ethical systems, many Christian biblical injunctions).
11. The sense of offense when particular instruments of market economic efficiency—such as the charging of interest for loans—violate religious (as in parts of the Muslim world today) or other ethical principles.
12. The loss of traditional tribal, religious and other historical cultures that are disrupted and otherwise swept aside by the forces of economic progress.
13. The overall sense of loss among those people who believe the world is captive to a heretical religion of economic progress that has taught many people to worship a false god.

Most mainstream economists, to be sure, do recognize at some level that such values—and associated costs to society—do exist. But they show little interest in taking these costs into explicit account in their own economic research and policy recommendations. They in effect argue implicitly that the transforming benefits of modern economic progress more than adequately justify the bearing of any such burdens of progress—that they are the necessary, if perhaps unfortunate, side effects that represent the "price of progress." All this, however, is never actually calculated by economists or scientifically demonstrated. Rather, the overriding benefits of progress are simply a core element of economic faith. If economic progress does in fact lead to a new heaven on earth, as "economic religion" implicitly (and sometimes explicitly) assumes, it does indeed follow logically enough that progress should be a transcendent value, superseding all other potentially competing values in society. In matters of salvation, this goal in western civilization has always come first.

Economic Religion versus Environmental Religion

A tension does not necessarily arise in every case between economists and environmentalists. While I was at the Interior Department, environmentalists were happy to put to good use technical economic arguments about the pork barrel failings of most proposals for new dams in the West—dams that they actually opposed as environmentally destructive. But more often—as, for example, in the case of the leasing of federally owned coal reserves in the West—economists and environmentalists found themselves on opposing sides of leading Interior policy debates relating to "the use of natural resources" (in progressive terms) or "the defense of nature" (in environmental terms).

As noted previously, I had seen a religious character to economics as early as my Princeton graduate school days. I now discovered in the late 1980s a large historical, philosophical, and theological literature about the growing role of secular religion in general in the twentieth century and about the religious character of belief in economic progress in particular. Indeed, the American progressive "gospel of efficiency" (as it has been described by a number of historians) was one among many modern forms of secular religion, a religion not only metaphorically but literally, as I now concluded. As an advocate in the Interior Department for progressive economic values of growth, progress, and efficiency, I had in effect been serving as an internal advocate for a particular religion (if one widely held by others in American life). According to the "theology" of this economic religion, to simplify a complex matter, past human lying, cheating, stealing, and other human "sinfulness" was a result of the severe material deprivation in which human beings had lived for almost all past history. By eliminating such material causes, however, modern economic progress would save the world, leading to a new heaven on earth (Nelson, 1991, 2001, 2010).

The material achievements of economic progress in the past 200 years are indeed extremely impressive—bordering on "miraculous" as they actually seem to me. The average person lives today materially at a higher standard of living than the member of a royal family a mere few hundred years ago. Life expectancies have doubled for ordinary people in developed nations in the past 100 years. Progressive religion, however, saw such remarkable economic progress not only in material terms but as the practical means to a much higher goal, the perfection of the human condition morally and spiritually on earth, as well as in terms of the levels of physical goods and services available for consumption. In this respect, as in some of the other respects noted above, progressive religion has failed to live up to the original very high hopes and expectations of its many true believers of the nineteenth and twentieth centuries.

I had also recognized a strong religious quality to environmentalism early in my Interior years but had not done much right away to explore this subject more fully in my own thinking and writing. By the late 1980s, however, I was now seeing Interior Department decision making as a new form of religious disagreement—literally. Even though I had no training in theology, and not much personal background in religion, I took the plunge to begin writing about the policy process in these terms. In a certain sense, this was in itself an ethical decision on my part. Despite the obvious intellectual risks for me of venturing into such uncharted waters, and the surprised reactions I often encountered from fellow economists (was I a traitor to the progressive cause or perhaps somehow even "losing it"?), I felt an obligation to try to "call it as I see it" in terms of describing the Interior Department policy process, even when this was taking me in such novel and surprising directions as the character and role of religion—secular religions as well as traditional ones—in American public life. It was to me simply a matter of maintaining basic intellectual integrity, another thing I like to think high in my overall value system.

At the beginning, I examined the contents of environmental religion and economic religion in separate writings. While I was still at the Interior Department, I published a 1990 article titled "Unoriginal Sin: The Judeo-Christian Roots of Ecotheology" and a 1991 book on *Reaching for Heaven on Earth: The Theological Meaning of Economics* (Nelson 1990, 1991). Although I left the Interior Department in 1993, I have continued over the past 20 years to write books and articles about progressive economic religion and environmental religion, including a 2001 book, *Economics as Religion*. This line of thinking culminated in a 2010 book in which I finally brought these two current powerful forms of secular religion together for comparative analysis and discussion, *The New Holy Wars: Economic Religion versus Environmental Religion in Contemporary America* (Nelson, 2010).

Another side of the role of the economic professional in government, it is hard to avoid concluding, is that of a religious advocate to influence Interior Department decision making. The Interior Department can be seen as an intellectual and religious policy battleground in a struggle between the two most influential secular belief systems of our time, economics, and environmentalism (Nelson, 2012*a*). By the early 1990s, I had thus moved even farther from the old progressive model of the role of the value-neutral professional economic expert in government. It was no longer a matter of my functioning as a professional economic advocate versus the forces of crass political expediency. I was instead also caught up during my Interior years in a religious struggle of economic religion versus environmental (and other noneconomic) religion. By the twenty-first century, I was not personally a strong advocate for any one religion. My intellectual interests thus shifted to the question of how strong true believers in competing religions can live among one another peacefully and prosperously in the same political jurisdiction. Given the intensity and frequency of destructive religious warfare in the history of western civilization, this is not an easy question to answer.

I also find myself asking these days how can one justify ethically the creation of government jobs and whole offices such as the Office of Policy Analysis in the Interior Department to argue internally the case for a particular form of religion (economic religion in the case of my old Office)? If all religions are to be treated equally, must all of them then have an entitlement to official representation in the in-house workings of government agencies such as the Interior Department? If not, and some religions are to be excluded, how would the possible eligibility of a specific religion for official internal representation in government deliberations be determined? One response might be to limit internal government representation to secular religions such as economics and environmentalism. It might be argued in defense of this view that secular religions are not actual religions, perhaps because they do not require the worship of any god or other supernatural force. I have concluded that this is not tenable, however. It has turned out on further study that a significant number of leading theologians and social scientists of the twentieth century fully agree with me. In any sophisticated theological understanding, religion must be understood more broadly than the traditional Jewish and Christian conceptions.

I recently explored this issue in a 2011 article in the *Pace Environmental Law Review* on "Rethinking Church and State: The Case of Environmental Religion" (Nelson, 2011). The article concludes, among other things, that secular religions—such as economic religion or environmental religion—should not be given preferential access to official government positions and roles (perhaps on the asserted grounds that they are not actual religions), relative to more traditional religions such as Judaism and Christianity. To do so would amount to a form of religious discrimination in favor of the secular and against the traditional faiths of Western history. The whole American idea of separation of church and state, as I suggest, will have to be reconceived to take account of the much greater religious diversity of contemporary America, including the presence of important secular and traditional religions alike. This is not likely to be an easy or uncontroversial intellectual task.

Another possibility, admittedly, is simply to argue for a privileged role for progressive economic religion on the following grounds. The American welfare and regulatory state is in essence an attempt to realize the progressive "gospel." Twentieth-century American government was in this sense the established church of a particular secular religion of economic progress. It would not make any sense to create a church and then to deny a full official role in the functioning of the church to its core beliefs and priesthood, the latter including prominently in this case the members of the American economics profession, along with other professional groups. Such a justification for the professional economist's dominant religious role in government would, however, require the abandonment of any conventional American understandings of the separation of church and state, certainly a radical prospect from the point of view of political theory.

I have been asked, given what I know now, how would I personally conceive my appropriate role as an economist working in the Interior Department? This is a mostly theoretical question, as my full explicit understand of the large role of religion in Interior policymaking was only developing in my last few years there. There is, it seems to me, no easy answer. It raises fundamental questions of the workings of the American political system, and how it might adapt to a "post-progressive" era (or "post-modern" era) in which fundamental progressive assumptions about the value neutrality of professional expertise, the proper relationship of politics and science, the role of religion in matters of state, the power of economic explanations of the world, and a number of others will have to be significantly reexamined. This is a basic task confronting the next generation of political thinkers in America. A first step, however, is to recognize the need for such an effort.

Conclusion

It now seems to me that the world must rediscover the methods and practice of theology, if now often including denominations of "secular theology" within the discussion. Since leaving the Interior Department in 1993, I have devoted increasing efforts to this task, including the critical evaluation of both the arguments and claims of economic religion and environmental religion (Nelson, 2001, 2004, 2010). Such writings have inevitably taken me well beyond the boundaries of conventional economic analysis and argument. Indeed, these writings have thus far attracted more interest and attention on the part of theologians than of my fellow economists and policy analysts (Farrell, 2011; Maidman, 2011; Rittenhouse, 2012). In principle, as I now believe, all religious are not alike; it is possible in concept to say that one current religion is "better" than another. This will never be, however, a matter for "scientific" resolution. Each religion, moreover, can be expected to evolve and perhaps "improve" as part of this process, a matter itself dependent on the quality of religious discussion. Equal treatment of religion does not mean equal results in terms of numbers of believers, political and intellectual influence, and in general the role of a religion in a given society but simply that each religion should be free to make its arguments. We may dismiss "heretics" but we should never again burn them.

Religion was dismissed by social scientists and policy analysts as an important factor in the public workings of society for much of the twentieth century. That belief now seems to have been part of a religion in and of itself. Public policy schools such as mine at the University of Maryland may soon have to introduce a course in religious thinking and argumentation to accompany the standard economics, political science, management, and other parts of the existing curriculum.

References

Akerlof, George A., and Robert J. Schiller. 2010. *Animal Spirits: How Human Psychology Drives the Economy and How It Matters for Global Capitalism*. Princeton, NJ: Princeton University Press.

Allen, William R. 1977. "Economics, Economists, and Economic Policy: Modern American Experiences." *History of Political Economy* 9(1): 48–88.

Autor, David. 2012. "*The Journal of Economic Perspectives* at 100 (Issues)." *Journal of Economic Perspectives* 26(2): 3–18.

Buchanan, James M., and Gordon Tullock. 1962. *The Calculus of Consent: Logical Foundations for Constitutional Democracy*. Ann Arbor: University of Michigan Press.

Carson, Rachel. 1962. *Silent Spring*. Boston: Houghton Mifflin.

DeMartino, George F. 2011. *The Economist's Oath: On the Need for and Content of Professional Economic Ethics*. New York: Oxford University Press.

Easterly, William Russell. 2007. *The White Man's Burden: Why the West's Efforts to Help the Rest Have Done So Much Ill and So Little Good*. New York: Penguin Books.

Farrell, Justin. 2011. *Review of The New Holy Wars: Economic Religion versus Environmental Religion in Contemporary America*, by Robert H. Nelson. *Journal for the Scientific Study of Religion* 50(3): 632–633.

Holcombe, Randall G. 2012. "Make Economics Policy Relevant: Depose the Omniscient Benevolent Dictator." *The Independent Review* 17(2): 165–176.

Jacoby, Karl. 2001. *Crimes against Nature: Squatters, Poachers, Thieves, and the Hidden History of American Conservation*. Berkeley: University of California Press.

Leman, Christopher K., and Robert H. Nelson. 1981. "Ten Commandments for Policy Economists." *Journal of Policy Analysis and Management* 1(1): 97–117.

Levinson, Sanford. 1988. *Constitutional Faith*. Princeton, NJ: Princeton University Press.

Lo, Andrew W. 2012. "Reading about the Financial Crisis: A Twenty-One-Book Review." *Journal of Economic Literature* 50(1): 151–178.

Maidman, Sarah. 2011. *Review of The New Holy Wars: Economic Religion versus Environmental Religion in Contemporary America*, by Robert H. Nelson. *Religion* 41(4): 709–713.

McCloskey, Deirdre N. 2007. *The Bourgeois Virtues: Ethics for an Age of Commerce*. Chicago: University of Chicago Press.

McCloskey, Deirdre N. 2011. *Bourgeois Dignity: Why Economics Cannot Explain the Modern World*. Chicago: University of Chicago Press.

Nelson, Robert H. 1977. *Zoning and Property Rights*. Cambridge, MA: MIT Press.

Nelson, Robert H. 1983. *The Making of Federal Coal Policy*. Durham, NC: Duke University Press.

Nelson, Robert H. 1984. "Why the Sagebrush Revolt Burned Out." *Regulation* 8(3): 27–35.

Nelson, Robert H. 1987. "The Economics Profession and the Making of Public Policy." *Journal of Economic Literature* 25(1): 49–91.

Nelson, Robert H. 1989*a*. "Introduction and Summary." In *The Role of the Economist in Government: An International Perspective*, edited by Joseph A. Pechman. New York: New York University Press, pp. 1–22.

Nelson, Robert H. 1989*b*. "The Office of Policy Analysis in the Department of the Interior." *Journal of Policy Analysis and Management* 8(3): 395–410.

Nelson, Robert H. 1990. "Unoriginal Sin: The Judeo-Christian Roots of Ecotheology." *Policy Review* 52: 52–60.

Nelson, Robert H. 1991. *Reaching for Heaven on Earth: The Theological Meaning of Economics*. Lanham, MD: Rowman & Littlefield.

Nelson, Robert H. 1995*a*. *How to Dismantle the Interior Department*. Washington, DC: Competitive Enterprise Institute.

Nelson, Robert H. 1995*b*. *Public Lands and Private Rights: The Failure of Scientific Management*. Lanham, MD: Rowman & Littlefield.

Nelson, Robert H. 2001. *Economics as Religion: From Samuelson to Chicago and Beyond*. University Park: Pennsylvania State University Press.

Nelson, Robert H. 2004. "Environmental Religion: A Theological Critique," *Case Western Reserve Law Review* 55(1): 51–80.

Nelson, Robert H. 2010. *The New Holy Wars: Economic Religion versus Environmental Religion in Contemporary America*. University Park: Pennsylvania State University Press.

Nelson, Robert H. 2011. "Rethinking Church and State: The Case of Environmental Religion," *Pace Environmental Law Review* 29(1): 121–217.

Nelson, Robert H. 2012*a*. "Economics and Environmentalism: Belief Systems at Odds." *The Independent Review* 17(1): 5–17.

Nelson, Robert H. 2012*b*. "Our Languishing Public Lands." *Policy Review* 171: 45–62.

Norton, Bryan G. 1991. "Thoreau's Insect Analogies: Or, Why Environmentalists Hate Mainstream Economists." *Environmental Ethics* 13: 235–251.

Olson, Mancur. 1965. *The Logic of Collective Action: Public Goods and the Theory of Groups*. Cambridge, MA: Harvard University Press.

Rittenhouse, Bruce P. 2012. *Review of The New Holy Wars: Economic Religion versus Environmental Religion in Contemporary America*, by Robert H. Nelson. *Journal of Religion* 92(2): 325–326.

Sanzillo, Tom. 2012. *The Great Giveaway: An Analysis of the United States' Long Term Trend of Selling Federally Owned Coal for Less than Fair Market Value*. Cambridge, MA: Institute for Energy Economic and Financial Analysis.

Schultze, Charles L. 1968. *The Politics and Economics of Public Spending*. Washington, DC: The Brookings Institution.

Schultze, Charles L. 1977. *The Public Use of Private Interest*. Washington, DC: Brookings Institution.

Schultze, Charles L. 1982. "The Role and Responsibilities of the Economist in Government." *American Economic Review* 72(2): 62–66.

Scott, James C. 1998. *Seeing Like a State: How Certain Schemes to Improve the Human Condition Have Failed*. New Haven, CT: Yale University Press.

Taylor, Timothy. 2012. "From the Desk of the Managing Editor," *Journal of Economic Perspectives* 26(2): 27–40.

United States. Commission on Fair Market Value Policy for Federal Coal Leasing. 1984. *Report of the Commission: Fair Market Value Policy for Federal Coal Leasing*. Washington, DC: Government Printing Office.

Wahl, Richard. 1989. *Markets for Federal Water: Subsidies, Property Rights and the Bureau of Reclamation*. Washington, DC: Resources for the Future.

Waldo, Dwight. [1948] 1984. *The Administrative State: A Study of the Political Theory of American Public Administration*. New York: Holmes and Meier.

CHAPTER 30

ETHICS AND THE GOVERNMENT ECONOMIST

SUSAN OFFUTT

Introduction

Public service is an aspiration of many economists. However, only a minority choose to pursue it by becoming public servants, working directly for government in support of public sector operations and decision making. Those economists who choose the academic or business or nonprofit world for a career certainly can and do act to advance the public interest, but in very different institutional settings from that of a public servant. The government of a representative democracy employs competent, nonpartisan professionals who are accountable to elected officials. This essentially political setting distinguishes the workplace and so the ethical challenges faced by the government economist.

Although the barrier between academic or business and government employment is permeable, relatively few professional economists move back and forth. Consequently, economists outside government may not be well informed about the challenges—and the rewards—of career public service simply because they have limited contact with those who have first-hand experience with it. This absence of knowledge can translate into a supposition that public service must be an inferior occupation. In particular, concern about constraints on a government economist's independence and objectivity may suggest the necessity of ethical compromise. Ethical dilemmas do indeed arise in a complex, political environment. But to eschew public service because of the potential for ethical challenge would be to forego a chance at a challenging and fulfilling career with policy impact. The issue is not how to avoid ethical challenge but how to address it thoughtfully.

As a basis for understanding the ethical issues that arise in public service, it is first necessary to be explicit about the context and what the work entails in order to understand how dilemmas may arise, as indeed they do. Toward this end, there are several questions to explore as a basis for considering the nature of public service.

- What are the terms of government service and what is the economist's role in government?
- How do politics cause ethical problems for economists?
- What knowledge and counsel would benefit a government economist faced with an ethical challenge?

The aim of this chapter is to explore the answers to these questions with the main purpose of elucidating the nature of ethical dilemmas that may arise in public service but also with the intention of helping economists outside of public service get a grasp of some of the realities of the government workplace.

The Nature of Career Public Service

The nature of career service as an economist in government will be fully explored in order to make clear the circumstances that may present ethical challenge. First, the terms of employment for civil servants include explicit prohibitions on financial and political conflict of interest. Second, the significance of economic arguments in policy debate has increased markedly, opening up new paths to policy influence. Third, because many economists in government expect to spend a career in federal service, their actions today are necessarily considered in light of their ability to continue to be influential in the future.

Terms of Career Service

In modern democracies, governments have at their heads officials elected for discrete terms who direct workers in the business of delivering public services. In this chapter, specific consideration is given to economists employed in the United States federal career civil service. Of course, economists also may hold term political positions to which they are appointed by elected officials, may function as paid consultants, or may provide uncompensated advice on a formal (as on an advisory committee) or informal basis. As the circumstances of such appointments are quite different from those of career staff, these economists face challenges peculiar to their temporary assignments (Henderson, 1977: 321). Those in the career civil service will find employment and the workplace governed by an established set of principles and procedures intended to ensure political neutrality and competence. In 2011, some 4300 economists were employed in the executive branch (U.S. Bureau of Labor Statistics), and most of these were in career positions, as the number of political appointees is limited.

All US civil servants, not just economists, are bound by an oath of office that requires a pledge to uphold the Constitution and specifically to "establish Justice, insure domestic tranquility, provide for the common defense, promote the general welfare, and secure the blessings of liberty." The Federal *Principles of Ethical Conduct* (Executive Order 12731) also stipulate that "public service is a public trust, requiring employees to place loyalty to the Constitution, the laws, and ethical principles above private gain." These general exhortations are accompanied by a code of conduct. Participation in partisan political activities is legally limited so as to preserve impartiality and neutrality in the performance of duties (US Office of Special Counsel). The Hatch Act, among other restrictions, bars a federal employee from standing for election as a partisan candidate and forbids participation in partisan campaigns and fundraising.

Under the code, civil servants are forbidden to hold financial interests or accept outside employment "that conflict with the conscientious performance of duty." These provisions are enforced through supervisory review of employees' annual financial disclosure statements and by a supervisor's approval of outside employment. The prohibition against conflict of interest (including the strictures on participation in partisan politics) goes further than the disclosure policy adopted by the American Economic Association (AEA) for articles published in its journals (American Economic Association, 2012). The AEA policy requires disclosure but will publish articles from authors receiving financial support from "interested" parties (those with a financial, ideological, or political stake) and/or with affiliation with a "relevant organization" (one with related policy positions, goals, or financial interests).

Economists in the federal government support decision making in the public sector and provide services to citizens and the private sector. In government, the choice of topics on which to work is mandated by the needs of policy and government operations; in that sense, there is little latitude to pursue a course independent of these imperatives. As a practical matter, applied economists in government are circumscribed in the scope of their analyses by the specific positions they accept. Though such an assignment might seem overly restrictive, the compensation for the economist in public service is that the stakes are likely to be high. Decisions with real-world consequences may very well be expected to follow from the analysis and advice provided. Indeed, that is why it is sought. Certainly, many economists choose public service because of this opportunity to confront the challenges that society, through its elected government, must address.

The federal bureaucracy is a hierarchy, and government economists are part of it. Different agencies have different numbers of layers of management, from relatively flat research organizations to those in program delivery that are more stepped. Wherever she is located, the economist is responsive to direction from policy officials, though there may be little face-to-face interaction. Career managers and supervisors mediate the assignment and production of economic statistics and analysis. Ethical challenges can arise anywhere in this chain.

The stereotype of the beaten-down bureaucrat hardly aligns with that of the noble public servant seeking to make a difference. Outside perceptions, particularly in academia, may well associate the government economist more strongly with the first image.

In the 1970s, Allen interviewed economists with government experience, mainly academics who had done tours at the Council of Economic Advisors. What they had to say about economists in career service was not flattering. Among their other deficiencies, career economists were seen as inevitably becoming "stale in their ideas" and being "kept in line" so as not to voice independent opinions. Allen himself supposed that most career economists were "essentially clerks and research assistants" but did allow, "Probably most and perhaps all of them earn their daily bread" (1977: 49).

In these days of political correctness, it is hard to imagine such observations finding their way into a peer-reviewed journal. Still, echoes of this stereotype are heard today in more informal settings. No doubt today there are those in federal service who would be recognizable to the observers of the 1970s. However, the root of the stereotype lies in the unfavorable comparison between the academic pursuit of research and the more applied work of government. The hallmarks of competent economists in government include intimate knowledge of institutions, an understanding of the currents of the political economy, familiarity with the context and the data associated with any given policy question, and an ability to characterize key relationships in policy analysis. These skills, like the ability to conduct insightful research, are acquired only with hard work, dedication, and a measure of intellectual rigor.

Federal economists aim to provide analysis and information that contributes constructively to decision making. However, they do realize that economic reasoning is not the sole determinant of policy outcomes. Schultze argued that there is good reason for economists' bias toward efficient solutions but that efficiency is "not an absolute criterion. Other points of view are legitimate" (1982: 63). He pointed specifically to the "tradeoff of overall efficiency against losses concentrated in specific groups" (1982: 63) as an example of the considerations in political decision making that transcend economics. Concerns about equity are accompanied by what Schultze termed "political opportunity costs" that should be "considered equally as real and important as economic opportunity costs" (1982: 63). In this political setting, the economist will be but one—albeit important—participant in the policy discussion.

Economists in government realize ultimately decisions are made by policy officials. However, they do have the expectation that their economic arguments will be heard, even if their conclusions or recommendations will not necessarily prevail. This outcome does not represent a failure of the application of economic reasoning but rather the reality of the significance of other criteria, those to which Schultze referred. Other criteria notwithstanding, economic data and analysis have contributed importantly to shaping argument and identifying solutions. Indeed, it can be argued that government economists exert far more influence over government decision making than one might predict given their relatively small numbers in the large bureaucracies where they work.

Economists in career service inevitably develop their own skills at handicapping the political reaction to policy and program decisions. Working in such a setting, it could hardly be otherwise. The terms of federal employment do not contemplate a role for economists as political advisors, though it would not be unusual for economic analysis to shed light on how a decision might affect the interests of various political actors. The

Hatch Act forbids involvement in partisan politics, but most economists—like other government employees—bring their political knowledge to the workplace. To the extent that cultural and institutional characteristics of the environment influence political views, it is the economist with the most intimate knowledge of them who is in a position to assist decision makers in assessing political feasibility. From their long experience with the particulars of programs and policies and knowledge of political economy, government economists are often those who are most familiar with the practical political constraints. Although these informed perspectives can be useful to policy officials, economists are aware that maintaining neutrality and objectivity requires vigilance.

By virtue of their graduate training, new government economists may not be very well prepared to assess political feasibility. But those who will be successful in government service necessarily learn this skill. Aaron wrote, "What the political system *can* do becomes at least as important a component of policy advice as what it *should* do" (1989: 12). But the track record of economists is surely mixed, as can be shown by a recent example. In considering how to restrict the quantity of carbon entering the atmosphere, academic researchers emphasized the use of an emissions trading regime over a tax because any tax increase was viewed as out of the question politically. Yet proposals for the carbon tax still surfaced, and it was presented as an expedient way to raise revenue for deficit reduction while garnering some benefit in mitigating global warming. The point is that politics are dynamic and complicated. It is hard for one outside the system (and even for those inside!) to reach definitive conclusions about what works. The occasional political savant aside, it seems prudent for economists to emphasize their expertise in economics while also attending to the political realities they confront.

Despite what may appear as an arms-length relationship with political decision making, government economists, like all others, do have an ethical obligation that arises out of the consequences that their work may have for others (DeMartino, 2011: 13). To discharge this obligation, economists ought first explore distributional effects of policy as referenced by Schultze in an analytical context. Hamilton, a former Congressman, chastised economists who, he said, "lose credibility with us [politicians] when they fail to take these distributional impacts seriously" (1992: 62). Analysts should be careful not simply to confirm or only to consider whether an action would confer benefit or impose costs on a target group. Unintended consequences for others in society, as well as those consequences that are politically inexpedient, are part of comprehensive analysis. It may not be sought explicitly but there is merit—if not an obligation—in providing it nonetheless.

In the 20th century progressive model of technocratic government, economists provide advice based on their professional expertise, but, once dispensed, economists have no further responsibility for how that advice might be used (Nelson, 1987). The National Research Council noted that scientists—social, physical, or otherwise—"do not tell policymakers what should interest them or what policy choices they should make" (2012: 9). In referring to the example of the development of the atom bomb, the report goes on to say "There was no scientific basis on which to say *whether* to drop the bomb" (Nelson, 1987: 9). True enough, but physicists and mathematicians of Los Alamos ultimately recognized ethical responsibility for the consequences of using the bomb. The atom bomb example is dramatic and tragic, but it does support the idea that the technocratic view is outmoded.

Consequences for other people are apparent in policy choices, and economists have a hand in identifying what they are. Economists as policy advisors have influence. Thompson (1983) has considered how moral responsibility arises in this context, suggesting three considerations in ascribing to an advisor the moral responsibility for a policymaker's decision.

- Would the decision maker have acted as she absent the advice she received?
- Could the advisor have reasonably foreseen any adverse consequences of the decision?
- Could foreseeable harm have been prevented if the advisor had taken an active, even public, role in criticizing the decision or the process by which it was reached?

Although answering these questions with certainty will be problematic, posing them underscores the broader scope for moral responsibility than that suggested by the limited technical advisor role.

Paths of Policy Influence

Economists in government have varied duties. Some are in applied research assignments, some produce national statistics, some analyze market developments, and some analyze policy design and impacts (DeMartino, 2011: 27–28). Whatever the specifics, their work takes place in an environment of complexity and ambiguity. Political decision making does not step rationally from problem definition, to information gathering, to identification and deliberation on alternatives, to final decision. In government, economists will often find themselves in what Weiss describes as "an interactive search for knowledge," characterized by a "disorderly set of interconnections and back-and-forthness that defies neat diagrams" (1979: 428). Rather than focus on identification of a solution to a well-defined problem, economists may more broadly influence how "policymakers and practitioners think about potential issues, problems, or solutions" (National Research Council, 2012: 38). The significance of the complexity of the environment is the many routes it creates for influence by economists, and so the potential for ethical challenge.

To highlight the intersection between political debate and what government economists do, it is useful to describe three key paths to policy influence. One path is to establish the facts that describe the world. Key indicators provide a shorthand means of gauging progress (or lack thereof) for policies and so are significant bits of evidence used in policy debate. A second path is the examination of causality in trying to understand the effects of government actions and interventions. A third path is sorting through the welter of assertions and supporting economic analyses that have become part of the landscape of political debate.

The statistical programs of the US government, indeed of any government, provide the basis for describing a nation's well-being. Economists perform key functions in developing measurement concepts, designing surveys, and making calculations and forecasts. In fact, many federal economists work in one of the principal statistical agencies, which include those that administer the national census, run employment and price surveys, compute gross domestic product (GDP), and forecast crop prices, among many other functions. Such information is valuable not only in public but also in private sector decision making.

Statistical indicators have political significance. As an example, measures of unemployment loom large as markers of a government's success or failure in managing the economy. Accusations have been made that the values of the measure have been tampered with for political reasons. The counter to that charge is the reliance on a prescribed set of procedures that career staff follows in compilation. These well-documented and reviewed processes provide protection against the loss of confidence in measures that would otherwise ensue. But the selection of which measures to produce may well be affected by politics. Political opposition has forestalled the creation of a measure of "green" GDP, the value of services flowing from the nation's natural resources. The inability to agree on an updated poverty measure is another example of controversy over how the world is to be described.

Harkening back to the themes of the progressive era, more recent efforts at government reform have stressed the use of evidence-based policy. Scientific evidence, in particular, is meant to underpin better and more defensible policy decisions (National Research Council, 2012: 50). Effectiveness of a policy or program is judged by whether its implementation has the intended consequences. Legislation requires agencies to report on effectiveness of their policies and programs. As a result, analysis of causality in government interventions has become a prominent part of discussion about policy design and selection. Economists are well positioned to address questions of effectiveness because of their discipline's orientation to discerning cause and effect. Through the application of theory and statistical analysis, empirical policy (mainly micro) economists provide what has become critical evidence about how government programs work.

In trying to determine cause and effect, economists must cope with imperfections in real-world data about the phenomena they are studying. Although the occasional "natural experiment" may be of benefit, usually economists must grapple with extracting signal from a noisy environment. Frequently, the historical record will provide only murky indications about the impact of a novel policy intervention. Models necessarily built on data from the past may not provide a good basis for prediction, and judgment must be applied to formulate a projection. In such circumstances, economists—within and outside of government—will attach significant qualifications to the conclusions they reach about policy impacts. When the results are brought to the policy arena, however, those qualifications often fall by the wayside. Point estimates are emphasized over confidence intervals. The analyst may have misgivings about the use to which her findings are put.

She may wonder whether putting forward a qualitative result would have served equally well. But the pressure to provide quantification is relentless. Is it better to provide an estimate knowing qualifications will be ignored or to advise that quantification will not yield a credible estimate?

Many in politics have strong views on the solutions they would like to see, but it is not always true that the favored solutions actually solve the problem or that they are without unintended consequences that may cause harm that outweighs the value of the solution. To be true in serving the public interest, the government economist ought not to be selective about the causal relationships to be studied. Only a comprehensive approach fully informs decision making. Indeed, this emphasis on identifying what might happen that was not explicitly meant is a key task of economists in government (Hamilton, 1992: 61).

Over the past 30 years or so, the significance of economic argument in public debate has increased markedly, and, as a consequence, the government economist is often looked to as an arbiter of the conflicting economic analysis coming to decision makers. The foundation for this rise was laid in the 1960s and 1970s with the move to more structured, first principles analysis such as zero-based budgeting. In the early 1980s, the Office of Management and Budget formalized the adoption of cost–benefit criteria as a means of evaluating policies and programs. As Nelson points out, "The fundamental question faced by OMB is an economic one—how to allocate scarce resources (federal funds) among a large number of competing claimants (federal programs)" (1987: 78). The use of economic reasoning to support policy decisions is found across the range of government programs.

As the foundation for government decision making shifted to include economic criteria explicitly, those wishing to influence government decisions also had to become more adept at economic argument. Simultaneously, the increased ease of computing made quantitative analyses key to measuring impact. Over time, more and more non-profit research and analytical organizations appeared on the Washington scene working on behalf of political factions, economic interests, and non-ideological foundations. Academic economists working for-hire joined the fray. The growth in what has been termed the "policy enterprise" is reflected in the expanding numbers of think-tanks, from only a handful after World War II to more than 1800 in 2010 (National Research Council, 2012: 29). Many are based in Washington, DC, and many have a distinct ideological orientation, from the Center for American Progress on the left to the conservative American Enterprise Institute. All employ economists and produce economic analysis that supports their policy stance.

Faced with a plethora of often conflicting findings, decision makers turn to in-house economists to sort through differing assumptions and methodologies to get at the root of the differences. This appropriation of economic research to serve ideological ends is the norm today. Weiss (1979: 429) identified this political use of social science research.

> It becomes ammunition for the side that finds its conclusions congenial and supportive. Partisans flourish the evidence in an attempt to neutralize opponents, convince

> waverers, and bolster supporters. Even if conclusions have to be ripped out of context (with suppression of qualifications and of evidence "on the other hand"), research becomes grist to the mill.

And it is also true that economists purposefully produce analyses meant to support political positions. Bombarded by economic studies in support of every conceivable position, policy makers often seek guidance in sorting and weighing such an abundance of evidence.

Government economists might best perform as honest brokers, but bias is easy to introduce in filtering conflicting policy views. DeMartino (2011) notes the influential role of government economists in selecting outside economic experts for testimony or research. He says that "the economist can take steps to ensure that an agency's (or a legislator's) bias is confirmed through nominally independent outside economic expertise, or the economist can instead subtly lean against this bias to ensure that opposing views are heard" (41). An economist who does a good job at providing balanced technical critique can help a decision maker anticipate reaction to policy proposals. The economist who pulls a punch may be found out when the policy official is surprised by an unlooked-for reaction.

Any of these paths may lead to policy influence. But how, exactly? The use of economic research (or indeed any social science or science) in the policy process is not well understood. Outcomes are rarely clearly related to any particular piece of information or analysis, even if the point at which it is provided as input is clear. Despite the emphasis on evidence-based policy (or perhaps more accurately evidence-influenced policy), little is known about how best to incorporate scientific knowledge into policy argument (National Research Council, 2012: 52). Research by psychologists and behavioral economists about the way people make decisions has debunked the notion that rationality rules the process. Fifty years ago, Lindblom (1959) described real-world, incremental policy decision processes as "the science of muddling through," contrasting them with the infeasible (for complex problems) "rational comprehensive" approach that starts from first principles each time.

The government economist cannot rely on the comforting notion that the policy decision maker seeks objective data and analysis that informs an orderly evaluation of options to achieve specified ends. Consequently, economists should have modest expectations about the prospect that their findings actually turn out to be the ultimate justification and motivation for policy choice. Still, the economist is aware that some impact on the decision may be felt and so have real-world consequences. Out of these consequences arise ethical obligations.

Career Management

Embarking on a career in government service means coming to grips with the conditions of employment that are distinctively (though not uniquely) associated with government service. One implication of government service is the motivated public servant's desire to remain effective in internal debate and discussions, especially when her analysis and findings are swimming against the political current. The other is the recognition (if not the acceptance) that the real-time nature of government decisions places constraints on the work economists would ideally like to do to support decisions. To some, these conditions mean inevitable (and, possibly, unacceptable) compromise in the quality of work an economist can do. Independence of thought and opinion may be constrained by considerations about longer-term influence in a role or in an agency. Time and data constraints may preclude careful use of economic concepts and theory and/or the application of appropriate methods of quantitative analysis.

An economist in government must be aware of her effectiveness—that is to say, her ability to be heard when decisions are contemplated so as to contribute constructively to the dialogue. Policy officials are not obligated to listen to what economists or any particular economist has to say, though there is a good government argument that suggests that they should do so. Political beliefs or ideologies may clash with the tenets of economics. An example is the rejection of the notion of valuation of life or of the natural world in evaluating environmental regulation (Nelson, 1987). To bring the benefit of economic reasoning to bear on policy, she must recognize—but not necessarily embrace—the positions and attitudes of those whom she advises.

Interpersonal skills may also determine how and whether an economist is heard. Some economists in government become skilled in explaining economics to non-economists. The most influential advisors understand the complexity of policy making and approach policy officials without condescension. The National Research Council emphasized the need to instruct public policy students on this point:

> Without such understanding, students may overestimate the persuasive power of scientific reasoning, and overlook the substantial barriers of institutional and cultural resistance to new research knowledge, unfamiliar policy framings, or solutions that challenge deeply held moral or ethical beliefs. (2012: 74)
>
> In a teaching role, government economists provide a valuable service. Hamilton writes, "There is an art to telling policymakers what they need to know but don't want to hear." (1992: 63)

An economist may be adept at her specialty but struggle to communicate the significance of her findings to a lay audience. It can be frustrating to find economic arguments fall on deaf or uncomprehending ears, but it should not be unexpected. Effective economists can translate their disciplinary findings into useful concepts for non-economist decision makers. Nelson observes that "Top policymakers are often confronted with overwhelming amounts of information and data," so that "the ability 'to tell a story' that makes sense, to 'paint a picture,' is at a premium in government" (1987: 86). Policy officials often seek out such economists as advisors, though others may be intimidated and simply avoid economists altogether.

The risk to the government economist is the sacrifice of objectivity and independence in trying to maintain a role in policy discussions. Being effective means delivering results that are unpopular without being ostracized. What that takes varies with politics and across policy officials. There is no doubt that career advancement can be threatened when conflict with policy officials occurs. Grappling with this tension comes with the territory for government economists, and it can take fortitude and possibly sacrifice to function with independence in a difficult environment.

Unavoidably, the government makes decisions in the face of uncertainty, complexity, and ambiguity. It often lacks the data that would ideally support good decision making. A time constraint is often present for practical or political reasons. In these circumstances, the economist will be asked to produce relevant analysis in a short time, working without adequate data and without time or resources to apply an elaborate methodology in analysis. In some cases, the nature of the decision does not require detailed analysis, while in other cases, it does. Deciding on the appropriate and necessary scope of analysis is a key step. The tradeoff between the virtues of completeness, relevance and timeliness is well recognized and often unavoidable. The careful analyst assesses the consequences of providing what she considers a poor estimate and attaches appropriate qualifications to her analysis. She may, however, find that to be an unsatisfactory approach, as such caveats are routinely ignored. In that situation, she must consider whether inadequate work should even go forward.

Working in a fraught political environment raises ethical questions for the applied economist in civil service. However, this fact is not a reflection of the imperfection of public service; it is simply an artifact of the institutional setting where winners and losers result from policy decisions. Certainly those with a preference to avoid ethical dilemmas altogether would be well advised to stay away from government service. Now, with an appreciation of context, discussion can turn to examine specific circumstances in which these ethical dilemmas evolve.

Challenges to Ethics

The most challenging ethical dilemmas arise out of the tension between political goals and interests and the economist's concern for independence and objectivity. Tension between politics and the findings of economics may arise when results are at odds with political aims and expediency. Different views on what constitutes the public interest can create conflict between the loyalty that the economist owes the government as an employee and her own sense of what will best serve the public. Conflict over ethics may arise in more ways than can be catalogued here, given the diversity of roles and settings in which government economists work. However, those that arise out of friction with politics are some of the most prominent. They include

- Suppression or alteration of results or analysis
- Direction to produce support for decisions already taken
- Disagreement over policy decisions

An appreciation of the circumstances in which these arise can help inform the development of resources and practices that can aid the economist who finds herself facing ethical questions.

Economists in the federal government often produce analyses and statistics for internal government deliberations. In this case, what is done is generally not meant by policy officials to enter the public domain. Such analyses appear in internal communications and presentations. This "pre-decisional" material is not to be released, though it may be when requested by those outside government under statutes that promote openness in government. At some agencies, these sensitive analyses may be designated "For Official Use Only" in order to reinforce that external release is prohibited. Particularly when analysis does not support a policy or program decision, though, an economist may try to find means to make the results public. Transparency might be the justification, but the economist also owes loyalty to the government as an employer.

In the case of work intended for publication, agencies generally have in place procedures that govern review and release. As discussed earlier, releases from statistical agencies follow specific guidelines that insulate the production of an estimate from political influence. Still, it is true that the government—policy officials, not the individual analyst—decides what to publish as an official document and what can be provided to the public. It is a bitter pill to swallow if work intended for an audience outside government is suppressed or if it is changed to make it more acceptable in political terms. An economist can argue that making all relevant analyses and data available to the public improves decision making and is a tenet of open government. But she may not prevail.

Today, no policy proposal or pronouncement is legitimate without an analysis that purports to show that it will be effective. The National Research Council (2012) report asserted, "Democracy rests on the obligations of rulers to give reasons for policy" (17). A scientific basis for policy, such as economic evidence would support, can be seen as "more dependable as well as more defensible reasons than unsupported presumption or speculation" (17). The penetration of policy discourse by economics over the past few decades reflects this dynamic. So, it is perhaps not surprising that circumstance can arise when a decision is made and the economic analytical support for it is sought after the fact. In that case, the economist may be directed to provide that support. This is a relatively clear case in which the economist's commitment to objectivity as a professional conflicts with the direction from superiors. Though it is not possible to know how often the attempt is made, most policy officials recognize the sensitivity—if not the impropriety—of fabricating evidence (should that be discovered) and do not usually take the risk. And there may be no need to do so. An analysis that confirms the decision may well be available from a source outside government, in which case it can be cited as support.

A related challenge arises when it seems clear that the analyses requested will not produce results that suit political purposes. Then, economists may try to avoid doing the work altogether or may explain up front that the results will not be pleasing. DeMartino (2011: 41) raises the concern that economists will conform to explicit or implicit pressure to produce results aligned with institutional interests. This pressure can result in self-censorship when results appear contrary to political expectations or desires.

In some cases, good quality analysis is done, nothing is suppressed, but the economist simply does not agree with the decision ultimately taken. Other considerations besides economics have, of course, likely factored into the decision. The economist cannot or should not be surprised by such an outcome nor have the expectation that economics will be the only thing that matters. Still, the decision may be antithetical to the economist's own values and view of what constitutes the public interest.

It is not unusual for federal economists to differ with policy decisions made, although these disagreements do not usually become public. Still, the temptation and the opportunity may exist, through what DeMartino terms "speaking strategically." By means of leaks and other back-channel communication, an economist may go beyond her authority when she believes that the political process ought to be redirected in some way (DeMartino, 2011: 49). Of course, such circumvention violates the obligation of the civil servant to be neutral in matters involving politics.

Supporting Ethical Behavior and Decision Making

What does an economist confronted with an ethical challenge do, exactly? The terms of employment provide no expectation that the economist's view will prevail in policy and program decisions. Even though she understands she may not prevail, she does expect that she will be heard. That is, her analysis will be treated as objective evidence in policy argument. When, instead, it is altered or suppressed for political expediency, what recourse does she have? To whom does she turn for advice and guidance?

There may be instances in which disagreement with the policy decision is so profound that she may contemplate leaving public service. What is the internal calculus that guides an economist's decision to stay or go when faced with an ethical challenge in federal service? Hirschman famously considered such a choice in *Exit, Voice, and Loyalty: Responses to Decline in Firms, Organizations, and States*. When an economist views the choice the agency has made as a decline in the quality of the institution, the decision to leave is conditioned by constraints on exit and by the likelihood that he or she can affect quality by remaining. Certainly, the availability of alternative employment is one consideration in exit, but so is the individuals' commitment to the institution, here the Federal government. Hirschman cites the possibility of "loyalist behavior," especially when the situation involves the production of public goods (in the current context, economic or social policy). The economist cares about policy outcomes whether or not he remains employed by his agency. In that case, Hirschman (1970: 98) writes,

> In deciding whether the time has come to leave an organization, members, *especially the more influential ones*, will sometimes be held back not so much by the moral and material sufferings they themselves would have to go through as a result of exit, but by the anticipation that the *organization to which they belong would go from bad to worse if they left*."

Such loyalist behavior is observed in civil servants, though there are those who regard the willingness to stay as an ethical dodge (Henderson, 1977).

The circumstances she confronts are presumably unlike any anticipated in her academic preparation, though there are pressures in university service, too. She may have sympathetic colleagues and, in some circumstances, a responsive supervisor. Agencies do have ethics officers, though their orientation is toward enforcement of the federal code of conduct. The more subtle issue having to do with treatment of economics in decision making is not generally within their scope. Mainly, she is on her own in deciding whether or how to voice concern or even whether to leave federal employment.

What might improve this situation? "Improve" is meant in the sense that an economist finds resources that allow her to express her concerns and also to elicit or understand the institutional response. Consider three complementary possibilities.

- Graduate economics curricula could include training in ethics, much as business schools have added ethics in the wake of financial crisis.
- Professional standards could provide recourse as justification for disagreement, as is an option in some fields.
- Expanded recognition of the existence of these dilemmas in the federal workplace could result in creation of recognized avenues for raising concerns with agency colleagues, supervisors, and policy officials.

Being prepared to think explicitly about ethics, having access to an external ethical standard, and legitimizing internal government dialogue on ethics would provide the basis for a constructive approach.

Other academic disciplines and programs that are closely aligned subject-matter-wise with economics have integrated ethics into university curricula. Schools of public policy offer courses that transmit the realities of public service to students. Of course, to add these elements to economics course offerings requires faculty who have experience as practitioners. Academic economists with experience in government are most often those who held short-term political appointments to offices such as the Council of Economic Advisors. Those with long, career experience are not likely to end up on university faculties. So, possibly outsourcing this aspect of graduate education to other schools in the university might be more feasible.

Another route for exposure to the terms of public service might be for graduate students in economics to seek internships in the federal government. And, indeed, some number does. Typically, government agencies market internships to undergraduates and often to those working towards master degrees in public policy. The supposition is that these students—and not those pursuing doctorates—are most likely to be interested and prepared to be practitioners. However, that does not mean that, for the motivated student, an internship should not be considered.

Professional fields comprising large numbers of practitioners, as opposed to academics, do have standards that provide guidance on ethics. For example, actuaries contemplate explicitly the possibility that an opinion may run counter to a client's preferences. Their professional standards provide published guidance on what should be done and also establish an ethical standards board, the American Academy of Actuaries, whose advice and counsel may be sought. The American Society for Public Administration (ASPA), for another, has had for many years a set of ethical standards for those in public service. These standards address explicitly the unique features of the government workplace, though they are not, at this point, tailored to circumstances of policy analysis.

Could the economics profession develop ethical standards that would be useful to career government economists? Possibly, but it is still the case that the majority of economists work or expect to work in academia. DeMartino reports that some 60 percent of recent, new doctorates expected to work at universities. By comparison, only about 16 percent were oriented to government employment (DeMartino, 2011: 20). In 2011, the American Economic Association had around 17,000 paid members, the vast majority of whom appear to be academics. So, the demand for such a standard might be limited, and the professional society's ability to supply it might be constrained by the relatively few practitioners among its members. Possibly economists in government should seek alliance with other practitioners, such as the ASPA or the Society of Government Economists.

Bolstering awareness and discussion of ethics for economists in the workplace would be an expedient and relevant approach. In the United States, federal policies on the maintenance of scientific integrity offer such an avenue. For an individual scientist, integrity encompasses dedication to intellectual honesty and to the responsible conduct of research, including accuracy in representing contributions to reports, fairness in peer review, and transparency in conflict of interest (National Research Council, 2002). In the federal workplace, protection of scientific integrity means, most importantly, that research findings not be suppressed or altered by political officials, as the Obama Administration has said (US Office of Science and Technology Policy, 2012). Beyond the value to the individual scientist's own sense of professional ethics, integrity in government science is key to maintaining public trust in the process of policy decision making.

Guidelines for federal agencies in the implementation of the principles of scientific integrity have been laid out by the White House science office. They contemplate the creation of both forums for discussion and exploration as well as institutional awareness and commitment to upholding practices that promote and protect scientific integrity. Their scope includes steps taken to protect against political interference, approaches to communicating scientific results to the public, and the professional development of scientists. Attention must be given as well to procedures that address the compromise of scientific integrity, including protection against retaliation toward those who assert violations. Taken together, and if taken to heart, the full framework of scientific integrity could provide a more hospitable environment for discussion about ethical challenges in the government workplace.

Conclusions

Public service is a calling distinct from academic education and research or business pursuits. The imperative to serve the public interest in a complex and ambiguous situation introduces ethical dilemmas unique to government. However, the existence of ethical challenge is not a defect of public service but rather part of its essence. Those who choose public service careers must recognize this reality. Those who prepare these economists and those who employ them must also do a better job of acknowledging the existence of these challenges and finding ways to address them, to the benefit of both the economist and the quality of government decision making.

References

Aaron, H. J. 1989. "Politics and the Professors Revisited." *American Economic Review* 79(2): 1–15.

Allen, W. R. "Economics, Economists, and Economic Policy: Modern American Experiences." *History of Political Economy* 9(1): 48–88.

American Academy of Actuaries. *Code of Professional Conduct*. Retrieved fromhttp://www.actuary.orgcontent/code-professional-conduct (cited October 18, 2013).

American Academy of Actuaries. Council on Professionalism. *The Profession's Responsibility to the Public*. Retrieved from http://www.actuary.org/pdf/062911_webinar_slides.pdf (cited June 29, 2011).

American Economic Association. 2012. "AEA Adopts Extensions to Principles for Author Disclosure of Conflict of Interest." Press release, January 5.

American Society for Public Administration. *Code of Ethics*. Retrieved from http://www.aspanet.org (cited September 19, 2011).

DeMartino, George F. 2011. *The Economist's Oath: On the Need for and Content of Professional Economic Ethics*. Oxford: Oxford University Press.

Hamilton, L. H. 1992. "Economists as Public Policy Advisors." *Journal of Economic Perspectives* 6(3): 61–64.

Henderson, J. B. 1977. "Professional Standards for the Performance of the Government Economist." *American Economic Review* 67: 321–325.

Hirschman, Albert O. 1970. *Exit, Voice, and Loyalty: Responses to Decline in Firms, Organizations, and States*. Cambridge, MA: Harvard University Press.

Lindblom, C. E. 1959. "The Science of Muddling Through." *Public Administration Review* 19(2): 79–88.

National Research Council. 2002. *Integrity in Scientific Research: Creating an Environment that Promotes Responsible Conduct*. Washington, DC: National Academies Press.

National Research Council. 2012. *Using Science as Evidence in Public Policy*. Washington, DC: National Academies Press.

Nelson, Robert H. 1987. "The Economics Profession and the Making of Public Policy." *Journal of Economic Literature* 25: 49–91.

Schultze, Charles L. 1982. "The Role and Responsibilities of the Economist in Government." *The American Economic Review* 72: 62–66.

Thompson, Dennis. 1983. "Ascribing Responsibility to Advisors in Government." *Ethics* 93: 546–560.

U.S. Bureau of Labor Statistics. *Occupational Outlook Handbook 2010-2011, Economists*. Retrieved from http://www.bls.gov/oco/ocos055.htm (cited August 1, 2011).

U.S. Office of Government Ethics. *Principles of Ethical Conduct. Executive Order 12731*. Retrieved from http://www.usoge.gov/Laws-and_Regulations/Employee-Standards-of-Conduct/Employee-Standards-of-Conduct (cited October 18, 2013).

U.S. Office of Personnel Management. *Constitution Initiative*. http://www.opm.gov/constitution_initiative/oath.asp (cited June 30, 2011).

U.S., Office of Science and Technology Policy "Scientific Integrity: Fueling Innovation, Building Public Trust." December 17, 2010. Retrieved from www.thewhitehouse.gov/blog/2010/12/17/scientific-integrity-fueling-innovation-building-public-trust-ostp (cited October 18, 2013).

U.S. Office of Special Counsel.*Hatch Act Frequently Asked Questions*. Retrieved from http://www.osc.gov/h3Federalfaq.htm (cited October 18, 2013).

Weiss, C. H. 1979. "The Many Meanings of Research Utilization." *Public Administration Review* 39(5): 426–431.

CHAPTER 31

THE ETHICS PROBLEM

Toward a Second-Best Solution to the Problem of Economic Expertise

DAVID M. LEVY AND SANDRA J. PEART

Introduction

While it is in the interest of society to obtain disinterested advice from experts, there may be strong private incentives for any one expert to provide biased advice. This is the collective action problem associated with expertise. In recognition of this problem, the American Economic Association (AEA) has recently implemented new publication guidelines (AEA, 2012) that ask for disclosure of financial rewards associated with research conducted by economists. On the occasion of a discussion of these new AEA publication guidelines (AEA, 2012) we ask whether they are sufficient to overcome the barrier to disinterested economic research and advice. We suggest that the guidelines are insufficient to solve the collective action problem associated with advice-giving and we sketch out a potential remedy to our continued concerns.

We approach the problem from the point of view of the consumer of expert advice. In a world of transparency, the sensible rule would be to trust experts. We'd make the same decision as they recommend had we spent our resources on obtaining their knowledge. However, when transparency fails that trust can be a catastrophe. We propose to think in terms of the general theory of the second-best in which we accept the existence of constraints that cannot be removed (Lipsey and Lancaster, 1956–57). In this world transparency is a pipedream, but what *is* possible is to make that nontransparency itself transparent. A code of ethics for experts might suggest to nonexperts that there is temptation to violate professional standards for private ends. Thus, the very existence of an ethical code is a warning. To serve this end the code of ethics needs to indicate where the dangers lie, what tempts the experts.

In what follows we review early discussions of the collective action problem associated with giving advice. Frank Knight's discussion of economic experts is particularly valuable because he held a view of governance by truth-seekers but he also realized that such governance wasn't incentive-compatible. Instead of falling into Knight's pessimism we take this view as a first-best situation and ask what constraint blocks the solution. Given that constraint, we can then think about a second-best solution.

We begin with Knight's important insights into "the reasons why economists write books and articles." Knight recognized, first, that economists should apply their models to themselves, thereby explicitly modeling researchers and advice-givers as self-interested. Second, he was acutely aware of the collective action problem in which the "competition for recognition and influence take the place of the effort to get things straight" (Knight, 1933: xxvii). Knight's sometimes intellectual opponent, A. C. Pigou, made the similar point that instead of seeking the truth, individual economists who are unconstrained by ethics simply posture and argue. The third section locates the Knightian enterprise in a first-best world in which governance is conducted as truth-seeking. Knight's truth-seeking view of governance is explicitly presupposed in John Rawls's magisterial *Theory of Justice*. The Knight–Rawls connection is even clearer when one examines Rawls' annotations to Knight's *Ethics of Competition*. The first-best supposition of truth-seeking can fail when economists act as advocates for predetermined systems of belief. The fourth section moves to econometrics and the problem of nontransparent specification search, an issue first raised by Rutledge Vining when he asked the Knightian question where is the econometrician in the econometrician's model. In the fifth section we suggest why the Knight–Rawls' notion of government with ethics, which is to say government by (fair) discussion, is fragile and we offer a suggestion to help better align private and public incentives in the arena of giving advice by making the nontransparent pursuit of private ends itself transparent. We close with a proposed addition to the AEA guidelines to help deal with the motivated economist.

The Expert Economist's Dilemma, Historically Considered

We know of two important treatments of the collective action problem from the early 20th century. The first was offered by Knight in the 1933 "Preface to the Re-Issue" of *Risk, Uncertainty and Profit* in the London School of Economics reprints series of "Scarce Tracts." A. C. Pigou offered a second treatment a year later in his London School of Economics lecture in which he flamboyantly described the issue.[1]

[1] Perhaps Knight and Pigou were inspired by considering what follows from failure of the motivational condition that J. Neville Keynes put forward when he described positive economics as the search for law. (We put the motivational condition in bold.) "We mean by a *law* a theorem, the statement of a uniformity, not a command enforced by sanctions. The law of supply and demand, the Ricardian law

Knight and Pigou are often correctly seen in oppositional terms. Knight's response to Pigou's road problem is rightly celebrated as the beginning of the London School of Economics (LSE)–Chicago analysis of the critical rule of property rights in a competitive economy (Pigou, 1918; Knight, 1924; Coase, 1993; Heckman, 1997). As Coase tells us, he selected the title of his most famous article, "The Problem of Social Cost," in tribute to Knight's "Fallacies in the Interpretation of Social Cost" (Coase, 1993: 250). But Knight and Pigou also share an important insight into the economics of economists as experts. Just as they hold that the individuals studied by economists confront collective action problems, so too do the economists themselves face these problems. This makes for a motivational homogeneity between theorist and theorized, something we take as foundational in analytical egalitarianism.

Frank Knight

Knight begins his "Preface" by proposing to address what needs to be done to develop and improve received economic doctrine (Knight, 1933: xi). Although there are very few specific targets of his preface—Pigou's treatment of uncertainty in an appendix of *Economics of Welfare* (xiv) and the confounding of firm and plant (xxi) are exceptions—his unhappiness with the larger classical enterprise is quite clear and not especially surprising given his other writings of the period.

What *is* a surprise comes in his two-paragraph exercise in the economics of economics. In the first of these he proposes to use the tools of economics to analyze the economist's own activity:

> The first and main suggestion, looking towards a more relevant economics, is that the inquiry into motives might well, like charity, begin at home, with a glance at the reasons why economists write books and articles. These things are also commodities, produced competitively for a market, . . . , the behaviour of economists provides evidence regarding the possibilities of settling questions—and of settling them rightly—by free discussion. (xxvi)

Then Knight describes the collective action problem in which "Economics finds itself in a vicious circle":

> To get recognition and have influence it descends to the public's level of thinking; then competition for recognition and influence take the place of the effort to get things straight; finally, success in this competition becomes the condition of membership in the profession itself. It is no doubt idle to say, now, that there "might

of rent, Gresham's law, and the like, may be given as examples of economic laws in the above sense. The validity of such laws is a purely theoretical question, **and our attitude towards them is not, nor at any rate should not be, affected by our ethical or political views"** Keynes (1891: 36). Keynes continues and describes such activity as advocacy.

> have been" an economics profession made up of minds exclusively devoted to the problem-solving interest and working co-operatively at this task, instead of more and more hawking their wares competitively to the public by way of settling their "scientific" differences. (xxvii–xxviii)

Knight's statement of the problem and his own solution to it were taken up by William Hutt in his 1936 *Economists and the Public* but they were otherwise largely ignored.

A. C. Pigou

Lecturing at the London School of Economics in late 1934 on the role of economists in society, A. C. Pigou comes to the matter of controversy. Those who thought he might respond to Knight's criticism were in for a surprise, as Pigou actually sharpened Knight's point. While "controversy up to a point serves, no doubt, to stimulate and clarify thought," Pigou argued that "controversy for its own sake is a prodigious waste of time" (Pigou, [1935] 1936: 22). He then quoted a verse from Rudyard Kipling without explanation: "There are nine and sixty ways of constructing tribal lays, / And every single one of them is right!"

Those in the audience who could place the verse in Kipling's poetic sketch of the hesitant steps away from a world of wars ("Neolithic Age") might have foreseen some of what followed. Pigou pointed to a rule that J. M. Keynes urged on the occasion of the official obituary notice for Alfred Marshall:

> It is not politic for us to lay down even the most general rules for one another: we may so soon be constrained to break those rules ourselves. Not so long ago one of my most distinguished colleagues urged his fellow-economists to "eschew the Treatise, pluck the day, fling pamphlets into the wind." A few years later he himself offered, and we gratefully received, a work with the title of Treatise and comprising two weighty tomes![2]

After offering a defense of Marshall's generosity to the classics, Pigou clarified the point of the verse:

> And there is yet another thing. Are we, in our secret hearts, wholly satisfied with the manner, or manners, in which some of our controversies are carried on? A year or two ago, after the publication of an important book, there appeared an elaborate and careful critique of a number of particular passages in it. The author's answer was, not to rebut the criticisms, but to attack with violence another book, which the critic had himself written several years before! Body-line bowling! The method of the duello! ([1935], 1936: 23–24)

[2] Pigou, [1935] 1936: 22–23.

The episode, now cited as witness to the decade-spanning dispute between Keynes and F. A. Hayek, is for Pigou an instance of the failure of economists to attain their collective goal as they understand it[3]:

> That kind of thing is surely a mistake. It is a mistake, not merely in general and in the abstract, but also for a solid reason of State. Economists in this country lack the influence which—in their own opinion—they ought to have, largely because the public believe that on all topics they are hopelessly divided. Controversies conducted in the manner of Kilkenny cats do not help to dissipate this opinion. And yet in truth the opinion is largely mistaken! ([1935], 1936: 24)

For Pigou, group influence depends upon unanimity but individual self-interest unconstrained by ethics leads to posturing and dissent. This was especially true in the arena of policy advice. Pigou described the demand for economic advice:

> . . .political partisans, I say, are accustomed to decide what they want to do first and to seek for arguments in favour of it afterwards. Economic reasoning is for them, not a means of arriving at the truth, but a kind of brickbat useful on occasions for inflicting injury on their opponents. ([1935], 1936: 8–9)

He continues with a story about an unnamed political figure who switched economic advice as policy changed and then another about his adventures in offering advice in the letters column of the *Times*. He moved from being in the judgment of the Prime Minister, "the great Cambridge economist" to a "mere academic theorist" in a twinkling of a policy shift! ([1935], 1936: 9–10). Then he reviews the private incentives facing economists to gain influence through the sale of their theories for the sake of policy results:

> Of course to students of detached mind this kind of thing is entertaining and quite harmless. But to a young man the ambition to play a part in great affairs is natural: and the temptation to make slight adjustments in his economic view, so that it shall conform to the policy of one political party or another, may be severe. As a conservative economist or a liberal economist or a labour economist he has much more chance of standing near the centre of action than he has as an economist without adjectives. But for the student to yield to that temptation is an intellectual crime. It is to sell his birthright in the household of truth for a mess of political pottage. ([1935], 1936: 10–11)

The only solution that Pigou proposed is what Kipling saw, a norm of toleration and awareness, from which it followed that the public would be skeptical of advice. Two stanzas provide a context to the lines quoted above:

> Then I stripped them, scalp from skull, and my hunting-dogs fed full,
> And their teeth I threaded neatly on a thong;

[3] F. A. Hayek (1994: 47) quotes the passage as evidence of Keynes's reaction to the review of *Treatise of Money*. Bruce Caldwell offers an extensive discussion (1995: 26).

And I wiped my mouth and said, "It is well that they are dead,
For I know my work is right and theirs was wrong."
But my Totem saw the shame; from his ridgepole-shrine he came,
And he told me in a vision of the night:—
"There are nine and sixty ways of constructing tribal lays,
And every single one of them is right!"[4]

Government by Truth-Seeking as First-Best

John Rawls depended upon Knight at the critical moment in which the question arose as to whether legislative discussion is aimed at discovering the correct answer or simply working out a compromise. Rawls then provided a framework to think about the fair conduct of those who are concerned with discovering the correct answer but who are aware that they and others have other motivations. Knight's view of governance is that it ought to be, but rarely is, an objective exercise to find the best solution to social problems. Governance for Knight is not about trading interests. It is instead a discussion about how best to obtain agreed-upon ends. In Justice Rawls is completely clear that his understanding of legislation was Knightian.

Government by discussion involves majority rule and decision making by experts. We quote the long passage in which Rawls takes legislation in a just constitution as a procedure to arrive at the "best policy as defined by the principles of justice":

> In the ideal procedure, the decision reached is not a compromise, a bargain struck between opposing parties trying to advance their ends. The legislative discussion must be conceived not as a contest between interests, but as an attempt to find the best policy as defined by the principles of justice. I suppose, then, as part of the theory of justice, that an impartial legislator's only desire is to make the correct decision in this regard, given the general facts known to him. He is to vote solely according to his judgment. The outcome of the vote gives an estimate of what is most in line with the conception of justice.
>
> If we ask how likely it is that the majority opinion will be correct, it is evident that the ideal procedure bears a certain analogy to the statistical problem of pooling the views of a group of experts to arrive at a best judgment. ([1971], 1999, 314).

[4] It perhaps intrigued readers, and certainly struck us as worthy of note that both Knight's and Pigou's reflections offered in the space of a year on the collective action problem of economists have an LSE address. Whether this is purely coincidental or not, there is an LSE tradition of the 1903s that considers the role of the economist in the economy that we find in William Beveridge's "Mock Trial of the Economists" (Levy and Peart, 2011*a*) and in William Hutt (1936).

Rawls's footnote reveals the complexity of the issue. After the citation to K. J. Arrow's *Social Choice* comes the reference to the critical argument in Knight: "For the notion of legislative discussion as an objective inquiry and not a contest between interests, see F. H. Knight, *The Ethics of Competition* (New York: Harper and Brothers, 1935), pp. 296, 345–347. In both cases see the footnotes."

The pages cited in *Justice* are marked for attention in Rawls's index in the rear inner lining of his copy *of Ethics of Competition*. These passages are from Knight's 1934 paper on nationalism which has been (unfortunately) read in isolation from the introduction to the LSE reprint except perhaps by W. H Hutt (1936). A small part of the index Rawls prepared for *Ethics* is reproduced in Figure 31.1.

The pages Rawls cites are also reproduced below. Rawls's use of red ink is apparently a mark of emphasis. He seems particularly taken by Knight's response to a skeptic who denies there is a "best" answer.

Knight clearly worried that discussion aimed at discovering the correct answer can degenerate into pursuit of one's interests. His proposed solution to the problem of partial interest corrupting the discussion of social goals was to appeal to fairness. The role of agreement is very subtly worked into Knight's argument. The background assumption in footnote 1 (345) is an appeal to impartiality (Figures 31.2 and 31.3).

We see in the extensive footnote to which Rawls paid close attention the doctrine that "expression of personal preferences is not discussion and indeed leads definitely toward conflict."

Knight famously worried that growing income inequality would corrupt government by discussion because those with more dollars would have a louder voice. The problem of interest—the individualization of ends—does not go away when we leave the government of a commercial society and move to the government of a philosophical one.

Knight's answer is precisely the same in philosophical discussions as it is in the government of a competitive order. The player, as Knight puts it, must be more concerned to have a good game, to play by agreed upon rules, than to win. The question as we see it is whether this is sufficient to ensure the discussion is "fair." Our worry, expounded in more detail in the fifth section, is that without a more expansive code of ethics, enforced by spectators who are aware of the nontransparency of advice, experts will be insufficiently wedded to a norm of fair play to take part willingly in a competitive discussion, to

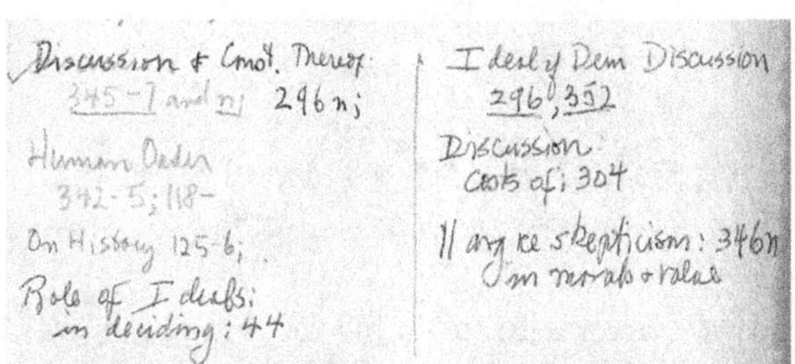
Discussion & Cmot. Theory: 345–7 and n1 296n;
Human Order 342–5; 118–
On History 125–6;
Role of Ideals: in deciding: 44
Ideal of Dem Discussion 296, 352
Discussion: costs of; 304
Il arg re skepticism: 346n in morals & values

FIGURE 31.1 A section of Rawls's index to Knight's *Ethics of Competition*.

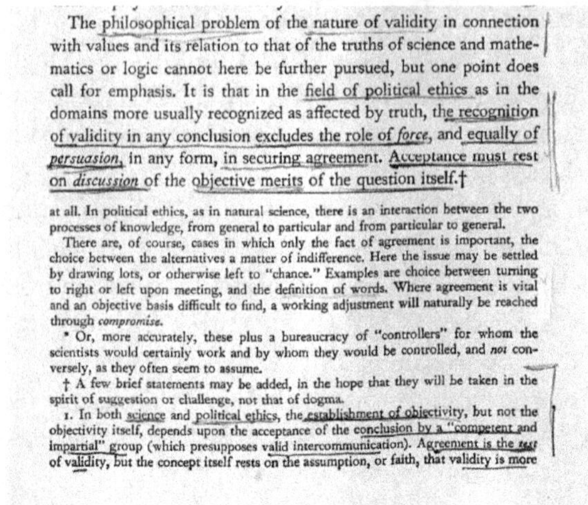

The philosophical problem of the nature of validity in connection with values and its relation to that of the truths of science and mathematics or logic cannot here be further pursued, but one point does call for emphasis. It is that in the field of political ethics as in the domains more usually recognized as affected by truth, the recognition of validity in any conclusion excludes the role of *force*, and equally of *persuasion*, in any form, in securing agreement. Acceptance must rest on *discussion* of the objective merits of the question itself.†

at all. In political ethics, as in natural science, there is an interaction between the two processes of knowledge, from general to particular and from particular to general.

There are, of course, cases in which only the fact of agreement is important, the choice between the alternatives a matter of indifference. Here the issue may be settled by drawing lots, or otherwise left to "chance." Examples are choice between turning to right or left upon meeting, and the definition of words. Where agreement is vital and an objective basis difficult to find, a working adjustment will naturally be reached through *compromise*.

* Or, more accurately, these plus a bureaucracy of "controllers" for whom the scientists would certainly work and by whom they would be controlled, and *not* conversely, as they often seem to assume.

† A few brief statements may be added, in the hope that they will be taken in the spirit of suggestion or challenge, not that of dogma.

1. In both science and political ethics, the establishment of objectivity, but not the objectivity itself, depends upon the acceptance of the conclusion by a "competent and impartial" group (which presupposes valid intercommunication). Agreement is the *test* of validity, but the concept itself rests on the assumption, or faith, that validity is more

FIGURE 31.2 Rawls's marking of Knight's *Ethics of Competition*, p. 345.

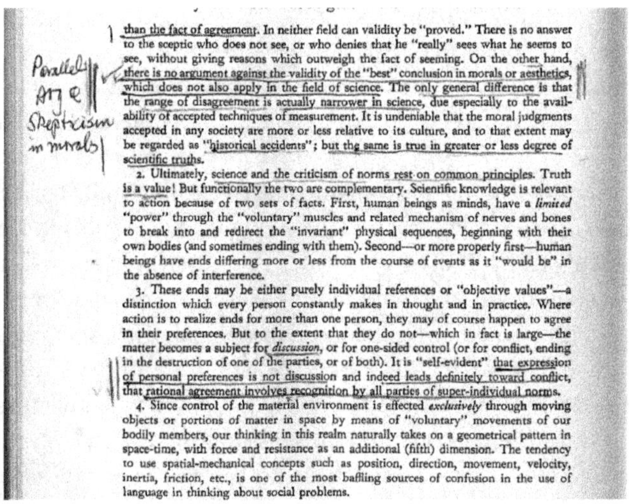

than the fact of agreement. In neither field can validity be "proved." There is no answer to the sceptic who does not see, or who denies that he "really" sees what he seems to see, without giving reasons which outweigh the fact of seeming. On the other hand, there is no argument against the validity of the "best" conclusion in morals or aesthetics, which does not also apply in the field of science. The only general difference is that the range of disagreement is actually narrower in science, due especially to the availability of accepted techniques of measurement. It is undeniable that the moral judgments accepted in any society are more or less relative to its culture, and to that extent may be regarded as "historical accidents"; but the same is true in greater or less degree of scientific truths.

2. Ultimately, science and the criticism of norms rest on common principles. Truth is a value! But functionally the two are complementary. Scientific knowledge is relevant to action because of two sets of facts. First, human beings as minds, have a *limited* "power" through the "voluntary" muscles and related mechanism of nerves and bones to break into and redirect the "invariant" physical sequences, beginning with their own bodies (and sometimes ending with them). Second—or more properly first—human beings have ends differing more or less from the course of events as it "would be" in the absence of interference.

3. These ends may be either purely individual references or "objective values"—a distinction which every person constantly makes in thought and in practice. Where action is to realize ends for more than one person, they may of course happen to agree in their preferences. But to the extent that they do not—which in fact is large—the matter becomes a subject for *discussion*, or for one-sided control (or for conflict, ending in the destruction of one of the parties, or of both). It is "self-evident" that expression of personal preferences is not discussion and indeed leads definitely toward conflict, that rational agreement involves recognition by all parties of super-individual norms.

4. Since control of the material environment is effected *exclusively* through moving objects or portions of matter in space by means of "voluntary" movements of our bodily members, our thinking in this realm naturally takes on a geometrical pattern in space-time, with force and resistance as an additional (fifth) dimension. The tendency to use spatial-mechanical concepts such as position, direction, movement, velocity, inertia, friction, etc., is one of the most baffling sources of confusion in the use of language in thinking about social problems.

FIGURE 31.3 Rawls's marking of Knight's *Ethics of Competition*, p. 346.

play by the rules and to abide by the outcome. Knight sees this too and despairs (Figures 31.4 and 31.5).

VINING EXPLAINS KNIGHT

Readers of Knight owe a great debt to Vining for a stream of publications in which Knightian themes were expounded (Vining, 1949, 1950, 1956). Vining's stress on the ethical obligations of researchers was particularly important in these publications. We begin with the 1949 exchange with Tjalling Koopmans, in which Vining defended the throughout history.

Discussion itself, moreover, is a social activity in the true sense, a "game" which has to be carried on in accord with rules, and these rules must be respected for "absolutistic" or "spiritual" reasons and not from individual utilitarian motives. The player must be more

FIGURE 31.4 Rawls's marking of Knight's *Ethics of Competition*, p. 352.

concerned to maintain the game and have it a good game than he is to win. But discussion seems to manifest in an especial degree the tendency of games to deteriorate, through "cheating," first into ill-will, and ultimately into disruption or even violence. From this point of view, the history of intellectual activity, in science, criticism, and philosophy, is surely far from encouraging. The specialized, professional intellectuals have shown little enough capacity to maintain the spirit of discussion, even in small groups and under what should be extremely favourable conditions; and of their ability to settle issues and solve serious problems by discussion among themselves, it is more pleasant not to speak. In the natural sciences, the issues finally get settled by unmistakable objective tests, the results of which are plain even to the non-specialist. In the field of morals and politics —to say nothing of religion—it is questionable whether the net result has been progress toward consensus or the multiplication of controversy.

FIGURE 31.5 Rawls's marking of Knight's *Ethics of Competition*, p. 353.

National Bureau of Economic Research (NBER) practice as "hypothesis seeking," something we might now call "exploratory data analysis" (Vining, 1949: 78). There Vining asked Koopmans to consider the econometrician's motivations in Koopmans's research program. If the econometrician was considered to be outside the chain of cause and effect then perhaps, Vining argued, we need to appeal to the sort of Kantian moral motivation that Knight presupposed (81). In his response Koopmans accepted "hypothesis seeking" as an open problem to be addressed by future technical developments.[5]

For our purposes the most helpful of Vining's statements is found in his 1956 pamphlet for UNESCO, *Economics in the United States*. The pamphlet speaks to the relationship between choice and individual obligation. Vining opens his section "The individual obligation implicit in the idea of individual freedom" with a statement familiar to Knight's readers, that one is ethically bound not to advocate in one's own interests:

> One can never propose an alteration in an economic system on the *explicit* grounds that he will gain personally from the alteration—at least he can never do so with any hope that he will be listened to. The proposal must be made on the grounds that the result will be generally more satisfying or else that what now exists is unfair. (1956: 18 [emphasis added])

[5] Koopmans (1949: 90): "This touches on unsolved problems at the very foundations of statistical theory, and I must confess that I do not see clearly through the issues involved. It is possible to take a formal view and argue that hypothesis-seeking and hypothesis-testing differ only in how wide a set of alternatives is taken into consideration."

We return later to the possibility of dropping "explicit" and pursuing personal interest, whether pecuniary or ideological, in a nontransparent manner. Vining's argument of course raises a puzzle concerning the sources of the ethical obligation:

> How is it that we say that social criticism in order to be valid must necessarily be devoid of personal motive? And how is it that the individuals constituting the society may feel a binding obligation to pursue the process until consensus is reached and to conform to the rules and constraints which are the outcome of the process? That is, what is the source of the obligation that may be felt by each member of the society to abide by the laws established by the group? (1956: 18)

The solution, Vining argues, comes from the very concept of "a free and rational individual," an explicit Kantian imperative (1956: 19).

The econometric literature moved on with rare backwards glances, two of which are of considerable importance. While in his 1972 *JEL* review article of Koopman's life work, Edmond Malinvaud regarded Vining as the "definite loser" as judged by professional acceptance (1972: 801), and he emphasized the "interesting distinction" between hypothesis seeking and the practice defended by Koopmans (Malinvaud, 1972: 801). Second, at the 50th anniversary of Cowles in 1983 Malinvaud began a serious reconsideration: "Notwithstanding this undisputable success of the probability approach, some of R. Vining's doubts have been recently echoed within the econometric literature. Some have argued that current econometric practice is often weak at the specification stage." (Malinvaud, [1983] 1988: 207). (Malinvaud cited the work of E. Leamer (1978), C. Sims (1980), and referred to the work of exploratory data analysis in mathematical statistics of J. Tukey.)

1983, the year that marked the 50th anniversary of the Cowles Commission, also saw the publication of Leamer's "Let's Take the Con Out of Econometrics" (Leamer, 1983) that developed the unhappy consequences of the hypothesis-seeking behavior Vining had laid out as a problem for Koopmans and his associates. Since then, 30 years of econometric work on specification search suggests that economists and other experts are indeed motivated by something other than truth itself (Leamer, 1983; Feigenbaum and Levy, 1996; Levy and Peart, 2007, 2008).

Toward a Solution to the Ethical Dilemmas of Expertise

We need to recognize that the problem of expert advice is more than just a worry about financial incentives; we take seriously Adam Smith's worries about the dangers of system (Levy and Peart, 2013). If we combine Smith with Knight and Rawls, the "objective inquiry" or the "best policy" may only be contingent upon a system. This would be akin to how Buchanan reads Knight (Buchanan, 1967) except that instead of preferences for policies we have preferences for a system.

"Best" answers that are far from the best are often the consequence of a false system. System-specific answers of course will generally be local to issues. Thus, if the system was a eugenic system in which the great "dangers" were race suicide and inherited criminality, a "best" policy might be the sterilization of the "unfit." If the system was a view of comparative growth of the American and the Soviet economy in which Soviet overtaking was a near-certainty, the "best" policy might be an early war against North Vietnam, a Soviet client state, as a way to prevent a later war against an "increasingly powerful" Soviet Union.[6]

It is common knowledge that Knight and Rawls worried about income going to those with extraordinary inherited abilities. For Knight, income inequality changes the rules of government by discussion; those with more income obtain a louder voice. Knight's concerns with bias via inequality is largely a question of transparency. He worried that the arguments advanced by interested parties could not be checked by their opponents. And because the bias in the system is nontransparent, regular people would not come to the conclusion that the discussion was unfair.[7] Consequently, the question of how the system is selected requires our attention.

The Knightian vision of a fair game in which all the players are tempted by their several goals to cheat poses the question of what makes playing the game of greater importance than winning one round. What induces experts to propose their best attempt at the correct answer instead of their best attempt at an answer that maximizes their several individual interests? There is, as we have argued previously, no easy answer to this question. But given individual and social interests so rarely fully align, knowing the question is one step, perhaps, toward a second best solution. As we argued elsewhere, experts function best when they are not fully trusted (Levy and Peart, 2010*a*).

A Rawlsian potential solution now presents itself. Suppose the experts put themselves behind a veil of ignorance in which their future clients are unknown. Why would they do this? Perhaps if the consumers of expertise know the tricks of argumentation (of expertise), it is harder for experts to impose a trick upon them (Levy and Peart, 2010*b*). But this would make the readers into experts of a sort. Making the nontransparency itself transparent is our second-best answer.

When economists act as expert witness in a case for monetary damages in trials before juries, the nontransparency of economic advocacy is itself transparent. It is

6 As illustration of the fragility with respect to false systems in the Knight–Rawls approach to politics, we can do no better than to notice that Rawls himself toyed with eugenic concerns (Rawls, [1971], 1999, 92–93) and Barry's important commentary asks whether we are willing to trade liberty for the higher growth and the more abundant future for the sort of direction provided by the Soviet Union (Barry, 1973: 73–74).

7 This is not to say that inequality concerns go away in our approach. Rather, they come to us in system specific fashion. In the eugenic era, poor girls were sterilized; in the Vietnam War, poor boys were drafted.

entirely implausible to presume that the jury members know what underlies the econometric models that are presented by the contending experts engaged by the opposing parties. Legal institutions have been developed so that presentations by experts are tightly constrained. The legal rules of discovery that mandate data and program sharing, along with sanctions for fraud, help ensure that the opposing estimates are replicable. Everyone involved in the procedure understands that the advocates will offer biased estimates but there will be contending experts. Thus, such a simple rule as splitting the difference offers a coherent way to reduce the bias (Froeb and Kobayashi, 1996; Posner, 1999). A modest change in procedure, introducing a statistical variation on final offer arbitration, would attenuate the incentives to offer biased testimony and thus help attenuate the economist's dilemma that Knight and Pigou described (Levy and Peart, 2008).

All these nice properties depend on the transparency of nontransparency. No one believes the jury will become expert so steps are taken to overcome their limitation. To reform economic advocacy we need to take the hardest step of all—to recognize, with Knight and Pigou, that we share motivation structure with those we study (Peart and Levy, 2003, 2005). The consequence of this is that we really need to put the economist in her model.

The dust has yet to settle on the consequences of the data error in the collection compiled by Carmen Reinhart and Kenneth Rogoff so we await a consensus judgment (Cowen, 2013). What does come as a surprise is that sophisticated spectators were surprised by the reported difficulties in obtaining data with which to do the statistical analysis.[8] Systematic data-sharing problems were reported in the economic literature at least since the 1986 study by William Dewald, Jerry Thursby, and Richard Anderson (1986). It came as a shock that the *editors* of the *Journal of Money, Credit and Banking* tried and often failed to get data from the authors who published in their journal! If the nontransparency of expert advice were itself transparent then we would simply ignore those who advocate policies without sharing their data.

Conclusion

The AEA ethics guidelines ask for disclosures of financial temptations to bias. This is surely a significant improvement over no disclosure. The temptation to bend one's results in favor of a client who financially supports the research is now perhaps an uncontroversial concern.[9] Our concern, however, is that there are other private reasons

[8] According to reporter who corresponded with the student who discovered the error (Weisenthal 2013) the raw data were published on the web but it wasn't until the spreadsheet, which wasn't publically available, came that the problem was discovered.

[9] The fact, however, that financial disclosure has only recently entered the economics discourse while there has long been a code of ethics in statistics (Levy and Peart, 2008) suggests that there has been rather more resistance to admitting that private interests might clash with the public interest in economics than other disciplines.

for bias. An advice giver might, for instance, have a nonmonetary ("sympathetic") connection with the advice seeker. Or, a researcher might hold with a particular "system" as Adam Smith put it. In today's parlance he or she might have ideological attachments or policy commitments, or commitments to governing principles for society. The commitment to "social justice" or "classical liberalism," for example, might influence an economist's model specification or choice of estimation technique which of course in turn yield specific conclusions in favor of the presupposed (but hidden) commitment. This is not to suggest that economists should refrain from having commitments—the impossible—but instead to maintain that the commitments themselves might constitute relevant information as the results (or advice) become public, are published in a journal or are otherwise dispersed to a more general audience. We suggest that such sympathetic connections will be revealed best by detailing the history of one's work, including not least one's consulting history, the policy positions one has advocated in consulting and academic work.

Economists have, indeed, occasionally recognized that they have enormous influence in the business of persuasion, which can entail diverse forms of reward. Paul Samuelson's remark about the rewards associated with making his conclusions widely known speaks directly to the potential for influence and the nonmonetary reward that accrues from writing textbooks: "Let those who will, write the nation's laws if I can write its textbooks" (quoted in Colander and Landreth, 1996: 28). For those whose expertise is prized, influence is gained by giving highly regarded advice. If the advice is regarded as ill-informed or wrong, then the expert loses face or influence. Thus the expert will be asymmetrically motivated to accept confirming evidence and reject contradictory evidence. There is consequently a certain stickiness of models with respect to falsifying evidence. We have documented this stickiness in the context of the leading textbook comparisons, including that of Samuelson, of Soviet and American growth after 1960 (Levy and Peart, 2011*b*).[10]

Interestingly, our concern about the nonmonetary connections between those who give and receive advice was shared by Ronald Coase. In 1968 Coase was accused of yielding to the sort of influence addressed in the AEA guidelines, of advocating for the Zenith Corporation as a result of financial incentives or being a hired advocate for Zenith. Coase responded with a letter that flatly denied that there was any monetary connection between himself and Zenith. But he then went on to recognize the second reason for bias we have identified, that of nonmonetary rewards that accrue from obtaining influence. Coase's letter suggested that many false arguments are circulated as a means to an end, advancing the "public interest," as he put it (Coase, 1968).

The foregoing has focused on two issues associated with the ethics of giving advice, problems that arise when there are nonmonetary incentives to bias one's advice, and

[10] In the context of a close examination of the methodology of economics, Blaug (1980) concludes that economists' empirical research "is like playing tennis with the net down: instead of attempting to refute testable predictions, modern economists all too frequently are satisfied to demonstrate that the real world conforms to their predictions . . . " (256).

those that arise when the expert has a commitment to particular principles or policy stances. We find these to be more intriguing and perhaps more difficult to deal with than simple financial incentives. First, it is likely the case that these nonmonetary inducements to bias are more pervasive than are financial ones; second, it may be harder to detect bias associated with prior ideological commitments. Here we find Pigou and Coase in agreement that the temptation especially occurs in the giving of advice, in public service. We propose in conclusion not that advisors should remain neutral with respect to their advisees but rather that they render more fully transparent non-monetary inducements to select evidence and estimation techniques. We propose an addendum to the AEA disclosure policy:

> *The authors should describe their consulting history in sufficient detail so that the reader can infer sympathetic connections.*

Acknowledgments

A conversation with James Buchanan helped us realize the importance of Rutledge Vining's methodological work for our project. We thank Eric Schliesser and Ross Emmett for comments on earlier versions and Jane Perry for careful proofreading. The mistakes that remain are our responsibility. In accord with the AEA requirements we assert that we have neither asked for nor received financial payment of any sort for the work reported in the paper. Nor, in accord with our concerns, do we have any history of paid consulting about econometric or statistical ethics. We do have a long history revealed in publications and committee membership of worry about statistical and econometric ethics.

References

Private Holding

Coase, Ronald. 1968. Letter to Dean Edward G. Barrett. William J. Baroody Collection, Manuscript Division, Library of Congress, Box 77.

Knight, Frank. [1935] 1951. *Ethics of Competition*. New York: Augustus Kelly. With John Rawls's Annotations.

Public Holdings

American Economics Association. 2012. American Economic Association adopts extensions to principles for author disclosure of conflict of interest. http://www.aeaweb.org/PDF_files/PR/AEA_Adopts_Extensions_to_Principles_for_Author_Disclosure_01-05-12.pdf.

Barry, Brian. 1973. *The Liberal Theory of Justice: A Critical Examination of the Principle Doctrines in Theory of Justice by John Rawls*. Oxford: Clarendon Press.

Blaug, Mark. 1980. *The Methodology of Economics*. Cambridge: Cambridge University Press.

Buchanan, James M. 1967. "Politics and Science: Reflections on Knight's Critique of Polanyi." *Ethics* 77: 303–310.

Caldwell, Bruce. 1995. Introduction. In F. A. Hayek, *Contra Keynes and Cambridge: Essays, Correspondence*, edited by Bruce Caldwell, pp. 1–48. Chicago: University of Chicago Press.

Coase, Ronald H. 1960. "The Problem of Social Cost." *Journal of Law and Economics* 3: 1–44.

Coase, Ronald H. 1993. "Law and Economics at Chicago." *Journal of Law and Economics* 36: 239–254.

Colander, David C., and Henry Landreth, eds. 1996. *The Coming of Keynesianism to America: Conversations with the Founders of Keynesian Economics*. Cheltenham, UK: Edward Elgar.

Cowen, Tyler. 2013. "An Update on the Reinhart Rogoff Critique and Some Observations." *Marginal Revolution*. http://marginalrevolution.com/marginalrevolution/2013/04/an-update-on-the-reinhart-and-rogoff-critique-and-some-observations.html

Dewald, William G., Thursby, Jerry G., and Anderson, Richard G. 1986. "Replication in Empirical Economics: The *Journal of Money, Credit and Banking* Project." *The American Economic Review* 76: 587–603.

Feigenbaum, Susan, and Levy, David M. 1996. "The Technological Obsolescence of Scientific Fraud." *Rationality and Society* 8: 261–276.

Froeb, Luke M., and Kobayashi, Bruce H. 1996. "Naive, Biased, Yet Bayesian: Can Juries Interpret Selectively Produced Evidence?" *The Journal of Law, Economics and Organization* 12: 257–276.

Hayek, F. A. 1994. *Hayek on Hayek: An Autobiographical Dialogue*, edited by Stephen Kresge and Leif Wenar. London: Routledge.

Heckman, James J. 1997. "The Intellectual Roots of the Law and Economics Movement." *Law and History Review* 15: 327–332.

Hutt, William H. 1936. *Economists and the Public*. London: Jonathan Cape.

Keynes, J. Neville. 1891. *The Scope and Method of Political Economy*. London and New York: Macmillan.

Kipling, Rudyard. 1895. "Neolithic Age." http://www.kipling.org.uk/poems_neolithic.htm

Knight, Frank H. 1924. "Some Fallacies in the Interpretation of Social Cost." *Quarterly Journal of Economics* 38 (4): 582–606.

Knight, Frank H. 1933. "Preface to the Re-Issue." In *Risk, Uncertainty and Profit*. London: London School of Economics and Political Science.

Koopmans, Tjalling. 1949. "Methodological Issues in Quantitative Economics: A Reply." *Review of Economics and Statistics* 31: 86–91.

Leamer, Edward S. 1978. *Specification Searches—Ad Hoc Inferences with Nonexperimental Data*. New York: John Wiley & Sons.

Leamer. Edward S. 1983. "Let's Take the Con out of Econometrics." *The American Economic Review* 71: 33–41.

Levy, David M., and Peart, Sandra J. 2008. "Inducing Greater Transparency: Towards the Establishment of Ethical Rules in Econometrics." *Eastern Economic Journal* 34: 103–114.

Levy, David M., and Peart, Sandra J. 2010*a*. "Prudence with Biased Experts: Rating Agencies and Regulators." http://papers.ssrn.com/sol3/papers.cfm?abstract_id=1681609.

Levy, David M., and Peart, Sandra J. 2010*b*. "Richard Whately and the Gospel of Transparency." *American Journal of Economics and Sociology* 69: 166–187.

Levy, David M., and Peart, Sandra J. 2011*a*. "The Mock Trial of the Economists." http://jepson.richmond.edu/conferences/adam-smith/paper11levy-peart.pdf

Levy, David M., and Peart, Sandra J. 2011*b*. "Soviet Growth and American Textbooks: An Endogenous Past." *Journal of Economic Behavior and Organization*. 76: 110–125.

Levy, David M., and Peart, Sandra J. 2013. "Adam Smith on the State: Language and Reform." *Oxford Handbook on Adam Smith*, edited by Christopher J. Berry, Maria Paganelli, and Craig Smith, pp. 372–392. Oxford: Oxford University Press.

Lipsey, R. G., and Lancaster, Kevin. 1956–57. "The General Theory of Second Best. *The Review of Economic Studies* 24: 11–32.

Malinvaud, Edmond. 1972. "The Scientific Papers of Tjalling C. Koopmans: A Review Article." *Journal of Economic Literature* 10: 798–802.

Malinvaud, Edmond. [1983] 1988. "Econometric Methodology at the Cowles Commission: Rise and Maturity' [Address to the 50th Anniversary Cowles Celebration: 1983]. *Econometric Theory* 4: 187–209.

Peart, Sandra J., and Levy, David M. 2003. "Denying Human Homogeneity: Eugenics and the Making of Post-classical Economics." *Journal of the History of Economic Thought* 25: 261–288.

Peart, Sandra J., and Levy, David M. 2005. *The "Vanity of the Philosopher": From Equality to Hierarchy in Post-Classical Economics*. Ann Arbor: University of Michigan Press.

Pigou, Arthur C. 1918. *The Economics of Welfare*. London: Macmillan.

Pigou, Arthur C. [1935] 1936. *Economics in Practice*. London: Macmillan.

Pigou, A. C. 1953. *Alfred Marshall and Current Thought*. London: Macmillan.

Posner, Richard A. 1999. "An Economic Approach to Legal Evidence." *Stanford Law Review* 51: 1477–1546.

Rawls, John. [1971] 1999. *A Theory of Justice*. Revised edition. Cambridge, MA: Harvard University Press.

Sims, C. A. 1980. "Macroeconomics and Reality." *Econometrica* 48: 1–48.

Vining, Rutledge. 1949. "Methodological Issues in Quantitative Economics." *Review of Economics and Statistics* 31: 77–86.

Vining, Rutledge. 1950. "Methodological Issues in Quantitative Economics: Variations on a Theme by F. H. Knight." *The American Economic Review* 40: 267–284.

Vining, Rutledge. 1956. *Economics in the United States of America*. Paris: UNESCO.

Vining, Rutledge. 1984. *On Appraising the Performance of an Economic System: What an Economic System Is, and the Norms Implied in Observers' Adverse Reactions to the Outcome of Its Working*. New York: Cambridge University Press.

Weisenthal, Joe. May 26, 2013. "The Grad Student Who Busted Reinhart and Rogoff Explains How Open They Really Were with their Data." *Business Insider*. http://www.businessinsider.com/thomas-herndon-on-reinhart-and-rogoffs-data-availability-2013-5.

CHAPTER 32

FIRST TELL NO UNTRUTH

ALAN FREEMAN

Pierre je veux tout savoir/dis-moi la vérité . . .

question stupide et grandiose

Pierre ne sait que répondre/il est perdu/il est prisonnier/coincé par ses promesses
on lui demande des comptes

en face de lui/une machine à compter/une machine à écrire des lettres d'amour/

une machine à souffrir/le saisit/s'accroche à lui
Pierre dis-moi la vérité

– Jacques Prévert, *Rue de Seine* (1946)

Introduction

This chapter argues that the precept "first tell no untruth" is the ethical equivalent, for an economist, of the Hippocratic injunction "first do no harm."[1] If economists unjustifiably claim truth for their statements, and if people act on these statements when different actions could have resulted in better outcomes, then harm has been done, to which the statements have contributed materially. If, moreover, there are known critical practices which, had they been employed, would have given grounds to doubt the claim of truth, this harm is avoidable. Economists therefore have an ethical duty to adopt such critical practices.

[1] Many pluralists from the AHE, FAPE, ICAPE, and WEA have influenced this document, in particular Ali Douai, Andy Denis, Radhika Desai, Edward Fullbrook, Andrew Kliman, Dany Lang, Fred Lee, Andrew Mearman, Jamie Morgan, Ioana Negru, and Erik Olsen. I am indebted to Victoria Chick and Serap Kayatekin, co-editors of the 2014 CJE special edition on Whig history and to George DeMartino's seminal work and patience. My 10 years as an economist with the Greater London Authority were as formative as my interactions with colleagues there. Students from the UK "Rethinking Economics" collective provided hope and inspiration in equal measure. All mistakes are my own.

This approach scrupulously avoids any special definition of truth. Its premise is the fact that economists produce statements which they claim to be true, basing such assertions on the further claim that economics equips them with sufficient special expertise and knowledge that the public may place confidence in these statements. This, I will show, does not stand up to an examination of what economists actually do. They are subject to systematic pressures, to which their profession has succumbed over time,[2] to make unjustifiable claims of truth.

This practice arises not from malign intent but from economists' function in modern society. They are in general employed to inform, justify, and influence decisions by means of arguments presented as truths. Contracts between economists and their employers impose, explicitly or implicitly, an expectation that they will certify information as true, irrespective of whether they are in a position to judge. This is the principal origin of the harm they cause.

Ethical responsibility for this harm is therefore mutual and collective. Employers abnegate responsibility for choices, using economic advice, in effect, to hide behind its authority and justify what are really either political decisions or decisions with political consequences by presenting them as unavoidable. Economists are expected to produce, on behalf of their employers, explanations and advice that suit the employers' purpose.

They do not always do so, and frequent ethical dilemmas arise precisely because they become aware that performance in their jobs depends on preferring persuasiveness over truth. But such constraints do not absolve the economist of ethical responsibility because obeying instructions is not an ethical defence. A range of ethical responses reduce culpability; they include warning the public, dissuading employers from demanding unjustifiable conclusions, qualifying economic judgments, explaining their presuppositions, and above all, presenting alternative conclusions which can legitimately be drawn.

Economists are dissuaded from such responses by systematic social pressure to present each judgment as the only one possible, thus allowing agents who act on their advice to claim that they have no choice. In place of truth, society both accepts and demands plausible simulacra, fostering what I term the "monotheoretic fallacy": the thesis that economics is equipped to provide a single answer, deduced from a single theoretical premise, to any question an economist may face. This, in turn, provides the rationale for "monotheoretic practice": economists are expected, trained, and enjoined to give single answers informed by single theories, which can be presented as true by denying the existence of alternatives.[3]

I deduce the need for a code of ethics for economics of an unusual type: it should be rooted in a *mutual and collective* responsibility to avoid untruth. The goal is to protect society against the harmful consequences of poor economic judgments and to protect economists and their profession against the monotheoretic pressure of society.

[2] Economics is not a profession in the strict sense of law or accountancy, but I describe it as one because it behaves and is treated as if it was (see Freeman, 2009).

[3] Denis (2009), Freeman (2007a), Lee (2007), Dow (2009), and Elsner (2009) are among many works that establish these points, first surfacing in a declaration by 44 economists, including four Riksbank Nobel Laureates, in the *American Economic Review* (Hodgson, Mäki, and McCloskey, 1992).

The chief critical constituent of this responsibility is what I term "systematic pluralism."[4] This is the requirement to consider a range of possible ways of answering each definite question based on a range of legitimate theories. Such a requirement is mutual in that economists should supply it, and employers should demand it. It is collective in that it holds individuals responsible for collective conduct by governing all practices which affect the output and capacities of the economics profession: hiring, promotion, selection for publication, recognition, or the allocation of funds.

Systematic pluralism, if adopted by sufficient numbers of economists, institutions, publications, employers, and students, would provide meaningful protection against monotheoretic practice, reconstituting economics as a scientific discipline which assumes a properly circumscribed role in placing valid economic information at society's disposal.

The Production of Economic Knowledge

The literature on pluralism is abundant but misunderstood. The most common misconception is that pluralism means a refusal to give an answer. Pluralism, however, governs not what the answer is, but how it should be produced.

Economics generally claims that in giving single answers it is behaving "like a real science."[5] This arises from a fundamental confusion about what scientists actually do. Many sciences indeed provide valid single answers; this does not make them monotheoretic. Whilst it may be true that if you ask a physicist where to point a rocket in order to land it at a certain point, she will not give a range of options, her single answer is only made possible by a community of experimenters who test a huge variety of hypotheses and theories, selecting those that best explain the entire range of observations at their disposal by applying systematic doubt. Successful science is thus "internally pluralist."

To clarify this point, I distinguish a *legitimate* from a *valid* theory. A legitimate theory is fit to be tested against others: it is internally consistent, relevant, and has not been conclusively refuted by evidence. A valid theory is one particular legitimate theory that best explains the facts. Scientists thus treat the relativistic and fixed-frame theories of space-time as legitimate even though relativistic theory is currently held to be valid because it best explains the results of the ever more sophisticated experiments they use to test these two theories. Any professional scientist must be well versed in both, even though only one is currently considered applicable when answering practical questions.

[4] Many other writers have proposed similar terms: for example Denis (2009) and Elsner (2009).

[5] See, for example, QAA (2007), see also the more recent debate on the revision of the UK curriculum (CORE (2013), Coyle (2012), INET (2011), Morgan et al. (2014)) which instantiates this approach, in combination with Freeman (2007*a*, 2009) which dissect it.

Though other sciences do produce single conclusions, then, pluralism is indispensable to their production: without taking account of many possible approaches, the single answer given could not be given; if given, it could not be relied on. The renunciation of pluralism by conventional economics is therefore profoundly antiscientific, and accounts for the dogmatic, religious character of many economic ideas (Freeman, 2007*b*). If any enquiry begins by ruling out as illegitimate theories that may have a bearing on the problem at hand, then the most basic prerequisite of good science—the testing of a variety of hypotheses—is absent from the start.

How, then, has economics succumbed to this antiscientific pressure? Materially, the explanation lies in its relation to society, assessed in the next section. The underlying theoretical problem, however, is the nature of economic knowledge. "Internal pluralism" works for rocket scientists because they can isolate and test all the factors which affect the outcome of a launch before it takes place. Economics cannot; by its nature, it cannot isolate the causes which affect the outcome of an economic action prior to undertaking the action.

To illustrate this point, consider the consequences of the "shock therapy" policies adopted by Russian and Polish policymakers, drawing on advice from economists like Sachs and Åslund. DeMartino (2011: 8, 147, 149–150) sets out considerable evidence that avoidable harm arose from these policies. Should the advice have been issued? Was it soundly based?

Contemporary judgments fall into four categories: shock therapy was right and did work; it was wrong and did not work; it was right, but frustrated by unforeseen events; or it was never really applied. We do not need to establish which of these is "correct" because the very fact of this disagreement proves the critical point: if historians cannot even agree in *hindsight* on the effects of these measures, how can economists claim to predict them *in advance*? As DeMartino (2011: 9) puts it "Given the absence of historical precedents for economic transformations of this scale, it is clear that the reformers subjected countries to economic experimentation without sufficient knowledge . . . "

Was shock therapy perhaps a special case, not normally encountered by economists? Closer consideration suggests not. Uncertainty about outcomes arises whenever single economic causes cannot be isolated from others—including, not least, the economic factors that were ignored when predicting the outcome. This applies to a wide range of economic judgments because of the sheer complexity of even small systems of economic interactions.[6]

This is precisely why economics, alone among the social sciences, deploys the mumbled absolution "*ceteris paribus*": economists know in their heart of hearts that factors

[6] A further point, which space prevents us exploring, is that economic causes include the effects of knowing about them: every economic action thus alters its own premises. Many sophisticated theories recoil from the obvious conclusion that no economic truth can be wholly known in advance of acting upon it. The very notion of complete, positive, advance knowledge of the effect of economic actions is as internally self-contradictory as pre-quantum mechanics; the failure to recognise this "role of the active observer" infuses conventional economics with a peculiarly ancient Victorian positivism which would be quaint were its consequences less barbaric.

other than those they fasten on will almost certainly intervene to produce results other than those predicted. This knowledge is also the original reason for econometrics itself—introduced precisely as a substitute for the isolation of causes available to the experimental scientist.

Nor does this reduce to problems of scale or even isolation as such: it arises from the inherent complexity of economic systems. The isolated province of Manitoba in which I live has a tiny population in comparison with many minor municipalities, yet has the full range of social classes and political institutions that characterize any major state. The very fact of a world market and the multiplicity of invisible bonds which this creates between humans the world over mean that even the most microeconomic action has complex effects which can never be fully isolated from each other.

In summary, the consequences of even the simplest economic actions cannot be reliably predicted in any way except by allowing them to happen. This does not mean there are no economic truths, nor that no economic hypothesis can be tested; it simply means that we cannot fully determine the validity of claims about the effects of economic action in advance. In consequence, economists themselves cannot conduct all the tests required to make a reliable judgment that an economic claim is true. The verification of the claim has to include the experience of those affected by it.

It follows that on scientific as well as democratic grounds, political and social actors must make, and be allowed to make, informed choices by selecting from a range of possible actions, by being informed of the presuppositions of each, and by monitoring the outcome of the actions chosen. That is to say, responsibility for validating most economic predictions is mutual, so that economic specialists, and society as a whole, must undertake it jointly. The monotheoretic fallacy, seen in this light, reduces to the idea that economic specialization is alone sufficient to produce valid economic knowledge: that economists can *preselect* a single theory and consequential action in advance of the test of practice.

How Do Economists Do Harm?

The previous section explained why unjustifiable claims of economic truth may occur. To what extent does this happen, what factors make it more likely, and what can counteract or mitigate these factors? To study this, we return to the mutual relation between society and its economists.

Society uses economists by employing them. This may seem a commonplace, but immediately distinguishes the ethical problems facing an economist from those facing, say, a parent or a private car driver. It leads to ethical responsibilities defined, essentially, by the job of an economist. The potential for "econogenic harm" to use DeMartino's terminology in this volume (pp. 71–97), arises when economists either carry out the duties of their employment or equip other economists to do so. What are these duties?

The specific function of economists, in modern society, is to provide information on the basis of which others will make decisions. The concept of information naturally includes advice, which is simply information of the special type "if you undertake policy A, it will lead to outcome B." A separation of decision-making functions is thus involved in the very existence of a distinct occupation or specialization of "economist." Even where economists directly make policy—as for example in a central bank or a planning board—their actions are invariably justified in terms of the information on which they are based, as anyone who has attended a Bank of England briefing can testify.

In nearly all modern cases, the outcome of economic advice is a decision to take an action. A bank might for example change interest rates, or conduct market operations; a producer might decide to enter a market, to invest, or to change a price; a government agency might decide to spend money, levy taxes, or set regulatory policies. Before doing so, they take economic advice in the expectation that their actions will be better informed.

The validity of the information provided to the actor is thus critical to the potential for harm. Defining unreliable information as that which, when acted on, may or does lead to harmful consequences that were not predicted, it is a syllogistic deduction that an economist risks causing harm by supplying unreliable information.

The risk arises not so much from demonstrably false information as from information for which the claim of truth is unjustifiably advanced. Decision makers who act on unreliable information are likely to take insufficient precautions against the risk of failure and, being wrongly certain, will fail to explore different decisions that, had they been properly informed, they would, could, and should have explored. Shock therapy would have been a considerably less likely choice if even the limited hindsight we now dispose of had been available at the time; alternative policies such as the Chinese road, slow adaptive change, or even the status quo would have been more likely. The harm thus arose because a conclusion for which economists had no business claiming certainty was presented, and accepted, as the only possible course of action.

This sheds further light on the ethical role of the advisor, studied in Dennis Thompson's (1983, 1987) analysis of the ethos of "moral insulation"—the widespread view that advisors are mere technocrats who present neutral facts, on the basis of which decision makers undertake actions for which they bear full and independent responsibility. This is rooted in the conventional positive-normative distinction, as noted by Amy (1984: 581, cited by DeMartino, 2011: 73)

Trained in positivist social science, analysts could draw a sharp distinction between normative questions and factual questions. In practice, this meant that analysts could focus on questions of means, while leaving questions of ends to policymakers.

Thompson explores several flaws in the idea that economists have no ethical responsibility for what is done with their advice. The concept of avoidable untruth adds a further dimension: if the information itself is unreliable, its provider bears responsibility for the effects of using it. This holds even if the fault lies with the user's insistence: if a builder demands numbers that lead ultimately to a bridge collapsing, or a fraudster commissions accounts to hide his misdemeanours, this does not absolve the architect or the accountant who provides what was requested.

Why does economics overlook this obvious connection between quality of information and ethical consequences? Essentially, because the positivist tradition treats provision of bad information as *negligence*, ignoring the far more serious consequences of *misleading*. This reduction of misleading to mere competence excludes the most serious danger of all; namely collective failure: the systematic production of misleading information.

Systemic Error and the Duty of Reform

The fact that economists can misinform is hardly controversial; the most self-satisfied economist will gleefully concede the mistakes of his or her colleagues. Indeed, DeMartino (2011) found that many economists are concerned ethically about their own mistakes.

More contested is the scale and cause of these mistakes. Objective scholars must consider Colander et al.'s (2009) well-evidenced claim that economics, by analogy with the so-called systemic crisis of financial markets that hit in 2007, itself underwent "systemic failure"

> If one browses through the academic macroeconomics and finance literature, "systemic crisis" appears like an otherworldly event that is absent from economic models. Most models, by design, offer no immediate handle on how to think about or deal with this recurring phenomenon. In our hour of greatest need, societies around the world are left to grope in the dark without a theory. That, to us, is a systemic failure of the economics profession.

It is a truth generally acknowledged that in the run-up to the crash, the great majority of those statements from economists, on which the public relied, were harmfully misleading. This diagnosis is supported by sources which most economists treat as impeccable. Thus, Alan Greenspan (Norris, 2008)

> In recent decades, a vast risk management and pricing system has evolved . . . A Nobel Prize was awarded for the discovery of the pricing model that underpins much of the advance in derivatives markets. This modern risk management paradigm held sway for decades. The whole intellectual edifice, however, collapsed in the summer of last year.

The International Monetary Fund's (IMF) independent evaluation office, in its investigation into the conduct of the IMF in the run-up to the crisis (IEO, 2011), found that

> The IMF's ability to correctly identify the mounting risks was hindered by a high degree of groupthink, intellectual capture, a general mind-set that a major financial crisis in large advanced economies was unlikely, and incomplete analytical approaches.

Both Greenspan and the IMF are widely recognized as sources of authority by economists, who are therefore in no position to reject these conclusions just because they are critical of their own profession. Economics, we must honestly conclude, is prone not merely to occasional error, but also to the systematic and repeated production of misleading information.

This fact, above all, calls into question the notion that the sole duty of an ethical economist is to be technically competent. When a discipline as a whole repeatedly misleads, the response "do the same thing but better" is not merely inadequate but counterproductive: conformity to an erroneous norm simply reinforces the errors. The point is to do something different. What might that "something" be? The obvious ethical answer is to put right whatever led to the systemic errors. So what, actually, did lead to these errors?

Bias and the Regulatory Capture of Economics

Even major errors do not necessarily prevent a discipline from correcting its own mistakes. Many sciences do this, some of them quite frequently. Can economics do so? The reason for skepticism on this front is the critical issue of *bias* and its origins.

Any systematic error in economics acts to the advantage of one class or part of society; this follows from the zero-sum nature of distribution. Econogenic harm is *selective*: when one group gains from misleading information, another loses. This has many ethical consequences, of which the most difficult is the complex question of ethical optimality. If an action will harm some, and benefit others, by what criterion do we adopt it?

This issue is not foreign to economics, which reflects a long tradition of inquiry into ethical truth. Starting with the Benthamite principle of the "greatest good of the greatest number," it has evolved not only welfare economics but optimality principles on which most of its doctrines rest. It is not my purpose here to question these doctrines, but rather to show that economics itself recognizes, implicitly or explicitly, the question "how may the least harm be done?"

The conventional presentation of this issue omits a vital point: the beneficiaries of misleading judgments have an interest in misleading advice. Anyone who employs an economist stands to gain from overstating the social benefits of a decision that also benefits the employer. The issue of "conflict of interest" is from this point of view a misdirected charge. The issue is one of *bias*. The risk is, simply put, that the material interest of securing selective benefits from the advice may outweigh intellectual interest in getting it right.

Particularly important here is that nearly all economic actions, even purely private ones, have public effects and will therefore be subject to public scrutiny and, potentially, regulation. It follows that any potential beneficiaries—financial interests, employers, regulated companies providing public services, or, for that matter, trade unions and nongovernmental organizations (NGOs)—have an interest in which economic judgments are presented as true.

The risk should be evident to any student of regulation theory. The goal of any rational actor whose interests are affected by political decisions is to influence those decisions to the benefit of the actor. If that actor employs economists, she or he will impose a rhetorical purpose: they will judge those economists, at least in part, by whether they produce successful and influential arguments that establish the public benefits of the employer's actions.

This does not mean that these arguments are never based on truth, since truth is itself a persuasive argument. It does however introduce a systematic bias toward selecting not only beneficially misleading information, but also economists who can supply it. Any practicing economist is familiar with the mechanisms involved. Who among us has been in a report preparation meeting at which either the question on the table—or the elephant in the room—is "will the boss accept what we are about to say?"

This directs our attention to a feature of economics specific to its postwar history in the United Kingdom and the United States, which is the increasing role and concentration of professional economists in government. A striking feature of DeMartino's (2011: 23–24) figures on graduate employment is the high proportion of nonteaching applied economists who work in a branch of government—nearly half, with a further 15–20 percent in financial institutions such as the IMF, which have significant policy functions. In the United Kingdom, the monotonic growth of government economists has produced a special branch of government—the Government Economic Service (GES)—which has become a mandarinate, recruiting economists early and retaining them for life. The GES also staffs the Bank of England. A further feature of the UK system is the exceptional influence of the Treasury—the only government department entitled to scrutinize the plans of other departments before they go to the minister concerned.

All the above appears to provide economists with exceptional power and influence within government. But it is for precisely this reason that the dangers of theoretical corruption are greater. It means that any economist outside the government, seeking to influence government policy, will begin from the requirement of influencing government economists.

This fact has profound consequences: it introduces a systematic material basis for theoretical bias and sheds profound light on what I (Freeman, 2009), Zingales (2013), and Turner (Tett, 2009); see also Ferguson (2012) describe as the "regulatory capture" of economics. Regulatory capture is, ironically, a term coined by economics itself to describe how an authority responsible for regulating an industry—such as electricity or telecommunications—becomes systematically biased in favor of those it regulates. However, economics *itself* functions as a regulatory institution, both because of its governmental role and because so many economic judgments, even in the private sector, are concerned with influencing the policies of governmental and paragovernmental institutions. As Zingales points out

> Regulatory capture is . . . driven by standard economic incentives, which push even the most well-intentioned regulators to cater to the interest of the regulated. These incentives are built in their positions.

Zingales and others cite a series of causal mechanisms of capture including information dependency, career incentive, and taxpayer interest to reach the reasonable conclusion that "[i]f these are the reasons why regulators are captured, it is not clear why economists are not captured as well."

The critical point for our analysis is this: given bias, and in the absence of any systematic corrective (such as a code of ethics), the tendency to capture is built into the present relation between employers and economists. Employers have a material interest in securing biased judgments—and economists have a material interest in providing them. This mutuality of interest is a red-light warning sign. It tells us that in the absence of a countervailing pressure, expressed precisely in the ethical commitment to truth, standard rational choice analysis as developed by economics itself—that these material forces will prevail.

And, in fact, a series of factors reinforce the direct pressures just cited, as Zingales notes. Career pressure extends beyond immediate employment, because careers are built through reputation, established from early years through acceptance into prestige institutions, research record, and publication. The institutions that monitor these markers of distinction are in turn subjected to pressures of selective funding, employer recognition, government recognition, and peer recognition thus constituting a complex set of mutually reinforcing mechanisms all of which point in a single direction.

By degrees, economics itself has yielded to the relentless pressure to produce definitive statements that sound good, but are not justifiable by good scientific practice. Its corrosive relationship to society has elevated criteria of authority and conformity (Freeman, 2009) to the status of adequate substitutes for logic, evidence, and systematic doubt. Systems for teaching, research, publication, promotion, recognition, and reward have evolved to make monotheoretic practice a professional norm, presented to the public as "correct" economics.

The result is "institutional monotheoreticism": the structures responsible for producing and certifying economic ideas have been pared down to the single function of efficiently implementing monotheoretic practice, thus eliminating all but the most minimally divergent thought and all but the most minimally critical practitioners and thinkers.

Monotheoreticism, I would argue, is a critical integrating factor. To the mass of career mechanisms which impel economists in the direction of bias and capture, it adds the deadening weight of the pressure to conform. A special edition of the *Cambridge Journal of Economics* (Freeman, Chick, and Kayatekin, 2014) spells out a decisive consequence: the human and intellectual capacity of economics, as a body, to recognize error and correct it has been depleted close to exhaustion by the systematic elimination of dissenting thought and the parallel depletion of dissenting, critical or creative thinkers.

The very possibility of "thinking differently" is serious diminished whenever the canon of legitimate theory becomes narrowed to a small range of "acceptable" ideas. One of the reasons that economics found it so hard to foresee the crisis is that it had stopped teaching—or even entertaining—the ideas of thinkers like Keynes, Marx, Veblen, or Polanyi, which might lead to the threatening deduction that something could go wrong.

The most typical mechanism of monotheoreticism is a systematic confusion between validity and legitimacy. When economics ceases to entertain Keynes's, Marx's, or Veblen's analysis of a capitalist economy, it does not merely demote them to the status of "possibly valid"—that is, legitimate—theories that students and researchers should be versed in, but also eliminates these theories from its thinking.

I summarize this by the term "institutional delegitimation." Research articles based on non-mainstream theories are rejected, promotions are denied, appointments become difficult, whole departments are eliminated. Alternative approaches vanish from the curriculum; journals carrying heterodox ideas are downgraded, thus rendering funding ever more difficult to secure. Ever more sophisticated reasons for rejecting discarded ideas are invented: entire industries emerge dedicated to disproving them.[7] This intellectual dissipation brings about a parallel depletion of sheer human capital because those who wish to learn, explore, or teach the abandoned ideas can no longer find employment.[8]

These two developments are inimical to any prospect of spontaneous self-reform. For economics, like a normal science, to "change its mind" and adopt new theories, it must contain within itself the capacity to do so. But the twin extirpation of dissenting ideas and dissenting thinkers destroys this capacity. Systematic pluralism is, therefore, something beyond a mere regularization of an existing practice; it is the only means to introduce, into the body politic of economics, the antidote to a self-inflicted wasting disease that has passed the point where remission is a likely event.

Can an Ethical Principle Be Enforced?

I propose a strategy to respond to the two critical features of the econogenic harm identified at the start of this chapter. It deals with the *mutual* character of this harm by recognizing the joint responsibility of economists and their employers and to its *collective* character by placing responsibility on the individual economist for the conduct of her whole profession. This framing, critically, confers *rights* on the economist, above all the right to dissent and the right to criticize.

At various times, various ways of securing ethical practice have been advanced: a simple prescription with no binding consequence, a voluntary but noncontractual

[7] See, for example, Kliman (2014) on the treatment of Marx, and Chick and Tily (2014) on the treatment of Keynes.

[8] See the exhaustive empirical studies in Lee (2007) and Lee and Harley (1998).

commitment, a professional obligation or professional code of conduct, or a regulatory system.

I advance a fifth, distinct strategy: "First tell no untruth" should be translated into verifiable requirements in contracts between economists and their employers whether public, private, or scholarly. By verifiable requirements, I mean generally acceptable tests, which can be objectively applied inorder to ascertain whether an economist has exercised due care to avoid presenting untrue statements as if they were true. This is neither a form of external regulation nor is it a code of practice. It simply means that, since the harm done by economists is an outcome of the social function of economics, a new kind of social contract is required if this harm is to be reduced. It should be noticed that there is actually a dual ethical precept involved. Economists should avoid untruth; however, society should also cease pressuring them to produce it. Therefore, economists should work with society to devise mutually agreed, verifiable tests that can be used to frustrate the operation of the monotheoretic fallacy by monitoring the operation of systematic pluralism.

This approach to the relation between an ethical principle and the action that can be taken to make it operational responds to the very welcome debate initiated by DeMartino (2011). Concern with ethical practice has different origins on the two sides of the Atlantic. In Britain and Europe—also, not unimportantly, in Australia—the preoccupation has been with regulatory methods and principles, whereas in North America it is more concerned with individual principles of conduct. I discovered some of the differences in the course of DeMartino's talk to the UK-based Association for Heterodox Economists (DeMartino, 2012) in which he made clear the argument already put forward in his book that ethics should not be enforceable by regulation or a formal code. I was quite surprised by this and have been reflecting on it ever since. The differences arise, I think, because of the different institutional circumstances of the two debates.

In Britain, economics is already regulated; the debate has arisen because of growing disquiet, both within and outside the economics profession, that the results of this regulation are adverse. The issue is thus reform: the rectification of a regulatory system already in place. The first line of inquiry is naturally therefore to try to change the regulations. By way of information, the state and academic system as a whole in Britain have entered into a formal agreement overseen by a quasi-public institution, known as the Quality Assurance Authority (QAA) whose function is described by its founder (Dearing, 1997) as a "compact between higher education and society." The QAA intervenes across the spectrum of scholarly activity to prescribe and bring into effect regulatory schemas that govern both the content and practice of what, with a certain linguistic ambiguity that is important enough for us to draw attention to it, is termed "good economics."

A long exercise, termed the Subject Benchmarking Statement Exercise (SBSE), has tried to standardize the economics curriculum, in parallel with an exercise to benchmark research against international standards. The initiative fed into a controversial procedure which governs the allocation of a significant volume of research funding in the United Kingdom, termed the Research Assessment Exercise (RAE, now superseded by the Research Excellence Framework or REF) by introducing metrics of research performance, for the most part based on journal publication.[9] Whereas, in almost all subjects other than economics, practitioners avoided prescriptive definitions and indeed wrote in explicit commitments to pluralism, economics proposed explicitly monotheoretic teaching benchmarks tied to research metrics based, fundamentally, on a list of journals selected only for their authority: that is, on the self-selecting basis of conformity to existing norms. These exercises merely reinforced the already narrow concept of the subject as practiced in most UK institutions recorded by Lee (2007) and Lee and Harley (1998), creating instrumental recruitment and promotion practices confined to achieving high scores by the very standards that had been created as a consequence of the previous phase of selection for conformity.

Different, but no less monotheoretic arrangements prevail in the United States and also in Canada. Being less familiar with them I restrict my comments on them, except to note that, whereas the primary concern east of the Atlantic has been inappropriate regulation, the west side appears more concerned about inappropriate commercial intrusion. Ethics in this context is more connected to the related notions of conflict of interest, and academic independence. The interrelation, and convergence, between these two debates should be self-evident, but it is important to begin with a clear understanding of the origin of the differences in approach and concerns.

The first point is to recognize that self-regulation cannot be expected to work; it cannot overcome the institutional bias that has been now built into the discipline of economics because the latter has become self-reinforcing. An institutionalized monotheoretic structure cannot reform itself.

I agree that a professional code of conduct, which provides guarantees of compliance with prevailing professional norms will not work, although for different reasons. The issue is not whether codes of conduct work in other professions, but that economics is not a normal profession. A code of conduct for economists, like an inquiry into best practice for the inquisition, would miss the point of the exercise. Ethical responsibility is required precisely because it is external to and may well conflict with pressures emanating from within the profession.

However, external regulation itself does not provide the answer: in the case of the QAA, it has been tried and has failed. The regulatory authority has merely reflected back to the discipline of economics the self-image which it has already constructed. Moreover, because the underlying problem is regulatory capture, stronger regulation is unlikely to do anything more than reinforce the existing adverse practices which led to this capture.

[9] Curiously, neither the QAA nor the RAE has developed or even discussed any proposals to verify the standards of the journals themselves. It should be evident that if a regulatory system is made to depend on acceptance of outputs by unregulated sources of authority, then a rational strategy for regulatory capture would be to acquire influence over the decisions of these sources. However, this conclusion appears to have escaped the regulatory authorities. The peer review system in science as a whole, with economics included as a subcategory, was itself the subject of a separate parliamentary inquiry (see AHE, 2011).

As a kind of codicil, this chapter would be incomplete without pointing out that heterodoxy is itself not the answer. Without pluralism, heterodoxy simply generates a system of competing orthodoxies. Working in UK government, I have seen an extraordinary procession of "theories in waiting" who line up during crises to present patent theories for the attention of government advisors. As a consequence, most so-called heterodoxies reproduce all the monotheoretic practices of orthodoxy with the added blight that they are not even subject to the minimal constraint of public attention. They therefore act as singularly effective policemen in weeding out, before alternative ideas can even reach the ears of the public, those especially dangerous theories that might stand in the way of being listened to. As Chick and Tily (2014), Freeman (2010), and Kliman (2014) meticulously document, the most effective suppression of Marx and Keynes has been conducted, respectively, by Marxists and Keynesians.

This is precisely why systematic pluralism does not simply mean a token monotheoretic Keynesian, Marxist, institutionalist, ecologist, or feminist in the ranks of otherwise respectable departments. The bar is much higher: every economist in the department should be familiar not only with mainstream ideas but also with their principal critics. Pluralism has to inform all aspects of teaching, research, publication, and funding, including the individual practice of the individual economist. If anything, systematic pluralism begins with the reform of heterodoxy.

How could such a contentious and difficult solution, which goes against the grain of 50 years of economic training, conceivably be implemented? The solution is suggested by the original cause of the problem: the relation between economists and society. The effect of the monotheoretic function of economics is that society loses the right to make informed choices between economic alternatives. The information deficit becomes a democratic deficit. Redress requires an alliance between pluralism and democracy; a social reclaiming of the right to make economic choices.

To this end I propose a *public contract* between economics and its users. Change will come about from a pincer movement. On the one hand, economists and their institutions, such as departments in higher education, journals, research units, and learned societies, can and should develop and promote examples of good pluralist practice, which they should promote. There are many examples of this, such as the actual practice of pluralist bodies like the UK Association for Heterodox Economics or the 10,000-strong World Economics Association,[10] or the growing body of work devoted to a pluralist economics in general and the curriculum in the United Kingdom and the United States in particular (see, e.g., Lawson, 2006; Fullbrook, 2008; Denis, 2009; Negru, 2010; Garnett and Mearman, 2011; Garnett and Reardon, 2011; Mearman 2011, AHE 2014).

From the other side, the users and certifiers of economics have to recognize—and reward—pluralism's true merits. A great deal would change if, for example, a demonstrated pluralist practice was made a precondition for admission to the notorious

[10] At www.worldeconomicsassociation.org

citation indexes which govern the publish-or-perish culture of modern academia or if journal editors and referees began systematically requiring, before accepting any submission as ready for publication, that it engage with, and recognize, the theories in the field that most directly conflict with those defended or used in the article.

When such pluralistic practices are codified and kitemarked so that good practice is recognized and rewarded not just by the community of practitioners but also by those who hire them and fund them; when it becomes a requirement for any submission to any government department, or any funding application for research, or any proposal for promotion, tenure, or appointment, to demonstrate how pluralism has been and will be applied: on that day, a truly scientific economics will be founded, and the way will be open for a society founded on genuine informed economic choice.

References

AHE. 2014. Redrafting project for the Subject Benchmark Statement in Economics. Available at http://hetecon.pbworks.com/pluralistSBSE

AHE. 2011. Submission to the Science and Technology Committee Enquiry into Peer Review. London: House of Commons.

Amy, D. J. 1984. "Why Policy Analysis and Ethics are Incompatible." *Journal of Policy Analysis and Management* 3(4): 573–591.

Chick, V. and G. Tily. 2014 "Whatever Happened to Keynes's Monetary Theory?" Forthcoming in Cambridge Journal of Economics.

Colander, D., H. Föllmer, A. Haas, M. Goldberg, K. Juselius, A. Kirman, T. Lux., and B. Sloth. 2009. "The Financial Crisis and the Systemic Failure of Academic Economics." Kiel working paper 1489, Kiel Institute for the World Economy.

CORE. 2013. "The INET CORE curriculum—Curriculum Open-access Resources in Economics: A project within INET's educational program." Mimeo supplied by the INET CORE project workshop at UK HM Treasury November 11, 2013.

Coyle, D. ed. 2012. *What's the Use of Economics?* London: London Publishing Partnership.

Dearing, R. 1997. Report of the National Committee of Inquiry into Higher Education ("The Dearing Report"). London: TSO.

Denis, A. 2009. "Pluralism in Economics Education." Editorial in *International Review of Economics Education* 8(2): 6–22.

DeMartino, G. 2011. *The Economist's Oath: On the Need for and Content of Professional Economic Ethics*. Oxford: Oxford University Press.

DeMartino, G. 2012. Speech to the Association for Heterodox Economics. Nottingham, July, 2012.

Dow, S. 2009. "History of Thought and Methodology in Pluralist Economics Education." *International Review of Economics Education* 8(2): 41–58.

Elsner, W. 2009. "Report on Peer Review in Economics." Presented to the European Workshop on "Assessing Heterodox Economics in a European Context." University of Bremen, June 26–27, 2009.

Ferguson, C. 2012. *Inside Job: The Financiers who Pulled off the Biggest Heist of the Century*. London: Oneworld Books.

Freeman, A. 2007*a*. "Catechism Versus Pluralism: the Heterodox Response to the National Undergraduate Curriculum Proposed by the UK Quality Assurance Authority." Available at http://mpra.ub.uni-muenchen.de/6832/

Freeman, A. 2007*b*. "Heavens Above: What Equilibrium Means for Economics." In *Equilibriam in Economics: Scope and Limits*, edited by V. Mosini, pp. 240–260. London: Routledge.

Freeman, A. 2009. "Towards a Pluralist Subject Benchmark Statement for Economics." *International Review of Economics Education* 8(2): 23–40.

Freeman, A. 2010. "Marxism Without Marx." *Capital and Class* 34(1): 84–97.

Freeman, A., V. Chick, and S. Kayatekin. 2014. "Whig History and the Reinterpretation of Economic Theory." Special edition of the *Cambridge Journal of Economics* 38(3): 519–529.

Fullbrook, E. 2008. *Pluralist Economics*. London: Zed Books.

Garnett, R., and A. Mearman. 2011. "Contending Perspectives Twenty Years on: What have our Students Learned?" *International Journal of Pluralism and Economics Education* 2(1): 2–18.

Garnett, R. F., Jr., and J. Reardon. 2011. "Pluralism in Economics Education." In *International Handbook on Teaching and Learning Economics*, edited by K. M. McGoldrick and Gail Hoyt. Aldershot: Edward Elgar.

Hodgson, G., U. Mäki, and D. McCloskey. 1992. "Plea for a Pluralistic and Rigorous Economics." *American Economic Review* 82(2): xxv.

IEO. 2011. "IMF Performance in the Run-Up to the Financial and Economic Crisis: IMF Surveillance in 2004–07." Washington, DC: IMF.

INET. 2011. "Building a global community of New Economic Thinkers: Inaugural Annual Report 2010-2011." New York: INET. Available at http://ineteconomics.org/sites/inet.civicactions.net/files/inet-annual-report-2010-2011.pdf

Kliman, A. 2014. "The Whiggish Foundations of Marxian and Sraffian Economics." *Cambridge Journal of Economics* 38(3): 643-661. doi: 10.1093/cje/bet045.

Lawson, T. 2006. "The Nature of Heterodox Economics." *Cambridge Journal of Economics* 30(4): 483–505.

Lee, F. 2007. "The Research Assessment Exercise, the State and the Dominance of Mainstream Economics in British Universities." *Cambridge Journal of Economics* 31(2): 309–325.

Lee, F., and S. Harley. 1998. "Peer Review, The Research Assessment Exercise and the Demise of Non-Mainstream Economics." *Capital and Class* 66: 23–53.

Mearman, A. 2011. "How Should Economics Curricula be Evaluated?" *International Review of Economics Education* 10(2): 50–62.

Morgan, J. (on behalf of the AHE). 2014. "Pluralism, Heterodoxy, and the Prospects for a New Economics Curriculum: Assessing the Potential of INET, *What's the Use of Economics*, and the CORE Project." Association for Heterodox Economics, Available at www.hetecon.net/documents/The_prospects_for_a_new_economic_curriculum.pdf

Negru, I. 2010. "Plurality to Pluralism in Economics Pedagogy: the Role of Critical Thinking." *International Journal for Pluralism in Economics Education* 1(3):185–193.

Norris, F. 2008, October 23. "Greenspan's Lament." *New York Times*. Available at http://economix.blogs.nytimes.com/2008/10/23/greenspans-lament/?_r=0?

Tett, G. 2009, August 27. "Could 'Tobin Tax' Reshape Financial Sector DNA?" *Financial Times*.

Thompson, D. F. 1983. "Ascribing Responsibility to Advisors in Government." *Ethics* 93(3): 546–560.

Thompson, D. F. 1987. *Political Ethics and Public Office*. Cambridge, MA: Harvard University Press.

QAA. 2007. "Economics." The Quality Assurance Agency for Higher Education. Available at http://www.qaa.ac.uk/Publications/InformationAndGuidance/Pages/Subject-benchmark-statement-Economics.aspx

World Economics Association (WEA). Available at worldeconomicsassociation.org.

Zingales, L. 2013. "Preventing Economists' Capture." In *Preventing Regulatory Capture: Special Interest Influence and How to Limit It*, edited by D. Carpenter and D. Moss, pp. 124-151. Cambridge: Cambridge University Press.

3. Forensic Economics

CHAPTER 33

ETHICAL ISSUES IN FORENSIC ECONOMICS

ROBERT J. THORNTON AND JOHN O. WARD

What Is Forensic Economics and Why Do Ethics Matter?

If one were to ask many people what the word "forensic" means, they might associate it with corpses, remembering the TV series of the 1970s and 1980s called *Quincy*. Played by Jack Klugman, Quincy was a forensic pathologist (a medical examiner) who used his physician skills to solve murders, often by performing autopsies. In fact, though, the word "forensic" has nothing to do with death, bodies, murders, or pathology. Its root is the Latin adjective *forensis* (itself related to *forum*), meaning "connected with the law-courts in Rome."[1]

So what is forensic economics and what do forensic economists do? Over the past several decades in the United States, the involvement of economists as consultants and expert witnesses in civil tort actions in courts of law has grown rapidly. This involvement has taken the form of economists being asked as "experts" to apply the methodology of economics to estimate damages in litigation most commonly involving personal injury and wrongful death, but also in other types of tort actions as well (as described in Types of Cases Handled by Forensic Economists). In most cases the forensic economist is asked by an attorney representing the plaintiff to undertake the necessary research and draw up a report in which the amount of damages is calculated. Sometimes the economist might later be called on to give a legal deposition or to testify in court on his or her estimates.

Parts of the first two sections have been adapted from Thornton and Ward (1999).

[1] *Oxford Latin Dictionary* (2004). One of the authors was a member of his high school debating club. The official name of the club was the "forensic society" but we never met in the morgue.

Not all who are asked to provide expert economic testimony on such matters are economists. Some are certified public accountants, some are actuaries, and some are vocational specialists. However, most often such experts are either academic economists associated with a university or economists working with a private consulting firm. Regardless of the credentials of the forensic economist, it is inevitable that at some point in their work the issue of ethics will be encountered.

Ethics are a concern in most professions—doctors, lawyers, engineers, accountants, and forensic economists. The Hippocratic Oath of physicians, the various codes of professional responsibility and ethical practices of attorneys and engineers, and the accrediting standards of CPAs all represent efforts to assure consumers of professional services of the quality, honesty, and fairness of those delivering those services. Forensic economists have developed similar standards of professional practice over the past several decades to assure attorneys and the legal system that those adopting such codes of behavior and practice are impartial, honest, and qualified to render their services as experts to the courts. The questions that we raise in this chapter are two. Do such statements of ethics really matter and, if so, how can they best be promoted?

Richard Posner has suggested that there is no compelling reason to believe either that such codes promote ethical behavior or that the courts should have any trust in self-professed standards of practice in judging the impartiality and honesty of the testimony of forensic economists. Posner instead presumes that the economist will serve as advocate for the party retaining him or her and that any pledged adherence to impartiality should be questioned. In his view, the adversarial nature of a tort and the competition of forensic economists for employment would promote bias in opinions of the forensic economist favorable to the party retaining him or her. Posner suggests that the way to obtain impartial economic opinion on economic damages in torts is to have the courts directly select forensic economists, preferably from a list maintained by an impartial third party such as the American Economic Association.[2]

On the other hand, the position of the National Association of Forensic Economics for the past 20 years has been that ethics for forensic economists do matter and that they can be promoted by personal adherence to a code of professional practice, by continuing education through participation in academic meetings, and through the development of a vigorous literature in the field of forensic economics. Some would add a system of enforcement to such a code, while others would rely on the market alone to police the profession. The majority of forensic economists appear to believe that the current system of selection of experts by adversaries in a tort action can produce impartial and honest testimony on economic damages and that a system of ethics can provide a path to impartiality within the existing legal framework.

[2] Remarks by Richard A. Posner presented at the panel discussion entitled "Ethics and the Economist as an Expert Witness in Litigation," Allied Social Science Association Meetings, Chicago IL, January 6, 2012. Judge Posner's remarks are summarized in George DeMartino, "Professional Economic Ethics: The Posnerian and Naïve Perspectives," *Journal of Forensic Economics* (2013).

We realize that this chapter may not provide definitive answers to the questions of whether ethics matter, whether a code of professional practice can produce impartial economic analysis, or whether the only way of obtaining impartial and honest economic testimony on damages in torts is for the courts to reform the system of selection and use of forensic economists. However, the chapter can provide a better understanding of what forensic economists do and what issues they face in addressing ethical issues.

Types of Cases Handled by Forensic Economists

In addition to cases involving personal injury and wrongful death, commercial litigation represents another area frequently calling for economic testimony on damages. Issues in commercial litigation typically involve claims of lost profits or destruction of a business because of breach of contract, patent or copyright infringement, or other such torts. Commercial litigation cases are usually more complex than personal injury/death cases and often involve many damages experts—economists, CPAs, and specialists in business valuation. Often, both the plaintiff(s) and defendant(s) in such cases will retain an expert.

Economists have also been retained in antitrust cases and public utility rate cases for more than half a century, but such areas of specialization involve far fewer economists than either personal injury/death or commercial litigation. The same is true of the use of economic experts in cases involving securities analysis or employment law, although wrongful employment termination cases are similar to personal injury cases with respect to the methodology that is employed.

The most common way by which economists become involved with the practice of forensic economics, however, continues to be via personal injury/death litigation; and ethical issues that arise in this type of litigation are the primary focus of this chapter. Decades ago, the first economists to engage in such litigation were typically academic economists with areas of specialization in labor economics, human resources, and/or econometrics. For most of these economists, their initial exposure to the subject began with a call from an attorney with a request to do a simple present value calculation of an injured or deceased individual's stream of lost earnings up to the age of retirement. The request was usually accompanied by an offer of a sizeable amount of compensation, which served as a strong inducement to become a forensic economist, at least until the economist encountered the sometimes gut-wrenching experience of depositions and trials. The field of legal combat sorted out the capable from the merely curious, or at least those with a thick skin from those without one. Also, 30 years ago the methods of loss calculation were very basic and could be performed simply with a financial calculator and a pad of paper. Guides on how to perform a lost earnings calculation were practically nonexistent, and only a few published papers on the subject existed. At that time the practice of forensic economics by academics was generally viewed with skepticism, if not outright disapproval, by fellow faculty, department chairs, deans, and tenure committees (although envy may also have been at work here). Nevertheless, the discipline of forensic economics did eventually generate a growing number of practitioners, a vigorous literature (including several journals, most notably the *Journal of Forensic Economics*), and a number of practical guides for computing economic damages (e.g., Gerald Martin, *Determining Economic Damages*). Today, academic economists still represent a plurality, if not a majority, of forensic economists. And the 800-member National Association of Forensic Economics (NAFE, the main association of forensic economists) consists of academic economists, full-time forensic economists, and CPAs—working as sole practitioners or in regional and national practices.

Long-time practitioners of forensic economics are witnesses to the fact that there are myriad ways, common and bizarre, in which people are injured or die and that a lawsuit to recover damages is likely to follow if someone else can be blamed. In such cases two attorneys (but sometimes more if there are additional persons at fault) will be employed to litigate the case. If the level of damages is expected to be large, an economist will usually be retained to calculate the dollar value of the damages suffered by the plaintiff. When such damages are large and the defense attorneys are skeptical about the damage calculations offered, they will also retain an economist.

A typical personal injury/death case will involve a "but for the harm" projection of lost earnings (or earnings capacity), incorporating past and future earnings growth as well as losses of certain types of fringe benefits. In an injury case where the injured person retains some ability to work, a second "post-injury earnings" or earnings capacity projection will be offered; and the difference between the two projections will serve as the measure of net earnings losses. Other losses that may be considered include a lost or reduced ability to perform certain services, such as household services, as well as future medical costs in the case of an injured person with significant future life care needs. All future losses are typically adjusted downward for the possibility that they would not occur for reasons (unrelated to the tort) of later death, disability, unemployment and, though not always, voluntary withdrawal from the labor force. Once the future loss projections are calculated, they are then reduced to present value at some rate of interest, often a Treasury bond rate. In a death case, losses to survivors may also be reduced by the decedent's own expected personal consumption of earnings, benefits, and services.

Although all of the above calculation procedures may seem fairly straightforward, they are complicated by the fact that various states impose rules on what methods can be used in projections, either through statute or by case law precedent. Such rules apply to earnings growth rates, discounting, taxes, elements of loss that may or may not be considered, personal consumption, and other variables used in the projections. For example, Pennsylvania requires the use of the "offset method" in discounting future earnings losses to present value. According to this reasoning, future inflation and the interest rate are assumed to be offsetting (they are not, of course), thereby allowing Pennsylvania courts and forensic economists to sidestep such problems as the appropriate interest rate to use and what projections of future earnings growth and inflation to assume. Pennsylvania and several other states also do not require that a decedent's expected future consumption be deducted in an award for lost future earnings, but instead only that the decedent's expected "personal maintenance costs" be deducted. The latter is a more restrictive deduction, referring to those costs a decedent would have been expected to incur in order to maintain his or her "earnings power." Other restrictions apply to the question of who is the plaintiff. In some states, the decedent remains the plaintiff even after death. It is also the case that, while standard lawsuits filed in federal court for jurisdictional reasons follow state law rules, federal tort claims, Federal Employment Liability cases, and cases involving longshoremen and railroad workers have their own sets of rules for calculating damages.

What the preceding discussion shows is that, even if forensic economists were to agree on a universal model of damages, there would still be differences in damage calculations arising from statutory and judicial restrictions. However, although the field of forensic economics has matured significantly over the past several decades, fundamental disagreements on methodology persist. For example, should work life expectancy or a "normal" retirement age be used in forecasts? Should earnings capacity or probable earnings be used to measure lost earnings? Should historical averages or current rates of earnings growth and interest rates be used in the projection? There may be more understanding of the implications of these questions today than 20 years ago, but there is certainly no consensus among forensic economists. As a result, two forensic economists approaching the same personal injury or death case with the same set of facts will most likely arrive at different estimates of the dollar magnitude of the loss. There are no simple right or wrong standards to apply in judging the "correctness" of a forecast. A major reason, of course, is that forensic economists—and economists in general—have a variety of models, methods, and data sources at their disposal. Professional judgment is ultimately involved. Furthermore, damages forecasts are made in the litigation arena where both plaintiffs and defendants have much riding on the outcome.

Does all this mean that forensic economists and their forecasts will necessarily be suspected of bias? Sitting through a deposition or trial would certainly suggest that such beliefs exist. To the extent that this is the case, it is in the interests of forensic economists to address issues of bias and unethical practice head on.

Ethical Dilemmas Faced by Forensic Economists: A Typical Case

How do ethical issues arise in the practice of forensic economics? As we noted previously, not only is there considerable variation and discretion possible in the methods and data sources used by forensic economists, there are also potential conflict of interest that exist. Take, for example, the hypothetical situation where an economist is approached by a lawyer hired by the husband of a 25-year-old woman who was killed in an automobile collision. The economist has been asked to draw up a report on the economic losses suffered by the survivor (the husband) of the decedent.[3] Is the economist expected to serve in the role of a neutral expert or rather as an advocate for the party doing the hiring? If the economist serves as an advocate for the party that has hired him (here the plaintiff), he may feel an inclination to make use of assumptions, methodologies, and data sources that would make the amount of damages high. For example, the economist might be asked by the plaintiff's attorney to assume that the young woman would have returned to college to pursue an MBA, when in fact there may be little or no evidence that she would have done so. On the other hand, if the economist serves as a neutral expert or as an expert hired by the defense, he is not likely to assume such a scenario in constructing his lost earnings report. What role—neutral or advocate—do personal injury lawyers expect their experts to assume? A survey taken of several hundred attorneys who had used economists as experts found that a majority (53 percent) preferred their expert to be an advocate, with advocacy defined as "presenting the best possible case for their client's interest" (Colella, Johnson, and Tinari, 1995: 18). But in the opinion of probably most forensic economists, economists ought to act as neutrals in the process.[4] Furthermore, according to the Statement of Ethical Principles first adopted by the National Association of Forensic Economics in 1992 (and later revised): "The forensic economist shall attempt to operate at all times from a position of neutrality with respect to his calculations and analysis. Whether he is engaged by the plaintiff or the defense, his approach, methodology and conclusions should in the end be essentially the same" (Statement on neutrality from NAFE Principles, 1992).

To continue our preceding example, assume that the facts of the case are that the decedent possessed a bachelor's degree and had earned $35,000 the year before her death on December 31, 2012. Suppose that her surviving husband had earned $25,000 in 2012. A general equation that could be used to forecast the present value (*PV*) of her earnings losses over her remaining work life can be written as follows:

$$PV = \sum_{t=1}^{WLE} W_0 \times A_t \times (1-U_t) \times (1-D_t) \times (1-C_t) \times \frac{(1+g)^t}{(1+d)^t}$$

where

- *WLE* is the number of years of remaining work life;
- W_0 is the earnings level in the base year;

[3] Some states allow recovery to the decedent as if he or she were still alive although most states only allow recovery to survivors of the decedent.

[4] Ireland (1997) makes an interesting argument that there are two different sets of ethical standards: the "ethics of neutrality" and the "ethics of advocacy." He suggests that when an economist is under oath at trial or is giving a deposition, he is required to serve as a neutral, but that at other times the forensic economist has an obligation to act as an agent of the employing attorney. He also claims that "the two systems of ethics have very clear lines of delineation" and that as a consequence "it is relatively easy for all parties to determine when each system applies."

- A_t is an age–earnings growth factor to account for the expected change in earnings due to human capital accumulation over time;
- U_t is the probability of experiencing unemployment in future year t;
- D_t is the probability of death in future year t;
- C_t is the decedent's personal consumption expenditures expressed as a proportion of earnings;
- g is the annual expected growth rate in earnings due to economy-wide productivity growth; and
- d is the discount rate used to reduce future earnings to present value. Often the earnings growth and discount rate factors ($1 + g$ and $1 + d$ respectively) are combined to form a "net discount rate."

The precise specification and even the question of the inclusion of some of these variables in the equation are subject to differences in professional judgment and data sources used.

To demonstrate just how much of an effect these differences can have on lost earnings calculations, in Table 33.1 a set of "plaintiff-favoring" assumptions is compared to a set of "defendant-favoring" assumptions, along with the resulting present values of lost earnings. In addition, a third set of assumptions and estimates is presented, based on guidelines laid out in the 2011 Victim Compensation Fund (VCF).[5] The VCF was created by an Act of Congress after 9/11 to compensate the victims of the attack and their families in return for their agreement not to sue the airlines involved.[6] The program was administered by the U.S. Department of Justice. The VCF assumptions were adopted by the Department after its review of the forensic economics literature and represent what some might call a "middle ground" view with respect to the level of damages.

The authors have seen all of the various assumptions in the three scenarios in Table 33.1 used in actual cases. Some of the assumptions are supported by statistical research (e.g., work-life expectancies, self-consumption rates, and age–earnings data) while others are just a matter of opinion (e.g., that the worker would have retired at age 65.) As can be seen in the table (line 9), when all of the plaintiff-favoring assumptions are used in the estimating equation, the result is a net earnings loss to the surviving spouse of about \$1.75 million. On the other hand, when the defendant-favoring assumptions are used in the estimating equation, the resulting loss estimate is only \$315, 408, about 18 percent of the plaintiff-favoring estimate. Finally, the VCF estimate of \$1,062,292 is approximately midway between the two estimates—about \$700,000 away from each.

The aforementioned case shows just how great differences in damages estimates can be if an economist would choose to represent the interests of either the plaintiff or defendant. Even so, the magnitudes of their loss estimates should not necessarily be used as evidence

[5] VCF guidelines at: http://www.vcf.gov/pdf/VCFFAQsFINAL20120727.pdf

[6] Kenneth Feinberg was appointed special master of the fund and developed the regulations governing the administration of the fund.

Table 33.1 Three Sets of Assumptions and Corresponding Estimates of the Present Value of Lost Earnings for a Deceased 25-Year-Old Married Female[7]

Variables	Plaintiff-Favoring Assumptions	2011 Victim's Compensation Fund Assumptions	Defendant-Favoring Assumptions
1. Base Earnings	$35,000 (earnings at time of death)	$30,000 (average over last three years)	$30,000 (average over last three years)
2. Age-earnings Profile (future wage adjustments based on age)[8]	Average age-earnings profile for males with bachelor's degree	Average age-earnings profile for all males	Average (median) age-earnings profile for females with bachelor's degree
3. Length of Work Life	To age 67 (current social security retirement age) adjusted by risk of death	Expected work life of all full-time-employed males (34.19 years to age 59.19)	Expected work life of females with bachelor's degree (33.2 years to age 58.2, reduced again by husband's survival probability)
4. Unemployment	3% (historical average for bachelor's degree holders, 25+ years old)	Historical population average of 6%	Historical population average of 6%
5. Personal Consumption (decedent's consumption of earnings)	25% of own earnings	25.7% of own earnings	30% of the average of the last three years of family earnings of $60,000 which equals $18,000 (60% of the decedent's average earnings).
6. Net discount rate (discount rate minus earnings growth rate)	0.0%	1.10%	2.50%
7. Present Value of Earnings	$2,342,738	$1,429,734	$788,521
8. Present Value of Personal Consumption	($585,685)	($367,442)	($473,113)
9. Net Earnings Loss (line 7 minus line 8)	$1,757,054	$1,062,292	$315,408

[7] Table 33.1 was constructed by Kurt Krueger.

[8] The U.S. Department of Labor publishes earnings data by age, gender, education, and race. These cross-sectional age–earnings profiles capture the earnings trend associated with increased age at a given point of time. Using such data allows the earnings loss projection to capture the life-cycle of earnings growth associated with age alone. Some forensic economists justify using age–earnings profiles for *men* in evaluating the lost earnings of women by arguing that doing so eliminates the effects of past discrimination still reflected in tables for women.

for characterizing forensic economists as biased toward the plaintiff or the defendant. For one thing, most forensic economists do both defense work and plaintiff work. Moreover, although there are some who do work exclusively for either the defense or for the plaintiff, as long as their estimates are not the product of intentional bias, it would be unfair to accuse such economists of unethical practice. It would be a different matter, though, if the economist is inconsistent from case to case and that the choice of assumptions and data is solely a function of who—plaintiff or defense—retains him. For example, an economist who uses a zero percent discount rate for plaintiff work but an 8 percent historical stock yield rate to discount damages for defense work could be considered to be acting unethically.

Consistency of approach in calculating damages in a personal injury/death case should be the goal of any forensic economist who wishes to maintain a neutral position with respect to the interests of plaintiffs and defendants. However, even the mere choice and specification of a particular variable in the calculation of damages may sometimes raise the *suspicion* of bias. To use one example, a forensic economist's decision to calculate self-consumption based on the decedent's earnings as opposed to basing it on family earnings may lead to a much higher estimate of net lost earnings (see Table 33.1, lines 5, 8, and 9). The question of just what is the appropriate measure of self-consumption to be used in reducing lost earnings has been examined in a number of papers published in both the *Journal of Forensic Economics* and the *Journal of Legal Economics*, and there are advocates for both approaches. Furthermore, the use of the decedent's earnings or family earnings as a base for self-consumption may be directed by state law. The bottom line is that, although the choice of one approach or another will significantly affect the loss calculation, the choice itself is not necessarily evidence of bias or unethical practice. Instead, the focus should again be on the *consistency* of the forensic economist's approach, as well as on the independence exercised by the economist in making assumptions and selecting data sets.

The National Association of Forensic Economics and the Ethics Question

The membership and leadership of the National Association of Forensic Economics (NAFE) have had a long-standing interest in ethics and related issues, such as appropriate qualifications for testifying economists. [9] The Association was organized in 1986 and as DeMartino states "is the only U.S.-based economics association to have adopted a code of conduct for its members."[10] Minutes of the NAFE annual membership meetings

[9] Parts of this section have been drawn from R. Thornton and M. Brookshire, "NAFE and the Ethics Question," *Journal of Forensic Economics*, 2013.

[10] DeMartino, *The Economist's Oath*, p. 41. DeMartino's observation is not quite accurate, for another smaller body of forensic economists (the American Academy of Economic and Financial Experts [AAEFE]) has also passed a code of conduct, which was modeled after the NAFE code. Many of its

indicate discussion of ethics-related issues in 1989, but the question of whether NAFE should function as a certifying body for forensic economists had been raised earlier and rejected. At the December 1989 NAFE membership meeting, the majority of those attending expressed the belief that instead of certification "it was more important to establish a code of ethics for forensic economists."

The next year (1990), the general membership recommended that a special issue of the *Journal of Forensic Economics* be devoted to the question of ethics. As a result of that recommendation, a symposium on ethics appeared in the Fall 1991 issue. The symposium consisted of contributions by Pauline Fox, Edward Sattler, Michael Piette, and symposium editor Walter Johnson. The symposium articles addressed such topics as whether the market works to weed out unethical economists as well as common types of unethical practices encountered in forensic economics. Also in 1990 the results of a survey of the NAFE membership appeared in the *Journal of Forensic Economics*, the first of nine such surveys to have been taken through 2012. The surveys have dealt mostly with issues that arise in practice, such as what discount rate or deduction for consumption one would use in a particular scenario. However, questions regarding ethics have occasionally been asked, and a 1993 survey was almost entirely devoted to issues of qualifications and ethics (Adams et al., 1993). Echoing the previous sentiment of the general membership, the majority of respondents disagreed with a proposal that NAFE should become a certifying body for forensic economists, but respondents were more supportive of the notion (41 percent were in favor) that NAFE should have a code of professional conduct that was a "binding condition of membership" (Adams et al., 1993: 17). The survey also revealed what types of conduct NAFE members considered to be ethical (such as paid advertising) and unethical (such as the acceptance of contingency fees).

In 1992 NAFE first adopted a "Statement of Ethical Principles," and these principles covered the categories of employment (or engagement), honesty, candor, fairness, neutrality, knowledge, and responsibility—and later disclosure. At the time, adherence to these principles was not made a condition of membership in NAFE. The principles have been amended several times since and subsequently approved by the NAFE membership. The latest version (see Table 33.2) with eight basic tenets—the Statement of Ethical Principles and Principles of Professional Practice (SEP/PPP)—was passed in 2004 and appears in each issue of the *Journal*. Various NAFE committees on ethics have also wrestled from time to time with the question of just how proactive NAFE should be in enforcing its ethical principles. For example, at the summer 1996 meeting of the Board of Directors, discussion arose as to whether NAFE should "police CVs, maintain 'bad practice files' on economists, [and] monitor the testimony of non-economists." Again, however, the consensus was that NAFE should not assume the role of a policeman. Rather, as the current SEP/PPP states, NAFE members are now asked to "pledge" to adhere to the principles "as a condition of membership," with the SEP/PPP appearing on the membership application.

members are also members of NAFE, and some individuals on the board of editors of its journal (the *Journal of Legal Economics)* are also members of the board of editors of the *Journal of Forensic Economics*.

Table 33.2 Statement of Ethical Principles and Principles of Professional Practice, National Association of Forensic Economics (NAFE) (Effective October 1, 2004)

When providing expert opinion for use as evidence by the trier of fact, a NAFE member pledges, as a condition of membership, adherence to the following:

1. Engagement
Practitioners of forensic economics should decline involvement in any litigation when they are asked to assume invalid representations of fact or alter their methodologies without foundation or compelling analytical reason.

2. Compensation
Practitioners of forensic economics should not accept contingency fee arrangements, or fee amounts associated with the size of a court award or out-of-court settlement.

3. Diligence
Practitioners of forensic economics should employ generally accepted and/or theoretically sound economic methodologies based on reliable economic data. Practitioners of forensic economics should attempt to provide accurate, fair and reasonable expert opinions, recognizing that it is not the responsibility of the practitioner to verify the accuracy or completeness of the case-specific information that has been provided.

4. Disclosure
Practitioners of forensic economics should stand ready to provide sufficient detail to allow replication of all numerical calculations, with reasonable effort, by other competent forensic economics experts, and be prepared to provide sufficient disclosure of sources of information and assumptions underpinning their opinions to make them understandable to others.

5. Consistency
While it is recognized that practitioners of forensic economics may be given a different assignment when engaged on behalf of the plaintiff than when engaged on behalf of the defense, for any given assignment, the basic assumptions, sources, and methods should not change regardless of the party who engages the expert to perform the assignment. There should be no change in methodology for purposes of favoring any party's claim. This requirement of consistency is not meant to preclude methodological changes as new knowledge evolves, nor is it meant to preclude performing requested calculations based upon a hypothetical—as long as its hypothetical nature is clearly disclosed in the expert's report and testimony.

6. Knowledge
Practitioners of forensic economics should strive to maintain a current knowledge base of their discipline.

7. Discourse
Open, uninhibited discussion is a desired educational feature of academic and professional forensic economic conferences. Therefore, to preserve and protect the educational environment, practitioners of forensic economics will refrain from the citation of oral remarks made in an educational environment, without permission from the speaker.

8. Responsibility
Practitioners of forensic economics are encouraged to make known the existence of, and their adherence to, these principles to those retaining them to perform economic analyses and to other participants in litigation. In addition, it is appropriate for practitioners of forensic economics to offer criticisms of breaches of these principles.

In five of the survey studies published in NAFE journals,[11] respondents have provided actual examples of ethical problems and dilemmas encountered in their forensic economics practices. We list the more commonly encountered ones in the following section. Other questions asked in the surveys have focused upon the NAFE SEP/PPP and its value to practitioners, as well as the most commonly used methods, data sources, and assumptions in forensic practice. The latter are also important to the issue of ethics, with most NAFE survey respondents holding the view that incompetent practice should itself be deemed a breach of ethics.[12].

How Much Unethical Practice Is Out There? What Have the Surveys Shown?

As noted previously, a number of the survey-of-forensic-practice studies published in NAFE journals have contained broad questions inviting respondents to describe ethical dilemmas or examples of unethical practice that they have encountered. Below we list examples of the types of comments most frequently expressed.

- "Some economists do whatever the employing attorney wants" (Brookshire, Luthy, and Slesnick, 2004: 41).
- "Too many reports don't allow another economist to understand how their opinion is arrived at" (Brookshire, Luthy, and Slesnick, 2004: 41).
- "I am increasingly dismayed by economists on both sides who work the numbers to achieve the maximum/minimum possible. They don't disclose their assumptions. Don't show their work" (Brookshire, Luthy, and Slesnick, 2004: 42).
- "FE's often provide what clients want rather than a professionally determined product" (Brookshire, Luthy, and Slesnick, 2004: 42).
- 'Forensic economists too readily [accept] assumptions from the hiring attorney" (Brookshire and Slesnick, 1999: 93).
- "Full-time faculty with research responsibilities [should not be engaged in] full-time consulting work" (Brookshire and Slesnick, 1993: 8).
- "Using university letterheads [on their reports and correspondence] since that can indicate [imply?] the expert represents the institution" (Brookshire and Slesnick, 1993: 8).
- "Tailoring assumptions based on which side of the fence you are working" (Brookshire and Slesnick, 1993: 8).

[11] In addition to the *Journal of Forensic Economics*, NAFE also published a second journal, the *Litigation Economics Digest* (later renamed the *Litigation Economics Review*) from 1995 to 2003.

[12] However, where one draws the line between incompetence and honest differences in preferred methodologies is not always clear. To quote Depperschmidt, "Experts may not [always] know or be able to define 'adequate and accepted procedures'. . ." (1994: 164).

- "When experts testify outside of their fields [of expertise]" (Brookshire and Slesnick, 1993: 8).
- "It is often impossible to duplicate results from information given in reports" (Brookshire, Luthy, and Slesnick, 2006: 55).
- "Use of methods when working for plaintiffs that differ from those used when working for the defense" (Brookshire, Luthy, and Slesnick, 2006: 56).
- "The preparation of reports which are based upon speculation and/or gross generalization continues . . . unabated" (Brookshire, Luthy, and Slesnick, 2010: 33).

Sometimes arguably unethical practices have been initiated by attorneys, as the following comments indicate.

- "I have been asked to produce a draft copy of my report but tell the defense that there was no draft copy" (Brookshire, Luthy, and Slesnick, 2010: 33).
- "I was asked by the plaintiff's attorney in a wrongful death case not to make a deduction for personal consumption expenses. I stupidly agreed to do this and was grilled during a deposition by the defense, who noted (correctly) that I had done so in past cases" (Brookshire, Luthy, and Slesnick, 2010: 32).
- "Making unreasonable assumptions based on the hiring attorney's request (and defending it by saying he/she told me to make this assumption)" (Brookshire, Luthy, and Slesnick, 2006: 56).
- "Attorneys list[ing] you as an expert without your knowledge or consent . . . [or who] fail to supply all the information to you regarding the economic issues" (Brookshire, Luthy, and Slesnick, 2004: 42).
- "Requests by retaining attorneys who want [the] expert to cut fees when [the] outcome in trial/settlement is below expectations" (Brookshire, Luthy, and Slesnick, 2004: 43).

But just how common are these and other examples of unethical behavior and incompetence in the practice of forensic economics? Is it restricted to just a few individuals or is the problem more severe than that? Thomas Depperschmidt has expressed strong doubts about the pervasiveness and gravity of the ethics problem in forensic practice. As Depperschmidt argued, "There is not much to get excited about from an ethics standpoint. Some inexperience is revealed, perhaps even some incompetence, not a little poaching by other disciplines on economic turf, and largely unsubstantiated allegations of 'manipulation' of award figures. . . . [but overall] ethics is not a problem in the profession" (1994: 168). In response to Depperschmidt, Walter Johnson countered with specific examples of unethical behavior, such as those mentioned above, as well as falsifying one's credentials. Johnson also asks rhetorically, "Just how widespread do these instances have to be . . . ?" (1995: 291) for Depperschmidt and others to be concerned.

More recent, though largely anecdotal, evidence from discussions at professional meetings and messages posted on the listserves of both NAFE and AAEFE would suggest that there may be more incompetent forensic economists than unethical ones. However, the numbers of both seem to be relatively small. Moreover, internet postings of court decisions involving forensic economic experts reveal few judicial rejections of economic experts on the basis of incompetence, and few economic experts have been barred from testimony in Daubert[13] hearings in Federal Court.[14] The Daubert process of making the judge the gatekeeper for expert testimony can be viewed as a reform in the sense that an adverse Daubert decision excluding an economic expert from testimony would represent a "black mark" on future testimony by the expert.

But again, is the fact that a forensic economist might, for example, discount lost earnings in an injury case using high-yield equities an ethics violation per se? The results would certainly favor the defense and not be supported by the forensic economics literature nor by sound general practice. Or could the results be a product of the economist's incompetence? On the other hand, as we noted earlier, incompetence itself is considered by many forensic economists to be an ethics transgression insofar as one's responsibility as a practicing forensic economist is to be knowledgeable of the literature and of practices of the field (see SEP/PPP principle 6). By this reasoning, a forensic economist who has used the same growth and discount rates over the past two decades, without regard to substantial changes in those rates over time, might be considered to be engaging in unethical practice because of the lack of due diligence in maintaining his skills.

Can Statements of Ethical Principles and Codes of Practice Make a Difference?

How much of an impact can a code of ethics such as the NAFE Statement of Ethical Principles and Standards of Professional Practice (SEP/PPP) have on the ethical practice of forensic economics? Again, the NAFE code is one of the only codes of its type to have been passed by an association of economists in the United States. As we have already noted, there are some who are skeptical of the potential of a code of ethics to make a difference.

In September 2011 the authors conducted a survey of the membership of NAFE on their attitudes regarding the Statement of Ethical Principles and Standards of Professional Practice (SEP/PPP) adopted by NAFE as a condition of membership. More

13 In the 1993 case of *Daubert v Merrell Dow Pharmaceuticals*, the U.S. Supreme Court encouraged federal judges to take a much more active role as gatekeepers in determining the admissibility of scientific experts. The *Daubert* decision also included a number of criteria for determining the scientific validity of the expert's testimony. See Thornton and Ward (1999: 109).

14 A listing of federal and state Appellate and Supreme Court decisions relating to the admissibility of economic experts can be found at http://www.umsl.edu/~irelandt/Decisions%20of%20Interest.htm.

specifically, the questionnaire was designed to ascertain the extent to which ethical problems have been encountered in the practice of forensic economics and the influence that NAFE's SEP/PPP has had in mitigating the problem. From the approximately 520 e-mails sent, 175 responses were received.

Below we have selected four questions from the survey.[15]

1. As a member of NAFE do you consider the current Statement of Ethical Principles and Standards of Professional Practice (SEP/PPP) to be an effective tool in promoting ethical behavior by forensic economists in their practice?
2. In which of the eight categories of the SEP/PPP have you found the most frequent violations of ethical behavior in forensic economics practice?
3. Do you believe that "the market" has helped to remove (weed out) unethical forensic economists from practice?
4. Overall, do you believe that the practice of forensic economics is characterized by a higher level of ethical behavior today than in the past (a decade or two ago)?

To briefly summarize the results of the survey, first of all a slight majority (55 percent) of respondents believe the SEP/PPP to be an effective tool in promoting the ethical practice of forensic economics, with only about 20 percent believing that it is not. As for the types of unethical behavior most frequently encountered in forensic practice, three categories stand out: (1) the lack of consistency—that is, the failure of the expert to use the same methods and data sources when employed by the plaintiff and when employed by the defense; (2) the lack of diligence—that is, the failure to employ generally accepted and sound economic methods based on reliable data; and (3) the lack of adequate disclosure—that is, the failure of the expert to provide sufficient detail to allow replication of numerical calculations. These three types of unethical behaviors were also frequently noted in previous NAFE surveys of professional practice. With respect to the question of whether the market has helped to remove unethical forensic economists from practice, 35 percent of respondents answered in the affirmative, with slightly fewer than half (49 percent) responding no. Finally, in answer to the question as to whether the practice of forensic economics is characterized by a higher level of ethical behavior today than in the past, the results were quite mixed. About 33 percent of respondents thought that it was, about 27 percent thought that it was not, while the modal response (40 percent) was "unsure."[16]

[15] More detailed information regarding the results and representative comments from those responding are included in the appendix to this chapter.

[16] The survey also asked four other questions that we have not discussed in this chapter:

- Have you ever been asked a question in deposition or at trial about whether you adhere to the NAFE SEP/PPP?
- In your opinion and based on your personal experience, approximately what percentage of forensic economists (including non-members of NAFE) adhere to the standards of the SEP/PPP in their professional practice?

Our general impression drawn from our survey results and from the additional observations offered is that the SEP/PPP has had a positive, though perhaps modest, impact on the levels of ethics and competency demonstrated by forensic economists. On the other hand, neither the market nor the SEP/PPP seems to have eliminated all of the "hired guns" in the profession. As one respondent noted, "There were rogues before and there are rogues today."

Nonetheless, evidence from the various surveys still suggests that few forensic economists would support a disciplinary process within NAFE that would expose and punish violations of an ethical code.

Alternative Remedies?

Is the quality of expert economic testimony in the courts biased to such an extent that it would require measures beyond the self-regulation provided by an ethics code such as that developed by NAFE? A review of Daubert hearings to strike such testimony suggests that this is not the case. Relatively few Daubert challenges to economic experts in general (not just forensic economic experts) have been successful; and often the causes for exclusion involve the economic expert's lack of specific expertise about a firm or industry being evaluated, rather than general incompetence or evidence of bias. Even so, what other alternatives to codes of ethics have been proposed to deal with those who do engage in unethical practices?

Both licensing and certification have at various times been suggested, but neither has gathered much support either from within or outside of the forensic economics profession. An occupational license is simply a government-issued "permit" allowing one to work in a particular occupation. If an occupation is licensed, a prospective practitioner of the occupation is usually required to have attained a specified level of education or training in the field, passed an examination, paid a fee to be given the license, and met certain additional requirements. Unlike licensing, certification (which can be either public or private) does not restrict the right of a person to practice in a field, but allows only individuals who have met certain requirements to use the "certified" designation or the job title. For example, certification laws prohibit individuals who have not met a minimum set of requirements from using the title "certified public accountant" (or CPA) in every state in the United States, but individuals are still allowed to perform the tasks of an accountant as long as they do not use the CPA title. Licensing laws are much more restrictive. Doctors, for example, are not permitted to *practice* in any state in the United States without obtaining a license. Both licensing and certification also require

- In your opinion, should any of the eight SEP/PPP principles be modified? If so, which one(s) and in what way?
- Do you believe that the SEP/PPP should be strengthened by an enforcement mechanism? If so, what type of enforcement mechanism would you suggest?

Copies of the survey findings regarding these additional questions are available from the authors upon request.

elaborate and costly administrative, regulatory, and enforcement systems. It would be naïve for us to argue that it is unlikely that a licensing or certification regime would someday be applied to forensic economists. For as Kleiner and Krueger (2010: 676) have shown, nearly 30 percent of workers in the United States are now in jobs that require a license to practice. And many of them work in jobs where the danger to the public of incompetent or unethical practitioners is small (e.g., barbers, massage therapists, athletic trainers, auctioneers, funeral attendants, and makeup artists, to name just a few).

Richard Posner, who is a skeptic on the potential for codes of ethics to raise the level of ethical forensic practice, has presented several criticisms of the current practice of selecting and using economist expert witnesses. For example, he argues that:

1. Expert witnesses hired by and paid for by the plaintiff and by the defense may act as partisans or "hired guns" (as we have seen, a criticism that several respondents to our survey have echoed).
2. Expert witnesses can mislead judges and juries more readily than can lay witnesses. The reason is that they are "more difficult to pick apart on cross examination" because of the esoteric nature of their knowledge.
3. Opposing experts often "cancel each other out." The reason is that some juries, unable to decide which expert to believe, simply ignore the testimony of both (Posner, 1999a: 93).

Interestingly, Posner feels that the first criticism—the hired gun charge—"does not seem . . . very grave with respect to economic witnesses" as long as they are testifying "in areas in which there is a substantial professional consensus." The reason is that most such expert witnesses are "repeat players" with a financial interest in maintaining an honest reputation both for themselves and the firms that employ them (Posner, 1999a: 93–94).

Instead of a code of ethics, Posner argues that more frequent use should be made of court-appointed experts. He notes that a provision of the Federal Rules of Evidence allows a judge to appoint an expert witness but that this provision is seldom used because judges "lack confidence in their ability to pick a neutral" (Posner, 1999a: 92). To circumvent this problem, Posner says that a roster should be maintained—he suggests by the American Economic Association—of all members who have provided economic testimony in the past, along with (perhaps) the testimony itself and any criticisms of the testimony by the trial judge, opposing attorneys, or other experts. In this way the profession would be able to monitor the level of ethical and competent testimony of its members (Posner, 1999a: 98).[17] Novel as this idea is, we think it is unlikely to be put

[17] In a *Stanford Law Review* article published in the same year, Posner (1999*b*) offers the same criticisms of expert witnesses as in his *Journal of Economic Perspectives* article (1999*a*). However, the tone of the former article is somewhat less critical toward expert witnesses in general than that of the latter. For example, in the *SLR* article, Posner suggests that professional associations from whom expert witnesses are selected "*could* maintain a roster of all testimonial appearances by members," whereas in the *JEP* article Posner suggests that the American Economic Association *should* maintain such a list. The same "could vs. should" distinction also applies to his recommendation that lawyers disclose how many experts were contacted before the one who was ultimately chosen. See Posner (1999*b*: 1541) and Posner (1999*a*: 98).

into practice any time soon. For one thing, a large number of practicing forensic economists are not members of the American Economic Association. And for another, the Association has shown a marked reluctance—an aversion even—to inquire into and engage in debate over what DeMartino calls the "myriad ethical issues that arise in the context of professional economic practice" (DeMartino, 2011: 66).

Posner also argues that lawyers should be required to divulge the names of all economists whom they may have contacted to serve as possible expert witnesses for a given case. In this way, courts could be alerted to the practice of "expert witness shopping." Presumably an attorney who had to contact many economists before being able to hire one to testify would have a weaker damages case than an opposing attorney who was able to hire the first economist who was interviewed (Posner, 1999a: 98). It should be noted, however, that Posner's criticisms of the use of economic experts are not directed solely or even mainly at forensic economists. Rather he argues that the use of economic experts is "most problematic" in the areas of economics where there is "no professional consensus"—for example, antitrust economics (Posner, 1999a: 96).

Conclusion

Overall, the substantial attention directed to ethical issues by NAFE—through its code of ethics, regular surveys of practice, and research—should not be surprising. After all, forensic economists are probably more likely to confront ethical issues in their work than are other professional economists. For over two decades, members of NAFE have debated the need for a code of professional practice for its members, and the code that has evolved from that process addresses a number of ethical issues such as transparency, objectivity, and conflict of interest. Although the NAFE code has no enforcement mechanism, a pledge to adhere to the code has been made a condition of membership in NAFE. Has the code succeeded in enhancing the levels of ethical behavior of forensic economists? The relatively few successful Daubert challenges to economic testimony in the courts and the results of various surveys suggest that the NAFE ethics code has indeed had a positive, although perhaps modest, effect on the objectivity and quality of forensic economic work.

Appendix

Survey of NAFE Membership on Ethical Principles and Practice: Detailed Results

As noted in the chapter, in September 2011 the authors conducted a survey of the membership of NAFE on their attitudes regarding the Statement of Ethical Principles and Standards of Professional Practice (SEP/PPP) adopted by NAFE as a condition of membership. The questionnaire was designed to ascertain the extent to which ethical problems have been encountered in the practice of forensic economics and the influence that NAFE's SEP/PPP has had in mitigating the problem. The survey was approved by the Board of Directors of NAFE at its August 2011 meeting. From the approximately 520 e-mails sent, 175 responses were received. Not all questions were answered in every survey returned, so response rates vary across questions. The results of the survey were first presented at the Allied Social Science Association meetings of NAFE in January 2012.

Below are four questions from the survey, along with the results and representative comments.

1. As a member of NAFE do you consider the current Statement of Ethical Principles and Standards of Professional Practice (SEP/PPP) to be an effective tool in promoting ethical behavior by forensic economists in their practice?

Responses	Response Percent	Response Count
Yes	55.2	91
No	21.2	35
Unsure	23.6	39

Selected comments regarding question 1:

- I have referred to the statement in litigation when the economist on the other side violates the disclosure principle and fails to provide information sufficient to evaluate their method/assumptions.
- Ethical actions are more likely to arise from ethical individuals rather than from some collective "code of action."
- Many FEs that I come across, especially out of the CPA field, do not appear to know of its existence and certainly don't abide by its standards.
- It's plausible that the NAFE Statement has helped, but I am not able to think of any single specific example where the existence of the Statement has been critical.
- I believe that publishing such principles is important, particularly for newcomers to the practice. I have occasionally encouraged my attorney clients to use the SEP/PPP as a tool when an opposing expert steps over the line. I believe this to be effective. Unfortunately, the rare expert that habitually steps way out of line is not fazed by such tactics.
- Many of whom would be considered unethical in the profession either ignore the principles or are not members of NAFE. That being said I like the statement of ethical principles and standards of professional practice.
- It's only a modest start. It lacks strong sanctions and ongoing monitoring/enforcement.

2. In which of the eight categories of the SEP/PPP have you found the most frequent violations of ethical behavior in forensic economics practice? Please identify by category number and provide specific examples below.

Those tenets of the SEP/PEP identified as being most frequently violated:

1. Engagement—11 responses
2. Compensation—6 responses

3. Diligence—34 responses
4. Disclosure—31 responses
5. Consistency—50 responses
6. Knowledge—12 responses
7. Discourse—no responses
8. Responsibility—1 response

Selected comments regarding question 2:

- [Disclosure] I often see forensic economist reports with little or no explanation, sometimes without even spreadsheets, even after being subpoenaed.
- [Consistency] I often see economists changing their methodology when retained by plaintiff v. defendant.
- [Knowledge] I know of one economist who uses a negative net discount rate and incorrectly claims that it is based on Missouri law. Also, I have seen testimony of economists who readily admit that they do not read any journals in the forensic area or go to conferences, etc.
- [Knowledge] I frequently review cases wherein the forensic economist clearly has not kept up with the literature in the field and is not aware of more up-to-date data that is available for use in analyses.
- [Disclosure] Many forensic economists do not provide enough information for me to replicate their calculations.
- [Diligence] Some of the reports I have seen are absolutely horrible either due to ignorance or just plain fraudulent practices. They don't know the legal parameters and/or don't know economics.
- [Disclosure] This is the biggest problem. You simply cannot duplicate what is in the report. As a quick example, the author simply gives a bottom-line number with no accompanying tables.

3. Do you believe that "the market" has helped to remove (weed out) unethical forensic economists from practice? If so, please provide ways in which the weeding out process has worked.

Responses	Response Percent	Response Count
Yes	35.0	57
No	49.1	80
Unsure	16.0	26

Selected comments regarding question 3:

- "Has helped to" is the right phrasing. It has not eliminated, but it has somewhat affected the list of practicing forensic economists.
- Getting skewered in testimony tends to reduce the demand for one's services.
- As long as lawyers continue to use them, these economists will continue deriving income from and giving a bad name to the profession.
- Hasn't weeded them out, because most cases don't go to trial and there is a continuing demand for figures that bolster the lawyer's case; but it has worked to align ethical lawyers with ethical experts, and unethical with unethical.

- Many attorneys will still pay for unethical evaluations if they will be told by the forensic economist what they want to hear.
- I have encountered few "unethical" economists in my 30 some years of practice. I have encountered many who lack the training and knowledge for the task. They are not unethical.
- I believe precedent rulings such as Frye and Daubert have made judges much more vigilant for instances in which unqualified individuals or otherwise qualified individuals have used methodologies that are not in keeping with industry standards.
- The legal discovery process is designed to do this very thing. With the assistance of a consulting economist, a competent attorney should be able to disqualify or competently cross examine an unethical expert.
- In my experience, economists whose assumptions are extreme (either to benefit plaintiff or defense) are recognized as such by attorneys and tend to be shunned over time. On the other hand, I have been told by many attorneys (both plaintiff and defense) that I was retained because of my reputation for being fair and reasonable in my approach.
- With a significant defense and plaintiff practice, I encounter dozens of other forensic economists each year and find unethical behavior to be rare. However, those few who are unethical do not seem to be removed from the market.
- Rank violation of general ethics is just not common in the jurisdictions in which I testify. Inexperience and sloppy documentation is more likely than outright unethical conduct.
- The market has not weeded out unethical forensic economists, but it does eliminate the incompetent ones.

4. Overall, do you believe that the practice of forensic economics is characterized by a higher level of ethical behavior today than in the past (a decade or two ago)? If yes, please note in the Comments section the way in which the level of ethical practice has improved and what you think is responsible for the change.

Responses	Response Percent	Response Count
Yes	32.7	54
No	27.3	45
Unsure	40.0	66

Selected comments regarding question 4:

- NAFE members have set good examples and have raised the bar of professional conduct.
- I'm not sure that "ethical" can be easily judged. I do not see experts switching their methods of analysis and assumptions, depending on whether they work for the plaintiff or the defense. They seem to use a consistent set of assumptions in their reports that I review. What I see is a "hardening" or rigidity of the assumptions used by particular economists and these assumptions, and their projection methods are consistently used case after case even for two decades or more!
- The increasingly common Daubert challenge has dramatically improved both ethics and competence. Bad apples are disqualified or never hired, while highly competent and ethical experts, aware of the potential risk to their careers of a successful challenge, redouble their efforts to excel.
- I have been practicing in this field for 15 years. It is my full-time job. I find the greatest improvement to be in the area of Disclosure. I find today's reports more detailed and

providing more information to allow work to be replicated. I find this to be true even with non-NAFE members who practice regularly in this field. I attribute that to the work of NAFE, courts demanding more information for reports, and the increasing number of CPA's expanding their practice to include litigation support. I feel the areas of least advancement are Diligence and Knowledge. I see too many experts relying on old data or not staying up to date with changes in our field. This is disappointing and shows complacency in some experts to not advance themselves or our field.

- Simply by establishing SEP/PPP and a trade journal (*JFE*), this starts to promote the exchange of ideas and scholarship, which raises the bar for everyone. If NAFE can promote the usefulness of the SEP/PPP to lawyers and judges, this will help enforce ethical behavior (ignoring for the moment that if one truly adheres to a standard of ethics, there should be no need for enforcement).
- I believe that AAEFE and NAFE have made the code of conduct more visible to all.
- In say the last 20 years (at least in Wisconsin), the range of final opinions between plaintiff and defense experts has narrowed considerably. Put another way, forensic reports with very expansive claims for the plaintiff are very rare these days.
- The availability today of a substantial literature about practically every topic in forensic economics is the primary reason for the more ethical behavior. It is no longer as easy for maverick experts to design unusual models on their own and exaggerate the economic damages in one direction or another.
- I don't know the reason, but I believe there has been more transparency in the work conducted by forensic economists (more provision of spreadsheets, backup information, etc.) and I believe that gives us incentive to remain ethical.

References

Adams, J., M. L. Brookshire, and F. Slesnick. 1992. "1993 Survey: Qualifications, Ethics and Procedures for Forensic Economics Practitioners." *Journal of Forensic Economics* 7(1): 1–24.

Brookshire, M. 2003. "A History of the National Association of Forensic Economics, 1986–2001." *Litigation Economics Review* 6(1): 22–32.

Brookshire, M., and F. Slesnick. 1991. "A 1990 Survey Study of Forensic Economists." *Journal of Forensic Economics* 4(2): 125–149.

Brookshire, M., and F. Slesnick. 1993. "1993 Survey of NAFE Members: A Follow-up Survey of Economic Methodology." *Journal of Forensic Economics* 7(1): 25–46.

Brookshire, M., and F. Slesnick. 1997. "A 1996 Study of 'Prevailing Practice' in Forensic Economics." *Journal of Forensic Economics* 10(1): 1–28.

Brookshire, M., and F. Slesnick. 1999. "A 1999 Survey Study of Forensic Economics—Their Methods and Their Estimates of Forecast Variables." *Litigation Economics Digest* 4(2): 65–96.

Brookshire, M., F. Slesnick, and R. Lessne. 1990. "The Emerging Industry of Forensic Economics: A Survey of NAFE Members." *Journal of Forensic Economics* 3(2): 15–29.

Brookshire, M., M. R. Luthy, and F. L. Slesnick. 2004. "Forensic Economists, Their Methods, and Estimates of Forecast Variables: A 2003 Survey." *Litigation Economics Digest* 6(2): 28–44.

Brookshire, M., M. R. Luthy, and F. L. Slesnick. 2006. "2006 Survey of Forensic Economists: Their Methods, Estimates, and Perspectives." *Journal of Forensic Economics* 19(1): 29–59.

Brookshire, M., M. R. Luthy, and F. L. Slesnick. 2010. "A 2009 Survey of Forensic Economists: Their Methods, Estimates, and Perspectives." *Journal of Forensic Economics* 21(1): 5–34.

Colella, F., and W.D. Johnson, and F.D. Tinari. 1995. "Attorney Perspectives on the Use of Economic Experts: Survey Results." *Journal of Forensic Economics* 8(1): 13–23.

DeMartino, G. 2011. *The Economist's Oath*. Oxford: Oxford University Press.

DeMartino, G. 2013. "Professional Economic Ethics: The Posnerian and Naïve Perspectives." *Journal of Forensic Economics* 24 (1): 3–18.

Depperschmidt, T. 1994. "Ethics in Forensic Economics: Evidence and Remedy Issues." *Journal of Forensic Economics* 7(2): 159–169.

Fox, P. 1991. "The Economic Expert in Wrongful Death and Personal Injury Cases: Workable Competition or Monopoly Power?" *Journal of Forensic Economics* 4(3): 255–262.

Ireland, T. 1997. "Ethics and Agency in Forensic Economics." Paper presented at the annual meetings of the Southern Economic Association.

Johnson, W. 1991. "Qualifications, Ethics, and Professional Responsibility in Forensic Economics." *Journal of Forensic Economics* 4(3): 277–285.

Johnson, W. 1995. "Ethics in Forensic Economics: A Reply to Depperschmidt." *Journal of Forensic Economics* 8(3): 289–291.

Kleiner, M. and A. Krueger. 2010. "The Prevalence and Effects of Occupational Licensing." *British Journal of Industrial Relations* 48(4): 676–687.

Martin, G., and M. Weinstein. 2012. *Determining Economic Damages*. Costa Mesa, CA: James Publishing.

National Association of Forensic Economics. Minutes of the General Membership Meetings. 1987–2011.

National Association of Forensic Economics. Minutes of the Board of Directors Meetings. 1987–2011.

Oxford Latin Dictionary. 2004. Oxford: Oxford University Press.

Piette, M. 1991. "Codes of Professional Ethics for Forensic Economists: Problems and Prospects." *Journal of Forensic Economics* 4(3): 269–276.

Posner, R. A. 1999*a*. "The Law and Economics of the Economic Expert Witness." *Journal of Economic Perspectives* 13(2): 91–99.

Posner, R. A. 1999*b*. "An Economic Approach to the Law of Evidence." *Stanford Law Review* 51(3): 1477–1546.

Sattler, E. 1991. "Economists, Ethics, and the Marketplace." *Journal of Forensic Economics* 4(3): 263–268.

Thornton, R., and J. Ward. 1999. "The Economist in Tort Litigation." *Journal of Economic Perspectives* 13(2): 101–112.

Thornton, R., and M. Brookshire. 2013. "NAFE and the Ethics Question." *Journal of Forensic Economics* 24 (1): 19–22.

PART VII

ETHICAL ISSUES IN ECONOMIC EDUCATION

CHAPTER 34

EXPOSURE AND DIALOGUE PROGRAMS IN THE TRAINING OF DEVELOPMENT ANALYSTS AND PRACTITIONERS

RAVI KANBUR

Introduction

A great and grotesque paradox stalks the development community. Those who work to advance the well-being of the poor and downtrodden seem to do rather well because of it themselves. The paradox has hardly gone unnoticed. The British newspaper *The Daily Telegraph* on September 30, 2012 published an article with the headline "Revealed: Taxpayer-Funded Aid Consultants on Six Figures a Year." The lead paragraph reads as follows:

> The top payee is a former middle-ranking British police officer, now based in Jamaica, who was given almost 20 percent more than the chief constable of his old force earned in the UK. Another British consultant receiving more than £200,000 a year from the aid budget is a former manager for the Timber Trade Federation, the trade association for the timber industry, who now runs a "sustainable forestries" programme in Indonesia.... The disclosures will worsen the political row about British "poverty barons" collecting large sums of money from the swelling aid budget.[1]

A quarter century earlier, Graham Hancock (1989) wrote a book entitled *The Lords of Poverty: The Power, Prestige and Corruption of the International Aid Business.*

[1] http://www.telegraph.co.uk/news/politics/9576104/Revealed-taxpayer-funded-aid-consultants-on-six-figures-a-year.html

And a decade before that, Ross Coggins (1976) wrote a famous poem called "The Development Set," whose opening lines set the tone:

> The Development Set is bright and noble
> Our thoughts are deep, our vision global;
> Although we move with the better classes
> Our thoughts are always with the masses.

Is the paradox real? Is it inherent and unavoidable in the development discourse? What, if anything, can be done about it? This chapter addresses these questions. Briefly stated, the answers are that the paradox is indeed real and inherent and needs to be negotiated as an ethical and practical matter. One response to it is for development professionals to engage in what have come to be called "Exposure and Dialogue Programs" (EDPs) or "Immersions," to keep them in touch with the realities of the lives of the people their work is supposed to help.

The plan of the chapter is as follows. The second section develops the nature of the paradox by examining the career paths of different types of development professionals, and it argues that these paths typically entail a progressive disconnect from the ground level realities of the lives of the poor in developing countries. The third section discusses the EDP methodology and illustrates with the specific case of the Cornell-SEWA-WIEGO EDPs. The fourth section then takes a broader perspective on the use of Immersions in a range of development agencies, and how best to design these activities. The fifth section concludes the chapter.

Development Professionals and the Disconnect

Robert Chambers once observed:

> ... it would seem that it is we the professionals, the powerful and the influential, and those who attend roundtables and summits, who have to reconstruct our reality, to change as people... (Chambers, 1995: 203–204).

So the presumed problem solvers are part of the problem. [2] The reality of their working lives are so far removed from the reality of the lives they analyze and prescribe for that questions must arise as to their assessments and their prescriptions.

[2] I include myself in this group, of course. This paper builds on my brief contribution to a Festschrift for Robert Chambers. See Kanbur (2011).

Who are these development professionals? Several main categories come to mind:

1. Academics who work on development across a range of disciplines, including economics, sociology, political science, anthropology, geography
2. National level civil servants who are directly charged with addressing the needs of the poorest, such as those in Ministries of Health, Education, Rural Development, Gender, Urban Development, Poverty Alleviation, and apex ministries such as Finance and Planning
3. Officials in multilateral and bilateral development agencies such as the World Bank, the Regional Development Banks, European Union Development and Cooperation Directorate, various United Nations agencies such as the United Nations Development Program (UNDP) and United Nations Children's Fund (UNICEF), the United Kingdom Department for International Development (DFID), the Swedish International Development Agency (SIDA)
4. Think tanks and networks such as the Center for Global Development (CGD), the Global Development network (GDN), the Overseas Development Institute (ODI)
5. Advocacy and Implementation nongovernmental organizations (NGOs) such Oxfam, Save the Children, CARE, Gender Action

Of course, these professionals are not a uniform lump. There is considerable heterogeneity among them in terms of disciplinary background, field exposure, and frameworks of analysis. For example, in terms analytical mindsets, in Kanbur (2001: 1084) I highlighted disagreements on economic policy as follows:

> Disagreements between whom? Any attempt at categorization and classification risks doing violence to a complex and richly textured reality. But the following grouping would be recognizable to many, and captures broad elements of policy disagreements. One group, call them Group A, could be labeled "Finance Ministry." In this group would obviously be some who worked in finance ministries in the North, and in the South. It would also include many economic analysts, economic policy managers and operational managers in the IFI's and the Regional Multilateral Banks. A key constituent would be the financial press, particularly in the North but also in the South. Finally, one would include many, though not all, academic economists trained in the Anglo-Saxon tradition. Another group, call them Group B, could be labeled "Civil Society." This group would obviously include analysts and advocates in the full range of advocacy and operational NGOs. There would also be people who worked in some of the UN specialized agencies, in aid ministries in the North and social sector ministries in the South. Among academics, noneconomists would tend to fall into this group.

However, in this chapter I want to focus more on the similarities between Groups A and B, and other groups in the development professionals' ecosystem. And, indeed, ecosystem might be the right term because in many ways the different groups need each other—to oppose or to support. Ross Coggins' passionate poem damns high-minded NGO critics as much as their supposed targets in international financial institutions:

> In Sheraton Hotels in scattered nations
> We damn multinational corporations. . . . . .
> Thus guaranteeing continued good eating
> By showing the need for another meeting.

What is it, then, that binds development professionals together, albeit seeming adversaries at times? I take my lead from anthropologist Annelise Riles's characterization of various groups she studied in the run up to the United Nations Fourth World Conference on Women (the "Beijing conference"):

> In describing the "networks" and "networking" as well as many other activities that captivated these persons' passions and commitments, I hope to understand the flurry of international activity, of which the UN women's conference is a part, as an effect of a certain aesthetic of information of which the world of NGOs, nation-states, international institutions, and networks is only one instantiation. (Riles, 2001: 2).

I want to examine how this common "aesthetic of information" comes about, starting with academics.

In my own discipline, economics, academic success is measured by publication of articles in the top journals. The same is true of my sub-discipline of development economics. There is a well-defined hierarchy of journals in the discipline and the sub-discipline. To get ahead, the young academic development economist must publish in the leading development economics journals, but the best is to get a development economics paper published in a top general economics journal. To get published, the paper has to be rigorous, by which is meant that it has to meet and conform to certain standards of exposition and proof. In economics, this means meeting the standards of quantitative and technical rigor. Although there may be some dispute on what this means, the most recent being the controversies surrounding the use of randomized controlled trials (RCTs), there is more agreement than disagreement on what falls within the canon and what lies beyond the pale. Within academic economics, certainly, even heated debates share "a certain aesthetic of information" that delineates what does and what does not constitute the acceptable mainstream.

Moving beyond economics to the broader social sciences, there are of course major methodological differences between economics, sociology, political science, anthropology, and so forth, not to mention differences within these disciplines, for example, between different branches of anthropology. Kanbur and Shaffer (2007) explore alternative epistemological approaches in poverty analysis and find that they cut across many disciplines, albeit that economics does fall squarely in the "positivist" camp. Kanbur, Rajaram, and Varshney (2011) consider applications of different disciplinary approaches to the analysis of ethnicity and ethnic strife and highlight the need for complementarity so as to build on the strengths of different approaches. However, what I wish to emphasize here is that academic success in other social science disciplines is broadly speaking on the same metric as for economics, namely, publishing articles in prestigious journals and (more so in the broader social sciences) books with prestigious academic presses. Just as development economists who are more persuaded or less persuaded by RCTs would nevertheless agree on a common core of what constitutes quantitative rigor, academics from anthropology who would criticize economists' analysis of development would nevertheless recognize and pay homage to common measures of academic success such as publication, awards, appointment in leading universities, and so forth. They too share this common aesthetic which cuts across academia.

The academic professors' aesthetic on what constitutes success also filters through, I believe, to the students they teach. Certainly the ones who plan to take up an academic career had better follow the standard battle plan and conform to what constitutes rigor, and even what constitutes innovation, according to the ruling aesthetic. And they do so, just as their teachers did so before them, and the aesthetic deepens like a coastal shelf, threatening to drown those who do not learn to swim in it. But even those who do not plan to follow an academic career are of course affected by their teachers. For economics, I have written about the core lessons that an economics graduate takes with him or her into the outside world (Kanbur, 2002). But all students, across the disciplines, cannot but be affected by the striving to achieve standards for rigor and the appreciation of abstract mode of thought and reason. And this, by and large, is the pool from which national and international civil servants, think tank researchers and policy analysts, and NGO activists are drawn.

Although a development economics student is perhaps less likely than an anthropology or a sociology student to have been exposed to the realities of development "on the ground" through field trips and the like, the exposure of either to the lives of the poor in developing countries is likely to be minimal if he or she joins an international development agency such as the World Bank or the other agencies in category (3) listed earlier. In an insightful commentary, Moises Naim (1994) wrote sharply about what he called the "G-4" syndrome. His observations are worth quoting at some length because they capture the generic issue in aid agencies and beyond:

> . . . The G-4 is not a grouping of countries. It is the designation of the US visa that non-US citizens on the Bank staff hold as long as they are employed by it. . . . Upon termination of their bank-sponsored residency they-and their family-have only a few weeks to leave the United States. . . . When the job loss also entails the instantaneous loss of the G-4 visa, the tax exemption status, education and health benefits and the rest of the prerequisites enjoyed by Bank staff, losing a job at the Bank becomes an event of catastrophic proportions. . . . The Bank pays very well and offers benefits that are not easily found elsewhere. Furthermore, for many, the Bank is one of the few places in the world where there is a demand for their highly specialized skills. . . . Staff "knows" that, in order to progress in the Bank, ideas are more important that actions, solid technical writing is more important than public eloquence, economic reasoning is respected while "soft," sociological-type analysis is belittled, and the opinion of colleagues and others in Washington matters more that the opinion of clients. . . . [V]ery few other organizations have the combination of extreme job-dependency, lack of competition and aloofness from the clients that allow the

> internal culture to be as self-absorbed as that of the Bank. . . . The implication of these observations is not that the Bank's performance can be improved by changing the visa status of its non-US employees. It is, rather, to use the G-4 effect to highlight the importance of subtle but powerful forces acting within the Bank and that are often ignored when discussing grand plans about the Bretton Woods institutions. (Naim, 1994)

It should be clear of course that although Naim develops the G-4 metaphor, his characterization applies also to US staff of the World Bank, and to staff of other international agencies the world over. More generally, his fundamental point is about the internal culture of aid agencies, and it extends equally to the culture of bilateral aid agencies as well. Further, although Naim points to the special role of economists and economic methodology, it is difficult to believe that the G-4 syndrome would not also infect non-economists in these organizations. The general point is that no matter how they entered the agencies, with whatever training and exposure and whatever roots of idealism, it is in the nature of these institutions as currently organized that individuals within them are bound to become more internally geared, rather than oriented toward helping the development of the poor in poor countries.

That which applies to the international civil service also applies to the civil service in developing countries. For high flying civil servants in developing countries there are in any case opportunities to move to positions in international agencies, and in some cases to move back and forth as a progression up the career ladder. But the same internal focus on the processes of a ministry, rather than outward orientation to the needs of the poor, is likely to dominate. Rather like academia, bureaucracy (domestic and international) has its own criteria of success, which may be different from those of academia but are equally distant from the reality of the lives of those that development professionals are meant to be serving.

Perhaps the most difficult case to discuss is that of NGO activists, those who have manifestly dedicated themselves to fight for the poorest of the poor, and indeed have perhaps turned down "cushy" aid agency appointments to do so, and in many cases are now battling the policies of these very same aid agencies. Surely there can be no gainsaying their connection with the ground level realities in developing countries? I would, however, like to highlight that, especially in advocacy NGOs based in the North, "civil service like" career structures can and do develop, and there are promotion paths to be followed. The world of within-NGO and cross-NGO coordination is as fraught with dangers of inward looking impetus as the G-4 culture of the World Bank as described by Naim. I would further note that many of the staff of these, especially Northern-based, NGOs are as much the product of the higher educational system in these countries as the staff of international aid agencies. It would not be surprising then if what Annelise Riles (2001) observed holds more widely, that they share "certain aesthetic of information." In the archetypal face off between International Financial Institutions (IFIs) and NGOs, opposed to each other though they are, the staffs of these institutions may be equally removed from the lived realities of the poor, about which they are arguing in what are often highly ritualized settings ("In Sheraton Hotels in scattered nations. . . . ").

So, I have argued that development professionals, in any of the major categories, are led inexorably to a greater and greater distance between their work and the reality of the lives of the poor in developing countries, whom their work is meant to be helping. For academics, the disconnect is caused by the currency of success in their field—publication according to certain standards and criteria. For aid agency workers, the cause is the pressure to be become inward looking and focus on the organizational processes to achieve security, promotion, and success. For the staff of NGO there are similar pressures, compounded by the fact that in effect the nature of the discourse with academics or aid agency officials is in a language and employs an aesthetic that makes it difficult to stay true to the lived reality of poor peoples' lives.

What can be done about this? Just as Moises Naim recognized that the solution to the World Bank's G-4 effect is not to rescind the G-4 visa category, in the same way there are no simple solutions to the dilemma of the disconnect between development professionals and the reality of poverty in developing countries, especially because being a professional means, almost by definition, a lifestyle removed from poverty. Further, professionalism and technical skills should indeed be deployed in the fight against poverty, and one should pay the going rate for these skills. It is too much to expect development professionals to don sack cloth and ashes to legitimate their contribution to the fight against poverty, even as we must be vigilant against them taking the moral ground too easily just because they are engaged in this fight, especially because many of them seem to do not too badly out of it for themselves and for their families.

One answer to this problem is to try and continuously update the connection between development professionals and the reality of the poor in developing countries. This can be presented purely from the point of view of efficiency and efficacy. Rather like sending a technician on a refresher course to keep up to date on the latest technical developments, there could be an attempt to sensitize development professionals to the changing realities of development, which may have altered quite a bit since they (or some of them) did their field work exposure as college students or young professionals. But it can equally well be a device for keeping fresh in the minds of development professionals why it is that they do what they do, make vivid for them the struggle against poverty, which their work is meant to help. In what follows I will describe and discuss such attempts and draw lessons from them. I begin in the next section with a specific exercise with which I have been involved—the Cornell-SEWA-WIEGO Exposure and Dialogue Program (EDP). The following section then considers a broader set of experiences from a range of agencies, and pulls together some design issues and recommendations.

The Cornell-SEWA-WIEGO Exposure and Dialogue Program

This section gives an account of a particular attempt by academics, analysts, and activists to ground their debates in poor peoples' lived reality. Imperfect as it is, the exercise may be helpful to others as a practical manifestation of the desire to reduce the disconnect between the working lives of development professionals and the lives of those they analyze, write about, and prescribe for. This EDP is one example of a broad movement in the development community to institute a practice of "Immersions." The next section looks at the broader experience and draws implications for the training of development practitioners.

Cornell University is of course a world famous Ivy League University. It has a highly ranked economics program and, within that, development economics is even more highly ranked. Its development economists have published in the leading journals and have held leading positions in developing country governments and in international agencies. They are among the leading economic analysts of labor and poverty in the developing world. SEWA, the Self Employed Women's Association, is an Indian organization that describes itself as follows:

> It is an organisation of poor, self-employed women workers. These are women who earn a living through their own labour or small businesses. They do not obtain regular salaried employment with welfare benefits like workers in the organised sector. They are the unprotected labour force of our country. Constituting 93% of the labour force, these are workers of the unorganised sector." (http://www.sewa.org/)

WIEGO, Women in Informal Employment: Globalizing and Organizing, is "a global action-research-policy network that seeks to improve the status of the working poor, especially women, in the informal economy" (www.wiego.org). Thus Cornell is primarily academic, SEWA is primarily activist, and WIEGO combines action, policy, and research.

A group of individuals from these three institutions came together in 2003 to build on previous discussions and interactions on differing perspectives on labor market and trade policy. In particular, the group was concerned about the gaps between mainstream economics on one side and heterodox economists, broader social scientists, and ground level activists on the other, on a range of issues in economic policy. One emblematic issue was that of the minimum wage. Paraphrasing somewhat the arguments of SEWA and WIEGO, they were surprised at the visceral opposition to minimum wage legislation among mainstream economists, especially because they tended to support a range of other interventions such as improved education opportunity for girls and improving property rights for women. For SEWA and WIEGO activists, all these proposals, including that on a minimum wage, flow from the same framework, and they were perplexed as to why the economists they deal with in government, in international agencies, and in academia have such a different reaction to minimum wages alone.

There was considerable interest in such a dialogue combined with significant good will among the individuals concerned, and discussions began to develop on how best to conduct the dialogue. The standard way would have been to meet, have presentations, discussants, critiques, and so on. And indeed, the group did do this. But at an early stage the group introduced a new feature, which was that before each dialogue there would be an exposure to the lives of poor working women in the informal sector that SEWA and WIEGO worked with directly, and whose lives the work of the economists and analysts was meant to improve.

Members of the group had been influenced by the work of Karl Osner, who had introduced the EDP approach to his work when he was a senior official of the German aid agency (BMZ). As Osner notes:

> The trigger for the BMZ's initiative was a cross-sectional evaluation of the 80 state-owned development banks. These had been promoted for many years under financial development cooperation with an annual amount equivalent to 150 million euros.... The result of the evaluation sent shock waves through the Government, forcing the BMZ to react....
>
> - changes in pro-poor development policy;
> - changes in promotional concepts or administrative regulations (i.e. **instruments**); and
> - changes in the daily **practice** of development cooperation, which depend in large part on the **mindset** and **behavior** of the 'bureaucrats' responsible for this policy. (Osner, 2007: 129)

A key part of the third leg of the strategy was the introduction of "immersions":

> During an immersion, people from developed countries or people who are relatively well off stay for a few days with people who live in poverty and are struggling to achieve a decent life by their own efforts. It is a short, in situ encounter with the reality of poverty and exclusion. (Osner, 2007: 129)

In fact, many of these immersions, which became the central part of a broader Exposure and Dialogue Program (see http://www.exposure-dialog.de/), had been hosted by SEWA and their members. Officials of BMZ, and German Parliamentarians and senior civil servants, would spend a few days experiencing the lives of the poor at close quarters. It was this component that the Cornell-SEWA-WIEGO dialogue wove into their interactions, making it an EDP.

The Cornell-SEWA-WIEGO group have held five EDPs between 2004 and 2011, in Ahmedabad, India (2004 and 2008), Durban, South Africa (2007 and 2011), and Oaxaca, Mexico (2009).[3] Each EDP lasted three to five days, roughly evenly divided between Exposure and Dialogue. Members of the group were divided into pairs and,

[3] The members of the group are Namrata Bali, Kaushik Basu, Suman Bery, Haroon Bhorat, Françoise Carré, Nancy Chau, Martha Chen, Gary Fields, Renana Jhabvala, Ravi Kanbur, Francie Lund, Karl Osner, Carol Richards, Jeemol Unni, and Imraan Valodia. Although "Cornell" is used as the shorthand for "mainstream economists," it should be noted that some mainstream economists in the group were not from Cornell. Further, the group was joined by Santiago Levy for the Mexico EDP.

together with facilitators from local organizations, stayed one or two nights with the families of hosts who earned their living in the informal sector. With a few exceptions, the lead hosts were women. Each EDP was focused around a specific set of questions, and hosts were selected by local organizations with these issues in mind (e.g., minimum wages, or trade liberalization, or organizations of the poor). After the Exposure, came the Dialogue around the issues. This dialogue could be fairly technical in nature, but was always informed by and tempered by the profound experience of the previous days of Exposure.

What was the outcome of this process? There are two sources of information. First, after each EDP, participants were asked to write up their experiences in the form of two short notes—one "personal" and one "technical." The compendium of notes for each EDP was put on the web. Second, the whole process underwent an assessment as part of an independent evaluation of WIEGO by their donors. The EDP component was evaluated by Professor Tony Addison, then of the University of Manchester and now at UNU-WIDER. This evaluation is also publicly available.[4] A summary and overview of the process, and the main lessons learned from it, is available in Bali, Chen, and Kanbur (2012b).

The notes are revealing about what the economists, in particular, felt they had learned from the EDP process. Thus Gary Fields, one of the world's leading economists of Labor and Development, said the following after the first EDP in Gujarat, India:

> Because of what I saw on the ground, my professional judgment about minimum wages and supplementary benefits changed. With the standard labour economics model in mind, I had worried that the minimum wage might hurt the very women it was meant to help, because of a loss of jobs. In this context though, the minimum wage does not act as a wage floor. It acts as an aspirational target. If bidi rollers earn 36 rupees per 1000 bidis and a minimum wage is set at 80 or 90 rupees, there would probably be major job losses. However, the SEWA team is astute enough to take this into account, and so they negotiate for minimum wages, expecting that they will not be paid, at least not now. However, the very fact that a minimum wage is set at so (relatively) high a level strengthens SEWA's negotiating position.... Set in this way by negotiators who take full account of possible job losses as well as earnings gains, the minimum wage and Provident Fund are meant to help all of the women in their respective occupations and not, as is often the case in other contexts, insiders at the expense of outsiders. This kind of "wage" increase is something that I favour. Without this experience on the ground, that is not something I would have said two days earlier.... I will conclude with one final thought. I have long thought that if I do my homework before I set off on a trip, nine out of ten notions that I had before are confirmed, but it is the tenth one that makes the trip worthwhile. That is exactly what happened this time. Truly, this was a life experience I will never forget. (Fields, 2012: 41–42)

[4] The Compendia have been brought together in Bali, Chen, and Kanbur (2012*a*), and Addison's evaluation is reproduced as an Appendix in the volume.

The technical and personal notes, by economists and noneconomists alike, are full of such self- revealing comments. Santiago Levy, Vice President of the Inter-American Development Bank and formerly an economics professor and a Deputy Minister of Finance in Mexico, joined us for the EDP in Oaxaca. His notes show the interplay in his mind between formal models and the lived reality of Rambo, the informal sector worker whose family was Santiago's host:

> Rambo told us that he left voluntarily his formal job as a security guard at the Club Med to get an informal salaried job as a waiter at a restaurant (also in Huatulco). On the other hand, Rambo was fired from the Home Depot firm (because he got into a fight). So Rambo's transits from formal to informal jobs have been both voluntary and involuntary. But note again that, from the perspective of the social goals of the government, it does not really matter whether Rambo's transits were voluntary or not. From that perspective, what matters is that at times Rambo was saving for a pension and for a house, and at times not; and at times was covered against death, health and disability risks, and at times not. Of course, the distinction between voluntary and involuntary transits does make a lot of difference for Rambo. In one case he thought he could improve his lot by moving from the Club Med to the restaurant; in the other he was fired, and he might have spent a while openly unemployed or in difficult circumstances until he found a new job. (Levy, 2012: 496–497)

Suman Bery, Director of the National Council of Applied Economics Research (NCAER) in Delhi at the time of the EDPs, a senior World Bank official before that and currently the Chief Economist of Shell, wrote a moving account of his experience in his column in *Business Times*, a leading Indian newspaper targeted to the business community, under the heading "Mother Courage and her Children":

> This was my first experience of an urban slum in India. Two things surprised me: the fact of an established urban "working class" culture; and the apparent extent of social capital in that environment. . . . I left with mixed emotions. I applaud the efforts of SEWA to establish the rights of vendors to ply their trade free from police harassment, and to elevate the dignity of women's work. . . . But I also left with a sense that the larger system was failing these poor people, despite their energy, civility, and enthusiasm. For the opportunity to put a face on urban poverty, and to see Indian cities in a truly different light, I will forever be in SEWA's debt-and that of my hosts. (Bery, 2012: 87–89)

For his independent evaluation, Tony Addison interviewed most members of the group. His report was focused as much on what participants learnt from each other as their learning from the informal sector hosts:

> The EDPs have provided what amounts to a training in economics for the SEWA/WIEGO team of an unusual and innovative kind. It is clear that the EDP has significantly strengthened the ability of the non-economists to engage mainstream economists in debate. . . . SEWA interviewees confirmed that they now have a much

> better understanding of mainstream economics than before the EDP. . . . What of the Cornell economists?. . . . Without exception, the Cornell economists all said that their time in the host households and their discussions with informal workers about their lives had given them a deeper understanding and had led to many new questions for debate in the subsequent dialogues and for later analytical work.. . . One economist, from a developing country, who felt he knew his own country well and was therefore sceptical about whether the EDP would provide him with anything new, said: "I now truly believe that there is so much that researchers can get out of these interactions, and it breaks down the hierarchies that we all operate with. . . . The fact that these processes of learning and analyzing take place outside of the normal academic environment is a key ingredient of the EDP's success. This came across clearly from every Cornell interviewee. One of the Cornell economists commented: ". . . the reality is so humbling that all the grandstanding just falls away that you see in conventional seminars.. . . and you are genuinely moved to understand their reality. (Addison, 2012: 629–630)

The Cornell-SEWA-WIEGO experience is one specific example of an EDP. I have focused on it not only because I have been involved with it, but because it highlights a particular type of interaction which is interesting and important—that between academic mainstream economists and other analysts and activists, especially when this takes place in the shadow of the interaction of both with the object of the analysis and prescription, namely, the poor themselves. Some lessons can be drawn from this type of EDP, and they are highlighted in Bali, Chen, and Kanbur (2012*b*). I return to these lessons in the next section, but in the context of the broader experience of EDPs in other settings and with other agencies.

Immersions and the Development Community

An alternative and broader term for EDP, perhaps equally as well recognized in the development community, is "Immersion." Surveying their development over the previous quarter century, Chambers (2007) noted the wide range of activities that fall under the rubric, albeit with a common theme:

> There is no template or formula. Some are self-organised or even spur-of-the-moment; some are organised with a programme. Some are open-ended for experiential learning; others are thematic, designed to focus on and learn about a topic or sector. Some are personal and individual; others more usually are in groups. An almost universal feature is, though, staying in a poor community, as a person, living with a host family, helping with tasks and sharing in their life. . . . For all this the term immersion has come to be used: the visitor is immersed in daily life, having left behind the baggage of role, organisation, and importance, and stays for days and nights in a community. (Chambers, 2007: 9)

The special issue of *Participatory Learning and Action* (2007), from which this quote is taken, is an extremely useful collation of experiences from which design lessons can be drawn. In this section I will first review some of the experiences and then move to questions of design.

Among the agencies listed at the start of this paper are multilateral and bilateral aid agencies. Indeed, Karl Osner began the EDP in the German aid agency BMZ. In their assessment of immersions in SIDA, the Swedish aid agency, Nilsson, Sandkull, and Sundberg (2007) raise an issue that is ever present:

> We know that some colleagues have questions – often unspoken – about immersions: about their relevance, the time required, the risks of "development tourism," and the possible threats to their personal safety and comfort. We also know that until they can really see their potential benefits, it will be hard to overcome these barriers. ... Slowly, people are becoming more convinced: initial scepticism is declining, and interest in conducting immersions is on the increase both at Sida headquarters and at the embassies. ... There is still a long way to go before immersions are truly institutionalised within Sida as common practice, but we have made progress. ... (Nilsson, Sandkull, and Sundberg, 2007: 120)

It is interesting that the challenges and experiences of an NGO, Action Aid, as elaborated by Ruparel (2007), are similar to those of bilateral (or multilateral) aid agencies:

> ... we are finding that it is not only governments and donors that are at risk of losing their links with communities; international NGOs such as ActionAid face the same challenge. ... There is some resistance to the idea of immersions, not by those who have experienced them, but by those who are reluctant to do so. The usual reason for not participating is: "I don't have the time." This usually means: "I can't, or won't, make this my priority for my time." We manage to make time for workshops in capital cities and for training courses, but we find it difficult to make time to spend with poor people, building relationships with them, and really listening to the voices that we don't usually hear. ... Another reason given for not doing immersions is: "I come from a village, I don't need to do this." While it is often the case that staff have such a background, an immersion offers an opportunity for them to stay with different communities that don't know them, their roles, and their status. (Ruparel, 2007: 39–40)

A central finding emerges from these and other experiences. Those who have experienced immersions are their greatest supporters. Those who have not are more likely to be skeptical. This skepticism has the potential to lead to a bad equilibrium where immersions are not done because they are not done. The only way this equilibrium can be broken is through outside action—for example, by a mandatory requirement from their management that all staff in all development agencies, whether official or nongovernmental, undertake an immersion at least once in their career and preferably at key points in their career such as at appointment and promotion. Indeed, participation in an immersion in the current position could be made a basic qualification for promotion.

I can of course see the objections to this—that it becomes yet another box-checking exercise on the career ladder. But we have such box-checking all over the place. For example, having taken certain courses, or attended certain seminars, are indeed often requirements for even being considered for promotion within these agencies. I can think of worse forms of box-checking than that staff in a development organization actually have spent a few nights living with those whose lives the organization seeks to improve. There are other objections such as cost, but there is cost to all forms of training of staff. The question is whether this form of training, if one can classify it as that, is essential to a development agency.

None of this to gainsay the argument that immersions need to be well designed, monitored, and followed through. The reason I have not spent more time on this issue is that each organization will need to design the immersion that best suits its needs and context. The Cornell-SEWA-WIEGO drew inspiration from the original EDP methodology of Karl Osner, but this was modified to fit our needs. As Osner notes in his reflection on these modifications:

> Unlike the classic EDP methodology as practised until now, the third phase of the Cornell-SEWA-WIEGO EDP, the phase of Dialogue was given its own conceptual basis... It was intended that the resulting Dialogue in the Cornell-SEWA-WIEGO EDP would be fed from two sources: from the ground-level experiences of the EDP participants during their Exposure and from the theoretical and conceptual inputs of the mainstream economists and the ground-level researchers and organizers participating in the Dialogue... The experience at SEWA can lead to a new type of "Business and Issue-related Exposure and Dialogue Programmes for key decision and policy-makers." This new type of EDP is meant to complement the existing types of EDPs, which are mainly concerned with sensitizing and motivating decision and policy-makers for shaping pro-poor policy. (Osner, 2012: 612–614).

Similarly, the immersions in different agencies will be done differently. Birch and Catani (2007) synthesize "elements of good practice," which include such general points as (1) adequate investment in preparation and orientation, (2) appropriate facilitation and interpretation, (3) willingness to embrace the personal and the unexpected, (4) legitimation from employers and managers, (5) addressing ethical dilemmas in immersions, and (6) impact assessment. These general principles need to be translated and implemented at the organization-specific level.

I want to finish this section on immersions in the broader development community by focusing on a population that is of central interest to me and to this volume—students of development economics. Their teachers, academics that is, cannot easily be structured into EDP training. Unlike for staff in development organizations, EDP training cannot be mandated for University Professors, especially those with tenure. For them, persuasion by those who have already had the EDP experience seems the only route. What about their students? The course curriculum can indeed be designed so as to include an element of EDP training. Many, but not all, graduate level courses in development economics, especially courses with titles like Master of Public Affairs (International

Development), have a practicum component that involves internship with a development agency. However, this is more likely than not to be with agencies in one of the Northern or Southern capitals (indeed universities located in these capitals boast of the proximity of these agencies and the opportunities this opens up for students). Although there are of course some opportunities for exposure to the lives of the poor themselves, there does not seem to be as much of an emphasis on this as on more conventional insertions into organizational internships. Similarly, at the PhD level, although those doing dissertations on micro level data that they collect themselves will indeed get exposure to ground level realities; those who do dissertations using macro level data and standard household surveys that are now downloadable from websites will not. Yet this latter group is as likely to be appointed to academic posts, where they will train the next generation, or to a range of development organizations where they will design and implement policies that will affect the lives of the poor.

Are EDPs feasible for development economics students? There are two issues—the time constraint and the financial constraint. On time, there are ever increasing demands on time to get students up to an ever advancing technical frontier. Given the current curriculum, and the current preferences of employers, my advice to students is to "tech themselves up" as much as they can. It would not be fair to any cohort to go against market trends, but I realize that in giving my advice I contribute to the current trap. What is needed is a systemic change, and in that context a tradeoff can indeed be made between the marginal specialized course in development economics and EDP training. In any event, the time costs of an EDP (10 days at most including travel time) are not significant, and the financial costs at the level of students (airfare and minimal living expenses) are not huge. It is all a matter of objectives and priorities.

Conclusion

Let me draw together the threads of the argument, which has three main components. First, it is inherent in the nature of the beast that there will be a progressive disconnect between the working lives of development professionals and the lives of those their work is meant to help. Across a range of professionals, from academics through aid agency officials to NGOs, the focus will increasingly be inward oriented and further removed from the lives of the poor. This is bad purely from a technical point of view. The efficacy and efficiency of interventions designed by such disconnected professionals is bound to be problematic. But it is a gross moral disconnect, too, where development professionals make a good living in the name of a phenomenon of which they have no ongoing experience.

Second, EDPs, or Immersions as they are also known, are a way of addressing this disconnect between development professionals and development reality. They involve exposure to the realities of the lives of the poor through staying with them and experiencing their lives for a period of time, however short. This is not perfect, and it is of course fraught with problems and dangers of its own. Most importantly, it might encourage a "development tourism" syndrome where EDPs are seen in the same vein as exotic vacations. This has not in fact been the experience documented by those who have engaged in EDPs, including in the Cornell-SEWA-WIEGO EDP exercise, but it is something to be watched out for. But because individual and institutional costs are often invoked as reasons for not doing EDPs by those who have not done them, and those who have done them find them to be valuable, the way of breaking out of the current equilibrium of minimal EDPs is to mandate them in organizations and build them into student curricula.

Third, although there are some general design principles that have emerged from experience, EDPs need to be fashioned for each context, taking into account the culture of each organization, and its specific needs. The Cornell-SEWA-WIEGO EDP, for example, was designed as a vehicle to bridge the gap between mainstream economists and those who often oppose them from the activist and noneconomist end of the spectrum. Immersions in aid agencies may naturally focus on areas where that agency has its operations. As experience has shown, clarity of objectives, prior preparation and facilitation, and ex post evaluation are all important. Immersions must be done well. The point, however, is that they must be done.

References

Addison, Tony. 2012. "Bridging Different Perspectives on Labour and Poverty: An Evaluation." In *The Cornell-SEWA-WIEGO Exposure Dialogue Programme on Labor, Informal Employment and Poverty*, edited by Namrata Bali, Martha Chen, and Ravi Kanbur, pp. 621–640. Gujarat, India: SEWA Academy.

Bali, Namrata, Martha Chen, and Ravi Kanbur, Eds. 2012*a*. *Bridging Perspectives: The Cornell-SEWA-WIEGO Exposure Dialogue Programme on Labor, Informal Employment and Poverty*. Gujarat, India: SEWA Academy.

Bali, Namrata, Martha Chen, and Ravi Kanbur. 2012*b*. "The Cornell-SEWA-WIEGO Exposure Dialogue Programme: An Overview of the Process and Main Outcomes." In *The Cornell-SEWA-WIEGO Exposure Dialogue Programme on Labor, Informal Employment and Poverty*, edited by Namrata Bali, Martha Chen, and Ravi Kanbur, pp. 621–640. Gujarat, India: SEWA Academy.

Bery, Suman. 2012. "An Ahmedabad Slum reveals Strong Social Capital but Little Interest in Education." In *The Cornell-SEWA-WIEGO Exposure Dialogue Programme on Labor, Informal Employment and Poverty*, edited by Namrata Bali, Martha Chen, and Ravi Kanbur, pp. 86–89. Gujarat, India: SEWA Academy.

Birch, Izzy, and Rafaella Catani. 2007. "Immersions: Reflections on Practice." *Participatory Learning and Action* No. 57:134–139.

Chambers, Robert. 1995, April. "Poverty and Livelihoods: Whose Reality Counts?" *Environment and Urbanization* 7(1): 173–204.

Chambers, Robert. 2007. "Overview Immersions; Something Is Happening." *Participatory Learning and Action* No. 57: 9–14.

Coggins, Ross. 1976, September. "The Development Set." *Adult Education and Development*, reprinted in *Adult Education and Development* (1988), p. 56.

Fields, Gary. 2012. "Reflections on My Immersion in India." In *The Cornell-SEWA-WIEGO Exposure Dialogue Programme on Labor, Informal Employment and Poverty*, edited by Namrata Bali, Martha Chen, and Ravi Kanbur, pp. 39–42. Gujarat, India: SEWA Academy.

Hancock, Graham. 1989. *The Lords of Poverty: The Power, Prestige and Corruption of the International Aid Business*. New York: Atlantic Monthly Press.

Kanbur, Ravi. 2001. "Economic Policy, Distribution and Poverty: The Nature of Disagreements." *World Development* 29(6): 1083–1094.

Kanbur, Ravi. 2002. "Economics, Social Science and Development." *World Development* 30(3): 477–486.

Kanbur, Ravi. 2011. "Poverty Professionals and Poverty." In *Revolutionizing Development*, edited by A. Cornwall and I. Scoones, pp. 211–216. London: Earthscan.

Kanbur, Ravi, P. Rajaram, and A. Varshney. 2011. "Ethnic Diversity and Ethnic Strife: An Interdisciplinary Perspective." *World Development* 39(2): 147–158.

Kanbur, Ravi, and Paul Shaffer. 2007. "Epistemology, Normative Theory and Poverty Analysis: Implications for Q-Squared in Practice." *World Development* 35(2): 183–196.

Levy, Santiago. 2012. "After a Few Days with a Poor Mexican Worker." In *The Cornell-SEWA-WIEGO Exposure Dialogue Programme on Labor, Informal Employment and Poverty*, edited by Namrata Bali, Martha Chen, and Ravi Kanbur, pp. 493–505. Gujarat, India: SEWA Academy.

Naim, Moises. 1994. "World Bank: Its Role, Governance and Organizational Culture." Carnegie Endowment for international Peace. Retrieved from http://www.carnegieendowment.org/1999/09/04/world-bank-its-role-governance-and-organizational-culture/2bkj. (Accessed October 29, 2012).

Nilsson, Esse, Olof Sandkull, and Molly Sundberg. 2007. "Taking Onboard Immersions within Sida." *Participatory Learning and Action* No. 57: 118–120.

Osner, Karl. 2007. "With the Strength of the Powerless: Using Immersions for Processes of Structural Change." *Participatory Learning and Action* No. 57: 128–132.

Osner, Karl. 2012. "Using Exposure Methodology for Dialogue on Key Issues." In *The Cornell-SEWA-WIEGO Exposure Dialogue Programme on Labor, Informal Employment and Poverty*, edited by Namrata Bali, Martha Chen, and Ravi Kanbur, pp. 607–620. Gujarat, India: SEWA Academy.

Riles, Anne. 2001. *The Network Inside Out*. Ann Arbor: University of Michigan Press.

Ruparel, Sonya. 2007. "Immersions in Action Aid." *Participatory Learning and Action* No. 57: 36–40.

CHAPTER 35

ETHICS AND LEARNING IN UNDERGRADUATE ECONOMICS EDUCATION

ROBERT F. GARNETT, JR.

Introduction

George DeMartino (2011) challenges professional economists to confront their ethical responsibilities, especially in areas where their expert roles and activities are marked by "epistemic insufficiency" and by "epistemic asymmetry" vis-à-vis those over whom they exert influence (105–116). In this chapter, I focus on the ethical duties of economists as undergraduate educators, a sphere of professional activity in which the problem of "influence without control" is pervasive yet underexamined.

Teachers of undergraduate economics generally receive little or no formal teacher training; yet their disciplinary expertise enables them to act as professionals in the classroom, to "enjoy authority and exercise influence over others by virtue of the intellectual monopoly [we] hold over a body of knowledge" (DeMartino, 2011: 106). The epistemic asymmetry between economics professors and students is particularly acute due to the "adult" nature of our worldly philosophy. As Deirdre McCloskey (2000: 180) observes,

> I think economics, like philosophy, cannot be taught to 19-year-olds. . . . You can teach a 19-year-old boy from a suburban, middle-class family all the math he can grasp, all the history he can read, all the Latin he can stand. But you cannot teach him a philosophical subject. For that he has to be, say, 25; or, better, 45. Or female.

The epistemic condition of the undergraduate instructor is further exacerbated by the limited and often erroneous knowledge with which we enact our expert role (DeMartino, 2011: 112). Notwithstanding our earnest efforts, student learning is constrained by the uncertainties inherent to the educational process (e.g., the difficulty of ascertaining the impact of a particular lesson, course, or degree program on students' knowledge and skills). The uncertainty-laced perils of teaching and learning are further multiplied by our expert-minded propensity to underestimate the gap between intentions and results.

Student learning often falls far short of instructors' perceptions due to what physics educator Carl Wieman (2007) calls the "curse of knowledge": the fact that "when you know something, it is extremely difficult to think about it from the perspective of someone who does not know it." The epistemic gap between expert and novice gives rise to mutual incomprehension and chronic frustration between teacher and student:

> Students can think about a topic in ways quite unimagined by the instructor, and so a lesson that is very carefully thought out and is beautifully clear and logical to experts may be interpreted totally differently (and incorrectly) by the student. (Wieman, 2007)

Wieman concludes that "it is dangerous, and often profoundly incorrect, to think about student learning based on what appears best to faculty members, as opposed to what has been verified with students."

DeMartino contends, and I agree, that the most effective way to address the ethical difficulties and blind spots in our professional work is through sustained scholarly inquiry (2011: 87). In this chapter, I submit a *prima facie* case for an ethical turn in the scholarship of economics education—to explore anew the problems we confront as teachers of undergraduate economics through the lens of the liberal tradition we share as economists and academic citizens.

The ideals of liberal education are widely if tacitly shared among economics educators. Despite many other disagreements, the goal of increasing students' capacity for cogent, self-directed thought—for example, "creative, critical thinking" (Shackelford, 1992: 522) or "independent problem-solving skills" (Fels, 1974: 404)—is applauded by economists of every stripe. Without suggesting that ethical matters are more important than other realms of educational inquiry, I believe we can improve undergraduate economics by employing educational ethics as a starting point or heuristic frame, to acknowledge and explore the liberal sensibilities that inspire and guide us as teachers and academic citizens. By focusing on the ethical dimensions of our craft, about which we agree more than we disagree, mainstream and heterodox economists can expand professional understanding of how and why undergraduate economics courses should foster liberal education outcomes such as the expansion of students' capacity for reflective judgment.

Ethical Duties of Undergraduate Educators

To identify a minimal set of ethical duties for all undergraduate educators, I turn to two sources: the Socratic tradition of liberal education as represented by the foundational writings of educational psychologist William Perry (1970), philosopher Martha Nussbaum (1997), and economist David Ellerman (2005); and the literature on undergraduate students' academic rights, drawing from the American Association of University Professors' principles of academic freedom (AAUP, 1915, 1940, 1967, 1970, 2005) and the incisive reflections of educational philosopher Kenneth Strike (1982).

Socratic Perspectives

Nussbaum (1997) argues that liberal education is the proper aim of all baccalaureate institutions. In her view, "Liberal education in our colleges and universities is and should be Socratic, committed to the activation of each student's independent mind and to the production of a community that can reason together about a problem, not just trade claims and counterclaims" (19). Education is liberal, Nussbaum argues, when it produces "citizens who are free not because of wealth or birth" but because they "can call their minds their own," because they "have looked into themselves and developed the ability to separate mere habit and convention from what they can defend by argument" and have gained thereby "ownership of their own thought and speech" (293). These essential capabilities prepare students for active participation in the communities that comprise their personal, civic, and professional lives.

The process of intellectual self-ownership—becoming an autonomous thinker—is classically described by Perry's nine stages of intellectual development (Perry, 1970), ranging from students who view education as the delivery of Truth from experts to novices, to students who are able to assume responsibility for their own minds and ideas despite the absence of absolute epistemic warrants for their positions. In Perry's words, "The liberally educated [person] . . . can take responsibility for [his or her] own stand and negotiate—with respect—with other men" (39–40). Liberal education names the developmental process by which students become intellectual free agents: responsible, self-directed subjects of knowledge.

The Socratic view of knowledge and liberal education as acts of intellectual (self-) ownership is neatly summarized by Hungarian philosopher Laszlo Versényi (1963: 117):

> Real education aims at imparting knowledge rather than opinion. . . . [K]nowledge cannot be handed over ready-made but has to be appropriated by the knower . . . [and] that appropriation is only possible through one's own search.

Taking Versényi's theme as his starting point, Ellerman (2005) foregrounds the ethical dimension of teaching and other forms of "autonomy-respecting help." Ellerman argues that, "Helpers can at best use indirect, enabling, and autonomy-respecting methods to bring doers to the threshold. [But] the doers have to do the rest on their own in order to make it their own. The doers will acquire [knowledge] only as the fruits of their own labor" (252). Autonomy-respecting help is a delicate art that requires vigilant attention to the paradox of "assisted autonomy":

> If the helpers are supplying help that directly influences the doers, then how can the doers really be 'helping themselves'? Autonomy cannot be externally supplied. (2005: 4).

In the undergraduate classroom, Ellerman's approach underscores the inherent indirectness of the teacher's role in the learning process: providing resources and opportunities that bring students to the threshold of discovery and learning but without overriding or undercutting their capacity for self-reliance. Indeed, Ellerman's rigorous commitment to the Socratic "labor theory of learning," whereby each student bears the inalienable task of appropriating new ideas by integrating them into his or her unique web of prior knowledge, crystallizes the *liberal* nature of the education ("education befitting a free person") to which every student is entitled under a Socratic view of undergraduate education.

Students' Academic Rights

The duties of faculty members in the provision of "autonomy-respecting help" are the principal focus of the AAUP's official statements on students' academic rights over the past century. The AAUP addressed students' academic rights in their founding document (AAUP, 1915), stipulating that the university teacher shall not "provide his students with ready-made conclusions" and must "guard against taking unfair advantage of the student's immaturity by indoctrinating him with the teacher's own opinions before the student has . . . sufficient knowledge and ripeness of judgment to be entitled to form any definitive opinion of his own." The AAUP enjoined faculty to "train (students) to think for themselves and to provide them access to those materials which they need if they are to think intelligently." In the illustrative words of the 1915 report:

> The university teacher . . . while he is under no obligation to hide his own opinion under a mountain of equivocal verbiage . . . should cause his students to become familiar with the best published expressions of the great historic types of doctrine upon the questions at issue . . . (including) the divergent opinions of other investigators.

In philosophical terms, the AAUP guidelines (1915, 1940, 1967, 1970, 2005) accord positive as well as negative academic rights to undergraduate students. Negative academic freedom ("freedom from") protects each student from improper coercion by academic peers or superiors. It requires instructors to provide learning environments in which students can question disciplinary assumptions and reasoning in academically appropriate ways without intimidation or ridicule from professors or fellow students and their work can be evaluated without prejudice. Positive academic freedom ("freedom to") requires faculty to "train (students) to think for themselves," to be self-directed intellectual agents (Nussbaum, 1997).[1]

The ethical rationale for these positive and negative freedoms is a matter of ongoing debate. Some critics argue that the very idea of students' academic rights is a normative non sequitur because the intellectual immaturity of undergraduate students means they "do not possess any rights except the right to competent instruction" (Fish, 2008: 123; Saito, 2003: 25). Strike (1982) offers a robust Socratic response to these critics, one that acknowledges the epistemic gap between expert teacher and novice student while invoking this very asymmetry as grounds for students' academic rights.

Strike agrees with Fish that undergraduate students *qua* students possess no civil or constitutional free speech rights:

> The rights of students in schools are not simply the civil rights of adults in society. Civil liberties are rooted in a presumption of equality between the parties. . . . [Postsecondary education] is not a marketplace of ideas where truth emerges from a multitude of tongues. It is a place where the student strives to master a rational enterprise under the guidance of an expert. Treating the expert-novice relationship as though it were governed by civil rights distorts its character. (Strike, 1982: 148)

At the same time, Strike defends students' academic rights on both moral and epistemological grounds. "Students do have rights," Strike argues, since "[t]hey are persons and moral agents, and must, therefore, be treated as objects of value and respect" (1982: 148). The moral equality of teacher and student, as persons who each bear moral responsibility "for what they choose and what they do," obliges teachers to respect the autonomy of students, "to give students reasons for what they are asked to believe, within students' capacity to grasp them, and to teach so as to expand the students' capacity to comprehend and assess reasons" (43).

Epistemically, however, the student–faculty relationship is marked by "a significant inequality between the student (as novice) and the teacher (as expert) in terms of their current capacity to understand and assess the ideas and arguments of a field" (Strike, 1982: 49). This epistemic asymmetry imparts to teachers an academic duty to honor and cultivate students' intellectual freedom. The teacher/expert is obliged to treat each student "as a junior member of a community united by a shared commitment to some intellectual enterprise" (51), to "secure for the student the right to participate in the intellectual affairs of the classroom in a way that assists the student in internalizing the standards and procedures of a discipline" (49), and to provide a set of educational resources and opportunities that "brings the student into a position of intellectual independence" (135).

[1] The terms negative and positive liberty were coined by political philosopher Isiah Berlin (2002[1958]). The subtlety of Berlin's thinking on these matters is not fully captured by popular translations of the negative/positive distinction as "freedom from" and "freedom to," but the latter will suffice for our purposes here.

A final issue regarding the epistemic rationale for students' academic rights is to clarify the precise nature of the teacher–student asymmetry, specifically, the nature of the knowledge teachers and students are presumed to acquire by means of their respective inquiries.

Strike's discussion is muddy on this crucial point. On one hand, he says teachers and students are engaged in two distinct modes of inquiry: the inquiry of experts, which has the potential to "add to human knowledge," versus the inquiry of the novice that "may be adding to his personal store of knowledge" but "is not likely to add to the general store of human knowledge" (1982: 53). On the other hand, he sees teachers and students as participants in a common process of inquiry, a process in which "new ideas must be assessed, accepted, modified or rejected on the basis of relevant evidence" (52) and conducted within "a community united by a shared commitment to some intellectual enterprise" (51).

At issue is the nature of student learning itself and whether the undergraduate classroom is understood as a locus of knowledge production or merely a site for the redistribution of expert knowledge produced elsewhere. Strike leaves open the latter possibility when he defines the teacher–student asymmetry in terms of expert versus novice inquiry. Yet the rest of his discussion eschews this demarcation, describing students and teachers as junior and senior participants within a single process of inquiry (recognizing, of course, the unequal value of student vs. expert knowledge within any disciplinary learning community). Student knowledge may not advance the frontiers of human knowledge in the conventional sense; but any act of intellectual appropriation by a unique human subject—creating a unique fusion of old and new ideas, the fruits of an inherently personal act of learning—constitutes new knowledge nonetheless.

Strike's epistemic defense of students' academic rights holds under either view of the teacher–student asymmetry. But the ethical force of his defense—the wrongness of treating students as educational objects rather than subjects—is greater if the college classroom is cast as a locus of knowledge production, as against the more restrictive premise that new knowledge is produced by disciplinary experts alone. In other words, the epistemic case for students' academic rights is more securely anchored in a vision of the educational process as *epistemically asymmetric but inclusive*, recognizing the limited but real sense in which student learning is an act of knowledge production.

On a Socratic view, therefore, our fundamental duty as undergraduate educators is to facilitate each student's achievement of a liberal education: an education that honors the student's negative and positive academic rights and brings him or her "into a position of intellectual independence" (Strike, 1982: 135; also Garnett and Butler, 2009; Garnett, 2011). The ethical/pedagogical problem facing the undergraduate educator is thus aptly described as a helper-doer conundrum, as the educator, despite chronic epistemic insufficiency, seeks to navigate the epistemic asymmetry of the student–teacher relationship in autonomy-respecting ways that enable students to exercise their reasoned agency, to become the owners of their own minds and ideas.

Samuelsonian Legacies

Undergraduate economics education has changed relatively little over the past half-century. One can find many departments whose course offerings or major requirements deviate from the mainline norm, sometimes radically so. But the typical experience of an economics student today is remarkably similar to what his or her economics professors encountered during their undergraduate days. These enduring norms are well described as Samuelsonian (Elzinga, 1992).

One hallmark of Samuelsonian economics is the notion of a singular scientific consensus, a core of foundational principles that comprises "the economic way of thinking" and is "accepted by all but a few extreme left-wing and right-wing writers" (Samuelson, 1967: 197–198). On this premise, the chief task of economics educators and degree programs becomes the inculcation of the prevailing orthodoxy because all relevant ideas from previous thinkers are assumed to be embodied in the prevailing mainstream consensus (Boulding, 1971). Courses on contending economic theories, economic history, or the history of economic thought are classified as "breadth" courses; that is, inessential (if not inimical) to undergraduate economics education.

Equally characteristic of Samuelsonian economics are tool-oriented, expert-centered pedagogies in which teachers and textbooks deliver "knowledge" to students in the form of predigested arguments and conclusions drawn from the work of other disciplinary experts. "Chalk and talk" (or "PowerPoint and talk") methods have been the go-to techniques in economics education for decades (Becker and Watts, 1996, 2001; Watts and Becker, 2008; Harter, Becker, and Watts, 2011; Watts and Schaur, 2011), despite growing evidence across the disciplines that even masterful lectures generate less student learning than subject-centered alternatives (Hake, 1998; Mazur, 2009; Campbell and Smith, 1997; Finkel, 2000; Fink, 2003; Tagg, 2003; Deslauriers, Schelew, and Wieman, 2011).

The patently illiberal practice of conveying a singular "economic way of thinking" via expert-centered pedagogies derives its legitimacy from the erstwhile norms of the natural sciences, according to which the undergraduate degree course is "a dogmatic initiation in a pre-established tradition that the student is not equipped to evaluate" (Kuhn, 1977: 229). The natural science connection is germane because it underscores the academic economist's self-image as "scientist" and recalls DeMartino's analysis of economists' ingrained resistance to codes of professional ethics of the sort commonly found in law, medicine, engineering, accounting, and other professions. By seeing their intellectual domain as a science (hence a "nonprofession"), economists believe they should be exempt from formal ethical rules because, as members of a scientific community, they are properly bound by the minimal ethics of scientific practice but nothing more (DeMartino, 2011: 123–139).

The ersatz ethics of "economic exceptionalism" extend to the undergraduate classroom. As products of a Samuelsonian culture, most economics professors take a narrow view of educational ethics. They observe codes of faculty conduct within their own institutions but give little thought to their students' moral-intellectual autonomy or to their special role as protectors and cultivators of this autonomy. They do not consider the possibility that standard economics courses and curricula may unwittingly undercut students' capacity for reflective judgment and self-directed inquiry. Some teach their whole careers without effectively confronting the ethical-pedagogical riddle at the heart of undergraduate education: the delicate dance of "teaching for freedom" (Finkel and Arney, 1995; also Finkel, 2000), of "helping people help themselves" as learners (Ellerman, 2005).

The Samuelsonian view of students' intellectual freedom as an ornamental extra is strikingly analogous to the way US development economists treated citizens' political and civil liberties in low-income nations in the 1950s and '60s—seeing such freedoms as luxury items, to be indulged only after threshold levels of gross domestic product (GDP) per capita had been achieved (Sen, 1999). The economics professorate since World War II has taken a similarly hard-nosed view of students' intellectual development. When students raise questions about the assumptions, logic, or implications of standard textbook arguments, the Socratic ethic says it is our duty "to give reasons" and to respect the student's right "to question and debate the conclusions reached by experts" (Strike, 1982: 49). The implicit Samuelsonian ethic conveys no such duty. Kinder souls may elect to give reasons, but no ethical line is crossed by the professor who illiberally responds, "Just learn the models; then we'll talk."

The Puzzling Persistence of Samuelsonian Norms

Why do these antiquated and arguably authoritarian norms persist, especially when there is so little evidence that they enhance student learning? Economics remains a popular course of study in the United States and across the globe, yet even our best and brightest majors are frequently unable to demonstrate retained understanding of basic economic principles (Walstad and Allgood, 1999) or to apply their economic knowledge to messy, real-life problems (Salemi and Siegfried, 1999; Hansen, Salemi, and Siegfried, 2002; Katz and Becker, 1999). Economics education is still mired in the same basic difficulty that has plagued the Samuelsonian enterprise since the 1950s, namely: the inability to generate "learning that lasts" (Stigler, 1963) via graphical-mathematical, chalk-and-talk renderings of the great ideas and debates of our discipline.

Sheer inertia is part of the story. As Paul Heyne observed two decades ago:

> None of this is the product of a conspiracy. We are caught in a kind of prisoner's dilemma where almost everyone prefers an outcome that is, unfortunately, in no one's interest to bring about. Teachers present what appears in the textbooks, the

textbooks offer what the teachers expect, and the teachers expect what has been in the textbooks for as long as they can remember. (Heyne, 1995: 150)

The intergenerational stalemate is exacerbated by the increased use of contingent faculty in introductory courses (instructors more likely to conduct textbook-driven, chalk-and-talk courses) and professional reward structures that generally afford greater recognition and compensation for research productivity than for teaching accomplishments (Walstad and Allgood, 2005).

The persistence of Samuelsonian norms also reflects how influential segments of our profession think about liberal education vis-à-vis undergraduate economics education. Some say, "Liberal education is not our job." They value liberal education learning outcomes but think they are better provided by a general education curriculum outside the major, simply feel unprepared to provide them in their own courses, or both (Solow, 1990; Colander, 1991, 2001). Others say, "Liberal education is our job, and we already do it well." These economists have few if any qualms with the Samuelsonian status quo because their disciplinary training persuades them that "the analytical nature of most economics courses inherently teaches students to think critically" (Borg and Borg, 2001: 20). They see themselves as liberal educators who *already* promote "independent and critical thought" (Siegfried et al., 1991: 199).

Many other economists say, "Liberal education is our job, and we do *not* do it well enough." Yet the pedagogical ideals of this "silent plurality" have never gained much professional standing, in part because the energies of its leading advocates—heterodox and mainstream—are perennially divided along the methodological and sociological fault lines of our profession. The breadth and strength of support for liberal education reforms to undergraduate education have thus been vitiated by a failure to articulate common ethical principles or projects to which all would-be reformers could subscribe.

Liberal Educators, Heterodox and Mainstream

Even as the structure, pedagogy, and tacit philosophy of undergraduate economics have remained predominantly Samuelsonian, a rich array of liberal education alternatives have flourished—for decades, across multiple schools of thought—in the interstices of the dominant approach.

As evidence of this "silent plurality," consider the vocal dissent that arose from multiple corners in response to the "Voluntary Economics Content Standards for Pre-College Economics Education" (National Council of Economic Education, 1997; Siegfried and Meszaros, 1997, 1998) and the complementary push for a "less is more" revision of micro- and macroeconomic principles courses (Frank, 1998; Hansen et al., 2002; Kennedy, 2006). The "content standards" were an effort to streamline and standardize the canon of principles taught in high school economics courses (Siegfried and Meszaros, 1997). However, the standards were derived from and have subsequently influenced revisions of material presented in most US college textbooks—textbooks whose influence over economics education reaches far beyond the United States (Ferber, 1999: 136). The "less is more" initiative sought to shift principles courses away from the "encyclopedic" approaches of standard textbooks toward a "short list of topics" in order to reallocate the "recovered course resources to help students apply the basic tools of economics to problems and questions they will face throughout their lives" (Salemi, 2009). Although not intentionally, both campaigns gave impetus to the development and marketing of Gregory Mankiw's *Principles of Economics* (1998), which came to be seen as the prototype for a new generation of "less is more" principles texts (Schneider and Shackelford, 2001).

Marianne Ferber, a leading feminist economist, delivered the sharpest initial criticism of the national content standards (Ferber, 1999). Taking vigorous exception to the claim that the standards "are, in fact, the fundamental propositions of economics" (Siegfried and Meszaros, 1997: 247), Ferber argued that, "It is difficult, if not impossible, to teach economics effectively while pretending that there is consensus in the discipline about either theory or policy. . . . Ignoring these issues deprives students of learning about the most thought-provoking discussions of the profession" (1999: 137–138). Similar criticisms followed from other feminist and heterodox economists (Lewis and McGoldrick, 2001; Schneider and Shackelford, 2001) and, most recently, from Stephen Marglin, who rejects the Samuelsonian thrust of these and other recent efforts to improve students' economic literacy. "Teaching a catechism," says Marglin (2012: 288), "is not how to cultivate the questioning and searching that is the end product we should be seeking."

These responses express heterodox economists' commitment to intellectual pluralism and critical thinking as necessary elements in economics education at all levels (Earl, 2000; Colander, 2001; Feiner, 2002; Fullbrook, 2003; Garnett and Klopfenstein, 2003). For these educators, the depiction of economics as a "single coherent view" is factually misleading, pedagogically counterproductive, and turns economics education into "illiberal education" (Marglin, 2009). Even at the introductory level, most heterodox economists favor introducing "competing views on recurring problems in economics" (Raveaud, 2003) as a means of enabling students to "learn how to think critically and independently—the essence of a liberal undergraduate education" (Moseley, Gunn, and Georges, 1991: 237; see also Barone, 1991; Feiner and Roberts, 1995; Knoedler and Underwood, 2003; Underwood, 2004; and O'Donnell, 2009). Other disagreements notwithstanding, all heterodox economics educators would find congenial George Shackle's Socratic vision of the undergraduate enterprise:

> The first task of the University teacher of any liberal art is surely to persuade his students that the most important things he will put before them are questions and not answers. He is going to put up for them a scaffolding, and leave them to build within it. He has to persuade them that they have not come to the University to learn as it were by heart things which are already hard-and-fast and cut-and-dried, but to

> watch and perhaps help in a process, the driving of a causeway which will be made gradually firmer by the traffic of many minds. (Shackle, 1953: 18)

Among mainstream economics educators, William Becker, former editor of the *Journal of Economic Education*, deplores the remedial, illiberal thrust of "less is more" and the national content standards:

> The dumbing down of economics to the dogmatic preaching of a few simple concepts, principles, and axioms of old misses the excitement of modern day economics and is a deceitful representation of the science of economics and a disservice to students seeking a higher education. (2007: 9; see also Becker, 2004)

Becker advocates a broader approach, even in introductory courses, to "show students that economics is a science that is innovating and evolving with social change" (2004: 58) and to expose them to the complexities of applying textbook principles whose underlying assumptions "are unlikely to be met in actual circumstances" (2007: 5).

Becker's objections resonate with the liberal education ethos of the mainstream economics education community, a tradition whose roots include Rendigs Fels's ambitious efforts to redirect undergraduate economics education toward the "development of independent problem-solving skills" (Fels, 1974: 404). Fels and his collaborators (Richard Leftwich, Ansel Sharp, Stephen Buckles, and Paul Grimes) created a problem-centered, case study approach to introductory economics, aiming to help students learn to think like liberally educated economists (Grimes, 2009). "Applying economic principles to new situations requires judgment," Fels argued, including normative value judgments (Fels and Buckles, 1981: 16). Even though the questions raised in a case often had "no clearly right or wrong answers," Fels believed the soundness of students' judgments could be improved with training and practice (1974: 405). In presenting these cases to students, Fels would explain that their purpose was "not to provide cut-and-dried answers for you to memorize but to train you . . . to think for yourself" (Fels and Buckles, 1981: 16), and "to highlight the role which values and norms must play in the formulation of policy" (Fels, 1974: 405). The integral place of liberal arts skills in undergraduate economics education is further echoed in the landmark report of Siegfried et al. (1991) in which the authors claim that the ultimate goal of the economics major is "to empower students with a self-sustaining capacity to think and learn" (201).

The educational perspectives of Ferber, Marglin, Becker, Fels, et al. hardly comprise a united front (e.g., a common conception of liberal education). Their approaches are diverse and in many ways divergent. But there are significant overlaps in their assumptions, aims, and values, and these overlaps offer grounds for conversation among heterodox and mainstream economists in which the *lingua franca* is educational ethics. For example, all of these writers are committed to the protection and cultivation of students' intellectual freedom (Garnett, 2009), including the positive capability John Dewey (1933) called reflective thinking: the art of formulating reasoned solutions to problems for which "there is no way to apply a formula to derive a correct solution and no way to prove definitively that a proposed solution is correct" (King and Kitchener, 1994: 6; Perry, 1970; Thoma, 1993; Nelson, 1997; Paul, 1999). This loose coalition of perspectives thus stands in support of liberal alternatives to the "algorithmic thinking" (Marglin, 2008: 128–146) and "complex correct thinking" (Nelson, 1997: 62) promoted by standard Samuelsonian textbooks in which problems are specified with high degrees of completeness and solvable with high degrees of certainty using deductive or inductive logic (McGoldrick and Garnett, 2013).

Activating the Silent Plurality: Economics Education as Freedom

Even as they are scattered across regions, nations, schools of thought, and academic ranks, this inchoate plurality of educators is drawn together by their congruent conceptions of the task at hand: a complex task that admits no panaceas and raises a host of fundamental questions about how "liberal education" capabilities should be defined and fostered. To spark and sustain dialogue across this nascent community, economics educators would be well served to craft a strategy analogous to Amartya Sen's "development as freedom" project (Sen, 1999), his reframing of economic and social development as "a process of expanding the real freedoms people enjoy" (3).

Sen embraced this strategy for intellectual reasons, in part: to foreground the multidimensionality of human freedom (e.g., procedural vs. substantive freedoms) and to cast human freedom as both "the primary end" and "principal means" of development" (1999: xii). He also saw "development as freedom" as a political strategy: using the language of freedom to promote dialogue and cooperation among diverse cultural, intellectual, and ideological groups in hopes of generating broader support—hence greater leverage—for addressing the most pressing forms of unfreedom (e.g., preventable morbidity or lack of access to basic education, especially for girls and women).

The field of economics education is already a rudimentary exemplar of professional-ethics-as-conversation, with practitioners engaged in dialogue across multiple journals and annual conferences about the ethics and pragmatics of their professional work (DeMartino, 2011: 87). However, the conversation is highly segregated along mainstream/heterodox lines, and its ethical content is limited, especially on the mainstream side. For economics educators to move in the direction of Sen's model, the next big step would be more explicit attention to ethical matters as such and more discussion among mainstream and heterodox economists; for example, more discussion of why the development of students' capacity to think for themselves is not an ornamental extra but an essential part of what economics education should and must be and an appraisal of pragmatic strategies for making it so.

The rich feminist literature on economics education offers one fruitful starting point for this endeavor. Leading feminist educators have long framed their agendas within the language and philosophy of liberal education (Bartlett and Feiner, 1992; Shackelford, 1992). David Colander and KimMarie McGoldrick employed a similar strategy in their recently published collection on "the economics major as part of a liberal education" (Colander and McGoldrick, 2009*a*), a volume framed neither as "a blue-ribbon report" nor a "set of best practices for the major" but as an inclusive discussion among mainstream and heterodox economists seeking "to raise questions, not to provide answers or conclusions" (Colander and McGoldrick, 2009*b*: xxviii–xxix).

Pace Sen, sustained discussion of the ethical precepts to which we subscribe as professional economic educators could eventually facilitate interparadigmatic agreements on the "low-hanging fruit" of educational reform. Apropos of the recent push for learning outcomes assessment across colleges and universities in the United States, the United Kingdom, and elsewhere, one opportune item would be a campaign to institute "reflective thinking" as a standard proficiency goal for the economics major (Freeman, 2007; Dekker and Klamer, 2016; Wight, 2016). Economics majors are currently expected to acquire threshold proficiencies in micro- and macroeconomic principles, probability and statistics, and certain forms of mathematics. These transferable skills are deemed essential because they enable students to understand, evaluate, construct, and communicate economic arguments. Reflective thinking would be a natural addition to this core set of skills, to enable economics majors "to engage differences of opinion, evaluate evidence and form their own grounded judgments about the relative value of competing perspectives" (AAC&U, 2006). Moreover, since there is no single, correct way to help students acquire reflective thinking skills, each department and instructor would retain the freedom to craft individual recipes for doing so.

Three additional sets of resources are already available to support an ethical turn in the formal and informal discourse of economics education.

- *The US tradition of academic freedom.* This evolving dialogue on the rights and duties of instructors and students is a neglected but defining rubric for US higher education. Its enumerated principles provide a basic ethical framework for college and university educators, specifying not a utopian set of ideal conditions for academic inquiry but "minimal standards . . . essential to any community of scholars" (AAUP, 1967). As such, the language and tradition of academic freedom offers a potential vehicle for curricular/pedagogical conversation and reform.
- *Our disciplinary commitment to intellectual freedom.* Intellectual freedom and reflective judgment were matters of considerable interest to Adam Smith. In his *Theory of Moral Sentiments* (1976[1759]), Smith describes intellectual autonomy as a form of "positive liberty" (self-mastery or self-command), the evaluative capacity to judge one's own conduct through dialogue with one's impartial spectator (Harpham, 2000). Such autonomy was, in Smith's view, a necessary condition for the exercise of other moral, civic, and intellectual virtues. According to philosopher Samuel Fleischacker (1999), this "freedom to judge" lies at the heart of Smith's thinking about human freedom. "Above all," Fleischacker argues, Smith

"construes freedom . . . as that which enables one to judge for oneself—unlike a child, who requires others to judge for her, who requires tutelage" (4).

- Smith's "freedom to judge" is repeatedly affirmed across the broad tradition of liberal economics. It figures prominently in John Stuart Mill's discussion of intellectual liberty and the "marketplace of ideas" (Mill, 1956[1859]: 26–78) and is equally visible in Friedrich Hayek's emphasis on the subjective character of human knowledge, understood as the individual appropriation of information via "learned and skillful judgment" (Lavoie, 1995; Boettke, 2002) and in Sen's emphasis on the substantive ability to exercise one's reasoned agency as an autonomous thinker as an essential human freedom (Sen, 1999: 293). None of these thinkers is an education theorist per se yet all offer keen insight into the perennial challenge facing the liberal educator, namely: how to help students learn to think for themselves (Ellerman, 2005) without overriding or undercutting their "self-sustaining capacity to think and learn" (Siegfried et al., 1991: 201).
- *The teacher and student within.* The increasingly technical nature of economics PhD training raises daunting questions about the feasibility of any liberal education reform in undergraduate economics education. However, our resources as undergraduate teachers are never limited to the knowledge and skills we acquire as graduate students. Educator Parker Palmer (1998) argues that our authority and effectiveness in the classroom flows from "the teacher within" (30–31), the intersection of diverse forces that constitute our identities as teachers (13), and that our inner teachers are profoundly shaped by our experiences as students, viz., by "subjects that chose us" (25) and "mentors who evoked us" (21). Palmer's thesis underscores the potency of professional-ethical dialogue. As DeMartino wisely observes, the efficacy of professional ethics-as-conversation lies in the formative and performative impacts of ethical talk itself on "all matters pertaining to the identity, character, and behavior of the professional" (2011: 85). As we acknowledge and explore the tacit ideas and values that inspire who we are and what we do as teachers and scholars, the "teacher within" can become a generative ally, individually and collaboratively.

Conclusion

Preaching professional ethics at a time of rising fears about the very future of our profession (e.g., unsustainable revenue/cost structures in private and public higher education and the specter of massive open online courses) may sound like a counsel of perfection. But these very perils underscore the urgency of keeping our eyes on the only ball that makes a higher education worth having: the perennial liberal challenge of helping students to help themselves become disciplined, creative, fair-minded, self-possessed thinkers.

In his manifesto for professional economic ethics, DeMartino (2011) emphasizes the duties of economics educators in view of our influence over how undergraduate economics students "will view economic expertise for the rest of their lives" (212). Echoing Joan Robinson's view that, "The purpose of studying economics is . . . to learn how to avoid being deceived by economists" (1978: 75), DeMartino declares that "the [economics] profession faces an acute obligation . . . to deflate its students and the public's mistaken presumptions about what economists can know and do" (2011: 216). Our larger duty, beyond inoculating our students against the false promises of economic expertise, is to provide our share of the conditions for their flourishing as free and responsible economic thinkers.

All who believe that "thinking like a liberally educated person" is and should be an integral part of "thinking like an economist" would be well served to pool our efforts—to acknowledge the rich resources already available within us and around us to become active consumers and producers of ideas and materials for the next generation of economics education. Indeed, our academic duties to our students and colleagues require nothing less. If we dodge our duties by accepting or ignoring the Samuelsonian status quo, we will leave our students ill-prepared to "grapple successfully with uncertainty, complexity, and conflicting perspectives and [to] still take stands that are based on evidence, analysis and compassion" (Nelson, 1997: 71). We will also leave ourselves vulnerable to the charge that our pricey institutions are exploiting students rather than educating them—treating them not as moral agents and junior apprentices but merely as means to our employers' revenue-generating ends. For the heirs of Adam Smith, John Stuart Mill, Friedrich Hayek, and Amartya Sen (not to mention Bill Perry and Socrates), such outcomes are both unacceptable and unnecessary.

Acknowledgments

I am grateful for inspiring conversations over many years with Susan Feiner, Robin Bartlett, Ted Burczak, George DeMartino, Paul King, Ed McNertney, Kristin Klopfenstein, Julie Graham, Mike Butler, Lisa Vanderlinden, Emily Chamlee-Wright, Steve Horwitz, David Ellerman, Lenore Ealy, and KimMarie McGoldrick. I owe special thanks to George DeMartino for his exceptional kindness and encouragement as I worked to complete this chapter.

References

American Association of University Professors (AAUP). 1915. *General Declaration of Principles.* New York: Columbia University.

American Association of University Professors (AAUP). 1940. *Statement of Principles on Academic Freedom and Tenure.* Washington, DC.

American Association of University Professors (AAUP). 1967. *Joint Statement on Rights and Freedoms of Students*. Washington, DC.

American Association of University Professors (AAUP). 1970. *Interpretive Comments on 1940 Statement of Principles on Academic Freedom and Tenure*. Washington, DC.

American Association of University Professors (AAUP). 2005. *AAUP Policies in the Classroom*. Washington, DC.

Association of American Colleges and Universities (AAC&U). 2006. *Academic Freedom and Educational Responsibility*. Washington, DC.

Barone, C. A. 1991. "Contending Perspectives: Curricular Reform in Economics." *Journal of Economic Education* 22(1): 15–26.

Bartlett, R. L., and S. F. Feiner. 1992. "Balancing the Economics Curriculum: Content, Method, and Pedagogy." *American Economic Review* 82(2): 559–564.

Becker, W. E. 2004. "Economics for a Higher Education." *International Review of Economics Education* 3(1): 52–62.

Becker, W. E. 2007. "Quit Lying and Address the Controversies: There Are No Dogmata, Laws, Rules, or Standards in the Science of Economics." *American Economist* 51(1): 3–14.

Becker, W. E., and M. Watts. 1996. "Chalk and Talk: A National Survey of Teaching Undergraduate Economics." *American Economic Review* 86(2): 448–454.

Becker, W. E., and M. Watts. 2001. "Teaching Economics at the Start of the 21st Century: Still Chalk and Talk." *American Economic Review* 91(2): 446–451.

Berlin, I. 2002[1958]. "Two Concepts of Liberty." In *Liberty*, edited by H. Hardy (pp. 166–217). Oxford: Oxford University Press.

Boettke, P. J. 2002. "Information and Knowledge: Austrian Economics in Search of Its Uniqueness." *Review of Austrian Economics* 15(4): 263–274.

Borg, J. R., and M. O. Borg. 2001. "Teaching Critical Thinking in Interdisciplinary Economics Courses." *College Teaching* 49(1): 20–29.

Boulding, K. E. 1971. "After Samuelson, Who Needs Adam Smith?" *History of Political Economy* 3(2): 225–237.

Campbell, W. E., and K. A. Smith (eds.). 1997. *New Paradigms for College Teaching*. Edina, MN: Interaction Books.

Colander, D. 1991. "A Consideration of the Economics Major in American Higher Education." *Journal of Economic Education* 22(3): 227–234.

Colander, D. 2001. *The Lost Art of Economics: Essays on Economics and the Economics Profession*. Northampton, MA: Edward Elgar.

Colander, D. and McGoldrick, K. (eds.). 2009*a*. *Educating Economists: The Teagle Discussion on Reevaluating the Undergraduate Economics Major*. Northampton, MA: Edward Elgar.

Colander, D. and K. McGoldrick. 2009*b*. "The Teagle Foundation Report: The Economics Major as Part of a Liberal Education." In *Educating Economists*, edited by D. Colander and K. McGoldrick (pp. 3–39). Northampton, MA: Edward Elgar.

Dekker, E. and A. Klamer. 2016. "About Doing the Right Thing as an Academic Economist. In *The Oxford Handbook of Professional Economic Ethics*, edited by G. DeMartino and D. McCloskey, pp. 101–115. New York: Oxford University Press.

DeMartino, G. F. 2011. *The Economist's Oath: On the Need for and Content of Professional Economic Ethics*. New York: Oxford University Press.

Deslauriers, L., E. Schelew, and C. Wieman. 2011. "Improved Learning in a Large-Enrollment Physics Class." *Science* 332(6031): 862–864.

Dewey, J. 1933. *How We Think: A Restatement of the Relation of Reflective Thinking to the Educative Process*. Lexington, MA: Heath.

Earl, P. E. 2000. "Indeterminacy in the Economics Classroom." In *Economics as an Art of Thought: Essays in Memory of G. L. S. Shackle*, edited by P. E. Earl and S. F. Frowen (pp. 25–50). London: Routledge.

Ellerman, D. 2005. *Helping People Help Themselves: From the World Bank to an Alternative Philosophy of Development Assistance*. Ann Arbor: University of Michigan Press.

Elzinga, K. G. 1992. "The Eleven Principles of Economics." *Southern Economic Journal* 58(4): 861–879.

Feiner, S. F. 2002. "Toward a Post-Autistic Economics Education." *Post-Autistic Economics Review* 12(March). http://www.paecon.net/PAEReview/wholeissues/issue12.htm

Feiner, S. F., and B. B. Roberts. 1995. "Using Alternative Paradigms to Teach About Race and Gender: A Critical Thinking Approach to Introductory Economics." *American Economic Review* 85(2): 367–371.

Fels, R. 1974. "Developing Independent Problem-Solving Ability in Elementary Economics." *American Economic Review* 64(2): 403–407.

Fels, R., and S. Buckles. 1981. *Casebook of Economic Problems and Policies: Practice in Thinking*, 5th edition. St. Paul, MN: West Publishing.

Ferber, M. A. 1999. "Guidelines for Pre-College Economics Education: A Critique." *Feminist Economics* 5(3): 135–142.

Fink, D. L. 2003. *Creating Significant Learning Experiences: An Integrated Approach to Designing College Courses*. San Francisco: Jossey-Bass.

Finkel, D. L. 2000. *Teaching with Your Mouth Shut*. Portsmouth, NH: Boynton/Cook.

Finkel, D. L., and W. R. Arney. 1995. *Educating for Freedom: The Paradox of Pedagogy*. New Brunswick: Rutgers University Press.

Fish, S. 2008. *Save the World on Your Own Time*. Oxford: Oxford University Press.

Fleischacker, S. F. 1999. *A Third Concept of Liberty*. Princeton: Princeton University Press.

Frank, R. 1998. "Some Thoughts on the Micro Principles Course." In *Teaching Undergraduate Economics: A Handbook for Instructors*, edited by W. B. Walstad and P. Saunders (pp. 13–20). New York: Irwin McGraw-Hill.

Freeman, A. 2007. "Catechism Versus Pluralism: The Heterodox Response to the National Undergraduate Curriculum Proposed by the UK Quality Assurance Agency." Unpublished paper. Available at [http://econpapers.repec.org/paper/pramprapa/6832.htm], accessed September 14, 2009.

Fullbrook, E. 2003. *The Crisis in Economics: The Post-Autistic Economics Movement*. London: Routledge.

Garnett, R. F. 2009. "Liberal Learning as Freedom: A Capabilities Approach to Undergraduate Education." *Studies in Philosophy and Education* 28(5): 437–447.

Garnett, R. F. 2011. "Rethinking the Pluralist Debate in Economics Education." *International Review of Economic Education* 8(2): 58–71.

Garnett, R. F., and M. R. Butler. 2009. "Should Economic Educators Care About Students' Academic Freedom?" *International Journal of Pluralism and Economics Education* 1(1/2): 148–160.

Garnett, R. F., and K. M. Klopfenstein. 2003. "Critical Thinking as an Interpersonal Experience: Rethinking Introductory Courses Across the Disciplines." *Inquiry: Critical Thinking Across the Disciplines* 23(1): 11–16.

Grimes, P. W. 2009. "Reflections on Introductory Course Structures." In *Educating Economists*, edited by D. Colander and K. McGoldrick (pp. 95–98). Northampton, MA: Edward Elgar.

Hansen, W. L., M. K. Salemi, and J. J. Siegfried. 2002. "Use It or Lose It: Teaching Literacy in the Economics Principles Course." *American Economic Review* 92(2): 463–472.

Hake, R. R. 1998. "Interactive-Engagement vs. Traditional Methods: A Six Thousand-Student Survey of Mechanics Test Data for Introductory Physics Courses." *American Journal of Physics* 66(1): 64–74.

Harpham, E. J. 2000. "The Problem of Liberty in the Thought of Adam Smith." *Journal of the History of Economic Thought* 22(2): 217–237.

Harter, C. L., W. E. Becker, and M. Watts. 2011. "Time Allocations and Reward Structures for U.S. Academic Economists from 1995–2005: Evidence from Three National Surveys." *International Review of Economics Education* 10(2): 6–27.

Heyne, P. 1995. "Teaching Introductory Economics." *Agenda* 2(2): 149–158.

Katz, A., and W. E. Becker. 1999. "Technology and the Teaching of Economics to Undergraduates." *Journal of Economic Education* 30(3): 194–199.

Kennedy, P. E. 2006. "The Macroeconomic Principles Course: What Should Be Done?" In *Teaching Economics: More Alternatives to Chalk and Talk*, edited by W. E. Becker, M. Watts, and S. R. Becker (pp. 89–107). Northampton, MA: Edward Elgar.

King, P. M., and K. S. Kitchener. 1994. *Developing Reflective Judgment: Understanding and Promoting Intellectual Growth and Critical Thinking in Adolescents and Adults*. San Francisco: Jossey-Bass.

Knoedler, J., and D. Underwood. 2003. "Teaching the Principles of Economics: A Proposal for a Multi-Paradigmatic Approach." *Journal of Economic Issues* 37(3): 697–725.

Kuhn, T. S. 1977. *The Essential Tension: Selected Studies in Scientific Tradition and Change*. Chicago: University of Chicago Press.

Lavoie, D. 1995. "The "Objectivity" of Scholarship and the Ideal of the University." *Advances in Austrian Economics* 2B: 371–403.

Lewis, M., and K. McGoldrick. 2001. "Moving Beyond the Masculine Neoclassical Classroom." *Feminist Economics* 7(2): 91–103.

Mankiw, N. G. 1998. *Principles of Economics*. Fort Worth, TX: Dryden Press, Harcourt Brace College Publishers.

Marglin, S. A. 2008. *The Dismal Science: How Thinking Like an Economist Undermines Community*. Cambridge: Harvard University Press.

Marglin, S. A. 2009. "The Economics Major as Illiberal Education." In *Educating Economists*, edited by D. Colander and K. McGoldrick (pp. 48–52). Northampton, MA: Edward Elgar.

Marglin, S. A. 2012. "Saving the Children—A Rant." *Journal of Economic Education* 43(3): 283–292.

Mazur, E. 2009. "Farewell, Lecture?" *Science* 2(1): 50–51.

McCloskey, D. N. 2000. "The Natural." In *How to be Human ** Though an Economist*, edited by D. N. McCloskey (pp. 178–181). Ann Arbor: University of Michigan Press.

McGoldrick, K., and R. Garnett. 2013. "Big Think: A Model for Critical Inquiry in Economics Courses." *Journal of Economic Education* 44(4): 389–398.

Mill, J. S. 1956[1859]. *On Liberty*, edited with introduction by C. V. Shields. Indianapolis: Bobbs-Merrill.

Moseley, F., C. Gunn, and C. Georges. 1991. "Emphasizing Controversy in the Economics Curriculum." *Journal of Economic Education* 22(3): 235–240.

National Council on Economic Education. 1997. *Voluntary National Content Standards in Economics*. New York: National Council on Economic Education.

Nelson, C. E. 1997. "Tools for Tampering with Teaching's Taboos." In *New Paradigms for College Teaching*, edited by W. E. Campbell and K. A. Smith (pp. 51–77). Edina, MN: Interaction Books.

Nussbaum, M. C. 1997. *Cultivating Humanity: A Classical Defense of Reform in Liberal Education*. Cambridge: Harvard University Press.

O'Donnell, R. 2009. "Economic Pluralism and Skill Formation: Adding Value to Students, Economies, and Societies." In *Economic Pluralism*, edited by R. Garnett, E. Olsen, and M. Starr (pp. 262–277). London: Routledge.

Palmer, P. 1998. *The Courage to Teach*. San Francisco: Jossey-Bass.

Paul, R. 1999. "Critical Thinking, Moral Integrity, and Citizenship: Teaching for the Intellectual Virtues." In *The Social Worlds of Higher Education*, edited by B. A. Pescosolido and R. Aminzade (pp. 128–136). Thousand Oaks, CA: Pine Forge Press.

Perry, W. G. Jr. 1970. *Forms of Intellectual and Ethical Development in the College Years: A Scheme*. New York: Holt, Rinehart and Winston.

Raveaud, G. 2003. "Teaching Economics Through Controversies." In *The Crisis in Economics*, edited by E. Fullbrook (pp. 62–69). London: Routledge.

Robinson, J. 1978. *Contributions to Modern Economics*. Oxford: Basil Blackwell.

Saito, M. 2003. "Amartya Sen's Capability Approach to Education: A Critical Exploration." *Journal of Philosophy of Education* 37(1): 17–33.

Salemi, M. K. 2009. "Economics and Liberal Education: Why, Where, and How. In *Educating Economists*, edited by D. Colander and K. McGoldrick (pp. 99–106). Northampton, MA: Edward Elgar.

Salemi, M. K., and J. J. Siegfried. 1999. "The State of Economic Education." *American Economic Review* 89(2): 355–361.

Samuelson, P. A. 1967. *Economics*, 7th edition. New York: McGraw-Hill.

Schneider, G., and Shackelford, J. 2001. "Economics Standards and Lists: Proposed Antidotes for Feminist Economists." *Feminist Economics* 7(2): 77–89.

Sen, A. K. 1999. *Development as Freedom*. New York: Anchor Books.

Shackelford, J. 1992. "Feminist Pedagogy: A Means for Bringing Critical Thinking and Creativity into the Economics Classroom." *American Economic Review* 82(2): 570–575.

Shackle, G. L. S. 1953. *What Makes an Economist?* Liverpool: Liverpool University Press.

Siegfried, J. J., R. L. Bartlett, W. L. Hansen, A. C. Kelley, D. N. McCloskey, and T. H. Tietenberg. 1991. "The Status and Prospects of the Economics Major." *Journal of Economic Education* 22(3): 197–224.

Siegfried, J. J., and B. Meszaros. 1997. "National Voluntary Content Standards for Pre-college Economics Education." *American Economic Review* 87(2): 247–253.

Siegfried, J. J., and B. Meszaros. 1998. "Voluntary Economics Content Standards for America's Schools: Rationale and Development." *Journal of Economic Education* 29(2): 139–149.

Smith, A. 1976[1759]. *The Theory of Moral Sentiments*, edited by D. D. Raphael and A. L. Macfie. Oxford: Oxford University Press.

Solow, R. 1990. "Discussion (Comments on W. Lee Hansen, Educating and Training New Economics PhDs: How Good a Job Are We Doing?)". *American Economic Review* 80(2): 448–450.

Stigler, G. J. 1963. "Elementary Economics Education." *American Economic Review* 53(2): 653–659.

Strike, K. A. 1982. *Liberty and Learning*. New York: St. Martin's Press.

Tagg, J. 2003. *The Learning Paradigm College*. Bolton, MA: Anker.

Thoma, G. A. 1993. "The Perry Framework and Tactics for Teaching Critical Thinking in Economics. *Journal of Economic Education* 24(2): 128–136.

Underwood, D. A. 2004. "Principles of Macroeconomics: Toward a Multiparadigmatic Approach." *Journal of Economic Issues* 38(2): 571–581.

Versényi, L. 1963. *Socratic Humanism*. Westport, CT: Greenwood Press.

Walstad, W., and S. Allgood. 1999. "What Do College Seniors Know About Economics?" *American Economic Review* 89(2): 350–354.

Walstad, W., and S. Allgood. 2005. "Views of Teaching and Research in Economics and Other Disciplines." *American Economic Review* 95(2): 177–183.

Watts, M., and W. E. Becker. 2008. "A Little More than Chalk and Talk: Results from a Third National Survey of Teaching Methods in Undergraduate Economics Courses." *Journal of Economic Education* 39(3): 273–286.

Watts, M., and G. Schaur. 2011. "Teaching and Assessment Methods in Undergraduate Economics: A Fourth National Quinquennial Survey." *Journal of Economic Education* 42(3): 294–309.

Wieman, C. 2007. "The 'Curse of Knowledge' or Why Intuition About Teaching Often Fails." *American Physical Society News* 16 (10): 8. Available at http://www.aps.org/publications/apsnews/200711/backpage.cfm, accessed April 21, 2012.

Wight, J. B. 2016. "The Ethical Economist: Duty and Virtue in the Scientific Process." In *The Oxford Handbook of Professional Economic Ethics*, edited by G. DeMartino and D. McCloskey, pp. 137–164. New York: Oxford University Press.

PART VIII

LOOKING AHEAD

CHAPTER 36

CREATING HUMBLE ECONOMISTS

A Code of Ethics for Economists

DAVID COLANDER

INTRODUCTION

FROM the movie *Inside Job*, one gets the sense that economists are ethically challenged because they take payments for writing papers that say what the funders of their research want them to say. The sense conveyed by the movie is that economists are for sale. In my view, that is far from the case; economists are not for-hire any more than a similar group of academic experts, and probably significantly less than many, because by academic standards, economists tend to be well paid. The money given to economists by groups that support the policy positions they are espousing, either in the form of honoraria for a talk, payment as a director or consultant to the company, or funding for research, is seldom the reason economists are supporting their policy positions. The causal link generally goes the other way around. Thus, though I support reasonable, minimally invasive measures that increase transparency of funding, I see such measures as having little effect on the ethical failings of the economics profession. Economists will espouse the positions they espouse whether or not the funding takes place. If academic economists were primarily interested in the money, they could earn significantly more income by leaving academia and entering business or finance. Money, or biased support of research, in my view, is not the most serious ethical issue facing the economics profession. The ethical problem of economists is deeper.

The more serious ethical problem of economics has little to do with the funding of economic research on either the right or the left. It has to do with lack of humility. By this I mean that we economists have a tendency to convey more scientific certainty in our policy positions than the theory and evidence objectively would allow. Too many economists are willing to make seemingly definitive scientific statements about policy based on models, that they know, or should know, are highly imperfect. It was that tendency that I (Colander et al., 2009) criticized the profession for in the recent crisis. Back in 1927, Lionel Robbins (Robbins, 1927) argued that "what precision economists can claim at this stage is largely a sham precision. In the present state of knowledge, the man who can claim for economic science much exactitude is a quack." (176). Despite the advances economic science has made, that remains true today. Yet, all too often economists allow lay people and policymakers to believe that our policy suggestions have far more scientific foundation than a neutral objective observer would give them.

Good economists recognize our tendency to do this, but too often allow other individuals and other economists to convey their findings and policy views in ways that make those views seem far more scientifically grounded than they are. This tendency is exacerbated by an ethical failing in the reporting profession, which, when looking for a good story, will gravitate to economists who most overstate the conclusions of policy. A newspaper article concluding with "This finding is at best suggestive, and goes far beyond what one can say with scientific certainty" does not endear a reporter to his or her editor. Thus, not only are economists as a group not humble enough, but what lay people are presented as economists' policy recommendations also are often the policy recommendations of the least humble economist. In summary, my argument is that lack of humility in conveying the limitations of their results is the most serious ethical problem facing economists; it played a much larger role in causing the recent financial crisis than did the type of payments highlighted by *Inside Job*. Thus, any new code of ethics for economists should deal with that humility problem.

Applied Science vs. Engineering

How does one go about creating humble economist? I don't have a complete answer to that, but one step toward doing so would involve a change in the self-image of applied economists. Currently applied economists see themselves as applied scientists. My argument in this chapter is that that needs to change. Applied economists should see themselves as engineers, not as applied scientists, as Howard Wolowitzes, rather than Sheldon Coopers or even Leonard Hofstadters. That change in self-image would be an important step toward creating a more humble economics profession and would bring about major changes in their method, which would contribute toward creating a more ethical economics profession.

I suspect that to many economists my argument that most economists should see themselves as engineers, not applied scientists, will seem strange. Isn't engineering just applied science? My answer is no, it isn't; if anything science is applied engineering. Engineering and applied science can be distinguished by their primary goals and methods.

The primary goal of science is finding the truth—understanding for the sake of understanding. Science's methods are consistent with that goal, and those methods have evolved into relatively formal prescriptions about methods that guide and limit scientists in their work. Back of the envelop calculations, value judgments, guestimates, heuristic models, rough generalizations from case studies, commonsense observation, and fudge factors are not the methods to establish scientific truths. The scientific method requires rigorous analysis and precise conventions to counter individuals' tendency toward fast pattern completion. A set of conventions about how to do empirical analysis; how to develop models; the appropriate level of statistical significance of empirical work such as appropriate *t* values; and the appropriate structure of experiments such as randomized, double blind, placebo-controlled experiments, become part of its method.

Doing good science is costly and time consuming, but the amount of time or effort it takes to resolve an issue is not deemed a legitimate consideration in establishing a scientific result. A scientific truth is timeless, and if your goal is true understanding, then anything less than the methodological gold standard is not good enough to establish the truth. Applied science involves the translation of scientific findings to solve real-world problems and, in principle, it holds itself up to the same standards as does science because the primary goal is scientific understanding. Applied science has science and the scientific method at its core.

Engineering is different than science. The primary goal of engineers is solving a specific problem with available resources, and an engineering solution can be judged only relative to its cost. Whereas the scientific method does not allow shortcuts to save time and money, the engineering method does. Engineering is by nature applied, and it need not have a scientific core, or general formal methodological prescriptions based on the scientific methods. Billy Vaughn Koen (2003), who has written what appears to be the current standard methodological treatise for engineering, defines the engineering method as "The strategy for causing the best change in a poorly understood or uncertain situation within the available resources" (7). He describes an engineer as an individual who solves problems using engineering heuristics. He argues that an engineer makes no pretense of having found the truth, or having found the "correct" model.[1] An engineer focuses on finding solutions that work, and uses whatever methods he or she finds best leads to finding a solution to the particular problem he or she is trying to solve. In the engineering field, there are no rigid prescriptions guiding method.

Engineering uses science when appropriate, but where science does not have an answer to a part of the question that is needed to come to a policy recommendation, an engineer finds the best answer he or she can, and uses that. An engineering method might involve back of the envelop calculations, input from other specialties, guestimates, and individual judgment—whatever is needed to provide the best answer an engineer can provide to the problem he or she is trying to solve. In providing an engineer's recommendation, an engineer follows the "weakest link principle"—and presents

[1] Koen argues that the engineering method, which he calls a universal method, predates the scientific method, and that the scientific method is simply an application of the engineering method when the research goal is to find the truth rather than to solve a particular problem.

his or her recommendation with no more certainty than he or she has in the weakest link of the analysis needed to arrive at a solution.

This difference in focus between applied science and engineering means that the engineering method can differ significantly from the applied science method. If a rule of thumb seems to work in similar cases, it will be incorporated even though it has no scientific foundation. If arriving at a policy recommendation involves making value judgments, the engineering method makes what it believes are reasonable value judgments. There is no need to shy away from them. If the data don't exist that meet appropriate levels of statistical significance, or if it doesn't seem cost effective to collect and analyze the data to that level of precision, the engineer uses the best data he or she can to arrive at the solution he or she believes appropriate.

I am not arguing that engineering uses an "anything goes" methodology. Acceptable heuristics, which is what engineers call methodology, develop endogenously within the engineering profession about which approaches are acceptable and which aren't. These state-of-the-art methods change over time (which is why "state of the art" is an important concept in any engineering methodology) and are developed by the engineering specialists in a particular field. Acceptable heuristics can differ in different branches of engineering, and there is no overarching methodogical requirement, other than "what seems to work."

I am fully aware of the ambiguity of the term "science," and I agree that, in principle, it makes no difference whether someone calls him- or herself an applied scientist or an engineer —it is just a name. But, as I hope I have made clear in the preceding text, the method that an applied researcher uses matters a lot, both in how an applied researchers goes about his or her research and in how he or she presents research findings. To the degree that self-classification affects method, it makes a big difference.

My argument is that most economists (and most applied natural scientists as well) are actually engineers, who, in practice often go about their research (and should go about their research) using an engineering method. The problem I see is that they don't use it enough, and they don't make it clear to others that they are using an engineering method, not a scientific method. Their self-classification as applied scientists leads them to contort their methodological approach to attempt to make it seem to fit a scientific method, and to present their research findings and conclusions as scientific truths, not as rough and ready engineering insights that can be useful in looking at particular problems. Seeing oneself as a scientist undermines the humility the actual practice of applied economics warrants.

Presenting findings as scientific findings give those findings an aura of validity that goes beyond the method used. An example of what I mean can be seen in econometric findings, which are often presented as having met scientific standards, when in fact the findings are often engineering guestimates based on reasonable proxies. Because even the reasonable proxies are often highly imperfect, the empirical results should be seen as highly questionable regardless of the statistical precision of the analysis. To present results as meeting a 95 percent confidence interval can lead nonspecialists to have more confidence in the results than is warranted. Applied economists data mine and choose models based on analytic tractability, not appropriateness to the process. That all makes sense, but to present results of work that uses these reasonable ad hoc engineering methods as scientific results, and not as engineering results, does not.

My argument is that most applied economics involves many of the same pragmatic methods as does engineering. But we economists tend to be less open about our actual methods because they seem to violate scientific methodology. We think of applied economics as applied science, which places scientific models and scientific facts at the center of our analysis. For example, we justify a Dynamic Stochastic General Equilibrium (DSGE) modeling strategy because it is more "scientific" than other modeling strategies even though it is forcing our macro models into a form that intuitively doesn't fit the macro reality. With sufficient gyrations, DSGE models can be made to fit, but from an engineering standpoint it is unclear what one has gained from the analytic contortions necessary to do so, and the loss of not using models that can better capture the likely problems faced by a macroeconomy likely overwhelm any gains from having a broad formal model. The situation is similar with standard macro models.

An engineer's approach to modeling such a complex system as the macro economy would likely focus much more on statistical models and methods of pulling patterns out of the data. It would explore a wide variety of formal models to gain analytic insight, and then would integrate the many variety of models with the statistical models to interpret the patterns. That would involve a fundamentally different way of doing macro and of thinking about macro problems. The situation is similar with micro models. Economists focus much of their applied micro policy discussion on Pareto optimal solutions even though we know that all actual policies will violate Pareto optimality. We can contort our micro policy models designed to provide Pareto optimal solutions to provide insight into non-Pareto optimal solutions, but, generally, that contortion comes at a cost. It means that we spend less time discussing other models that better fit non-Pareto optimal solutions. They lead us away from "reasonable person solutions" that more closely reflect society's value judgments. An engineering applied microeconomics would likely have an entire branch devoted to measuring society's value judgments and integrating those judgments into applied policy instruments. Our scientific applied micro leaves the topic almost totally undiscussed.

My interest in this chapter is not in how economists' research methods and applied economics would change if economists saw themselves as engineers; it is in how economists' view of themselves and presentations of their findings would change if they saw themselves as engineers. My argument is that economists who see themselves as engineers would be much more humble in their presentation of results than are economists who see themselves as applied scientists. Because the engineering method is by nature pragmatic and often scientifically unjustified, and makes no claim to being the truth, an "economic engineer" would tend to be more modest about his or her work. Accepting that economists are engineers, not applied scientists, would take economic policy out of the realm of science and put it in the realm of engineering or art, where uncertainty reigns, and where the need for judgments is explicitly acknowledged. Debates in economic policy would move outside of economics, and the role that economic models play would change.

Applied economists as engineers would not claim scientific status for our policy pronouncements, and heuristics would develop to compare various policy pronouncements of different economists. Those heuristics would recognize that the judgments underlying policy pronouncements are subject to legitimate debate, and that debate about nuance would tend to make our policy pronouncements more humble.

A Code of Ethics for Economists

My goal in this chapter is not to make the argument for economists seeing themselves as engineers; I have dealt with that in another paper (Colander, 2013). My goal here is to explain how seeing ourselves as engineers, not applied scientists, would help us arrive at a code of ethics for economists. My hypothesis is the following: If it is true that economics is essentially engineering, then a code of ethics for engineers should nicely translate into a code of ethics for economists. I believe it does so. To demonstrate that, I went to the National Society of Professional Engineers and found their code of ethics. (http://www.nspe.org/Ethics/CodeofEthics/index.html). I then did a global change of the word "engineer" to "economist," and arrived at the following code, which I believe would make a good first effort at a code of ethics for the economics profession.

Code of Ethics for Economists (Adapted from the Code of Ethics for Engineers)

Preamble

Economics is an important and learned profession. As members of this profession, economists are expected to exhibit the highest standards of honesty and integrity. Economics has a direct and vital impact on the quality of life for all people. Accordingly, the services provided by economists require honesty, impartiality, fairness, and equity, and must be dedicated to the protection of the public health, safety, and welfare. Economists must perform under a standard of professional behavior that requires adherence to the highest principles of ethical conduct.

I. Fundamental Canons

Economists, in the fulfillment of their professional duties, shall:

1. Hold paramount the safety, health, and welfare of the public.
2. Perform services only in areas of their competence.
3. Issue public statements only in an objective and truthful manner.

4. Act for each employer or client as faithful agents or trustees.
5. Avoid deceptive acts.
6. Conduct themselves honorably, responsibly, ethically, and lawfully so as to enhance the honor, reputation, and usefulness of the profession.

II. Rules of Practice

1. Economists shall hold paramount the safety, health, and welfare of the public.
   a. If economists' judgment is overruled under circumstances that endanger life or property, they shall notify their employer or client and such other authority as may be appropriate.
   b. Economists shall approve only those economics documents that are in conformity with applicable standards.
   c. Economists shall not reveal facts, data, or information without the prior consent of the client or employer except as authorized or required by law or this Code.
   d. Economists shall not permit the use of their name or associate in business ventures with any person or firm that they believe is engaged in fraudulent or dishonest enterprise.
   e. Economists shall not aid or abet the unlawful practice of economics by a person or firm.
   f. Economists having knowledge of any alleged violation of this Code shall report thereon to appropriate professional bodies and, when relevant, also to public authorities, and cooperate with the proper authorities in furnishing such information or assistance as may be required.
2. Economists shall perform services only in the areas of their competence.
   a. Economists shall undertake assignments only when qualified by education or experience in the specific technical fields involved.
   b. Economists shall not affix their signatures to any plans or documents dealing with subject matter in which they lack competence, nor to any plan or document not prepared under their direction and control.
   c. Economists may accept assignments and assume responsibility for coordination of an entire project and sign and seal the economics documents for the entire project, provided that each technical segment is signed and sealed only by the qualified Economists who prepared the segment.
3. Economists shall issue public statements only in an objective and truthful manner.
   a. Economists shall be objective and truthful in professional reports, statements, or testimony. They shall include all relevant and pertinent information in such reports, statements, or testimony, which should bear the date indicating when it was current.
   b. Economists may express publicly technical opinions that are founded upon knowledge of the facts and competence in the subject matter.

   c. Economists shall issue no statements, criticisms, or arguments on technical matters that are inspired or paid for by interested parties, unless they have prefaced their comments by explicitly identifying the interested parties on whose behalf they are speaking, and by revealing the existence of any interest the economists may have in the matters.
4. Economists shall act for each employer or client as faithful agents or trustees.
   a. Economists shall disclose all known or potential conflict of interest that could influence or appear to influence their judgment or the quality of their services.
   b. Economists shall not accept compensation, financial or otherwise, from more than one party for services on the same project, or for services pertaining to the same project, unless the circumstances are fully disclosed and agreed to by all interested parties.
   c. Economists shall not solicit or accept financial or other valuable consideration, directly or indirectly, from outside agents in connection with the work for which they are responsible.
   d. Economists in public service as members, advisors, or employees of a governmental or quasi-governmental body or department shall not participate in decisions with respect to services solicited or provided by them or their organizations in private or public economics practice.
   e. Economists shall not solicit or accept a contract from a governmental body on which a principal or officer of their organization serves as a member.
5. Economists shall avoid deceptive acts.
   a. Economists shall not falsify their qualifications or permit misrepresentation of their or their associates' qualifications. They shall not misrepresent or exaggerate their responsibility in or for the subject matter of prior assignments. Brochures or other presentations incident to the solicitation of employment shall not misrepresent pertinent facts concerning employers, employees, associates, joint venturers, or past accomplishments.
   b. Economists shall not offer, give, solicit, or receive, either directly or indirectly, any contribution to influence the award of a contract by public authority, or which may be reasonably construed by the public as having the effect or intent of influencing the awarding of a contract. They shall not offer any gift or other valuable consideration in order to secure work. They shall not pay a commission, percentage, or brokerage fee in order to secure work, except to a bona fide employee or bona fide established commercial or marketing agencies retained by them.

III. Professional Obligations

1. Economists shall be guided in all their relations by the highest standards of honesty and integrity.
   a. Economists shall acknowledge their errors and shall not distort or alter the facts.

   b. Economists shall advise their clients or employers when they believe a project will not be successful.
   c. Economists shall not accept outside employment to the detriment of their regular work or interest. Before accepting any outside economics employment, they will notify their employers.
   d. Economists shall not attempt to attract an economist from another employer by false or misleading pretenses.
   e. Economists shall not promote their own interest at the expense of the dignity and integrity of the profession.
2. Economists shall at all times strive to serve the public interest.
   a. Economists are encouraged to participate in civic affairs; career guidance for youths; and work for the advancement of the safety, health, and well-being of their community.
   b. Economists shall not complete, sign, or seal plans and/or specifications that are not in conformity with applicable economics standards. If the client or employer insists on such unprofessional conduct, they shall notify the proper authorities and withdraw from further service on the project.
   c. Economists are encouraged to extend public knowledge and appreciation of economics and its achievements.
   d. Economists are encouraged to adhere to the principles of sustainable development in order to protect the environment for future generations.
3. Economists shall avoid all conduct or practice that deceives the public.
   a. Economists shall avoid the use of statements containing a material misrepresentation of fact or omitting a material fact.
   b. Consistent with the foregoing, economists may advertise for recruitment of personnel.
   c. Consistent with the foregoing, economists may prepare articles for the lay or technical press, but such articles shall not imply credit to the author for work performed by others.
4. Economists shall not disclose, without consent, confidential information concerning the business affairs or technical processes of any present or former client or employer, or public body on which they serve.
   a. Economists shall not, without the consent of all interested parties, promote or arrange for new employment or practice in connection with a specific project for which the economist has gained particular and specialized knowledge.
   b. Economists shall not, without the consent of all interested parties, participate in or represent an adversary interest in connection with a specific project or proceeding in which the economist has gained particular specialized knowledge on behalf of a former client or employer.
5. Economists shall not be influenced in their professional duties by conflicting interests.
   a. Economists shall not accept financial or other considerations, including free economic designs, from material or equipment suppliers for specifying their product.

  b. Economists shall not accept commissions or allowances, directly or indirectly, from contractors or other parties dealing with clients or employers of the economist in connection with work for which the economist is responsible.
6. Economists shall not attempt to obtain employment or advancement or professional engagements by untruthfully criticizing other economists, or by other improper or questionable methods.
   a. Economists shall not request, propose, or accept a commission on a contingent basis under circumstances in which their judgment may be compromised.
   b. Economists in salaried positions shall accept part-time economics work only to the extent consistent with policies of the employer and in accordance with ethical considerations.
   c. Economists shall not, without consent, use equipment, supplies, laboratory, or office facilities of an employer to carry on outside private practice.
7. Economists shall not attempt to injure, maliciously or falsely, directly or indirectly, the professional reputation, prospects, practice, or employment of other economists. Economists who believe others are guilty of unethical or illegal practice shall present such information to the proper authority for action.
   a. Economists in private practice shall not review the work of another economist for the same client, except with the knowledge of such economist, or unless the connection of such economist with the work has been terminated.
   b. Economists in governmental, industrial, or educational employ are entitled to review and evaluate the work of other economists when so required by their employment duties.
   c. Economists in sales or industrial employ are entitled to make economics comparisons of represented products with products of other suppliers.
8. Economists shall accept personal responsibility for their professional activities, provided, however, that Economists may seek indemnification for services arising out of their practice for other than gross negligence, where the economist's interests cannot otherwise be protected.
   a. Economists shall conform with state registration laws in the practice of economics.
   b. Economists shall not use association with a noneconomist, a corporation, or partnership as a "cloak" for unethical acts.
9. Economists shall give credit for economics work to those to whom credit is due, and will recognize the proprietary interests of others.
   a. Economists shall, whenever possible, name the person or persons who may be individually responsible for designs, inventions, writings, or other accomplishments.
   b. Economists using designs supplied by a client recognize that the designs remain the property of the client and may not be duplicated by the economist for others without express permission.

c. Economists, before undertaking work for others in connection with which the economist may make improvements, plans, designs, inventions, or other records that may justify copyrights or patents, should enter into a positive agreement regarding ownership.
d. Economists' designs, data, records, and notes referring exclusively to an employer's work are the employer's property. The employer should indemnify the economist for use of the information for any purpose other than the original purpose.
e. Economists shall continue their professional development throughout their careers and should keep current in their specialty fields by engaging in professional practice, participating in continuing education courses, reading in the technical literature, and attending professional meetings and seminars.

Discussion

In adapting the code, I specifically only changed the terms "engineer" and "economist," and made no other changes. What was amazing to me is how little I saw that seemed inappropriate to me. In fact there was only one statement in the entire code that I found objectionable, and that was Statement 7-a.[2] This is in stark contrast to other codes of ethics that I explored for other groups such as lawyers or for subgroups of economists who have developed explicit codes. I even have more differences with George DeMartino's short "Economist's Oath" than I do with this engineer's code of ethics. For example, I would question DeMartino's paragraph in his Oath about "exposing oppression" and "giving voice to the needs and aspirations of the dispossessed," and his statement in favor of pluralism (DeMartino, 2011: 232).

It is not that I necessarily disagree with ethical sentiments behind these statements, but I have a serious problem with their ambiguity and the way in which they may be interpreted. For example, what if one believes that other's theoretical perspective is totally wrong? Then I would believe that one has a responsibility to point that out, and not be pluralistic. Similarly, how are we to say what "oppression" is, or what a "self-serving argument of the privileged" is? (DeMartino, 2011: 232). In my view, any oath or code of ethics should avoid such references to terms that are subject to ambiguous interpretation as much as possible.

[2] The statement is "Engineers in private practice shall not review the work of another engineer for the same client, except with the knowledge of such engineer, or unless the connection of such engineer with the work has been terminated." That statement provided more protection than I would believe is appropriate. But I see this as inappropriate for both economists and engineering. There should, in my view, be a general presumption that others will review and criticize one's work and no requirement that the person be informed that that is happening.

What was amazing to me is how well the engineer's code of ethics comported with my implicit code. This consistency of code exists even though the engineering profession operates quite differently than the economics profession in that engineering is generally private sector based, and economics more academic or public sector based. But the sentiments conveyed were consistent with the methodology I see as appropriate for applied economists.

Let me now turn to the question: Would adopting a variation of an engineering code of ethics make a difference? In practice, I suspect not, simply because I don't see codes of ethics as significantly affecting behavior. But were economists to accept that they were engineers, not scientists, and change their methodology and presentation of research results accordingly, it would make a major difference. To demonstrate the differences it would make, in the following I suggest some places where I believe economists would be required to change what they do to meet this ethical code.

- Rule II 1a (If economists' judgment is overruled under circumstances that endanger life or property, they shall notify their employer or client and such other authority as may be appropriate.) should have led the economists developing financial derivative models to warn the public. (It was this ethical failing that we highlighted in Colander et al., 2009.)
- Rule II 2a (Economists shall undertake assignments only when qualified by education or experience in the specific technical fields involved.) should have stopped many economists from making pronouncements about policy as economists, rather than making pronouncements as private individuals, which they are free to do.
- Rule II 2b (Economists shall not affix their signatures to any plans or documents dealing with subject matter in which they lack competence, nor to any plan or document not prepared under their direction and control.) should stop economists from advocating policy solutions outside of their specific area of expertise.
- Rule II 3a (Economists shall be objective and truthful in professional reports, statements, or testimony. They shall include all relevant and pertinent information in such reports, statements, or testimony, which should bear the date indicating when it was current.) should lead economists to emphasize more than they do how much economic theory changes over time, and does not reflect scientific truth, but rather engineering truth.
- Rule II 3c (Economists shall issue no statements, criticisms, or arguments on technical matters that are inspired or paid for by interested parties, unless they have prefaced their comments by explicitly identifying the interested parties on whose behalf they are speaking, and by revealing the existence of any interest the economists may have in the matters.) would catch the funding issues that *Inside Job* highlighted.
- Rule II 4a (Economists shall disclose all known or potential conflict of interest that could influence or appear to influence their judgment or the quality of their

services.) goes beyond Rule 3c and places a restriction on broader conflict of interests that often are more important than financial ones.

- Rule III 1b (Economists shall advise their clients or employers when they believe a project will not be successful.) is another important rule that would affect many economic consulting jobs, where it seems all too often economists come up with conclusions that fit the client wants to hear—conclusions that are sometimes referred to as "stadium project" conclusions because in studies these projects tend to have much bigger positive impacts than they have in practice.
- Rule III 6 (Economists shall not attempt to obtain employment or advancement or professional engagements by untruthfully criticizing other economists, or by other improper or questionable methods.) would call into question certain comments by some economists about other economists' proposals.

I could go on, but these examples should make my point. Adoption of a variation of the Engineer's Code of Ethics would have a much broader reach than would DeMartino's Economist's Oath, or would a code designed to deal with the ethical problems highlighted by *Inside Job*. Perhaps the aspect I find most appealing about the engineering code of ethics is that it expresses a humility about one's goals. It makes no sweeping claims about goals, but rather focuses on the economic engineer's individual actions. In my view such an individual action-oriented code creates a professional ethic that is stronger than a more inclusive oath or code that deals with moral judgments such as "opposing oppression" and "giving voice to the needs and aspirations of the dispossessed."

By being limited about the nature of the code, we can be more humble. In a well-known passage, Keynes wrote that "If economists could manage to get themselves thought of as humble, competent people on a level with dentists, that would be splendid." I never quite understood Keynes' dentist allusion, but I would suggest if we could replace "dentist" in the quotation with "engineer," that would indeed be splendid.

References

Colander, David. 2013. "The Systemic Failure of Economic Methodologists." *Journal of Economic Methodology* 20(1), 56–68.

Colander, David, Alan Kirman, Michael Goldberg, Brigitte Sloth, Katarina Juselius, Armin Haas, and Thomas Lux. 2009. "The Financial Crisis and the Systemic Failure of the Economics Profession." *Critical Review* 21(2–3), 249–267.

DeMartino, George. 2011. *The Economist's Oath*. Oxford: Oxford University Press.

Koen, Billy Vaughn. 2003. *Discussion of the Method*. Oxford: Oxford University Press.

Robbins, Lionel. 1927. "Mr. Hawtrey on the Scope of Economics." *Economica* 172–178.

CHAPTER 37

CODES OF ETHICS FOR ECONOMISTS, PLURALISM, AND THE NATURE OF ECONOMIC KNOWLEDGE[1]

SHEILA C. DOW

INTRODUCTION

THE financial and economic crisis that emerged in 2008 has brought the issue of ethics and economics into the public discourse. Though much of the public opprobrium has centered on bankers, economists too have been blamed, not only for failing to predict the crisis but also for helping to bring it about. Many perceive the source of the crisis in a sustained policy of deregulation of financial markets that had been supported by economic analysis. Yet there is scant mechanism for calling the profession to account, a notable exception being the question raised with London School of Economics (LSE) economists by the British Queen.[2] But in any case the notion of attaching blame to economists is in itself controversial, not least because economics is often presented as a purely technical discipline.

Any calling to account requires a procedure, but also a set of criteria. Although many professions proceed according to a code of ethics, neither bankers nor economists do so. It is reasonable therefore to consider the possibility of a code of ethics for economists. Such a code could be justified more generally, but any justification takes on particular piquancy in light of the crisis.

[1] This chapter has benefited from comments from George DeMartino and discussions with Alexander Dow.

[2] See Earl (2010) for a discussion of the issues raised by her question as to why economists had failed to predict the crisis and the various responses offered.

The possibility of such a code has been discussed for some time (DeMartino, 2007; Bartlett, 2009). A range of ethical standards has been considered for a code of ethics. Of these, the most straightforward seem to be standards of competence and of declaration of interests. Such principles as "do no harm" appear more complex because of the difficulty of predicting the consequences of policy advice, and indeed because of differences of view as to what that difficulty entails. But in fact potentially all of these principles are complex: competence must be defined according to some methodological principles and the notion of personal interest presumes a particular relation between individual and society. Finally the whole notion of a code of ethics raises questions about the nature of economics itself.

There are differences among economists both as to subject matter and economic knowledge (how it should be built up and what its status is). For many economists there are no particular ethical issues beyond the generic academic ones (such as plagiarism and conflict of interest, for example) because economics is regarded as a positive science. Even then, as DeMartino (2011: chapter 5) explains, the inattention by economists even to these issues can be understood in terms of the mainstream inattention to ethics among economic agents. But, even where there is agreement that a code of professional ethics is required for economics and even if there were agreement on ethical standards in the abstract, differences as to the nature of the economy and of economic knowledge would make it difficult for economists to agree on the practical implementation of ethical standards.

There is a particular problem for economics that the organization of the discipline is dominated by a view that no such differences legitimately exist, a monist view of economics. This entry rather explores a pluralist approach to economics, recognizing the legitimacy of a range of approaches to the subject, including a range of understandings of the subject matter. Although this is not the dominant view, it is one shared by an increasing number of economists, as evidenced by the existence of the International Confederation of Associations for Pluralism in Economics (ICAPE), an umbrella organization for more than 30 individual economics organizations.

The argument to be developed here accords well with, and draws on, DeMartino's (2011) full discussion of the importance of professional ethics even though a code of ethics would be highly problematic. In particular we approach the subject from a pluralist standpoint. We argue that professional ethics with respect to policy advice are much more demanding from a pluralist perspective than a monist perspective. We also explore the ethical content of the pluralist position itself for the behavior of economists among themselves.

We start by exploring the pluralist approach to economics and what that implies for possible ethical standards for economists, focusing particularly on standards of competence and the "do no harm" principle. We then explore the range of understandings of economic behavior (and thus also the behavior of economists) which is associated with this pluralist approach, including the role of ethics. We consider the relevance of pluralism for ethical standards, particularly in terms of self-interest. These considerations will show how difficult it would be to establish a common specification of ethical standards for economists. They also demonstrate how demanding professional ethics are, particularly for pluralists.

The entry concludes with a discussion of what might still be possible for a pluralist code of ethics for economists. What is suggested in terms of pluralism itself accords with the principles for good academic behavior. But we go further in advocating the positive requirement on economists to justify arguments from their own approach and to justify judgment specifically about the consequences of policy advice. Finally we go further still than much of the existing discussion in recognizing the performativity of economics, that is, the potential for economics to change its own subject matter, and to change it in a way that might challenge wider ethical standards in society.

A Pluralist Understanding of Economics

A pluralist understanding of economics involves, first of all, a recognition of a range of approaches to the subject. By approach is meant not just different theories or even different methods, but something much more fundamental. It stems from the ontological view of the nature of the economic system as being open. Such a system does not yield universal principles for scientific enquiry at the methodological level or universal laws at the theoretical level. Inevitably therefore there will be a range of modes of scientific enquiry and also different theories, that is, an open-system ontology entails an open-system epistemology. As we shall discuss further in the text that follows, this range of approaches makes it virtually impossible to establish a meaningful universal code of ethics for economists.

The easiest way of understanding system openness is in counterpart to closure. This is particularly the case for economics, where the familiar, dominant mainstream approach is one of closure.[3] A closed system is one in which all relevant variables can be identified and defined to be endogenous or exogenous, in which the structure of the system (possibly including dynamic evolution) can be pre-specified, and in which atomic elements are independent and their interrelations can be pre-specified. Because such a system at the ontological level yields law-like behavior, a scientific system can be built up to identify these laws. Because this behavior is regarded as universal, it is independent of knowledge systems and is therefore independent also of any issues as to meaning, including the meaning of evidence.

It was this understanding of reality as yielding universal laws that underpinned logical positivism, whereby independent facts were the arbiter of theory. Logical positivism put forward a universal approach to scientific enquiry built around the principle of empirical testing. Such a scientific system is well represented by general equilibrium

[3] See Chick and Dow (2005) for a full specification of system openness and closure.

theory, built on the axioms of rational choice, on the understanding that the resulting propositions could be assessed against the facts (at least in principle). Because the meaning of the facts and the terms of theory were regarded as independent of theory itself, mathematics was regarded as a neutral language within which to express, develop, and assess theory. The appropriate method for such a system is thus formal deductivist mathematics. Even though mainstream economics includes theoretical approaches that take a more partial approach than general equilibrium theory, it retains the requirement that arguments be expressed in terms of formal deductivist mathematics and that the rational choice axioms be the benchmark.

Indeed it seems that, for many mainstream economists, the discipline of economics is actually defined by this methodology rather than its content. Any theory based on a different approach thus falls outside the classification of economics. There is no scope for even recognizing a range of approaches, far less for forming a view about such a range. Any ethical code of competence, then, is straightforward in that it would refer to competence with respect to the recognized preferred methodology. Such standards are represented by the assessment procedures in graduate schools in mainstream economics departments.

Non-mainstream economics can similarly be characterized in methodological terms, where that methodology stems from a particular epistemology which in turn stems from a particular ontology. Thus Lawson (1997) identifies non-mainstream economics with an open-system understanding of the economics system (just as Lee, 2009, identifies it with pluralism). It is important to recognize that the commonality is openness as such, or a denial of closure. This need not be seen as unduly negative, as denial of closure opens the way to open-system thinking. But these are not duals because there is a range of possibilities for open-system thinking. In particular, it requires only one of the conditions of closure to be violated for a system to be open. The different schools of thought outside the mainstream can therefore be identified in terms of the particular form of openness they adopt, depending on their particular open-system ontology. Each school of thought has its own approach to building knowledge depending on its ontology. Some schools include mathematical modeling as one among a range of methods. But it is a distinguishing characteristic of open-system approaches that they regard formal mathematical argument as only a partial contributor to theory; only if the economic system is closed can deductivist mathematics be sufficient. Corresponding to the varying degrees of willingness in different schools of thought to include mathematical methods is a view as to how far to invoke partial, provisional closures as a way of segmenting knowledge systems.

If the subject matter is understood to be open, then its complexity and potential for indeterminate evolution precludes the possibility of capture by any one theoretical system. There is inevitably a recognition of a range of approaches. Within non-mainstream economics there are some who deny this, preferring to argue that their particular approach is the best and in particular that the mainstream approach is wrongheaded. But it is so natural for non-mainstream economists to recognize the existence of mainstream economics (this approach being dominant, such recognition is hard to avoid), that the contrast with the mainstream refusal to recognize alternative approaches is not fully appreciated. Any open-system approach is pluralist in the sense of recognizing alternatives (whatever view is taken of them).

But pluralism in its fullest sense goes further than recognition, encompassing tolerance of a range of approaches and indeed cultivation of such a range. Both are implied by an open-system ontology. This is where there is debate within non-mainstream economics (Davis, 2006; Garnett, 2006; Garnett, Olsen, and Starr, 2009; Lee, 2009). Where the recognition of difference extends only from the chosen approach to the mainstream approach that is being rejected, there is little tolerance, and far less cultivation, of difference (Chick, 1995). In fact, from this perspective there is suspicion of a code of ethics establishing standards of competence, for example, because of the danger that it would be set by the mainstream establishment as a further mechanism for exerting power over alternative approaches (DeMartino, 2011: chapter 5). Were the relevant non-mainstream approach to become mainstream, it is not clear that this objection to a code of ethics would be carried over.

The particular position on pluralism taken forward here is that an open-system ontology necessarily involves pluralism in a more full meaning. If no one system of knowledge can be demonstrated to be the best then tolerance of a range of approaches is warranted. Further, if different systems of knowledge shed light on different aspects of the open system, then the scope for understanding an open system that is evolving in unpredictable ways will be enhanced if a range of approaches has been cultivated. An economic crisis provides a good case in point. The mainstream approach ignores alternative approaches that offer explanations for the crisis insofar as they are not recognized as economics, yet the cultivation of a range of approaches would have provided a rich seam to mine for new developments in economic theory in light of the crisis.

A pluralist approach, however, undermines any scope for establishing universal principles for economists' competence, as by definition different schools of thought proceed according to different methodologies. Different methods are used and combined in different ways, different meanings are employed and different standards applied to assessment of theoretical developments. Non-mainstream economics generally assesses theory on realist grounds. But because the understanding of reality differs among them, no universal principles of assessment are feasible (Radford, 2011).

But it is important to clarify what pluralism implies for professional ethics with respect to competence. Pluralism is often misunderstood as nihilism. But, as DeMartino (2011: chapter 1) argues, the impossibility of establishing a code of ethics (e.g., with respect to competence) does not constitute an argument against promoting professional ethics. Pluralism means that there is no universal set of standards, but it does not mean that anything goes.[4] Rather, pluralism requires that economists are able and willing to set out the arguments in favor of the particular approach they have chosen, arguing why they regard this approach as best, but doing so with reference to alternative possible

[4] Although this "pure pluralism" was epitomized by Feyerabend's (1975) initial work, he later moderated his position to something more workable (Feyerabend, 1978).

approaches. This ethic requires not only tolerance of alternative approaches but, further, an understanding sufficient for a justification of the preferred approach to be meaningful. Competence can be discussed in its technical sense only within one methodological approach. Competence more widely must refer to judgments as to different ways of understanding a complex reality. Pluralist professional ethics of competence are thus much more demanding than either monism or nihilism.

DeMartino (2007) has explored another possible ethical standard for economists: the "do no harm" principle. This requires prediction of the outcome of the application of economic theory. Clearly this principle also encounters particular difficulties with pluralism. If there is a range of understandings of the economic system, of methodologies and of theories, then there will inevitably be a range of predictions of the outcome of particular policies. There is no scope for a universal standard other than in very abstract terms. But again there may be scope for a professional ethic whereby economists undertake to "do no harm" by the lights of their own approach.

But different approaches will have different understandings of what "do no harm" might mean and how the principle should be applied. There is a key difference between open-system and closed-system approaches as regards the scope for predicting policy outcomes. As DeMartino argues, the application of the "maxi-max" principle has presumed that outcomes can be predicted within probability distributions. This distracts from low-probability high-loss outcomes. But even the monetary policy literature that adopts a loss-minimization approach presumes that the outcomes are stochastically predictable. The scope for harm is something that is constrained within a known range and is therefore open to calculation.

But open-system epistemology embodies the uncertainty attached to prediction on the basis of (inevitably) partial knowledge, such that quantifiable probability distributions of outcomes cannot in general be known. This insight is central in particular to Post Keynesian theory. But again, outside a dualistic closed-system framework, such uncertainty is not tantamount to ignorance. Indeed Post Keynesian theory explores the basis on which actions are taken in spite of uncertainty.[5] All prediction is imprecise and is based on judgment applied to the range of relevant knowledge available. This includes judgment as to the potential for harm. Although "do no harm" sets an impossible standard under uncertainty, there is still scope for a professional ethic such that harm is to be avoided. Again we find that the demands of professional ethics are much greater for the pluralist, as it requires, first, judgment as to policy outcomes and, second, the ability to argue for the relative merits of the approach by which that judgment is made. Third, it requires the economist to refer to value judgments with respect to the nature, scale, and distribution of the benefits expected from policy measures and any harm that is likely to ensue. This requirement opens up the more fundamental issues of ethics and economics that we explore in the next section.

[5] See, e.g., Dow (2013). O'Donnell (1989) explicitly addresses Keynes's willingness to give policy advice in spite of his views on the fundamental importance of uncertainty.

Economic Behavior and the Behavior of Economists

We have discussed the different, pluralist and non-pluralist, approaches to economics in terms of their ontological foundations. The former were discussed in terms of understanding the economic system and its constituent parts as being open, while the dominant mainstream approach is based on a closed-system understanding. So far we have considered the implications of these differences for the epistemology and methodology of economics, and thus for the scope for identifying standards with respect to competence and also for predicting the consequences of policy advice. But these differences are also important for what they imply about how we discuss the ethics of individual behavior and indeed whether such a discussion is relevant to economics at all.

Taking first the mainstream approach, economics is regarded primarily as a technical subject whereby deductive logic generates conclusions independent of any value system. The scientific method is seen as demonstrating on the basis of independent facts the validity of conclusions deduced with respect to law-like behavior. Policy proposals are put forward contingent on the introduction of one set of values or another. Colander (2002) points out that, to be useful, such advice should draw also on institutional knowledge relevant to the context, as well as noneconomic considerations. But he differentiates between the methods and skills this would require and the quite different scientific method employed to generate the policy conclusions in the first place. The deductivist method of building theory is not challenged.[6] "Do no harm" is therefore not regarded as a relevant consideration insofar as it refers to separate value judgments applied by others to the technical advice from economists based on theories deductively established. It can be relevant only to the generic ethical considerations for any scientist: to be competent in producing expert advice and to be truthful about its meaning (and thus implicitly about the consequences of applying different sets of values).

Moreover, mainstream economics does not seek to comment on the ethical content of individual behavior in the economy. Following the influence of Robbins (1932), the content of personal preferences is not to be discussed, only their consequences, under scarcity. Nevertheless, the axioms of rational choice do depict behavior in a particular way. While behavioral theory is increasingly incorporating the possibility of other-regarding behavior, the benchmark is still self-interested behavior among atomistic individuals. There is a long history of debate as to how far this depiction of behavior is positive or normative and how far it is complete or partial, and if partial how far it is separable from

[6] Colander (2005) traces the evolution of thinking on pure and applied economics, identifying the encroachment in textbooks of value judgments that blur the distinction between theory and the necessary "muddling through" process of application. He concludes (p. 291) that "the role of the economic theorist is not to give answers but to provide input into a broader policy decision process that goes far beyond economics."

noneconomic behavior (Drakopoulos, 1991). But insofar as rational economic man is the benchmark, for economists theorizing about economic agents, it must also be the benchmark for economists themselves.

In these terms, then, if behavior is normally opportunistic, a consideration of economists' own behavior must address the possibility that there are incentives for them to behave in an unethical manner themselves. Not only should a code of ethics address areas where such incentives exist, but also it must be the case that a code in itself would be insufficient to counteract these incentives. As DeMartino (2011: chapter 5) points out, codes are easily ignored. What would be required would be a change to the incentives faced by economists. Such incentives exist to some degree in that academic success depends on publications and the award of grants, and these are organized in such a way as to discourage such unethical behavior as plagiarism, conflict of interest, and misrepresentation. But ultimately the only sanction lies in the legal system. Even if we were to take the mainstream approach at face value and even if it were possible to agree on a code of ethics, it is hard to see the profession setting up a system of financial penalties in order to enforce such a code. Yet that is what mainstream theory would suggest.

It is instructive to consider the economic discussion of moral hazard, that is, the situation where insurance encourages the insured to take on excessive risk (a common way of understanding the basis of the banking crisis). The concept first entered into the economics literature in an article by Arrow (1963) about health insurance. Arrow argued that where health professionals had the advantage of expertise over patients and where the outcome of treatment was subject to uncertainty, health professionals should be required to abide by a code of professional ethics. Curiously the moral hazard was not that insured patients would seek excessive treatment but that the providers would provide excessive treatment, acting against the patients' interests. But the notion of morality and the relevance of uncertainty were subsequently dropped from the mainstream literature on moral hazard. Pauly (1968), for example, argued that the issue was simply one of incentives with respect to rational individual behavior. Indeed while much of the public discussion of banks' behavior in the run-up to the banking crisis has had a strong ethical dimension, the discussion by mainstream economists has referred rather to rational response to incentives.

But the pluralist approaches to economics trace their history to explicit understanding of economics as a moral science, such that any discussion of moral hazard, for example, has an ethical dimension (Dow, 2012a). According to this view, values are embedded in any economic theory; far from being value-free, mainstream economics, for example, is founded on hedonistic philosophy (Drakopoulos, 1991). Different approaches espouse different values: neo-Austrian economics puts a high value on individual liberty, for example, while institutionalist theory rather values social cohesion embodied in institutions. Because these values are not separable from the theory that yields policy conclusions, the economic advisor is already taking an ethical position with respect to policy. In support of professional ethics with respect to honesty therefore, the economic advisor should be obliged to explain the values embedded in her theory and their implications for policy. This is no simple matter and again puts much higher demands on the pluralist economist than would any mainstream professional ethic.

The different open-system ontologies of pluralist approaches to economics do not separate economic behavior from noneconomic behavior.[7] This pluralist approach to the abstractions inevitably required of theorizing reflects the privileging of ontology. This abstraction follows the principle of selective simplification rather than fictionalization, where the latter involves directly contradicting real experience. Thus, for example, a Marxist might simplify by focusing on the common social forces behind behavior within a particular class, disregarding differences that exist but are regarded as secondary. A mainstream economist builds theory on the core assumption that individuals are isolated and rational with access in principle to complete information, something known to be false.

The open-system approach in turn requires a pluralist methodology—recourse to a range of methods—in order to understand what is to be simplified. The ontology that leads to a pluralist epistemology is one of individuals and social groupings who attempt to build knowledge about an open system, as a basis for action. The system is open partly because of human creativity; if all possibilities are not known in advance then probabilistic forecasts cannot be quantified—there is uncertainty. Further, given the uncertainty of knowledge, society over time evolves conventions and institutions to provide a relatively stable basis for action (Hodgson, 1988). This argument goes back to the Scottish Enlightenment, when it was argued that, rather than being exogenous abstract standards, ethical norms are embedded in conventions and institutions, evolving together. Rather than being a rational response to financial incentives, much behavior is governed by convention and both enabled and constrained by institutions.

Perhaps most significantly for any consideration of ethics for economists, these pluralist approaches (including the individualistic neo-Austrian approach) all incorporate to a greater or lesser degree the social nature of human behavior. This is evident on epistemological grounds, but more fundamentally at the level of the nature of identity (Davis, 2011). All behavior therefore is regarded as being to some degree other-regarding. Both ethics and a flouting of ethics are part and parcel of individual behavior, and the strength of social norms is important for defining and promoting ethical standards.

Again it is instructive to consider the example of the banking crisis. It is widely understood that there was a failure of ethics in banking. Initially the response was governed by the mainstream approach, to seek an alternative set of incentives in order to change bankers' behavior. Yet time and again such efforts have backfired. For example, executive remuneration by stock options had been introduced to incentivize an alignment of the interests of the executives and their companies. But what transpired was a prioritization of short-term stock value at the expense of companies' long-term health (Lazonick, 2009). Specifically in terms of bank regulation, Chick (2008) shows that the practices of securitization and banks' increasing activities in derivatives markets were the result

[7] See further Hausman (1992) on the issues raised by the separateness of (mainstream) economics.

of the capital adequacy requirements that had been designed to curtail excessive bank lending. Given this experience, the policy discussion is increasingly focusing on efforts to change banking culture, including ethical standards. Because a fundamental problem has been identified as the loss of trust in banking, efforts are required to restore trust (Dow, 2012b). But if, outside a mainstream framework, trust is noncalculative, then its building-up requires enough social experience, and possibly institutional development, for a trusting convention to be reestablished. Further, much will depend on the local context: how trust had historically been reinforced by experience and how institutions had evolved, and how trust had broken down.

A similar argument may be applied to economists. The ethics of economists have evolved over a long period as a social convention within the profession, or institutionalized, for example, in the rules of professional societies and journal editorial boards. The discipline is increasingly globalized. This globalization is due not only to academic labor mobility but also to the power exercised by particular groupings, such as the top US journals, in influencing ranking within national labor markets, within national grant awarding bodies, and indeed in other journals. Nevertheless national differences persist, such that ethical standards are colored by local conventions and institutions. This alone would make it difficult to operationalize any common international ethical standards. Rather a pluralist analysis of behavior of economists, just as of economic agents, would suggest that the focus of any attempt to promote professional ethics should address current institutions and conventions in the particular context being addressed. More generally, the focus should be on the culture of the economics profession. Of course this is easier said than done. All that is intended here is to point in a direction that accords with pluralism and in particular gets away from any idea of universal incentivization.

There is a final consideration regarding the pluralist view of human behavior. Far from taking preferences as given, as in mainstream economics, pluralist economics sees preferences as being socially influenced. This influence may be helpful in allowing individuals to function under uncertainty. But it may also be the result of the exercise of power. Economists themselves may exercise power, presenting themselves merely as technical experts and yet influencing behavior. In particular, mainstream economics employs a very particular meaning of the term "rational," classifying as irrational anything which falls outside that definition. Thus the noncalculative behavior that pluralist economists see as inevitable under uncertainty is deemed undesirable and, as in the context of the financial crisis, positively damaging. This calculative individualistic culture reached its height in the 1980s (with the "me" generation) and appears to have persisted to a considerable degree, notably in the financial sector.[8]

Mainstream economics may have been promoted in the 1980s because it lent support to such a culture, but it also has to take responsibility for itself promoting the idea that such "rational" behavior is positively desirable. This role persists in efforts to "nudge"

[8] Nevertheless the financial sector is profoundly social, not only in terms of its institutional arrangements, but more fundamentally in terms of the importance of conventional knowledge in the absence of any basis for "true" prices.

individuals to be rational. Mainstream economics can be seen to be attempting to mould the real world into a form which is closer to its own fictional abstraction. Most economists therefore may reasonably be held to account both for failing to predict the possibility of crisis and for having promoted policies that made crisis more likely. But they may also be held responsible for promoting the kind of culture that it is now going to be so hard to reverse. The exercise of this power was all the more unethical for being hidden under a cloak of technical expertise.

Conclusion: Some Ethical Standards for a Pluralist Economics

Given such differences between the mainstream view of the economy, economics and economists and that outside the mainstream, the preceding discussion implies that there is little scope for agreement on ethical principles with respect to such matters as competence and "doing no harm," far less an operational code of ethics. But this is no reason to abandon any discussion of professional ethics. On the contrary, the discussion in this chapter has shown that the scope for unethical behavior and the need for addressing professional ethics are much more extensive than the conventional discussion of economists' ethics might imply.

A pluralist approach to professional ethics would address first of all the ethics of relations among economists themselves. Openness to other viewpoints has been central to the modern rhetoric literature (McCloskey, 1994), whereby "good conversation" requires a basic level of tolerance. Similarly Screpanti (1997) concluded a volume on pluralism in economics with the ethical argument for pluralism. He advocated tolerance of a range of perspectives on the grounds that no one perspective could be demonstrated to be superior to the rest. Critical rationalism similarly espouses ethical standards for economists that include tolerance, along with "honesty, commitment to the advance of science above personal advance and to the freedom to exercise criticism, a willingness to listen and learn from others, and so on" (Redman, 1991: 173). The ethics of pluralism thus require the fostering of a culture where different viewpoints are not rejected out of hand.

More widespread civil behavior, whereby alternative viewpoints are treated with respect, would represent ethical progress in economics. But pluralist ethics require more. Pluralism is often misunderstood as an open season on any viewpoint at all, or "anything goes," something that comes perilously close to nihilism. From a logistical point of view, there is a limit to the number of approaches to economics that can be sustained, given that knowledge activities are pursued within knowledge communities. So pluralist economics would be structured roughly (and provisionally) around a range of such communities (Dow, 2004). This more limited pluralism allows economists from different perspectives to understand something of each other's viewpoints, and thus also allows scope for potentially constructive engagement across approaches.

Pluralism does not involve operating within several approaches at once, but rather being well enough informed about other approaches to be able to communicate. It also means being equipped to justify one's own approach relative to others.

This ability to justify one's position is important not just to the ethics of interactions between economists but also to the ethics of interactions with policymakers. If economists are being honest with policymakers, then they have to accept that their own approach to policy questions is only one among several and therefore needs to be justified. Honesty with policymakers requires that economists are open about the limits to their capacity to explain and predict, but nevertheless able to explain the merits of their own approach for (limited) explanation and prediction relative to others. Part of this justification also requires openness as to the value judgments embedded in theory and the implications of these judgments for policy advice and how different groups in society are affected by policy. Finally, given that any economic approach can only yield partial understanding, any economist must exercise judgment in arriving at policy advice and be able to justify the way in which that judgment was arrived at. From a pluralist view of knowledge, no policy can be guaranteed to do no harm, but arguments can be presented for the degree of harm to be expected relative to good, which groups are likely to benefit and which to lose out, and the degree of confidence with which such judgments can be arrived at.

But the power of economics and its capacity for good or ill are not limited to specific theories and policy advice. Economics has the capacity for influencing behavior and institutional design more broadly by influencing the way in which different groups in society understand the economy and their place in it. Pluralist economics recognizes the role of power in the dominance of one approach to economics over others and the interdependence between that power and political power more generally. A professional ethic for economics would require awareness of how a particular approach to economics might itself influence how others understand the economy and how behavior and the evolution of institutions might change accordingly. Such an awareness can be built on more explicit statements about the value judgments embedded in theory and how far they are shared in society.

We have argued against the cementing of ethics (pluralist or otherwise) in a code, arguing instead for efforts in promoting a culture of ethical behavior within economics. The pluralist ethics proposed here require the evolution of the conventions of even-handedness which were more prevalent, for example, in the United States before the second half of the twentieth century (Morgan and Rutherford, 1998). Promotion of such conventions could be supported further with institutional support, in the criteria for peer review of publications, awarding of research grants, and promotion within academic departments, for example. Freeman (2012) argues that this would require a much higher degree of independent scrutiny than at present. But until economists as a group develop a pluralist ethic that requires them to be more modest about the scope of their expertise, independent scrutiny is likely to lack sufficient assurance.

Ultimately, developing pluralist ethics in economics requires that they be embedded in the teaching of economics, so that young economists enter the profession well-informed about the range of approaches to economics and equipped both to form their own judgments and to justify them. There has been considerable attention paid to the teaching of pluralist economics (Groenewegen, 2007; Reardon, 2009). But further, DeMartino (2011: chapter 12) and Earl (2012) have demonstrated the importance of education not only for pluralism but also for the ethics required for the effective operation of pluralism. While pluralist teaching would be performative in encouraging pluralism, it would be part of the ethics of pluralism to be open and honest about attempts to influence behavior and conventions. But the influence would be in the direction of promoting professional ethics themselves and making them a matter for open and informed discussion.

References

Arrow, K. J. 1963. "Uncertainty and the Welfare Economics of Medical Care." *American Economic Review* 53(5): 941–969.

Bartlett, R. L. 2009. "Code of Ethics for Economics." In *Handbook of Economics and Ethics*, edited by J. Peil and I. van Staveren, pp. 54–61. Cheltenham: Edward Elgar.

Chick, V. 1995. "Order Out of Chaos in Economics." In *Keynes, Knowledge and Uncertainty*, edited by S. C. Dow and J. Hillard, pp. 25–42. Aldershot, UK: Edward Elgar.

Chick, V. 2008. "Could the Crisis at Northern Rock have been Predicted? An Evolutionary Approach." *Contributions to Political Economy* 27(1): 115–124.

Chick, V., and S. C. Dow. 2005. "The Meaning of Open Systems." *Journal of Economic Methodology* 12: 363–381, reprinted in S. C. Dow, *Foundations for New Economic Thinking: A collection of essays*. London: Palgrave Macmillan, 2012.

Colander, D. 2002. "The Lost Art of Economics." *Journal of Economic Perspectives* 6(3): 191–198.

Colander, D. 2005. "From Muddling Through to the Economics of Control: Views of Applied Policy from J. N. Keynes to Abba Lerner." *History of Political Economy* 37 (Suppl. 1): 277–291.

Davis, J. B. 2006. "The Turn in Economics: Neoclassical Dominance to Mainstream Pluralism?" *Journal of Institutional Economics* 2(1): 1–20.

Davis, J. B. 2011. *Individuals and Identity in Economics*. Cambridge, UK: Cambridge University Press.

DeMartino, G. 2007. "A Hippocratic Oath for Economics? On the Need for and Content of a Professional Economic Ethics." In *Future Directions for Heterodox Economics*, edited by J. T. Harvey and R. F. Garnett, pp. 116–124. Ann Arbor: University of Michigan Press.

DeMartino, G. 2011. *The Economist's Oath: On the Need for and Content of Professional Economic Ethics*. Oxford: Oxford University Press.

Dow, S. C. 2004. "Structured Pluralism." *Journal of Economic Methodology* 11(3): 275–290, reprinted in S. C. Dow, *Foundations for New Economic Thinking: A Collection of Essays*. London: Palgrave Macmillan, 2012.

Dow, S. C. 2012a. "Economics and Moral Sentiments: The Case of Moral Hazard." In *Facts, Values and Objectivity*, edited by V. Neves and J. C. Caldas, pp. 17–32. London: Routledge.

Dow, S. C. 2012b. "What Are Banks and Bank Regulation for? A Consideration of the Foundations for Reform." *Intervention* 9(1): 39–56.

Dow, S. C. 2013. "Keynes on Knowledge, Expectations and Rationality." In *Rethinking Expectations: The Way Forward for Macroeconomics*, edited by E. S. Phelps and R. Frydman, pp. 112–129. Princeton, NJ: Princeton University Press

Drakopoulos, S. 1991. *Values in Economic Theory*. Aldershot, UK: Avebury.

Earl, P. E. 2010. "Economics Fit for the Queen: A Pessimistic Assessment of Its prospects." *Prometheus* 28(3): 209–225.

Earl, P. E. 2012. "Real-World Economics and the Ethics of Teaching." In World Economics Association (WEA) Conference on Economics and Society: The Ethical Dimension.

Feyerabend, P. K. 1975. *Against Method: Outline of an Anarchist Theory of Knowledge*. London: New Left Books.

Feyerabend, P. K. 1978. *Science in a Free Society*. London: New Left Books.

Freeman, A. 2012. "Towards an Assertive Pluralist Code of Conduct for Economists," World Economics Association (WEA) Conference on Economics and Society: The Ethical Dimension.

Garnett, R. F., Jr. 2006, Fall. "Paradigms and Pluralism in Heterodox Economics." *Review of Political Economy* 18: 521–546.

Garnett, R. F. Jr., E. Olsen, and M. Starr Eds. 2009. *Economic Pluralism*. London: Routledge.

Groenewegen, J., Ed. 2007. *Teaching Pluralism in Economics*. Cheltenham, UK: Edward Elgar.

Hausman, D. M. 1992. *The Inexact and Separate Science of Economics*. Cambridge, UK: Cambridge University Press.

Hodgson, G. M. 1988. *Economics and Institutions*. Cambridge, UK: Polity Press.

Lawson, T. 1997. *Economics and Reality*. London: Routledge.

Lazonick, W. 2009. "The New Economy Business Model and the Crisis of U.S. Capitalism." *Capitalism and Society* 4(2): article 4.

Lee, F. 2009. *A History of Heterodox Economics: Challenging the Mainstream in the Twentieth Century*. London: Routledge.

McCloskey, D. N. 1994. *Knowledge and Persuasion in Economics*. Cambridge, UK: Cambridge University Press.

Morgan, M. S., and M. Rutherford. 1998. "American Economics: The Character of the Transformation." In *From Interwar Pluralism to Postwar Neoclassicism*, edited by M. S. Morgan and M. Rutherford, pp. 1–28. Durham, NC: Duke University Press.

O'Donnell, R. M. 1989. *Keynes's Philosophy, Economics and Politics: The Philosophical Foundations of Keynes's Thought and Their Influence on His Economics and Politics*. London: Macmillan.

Pauly, M. V. 1968. "The Economics of Moral Hazard: Comment." *American Economic Review* 53(5): 531–537.

Radford, P. 2011. "Ethics in Economics—Where Is It?" *Real-World Economics Review* no. 58: 2–8. Retrieved from http://www.paecon.net/PAEReview/issue58/Radford58.pdf

Reardon, J., Ed. 2009. *A Pluralist Handbook for Economics Education*. London: Routledge.

Redman, D. A. 1991. *Economics and the Philosophy of Science*. Oxford: Oxford University Press.

Robbins, L. 1932. *An Essay on the Nature and Significance of Economic Science*. London: Macmillan.

Screpanti, E. 1997. "Afterword: Can Methodological Pluralism be a Methodological Canon?" In *Pluralism in Economics: Theory, History and Methodology*, edited by A. Salanti and E. Screpanti, pp. 298–307 Aldershot, UK: Edward Elgar.

Author Index

CPSIA information can be obtained
at www.ICGtesting.com
Printed in the USA
BVHW011405071019
560172BV00033B/101/P

9 780199 766635